1/14

THE ROUGH GUIDE TO

Argentina

written and researched by

Danny Aeberhard, Andrew Benson, Shafik Meghji,
Rosalba O'Brien and Lucy Phillips

ROUGH GUIDES

roughguides.com

Contents

OPPOSITE LAGO ARGENTINO, EL CALAFATE **PREVIOUS PAGE** CATHEDRAL, CÓRDOBA

Introduction to
Argentina

Studded with outstanding natural wonders and endowed with one of the world's hot-list cities, Argentina is a vast and varied land. Tapering from the Tropic of Capricorn towards the tip of Antarctica it encompasses a staggering diversity of terrains, from the lush wetlands of the Litoral and the bone-dry Andean plateaux of the Northwest to the end-of-the-world archipelago of Tierra del Fuego. Its most emblematic landscapes are the verdant flatlands of the Pampas and the dramatic steppe of Patagonia, whose very name evokes windswept plains inhabited by hardy pioneers.

At first glance, Argentina may seem less "exotic" than the rest of South America and its inhabitants will readily, and rightly, tell you how powerful an influence Europe has been on their nation. It has been quipped that Argentina is the most American of all European countries and the most European of all American countries, but it actually has a very special character all of its own, distilled into the national ideal of **Argentinidad**, characterized by proud, defiant passion. While there is a lot of truth in the clichés – Argentine society really is dominated by **football**, politics and living life in the fast lane (literally, when it comes to driving) – not everyone dances the **tango**, or is obsessed with **Evita** or gallops around on a horse. Wherever you go, though, you're bound to be wowed by Argentines' zeal for so many aspects of their own culture and curiosity about the outside world.

One of Argentina's top attractions is the leviathan metropolis of **Buenos Aires**, the most fascinating of all South American capitals. It's a riveting place just to wander about, people-watching, shopping or simply soaking up the unique atmosphere. Its many barrios (neighbourhoods) are startlingly different – some are decadently old-fashioned, others daringly modern – but all of them ooze character. The other main cities worth visiting are colonial **Salta** in the Northwest, beguiling **Rosario** – the birthplace of Che Guevara – and **Ushuaia**, which, in addition to being the world's most southerly city, enjoys a fabulous waterfront setting on the Beagle Channel.

ABOVE FIELD OF SUGAR CANE, GRAN CHACO

FACT FILE

• Argentina is the world's eighth-largest country by area, though with a population of just over 40 million – one-third of whom live in Greater Buenos Aires – it is one of the least densely populated countries on the planet.

• Some 97 percent of Argentines are of European origin, largely of Spanish or Italian descent. Most citizens are nominally Catholic, but under a fifth are practising. Although abortion is still restricted, Argentina has some of the world's most progressive laws on matters like same-sex marriage and death with dignity.

• Best known for its beef, Argentina is also a leading producer of wine, wheat, fruits and vegetables. In recent years much of the country's land has been turned over to soya and exports of animal feed to China have helped to drive its strong economic growth since the 2001 crisis.

• Argentines have long been distinguished in the field of science, with Dr Luis Agote carrying out one of the earliest successful blood transfusions in 1914, and three Argentines receiving Nobel prizes for medicine or chemistry in the twentieth century. Argentines have twice been awarded the Nobel Peace Prize: Carlos de Saavedra Lamas, in 1936, for his peace efforts in South America, and Adolfo Pérez Esquivel, in 1980, for his defence of human rights in the 1970s.

• Argentina has a vibrant film industry and has twice carried off an Oscar for best foreign language film: *La historia oficial* (The Official Story) in 1985 and *El secreto de sus ojos* (The Secret in Their Eyes) in 2010; both movies deal with the "Dirty War" and its aftermath (see box, p.563).

But the country's real trump cards outside the capital are the sheer size of the **land** and the diverse **wildlife** inhabiting it. In theory, by hopping on a plane or two you could spot howler monkeys and toucans in northern jungles in the morning, then watch the antics of penguins tobogganing into the icy South Atlantic in the afternoon. Argentina hosts hundreds of bird species – including the Andean condor and three varieties of flamingo – plus pumas, armadillos, llamas, foxes and tapirs roaming the country's forests and mountainsides and the dizzying heights of the altiplano, or *puna*. Lush tea plantations and parched salt-flats, palm groves and icebergs, plus the world's mightiest waterfalls, are just some of the scenes that will catch you unawares if you were expecting Argentina to be one big cattle ranch. Dozens of these biosystems are protected by an extensive network of national and provincial **parks and reserves**.

For **getting around** and seeing these marvels, you can generally rely on a well-developed infrastructure inherited from decades of domestic tourism. Thanks in part to an increasing number of boutique hotels, the range and quality of **accommodation** has improved no end in the last decade. Among the best lodgings are the beautiful ranches known as **estancias** – or *fincas* in the north – that function as luxury resorts. In most places, you'll be able to rely on the services of top-notch tour operators, who will not only show you the sights but also fix you up with a staggering range of **outdoor adventures**: horseriding, trekking, whitewater rafting, kayaking, skiing and hang-gliding, along with more relaxing pursuits such as wine tasting, birdwatching or photography safaris. Argentina offers such a hallucinating variety it's all but impossible to take in on one trip – don't be surprised if you find yourself longing to return to explore the bits you didn't get to see the first time around.

RIGHT PARQUE PROVINCIAL ISCHIGUALASTO

Where to go

Argentina has many attractions that could claim the title of natural wonders of the world: the prodigious waterfalls of **Iguazú**; the spectacular **Glaciar Perito Moreno**; unforgettable whale-watching off **Península Valdés**; or the handsome lakes and mountains around **Bariloche** – indeed, **Patagonia** in general. Yet many of the country's most rewarding destinations are also its least known, such as the **Esteros del Iberá**, a huge reserve of lily-carpeted lagoons offering close-up encounters with cormorants and caimans; or **Antofagasta de la Sierra**, a remote village set amid frozen lakes mottled pink with flamingoes; or **Laguna Diamante**, a high-altitude mirror of sapphire water reflecting a wondrous volcano. In any case, climate and distance will rule out any attempt to see every corner; it's more sensible and rewarding to concentrate on one or two sections of the country.

Unless you're visiting Argentina as part of a South American tour, **Buenos Aires** is likely to be your point of entry, as it has the country's only *bona fide* international airport, Ezeiza. It is one of the world's top urban experiences, with an intriguing blend of European architecture and a vernacular flair that includes houses painted in the colours of legendary football team Boca Juniors. The city's museums are eclectic enough to suit all interests – Latin American art, colonial silverware, dinosaurs and ethnography are just four subjects on offer – and you can round off a day's sightseeing with a tango show, a bar tour or a meal at one of the dozens of fabulous restaurants.

CRIOLLO CULTURE

Most closely translated as "creole", **criollo** refers to a way of life born in the Americas, but with Old World roots. In Argentina, it is a byword for that which is absolutely Argentine – the culture of the countryside and the gaucho. Key aspects of this include the food – *asado* barbecues, of course, but also maize-based stews like *locro*; clothing – such as baggy riding trousers called *bombachas* and the espadrille-like *alpargatas*; horses – be they for rounding up cattle or playing polo; and a decidedly anti-authoritarian streak in the national character. Even the wealthiest city-dweller is usually keen to prove that he or she is fundamentally a *criollo*, never happier than when sipping a *mate* by the fire.

Due north lies the **Litoral**, an expanse of subtropical watery landscapes that shares borders with Uruguay, Brazil and Paraguay. Here are the photogenic **Iguazú waterfalls** and Jesuit missions whose once-noble ruins are crumbling into the jungle – with the exception of well-groomed **San Ignacio Miní**. Immediately west of the Litoral extends the **Chaco**, one of Argentina's most infrequently visited regions, reserved for those with an ardent interest in **wildlife**, so be prepared for fierce summer heat and poor infrastructure. A highlight in the country's landlocked **Northwest** is the **Quebrada de Humahuaca**, a fabulous gorge lined with rainbow-hued rocks; it winds up to the oxygen-starved altiplano, where llamas and their wild relatives munch wiry grass. Nearby, in the **Valles Calchaquíes**, a chain of stunningly scenic valleys, high-altitude vineyards produce the delightfully flowery torrontés wine.

Sprawling across Argentina's broad midriff to the west and immediately south of Buenos Aires are **the Pampas**, arguably the country's most archetypal landscape. Formed by horizon-to-horizon plains interspersed with the odd low sierra, this subtly beautiful scenery is punctuated by small towns, the occasional ranch and countless clumps of pampas grass (*cortaderas*). Part arid, part wetland, the Pampas are grazed by millions of cattle and planted with soya and wheat fields of incomprehensible size. The Pampas are also where you'll glimpse traditional **gaucho culture**, most famously in the charming pueblo of **San Antonio de Areco**. Here, too, are some of the classiest estancias, offering a combination of hedonistic luxury and horseback adventures. On the Atlantic Coast a string of fun beach resorts includes long-standing favourite **Mar del Plata**.

As you head further west, the Central Sierras loom: the mild climate, clear brooks and sylvan idylls of these ancient highlands have attracted holiday-makers since the late nineteenth century, and within reach of **Córdoba**, the country's colonial-era second city, are some of the oldest resorts on the continent. Keep going west and you'll get to the **Cuyo**, with the highest Andean peaks as a snow-capped backdrop; here you can discover one of Argentina's most enjoyable cities, the regional capital of **Mendoza**, also the country's **wine capital**. From here, the scenic **Alta Montaña** route climbs steeply to the Chilean border, passing **Cerro Aconcagua**, now well established as a fantasy challenge for mountaineers worldwide. Just south, **Las Leñas** is a ski-and-snowboard resort where

Author picks

Rough Guides authors covered every corner of Argentina for this new edition, from the gale-swept shores of the Beagle Channel to the spray-drenched viewing-platforms at the Iguazú Falls. These are their personal picks.

Road trips The world's eighth largest country is laced by roads that pass through an astonishing variety of landscapes. Most famously, Ruta 40 (p.488) skirts the Andes to zip through Patagonia and beyond. We also like the two-day Cafayate–Cachi circuit (p.312) and the polychrome Quebrada de Humahuaca (p.297).

Meet the ancestors Argentina is a country of immigrants. Follow Old World traditions and enjoy cakes in the Welsh teahouses of Gaiman (p.457) and Trevelin (p.415), wander through colourful Genoese Boca (p.82), and sup locally brewed beer in Germanic Villa General Belgrano (p.201) and Bariloche (p.395).

Breathtaking views Picking Argentina's finest view is an impossible task, but our favourites include Glaciar Perito Moreno (p.472) and Monte Fitz Roy (p.480) in Patagonia, Cerro Catedral (p.404) in the Lake District, and, of course, the Iguazú Falls (p.236) in the Northeast.

Wildlife encounters Argentina is a wildlife haven with whales off Península Valdés (p.448), Magellanic penguins at Punta Tombo (p.459) and vicuñas in the Northwest (p.326) – just make sure the coatis don't steal your lunch at the Iguazú Falls (p.236).

Favourite wines Argentina is one of the world's leading producers of vino and the quality improves every harvest. Vineyard tours are highpoints of any visit to the Lake District (p.437), Salta Province (p.314) or El Cuyo (p.346). Or else crack open a bottle of malbec or torrontés at a top restaurant in Buenos Aires (p.113).

Most romantic estancia The marvellous estancia of *La Bamba* (p.141) may have been the setting for a film about a tragic love story but that shouldn't put off honeymooners. The wild isolation of Patagonia (p.522) or the colonial charms of the Northwest (p.291) also lend themselves to memorable holiday trysts.

> Our author recommendations don't end here. We've flagged up our favourite places – a perfectly sited hotel, an atmospheric café, a special restaurant – throughout the guide, highlighted with the ★ symbol.

FROM TOP MAGELLAN PENGUINS AT PUNTA TOMBO (P.459); WOMAN CYCLING ON RUTA 40 (P.488); *CIERVO ROJO*, VILLA GENERAL BELGRANO (P.201)

TANGO, ARGENTINA'S BLUES

Tango is not only a dance, or even an art form, it is a powerful symbol, closely associated with Argentina around the world. Essentially and intrinsically linked to Buenos Aires and its multicultural history, it nonetheless has ardent fans all around the country. Rosario and, to a lesser extent, Córdoba, the country's two biggest cities after the capital, have a strong tango culture, complete with **milongas** (tango dance halls) and shops to buy the right garb and footwear. And don't be surprised to find villagers in some remote hamlet, hundreds of miles from Buenos Aires, listening to a scratchy recording of **Carlos Gardel** – the 1930s heart-throb still regarded as the best tango singer. Some experts argue that tango's success can be put down to its perfect representation of the Argentine psyche: a unique blend of nostalgia, resignation and heartbroken passion.

celebrities show off their winter wear, while the nearby black-and-red lava wastes of **La Payunia**, one of the country's hidden jewels, are all but overlooked. Likewise, **San Juan** and **La Rioja** provinces are relatively uncharted territories, but their marvellous hill-and-dale landscapes reward exploration, along with their underrated wineries. The star attractions are a brace of parks: **Parque Nacional Talampaya**, with its giant red cliffs, and the nearby **Parque Provincial Ischigualasto**, usually known as the **Valle de la Luna** on account of its intriguing moonscapes.

Argentina cherishes the lion's share of the wild, sparsely populated expanses of **Patagonia** (the rest belongs to Chile) and possesses by far the more worthwhile half of the remote archipelago of **Tierra del Fuego**. These are lands of seemingly endless arid steppe hemmed in for the most part by the southern leg of the Andes, a row of majestic volcanoes and craggy peaks interspersed by deep glacial lakes. An almost unbroken series of national parks running along these Patagonian and Fuegian cordilleras makes for some of the best trekking anywhere on the planet. You should certainly include the savage granite peaks of the Fitz Roy massif in **Parque Nacional Los Glaciares** in your itinerary, but consider also the less frequently visited araucaria (monkey puzzle) forests of **Parque Nacional Lanín** or

the peerless trail network of **Parque Nacional Nahuel Huapi**. On the Atlantic side of
Patagonia, **Península Valdés** is a must-see for its world-class marine fauna, including
sea elephants and orcas. If you have a historical bent, you may like to trace the region's
associations with Darwin and his captain Fitz Roy in the choppy **Beagle Channel** off
Ushuaia, or track down the legacy of Butch Cassidy, who lived near Cholila, or of the
Welsh settlers whose influence can still be felt in communities like **Gaiman** and **Trevelin**.

When to go

Given the size of Argentina, you're unlikely to flit from region to region and, if you can,
you should try and visit each area at the optimal time of year. Roughly falling from
September to November, the Argentine **spring** is perfect just about everywhere, although
in the far south icy gales may blow. **Summer** (Dec–Feb) is the only time to climb the
highest Andean peaks, such as Aconcagua, and also the most reliable time of year to head
for Tierra del Fuego, though it can snow there any time of year. Buenos Aires is liable to
be very hot and sticky in December and January, and you should certainly avoid the
lowland parts of the North at this time of year, as temperatures can be scorching and roads
flooded by heavy storms. **Autumn** (March and April) is a great time to visit Mendoza and
San Juan provinces for the wine harvests, and Patagonia and Tierra del Fuego to witness
the eye-catching red and orange hues of the beech groves. The **winter** months of June,
July and August are obviously the time to head for the Andean ski resorts, but blizzards
can cut off towns in Patagonia and many places close from Easter through to October,
so it's not a good time to tour the southerly region. Temperatures in the north of the
country should be pleasant at this time of year, though Buenos Aires can come across as
somewhat bleak in July and August, despite a plethora of indoors attractions.

A final point to bear in mind: the **national holiday seasons** are roughly January, Easter
and July, when transport and accommodation can get booked up and rates are hiked,
sometimes almost doubling.

AVERAGE TEMPERATURES AND RAINFALL

	Jan	Feb	Mar	Apr	May	Jun	Jul	Aug	Sep	Oct	Nov	Dec
BARILOCHE												
Max/Min (°C)	22/6	22/6	19/4	15/2	10/1	7/-1	6/-1	8/-1	11/0	14/1	17/4	20/5
Rainfall (mm)	22	22	29	54	134	141	129	116	58	39	25	32
BUENOS AIRES												
Max/Min (°C)	30/20	28/19	26/17	22/13	19/10	15/7	14/7	17/8	18/9	22/13	25/15	28/18
Rainfall (mm)	121	122	153	106	92	50	52	63	77	139	131	103
SALTA												
Max/Min (°C)	27/16	26/16	25/15	23/12	21/8	19/4	20/3	22/4	24/7	26/11	27/14	28/16
Rainfall (mm)	182	163	118	37	9	3	3	4	7	26	65	138
USHUAIA												
Max/Min (°C)	15/5	14/5	12/3	9/2	6/0	4/-1	4/-1	6/-1	8/0	11/2	12/3	13/4
Rainfall (mm)	30	33	47	49	54	54	46	60	39	34	35	41

25

things not to miss

It's not possible to see everything Argentina has to offer in one trip – and we don't suggest you try. What follows, in no particular order, is a selective taste of the country's highlights: vibrant cities, dramatic landscapes, spectacular wildlife and more. Each one has a page reference to take you straight into the Guide, where you can find out more. Coloured numbers refer to chapters in the Guide.

1 RUTA DE LOS SIETE LAGOS
Page 408

Seven Patagonian lakes – their sparkling waters emerald, ultramarine, cobalt, turquoise, cerulean, sapphire and indigo – linked by a rugged mountain road: a magical route best explored in a 4WD.

2 CARNIVAL IN THE LITORAL
Page 214

Like their neighbours across the river in Uruguay and Brazil, the people of the Northeast do know how to party, not least in Gualeguaychú in the lead-up to Lent.

3 TALAMPAYA
Page 384

The undisputed highlight of La Rioja Province is a World Heritage Site dominated by giant cliffs of deep pink sandstone – once home to dinosaurs, now the protected habitat of condors, guanacos and foxes.

4 GLACIAR PERITO MORENO
Page 472

A visit to one of the world's last advancing glaciers is a treat for the eyes and the ears; count impossible shades of blue as you listen to a chorus of cracks, thuds and whines.

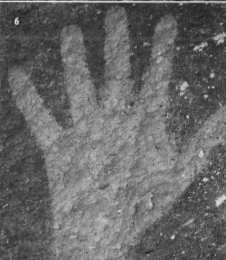

14

11 THE PAMPAS
Page 136

Rugged gauchos, nodding pampas grass and herds of contented cattle are the famous inhabitants of Argentina's most archetypal landscape.

12 TIGRE AND THE PARANÁ DELTA
Page 133

Take a boat or paddle a kayak around the swampy islets and muddy creeks of Tigre – a subtropical Venice right on the capital's doorstep.

13 VOLCÁN LANÍN
Page 430

Despite the unappealing meaning of its native name – "he who choked himself to death" – this perfect symmetrical cone of a volcano is both a beauty to behold and a treat to climb.

14 DINOSAUR FOSSILS IN NEUQUÉN
Page 436

The world's biggest dinosaurs once roamed Neuquén Province – nothing will convey their immensity more than standing underneath their skeletons or seeing their giant footprints in the rock.

15 ANDEAN CAMELIDS
Page 553

Shaggy llamas and silky-fleeced alpacas, imposing guanacos and delicate vicuñas – all four distant relatives of the camel can be spotted along Argentina's cordillera.

16 QUEBRADA DE HUMAHUACA
Page 297

Whitewashed settlements nestled against polychrome mountains, dazzling salt-flats, lush valleys and cactus forests, windswept steppe and deep gorges – some of the planet's most incredible scenery.

15

16

17 USHUAIA
Page 505

Once Argentina's most feared penal colony, now vaunted as the world's southernmost city, Ushuaia sits proudly on the Beagle Channel, backed by serrated peaks and a bijou glacier.

18 FOOTBALL
Page 38

It is no exaggeration to say that nothing else holds the same grip on Argentine society as football – some say no trip to the country is complete without attending a match.

19 WINES OF MENDOZA
Page 346

What better to accompany a juicy grilled *bife de chorizo* than one of the province's award-winning malbecs or syrahs?

20 ASADOS
Page 33

The local answer to the barbecue, and inseparable from Argentinidad (the national identity), these meat-roasting rituals are prepared with the utmost pride and devoured in carnivorous bliss.

21 ESTANCIAS
Page 31

Try your hand at cattle-herding or sheep-shearing at a working estancia – one of the great Argentine institutions – and get an authentic taste of the gaucho way of life.

Itineraries

The following itineraries will take you to every corner of the country, via both well-known sights and less visited ones, from the crashing Patagonia glaciers to off-the-beaten-track villages. Given the size of the country and cost of internal flights, don't worry if you can't complete the list – just visiting some will give you a good flavour of what Argentina has to offer.

WONDERS OF NATURE

Much of Argentina's "wow" nature highlights are in Patagonia, but there are unmissable sights further north, too, if you can spare a month or so.

❶ **Península Valdés** Watch whales, seals and sea lions basking in the rich, cool waters off this peninsula in Chubut, northern Patagonia. **See p.448**

❷ **Punta Tombo** The biggest colony of penguins in South America is a delightful sight, and the trip there will likely take you past guanacos, armadillos and more. **See p.459**

❸ **Ushuaia** At the very end of the road, Ushuaia sits on the Beagle Channel, teeming with birds, sea lions and giant crabs, and provides a base for exploring nearby Tierra del Fuego national park. **See p.505**

❹ **Glaciar Perito Moreno** Justifiably one of Argentina's most visited sights. Watch enormous chunks of blue ice carve off the city-sized glacier and even don crampons to walk on top of it. **See p.472**

❺ **Fitz Roy** The northern part of Los Glaciares national park provides some of the country's best trekking, among jagged peaks and turquoise lakes. **See p.480**

❻ **Quebrada de Humahuaca** Up in the dry northwest, the multicoloured hues of the pinnacles and strata of Humahuaca make it the pick of the region's sights. **See p.297**

❼ **Iguazú** The enormous Iguazú waterfalls by the Brazilian border, set in subtropical rainforest, make a steamy, stunning contrast to the icy southern sights. **See p.236**

❽ **The Delta** A surprisingly verdant riverine community, right on Buenos Aires' doorstep, makes for a gentle but impressive end to a tour of Argentina's natural highlights. **See p.132**

RUTA 40

Like Route 66 in the US, Argentina's Ruta 40 – the country's longest highway, running from Patagonia to Bolivia – has a legendary status, inspiring songs, books and of course road trips. Count on six weeks if you want to take in all 5224km.

❶ **Cabo Vírgenes** La Cuarenta's beginning by the Straits of Magellan, marked by a lighthouse, heralds the start of a zigzagging route through the windswept Patagonian steppe.

❷ **Estancia Lagos del Furioso** Consider splurging at this Santa Cruz estancia, where you'll find glorious views, excellent fishing and every creature comfort. **See p.493**

ABOVE VOLCANO, LA PAYUNA

❸ Bariloche Gateway to the Nahuel Huapi park, Argentina's Lake District has pristine alpine-like scenery, dramatic mountain lakes and ancient trees. **See p.395**

❹ La Payunia A remote land of rosy lava, ebony gorges, deep karstic caves and flamingo-flecked lagoons in Mendoza Province. **See p.367**

❺ Laguna Diamante Often inaccessible, this lagoon rewards the adventurous. Enjoy a picnic on the banks of a crystalline brook as you admire the silhouette of Volcán Maipo. **See p.358**

❻ Cuesta de Miranda The road in La Rioja Province winds through polychrome mountains that contrast with the verdant vegetation along the riverbanks below. **See p.384**

❼ Belén Stop off at this Catamarca highland village for a top-notch poncho – methods of weaving have been maintained since pre-Hispanic times. **See p.323**

❽ Salinas Grandes Ringed by mountains, this area of snow-white salt flats is a good place to spot llamas and vicuñas. **See p.293**

WINE AND DINE

Wherever you travel in Argentina, you can find excellent-quality food and drink. Beef plays a part of course, but there's more to the country's culinary offering. Allow two to three weeks.

❶ Buenos Aires The country's capital has, unsurprisingly, the most cosmopolitan selection of restaurants, with inventive cooking at reasonable prices easy to track down. **See p.113**

❷ The Pampas Stay on an estancia to enjoy the best barbecued beef you're likely to taste anywhere, right in the fertile heartland where it comes from. **See p.141**

❸ Mendoza Spend your days – and nights if you wish – at a bodega, tasting fine malbec wines with the snow-capped Andes as a backdrop. **See p.346**

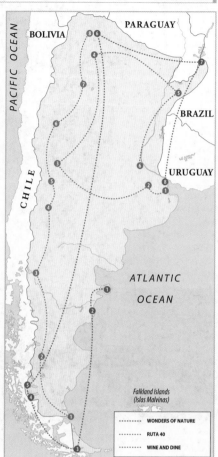

Falkland Islands
(Islas Malvinas)

·········· WONDERS OF NATURE
·········· RUTA 40
·········· WINE AND DINE

❹ Salta A good place to try the distinctive northwestern cuisine, including the classic empanada, a pasty filled with meat or vegetables, or *locro* stew. **See p.288**

❺ Estancia Santa Inés Set among plantations of *mate*, the tea-like beverage drunk avidly throughout Argentina, this estancia in verdant Misiones also serves delicious food. **See p.232**

❻ Rosario Vibrant and stylish Rosario overlooks the Río Paraná and is an excellent place to dine on the local river fish, such as *dorado*, *boga* and *surubí*. **See p.256**

DRIVING TOWARDS FITZ ROY, EL CHALTÉN, PATAGONIA

Basics

Getting there

Though some visitors reach Argentina overland from a neighbouring country and a tiny handful arrive by boat, the overwhelming majority of travellers first set foot on Argentine soil at Buenos Aires' international airport, Ezeiza.

In general, airfares to Argentina tend to be quite high, but they do vary widely depending on the routing and the **season**. The highest fares are between December and February, around Easter and in July and August. You'll get the best prices during the low season: March to June and September to November. Note also that flying on weekends often hikes return fares; price ranges quoted in this section assume midweek travel.

Flights from the UK and Ireland

Several airlines offer regular scheduled flights **from the UK** to Buenos Aires, via another European city, São Paulo or the US (the latter trips can be marginally less expensive, but are usually longer). British Airways (@ba.com) is currently the only airline to fly direct from London, refuelling in São Paulo. Iberia (@iberia.com) via Madrid skimps on the creature comforts but is often the cheapest. Adult **fares** from London to Buenos Aires usually start at around £650 in the low season, rising to well over £1000 in the high season.

There are no direct flights **from Ireland** to Argentina. If you're trying to keep costs down, consider flying to London with an economy airline and making a connection there. For less hassle, though, and only a fraction more money, you're better off flying direct to New York or Miami and catching an onward flight from there.

In addition to fares, it's worth paying attention to the **routes** used by different airlines. The shortest and most convenient routes from London, often via São Paulo or Madrid, entail a total travelling time of around sixteen hours. Apart from minimizing the length of the flight, another reason to check the routes is that many airlines allow you to take **stopovers** on the way — sometimes for free,

sometimes for a surcharge of around ten percent. Potential stopovers include Bogotá, Rio and São Paulo in South America; Boston, Chicago, Dallas, Houston, Miami, Newark and Washington DC in the US; and Frankfurt, Madrid, Milan, Paris and Rome in Europe.

Flights from the US and Canada

Several airlines, including American Airlines (@aa.com), United (@united.com) and Aerolíneas Argentinas (@aerolineas.com.ar), offer daily nonstop **flights from the US** to Buenos Aires. Typical **fares** start at around US$1100 from New York, Chicago or Washington in low season, rising to US$1600 in the high season. Flying times to Buenos Aires are around eleven hours from New York and Chicago, and nine from Miami.

There's less choice if you're flying **from Canada**, with Air Canada (@aircanada.com) offering the only direct flight into the country – from Toronto via São Paulo (with connections from other major Canadian cities). You'll be able to put together a considerably more flexible itinerary if you look for connecting flights with a US carrier. Direct flights from Toronto take around thirteen hours and **prices** start at Can$1200 in low season; from Vancouver the journey time is at least eighteen hours, at a similar fare.

Note that reciprocity fees charged to Americans and Canadians (see p.47) are only payable when entering Buenos Aires on an international flight, so if you're travelling to other South American countries anyway it may be worth considering entering Argentina another way – via the land border with Brazil (see p.243), for example, or on a flight from Santiago in Chile to Mendoza (see p.335).

Flights from Australia, New Zealand and South Africa

The best flight deals to Argentina from Australia and New Zealand are offered by Aerolíneas Argentinas (@aerolineas.com) and LAN (@lan.com) in conjunction with Qantas (@qantas.com.au) and Air New Zealand (@airnz.co.nz), either direct to Buenos Aires or via a stopover in Santiago. **In Australia**, flights to

---

ROUND-THE-WORLD TICKETS

If Argentina is only one stop on a longer journey, you might want to consider buying a **round-the-world (RTW)** ticket. Some travel agents can sell you an "off-the-shelf" RTW ticket that will have you touching down in about half a dozen cities (Buenos Aires is on many itineraries). Alternatively, you can have a travel agent assemble an RTW ticket for you; in this case the ticket can be tailored to your needs but is usually more expensive.

Argentina leave from Sydney, plus a couple a week that depart from Brisbane and Melbourne. There are no direct flights from New Zealand, so you will need to go either via Sydney or with LAN via Santiago. Flights **from South Africa** to Argentina leave from Cape Town and Johannesburg and usually go via São Paulo, taking sixteen or seventeen hours. South African Airways (**W** flysaa.com) has direct flights from Johannesburg.

Airfares depend on both the season and duration of stay. Fares from Australia normally start around Aus$2200 in low season. The lowest return fares from Cape Town or Johannesburg cost around ZAR9000.

DISCOUNT AGENTS

Adventure World Australia **T** 02 8913 0755, **W** adventureworld .com.au; New Zealand **T** 09 524 5118, **W** adventureworld.co.nz. Agents for a vast array of international adventure travel companies that operate trips to South America.

Bridge the World UK **T** 0870 443 2399, **W** bridgetheworld.com. Specializing in RTW tickets, with good deals aimed at backpackers.

North South Travel UK **T** 01245 608 291, **W** northsouthtravel .co.uk. Friendly, competitive travel agency, offering discounted fares worldwide. Profits are used to support projects in the developing world, especially the promotion of sustainable tourism.

STA Travel UK **T** 0871 2300 040, US **T** 1 800 781 4040, Australia **T** 134 782, New Zealand **T** 0800 474 400, South Africa **T** 0861 781 781; **W** statravel.com. Worldwide specialists in independent travel; also student IDs, travel insurance, car rental, rail passes and more. Good discounts for students and under-26s.

Trailfinders UK **T** 0845 058 5858, Ireland **T** 01 677 7888, Australia **T** 1300 780 212; **W** trailfinders.com. One of the best-informed and most efficient agents for independent travellers.

Travel Cuts Canada **T** 1 866 246 9762, US **T** 1 800 592 2887; **W** travelcuts.com. Canadian youth and student travel firm.

USIT Ireland **T** 01 602 1906, Northern Ireland **T** 028 9032 7111; **W** usit.ie. Ireland's main student and youth travel specialist tour operator.

A BETTER KIND OF TRAVEL

At Rough Guides we are passionately committed to travel. We believe it helps us understand the world we live in and the people we share it with – and of course tourism is vital to many developing economies. But the scale of modern tourism has also damaged some places irreparably, and climate change is accelerated by most forms of transport, especially flying. All Rough Guides' flights are carbon-offset, and every year we donate money to a variety of environmental charities.

ADVENTURE TOUR SPECIALISTS

Adventure Center US **T** 1 800 228 8747, **W** adventurecenter .com. Hiking and "soft adventure". Offers a wide range of Argentina tours.

Adventures Abroad US & Canada **T** 1 800 665 3998, **W** adventures-abroad.com. Adventure specialist offering mainly cultural tours to Argentina, combined with Chile or Brazil.

Contours Australia **T** 1300 135 391, **W** contourstravel.com.au. Specialists in tailored city stopover packages and tours, including self-drive tours through the Lake District and Mendoza wine tours.

Dragoman UK **T** 0870 499 4478, **W** dragoman.co.uk. Extended overland journeys; shorter camping and hotel-based safaris, too.

Exodus UK **T** 0870 240 5550, **W** exodus.co.uk. Adventure-tour operator taking small groups for specialist programmes, including walking, biking, overland, adventure and cultural trips. Among its tours is a three-week Fitz Roy and Torres del Paine trip.

Explore Worldwide UK **T** 01252 760 000, **W** explore.co.uk. Small-group tours, treks, expeditions and safaris. Offers three-week tours of the fjords and Patagonia.

Journey Latin America UK **T** 020 8747 3108, **W** journeylatin america.co.uk. Specialist in flights, packages and tailor-made trips to Latin America, including a two-week Salta hiking and biking trip.

Tucan Travel UK **T** 020 8896 1600, **W** tucantravel.com. Group holidays in Argentina, plus a range of overland expeditions in the rest of South America.

Wilderness Travel US **T** 1 800 368 2794, **W** wildernesstravel .com. Specialist in hiking, cultural and wildlife adventures. Offers tours of Mendoza, the Northwest and Patagonia.

Wildlife Worldwide UK **T** 020 8667 9158, **W** wildlifeworldwide .com. Tailor-made trips for wildlife and wilderness enthusiasts. Nineteen-day southern Patagonia and Iguazú trip.

World Expeditions UK **T** 020 8870 2600, **W** worldexpeditions .co.uk; Australia **T** 1300 720 000, **W** worldexpeditions.com.au. Australian-owned adventure company whose trips include an Aconcagua ascent for hardcore adventurers and special tours for travellers over 55.

Getting around

Distances are immense in Argentina, and you are likely to spend a considerable portion of your budget on travel. Ground transport (mostly bus) is best for giving a true impression of the scale of the country and for appreciating the landscape. However, you may want to cover some big legs, particularly to and around Patagonia, in which case travelling by domestic flights can often save a day or more. The inter-city bus network is extensive but services in remote areas can be poor and infrequent; in these places, it is worth considering car rental. Train services are run-down and limited and not generally a viable method of getting around.

By bus

By far the most common and straightforward method of transport in Argentina is the **bus** (*omnibus*, *bus* or *micro*). There are hundreds of private companies, most of which concentrate on one particular region, although a few, such as TAC and Cruz del Sur, run essentially nationwide.

Many buses are modern, plush Brazilian-built models designed for long-distance travel. Breakdowns do happen, but in general your biggest worry will be what movie the driver has chosen to "entertain" you with (usually subtitled Hollywood action flicks, played with the sound either turned off or at thunderous volume). On longer journeys, snacks and even hot meals are served (included in the ticket price), although these vary considerably in quality and tend towards sweet-toothed tastes. *Coche cama*, *ejecutivo* and *pullman* are the luxury services, with wide, fully reclinable seats; *semi-cama* services are not far behind in terms of seat comfort. These services usually cost twenty to forty percent more than the *común* (regular) services, but are well worth the extra, particularly over long distances. On minor routes, you'll have less choice of buses, though most are decent with plenty of legroom. Many services turn the air conditioning up beyond most people's levels of endurance; take a sweater on board.

Buying tickets (*boletos*) is normally a simple on-the-spot matter, but you must plan in advance if travelling in the high season (mid-Dec to Feb) or around long weekends, especially if you're taking a long-distance bus from Buenos Aires or any other major city to a particularly popular holiday destination. In these cases you should buy your ticket two to three days beforehand; note that prices rise during peak times. Some destinations have both direct (*directo* or *rápido*) and slower services that stop at all intermediary points, and though most services call into the bus terminal (*terminal de omnibus*), this is not always the case: some drop you on the road outside the centre. Similarly, when heading to Buenos Aires, check that the bus goes to **Retiro**, the central bus terminal (see p.105).

There's usually some kind of **left-luggage office** (*guardamaleta* or *guardaequipaje*) at terminals, or, if you have a few hours to kill between connections, the company with whom you have your onward ticket will usually store your pack free of charge, enabling you to look around town unencumbered.

If you are planning to travel a lot by bus, it may be worth investing in a **South Pass**, which allows unlimited travel in the Southern Cone and Andean countries over a set number of days, though you will have to be clocking up quite a few miles to make it worthwhile, with prices starting at US\$80 per trip and a minimum of five trips (☎011 4724 7878, ⊛argentinabybus.com).

By air

Argentina's most important domestic **airport** is Buenos Aires' Aeroparque Jorge Newbery, which has **flights** to all the country's provincial capitals and major tourist centres. People who want to get an overview of Argentina's tremendous variety in a limited time may rely heavily on domestic flights to combat the vast distances involved – what takes twenty or more hours by bus might take only one or two by plane. As a rule, you'll find **prices** are the same whether you buy your ticket direct from the airline office or from the plentiful travel agencies in most towns and cities. Availability can be a problem on tourist routes such as those around Patagonia or during the holidays, and if these feature in your itinerary you are advised to book as far in advance as possible. Some deals booked in advance are good value, although non-residents usually pay a considerably higher tariff than Argentines. Domestic **departure taxes** are always included in the price of the ticket.

Aerolíneas Argentinas (☎0810 2228 6527, ⊛aerolineas.com.ar) is the national flag carrier, with the biggest destination network. The company has faced many problems over the past decade or so and its once excellent reputation has been tarnished, but in many places it will be your only option. Its main rival in Argentina these days is Chilean flag carrier **LAN** (☎0810 999 9526, ⊛lan .com), which has an Argentine subsidiary (LAN Argentina) operating flights to the country's major tourist destinations.

The military also provides civilian services – the Air Force's **LADE** (☎0810 810 5233, ⊛lade.com.ar) is one of the cheapest methods of travel in the country and flies to isolated, often unexpected places, mostly destinations in Patagonia. However, routings can be convoluted, and you might find a flight stops four or five times between its original departure point and final destination. Timetables change frequently (up to once a month) and services can be cancelled at the last moment if the Air Force needs the plane. That said, it's worth asking at LADE offices as you travel round just in case they've something useful.

Other small airlines in operation are Salta-based Andes (☎0810 7772 6337, ⊛andesonline.com), which connects the city with several destinations, including Buenos Aires and Iguazú, and Sol (☎0810 444 765, ⓦsol.com.ar), a Rosario-based low-cost airline that serves destinations in the centre of the country such as Córdoba and Santa Fe, as well as some coastal and Uruguayan destinations.

One factor to bear in mind is the possible disruption caused by **volcanic eruptions** in the Andes. Huge clouds of ash billowed out of a Chilean volcano throughout much of 2011, showering grit and dust onto the Lake District and causing havoc farther afield. Bariloche airport was closed for several months while other airports around the country, including both of the capital's, were repeatedly shut down as a precaution, sometimes for a couple of days at a time.

By car

You are unlikely to want or need a **car** for your whole stay in Argentina, but you'll find one pretty indispensable if you want to explore some of the more isolated areas of Patagonia, Tierra del Fuego, the Northwest, Mendoza or San Juan. If possible, it makes sense to get a group together, not just to keep costs down but also to share the driving, which can be arduous and potentially dangerous, especially on unsealed roads. Approximately thirty percent of roads are paved in Argentina, but some of the less important of these routes are littered with potholes. Unsealed roads can be extremely muddy after rain, and may be impassable, even to 4WDs, after prolonged wet spells. A 4WD is not usually

necessary, but can be useful on minor roads in mountainous areas, when you're likely to encounter snow, or on Ruta 40 in Patagonia. Outside major cities, most accidents (often the most serious ones) occur on unsurfaced gravel roads (*ripio*).

Altitude can also be a problem in the high Andes – you may need to adjust the fuel intake. One thing worth noting: flashing your lights when driving is a warning to other vehicles *not* to do something, as opposed to the British system, where it is used to signal concession of right of way. You can be fined for not wearing **seatbelts** (both in the front and back), although many Argentines display a cavalier disregard of this law.

Car rental

To **rent a car**, you need to be over 21 (25 with some agencies) and hold a driver's licence – an international one is not usually necessary. Bring a credit card and your passport for the **deposit**. Before you drive off, check that you've been given insurance, tax and ownership papers, check carefully for dents and paintwork damage and get hold of a 24hr emergency telephone number. Also, pay close attention to the small print, most notably what you're liable for in the event of an accident: the list of people with grievances after renting a car and spending considerably more than they intended is a long one. Your insurance will not normally cover you for flipping the car, or smashed windscreens or headlights.

Car-rental **costs** are relatively high in Argentina, though rates between different agencies can vary

---

DRIVING ON DIRT ROADS

Driving on gravel is much like driving on snow – fine in a straight line but difficult on bends or when braking. To keep safe, stick to the Highway Code and follow this **advice**:

- On unpaved sections, follow the most recently used tracks and never exceed 70km/hr (you'll often creep along at 40km/hr).
- Slow down and move as far right as possible when approaching an oncoming vehicle to avoid windscreen or headlight damage.
- Overtake with caution – dust and stones thrown up will obscure visibility.
- Go downhill in a low gear – the rear will skid if you go too fast.
- Slow down in strong winds, especially crosswinds – in a high-clearance 4WD the wind may get underneath – and be careful opening doors, as they can be wrenched from their hinges.
- Give help if you see someone has broken down: offering to give them a lift or taking a message to the next town could be vital.
- Refuel whenever you see a pump – the next may be hundreds of kilometres away.
- Take plenty of provisions with you (especially drinking water), plus warm clothing in case you are stranded overnight.
- Always allow more time than you need to get from A to B, as the distances are huge.

ADDRESSES

Addresses are nearly always written with the street name followed by the street number – thus, San Martín 2443; with avenues (avenidas), the abbreviation "**Av**" or "**Avda**" appears before the name – thus, Av San Martín 2443. The relatively rare abbreviation "**c/**" for calle (street) is used only to avoid confusion in a city that has streets named after other cities: thus c/Tucumán 564, Salta or c/Salta 1097, Tucumán. If the name is followed by "**s/n**" (sin número), it means the building is numberless, frequently the case in small villages and for larger buildings such as hotels or town halls. Sometimes streets whose names have been officially changed continue to be referred to by their former names, even in written addresses. In most cities, **blocks** (*cuadras*) go up in 100s, making it relatively easy to work out on a map where a hotel at no. 977 or a restaurant at no. 2233 is located.

considerably. Small, local firms often give very good deals – up to half the price of the global rental names – and it doesn't necessarily hold that the local branch of an international agency will be up to the standards you expect. The main cities offer the most economical prices, while costs are highest in Patagonia; **unlimited mileage** deals are usually your best option, as per-kilometre charges can otherwise exceed your daily rental cost many times over. Unfortunately, there are relatively few places in Argentina where you can rent a vehicle and drop it in another specified town without being clobbered with a high relocation fee. Book as early as possible if you're travelling in high season to popular holiday destinations, as demand usually outstrips supply. It's fairly straightforward to take a vehicle into **Chile** but it is essential to have the correct paperwork from the rental firm. Many provide this free of charge, particularly those in towns near the border.

If you plan to do a lot of driving, consider a membership with the **Automóvil Club Argentino (ACA)**, which has a useful **emergency breakdown** towing and repair service and offers discounts at a series of lodges across the country (many of which are in need of an overhaul). You can join in Buenos Aires at Av del Libertador 1850 (Mon–Fri 10am–6pm; ☎011 4808 4000, Ⓦaca.org.ar), or at any of the ACA service stations.

Taxis

There are two main types of taxi in Argentina: regular **urban taxis** that you can flag down in the street; and **remises**, or minicab radio taxis, that you must book by phone or at their central booking booth. Urban taxis are fitted with meters – make sure they use them – and each municipality has its own rates. *Remises* operate with rates fixed according to the destination and are less expensive than taxis for out-of-town and long-distance trips. Often, it makes more sense to hire a *remise* for a day than to rent your own car: it can be more economical, you save

yourself the hassle of driving and you'll normally get the sights pointed out for you along the way.

In some places, **shared taxis** (*taxis colectivos*) also run on fixed routes between towns: they wait at a given collection point, each passenger pays a set fee and the *colectivos* leave when full (some carry destination signs on their windscreen, others don't, so always ask around). They often drop you at a place of your choice at the other end, making them a faster and more convenient alternative to buses, often for only marginally more money. *Taxis colectivos* also drive up and down fixed routes within certain cities: flag one down and pay your share (usually posted on the windscreen).

By boat

Boat services in Argentina fall into two broad categories: those that serve as a functional form of transport, and (with some overlap) those that you take to enjoy tourist sights. The two **ferry services** you are most likely to use are the comfortable ones from Buenos Aires to Colonia del Sacramento in Uruguay (also served by the speedier hydrofoil) and the much more spartan Chilean ones that transport foot passengers and vehicles across the Magellan Straits into Tierra del Fuego at Punta Delgada and Porvenir. There are also several practical river crossings throughout the Litoral region, connecting towns such as Concordia with Salto in Uruguay and Goya in Corrientes with Reconquista in Santa Fe, as well as numerous crossings from Misiones to neighbouring Paraguay and Brazil. Tigre, just north-west of the capital, tends towards the pleasure-trips end of the market, and offers boat trips around the Delta and to Isla Martín García.

In Patagonia, most **boat trips** are designed purely for their scenic value, including ones that give access to the polar scenery of the Parque Nacional Los Glaciares and the alpine Parque Nacional Nahuel Huapi.

By rail

Argentina's **train network**, developed through British investment in the late nineteenth century and nationalized by the Perón administration in 1948, collapsed in 1993 when government subsidies were withdrawn. The railways are now in a pitiful state, with very little in the way of long-distance services – just a handful in Buenos Aires Province (see p.157 & p.167), which are cheaper than the bus but considerably less savoury. The government has announced a plethora of measures and licences intended to reinvigorate the system and introduce new, modern services, most notably a controversial US$4 billion bullet train connecting Buenos Aires, Rosario and Córdoba, the licence for which has been awarded but which is still on hold indefinitely at the time of writing.

You're far less likely to want to use Argentine trains as a method of getting from place to place, however, than you are to try one of the country's **tourist trains**, where the aim is simply to travel for the fun of it. There are two principal lines: La Trochita (see p.415), the Old Patagonian Express from Esquel; and the Tren a las Nubes (see p.292), one of the highest railways in the world, climbing through the mountains from Salta towards the Chilean border.

Cycling

Most towns with a tourist infrastructure have at least one place that rents out **bicycles** for half- or full-day visits to sights at very reasonable prices. These excursions can be great fun, but remember to bring spare inner tubes and a pump, especially if you're cycling off sealed roads, and check that the brakes and seat height are properly adjusted. Dedicated bike paths are rare, though more are appearing all the time, particularly in Buenos Aires. Don't expect much consideration from other vehicles on the road, though. There are almost no places that rent out **motorbikes**.

Argentina is also a popular destination for more serious cyclists, and expeditions along routes such as the arduous, partly unsurfaced RN-40 attract mountain-biking devotees who often value physical endurance above the need to see sights (most points of interest off RN-40 lie a good way west along branch roads, which deters most people from visiting more than one or two). Trips such as these need to be planned thoroughly, and should only be attempted by experienced expedition cyclists with top-quality equipment and plenty of spares.

Hitchhiking

Hitchhiking always involves an element of risk, but it can also be one of the most rewarding ways to travel, especially if you can speak at least elementary conversational Spanish. It is getting trickier to hitchhike in Argentina: some truck drivers are prohibited by company rules from picking you up, others are reluctant as it often invalidates car insurance or you become the liability of the driver. And in general, it is not advisable for women travelling on their own to hitchhike, or for anyone to head out of large urban areas by hitchhiking: you're far better off catching a local bus out to an outlying service station or road checkpoint and trying from there. In the south of the country, hitching is still generally very safe. In places such as Patagonia, where roads are few and traffic sparse, you'll often find yourself part of a queue, especially in summer. If you do try to hitchhike, always travel with sufficient reserves of water, food, clothes and shelter; you can get stranded for days in some of the more isolated spots.

Accommodation

Accommodation in Argentina runs the gamut from campsites and youth hostels to fabulously luxurious estancias (ranches) and opulent hotels offering every conceivable amenity. Between these two extremes you'll find a whole variety of establishments, including charming old colonial houses with balconies and dark and seedy hotels that lack so much as a window. Informal room rental is also common in towns with seasonal influxes of tourists but too few hotels to cope.

Prices vary considerably depending on where you are in the country. Areas receiving large numbers of foreign visitors, particularly Buenos Aires and Patagonia, have seen prices rise sharply in recent years; less-visited areas offer less variety but also much better bargains. Even in the capital, however, you can expect to pay slightly less for comparable accommodation than you would in most European countries or North America. Single travellers on a budget and seeking more privacy than is available at a youth hostel will find things harder, although the number of places offering per-person prices appears to be on the rise, especially at resorts and estancias where meals or activities are included. Discounts can sometimes be negotiated, particularly if you are staying for a longer period. Bear in mind that taxes are often not included in quoted prices, while places aimed at foreigners may quote in US$ rather than pesos. If paying with cash dollars, you may be able to strike a deal on the exchange rate (see "Costs", p.44).

Hotels

Most towns in Argentina will have at least one **hotel**, though in many places these are unimaginative, rather drab places. If you are on a budget, and the option is available, you might do better to head for a hostel, most of which provide good-value private rooms as well as dorms. Posadas and bed and breakfasts can be more attractive in the middle of the range, while small boutique or designer hotels – which have popped up in significant numbers in Argentina in the last few years – often have a lot more individuality than the standard plush but monotonous five-star places aimed at business travellers.

Posadas, hosterías and B&Bs

The use of the term **posada** usually denotes a fairly idiosyncratic place, often with a slightly rustic feel, but generally comfortable or even luxurious. In a similar vein, the term **hostería** is frequently used for smallish, upmarket hotels – oriented towards tourists rather than businessmen.

A similar type of accommodation, particularly common around Buenos Aires, is **B&Bs** (the English term is used), which tend to be chic, converted townhouses with an exclusive but cosy atmosphere – price-wise they tend to be mid- to top-range options, and generally offer far more attractive surroundings than standard hotels at the same price.

Hostels

Youth hostels are known as *albergues juveniles* or *albergues de la juventud* in Argentina, though the term "(youth) hostel" is frequently used instead – *albergue* is normally taken to mean *albergue transitorio* (short-stay hotels where rooms are rented by the hour). There is an extensive chain of mostly reliable hostels in Argentina affiliated with Hostelling International (HI), as well as a good number of independent hostels, which vary more in quality, but when they are good – particularly in Buenos Aires, Mendoza and Salta – they are among the country's best. Accommodation is generally in **dormitories**, though most

places also have several double **rooms**, often en suite. Facilities vary, too, from next to nothing to swimming pools, internet access, washing machines, cable TV and patios with barbecue equipment.

Note you sometimes see the term "**hostal**" used as a seemingly general term for hotels – both youth hostels and high-rise modern hotels call themselves *hostales*.

Youth hostel associations

The local office of Hostelling International is in Buenos Aires, at Florida 835 (☎011 4511 8723, ⓦ hostels.org.ar). Associated hostels give discounts – usually a few pesos a night – to holders of HI cards but they rarely require that you possess a card in order to stay there. Membership for non-Argentines is US$20 a year, and also gives you discounts with some bus companies and other businesses.

Residenciales and hospedajes

Basic **hospedajes** and **residenciales** have low prestige in Argentina and often are not recommended by tourist offices, but they can be far more welcoming, clean and secure than one-star hotels; a few of them stand out as some of Argentina's best budget accommodation. Furnishings tend to be basic, with little more than a bed, perhaps a desk and chair and a fan in each room – though some are far less spartan than others and there is even the odd one with cable TV. Most places offer private bathrooms. There's little difference between *residenciales* and *hospedajes* – indeed, the same establishment may be described in different accommodation lists as both, or even as a hotel or hostel. The only real difference is that *hospedajes* tend to be part of a family house.

Estancias

A very different experience to staying in a hotel is provided by Argentina's many **estancias** (ranches, or **fincas** as they are known in the North) that are open to visitors. Guests usually stay in the *casco*, or farmhouse, which can be anything from a simple family home to an extravagant castle-like residence. Estancias are nearly always family-run, the income from tourism tending to serve as a supplement to the declining profits earned from the land itself. Accommodation is generally luxurious, with bags of character, and a stay is a mini-vacation in itself; for about US$300–700 a day you are given four meals, invariably including a traditional *asado*, with activities such as horseriding and swimming also usually part of the price. Many places offer experiences that reflect the local area, from cattle herding and branding in the pampas to wine tasting at Mendoza to observing caymans in the Litoral.

You can **book** your estancia accommodation either by approaching them directly or through certain travel agencies; a comprehensive one in Buenos Aires is Estancias Argentinas, at Roque Sáenz Peña 616, 9th floor (☏011 4343 2366, ⓦestanciasargentinas.com).

Cabañas

Popular in resort towns, self-catering *cabañas* are small, chalet-style buildings that can vary from miniature suburban villas with cable TV and micro-waves to pleasingly simple and rustic wooden constructions. If you have been staying in a lot of hotels or doing some hardcore camping, *cabañas* can be fun and relaxing places to take a break for a few days. They are often very good value for money for small groups, although a few of the simpler ones can also be surprisingly affordable options for couples or even single travellers. They are usually grouped together in outfits of between two and ten cabins; many campsites also offer basic ones as an alternative to tents.

Camping

There are plenty of places to camp throughout Argentina, with most towns and villages having their own municipal **campsites** (*campings*), but standards vary wildly. At the major resorts, there are usually plenty of privately owned, well-organized sites, with facilities ranging from provisions stores to volleyball courts and TV rooms. Some are attrac-tive, but mostly they seem to take the fun out of camping and you're more likely to wake up to a view of next door's 4WD than the surrounding countryside. They are, however, good places to meet other travellers and generally offer a high degree of security. There are also simpler campsites, though at nearly all of them showers, electric light and barbecue facilities are standard. A campsite with no, or very limited, facilities is referred to as a *camping libre*. Municipal sites can be rather desolate and sometimes not particularly safe: it's usually a good idea to check with locals as to the security of the place before pitching a tent. The price and pricing system vary greatly from place to place but expect to pay around $30–70 per person; the price given is usually per person pitching your own tent, unless otherwise specified.

Food and drink

Argentine food can be summed up by one word: beef. And not just any beef, but the best in the world – succulent, cherry-red and healthy, meat raised on some of the greenest, most extensive pastures known to cattle. The asado, or barbecue, is an institution, every bit a part of the Argentine way of life as football, fast driving and tango.

Where to eat

Apart from generic *restaurantes* (or *restoranes*), you will come across *parrillas* (for steak and beef), *maris-querías* (for seafood), *confiterías* (cafés for coffee, cakes, snacks or simple meals), *comedores* (simple local canteens), *pizzerías*, *bodegones* (unpretentious restaurants that theoretically serve a house wine) and *cantinas* (neighbourhood places often dishing up Italian food, such as home-made pasta). By South American standards the quality of restaurants is high, and though by international standards they are not always cheap, they often represent good value. If you're on a tight budget make lunch your main meal, and take advantage of the **menú del día** or **menú ejecutivo** – usually set meals for about $60 – and in the evening try **tenedor libre** restaurants where you can eat as much as you like for a set price at self-service buffets. Up your budget to $120 or so a head and you can dine à la carte at most mid-range restaurants, wine included. Argentina also has a fair sprinkling of gourmet locales (*restaurantes de autor*), concentrated in, but by no means limited to, Buenos Aires. In these your per-head bill will be more like $200 or even more, though this still compares well with cities in other industrialized countries and you get fabulous food, wine, ambience and service. You should try and splash out at least once during your visit.

When to eat

Breakfast is usually served up until around 10am, and **lunch** from around noon until 3pm. Hardly any restaurant opens for **dinner** before 8pm, and in the hotter months – and all year round in Buenos Aires – few people turn up before 10 or even 11pm. Don't be surprised to see people pouring into restaurants well after midnight: Argentines, and Porteños in particular, are night owls. If you think you're going to be starving by 7pm, do like the locals and either have a hearty lunch or take merienda – tea and snacks – at a café or *confitería* in the late afternoon.

What to eat

While beef is the most prominent feature on many menus, it's by no means the whole story. In general, you seldom have a bad meal in Argentina. That said, imagination, innovation and a sense of subtle flavour are sometimes lacking, with Argentines preferring to eat the wholesome but often bland dishes their immigrant forebears cooked. At the other end of the spectrum, there is some very (some might say overly) inventive *cordon bleu* cooking being concocted by daring young chefs across the country. Fast food is extremely popular, but you can also snack on delicious local specialities such as empanadas or home-made pizza if you want to avoid the ubiquitous multinational chains.

Snacks

If you're feeling peckish during the day there are plenty of **minutas** (snacks) to choose from. The **lomito** (as opposed to *lomo* – the name of the steak cut itself) is a nourishing sandwich filled with a juicy slice of steak, often made with delicious **pan árabe** (pitta bread); the **chivito** (originally Uruguayan) refers to a similar kind of sandwich made with a less tender cut, though it literally means "kid", or baby goat. Other street food includes the **choripán**, a local version of the hot dog made with natural meaty sausages (*chorizos*), while at cafés a popular snack is the **tostado** (or *tostado mixto*), a toasted cheese and ham sandwich, often daintily thin and sometimes (in the provinces) called a *carlitos*. **Barrolucas** are beef and cheese sandwiches, a local variant on the cheeseburger, and very popular around Mendoza. **Milanesas** refer to breaded veal escalopes served in a sandwich, hamburger-style. **Empanadas** are small pastries with savoury fillings, usually stuffed with beef, cheese and/or vegetables, although the fillings are as varied as the cook's imagination.

Parrillas, pizza and pasta

Parrillas, pizza and pasta are the mainstays of Argentine cuisine, both at home and in restaurants. **Parrillas** are simply barbecues (or the restaurants

---

ASADO BASICS

The term **asado** (from *asar*, to roast) originally referred specifically to a particular cut of beef, the brisket, meant to be slowly grilled or roasted, but now is applied to any **barbecued meat**. Since barbecues are an integral part of life in Argentina, it's good to know your way around the vocabulary of beef-eating, especially as beef in Argentina isn't cut in the same way as in the rest of the world – cuts are sliced through bone and muscle rather than across them.

Argentines like their meat **well done** (*cocido*), and indeed, some cuts are better cooked through. If you prefer your meat medium, ask for *a punto*, and for rare – which really requires some insistence – *jugoso*. Before you get to the steaks, you'll be offered **achuras**, or offal, and different types of sausage. **Chorizos** are excellent beef sausages, while **morcilla**, blood sausage, is an acquired taste. Sometimes **provoletta**, sliced provolone cheese, grilled on the barbecue till crispy on the edges, will be on the menu. Otherwise, it's beef all the way.

After these "appetizers" – which you can always skip, since Argentine *parrillas* are much more meat-generous than their Brazilian counterparts – you move on to the **asado** cut, followed by the **tira de asado** (ribs; also called *costillar* or *asado a secas*). There's not much meat on them, but they explode with a meaty taste. Next is the muscly but delicious **vacío** (flank). But save some room for the prime cuts: **bife ancho** is entrecôte; **bife angosto** or **lomito** is the sirloin (referred to as **medallones** when cut into slices); **cuadril** is a lump of rumpsteak, often preferred by home barbecue masters; **lomo**, one of the luxury cuts and often kept in reserve, is fillet steak; **bife de chorizo** (not to be confused with *chorizo* sausage) is what the French call a *pavé*, a slab of meat, cut from either the sirloin or entrecôte. The **entraña**, a sinewy cut from inside the beast, is a love-it-or-hate-it cut; aficionados claim it's the main delicacy. Rarely barbecued, the **peceto** (eye round steak) is a tender lump of flesh, often braised (*estufado*) and served on top of pasta, roasted with potatoes (*peceto al horno con papas*) or sliced cold for *vittel tonne* – a classic Argentine starter made with tuna and mayonnaise.

Mustard (*mostaza*) may be available, but the lightly salted meat is usually best served with nothing on it but the traditional condiments of **chimichurri** – olive oil shaken in a bottle with salt, garlic, chilli pepper, vinegar and bay leaf – and **salsa criolla**, similar but with onion and tomato as well; everyone jealously guards their secret formulas for both these "magic" dressings.

that employ them) where you can try the traditional *asado* (see box, p.33). Usually there's a set menu (the **parrillada**), though the establishments themselves vary enormously. At many, especially in big cities, the decor is stylish, the staff laidback, the crockery delicate and the meat served tidily. Elsewhere, especially in smaller towns, *parrillas* are more basic, and you're likely to be served by burly, sweaty grill-men who spend all their time carving hunks of flesh and hurling them onto wooden platters. Portions in *parrillas* are generally very large, intended for sharing, and accompaniments like fries or salad are ordered separately, again served on large platters to share.

Mass immigration from Italy since the middle of the nineteenth century has had a profound influence on Argentine food and drink – the abundance of **fresh pasta** (*pasta casera*) is just one example. The fillings tend to be a little unexciting (lots of cheese, including ricotta, but seldom meat), the sauces are not exactly memorable (mostly tomato and onion) and the pasta itself cooked beyond *al dente*, yet it's a reliable staple and rarely downright bad. **Pizzas** are very good on the whole, though the toppings tend to lack originality, especially away from the capital. One popular ingredient regularly used as a garnish may be unfamiliar to visitors: the **palmito (palm heart)**, a sweet, crunchy vegetable resembling something between asparagus and celery. Argentine pizzas are nearly always of the thick-crust variety, wood-oven baked and very big, meant to be divided between a number of diners.

Regional cuisine

Although you will find *parrillas* throughout Argentina, different regions have their own specialities, too. Probably the most noteworthy regional cuisine is found in the Argentine **Northwest**, where as well as the juiciest empanadas, you can find *humitas* – steamed creamed sweetcorn, served in parcels made from corncob husks, and *locro*, a substantial stew based on maize, with onions, beans and meat thrown in. **Andean** *quinoa* is a frequent ingredient in everything from soups to empanadas. **Patagonia**, meanwhile, is famed for its barbecued lamb, staked around the fire, and jams made from local fruit such as *calafate*.

Other cuisines

In addition to the Italian cooking available all over the country, **Spanish** restaurants serve tapas and familiar dishes such as *paella*, while specifically Basque restaurants are also fairly commonplace; these are often the places to head for fish or seafood. **Chinese** and, increasingly, **Korean** restaurants are found in many Argentine cities, but they rarely serve anything remotely like authentic Asian food and specialize in *tenedor libre* buffet diners. You can find excellent **sushi and Peruvian food** in Buenos Aires, where nearly every national cuisine from Armenian to Vietnamese via Mexican, Polish and Thai is also available, but such variety is rare in the provinces.

Arab and **Middle Eastern** food, including specialities such as kebabs and *kepe*, seasoned ground raw meat, is far more widespread, as is **German** fare, such as sauerkraut (*chucrút*) and frankfurters, along with Central and Eastern European food, often served in *choperías*, or beer gardens. **Welsh tearooms** are a speciality of Patagonia.

Vegetarian food

As a **vegetarian** in Argentina you shouldn't have too many problems in the capital, the larger cities or the Patagonian resorts, all of which are relatively cosmopolitan. A number of **restaurants** completely dedicated to non-meat-eaters do exist and many places have a few good non-meat alternatives. The exceptions are the *parrillas*, though the sight and smell of entire animals roasting on the grill is unlikely to appeal to vegetarians anyway.

In the smaller provincial towns, however, vegetarian fare tends to be a lot simpler and you will likely have to adjust to a diet of pizza, pasta, empanadas and salads, with very little variety in the toppings and fillings. The good news is that these fillings are often options such as spinach, **acelga** (Swiss chard – similar to spinach, but slightly more bitter) and ricotta. Other foods to keep an eye out for are **fainá**, a fairly bland but agreeable Genovese speciality made with chickpea dough, and **milanesas de soja** (breaded soya "cutlets") while *milanesas* of vegetables like **berenjena** (aubergine) and **calabaza** (pumpkin) are also quite popular.

When all the cheese gets a bit much, look out for the popular Chinese-ish *tenedor libres*, which usually feature a good smattering of veggies, as do Middle Eastern restaurants. Another possibility would be to self-cater – supermarkets are usually fairly well stocked with vegetables, seasonings and soy products.

You should always check the ingredients of a dish before ordering, as the addition of small amounts of meat is not always referred to on menus. Don't be surprised if your "*no como carne*" (I don't eat meat) is dismissed with a glib "*no tiene mucha*" (It doesn't contain much) and be particularly on your guard for the seemingly ever-present **jamón** (ham).

Vegans will have a hard time outside of Buenos Aires, as pretty much everything that doesn't contain meat contains cheese or pastry. Waiters will rarely be familiar with veganism, but will usually try to accommodate your requests.

Desserts

Argentines have a fairly sweet tooth and love anything with sugar, especially *dulce de leche* (see box below). Even breakfast tends to be dominated by sweet things such as sticky croissants (*medialunas*) or **chocolate con churros**, Andalucían-style hot chocolate with fritters, sometimes filled with *dulce de leche*. All kinds of cakes and biscuits, including *alfajores* (maize-flour cookie sandwiches, filled with jam or *dulce de leche*, sometimes coated with chocolate), pastries called **facturas** and other candies and sweets are popular with Argentines of all ages.

However, for dessert you'll seldom be offered anything other than the tired trio of **flan** (a kind of crème caramel, religiously served with a thick custard or *dulce de leche*), **budín de pan** (a syrupy version of bread pudding) and fresh fruit salad (*ensalada de fruta*). In Andean regions, or in *criollo* eateries, you'll most likely be served **dulce vigilante**, a slab of neutral, pallid cheese called *quesillo* eaten with candied fruit such as sweet potato (*batata*), quince (*membrillo*), (*al*)*cayote* (a kind of spaghetti squash), pumpkin (*zapallo*) or lime (*lima*). *Panqueques*, or crêpes, are also popular.

With such a large Italian community it is not surprising that superb *helado* (**ice cream**) is easy to come by in Argentina. Even the tiniest village has at least one *heladería artesanal*. If you're feeling really self-indulgent you might like to have your cone dipped in chocolate (*bañado*). Some of the leading ice-cream makers offer an overwhelming range of flavours (*sabores*). Chocolate chip (*granizado*) is

a favourite, and raspberry mousse (*mousse de frambuesa*) is also delicious.

Drinks

Fizzy drinks (*gaseosas*) are popular with people of all ages and often accompany meals. All the big brand names are available, along with local brands such as Paso de los Toros, which makes tonic water and fizzy grapefruit (*pomelo*) drinks. You will often be asked if you want **mineral water** – either still (*agua sin gas*) or carbonated – (*agua con gas* or *soda*) – with your meal, but you can ask for **tap water** (*agua de la llave*), which is safe to drink in most places, though this may raise eyebrows. Although little is grown in the country, good **coffee** is easy to come by. You will find very decent espressos, or delicious *café con leche*, in most cafés. **Tea** is usually made from teabags; Argentine tea is strong rather than subtle, and is served with either milk or lemon. **Herbal teas** (*infusiones*) are all the rage, camomile (*manzanilla*) being the most common. **Mate** is a whole world unto itself and is explained, along with the etiquette and ritual involved, on p.229. **Fruit juices** (*jugos*) and **shakes** (*licuados*) can be excellent, though freshly squeezed orange juice is often sold at ridiculously high prices.

Beer

Argentina's **beer** is more thirst-quenching than alcoholic and mostly comes as fairly bland lager, with Quilmes dominating the market and Heineken producing a big-selling beer in the country; imported brands are fairly common in the cities, though more expensive. Regional brews are sometimes worth trying: in Mendoza, the Andes brand crops up all over, while Salta's own brand is also good, and a kind of stout (*cerveza negra*)

DULCE DE LECHE

Dulce de leche, a sticky, sweet goo made by laboriously boiling large quantities of vanilla-flavoured milk and sugar until they almost disappear, is claimed by Argentines as a national invention, although similar concoctions are made in Brazil, France and Italy. Something called *manjar* is produced in Chile, but Argentines rightly regard it as far inferior. The thick caramel is eaten with a spoon, spread on bread or biscuits, used to fill cakes, biscuits and fritters or dolloped onto other desserts. Some of the best flavours of ice cream are variations on the *dulce de leche* theme. Although some people still make their own, most people buy it ready-made, in jars. While all Argentines agree that *dulce de leche* is fabulous, there is no consensus on a particular brand: the divisions between those who favour Havanna and those who would only buy Chimbote run almost as deep as those between supporters of Boca Juniors and River Plate. Foreigners are advised to maintain a diplomatic neutrality on the issue.

can sometimes be obtained in the Northwest. **Home-brewed beer** (*cerveza artesanal*) is increasingly available, particularly around Bariloche and El Bolsón, often coming in a surprising array of flavours and served at dedicated bars (*cervecerías*). Usually when you ask for a beer, it comes in large litre bottles, meant for sharing; a small bottle is known as a *porrón*. If you want draught beer ask for a *chopp* (or a *liso* in Santa Fe province).

Wine

The produce of Argentina's **vineyards**, ranging from gutsy plonk to some of the world's prize-winning **wines**, is widely available both in the country and abroad. Most vintages are excellent and not too expensive. Unfortunately, many restaurants still have limited, unimaginative wine lists, which don't reflect Argentina's drift away from mass-produced table wines to far superior single or multi-varietals (for more on wine, see box, p.349). It is also quite difficult to get wine by the glass, and half-bottles too are rare but on the increase. Cheaper wine is commonly made into **sangría** or its fruitier, white wine equivalent, **clericó**.

Spirits

Don't be surprised to see home-grown variants (*nacionales*) of whisky, gin, brandy, port, sherry and rum, none of which is that good; familiar imported brands (*importados*) can be very dear, however. It's far better to stick to the locally distilled **aguardientes**, or firewaters, some of which (from Catamarca, for example) are deliciously grapey. **Fernet Branca** is the most popular, a demonic-looking brew the colour of molasses with a medicinal taste, invariably combined with Coke and consumed in huge quantities – it's generally regarded as the gaucho's favourite tipple.

The media

In terms of newspaper circulation, Argentina is Latin America's most literate nation, and it has a diverse and generally high-quality press. Its television programming is a rather chaotic amalgam of light-entertainment shows and sports, and its radio services tend to fall into one of two categories: urban mainstream commercial channels or amateur ones designed to serve the needs of local rural communities.

Newspapers and magazines

In the past, the fortunes of the print **press** in Argentina have varied greatly, depending on the prevailing political situation. Overbearing state control and censorship characterized much of the twentieth century, but the current situation is much more dynamic, and a resilient streak of investigative journalism provides a constant stream of stories revolving around official corruption. Self-censorship, though, is fairly widespread, and deep criticism of the country's institutions is pretty muted in favour of a generally patriotic stance.

The *Buenos Aires Herald* (Ⓦ buenosairesherald .com) is South America's most prestigious **English-language daily** and dates back to 1876. Although the quality of the writing and editing is a little inconsistent, the *Herald* is useful for getting the low-down on current events in Argentina and for catching up on international news and sports, as it features stories from the wires as well as syndicated articles from the likes of *The New York Times* and Britain's *Independent*. It is still associated in many minds with the old-style Anglo-Argentine elite, but it won international plaudits for its stand on human rights issues in the years of the military dictatorship. The *Herald* is easily available in the capital, but don't expect to find it outside major cities and tourist centres. Look out also for the *Argentina Independent* (Ⓦ argentinaindependent.com), a free monthly English-language publication written by and aimed at young expats and visitors, with articles on aspects of life and travel in Argentina.

If you have some Spanish, the most accessible of the **national dailies** is *Clarín* (Ⓦ clarin.com.ar), the paper with the highest circulation. Despite its mass-market appeal, it is surprisingly highbrow, with politics on page three, followed by a fair-sized economics section, with celebrities usually kept in their place – that is, the "*Espectáculos*" supplement, which also has good listings of what's on. The country's major **broadsheet** is *La Nación* (Ⓦ lanacion .com.ar), the favoured reading of the upper and educated classes. Conservative in some ways, it is also the most international, outward-looking and arguably best written of the Spanish-language newspapers. At the other extreme, *Página 12* (Ⓦ pagina12.com.ar) is a left-leaning paper, originally anti-establishment, that has become the Fernández government's biggest fan. Popular with students and intellectuals, it requires a pretty good knowledge of the Spanish language and Argentine politics.

Argentina's **regional press** is also strong, though the quality varies enormously across the country.

A handful of local dailies, such as Mendoza's *Los Andes* (Ⓦlosandes.com.ar), Córdoba's *La Voz del Interior* (Ⓦlavozdelinterior.com.ar) and Rosario's *La Capital* (lacapital.com.ar), are every bit as informative and well-written as the leading national newspapers, and they contain vital information about tourist attractions, cultural events and travel news. Outside Buenos Aires, you pay a supplement for the nationals, and dailies often don't arrive till late in the day.

International publications such as *Time*, *Newsweek*, *The Economist*, the *Miami Herald* and the *Daily Telegraph* are sold at the kiosks on Calle Florida and in Recoleta in Buenos Aires, and at the capital's airports, as are some imported European and US magazines. However, check the cover as they can often be long past their publication date; they are also usually so expensive that unless you're really desperate you're probably better off with the *BA Herald*.

Radio

Argentina's most popular **radio** station, La 100 (99.9FM), plays a fairly standard formula of Latin pop, whereas Rock & Pop (95.9FM) veers, as its name would imply, toward rock and blues. Classical can be heard on Radio Clasica (96.7FM). Neither the **BBC World Service** nor the Voice of America now broadcast on shortwave to Argentina. Towns are blessed with a remarkable number of small-time radio stations, which are listened to avidly by locals, though they're rarely likely to appeal to foreign visitors.

Television

There are five national free-to-air **television stations**, mostly showing a mix of football, soap operas (*telenovelas*) and chat shows. Even if you can't understand much, these shows can provide a fascinating glimpse into certain aspects of society. Cable TV, offering many more channels, is common in many mid-range and even budget hotels; the channels you get depend on the cable provider, but often include CNN or BBC World in English, with a myriad of channels playing movies, sports and (mostly American) TV shows, frequently subtitled. Argentine cable news channels include Clarín's TN (*Telenoticias*) and the unique Crónica, a budget Buenos Aires-based news channel that provides live, unedited coverage of anything that happens in the city; indeed, it is said that the Crónica vans often arrive before the police do.

Festivals

The bulk of Argentina's festivals are found in the Northwest, owing to its attachment to tradition and its high proportion of ethnic communities. Pre-Columbian revivals, Catholic and secular celebrations are observed that are a blend of indigenous and imported customs, so subtly melded that the elements are indistinguishable. On the whole, holidays such as Christmas and Easter are more religious, family-focused occasions than they are in Europe and the US. Although some traditions – such as the European custom of eating chocolate eggs at Easter – are starting to take off, the festivals are generally a lot less commercial, and the run-up to them doesn't start two months beforehand.

What follows is a selective list of some of the major festivals, though wherever you travel you'll come across events celebrating minor saints or local produce; public holidays are observed nationwide (see box, p.53).

A festival calendar

JANUARY

6: Procession in honour of the Virgin Mary, Belén. A pilgrimage procession up to a hilltop statue of the Virgin.
Last week: Festival de Cosquín. Large folklore music festival. A rock music version takes places a couple of weeks later.

FEBRUARY

2: Virgen de Candelaria, Humahuaca.
Early Feb: Fiesta Nacional del Queso, Tafí del Valle. A lively celebration of the country's cheeses.
6: Pachamama festival, Purmamarca and Amaicha. Pachamama, the Mother Earth deity dear to the indigenous peoples of the Northwest, is celebrated in these festivities.
First weekend: Fiesta de la Manzana y la Semilla, Rodeo. A major regional folk festival.
Mid Feb: Feria Artesanal y Ganadera de la Puna, Antofagasta de la Sierra. Vibrant Northwest craft festival.
Five days preceding Ash Wednesday: Carnaval, nationwide. Celebrated throughout Argentina, especially in Gualeguaychú, which hosts the country's premier parades.
Weekend following Shrove Tuesday: Serenata Cafayateña, Cafayate. Popular folk jamboree.

MARCH

First weekend: Fiesta de la Vendimia, Mendoza. Grape harvest festival in the country's main wine region.

17: St Patrick's Day, Buenos Aires. The Irish saint's day, celebrated with much gusto in the capital.

18 & 19: Pilgrimage of Puerta de San José, near Belén. A major pilgrimage, with night vigils and processions, converges on this tiny village.

19: St Joseph's Day, Cachi.

APRIL

Variable (sometimes in March): Semana Santa (Holy Week), nationwide. Celebrated throughout Argentina; highlights include the pilgrimage to El Señor de la Peña, Aimogasta, La Rioja, the procession of the Virgen de Punta Corral, from Punta Corral to Tumbaya, and Maundy Thursday in Yavi.

MAY

4: Santa Cruz celebrations, Uquía.

JUNE

10: Día de las Malvinas, nationwide. Ceremonies to remember the Falklands conflict are held throughout Argentina.

24: St John's Day, Northwest. A major feast day throughout the region.

JULY

25: St James' Day, Humahuaca.

AUGUST

Early Aug: Fiesta Nacional de la Nieve, Bariloche. A five-day festival of snow, with parades, races and evening skiing.

15: Assumption, Casabindo. Festivities culminate in Argentina's only bullfight, a bloodless *corrida*.

Mid-Aug: World Tango Festival, Buenos Aires. Lasting around two weeks, the world's largest tango festival attracts aficionados from all over.

30: Santa Rosa de Lima, Purmamarca.

SEPTEMBER

6–15 Fiesta del Milagro, Salta. Major religious event climaxing in a huge procession.

OCTOBER

Early: Oktoberfest, Villa General Belgrano. For ten days at the beginning of October, Villa General Belgrano is awash with beer in this answer to the famous German festival.

First Sun: Our Lady of the Rosary, Iruya. Highly photogenic masked event that's one of the most fascinating in the Northwest region.

20 (approx): Fiesta de la Ollas, or "Manca Fiesta", La Quiaca. Literally, a "cooking-pot" festival with crafts and music.

NOVEMBER

1 & 2 All Souls' Day and the Day of the Dead, Quebrada de Humahuaca and Antofagasta de la Sierra.

10: Fiesta de la Tradición, San Antonio de Areco. Lively gaucho festival.

DECEMBER

24: Christmas Eve, Buenos Aires. A great time to be in the capital, when the sky explodes with fireworks.

Sports

Argentines suffer an incurable addiction to sport; many go rigid at the thought of even one week without football (soccer), and you'll hear informed and spirited debate in bars on subjects as diverse as tennis, rugby, basketball and the uniquely Argentine equestrian sport of pato.

Football

Ever since two teams of British merchants lined up against each other at the Buenos Aires Cricket Club for a kick-about in 1867, *fútbol* has been an integral part of Argentine identity. The incredible atmosphere generated by the passion of the fans makes attending a match one of the highlights of many people's visits to Argentina, and it is certainly worth setting aside time to do so, even if you're not normally a fan. There are twenty teams in the Primera División, the country's top flight, including the "Big Five": River Plate, Boca Juniors, Independiente, San Lorenzo and Racing Club (all based in Buenos Aires but supported around the country). If you can catch the *super-clásico*, the derby between Boca and River, then you're in for a real treat.

The domestic league's year is split into two **seasons** – allowing for two champions and two sets of celebrations. The first season runs from August to December and is known as the *apertura* (opening); the second, from February to June, is the *clausura* (closing); fixtures are mostly played on Sunday afternoons. In addition, there are two South American club championships – the Copa Libertadores and Copa Sudamericana, roughly equivalent to Europe's UEFA Champions League and Europa League, respectively. These are generally dominated by teams from Argentina, Brazil and Colombia, with a leg played in each country, usually a midweek fixture. If you're lucky, you may even get the chance to see the national side (*la selección*) strutting their stuff in a friendly or World Cup qualifier.

You can usually buy **tickets** at the grounds on match day, although some games sell out in advance, notably the matches between the big five and top-of-the-table clashes. For these, you can get tickets two days before the game at the stadium (be prepared for a scrum) or further in advance for some games from Ticketek (☎ 011 5237 7200, ⓦ ticketek.com.ar). Many Buenos Aires-based tour agencies, hotels and hostels provide a service of ticket and transfer, for a premium.

Tickets for spectators are either in the *popular* or the more expensive *platea*, with the price depending on your vantage point and the game's importance, although it always compares favourably with the cost of European match tickets. The *popular* are the standing-only **terraces**, where the young men, the hardcore home fans, sing and swear their way through the match. This is the most colourful part of the stadium, but it's also the area where you're most likely to be pickpocketed, charged by police or faced with the wrath of the equally hardcore away fans (in the *visitantes* section, where you can often buy the cheapest tickets, though it's standing room only). Unless you're pretty confident, or with someone who is, you may be better off heading to the relative safety of the *platea* **seats**, from where you can photograph the *popular* and enjoy the match sitting down. Don't be surprised if someone's in the seat allocated to you on the ticket – locals pay scant regard to official seating arrangements. After major wins, the Obelisco in central Buenos Aires is the epicentre of raucous **celebrations**.

It's advisable to turn up forty minutes or so before the match in order to avoid the rush, and not to hang around the stadium afterwards, when trouble sometimes brews. Dress down, avoid flaunting the colours of either side and take the minimum of valuables.

Polo and pato

Although it's mainly a game for *estancieros* and wealthy families from Barrio Norte, **polo** is nonetheless far less snobbish or exclusive in Argentina than in Britain or the US; there are some 150 teams and 5000 club members nationwide. You don't need an invitation from a member or a double-barrelled surname to see the world's top polo players; simply turn up and buy a ticket during the open championship in November and December, played at the **Campo de Polo** in Palermo, Buenos Aires. Even if the rules go over your head, the game is exciting and aesthetically pleasing, with hooves galloping over impeccably trimmed grass.

The sport is at least as hard as it looks, but if you're confident on horseback and determined to have a go, many estancias (listed throughout the text) offer lessons as part of their accommodation and activity packages. Alternatively, contact the

Asociación Argentina de Polo at Arévalo 3065, Buenos Aires (☎011 4777 6444, ☻aapolo.com), which can also provide match information.

Less glamorous, the curious sport of **pato** has been played by gauchos since the early 1600s. Named after the trussed duck that once served as the "ball" – a leather version with six handles is now used – pato is a sort of lacrosse on horseback, which also has its national tournament in November and December each year, played at the **Campo Argentino de Pato** in San Miguel, just outside the city limits. For more information on pato and a fixture list, see the national federation's website, ☻pato.org.ar.

Rugby

Argentina's national **rugby** squad, the Pumas, is currently ranked eighth in the world and in 2012 took part in the southern hemisphere Rugby Championship (formerly the Tri Nations) for the first time; this success has seen the sport's popularity rise significantly. You may be able to catch the burly Pumas playing test series at home (all over the country) or in World Cup qualifiers. See the website of the Unión Argentina de Rugby (☻uar.com.ar) for upcoming fixtures.

Outdoor activities

Argentina is a highly exciting destination for outdoors enthusiasts: world-class fly-fishing, horseriding, trekking and rock-climbing opportunities abound, as do options for whitewater rafting, skiing, ice climbing and even – for those with sufficient stamina and preparation – expeditions onto the Southern Patagonian Ice Cap.

Nature tourism

Argentina's network of national and provincial parks offers wonderful opportunities for nature tourism across this country's range of ecosystems (see pp.551–555). **Highlights for wildlife viewing** include the Península Valdés, a superb destination for marine wildlife and fauna of the Patagonian steppe (see p.448), the humid swamplands of Esteros de Iberá (see p.222), and the subtropical jungles of Iguazú (see p.236).

For an overview of the national park system, visit the **National Park Headquarters** in Buenos Aires at Santa Fe 690 (Mon–Fri 10am–5pm; ☎011 4311 0303, Ⓦparquesnacionales.gov.ar). There is an underfunded and not terribly helpful information office on the ground floor that may be able to provide some introductory leaflets, and they can give you tips if you're intending to visit some of the more isolated places like Baritú, Perito Moreno, San Guillermo and Santiago del Estero's Copo, which have limited infrastructure and require some prior planning. A wider range of free material is available at each individual park, but these are of variable quality – many only have a basic map and a brief park description. Each national park has its own **intendencia**, or park administration, although these are often in the principal access town, not within the park itself. An information office or visitors' centre is often attached. Argentina's **guardaparques**, or national park rangers, are some of the most professional on the continent: generally friendly, they are well trained and dedicated to jobs that are demanding and often extremely isolated. All have a good grounding in the wildlife of the region and are happy to share their knowledge, although don't expect them all to be professional naturalists – some are, but ranger duties often involve more contact with the general public than with the wildlife.

A good port of call in the capital for nature enthusiasts is the **Fundación Vida Silvestre**, located at Defensa 251, 6th floor, Buenos Aires (Mon–Fri 10am–1pm & 2–6pm; ☎011 4343 4086, Ⓦvida silvestre.org.ar), a committed and highly professional environmental organization, and an associate of the WWF. Visit its shop for back issues of its beautiful magazine (in Spanish) and for books and leaflets on wildlife and ecological issues, as well as for information on its nature reserves.

Argentina has an incredible diversity of birdlife – you can see some ten percent of all the world's bird species here. **Birdwatchers** should visit the headquarters of the country's well-respected birding organization, **Aves Argentinas**, at Matheu 1246, Buenos Aires (nearest subte station is Pichincha on Linea E; Mon–Fri 10.30am–1.30pm & 2.30–8.30pm; ☎011 4943 7216, Ⓦavesargentinas .org.ar). It has an excellent library and a shop, and organizes regular outings and **birding safaris**.

Trekking

Argentina offers some truly marvellous **trekking**, and it is still possible to find areas where you can trek for days without seeing a soul. Trail quality varies considerably, and many are difficult to follow,

so always get hold of the best **map** available and ask for information as you go; the Club Andino in Bariloche (see p.397) can offer excellent advice, as well as sell you maps. Most of the best treks are in the national parks – especially the ones in Patagonia – but you can often find lesser-known but equally superb options in the lands bordering them. Most people head for the savage granite spires of the **Fitz Roy** region around El Chaltén, an area whose fame has spread so rapidly over the last ten years that it now holds a similar status to Chile's renowned Torres del Paine. Tourist pressures are starting to tell, however, at least in the high season (late Dec to Feb), when campsites are packed. The other principal trekking destination is the mountainous area of **Parque Nacional Nahuel Huapi**, south of Bariloche. This area has the best infrastructure, with a network of generally well-marked trails and mountain refuges. In the north of the country, some of the best trekking is in **Jujuy Province**, especially in Calilegua, where the habitat ranges from subtropical to bald mountain landscape.

Camping is possible in many national parks, and sites are graded according to three categories: *camping libre* sites, which are free but have no or very few services (perhaps a latrine and sometimes a shower block); *camping agreste* sites, which are run as concessions and usually provide hot water, showers, toilets, places for lighting a campfire and some sort of small shop; and *camping organizado* sites, which have more services, including electricity and often some sort of restaurant.

TREKKING ROUTES

Please refer to the following pages in the guide for further information on specific treks and trails:

PROTECTING ARGENTINA'S NATURAL WONDERS

When visiting natural parks and wild areas, always try to be **environmentally responsible**. Stick to marked trails, camp only at authorized sites, take all litter with you (don't burn it), bury toilet waste at least 30m away from all water sources and use detergents and toothpastes as sparingly as possible, choosing biodegradable options such as glycerine soap. Above all, pay particular respect to the fire risk. Every year, fires destroy huge swathes of forest, and virtually all of these are started by hand: some deliberately, but most because of unpardonable negligence. As ever, one of the prime culprits is the cigarette butt, often casually tossed out of a car window, but just as bad are campfires, both those that are poorly tended and those that are poorly extinguished. Woodland becomes tinder-dry in summer droughts, and, especially in places such as Patagonia, it is vulnerable to sparks carried by the strong winds. Once started, winds, inaccessibility and limited water resources can turn fires into infernos that blaze for weeks on end, and much fire-damaged land never regenerates its growth. Many parks have a complete ban on lighting campfires and trekkers are asked to take stoves on which to do their cooking; please respect this. Others ban fires during high-risk periods. The most environmentally responsible approach is to avoid lighting campfires at all: even dead wood has a role to play in often-fragile ecosystems. If you do need to light one, never choose a spot on peaty soil, as peat, once it has caught, becomes virtually impossible to put out. Choose a spot on stony or sandy soil, use only fallen wood and always extinguish the fire with water, not earth, stirring up the ashes to ensure all embers are quenched.

You should always be well prepared for your trips, even for half-day hikes. Good-quality, **water- and windproof clothing** is vital: temperatures plummet at night and often with little warning during the day. Keep spare dry layers of clothing and socks in a plastic bag in your pack. **Boots** should provide firm ankle support and have the toughest soles possible (Vibram soles are recommended). Gore-Tex boots will not stay dry when you have to cross swampland. A **balaclava** is sometimes more useful than a woollen hat. Make sure that your **tent** is properly waterproofed and that it can cope with high winds (especially for Patagonia). You'll need a minimum of a three-season sleeping bag, to be used in conjunction with a solid or semi-inflatable foam mattress (essential, as the ground will otherwise suck out all your body heat). Also bring high-factor **sunblock** and lipsalve, plus good **sunglasses** and headgear.

Park authorities often require you to carry a **stove** for cooking. The Camping Gaz models that run on butane cylinders (refills are fairly widely available in *ferretería* hardware shops) are not so useful in exposed areas, where you're better off with a high-pressure petrol stove such as an MSR, although these are liable to clog with impurities in the fuel, so filter it first. Telescopic hiking poles save your knees from a lot of strain and are useful for balance. Miner-style head **torches** are preferable to regular hand-held ones, and gaffer tape makes an excellent all-purpose emergency repair tool. Carry a **first-aid kit** and a **compass**, and know how to use both. And always carry plenty of **water** – aim to have at least two litres on you at all times. Pump-action **water filters** can be very handy, as you can thus avoid the hassle of having to boil suspect water.

Note also that, in the national parks, especially on the less-travelled and overnight routes, you should inform the **park ranger** (*guardaparque*) of your plans, not forgetting to report your safe arrival at your destination – the ranger will send a search party out for you if you do not arrive. You'd be advised to buy all your camping equipment before you leave home: quality gear is relatively expensive in Argentina, and there are few places that rent decent equipment, even in some of the key trekking areas.

Climbing

For **climbers**, the Andes offer incredible variety. You do not always have to be a technical expert, but you should always take preparations seriously. You can often arrange a climb close to the date – though it's best to bring as much high-quality gear with you as you can. The climbing season is fairly short – November to March in some places, though December to February is the best time. The best-known challenge is South America's highest peak, **Aconcagua** (6962m), accessed from the city of Mendoza (see p.356). Not considered the most technical challenge, this peak nevertheless merits top-level expedition status, as the altitude and storms claim several victims a year. Only slightly less lofty are nearby Tupungato (6750m), just to the south; Mercedario (6770m), just to the north; Cerro Bonete (6872m) and Pissis (6793m) on the provincial border between La Rioja and Catamarca; and Ojos del Salado, the highest active volcano in the world (6885m), a little further north into Catamarca. The last three can be climbed from Fiambalá, but Ojos is most normally climbed from the Chilean side of the border. The most famous volcano to climb is the elegant cone of **Lanín** (3776m), which can be ascended in two days via the relatively straightforward northeastern route (see p.430). Parque Nacional Nahuel Huapi, near Bariloche, offers the **Cerro Catedral** massif and **Cerro Tronador** (3554m). Southern Patagonia is also a highly prized climbing destination. One testing summit is **San Lorenzo** (3706m), which, from the Argentine side, can best be approached along the valley of the Río Oro, although the summit itself is usually climbed from across the border in Chile. Further south are the inspirational granite spires of the Fitz Roy massif and Cerro Torre, which have few equals on the planet in terms of technical difficulty and scenic grandeur.

On all of these climbs, but especially those over 4000m, make sure to acclimatize thoroughly, and be fully aware of the dangers of *puna*, or altitude sickness (see p.48).

CLIMBING CONTACTS IN ARGENTINA

Centro Andino Buenos Aires Rivadavia 1255, Buenos Aires ☎ 011 4381 1566, ⓦ caba.org.ar. Offers climbing courses, talks and slideshows. Its website has a useful page of links to other Argentine climbing clubs.

Club Andino Bariloche (CAB) 20 de Febrero 30, Bariloche, Río Negro ☎ 02944 422266, ⓦ clubandino.com.ar. The country's oldest and most famous mountaineering club, with excellent specialist knowledge of guides and Patagonian challenges.

Fishing

As a destination for **fly-fishing** (*pesca con mosca*), Argentina is unparallelled, with Patagonia drawing in professionals from around the globe. Trout, introduced in the early twentieth century, is the sport's mainstay, but there is also fishing for landlocked and even Pacific salmon. The most famous places to go are those where the world's largest sea-running brown trout (*trucha marrón*) are found: principally the **Río Grande** and other rivers of eastern and central Tierra del Fuego, and the Río Gallegos on the mainland. The reaches of the Río Santa Cruz near Comandante Luís Piedra Buena have some impressive specimens of steelhead trout (sea-running rainbows, or *trucha arco iris*), and the area around Río Pico is famous for its brook trout. The Patagonian **Lake District** – around Junín de los Andes, San Martín de los Andes, Bariloche and Esquel – is the country's most popular trout-fishing destination, offering superb angling in delightful scenery.

The **trout-fishing season** runs from mid-November to Easter. Regulations change slightly from year to year, but **permits** are valid country-wide. They can be purchased at national park offices, some *guardaparque* posts, tourist offices and at fishing equipment shops, which are fairly plentiful – especially in places like the north Patagonian Lake District. With your permit, you are issued a **booklet** detailing the regulations of the type of fishing allowed in each river and lake in the region, the restrictions on catch-and-release and the number of specimens you are allowed to take for eating. Argentine law states that permit holders are allowed to fish any waters they can reach without crossing private land. You are, in theory at least, allowed to walk along the bank as far as you like from any public road, although in practice you may find that owners of some of the more prestigious beats try to obstruct you from doing this.

For more **information** on fly-fishing in Argentina, contact the Asociación Argentina de Pesca con Mosca, Lerma 452, Buenos Aires (☎ 011 4773 0821, ⓦ aapm.org.ar).

Skiing

Argentina's **ski resorts** are not on the same scale as those of Europe or North America and attract mainly domestic and Latin American tourists (from Chile and Brazil), as well as a smattering of foreigners who are looking to ski during the northern summer. However, infrastructure is constantly being upgraded and it's easy to rent gear. The main **skiing season** is July and August, although in some resorts it is possible to ski from late May to early October. Snow conditions vary from year to year, but you can often find excellent powder.

The most prestigious resort for downhill skiing is modern **Las Leñas** (see p.363), which also offers the most challenging skiing and once hosted World Cup races. Following this are **Chapelco**, near San Martín de los Andes (see p.420), where you also have extensive cross-country options, and the Bariloche resorts of **Cerro Catedral** and **Cerro Otto** (see p.404), which are the longest-running in the country, with wonderful panoramas of the Nahuel Huapi region, albeit with rather too many people. **Ushuaia** (see p.505) is an up-and-coming resort, with some fantastic cross-country possibilities and expanding – if still relatively limited – downhill facilities; the resort's right by the scenic town, so it's a good choice if you want to combine skiing with sightseeing. Bariloche and Las Leñas are the best destinations for those interested in après-ski.

Rafting

Though it does not have the same range of extreme options as neighbouring Chile, Argentina nevertheless has some beautiful **whitewater rafting** possibilities, ranging from grades II to V. Many of these are offered as day-trips, and include journeys through enchanting monkey-puzzle-tree scenery on the generally sedate Río Aluminé (see p.431); along the turbulent and often silty Río Mendoza (p.363); through deep canyons carved by the Río Juramento in Salta (p.286); on the Río Manso in the Alpine-like country south of Parque Nacional Nahuel Huapi; and along the similar but less-visited Río Corcovado, south of Esquel (p.413). Esquel can also be used as a base for rafting on Chile's fabulous, world-famous Río Futaleufú, a turquoise river that flows through temperate rainforest and tests rafters with rapids of grade V. You do not need previous rafting experience to enjoy these, but you should obviously be able to swim. Pay heed to operators' safety instructions, and ensure your safety gear (especially helmets and life-jackets) fits well.

Culture and etiquette

Argentina's mores reflect its overwhelmingly European ancestry, and, apart from getting used to the late dining hours, most travellers from the West will have little trouble fitting in.

Society generally displays a pleasing balance between formal politeness and casual tolerance. When it comes to dress, Argentines are quite conservative, and take great pride in their appearance, but in the bigger cities in particular you will see examples of many different styles and subcultures. Particularly outlandish clothing might raise eyebrows out in the provinces, but probably no more than it would in, say, deepest Wisconsin

or Wiltshire. One area of etiquette that will probably be new to you is the very Argentine custom of drinking *mate*, which comes with its own set of rules (see box, p.229), but foreigners will be given lots of leeway here, as in other areas of social custom – *faux pas* are more likely to cause amusement than offence.

Rules, regulations and bureaucracy

Argentines' rather cavalier attitude towards **rules** and considerations of health and safety is probably the biggest culture shock many foreigners have to deal with; the most obvious example of this is the anarchy you'll see on the roads, but you will also likely come across things such as loose wiring in hotels or wobbly cliff-top fencing. A complaint will probably get you no more than a shrug of the shoulders, though there are signs of a change in attitudes. Many visitors actually find the lack of regulations liberating.

Another difference is the Kafka-esque **bureaucracy** that you will encounter if you're in the country for any length of time – when obtaining a visa, say, or picking up a parcel from the post office. Do not lose your temper if faced with red tape – this will hinder rather than help.

Sexual harassment and discrimination

Women planning on travelling alone to the country can do so with confidence. Some **machista** attitudes do persist but the younger generation seems to be shedding gender differences with alacrity and few people will find it strange that you are travelling unaccompanied. You will probably find you are the target of comments in the street and chat-up lines more frequently than you are accustomed to, but those responsible will not persist if you make it clear you're not interested. Such attentions are almost never hostile or physical – Italian-style bottom pinching is very rare here.

Greetings

When **greeting** people or taking your leave, it is normal to kiss everyone present on the cheek (just once, always the right cheek), even among men, who may emphasize their masculinity by slapping each other on the back. Shaking hands tends to be the preserve of conservative businessmen or very formal situations; if in doubt, watch the locals.

Drinking and smoking

Argentine attitudes to **drinking** tend to be similar to those in southern Europe: alcohol is fine in moderation, and usually taken with food. Public drunkenness remains rare and frowned upon, though it occurs more frequently among the young than it used to. **Smoking** is fairly common among both sexes and all classes, although it is illegal to smoke in enclosed public areas throughout the country.

Shopping

You will find no real tradition of **haggling** in Argentina, although you can always try it when buying pricey artwork, antiques, etc. Expensive services such as excursions and car rental are also obvious candidates for bargaining, while hotel rates can be beaten down off-season, late at night or if you're paying cash (*efectivo*). But try and be reasonable, especially in the case of already low-priced crafts or high-quality goods and services that are obviously worth every centavo.

Tipping

Tipping is not widespread in Argentina, with a couple of exceptions. It's normal to give hairdressers and the like a few pesos and you should add a small gratuity to restaurant bills if service is not included. The unofficial assistants who hang around taxi ranks to open and close doors also expect a small amount, as do hotel porters and the people who load and unload long-distance bus luggage.

Travel essentials

Children

Argentines love children and you will generally find them helpful and understanding if you're travelling as a family. Most hotels have triple rooms or suites with connecting rooms to accommodate families and will be able to provide a cot if you have a small child (ask when you reserve).

When it comes to **eating out**, only the very snootiest restaurants will turn children away or look pained when you walk in; the vast majority will do their best to make sure you and your offspring are comfortable and entertained. Highchairs are sometimes, but not always, provided. It is quite normal to see children out with their parents until late – you may well see families strolling home at 1 or 2am, especially in summer. Bring any **children's medicines** that you are likely to need with you and if your child gets sick, go to a private hospital, preferably in one of the larger cities, where you will be attended by a pediatrician rapidly and professionally. Discreet **breastfeeding** in public is fine. Supplies such as nappies/diapers are widely available, but changing facilities are practically nonexistent, so you will have to get used to changing on the move.

Argentina's **natural attractions** may be your best bet for entertaining your kids – the country has little in the way of amusement parks or specific family destinations, and the ones that do exist are generally rather poor. Consider the waterfalls and jungle critters at Iguazú, the boat rides and glaciers of Parque Nacional Los Glaciares or the whales and penguins near Península Valdés. Areas that provide sports such as skiing and rafting may also be worth considering. Buenos Aires' somewhat sophisticated attractions will mostly appeal more to adults, but there is enough to keep younger ones amused for a couple of days, including a zoo (p.99), a planetarium (p.100) and a natural history museum (p.103). Rosario (p.254) is unusual among Argentine cities for the amount of child-centred attractions it has – and it's fun for their parents too. Wherever you go, remember the distances in Argentina are vast and travel times can be lengthy – do not be too ambitious in planning your itinerary. Avoid the summer heat unless you will be spending most of your time in Patagonia.

Costs

Argentina cannot really be described as a cheap destination, and with inflation unofficially estimated at around thirty percent it's getting rapidly more expensive all the time. But the quality of what is on offer is mostly pretty good, and outside Buenos Aires and the main tourist destinations you can find real bargains in shops and hotels.

Adhering to a reasonable **daily budget** is not impossible, but there are considerable regional variations. As a rule of thumb, the further south you travel the more you will need to stretch your budget. Roughly speaking, on average you'll need to plan on spending at least $1400/US$280/£180 a week on a tight budget (sharing a dorm, eating snacks, limiting other spending), double that if staying in budget accommodation but not stinting, while to live in the lap of luxury you could easily burn through $14000/US$2800/£1800 in a week.

Camping and self-catering are good ways of **saving money**, though the now-extensive network of youth hostels enables you to pay little without sleeping rough. Out of season, at weekends and during slow periods it is a good idea to bargain hotel prices down. You can save money on **food** by having your main meal at lunchtime – especially by opting for the set menu (usually called *menú ejecutivo*). Picnicking is another option; local produce is often world-class and an alfresco meal of bread, cheese, ham or salami with fresh fruit and a bottle of table wine in a great location is a match for any restaurant feast.

Long-distance **transport** will eat up a considerable chunk of your expenses, particularly if you use internal flights; buses are usually (but not always) cheaper but take far longer. They vary greatly in condition and price from one category to another, though you may find the cheaper fares are a false economy – the better companies usually give you free food and drink (of varying quality) on lengthy journeys, while spacious *coche cama* comfort overnight enables you to save the price of a room and is worthwhile for covering the longest distances over less interesting terrain. City transport – including taxis and *remises* (radio taxis) – is inexpensive, but then most cities are compact enough to walk around anyway.

Hotels, restaurants and big stores may ask for a hefty handling fee for credit-card payments (as high as twenty percent), while many businesses – and hotels in particular – will give you a fair-sized **discount for cash payments** (*efectivo* or *contado*) on the quoted price, though they may need prompting. Be aware that some costs, such as air

EXCHANGE RATES

The economic/currency situation in Argentina is volatile, and it is advisable to check the latest before you travel. At the time of writing, there were two exchange rates – an **official rate** (around five pesos to the US dollar), which you will get from ATMs and exchange offices, and a **black market** ("blue") rate (nudging eight pesos to the dollar) that you will be offered (illegally) in the street by those working for clandestine **cambios**, known as *"cuevas"* or caves. If you offer to pay for services such as hotels and tours in cash dollars, you may be able to obtain it at an exchange rate just short of the "blue" one (say, 7), which can equate to a significant discount compared to paying in pesos or with a credit card. Note that hotels and other types of commerce, especially at the luxury end of the market sometimes quote in dollars, rather than Argentine pesos.

travel and entrance fees, operate on a **dual pricing structure** – one price for Argentine residents (including foreigners) and another, often as much as three times more, for non-residents.

All prices in this book are quoted in Argentine pesos ($) unless noted otherwise.

Crime and personal safety

With the effects of economic crises in 2001 and 2009 still lingering, Argentina has lost the reputation it enjoyed for many years as a totally safe destination. However, any concern you have should be kept in perspective – the likelihood of being a victim of crime remains small, because most of the more violent crime (concentrated in the big cities) tends to be directed at wealthy locals rather than foreign visitors.

In Buenos Aires, highly publicized incidents of violence and armed robbery have increased over the years but the vast majority of visitors have no problems. Some potential pitfalls are outlined here – not to induce paranoia, but on the principle that to be forewarned is to be forearmed.

The usual precautions should be taken, particularly in the capital, cities like Rosario and Córdoba, and some of the northern border towns (near the frontiers with Paraguay and Brazil). A basic rule is to carry only what you need for that day, and conceal valuable items such as cameras and jewellery. Be cautious when withdrawing cash from ATMs.

STUDENT CARDS

These are not as useful as they can be in some countries, as museums and the like often refuse to give **student discounts**. Some bus companies, however, do give a ten- to fifteen-percent discount for holders of **ISIC cards**, as do certain hotels, laundries and outdoor gear shops, and even one or two ice-cream parlours. ASATEJ, Argentina's student travel agency, issues a booklet that lists partners throughout the country. The international student card often suffices for a discount at youth hostels in the country, though membership of the Youth Hostelling Association may entitle you to even lower rates (see p.31).

If you're not sure about the wisdom of walking somewhere, play it safe and take a cab – but call radio taxis or hail them in the street, rather than taking a waiting one. Remember that pickpockets most commonly hang around subte stations and bus terminals (particularly Retiro in the capital), and on crowded trains and buses.

Theft from **hotels** is rare, but do not leave valuables lying around. Use the hotel safe if there is one. Compared with other Latin American countries, you're unlikely to have things stolen on long-distance **buses** (luggage is checked in and you should get a ticket for each item), but it makes sense to take your daypack with you when you disembark for meal stops, and, particularly at night, to keep your bag by your feet rather than on the overhead rack. Pilfering from checked-in luggage on **flights** is quite common – don't leave anything of value in outside pockets, and lock your bag where possible. **Car theft** has become a very common occurrence; if you are renting a car, check that the insurance will cover you, and always park in a car park or where someone will keep an eye on it. When driving in the city, keep windows closed and doors locked.

Drugs are frowned upon, although perhaps not as much as in other parts of South America. Drug use, particularly of marijuana and cocaine, is fairly common among the younger generation, and quite openly celebrated in some popular song lyrics. Despite court rulings in 2009 interpreted as a step towards decriminalization, Argentine society at large, and the police, don't draw much of a line between soft drugs and hard drugs, and the penalties for either can be stiff if you get caught. As everywhere else, there are many slang words for drugs: common ones for marijuana include *porro*, *maconia* and *yerba;* for cocaine, *merca* and *papa*.

If you are unlucky enough to be the victim of a **robbery** (*asalto*) or lose anything of value, you will need to make a report at the nearest police station for insurance purposes. This is usually a time-consuming but fairly straightforward process. Check that the report includes a comprehensive account of everything lost and its value, and that the police add the date and an official stamp (*sello*). These reports do not cost anything.

Scams

As elsewhere in Latin America, you should be aware of the possibility of **scams**. A popular one, especially in the tourist areas of Buenos Aires, is having mustard, ice cream or some similar substance "spilt" over you. Some person then offers to help clean it off – cleaning you out at the same time. If this happens to you, push them off, get away from them fast and make as much noise as possible, shouting "thief!" ("*ladrón!*"), "police!" ("*policia!*") or for help ("*socorro!*"). Another well-worked scam involves a regular cab picking you up from the taxi rank outside the airport, driving off the airport grounds (so they're no longer on CCTV), then the driver taking a call on his mobile phone and suddenly saying that he has to drop you off and can't take you to your destination. He leaves you stranded at the side of the road to be picked up by a "random" cab he's in league with, who'll fleece you. Easily avoided: always make sure you take an official, booked *remise* rather than waiting for a regular cab.

Note, too, that though the police are entitled to check your documents, they have no right to inspect your money or travellers' cheques: anyone who does is a con artist, and you should ask for their identification or offer to be taken to the police station (*gendarmería*). If you ever do get "arrested", never get into a vehicle other than an official police car.

Electricity

220V/50Hz is standard throughout the country. Two different types of sockets are found: increasingly rare two-pronged with round pins, but which are different to the two-pin European plugs; and three-pronged, with flat pins, two of which are slanted (Australian adaptors usually work ok with these). Electrical shops along Calle Talcahuano, in Buenos Aires, sell adaptors if you haven't brought one with you.

Entry requirements

Citizens of the US, Canada, the UK, Ireland, Australia, New Zealand and most European countries do not currently need a **visa** for tourist trips to Argentina of up to ninety days. All visitors need a valid **passport** and, at international airports, have their thumbprint and photo digitally recorded on arrival; passports are stamped on arrival wherever you enter. In theory, this could be for thirty or sixty days, but in practice it's almost always ninety. If you are travelling alone with a child you must obtain a notarized document before travel certifying both parents' permission for the child to travel (check with the embassy).

Citizens of Australia, Canada and the US must pay a reciprocity fee (because Argentines are charged a fee or must obtain a visa to visit their countries) of US$100, 70 or 160 respectively if they are entering Argentina at either of the Buenos Aires airports (you do not need to pay if you enter at a land crossing or any other airport, including on an international flight). In the case of US travellers the payment is valid for ten years, but only one entry for the others. Anyone needing to pay must do so online in advance at ⓦ https://virtual.provinciapagos.com.ar /ArgentineTaxes. The rules do change frequently, so it's best to check the government website for the latest (ⓦ argentina.gob.ar).

On entering the country, you will also be given a **customs declaration form** to fill in and all luggage is scanned on arrival at international airports. Duty is not charged on used personal effects, books and other articles for noncommercial purposes, up to the value of US$300. You might be required to declare any valuable electronic items such as laptop computers or fancy mobile phones but Customs are really looking for large quantities of goods or illicit items.

You can **extend your stay** for a further ninety days by presenting your passport at the main immigration department, Dirección de Migraciones in Buenos Aires, at Av Antártida Argentina 1350, Retiro (ⓣ011 4317 0237). This costs $100 and must be done on weekdays between 8am and 1pm; be prepared for a possible lengthy wait. You can do this extension, called a *prórroga*, once only. Alternatively, you could try leaving the country (the short hop to Colonia del Sacramento in Uruguay is a good option) and returning to get a fresh stamp. This usually works, but may be frowned upon if done repeatedly, and the provision of an extra stamp is totally at the discretion of the border guards. If you do overshoot your stay, you pay a moderate fine at Migraciones, who will give you a form that allows you to leave the country within ten days. This was a fairly common practice at the time of publication, but bear in mind that if you do this your stay in the country will be illegal and could potentially cause you problems. If you are crossing into **Chile**, make sure your papers are in order, as Chilean officials are considerably more scrupulous.

When leaving the country, you must obtain an **exit stamp**. At certain border controls, particularly in the north of the country, it is often up to you to ensure that the bus driver stops and waits while you get this – otherwise drivers may not stop, assuming that all passengers are Argentine nationals and don't need stamps. In some places

(for example, Clorinda) your Argentine exit stamp is actually given on the far side of the border, but check this with the driver beforehand.

Visas for work or study must be obtained in advance from your consulate. Extensive paperwork, much of which must be translated into Spanish by a certified translator, is required; allow plenty of time before departure to start the process. The websites listed below have details of what documentation is needed, or contact the consulate directly.

Although checks are extremely rare, visitors are legally obliged to carry their passport as ID. You might get away with carrying a photocopy, but don't forget to copy your entrance stamp and landing card as well.

ARGENTINE EMBASSIES AND CONSULATES ABROAD

Australia Embassy: John McEwan House, Level 2, 7 National Circuit, Barton ACT 2600 ⓣ 02 6273 9111, ⓦ argentina.org.au; Consulate: 44 Market St, Piso 20, Sydney, NSW ⓣ 02 9262 2933, ⓦ argentina.org.au/consulado.

Canada Embassy: 90 Sparks St, Suite 910, Ottawa, ON K1P 5B4 ⓣ 613 236 2351, ⓦ argentina-canada.net; Consulates: 2000 Peel St, 7th floor, Suite 600, Montréal, PQ H3A 2W5 ⓣ 514 842 6582, ⓦ consargenmtl.com; 5001 Yonge St, Suite 201, Toronto, ON M2N 6P6 ⓣ 416 955 9190, ⓦ consargtoro.ca.

New Zealand Embassy: Sovereign Assurance Building, Level 14, 142 Lambton Quay, PO Box 5430, Wellington ⓣ 04 472 8330, ⓦ arg.org.nz.

UK Embassy: 65 Brook St, London W1K 4AH ⓣ 020 7318 1300, ⓦ argentine-embassy-uk.org; Consulate: 27 Three Kings Yard, London W1K 4DF ⓣ 020 7318 1340, ⓔ fclond@mrecic.gov.ar.

US Embassy: 1600 New Hampshire Ave NW, Washington DC 20009 ⓣ 202 238 6401, ⓦ embajadaargentinaeeuu.org. Consulates: 245 Peachtree Center Ave, Suite 2101, Atlanta, GA 30303 ⓣ 404 880 0805, ⓦ consuladoargentinoatlanta.org; 205 N Michigan Ave, Suite 4209, Chicago, IL 60601 ⓣ 312 819 2610, ⓔ argchic@aol.com; 3050 Post Oak Blvd, Suite 1625, Houston, TX 77056 ⓣ 713 871 8935, ⓔ chous_ar@hotmail.com; 5055 Wilshire Blvd Suite 210, Los Angeles, CA 90036 ⓣ 323 954 9155, ⓦ consuladoargentino-losangeles.org; 800 Brickell Ave, Penthouse 1, Miami, FL 33131 ⓣ 305 373 1889, ⓦ consuladoargentinoenmiami.com; 12 W 56th St, New York, NY 10019 ⓣ 212 603 0400, ⓦ congenargentinany.com.

EMBASSIES IN ARGENTINA

Australia Buenos Aires Villanueva 1400, C1426BMJ ⓣ 011 4779 3500.

Canada Buenos Aires Tagle 2828, C1425EEH ⓣ 011 4808 1000.

New Zealand Buenos Aires Carlos Pellegrini 1427, 5th floor, CP1011 ⓣ 011 4328 0747.

UK Buenos Aires Dr Luis Agote 2412, C1425EOF ⓣ 011 4808 2200.

US Buenos Aires Av Colombia 4300, C1425GMN ⓣ 011 5777 4533.

Gay and lesbian travellers

Despite remarkable progress in recent years, the attitude in Argentina towards homosexuals is generally ambivalent. **Discreet relationships** are tolerated, but in this overwhelmingly Roman Catholic nation any "deviance", including any explicit physical contact between members of the same sex (let alone transvestism or overtly intimate behaviour) will be almost universally disapproved of. Violent manifestations of **homophobia** are rare, however, especially now that the Church and the military exert less influence; homosexual acts between consenting adults have long been legal.

Gay and lesbian **associations** are springing up in the major cities, notably in Buenos Aires, where nightlife and meeting places are increasingly open (see p.120), but rural areas still do their best to act as if homosexuality doesn't exist. Yet a piece of legislation passed by parliament in 2003 afforded all citizens protection from discrimination, making a specific reference to sexual orientation (and making it illegal for hoteliers to turn away same-sex couples, for example). Same-sex marriage with full adoption rights was legalized by constitutional amendment in 2010.

CONTACTS FOR GAY AND LESBIAN TRAVELLERS IN ARGENTINA

Bue Gay Argentina Pueyrredón 2031, 1st floor, B, Buenos Aires ☎ 011 4805 1401, ⓦ buegay.com.ar. Young company concentrating on city tours and activity vacations around the country, accompanied by gay tour guides.

Pride Travel Paraguay 523, 2nd floor, E, Buenos Aires ☎ 011 5218 6556, ⓦ pride-travel.com. Argentine travel agent offering air tickets, day-trips, tours and adventure tourism aimed at gay and lesbian travellers.

GAY RESOURCES ONLINE

Ba4uapartments Santa Fe 2630, 7th floor, E, Buenos Aires ☎ 011 4827 5293, ⓦ ba4uapartments.com.ar. In addition to a variety of excellent apartments for rent (usually 3 nights minimum), this dynamic team also offers other services including Spanish classes, massages, etc.

Gay Places to Stay ⓦ gayplaces2stay.com. Information about gay-friendly accommodation worldwide.

Gay Travel ⓦ gaytravel.com. The most helpful site for trip planning, bookings and general information about international travel.

Nexo ⓦ nexo.org. The best site for finding out latest news and venues in Argentina.

Health

Travel to Argentina doesn't raise any major **health** worries and with a small dose of precaution and a handful of standard vaccinations or updates (tetanus, polio, typhoid and hepatitis A) you are unlikely to encounter any serious problems. There have been highly publicized outbreaks of **dengue fever** in the far north and there were a large number of (again, much publicized) cases of swine flu in mid-2009. Yet a bout of **travellers' diarrhoea**, as your body adjusts to local microorganisms in the food and water, is the most you're likely to have to worry about. The **tap water** in Argentina is generally safe to drink, if sometimes heavily chlorinated, but you may prefer to err on the side of caution in rural areas in the north of the country. Mineral water is good and widely available.

Argentine **pharmacies** are plentiful, well-stocked and a useful port of call for help with minor medical problems; the staff may offer simple diagnostic advice and will often help dress wounds, but if in doubt consult a doctor. Medicines and cosmetic products are fairly expensive, however, as they are mostly imported, so if you have room, take plenty of supplies.

The easiest way to get treatment for more serious ailments is to visit the outpatient department of a **hospital**, where treatment will usually be free. In Buenos Aires, the Hospital de Clínicas, at José de San Martín, Av Córdoba 2351 (☎ 011 4961 6001), is a particularly efficient place to receive medical advice and prescriptions; you can simply walk in and, for a small fee, make an on-the-spot appointment with the relevant specialist department – English-speaking doctors can usually be found. For a list of English-speaking doctors throughout the country, contact your embassy in Buenos Aires. For **emergencies or ambulances** in Argentina, dial ☎ 107.

Among the nasty complaints that exist on Argentine territory are Chagas' disease, cholera, malaria, dengue, hantavirus, yellow fever and rabies, though are all rare, mostly confined to remote locations off the tourist trail. That said, each is sufficiently serious that you should be aware of their existence and of measures you should take to avoid infection. For up-to-date information on current health risks in Argentina, check ⓦ cdc.gov and ⓦ medicineplanet.com.

The incidence of **HIV/AIDS** is similar to that in most developed countries. As some of the condoms sold in Argentina are of pretty poor quality, it's wise to bring a reliable brand with you.

Puna (altitude sickness)

Altitude sickness is a potentially – if very rarely – fatal condition encountered at anything over

2000m, but likeliest and most serious at altitudes of 4000m and above. It can cause severe difficulties, but a little preparation should help you avoid the worst of its effects. In many South American countries it is known by the Quichoa word *soroche*, but in Argentina it is most commonly, and confusingly, called *puna* (the local word for altiplano, or high Andean steppes). You'll also hear the verb *apunar* and the word *apunamiento*, referring to the state of suffering from *puna*, whether affecting humans or vehicles (which also need to be adjusted for these heights).

First, to avoid the effects of the *puna*, don't rush anywhere – walk slowly and breathe steadily – and make things easier on yourself by not smoking. Whenever possible, **acclimatize**: it's better to spend a day or two at around 2000m and then 3000–3500m before climbing to 4000m or more rather than force the body to cope with a sudden reduction in oxygen levels. Make sure you're fully **rested**; an all-night party isn't the best preparation for a trip up into the Andes. Alcohol is also best avoided both prior to and during high-altitude travel; the best thing to **drink** is plenty of still water – never fizzy because it froths over and can even explode at high altitudes – or tea. **Eating**, too, needs some consideration: digestion uses up considerable quantities of oxygen, so snacking is preferable to copious meals. Carry supplies of high-energy cereal bars, chocolate, dried fruit (the local raisins, prunes and dried apricots are delicious), walnuts or cashews, crackers and biscuits, and avoid anything that ferments in the stomach, such as milk, fresh fruit and juices, vegetables or acidic food – they're guaranteed to make you throw up if you're affected. The best form of sugar to ingest is honey, because it's the least acidic. Grilled meat is fine, so *asados* are all right, but don't over-indulge.

Minor symptoms of the *puna*, such as headaches or a strange feeling of pressure inside the skull, nausea, loss of appetite, insomnia or dizziness, are nothing to worry about, but more severe problems, such as persistent migraines, repeated vomiting, severe breathing difficulties, excessive fatigue and a marked reduction in the need to urinate are of more concern. If you suffer from any of these, return to a lower altitude and seek out medical advice at once. Severe respiratory problems should be treated immediately with oxygen, carried by tour operators on excursions to 3000m or more as a legal requirement, but you're unlikely ever to need it.

Sunstroke and sunburn

You should take the sun very seriously in Argentina. The north of the country, especially the Chaco region and La Rioja Province, is one of the hottest regions of Latin America in summer – temperatures regularly rocket above 40ºC; the extended siestas taken by locals are wise precautions against the debilitating effects of the midday heat. Where possible, avoid excessive activity between about 11am and 4pm and when you do have to be out in the sun, wear sunscreen and a hat. You should also drink plenty of liquids – but not alcohol – and always make sure you have a sufficient supply of water when embarking on a hike. Throughout the country, the sun can be extremely fierce and even people with darker skin should use a much higher factor sunscreen than they might normally: using factor 15 or above is a sensible precaution. Remember that the cooler temperatures in the south are deceptive – ozone depletion and long summer days here can be more hazardous than the fierce heat of the north.

MEDICAL RESOURCES FOR TRAVELLERS

Canadian Society for International Health ☎ 613 241 5785, Ⓦ csih.org. Extensive list of travel health centres.
CDC ☎ 1 800 232 4636, Ⓦ cdc.gov/travel. Official US government travel health site.
International Society for Travel Medicine ☎ 1 770 736 7060, Ⓦ istm.org. Has a full list of travel health clinics.
Hospital for Tropical Diseases Travel Clinic UK ☎ 0845 155 5000, ☎ 020 7388 9600 (Travel Clinic), Ⓦ thehtd.org.
MASTA (Medical Advisory Service for Travellers Abroad) UK ☎ 0870 606 2782, Ⓦ masta.org for the nearest clinic.
Tropical Medical Bureau Ireland ☎ 1850 487 674, Ⓦ tmb.ie.
Travellers' Medical and Vaccination Centre ☎ 1300 658 844, Ⓦ tmvc.com.au. Lists travel clinics in Australia, New Zealand and South Africa.

Insurance

It is a good idea to take out an **insurance policy** before travelling, though always check first to see whether you are already covered by your home insurance, provincial health plan or student/ employment insurance. In Argentina, insurance is more important to cover theft or loss of belongings and repatriation than medical treatment – the country has a state medical system that is free for emergencies. It is perfectly adequate, though the technology is not the latest and waits can be long. Most well-off Argentines use private healthcare, which is very good and far cheaper than the equivalent in the US or Europe. Make sure your travel insurance policy includes coverage for any adventure sports you may be planning, such as scuba diving, whitewater rafting, or skiing – you will probably have to pay a premium to have this included. If you need to make a claim, you should keep all receipts, and in the event you have anything stolen, you must obtain an official statement from the police.

Internet

Virtually all upmarket hotels offer wi-fi, and most hostels and mid-market hotels now do as well. Cafés with wi-fi are common in Buenos Aires, less so in the interior – try Ⓦnavegawifi.com for a hotspot list. Otherwise, you can access the internet via internet cafés, or in *locutorios* (see p.54), found in most towns. Rates vary considerably, from $4 to $15 an hour, with the highest rates in Patagonia.

The Spanish keyboard is prevalent; if you have problems locating the "@" symbol (called *arroba* in Spanish), try holding the "Alt" key down and type 64.

Laundry

Most towns and cities have a plentiful supply of **laundries** (*lavanderías* or *lavaderos*), especially since not everyone has a washing machine. Some also do dry-cleaning, though you may have to go to a *tintorería*. Self-service places are almost unheard of; you normally give your name and leave your

washing to pick it up later (the service is fast by European standards); some places will deliver to wherever you're staying. Laundry is either charged by weight or itemized, but **rates** are not excessive, especially compared with the high prices charged by most hotels. Furthermore, the quality is good and the service is usually reliable. One important word of vocabulary to know is **planchado** (ironed).

Living and working in Argentina

Many foreigners choose to stay in Argentina long-term, and if you want to take the plunge you will be in good company, particularly if you settle in Buenos Aires or one of the key travel destinations such as Ushuaia or Mendoza. **Organizations** that cater to expats include the South American Explorers' Club (see p.55), the lively internet forum Ⓦbaexpats .org and the website Ⓦlivinginargentina.com.

Tourist **visas** are valid for ninety days. You are usually allowed to renew your visa once, although this does mean an encounter with the bureaucratic immigration services. Many medium-term residents simply leave the country every three months (usually hopping across to Colonia, in Uruguay), to get a new stamp, but this approach might not be tolerated over many years. Obtaining a **residence permit** is time-consuming and is usually granted only if you have an Argentine spouse or child, or make a sizeable investment in the national economy.

As far as **working** is concerned, remember Argentines themselves compete for the few jobs on offer and your entry into the employment market may not be looked on kindly; also, unless you are on a contract with an international firm or organization, you will be paid in pesos, which will inevitably add up to a pretty low salary by global standards, while currency controls implemented in 2011 mean that you cannot easily change your income into dollars. If you're determined anyway, many English-speaking foreigners do the obvious thing and **teach English**. Training in this is an advantage but by no means necessary; the demand for native English-speaking teachers is so high that many soon build up a roster of students via the odd newspaper ad and word of mouth. **Working in tourism** is another possibility – a fair proportion of agencies and hotels are run by foreigners. Consider also translation if you have the language ability.

If you need a **place to live**, there are plenty of agencies aimed at foreigners – one is Ⓦalojargentina .com – offering accommodation in apartments, university residences and B&B-type establishments; more are listed on the forums mentioned above, or you could try ⓦcraigslist.com. Apartments aimed at locals are advertised in newspapers or rented by *inmobiliarías* (estate agents) and are cheaper, but you will need somebody who owns property to be your guarantor and be prepared to sign a two-year contract.

Mail

Argentina's rather unreliable **postal service**, Correo Argentino (☎011 4891 9191) is the *bête noire* of many a hapless expat. Not only is it costly to send post to North America or Europe (starting at $14 for a postcard), but many items also never arrive. If you want to **send mail abroad**, always use the *certificado* (registered post) system, which costs about $40 for a letter, but increases chances of arrival. Safer still is Correo Argentino's *encomienda* system (around $200 for a package under 1kg to North America or Europe), a **courier-style** service; if you are sending something important or irreplaceable, it is highly recommended that you use this service or a similar international one such as UPS (☎0800 222 2877) or DHL (☎0810 222 2345). Packets over 2kg need to be examined by the customs (*Aduana*) at the Centro Postal Internacional at Antártida Argentina 1900 y Comodoro Py in Retiro, Buenos Aires (Mon–Fri 10am–5pm). For regular airmail, expect delivery times of one to two weeks – the quickest deliveries, unsurprisingly, are those out of Buenos Aires. You are not permitted to seal envelopes with sticky tape: they must be gummed down (glue is usually available at the counter). The good news is that as well as post offices, many *locutorios*, lottery kiosks and small stores deal with mail, which means you don't usually have to go very far to find somewhere open.

Receiving mail is generally even more fraught with difficulties than sending it. Again, a courier-style service is your best bet; if not, make sure the sender at least registers the letter or parcel. All **parcels** go to the international post office at Antártida Argentina 1900 in Retiro, and you will receive a card informing you that it is there; you will have to pay customs duties and should expect a long wait. If you are elsewhere in the country you must find out where your nearest customs office is. All post offices keep **poste restante** for at least a month. Items should be addressed clearly, with the recipient's surname in capital letters and underlined, followed by their first name in regular script, then "Poste Restante" or "Lista de Correos", Correo Central, followed by the rest of the address. Buenos Aires city is normally referred to as Capital Federal to distinguish it from its neighbouring province. Bring your passport to collect items ($6 fee per item).

To send **packages within Argentina**, your best bet it to use the *encomienda* services offered by bus companies (seal boxes in brown paper to prevent casual theft). This isn't a door-to-door service like the post: the recipient must collect the package from its end destination (bring suitable ID). By addressing the package to yourself, this system makes an excellent and remarkably good-value way of reducing the weight in your pack while travelling, but be aware that companies usually keep an *encomienda* for only one month before returning it to its original sender. If sending an *encomienda* to Buenos Aires, check whether it gets held at the Retiro bus station (the most convenient) or at a bus depot elsewhere in the capital.

Maps

There are a number of **country maps** available outside Argentina, including the **Rough Guides'** detailed, indestructible Argentina map. Other than that and the maps in this book, the best city map of Buenos Aires is the brilliant Insight Fleximap, which is clear, reliable and easy to fold.

Within Argentina, **road maps** can be obtained at bookshops and kiosks in all big towns and cities or at service stations. Many maps aren't up to date: it's often a good idea to buy a couple of maps and compare them as you go along, always checking with the locals to see whether a given road does exist and is passable, especially with the vehicle you intend to use. The most reliable maps are those produced by **ACA** (Automóvil Club), which does individual maps for each province, to varying degrees of accuracy. These are widely available at ACA offices, kiosks on Calle Florida in the capital and service stations. Glossy and fairly clear – but at times erratic – regional road maps (Cuyo, Northwest, Lake District, etc) are produced by **AutoMapa** and are often available at petrol stations and bookshops. Slightly more detailed but a tad less accurate is the mini-atlas *Atlas Vial* published by **YPF**, the national petrol company, which is sold at its service stations.

For 1:100,000 Ordnance Survey-style maps, the Instituto Geográfico Nacional at Av Cabildo 381 in Buenos Aires is the place to go (Mon–Fri 8.30am–4pm; ☎011 4576 5576 ext 152, ⓦigm.gov.ar). These topographical and colour satellite maps are great to look at and very detailed, but they are only really practical for trekkers who are used to maps of this type.

Country maps can be found at the University of Texas's Perry–Castañeda Library: Ⓦlib.utexas.edu/maps/argentina.html. A good interactive map of Buenos Aires capital can be found at Ⓦmapa.buenosaires.gov.ar.

Money

Notes come in 2, 5, 10, 20, 50 and 100 denominations, while 1 and 2 peso and (rare) 5, 10, 25 and 50 centavo coins are in circulation. Sometimes people are loath to give change, as coins can be in short supply, so it's a good idea to have plenty of loose change on your person. Ask for small denomination notes when exchanging if possible, break bigger ones up at places where they obviously have plenty of change (busy shops, supermarkets and post offices), and withdraw odd amounts from ATMs ($190, $340, etc) to avoid getting your cash dispensed in $100 bills only – trying to buy a drink, an empanada or a postcard with a crisp $100 note can be a frustrating ordeal and won't make you many friends. Since strict currency controls were introduced in 2011, it has become virtually impossible to change pesos back into dollars inside Argentina, let alone outside, so change into pesos only the amounts you need for your stay so that you are not left with unwanted local currency at the end.

Taxes

IVA (*Impuesto de Valor Agregado*) is the Argentine equivalent of VAT or **sales tax** and is usually included in the price for goods and services except food or medicines. The major exceptions are some hotels, which quote their rates before tax, plus airfares and car rental fees. IVA is currently a hefty **21 percent** and is added to everything except food and medicines. It is worth knowing that foreigners can often get IVA reimbursed on many purchases, though this is practical only for bigger transactions (over $100) and subject to all kinds of limits and complications. Shops in the more touristy areas will volunteer information and provide the necessary

---

CURRENCY NOTATION

When you see the $ sign in Argentina – and throughout this book – you can safely assume that the currency being referred to is the Argentine peso. Where a price is quoted in US dollars, the normal notation in Argentina – and the notation we use – is US$.

---

forms, but finding the right place to go to have the final paperwork completed, signed and stamped and to get your money back, at your point of exit (international airports), is a much taller order; ask for instructions when you check in, as you must display your purchases before check-in and then go through the often frustratingly slow formalities once you've been given your boarding pass.

ATMs and credit and debit cards

ATMs (*cajeros automáticos*) are plentiful in Argentina. It's rare that you'll find a town or even a village without one, though you can sometimes be caught out in very remote places, especially in the Northwest, so never rely completely on them. Most machines take all credit cards or display those that can be used: you can nearly always get money out with Visa or MasterCard, or with any cards linked to the Plus or Cirrus systems. Most ATMs are either Banelco or LINK – test the networks to see which works best with your card. Machines are mostly multilingual though some of them use Spanish only, so you might need to have a phrase book or a Spanish-speaker handy.

Credit cards (*tarjetas de crédito*) are a very handy source of funds, and can be used either in the abundant ATMs (this can be expensive) or for purchases. Visa, MasterCard and American Express are all widely used and recognized. Be warned that you might have to show your ID when making a purchase with plastic, and, especially in small establishments in remote areas, the authorization process can take ages and may not succeed at all. Using your **debit card**, which is not liable to interest payments like credit cards, is usually the best method to get cash and the flat transaction fee is generally quite small – your bank will able to advise on this. Make sure you have a card and PIN that are designed to work overseas and advise your bank before you depart. Bear in mind that all use of credit cards and ATMs will be at the disadvantageous official exchange rate (see p.45).

Opening hours

Most **shops and services** are open Monday to Friday 9am to 7pm, and Saturday 9am to 2pm. Outside the capital, they may close at some point during the afternoon for between one and five hours. As a rule, the further north you go, the longer the siesta – often offset by later closing times in the evening. Supermarkets seldom close during the day and are generally open much later, often until 8 or even 10pm, and on Saturday afternoons. Large

PUBLIC HOLIDAYS

Argentina has no shortage of public holidays dotted throughout the calendar, several of which have been introduced or had their names made more politically correct since 2003. Most services run even on these *feriados*, with the possible exception of Christmas Day and May Day. Bear in mind that some of these holidays move to the following Monday (or sometimes to another convenient date) and that "bridges" are conceded when certain holidays fall on a Tuesday or Thursday, to form long weekends. There are also several local public holidays, specific to a city or province, throughout the year (those specific to certain communities and non-Christian faiths are also respected by state-run services). Many offices close for the whole of Semana Santa (Holy Week), the week leading up to Easter, while the Thursday is optional, as is New Year's Eve. Easter Monday is not normally a holiday.

January 1 New Year's Day
Carnival Final Monday and Tuesday before Lent (usually Feb)
Good Friday Friday before Easter
March 24 Truth and Justice Day, in commemoration of the 1976 coup
April 2 Malvinas Veterans' Day
May 1 Labour Day
May 25 Day of the Revolution

June 20 Day of the Flag (anniversary of General Belgrano's death)
July 9 Independence Day
August 17 Anniversary of San Martín's death
October 12 Day of Respect for Cultural Diversity
November 20 Day of National Sovereignty
December 8 Immaculate Conception
December 25 Christmas Day

shopping malls don't close before 10pm and their food and drink sections (*patios de comida*) may stay open as late as midnight. Many of them open on Sundays too. *Casas de cambio* more or less follow shop hours. However, **banks** tend to open only on weekdays: opening times depend on the region. In hotter regions, banks open as early as 7am or 8am, but close by noon or 1pm; whereas in many other areas, including Buenos Aires, they're open from 10am to 3 or 4pm.

The opening hours of **attractions** are indicated in the text; however, bear in mind that these often change from one season to another. If you are going out of your way to visit something, it is best to check if its opening times have changed. **Museums** are a law unto themselves, each one having its own timetable, but all commonly close one day a week, usually Monday. Several Buenos Aires museums are also closed for at least a month in January and February. **Tourist offices** are forever adjusting their opening times, but the trend is towards longer hours and opening daily. **Post offices'** hours vary; most should be open between 9am and 6pm on weekdays, with siestas in the hottest places, and 9am to 1pm on Saturdays. Outside these hours, many *locutorios* will deal with mail.

Phones

Argentina operates a GSM 850/1900 **mobile phone** network, in common with much of Latin America. Most modern mobile phones are tri- or quad-band

so should work fine, but if yours is older you should check with your phone provider to confirm it will work. Local mobile numbers are prefixed by the area code, like fixed lines, and then 15. If you are dialling an Argentine mobile number from abroad, omit the 15 and dial 9 before the area code. If you're likely to use your phone a lot, it may be worth getting an **Argentine SIM card** to keep costs down. These can be obtained before you travel from various providers, or, cheaper still – though you'll need some Spanish here – is to get a pre-paid SIM (*chip*) from a local operator such as Movistar (Ⓦmovistar.com.ar) or Personal (Ⓦpersonal.com.ar). Movistar is preferable as it will activate your service straight away, whereas you may have to wait a day

CALLING HOME FROM ABROAD

Note that the initial zero is omitted from the area code when dialling the UK, Ireland, Australia and New Zealand from abroad.
Australia international access code + 61
New Zealand international access code + 64
UK international access code + 44
US and Canada international access code + 1
Ireland international access code + 353
South Africa international access code + 27

or two with other providers. It has a large customer service centre in Buenos Aires at Santa Fe 1844 (Mon–Fri 9am–6pm).

In many ways it's just as cheap and straightforward to make calls from the public call centres known as **locutorios**. Although they are not as ubiquitous as they once were, they are still widely found throughout the country. You'll be assigned a cabin with a meter, with which you can monitor your expenditure. Make as many calls as you want and then pay at the counter. You can get significant discounts on international calls with pre-paid phonecards, available at the *locutorios*. If you are travelling with a laptop, tablet or smartphone, it is even cheaper to use an internet phone service such as Skype, utilizing the free wi-fi provided by most hotels.

Photography

Digital memory cards are widely available, although generally more expensive than in places like the US and Europe, especially in the more remote locations and for the larger-memory cards. Most mid-size towns have places where you can burn photos onto DVDs or CDs. Standard photographic **film** is also still available, but you're advised to bring specialist films (eg slide film, black-and-white, low-light ASA ratings) from home. The same goes for all camera spares and supplies. **Developing** and printing are usually of decent quality but are also quite expensive and outside Buenos Aires the situation is erratic. A constant, however, is that you should watch out where you take photos: sensitive border areas and all military installations, including many civilian airports, are camera **no-go areas**, so watch out for signs and take no risks.

Time

Argentina hasn't – it seems – settled on a stable pattern of **time zones**. Officially, there's supposed to be a unified national time zone (3hr behind GMT), but some provinces have been known to operate separate systems. For the latest information you're best off checking on Ⓦen.wikipedia.org /wiki/Time_in_Argentina and the official government site at Ⓦ hidro.gov.ar.

Tourist information

The main **national tourist board** (Ⓦturismo.gov .ar) is in Buenos Aires and is a fairly useful stop for maps and general information. Piles of leaflets,

glossy brochures and maps are dished out at provincial and municipal **tourist offices** (*oficinas de turismo*) across the country, which vary enormously in quality of service and quantity of information. Don't rely on staff speaking any language other than Spanish, or on the printed info being translated into foreign languages. In addition, every province maintains a **casa de provincia** (provincial tourist office) in Buenos Aires.

CASAS DE PROVINCIAS IN BUENOS AIRES

Buenos Aires Av Callao 237 (Mon–Fri 9am–5pm; ☎ 011 4371 3587).

Catamarca Av Córdoba 2080 (Mon–Fri 8am–6pm; ☎ 011 4374 6891 ext 30).

Chaco Av Callao 328 (Mon–Fri 9am–3pm; ☎ 011 4372 0961 ext 1029).

Córdoba Av Callao 332 (Mon–Fri 8am–6pm; ☎ 011 4372 8859).

Corrientes San Martín 333, 4th floor (Mon–Fri 8am–2pm; ☎ 011 4394 7418).

Chubut Sarmiento 1172 (Mon–Fri 10am–5.30pm; ☎ 011 4383 7458).

Entre Ríos Suipacha 844 (Mon–Fri 9am–5pm; ☎ 011 4326 2573).

Formosa H. Yrigoyen 1429 (Mon–Fri 9am–3pm; ☎ 011 4381 2037).

Jujuy Av Santa Fe 967 (Mon–Fri 10am–7pm; ☎ 011 4393 6096).

La Pampa Suipacha 346 (Jan & Feb Mon–Fri 9am–3pm; rest of year same days 8am–6pm; ☎ 011 4326 0511).

La Rioja Callao 745 (Mon–Fri 9am–6pm; ☎ 011 4813 3417).

Mendoza Av Callao 445 (Mon–Fri 9am–5pm; ☎ 011 4371 0835).

Misiones Santa Fe 989 (Mon–Fri 9am–6pm; ☎ 011 4317 3722).

Neuquén Maipú 48 (Mon–Fri 9.30am–4pm; ☎ 011 4343 2324).

Río Negro Tucumán 1916 (Mon–Fri 10am–4pm; ☎ 011 4371 7273).

Salta Av Pte Roque S. Peña 933 (Mon–Fri 10am–6pm; ☎ 011 4326 2456).

San Juan Sarmiento 1251 (Mon–Fri 9am–5pm; ☎ 011 4382 9241).

San Luís Azcuénaga 1087 (Mon–Fri 9am–6pm; ☎ 011 5778 1665).

Santa Cruz Suipacha 927 (Mon–Fri 10am–5pm; ☎ 011 4313 4880).

Santa Fe 25 de Mayo 178 (Mon–Fri 9.30am–6pm; ☎ 011 4342 0408).

Santiago del Estero Florida 274 (Mon–Fri 10am–6pm; ☎ 011 4326 7739).

Tierra del Fuego Esmeralda 783 (Mon–Fri 9am–5pm; ☎ 011 4328 7040 ext 108).

Tucumán Suipacha 140 (Mon–Fri 9am–5pm; ☎ 011 432 0010 ext 124).

USEFUL WEBSITES

Argentina – LANIC Ⓦ lanic.utexas.edu/la/argentina. The most complete resource of links to every imaginable aspect of life in Argentina, invaluable both to travellers and researchers.

Argentina Parques Nacionales Ⓦ parquesnacionales.gov.ar. Spanish-only site for the country's national park system, with information and news on all the parks.

Ciudad de Buenos Aires Ⓦ bue.gov.ar. The official city site, with listings for bars, clubs, restaurants, shops, theatres, all searchable by genre and area. A good section on tours, including suggested circuits designed around famous literary, cultural and historical figures linked to the capital.

Directorio de Museos Argentinas Ⓦ museosargentinos.org.ar. Useful searchable database of most of the country's museums, including practicalities.

Literatura Argentina Contemporánea Ⓦ literatura.org. Site dedicated to Argentine writers, with a biography and bibliography for all the major authors, plus extracts of their work. Mostly Spanish, but with some English links.

Planeta Argentina Ⓦ planeta.com/argentina.html. Articles and advice relating to ecotourism in Argentina.

El Portal del Tango Ⓦ elportaldeltango.com. Lots of background on the national dance.

South American Explorers Ⓦ saexplorers.org. Useful site set up by the experienced nonprofit organization South American Explorers aimed at scientists, explorers and travellers to South America. Includes travel-related news, descriptions of individual trips, a bulletin board and links to other websites.

Travel Blog Ⓦ travelblog.org/South-America/Argentina/ and **Travel Pod** Ⓦ travelpod.com/travel-blog-country/Argentina/tpod .html. Two good travel sites with forums, photos, hotel options etc.

Travellers with disabilities

Argentina does not have a particularly sophisticated infrastructure for travellers with disabilities, but most Argentines are extremely willing to help anyone experiencing problems and this helpful attitude goes some way to making up for deficiencies in facilities.

Things are beginning to improve, and it is in Buenos Aires that you will find the most notable changes: a recent welcome innovation has been the introduction of wheelchair **ramps** on the city's pavements – though unfortunately the pavements are not great. Public transport is less problematic, with many of the new buses that now circulate in the city offering low-floor access. Laws demand that all new hotels now provide at least one room that is accessible for those in wheelchairs, but the only sure-fire option for those with severe mobility problems is at the top end of the price range: many five-star hotels have full wheelchair access, including wide doorways and roll-in showers. Those who have some mobility problems, but do not require full wheelchair access, will find most mid-range hotels are adequate, offering spacious accommodation and lifts.

Outside Buenos Aires, finding facilities for the disabled is pretty much a hit-and-miss affair, although there have been some notable improvements at major **tourist attractions** such as the Iguazú Falls, where new ramps and catwalks have been constructed, making the vast majority of the falls area accessible by wheelchair. The local branch of Hostelling International (see p.31) can offer information on access at its hostels.

CONTACTS FOR TRAVELLERS WITH DISABILITIES

Access-Able Ⓦ access-able.com. Online resource for travellers with disabilities.

Accessible Journeys US ☎ 800 846 4537, Ⓦ disabilitytravel.com. Travel tips and programmes for groups or individuals.

Irish Wheelchair Association Ireland ☎ 01 818 6400, Ⓦ iwa.ie. Information and listings for wheelchair users travelling abroad.

Society for the Advancement of Travellers with Handicaps (SATH) US ☎ 212 447 7284, Ⓦ sath.org. Information on the accessibility of specific airlines and advice on travelling with certain conditions.

Tourism for All Vitalise UK ☎ 0845 124 9971, Ⓦ tourismforall .org.uk. Free lists of accessible accommodation abroad and information on financial help for holidays.

Buenos Aires

PAINTED BUILDINGS, CAMINITO, BOCA

1

Buenos Aires

Of all South America's capitals, Buenos Aires – aka Capital Federal, Baires, BsAs or simply BA – has the most going for it. Seductive and cultured, sophisticated yet earthy, eclectic but with a strong identity, it never bores, seldom sleeps and invariably mesmerizes its visitors. Influenced by the great European cities, Buenos Aires nonetheless has it own distinct personality enhanced by proud traditions, including football, tango and *mate*. On one flank lap the caramel-hued waters of the Río de la Plata, the world's widest estuary: signs of BA's regained prosperity include the wharves stacked high with containers and the ever-busier cruise-ship terminus. To the west and south, the verdant Pampas – historically the source of the city's food and wealth – meld seamlessly into its vast suburbs.

Modern Buenos Aires enjoys an incomparable **lifestyle**. Elegant restaurants, glamorous bars, historic cafés and heaving nightclubs, plus a world-class opera house, countless theatres, multiscreen cinemas, avant-garde galleries and French-style palaces all underscore its attachment to the arts and its eternal sense of style. Its proud inhabitants, known as Porteños, are notoriously extravagant and well groomed but they are also hospitable and eager to show visitors around. Another boon are the **parks and gardens** and the abundance of **trees** lining the streets and providing shade in the many lively **plazas** that dot the huge conurbation; they add welcome splashes of colour, particularly when ablaze with yellow, pink and mauve blooms in spring and, in some cases, autumn, too. The squadrons of squawky parrots and vociferous songbirds that populate the greenery help visitors forget that this is the fifth largest conurbation in the Americas: there are nearly fourteen million inhabitants in the **Gran Buenos Aires** area, which spills well beyond the city's defining boundary of multi-lane ring roads into Buenos Aires Province (see Chapter 2).

On the map and from the air the metropolis does look dauntingly huge, yet the compact centre and relative proximity of all the main sights mean that you don't have to travel that much to gain an overview. Of the city's 48 **barrios** you will most probably be visiting only the half-dozen most central. The **city centre** (basically San Nicolás and Monserrat) is mostly a hectic place, particularly during the week and along pedestrianized Calle Florida, but the *fin-de-siècle* elegance of **Avenida de Mayo** and the bohemian café culture of **Avenida Corrientes** offer a contrasting atmosphere. Beyond the converted docklands of **Puerto Madero**, east of downtown, lies the unexpectedly wild **Reserva Ecológica**, one of the city's green lungs.

KIDS PLAYING FOOTBALL IN THE BOCA NEIGHBOURHOOD

Highlights

❶ San Telmo Historic barrio, appreciated for its mellow charm and seductive ambience. Every Sunday impromptu tango provides the soundtrack for visits to treasure-packed antique stalls. **See p.78**

❷ Football Tricky footwork and colourful passion is on display at Boca Juniors' Bombonera or River Plate's Monumental – and in the surrounding streets. **See p.83 & p.101**

❸ La Recoleta Cemetery Join the feral cats and prowl around one of the world's most exclusive cemeteries, where Evita's final (for now) resting place lurks discreetly among eminent tombs, extravagant mausoleums and elaborate sculptures. **See p.91**

❹ MALBA Ogle the best of contemporary Latin American painting and sculpture showcased in a stunning example of cutting-edge architecture. **See p.95**

❺ Palermo Viejo Argentina's most famous writer, Borges, loved its authentic lowlife, but today's glitterati flock here for trendy shops, gourmet restaurants and boutique guesthouses. **See p.99**

❻ Tango Listen to alfresco *bandoneón* players, admire a showcase extravaganza at a glitzy venue or attend a humble neighbourhood *milonga* and learn the basic eight steps. **See p.121**

HIGHLIGHTS ARE MARKED ON THE MAP ON P.60

BUENOS AIRES & AROUND

N

0   kilometres   10

URUGUAY

Colonia del Sacramento

Isla Martín García (Argentina)

Río de la Plata

Delta del Paraná

Río Luján

Tigre

San Isidro

Olivos

Vicente López

Aeroparque Jorge Newbery (Domestic Airport)

Avellaneda

Quilmes

BUENOS AIRES

CAPITAL FEDERAL

SEE INSET FOR DETAIL

Ezeiza (International Airport)

Ezeiza

La Plata

HIGHLIGHTS

1 San Telmo
2 Football
3 La Recoleta Cemetery
4 MALBA
5 Palermo Viejo
6 Tango

CAPITAL FEDERAL

N

0   kilometres   2

Río de la Plata

Retiro Bus Terminal

Uruguay Ferry Terminal

RESERVA ECOLÓGICA COSTANERA SUR

PUERTO MADERO

Aeroparque (Jorge Newbery) (Domestic Airport)

RETIRO

RECOLETA

PALERMO

BELGRANO

NÚÑEZ

SAAVEDRA

VILLA URQUIZA

VILLA PUEYRREDÓN

AGRONOMÍA

CHACARITA

COLEGIALES

VILLA CRESPO

CABALLITO

FLORES

PARQUE CHACABUCO

BOEDO

ALMAGRO

BALVANERA

SAN NICOLÁS

MONSERRAT

SAN CRISTÓBAL

CONSTITUCIÓN

PARQUE PATRICIOS

NUEVA POMPEYA

BARRACAS

BOCA

SAN TELMO

LA BOCA

AVELLANEDA

LANÚS

VILLA LUGANO

VILLA SOLDATI

PARQUE AVELLANEDA

VÉLEZ SÁRSFIELD

VILLA DEL PARQUE

FLORESTA

MONTE CASTRO

LINIERS

LA MATANZA

SAN MARTÍN

VICENTE LÓPEZ

The older **south** of the city begins just beyond the central Plaza de Mayo. The narrow streets are lined with some of the capital's finest architecture, typified by late nineteenth-century townhouses with ornate Italianate facades. Increasingly gentrified, **San Telmo** is primarily known for its cutting-edge artists, lively antiques fair and touristy tango haunts, while resolutely working-class **Boca**, further south, is so inextricably linked with its football team, Boca Juniors, that many of its buildings are painted blue and yellow. The **north** of the city is leafier and wealthier; you can ogle the French-style palaces of **Retiro**, stay in one of the top-end hotels of **Recoleta** or head to **Palermo** to shop or dine or just to wander the streets. Most of the city **museums** are clustered in the northern barrios, with themes as varied as Latin American art, *mate* cups and Eva Perón.

Brief history

Buenos Aires was named in honour of **Nuestra Señora de Santa María de los Buenos Ayres**, provider of the good wind, the patron saint of the Spanish sailors who first landed on the banks of the Río de la Plata estuary in 1516. The first successful settlement came in 1580, but though the Spanish found the horses and cattle that they brought over from Europe thrived, the fertility of the land made little impression on them. They were more interested in precious metals, and named the settlement's river the **Plata** (silver) in the belief that it flowed from the lands of silver and gold in the Andes.

Expansion was slow, however, and Buenos Aires remained a distant outpost of the Spanish-American empire for the next two centuries, with **smuggling** being the mainstay of the local economy. In 1776, in an attempt to shore up its empire, Spain gave the Argentine territories **Viceroyalty status**, with Buenos Aires as the capital. It was too little, too late: boosted by the defeat of two attempted British invasions, the people of the Viceroyalty declared **independence** in 1810, freeing the area from the last vestiges of colonial hindrance.

Immigration and growth

The industrial revolution gave Buenos Aires the opportunity to exploit and export the great riches of the Pampas, thanks to technological advances such as railways and refrigeration – which enabled Europeans to dine on Argentine beef for the first time. Few cities in the world have experienced a period of such astonishing **growth** as that which spurred Buenos Aires between 1870 and 1914. Massive foreign investment – most notably from the British – poured into the city and Buenos Aires' stature leapt accordingly. European **immigrants**, over half of whom were Italians, flocked to the capital, and the city's population doubled between 1880 and 1890. Most of the old town was razed and an eclectic range of new buildings went up in a huge grid pattern. The standard of living of Buenos Aires' middle class equalled or surpassed that of many European countries, while the incredible wealth of the city's elite was almost without parallel anywhere. At the same time, however, much of the large working-class community endured appalling conditions in the city's overcrowded *conventillos*, or tenement buildings.

Modern troubles

By the mid-twentieth century the period of breakneck development had come to a close as the country slid into political turmoil and economic **crisis**. In September 1945, Buenos Aires saw the first of what was to become a regular fixture – a massive **demonstration** that filled the city centre. Rallies of almost religious fervour in support of Perón and his wife **Evita**, who came out onto the balcony of the Casa Rosada to deliver their speeches, followed at regular intervals until Evita's death and Perón's deposition. The long years of military dictatorship that followed saw the city in lockdown, with the mothers of the disappeared (see box, p.66) one of the few visible signs of the turmoil underneath the surface. Since the return to democracy in 1982, Buenos Aires has been the most visible face of the country's economic rollercoaster. The temporary stabilization of the currency in the 1990s brought a new upsurge in

1

spending by those who could afford it – smart new shopping malls, restaurants and cinema complexes sprung up around the city. But Buenos Aires entered the twenty-first century in retreat, as a grinding **recession** led to weeks of protests and looting that came to a horrendous head in December 2001, when widespread rioting led to dozens of deaths. Demonstrations and roadblocks by unemployed *piqueteros* became part of the fabric of everyday life in the city during the messy recovery that followed, with the sad sight of *cartoneros* rooting through rubbish the most obvious example of the economic problems, and growing crime an inevitable offshoot of this rise in poverty.

As the focus of national **bicentenary** celebrations in 2010 – and despite some backwash from the global financial crisis – Buenos Aires is mostly in good shape. Long overdue repairs have been carried out, welfare plans have reduced (though not eradicated) the worst poverty and **international tourism** continues to be an engine of growth, leading to the opening of new gourmet restaurants and boutique hotels every week. Problems remain – traffic, crime, shantytowns, flooding in big storms, power outages and the still frequent roadblocks – but Buenos Aires seems confident of its future, led by an ambitious mayor who has his eye on the presidency.

The city centre

A sometimes chaotic mix of old-fashioned cafés, grand nineteenth-century public edifices, high-rise office blocks and tearing traffic, Buenos Aires' **city centre** exudes energy and elegance – though it can be shabby and downright dingy in parts. Its heart is the spacious, palm-dotted **Plaza de Mayo**, the ideal place to begin a tour of the area and explore its historical and political connections; its mismatched medley of buildings includes the famous **Casa Rosada**, or government house. An amble westwards from the plaza will take you along **Avenida de Mayo**, the city's major boulevard, offering an impressive display of Art Nouveau and Art Deco architecture. At its western end, Avenida de Mayo opens onto the **Plaza del Congreso**, presided over by the **Congreso Nacional** building, the seat of the federal parliament.

From Plaza del Congreso, Avenida Callao will take you northwards to **Avenida Corrientes**. Now a busy commerical artery, Corrientes was famous in the twentieth century as the hub of the city's left-leaning café society. Though there's less plotting going on here today, it's still the place to get some culture, lined as it is with no end of bookstores, music shops, cinemas and theatres. A short detour north from Corrientes will take you to **Plaza Lavalle**, a long, grassy square most notable for the magnificent opera house that looms over its eastern edge, the regal **Teatro Colón**.

East from Plaza Lavalle, you'll hit the jarring and enormous **Avenida 9 de Julio** – the city's multilane central nerve. Presiding at its heart is the stark white **Obelisco**, a 67m stake through the intersection of avenidas 9 de Julio and Corrientes. Crossing east over 9 de Julio, you head into a densely packed and busy block known as the **microcentro** (the Argentine term for downtown), whose two main streets are pedestrianized **Lavalle** and **Florida**, where you'll be swept along by a stream of human traffic past elegant *galerías* (arcades) and stores of every kind. Buenos Aires' small financial district – called, in homage to London, "**La City**" – makes up the southeast corner of the microcentro, while to the northeast sits the quieter "**El Bajo**", home to yet more downtown bars and restaurants.

Plaza de Mayo

Packed with some of Buenos Aires' best known historical landmarks, not least the presidential palace, the **Plaza de Mayo** is a microcosm of the city's past: it's been bombed by the military and crowded with Evita's *descamisados* (literally "the shirtless ones", or manual workers), while for many years it was the scene of the Madres de Plaza de Mayo's weekly demonstration (see box, p.66). Although it still often attracts small, noisy protests, including an eternal group of Malvinas/Falklands veterans demanding greater compensation, more often than not it's sedately filled with gossiping old men batting away flocks of squawking pigeons while hawkers sell candied peanuts and Argentine flags. At its centre stands the **Pirámide de Mayo**, a snow-white obelisk erected in 1811 to mark the first anniversary of the May 25 Revolution, when a junta overthrew the Spanish viceroy, declared Buenos Aires' independence from Spain and set about establishing the city's jurisdiction over the rest of the territory. The headscarves painted on the ground around the pyramid echo those worn by the **Madres**. The plaza's towering palm trees lend it all a wonderfully tropical feel.

Casa Rosada

Balcarce 50 • Tours on Sat, Sun & public holidays 10am–6pm • Free • Take ID

Perón, Evita, Maradona and Galtieri have all addressed the crowds from the balcony of the unmissable **Casa de Gobierno**, otherwise known as the **Casa Rosada**, or "Pink House", the rose-hued government palace that occupies the eastern end of the square. The practice of painting buildings pink was common in the nineteenth century, particularly in the countryside, where you'll still see many estancias this colour, and was originally achieved with the use of ox blood, for both decorative and practical reasons – the blood acted as a fixative for the whitewash to which it was added. After being a muted rose for many years, followed by a brief phase in a shocking pink – a legacy of the flamboyant Menem era – the building was restored in 2007 to a deep puce colour, patented as "Casa de Gobierno pink" in a probably fruitless attempt to prevent any more tampering with the tone. It has been strikingly lit at night since the bicentenary celebrations in 2010 (see box below).

The present structure, a typically Argentine blend of French and Italian Renaissance styles, developed in a fairly organic fashion. It stands on the site of the city's Spanish fort, begun in 1594 and converted in 1776 to the viceroy's palace. In 1862, President Bartolomé Mitre moved the government ministries to the building, remodelling it once again. The final touch was added in 1885, when the central arch was added, unifying the facade. Multilingual guided tours leave the main entrance every ten minutes at weekends and last around one hour – taking in the presidential office (where lingering is forbidden) and most of the palace's opulent rooms, these are well worth it; dashing grenadiers in their nineteenth-century uniforms act as guides.

CENTENARY AND BICENTENARY

On May 25, 1810, locals gathered in the **Plaza de Mayo** to demand the withdrawal of the viceroy and to form the **Primera Junta** – the first move in throwing off the yoke of Spanish rule and creating an independent nation.

The centenary in 1910 was cause for great celebration: in its first hundred years Argentina had gone from being a fairly small colonial backwater to one of the world's richest countries, still in the throes of an unprecedented immigration and building boom, and bursting with confidence that it was destined to be a great country, perhaps even challenging US hegemony in the western hemisphere. Several foreign nations gifted **monuments**, many of which are still standing in Buenos Aires, including the Torre Monumental (Britain; see p.88) and the Monumento de los Españoles (Spain; see p.101).

Argentina has failed to live up to its original heady promise, but in 2010 its citizens nonetheless passionately celebrated their two-hundredth birthday. In Buenos Aires, lasting legacies of the party include a new museum (see p.66), behind the Casa Rosada, and the **Casa del Bicentenario**, at Riobamba 983 (☎011 4129 2400, ⓦbicentenario.gov.ar), which holds exhibitions on different aspects of Argentine identity. The huge main post office, the Correo Central, at Sarmiento 189, near the beginning of Avenida Corrientes, is slowly being restored and transformed into a cultural centre. It is to be the seat of the national symphony orchestra and host more exhibitions – and might just be ready in time for the next bicentenary, that of the declaration of independence: July 9, 2016.

1

Recoleta

Callao

Teatro Nacional
Cervantes

AVENIDA CORDOBA

Museo Judío

Sinagoga
Central

Palacio de las
Aguas Corrientes

DEL CARMEN

DELLEPIANE

PLAZA
LAVALLE

Teatro
Colón

AVENIDA CALLAO

Palacio de
Justicia

Tribunales

CERRITO

9 DE JULIO

Lavalle

CARLOS PELLEGRINI

Callao

Centro Cultural
Ricardo Rojas

Callao

Teatro
General
San Martín

Uruguay

TALCAHUANO

Arteplex
Centro

AVENIDA CORRIENTES

Obelisco

Carlos
Pellegrini

SUIPACHA

Teatro Ópera

Centro Cultural
San Martín

AYACUCHO

RODRIGUEZ PEÑA

MONTEVIDEO

PARANA

URUGUAY

RIVADILA

LIBERTAD

AVENIDA

MITRE

RIOBAMBA

Congreso

PLAZA
DEL CONGRESO

Gaumont

RIVADAVIA

Museo
Mundial
del Tango

Congreso
Nacional

Saenz Peña

Edificio
Barolo

Teatro
Avenida

AVENIDA DE MAYO

Av. De Mayo

ALSINA

CEBALLOS

PEÑA

ALSINA

LIMA

MONSERRAT

MORENO

MORENO

AVENIDA BELGRANO

Moreno

VENEZUELA

SOLIS

SARANDI

COMBATE DE LOS POZOS

AVENIDA ENTRE RIOS

VIRREY

PTE. SAENZ

SAN JOSE

SANTIAGO DEL ESTERO

SALTA

BERNARDO DE IRIGOYEN

TACUARI

CONSTITUCIÓN

AVENIDA INDEPENDENCIA

**CENTRAL
BUENOS AIRES**

ESTADOS UNIDOS

Bahavnera, Abasto Mall & Once

Ezeiza Airport

◼ ACCOMMODATION			
725 Buenos Aires	5	Ibis Buenos Aires	11
Boquitas Pintadas	16	Milhouse	10
Castelar	9	Moreno	13
La Cayetana	15	NH Jousten	4
Chile	8	O'Rei	3
Esplendor	1	Sportsman	7
Faena Hotel & Universe	14	V&S Youth Hostel	2
Gran Hotel España	12		
Hotel de los Dos Congresos	6		

● RESTAURANTS AND CAFÉS			
La Americana	19	Confitería Ideal	13
Arturito	11	Las Cuartetas	12
Bice	5	La Giralda	9
Brasserie Petanque	24	El Globo	21
Cabaña Las Lilas	16	Granix	18
Cadore	7	Güerrín	10
Café Tortoni	20	"i" Fresh Market	22
Chiquilín	14	Laurak-Bat	23
El Claustro	2	New Brighton	15

			BARS, CLUBS, LIVE-MUSIC AND TANGO VENUES			**SHOPS**	
Nsalad	4	Alsina Buenos Aires	10	Fantástico Bailable	7	Bailarín Porteño	7
Parrilla Peña	3	Amérika	6	Maluco Beleza	4	Galerías Pacífico	1
Patio San Ramón	17	Asia de Cuba	15	Niño Bien	13	El Gauchito	4
La Paz	8	Bahrein	2	Pan y Teatro	16	Liberarte	2
Siga La Vaca	25	Celta Bar	5	Piazzola Centro de Artes	9	Librería de Ávila	6
Tomo 1	6	Confitería Ideal	3	Señor Tango	14	Musimundo	5
Winery	1	Club Gricel	17	La Trastienda	11	Zival's	3
		El Chino	12	Vaca Profana	8		
		Estadio Luna Park	1				

1

Behind the Casa Rosada, the Plaza Colón features a gigantic Argentine flag and a Carrara marble statue of **Cristóbal Colón** (Christopher Columbus), looking out to the river and towards the Old World.

Museo del Bicentenario

Paseo Colón 100 • Wed–Sun 10am–6pm • Free • ☎ 011 4344 3802, ⓦ museo.gov.ar

Uniformed grenadiers guard the Casa Rosada's own museum, the **Museo del Bicentenario**, which opened in May 2011, a year after the national bicentenary it was intended to celebrate (see box, p.63). An impressive subterranean structure behind the presidential palace, enhanced by handsome brick arches, it covers the role of the Casa Rosada in the city's history, highlighting the various constructions occupying the site and the presidency past and present – with carefully chosen film footage relating Argentine political history from a Peronist and, above all, Kirchnerist slant. Posters of the Peróns, plus clothing, furniture, writing instruments and even porcelain and carriages used by various holders of the office since 1810 help illustrate this slick propaganda.

MADRES DE LA PLAZA DE MAYO

Many of those arrested – and, in many cases, tortured and executed – during the **1976–83 dictatorship** (see Contexts, p.540) were young people in their teens and 20s who were kidnapped from their homes and streets with no acknowledgement from the authorities as to their whereabouts. In 1976 some of their mothers, frustrated by the intimidating silence they were met with when they tried to find out what had happened to their children, started what would become the **Madres de la Plaza de Mayo (Mothers of the Plaza de Mayo) movement**.

At first just a handful of women, the Madres met weekly in the **Plaza de Mayo**, the historical centre of the city, as much to support each other as to embarrass the regime into providing answers; the wearing of white headscarves emerged as a means of identification. As their numbers grew, so did their defiance – standing their ground and challenging the military to carry out its threat to fire on them in front of foreign journalists, for instance. Some disappeared themselves after the notorious torturer known as the "Blond Angel of Death", Alfredo Astiz, infiltrated the group, posing as the brother of a *desaparecido* (disappeared). He was sentenced to life imprisonment in October 2011.

In 1982, during the Malvinas/Falklands crisis, the Madres were accused of being anti-patriotic for their stance **against the war**, a conflict that they rightly claimed was an attempt by the regime to divert attention away from its murderous acts. With the return to democracy in 1983, the Madres were disappointed by the Alfonsín government's reluctance to delve too deeply into what had happened during the "Dirty War", as well as by the later granting of immunity to many of those accused of kidnap, torture and murder. The group rejected monetary "compensation" and both the Madres and the respect in which they are held were key in finally getting the amnesty laws overturned in 2005. The Madres continued to protest at the Pirámide de Mayo weekly until January 2006, when, after around 1500 protests, the Madres finally brought their long vigil to an end, citing confidence in President Néstor Kirchner. Now some of the Madres have branched into other areas of social protest: the emblem of the white headscarf was at the forefront of the movement to demand the **non-payment of the country's foreign debt**, among other issues.

The Madres were mixed up in an extremely embarrassing scandal in 2011, when Sergio Schoklender, a lawyer employed by their association, was accused of embezzlement; he was charged in early 2012. Jailed in the 1980s with his brother, Pablo, after they were found guilty of murdering their parents, whom they accused of abuse, he was taken under the wing of the current president of the Madres, Hebe de Bonafini, when he emerged as a leading defender of prisoners' rights in the dying months of the junta. According to the allegations, Schoklender had amassed a huge fortune by siphoning off funds intended to build low-price housing for the poor. De Bonafini is no stranger to scandal (indeed her daughter Alejandra was accused of involvement in the Schoklender corruption case). Most notably she publicly expressed support for the 9/11 attacks, saying that they were acts of revenge for global repression by the United States and NATO.

1

Along with temporary exhibitions, the museum hosts *Ejercicio Plástico* ("Plastic Exercise"), a sensual mural painted in 1933 by the Mexican artist David Alfaro Siqueiros, assisted by the Argentine painters Spilimbergo, Berni and Castagnino (all three of whom contributed to the fantastic frescoes that decorate the Galerías Pacífico mall in the microcentro; see p.72) and the Uruguayan Enrique Lázaro. To enter the capsule containing it you must don protective footwear covers. At the far end of the museum there is a decent café and a gift shop where you can treat yourself to dolls of the Peróns and the Kirchners and other Casa Rosada-related souvenirs.

Cabildo

Bolívar 65 • Wed–Fri 10am–5pm, Sat & Sun 11.30am–6pm • $6 • ☎ 011 4334 1782, ⓦ cabildonacional.com.ar

At the opposite end of the square from the Casa Rosada is the **Cabildo**, the only colonial-era civil construction to survive the rebuilding craze of the 1880s. Its simple, unadorned lines, green and white shuttered facade and colonnaded front, dating from the mid-eighteenth century, stand in stark contrast to the more ornate nineteenth-century buildings around it. The Spanish administrative headquarters, it now houses a small **museum** whose modest collection includes standards captured during the 1806 British invasion, some delicate watercolours by Enrique Pellegrini and original plans of the city and the fort. Although the museum was painstakingly restored at great cost in time for the 2010 bicentenary (aptly so since it is dedicated to the May Revolution) it is the building's interior that makes a visit worthwhile, in particular the upper galleries lined with an assortment of relics from the colonial period onwards, such as huge keys and sturdy wooden doors. Behind the Cabildo, a patio area with an ornamental well hosts a café and small artisans' fair (Thurs & Fri 11am–4pm).

Catedral Metropolitana

San Martín 27 • Daily 9am–7pm • Free guided tours Mon–Fri 11.30am & 4pm, Sat & Sun 4pm • ⓦ catedralbuenosaires.org.ar

The **Catedral Metropolitana**, with its severe Neoclassical facade, is not a particularly beautiful or impressive church. However, it is assured a steady stream of visitors, owing partly to its location, partly to its status as Buenos Aires' main cathedral and partly to the **mausoleum** to Independence hero General San Martín (see Contexts, p.530) inside, solemnly guarded and frequently mobbed by schoolchildren on history trips.

The cathedral assumed its final form over many years; built and rebuilt since the sixteenth century, the present building was completed in the mid-nineteenth century, complete with Venetian mosaic floors, gilded columns and a silver-plated altar. The twelve columns that front the entrance represent the twelve apostles; above them sits a carved tympanum whose bas-relief depicts the arrival of Jacob and his family in Egypt.

In 2013, the cathedral became the focus of jubilant celebrations and international attention when Jorge Bergoglio, ex-Archbishop of Buenos Aires, was named **Pope Francis I**. Bergoglio is the first Latin American pontiff and the first to hail from outside Europe in around 1300 years.

Avenida de Mayo

An amble west from Plaza de Mayo takes you along one of the capital's grandest thoroughfares, **Avenida de Mayo**, a wide, tree-lined boulevard flanked with ornamental street lamps and offering a stunning ten-block vista between Plaza de Mayo and Plaza del Congreso. Part of an 1880s project to remodel the city along the lines of Haussmann's Paris, Avenida de Mayo is notable for its architectural melange; many of its buildings are topped with decorative domes and ornamented with elaborate balustrades and sinuous caryatids. Unimpressed with the city's European pretensions, Borges called it one of the saddest places in Buenos Aires, yet even he couldn't resist the charm of its **confiterías** and traditional restaurants, a handful of which remain open.

1

Casa de la Cultura

Av de Mayo 567 • Free guided tours Sat 4pm & 5pm, Sun hourly 11am–4pm

Just half a block west of Plaza de Mayo, there's the magnificent, French-influenced **La Prensa** building, an extravaganza of grand wrought-iron doors, curvaceous lamps and a steep mansard roof. The building – now the headquarters of the city's culture secretariat and renamed the **Casa de la Cultura** – was originally built as the head office of the once-influential national newspaper *La Prensa*. You can take a peek at the opulent interior – all ornamental glass and elaborate woodwork – or take advantage of one of the free guided tours organized by the city government at the weekend. Occasional concerts and other events are held in the opulent Salón Dorado ("Gilded Hall").

Café Tortoni

Av de Mayo 829 • ☎ 011 4342 4328, ⓦ cafetortoni.com.ar

The fact that the **Café Tortoni** (see p.116) is on every tourist's must-visit list – some days you even have to queue to get in – has spoilt the atmosphere a little and hiked the prices a lot, but the *Tortoni*, which has existed in some form or other for over 150 years, is still worth stopping by for a *cafecito*. Famous for its literary and artistic connections – notable habitués included poets Alfonsina Storni and Rubén Darío, writer Jorge Luis Borges and tango singer Carlos Gardel – its heavy brown columns and Art Nouveau-mirrored walls undeniably exude an elegance no longer found in many of its rivals.

Museo Mundial del Tango

Av de Mayo 833 (entrance Rivadavia 830, 1st floor) • Museum Mon–Fri 2.30–7.30pm • $5 • ⓦ anacdeltango.org.ar/museo_interior.asp

The fine **Palacio Carlos Gardel** is home to the Academia Nacional del Tango; and the ambitiously named **Museo Mundial del Tango**. The musty museum traces the history of tango (in Spanish, though an English-speaking guide may be available) through interesting displays such as Tita Merello's glittering dress and a photo of men dancing tango together in 1910 – women were rarely allowed to dance in those days, except in brothels.

Edificio Barolo

Av 9 de Julio 1370 • Tours Mon & Thurs 2pm & 7pm • $40 • ⓦ pbarolo.com.ar

Continuing down Avenida de Mayo will take you over the wide Avenida 9 de Julio and past a clutch of old-fashioned hotels, cafés and government institutions dressed in *belle époque* Art Deco splendour. On the south side of the street stands the avenue's most fantastical building, the **Edificio Barolo** – named after the extremely wealthy farmer of Italian origin who had it built. Designed by the Italian architect Mario Palanti and constructed between 1919 and 1923, its unusual top-heavy form is an example of the eclectic style popular at the time. Created as a monument to Dante's *Divine Comedy* (of which Barolo was a great admirer) it is full of references to the epic poem – its different sections represent Hell, Purgatory and Heaven, its height in metres equals the number of songs (100) and it has 22 floors, the same as the number of stanzas in each canto. Moreover, in early June, the roof's tip aligns with the Southern Cross constellation – said to represent the "entrance to heaven". Try and catch one of the fascinating guided tours of the building (mostly taken up by offices) for a detailed explanation of its history and symbolism.

Plaza del Congreso

At its western extremity, Avenida de Mayo opens up to encircle the **Plaza del Congreso**, a three-block-long wedge of grass dotted with statues, a fountain, swooping pigeons and a number of benches. It is dominated by the grandiose building of the Congreso Nacional, the federal parliament. There is also an allegorical monument to Argentina's history as a republic and its parliamentary institutions.

1

Congreso Nacional
Hipólito Yrigoyen 1849 • Guided visits in English Mon, Tues, Thurs & Fri 11am & 4pm • Free • Ⓦ senado.gov.ar/web/museo/visitaguiada.php

Plaza del Congreso's western end is presided over by the Greco-Roman **Congreso Nacional** building, inaugurated in 1906 and designed by Vittorio Meano, who was also one of the architects of the Teatro Colón (see p.70). The northern wing is where the Lower Chamber (the Diputados or Members of Parliament) sits, while the southern wing is used by the Upper Chamber of senators. The tours include a visit to the marble Salón Azul, right in the centre of the building under the copper cupola; look up to see the giant 2000kg chandelier featuring figures representing the Republic and all its provinces.

Monumento a los dos Congresos
Plaza del Congreso's most striking monument is the exuberant **Monumento a los dos Congresos**, a series of sculptural allegories atop heavy granite steps and crowned by the triumphant figure of the Republic, erected to commemorate the 1813 Assembly and the 1816 Declaration of Independence. The plaza has traditionally been the final rallying point for many political demonstrations – it was the site of a mass illegal encampment of farmers protesting the government's increase in export taxes in 2008 – and the sculpture has now been surrounded by a high fence to try to prevent the constant reappearance of fresh graffiti. You'll also see a greening bronze statue in the square, a somewhat rain-streaked version of Rodin's *The Thinker*. Next to it, a white block marks *kilómetro cero* – the point from which all roads that lead from Buenos Aires are measured.

Avenida Corrientes
Running parallel to Avenida de Mayo, four blocks north of Plaza Congreso, **Avenida Corrientes** is another of the city's principal arteries, sweeping down to the lower grounds of El Bajo. It's not so much the architecture that is of note but the atmosphere generated by its bustling mix of cafés, bookstores, cinemas, theatres and pizzerias. For years, **cafés** such as *La Paz*, on the corner of Corrientes and Montevideo, and the austere *La Giralda*, two blocks west, have been the favoured meeting places of left-wing intellectuals and bohemians – and good places to observe the Porteño talent for whiling away hours over a single tiny coffee.

Corrientes' **bookstores**, many of which stay open till the wee hours, have always been as much places to hang out in as to buy from – in marked contrast to almost every other type of shop in the city, where you'll be accosted by sales assistants as soon as you cross the threshold. The most basic places are simply one long room open to the street with piles of books slung on tables and huge handwritten price labels, whereas the leftish, alternative Liberarte at no. 1555 and its ilk take literature more seriously. Almost as comprehensive as the bookstores are the street's numerous pavement kiosks, proffering a mind-boggling range of newspapers, magazines and books on subjects from psychology and sex to tango and politics.

Teatro General San Martín
Av Corrientes 1530/Sarmiento 2715 • Box office daily 10am–10pm • Ⓦ complejoteatral.gob.ar

The glass front of the **Teatro General San Martín** (see p.123) on Avenida Corrientes signals one of the city's most important cultural spaces. As well as the namesake theatre, this municipal complex includes an art-house cinema and a small free gallery that often has worthwhile exhibitions showcasing Argentine photographers, among other subjects. At the back of the theatre is a large and rather shabby 1960s building, inaugurated by Perón, that is home to the eclectic **Centro Cultural General San Martín**, a space for cutting-edge art, theatre and dance, and also a major venue for conventions and academic debates.

1

Obelisco

The much-photographed centrepiece of Buenos Aires' cityscape, the iconic 67m-tall **Obelisco** dominates the busy intersection between Corrientes and Avenida 9 de Julio. Erected in 1936 in just 31 days, it commemorates four key events in the city's history: the first and second foundings; the first raising of the flag in 1812; and the naming of Buenos Aires as Capital Federal in 1880. Its giant scale and strategic location also make it a magnet for carloads of celebrating fans after a major football victory. The obelisk stands on the Plaza de República, where you will also see representations in bronze of the country's provinces and the flags of Buenos Aires and Argentina, raised in 2008 to commemorate 25 years since the return to democracy.

Plaza Lavalle

A short walk northwest from the Obelisco along Diagonal Roque Sáenz Peña takes you past a row of fountains and patio cafés – popular places to take a coffee break or eat lunch – to **Plaza Lavalle**. Stretching for three blocks, the plaza is a pleasant green space, notable for its fine collection of native and exotic trees, many of them over a hundred years old. Among the pines, magnolias and jacarandas stands an ancient *ceibo*, a tall tree with a twisted trunk whose bright red spring blossom resembling coral is Argentina's national flower.

The plaza began life as a public park, inaugurated in 1827 by British immigrants, and thirty years later was the departure point for the first Argentine train journey, made by the locomotive *La Porteña* to Floresta in the west of the capital; the original locomotive can still be seen in the Complejo Museográfico in Luján (see p.143). Nowadays the plaza is practically synonymous with the law courts that surround it; this part of the city is often referred to as **Tribunales**.

Palacio de Justicia

The western end of Plaza Lavalle is dominated by the **Palacio de Justicia**, seat of the Supreme Court. In a loose and heavy-handed interpretation of Neoclassicism, heavily adorned with pillars, the building stands as something of a monument to architectural uncertainty, which some see as a metaphor for Argentina's state of justice. The needs of the lawyers who rush to and from the court are catered for by numerous stallholders who set up tables spread with pamphlets and secondhand books explaining every conceivable aspect of Argentine law.

Teatro Colón

Cerrito 628 • Tours daily 9am–5pm • $110 • ⓦ teatrocolon.org.ar

The handsome **Teatro Colón**, resplendent with its grand but restrained French Renaissance exterior, stands on the eastern side of Plaza Lavalle, between Viamonte and Tucumán, with its main entrance on the plaza. Famed as an opera house – though it also hosts ballet and classical recitals – the Teatro Colón (named for Christopher Columbus) is Argentina's most prestigious cultural institution and is considered to have some of the best acoustics of any opera house in the world (Luciano Pavarotti was a big fan). Most of the twentieth century's major opera and ballet stars appeared here, from Caruso and Callas to Nijinsky and Nureyev, while classical music recitals were given by the likes of Toscanini and Rubinstein. More recent performers have included Plácido Domingo, Lang Lang, Joshua Bell and Daniel Barenboim. The interior features an Italian Renaissance-style central hall, the beautiful gilded and mirrored Salón Dorado (allegedly inspired by Versailles) and the stunning auditorium itself, whose five tiers of balconies culminate in a huge dome decorated with frescoes by Raúl Soldi during the 1966 restoration of the theatre.

The theatre, first inaugurated on May 25, 1908, was again closed for an extensive and extremely costly refurbishment in 2006 and reopened for the 2010 bicentenary, complete with air conditioning and impeccably restored gold leaf. The celebratory

1

JEWISH BUENOS AIRES

Argentina is home to one of the largest **Jewish communities** in the world, currently estimated at around 185,000, although this is around one third of its peak figure in the 1950s, since when many have migrated to Israel, Europe and the United States. The majority live in Buenos Aires; the more well-to-do in Belgrano, and the lower middle classes in Once. The latter is where you'll find most of the city's kosher restaurants, especially on the streets around Pueyrredón between Córdoba and Corrientes. Approximately eighty synagogues dot the city, including the large Central Synagogue (see below), along with more than seventy Jewish educational institutions.

The first Jewish **immigrants** arrived in Argentina in the early seventeenth century but were officially excluded from colonial society by the Spanish authorities. Following independence Jews were openly allowed to settle and began moving in from France and other Western European countries in the early nineteenth century; Jewish refugees later fled here in large numbers from pogroms and persecution in Russia and Eastern Europe, and were commonly known as "rusos", a term still often used erroneously to refer to all Jews (two-thirds of whom are Ashkenazi).

In 1938 the foreign minister under President Ortiz signed an infamous circular that effectively instructed Argentine consulates not to issue visas to Jews seeking asylum from Nazi Germany. Perón's government was one of the first to recognize the State of Israel, but he openly admired Mussolini, covertly hampered Jewish immigration and notoriously allowed Nazi war criminals to settle in Argentina, including Adolf Eichmann, an SS officer who masterminded the systematic massacre of Jews in Central Europe. In 1960 Eichmann was abducted from a Buenos Aires suburb, where he worked for Mercedes Benz, by Mossad and Shin Bet agents and whisked off for trial and execution in Jerusalem.

The Jewish community was the target of two of the country's most murderous **terrorist attacks**: a bomb explosion at the Israeli Embassy in 1992, in which 29 people died, and another at the headquarters of AMIA, the Argentine Jewish association, in 1994, which killed 85 people. In 2006, Argentine prosecutors officially accused the Iranian government and Hezbollah of ordering the bombings, a charge Teheran adamantly denies, but the crimes have never been properly resolved. A monument in Plaza Lavalle remembers those who lost their lives in both attacks – another in the Plaza Embajada de Israel, at the corner of Arroyo and Suipacha, Retiro, focuses on the loss of life in the 1992 atrocity, with one lime tree representing each victim.

concert held on May 24 featured *Swan Lake* and the second act of Puccini's *La Bohème*. Check the website or enquire at the box office (*boletería*) for both guided visits and tickets for performances; it is located in the narrow passageway, Pasaje de Carruajes (formerly used for carriages), that cuts sideways through the building at Tucumán 1171.

Sinagoga Central and Museo Judío

Libertad 761–769 • Tues–Thurs 11am–6pm, Fri 11am–5pm (tours last 45min) • $35 • Take ID • ⓦ museojudio.org.ar

At the northeastern end of the plaza near Avenida Córdoba is the **Sinagoga Central**, a neo-Byzantine edifice housing the main synagogue of Argentina's Jewish community. Well-informed guides (English speakers available) will take you around the handsome interior of the synagogue (men are provided with a kippa) and the **Museo Judío**, a small museum of religious artefacts, mostly imported from Europe, providing an explanation of the history of Argentina's large Jewish community (see box above). Some of the finest objects are two sixteenth-century torahs from Morocco and a set of paintings depicting Polish Jews on their arrival in the Pampas. The museum holds the occasional exhibition of Judaism-related contemporary art, too. You might like to sample Jewish specialities at the on-site kosher bar-restaurant, *Hamakom* (Mon–Thurs 11am–8pm, Fri 11am–2pm).

The microcentro

The **microcentro** – bounded by avenidas Corrientes, Além, de Mayo and 9 de Julio – is the core of downtown, the central nerve system of the modern city,

1

a fast-moving, noisy, traffic-filled district packed with offices, banks, bars, hotels and stores. Few people other than business visitors opt to stay here, but you're bound to come here at least once or twice to eat or drink, make travel arrangements, shop and take in the sights. The microcentro's key thoroughfares are pedestrianized **Calle Florida**, which runs from Plaza de Mayo to Plaza San Martín in Retiro (see p.87), and partly pedestrianized, cheap and cheerful **Calle Lavalle**, which bisects Florida halfway along its length.

Calle Florida

At the beginning of the twentieth century, **Florida** was one of the city's most elegant streets – the obligatory route for a stroll following tea at its very own branch of Harrods. Nowadays over a million people a day tramp its length, and cutting your way through its stream of foot traffic requires considerable determination. But this traffic is Florida's most appealing quality; there's always a lively buzz about the place, as a handful of street performers do their best to charm a few pesos from the passers-by. Unofficial vendors have been controversially banned from peddling their wares by city decree but some still try and sell bootleg CDs or cheap leather wallets.

Florida commences at Plaza de Mayo and, save for the elegant facade of the Standard Bank (formerly the **Banco de Boston**) at no. 99, which is particularly impressive when lit up at night, its initial blocks are mostly taken up with bookstores, clothes stores, exchange offices and fast-food outlets, packed with office workers at lunch time. Vestiges of Florida's more sophisticated past remain in its **galerías**, or shopping arcades, such as the Art Nouveau **Galería Güemes** at no. 165, which features a series of beautiful glass cupolas, or in its cafés – though the historic **Richmond confitería** at Florida 468 closed to widespread consternation in 2011.

Towards the northern (Retiro) end of Florida, the crowds become thinner and the stores more upmarket – at no. 877 you'll see the impressive shell that once housed the local Harrods branch. Until the 1960s, this was a fully operational branch of the famous British department store, with visitors flocking to marvel at its full-size double-decker bus and (possibly apocryphal) live Indian elephant. Despite occasional rumblings that it is to be reopened, and its intermittent use as an exposition hall and arts venue, it has been shuttered for years.

Galerías Pacífico

Florida 753 • W galeriaspacifico.com.ar

The most notable of Florida's *galerías*, the **Galerías Pacífico** offers a glitzy retailing opportunity within a vaulted and attractively frescoed building built as a branch of the Paris department store Le Bon Marché at the end of the nineteenth century. The first floor is home to the **Centro Cultural Borges** (see p.124), a large space offering a worthwhile selection of photography and painting exhibitions from both Argentine and foreign artists. Florida's last two blocks before it spills into Plaza San Martín are filled with leather and handicraft stores; look out also for the fine decorative facade and door of the Centro Naval on the corner of Avenida Córdoba.

La City

Buenos Aires' financial district, **La City**, takes up the southeastern quarter of the microcentro's grid of streets. Its atmosphere serves as a barometer of the country's economic ups and downs – from frantic money changing during hyperinflation in the 1980s, via the noisy pot-banging demonstrations that followed the savings withdrawal freeze in 2001–02, to the renewed currency speculation of 2012; you can still see the scars of the crisis protests on the battered bank shutters. The tight confines and endless foot traffic make it difficult to look up, but if you do you'll be rewarded with an impressive spread of grand facades crowned with domes and towers. La City was once known as the *barrio inglés*, in reference to the large number of British immigrants who set up business here. Indeed, the first financial institutions were built in a rather Victorian style; it seems that the Porteño elite thought their houses should be French and their banks British.

Basílica and Convento de San Ramón

Reconquista 269 • Mon–Fri 10.30am–6pm • Free • ⓦ conventosanramon.org.ar

The City district hosts one of the most beautiful churches in Buenos Aires, the **Basílica de Nuestra Señora de la Merced** at Reconquista and Perón, which has been favoured by important political and military figures through the ages. The main structure dates from 1783, while the sandy coloured facade – the tympanum shows General Belgrano after he defeated the Spanish in battle in 1812 – was added in 1905. Every inch of the sombre interior is ornamented with gilt or tiles. Attached to the basilica is one of the city's best-kept secrets, the **Convento de San Ramón**. At its heart is a charming courtyard where you can eat in the restaurant under the arches, or just take a break from elbowing your way through the crowds outside.

Puerto Madero

More water than dry land, **Puerto Madero**, Buenos Aires' newest and glossiest barrio, centres on a defunct port directly to the east of the historical centre. Here four enormous oblong *diques*, or docks, run parallel to the Río de la Plata, connecting on either side to the Dársena Sur (Southern Harbour), near Boca, and the Dársena Norte (Northern Harbour), near Retiro, from where ferries depart for Uruguay. Lining these docks – which are officially numbered one to four, Dock One being the most southerly – are a series of preserved and restored brick and iron warehouses, originally used to hold grain from the Pampas before it was shipped around the world. By 1898, before the port was even fully finished, it was already insufficient in scale to cope with the volume of maritime traffic, and a new port was constructed to the north. For most of the twentieth century, Puerto Madero sat as a forlorn industrial relic, but in the 1990s private money was injected and it began to be converted into a voguish mix of restaurants, luxury apartments and offices. While this dockside development is decidedly upmarket and somewhat lacking in colour, it's nonetheless a relaxing place to stroll, and there are far worse ways to spend a lazy summer afternoon than sitting on a terrace here, sipping a *clericó*, watching the yachts bob on the water and enjoying the gentle breeze off the river. Docks Three and Four host the pick of the barrio's restaurants and bars.

GETTING AROUND   PUERTO MADERO

On foot Puerto Madero is within easy walking distance from downtown – just head east along Av Belgrano, c/Juan Domingo Perón or c/Viamonte – though the train tracks sandwiched between avenidas Alicia Moreau de Justo and Eduardo Madero can be awkward to cross on foot.

By tram Since the 1960s the harbourside railway lines had been used only by freight trains, but in 2007 the Tranvía del Este, a shiny, silent and smooth passenger tram, began

operating along the old tracks, connecting Av Córdoba with Av Independencia (approx every 20min; Mon–Sat 8am–11pm, Sun 9am–10pm; $1; ⓦ tranviadeleste.com.ar). With two intermediate stops where it crosses avenidas Corrientes and Belgrano, it's an excellent way to give your legs a break if they begin to falter midway along the barrio's 24-block length; you will need change to use the ticket machines but you might be able to buy tickets on board.

The docks

It's logical to begin your tour of Puerto Madero on the western (or city) side of the docks, which is flanked by a walkway along its entire length. The focal point – and best way to cross to the eastern side of the docks – is Spanish architect Santiago Calatrava's striking white bridge, dubbed the **Puente de la Mujer** (the "women's bridge"). Unveiled in 2001, its graceful curve – said to echo the outstretched leg

1

of a tango dancer – is a mesmerizing sight, especially when beautifully lit at night. The area's main attraction is the splendid collection of national and international art on display at the Colección Fortabat, at the northernmost end of the docks.

Museum ships

Av Alicia Moreau de Justo 500 and 980 • Daily 10am–7pm • $2 each • Ⓦ ara.mil.ar

Two of the handsomest sights in docks Four and Three respectively are two well-maintained **museum ships** – the *Buque Museo Corbeta ARA Uruguay*, built at the Cammell Laird shipyard in Birkenhead in 1874, and the Argentine navy's first training ship; and the *Buque Museo Fragata ARA Presidente Sarmiento*, built at the same British shipyards and the Argentine navy's flagship from 1899 to 1938. Both sailing ships (a corvette and a frigate, to give them their English names) have justifiably been declared historic monuments, though the bit about their being built in Britain is often skimmed over.

Colección de Arte Amalia Lacroze de Fortabat

Olga Cossettini 141 • Tues–Sun noon–9pm • $25 • ☎ 011 4310 6600, Ⓦ coleccionfortabat.org.ar

Since opening in 2008, the **Colección de Arte Amalia Lacroze de Fortabat** has become the barrio's star attraction. Located at the far northern end of Dock Four, it is housed in a purpose-built pavilion that looks rather like a giant sliding-top bread bin. A state-of-the-art blend of glass and aluminium (the sliding top is a retractable roof with protective panels that open as sunlight diminishes), the pavilion is in fact only the tip of the iceberg: below water level is a breathtakingly huge space showcasing the best private art collection on display in Latin America.

The museum was founded by Amalia Lacroze de Fortabat, who married well, twice – first an Argentine lawyer and later a cement magnate, Alfredo Fortabat, whose immense fortune she inherited in the 1970s. She sold the Loma Negra cement works in 2005, partly in order to set up the art museum.

Although the art collection is dominated by Argentine works, a number of European and US artists are also represented.

The foreign works

Perhaps the surest sign of Amalia Lacroze de Fortabat's importance both as a personality and art collector is her 1960 portrait by Andy Warhol that kicks off the display, alongside two earlier portraits by Catalan painter Vidal-Quadras. The place of honour must go to *Juliet and her Nurse*, a magnificent oil by Turner depicting Venice's St Mark's Square, which manages to dominate the main exhibition room, a splendid unadorned space the length of a city block.

The Argentine and Uruguayan works

Many of Argentina's major nineteenth- and twentieth-century artists are represented, many of them strongly influenced by European artistic movements such as Impressionism (for example, Fernando Fader's *Entre duraznos floridos* – "Among peach trees in blossom", 1915) and Symbolism (several works by Xul Solar). Like the Turner, many of the works depict famous sights in Europe such as Venice (see Rómulo Macció's *Puente de los Suspiros* – "Bridge of Sighs", 1998) or London (Nicolás García Uriburu's *Coloration of Trafalgar Square Fountains*, 1974). Several Argentine artists developed their own idiosyncratic styles, though – especially as the twentieth century advanced: many of the works by leading artist Antonio Berni (1905–81) are typically *criollo* (native), depicting among other things a rustic lunch or a country girl fondling a pumpkin. Uruguayans Blanes and Figari also get a look-in: the former's *La cautiva* ("The captive girl", 1880) is a scene from Argentina's own Wild West, while the latter's *En el patio* ("In the patio", undated) is a colonial vignette.

CLOCKWISE FROM TOP LEFT CASA ROSADA (P.63); BOUTIQUE IN PALERMO VIEJO (P.99); PIRÁMIDE DE MAYO, PLAZA DE MAYO (P.62); PLAZA DORREGO BAR, SAN TELMO (P.80) >

1

Costanera Sur

Running along Puerto Madero Este's eastern edge, the **Costanera Sur** is a sweeping avenue flanked by elegant balustrades, originally built as a riverside promenade at the beginning of the twentieth century. The avenue essentially lost its *raison d'être* in the 1970s when the government devised a project to reclaim land from the river. Dykes were constructed and the water drawn off but the project was never completed, leaving the suddenly inaptly named Costanera cut off from the river. However, the drained land unexpectedly became a haven for wildlife – now the Reserva Ecológica (see below). Just outside the reserve, it's worth pausing to see the flamboyant **Fuente de las Nereidas**, a large and elaborate marble fountain created by Tucumán sculptress Lola Mora in 1902. The fountain depicts a naked Venus perched coquettishly on the edge of a shell supported by two straining sea nymphs. The fountain was originally destined for the Plaza de Mayo, but its seductive display was thought too risqué to be in such proximity to the cathedral.

Reserva Ecológica

Av Tristán Achaval Rodríguez 1550 • Tues–Sun: April–Oct 8am–6pm; Nov–March 8am–7pm • Free • ☎ 011 4315 4129, ⊛ buenosaires .gov.ar/areas/med_ambiente/reserva

The **Reserva Ecológica** is a strange but wonderful place, a fragment of wild and watery grassland stretching for 2km alongside the Costanera. Having self-seeded with grassland after the landfill project was abandoned in 1984, the reserve offers a juxtaposition of urban and natural scenes, whether factory chimneys glimpsed through fronds of pampas or the city skyline over a lake populated by ducks and herons. Inside the reserve, near the entrance, the visitors' centre displays panels explaining the park's development and serves as the starting point for ranger-guided walks along the park's many trails (Sat & Sun 10.30am & 3.30pm). Full-moon nocturnal tours (weather permitting; dates of tours and sign-up deadlines are listed on the website) allow you to spot all manner of creatures, mainly birds, which keep a low daytime profile. There is a surprising diversity of flora and fauna in the park, with over two hundred species of bird visiting during the year. Aquatic species include ducks, herons, elegant black-necked swans, skittish coots, the common gallinule and the snail hawk, a bird of prey that uses its hooked beak to pluck freshwater snails out of their shells. The park is also home to small mammals, such as the easily spotted coypu, an aquatic rodent, and reptiles such as monitor lizards. The reserve's vegetation includes the bright red *ceibo*, but the most dominant plant is the *cortadera*, or pampas grass.

The south

Described by Borges as "an older, more solid world", **the south** is where Buenos Aires best preserves its traditions. Immediately south of the Plaza de Mayo lies the barrio of **Monserrat**, packed with historic buildings, churches and a couple of noteworthy museums. Heading south through Monserrat, you'll emerge into the cobbled streets and alleyways of **San Telmo**, where grand nineteenth-century mansions testify to the days when the barrio was home to wealthy landowners. San Telmo is best visited on a Sunday, when its central square, Plaza Dorrego, is the scene of a fascinating **antiques fair**, although there are plenty of antiques stores also open during the week. At the southern end of the barrio, there's the tranquil **Parque Lezama** – a good spot for observing local life, and home to an important history museum. Beyond Parque Lezama, and stretching all the way to the city's southern boundary, the Río Riachuelo, the quirky barrio of **La Boca** is a great place to spend an hour or two, wandering its colourful streets and soaking up its idiosyncratic atmosphere.

Monserrat

Monserrat, sometimes known as Barrio Sur, is the city's oldest district and, together with neighbouring San Telmo, is one of the most rewarding areas to explore on foot. A good starting point for delving into its grid of narrow streets and historic buildings is along **Calle Defensa**, named in honour of the barrio's residents, who, during the British invasions of 1806 and 1807, defended the city from the British troops by pouring boiling water and oil on them as they marched down the street.

Basílica de San Francisco de Asís

Alsina 380 • Mon–Fri 8am–7pm • Free • ☎ 011 4331 0625

On the corner of Alsina and Defensa stands the neo-Baroque **Basílica de San Francisco de Asís**. Dating from 1754, it was one of a number of churches burnt by angry Peronists in March 1955 in reaction to the navy's murderous bombing of an anti-Church, pro-Perón trade union rally in the Plaza de Mayo. The basilica was eventually restored, reconsecrated and reopened in 1967. An oak column from the original altarpiece, destroyed by the fire, is preserved in the adjoining Franciscan monastery, where monks sell bee-derived products, including honey and soap.

Museo de la Ciudad

Defensa 219 • Mon–Fri 11am–7pm, Sat & Sun 10am–8pm • $1, Mon & Wed free • ⓦ museodelaciudad.buenosaires.gov.ar

Half a block west of the Basilica de San Francisco de Asís, on the first floor of a handsome private residence, is the imaginative **Museo de la Ciudad**. Half the museum is given over to a permanent display of children's toys through the ages, so it's particularly worthwhile if you have youngsters to entertain. Look out for the toy farm reinvented as an Argentine estancia – dancing gauchos, bucking broncos and all. The rest of the museum is devoted to regularly changing exhibitions designed to illustrate everyday aspects of Porteño life, such as holidays or football. The objects are accompanied by witty descriptions, in Spanish only. Downstairs, a salón open to the street holds larger items, such as rescued doors and a traditional barrow from which *ambulantes* (hawkers) would have sold their wares, decorated in the *filete* style (see box, p.80).

Farmacia de la Estrella

Defensa 201 • Mon–Fri 8am–7pm • Free

At the corner with Alsina, the **Farmacia de la Estrella**, a beautifully preserved old pharmacy, describes itself as a living museum and is considered part of the Museo de la Ciudad, yet it is a working chemist's, specializing in homeopathy. Founded in 1834, it boasts an opulent interior of heavy walnut fittings and quirky old-fashioned medical murals and mirrors, finished off with a stunning frescoed ceiling.

Basílica de Santo Domingo

Defensa 422 • Mon–Fri 8am–7pm • Free • ☎ 011 4331 1668

Along Defensa, on the corner of Avenida Belgrano, you'll find the **Basílica de Santo Domingo**, an austere twin-towered structure whose glory is somewhat overshadowed by the elevated mausoleum to General Belgrano that dominates the tiled patio at its front. The square on which the basilica stands was taken by the British on June 27, 1806, on which date Catholicism was outlawed (briefly, as it turned out). In the corner to the left of the altar as you enter, you can see the flags from British regiments captured by General Liniers when the city was retaken two months later.

Manzana de las Luces

Perú 272 • Guided visits Mon–Fri 3pm, Sat & Sun 3pm, 4.30pm & 6pm • $12 • ⓦ manzanadelasluces.gov.ar

Taking up the whole block bounded by Alsina, Perú, Moreno and Bolívar – the latter one block west of Defensa – is the complex of buildings known as the **Manzana de las Luces**,

1

or "block of enlightenment". Dating from 1662, the complex originally housed a Jesuit community, and has been home to numerous official institutions throughout its history. The forty-minute tour (in Spanish, with summary explanations given in English) generally visits the inner patio, tunnels constructed to connect the churches (and later used for smuggling), some of the surrounding chambers – including one that hosted a nineteenth-century political assassination – and the reconstructed **Sala de Representantes**, a semicircular chamber where the first provincial legislature sat. Opposite the statue of General Roca at Av Julio Roca 600, the **Mercado de las Luces** (Mon–Fri 10.30am–7.30pm, Sun 2–7.30pm) has stalls set up in one of the Jesuit corridors, selling antiques, crystals, candles and other artisan products.

The block also encompasses the elite Colegio Nacional, where the nation's future politicians are schooled, and Buenos Aires' oldest church, **San Ignacio**, on the corner of Bolívar and Alsina, which dates from 1675. Apart from the rather Baroque Altar Mayor, the church's interior is fairly simple, an arrangement that makes one of its most notable icons, the beautiful seventeenth-century Nuestra Señora de las Nieves, all the more arresting. Check the website for details of visits – they vary from day to day and you might also book a guided tour in English.

Museo Etnográfico Juan Bautista Ambrosetti

Moreno 350 • Tues–Fri 1–7pm, Sat & Sun 3–7pm, guided visits Sat & Sun 4pm, closed Jan • $3 voluntary donation • Ⓦ museoetnografico.filo.uba.ar

Part of the Universidad de Buenos Aires, the fascinating **Museo Etnográfico Juan Bautista Ambrosetti** has some international anthropological exhibits, though its real interest lies in its well-displayed collection from pre-Columbian South America. Ambrosetti himself gained fame by discovering the pre-Incan ruins of Tilcara (see p.300) in 1908.

Ground floor

The ground-floor rooms display the impressive jewellery, pots and tools of the few native groups who lived on what is now Argentine territory, such as the Mapuche, whose territory reached from modern Chile as far as the pampas. For hundreds of years the Mapuche successfully resisted both Inca and Spanish attempts to conquer their territory; their textiles and jewellery are particularly noteworthy, with distinctive headbands and chest pieces featuring heavy silver frills. There are also exhibits on the Yámana and other peoples of Tierra del Fuego, whose societies were less developed (see box, p.521). Panels (and pamphlets in English) provide the exhibits with some context.

Upper floor

The upper floor deals with different themes relating to the culture, religion and trade of various other pre-Columbian South American peoples, including the Inca. Of particular note are a fine Huari tunic covered in the symbols used instead of a written language and religious costumes from present-day Bolivia made of jaguar skin, an animal that represented power and wisdom. There are many fascinating examples of the gradual Hispanicization of the indigenous people, where Christian motifs and European materials were melded with native American beliefs – look out for the wooden statue of Jesus wearing a jaguar pelt.

San Telmo

You have to be very hard-hearted not to be seduced by the romantically crumbling facades and cobbled streets of **San Telmo**, a neighbourhood proud of its reputation as the guardian of the city's traditions. A small, roughly square-shaped barrio, San Telmo is bounded to the north by Avenida Chile (six blocks south of Plaza de Mayo), to the west by Calle Piedras, to the east by Paseo Colón and to the south by Parque Lezama. Like neighbouring Monserrat, its main artery is **Calle Defensa**, once the main throughfare between the Plaza de Mayo and the city's port.

The barrio's appearance of decaying luxury is the result of a kind of reverse gentrification. When the city's grand mansions were abandoned by their patrician owners after a yellow fever epidemic in 1871, they were soon converted into *conventillos* (tenements) by landlords keen to make a quick buck from newly arrived immigrants. This sudden loss of cachet preserved many of the barrio's original features: whereas much of the north, centre and west of the city was variously torn down, smartened up or otherwise modernized, San Telmo's inhabitants simply adapted the neighbourhood's buildings to their needs. It's still largely a working-class area, and well-heeled Palermo-dwellers may warn you off coming here, but the area's superb architecture also attracts bohemians, students, backpackers and artists, from Argentina and abroad. Together with rising rents, the recent appearance of designer clothing and homewares stores among the traditional antiques shops is an indication that San Telmo may once again be going up in the world – though this latterday gentrification is not a development that everyone welcomes.

1

FILETEADO OR FILETE ART

As you wander around the city, look out for examples of **fileteado** or **filete art**, particularly on shop signs. Characterized by ornate lettering, heavy shading and the use of scrolls and flowers entwined with the azure and white of the national flag, this distinctive art form first made its appearance on the city transport system in the early twentieth century. Often associated with tango, its actual origins are a little murky, but it seems to have been introduced by Italian immigrants. Banned from public transport in 1975 – the authorities felt bus destinations and numbers should be unadorned – it moved onto signs above stores and cafés as well as more traditional canvases. Today it is synonymous with Porteño identity, particularly in the south of the city. As well as tango stars, a popular subject is the pithy saying, including the classic *si bebe para olvidar paga antes de tomar* ("if you drink to forget, pay first") and the more obscure *si querés la leche fresca, atá la vaca a la sombre* ("if you want fresh milk, tie the cow up in the shade").

San Telmo is one of Buenos Aires' major tourist attractions per se, particularly for its Sunday antiques market, the **Feria de San Telmo**, held in the neighbourhood's central square, Plaza Dorrego; there's usually a smaller version on Saturdays. It's also the barrio most closely associated with **tango**, and the place where many of the best-known tango shows and bars have their home. At the southern end of the barrio, the small, palm-lined Parque Lezama, containing the city's well-organized **Museo Histórico Nacional**, makes a restful spot to end a tour of the neighbourhood.

Calle Defensa

Leading south from Plaza de Mayo, Defensa runs through Monserrat (see p.77) and then straight on through San Telmo to Parque Lezama. On weekends, vehicles are banned and replaced with solely human traffic as visitors wend their way past performance artists and buskers to visit the cobbled lane's antiques stores and bars. A stroll along here is more about soaking up the atmosphere than visiting specific sites – musicians, mainly playing tango, naturally, eccentric buskers and inventive puppeteers add to the ambience.

Mercado Municipal

Mon–Sat 7am–2pm & 4.30–9pm, Sun 7am–2pm

Don't miss the fabulous iron-roofed **Mercado Municipal** between Carlos Calvo and Estados Unidos, a thriving city-centre food market and one of the few of its kind left in the city. In addition to piles of colourful fruit and veg, a number of old-fashioned butcher stalls and other food vendors, the market also features all manner of curios, minor antiques and junk, plus interesting items such as vintage clothing and collectables like old gramophone records, coins and posters.

El Zanjón

Defensa 755 • Guided visits Mon–Fri hourly 11am–4pm • $60 (shorter tours Sun every 30min 1–6pm, $40) • Reservations advisable on ☎ 011 4361 3002, ⓦ elzanjon.com.ar

El Zanjón is a typical example of a pre-yellow-fever-era mansion that was turned into a *conventillo* or tenement building. The well-run visits take you underground through layers of history to see the reconstructed and tastefully lit tunnels where the city's water once flowed, and the cisterns the inhabitants used, though the tour price might seem a bit steep to see what are essentially little more than foundations and old water tanks.

Plaza Dorrego

At the core of San Telmo on the corner of Defensa and Humberto 1°, **Plaza Dorrego** is a tiny square surrounded by elegant mansions, most of them now converted into bars and antiques shops. During the week, cafés set up tables in the square, and on Sunday it becomes the setting for the city's long-running antiques market, the **Feria de San Pedro Telmo** (10am–5pm; ⓦferiadesantelmo.com). Overflowing with antique *mates*, jewel-coloured soda syphons, vintage watches and ancient ticket machines from the city's buses, the two dozen tightly packed stalls make for fascinating browsing, albeit through occasionally heavy crowds. There are no real bargains to be had – the stallholders and habitués are far too canny to let a gem slip through their fingers – but among the jumble you may find your own souvenir of Buenos Aires. The market's pickpockets are also very canny – one famously swiped the bag of former US President George W. Bush's daughter despite the presence of six security guards – so be careful with your belongings.

As the stallholders start to pack away their wares on Sunday afternoons, Plaza Dorrego becomes – weather permitting – the setting of a free outdoor **milonga** (tango dance; see box, p.122). There's a refreshing informality to this regular event, frequented by tourists, locals and tango fanatics alike, which might encourage even those with only a rudimentary knowledge of tango to take the plunge.

Museo de Arte Moderno de Buenos Aires (MAMBA)

Av San Juan 350 • Tues–Fri 11am–7pm, Sat, Sun & public hols (including Mon) 11am–8pm • $2, free on Tues • ☎ 011 4342 3001, ⓦmuseos.buenosaires.gob.ar/mam2.htm

At the corner of Calle Defensa and Avenida San Juan, one of the main east–west arteries of the city, the **Museo de Arte Moderno de Buenos Aires** showcases a permanent collection of mostly Argentine art from the 1920s to the present day. Housed in the late nineteenth-century Nobleza Picardo tobacco factory, with a distinctive brick facade adorned with elegant arches, the collection features big national names, such as Enio Iommi, Emilio Pettoruti, Guillermo Kuitca and Xul Solar. After many years of closure for renovation, it reopened in late 2010, since when it has shown off national and international treasures by the likes of Paul Klee, Julio Le Parc, Henri Matisse and Juan del Prete. Further exhibition space was inaugurated in 2011 and when complete the museum will also feature a sculpture patio, bookshop, café and auditorium. One of the most outstanding architectural details is a futuristic staircase that resembles the charred skeleton of some mythical beast.

Parque Lezama and the Museo Histórico Nacional

The southern stretch of Defensa takes you through a slightly more run-down though perhaps more authentic part of San Telmo, with its own neighbourhood cafés and stores, though there are some outstanding antiques shops, too. Four blocks on from Plaza Dorrego, you will reach the classic 24-hour café *Bar Británico* (see p.118), overlooking the **Parque Lezama**, a lively green expanse. On a bluff towering over Paseo Colón, the park is generally regarded as the site of Buenos Aires' founding by **Pedro de Mendoza** in 1536. The conquistador's statue looms over you as you enter the park from the corner of Defensa and Brasil; a bronze of Mendoza thrusts his sword into the ground, while behind him a bas-relief shows an indigenous man, throwing up his hands in surrender. The park looks at its best in early evening, when the sun filters through its trees, children run along its paths and groups of old men play cards or chess at stone tables.

Iglesia Ortodoxa Rusa

Brasil 313 • Sat 5–8pm, Sun 10am–12.30pm, guided visits every second Sun of month at 4pm ($10) • Women must wear long skirts to be allowed entry • ☎ 011 4361 4274, ⓦ iglesiarusa.org.ar

Overlooking the north end of the park is the exotic-looking **Iglesia Ortodoxa Rusa**, conspicuous for its crown of five bright-blue curvaceous onion domes, typical of Russian Orthodox churches. Dedicated to the Holy Trinity, it was built in 1899 and contains a large set of valuable icons donated by Tsar Nicolas II just as his empire was falling into terminal decline.

1

Museo Histórico Nacional

Defensa 1600 • Wed–Sun 11am–6pm • Free • ☎ 011 4307 1182

Within the park, though entered via Defensa 1600, the **Museo Histórico Nacional**, founded in 1887, is housed in a magnificent colonial building painted a startling deep red and covered with elaborate white mouldings that resemble piped cake-icing. The museum takes a tour through Argentina's history, concentrating mainly on the tumultuous nineteenth century, featuring portraits of all the big names from Argentina's formative years as well as maps and a number of important paintings of historical, rather than artistic, interest. But, when it is on display, the high point of the collection is the stunning **Tarja de Potosí**, an elaborate silver and gold shield given to General Belgrano in 1813 by the women of Potosí (a silver-mining town in Upper Perú, now Bolivia) in recognition of his role in their country's struggle for independence from Spain. Almost as tall as a man, it's a delicately worked and intricate piece complete with tiny figures symbolizing the discovery of America.

Boca

The barrio is easily reached on foot from Parque Lezama or by bus #86 from Plaza de Mayo or #53 from Constitución; it's also on the route of the city government's tour bus (see p.106)

More than any other barrio in Buenos Aires, **Boca** (or "La Boca") and its inhabitants seem to flaunt their idiosyncrasies. Located in the capital's southeastern corner, this working-class riverside neighbourhood has been nicknamed the "República de la Boca" since 1882, when a group of local youths declared the barrio's secession from the country. Even today, its residents – many new immigrants from other South American countries – have a reputation for playing by their own rules and are most famous for their brightly coloured wooden and corrugated-iron houses. The district was originally

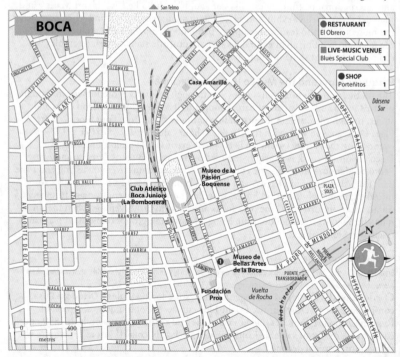

the favoured destination for Italian immigrants, and the colours of the houses derive from the Genoese custom of painting homes with the paint left over from boats. Boca's other most characteristic emblem is its football team, **Boca Juniors**, the country's most popular club and probably the most famous one abroad.

Named after the *boca*, or mouth, of the Río Riachuelo, which snakes along its southern border, Boca is an irregularly shaped barrio, longer than it is wide. Its main thoroughfare is Avenida Almirante Brown, which cuts through the neighbourhood from Parque Lezama to the towering iron **Puente Transbordador** that straddles the Riachuelo. Apart from some excellent pizzerias, there's little to detain you along the avenue: the majority of Boca's attractions are packed into the grids of streets on either side. Even then, there's not a great deal to see as such, and unless you plan to visit all the museums an hour or two will suffice; morning is the ideal time to go, when the light best captures the district's bright hues and before the tour buses arrive.

Be warned that Boca remains a poor neighbourhood and has an unfortunate reputation for crime, with muggings a fairly common occurrence. There's no need to be paranoid, but it is advisable to stick strictly to the main tourist district and follow the advice of the police who patrol the area; keep expensive watches and cameras out of sight.

La Bombonera

Brandsen 805 · ☎ 011 4362 2260, ⓦ bocajuniors.com.ar/la-bombonera

The true heart of Boca is Boca Juniors' stadium, **La Bombonera**. Built in 1940, it was remodelled in the 1990s and the name – literally "the chocolate box" – refers to its compact structure; although Boca has more fans than any other Argentine team, the stadium's capacity is smaller than that of most of its rivals. This is the place where many of the country's best young players cut their teeth before heading to Europe on lucrative deals – the Bombonera's most famous veteran is Diego Maradona (see box, p.84), who retains a VIP seat at the stadium. Seeing a game here is an incredible experience, even for non-soccer fans.

Just inside the stadium entrance, there's a large painting by famous local artist Benito Quinquela Martín (see p.84) entitled *Orígen de la bandera de Boca* ("the origin of Boca's flag"), which illustrates one of the club's most famous anecdotes. Though the exact date and circumstances of the event are disputed, all agree that Boca Juniors chose the colours of its strip from the flag of the next ship to pass through its then busy port. As the boat was Swedish, the distinctive blue and yellow strip was selected.

Around the stadium, a huddle of stalls and shops sell Boca souvenirs while, on the pavement outside the stadium, stars with the names of Boca players past and present, some featuring their footprints, were laid as part of the club's centenary celebrations in 2005. Some of the neighbouring houses have taken up the blue and yellow theme, too, with facades painted like giant football shirts.

Museo de la Pasión Boquense

Daily 10am–6pm · $40 for museum visit only, $50 for museum and brief tour, $55 for museum and full tour · ⓦ museoboquense.com

If you don't get the opportunity to watch a match, check out the **Museo de la Pasión Boquense** and its **stadium tour**. The museum, built into the stadium structure, offers a modern audiovisual experience, including a 360-degree film that puts you in the boots of a Boca player and a charming model of how La Boca would have looked and sounded in the 1930s. The full tour (usually in Spanish, English and Portuguese) includes the stands, pitch and press conference room and even takes in the players' jacuzzi and dressing room, complete with statues of the Virgin Mary.

Caminito and around

From La Bombonera it's a short walk southwards to La Boca's other nerve centre: **Caminito**. A former train siding now transformed into a pedestrian street and open-air

1

EL DIEGO

Few people have captured the imagination of the Argentine public as much as **Diego Armando Maradona**. A bull of a player with exceptional close control, balance and on-field vision, the diminutive no. 10 was the finest footballer of his generation and arguably of all time – though the latter title is now seriously contested by his compatriot, Lionel Messi. Born in a poor neighbourhood on the outskirts of Buenos Aires, Maradona's playing career (1976–97) was peerless. He made his first-team, first-division debut for club **Argentinos Juniors** in 1976, when he was just 15. Maradona wore the colours of seven clubs in total, including **Boca Juniors**, **Barcelona** and, most famously, **Napoli**, where he is still venerated as the player who brought southern Italy's poorer brother glory and silverware. He also led Argentina to win the World Cup in 1986, a campaign that included one of the most celebrated of all World Cup games, the quarter-final played against England, just four years after the South Atlantic conflict. Maradona scored two goals, including the infamous "Hand of God" goal, in which he tapped the ball in with his hand, and a second, legitimate goal considered to be one of the finest ever scored.

Like many geniuses, though, Maradona was flawed – in his case, by the excesses of alcohol and, particularly, drugs. He was suspended in 1991 for testing positive for cocaine, and then again for the banned substance ephedrine during the 1994 World Cup. After a low point in 2004 where he was hospitalized following a cocaine-induced heart attack, he bounced back to host his own talk show in 2005, where guests included Pele and Maradona's friend Fidel Castro. In 2008 he surprised many when he took over as coach of the Argentine national side and during qualifications for the 2010 World Cup was strongly criticized for his tactics (or lack of them) – which led him to more notoriety, this time when he launched an obscenity-laden tirade against the press following Argentina's qualification. He lost his job after a humiliating 4-0 defeat by Germany in the South Africa finals, but was soon after appointed manager of Al-Wasl FC, based in Dubai, earning €3.5 million a year.

art museum, Caminito, which runs diagonally between the riverfront and Calle Lamadrid, is the barrio's (and possibly the city's) most famous street. Lined with the best-kept examples of Boca's coloured houses, it's very photogenic but not very lived-in – a life-size museum or a tourist trap, depending on your point of view. The street was "founded" by the barrio's most famous artist, **Benito Quinquela Martín**, who painted epic and expressive scenes of the neighbourhood's daily life. Quinquela Martín rescued the old siding from oblivion after the rail company removed the tracks in 1954. He encouraged the immigrants' tradition of painting their houses in bright colours and took the name for the street from a famous 1920s tango.

The Caminito may have lost its original charm, but the bold blocks of rainbow-coloured walls, set off with contrasting window frames and balconies, are still an arresting sight. Down the middle of the street, there's an **arts and crafts fair**, dominated by garish paintings of the area. Tango musicians frequently perform along the street, too, accompanied by the sound of cameras clicking. At the western end of Caminito, Calle Garibaldi runs past and on south, a charmingly ramshackle street with a slew of coloured corrugated-iron buildings, less done up than those of Caminito.

Vuelta de Rocha and Puente Transbordador

The eastern end of Caminito leads to Avenida Pedro de Mendoza and the Riachuelo, which bulges dramatically at this point, creating a curvaceous but often malodorous inlet known as the **Vuelta de Rocha**. The view from Avenida Pedro de Mendoza is of a jumbled but majestic mass of boats, factories and bridges: directly south, across the river, there's the working-class suburb of Avellaneda while to your left there's one of Buenos Aires' major landmarks, the massive iron **Puente Transbordador**, or transport bridge, built in the early years of the twentieth century and now out of use. Next to the transport bridge is Puente Nicolás Avellaneda – a very similar construction built in

1939. This functioning bridge is one of the major causeways in and out of the city. Far below it, small rowing boats still ferry passengers to and from Avellaneda. Avenida Pedro de Mendoza itself is lined with cafés catering to the hordes of visiting tourists, and there are also two excellent **art museums**.

Fundación Proa

Av Pedro de Mendoza 1929 • Tues–Sun 11am–7pm, guided visits Sat & Sun noon–6pm in Spanish • $12 • ☎ 011 4104 1000,
Ⓦ proa.org

The first of the art museums on Avenida Pedro de Mendoza is the **Fundación Proa**. Set inside a converted mansion – all Italianate elegance outside and modern, angular galleries within – Proa has no permanent collection but hosts some fascinating and diverse exhibitions, usually with a Latin American theme, ranging from 1980s Argentine art to pre-Columbian Aztec sculpture. There have also been shows dedicated to non-Latin American artists, such as Louise Bourgeois and Marcel Duchamp.

Museo de Bellas Artes de La Boca

Av Pedro de Mendoza 1835 • Tues–Sun 10am–6pm • $8 • ☎ 011 4301 1080

A short stroll east along Avenida Pedro de Mendoza from the Fundación Proa brings you to another art museum, the long-established **Museo de Bellas Artes de La Boca**. Founded in 1938 by local lad Benito Quinquela Martín on the site of his studio (now also a school), it houses many of his major works, as well as those of contemporary Argentine artists. It's the perfect setting for a display of Quinquela Martín's work, since you can actually see much of his subject matter simply by peering out of the windows of the gallery or climbing up to the viewpoint on the roof. More than anyone, Quinquela Martín conveyed the industrial grandeur of La Boca, dedicating himself to painting scenes of everyday life. Indeed, he was so associated with the city's least salubrious neighbourhood that, like the tango, he did not garner respect with the Argentine establishment until he had become famous abroad.

The north

A combination of extravagant elegance and an authentic lived-in feel pervades **the north** of Buenos Aires, where the four residential barrios of most interest to visitors – Retiro, Recoleta, Palermo and Belgrano – each retain a distinctive character. Nearest to the centre, **Retiro** and **Recoleta** – known jointly as **Barrio Norte** – have chic streets lined with boutiques, art galleries and smart cafés, although the dockside fringes and the highly insalubrious bits near the city's biggest train station, also called Retiro, are just as down at heel as parts of the southern barrios, if not more so. Recoleta is associated primarily with its magnificent **cemetery** where, among other national celebrities, Evita is buried. Both barrios also share an extraordinary concentration of French-style **palaces**, tangible proof of the obsession of the city's elite at the beginning of the twentieth century with established European cities. Many of these palaces can be visited and some of them house the area's opulent museum collections, but they are also sights in themselves.

   Palermo and **Belgrano**, further north, are large districts composed of a mixture of tall apartment buildings, tree-lined boulevards, little cobbled streets and grandiose neocolonial houses. Many of Buenos Aires' best **restaurants** and **shops** are here, so you should plan a visit in this direction at least once. It's worth making a day of it to check out the beautiful **parks** and **gardens**, attend a game of polo (see p.39), or to see another beguiling side of the city in, for example, Palermo Soho, a district of lively cafés-cum-art galleries.

1

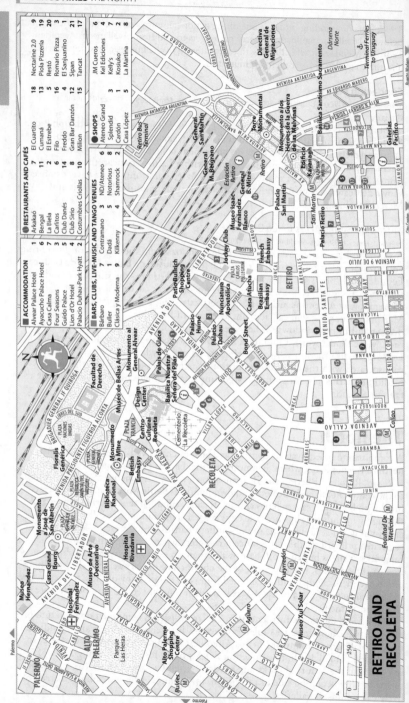

RETIRO AND RECOLETA

■ **ACCOMMODATION**

Alvear Palace Hotel	1
Ayacucho Palace Hotel	6
Casa Calma	3
Four Seasons	7
Guido Palace	5
Lion d'Or Hotel	4
Palacio Duhau–Park Hyatt	2

● **RESTAURANTS AND CAFÉS**

Arkakao	1	El Cuartito	18	Nectarine 2.0	9
Bengal	11	Cumaná	13	Piola Pizzeria	19
La Biela	7	El Estrebe	2	Restó	20
Carlitos	3	Filo	6	Romario Pizza	3
Club Danés	14	Freddo	4	El Sanjuanino	1
Club Sirio	4	Gran Bar Danzón	12	Sipan	21
Costumbres Criollas	10	Million	15	Tancat	17

■ **BARS, CLUBS, LIVE-MUSIC AND TANGO VENUES**

Bárbaro	7	Contramano	3	ND/Ateneo	6
Buller	1	Dadá	5	Notorious	8
Clásica y Moderna	9	Kilkenny	4	Shamrock	2

● **SHOPS**

Ateneo Grand		JM Cueros	6
Splendid	3	Kel Ediciones	4
Cardón	8	Kelly's	7
Casa López	5	Kosiuko	2
		La Martina	8

Retiro

Retiro is easily reached on foot from the city centre, and is connected to the subte via San Martín and Retiro stations, both on Line C

Squeezed between the city centre to the south, Recoleta to the west and mostly inhospitable docklands to the north and east, **Retiro** gets its name from a hermit's *retiro* (retreat) that was hidden among dense woodland here in the sixteenth century, when Buenos Aires was little more than a village. Today it's surprisingly varied for such a small barrio: commercial **art galleries** and airline offices outnumber other businesses along the busy streets around the end of Calle Florida near the barrio's focal point, Plaza San Martín, while west of busy Avenida 9 de Julio lies a smart, quiet residential area.

Lying at Retiro's aristocratic heart, **Plaza San Martín** is one of the city's most enticing green spaces, flanked by opulent patrician buildings. More outstanding examples of the barrio's palaces, which reflect how wealthy Porteños of the late nineteenth century yearned for their city to be a New World version of Paris, are clustered around **Plaza Carlos Pellegrini**, one of the city's most elegant squares. For most Porteños, the barrio's name has become synonymous with the once grand but now mostly decrepit train terminal, the **Estación Retiro**, which still retains some original Edwardian features. Next to it is the city's major bus terminal, a modern and fairly efficient complex, and beyond that urban wasteland and a shantytown.

Estación Retiro

Av del Libertador 50

A massive complex of rail terminals, **Estación Retiro** is in fact three train stations in one: General San Martín, General Belgrano and General Mitre. The third of these is also by far the most impressive, a massive stone and metal structure completed in 1915 by Charles John Dudley, a British constructor based in Liverpool. Decorated with Royal Doulton porcelain tiles, it is a majestic, airy edifice with an iron roof that, at the time, was the largest of its kind in the world. Recently restored to its former glory, it's worth a visit for its splendid café, *Café Retiro*. This is also the place to come if you plan to take the train to Tigre (see p.133).

Plaza San Martín

Immediately southeast of the train stations, the leafy **Plaza San Martín** plays many roles: romantic meeting-place, picnic area for office workers, children's playground and many people's arrival point in downtown Buenos Aires, owing to the main train and bus terminals nearby. Plaza San Martín was designed by Argentina's most important landscape architect, Frenchman **Charles Thays** (see box, p.88), and created especially for a monument to **General San Martín** that was moved to its southwestern corner in 1910 for the country's centenary. Aligned with Avenida Santa Fe, the imposing bronze equestrian statue stands proudly on a high marble pedestal decorated with scenes representing national liberation. The Libertador points west, showing the way across the Andes. The plaza's lush lawns are a favourite sunbathing spot in the warmer months, but when it gets baking hot you can always cool down on a bench beneath the luxuriant palms, *ceibos*, monkey puzzles, lime trees and acacias.

Monumento a los Héroes de la Guerra de las Malvinas

The more open, northern half of Plaza San Martín slopes down to Avenida del Libertador, which runs through northern Buenos Aires all the way to Tigre. The **Monumento a los Héroes de la Guerra de las Malvinas** stands on the brow of the slope, a sombre cenotaph comprising 25 black marble plaques inscribed with the 649 names of the country's fallen during the 1982 Falklands conflict, its eternal flame partly symbolizing Argentina's persistent claim over the South Atlantic islands. It is permanently guarded by a rotation of the army, navy and air force, and is the scene of both remembrance ceremonies and demonstrations on April 2 each year, the day on

1

CHARLES THAYS: BUENOS AIRES' LANDSCAPE ARTIST

In the 1880s, French botanist and **landscape architect Charles Thays** (1849–1934) travelled to South America to study its rich flora, particularly the continent's hundreds of endemic tree species. He initially settled in Argentina, where his services were in great demand as municipal authorities across the country sought to smarten their cities up. They, like their European and North American counterparts, were spurred by the realization that the country's fast-growing urban sprawls needed parks and gardens to provide vital breathing spaces and recreational areas.

In 1890, Thays was appointed director of parks and gardens in Buenos Aires, in no small part due to his adeptness at transforming open plazas formerly used for military parades, or *plazas secas*, into shady *plazas verdes*, or green squares, such as Plaza San Martín. He also designed the capital's botanical garden and the zoo – which he planted with dozens of *tipas* (also known as *palo rosa*, or rosewood) – as well as Palermo's Parque 3 de Febrero, Belgrano's Barrancas, Córdoba's Parque Sarmiento and Parque San Martín, Tucumán's Parque 9 de Julio and, most impressive of them all, Mendoza's Parque General San Martín. Thays received countless private commissions, too, including the garden of Palacio Hume, on Avenida Alvear in Recoleta, and the layout of the exclusive residential estate known as Barrio Parque, in Palermo Chico.

Despite his French origins, he preferred the informal English style of landscaping, and also experimented with combinations of native plants such as jacarandas, *tipas* and *palo borracho* (a spiky-trunked relative of the *ceibo* with handsome pink flowers) with Canary Island palms, planes and lime trees. Oddly enough, given the high regard in which he was held and his contributions to the greening of Buenos Aires, the lone plaza named in his honour, Plaza Carlos Thays, in Palermo, is disappointingly barren, and definitely not the best example of landscaping the city has to offer.

which Argentina began its brief occupation of the islands. The monument was deliberately placed opposite the former Plaza Británica – called the Plaza Fuerza Aérea Argentina since 1982.

Torre Monumental (Torre de los Ingleses)

Plaza Fuerza Aérea Argentina • Mon–Fri noon–6pm, Sat & Sun 9am–6pm • Free

At the centre of the Plaza Fuerza Aérea Argentina there are echoes of London's Big Ben in the 76m-high **Torre de los Ingleses**, the Anglo-Argentine community's contribution to the city's 1910 centenary celebrations. During and after the 1982 conflict there was talk of demolishing the tower, and it was officially renamed Torre Monumental, though no one calls it that. The lift that used to carry visitors to the top has been out of operation for some years, but it is still worth going inside to see the collections of interesting old photos of Retiro or to chat to the tower's caretaker – a fount of knowledge on local history and museums throughout the city.

Basílica del Santísimo Sacramento

San Martín 1039 • Daily 8am–10pm • Free

The **Basílica del Santísimo Sacramento** lurks east of the Plaza San Martín, at the end of a narrow *pasaje* and rather dwarfed by the skyscrapers surrounding it. It was built with some of the vast fortune of Mercedes Castellanos de Anchorena, a matriarchal figure who married into one of Argentina's wealthiest and most influential landowning clans (hence the Argentine expression "as rich as an Anchorena"). Consecrated in 1916, the basilica is still regarded as the smartest place to get married in Buenos Aires. It was designed by French architects, with a white marble dome and five slender turrets; it's no coincidence that it looks so much like Paris's Sacré Coeur. Inside, no expense was spared: red onyx from Morocco, marble from Verona and Carrara, red sandstone from the Vosges, glazed mosaic tiles from Venice and bronze from France were imported to decorate Mercedes' monument to devotion. Down in the crypt and behind a protective grille is her **mausoleum**, an ostentatious yet doleful concoction of marble angels guarded by a demure Virgin Mary.

Edificio Kavanagh

San Martín and Florida 1065

The **Edificio Kavanagh** sums up the social – and architectural – evolution in twentieth-century Buenos Aires. It is rumoured that Corina Kavanagh sold most of her property in the country to erect what, when it went up in 1935, was to be the tallest building (120m) in South America. It is also rumoured that she deliberately built it in front of the Basílica del Santísimo Sacramento to conceal her bitter rival's masterpiece. The two facades of its distinctive flat-iron shape – it's built in a wedge formed by the two streets – were hailed at the time by the American Institute of Architects as the world's best example of Rationalist architecture. Over the years the apartment building has been inhabited by many of the city's rich and famous; it is not open to the public.

Palacio Retiro

Av Santa Fe 750 • Guided visits only, in English Wed & Thurs 3.30pm; in Spanish Tues 3pm, Wed–Fri 11am & 3pm, Sat 11am • $35 • ⓦ palaciopaz.com.ar

Press baron José Paz, founder of daily newspaper *La Prensa* and related by marriage to the Anchorenas, wanted his Buenos Aires home to look like the Louvre in Paris, so he commissioned the **Palacio Retiro** – previously known as the Palacio Paz – to be built by a French architect between 1902 and 1914. Sadly, however, Paz died in 1912, without ever seeing the finished product. The palace runs along the southwest side of Plaza San Martín, and access is via magnificent wrought-iron gates at Av Santa Fe 750. It remains the largest single house ever built in Argentina, and its main facade is an uncanny replica of the Sully wing of the Louvre, with steeply stacked slate roofs, a double row of tiny windows and a colonnaded ground floor.

Inside, the eighteen rooms open to the public – less than one-sixth of the whole building – are decorated in an eclectic range of French styles, from Gothic to Empire, including a scaled-down copy of the Hall of Mirrors in Versailles, but the *pièce de résistance* is the great Hall of Honour, a cavernous, circular room lined with several types of European marble and crowned with a stained-glass dome from which the Sun King beams down. Artur Rubinstein entertained guests in the little music room and the Prince of Wales dined here during his visit to the city in 1925, but the Paz family fell on hard times in the late 1930s, most of the original furniture was sold off and the palace was divided between the Círculo Militar, an officers' club, and the **Museo de Armas de la Nación** (Mon–Fri 1–7pm; $10). The latter now houses an exhibition of armour, weapons and military uniforms, some dating back to the Wars of Independence.

Palacio San Martín

Arenales 761 • Guided visits in English and Spanish Mon & Wed 2.30pm • Free • ☎ 011 4819 8092

Just north of the Palacio Retiro and northwest of Plaza San Martín, at Arenales and Esmeralda, **Palacio San Martín** is a particularly extravagant example of the city's ostentatious palaces. Built in 1905 for the **Anchorena** family, it was originally known as the Palacio Anchorena. Mercedes Castellanos de Anchorena lived here with her family for twenty years, until the Great Depression left them penniless. The enormous building is actually divided up into three subtly different palaces, all sharing a huge Neoclassical entrance and ceremonial courtyard. Its overall structure is based on a nineteenth-century Parisian banker's mansion, with slate mansard roofs, colonnades and domed attics, while the neo-Baroque interior is inspired by the eighteenth-century Hotel de Condé, also in Paris. Fashionable Art Nouveau details, such as ornate stained-glass windows and wrought-iron staircases, were also incorporated.

After the palace and its accumulated treasures were hurriedly sold off in 1927, the government turned it into the Ministry of Foreign Affairs, International Trade and Worship, and renamed it Palacio San Martín. Since the 1980s, when the ministry moved into the larger plate-glass building across Calle Esmeralda, the palace has been

1

reserved for state ceremonies, and is open to the public for tours only. Some of the original furniture and paintings have been recovered, but the guided visits are above all a rare opportunity to witness the opulent interior of a Porteño palace. The gilt mirrors, marble fireplaces and chandeliers are all on a grandiose scale, yet they still look lost in the cavernous rooms, with their polished parquet floors, inlaid wooden panelling and ceilings richly decorated with oil paintings.

Museo de Arte Hispanoamericano Isaac Fernández Blanco

Suipacha 1422 • Tues–Fri 2–7pm, Sat & Sun 11am–7pm • $1 • ⓦ museofernandezblanco.buenosaires.gov.ar

Two blocks north and one west of Palacio San Martín, the **Museo de Arte Hispanoamericano Isaac Fernández Blanco** is one of the city's undisputed cultural highlights. The museum occupies the **Palacio Noel**, a stunning Neocolonial house built in the 1920s by architect Martín Noel, who later donated it to the city. Its style imitates eighteenth-century Lima Baroque, a backlash against the slavish imitation of Parisian palaces fashionable at the time. With plain white walls, lace-like window-grilles, dark wooden bow windows and wrought-iron balconies, it's the perfect residence for the superb collection of **Spanish-American art** on display inside. Most of the artefacts on display, all favourably presented, were produced in the seventeenth and early eighteenth centuries, in Perú or Alto Perú (present-day Bolivia).

The collection, spread over three floors, highlights the culture of many of the peoples who made up early South America, from Jesuits in the jungle to prosperous colonial *criollos* (Spanish-Americans). One of the most striking pieces, on the ground floor, is a fantastic eighteenth-century silver sacrarium, embellished with a portrait of Christ on a copper plaque. Other high points of this huge and varied collection include a Luso-Brazilian silver votive lamp, polychrome furniture – the work of Bolivian craftsmen – and fine Jesuit/Guaraní statues, all carved from wood. There's also an extensive display of anonymous paintings from the **Cusqueña School** – one of the most prodigious in colonial South America. Its masters, based in the Peruvian city of Cusco and especially active in the eighteenth century, produced subtle oil paintings, mostly of religious, devotional subjects, which combined sombre understatement with a startling vitality and mixed traditional Catholic imagery with indigenous motifs.

Plaza Carlos Pellegrini and around

The elegant triangle of **Plaza Carlos Pellegrini** is a centre of Retiro's well-heeled residential streets west of Avenida 9 de Julio, and near it you'll find a variety of spectacular buildings that share a common theme: their meticulous French style. Between 1910 and 1925, the obsession with turning Buenos Aires into the "Paris of the South" reached a fever pitch in this part of the city, making this neighbourhood one of the more exclusive, something it remains to this day. The many feats of **Carlos Pellegrini**, president in the 1890s and the plaza's namesake, include founding both the Banco Nación and Argentina's influential **Jockey Club**; the latter's national headquarters occupies the massive honey-coloured **Palacio Unzué de Casares**, on the north side of the plaza at Av Alvear 1345. Opposite, on the south side of the plaza, stands the **Palacio Celedonio Pereda**, named after a member of the oligarchy who wanted a carbon copy of the Palais Jacquemart-André in Paris. The Porteño palace, now occupied by the Brazilian Embassy and undergoing refurbishment at the time of writing, is a uniformly successful replica, classical columns and all.

Half a block north, at Cerrito 1455, the **Mansion Alzaga Unzué** now forms a luxurious annexe of the *Four Seasons* hotel (see p.112). It's a faultless duplicate of a Loire chateau, built in attractive red brick and cream limestone and topped with a shiny slate mansard roof. Back up on the other side of Arroyo, the Louis XIV-style **Palacio Ortiz Basualdo** has been the location of the French Embassy since 1925. This magnificent palace with slightly incongruous detailing, including Art Nouveau balconies, monumental Ionic pilasters and bulging Second Empire corner turrets, mercifully escaped demolition in the 1950s when Avenida 9 de Julio was widened, though it did have to be altered considerably to accommodate the highway. From Plaza Carlos Pellegrini, Avenida Alvear leads due northwest to Recoleta.

Recoleta

The subte skirts the southern edge of Recoleta, but the barrio is walking distance (or a short cab ride) from the city centre

The well-heeled barrio of **Recoleta** is, for most Porteños, intrinsically tied to the magnificent **La Recoleta Cemetery** at its heart. In around 1720, drawn to the area's tranquillity, which was deemed perfect for meditation or "recollection" (hence the name), Franciscan monks set up a monastery here. It wasn't until the cholera and yellow fever epidemics of 1867 and 1871 that the city's wealthy moved to Recoleta, from hitherto fashionable San Telmo. Although many of its residents have left for the northern suburbs in recent years, a Recoleta address still has cachet. **Avenida Alvear** is Buenos Aires' swankiest street: along it you'll find stately **palaces**, plus designer **boutiques**, swish art galleries and one of the city's most prestigious hotels. Scattered throughout the barrio are a host of **restaurants** and bars, ranging from some of the city's most traditional to trendy joints that come and go.

Recoleta's other notable attractions include one of the capital's few remaining colonial buildings, the gleaming white **Basílica Nuestra Señora del Pilar**; the **Centro Cultural de Recoleta**; and the country's biggest and richest collection of nineteenth- and twentieth-century art at the **Museo Nacional de Bellas Artes**.

Avenida Alvear

Only five blocks in length, stretching from Plaza Carlos Pellegrini to Plaza San Martín de Tours, Avenida Alvear is one of the city's shortest but most exclusive avenues, lined with expensive **art galleries**. For many years it has also been home to international designer boutiques like Louis Vuitton and Emporio Armani, although government import restrictions imposed in 2012 left many of these stock-less and shuttered. At the corner of Ayacucho lies the city's most famous and traditional luxury hotel, the French Art Deco **Alvear Palace** (see p.112), built in 1932.

Two blocks south, opposite elegant apartment buildings between Montevideo and Rodriguez Peña, are three palaces that were home to some of Argentina's wealthiest families at the beginning of the twentieth century. Although none is open to the public, the exteriors are worth a peek for their splendid architecture. The northernmost, behind a Charles Thays-designed garden, is the **Palacio Hume**. This perfectly symmetrical Art Nouveau creation, embellished with intricate wrought-iron work, now looks a little the worse for wear. It was originally built for British rail-engineer Alexander Hume, but was sold to the Duhau family in the 1920s, who staged the city's first-ever art exhibition inside. The Duhau family also built the middle palace, the **Palacio Duhau**, now the *Park Hyatt* (see p.112), an austere imitation of an eighteenth-century French Neoclassical *palais*. The third palace, the severely Neoclassical **Nunciatura Apostólica** on the corner of Montevideo, was designed by a French architect for a member of the Anchorena family. Nowadays it's the seat of the Vatican's Argentina representative, and was used by Pope John Paul II during his visits to the country.

La Recoleta Cemetery

Av Quintana and Junín • Daily 7am–5pm; guided tours in English Tues & Thurs 11am • Free

One of the world's most remarkable burial grounds, **La Recoleta Cemetery** presents an exhilarating mixture of architectural whimsy and a panorama of Argentine history. The giant vaults, stacked along avenues inside the high walls, resemble the rooftops of a fanciful Utopian town from above. The necropolis is a city within a city, a lesson in architectural styles and fashions, and a great place to wander, exploring its narrow streets and wide avenues of yews and cypress trees.

1

The **tombs** themselves range from simple headstones to bombastic masterpieces built in a variety of styles including Art Nouveau, Art Deco, Secessionist, Neoclassical, neo-Byzantine and even neo-Babylonian. The oldest monumental grave, dating from 1836, is that of **Juan Facundo Quiroga**, the much-feared La Rioja *caudillo* (local leader) immortalized in the Latin American classic *Facundo* by Argentine statesman and writer Domingo Sarmiento, also buried here. Facundo's tomb stands straight ahead of the gateway. Next to it, inscribed with a Borges poem, stands the solemn granite mausoleum occupied by several generations of the eminent Alvear family. The vast majority of tombs in Recoleta belong to similar patrician families of significant means – but not all. Perhaps the most incongruous statue in the cemetery is that of a boxer, in the northwest sector – the final resting place of **Angel Firpo**, who fought Jack Dempsey for the world heavyweight title in 1923. Military heroes, many of them Irish or British seafarers who played a key part in Argentina's struggle for independence, are also buried here, such as **Admiral William Brown**. An Argentine hero of Irish origins, at the beginning of the nineteenth century Brown decimated the Spanish fleet in the River Plate estuary. An unusual monument decorated with a beautiful miniature of his frigate, the *Hercules*, is a highlight of the cemetery's central plaza.

Basílica Nuestra Señora del Pilar

Mon–Sat 10.30am–6.15pm, Sun 2.30–6.15pm • Free • ⓦ basilicadelpilar.org.ar

Just north of the cemetery gates is the stark white silhouette of the **Basílica Nuestra Señora del Pilar**. Built in the early eighteenth century by Jesuits, it's the second oldest church in Buenos Aires and effectively the parish church for the Recoleta elite. The sky-blue Pas-de-Calais ceramic tiles atop its single slender turret were restored in the 1930s, along with the plain facade. The interior was also remodelled, and the monks' cells turned into side chapels, each decorated with a gilded reredos and polychrome wooden saints. These include a statue of San Pedro de Alcántara, the Virgen de la Merced and the Casa de Ejercicios, all attributed to a native artist known simply as "José". The magnificent Baroque silver altarpiece, embellished with an Inca sun and other pre-Hispanic details, was made by craftsmen from Alto Perú. Equally admirable is the fine altar crucifix allegedly donated to the city by King Carlos III of Spain. It is possible to visit the cloisters above the church (same hours as church; free) via the staircase three altars to the left. The rooms, once home to the Franciscan monks, now hold a collection of religious paintings and artefacts, including some impressive colonial and *criollo* silverware. From the windows you get a good view over La Recoleta Cemetery.

Centro Cultural Recoleta

Junín 1930 • Tues–Fri 2–9pm, Sat & Sun noon–9pm • Free

Immediately north of Basílica Nuestra Señora del Pilar, the **Centro Cultural Recoleta** is one of the city's leading **arts centres**, a good deal bigger and more impressive inside than its modest front suggests. The building, which dates from the 1730s, is one of Buenos Aires' oldest, and originally housed the area's Franciscan monks. The building was extensively, but tastefully, remodelled in the 1980s and retains its former cloisters. These cool, white, arched hallways and simple rooms make an excellent setting for the changing art, photography and audiovisual exhibitions the centre hosts. There are also a number of auditoriums for theatre, dance and music, including the **Sala Villa Villa**, the occasional home of the internationally renowned, anarchic theatre troupe De La Guarda/Fuerza Bruta.

Plaza San Martín de Tours and Feria Plaza Francia

Opposite the Centro Cultural Recoleta, grassy **Plaza San Martín de Tours** is shaded by three of the biggest rubber trees in the city, an impressive sight with their huge buttress-roots, contorted like arthritic limbs. A 100-year-old rubber tree, the famous Gran Gomero, shelters the terrace of nearby *La Biela*, on the corner of Avenida Quintana. One of the city's most traditional *confiterías*, *La Biela* gets its name, which means "connecting-rod", from being the favourite haunt of racing drivers in the 1940s and 50s, and was a frequent guerrilla target in the 1970s, owing to its conspicuously wealthy patrons. On the other side of the cultural centre in Plaza Francia, buskers, jugglers and groups practising the fluid Brazilian martial art of *capoeira* entertain crowds during the **Feria Plaza Francia**, also known as the Feria Hippy, at weekends (9am–7pm; free), while artisans sell hand-crafted wares including *mate* gourds, jewellery and ceramics at stalls arranged along the wide paths.

Museo Nacional de Bellas Artes

Av del Libertador 1473 • Tues–Fri 12.30–8.30pm, Sat & Sun 9.30am–8.30pm • Free • Ⓦ mnba.org.ar

Argentina's principal art museum, the **Museo Nacional de Bellas Artes** occupies an unassuming, slightly gloomy, brick-red Neoclassical building half a kilometre due north of La Recoleta Cemetery. Like the barrio's architecture, the museum's contents, comprising mostly nineteenth- and twentieth-century paintings and some sculpture, are resoundingly European, while the Old World influences on the Argentine art on display are clearly evident.

Only about a tenth of the museum's collection of 11,000 exhibits is on display at any time. The whole of the ground floor is given over to **international art**, dominated by French, Dutch and Italian masters such as Degas and Rubens. Later masters as varied as Pollock, Picasso and Italo-Argentine Lucio Fontana also feature. In a room by itself, the wide-ranging **Hirsch bequest** – left to the nation by the wealthy Belgrano landowners and art collectors – includes some fabulous European paintings, sculptures, furniture and other art objects spanning several centuries, including a Spanish retable (an ornamental screen behind the altar) and a portrait by Rembrandt of his sister.

The upper-floor galleries are an excellent introduction to **Argentine art**, containing a selection of the country's major artists. The works span from pre-Columbian terracotta and textiles, through nineteenth-century European imitators such as Prilidiano Pueyrredón and Eduardo Sívori to the Argentine artists in the twentieth century who tried to break away from this imitative tendency and create a movement of their own. Accessed via a short staircase, vast Room 107 covers Argentine art from the 1920s, featuring contemporay masters such as Guillermo Kuitca and Xul Solar (who has a museum dedicated to his works in Recoleta; see p.94).

Floralis Genérica

Av Figueroa Alcorta 2263

Behind the Museo Nacional de Bellas Artes lurks the massive Doric columns of the Facultad de Derecho (Law Faculty), next to which it's hard to miss the 25m-high aluminium- and steel-bloom named **Floralis Genérica**, one of the city's newest sculptures. Argentine architect **Eduardo Catalano** donated this work to the city as a tribute to all flowers and a symbol of "hope for the country's new spring". A system of light sensors and hydraulics closes the petals at sunset and opens them again at 8am, but they stay open on May 25, September 21 (the beginning of spring), Christmas Eve and New Year's Eve.

Museo Xul Solar

Laprida 1212 • Tues–Fri noon–8pm, Sat noon–7pm, closed Jan • $15 • ⓦ xulsolar.org.ar

The **Museo Xul Solar**, deep in residential Recoleta, is housed in the "Fundación Pan Klub", an early twentieth-century townhouse where, for the last twenty years of his life, eccentric Porteño artist Xul Solar (1888–1963) lived. The house was remodelled in the 1990s, and its award-winning design is as exciting as the display of Solar's paintings and other works. The space contains work spanning nearly five decades and is on several different levels, built of timber and glass, each dedicated to a specific period in the artist's career. As well as paintings, there's a set of "Pan Altars", multicoloured mini-retables designed for his "universal religions" – Solar once told Borges that he had "founded twelve new religions since lunch". Other curiosities include a piano whose keyboard he replaced with three rows of painted keys with textured surfaces, created both for blind pianists and to implement his notion of the correspondence of colour and music.

Palermo

Part of subte Line D runs underneath Avenida Santa Fe, one of Palermo's main arteries, and where appropriate the nearest station is indicated in the text. Otherwise, take one of the many buses that go up avenidas Las Heras and Del Libertador, such as #10 or #38

Much of **Palermo**, Buenos Aires' largest barrio, is vibrantly green and appealingly well kempt: ornate balconies overflow with jasmine and roses, grand apartment blocks line wide avenues, and plane trees, palms and jacarandas shade older, cobbled streets; its beautifully landscaped parks, some of the biggest in the world, come alive with locals practising in-line skating, playing football or walking their dogs.

Palermo takes its name from an Italian farmer, Giovanni Palermo, who in 1590 turned these former flood plains into vineyards and orchards. The barrio began to take on its present-day appearance when large parks and gardens were laid out at the end of the nineteenth century; the process of gentrification continued and Palermo is now regarded as a distinctly classy place to live.

Given its sizeable proportions – it stretches all the way from Avenida Coronel Díaz, on the border with Recoleta, to Colegiales and Belgrano, to the north – it's not surprising that the barrio isn't completely homogeneous. The bit of Palermo around Plaza República de Chile that juts into Recoleta is known as **Palermo Chico** and contains some significant museums, including the **Museo de Arte Decorativo**. Nearby, the **Museo de Arte Latinoamericano de Buenos Aires** (**MALBA**) is a must for fans of modern art. About ten blocks west, **Palermo Viejo** is a traditional neighbourhood with lovely old houses along cobbled streets, but it's become such a trendy place, full of

---

DOG WALKERS

Along the wide avenues and in the many parks of Barrio Norte and Palermo, you'll often be treated to one of Buenos Aires' more characteristic sights: the *paseaperros*, or professional **dog walkers**. Joggers holding seven or eight prized pedigrees on leashes are surprising enough, but these dilettantes are rightly held in contempt by the beefy specialists who confidently swagger along towed by twenty to thirty dogs. These invariably athletic young men (or, occasionally, women) are not paid just to take all manner of aristocratic breeds for a stroll, with the inevitable pit stops along the way, but must brush and groom them and look out for signs of ill health; many dog walkers have veterinary training. They perform these vital duties every weekday – the dogs' owners usually manage such chores themselves on the weekends.

funky cafés and avant-garde art galleries, that the area around Plaza Cortázar is now known as **Soho**. Across the rail tracks, people in the media work, eat and drink in a cluster of TV studios, restaurants and bars that have been christened **Hollywood**. Much of the north of Palermo is taken up by parks and gardens, such as the grand **Parque 3 de Febrero**, giving the area its soubriquet the "**bosques de Palermo**" (Palermo woods). At the barrio's northern edge is **Las Cañitas**, a zone of upmarket bars and restaurants, focused on the corner of Báez and Arévalo.

Museo de Arte Decorativo

Av del Libertador 1902 • Tues–Sun 2–6.45pm • $5, free Tues • Free guided visits in English 2.30pm Tues–Sat • W mnad.org.ar

There's no finer example of the decadent decor money could buy in early twentieth-century Buenos Aires than that on display in the **Museo de Arte Decorativo** with its remarkable collection of art and furniture. The museum is housed in **Palacio Errázuriz**, one of the city's most original private mansions, albeit of typically French design. The two-storey palace was built in 1911 for a Chilean diplomat and his patrician Argentine wife, and was turned into a museum in 1937. Designed by René Sergent, a French architect and proponent of the Academic style, it has three contrasting facades. The western one, on Sanchez de Bustamante, is inspired by the Petit Trianon at Versailles; the long northern side of the building with its Corinthian pillars, on Avenida del Libertador, is based on the palaces on Paris's Place de la Concorde; and the eastern end, near the entrance, is dominated by an enormous semicircular stone porch, supported by four Tuscan columns. The coach house, now a restaurant and tearoom, *Croque Madame*, sits just beyond the monumental wrought-iron and bronze gates, in the style of Louis XVI.

The interior is as French as the exterior, especially the Regency ballroom, lined with gilded Rococo panels and huge mirrors, all stripped from a Parisian house. The couple's extravagant taste in **art** – Flemish furniture and French clocks, Sèvres porcelain, bronzes by Bourdelle, and paintings, old and modern, ranging from El Greco (*Christ Bearing the Cross*) to Manet (*The Sacrifice of the Rose*) – is reflected and preserved. In the basement resides a Gothic chapel, transferred from the Château de Champagnette in France. Temporary exhibitions of ancient and contemporary art are also held down here, or in the garden in the summer, as are classical concerts.

Museo de Arte Popular José Hernández

Av del Libertador 2373 • Wed–Fri 1–7pm, Sat & Sun 10am–8pm • $1 • W museohernandez.org.ar

A very different kind of art from that on display at the Museo de Arte Decorativo can be found further along Avenida del Libertador, in a rambling Neocolonial house, home to the **Museo de Arte Popular José Hernández**. José Hernández wrote the great gaucho classic *Martín Fierro* (1872), a revolutionary epic poem that made *campo* (peasant) culture respectable, and in this vein the museum's purpose is to highlight the value of **popular crafts**, housed in two buildings separated by a shady patio. In the basement of the first building is an impressive but unimaginatively presented display of mostly nineteenth-century rural silverware; spurs, stirrups, saddles, knives and gaucho weaponry stand side by side with a large collection of fine silver *mate* ware. Upstairs, and across the courtyard, changing exhibits of lovingly made crafts such as tablecloths, jewellery, ceramic figures and the like are displayed, many with a strong Catholic influence.

Museo de Arte Latinoamericano de Buenos Aires (MALBA)

Av Figueroa Alcorta 3415 • Mon, Tues & Thurs–Sun noon–8pm, Wed noon–9pm • $30, Wed $15 • W malba.org.ar

One of the city's best museums, the **Museo de Arte Latinoamericano de Buenos Aires (MALBA)**, two blocks north of the Museo de Arte Popular, is housed in a modern, glass-fronted, purpose-built building that is an attraction in its own right, its airy, spacious galleries contrasting with the dark nooks and crannies of the city's more traditional art museums.

1

PALERMO

Palermo Club de Pescadores

Complejo Costa Salguero

Museo Nacional de Aeronautica

Aeroparque

AVENIDA COSTANERA RAFAEL OBLIGADO

AUTOPISTA ARTURO U ILLIA

AVENIDA J. SALGUERO

BARRIO PARQUE

PALERMO CHICO

SAN MARTIN DE TOURS

Paseo Alcorta Shopping Centre

MALBA

Museo de Arte Popular

AVENIDA DEL LIBERTADOR

AVENIDA CASARES

Parque Jorge Newbery

Planetario Galileo Galilei

Tennis Club Argentina

AVENIDA SARMIENTO

AVENIDA ADOLFO BERRO

Jardín Japonés

Plaza Alemania

AVENIDA CASARES

Monumento a Sarmiento

AVENIDA PRESIDENTE FIGUEROA ALCORTA

Velodromo Municipal

AVENIDA BELISARIO ROLDAN

AVENIDA ALSINA

Museo Sivori

AVENIDA INFANTA ISABEL

Lago de Palermo

Patio Andaluz

Parque 3 de Febrero

AVENIDA BERRO

Monumento de los Españoles

Jardín Zoológico

AVENIDA SARMIENTO

N

AVENIDA INTENDENTE CANTILO

Club Alemán de Equitación

AVENIDA DORREGO

Club Gimnasia y Esgrima

AVENIDA PRESIDENTE PEDRO MONTT

Paseo del Rosedal

Plaza Intendente Seeber

AVENIDA COLOMBIA

BERUTI

Argentino

Hipodromo

AVENIDA DORREGO

Campo Hípico Militar

Campo Argentino de Polo

Centro Cultural Islámico Rey Fahd

AVENIDA INTENDENTE BULLRICH

CERVIÑO

SINCLAIR

GODOY CRUZ

PEÑA RTA

CERVIÑO

L.SEGUI

US Embassy

Sociedad Rural Argentina

DEMARIA

(M) Palermo

Estación Palermo

Buenos Aires Lawn Tennis Club

AUGUSTIN MENDEZ

AVENIDA DEL LIBERTADOR

LAS CAÑITAS

AVENIDA CHENAUT

ARAOZ

M CAMPOS

AVENIDA SANTA FE

CHARCAS

PARAGUAY

(M) Carranza

AVENIDA DORREGO

Belgrano

1

The permanent **Constantini collection**, on the first floor up, concentrates on the best Latin American art of the twentieth century. It is arranged chronologically, beginning around 1910, when the Modernist movement in Latin America heralded the start of a real sense of regional identity. This is exemplified in paintings such as a series by Argentine master Xul Solar, a Frida Kahlo self-portrait and Brazilian Tarsila do Amaral's Mexican-influenced *Abaporu*. Dark political undercurrents run through the 1930s to 1950s and the work of Antonio Berni and the Chilean

BORGES AND BUENOS AIRES

This city that I believed was my past,
is my future, my present;
the years I have spent in Europe are an illusion,
I always was (and will be) in Buenos Aires.

Jorge Luis Borges, "Arrabal", from Fervor de Buenos Aires (1921)

There's no shortage of literary works inspired by Argentina's capital city, but no writer has written so passionately about it as **Jorge Luis Borges**. Though he was born in the heart of Buenos Aires, in 1898, it was the city's humbler barrios that most captivated Borges' imagination. His early childhood was spent in **Palermo**, now one of Buenos Aires' more exclusive neighbourhoods, but a somewhat marginal barrio at the start of the twentieth century. Borges' middle-class family inhabited one of the few two-storey houses on their street, **Calle Serrano** (now officially renamed Calle J. L. Borges), and, though his excursions were strictly controlled, from behind the garden wall Borges observed the colourful street life that was kept tantalizingly out of his reach. In particular, his attention was caught by the men who gathered to drink and play cards in the local *almacén* (a sort of store-cum-bar) at his street corner. With their tales of knife fights and air of lawlessness, these men appeared time and again in Borges' early short stories, and, later, in *Doctor Brodie's Report*, a collection published in 1970.

Borges' writing talent surfaced at a precocious age: at 6 he wrote his first short story and when he was 11, the newspaper *El País* published his translation of Oscar Wilde's *The Happy Prince*. However, it was not until he returned from Europe in 1921, where he had been stranded with his family during World War I, that Borges published his first book, *Fervor de Buenos Aires*, a collection of **poems** that attempted to capture the essence of the city. Enthused by his re-encounter with Buenos Aires at an age at which he was free to go where he wanted, Borges set out to explore the marginal corners of the city. His wanderings took him to the outlying barrios, where streets lined with simple one-storey buildings blended with the surrounding Pampas, or to the poorer areas of the city centre with their tenement buildings and bars frequented by prostitutes. With the notable exception of La Boca, which he appears to have regarded as too idiosyncratic – and perhaps, too obviously picturesque – Borges felt greatest affection for the **south** of Buenos Aires. His exploration of the area that he regarded as representing the heart of the city took in not only the traditional houses of San Telmo and Monserrat, with their patios and decorative facades, but also the humbler streets of Barracas, a largely industrial working-class neighbourhood, and Constitución, where, in a gloomy basement in Avenida Juan de Garay, he set one of his most famous short stories, *El Aleph*.

For a writer as sensitive to visual subtlety as Borges – many of his early poems focus on the city's atmospheric evening light – it seems particularly tragic that he should have gone virtually blind in his 50s. Nonetheless, from 1955 to 1973, Borges was **Director of the National Library**, then located in Monserrat, where his pleasure at being surrounded by books – even if he could no longer read them – was heightened by the fact that his daily journey to work took him through one of his favourite parts of the city, from his apartment in Maipú along pedestrianized Florida. As Borges' fame grew, he spent considerable periods of time away from Argentina, travelling to Europe, the US and other Latin American countries – though he claimed always to return to Buenos Aires in his dreams. Borges died in 1986 in Geneva, where he is buried in the Plainpalais cemetery. Borges pilgrims in Buenos Aires will find a commemorative plaque at no. 2108 on Calle Serrano, inscribed with a stanza from his *Mythical Foundation of Buenos Aires*.

Roberto Matta, while Catholic traditions are given a Surrealist twist in Remedios Varo's votive box *Icono*. Things get more conceptual from the 1960s on, with the moving installations of Julio Le Parc and the LSD-splashed "end of art" collages by the "Nueva Figuración" movement.

Upstairs, temporary exhibitions generally feature the collected works of a prominent modern or contemporary artist, often an Argentine. MALBA also has its own small art-house cinema (see website for programme), a café (daily 9am–9pm), a bookstore and a fun gift-shop.

Palermo Viejo

The nearest subte stations to Palermo Viejo are Scalabrini Ortíz and Plaza Italia

Palermo Viejo is Buenos Aires' most fashionable place to live, shop or have an evening out. The part of the city most closely linked to Borges, where he lived and began writing poetry in the 1920s, its architecture has changed little since then. Bounded by avenidas Santa Fe, Córdoba, Juan B. Justo and Raúl Scalabrini Ortíz, it's a compact oblong of narrow streets, most of them still cobbled and lined with brightly painted one- or two-storey Neocolonial villas and townhouses, many of them recently restored, some of them hidden behind luxuriant gardens full of bougainvillea and jasmine. Part run-down, part gentrified, it's a leafy district with a laidback bohemian ambience, and many of its stylish houses have been converted into bars, cafés and boutiques. Large communities from Poland, Ukraine, Lebanon and Armenia live here, alongside an Italian contingent and some old Spanish families, and they all have their shops, churches and clubs, adding to the district's colour. The area also boasts a dazzling blend of outstanding **restaurants**, serving cuisines as varied as Armenian and Vietnamese, and has succeeded in luring the city's residents and visitors alike away from more superficial districts such as Puerto Madero and Las Cañitas.

Palermo Viejo's official epicentre is **Plaza Palermo Viejo**, a wide, park-like square dominated by a children's playground and some huge lime trees, but the barrio's cultural and social focal point is nearby **Plaza Serrano**. The plaza's official name (used on maps but unknown by most taxi drivers) is Plaza Cortázar, after Argentine novelist Julio Cortázar, who frequented this part of the city in the 1960s and set his Surrealist novel *Hopscotch* (see p.564) here. The plaza centre becomes the site of a crafts fair at weekends (Sat & Sun 10am–8pm), while more permanently it is surrounded by trattorias, cafés and bars, some doubling as arts centres and galleries. Among them, a rash of independent designer shops sell upmarket bohemian clothes, jewellery and furnishings – hence the **Soho** nickname.

Jardín Botánico

Av Santa Fe 3951 • Mon–Fri 8am–6pm, Sat & Sun 9.30am–6pm • Free • ⓦ jardinbotanico.gov.ar

The entrance to Buenos Aires' charming **botanical garden** is at Plaza Italia, east of Palermo Viejo and near the Plaza Italia subte station. Established at the end of the nineteenth century, the layout was completed by Charles Thays in 1902 and is now named after the ubiquitous landscape artist (see p.88). He divided the garden into distinct areas representing the regions of Argentina and further afield. Most of the trees are labelled with their Latin and common names, as well as where they are found.

Jardín Zoológico

Sarmiento and Las Heras • Tues–Sun 10am–6pm • $30, or $47 for a "pasaporte", entitling you to all the attractions and activities, under-12s free • ⓦ zoobuenosaires.com.ar

Just over the road from the botanical garden, Buenos Aires' **zoo** offers the chance to see a variety of South American fauna close up, including the four native camelids (guanacos, llamas, vicuñas and alpacas), as well as condors, maras ("Patagonian hares", actually a type of rodent) and capybaras. It was also landscaped by Thays and its

1

monumental pavilions and cages, built around 1905, include a fabulous replica of the temple to the goddess Lakshmi in Mumbai, a Chinese temple, a Byzantine portico and a Japanese pagoda. Borges fondly wrote that the zoo "smelled of toffee and tiger", a description that still holds true. Generally the animals are kept in reasonable conditions for a city zoo, but if you skip the added "pasaporte" attractions, such as the poor "jungle house" and seal show, you won't miss much.

Outside the zoo, traditional **mateos** (horse and carriages), decorated with the ribbons and swirls of *filete* art (see box, p.80), cart off the romantically minded on trips around Palermo's parks.

Museo Evita

Lafinur 2988 • Tues–Sun 11am–7pm • $15 • ⓦ museoevita.org

For many Argentines, the **Museo Evita**, opened in 2003, was a long time coming. Located a block east from the zoo, in an attractive early twentieth-century building that was once a hotel, it was bought in 1948 by Evita's Social Aid Foundation to be set up as emergency temporary accommodation for homeless families. The well-laid-out museum traces Evita's life and passions, as well as the daily life of the families who were given shelter here, with helpful info sheets in English in each room. Despite its uncritical stance and glossing over of the less salubrious facts in Evita's life, such as her Nazi sympathies, the museum has some interesting pieces, including magazines featuring her when she was Eva Duarte the radio star, and videos of the extraordinary scenes in the city after she died. A small space on the ground floor is given over to minor temporary exhibitions, while – with a separate entrance next door – an excellent **café** serves coffee, cakes and meals.

Parque 3 de Febrero and around

Avenidas Libertador and Sarmiento • ⓦ parquetresdefebrero.gov.ar

Parque 3 de Febrero is one of the biggest and most popular parks in the city, a wonderful place to stroll on a sunny afternoon. Another Palermo fixture designed by Thays, it was originally envisioned by President Sarmiento, who believed that parks were a civilizing influence and wanted something for Buenos Aires that would be on the scale of New York's Central Park or London's Hyde Park. With its beautifully tended trees, lawns and patios, it's at its most serene during the week. Although the wide pathways running along the banks of the boating lake become rather crowded with joggers, cyclists and in-line skaters on weekends and public holidays, that's also the time to see Porteños at play. You'll see typical scenes of families drinking *mate* under the shade of palms or rubber trees, but perhaps also less expected sights, such as tai chi classes, or transvestite volleyball games.

The park's features include an **Andalucian patio**, decorated with vibrant ceramic tiles and donated by the city of Seville, and a **Rosedal** (rose garden) that showcases new and colourful varieties of the flower.

Planetario Galileo Galilei

Shows Tues–Sun, box office opens at 10.30am, see website for schedule • $20 • ⓦ planetario.gov.ar

The far northeastern tip of Parque 3 de Febrero, at Avenida Sarmiento, serves as the setting for the UFO-shaped **Planetario Galileo Galilei**. In the entrance hall, you can see an alarmingly huge metal meteorite, discovered in the Chaco in the 1960s (see p.270), and in the evenings from around 7pm (weather permitting) local astronomy enthusiasts cluster around telescopes to peer at the night sky.

Jardín Japonés

Daily 10am–6pm • $8 • ⓦ jardinjapones.org.ar

To the east of the park, and with its own entrance on Plaza de la República Islámica de Irán, the **Jardín Japonés** was donated to the city by Buenos Aires' small Japanese community in 1979 and contains beautifully landscaped gardens, including a bonsai section, a lake of huge koi carp, and a temple-like café. It is at its best in the springtime, when the almond trees are in blossom and the azaleas are out.

Monumento de los Españoles

The busy rotunda to the park's southeast, at the junction of avenidas del Libertador and Sarmiento, is taken up by the most glorious monument in the city, the **Monumento de los Españoles**, whose fine bronze sculptures symbolize the Andes, the Chaco, the Pampas and the Río de la Plata. Its allegorical figures, including the dainty angel at the top, are sculpted from Carrara marble.

Belgrano

Belgrano can be reached via the subte Line D (Juramento stop), or by train from Retiro (stops Belgrano C or Belgrano R)

North of Palermo, leafy **Belgrano** is largely residential, apart from the lively shopping streets on either side of its main artery, Avenida Cabildo. Named after General Manuel Belgrano, hero of Argentina's struggle for independence, it was founded as a separate town in 1855. Over the next decade or two lots of wealthy Porteños built their summer or weekend homes here, and it was incorporated into Buenos Aires during the city's whirlwind expansion in the 1880s. Many Anglo-Argentines settled in the barrio in those years, and it became popular with the city's sizeable Jewish community in the 1950s. More recently Taiwanese and Korean immigrants have settled in **Barrio Chino**, Buenos Aires' small Chinatown, which stretches along Arribeños between Juramento and Olazába. The central part of the barrio is known as **Belgrano C**, whose nucleus lies at the junction of avenidas Cabildo and Justamento. As well as stores, cafés and galleries, there's a clutch of minor museums here.

Museo de Arte Español

Juramento 2291 • Mon–Fri 1–7pm, Sat & Sun 10am–8pm • $1 • ⓦ museolarreta.buenosaires.gov.ar • Juramento station

The **Museo de Arte Español**, located in a well-restored, whitewashed colonial building, is home to a priceless collection of **Spanish art** amassed by an aristocratic Uruguayan exile, **Enrique Larreta**. From around 1900 to 1916, the dandyish Larreta spent many of his days in Spain; during that time he visited churches and monasteries, buying up artwork for his Belgrano home, most of them from the Renaissance – statues and paintings of saints, but also furniture, porcelain, silverware and tapestries, all of which are displayed in this house, which he bequeathed to the city.

El Monumental

Av Pte Figueroa Alcorta 7597 • Museum: daily 10am–7pm, closes early on match days; tours hourly 11am–5pm • $45, or $55 with tour • ⓦ museoriver.com

The huge concrete stands of **El Monumental**, the country's largest sporting stadium, rise up on the eastern edge of Belgrano, on the border with residential barrio Nuñez. Home to Boca Juniors' bitter rivals, **River Plate** football club, it was remodelled for the 1978 World Cup and can seat 70,000. Matches at the Monumental are a glorious riot of red and white shirts, banners and streamers (for more on attending a match, see p.38).

River has its own **museum**, an audiovisual experience that makes every effort to be bigger and better than the Boca museum in the Bombonera (see p.83), although it's less tourist-friendly – both the tour and museum are in Spanish only. Highlights are a "time machine" that takes you through a tunnel relating the history of the club through the twentieth century, with plenty of fascinating historical and cultural context, and era-appropriate TVs showing River's greatest goals. On site there is also a comprehensive souvenir shop, and a surprisingly upmarket café.

The west

West of central Buenos Aires a vast, mostly residential area spreads out for over a dozen kilometres towards Avenida General Paz. Sights here are scattered; perhaps the neighbourhoods' greatest appeal lies in their relative lack of tourists, offering a prize glimpse into the lives of ordinary working- and middle-class Porteños. Architecture fans shouldn't miss the stunning **Palacio de las Aguas Corrientes** in the barrio of **Balvanera**, the neighbourhood just south of Recoleta. Northwest of Palermo, the barrio of **Chacarita** is best known for its namesake **cemetery**, where tango singer Carlos Gardel is buried. **Caballito**, right in the heart of the city, has an entertaining natural history museum. Finally, right at Buenos Aires' fringes, the hugely enjoyable gaucho fair, the **Feria de Mataderos**, provides one of the best days out in the city.

Balvanera

Balvanera is well connected to the subte network; get off at Plaza de Miserere on lines A or H, or Corrientes on lines B or H

Just west of the city centre, **Balvanera** is a commercial, somewhat downmarket barrio, home to many of the city's recent South American immigrants. It has two focal points: **Once**, a noisy shopping area around the Once (de Septiembre) train station, traditionally patronized by the city's less-well-heeled Jewish community and a good place to pick up bargains, including football shirts, *chamamé* CDs and carnival gear; and **Abasto**, focused on the enormous Abasto shopping centre (see p.125).

Palacio de las Aguas Corrientes

Avenidas Córdoba and Riobamba • Museum Mon–Fri 9am–1pm • Free

Other than shopping, the main point of interest in Balvanera is the spectacular **Palacio de las Aguas Corrientes**, right on the Recoleta border. Every bit as palatial as the name suggests, it has been described quite accurately as a cross between London's Victoria and Albert Museum and the Uffizi in Florence. Somewhat incongruously, it is home to twelve giant tanks that supplied Buenos Aires with water from 1894 until 1978. An impressive feat of engineering, it was planned and built in Europe, down to the glazed coloured ceramics that dot the facade, all manufactured by Royal Doulton of London, but painted in Buenos Aires. Inside, there is a small museum explaining the building's history.

Chacarita

Dominated by railway lines, **Chacarita** takes its name from the days when the barrio was home to a small farm (*chacra*) run by Jesuits. Nowadays, the neighbourhood is synonymous with the enormous **Cementerio de Chacarita**.

Cementerio de Chacarita

Av Guzmán 780 • Daily 7am–6pm • Free • Subte station Federico Lacroze, Line B

Less aristocratic than Recoleta's cemetery, but impressive nonetheless, the **Cementerio de Chacarita** contains the city's other most-visited tomb, that of **Carlos Gardel**, the greatest of all tango singers (see box, p.557). Lying at the northern end of Avenida Corrientes, with the monumental main entrance at Av Guzmán 780, the cemetery covers a good third of the barrio; at one square kilometre, it's Argentina's largest. Immediately facing the entrance, a section of grand mausoleums comes quite close to the Baroque splendour of Recoleta.

Gardel's tomb

By far the best sight in the cemetery is **Gardel's tomb**, on the corner of calles 6 and 33, a brisk five-minute walk to the left of the entrance and a little towards the middle. It is topped by a life-sized statue of the singer in typical rakish pose: hand in pocket, hair slicked back and with characteristic wide grin. Every inch of the surrounding stonework is plastered with plaques of gratitude and flowers placed there by the singer's devotees. There is a pilgrimage to his graveside every year on the anniversary of his death (June 24). Many visitors light a cigarette and place it between the statue's fingers; you will often see a dog-end still dangling between his index and forefinger.

Caballito

An unassuming, mostly middle-class barrio, **Caballito** lies at the very centre of the metropolis. Narrow Plaza Primera Junta, on Line A of the subte, is the barrio's core, while Avenida Rivadavia, flanked by high-rise apartment blocks and shopping malls, runs east–west through it.

Museo Argentino de Ciencias Naturales

Angel Gallardo 490 • Daily 2–7pm • $10 • ⓦ macn.secyt.gov.ar

Caballito's main attraction is the natural science museum, the **Museo Argentino de Ciencias Naturales**, in the circular Parque del Centenario. The museum is of note for its impressive **paleontological** collection, with many specimens from Argentina – you can see a spiky-necked amargasaurus from Neuquén and a 15m patagosaurus sauropod from Chubút. There is also a host of the later **megafauna** – giant herbivorous mammals that evolved in South America when the region broke away from other continents – such as giant sloths and creepy glyptodonts, a forerunner of today's armadillo. These megafauna were wiped out around three million years ago, after South America reconnected with North America and more successful fauna such as the sabre-toothed tiger and, later, humans arrived.

Mataderos

Lying just inside the boundary of Capital Federal, around 6km southwest of Caballito, **Mataderos** is a barrio with a gory past. For many years, people came to Mataderos to drink the fresh blood of animals killed in the slaughterhouses from which the area takes its name, in the belief that this would cure such illnesses as tuberculosis. The slaughterhouses have long gone, but Mataderos is still home to the **Mercado Nacional de Hacienda**, or livestock market, set back from the intersection of Lisandro de la Torre and Avenida de los Corrales, whose faded pink walls and arcades provide the backdrop for one of Buenos Aires' most fabulous weekend events, the **Feria de Mataderos** (see box below).

FERIA DE MATADEROS

The Sunday **Feria de Mataderos** (11am–sunset; ⓦ feriademataderos.com.ar; buses #92 & #12) is a celebration of Argentina's rural traditions. This busy fair attracts thousands of locals and tourists for its blend of folk music, traditional crafts and regional food such as *locro*, empanadas and *tortas fritas*, mouthwatering fried cakes. You can also try your hand at regional dances such as the *chamamé* and *chacarera*. The undoubted highpoint, however, is the display of **gaucho skills** in which riders participate in events such as the *sortija*, in which, galloping at breakneck speed and standing rigid in their stirrups, they attempt to spear a small ring strung on a ribbon. Take plenty of cash – the artisan wares here are often good quality and cheaper than in the central stores, but the stallholders do not take credit cards – and make sure the fair is actually on before setting out, as it sometimes closes or moves to Saturday evenings, especially during the summer months; the city's tourist kiosks (see p.106) should be able to advise.

1

DAY-TRIPS FROM BUENOS AIRES

For all its parks and tree-lined avenues, Buenos Aires is nonetheless predominantly urban, and it can be nice to get away from the hectic tumult for a day or two. Immediately surrounding the city limits as you cross the Avenida General Paz ring road, the Capital Federal spreads into greater Buenos Aires. Largely residential, the most appealing suburbs are those to the city's north – the **Zona Norte**, an affluent suburban world of riverine villas where the subtropical heart that lies beneath Buenos Aires' European veneer starts to show through. Most worth visiting is San Isidro, which preserves a villagey charm and worthwhile historic quarter that can be accessed via the Tren de la Costa (see p.135) or taxi (about $100). Further on but still easily in day-trip territory you will reach **Tigre**, a kind of cross between Venice and the Everglades, at the edge of the verdant **Paraná Delta** (see p.132).

To the east of the city, meanwhile, boats cross the Río de la Plata to the small **Isla Martín García**, a steamy island that appears to have walked off the pages of a children's adventure story. Once used as a penal colony, it is now mostly given over to a nature reserve (visits via Cacciola Turismo in Tigre; ☎ 011 4749 0931, ⊛ cacciolaviajes.com). You can also reach the Portuguese colonial historic town of **Colonia** in Uruguay or even visit pleasant **Montevideo**, the capital of Argentina's *rioplatense* neighbour – both destinations are served by Buquebus, whose ferries and catamarans depart regularly from Puerto Madero (☎ 011 4316 6500, ⊛ buquebus.com).

Go a little further beyond the city in any other direction and you will swiftly emerge in the emerald green **pampas**, Argentina's heartlands (see p.136). Magnificent estancias (farmsteads or ranches) and traditional Pampean villages are close enough to reach as a day-trip, though if possible they really warrant at least one overnight stay. The capital of Buenos Aires Province, **La Plata**, an orderly city with a large, old-fashioned natural history museum, is also only an hour or so on the bus from Retiro (see p.153).

ARRIVAL AND DEPARTURE

BUENOS AIRES

Buenos Aires is well served by numerous international and domestic **flights**. It is also a transport hub for the rest of the country, with frequent daily **bus** services to and from most towns and cities. Limited **train** services join the capital to the provinces, while fast and slow **ferries** cross the Río de la Plata to neighbouring Uruguay.

BY PLANE

Airport enquiries ☎ 011 5480 6111.

EZEIZA AIRPORT

All international flights, with the exception of a few from neighbouring countries, arrive 22km southwest of the city centre at Ministro Pistarini Airport or – as it is actually referred to by everyone – Ezeiza, in reference to the outlying neighbourhood in which it is situated. In comparison with some Latin American airports, arriving at Ezeiza is relatively stress-free: touting for taxis is banned inside the airport and the tourist information stand (daily 8am–8pm) has good information on accommodation in the city. Ignore the privately run exchange booths strategically placed before you exit Arrivals – change money instead at the small branch of Banco Nación in the airport arrivals hall, where you may face longer lines at busy times but will get a much better rate. Change most of your money in the city, if you can. ATMs are also available (you will get the official rate).

Taxis and remises If you want to take a taxi or *remise* (radio cab) into the city (around $220–270), ask at one of the official taxi/*remise* stands immediately outside the arrivals exit. It may be worth comparing prices. Unofficial taxi drivers congregate outside the terminal (they are not allowed inside) and, while these offer cheaper rates – as low as half the *remise* rate – they tend to be less secure and scams of various descriptions have been reported, so they are best avoided, especially by first-time visitors with no Spanish.

Express buses Buses are operated by Manuel Tienda León (☎ 011 4314 3636, ⊛ tiendaleon.com.ar). Running non-stop between Ezeiza and the centre every 30min during the day and hourly at night, these cost $70 and take approximately 40min (much longer at rush hour), making them fair value for solo travellers. They drop you at the company's main terminal at San Martín and Madero; for an extra $5–10 you can get a transfer from there to anywhere downtown or the inner barrios. If you are transferring to a domestic flight (for some destinations these also leave from Ezeiza; check first), you could get a Manuel Tienda León bus ($80; 9am–midnight) to the Aeroparque Metropolitano Jorge Newbery. If you are staying in a part of the city near the domestic airport, such as Palermo or Belgrano, you might consider using this service and taking a taxi for the final stretch. Finally, there's the local bus #86 ($1.35), which runs between Ezeiza and Boca, entering the city via Rivadavia and continuing past Congreso, Plaza de Mayo and San Telmo; it takes at least 2hr, and leaves just beyond the entrance to the airport. Make sure you have change for the ticket machines, as notes are not accepted, and be warned that the buses can become very full (not advisable if you have lots of luggage) and obvious tourists may be easy targets for pickpockets.

AEROPARQUE

Buenos Aires' other airport is Aeroparque Metropolitano Jorge Newbery, usually known as Aeroparque, on the Costanera Norte, around 6km north of the city centre. Most domestic flights and some flights from Brazil and Uruguay arrive here. Manuel Tienda Léon also runs a bus service from here to the centre ($30; 9am–midnight); a taxi will set you back about $25 (again, it's better to go with an official, booked car rather than take one from the rank outside), or you could catch the local bus ($1.20; the #33 will take you to Paseo Colón). Aeroparque also has a tourist information booth (daily 8am–8pm).

Destinations Bariloche (up to 10 daily; 2hr 20min); Catamarca (1 daily; 2hr 30min); Córdoba (10 daily; 1hr 15min); Corrientes (1 daily; 1hr 20min); El Calafate (10 daily; 3hr 20min); Formosa (1 daily; 1hr 45min); Jujuy (2 daily; 2hr 10min); La Rioja (1 daily; 3hr); Mar del Plata (up to 5 daily; 1hr 15min); Mendoza (up to 7–9 daily; 1hr 50min); Neuquén (4 daily; 1hr 40min); Posadas (1 daily; 1hr 30min); Puerto Iguazú (up to 10–12 daily; 1hr 50min); Resistencia (1 daily; 1hr 30min); Río Gallegos (3 daily; 3hr 15min); Salta (3 daily; 2hr); San Juan (1 daily; 1hr 50min); San Luís (1 daily; 1hr 30min); San Martín de los Andes (3 weekly; 2hr 35min); San Rafael (1 daily; 2hr 35min); Santiago del Estero (1 daily; 1hr 40min); Trelew (4 daily; 2hr); Tucumán (5 daily; 1hr 50min); Ushuaia (6 daily; 3hr 40min).

AIRLINES

Aerolíneas Argentinas, Perú 2 ☎011 4340 7777 or ☎0810 222 86527; Air Canada, Av Córdoba 656 ☎011 4327 3640; Air France, San Martín 334, 23rd floor ☎011 4317 4711; Alitalia, Suipacha 1111, 28th floor ☎011 4310 9999; American Airlines, Santa Fe 881 ☎011 4318 1111; Andes, Av Córdoba 966, 8th floor ☎0810 1222 6337; Avianca, Carlos Pellegrini 1163, 4th floor ☎011 4322 2731; British Airways, Libertador 498, 13th floor ☎0800 666 1459; Delta, Reconquista 737, 3rd floor ☎011 4312 1200; Gol ☎0810 266 3131; Iberia, Carlos Pellegrini 1163, 1st floor ☎011 4131 1000; KLM, Suipacha 268, 9th floor ☎0880 122 3014; LADE, Perú 714 ☎011 5129 9001; LAN, Cerrito 866 ☎0810 999 9526; Lufthansa, Marcelo T. de Alvear 636 ☎011 4319 0600; Qantas, Av Córdoba 673, 13th floor ☎011 4114 5800; Sol ☎0810 444 4765; South African Airways, Suipacha 1067, 2nd floor ☎011 4319 0099; TAM,

Cerrito 1026 ☎011 4819 6950; United Airlines, Av Madero 900, 9th floor ☎0810 777 8648.

BY TRAIN

Few tourists arrive in Buenos Aires by train these days; although plans are afoot to reinstate long-distance services (possibly with high-speed connections), currently most trains are suburban only. The main exceptions are trains from the Atlantic coast and some towns in Buenos Aires Province, such as Tandil or Azul, which arrive at Constitución, in the south of the city at General Hornos 11 (Ferrobaires ☎011 4304 0028, ⓦferrobaires.gba.gov.ar); and trains from Rosario, which arrive at Retiro on Av Ramos Mejía (TBA ☎0800 3333 822, ⓦtbanet.com.ar). Both terminals have subte stations and are served by numerous local bus routes.

Destinations La Plata (every 30min; 1hr); Mar del Plata (3 daily; 6hr); Rosario (1 daily; 4hr).

BY BUS

Retiro terminal If you are travelling to Buenos Aires by bus from other points in Argentina, or on international services from neighbouring countries, you will arrive at Buenos Aires' huge long-distance bus terminal (☎011 4310 0700, ⓦtebasa.com.ar), known as Retiro, located in the barrio of that name at the corner of Av Antártida and Ramos Mejía. There are good facilities at the terminal, including toilets, shops, cafés and left luggage. Retiro is very centrally placed and nobody with a reasonable amount of energy will find it too strenuous to walk to hotels in the Florida/Retiro area of the city, although at night this is not recommended – there is a shantytown close by and robberies are fairly common.

Taxis Taxis are plentiful and the Retiro subte station is just a block away, outside the adjoining train station (see p.108).

Local buses There are also plenty of local buses leaving from stands along Ramos Mejía, though actually finding the one you want might be a rather daunting first taste of local bus transport. Buses #5 or #50 will take you to Congreso and the upper end of Avenida de Mayo, a fairly promising hunting ground for accommodation if you haven't booked ahead.

Information If you are departing from Retiro, you can call the general number for information – it takes you to a recorded message that will ask for your province and destination and provide you with the numbers of the appropriate companies (Spanish only). The website will also let you check companies, destinations and timetables. You can then call the individual companies to check times and, in most cases, make a reservation. Alternatively, visit the terminal itself, where the 150 or so companies all have conveniently numbered ticket booths and there is a useful information booth.

1

Destinations Asunción, Paraguay (hourly; 18–22hr); Bahía Blanca (every 2hr; 9hr); Bariloche (7 daily; 21–23hr); Carmen de Patagones (4 daily; 12hr); Catamarca (daily; 15hr); Córdoba (hourly; 11hr); Corrientes (6 daily; 12hr); Formosa (5 daily; 14–15hr); Jujuy (hourly; 22hr); La Rioja (4 daily; 17hr); Lima, Perú (2 daily; 72hr); Mar del Plata (hourly; 7hr); Mendoza (hourly; 17hr); Merlo (6 daily; 12hr); Neuquén (4 daily; 15hr); Paraná (8 daily; 7hr); Posadas (8 daily; 13hr); Puerto Iguazú (7 daily; 14hr 30min–19hr); Resistencia (every 2hr; 13hr); Río de Janeiro, Brazil (2 daily; 40hr); Río Gallegos (5 daily; 36hr); Rosario (hourly; 4hr); Salta (hourly; 22hr); San Juan (10 daily; 16hr); San Luís (9 daily; 12hr); San Rafael (4 daily; 13hr); Santa Rosa (every 2hr; 8–10hr); Santiago de Chile, Chile (daily; 19hr); Santiago del Estero (11 daily; 13hr); Trelew (twice weekly; 20hr); Tucumán (every 2hr; 15hr); Zapala (3 daily; 17–18hr).

INFORMATION AND TOURS

INFORMATION

Tourist kiosks For information, head to one of the city's numerous tourist kiosks; the staff do not generally have much specialist knowledge but can usually provide maps and a few leaflets. The most central kiosk is just off the Plaza de Mayo at Av Diagonal Roque Sáenz Peña and Florida (Mon–Fri 10am–6pm, Sat 10am–4pm). There are other kiosks at the Retiro bus terminal, at c/10 local 83 (Mon–Sat 7.30am–1pm); in Recoleta, on avenidas Quintana and Ortíz, near the cemetery (daily 10am–6pm); in Puerto Madero, by Dock 4, also offering information on Montevideo (daily 10am–7pm); and in San Telmo at Defensa 1250 (Sat & Sun 10am–6pm only).

Websites There's a general telephone line (☎011 4313 0187; daily 7.30am–7pm; English spoken) and a comprehensive website with ideas of where to go and what to do (🖥bue.gov.ar).

English-language information An excellent source of English-language information is the ever-reliable South American Explorers (🖥saexplorers.org). Membership (US$60/yr) gives you access to their clubhouses in various Latin American capitals (virtual only in Buenos Aires), where you can store gear, use the computers, consult trip reports, chat with the knowledgeable staff, borrow books, find out about local volunteer opportunities, get discounts on hostels and other services, and generally chill out.

BY BOAT

Cruise ships aside, most people arriving in Buenos Aires by boat come aboard one of the ferries or faster catamarans (☎011 4316 6500, 🖥buquebus.com or ☎011 4317 4100, 🖥coloniaexpress.com.ar) that cross the Río de la Plata estuary from Uruguay, both from the capital Montevideo and the historic town of Colonia. Boats arrive at a gleaming new terminal at Dársena Norte at the bottom of Avenida Córdoba. Although within walking distance of downtown, the route involves negotiating a rather bewildering skein of busy roads and overgrown rail-tracks, so it is advisable to take a taxi from the rank outside. The terminal is not connected to the city's public transport system.

Destinations Colonia, Uruguay (4–5 daily; 55min–2hr 45min); Montevideo, Uruguay (2 daily; 2hr 35min); Punta del Este, Uruguay (2 daily; 2hr with bus).

Maps If you are planning to stay in the city a while and make use of the public transport, a combined street map and bus atlas such as *Guía Lumi* or *Guía "T"* is a useful accessory. Both are widely available from central kiosks and occasionally, at knockdown prices, from hawkers on the buses or trains. You can find an excellent city map online at 🖥mapa.buenosaires.gob.ar.

TOURS

Bus tours The city government runs daily bus tours with audio in a variety of languages, including English, beginning in Roque Sáenz Peña and Suipacha (9am–5.30pm, every 20 min) and stopping at various points of interest, such as Monserrat, Boca, the Reserva Ecológica and the Rosedal in Palermo. It costs $120 per day or $160 for two days and you can get on and off as many times as you like, so if you're planning to cover a lot of ground it represents good value compared to taxis.

Walking tours The tourism secretariat organizes free walking tours, in English and Spanish, usually around a given barrio, but sometimes with themes such as Evita or Carlos Gardel – ask for the current schedule. ANDA tours (🖥andatravel.com.ar) organizes responsible-tourism visits with a difference, such as its "Beyond the Caminito" walking tour of Boca, which includes stopoffs at local art collectives and community organizations.

GETTING AROUND

Buenos Aires may seem like a daunting city to get around, but it's actually served by an extensive, inexpensive and generally efficient **public transport** service – albeit not the world's cleanest, quietest or most modern. The easiest part of this system to come to grips with is undoubtedly the underground rail system, or **subte**, which serves most of the city centre and the north of the city. You may also want to familiarize yourself with a few bus routes, as **buses** are the only form of public transport that serve the outlying barrios and the south of the city. That said, with **taxis** being plentiful and relatively cheap, you'll likely find them the most convenient means to get you where you want to go.

FROM TOP PARQUE 3 DE FEBRERO (P.100); RETIRO (P.87) >

1

THE SUBTE

Buenos Aires' underground rail system, or subte (see box below), is a reasonably efficient system and certainly the quickest way to get from the centre to outlying points such as Caballito, Plaza Italia (Palermo) or Chacarita, though it's often dirty and hot in the summer. The main flaw in the subte's design is that it's shaped like a fork, meaning that journeys across town involve going down one "prong" and changing at least once before heading back up to your final destination. However, the network is being gradually extended, with work under way on new north–south lines as well as extensions to the existing lines.

Lines Using the subte is a fairly straightforward business. There are six lines, plus a "premetro" system which serves the far southwestern corner of the city, linking up with the subte at the end of line E. Lines A, B, D and E run from the city centre outwards, while line C, which runs north–south between Retiro and Constitución, connects them all. Line H is a new north–south line running south from Once, part of which is still under construction. Check the name of the last station on the line you are travelling on in order to make sure you're heading in the right direction; directions to station platforms are given by this final destination.

Tickets Tickets can be purchased from the *boleterías* (ticket booths) at each station. A single trip (*viaje*) ticket ($3.50) will take you anywhere on the system. If you are going to be in the city a while, you might want to get a "SUBE" magnetic card, which costs $15 from the ticket booths. You load it up with cash in advance and can use it on the subte or buses, saving you the hassle of finding the correct change.

BUSES

Peak hours aside, when traffic is increasingly gridlocked, Buenos Aires' **buses** (*colectivos*) are a useful way of getting to many of the outlying barrios for those on a limited budget. Unfortunately, they are also noisy, prone to belching out clouds of exhaust and are driven with scant regard for traffic laws – standing, or even sitting, can be an ordeal, and is certainly an experience. From a visitor's point of view, possibly the most daunting thing about them is the sheer number of routes – almost two hundred wend their way around the vast capital. Invest in a combined street and bus-route map (see p.106), however, and you shouldn't have too much trouble.

Tickets Trips within the city cost $2; once beyond the centre and into Gran Buenos Aires, fares increase slightly. Tickets are acquired on board from a machine, which gives change for coins, though not for notes, or you can use a SUBE card. Don't expect the driver to be helpful if you're not sure where you're going, nor to wait for you to take your seat before accelerating away.

TAXIS AND REMISES

Taxis The sheer volume of black-and-yellow taxis touting their business on Buenos Aires' streets is one of the city's most characteristic sights and – other than during sudden downpours or in the outer barrios – it's rare that it takes more than a few minutes, or even seconds, to flag down a cab. The meter starts at $9 and clocks up a peso every couple of blocks, still making it a fairly affordable way of getting around the central neighbourhoods, though it starts to add up if your journey takes you across several barrios. Note also that, thanks to Argentina's rampant inflation, the price goes up every few months. Taxi rides are sometimes white-knuckle affairs – drivers range from amiable characters who drive carefully and engage in lively conversation to maniacs who seem to want to involve you and others on the streets in some road-borne suicide pact. Regardless of road skills, drivers are generally trustworthy, despite occasional reports of accomplices being used to rob passengers. Radio taxis are regarded as more secure and better quality than the unaffiliated type – they are distinguished by the company name on the side and can be hailed in the street or ordered by telephone. Premium (☏ 011 4374 6666, ⌨ taxipremium.com) has good-quality cars, all with air conditioning, at the same price as other taxis.

Remises *Remises* are plain cars that can be booked through an office. They're cheaper and usually more comfortable than taxis for getting to the airport (and they tend to have larger boots). *Remise* companies include Reminor (☏ 011 4639 1101) and Tres Sargentos (☏ 011 4311 4832).

SUBTE HERITAGE

Inaugurated in 1913, Buenos Aires' **subte** (short for *subterráneo*) is the oldest in the Spanish-speaking world. Sometimes it shows, but not always in a bad way: many of the stations along renovated Line A, which runs between Plaza de Mayo and the residential neighbourhood of Flores, are beautifully decorated with tile murals, depicting anything from famous battles to Gaudí masterpieces; Perú station, on Avenida de Mayo, has been decorated to look like it did a century ago, complete with Victorian lamps and adverts for long-gone products. Ancient carriages with elegantly lit wood-framed interiors trundled along Line A for decades but in early 2013 were replaced by modern Chinese models fitted with air conditioning and automatic doors; the disused rolling stock is due to be displayed in a museum.

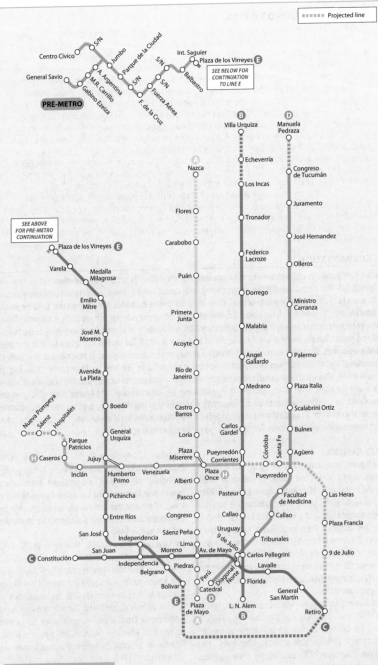

Projected line

Centro Cívico
S/N
Jumbo
Parque de la Ciudad
General Savio
A. Argentina
M.R. Carrillo
Gabino Ezeiza
PRE-METRO
S/N
S/N
F. de la Cruz
Fuerza Aérea
S/N
Int. Saguier
Plaza de los Virreyes **E**
Balbastro

SEE BELOW FOR CONTINUATION TO LINE E

B Villa Urquiza
D Manuela Pedraza

A Nazca

Echeverría
Congreso de Tucumán

Los Incas

Flores
Tronador
Juramento

Carabobo
José Hernández

Federico Lacroze
Olleros

Puán
Dorrego
Ministro Carranza

Primera Junta
Malabia

Acoyte
Angel Gallardo
Palermo

Río de Janeiro
Medrano
Plaza Italia

SEE ABOVE FOR PRE-METRO CONTINUATION

Plaza de los Virreyes **E**

Varela
Medalla Milagrosa

Emilio Mitre

José M. Moreno

Avenida La Plata
Boedo
Castro Barros
Scalabrini Ortiz

Nueva Pompeya
Sáenz
Hospitales
H Caseros

Parque Patricios
General Urquiza
Carlos Gardel
Córdoba
Santa Fe
Bulnes

Loria
Pueyrredón
Agüero

Jujuy
Plaza Miserere
Corrientes

Inclán
Humberto Primo
Venezuela
Plaza Once **H**
Pueyrredón

Pichincha
Alberti
Pasteur
Facultad de Medicina
Las Heras

Entre Ríos
Pasco
Callao
Callao

Congreso
Uruguay
Plaza Francia

San José
Sáenz Peña
9 de Julio
Tribunales
9 de Julio

Independencia
Lima
Av. de Mayo
Carlos Pellegrini

C Constitución
San Juan
Moreno
Lavalle
General San Martín

Independencia
Piedras
Florida
Retiro **C**

Belgrano
Perú
Diagonal Norte

Bolívar
D Catedral
B L. N. Alem

E Plaza de Mayo
A

THE SUBTE

1

DRIVING IN BUENOS AIRES

Make no mistake, **driving** in Buenos Aires demands nerves of steel: traffic hurtles around like in a Formula One race, with high-speed weaving common and even split-second hesitation punished by a fusillade of honking. The good news is that the city is simple to navigate once you've got the hang of the street system. With a few exceptions – notably avenidas 9 de Julio and Del Libertador – the streets are one way, with the direction (which mostly alternates street by street) marked on the street signs with an arrow. Some streets within the centre, mostly around the financial district, are closed to private traffic during the day.

The local technique for crossing the city's numerous traffic-light-less intersections at night is to slow down and flash your lights to warn drivers of your approach. In theory the vehicle coming from the right has the right of way, at all times, but be prepared to give way if the other driver looks more determined and never take it for granted that a speeding bus will respect your trajectory: accidents involving buses regularly make the headlines. Parking in the street, wherever the curb is not painted yellow, is allowed. However, car theft has risen sharply in recent years and you may prefer the relative security of an *estacionamiento* (car park) – look out for the large "E" signs.

A number of both international and national **car rental** companies (see p.28) operate in Buenos Aires. Be prepared to book some time ahead if you're planning to rent a car over a long weekend or holiday period. Given the comprehensive public transport system and the abundance of taxis, however, there's really little point in renting a car simply to tour the city.

ACCOMMODATION

Buenos Aires' popularity with international visitors means that many of the city's best **accommodation** – at all levels – is frequently full. With around half of all the country's hotels in the capital, you will always be able to find somewhere to stay, but if you're fussy about where you lay your head, you're advised to reserve in advance. At the budget end, there are dozens of **hostels**, mostly cheerful, well-run places in converted nineteenth-century mansions. If you baulk at dormitory living, consider a private room at a hostel or a costlier but homely **B&B**, which tend to be a better deal than the city-centre budget and mid-market **hotels**, many of which can be dull at best, grim at worst. The city has also seen a surge in upmarket **boutique hotels**, altogether more pleasant (though naturally more expensive) places to stay, catering principally to international visitors and scattered throughout the central neighbourhoods. The label boutique can be misleading, as anywhere else; often it just means small and vaguely trendy, but is no guarantee of comfort or quality of service. Wherever you spend the night, a fan or air conditioning is really a requirement in summer, and heating a big plus in winter. **Discounts** can sometimes be negotiated, particularly if you are staying for more than a few days, but note that credit cards may entail a surcharge. **Breakfast** is not always included at the budget hotels, but in any case you'll probably get a better start to the day in a nearby *confitería*. For advice on long-term accommodation, see p.50.

CITY CENTRE

The biggest concentration of accommodation is in the city centre, mostly hostels and budget to mid-range hotels on and around Av de Mayo and Congreso, plus a sprinkling of top-range places in the streets surrounding busy but pedestrianized Florida. It is not a laidback area in which to stay, and in many of the more traditional hotels you face a choice of internal windowless rooms, or front rooms where it can be hard to escape the noise of the city-centre traffic. However, there are plenty of exceptions, and the area has excellent transport links and is handy for its abundance of shopping and banks.

725 Buenos Aires Roque Sáenz Peña 725 ☎ 011 4131 8000, ⓦ hotel725buenosaires.com; map pp.64–65. A swish bar, trendy restaurant, spa and swimming pool are just some of the attractions at this fabulous hotel, in an equally remarkable 1920s building; the decor combines dark wood with vibrant colour schemes, with gorgeous results. US$330

Castelar Av de Mayo 1152 ☎ 011 4383 5000, ⓦ castelarhotel.com.ar; map pp.64–65. A Buenos Aires institution, this pleasant, old-fashioned hotel, where Spanish poet Federico García Lorca stayed when he was in town, offers attractive and soundproof rooms with big comfortable beds. There's also a glamorous bar downstairs and a sauna/spa. $400

La Cayetana México 1330, Monserrat ☎ 011 4383 2230, ⓦ lacayetanahotel.com.ar; map pp.64–65. Beautifully renovated nineteenth-century townhouse, with a huge, sunlit central patio and much of the original furniture worked harmoniously into the rooms, each of which is individually decorated. The only drawback is the location near Constitución – a good seven blocks from anywhere of interest – but taxis are always available. Reservations essential; the hotel won't accept anyone who just turns up. US$105

Chile Av de Mayo 1297 ☎ 011 4383 7877; map pp.64–65. Well-known hotel opened in 1906 with a beautiful Art

Nouveau facade; some rooms have balconies overlooking a side street and others have great views of Av de Mayo. All are spacious, with central heating, a/c and TV. **US$250**

Esplendor San Martín 780 ☎011 5256 8800, ⓦesplendorbuenosaires.com; map pp.64–65. In this boutique hotel 52 rooms, including very spacious suites, are arranged around a luminous atrium, on a corner of the beautiful, late nineteenth-century building mostly occupied by Galerías Pacifico (see p.72). Avant-garde works adorn the immaculate walls and each room has its own luxurious decor. **US$350**

Gran Hotel España Tacuarí 80 ☎011 4343 5541; map pp.64–65. Good budget option in a central yet quiet location, with clean, basic rooms, helpful staff and a lovely antique, manually operated elevator. It's worth paying more for the front rooms with little balconies. **$280**

Hotel de los Dos Congresos Rivadavia 1777 ☎011 4371 0072, ⓦhoteldoscongresos.com; map pp.64–65. Well-maintained hotel in a late nineteenth-century building. The best rooms at the front overlook the Congreso building and have a spiral staircase and mezzanine within them. All are decorated in a clean, modern style with a/c, TV and minibar, although the interior rooms can be on the stuffy side. **$350**

Ibis Buenos Aires Hipólito Yrigoyen 1592 ☎011 5300 5555, ⓦibishotel.com; map pp.64–65. Part of the Accor chain, the *Ibis* is a good-value hotel, offering clean, simple comfort and a friendly welcome in the city centre, near the Congreso building. **$400**

Milhouse Hipólito Yrigoyen 959 ☎011 4345 9604, ⓦmilhousehostel.com; map pp.64–65. Large, popular hostel, part of the HI chain, in a three-storey nineteenth-century house a block from Av de Mayo. The hostel arranges daily entertainment, both in-house events such as tango lessons and trips to football matches and nightclubs, and has expanded to a second locale at Av de Mayo 1245. Dorms **$80**, doubles **$300**

Moreno Moreno 376, Monserrat ☎011 6091 2000, ⓦmorenobuenosaires.com; map pp.64–65. The stunning Art Deco facade tells you this is something special – the forty sumptuous rooms inside range from large room to the jacuzzi loft. There is also a tango lounge and a wonderful deck terrace, offering amazing views. **US$210**

NH Jousten Av Corrientes 280 ☎011 4321 6750, ⓦnh-hoteles.com; map pp.64–65. Very comfortable accommodation in a beautiful, early twentieth-century building popular with business travellers but with appeal for all; it also has an excellent restaurant serving modern Spanish cuisine. One of several central hotels run by the Spanish NH designer hotel chain. **US$95**

O'Rei Lavalle 733 ☎011 4393 7186, ⓦhotelorei.com. ar; map pp.64–65. The high-ceilinged rooms are a bit gloomy and basic, but the *O'Rei* has two things really going for it – it's very central, and very cheap. **$225**

TOP 5 HISTORIC HOTELS
Alvear Palace Hotel See p.112
Castelar See opposite
Chile See opposite
Gran Hotel América See p.112
Palacio Duhau-Park Hyatt See p.112

Sportsman Rivadavia 1425 ☎011 4381 8021, ⓦhotel sportsman.com.ar; map pp.64–65. Popular budget hotel in a rambling old building with lots of character, though the interior is beginning to show its age. There's a range of rooms, all with fans and some with shared bathrooms; the nicest are the en-suite doubles at the front, which have balconies. Dorms **$75**, doubles **$300**

★**V&S Youth Hostel** Viamonte 887 ☎011 4322 0994, ⓦhostelclub.com; map pp.64–65. The most luxurious hostel in Buenos Aires, the *V&S* is centrally located in a 1910 French-style mansion. A bar and giant TV top the list of amenities, as well as all kinds of interesting organized excursions to keep you occupied. In addition to dormitory accommodation there are three great-value double rooms with private bathrooms and balconies. Dorms **$90**, doubles **$400**

SAN TELMO, PUERTO MADERO AND CONSTITUCIÓN
Most accommodation in the south is in the barrio of San Telmo, a magnet for travellers as much for its cobbled streets and prettily crumbling buildings as for its budget hotels and youth hostels. Puerto Madero has a handful of upmarket places to stay, while the area around Constitución station has some interesting accommodation options, as well as plenty of less-salubrious budget joints.

★**Boquitas Pintadas** Estados Unidos 1393, Constitución ☎011 4381 6064, ⓦboquitas-pintadas .com.ar; map pp.64–65. An ordinary-looking building in a rather run-down neighbourhood is the surprising home to a small offbeat hotel, where each of the five rooms is decorated differently (and comes at a different price), with an artist's touch. All guests have use of the flower-filled sun terrace, and there's a bar downstairs that hosts DJ nights and art happenings. **US$100**

★**Circus Hostel** Chacabuco 1020, San Telmo ☎011 4878 7786, ⓦhostelcircus.com; map p.79. *Circus* success-fully bridges the gap between hostel and hotel, offering the ambience and friendliness of the former with the comforts of the latter – the beds have decent mattresses, each room has its own bathroom, and there is even a smart decked pool. The street has other hostels, so is a good place to try your luck if you haven't anything booked. Dorms **US$16**

Faena Hotel & Universe Marta Salotti 445, Puerto Madero Este ☎011 4010 9000, ⓦfaenahoteland universe.com; map pp.64–65. Buenos Aires' hotel for the

1

in-crowd, this former grain-storage building has been given a serious Philippe Starck makeover and now has a *belle époque* jazz bar, a café stuffed with kitsch antiques, a floor-to-ceiling white restaurant with unicorn heads on the walls, an oriental spa and, of course, swish rooms. It's the kind of place that's too cool for a reception – you get an "experience manager". This is where movie producers and celebrities like to stay. US$600

Gran Hotel América Bernardo de Irigoyen 1608, San Telmo ☎011 4307 8785, ⍟granhotelamerica.com.ar; map p.79. A stone's throw from Constitución station, this reasonably priced hotel was where famous tango composer Angel Villoldo entertained his lady friends. Some of the rooms are a bit gloomy and noisy but the large, airy triples are a good deal. $200

RETIRO AND RECOLETA

These two barrios, jointly known as Barrio Norte, are where the city's top-flight luxury hotels tend to be located, although some cheaper options exist too. Recoleta is the perfect location, with plenty to offer – restaurants, bars and shops – and still within walking distance (about 20min) of the microcentro, but with less hustle and bustle.

Alvear Palace Hotel Av Alvear 1891, Recoleta ☎011 4804 7777, ⍟alvearpalace.com; map p.86. Once the choice of wealthy landowners and now the favourite of politicians and royalty, the *Alvear* is still BA's luxury hotel par excellence, despite the trendy new upstarts. It offers fabulously decorated rooms in Louis XV style and all the extras you would expect, including a personal butler. Excellent restaurants, too. US$590

Ayacucho Palace Hotel Ayacucho 1408, Recoleta ☎011 4806 1815, ⍟ayacuchohotel.com.ar; map p.86. Housed in a smart French-style building, the rooms in this hotel are clean, comfortable and come with a/c in a good location near the centre of Recoleta. $440

Casa Calma Suipacha 1015, Retiro ☎011 5199 2800, ⍟casacalma.com.ar; map p.86. One of the few boutique hotels in the area, *Casa Calma* lives up to its "quiet house" name, and takes a decidedly ecological approach, with hanging gardens and environmentally friendly toiletries. Many bathrooms have jacuzzis, while you can ask for massages in your room. There's also an honesty bar. US$255

Four Seasons Posadas 1086, Retiro ☎011 4321 1200, ⍟fourseasons.com/buenosaires; map p.86. Part of the international chain, this fantastically luxurious hotel is divided between a modern block and a *belle époque* mansion, which looks like a French chateau inside and out. Sunday brunch, open to the public, is served in the latter. US$525

Guido Palace Guido 1780, Recoleta ☎011 4812 0341; map p.86. Not exactly a palace, more a functional hotel, slightly worn at the edges, but cheap for the area. Its location in the heart of Recoleta is its big selling point. $350

Lion d'Or Hotel Pacheco de Melo 2019, Recoleta ☎011 4803 8992, ⍟hotel-liondor.com.ar; map p.86. Homely and friendly place, with a variety of appealing, tastefully decorated rooms. Rooms vary considerably in size, style and price, ranging from an internal single with shared bath to a lovely, spacious triple with a fireplace and balcony. $350

Palacio Duhau-Park Hyatt Av Alvear 1661, Recoleta ☎011 5171 1234, ⍟buenosaires.park.hyatt.com; map p.86. The Duhau family home on the city's most desirable street (see p.91) is now a hyper-luxury hotel, with huge rooms decorated with soothing woods and marble baths. The giant, superbly lit swimming pool, restaurant, *vinoteca* and *Oak Bar* mean you never need to leave the building. US$560

PALERMO

Away from the blasting horns and spluttering buses of the centre, Palermo is a greener, more relaxed neighbourhood in which to stay. There are some fabulous, if expensive, small hotels, extremely agreeable B&Bs and fun hostels, all with the added benefit of being close to the city's most interesting bars, restaurants and boutiques. A taxi to the centre costs about $50.

Casa Esmeralda Honduras 5765 ☎011 4772 2446, ⍟casaesmeralda.com.ar; map pp.96–97. Wonderful Franco-Argentine-run guesthouse smack in the middle of Palermo Hollywood, with a green garden and friendly service. $210

Craft Nicaragua 4583 ☎011 4833 0060, ⍟crafthotel .com; map pp.96–97. Overlooking the beautiful Plaza Armenia at the heart of Palermo Viejo, this trendy little hotel revels in its minimalistic decor that includes functional shower cubicles divided from the bedroom by a curtain. The cheapest room, Song, includes a vinyl record player (choose from a collection at reception). The excellent self-service breakfast is served on the top floor, where a sunny roof-terrace includes four-poster beds. US$144

Eco Pampa Hostel Guatemala 4778 ☎011 4831 2435, ⍟hostelpampa.com; map pp.96–97. Dubbing itself the city's first green hostel – the vibrant lime-hued facade sets the tone – *Eco Pampa* is comfortable as well as ecofriendly, with its leafy terrace and low-energy computers. Dorms US$15, doubles US$80

Home Honduras 5860 ☎011 4778 1008, ⍟home buenosaires.com; map pp.96–97. Owned and run by a British record producer and his Irish-Argentine wife, this masterpiece of modern architecture and hotel design is simply incredible: from the wallpaper in each room to the swimming pool and deck, the attention to detail is breathtaking. US$145

Legado Mítico Gurruchaga 1848 ☎011 4833 1300, ⍟legadomitico.com; map pp.96–97. Like its sister hotel in Salta (see p.287), this remarkable boutique hotel goes in for themed rooms. You can choose between Argentine heroes like San Martín and Evita or arty types like Borges and Tita Merello.

Each is spacious and stylishly decorated and furnished, with all manner of memorabilia recalling each historical figure. The breakfast room resembles the library of a gentleman's club. **US$300**

Magnolia Julián Álvarez 1746 ☎011 4867 4900, Ⓦ magnoliahotel.com.ar; map pp.96–97. At this gorgeous Art Nouveau townhouse with period furnishings, nothing is too much trouble – from the welcome glass of wine on arrival to help with all you need during your stay. Breakfast is excellent and copious. **US$250**

Nuss El Salvador 4916 ☎011 4833 6222, Ⓦ nusshotel .com; map pp.96–97. This utterly classy boutique hotel in a converted convent at the corner of Serrano houses a range of 22 beautiful rooms, ranging from spacious superior category to sizeable suites. The convent's inner courtyard has been preserved, adding to the sense of space and airiness, while the top-floor deck with its plunge pool and a small gym and spa is refreshed by the majestic plane trees in the neighbouring street. **US$220**

Posada Palermo Salguero 1655 ☎011 4826 8792, Ⓦ posadapalermo.com; map pp.96–97. Wonderful B&B in a more residential corner of Palermo, away, but not far, from the nerve centre of Soho; this typical *casa chorizo* (kind of elongated townhouse found in most Argentine cities), offers smart rooms, a homely atmosphere and a great breakfast, including home-made preserves. **US$140**

EATING

Buenos Aires is Latin America's **gastronomic capital** and, with many places offering excellent quality for the price, eating out here must count as a highlight of any visit to Argentina. In addition to the ubiquitous **pizza** and **pasta** restaurants common to the country as a whole, the capital offers a number of **cosmopolitan** cuisines, ranging from Armenian and Basque to Thai and Vietnamese. Foodie fashions are enthusiastically adopted; Peruvian haute cuisine and mini-gourmet restaurants in the intimate space of someone's house are currently all the rage. The city's crowning glory, however – though you have to be a meat eater – are its **parrillas**, whose top-end representatives offer the country's choicest beef cooked on an *asador criollo* – staked around an open fire. There are plenty of humbler places, too, where you can enjoy a succulent *parrillada* in a lively atmosphere.

OPENING HOURS

Though most restaurants open in the evening at around 8pm, it's worth bearing in mind that Porteños don't normally go out to eat until a couple of hours later; many restaurants suddenly go from empty to full between 9.30pm and 10pm. Kitchens generally close around midnight during the week, though at weekends many keep serving till the small hours. There are also plenty of *confiterías* and pizzerias open throughout the night, so you shouldn't have trouble satisfying your hunger at any time.

RESTAURANTS

Excellent meals can be had throughout Buenos Aires but, with some exceptions, the centre and the south are best for the city's most traditional restaurants, while the north is the place for more innovative or exotic cooking. Puerto Madero, the recently renovated port area, is knee-deep in big, glitzy themed restaurants, though – a couple of decent places notwithstanding – these are hardly the capital's most exciting eating options. You'll find a far more original crop of restaurants in Palermo, in three clusters – Soho around Plaza Cortázar/Serrano; Hollywood around Honduras and Fitzroy; and Las Cañitas around Báez and Chenaut.

CITY CENTRE

Arturito Corrientes 1124 ☎011 4382 0227; map pp.64–65. An old-fashioned haven reigned over by courteous white-jacketed waiters, *Arturito* is a Corrientes landmark, and its *bife de chorizo con papas* (rump steak and chips) is an unquestionably good deal. Daily noon–4pm & 7pm–1am.

Brasserie Petanque Defensa and Mexico, Monserrat ☎011 4342 7930; map pp.64–65. Classic French food such as *boeuf bourguignon*, *moules*, steak tartare and *crème brûlée*, with a particularly good-value lunchtime *menu du jour*; slightly uppity classic French service to match at times. Mon–Fri noon–3pm & 7pm–midnight, Sat 7pm–1am, Sun noon–2.30pm & 7.30–11pm.

Chiquilín Sarmiento 1599 ☎011 4373 5163; map pp.64–65. A classic Porteño restaurant, popular with tourists, serving traditional dishes in a friendly and stylish atmosphere. The *pollo al verdeo* (chicken with spring onions) is good, but it's the revered *bife* ($40) that brings most people in. Daily noon–4pm & 7–11.30pm.

El Claustro San Martín 705 ☎011 4312 0235; map pp.64–65. The vaulted dining room was part of the Santa Catalina convent, making it a haven of peace and quiet amid the frantic financial district. Considering the inventiveness of the cuisine – such as a tajine-like lamb dish or pears with lemongrass – the two-course lunch served on weekdays is quite reasonably priced. Mon–Fri noon–4pm.

Las Cuartetas Corrientes 838; map pp.64–65. A pared-down pizza and empanada joint where you can grab a slice of delicious and cheap pizza at the counter and while away a few hours after the cinema over a cold Quilmes. Mon–Sat noon–1am, Sun 7–11.30pm.

El Globo Hipólito Yrigoyen 1199 ☎011 4381 3926; map pp.64–65. One of several Spanish restaurants in the area, *El Globo* has a gorgeously old-fashioned interior and serves generous portions of classic dishes

1

FIVE GREAT PARRILLAS

Cabaña Las Lilas See below
La Cabrera See p.116
Chori & Wine See p.116
Desnivel See below
Parrilla Peña See below

---

such as *gambas al ajillo* (spicy prawns) and *puchero*. About $70 for a two-course meal. Daily noon–3.30pm & 7pm–midnight.

★ **Granix** Florida 165, Galería Güemes, Entrada Mitre, 1st floor; map pp.64–65. You pay a small fixed charge on entry at this large, airy, self-service vegetarian restaurant located in one of Florida's magnificent shopping arcades, and then eat as much as you want. Salads are straight-from-the-market fresh and the variety of soft drinks, warm dishes and delicious desserts, including some unusual options, is overwhelming. Mon–Fri noon–4pm.

Güerrín Corrientes 1368; map pp.64–65. A quint-essential Porteño pizza experience, the traditional order here is a portion of *muzzarella* and *fainá* eaten at the counter and accompanied by a glass of sweet Moscato. Some locals hold that the pizzas served in the proper dining area are a notch above the counter versions; however, all are inexpensive. Daily noon–1am.

Laurak-Bat Belgrano 1144, Monserrat ☎011 4381 0682; map pp.64–65. A moderately priced Basque restaurant within *Club Vasco* boasting specialities such as *bacalao al pil-pil* (salt cod in a garlic sauce). Mon–Sat noon–4pm & 7pm–midnight.

★ **Parrilla Peña** Rodríguez Peña 682 ☎011 4371 5643; map pp.64–65. Knowledgeable liveried waiters serve up some of the juiciest meat in town, as well as fine wines and mouthwatering salads at this great-value, no-nonsense *parrilla*. Mon–Sat noon–4pm & 7pm–midnight, Sun noon–4pm.

Patio San Ramón Reconquista 269; map pp.64–65. Generously portioned, well-cooked and inexpensive food with daily specials such as *pollo al horno con puré de batata* (roast chicken with sweet potato purée). The real attraction, however, is the stunning location – the patio of an old convent where, among palm trees and birdsong, you might even forget you're at the heart of Buenos Aires' financial district. Mon–Fri noon–4.30pm.

★ **Tomo 1** Carlos Pellegrini 525, in Hotel Panamericano ☎011 4326 6695; map pp.64–65. Considered by many to be Buenos Aires' best haute cuisine restaurant, this is an elegant but refreshingly unpretentious place where the emphasis is squarely placed on the exquisitely cooked food, such as chilled melon soup and quail with pistachios. Not cheap, but good value, particularly if you go for the set menus (around $180). Mon–Fri noon–4pm & 7–11.30pm, Sat 7.30pm–midnight.

Winery Av Alem 880 ☎011 4314 2639; map pp.64–65. As well as a store that holds regular tastings of all the best Argentine wines, *Winery* – a growing BA chain – has a restaurant serving cheeses, gourmet sandwiches and unusual specialities such as braised goat. About $100 for two courses. Mon–Sat noon–11.30pm.

PUERTO MADERO

Bice Av Alicia M. de Justo 192 ☎011 4315 6216; map pp.64–65. Style often triumphs over content in Puerto Madero, but the excellent pasta and gnocchi at this highly regarded, if expensive, Italian restaurant will not disappoint. Daily noon–4pm & 7pm–1am.

Cabaña Las Lilas Av Alicia M. de Justo 516 ☎011 4313 1336; map pp.64–65. The place to head if you want to splurge on just about the finest steak around; an *ojo de bife*, best savoured from a shaded veranda on the waterfront, will set you back what it would cost to eat for a week in a standard *parrilla*. Very popular with tourists; reservations advisable. Daily noon–3pm & 8pm–midnight.

"i" Fresh Market Azucena Villaflor and Olga Cossettini; map pp.64–65. By Dique 3, the pick of the chic new places in Puerto Madero Este. A great place for lunch or *merienda*, with a selection of inventive sandwiches, salads and bruschettas, plus a range of yummy *licuados* (fruit shakes) and herbal teas to accompany; meals such as pasta and steak are also available. Slightly pricey but not outrageous. Daily noon–4pm & 7.30–11.30pm.

Siga La Vaca Av Alicia M. de Justo 1714 ☎011 4315 6801; map pp.64–65. At this upmarket *tenedor libre* you can eat till you drop for a reasonable sum; the fixed rate (about $70, less at lunchtime) includes a carafe of wine, a dazzling choice of salads and, of course, a mountain of meat. As with all *tenedor libres*, go for quantity, variety and speed, rather than quality. Daily noon–1.30am.

SAN TELMO AND BOCA

El Baqueano Bolívar and Chile, San Telmo ☎011 4342 0802; map p.79. Unusual restaurant that uses local ingredients, particularly indigenous animals, to create gourmet dishes such as *Provençale* cayman tails and *ñandú* stuffed with liquor-soaked fruit. Relatively normal meats such as pheasant are also served, but it's not a place for vegetarians or the squeamish. Tasting menu with five dishes $105. Tues–Sat 7.30–11.30pm.

★ **Café San Juan** Av San Juan 450, San Telmo ☎011 4300 1112; map p.79. A small, good-value, family-run joint whose huge portions and fresh-from-the-market meals mean it's always full. Try the "hunter's-style" rabbit. Tues–Sun 12.30–4pm & 7pm–midnight.

Desnivel Defensa 855, San Telmo ☎011 4399 9081; map p.79. The backpackers pile in to this no-frills *parrilla*, which offers meat-laden dishes at rock-bottom prices. Mon 8pm–late, Tues–Sun 8am–4pm & 8pm–late.

El Obrero Caffarena 64, Boca ☎011 4362 9912; map p.82. With Boca Juniors souvenirs decorating the walls and tango musicians sauntering from table to table at weekends, the atmosphere at the hugely popular and moderately priced *El Obrero* is as much a part of its appeal as the simple home-cooked food, including great *milanesas*. Tues–Sun 12.30–4.30pm & 7.30pm–midnight.

RETIRO AND RECOLETA

Bengal Arenales 837, Retiro ☎011 4314 2926; map p.86. Although, as the name suggests, this smart restaurant offers Indian specialities, including a perfectly passable *rogan josh*, it really excels in its Mediterranean Italian dishes, with a strong focus on fish. The decor and ambience are decidedly posh but the highly attentive service is not snobbish, and the wine and food, albeit not budget-priced, are impeccable, down to all the nibbly bits they serve before and after. Mon–Fri noon–4pm & 8pm–late, Sat 8pm–late.

Club Danés Alem 1074 12th floor, Retiro ☎011 4312 9266; map p.86. This lunch-only Danish restaurant serves a mean *smörrebrod* – lots of herrings, anchovies and blue cheese – and other specialities in a suitably airy dining room with great river views, with change from $70. Brown ale brewed in Buenos Aires Province is available. Mon–Fri noon–3pm.

Club Sírio Ayacucho 1496, Recoleta ☎011 4806 5764; map p.86. Every major Argentine city has its Syrian club-restaurant, and this palatial place is one of the best, with an excellent and varied menu of starters. About $125 for dinner. Mon–Sat 8.30pm–1am.

El Cuartito Talcahuano 937, Retiro ☎011 4816 1758; map p.86. Classic budget BA pizzeria, famed for its delicious dough and *fugazzeta* – local pizza made with lots of onions and cheese, but no tomatoes. The seats are uncomfortable and the atmosphere noisy, but that's all part of the experience. Daily noon–1am.

El Estrebe Peña 2475, Recoleta ☎011 4803 0282; map p.86. What eating out in Buenos Aires is all about – white tablecloths, pictures by gaucho artist Molino Campos on the walls, enormous *copas* of velvety red Malbec, and thick, tender steaks at fairly reasonable prices. Daily noon–4pm & 8pm–late.

Filo San Martín 975, Retiro ☎011 4311 0312; map p.86. Some of the centre's best salads, if not the cheapest, featuring less common ingredients such as rocket, radishes and sultanas soaked in wine, in addition to imaginative pizzas, pastas and other Italian-inspired fusion dishes such as Venetian mussel soup with Patagonian clams. Daily noon–late.

Milion Paraná 1048, Recoleta ☎011 4815 9925; map p.86. A beautifully converted mansion, with a host of candlelit rooms. Cocktails and modern Argentine cuisine served, such as *pacu* river fish with orange and parsley sauce, or pasta with goat's cheese and sweet pumpkin. It's really more about the very cool ambience than the gastronomy, though. Mon–Fri 10am–late, Sat noon–6pm & 8pm–late, Sun 8pm–late.

Nectarine 2.0 Vicente López 1661, Recoleta ☎011 4813 6993; map p.86. A classical dining room is the setting for what some locals say is the city's best cordon bleu food: foie gras and duck grace the menu, with expensive wines to accompany them. Mon–Fri noon–3.30pm & 8pm–midnight, Sat 8pm–midnight.

Piola Pizzería Libertad 1078, Retiro ☎011 4812 0690; map p.86. You'll find dozens of toppings to choose from at this huge, hip, gay-friendly pizza joint, where thin crusts meet the city's upper crust. Prices are higher than usual for pizza. Mon–Fri noon–4pm & 8pm–late, Sat & Sun 8pm–late.

Restó Montevideo 938, Recoleta ☎011 4816 6711; map p.86. Set back from the street in the building housing the Central Society of Architects, this appropriately stylish little French restaurant serves quail, duck and other less common ingredients, while puddings include the likes of muscovado sugar ice cream. The three-course set menus cost around $150. Mon–Wed noon–3pm, Thurs & Fri noon–3pm & 8–11pm.

Romario Pizza Vicente López 2102, Recoleta ☎011 4511 4444; map p.86. You can savour *Romario's* great, reasonably priced pizzas in a small, outdoor seating area from where Recoleta in full swing can be observed; part of an excellent chain famed for its roller-skating delivery boys and girls. Daily noon–4pm & 8pm–late.

El Sanjuanino Posadas 1515, Recoleta ☎011 4804 2909; map p.86. The place to try empanadas, this inexpensive restaurant also has other regional fare such as *locro* and *humitas*, as well as more exotic dishes like pickled *vizcacha*. Tues–Sun noon–4pm & 8pm–late.

Sipan Paraguay 624, Retiro ☎011 4315 0763; map p.86. Stylish and pricey Peruvian–Japanese fusion cooking, offering ultra-fresh ceviche and sushi, as well as a number of delicious takes on the classic Peruvian sautéed beef dish *lomo saltado* – try the one with calamari. Mon–Wed noon–4pm & 8pm–midnight, Thurs–Sat noon–4pm & 8pm–1am.

Tancat Paraguay 645, Retiro ☎011 4312 5442; map p.86. A beautifully decorated and lit Spanish–Catalan *tasca*, where the *cañas* (small glasses of draft beer), varied tapas and other mainstays, like grilled baby squid, are totally genuine; the service is brisk, it gets very busy (bookings recommended) and can be noisy, but that only adds to the authenticity. Moderately priced, unless you opt for seafood. Mon–Sat noon–late.

PALERMO

Artemisia Cabrera 3877 ☎011 4863 4242; map pp.96–97. Probably BA's best non-meat restaurant, the vegetarian and fish dishes here make no sacrifices flavour-wise. Even die-hard carnivores will enjoy *Artemisia's* twist

1

on polenta lasagne or lime- and cilantro-spiked *abadejo* (pollock). The food is freshly cooked, so it's not the place to go if you're in a hurry – but it's worth the wait. About $100 for dinner. Tues–Sat 8.30pm–late.

Bio Humboldt 2192 ☎011 4774 3880; map pp.96–97. Vegetarian restaurant with lots of wholesome ingredients – wholemeal empanadas, quinoa risotto, tofu salad and so on – with a good-value ($55) lunch with drink. Organic wine and beer are also served. Daily 9am–1am.

★ **La Cabrera** Cabrera 5099 & 5127 ☎011 4831 7002; map pp.96–97. This fabulous, down-to-earth *parrilla* serves hard-to-beat *bifes de chorizo* (the half portion can feed two) with an array of delicious tapa garnishes; it's so popular the owners had to open a second restaurant just up the road. Mon, Sat & Sun 12.30–4.30pm & 8.30pm–1am, Tues–Thurs 8.30pm–1am, Fri 8.30pm–2am.

Casa Cruz Uriarte 1658 ☎011 4833 1112; map pp.96–97. The glossy red mahogany panelling and perfect portions at this trendy restaurant make you feel as if you're dining inside a Chinese lacquered box, while the food is eclectic, sumptuously presented and absolutely delicious – try the warm oysters served with tapioca caviar and a pear salad. Faultless service, but the bill is steep – don't expect much change from $300. Mon–Sat 8.30pm–late.

Chori & Wine Costa Rica 5198 esq. Godoy Cruz, Palermo Soho ☎011 4773 0954; map pp.96–97. A clear step above most *parrillas*, this intimate, moderately expensive restaurant serves truly exceptional, export-quality meat, cooked to perfection by an internationally trained chef. The wine list and desserts are excellent, complemented by attentive, friendly service. Tues–Sat 8pm–late.

La Fondue J.F. Segui 4674 ☎011 4778 0110; map pp.96–97. This small, friendly side-street bistro uses home-made ingredients to make unbeatable pasta and fondue. Fairly expensive. Mon–Sat 8am–late, Sun 8pm–late.

El Manto Costa Rica 5801 ☎011 4774 2409; map pp.96–97. Lamb, yogurt and mint dominate the menu at this authentic Armenian restaurant, where a Carrara marble statue of the Virgin presides over dinner. About $120 for two courses. Daily 8pm–late.

Ølsen Gorriti 5870 ☎011 4776 7677; map pp.96–97. This large, modern restaurant serves exciting cuisine with a Scandinavian touch, such as salmon pizza or goat-cheese ravioli. There are around forty different kinds of vodka and all manner of cocktails to kick things off, as well as an admirable wine cellar. About $180 for two courses. Tues–Thurs noon–1am, Fri & Sat noon–2am, Sun 10.30am–1am, closed Mon.

Ña Serapia Las Heras 3357 ☎011 4801 5307; map pp.96–97. An unexpectedly traditional and rustic restaurant in the heart of upmarket Palermo, *Ña Serapia* styles itself as a *pulpería* and bar and serves delicious regional dishes including *locro* and tamales at very reasonable prices. Daily noon–4pm & 8pm–late.

Las Pizarras Thames 2296 ☎011 4775 0625; map pp.96–97. Informal restaurant that's all about the fabulous (and reasonably priced) food. Run by a chef who has worked in top London restaurants, the menu varies according to what's available and is written up on black-boards (*pizarras*), so it's a bit of a lottery – but that's all part of the fun. Tues–Sun 8pm–midnight.

Sarkis Thames 1101 ☎011 4772 4911; map pp.96–97. Spartan decor, but excellent tabbouleh, *keppe crudo* (raw meat with onion – much better than it sounds) and falafel at this popular budget restaurant serving a fusion of Armenian, Arab and Turkish cuisines. Daily noon–3pm & 8pm–1am.

Sudestada Guatemala and Fitzroy ☎011 4776 3777; map pp.96–97. Smart noodle bar with a Vietnamese chef who prepares tasty curries and other Southeast Asian food at reasonable prices, all in modern, minimalist surroundings. Mon–Sat noon–4pm & 8pm–late.

Xalapa Gurruchaga and El Salvador ☎011 4833 6102; map pp.96–97. Argentines usually shy away from hot and spicy food, but this place, which has the most authentic and tasty Mexican fare in the city, is packed even midweek. Proceed with caution, lest you torch your taste buds, especially when sampling the stuffed *chiles*. About $90 for two courses. Mon–Thurs 8pm–midnight, Fri 8pm–1am, Sat 1–4pm & 8pm–1am, Sun 1–4pm & 8pm–midnight.

CAFÉS, CONFITERÍAS AND SNACKS

You can learn a lot about Porteños from a little discreet people-watching in the city's cafés. People stream through all day, from office workers grabbing a quick *medialuna* in the morning to ladies of leisure taking afternoon tea to students gossiping over a beer or juice in the evenings. They're not quite the hotbed of revolutionary activity they were in the 1970s, but they're still in many ways where you'll find authentic Buenos Aires – over an excellent espresso, usually served with a welcomingly hydrating glass of water. *Confiterías* are traditional tearooms that also specialize in biscuits, cakes and pastries to accompany the tea and coffee, although the dividing line between these, regular cafés and even restaurants (many serve full-blown meals, at very reasonable prices) can be quite blurred.

CITY CENTRE

★ **La Americana** Callao 83–99; map pp.64–65. A Callao landmark, serving up juicy empanadas – some say they're the city's best – to be consumed standing up at metal counters. Daily 8am–late.

Café Tortoni Av de Mayo 825 ☎011 4342 4328; map pp.64–65. Buenos Aires' most famous café (see p.68) exudes pure elegance, but is in grave danger of turning into a tourist trap. Some evenings it hosts live jazz or tango in *La Bodega* downstairs, but there are many far more authentic venues around. Daily 8am–late.

HELADERÍAS

More than anything else, one institution in Buenos Aires, and indeed the rest of the country, serves as a constant reminder of Argentina's strong Italian inheritance: the **heladería**, or ice-cream parlour. Ubiquitous, varied, extremely popular and the subject of fierce debate as to which is the best, these minefields of temptation serve millions of cones and cups daily, and dispatch hundreds of delivery boys on motorbikes to satisfy the needs of those who cannot be bothered to go out and buy in person (or are averse to queuing).

Arkakaó Av Quintana 188, Recoleta; map p.86. Originating in Aosta, northern Italy, as *Kakaó*, this international chain (with a branch in Rosario, too) now has a smart establishment in a Recoleta townhouse and prides itself on serving authentic cappuccinos along with creamy gelato made with Sicilian pistachios and other top-notch ingredients. Daily noon–late.

Cadore Corrientes 1695, city centre; map pp.64–65. Some experts have declared this the best place for ice cream in the city – despite much competition – and the *dulce de leche* flavour above all. It is certainly one of the most traditional and there are no other branches. Daily noon–late.

Freddo Guido and Junín, Recoleta ☎ 0810 3337 3336; map p.86. The quality at Buenos Aires' popular ice-cream chain has gone up and down over the years, and seems to be on a high at present – *dulce de leche* aficionados will be in heaven, and few will fail to be seduced by the banana split or *sambayon*. You get to choose two flavours with your cone, but almost inevitably you'll want to try more. One of many branches throughout the city (see ⓦ freddo.com.ar for others). Daily noon–late.

Jauja Cerviño 3901, Palermo; map pp.96–97. Buenos Aires is now blessed with a branch of Patagonia's pride and joy ice-cream parlour in El Bolsón (see p.412). The wild berry flavours, including unusual ones such as elderberry, are especially good. Daily noon–late.

★ **Persicco** Salguero 2591 and Cabello, Palermo ☎ 0810 3337 377, plus other branches; map pp.96–97. This small, family-run chain of stylish parlours – part modern, part retro – dish out fabulous ice creams and sorbets, with emphasis on chocolate flavours; they also serve excellent cakes, croissants, coffees, while the toast and jam served for breakfast are delicious. Mon–Fri 8am–1am, Sat & Sun 9am–1am.

★ **Confitería Ideal** Suipacha 384; map pp.64–65. It's not quite as famous as the *Tortoni*, and therefore less frequented, though it is just as beautiful, if a little worn at the edges. The main reason to go here is to see a *milonga* in the upstairs tango salon (see p.123). Don't be put off by the dusty, smelly entrance. Daily 8.30am–8pm.

La Giralda Av Corrientes and Uruguay; map pp.64–65. Brightly lit and austerely decorated Corrientes café famous for its *chocolate con churros*. A perennial hangout for students and intellectuals and a good place to experience the Porteño passion for conversation. Daily 8am–late.

New Brighton Sarmiento 645; map pp.64–65. The classic Anglo–Porteño *Brighton*, which first opened its doors in 1908, was recently renovated and reopened, retaining many of its original features. Wood panelling and stained glass help re-create a *belle époque* atmosphere, with a café area at the front and expensive restaurant at the back. Mon–Sat noon–4pm & 8pm–late.

Nsalad Tucumán 269; map pp.64–65. A great option for a quick and healthy lunch, to eat in or take away. *Nsalad* does, as you might expect, a variety of healthy salads, as well as filled tortillas and – a rarity in BA – bagels. Mon–Fri 9am–5pm.

La Paz Av Corrientes 1599; map pp.64–65. The classic Corrientes (and Porteño) café; less sumptuous but also with fewer tourists than the *Tortoni*. *La Paz* was once the favourite hangout of left-wing intellectuals and writers and it's still a good place to meet a friend or read a book over a coffee, especially when it's raining outside and the windows steam up. Daily 8am–late.

SAN TELMO

Abuela Pan Bolívar 707, San Telmo; map p.79. Homely vegetarian café and wholefood store offering a daily menu with options such as tofu burgers, stuffed aubergines and vegetarian sushi. Mon–Fri 8am–7pm.

La Poesía Bolívar and Chile, San Telmo; map p.79. Self-consciously traditional San Telmo café-bar with wooden tables and a mind-boggling choice of sandwiches and *picadas*. Tango is the usual backdrop. Daily 8am–late.

RETIRO, RECOLETA AND PALERMO

La Biela Quintana 600, Recoleta; map p.86. Institutional *confitería* perhaps more appealing for its history and location than for its average *lomitos* and coffee, served in the elegant bistro interior or in the shade of a gigantic gum tree on the terrace. Daily 8am–late.

Café Martínez Libertador 3598, Palermo; map pp.96–97. One of several branches of this 70-year-old, upmarket café. Its enticing speciality drinks include iced cappuccino with *dulce de leche*, while its *cappuccino miel* is a rich mix of chocolate, honey, steamed milk, cream, cinnamon – and a little coffee. Daily 8am–late.

Carlitos Guido 1962, Recoleta; map p.86. Classic neighbourhood café that's BA's branch of the famous *Carlitos*, "king of the pancakes" in Villa Gesell (see p.162). Choose from over one hundred different generous savoury and sweet fillings; the caramelized apple pancake is particularly noteworthy. Daily 8am–midnight.

Costumbres Criollas Libertador 308, Retiro; map p.86. A small restaurant specializing in excellent *empanadas tucumanas* and regional dishes such as *locro* and tamales. Worth seeking out for a snack if you have an hour or two to kill in the vicinity of Retiro. Daily 11am–4pm and 7pm–midnight.

Cumaná Rodríguez Peña 1149, Retiro; map p.86. Popular with students and office workers, this is a good place to try *mate*, served from 4pm to 7.30pm with a basket of crackers. There's also a selection of provincial food, such as empanadas and *cazuelas* (casseroles), on the menu. Daily noon–late.

OUTER BARRIOS

★ **Las Violetas** Av Rivadavia 3899, Almagro; subte Castro Barros. Rescued from closure by popular demand, this *confitería*-restaurant is a monument to the Porteño heyday of the 1920s, with its fine wood panelling, gorgeous stained glass, Carrara marble tabletops and impressive columns; it was a favourite hangout of writers such as Roberto Arlt. The *confitería* is justly famed for its breads, cakes and pastries, while the restaurant combines attentive service with copious and refined cuisine – try the delicious *agnelottis* (pasta) filled with ricotta, ham and walnuts. 8am–late; closed Sat.

DRINKING AND NIGHTLIFE

If you've come to Buenos Aires eager to experience the city after dark you will not leave disappointed. Porteños are consummate night owls and though nightlife peaks from Thursday to Saturday, you'll find plenty of things to do during the rest of the week too. Worthwhile venues are spread all over the city, but certain areas offer an especially large selection of night-time diversions. The city's young and affluent head to Palermo's **Soho** and **Hollywood** to strut their stuff year-round, and the **Costanera Norte** as well as in the summer. **El Bajo**, as the streets around Reconquista and 25 de Mayo are known, offers a walkable circuit of bars and restaurants as well as the odd Irish pub, while **San Telmo** harbours some eclectic and charismatic bars in among the tango spectacles. Though some bars open all day, most don't really get going until around midnight. Increasingly, the smoother bars run so-called *after offices* on weekdays to fill the early evening slot, but these are almost invariably rather sleazy. Websites with worthwhile **listings** include ⓦ adondevamos.com and ⓦ wipe.com.ar; for dance clubs, the best listings website is ⓦ buenosaliens.com.

BARS AND PUBS

Buenos Aires has no shortage of great **bars**, ranging from noisy Irish **pubs** to eminently cool places where the young and chic sip wine, cocktails and imported beers. Most of the former and their ilk are clustered in El Bajo (downtown, although technically in Retiro) or in San Telmo; while the latter variety are easiest to find – there are dozens – in any part of Palermo Viejo, Soho or Hollywood. Note that smoking is banned in public spaces, including bars and restaurants.

CITY CENTRE

★ **Celta Bar** Sarmiento 1702; map pp.64–65. Popular with a friendly and relaxed crowd, this attractive bar with big wooden tables is a good place for an early-evening drink. There's often live music, including Argentine rock and Brazilian MPB (Música Popular Brasileira) in the basement. Daily 8am–2am.

SAN TELMO

★ **Bar Británico** Defensa & Brasil; map p.79. Long-established bohemian bar overlooking Parque Lezama, reopened in 2007 after a sustained neighbourhood campaign to save it from closure. Freshly renovated, it retains both the table where Ernesto Sábato wrote *On Heroes and Tombs* and its 24hr opening policy. Daily 24hr.

Gibraltar Perú 895; map p.79. Popular both with expats and locals who like to hang out with expats, *Gibraltar* is a British-style pub that's a bit more relaxed than *Kilkenny* (see opposite), with a friendly atmosphere, bar service and great bar food, including fish and chips and Thai curry. Daily 6pm–4am.

Plaza Dorrego Bar Defensa 1098; map p.79. Most traditional of the bars around Plaza Dorrego, a sober wood-panelled place where the names of countless customers have been etched on its wooden tables and walls, and piles of empty peanut shells adorn the tables; mostly frequented by foreign tourists these days. Daily 8am–1am.

RETIRO AND RECOLETA

Bárbaro Tres Sargentos 415, Retiro; map p.86. This cosy bar, a long-standing institution tucked down a side street, regularly puts on live jazz. Mon–Sat 8am–late.

Buller Pres. Ortíz 1827, Recoleta ☎011 4808 9061; map p.86. The shiny stainless-steel vats and whiff of malt tell you that this brasserie brews its own excellent beer, which runs the gamut from pale ale to creamy stout. Daily noon–late.

Dadá San Martín 941, Retiro; map p.86. Small, hip and attractive bar, playing jazz soundtracks, serving reasonable food and offering a laidback alternative to the nearby Irish joints. Mon–Sat 8am–late.

Gran Bar Danzón Libertad 1161, 1st floor, Retiro; map p.86. Fashionable after-office bar and restaurant with sharply dressed staff and a very comprehensive wine list. Elegant and popular, even midweek. Mon–Fri 7pm–late, Sat & Sun 8pm–late.

Kilkenny Reconquista and Paraguay, Retiro; map p.86. The boisterous *Kilkenny* is one of the few bars heaving well before midnight and is an established favourite of both visiting foreigners and Guinness-drinking Porteños, though it can be a bit on the sleazy side. The bar – one of several Irish-themed pubs in the area – is the focus for the uproarious St Patrick's Day celebrations in the microcentro. Mon–Fri noon–5am, Sat & Sun 8pm–5am.

Notorious Av Callao 966, Recoleta ☎011 4815 8473; map p.86. Friendly bar selling CDs that you can listen to on headphones. There's also a great garden at the back where you can chill out over a cold beer. Interesting, small-scale concerts given – blues, jazz, tango, Latin – throughout the year. Mon–Sat noon–4pm & 9pm–1am, Sun 9pm–midnight.

Shamrock Rodríguez Peña 1220 ☎011 4812 3584;

map p.86. Irish bar with a Porteño touch. A good place to meet foreigners, with a small club downstairs. Mon–Fri 6pm–late, Sat 8pm–late.

PALERMO

Antares Armenia 1447 ☎011 4833 9611; map pp.96–97. Home-brewed Kölsch, porter, stout and barley beer, to name just a few, to accompany tapas and simple dishes, in a roomy, converted storehouse; jazz, blues and Irish music add to the ambience. Daily 8pm–late.

Carnal Coronel Niceto Vega 5511 ☎011 4772 7582; map pp.96–97. This bar, right opposite *Niceto* (see p.120), has a large upstairs terrace that fills quickly during the warmer months, when a DJ plays laidback dance grooves for a young, trendy crowd. Tues–Sun 8pm–late.

Mundo Bizarro Serrano 1222 ☎011 4773 1967; map pp.96–97. The name means "strange world" and this bar is definitely a bit different for super-trendy Palermo: expect low lighting, good cocktails and a relaxed crowd. Daily 8pm–late.

Único Honduras and Fitzroy ☎011 4775 6693; map pp.96–97. At the very centre of Hollywood, a lively crowd is always guaranteed at this well-known bar, which also does reasonable food; it fills early but is more laidback after 1am or so. Daily 8.30pm–5am.

LIVE MUSIC

Places offering **live music**, including folk, jazz, tango and rock, are scattered all over the city and differ enormously in style and ambience, though the quality is invariably high. For recitals by local bands, check the *Sí* supplement in *Clarín* on Fridays (⊚si.clarin.com) and the oppositionally named *No* supplement in *Página 12* on Thursdays (⊚pagina12.com.ar /diario/suplementos/no). As well as the larger venues like Luna Park, international stars often play at the football stadiums, particularly River Plate's Monumental – these gigs are widely advertised and are usually best booked through a ticket agency (see p.121). Tickets are generally sold on the door at the smaller venues, or from ticket agencies such as Ticketek for bigger gigs. If folk music is your thing, check out ⊚folkloreclub.com.ar. Classical music and opera are accounted for on p.124.

Blues Special Club Av Almirante Brown 102, Boca ☎011 4854 2338; map p.82. The name says it all: special blues acts, including those from the US, perform Fri–Sun, while most Fridays there is also a *zapada blusera*, or jam session. It's also a venue for *rock nacional* acts. Fri–Sun 8pm–late.

Estadio Luna Park Bouchard 465, city centre ☎011 5279 5279, ⊚lunapark.com.ar; map pp.64–65. Wonderful Art Deco edifice whose huge capacity lends itself to big sell-out events like boxing fights, the Chinese state circus and acts ranging from well-known international names like the Pet Shop Boys to big Argentine folk stars like Horacio Guarany. Make sure you don't get a "poor visibility" seat. Fri–Sun 8pm–late.

Mitos Argentinos Humberto 1° 489, San Telmo ☎011 4362 7810, ⊚mitosargentinos.com.ar; map p.79. The main attraction of this old mansion is the offbeat nature of the bands playing here, with Argentine tribute

bands often the star act. The format is *cena show*, starting at around $55. Fri–Sun 8pm–late.

★ **ND/Ateneo** Paraguay 918, Retiro ☎011 4328 2888, ⊚ndateneo.com.ar; map p.86. Folk, rock, tango, jazz, modern classical – all the big national and South American names play here at some point. The medium-sized theatre also hosts film screenings and recitals. Check website for schedule and times.

★ **No Avestruz** Humboldt 1857, Palermo Viejo ☎011 4777 6956, ⊚noavestruz.com.ar; map pp.96–97. Outstanding venue hosting emerging and established artists focusing on jazz and Latin sounds from Buenos Aires and further afield. Delicious food too. Wed–Sun 8pm–late.

Pan y Teatro Muñiz and Las Casas, Boedo ☎011 4924 6920, ⊚panyteatro.com.ar; map pp.64–65. This beautifully restored grocer's shop serves an original blend of Italian and *criollo* food and puts on shows, including tango, classical music and jazz. Tues–Sun 8am–late.

1

★ **Peña del Colorado** Güemes 3657, Palermo ☎ 011 4822 1038, ⓦ lapeniadelcolorado.com.ar; map pp.96–97. Famed for its past-midnight *guitarreadas* (bring your guitar, play and sing) that "finish when the candles burn out", the *Colorado* is the city's most traditional folk venue – there is also a *mate* bar, a restaurant and occasional folk and even tango shows. Daily 8pm–4am.

Thelonious Salguero 1884, Palermo ☎ 011 4829 1562, ⓦ thelonious.com.ar; map pp.96–97. The odd soul or blues concert is given here, but as the name implies, this is a jazz club, and generally regarded as the top; the music is always mesmerizing, the acoustics are faultless and the food isn't bad. Wed–Sun 8pm–late.

La Trastienda Balcarce 460, Monserrat ☎ 011 4342 7650, ⓦ latrastienda.com; map pp.64–65. Trendy live music in a late nineteenth-century mansion, with a wide-ranging roster of acts including rock, jazz, salsa and tango. Wed–Sun 8pm–late.

Vaca Profana Lavalle 3683, Balvanera ☎ 011 4867 0934, ⓦ vacaprofana.com.ar; map pp.64–65. Ground-breaking joint serving a delicious vegetarian *picada* (mixed platter) and all manner of food and drinks, but more interesting for its avant-garde music and occasionally theatre – new South American sounds including neo-ethnic. Wed–Sun 8pm–late.

NIGHTCLUBS

In terms of nightclubs, Buenos Aires stands head and shoulders above any other city in Argentina. Music in dance clubs varies from the cheesiest commercial house and Eighties pop to cutting-edge tunes mixed by DJs of international standing. Although Buenos Aires has some great home-grown DJs, trends in dance music tend to follow those of Europe and the US (particularly London) and clubbers are almost always young and affluent. If you're in town in November, don't miss the big annual Creamfields shindig (ⓦ creamfieldsba.com). At the other end of the spectrum, *bailantas* are events where the predominant music is *cumbia villera* – a version of Colombia's famous, repetitive *cumbia* rhythm that's the Argentine equivalent of gangsta rap, glorifying drugs and crime. Cheap, alcoholic and rowdy, *bailantas* can be fun but are not really recommendable unless you go in the company of a regular. Drunkenness and drug-taking are frowned upon by wider society but pretty common in clubs.

Costs Prices range wildly from free (particularly for women) to $100 or more, with prices sometimes including a drink.

Opening hours Traditionally clubs don't get going until around 3am but – to the relief of those who like to get at least some sleep, perhaps – there has been a tendency in BA to go out a bit earlier in recent times.

Asia de Cuba Pierina de Alessi Cossentini 750, Puerto Madero ⓦ asiadecuba.com.ar; map pp.64–65. Famous for its fashion model and VIP crowd, this place starts off the night as a sushi bar and then turns into an exclusive disco. Mon, Tues & Sun 12.30pm–1am, Wed–Sat 12.30pm–late.

Bahrein Lavalle 345, city centre ⓦ bahreinba.com; map pp.64–65. Uber-cool club in a beautifully renovated townhouse dripping with antique furnishings. Drum'n'bass on Tues, house and techno on Fri and Sat. Fri–Sun midnight–late.

Crobar Paseo de la Infanta Isabel, Palermo ☎ 011 4778 1500, ⓦ crobar.com.ar; map pp.96–97. Large and flashy complex of bars and dancefloors playing mainstream dance music that attracts a smartly dressed clientele. Fri & Sat 10pm–late.

Fantástico Bailable Rivadavia and Sánchez de Loria, Once (Loria subte) ⓦ fantasticodeonce.com; map pp.64–65. The best known *bailanta* – and a good place to try the heady mix of nonstop dancing and full-on flirting that goes with the territory. Fri–Sun 10pm–late.

★ **Maluco Beleza** Sarmiento 1728, city centre ☎ 011 4372 1737, ⓦ malucobeleza.com.ar; map pp.64–65. Long-running Brazilian club, playing a mix of lambada, afro, samba and reggae to a lively crowd of Brazilians and Brazilophiles. Wednesday is Brazilian music only, with a *feijoada* (traditional stew) served; book ahead. Wed, Sat & Sun 10pm–late.

★ **Niceto** Niceto Vega 5510, Palermo ☎ 011 4779 9396, ⓦ nicetoclub.com; map pp.96–97. Most famous for its Thursday night *Club 69* party (ⓦ club69.com.ar), complete with friendly, diverse crowd, outlandish podium dancers and house music played by the city's most acclaimed resident DJs. Thurs–Sat 8.30pm–4am.

Pacha Costanera Norte and La Pampa, Puerto Madero ⓦ pachabuenosaires.com; map pp.96–97. Big and glitzy like its Ibiza namesake, *Pacha* attracts a lively crowd, including a sprinkling of Argentine celebrities, and its Saturday "Clubland" nights just keep on going. Dance DJs of international standing often play here. Sat midnight–late.

GAY AND LESBIAN NIGHTLIFE

Buenos Aires is increasingly considered the major urban gay tourist destination in Latin America. Although the scene can be a disappointment for those looking for specifically gay and lesbian locales, for a lot of gay and lesbian tourists the very attraction is a lack of any "ghetto", with San Telmo the nearest the city comes to such a phenomenon. As in many Latin American cities, exclusively gay places are not always the best places to go out in any case, especially when it comes to restaurants; anywhere fashionable, with a "mixed" crowd, will most likely prove a better option. There is also an increasing open-mindedness on the part of its inhabitants and authorities – in 2010 Argentina became the first country in Latin America to sanction same-sex marriage at the national level. The streets, plazas and parks of Buenos Aires can be very cruisy, making them likelier places to meet people than bars or discos, where people tend to go out in groups of friends.

Information *Gay Buenos Aires* (🌐 gay-ba.com) is a booklet and website in English and Spanish; it carries comprehensive details of meeting-points, clubs, restaurants, hotels, travel agencies, gay-friendly shops and so forth. Most venues will also hand out a free gay city map, *BSASGay* (🌐 mapabsasgay.com.ar), with all the latest locales. Women are far less well catered for than men, but information about events and venues for lesbians can be found at the website 🌐 lafulana.org.ar.

Locales The long-established heart of gay Buenos Aires is the corner of avenidas Pueyrredón and Santa Fe, where nondescript *Confitería El Olmo* is still the place to hang out on Friday and Saturday evenings for free entrance flyers or discount vouchers, and to find out where to go. Palermo has increasingly become the main magnet, especially Palermo Hollywood, while San Telmo has ambitions to become the Porteño "Village". For gay *milongas*, try *La Marshall* (☎ 011 4912 9043, 🌐 lamarshall .com.ar), which holds one at Maipú 444 in the centre at 10pm on Wednesdays – though, as with all *milongas*, you should check it hasn't moved on before setting out.

★ **Alsina Buenos Aires** Alsina 934, city centre 🌐 alsinabuenosaires.com.ar; map pp.64–65. This palatial converted industrial building stages gay nights on Fri and Sun, usually starting around midnight and attracting some of the most beautiful people in the city. All ages and tastes come to dance to varied music, everything from house to 1970s disco. Fri & Sun midnight–late.

Amerika Gascón 1040, Almagro 🌐 ameri-k.com.ar; map pp.64–65. One of the city's biggest and best-known gay discos, with three dancefloors playing house and Latin music. Thurs–Sun midnight–late.

Bach Bar Cabrera 4390, Palermo 🌐 bach-bar.com.ar; map pp.96–97. Fairly mixed bar, with shows on Fri and Sat and karaoke on Sun, all starting very late, even though it is a pre-disco venue. Fri–Sun midnight–late.

Bulnes Class Bulnes 1250, Palermo; map pp.96–97. This laidback bar often features singers and is frequented by professional types. It stays open late on Fri and Sat. Daily 7pm–late.

Contramano Rodríguez Peña 1082, Recoleta 🌐 contramano.com; map p.86. One of the longest-running discos, attracting an older crowd, with bears night on Sun and shows on Sat. Fri–Sun midnight–late.

Sitges Av Córdoba 4119, corner of Pringles, Palermo 🌐 sitgesonline.com.ar; map pp.96–97. Large, bright trendy bar, frequented by a mixed but invariably young crowd. Bursting at the seams, with late-night weekend shows. Thurs–Sun 6pm–late.

THE ARTS AND ENTERTAINMENT

There's a superb range of **cultural events** on offer in Argentina's capital, ranging from avant-garde theatre to blockbuster movies and grand opera with a wealth of options in between. One of the best features of Porteño cultural life is the strong tradition of free or very cheap events, including film showings at the city's museums and cultural centres, tango and a series of enthusiastically attended outdoor events put on by the city government every summer; street performers are also of very high quality.

LISTINGS

A plethora of listings are given in the entertainment sections of both *Clarín* and *La Nación*. Numerous independent listings sheets are also available in bars, bookshops and kiosks throughout the city; it's always worth trying the tourist kiosks for pamphlets and magazines. *Arte al Día* (🌐 artealdia.com) is a monthly newspaper with details of art exhibitions, available from newspaper stands. The website 🌐 mundoteatral.com.ar is an excellent source of info on shows going on around the city, with a focus on offbeat stuff.

TICKETS

You can buy tickets at discounted prices for theatre, cinema and music events at the various centralized *carteleras* (ticket agencies) in the centre, such as Cartelera Baires, Av Corrientes 1382, local 24 (Mon–Thurs 10am–10pm, Fri 10am–11pm, Sat 10am–midnight, Sun 2–10pm; ☎ 011 4372 5058, 🌐 cartelerabaires.com). Alternatively Ticketek (☎ 011 5237 7200, 🌐 ticketek.com.ar) sells tickets to many upcoming concerts, plays and sporting events, bookable over the phone or online with a credit card. The most central of their outlets is at Viamonte 560 (Mon–Sat 9am–8.30pm).

TANGO

Tango is so strongly associated with Buenos Aires that a visit to the city really isn't complete unless you immerse yourself in it at least once. The most accessible way for visitors to experience tango is via the *tango espectáculos*. These generally rather expensive *cena shows* (dinner followed by a show) are performed by professionals who put on a highly skilled and choreographed display. Many hotels and hostels offer excursions to them, and they're mostly attended by foreign visitors, though there's usually a smattering of locals too. Porteños who are tango fans tend to prefer to go either to music recitals – with no dancing – or to *milongas* (see box, p.122) to dance themselves. A *milonga* refers to a moveable event rather than a specific venue, so the days, times and locations of these change frequently; many are situated in the city's outer barrios. *El Tangauta* (🌐 eltangauta.com) is a free magazine with listings, which can generally be picked up at tourist kiosks, hotels, cultural centres and record stores.

There are also regular tango festivals, with a host of free shows and hundreds of classes and *milongas* – the biggest is the Tango World Championship and Festival, held in August in recent years.

1

Bar Sur Estados Unidos 299, San Telmo ☎011 4362 6086, ⓦbar-sur.com.ar; map p.79. One of San Telmo's more reasonably priced tango shows (about $220 with dinner). The quality of the shows can vary but it's an intimate space where audience participation is encouraged towards the end of the evening. Daily 8pm–2am.

Centro Cultural Torquato Tasso Defensa 1575, San Telmo ☎011 4307 6506, ⓦtorquatotasso.com.ar; map p.79. This friendly San Telmo neighbourhood cultural centre has top-quality tango recitals, some of them free. See the website for details and times.

El Chino Beazley 3566, Pompeya ☎011 4911 0215; map pp.64–65. This bar and *parrilla* in traditional

Pompeya in the southwest of the city is probably the most authentic place to hear tango sung by the talented staff and a crowd of locals and regulars. It's even been the subject of a movie, *Bar El Chino*. Fri & Sat from 10pm.

Clásica y Moderna Callao 892, Recoleta ⓦclasicaymoderna.com; map p.86. The dark, brick interior has been converted from a bookstore into a café-restaurant with great food and live tango and other acts, including many top names. Daily from around 9.30pm.

Club Gricel La Rioja 1180, San Cristóbal (Urquiza subte) ☎011 4957 7157; map pp.64–65. Small, friendly, authentic club holding daily classes and *milongas*. Fri & Sat from 11pm, Sun from 9pm.

MILONGAS

Tango has gained a whole new audience in recent times, with an increasing number of young people filling the floors of social clubs, *confiterías* and traditional dancehalls for regular events known as **milongas**. Even if you don't dance yourself, it's still worth going to see one: the spectacle of couples slipping almost trance-like around the dancefloor is a captivating sight. Apart from the skill and composure of the dancers, one of the most appealing aspects of the *milonga* is the absence of class – and, especially, age – divisions; indeed, most younger dancers regard it as an honour to be partnered by older and more experienced dancers.

STRUCTURE AND ETIQUETTE

While the setting for a *milonga* can range from a sports hall to an elegant salon, the **structure** – and **etiquette** – of the dances varies little. In many cases, classes are given first. Once the event gets underway, it is divided into musical sets, known as **tandas**, which will cover the three subgenres of tango: tango "proper"; *milonga* – a more uptempo sound; and waltz. Each is danced differently and occasionally there will also be an isolated interval of salsa, rock or jazz. The invitation to dance comes from the man, who will nod towards the woman whom he wishes to partner. She signals her acceptance with an equally subtle gesture and only then will her new partner approach her table. Once on the dancefloor, the couple waits eight *compases*, or bars, and then begins to dance, circulating in a counter-clockwise direction around the dancefloor. The woman follows the man's lead by responding to *marcas*, or signs, to indicate the move he wishes her to make. The more competent she is, the greater number of variations and personal touches she will add. Though the basic steps of the tango may not look very difficult, it entails a rigorous attention to posture and a subtle shifting of weight from leg to leg, essential to avoid losing balance. The couple will normally dance together until the end of a set, which lasts for four or five melodies. Once the set is finished, it is good tango etiquette for the woman to thank her partner who, if the experience has been successful and enjoyable, is likely to ask her to dance again later in the evening.

CLASSES AND CLOTHING

Watching real tango danced is the kind of experience that makes people long to do it themselves. Unfortunately, a *milonga* is not the best place to take your first plunge; unlike, say, salsa, even the best partner in the world will find it hard to carry a complete novice through a tango. In short, if you can't bear the thought of attending a *milonga* without dancing, the answer is to take some **classes** – reckon on taking about six to be able to hold your own on the dancefloor. There are innumerable places in Buenos Aires offering classes, including cultural centres, bars and *confiterías* and, for the impatient or shy, there are private teachers. If you're going to take classes, it's important to have an appropriate pair of **shoes** with a sole that allows you to swivel (no rubber soles). For women, it's not necessary to wear heels but it is important that the shoes support the instep. At a *milonga*, however, a pair of well-polished heels is the norm, and will act as a signal that you are there to dance. Any woman going to a *milonga*, but not intending to dance, should make that clear in her choice of dress and footwear; go dressed to kill and you'll spend the night turning down invitations from bemused-looking men.

★ **Confitería Ideal** Suipacha 384, 1st floor, city centre ☎ 011 5265 8069, ⓦ confiteriaideal.com; map pp.64–65. An oasis of elegance just a few blocks from busy Corrientes, the *Ideal* has a stunning salon, which is undoubtedly one of the most traditional and consistently popular places to dance. There is an exhaustive programme of classes and *milongas* in both the afternoons and evenings every day. See the website for details and times.

Niño Bien Centro Región Leonesa, Humberto 1° 1462, Constitución (San José subte) ☎ 011 4305 7310; map pp.64–65. Popular *milonga* with both locals and foreign "tango tourists", and with a great atmosphere. Thurs from 11.30pm.

★ **Parakultural** ⓦ parakultural.com.ar. Young, bohemian organization that puts on the coolest *milongas* and shows in town at a rotating and eclectic set of venues, including the huge Salón Canning at Scalabrini Ortiz 1331, Palermo. Classes are also offered. See the website for details and times.

Piazzola Centro de Artes Galería Güemes, Florida 165, city centre ☎ 011 4344 8201, ⓦ piazzollatango show.com; map pp.64–65. In a renovated theatre in the lovely Galería Güemes, this is one of the most central *tango show* locations, with a dinner and exciting programme for around $280. Daily from 8.30pm.

Señor Tango Vieytes 1655, Barracas ☎ 011 4303 0231, ⓦ senortango.com.ar; map pp.64–65. Large and very professional *tanguería* in the quiet southern barrio of Barracas. Daily dinner and a real spectacle of a show that traces the history of tango and incorporates trapezes, 1980s tango fusion and even horses; $350 for dinner, drinks and show, or $90 for the show only. Daily from 8.30pm.

Taconeando Balcarce 725, San Telmo ☎ 011 4307 6696, ⓦ taconeando.com; map p.79. Smaller, more informal *tango cena* show; a good option if you want to see a show rather than a *milonga* but also want to avoid the larger, more commercial options; $180 with dinner, $140 without. See the website for details and times.

El Viejo Almacén Av Independencia and Balcarce, San Telmo ☎ 011 4307 6689; map p.79. Probably the most famous of San Telmo's *tanguerías*, housed in an attractive nineteenth-century building. Occasionally hosts nationally famous tango singers, otherwise slickly executed dinner and dance shows. $300 with dinner, $180 without. Daily from 8pm.

★ **La Viruta** Armenia 1366, Palermo ☎ 011 4779 0030, ⓦ lavirutatango.com; map pp.96–97. Huge, long-running institution with *milongas* (Sat & Sun) and shows (Thurs & Fri) that mix tango with folklore, salsa and even rock'n' roll. The action begins at midnight, with classes during the afternoon and evening. Thurs–Sun; times vary.

CINEMA

Porteños are keen and knowledgeable cinema-goers and there are dozens of cinemas in the city showing everything from the latest Hollywood releases to Argentine films and art-house cinema. Foreign films are usually subtitled. Traditionally, cinemas showing purely mainstream stuff were concentrated on Calle Lavalle, while art-house flicks were more common on Avenida Corrientes. However, both are increasingly losing out to the multiplex cinemas in the city's various shopping malls, which offer excellent visuals and acoustics, though in a blander atmosphere. Ticket prices vary but generally cost $30–60. You can also find free or very cheap showings at museums and cultural centres.

Abasto Shopping Av Corrientes 3200, Balvanera ⓦ abasto-shopping.com.ar. Enormous modern cinema at the Abasto shopping centre, featuring a good mix of international and local movies; usually one of the main hosts of April's enthusiastically attended international film festival.

Arteplex Centro Av Corrientes 1145, city centre ⓦ cines arteplex.com. The most central of a small local chain of art-house cinemas, and one of the last remaining cinemas on Corrientes; there's a bar and DVD store inside too.

Gaumont Rivadavia 1633, Balvanera ☎ 011 4371 3050. One of several "Espacio INCAA" showcase cinemas run by the Instituto Nacional de Cine y Artes Audiovisuales, the Argentine national cinema institute. If your Spanish is up to it, this is the place to catch the best examples of the country's strong national film industry.

THEATRE

Theatre is very strongly represented, with Avenida Corrientes standing up well in comparison to New York's Broadway and London's West End – although obviously almost all plays are in Spanish. Away from the major theatrical venues – where you'll find a good spread of international and Argentine theatre, both classic and contemporary, ranging from serious drama to reviews and musicals – the city is dotted with innumerable independent venues, with stages in bars and tiny auditoriums at the back of shopping centres; the terms "Off Corrientes" and "Off Off Corrientes" found in press listings are based on those used in New York and London. Tickets tend to cost around $50; some theatres will do a half-price show midweek. Some of the more noteworthy theatres are listed below; for what's on, consult the listings sections of *Clarín* or *La Nación*.

Teatro General San Martín Corrientes 1500, city centre ☎ 011 4371 0111, ⓦ teatrosanmartin.com.ar. Excellent modern venue with several auditoriums and a varied programme that usually includes one or two Argentine plays as well as international standards such as Pinter or Brecht. Also hosts contemporary dance events, ballet, children's theatre and art-house cinema in the Sala Leopoldo Lugones, while a cultural centre with free exhibitions is tucked behind.

Teatro Nacional Cervantes Libertad 815, city centre ⓦ teatrocervantes.gov.ar. This grand old-fashioned theatre, superb inside and out, presents a broad programme of old

1

and new Argentine and foreign works, with a particular emphasis on plays from Spain.

Teatro Ópera Corrientes 860, city centre ⓦoperaciti -teatro.com.ar. This fabulous Art Deco theatre, which in its heyday billed Edith Piaf and Josephine Baker, has undergone a recent revival focusing on a music and dance programme, usually of a very high quality.

CULTURAL CENTRES AND ART GALLERIES

Buenos Aires' numerous cultural centres are one of the city's greatest assets. Every neighbourhood has its own modest centre – good places to find out about free tango classes and generally offering a mixture of art exhibitions, film and cafés – while the major institutions such as the Centro Cultural Borges and the Centro Cultural Recoleta put on some of the city's best exhibitions. Buenos Aires also has some prestigious commercial art galleries, the majority of which are based in Retiro and Recoleta, particularly around Plaza San Martín and nearby Suipacha and Arenales. During May or June, the art fair ARTE BA (ⓦarteba.com), held in La Rural exhibition centre in Palermo, showcases work from Buenos Aires' most important galleries.

British Arts Centre (BAC) Suipacha 1333, Retiro ☎011 4393 6941, ⓦbritishartscentre.org.ar. The place to head for if you're nostalgic for a bit of Hitchcock or Monty Python – regular English-language film and video showings, as well as plays by the likes of Harold Pinter. Free entry. Mon–Fri 3–9pm.

Centro Cultural Borges Viamonte and San Martín, Retiro ☎011 5555 5359, ⓦccborges.org.ar. Large space above the Galerías Pacífico shopping centre. Excellent photography exhibitions in spacious galleries, as well as painting, theatre, dance, and art-house cinema. $15. Mon–Sat 10am–9pm, Sun noon–9pm.

Centro Cultural Recoleta Junín 1930, Recoleta ☎011 4803 1040, ⓦcentroculturalrecoleta.org. One of the city's best cultural centres – see p.92. Free entry. Tues–Fri 2–9pm, Sat & Sun noon–9pm.

Centro Cultural Ricardo Rojas Corrientes 2038 ☎011 4954 5521, ⓦrojas.uba.ar. Affiliated with the University of Buenos Aires, this friendly cultural centre and gallery space offers free events including live music and bargain film showings, usually alternative or art house. Free entry. Tues–Fri 1–9pm, Sat & Sun noon–10pm.

Espacio Fundación Telefónica Arenales 1540, Recoleta ☎011 4333 1300, ⓦfundacion.telefonica.com .ar/espacio. A high-tech art centre that lays emphasis on communications media, as you would expect for a founda-tion run by a telecoms company. This sleek, modern space stages small, mostly avant-garde exhibitions of work by contemporary Argentine artists, and houses an excellent media library. Free entry. Mon–Sat 2–8.30pm.

Fundación Federico J. Klemm Marcelo T. de Alvear 626, Retiro ⓦfundacionfjklemm.org. The late Argentine

art maverick Federico Klemm was a kind of self-fashioned Andy Warhol, producing bizarre portraits of modern-day Argentine celebrities in mythic and homoerotic poses. Klemm was also a collector of modern art and on a display here there is a serious collection of works by Picasso, Dalí, Mapplethorpe and Warhol himself – to name just a few – as well as major Argentine artists such as Berni and Kuitca. Free entry. Mon–Fri 11am–8pm.

Goethe Institut Corrientes 319, city centre ☎011 4318 5600, ⓦgoethe.de/hs/bue. Smart German cultural institute that has a good library for German and English books, as well as German movies and plays on offer. Free entry. Mon–Fri 9am–6pm; closed during summer.

Ruth Benzacar Gallery Florida 1000, Retiro ☎011 4313 8480, ⓦruthbenzacar.com. Rather unexpectedly reached through an underground entrance at the end of Florida, this prestigious gallery has temporary exhibitions featuring international artists as well as Argentines. Free entry. Mon–Fri 11.30am–8pm.

CLASSICAL MUSIC, OPERA AND BALLET

Argentina has a number of excellent classical performers, including opera singers, such as tenors Marcelo Álvarez and soprano María Cristina Kiehr, ballet dancers like Iñaki Urlezaga, and musicians, such as pianist and conductor Daniel Barenboim. Keeping a much lower media profile, but equally acclaimed, is concert pianist and multiple Grammy Award winner Martha Argerich; she presides over her own international piano competition in Buenos Aires. Classical performances in Buenos Aires have seen some-thing of a revival in recent years, boosted by frequent free and outdoor performances, especially in the summer. Some of the best concerts are small-scale affairs held at museums, churches and the like, such as those held at the Museo de Arte Hispanoamericano Isaac Fernández Blanco (see p.90), though the larger venues are also exciting, and none is more spectacular than the Teatro Colón. For news of concerts, consult ⓦmusicaclasicaargentina.com.

Casa de la Cultura Av de Mayo 575, city centre. Free classical concerts, mostly chamber music, are given from time to time in the marvellous Salón Dorado in the *La Prensa* building; look out for flyers and posters.

★ **La Scala de San Telmo** Pasaje Giuffra 371 (Defensa 800), San Telmo ☎011 4362 1187, ⓦlascala .org.ar. Not Milan, but this sumptuous bijou theatre hosts tango, jazz and other music genres, plus some excellent operas and classical concerts.

Teatro Avenida Av de Mayo 1222, city centre ☎011 4381 0662, ⓦbalirica.org.ar. This stylish theatre, opened only a few months after the Colón in 1908, is the home to Buenos Aires Lírica, which puts on a number of operas here every season.

Teatro Coliseo Marcelo T. de Alvear 1125, Retiro ☎011 4816 3789. The most important venue for ballet, musicals and classical music after the Colón, which it replaced during the latter's renovation; also offers occasional free recitals.

★ **Teatro Colón** Libertad 621, city centre ⓦteatro colon.org.ar. Buenos Aires' most glamorous venue is one of the world's great opera houses – acoustically in the top five, showcasing world-class opera, ballet and classical music. Since it reopened for the bicentenary it has been attracting top international performers, including Joshua Bell, Riccardo Muti and Renée Fleming. See p.70.

SHOPPING

Shopping in Buenos Aires is a pleasure unmatched elsewhere in South America. While goods tend to be more Western and familiar than those you will come across in, say, Bolivia or Perú, you can nonetheless count on finding some highly original items to take home. The best **handicrafts** are found in their home provinces rather than in Buenos Aires, but if you miss out on your trip around the country there are good craft markets in the capital. Typically Argentine goods include *mate* paraphernalia, polo wear, wine and world-class leatherware. A box of widely available Havanna *alfajores* (see p.35) makes a good present, or take a jar or two of *dulce de leche* away with you to satisfy cravings. **Opening hours** are usually around 10am–7pm Monday to Friday, with stores closed Saturday afternoon and Sunday.

SHOPPING MALLS

Over the past decade or two, shopping malls have partly superseded small shops and street markets, but those in Buenos Aires are among the most tastefully appointed in the world. Several of the malls, like Abasto, are housed in revamped buildings of historical and architectural interest in their own right. On a practical level, the malls are air-conditioned and the places where you'll find that rarity in Buenos Aires, public toilets.

Abasto Av Corrientes 3200, Balvanera (subte Carlos Garde) ⓦabasto-shopping.com.ar; map pp.64–65. This grand building, dating from the 1880s, was once the city food market; now it's the daddy of all the central malls. As well as a ten-screen cinema, it has hundreds of designer and cheaper stores, an enormous food hall, an amusement arcade and a hands-on museum for children, the Museo de los Niños (Tues–Sun 1–8pm; $20 for adults, $60 for children; ⓦmuseoabasto.org.ar). Daily 10am–10pm.

Bond Street Av Santa Fe 1670, Recoleta ⓦgaleria bondstreet.com; map p.86. The alternative mall, full of local teenagers skulking around skate stores and tattoo parlours; there's also a few surf shops in the surrounding streets. A good place to pick up flyers for live music and clubs. Daily 10am–10pm.

Buenos Aires Design Center Plaza Intendente Alvear, Recoleta ⓦdesignrecoleta.com.ar; map p.86. Right next to the Centro Cultural de Recoleta, this mall is dedicated to shops selling the latest designs, mostly for the home, from Argentina and elsewhere. Mon–Sat 10am–9pm, Sun noon–9pm.

Galerías Pacífico Florida 750, city centre ⓦgalerias pacifico.com.ar; map pp.64–65. BA's most central mall, with fashion boutiques and bookshops in a beautiful building decorated with murals by leading Argentine artists, plus the Centro Cultural Borges at the top and a food court and children's play area in the basement. Mon–Sat 10am–9pm, Sun noon–9pm.

Patio Bullrich Libertador 750, Retiro ⓦshopping bullrich.com.ar; map p.86. Once a thoroughbred horse market, this is one of the most upmarket malls, and

---

WHERE TO SHOP

Avenida Santa Fe, which runs from Plaza San Martín through Recoleta and Palermo, is one of the city's main shopping streets, with a good mix of stores to suit all budgets. **Palermo Soho** is the place to head for independent **designer clothing** stores, while **malls** scattered throughout the city house both Argentine and international chains. For **leather goods**, head to **Centro del Cuero**, Murillo 500–700, Villa Crespo (Malabia subte), a three-block stretch of around thirty warehouse stores and some boutiques selling leather clothing both wholesale and direct to the public; this is the place to go for a bargain, but prices are mostly unmarked so be prepared to haggle.

Shops selling **books** and **music** are strung along **Avenida Corrientes** between 9 de Julio and Callao. Others stretch out on Florida north of **Avenida Córdoba**, together with a bevy of craft, T-shirt and leather stores aimed at tourists, many of them in covered arcades or *galerías*. Contemporary **art** is on sale at the scores of smart galleries that line **Retiro**, with several along **Avenida Alvear**, while anyone looking for colonial paintings and **antiques** should head for **San Telmo**. For outdoor gear, there is a whole row of **camping** and **fishing** shops along the 100 to 200 block of **Calle Paraná**, just off Corrientes. If you're heading south, bear in mind Ushuaia and many Patagonian towns are just as well stocked as Buenos Aires, although prices may be higher down there.

1

a good place to find designer clothes and leather. Daily 10am–9pm.

CLOTHING AND ACCESSORIES

Buenos Aires has plenty of inventive designers, selling both unique off-the-peg designs and more classic attire. However, prices are often eye-watering these days, and the quality of domestic goods, except at the highest end, is not always the best – don't expect your nifty Buenos Aires outfits to hold together for long. On the upside, you can get better bargains by shopping at the increasing number of outlets clustering around Villa Crespo, near Palermo Soho – see ⓦ espaciooutlet.com.ar for a full list – while leather continues to be good value at all price levels. You can find high-quality leather boots, jackets and wallets – and bags to take it all home in.

Bailarín Porteño Suipacha 251, city centre; map pp.64–65. Everything a tango dancer needs, from head to toe – hats, shirts, jackets, shoes, and even jewellery with a *milonga* touch. One of a number of tango-ware stores in the same street. Mon–Sat 10am–7.30pm.

Bolivia Gurruchaga 1581, Palermo ☎ 011 4775 0896, ⓦ boliviaparatodos.com.ar; map pp.96–97. Hip men's clothes, perfect for all-night dancing. Floral shirts, grungy tops, zipped jackets and other clothes for guys who prefer not to take things too seriously. Mon–Fri 10am–7pm.

Cardón Sante Fe 1399, Recoleta ☎ 011 4813 8983, ⓦ cardon.com.ar; map p.86. With the slogan "*cosas nuestras*" ("our things") Cardón, beloved of the Argentine land-owning classes, sells smart khaki and white clothing and *carpincho* (capybara) leather shoes, jackets and belts. Perfect for polo matches or estancia stays – just don't get too muddy. Other branches are listed on the website. Mon–Fri 10am–7pm.

Casa López Marcelo T. de Alvear 640, Retiro ⓦ casa lopez.com.ar; map p.86. Regarded as the city's very best exporter of classic leather goods – bags, wallets, briefcases and clothing – the quality is excellent but it has prices to match. Mon–Fri 10am–7pm.

Deporcamping Santa Fe 4830, Palermo ☎ 011 4772 0534, ⓦ deporcamping.com.ar; map pp.96–97. Limited but decent-quality range of trekking clothes and boots, as well as other camping gear such as tents, mats, sleeping bags and stoves. Mon–Sat 9.30am–8.30pm.

Jazmín Chebar El Salvador 4702, Palermo ☎ 011 4833 4242, ⓦ jazminchebar.com.ar; map pp.96–97. One of the country's best-known designers, creating clothes for women that are simultaneously voguish yet soft and feminine. Expensive but top quality. Mon–Sat 10am–8.30pm, Sun 1–7pm.

JM Cueros Marcelo T. de Alvear 628, Retiro ☎ 011 4312 7104, ⓦ jmcueros.com; map p.86. Traditional *tabalartería* (leatherware shop) selling shoes, bags and accessories, some leather and some made from the soft,

attractively mottled skin of the *carpincho*. Many items also feature the geometric designs characteristic of the Pampas region. Branches at Paraguay 616 and Santa Fe 1240, both in Retiro. Mon–Fri 10am–7pm.

Kosiuko Santa Fe 1779, Recoleta ☎ 011 4815 2555, ⓦ kosiuko.com.ar; map p.86. Very cool shop (there are branches at most malls too) where affluent young Porteños go to get gear for the weekend's hanging out. Lots of individual items made with a real flair – you're bound to find something irresistible. Women's, men's and children's ranges. Mon–Fri 10am–7pm.

La Martina Paraguay 661, Retiro ⓦ lamartina.com; map p.86. Well-established Argentine polo brand that sponsors the national teams. As well as polo equipment, stores carry the kind of clothes that people wear to matches (think pastel blouses and lozenge-patterned sweaters). The floor spaces are laid out beautifully, with the polo boots and piles of cashmere set off by dark wood fittings and leather sofas. Mon–Fri 10am–7pm.

Rapsodia Honduras 4872, Palermo ☎ 011 4831 6333, ⓦ rapsodia.com.ar; map pp.96–97. Although it markets a variety of clothes, many with a bohemian twist, Rapsodia is most famous for its range of jeans, which are cut in ways that seem to flatter all shapes and sizes. Branches in most of the malls. Daily 10am–9pm.

BOOKS AND MUSIC

Corrientes is the traditional place to head for books and music, though there are also a number of antique bookstores housed on the ground floors of Av de Mayo's Art Nouveau concoctions. Upmarket bookstores, with good foreign-language and glossy coffee-table sections, can be found around Florida, Córdoba and Santa Fe.

Ateneo Grand Splendid Santa Fe 1860, Recoleta; map p.86. Easily the largest bookshop in Latin America and surely a strong contender for the most beautiful bookshop in the world, this store is housed in a former cinema, built in 1919 and inspired by the Opéra Garnier in Paris. A branch of the Ateneo/Yenny chain, it is particularly strong on art and architecture books, with an array of collectable albums of photos of Buenos Aires and the rest of the country. There is a small café on the ground floor, from where you can admire the sumptuousness of it all and browse before you buy. Daily 10am–10pm.

Kel Ediciones Marcelo T. de Alvear 1369, Recoleta ☎ 011 4814 3788, ⓦ kel-ediciones.com; map p.86. This long-running all-English bookstore has mostly fairly mainstream stock but it's big enough for anyone to find that perfect accompaniment to a long-distance bus journey. Daily 10am–9pm.

Liberarte Av Corrientes 1555, city centre ☎ 011 4375 2341; map pp.64–65. An emporium of the assorted interests of the Porteño left-wing intelligentsia. Loads of offbeat periodicals. Mon–Sat 10am–10pm.

Librería de Ávila Alsina 500, Monserrat ☎011 4331 8989; map pp.64–65. Allegedly the site of the city's first bookshop, this wonderful sprawling antique bookshop is worth a visit as much for the ambience as the books – which include a great selection on Argentina. Daily 10am–7pm.

Musimundo Florida 267, city centre ☎0810 888 5555, ⓦmusimundo.com; map pp.64–65. Argentina's major record chain, stocking everything from techno to tango. Branches throughout the city, and online delivery also possible. Mon–Sat 10am–10pm.

Walrus Books Estados Unidos 617, San Telmo ☎011 4300 7135; map p.79. Excellent English-language new and secondhand bookstore, with the emphasis on quality literature and nonfiction from around the world. Tues–Sun noon–8pm; restricted opening hours in summer.

Zival's Av Callao 395, city centre ☎011 4371 6978, ⓦtangostore.com; map pp.64–65. Small but well-stocked music store, particularly good for tango. There's a strong selection of CDs and DVDs as well as books and sheet music, and the staff are very knowledgeable on the best tango recordings. Daily 10am–10.30pm.

ARTS AND CRAFTS

The city's markets – such as the Sunday fairs in Recoleta, San Telmo and Mataderos, along with some of the *casas de provincia* (see p.54), are where you'll find handicrafts, including unique ceramics, wooden masks or alpaca-wool items, usually at far better value than the mass-produced alternatives. Local arts and crafts are also available at a number of central stores.

Arte Etnico Argentino El Salvador 4656, Palermo ☎011 4833 5111, ⓦarteetnicoargentino.com; map pp.96–97. Mostly pricey rugs and tapestries from the North, plus rustic furniture made from native wood. A fantastic shop – just go and look at the chairs hanging from the main ceiling like wooden bats – in every sense. Daily noon–9pm.

El Gauchito Carabelas 306, city centre ☎011 4326 8503; map pp.64–65. A stone's throw from the Obelisco, this reassuringly long-running store is an authentic vendor of gaucho clothing, artwork, antique and modern crafts for the home and many other goods emanating from Argentina's pampas heartlands. Mon–Sat 10am–8pm.

Kelly's Paraguay 431, Retiro ☎011 4311 9189; map p.86. Colourful store that sells a variety of ponchos from different provinces, ceramics and, of course, *mates*. Mon–Sat 10.30am–7.30pm.

Porteñitos Iberlucea 98, Boca ☎011 4302 2800; map p.82. Just around the corner from the Caminito, this co-operative gives work skills to young people by employing them in making and selling delicious *alfajores*, sold in pretty colourful boxes that echo the designs of the area without being garish. Call ahead for opening hours.

DIRECTORY

Banks and exchange There is an entire row of bureaux de change in the financial district, near the corner of San Martín and Sarmiento – rates are similar and opening hours are generally Mon–Fri 9am–6pm. This is also where you'll find the central bank branches, with similar hours. At other times, look out for the branches of exchange company Metropolis at Corrientes 2557, Florida 506 and Quintana 576, which are also open at weekends. ATMs are widespread.

Embassies and consulates Australia, Villanueva 1400 ☎011 4779 3500; Brazil, Carlos Pellegrini 1363, 5th floor ☎011 4515 6500; Canada, Tagle 2828 ☎011 4808 1000; Chile, San Martín 439, 9th floor ☎011 4394 6582; Ireland, Suipacha 1380, 2nd floor ☎011 5787 0801; New Zealand, Carlos Pellegrini 1427, 5th floor ☎011 4328 0747; Perú, Florida 165, 2nd floor ☎011 4334 0970; South Africa, Marcelo T. de Alvear 590, 8th floor ☎011 4317 2900; UK, Dr Luis Agote 2412 ☎011 4803 7070; Uruguay, Las Heras 1907, 4th floor ☎011 4807 3045; US, Av Colombia 4300 ☎011 5777 4533.

Hospitals Consultorio de Medicina del Viajero, Hospital de Infecciosas F.J. Muñiz, Uspallata ☎011 4304 2180; Hospital Británico, Perdriel 74 ☎011 4309 6400; Hospital Italiano ☎011 4959 0200. The Argentine medical emergency number is ☎107.

Language learning There are a number of organizations which provide Spanish immersion programmes, often with cultural and social activities as part of the language learning. These include EleBaires, Av de Mayo 1370, 3rd floor office 10 (☎011 4383 7706, ⓦelebaires.com), and Amauta, Federico Lacroze 2129 (☎011 4777 2130, ⓦamautaspanishschool.com).

Laundry Laverap, Suipacha 722 ☎011 4322 3458 or Av Córdoba 466 ☎011 4312 5460, plus many others across the city. Most Laveraps will also pick up and deliver free of charge.

Pharmacies There are plenty of pharmacies in the city, including the 24hr Farmacity, Corrientes 1820; for more branches see ⓦfarmacity.com.ar.

Police Tourist police Corrientes 436 ☎011 4346 5748, emergencies ☎101. There's a special number that visitors can call if they have been robbed or need other emergency assistance – ☎0800 999 2838.

Post office Correo Central, Sarmiento 189 (Mon–Fri 10am–8pm). There are numerous smaller branches throughout the city, open from 10am to 6pm. Outside these hours, there are many post office counters within stationery shops (*papelerías*), at *locutorios* and at kiosks.

Buenos Aires Province

FIELD OF SUNFLOWERS ON THE OUTSKIRTS OF
THE SIERRA DE LA VENTANA

Buenos Aires Province

Marvellous though Buenos Aires is, you may wish to follow the example of the Porteños and escape the urban mêlée for a few days. Immediately north of the city, and understandably a favourite getaway destination, is the watery labyrinth of the Paraná Delta. Unfolding westwards and southwards, the famed Pampas of Buenos Aires Province form the country's agricultural heartland; unfairly neglected by most tourists, these fertile grassy plains offer a fascinating window into Argentina's traditional gaucho culture and rural life. The country's beaches are not exactly world famous, but two dozen popular oceanside resorts fringe the province's Atlantic coast; some are worth checking out for their restful tranquillity, others for their frenetic nightlife.

The Paraná Delta's main town, **Tigre**, is often described as a subtropical Little Venice; wooden launches chug along opaque canals lined with timber bungalows and subtropical thickets instead of Renaissance palaces and piazzas.

The province's inland landscape is dominated by farmland – providing the bulk of the country's exports – peppered with picturesque gaucho settlements: **San Antonio de Areco** a charmingly old-fashioned example with cobbled streets and well-preserved nineteenth-century architecture, within striking distance of several traditional and luxurious **estancias** (see box, p.141); **Tandil**, whose museums and rugged setting make it a highly worthwhile stopping-place en route to Patagonia overland; and the appealingly quiet town of **Mercedes**, famed for its authentic *pulpería* (a traditional bar-cum-store). Closer to Buenos Aires, the mini-city of **Luján** exposes the country's spiritual heart, with a mass display of religious devotion in honour of Argentina's patron saint, the Virgin of Luján. In a predominantly flat province, to reach anything approaching a mountain, you will need to head for the western reaches, where you'll find the Pampas' most dramatic relief, the **Sierra de la Ventana** range, 580km southwest of Buenos Aires.

The coastal route starts just south of **La Plata**, the pleasant provincial capital. Another 260km southeast, the point where the silty Río de la Plata flows out into the cool waters of the South Atlantic Ocean marks the beginning of the country's seaside **resorts**, hugely popular with local families in the summer. In January and February much of the national capital pulls down its shutters and heads en masse for the coast; if crowds and 24-hour parties aren't your thing, visit in December or March when hotel prices can drop by half or more. Two of the major resorts along the so-called Interbalnearia, **Pinamar** and **Villa Gesell** tend to attract younger holiday-makers, while **Mar del Plata** is the liveliest of all, with vast crowds packing its beaches by day and flocking to its numerous clubs and restaurants at night. If you hanker after peace and quiet, there are more isolated spots, though, such as exclusive **Cariló**, bucolic **Mar de las Pampas** or sleepy **Mar del Sud**. Of course, if it's pristine white sands, shady palms and warm seas you're after, you'd be better off heading north to Brazil.

A LANCHA COLECTIVA ON THE PARANÁ DELTA

Highlights

❶ **Tigre and the Paraná Delta** Like having the Everglades on the doorstep of Manhattan – Tigre and the nearby islets offer a vivid green reminder that Buenos Aires is a subtropical city. See p.133

❷ **San Antonio de Areco** This postcard-perfect pampas town is a goldmine of rural culture and traditional crafts – and home to one of the country's main gaucho festivals. See p.137

❸ **Estancias** The fertile Pampas provide the ideal setting for many of the country's best-appointed and most famous ranches,

giving visitors a taste of country life within easy access of Buenos Aires. See p.141

❹ **Sierra de la Ventana** The craggy Sierra de la Ventana range in the west of the province has a well-earned reputation for enjoyable riding, cosy but rustic chalets and delicious *picada* platters. See p.151

❺ **Small beach resorts** The intimate yet fashionable resorts of Cariló, Mar de las Pampas and Mar del Sud offer quiet sands, aromatic pine forests and long walks along the oceanfront. See p.159, p.162 & p.170

HIGHLIGHTS ARE MARKED ON THE MAP ON P.132

GETTING AROUND

Buenos Aires is one of Argentina's easiest provinces to get around: it is crisscrossed with a dense network of roads and railways, making it straightforward to negotiate using public transport. Bear in mind, though, that bus services to the coast are greatly reduced out of season.

The Paraná Delta

One of the world's most beautiful and unusual suburban landscapes, the **Paraná Delta** lies just a few kilometres north of Avenida General Paz, the ring road that divides the city of Buenos Aires from its namesake province. Constantly shifting as sediment from tropical Brazil is deposited by the mighty Río Paraná, the Delta region is a wonderfully seductive maze of lush, green islands separated by rivers and streams. Lining the banks, traditional houses on stilts peep out from behind screens of subtropical vegetation. The

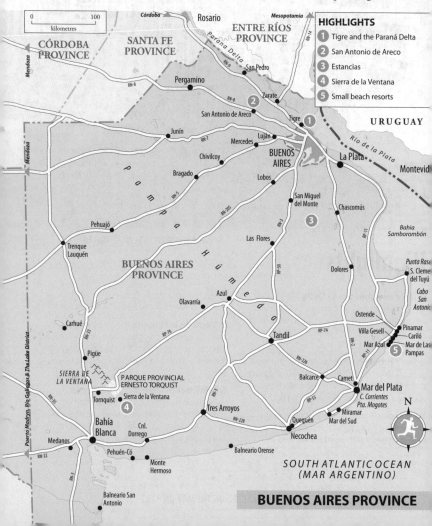

HIGHLIGHTS

1. Tigre and the Paraná Delta
2. San Antonio de Areco
3. Estancias
4. Sierra de la Ventana
5. Small beach resorts

BUENOS AIRES PROVINCE

Delta actually begins at the port of Diamante in Entre Ríos Province, some 450km to the northwest of the city, and its one thousand square kilometres are divided into three administrative sections. By far the most visited area is the first section, most of which lies within a ninety-minute boat trip from the picturesque town of **Tigre**, itself just 25km northwest of Capital Federal. Travel beyond here into the wide Río Paraná de las Palmas, and you may be forgiven for thinking that you've stumbled onto a tributary of the Amazon. At this point the Delta widens, inhabitants and amenities are much more dispersed and *isleños* (as island dwellers are known) rely on electric generators and kerosene lamps. The abundance of water and warm climate mean that mosquitoes are a real problem in and around the Delta, so come prepared.

Tigre

Sitting on an island bounded by the ríos Luján, Reconquista and Tigre, **TIGRE** owes its poetic name to the jaguars – popularly known as *tigres* in Latin America – that inhabited the Delta region until the beginning of the twentieth century. Primarily seen as a departure point for excursions to the Delta, the town itself is sometimes overlooked by tourists. At first glance, it's a bit of a hotchpotch but don't be put off by initial impressions – Tigre offers a vivacious mix of faded glamour and day-trip brashness. The bars and restaurants around the refurbished riverside area provide perfect vantage points for an unhurried contemplation of the comings and goings of Delta life.

El Tigre (as it also known) lies along the western bank of the Río Luján, one of the Delta's main arteries, and the town is divided in half by the smaller Río Tigre, which runs north–south through its centre. Riverside avenues flank both sides of the Río Tigre,

---

DELTA BOAT TRIPS AND OTHER ACTIVITIES

There are many ways to go messing about on the Delta, particularly in the summer months (Dec–Feb) when you should plan ahead and make reservations. In the capital, various tour companies organize day-trips, including Tangol (☏011 4312 7276, ⓦtangol.com), while companies in Tigre itself offer **paseos**, or round-trip tours. They generally last around an hour and inevitably don't go far into the Delta, but if you're pressed for time they do at least give a taste of river life. Rather touristy catamarans as well as the better, smaller *lanchas* (launches) run regular *paseos* (11am–5pm; from $40), some from the Estación Fluvial and some from around the international terminal opposite at Lavalle 520.

A second option is the frequent **passenger services**, known as *lanchas colectivas*, run by three companies – Interisleña, Delta and Jilgüero; these are used by Delta residents to go about their daily business – picking up supplies, taking children to school – and go to all points in it. If you have a specific destination in mind, phone the tourist office (not the companies themselves) for the timetable. Most routes are one way, but all three companies also do round trips to the Paraná de las Palmas in the second section, lasting about four hours (Delta 10.30am; Jilgüero 12.30pm; Interisleña 2.30pm). All cost $50–90; again, confirm the timetable with the tourist office in Tigre and, if possible, avoid the weekends, when the boats are packed and the trips take much longer. If you want to do some **walking**, you will need to take one of the regular services to Rama Negra and/or Tres Bocas ($40 & $35 return), where you can disembark and wander for a considerable distance thanks to a public riverside path and wooden footbridges that cross from island to island.

There are various places around Tigre where you can practise **watersports**. Buenos Aires Outdoors, based in Capital Federal (☏011 5258 5383, ⓦbuenosairesoutdoors.com), offers guided tours in **kayaks**, while Puro Remo, at Lavalle 945 (☏15 5808 2237, ⓦpuroremo.com.ar), gives you the choice of kayaks or rowing boats with wooden oars. Note that you must take a guide or instructor with you for safety reasons and should ring ahead and reserve. There's also a **wake-boarding school** run by South American champion Gabriela Díaz (☏011 4728 0031, ⓦwakeschool.com.ar).

while the broad Paseo Victorica runs along the Río Luján on the western side of town. A good place to begin a tour of the area is around the **Estación Fluvial**, immediately north of the bridge over the Río Tigre. The point of contact between island and mainland life, the Estación bustles with activity, particularly at weekends.

Brief history

The town was first documented in 1635 under the name of El Pueblo de las Conchas ("Seashell Village"), a small settlement that functioned as a defensive outpost against Portuguese invasions. The town became a favoured summer retreat of the Porteño elite in the late nineteenth and early twentieth centuries, from when its sumptuous mansions and palatial rowing clubs mostly date. Back then social life revolved around events at the Tigre Club, home to Argentina's first casino, and the grand Tigre Hotel, whose clientele included Enrico Caruso and the Prince of Wales. The town's decline as a glamorous destination was partly due to the closure of the casino (shut in 1933 through a law which prohibited casinos in the vicinity of the capital) and in part a result of the growing popularity of Mar del Plata (see p.163), made ever more accessible thanks to the arrival of the railway and improved roads. The Tigre Hotel was demolished in 1940, although the elegant Tigre Club still stands at the apex of the island and has now been reinvented as the excellent Museo de Arte Tigre.

Parque de la Costa

Vivanco 1509 • Jan & Feb Tues–Sun 11am–9pm; March–Dec Sat & Sun 11am–7pm • $66–100 (varies according to age, season and ticket type) • ☎ 011 4002 6000, ⓦ parquedelacosta.com.ar

On the same side of the river as the Estación Fluvial you'll find the **Parque de la Costa**, one of Latin America's largest amusement parks, with roller coasters, carousels and arcades. Major European fairy tales like Cinderella and Sleeping Beauty provide some of the themes.

Puerto de Frutos

Mon–Fri 10am–6pm, Sat & Sun 10am–7pm

A couple of blocks west of the Parque de la Costa, alongside the Río Luján, there's a rather more serene attraction, the **Puerto de Frutos**. A Tigre institution, the "Fruit Port" has declined somewhat in importance since the days when fruit cultivation was the region's main source of income. Even so it's still a working port, where you can watch boats being unloaded with wood, wicker – which grows in abundance in the Delta – and other goods in the small docks. The port also operates as a craft market, with rustic furniture and wickerwork the chief products.

Museo Naval de la Nación

Paseo Victorica 602 • Mon–Fri 8.30am–5.30pm, Sat & Sun 10.30am–6.30pm • $3 • ☎ 011 4749 0608

The most enjoyable part of Tigre to explore on foot is on the western side of the Río Tigre. Over the bridge, follow riverside Avenida Lavalle north to the confluence of the river with the Río Luján, where Lavalle merges with **Paseo Victorica**, a delightful riverside avenue lined with bars and restaurants. The **Museo Naval de la Nación** is housed in the old naval workshops and holds exhibits relating to the country's maritime history, as well as to Argentine naval history from the British invasions of 1806 to the Falklands/Malvinas conflict of 1982.

Museo de Arte Tigre (MAT)

Paseo Victorica 972 • Wed–Fri 9am–7pm, Sat & Sun noon–7pm; guided tours hourly • $12 • ☎ 011 4512 4528, ⓦ mat.gov.ar

At the far end of Paseo Victorica is the **Museo de Arte Tigre** or **MAT**, housed in a vast turreted and balustraded structure dating from between 1910 and 1927. The building (formerly the Tigre Club casino) was influenced by grand European hotels of the same period. Inside, the opulent mansion – with its marble staircase, wrought-iron banisters, gigantic chandeliers and delicate ceiling frescoes – is a setting to rival any of the capital's art museums. The art itself – mostly by Argentines or on Argentine themes, with many gauchos in evidence – is arranged into themes such as Tigre, the human figure and architecture. The interesting temporary exhibitions have included loans from the prestigious MALBA in Palermo (see p.95).

TIGRE

ARRIVAL AND INFORMATION

By train Trains depart regularly for Tigre from Retiro station (Línea Mitre); the hour's journey costs $2 and terminates at Tigre's train station on the riverbank, just a block south of the Estación Fluvial, where you'll find one of Tigre's five tourist offices, a number of kiosks representing assorted hotels and restaurants, and various boat companies' ticket offices. For a few pesos more, you can transfer to the Tren de la Costa at Olivos, which drops you at the portals of the Parque de la Costa.

Tourist information There are so many ways of seeing the Delta that it can seem slightly bewildering, and not surprisingly the excellent Estación Fluvial tourist office (daily 8am–6pm; ☎011 4512 4498, ⓦ tigre.gov.ar) is often busy, especially at weekends. They have good maps and can help you find your way through the labyrinth of trips available.

ACCOMMODATION

The Delta can easily be visited on a day-trip but an overnight stay offers a full break from the hectic pace of Buenos Aires. There are some attractive options both in Tigre and in the Delta itself; note that the first section, closer to Tigre, is easier to get to, but for more peace and quiet go farther out into the second section. Getting to most Delta destinations requires a bit of forward planning, so you should ring ahead for a reservation and transport arrangements. One of the most accessible places to stay is the area known as **Tres Bocas**, a 30min boat trip from the Estación Fluvial. However, to really appreciate the wild charm of the Delta, you should head further out to its more isolated areas like Arroyo Las Cañas. In addition to the hotels detailed below, there are plenty of houses and *cabañas* available to rent for weekends or longer stays – see ⓦ tigre.gov.ar or ⓦ vivitigre.gov.ar for a list.

THE TREN DE LA COSTA

The **Tren de la Costa** (daily; $16 for a *boleto turístico* one way, allowing you to get off and on as many times as you like – tickets can be bought on board; every 30min 7.20am–9pm; ☎011 4794 9159, ⓦ trendelacosta.com.ar) runs north from the leafy suburb of Olivos to Tigre in the Paraná Delta, a 25-minute trip if you do it in one go. It's one of the most attractive options for getting to Tigre – it runs parallel to the waterfront, mostly through green parkland and past grandiose suburban mansions and villas – and also presents a number of enticing stopoffs, with eleven restored or purpose-built stations along the route. Originally part of the state-run Tren del Bajo line, built in 1891, the service fell into disuse in the 1960s. In 1995 the northernmost section reopened as this privately run, scenic railway, with luxurious mock-Victorian carriages running smoothly and silently along electrified tracks.

To get to the Olivos terminus, known as **Estación Maipú**, first take a commuter train from Retiro (see p.105) to Olivos' Estación Mitre, a thirty-minute journey. From here, take the walkway across Avenida Maipú to the red-brick station (many of the stations are modelled on those of the British Victorian era).

As well as hopping-off points for the wealthy suburbs of Olivos and San Isidro, many of the Tren de la Costa's stations hold their own appeal. **Estación Borges**, the nearest to Olivos' marina, is referred to as the "station of the arts" – it's home to an art café with open-air sculptures. **Libertador** station has a shopping centre comprised of outlets for many of the most popular Argentine designer stores, while **Anchorena** station has been christened "Estación Tango" and sits alongside a cultural centre that puts on tango shows and classes; it's also the station closest to the river, and borders a riverside park. **Estación Barrancas** hosts an antiques fair (Sat & Sun 10am–6pm) and provides access to a cycling path, which runs north to San Isidro. **Estación San Isidro**, with its upmarket shopping mall, is located conveniently near the suburb's historic quarter. North of here, you pass through four more riverside stations – Punta Chica, Marina Nueva, San Fernando and Canal – before arriving at the northern terminus, **Estación Delta**, close to Tigre's fruit market (see opposite) and opposite the entrance to the Parque de la Costa.

La Becasina ☎011 4728 1253, ⓦlabecasina.com.ar. In the second, quieter section on Arroyo Las Canas, these thoroughly luxurious bungalows are the Delta's closest approximation to a jungle lodge. US$290

Bonanza Deltaventura ☎011 4728 1674, ⓦdeltaventura.com. At an isolated spot on the Carapachay river, *Deltaventura* is the place to go for serious peace and quiet, with only three rooms and around 3km worth of trails, where you can trek, birdwatch and canoe. It can also be visited as a day-trip ($300, including lunch). $1000

★ **Casona La Ruchi** Lavalle 557, Tigre ☎011 4749 2499, ⓦcasonalaruchi.com.ar. A fabulous old family house with enormous wood-floored bedrooms, huge balconies, a swimming pool in the garden and exceptionally friendly owners, though only shared bathrooms are available. $500

Hotel Fundación Agustín García Av Liniers 1547, Tigre ☎011 4749 0140, ⓔfundaciongarcia@yahoo.com.ar.

Simple, old-fashioned town hotel, with rooms sleeping one to five people. Also has its own restaurant. $390

l'Marangatu ☎011 4728 0752, ⓦi-marangatu.com .ar. Well-known place on the Río San Antonio close to the Tres Bocas part of the Delta, complete with swimming pool, sports pitches and even a heliport. $490

Los Pecanes Felicaria and Canal Dos ☎011 4728 1932, ⓦhosterialospecanes.com. An appealing, family-run *hostería* out on the Arroyo Felicaria in the second section of the Delta, away from the roar of the jet skis. $750

★ **Villa Julia** Paseo Victorica 800 ☎011 4749 0242, ⓦvillajuliaresort.com.ar. A 1910 house carefully converted into a luxury hotel, using many of the original floors, fittings and furniture alongside modern comforts such as soft pillows and a/c. The suites' wide balconies look out over the river, and the hotel has its own elegant restaurant. $800

EATING AND DRINKING

There are plenty of **restaurants** in Tigre, the pick of them along Paseo Victorica. You'll also find lots of cheap and cheerful *parrillas* near the entrance to the Parque de la Costa, while the above-average café at the Estación Fluvial prepares imaginative sandwiches. On the Delta itself, there are a number of eating options including some quite upmarket ones. However, there's not much in the way of **nightlife** in the Delta – which is kind of the point – although some restaurants, including *La Riviera*, double up as a bar if you fancy a contemplative beer or two.

Alpenhaus Ram Negra ☎011 4728 0422, ⓦalpenhaus .com.ar. As the name suggests this places serves up classic Germanic dishes, such as hams and sauerkraut, with plenty of tarts and strudels on offer for the sweet-toothed. Daily noon–5pm & 8.30pm–midnight.

Gato Blanco Río Capitán ☎011 4728 0390. One of the most upmarket restaurants in the whole Delta, its *ojo de bife* (a tender steak) is famous, as is the sole. Make sure you check the times of launches to get back or you might find yourself stranded after your leisurely lunch. Daily noon–4pm & 8pm–midnight.

Novo María Paseo Victorica 611. Tigre's most upmarket restaurant is situated in an elegant dining room on the riverbank. Soothing peach-hued decor offers a pleasant setting and the service is good except at the very busiest times when it can be slow. The extensive menu features

river fish and an array of well-prepared meat dishes. Daily noon–4.30pm & 7.30pm–midnight.

La Riviera Tres Bocas ☎011 4728 0177, ⓦla-riviera .com.ar. This simple, pretty place right by the jetty doubles up as a *hostería* and is one of the Delta's oldest restaurants, with a typical *parrilla* menu and lots of favourite desserts. Daily noon–3pm & 8pm–midnight.

La Terraza Paseo Victorica 134. This classy *parrilla* has an outside seating area both on the pavement and on the first floor, where you get great views. The meat has a good reputation and there is an excellent wine list to match. Daily noon–4pm & 8pm–midnight.

Vía Toscana Paseo Victorica 470. This home-made ice cream parlour has a lovely Victorian-style garden area from where you can enjoy cones and tubs and idly watch river life. Daily noon–midnight.

The Pampa Húmeda

Stretching for a couple of hundred kilometres west and northwest of Buenos Aires city, the **Pampa Húmeda** ("wet pampa") is the country's most fertile and valuable land. It is dotted with several sites of interest, including **Luján**, at the very beginning of the RN-5, less than 70km west of the federal capital. This is Argentina's leading religious site, thanks to its vast basilica, purpose-built to house an image of the country's patron saint, the Virgin of Luján. Further along the RN-5, **Mercedes** stands out for its authentic *pulpería* largely untouched since the nineteenth century. *Pulperías*, essentially provisions stores with a bar attached, performed an important social role in rural Argentina (rather like Wild West saloons or British village pubs) and enjoy an almost mythical status in gaucho folklore.

THE GAUCHO

The pampas, the vast expanse of flat grassland that radiates out from Buenos Aires, forms one of the country's most famous features. Similarly, the **gaucho**, who once roamed them on horseback, *facón* (knife) clenched between his teeth, leaving a trail of broken hearts and gnawed steak bones behind him, is as important a part of the collective romantic imagination of Argentina as the Wild West cowboy is in the US. The popular depiction of this splendid, freedom-loving figure – whose real life must actually have been rather lonely and extremely brutal – was crystallized in José Hernández's epic poem *Martín Fierro*, from which just about every Argentine can quote (they learn it by heart at school). It's a way of life whose time has passed, but the gaucho's legacy remains. You're unlikely to witness knife fights over a woman, but you can still visit well-preserved *pulperías* (traditional bars), stay at estancias and watch weather-beaten old *paisanos* (countrymen) playing cards and chuckling behind their huge handlebar moustaches. The term "gaucho" is still a compliment while gaucho garb – beret or sombrero, knotted scarf, checked shirt, ornate belt (*tirador*), baggy trousers (*bombachas*), boots or espadrilles (*alpargatas*) and a poncho – is considered almost chic. A *gauchada* means a good deed or an act of macho heroism, altruistic courage or, at least, heartfelt generosity. Shrines of red flags dedicated to the semi-mythical Gauchito Gil (see box, p.223), one of the most famous gauchos of all, are often seen by the roadside throughout the country.

2

The small town of **Lobos**, to the capital's southwest, is another popular weekend destination for Porteños, primarily for its lakeside setting. The most notable destination hereabouts, though, is **San Antonio de Areco**, a charming market town to the capital's northwest, along the RN-8. Known colloquially as Areco, it has retained a remarkably authentic feel despite its popularity with tourists; if you visit only one pampas town during your stay in Argentina, this is the one to head for. As the recognized centre of pampas tradition, Areco puts on a popular gaucho festival in November and has some highly respected artisans and an extremely attractive and unusually well preserved historic centre. Like other destinations in the Pampa Húmeda, it is close to Buenos Aires and a potential day-trip from the capital, but spending a night – especially at an estancia – will give you a better feel for the much slower pace of life in the interior. Areco and its neighbours are also useful stopping-off points on the way to the Litoral, Córdoba or the Northwest. Further afield and better suited for a longer stay (or a stopover on the way to Patagonia), **Tandil** is an appealing town of cobbled streets with its own tradition of pampas culture. The main attraction is the nearby mountain scenery, perfect for riding and long rambles.

San Antonio de Areco

Delightful **SAN ANTONIO DE ARECO**, the national capital of gaucho traditions, hosts the annual **Fiesta de la Tradición** (see box, p.139), the country's most important festival celebrating pampas culture. Despite its modest promotion as a tourist destination, playing on its appealing setting by the banks of the tranquil Río Areco, the town has retained a surprisingly genuine feel. You may not find Areco full of galloping gauchos outside festival week, but you still have a good chance of spotting estancia workers on horseback, sporting traditional berets and rakishly knotted scarves, or of coming across *paisanos* propping up the bar of a traditional *boliche* establishment. Areco has a prestigious literary connection: the town was the setting for Ricardo Güiraldes' Argentine classic *Don Segundo Sombra* (1926), a novel that was influential in changing the image of the gaucho from that of an undesirable outlaw to a symbol of national values.

The town's only real sights are a couple of museums, the most important of which is the **Museo Gauchesco Ricardo Güiraldes**. But what really makes Areco memorable is the harmonious architectural character of the town's centre: all cobbled streets and faded Italianate and colonial facades punctuated by elaborate wrought-iron grilles and

SAN ANTONIO DE ARECO

Pergamino & Rosario

0   200 metres

El Ombú, La Pampa & Buenos Aires

BARS AND CLUBS

Bar San Martin	3
Barril 990	2
Puesto La Lechuza	1

ACCOMMODATION

Los Abuelos	3	Hostal de Areco	4	
Antigua Casona	5	Hostel Gaucho	2	
Camping Club River	1	Patio de Moreno	6	
		Solar del Pago	7	

RESTAURANTS AND CAFÉS

Almacén de Ramos		La Costa	2	Tragame Tierra	1
Generales	5	La Esquina de Merti	6	La Vieja Sodería	7
Café de las Artes	4	La Olla de Cobre	3		

delicately arching lamps. There are also some excellent **artisans** working in the town in *talleres* (workshops). Weaving and leatherwork are well represented, but the silversmiths are the highlight.

Areco's traditional gaucho atmosphere extends to the surrounding area, where you will find some of Argentina's most famous **estancias**, offering a luxurious accommodation alternative to staying in Areco itself. The town and its surroundings were badly hit by terrible floods in late 2009, and many sights have only just recovered, having required extensive and costly restoration work.

Plaza Ruiz de Arellane

Areco's main square, the leafy **Plaza Ruiz de Arellano**, six blocks west of the bus terminal, is named after José Ruiz de Arellano, whose estancia stood on the site now occupied by the town and who built Areco's founding chapel, the **Iglesia Parroquial San Antonio de Padua**, on the south side of the square. The original chapel, a simple adobe construction, was declared a parish church in 1730, and was rebuilt in 1792 and then again in 1870 in keeping with the town's growing importance. Of no great architectural note, the current version is nonetheless a pleasingly simple white construction, with clear Italian influences. The exterior is dominated by a sculpture of St Anthony himself, who stands within a niche clad with blue-and-white tiles that echo those of the church's small bell-shaped dome. The inside is admittedly impressive, with a high vaulted ceiling.

Among the elegant *fin-de-siècle* residences that flank the plaza, there is the Italianate **municipalidad**, to the north, painted a particularly delicate version of the pink that characterizes so many of Areco's buildings. On the northwest corner of the square stands a typically colonial two-storey construction known as the **Casa de los Martínez**, after the local family who once inhabited it. The building's handsome but rather plain green-and-white exterior is dominated by the original railings of a balcony, which runs all the way around the first floor.

Centro Cultural y Museo Taller Draghi

Lavalle 387 • Mon–Sat 9am–1pm & 3.30–7.30pm, Sun 10am–1pm; free guided visits 11am, 5pm & 6pm • $20 • ☎ 02326 455583, ⓦ draghiplaterosorfebres.com

Bang opposite the church, one of Areco's most renowned silversmith families runs the **Centro Cultural y Museo Taller Draghi**. The centre displays some fine pieces made in the style of *platería criolla*, which first emerged around 1750 when local craftsmen, who had previously worked according to Spanish and Portuguese tradition, began to develop their own style. Fantastically ornate yet sturdy, in keeping with the practical use to which the items are put – at least in theory – the style is still commonly used to produce gaucho knives (*facones*), belts (*rastras*), *mates* and stirrups. The museum/workshop mixes the creations of the late Juan José Draghi – who produced pieces for various international figures, including the king and queen of Spain – with a collection of nineteenth-century silver spurs, bridles and swords that have been his inspiration. As there's little in the way of labels, it's hard to tell which is antique and which modern, but the helpful guide will put you straight. Draghi died in 2008 at the age of 64 but his sons Mariano and Patricio inherited his skills and now run the workshop. Among Draghi's finest work are the *mates*, which come in their original chalice shape (based on those used in churches) with finely wrought silver stems of cherubs and flowers. Such *mates* are now for decoration only, being expensive – not to mention likely to scald your fingers if filled with hot water. The Draghi family also has very pleasant rooms ($200) available in a *parador* (inn) behind the workshop in Calle Matheu – enquire at the museum.

Centro Cultural Usina Vieja

Alsina 66 • Tues–Sun 11.15am–4.45pm • $5

A block north of Plaza Ruiz de Arellano is the **Centro Cultural Usina Vieja**. The restored building originally housed Areco's first electrical generator and has been declared a national industrial monument. Now housing a cultural centre, the building also contains the **Museo de la Ciudad**, an eclectic collection – mainly supplied through local donations – of everyday items, from clothing to record players and even the town's old telephone switchboard, plus occasional temporary exhibitions, focusing mainly on subjects related to rural Argentine life. There's also a good display of the nationally famous **gaucho cartoons** of Florencia Molino Campos, first published in almanacs and now adorning hotel walls the length of the country.

FIESTA DE LA TRADICIÓN

One of Argentina's most original and enjoyable festivals, San Antonio de Areco's **Fiesta de la Tradición** began in 1939 on an initiative of then-mayor José Antonio Güiraldes. The actual Día de la Tradición is November 10 – the birthday of José Hernández, author of Argentina's gaucho text par excellence, *Martín Fierro* – but the celebrations last for a week and are organized to run from weekend to weekend, either the first or second week in November, depending on the weather forecast. Activities, including exhibitions, dances, music recitals and shows of gaucho skills, last throughout the week, although the high point is the final Sunday, which begins with dancing and a procession of gauchos dressed in their traditional loose trousers (*bombachas*), ornamented belts and wide-brimmed hats or berets. An *asado con cuero*, at which meat – primarily beef – is cooked around a fire with its skin on, takes place at midday in the Parque Criollo (at a reduced price for gauchos) and is followed by an extensive display of gaucho skills, including *jineteadas*, Argentine bronco riding.

Parque Criollo and Museo Gauchesco Ricardo Güiraldes

Ricardo Güiraldes s/n • Museum daily except Tues 11am–5pm • $12 • ⊕ blogmuseoguiraldes.com.ar

After crossing the simple brick **Puente Viejo** you reach the rather scrubby **Parque Criollo**, less a park than a kind of exhibition ground, used during the Fiesta de la Tradición as the setting for the main displays of gaucho skills, and within the grounds is the **Museo Gauchesco Ricardo Güiraldes**. The entrance to the park and the museum is via the *Pulpería La Blanqueada*, once a staging post on the old Camino Real, which linked Buenos Aires with Alto Perú. It was the setting for the first encounter between Fabio, the young hero of Güiraldes' novel – a sort of South American Huckleberry Finn – and his mentor, Don Segundo Sombra. The *pulpería* was closed in the 1930s but its original features have been retained, including the traditional grille that separated the owner from his customers and their knives and light fingers.

The museum is housed in a 1930s reproduction of an old estancia. Its collection mixes gaucho paraphernalia – *mate* gourds, silverware and *boleadoras* (lasso balls) – with objects deemed to be interesting largely because of their famous owners – General Rosas' bed, W.H. Hudson's books, and so on. Of particular interest are the black-and-white photos of the original gauchos who were the inspiration for Güiraldes, and the branding irons they used – each landowner had his own, somewhat cabalistic symbol, worn in various forms as a badge of pride by his men as well as his cattle.

ARRIVAL AND INFORMATION   SAN ANTONIO DE ARECO

By bus Most buses from Buenos Aires and Rosario stop at the pink Chevallier terminal at General Paz and Av Dr Smith, six blocks east of Areco's town centre. It's an easy and enjoyable stroll into town along Segundo Sombra, which brings you to Areco's main square, Plaza Ruiz de Arellano. If you're carrying a lot of luggage – or heading for an estancia – take a *remise* (☎02326 456225).

Tourist information The tourist office on the corner of Arellano and Zerboni (daily 8am–7pm; ☎02326 453165) has useful information, including maps, lists of hotels and artisan workshops. There's also a small office in the municipalidad building (Sat & Sun 9am–8pm) on Plaza Ruiz de Arellano, to cope with the extra influx of Porteños on weekends.

ACCOMMODATION

Areco is easily visited as a day-trip from Buenos Aires, but many museums and workshops close during the afternoon, so this can be a frustrating experience. Staying overnight gives you the chance to explore the town at a more leisurely pace and enjoy it at its best, in the morning and evening. Several cafés also double up as simple *hospedajes* (see p.31). If you plan on visiting during the Fiesta de la Tradición celebrations, book at least two weeks in advance; once the hotels are full, the tourist office can provide information on homestays. The countryside around Areco is home to a couple of the province's most traditional **estancias** (see box opposite).

Los Abuelos Zapiola and Zeboni ☎02326 456390. A decent option if you're after a more modern type of hotel, and reasonably priced. Rooms have TV and fans (extra for a/c) with balconies looking out over the Río Areco. $350

Antigua Casona Segunda Sombra 495 ☎02326 456600, ⊕antiguacasona.com. A B&B with a rustic edge and a lovely patio where a good breakfast is served. $450

Camping Club River Costanera s/n ☎02326 453590. The best campsite within easy reach of Areco is approached by following Zerboni west out of town. There's a large swimming pool within the grounds. $80

Hostal de Areco Zapiola 25 ☎02326 456118, ⊕hostal deareco.com.ar. One of the most attractive accommodation options in town: a traditional rose-coloured

building with farmhouse-style decor. The hotel has a bar and comfortable communal area with a fireplace. $340

Hostel Gaucho Zerboni 308 ☎02326 453625, ⊕hostel gaucho.com.ar. Hostel with decent communal area and a garden equipped with *parrilla*. Dorms $90, doubles $310

★ **Patio de Moreno** Moreno and San Martín ☎02326 455197, ⊕patiodemoreno.com. Stylish, centrally located boutique hotel with modern rooms, many with views onto a pretty garden. There's also a heated swimming pool and a wine bar serving local produce. $1100

Solar del Pago Hipólito G. Fiore 232 ☎02326 1541 0252, ⊕solardelpago.com. Located out of town on the RP-41 in the direction of San Andrés de Giles, this hotel affords stunning views of the nearby pampas. The hotel has a restaurant and spa, as well as disabled access. $710

THE ESTANCIAS OF BUENOS AIRES PROVINCE

Estancias are Argentina's haciendas or ranches, mostly wealthy farms set up to raise livestock on extensive swathes of green pasture, dotted with the odd ombú. The owners, or *estancieros*, effectively make up the country's aristocracy, and still employ large numbers of *peones* (ranch hands), some of them regarded as latter-day gauchos, to look after their cattle and, occasionally, sheep. The main buildings, known as *cascos*, range from simple colonial-style farmsteads to ornate mansions, with architecture inspired by French chateaux, English country homes or Italianate palaces. Scattered all over the country, but with the greatest concentration in Buenos Aires Province, above all around San Antonio de Areco, many of them take in paying guests; this can be either for *días de campo*, during which visitors take part in outdoor activities, such as horseriding or even polo, and enjoy three or four hearty meals, or overnight stays in often luxurious rooms for a complete estancia experience.

La Bamba Areco ☎ 011 15 5316 1200, �🌐 labamba deareco.com. Around 12km from Areco, *La Bamba* was used in María Luisa Bemberg's film *Camila* – the story of the ill-fated romance between Camila O'Gorman and a priest – and is one of Argentina's most distinctive estancias. The Río Areco runs through the grounds, so guests can fish as well as ride, although the "shows" in the recently built *pulpería* and immaculate living rooms make the place seem a bit Disneyfied. Day-trips at US$110. US$460

La Cinacina Areco; follow Bartolomé Mitre five blocks west of the main plaza to the end of the street ☎ 02326 452773, �🌐 lacinacina.com.ar. Offers relatively affordable "days in the country", a full day of *asado*, horseriding and a display of gaucho skills for $230, or $360 with transport from the centre of town included (Tues, Fri & Sun). You can also stay the night, in pretty, light, country-style rooms. $850

El Ombú Ruta 31, Areco ☎ 02326 492080, �🌐 estanciaelombu.com. Arguably the most luxurious estancia near Areco, with sumptuously decorated rooms and a lovely tiled and ivy-covered veranda. As well as offering horseriding, *El Ombú* has a small but well-maintained swimming pool and a games room. Other activities include helping out with – or at least observing – farm tasks and, of course, eating delicious *asados*, sometimes served under the shade of the large ombú tree that gives the estancia its name. Directions are on the website; the estancia will arrange a transfer from Buenos Aires. US$100 as a day-visit. US$400

Santa Rita Just beyond the tiny village of Carboni not far from Lobos ☎ 02227 495026, ⌀ santa-rita .com.ar. The faded, pink main building has been renovated with great taste by its owners and the rooms are gorgeous – choose between fresh, clean Caribbean decor or darker Old World antique elegance; all have views over the estate. A day at the estancia with *asado* included costs $360 per person. You can reach the estancia by train from Buenos Aires (Constitución); the train tracks run right past it and, with prior notice, you can arrange to get off in Carboni, from where the estancia's friendly, English-speaking owners will pick you up. $1500

La Sofía Polo 14km from Areco ☎ 011 6091 9266, ⌀ lasofiapolo.com.ar. Run by a German–Argentine couple, *La Sofía* is primarily a place for those wanting to improve their polo game; husband Marcos Antin has taught polo around Argentina and Europe and is also a qualified referee; lessons cater to all levels, including beginners. However, you don't have to be a polo player or even a fan to stay here – it's a beautiful, tranquil place and the room price includes food, drink and one horse-ride a day. There are additional costs for polo lessons and playing matches. US$380

EATING, DRINKING AND NIGHTLIFE

Most of Areco's locals tend to go in for simple, rustic food and, true to their gaucho roots, regard a pizza as the most exotic dish they are willing to try. That said, you can find some sophisticated **restaurants** in this prosperous town, catering for tourists and natives alike. Great for a beer and a plate of peanuts, traditional *pulperías* and *almacenes* abound, again partly as tourist attractions but maintaining an authentic aura nonetheless. The best **bars** in Areco are *boliches* – traditional places where estancia workers drink Fernet and play cards. Most *boliches* in the modern sense of the word – **nightclubs** – are out on Avenida Dr Smith, near the bus terminal (usually Fri & Sat only).

RESTAURANTS AND CAFÉS

Almacén de Ramos Generales Zapiola 143 ☎ 02326 456376, ⌀ ramosgeneralesareco.com.ar. A converted old *almacén* (general store) this bustling place serves *parrilla*, *picadas* and popular specials such as trout in Roquefort sauce with boiled potatoes. Daily noon–3.30pm & 8.30pm–midnight.

Café de las Artes Bolívar 68. This arty café – as the name suggests – does tasty handmade pasta that even Italians would find authentic, along with meat dishes such as the unusual but delicious pork in blackberry sauce. Summer daily noon–4pm & 8pm–midnight; winter Wed–Sun same hours.

La Costa Zerboni and Belgrano. This no-nonsense *parrilla* is popular with the locals for its keenly priced, generous servings of grilled meat, salads and hearty desserts like *budín de pan* (bread pudding). Daily noon–4pm & 8pm–midnight.

La Esquina de Merti Lavalle and Arellano ☎02326 456705, ⓦesquinademerti.com.ar. A much-loved place on the main plaza whose walls are adorned with old signs, ads and bottles, making it a tasteful re-creation of a *pulpería*. It serves straightforward Argentine classics and offers a very decent set lunch with drinks included. Daily noon–3pm & 8pm–1am.

La Olla de Cobre Matheu 433 ☎02326 453105, ⓦlaolladecobre.com.ar. A small but highly renowned chocolate factory and sweet shop where you can try handmade chocolates and particularly delicious *alfajores* before buying. Daily 10am–1pm & 3.30–8.30pm.

Tragame Tierra Calle Martínez. This down-to-earth haunt by the river does *panchos* (hotdogs) and *picadas* (meat and cheese platters), best accompanied by a cold beer, has basic rooms available and also rents out *piraguas* (boats) and mountain bikes. Daily noon–4pm & 8pm–midnight.

★ **La Vieja Sodería** Bolívar and General Paz. The pick of Areco's old-style establishments: with wall lined with coloured soda bottles this *pulpería* serves a wide range of teas and beers, and snacks including sandwiches and *picadas*. Daily noon–midnight.

BARS AND CLUBS

Bar San Martín Moreno and Alvear. This is a classic *boliche* – and hence a good bet for spotting local characters meeting up for a chat over a Fernet or two. Daily noon–late.

Barril 990 San Martín 381. More a modern pub than a classic *boliche* but occasionally you can hear live music here. Daily noon–late.

Puesto La Lechuza Victorino Althaparro 423. Down by the riverside, the "Owl" is one of the typical *boliches* and a likely place to catch folk music and dancing. Daily 7pm–1am.

Luján

Founded in 1756 on the site of a shrine containing a tiny ceramic figure of the Virgin Mary, **LUJÁN**, about 70km west of Buenos Aires, is now one of the major religious centres in Latin America. The **Virgin of Luján** (see box below) is the patron saint of Argentina and the epic basilica erected in her honour in 1887 in Luján attracts around

---

THE MIRACLE OF THE VIRGIN OF LUJÁN

In 1630, a Portuguese ship that docked in Buenos Aires on its way from Brazil contained a simple terracotta image of the **Virgin** made by an anonymous Brazilian craftsman. The icon had been ordered by a merchant from Santiago del Estero and, after unloading, it was transported by cart towards his estancia. After the cart paused near **Luján**, so the story goes, it could not be moved. Packages were taken off the cart in an attempt to lighten the load but only when the tiny package containing the Virgin was removed would the cart budge. This was taken as a sign that the Virgin had decided on her own destination. A small chapel was built and the first pilgrims began to arrive.

The Virgin has been moved over the centuries, although according to legend it took three attempts and several days of prayer the first time. In 1872, Luján's Lazarist order – a religious body founded in Paris in 1625 with the emphasis on preaching to the rural poor – was entrusted with the care of the Virgin by the archbishop of Buenos Aires. In 1875, a member of the order, **Padre Jorge María Salvaire**, was almost killed in one of the last Indian raids on Azul. Praying to the Virgin, he promised that if he survived he would promote her cult, write her history and build a temple in her name. He survived and the foundation stone to the basilica was laid in 1887.

The original terracotta Virgin is now barely recognizable: a protective bell-shaped silver casing was placed around it in the late nineteenth century. Sky-blue and white robes, the colours of the Argentine flag, were added as well as a Gothic golden surround. The face of the original statue can now just about be seen, peering through a tiny gap in the casing. Even if you don't visit Luján itself, you cannot avoid seeing images of the Virgin: she is the patron saint of roads and paths, and almost every bus and many other vehicles all over the country sport Luján figures and stickers.

eight million visitors a year. This Neo-Gothic edifice is one of the most memorable – though not the most beautiful – churches in Argentina. The town's other major attraction, the vast **Complejo Museográfico Enrique Udaondo**, is a multiplex museum with an important historical section, as well as being Argentina's largest transport museum. Away from the museums and the basilica, all grouped around the central square, Luján is pretty much like any other provincial town, with some elegant, early twentieth-century townhouses and less-elegant modern buildings.

For a real flavour of Luján in full religious swing, you should visit at the weekend, when as many as eight Masses are held a day – but, unless you desperately want to take part, avoid visiting during the annual **pilgrimages**, when the town is seriously overcrowded. These take place on May 8, the day of the Coronation of the Virgin; the last Sunday of September for the Gaucho pilgrimage, when up to a million gauchos come to honour the Virgin of Luján; the first Sunday of October, when young people walk here from Buenos Aires; and December 8, when smaller pilgrimages mark the Immaculate Conception, a national holiday.

Basílica de Nuestra Señora de Luján

Plaza Belgrano • Daily 8am–8pm: Mass Mon–Sat 8am, 9am, 10am, 11am, 5pm & 7pm, Sun also at 12.30pm & 3.30pm; crypt Mon–Fri 10am–5pm, Sat & Sun 10am–6.30pm • $10

The town's main drag, Avenida Nuestra Señora de Luján, rolls up like a tarmac carpet to the door of the **Basílica de Nuestra Señora de Luján**, at the far end of Luján's main square, Plaza Belgrano. At busy times, all you need to do to visit the Virgin is go with the flow. Begun in 1887 but not completed until 1937, the basilica is a mammoth edifice, built using a pinkish stone quarried in Entre Ríos. In true Neo-Gothic style, everything about the basilica points heavenwards, from its remarkably elongated twin spires, which stand 106m tall, to the acute angles of the architraves surrounding the three main doors. At the very centre of the facade there is a large circular stained-glass window depicting the Virgin. The basilica's nineteen bells were cast in Milan from the bronze of World War I cannons. One of the two heavy crosses on the spires fell from a height of 100m at midnight on June 13, 2000; no one was harmed, but both crosses were replaced for safety reasons.

On busy days, entering through one of the heavy bronze doors is a bit like stepping onto a religious conveyor belt, as you get caught up in a seemingly endless stream of pilgrims, some on their knees, making their way to the **Camarín de la Virgen**. For a closer look at the Virgin, head up the stairs to the chamber behind the main altar, where you can observe her from behind. Positioned on a marble pedestal and swathed in robes and adornments, the statue at the centre of all the fuss is rather hard to see; most people gather around the replica in front of the altar below. The outside wall of the chamber is covered with dozens of plaques of all shapes and sizes – including heart-shaped ex votos – thanking the "Virgencita" for prayers answered. The **crypt** below the basilica holds another replica, explains the history and harbours reproductions of Virgins from all over the world, in particular from Latin America and Eastern Europe.

Complejo Museográfico Enrique Udaondo

Plaza Belgrano • Wed–Fri 11am–5pm, Sat & Sun 11am–6pm • $3

West of the plaza in a cluster of mustard-and-white colonial buildings the **Complejo Museográfico Enrique Udaondo** claims to be the most important museum complex in South America. This is debatable, but it's certainly one of the continent's biggest. Its principal collections are housed within the Museo Histórico Colonial, inside the Casa del Virrey and the Cabildo on the western side of Plaza Belgrano, and the Museo de Transportes, at the northern end of the plaza, between Avenida Nuestra Señora de Luján and Lezica y Torrezuri.

2

Museo Histórico Colonial

The **Museo Histórico Colonial** is misleadingly named, since its exhibits cover a much wider period. Access to the main collection is via the admittedly totally colonial **Cabildo** next door, a two-storey galleried building dating from 1772. The leaders of the short-lived British invasion, General William Beresford and Colonel Dennis Pack, were held here after their surrender in August 1806. Trophies captured during the quashing of the invasion, notably the staff of the 71st Highland Regiment, are prominently displayed. An internal door leads onto a pretty courtyard with a marble well in the centre and an elegant wooden balustrade around the first floor of its green-and-white walls. Other rooms here feature displays on the gaucho (including some fine silver *mate* vessels), nineteenth-century fashion, and the disastrous and bloody War of the Triple Alliance against Paraguay.

Museo de Transportes

Argentina's largest transport museum, the **Museo de Transportes** offers less a chronology of the evolution of transport than a display of some of the country's most historically significant planes, trains and carriages. The museum's two most outstanding exhibits are *La Porteña*, Argentina's first steam locomotive, whose maiden journey between Plaza Lavalle and Floresta in Buenos Aires took place in 1857, and the *Plus Ultra*, the hydroplane with which Ramón Franco, General Franco's brother, made the first crossing of the South Atlantic in 1926 (he later died when another hydroplane he was piloting crashed off Mallorca during the Spanish Civil War, in what are regarded as suspicious circumstances).

ARRIVAL AND INFORMATION   LUJÁN

By bus Regular buses to Luján from Buenos Aires arrive at the bus terminal on Av Nuestra Señora de Luján 600 (📞02323 420044), a couple of blocks north of Plaza Belgrano.

By train There are frequent trains from the capital (Once station), changing at Moreno and terminating at Luján's train station, a couple of kilometres southeast of the centre at Av España and Belgrano.

Tourist information The town's tourist office is housed in a building known as La Cúpula, which stands in a park area on the riverbank between Lavalle and San Martín, a block west of Plaza Belgrano (Mon–Fri 9am–5pm, Sat & Sun 10am–6pm; 📞02323 427082, 🌐lujanargentina .com). In addition to maps and hotel lists, it has detailed info on the phenomenon of the Virgin and the basilica's history and importance.

EATING AND DRINKING

La Chakana Defensa y Cortínez 📞02323 15 4042 1235. A Colombian chef offers a refreshing mix of traditional Argentine dishes and international classics at this delightful restaurant set among woods. Fri–Sun noon–3.30pm & 8.30pm–midnight.

L'Eau Vive Constitución 2112 📞02323 421774. Luján's most famous restaurant is a long way out of the centre, fifteen blocks east along Av San Martín from Plaza Colón and most easily reached by taxi. The restaurant's main claim to fame is that it is run exclusively by nuns. The cooking, based on a traditional French menu with an emphasis on rich meat dishes, is generally excellent. Tues–Sat noon–3.30pm & 8.30pm–midnight.

La Recova San Martín 1 📞02323 422280. Conveniently located next to the tourist office, this pleasant restaurant offers outdoor seating and a simple, reasonably priced menu that focuses on pasta. Daily 12.30–3.30pm & 8pm–midnight.

Mercedes

Tranquil and cultured, the well-preserved provincial town of **MERCEDES**, 37km southwest of Luján along the RN-5, was founded in 1752 as a fortress to protect that city from Indian attacks. It's easy to find your way around – the main drag, Avenida 29, crosses central **Plaza San Martín**, which plays host to the grand Italianate **Palacio Municipal** and large Gothic **Basílica Catedral Nuestra Señora de Mercedes** and is a real hub of activity – especially in the evening, when locals fill the tables that spill out of its inviting *confiterías*. Mercedes' main draw, though, is its unmissable *pulpería*.

Pulpería "Lo de Cacho"

At the end of Av 29, two dozen blocks north of Plaza San Martín

The sign outside Mercedes' big attraction claims this to be the last *pulpería*. Known locally as "*Lo de Cacho*" (Cacho's place), it was run, until his death in 2009 at the age of 70, by the self-styled last *pulpero*, Cacho Di Catarina. The gloomy interior, which has hardly changed since it opened its doors in 1850, harbours a collection of dusty bottles, handwritten notices – included an original wanted poster for the biggest gaucho outlaw of them all, Juan Moreira, who was killed by a police posse in nearby Lobos – and gaucho paraphernalia: it doesn't require much imagination to conjure up visions of the knife fights that the late Cacho claimed to have witnessed in his youth. His family still runs the bar in his name and musicians frequently drop in for a glass of Vasco Viejo and impromptu singing and guitar playing, much of it dedicated to the sorely missed Cacho. To get to the *pulpería*, best visited in the evening for a beer and a *picada* featuring some of the renowned local salami, take a *remise* or the local bus that runs towards the park from Avenida 29. A couple of blocks beyond the last stop, the road becomes unsealed and on the left-hand corner you'll see the simple white building, a sign saying "*pulpería*" painted on its side.

ARRIVAL AND INFORMATION

MERCEDES

By bus Mercedes' bus terminal, served by regular buses from the capital, is south of the town centre, from where it's a 20min walk to Plaza San Martín. There's an infrequent local bus from the terminal to the centre, so if you don't fancy the walk you may be better off taking one of the terminal taxis (☎ 02324 420651).

By train There are regular trains from the capital's Once station; the train station is along Av España, eight blocks

north of the centre.

Tourist information The tourist office, on the corner of Av 29 and c/26 (Mon 7am–1pm, Tues–Fri 7am–6pm, Sat & Sun 10am–5pm; ☎ 02324 421080, ⊛ mercedes.gba.gov .ar), doesn't have much in the way of printed information, but the staff are enthusiastic and knowledgeable, and can provide you with a town map.

ACCOMMODATION

There's a free municipal **campsite** in the park on the edge of town; take any local bus from Avenida 29. Note that Mercedes hosts a motorbike rally at the end of March, which is the only time you might have trouble finding space to pitch your tent.

Gran Hotel Mercedes Av 29 and c/16 ☎ 02324 425987. It looks stern and unpromising from the outside, but inside the rooms are quite comfortable and have a/c and TV, while facilities include a restaurant and bar area. **$370**

Hostal del Sol Avenidas 2 and 3 ☎ 02324 433400, ⊛ hotelhostaldelsol.com. This good-value place on the western edge of town offers large comfortable rooms in a tranquil setting. **$340**

EATING AND DRINKING

Mercedes is the national capital of **salami** and even hosts a salami festival in September. You should certainly try some while you are here – the *salamín picado grueso* is favoured by locals, although its high fat content might be off-putting; the *pulpería Lo de Cacho* (see above) is one of the best places to sample some. Otherwise, the town is not exactly overflowing with places to eat and drink – and don't expect any gastronomic wonders, but there are a couple of decent places to keep hunger at bay or quench your thirst.

La Recova Plaza San Martín s/n. Of the *confiterías* around the plaza – all good for coffee, sandwiches and snacks – this is one of the nicest, housed in the only building in the square to retain an old-fashioned *revoca* (arcade). Daily noon–5.30pm & 8.30pm–midnight.

La Vieja Esquina Calles 25 and 28. A charming traditional corner bar that also sells deli produce, and is famed for its excellent *picadas* (platters of cheese and cold meats). Daily noon–11.30pm.

Lobos

LOBOS, an old-fashioned country town with picturesque, slightly crumbling houses, is best known for its famous son – Juan Domingo Perón – who was born here in 1895 at the house which now bears the address Perón 482; an archive of his letters and photos is stored there (Wed–Sun 10am–noon & 3–6pm; free; ☎ 02227 422843). About 100km southwest of the capital on RN-205, Lobos is also reachable from Mercedes via RP-41.

Laguna de Lobos

Near Lobos is a series of lakes known as *lagunas* (lagoons), the area's main attraction; the biggest is the **Laguna de Lobos**, thought to have been named after the resident otters, *lobos de agua* ("river wolves") in Spanish, hence the name of the town. Excellent fishing, boating and windsurfing are all possible; equipment can be rented from several spots around the lake, where there are also picnic spots shaded by pines and eucalyptus. To get to the quiet lakeside area, around 15km southwest of Lobos, take the local bus that runs every couple of hours from the corner of Alem and 9 de Julio, opposite the train station.

ARRIVAL, INFORMATION AND ACTIVITIES LOBOS

By bus Lobos' new main bus station is on the corner of Héroes de Malvinas and Perón, while the smaller bus terminal faces the train terminal. There are departures to Buenos Aires every 30min (2hr).

By train The train terminal is on the corner of 9 de Julio and Alem, around six blocks east of the town's central square, Plaza 1810. There are two-hourly services to and from Buenos Aires (2hr 30min).

Tourist information Lobos' useful tourist office (Mon–Fri 8am–2pm) is in the Edificio Bicentenario, by the train station on Av Alem 149. Smaller, weekend-only information centres can be found by the entrance of the Lagunas, and in the train station (Sat & Sun 9.30am–6.30pm; ☎ 02227 422275, ⊛ lobos.gov.ar).

Activities Lobos is a centre for both parachuting and polo, with the latter taught at a number of nearby estancias. There is a large and well-equipped skydiving school, CEPA (☎ 02227 1561 3722, ⊛ paracaidismolobos.com.ar), on the RP-205 at Km105, just outside Lobos; all levels are catered for, and tandem jumps with instructors are available.

ACCOMMODATION

Camping Club de Pesca ☎ 02227 494089. Best of the lakeside campsites – rent boats or fish from the jetty. $45
Class Hotel Belgrano and Almafuerte ☎ 02227 430090. This is the pick of a poor bunch of hotels in the centre but it does provide large rooms, an all-hours café and a decent buffet breakfast. $210

Tandil

Birthplace of Argentina's top two tennis players, Juan Martín del Potro and Juan Mónaco, the attractive town of **TANDIL**, many of whose streets are cobbled with stones quarried from nearby, is set among the central section of the **Sistema de Tandilia**, a long range of granite hills. Beginning around 150km northwest of the town and running across the province to Mar del Plata, they seldom rise above 200m; close to Tandil, however, there are craggy peaks of up to 504m. Although this is not wild trekking country, the sierras are ideal for **horseriding** and **mountain biking**. The town itself is well geared for the holiday-makers who come all year on weekend breaks, with some excellent accommodation plus enticing delicatessens and restaurants and a lively, bustling feel in the evening. Tandil is particularly popular during Holy Week, when the Vía Crucis (Stations of the Cross) processions take place; they end at Monte Calvario, a small hillock topped by a giant cross, to the east of the town centre.

Plaza Independencia

The central square, **Plaza Independencia**, on the site of the old fort, is overlooked by the rather grand municipalidad and the overblown **Iglesia del Santísimo Sacramento**. Neo-Romanesque in style, this church was inspired by Paris's Sacré Coeur – hence the unusual elongated domes that top the three towers. A block back at 25 de Mayo and Rodríguez, the far more attractive **Iglesia Luterana Danesa**, built in the 1870s, stands among cypress trees, with a simple white facade that wouldn't look out of place in Jutland – and a reminder of the multiethnic nature of immigration into Buenos Aires in the late nineteenth century. The streets surrounding the plaza, especially 9 de Julio,

have a pleasant, bustling feel, particularly in the evenings, when they are filled with people out for a stroll, or sitting outside the cafés and ice-cream parlours.

Museo Municipal de Bellas Artes

Chacabuco 353 • Tues–Fri 8.30am–12.30pm & Tues–Sun 4–8pm • Free

In a splendid Art Nouveau palace just around the corner from the municipalidad, the surprisingly good **Museo Municipal de Bellas Artes** houses a very worthwhile collection of works by some major names in Argentine art, including Noé, Gorriarena, Quirós and Ferrari, all belonging to the prestigious Santamarina collection, part of which was bequeathed to the museum's national counterpart in Buenos Aires.

Parque Independencia

To the south, Tandil's streets slope down towards **Parque Independencia**, not to be confused with the plaza of the same name. The park's entrance, on Avenida Avellaneda, is marked by the twin towers of a mock-Venetian palazzo, while its central wooded hill is topped by a kitsch Moorish castle. A road snakes around to the summit of the hill, which affords a clear view over the city, and an equally kitsch Moorish bar and restaurant, the *Luz de Luna*, complete with belly dancers.

Museo Tradicionalista

4 de Abril 845 • Tues–Sun 2–6pm • $5

North of the town centre, the **Museo Tradicionalista** occupies a handsome old building and consists of a staggeringly large collection of artefacts donated by locals. Although slightly disorganized, the museum is pleasant to wander around and features some

2

interesting curiosities, including photos of the enormous **Piedra La Movediza** (literally "the moving stone"), which rested at an inconceivably steep angle on one of the town's many rocky outcrops, before finally smashing to the valley floor in 1912. Thought to have given the town its Mapuche name ("Falling Rock"), the stone is so famous nationally that many Argentines are disappointed to arrive and find that it's no longer there; a cement replica now stands in the place where the original once teetered. The museum's warehouses contain many valuable examples of the huge carts, or *chatas*, once used to transport cereals around Argentina; the enormous wheels in the courtyard, the largest in the country, come from a *chata* that needed fifteen horses to pull it. Look out also for the *materas* – huge country hearths – where the gaucho and his clan would take their *mate*, roast their *asado*, stay warm, wash their clothes and do just about everything else.

ARRIVAL AND DEPARTURE   TANDIL

By bus Tandil's bus terminal (☎02293 432092) is around fifteen blocks east of the main square, at Buzón 650; there are usually plenty of taxis (☎02293 422466) waiting at the terminal to take you into town, or you could take local bus #501.

Destinations Azul (6 daily; 2hr); Buenos Aires (hourly; 5hr); Mar del Plata (hourly; 3hr); Necochea (4 daily; 3hr);

San Miguel del Monte (3 daily; 3hr).

By train The train station (☎0800 2228736) is at Av Machado and Colón, around twenty blocks northeast of the main square – trains leave weekly from Buenos Aires on Fridays and return on Sundays, taking 7hr. The return is not recommended as it gets you into dodgy Constitución station late at night.

INFORMATION AND ACTIVITIES

Tourist information The main tourist office is east of the city centre, on the main route in at Av Espora 1120 (summer Mon–Fri 8am–7pm, Sat 10am–7pm, Sun 9am–1pm; winter Mon–Fri 8am–6pm, Sat 10am–6pm, Sun 9am–1pm; ☎02293 432073, ⍵tandil.gov.ar), but there are also smaller, helpful offices at the bus terminal and on Plaza Independencia.

Adventure tour operators Perhaps the best way to explore the region is with the growing number of

companies offering adventure tourism opportunities: Nido de Condores, Necochea 166 ☎02293 426519, ⍵nidode condores.com.ar), runs a range of activities including trekking, abseiling, canoeing and mountain biking; Gabriel Barletta, Avellaneda 673 (☎02293 427725, ⊜cabalgatas barletta@yahoo.com.ar), offers adventurous half-day horse rides around the sierras, and regular group swimming sessions. Mountain bikes can be rented at Av Alvear 121 (☎02293 434313).

ACCOMMODATION

Popular for short breaks throughout the year, Tandil is absolutely inundated in January and even more so at Easter, when most **hotels** substantially increase their prices and are often fully booked up to a month beforehand; otherwise, there is generally a good choice of mid-range accommodation. There are also numerous **cabañas** on the outskirts of the town (the tourist office has plenty of leaflets), although you'll need your own transport to reach most of them. **Campsites** are also numerous.

★ **Albergue Casa Chango** 25 de Mayo 451 ☎02293 422260, ⍵casa-chango.com.ar. Youth hostel in a large, attractive house, colourfully decorated with an artistic touch. Scattered throughout the house are a series of pretty patios perfect for playing chess or chatting with one of the many Argentine students who make up the bulk of the guests. Decent dorms or double rooms. Dorms $50, doubles $270

Camping Chacra El Centinela Av Estrada ☎02293 433475, ⍵chacraelcentinela.com.ar. A quiet and attractive wooded site 4km west of town along the road out towards Cerro El Centinela, with hot water

round the clock and fire pits. Log cabins are also available. $75

★ **Hostería Ave María** Circuito Turístico Paraje La Porteña ☎0249 4422843, ⍵avemariatandil.com.ar One of the best accommodation options in the province, this gorgeous country lodge, some 7km southwest of the centre, is set among stunning grounds, with an avenue of monkey puzzle trees leading down to a walnut grove. Service is excellent and tranquillity is guaranteed – apart from the odd burst of birdsong. Thanks to a prolific kitchen garden the cook can offer guests delicious and generous breakfasts and dinners (the deal is half-board; you can

2

order a *picada* or salad for lunch, too), while you can explore the picturesque surroundings on horseback or in a carriage. A swimming pool is overlooked by fragrant eucalytus, while the dozen charming, comfortable rooms afford sweeping views towards the famed sierras. $1200

Hostería Casa Grande Bolívar 557 ☎02293 431719, ⓦhosteriacasagrande.com.ar. Very comfortable *hostería* in a one-storey stone building with its own decent-sized pool. There's a recreation area with a bar, pool table and, unusually for Argentina, a dartboard. $720

Hostería Lo de Olga Gandolfi Chacabuco 977 ☎02293 440258, ⓦlodeolgagandolfi.com.ar. A lovely rambling old building with a garden and *parrilla*. The furniture's a bit old and creaky, but the rooms are still good value; there are only a few of them and the place

is particularly popular with families, so try to reserve in advance. $400

Hotel Austral 9 de Julio 725 ☎02293 425606, ⓦhotel australtandil.com.ar. A friendly hotel in a modern building. The en-suite rooms are equipped with TV and telephone; the hotel does not offer breakfast but there is an adjoining *confitería*. $280

Plaza Hotel General Pinto 438 ☎02293 427160, ⓦplazahoteldetandil.com.ar. A three-star hotel with slightly sterile but comfortable a/c rooms and restaurant; rooms at the front overlook the plaza. $620

Viñas del Rosario Paz 625 ☎02293 444776, ⓦvinas delrosario.com. An attractive boutique hotel in the centre of town, decorated in Spanish colonial style, with jacuzzis and a garden. Extras include massages. $755

EATING AND DRINKING

There are plenty of good **restaurants** in Tandil, most of them within a few blocks of Plaza Independencia. When all else fails, *La Giralda* and *Eulogia*, on opposite sides of the intersection of Constitución and General Rodríguez, are attractive, old-fashioned places that both do classic, well-priced *parrilladas*. On warm evenings, you'll find plenty of people sitting outside **bars** in the centre of town.

Epoca de Quesos San Martín and 14 de Julio ⓦepocadequesos.com. Northwest of the plaza, this delicatessen-cum-pub is one of Tandil's oldest buildings, a simple, white construction that originally functioned as a staging post and now houses one of the region's major tourist attractions. You can buy local specialities, including every conceivable kind of salami, delicious garlic and herb cheeses, strong whisky cheddar, berry conserves and artisan dark stout. The house behind the deli has been as beautifully preserved as the jams and you can wander its tiny, antique rooms, with their homely little hearths straight out of a Hans Christian Andersen tale. There is a charming terrace shaded by vines but the chairs are

extremely uncomfortable. Daily 9am–11pm.

Liverpool 9 de Julio and San Martín. One of the classic bars on the main plaza; its Anglo-inspired interior comes complete with a red phone box and photos of England. Daily 7pm–late.

Lo de Martín Pinto 965 ☎02293 446050. This upmarket *tenedor libre* serves an impressive range of meats, salads and international dishes. The sucking pig (*lechón*) and lamb have especially good reputations. Daily noon–4pm & 8pm–late.

Paca Bar San Martín 775. For late-night drinking, try the centrally located *Paca Bar*, which sometimes hosts karaoke nights. Daily 7pm–1am.

The Sistema de Tandilia sierras

Opportunities for independent trekking in **Tandil's sierras** are limited, as much of the land is privately owned. The highest peak is the **Sierra Las Animas** (504m), southeast of the town centre, not far from the end of Avenida Brasil. It's a two- to three-hour scramble over rocks to the top, but the peak lies on private land and you must go with a guide – the tourist office has a list. More accessible is **Cerro El Centinela**, a smaller peak topped by an upright 7m rock balanced on an unfeasibly tiny base. To get there, head southwest along Avenida J.M. Estrada, the continuation of Avenida Avellaneda; the signposted track to the Cerro lies to the left, about 6km out of town. As the Cerro has been turned into a complex (ⓦcerroelcentinela.com.ar) with all kinds of attractions, it is rather too developed for some tastes. The road stops just a few metres short of the summit, and – should you feeling hungry – there's a *parrilla*. Nearby is the base of the *aerosilla*, or chairlift (noon–dusk; $35 return), a fifteen-minute ride over the pines of the valley to another, higher peak from where you can enjoy views over the hills as well as waffles and milkshakes at the *Salón de la Cumbre confitería*. You can go on short walks near the chairlift.

Reserva Natural Sierra del Tigre

Don Bosco and Suiza • Daily: summer 9am–6pm; winter 9am–5pm • $10

Several blocks south of town, the **Reserva Natural Sierra del Tigre** is a privately run patch of sierra where you can see indigenous species such as guanaco (cousins to the llama) as well as introduced deer, antelope and wild boar. The *yaguaraté*, a wild cat that gave the sierra its name, no longer prowls around but the hills are home to the tiny striped *marí marí* frog, barely the size of a thumb and found only here and a few other locations in Argentina and Paraguay.

The reserve's highest point is **Cerro Venado** (389m), an easy walk along the unsealed road that winds to the top, from where there are fine views over the surrounding sierra. Near the entrance to the reserve there is a small zoo housing pumas, grey foxes and ñandús (rheas or South American ostriches).

2

The Western Pampas

In the **Western Pampas** towards the border with La Pampa Province, the unremittingly flat landscape is given welcome relief by the modest mountain range of **Sierra de la Ventana**. At the same time, the drier, more desert-like features of the *pampa seca* (dry pampa) herald the start of the long route south into Patagonia. Increasingly popular with domestic visitors, the mountains of the Ventana range offer enjoyable trekking near an attractive settlement – the small town of Sierra de la Ventana, whose many well-equipped *cabañas* are perfect as a base for exploring the area.

Sierra de la Ventana

The rugged **Sierra de la Ventana** mountain range, 550km southwest of Buenos Aires, is the principal attraction of southern Buenos Aires Province. Running from northeast to southwest for 100km or so, the sierras' craggy spine forms a surprising backdrop to the serene pampas and provides the best opportunities in the province for walking and climbing. The range is named after one of its highest points, the **Cerro de la Ventana**, a 1136m peak pierced by a small "window" (*ventana* in Spanish); it's located within the **Parque Provincial Ernesto Tornquist**, bisected by the RP-76, the main highway through the sierras. There are plenty of options for accommodation in the area: as well as a base camp within the park, the nearby village of **Sierra de la Ventana** offers the best setup for visitors; it is situated around 30km southeast of the main park entrance.

Formed principally of sedimentary rock created during the Paleozoic period, the range is notable for its intensely folded appearance and its subtle grey-blue and pink hues. Though the harsh peaks may appear barren, the area supports an amazing range of **wildlife**, including pumas, foxes, guanacos, armadillos, *vizcachas* (rabbit-like rodents appreciated for their meat) and copper iguanas. The latter are named for their distinctive colour and are one of over forty species endemic to the region.

The province's highest peak, **Cerro Tres Picos** (1239m), juts from private land 6km south of Villa Ventana. It is less photogenic than Cerro de la Ventana, but its height, combined with its distance from the nearest base, makes it a more substantial hike. It is usually done as a two-day trek, overnighting in a cave on the way up. The route passes through land belonging to the Germanic *Estancia Funke* (☎0291 494 0058, ⓦfunketurismo.com) and you must go with a guide provided by the owners.

GETTING AROUND	SIERRA DE LA VENTANA

The easiest way of **getting around** the sierras is with your own transport; otherwise, the local La Estrella service runs along the RP-76, stopping anywhere along the route, including at both park entrances and the turn-off to Sierra de la Ventana. Buses travel twice a day in either direction.

2

Parque Provincial Ernesto Tornquist

Summer 8am–6pm; winter 9am–5pm • $20

Most walking and climbing activities take place within a relatively small section of the sierra, largely contained within the 65 square kilometres of **Parque Provincial Ernesto Tornquist**. There are two **entrances** to the park, both just off the RP-76. The Bahía Blanca entrance is around 22km from Sierra de la Ventana village, signposted "Acceso a Reserva Provincial". From the Centro de Visitantes you can also visit the **Reserva Natural Integral**, a strictly controlled sector of the park, where you can see herds of feral horses or explore caves, including one with ancient paintings.

The rest of the park's treks are within the **Monumento Natural**, an area of the park that includes the much-photographed national monument of Cerro Ventana; the entrance is 5km or so west of the main entrance. A well-marked trail to the summit of 1134m **Cerro Ventana** leads northeast from the post. Though the climb to the summit (5hr return trip; access 8am/9am–11am; $25) is not overly demanding, you do need to be quite fit. Follow the park keepers' guidelines and remember that weather conditions can change quickly and dramatically.

ARRIVAL AND INFORMATION   PARQUE PROVINCIAL ERNESTO TORNQUIST

You can visit the reserve in your own vehicle, accompanied by a guide ($70), twice a day, every day, in high season (Dec–Feb) but at weekends only for the rest of the year – enquire at the Centro de Visitantes, which has a good display of photos of the region's flora and fauna and a useful 3D topographical map. There is a helpful *guardaparques'* post (☎0291 491 0039) here, which can usually provide you with a sketchy map of the main attractions, as well as indications of the distance, direction and estimated duration of the walks.

ACCOMMODATION AND EATING

Campamento Base ☎0291 494 0999, ✉rhperrando @yahoo.com.ar. A few minutes' walk west of the *guardaparques'* post, and recognizable from the road by its iron gate, this is the best place to stay if you want to start out early for the park. As well as a shady campsite, the site provides dormitory accommodation and some cabins with wood-burning stoves for up to six people. You'll need to bring sleeping bags for all accommodation options. Cooking facilities and hot showers are provided and there is a small shop with a few basics. Camping $80, dorms $65, cabins $390

Hotel El Mirador ☎0291 494 1338, ⊛complejoel mirador.com.ar. Just outside the park, the hotel offers pleasant rooms overlooking the sierras as well as attractive and well-equipped wooden cabins that hold from four to eight people. It also has a good restaurant and swimming pool. $620

Ich-Hutu This restaurant, whose specialities include rabbit with peppers and onions in *escabeche* (a vinegar-based sauce), is just a few kilometres west of the *Hotel El Mirador* along the RP-76. Daily noon–midnight.

Sierra de la Ventana village

Away from its rather drab main street, Avenida San Martín, **SIERRA DE LA VENTANA** is a delightfully quiet little village with sandy lanes crisscrossed by streams. Divided into several barrios and dissected by both a railway line and the Río Sauce Grande, the village has a rather disjointed layout. Its centre is **Villa Tivoli**, west of the railway tracks; here you'll find most shops and restaurants. By following San Martín east over the rail tracks, you'll come first to **Barrio Parque Golf**, a mostly residential area of curving streets and chalet-style buildings. Most appealing of all is the aptly named **Villa Arcadia** to the north, separated from Barrio Parque Golf by a bridge over the Río Sauce Grande (note that, technically, Villa Arcadia is a different district, so the main tourist office has no information on it). There are various swimming spots throughout the village, mostly to the north of Avenida San Martín, along the banks of the Río Sauce Grande.

ARRIVAL AND INFORMATION   SIERRA DE LA VENTANA VILLAGE

By bus Buses drop you at the small bus terminal on Av San Martín. For return journeys to the capital, it's best to buy tickets in advance.

Destinations Azul (Mon–Fri & Sun 1 daily; 4hr); Buenos Aires (Mon–Fri & Sun 1 daily; 8hr); La Plata (Mon–Fri & Sun 1 daily; 7hr).

By train The train station, with services to and from Buenos Aires (5 weekly; 9hr 45min), is at the intersection of avenidas Roca and San Martín.

Tourist information The busy tourist office is right by the train station on Av del Golf, s/n (daily 8am–8pm, although hours may vary slightly according to the season; ☎0291 491 5303, ⊛sierradelaventana.org.ar).

ACCOMMODATION AND EATING

There is only one hotel to speak of in the vicinity but there are many **campsites** around the village. The most popular accommodation, on both sides of the river, are **cabañas**, which can represent good value for money, and are usually quite cosy and come fully equipped; the tourist office has a complete list. There are few **restaurants** in the village, although there's one very good *parrilla*. A good alternative, especially if you're staying in a *cabaña*, is to visit the popular La Rueda deli, at San Martín 250, and arm your own *picada* from its range of delicious salamis and cheeses.

Balcón del Golf ☎0291 491 5222, ⊛balcondelgolf.com. *Cabañas* with all mod cons as well as a sauna and pool. To get there, head over the bridge into Villa Arcadia and follow the road straight for about 300m. $500

Pillahuincó Parque Hotel Av Raíces 161, Villa La Arcadia ☎0291 491 5423, ⊛hotelpillahuinco.com.ar. This enormous but attractive hotel is set in beautiful grounds with a swimming pool. It organizes trekking and biking excursions in the area and offers half-board, a good idea in view of the lack of restaurants nearby. $500

Rali-Hue San Martín 307. This great little *parrilla* does an excellent and good-value *parrillada* for two people and is well worth a visit. Daily noon–3pm & 8pm–midnight.

La Plata

The pleasant and spacious city of **LA PLATA**, the purpose-built provincial capital, was essentially conceived as an administrative centre and in many ways it shows. For many locals it is simply somewhere to go to carry out the dreaded *trámites*, or bureaucratic procedures. In terms of identity, the city undoubtedly suffers from being so close to Buenos Aires, whose seemingly endless sprawl now laps at its outskirts, practically turning the city that was created as a counterbalance to the capital into its suburb. Nevertheless La Plata boasts a rich cultural life, partly because it is an important **university town**, with three major institutes drawing students from all over the country. One of the city's chief attractions is its bushy park, the **Paseo del Bosque**, ten blocks northeast of the centre, where you will find the **Museo de La Plata**, famed for some remarkable dinosaur skeletons. You won't need to stay overnight, but it makes for an enjoyable excursion from the city.

Brief history

When Buenos Aires became the federal capital in 1880, Buenos Aires Province – by far the wealthiest and most powerful in the republic – was deprived of a centre of government. A year later, the province's newly nominated governor, Dardo Rocha, proposed that a provincial capital be created 50km southeast of the federal capital. The new city's layout was based on an absolutely regular numbered street plan within a 5km square and was designed by the French architect Pedro Benoit. An international competition was held to choose designs for the most important public buildings, and the winning architects included Germans and Italians as well as Argentines, a mix of nationalities reflected in the city's impressive civic architecture. Argentina's first entirely planned city, **La Plata** was officially founded on November 19, 1882. Electric streetlights were installed in 1884 – the first in Latin America. Unfortunately, however, much of La Plata's carefully conceived architectural identity was lost during the twentieth century, as anonymous modern constructions replaced many of the city's original buildings. On a brighter note, there have been some successful attempts to preserve what's left – above all, the old train station, now the wonderful setting for the **Pasaje Dardo Rocha** arts centre, notable not only for its contemporary art museum but also for its stunning interior. The 1990s saw the final

2

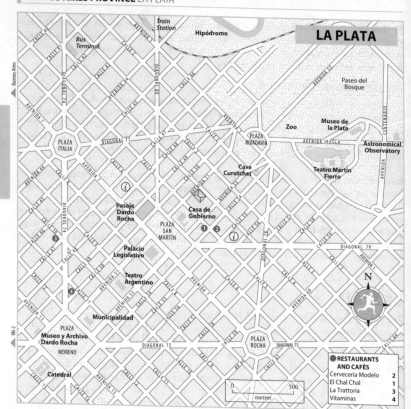

completion of the city's grandiose Neo-Gothic cathedral, over a century after its foundation stone was laid; it dominates Plaza Moreno at the very heart of the city. Another project that took decades to complete, the **Estadio Único** was finally inaugurated in 2011, in time for the Copa América soccer tournament won by Uruguay; the city's new pride and joy, in addition to football and other sporting events the stadium hosts major music concerts.

Plaza Moreno and around

La Plata's official centre is **Plaza Moreno**, a vast open square covering four blocks. The city's foundation stone was laid in the centre of the square in 1882, together with a time capsule containing documents and medals relating to the founding of the city. Over the years, a handful of theories circulated claiming the buried documents offered proof that La Plata was founded according to a secret Masonic scheme. When the capsule was unearthed on the city's centenary, however, the papers were too damaged to bear out the theory. The contents of the exhumed time capsule can be viewed in the **Museo y Archivo Dardo Rocha** (Mon–Fri 9am–5pm, Sat & Sun 3–6pm; free; ☎0221 427 5591), located in the residence once occupied by La Plata's founder on the western side of the square at Calle 50 no. 933. On the northeastern end of the square is the Germanic **municipalidad**, a broad white edifice dominated by a lofty central clock tower and elegant, arched stained-glass windows.

Catedral de la Inmaculada Concepción

Calles 14 and 51 y 53 • Daily 9am–7pm, closed 1–4pm in summer; museum Tues–Sun 10am–7pm • $15 (Sat & Sun $20)

At the southwestern end of Plaza Moreno you can't miss the gigantic, forbidding **Catedral de la Inmaculada Concepción**, which holds the dubious title of South America's largest Neo-Gothic church. Designed by Pedro Benoit, and loosely based on the cathedrals of Amiens and Cologne, it features a pinkish brick facade and steep slate roofs. The foundation stone was laid in 1884 but the cathedral was not completed until 1932, with its two principal towers not finished until 1999. If the cathedral doesn't strike you as exactly beautiful, it is certainly tremendously imposing, with its soaring, vertigo-inducing interior punctuated by austere ribbed columns, while its high windows make it surprisingly light and airy. The **museum** in the atmospheric crypt is entered via the *confitería*-cum-*santería* (shop selling religious objects) accessed on either side of the main steps. Along with temporary exhibitions of religious art, it features some excellent photographs documenting the cathedral's construction and also gives access to a *mirador* (viewpoint), in the **Torre de Jesús**, the south tower; 63m high and accessed by two lifts, it offers great views of La Plata and its distinctive urban plan.

Teatro Argentino de La Plata

Calles 51 and 9 y 10 • Tues–Sun 10am–8pm • ☏ 0221 429 1732, ⓦ teatroargentino.ic.gba.gov.ar

Two blocks northeast of Plaza Moreno is the site where the grand Italianate **Teatro Argentino de La Plata**, second in national importance after Buenos Aires' Teatro Colón, once stood. Sadly, it was razed to the ground after it was destroyed by a suspicious fire in the 1970s and rebuilt as an octagonal concrete monolith. Undeniably hideous, the structure is impressively vast and the theatre puts on a decent selection of concerts, operas and plays – contact the box office or consult the website for programme details.

Plaza San Martín

Avenidas 51 and 53 lead from Plaza Moreno to **Plaza San Martín**, the real hub of city life. This square is more intimate than Plaza Moreno, though it too is flanked by government buildings. At the northeastern end there's the **Casa de Gobierno**, a sturdy, mock Flemish-Renaissance building with a central slate-roofed dome; to the southwest you'll find the **Palacio Legislativo**, designed in the style of the German Renaissance – its grand Neoclassical entrance sitting slightly awkwardly on a more restrained facade.

Pasaje Dardo Rocha

Plaza San Martín s/n • Daily 9am–10pm • Free

More interesting than the square's civic edifices is the **Pasaje Dardo Rocha**, on its northwestern side. This elegant pitched-roof building, whose three-storey facade mixes French and Italian influences, was built in 1883 as the city's first train station. After the station moved to its current site, the Pasaje was remodelled and it now functions as an important **cultural centre** comprising a small cinema and various art museums, including the very worthwhile **Museo de Arte Contemporáneo Latinoamericano**, or **MACLA** (daily 9am–10pm; free). The galleries are located around a stunning Doric-columned central hall, where natural light (enhanced by a discreet modern lighting system) filters down through a high glass roof onto a vast sweep of black-and-white-tiled floor.

Paseo del Bosque and around

From Plaza San Martín, Avenida 53 heads northeast past the Casa de Gobierno. After four blocks you come to the monumental Plaza Rivadavia, next to the **Paseo del Bosque**, La Plata's major green space. Before crossing busy Avenida 1 and entering the

2

park, take a small detour along Boulevard 53, a short diagonal road curving off to the right of the plaza. The beautifully laid-out park features an artificial lake, a sad zoo and a botanical garden, but the main attraction is the city's main museum.

Casa Curutchet

Blvd 53 no. 320 • Tues–Fri hourly visits 10.30am–1.30pm; closed public holidays & Jan • $40 • ☎ 0221 482 2631, ⓦ capba.org.ar/curutchet/casa-curutchet-presentacion.htm

Halfway along Boulevard 53 stands the angular **Casa Curutchet**, the only Le Corbusier-designed residence built in Latin America (another, Chile's Maison Errazuriz, was commissioned but never erected). Commissioned by local surgeon Pedro Curutchet in 1948, the house is a typical Le Corbusier construction, combining functionality with a playful use of colour and perspective, and was the setting for the 2010 Argentine film *El hombre de al lado* ("The Man Next Door"). The building now houses the Colegio de Arquitectos de la Provincia de Buenos Aires and is open to visitors.

Museo de La Plata (Museo de Ciencias Naturales)

Paseo del Bosque s/n • Tues–Sun 10am–6pm; open Mon on public holidays • $6; free Tues (except public holidays) • ⓦ fcnym.unlp.edu.ar/indexmuseo.html

Within the Paseo del Bosque is the first purpose-built museum in Latin America (and something of a relic in itself), the **Museo de La Plata**. Housed in the Universidad Nacional de La Plata's natural science faculty, it is sometimes known as the **Museo de Ciencias Naturales** and is a real treat for anyone with a fondness for old-fashioned museums. Run by the university, the city's only worthwhile museum struggles to live up to its self-proclaimed reputation as one of the world's major natural history collections, but is certainly worth a visit for its picturesque presentation and fascinating contents, including some fabulous dinosaur remains. The exterior is very grand: the Neoclassical architecture is set off by a colonnaded entrance and a staircase lined with sculptures of sabre-toothed cats. Inside the museum is gradually being remodelled and modern audiovisuals make a brief and rather shaky appearance in the first rooms. However, later rooms, such as the six dedicated to zoology, have been deliberately preserved to look just as they did when the museum was first opened in 1888, with the embalmed birds and animals exhibited in glass cases, albeit with new easy-to-read labels.

The museum has 21 rooms, all chronologically ordered, including an impressive **paleontological section** that contains a reproduction of a gigantic diplodocus skeleton, and the original skeleton of a neuquensaurus, a herbivorous dinosaur common in northern Patagonia towards the end of the Cretaceous Period. Room VI is dedicated to the beginnings of the **Cenozoic Period**, also known as the Age of Mammals, which extends from around 65 million years ago to the present day. It houses the museum's most important collection: the megafauna, a group of giant herbivorous mammals that evolved in South America at the time when the region was separated from the other continents. The room's striking collection of skeletons includes the creepy gliptodon, forerunner of today's armadillo, and the enormous megatherium, largest of the megafauna, which, when standing upright on its powerful two hind legs, would have reached almost double its already impressive six metres.

Upstairs, a **Latin American ethnology and anthropology** section showcases items used by the continent's main indigenous groups, from the colourful, feathered headdresses of Bolivian carnival participants to the simple wood and leather articles of Tierra del Fuego's Onas. A sizeable collection of marvellous Pre-Columbian ceramics is let down by the lacklustre display.

ARRIVAL AND INFORMATION   LA PLATA

For a place designed along ultra-rational lines, La Plata can be quite a challenge to navigate. The prevalence of streets cutting across the blocks is very disorienting, and you won't need to walk around for very long to see why it's known as the "**city of diagonals**". While the convergence of similar-looking streets can be confusing, the city is small enough that you're unlikely to go too far off track. It helps to know that all of La Plata's major points of interest lie along or just off avenidas 51 and 53. A brisk walk will get you to all the sights, without any need for public transport.

By bus At the bus terminal, on the corner of calles 4 and 42, you can catch frequent, quick and safe buses to and from the capital (every 15min; 1hr; $25) and most major cities throughout the country.

By train Theoretically, the most appealing place to arrive in La Plata is at the beautiful *fin-de-siècle* train station, on the corner of avenidas 1 and 44, a dozen blocks northwest of the town centre; the train itself, however, which shuttles between here and Constitución in Buenos Aires (every 30min; 1hr 15min), is far from beautiful – in fact it is dirty and, at times, downright dangerous.

Tourist information La Plata's tourist office (Mon–Fri 9am–5pm; ☎0221 422 9764, ⓦ laplata.gov.ar) is in the Palacio Campodónico on Diagonal 79 between calles 5 and 56; there's also an information centre in the Pasaje Dardo Rocha (daily 10am–5pm; ☎0221 427 1535).

EATING AND DRINKING

As provincial capital, La Plata is large and sophisticated enough to have some culinary breadth. There are some very decent **restaurants**, mostly aimed at businessmen, although you'll find local hangouts more convivial – the bulk of these are located around the intersection of calles 10 and 47 along Diagonal 74.

Cervecería Modelo Calles 5 and 54 ☎0221 421 1321, ⓦ cerveceriamodelo.com.ar. The vast wood-panelled interior of the city's best-known bar-restaurant is hung with hams, Iberian-style. The seemingly endless menu includes everything from hamburgers and liverwurst sandwiches to *bife de chorizo* and seafood. The food and service are run-of-the-mill but prices are moderate. Daily 8am–1am.

El Chal Chal Calle 54 no. 507 ☎0221 483 0077. Diagonally opposite the Modelo, this place named after a native tree is an upmarket *parrilla*, serving fine cuts of meat and decent wines – though the service can be very slow.

The generous *parrilla* for two is good value. Mon–Sat 11am–4pm & 8pm–1am, Sun 11am–4pm.

La Trattoria Intersection of calles 10, 47 and Diagonal 74 ☎0221 422 6135. This restaurant-cum-café offers great views of the to and fro of La Plata life from its wooden tables and small but lively terrace. The mainstays are pizza and pasta but you can also have breakfast and tea here – the cakes and pastries are not bad at all. Daily 8am–1am.

Vitaminas Diagonal 74 no. 1640 ☎0221 482 1106. A colourful restaurant and bar, serving healthy vegetarian dishes and excellent-value lunchtime specials. Mon–Sat 11am–2.30pm & 7.30pm–midnight, Sun 11.30am–4pm.

The Interbalnearia

The endless string of resorts along the easternmost coast of Buenos Aires Province are connected by the RP-11, known as the **Interbalnearia** (literally, the inter-resort road). They include the trendy pair of **Pinamar** and **Villa Gesell** and their smaller, but rapidly growing, satellites **Cariló** and **Mar de las Pampas**, around which sand dunes and pine forests dominate the landscape. The route from La Plata runs southeast along the RP-36, threading through flat pampas, dotted with cows and divided at intervals by tree-lined drives leading to estancias. Tall metal wind-pumps, which extract irrigation water from beneath the surface of the land, inject a little drama into the scene, while giant cardoon thistles – a desiccated brown in summer – sprout in clusters like outsize bouquets. The RP-36 joins the RP-11 around 90km southeast of La Plata.

Pinamar

PINAMAR gets its name from the surrounding pinewoods planted among dunes by the town's founder, Jorge Bunge, in the 1930s; this attractive setting is now rather spoiled by a mix of high-rise buildings and ostentatious chalet-style constructions. Pinamar stretches southwards along the coast, swallowing up the neighbouring resorts of **Ostende** and **Valeria del Mar**, tranquil places that can be easily reached as a day-trip, albeit with their own accommodation options. Long the favourite resort of the Porteño

2

elite, in the 1990s the resort symbolized the high-living lifestyle of the Menem era, and the exploits of the politicians and celebrities who holidayed here were staples of the gossip mags. Pinamar fell out of popularity for a while following the high-profile murder of an investigative journalist here in 1997 and the post-2001 economic recession, but has bounced back with a vengeance. It remains a hugely popular summer holiday spot and, although it has lost its exclusive crown to places like Cariló, it is more expensive than many other Argentine seaside resorts.

Avenida Bunge and the beach

Pinamar's broad main street, **Avenida Bunge**, is flanked by restaurants and branches of the same boutiques that fill most of the capital's malls. Bunge runs east to west through the town centre, ending at beachfront Avenida del Mar. The attractive **beach** is the town's big draw, its pale sands dotted with delicate shells and, to the north and south of the town centre, bordered by high dunes. Various companies offer excursions by jeep to the most dramatic section of dunes, where, during the summer, you can have a go at **sandboarding**; ask at the tourist office for details.

ARRIVAL AND INFORMATION

By plane The closest airport to Pinamar is at Villa Gesell (see p.160).

By bus All long-distance buses arrive at the terminal at Jason 2250, several blocks west of the town centre, just off Av Bunge.

Destinations Buenos Aires (10 daily; 5hr); Mar del Plata (hourly; 2hr).

By train The train station, served by Ferrobaires (☎011 4305 0157), which runs trains to and from Buenos Aires'

Constitución station (3 weekly; 5hr 15min), is a couple of kilometres west of town, a short taxi ride away.

Tourist information With glossy brochures advertising golf courses, spas and estate agencies, the tourist office, at Av Shaw 18 (Jan & Feb daily 8am–9pm; March–Dec Mon–Sat 8am–8pm, Sun 10am–6pm; ☎02254 491680, ⍟pinamar.gov.ar), is heavily geared towards Pinamar's well-off visitors, but also provides decent maps and guides.

ACCOMMODATION

Hotels in Pinamar and its satellite resorts are plentiful, if generally expensive, with little in the way of decent budget accommodation (there aren't many campsites, either). As in all resorts, reservations are advisable in high season.

Algeciras Hotel Av del Libertador 75 ☎02254 485550, ⍟algecirashotel.com.ar. A large and off-puttingly ugly building houses this luxurious, top-of-the-range place, which has a swimming pool, sauna and nursery. $830

Las Calas Hotel Boutique Av Bunge 560 ☎02254 405999, ⍟lascalashotel.com.ar. Predominantly designed from wood, this highly regarded designer hotel has an intimate interior courtyard (smoke-free) and spacious rooms. $720

Camping Quimey Lemú 250m north of the entrance to town along the RP-11 ☎02254 484949, ⍟quimey lemu.com.ar. One of the best campsites hereabouts is set in attractive wooded grounds with plenty of facilities. It also has some basic cabins for rent – and tents for rent, too. Camping $40, cabins $280

Camping Saint Tropez Quintana 138 ☎02254 482498, ⍟sainttropezpinamar.com.ar. On the border with Ostende, this small but conveniently located campsite also rents out apartments. $35

Hotel Casablanca Av de los Tritones 258 ☎02254 482474, ⍟casablancapinamar.com.ar. A block from the

beach, the *Casablanca* offers light, airy rooms, some with balconies. Closed April–Nov, except Semana Santa. $480

Hotel Viejo Ostende Biarritz 799, Ostende ☎02254 486081, ⍟hotelostende.com.ar. A beautifully preserved reminder of the days when this pioneer resort hosted literary figures such as Argentine author Adolfo Bioy Casares and French writer Antoine de St-Exupéry. The rooms are quite simple and you do pay over the odds for the ambience, but the price includes breakfast and dinner, access to the hotel swimming pool, a beach tent at the *balneario* and a nursery, so it is actually a good deal. $1000

Playas Hotel Av Bunge 250 ☎02254 482236, ⍟playas hotel.com.ar. *Playas* is Pinamar's longest-established hotel, housed in a stately white building. It generally attracts a more mature clientele, with its elegant rooms and bar and quiet grounds. There's a swimming pool and a nine-hole golf course. $900

Posada Pecos Odiseo and Silenios ☎02254 484386, ⍟posadapecos.com.ar. This charmingly relaxed place has attractive tiled floors and whitewashed walls that lend it a slightly rustic feel. The rooms are perfectly comfortable, though, and very good value. $620

EATING, DRINKING AND NIGHTLIFE

The majority of Pinamar's **restaurants** are bunched around Avenida Bunge and along the seafront. Several of them specialize in fresh seafood and fish. **Nightlife** is mostly centred on a handful of bars along Avenida Bunge and the seafront. Pinamar's biggest nightclubs are *Ku* and *El Alma*, on Quintana and Nuestras Malvinas respectively, which play everything from dance to rock and salsa.

Paco Bar Av de las Artes 156. A good, traditional-style bar, its walls and counters stuffed with memorabilia. Daily 7pm–1am.

Paxapoga Avenidas del Mar and Bunge ☎02254 405098. This traditional upmarket restaurant offers good-value Argentine fare plus pricier but well-prepared fish and seafood, including excellent squid. Daily noon–3pm & 9pm–late.

Tante De las Artes 35 ☎02254 482735 (branch at Av Bunge 400). The best of Pinamar's cooking is undoubtedly found at this teahouse and restaurant. The wide-ranging menu offers elaborate, mostly Germanic, dishes, including some good vegetarian options, and at teatime there's a number of exotic tea blends with which to wash down some exceptionally good cakes. Daily noon–11.30pm.

Tulumei Bunge 64. A small and friendly place with a laidback atmosphere, good music and imaginative seafood dishes. Daily noon–3.30pm & 8pm–late.

UFO Point Av del Mar and Tobías. This beachfront bar is one of the most consistently cool places in town, and where you'll find the best DJs. Daily 7pm–1am.

Viejo Lobo Avenidas del Mar and Bunge. This Pinamar classic – the name means "old salt" – pleases locals, regulars and newcomers alike with a wide-ranging menu focusing on fish and seafood. Daily noon–4pm & 8.30pm–late.

Cariló

Pinamar merges seamlessly with **Ostende**, **Valeria del Mar** and finally **CARILÓ**, the area's most exclusive resort. While Ostende and Valeria del Mar are effectively quieter suburbs of Pinamar, Cariló has more of a separate personality, a fact made clear as Calle Bathurst, the paved main street of Valeria del Mar, abruptly turns to a sand track with a sign announcing the entrance to Cariló's exclusive "parque" on Calle Divisadero. An idyllic pine forest dotted with luxury hotels, spas and designer shops, this is where Argentina's rich and powerful come to get pampered, hidden away from the rest of society. While aparthotels and rental homes maintain a tasteful distance from each other, and development in the village is controlled by tight laws, the amount of new construction spiralled in the new millennium – too fast for some locals – and you're still likely to hear the distant hubbub of building work among the tweeting birds. Cariló nevertheless remains a tranquil place, albeit one significantly more expensive than other resorts nearby. If you can afford it, and don't mind the often snooty attitude of some of its regulars, its varied and thick vegetation, quiet, sandy streets and gourmet restaurants can make it a very agreeable destination. Stressed-out professional Porteños come to Cariló to *desenchufarse* ("unplug themselves"), but if you fancy some activity, **horseriding** and **polo** lessons are possible at the Estancia Dos Montes (☎02254 480045), just west of the village. Alternatively you can organize **sandboarding** on the plentiful dunes through Turismo Aventura (☎02267 1567 6835) or whizz around the sand on a 4WD buggy with Buggycar (office in Pinamar; ☎02254 492809).

ARRIVAL AND INFORMATION   CARILÓ

By bus Cariló is connected by the local Montemar bus to Valeria del Mar, Ostende and Pinamar, where the nearest long-distance bus terminal is located. Alternatively you can simply stroll along the beach, which runs for 10km or so without interruptions past all of them.

Tourist information Cariló's tourist board, a small wooden hut on the corner of Boyero and Castaño (☎02254 570773), has minimal information, probably since the main office in Pinamar covers all the satellite resorts.

ACCOMMODATION

Accommodation is all high-end luxury, with nothing near a budget option in sight. Most places – whether hotel, self-catering apartment or *cabaña* – include a wide range of excellent services.

La Estación Bandurria and Cerezo ☎ 02254 570829, ⓦ laestaciondecarilo.com.ar. Set among the woods, this charming *hostería* also offers well-equipped apartments; breakfast is served in your room. **$750**

La Hostería Cariló Jacarandé 7167 ☎ 02254 570704, ⓦ hosteriacarilo.com.ar. Decorated with the owner's photography, this outstanding boutique hotel puts on film screenings in its small underground cinema and there are thousands of DVDs behind reception. There's also a swimming pool and the enticing *Tiramisú* restaurant. **$800**

Marcin Hotel Laurel and Albatros ☎ 02254 570888, ⓦ hotelmarcin.com.ar. A modern hotel in a multistorey block, nevertheless offering charming mellow-hued rooms commanding ocean views. **$550**

EATING AND DRINKING

Cattalina Boyero and Castaño ☎ 02254 571922. Located in the upmarket Feria del Bosque shopping centre, this is the place to come for excellent Italian pasta dishes served with delicious sauces. Daily noon–4pm & 8pm–late.

Hemingway Lambertiana s/n ☎ 02254 571585. A local classic with great ocean views, this trendy haunt in a wooden building serves up sushi and other fish dishes during summer months. Oozing luxury, the place even boasts a downstairs spa. Daily noon–late.

Villa Gesell and around

Separated from Cariló by a strictly off-limits nature reserve, **VILLA GESELL** is reached by taking the RP-11 a further 10km or so south. The town is named after its founder, Carlos Gesell, a mildly eccentric Porteño of German descent. In 1931, Gesell bought a large swathe of coastal land, largely dominated by still-moving sand dunes. Inspired by methods used in Australia, Gesell managed to stabilize the dunes by planting a mixture of vegetation including tamarisk, acacia and esparto grass. He sold lots, many of which were bought by Germans and Central Europeans escaping World War II. Favoured by hippies in the 1960s and 70s, Gesell has a more laidback feel than some of its smarter neighbours and teeters on the edge of being run down. The resort remains popular with Argentina's middle and working classes, plus teenage groups enjoying holidays away from their parents. If you fancy something a bit livelier, head for one of Villa Gesell's popular **balnearios** spread out along the length of the beach, such as *Amy*, *AfriKa* or *13 al Sur*, which vie with each other every year to become the season's show-off spot.

The winding streets – many of them unsealed – do their best to defeat the Teutonic order imposed by a complex system of numbered avenidas (which run parallel to the sea), paseos, calles and alamedas, designed by Gesell to follow the natural course of the land. The town's main street is Avenida 3, the centre of its lively nightlife.

Reserva Parque Cultural and Museo Histórico Municipal

At the northern end of town, and entered from Alameda 202, lies the **Reserva Parque Cultural**. Designed by Gesell, the park's wooded walkways offer welcome shade on hot days, and the dunes that separate it from the beach to the east are particularly good for sunbathing or picnicking. The house used by Gesell has been turned into a small **Museo Histórico Municipal** (summer daily 10am–8pm; winter Tues–Sat 10am–4pm, Sun 2–5pm; $5); it is dedicated to Carlos and his father, Silvio, a leading economist.

ARRIVAL AND DEPARTURE VILLA GESELL

By plane Villa Gesell's airport (☎ 02255 458345) is 3km south from the turn-off to town on the RP-11, with regular flights during the summer to and from Buenos Aires with Sol (4 daily, summer only; 1hr; ☎ 011 503 14212, ⓦ sol.com.ar). A shuttle runs from the airport to the town, dropping off at central hotels.

By bus The town's main bus terminal is around 3km south of the centre, at Av 3 and Paseo 140; you'll probably want to get a local bus (#504, which will drop you off close to Av 3) or taxi to the centre.

Destinations Bariloche (1 daily; 22hr); Buenos Aires (hourly; 6hr); Córdoba (1 daily; 17hr); Mar del Plata (5 daily; 2hr).

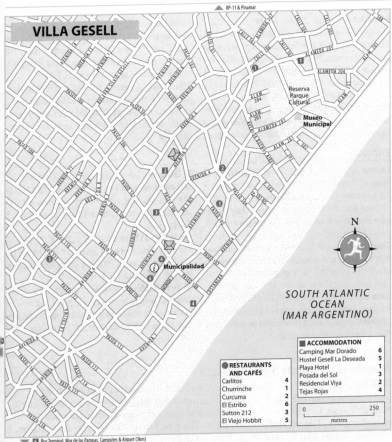

RESTAURANTS AND CAFÉS

Carlitos	4
Churrinche	1
Curcuma	2
El Estribo	6
Sutton 212	3
El Viejo Hobbit	5

ACCOMMODATION

Camping Mar Dorado	6
Hostel Gesell La Deseada	5
Playa Hotel	1
Posada del Sol	3
Residencial Viya	2
Tejas Rojas	4

INFORMATION

Tourist information The popularity of Gesell is reflected by its five tourist offices. The most central one is at Av 3 no. 820 (summer daily 8am–midnight; winter daily 9am–8pm; ☎02255 478042, ⓦgesell.gov.ar). Other useful ones are at the bus terminal (summer only 6am–1pm & 5pm–1am), and further out on the road towards Mar de las Pampas at Av 3 and Paseo 174 (Fri–Sun 10am–5pm).

Bike rental There are various places to rent bikes in town; try Casa Macca, on Av Buenos Aires between Paseo 101 and Av 5 (☎02255 468013), or Rodados Luis, on Paseo 107 between avenidas 4 and 5 (☎02255 463897).

ACCOMMODATION

As with the other coastal resorts, the cost of accommodation varies considerably according to the season. Many places cut prices by at least fifty percent out of season; others close altogether. It is easier to find budget accommodation here than in Pinamar and the tourist office holds a complete list of these as well as Villa Gesell's numerous **campsites**, all of which are some distance from the centre, with some of the nicest among the dunes at the southern end of town.

Camping Mar Dorado Av 3 and Paseo 170 ☎02255 470963, ⓦmardorado.com.ar. Set among woods and with its own beach, this is the best campsite in the resort – plenty of activities laid on and you can rent a tent, too, if you don't have your own. $75

Hostel Gesell La Deseada Av 6 no. 1183 ☎02255 473276, ⓦladeseadahostel.com.ar. Modern hostel with six shared dorms and some doubles outside high season. Great views of woodland and a spacious communal living room. Dorms $140, doubles $390

2

Playa Hotel Alameda 205 and 303 ☎02255 458027, ⓦgesell.com.ar/playahotel. Villa Gesell's oldest hotel is set in wooded grounds near the nature reserve, far from the bustle of the centre. The pretty whitewashed building has pleasant, simply decorated rooms. Closed April–Oct. $480

Posada del Sol Av 4 no. 642 ☎02255 462086, ⓦgesell .com.ar/posadadelsol. Definitely the most unusual place in town, this very friendly posada has a mini-zoo in its garden in which parrots, flamingoes and rabbits wander freely. Rooms are small but comfortable and well equipped.

Closed April–Nov. $510

Residencial Viya Av 5 no. 582 ☎02255 462757, ⓦgesell .com.ar/viya. The best of the town's budget places, this charming *residencial* has a pleasant garden and seating area, along with plain but very well kept rooms. $320

Tejas Rojas Costanera no. 848 ☎02255 462565, ⓦhoteltejasrojas.com.ar. This beachfront hotel is in a cool, tiled and spacious building and has a swimming pool. Rooms with sea views cost slightly more. Closed Easter–Oct. $760

EATING

Carlitos Av 3 no. 184 ☎02255 464611. The self-styled "King of Pancakes" makes them with an exhaustive range of savoury and sweet fillings. A super-sweet *dulce de leche* pancake following on from a fully loaded hamburger should satisfy even the hungriest punters. Daily 11am–11pm.

Churrinche Alameda 205. This European-style teahouse with a beautiful garden and delicious cakes also sells jars of artisanal *dulces* that make great souvenirs. Summer daily 8am–4pm; winter Fri–Sun 3pm–midnight.

Curcuma Paseo 104 and Av 4 ☎02255 473989. A homely restaurant packing everything from beef brochettes to chop suey into its menu, as well as an exhaustive range of desserts. Daily noon–3pm & 8pm–midnight.

El Estribo Av 3 and Paseo 109 ☎02255 466357. The best traditional *parrilla* in town serves delicious *bifes de chorizo* as well as all manner of fish, including sole with boiled potatoes, for the meat-shy. Daily noon–3.30pm & 7.30pm–1am.

★ **Sutton 212** Paseo 105 no. 212 ☎02255 460674. The funky decor gives it the feeling of a laidback bar, but the kitchen serves up great mid-priced food. Summer daily 10–5am; winter Fri & Sat 5pm–5am.

El Viejo Hobbit Av 8 between paseos 111 and 112. Countless pints of home-brew are pulled and delicious platters of farmhouse cheeses dished up in enjoyable faux-Middle Earth surroundings. Daily 6pm–late; closed April–Dec.

Mar de las Pampas and Mar Azul

MAR DE LAS PAMPAS, just south of Villa Gesell, is a haven of tranquil pine forests and pampas grass. The beach is not as deserted as you might expect, since it is easily accessible from Gesell, but inland you can lose yourself along sandy tracks that meander around dunes and woody valleys. The pine forest setting is not dissimilar to Cariló's, though Mar de las Pampas has a more down-to-earth feel – for now. There is no real division between it and **MAR AZUL**, a short way south and distinguished from its neighbour only by its more regular lanes and lesser development. The pair are currently enjoying a reputation for maintaining the bohemian spirit of Villa Gesell, with blues musicians playing at local pub *Mr Gone* on Mar Azul's main drag, Avenida Mar del Plata, and *Blue Beach*, a *balneario* cultivating a chilled-out atmosphere.

ARRIVAL AND INFORMATION   MAR DE LAS PAMPAS AND MAR AZUL

By plane/train/bus The nearest airport is at Villa Gesell (see p.160) and Pinamar has the closest train station. To reach either resort by bus from Buenos Aires, you will usually have to go to Pinamar and change. Both can be reached on foot from Villa Gesell, either along the beach or via Avenida 3, but it's a hefty walk. Alternatively,

take the local bus, which leaves every half-hour from behind the bus terminal on Avenida 4 and passes through both villages.

Tourist information Gesell's tourist offices have maps and accommodation information for both Mar de las Pampas and Mar Azul.

ACCOMMODATION

Aqui me Quedo Cuyo and Roca, Mar de las Pampas ☎02255 479884, ⓦaquimequedonet.com.ar. The best of the typical Mar de las Pampas *cabañas* complexes, with a heated pool, solarium and gym surrounded by exuberant vegetation. $760

Camping del Sur Av Mar del Plata and c/47, two blocks from Mar Azul's beach ☎02255 479502, ⓦcampingdel sur.com.ar. The twin resorts' best campsite nestles among fragrant pine woods just two blocks from Mar Azul's beach. You can sleep in dorms, too. Camping $65, dorms $70

Hostal de las Piedras Intersection of Cuyo, Virazón and Mercedes Sosa, Mar de las Pampas ☎02255 454220, ⓦhostaldelaspiedras.com. This upmarket *hostal* has large rooms each with private outdoor spaces. The decor is deliberately rustic, with bare brick walls and cool floor tiles. **$690**

Hostería Alamos Av Mar del Plata and c/35, Mar Azul ☎02255 479631, ⓦalamoshosteria.com.ar. Mar Azul's

only hotel, just one block from the oceanfront, has pleasantly simple doubles and suites in a Swiss-style building. There is a swimming pool and private parking. **$770**

Poetas del Bosque Copacabana y c/45, Mar Azul ☎011 4822 6686, ⓦpoetasdelbosque.com.ar. This decidedly poetic *cabañas* complex, with rooms for two to six people, is idyllically located in the woods suggested by the name. **$600**

Mar del Plata and around

Big, busy and brash, **MAR DEL PLATA** (or Mardel to initiates) dwarfs every other resort on Argentina's Atlantic coast. Around six million mostly Argentine tourists holiday here every year, drawn by its bustling beaches and lively entertainment, earning it the nickname La Feliz, or the Happy City. The seventh biggest city in Argentina, Mardel's primarily a place where the Argentine working classes go to forget their daily grind and chill out for two or three weeks every summer. If the thought of seeking an unoccupied towel-sized scrap of sand every morning or queuing for a restaurant every evening makes you shudder, you're better off avoiding the resort in January and February. On the other hand, if you quite like mixing your trips to the beach with a spot of culture, nightlife or shopping, you may appreciate the city's cheeky charm. Physically Mar del Plata is favoured by the gentle drama of a sweeping coastline and hilly terrain, and while its rather urban beaches may lack the unspoilt tranquillity of some other resorts, they are certainly fun places to hang out and great for people-watching.

Furthermore Mar del Plata is the only resort really worth visiting out of season – while the city folk may breathe a sigh of relief when the last of the tourists leave at the end of the summer, it certainly doesn't close down. The city enjoys a rich cultural life that includes a number of modest but interesting **museums** and **galleries**, and one of Argentina's most important **ports**, appealing for its colourful traditional fishing boats and seafood restaurants. The oceanfront is dominated by haphazard modern developments but scattered here and there are some wonderfully quirky buildings, built in a decorative – even fantastical – style known as *pintoresquista*, an eclectic brew of mostly Neo-Norman and mock-Tudor architecture.

The official centre is **Plaza San Martín** but on summer days the city's true heart lies further south, around **Playa Bristol** and the **Rambla Casino**, a pedestrian promenade flanking the grand casino and landmark *Gran Hotel Provincial* (see p.168). Aside from the beaches and away from the quiet neighbourhood of **La Perla**, there's little in the way of sightseeing in the city centre. Culture vultures will want to head south to the rollercoaster streets of **Loma Stella Maris**, where they'll find the Museo Municipal de Arte Juan Carlos Castagnino, or to the quiet residential area of **Divino Rostro**, home to the Villa Victoria cultural centre and the Archivo Museo Histórico Municipal. South along the coast, a visit to the colourful fishing **port** makes a fine way to end the day – for both the lively bustle of returning fishermen and the majestic (but noisy and smelly) sea lions who have made their home at the port's southern end.

Brief history

Founded in 1874, Mar del Plata was soon developed into a European-style bathing resort, following the vision of Pedro Luro, a successful Basque merchant. As the railway began to expand into Buenos Aires Province, Mar del Plata became accessible to visitors from the capital, with the first passenger train arriving in September 1886. The subsequent opening of the town's first hotel in 1888 – the luxurious, long-gone **Hotel Bristol** – was a great occasion for the Buenos Aires elite, many of whom travelled down for the opening on an overnight train.

Nevertheless the richest of Argentina's very rich continued to make their regular pilgrimages to Europe and it took the outbreak of World War I to dampen Argentine enthusiasm for the journey across the Atlantic and to firmly establish Mar del Plata as an exclusive resort. **Mass tourism** began to arrive in the 1930s, helped by improved roads, but took off in the 1940s and 1950s, when the development of union-run hotels under Perón finally put the city within the reach of Argentina's middle and working classes. The horrified rich then abandoned it for the more genteel Pinamar and Uruguay's Punta del Este, while Menem's peso–dollar parity in the 1990s meant the

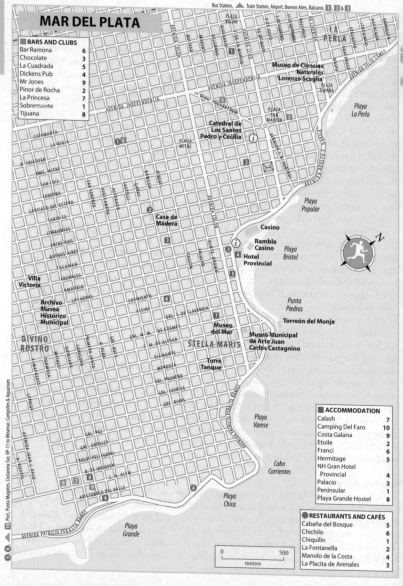

MAR DEL PLATA

■ BARS AND CLUBS	
Bar Ramona	6
Chocolate	3
La Cuadrada	5
Dickens Pub	4
Mr Jones	9
Pinor de Rocha	2
La Princesa	7
Sobremonte	1
Tijuana	8

■ ACCOMMODATION	
Calash	7
Camping Del Faro	10
Costa Galana	9
Etoile	2
Franci	6
Hermitage	5
NH Gran Hotel Provincial	4
Palacio	3
Peninsular	1
Playa Grande Hostel	8

● RESTAURANTS AND CAFÉS	
Cabaña del Bosque	5
Chichilo	6
Chiquilin	1
La Fontanella	2
Manolo de la Costa	4
La Placita de Arenales	3

middle classes found it cheaper to sunbathe in Florida and the Caribbean than on the Argentine coast. The 2001 crisis and devaluation led to a resurgence in Mardel's popularity; in 2009 the *Gran Hotel Provincial* reopened after lengthy restoration.

Plaza San Martín and the microcentro

Plaza San Martín, Mar del Plata's spacious main square, covers four blocks. The inevitable statue of San Martín, by sculptor Luis Perlotti, unusually depicts the general in his old age. At the southern end of the square, the Neo-Gothic **Catedral de los Santos Pedro y Cecilia** with its French stained-glass windows was designed by Pedro Benoit, chief architect of La Plata (see p.153).

To the south of the square extends the hectic **microcentro**; its main thoroughfare, pedestrianized Calle San Martín, gets so packed with holiday-makers and street performers on summer evenings that it can be difficult to weave your way through. Easier to negotiate is Avenida Pedro Luro: eight blocks northwest of Plaza San Martín it brings you to **Plaza Rocha**, where there is a small **fair** (Tues & Sat 9am–1pm) selling organic vegetables, honey, jams and other produce from local farms that might help you put a picnic together.

La Perla

Heading northeast from Plaza San Martín along Bartolomé Mitre takes you through the relatively quiet neighbourhood of **La Perla**. Just one block away at Mitre and 9 de Julio you'll find the atmospheric *La Cuadrada* café (see p.169) and following Mitre another three blocks will bring you to La Perla **beach**, almost as busy as the main beaches but regarded as slightly more upmarket.

Inland is La Perla's main square, the Plaza España, where you can visit the **Museo de Ciencias Naturales Lorenzo Scaglia** (Tues–Fri 9am–4.30pm, Sat & Sun 3–6.30pm; $10). It houses a decent collection of fossils from all over the world, including Patagonian dinosaurs, as well as a salt- and fresh-water aquarium.

Playa Bristol and Rambla Casino

Playa Bristol, Mar del Plata's iconic beach, lies half a dozen blocks southeast of Plaza San Martín. Together with neighbouring Playa Popular, just to the north, these are by far the city's busiest beaches and in high season their blanket coverage of multicoloured beach tents and shades resembles a strange nomadic settlement. Dominating the scene are the city's much loved duo of buildings by leading Argentine architect, Alejandro Bustillo (he notably worked on Bariloche's Centro Cívico; see p.396). The *Gran Hotel Provincial* and Casino Central were the country's biggest hotel and the world's biggest casino building when they were inaugurated in 1950. Inspired by the imperial Hôtel du Palais in Biarritz, they form a majestic architectural complex, set off by a harmonious esplanade, the **Rambla Casino**, and a monumental staircase guarded on either side by much-photographed stone sea lions.

Punta Piedras and Torreón del Monje

Follow the bay round to the southeast and you will come to a promontory known as **Punta Piedras**, crowned by another of the city's landmark buildings, the **Torreón del Monje**. This "monk's tower" is a perfect example of Mar del Plata's peculiar brand of fantasy architecture, which at times makes the city look like a toy village. Built as a folly in 1904 by Ernesto Tornquist, the mock medieval tower is a little overwhelmed by its skyscraper neighbours these days, but it still gives you great views of Playa Bristol and the Rambla Casino from its *confitería*. It is partly accessible by a pedestrian bridge.

2

2

Loma Stella Maris

One block inland from Playa Bristol, wide Avenida Colón begins to clamber to the hill known as **Loma Stella Maris**, just inland from the Torreón del Monje. This residential area affords fine vistas over the city, particularly from the crest of the hill back down the straight Avenida Colón, while Güemes, which branches off Colón and heads west towards Divino Rostro, has some of the city's most upmarket **shopping**. The barrio is a pleasant place to wander if you're interested in Mar del Plata's *pintoresquista* architecture – dominated by mock-Tudor villas that would not look out of place in Bournemouth. Beyond Stella Maris, the serpentine Avenida Patricio Peralta Ramos winds south along cliffs towards the fishing port (see box opposite), past three rocky beaches known as Playa Varese, Playa Chica and Playa Grande.

Museo Municipal de Arte Juan Carlos Castagnino

Colón 1189 • Daily except Tues: summer 5–10pm; winter noon–6pm • $10

The imposing Villa Ortiz Basualdo, an exuberantly turreted and half-timbered Anglo-Norman mansion, houses the **Museo Municipal de Arte Juan Carlos Castagnino**. Local artist Castagnino, born in 1908, painted colourful Expressionist scenes of Mar del Plata. His work forms the basis of the permanent collection, which has also been boosted in recent years by a growing number of contemporary Argentine works.

Museo del Mar

Colón 1114 • Mon & Thurs–Sun 10am–7pm • $30 • ⓦ museodelmar.org

Opposite the Museo Municipal, the **Museo del Mar** is a modern aquarium complex built around the sea-shell obsession of Benjamin Sisterna, who spent over sixty years amassing thirty thousand shells, which the museum claims is one of the world's largest such collections on display.

Mirador de la Torre Tanque

Falucho 995 • Mon–Fri 8am–3pm • Free

Two blocks south and two west of the Museo del Mar, at the very highest point of Stella Maris, you can climb 194 steps to the top of the bizarre, castle-like **Mirador de la Torre Tanque**, a mock-Tudor water tower built in the 1940s, from where there are great views over the city.

Divino Rostro

Some 3km southwest of Plaza San Martín is the leafy and well-heeled neighbourhood of **Divino Rostro**. The area is almost exclusively residential, with little in the way of cafés or bars, but is worth the detour to see the **Villa Victoria**, which houses the **Centro Cultural Victoria Ocampo**, dedicated to one of Argentina's great *dames de lettres* of the twentieth century.

Centro Cultural Victoria Ocampo

Matheu 1851, between Lamadrid and Arenales • Summer daily 10am–1pm & 5–9pm; winter Tues–Sun noon–6pm • $30 • ☎ 0223 492 0569 (call to check opening times) • Take bus #511 from Av Luro or the Blvd Marítimo and get off on the corner of Alsinas and Formosa

The site of some lively exhibitions and events, the **Centro Cultural Victoria Ocampo** is an architectural curiosity in its own right. Built of Norwegian wood, it is a fine example of the prefabricated housing that the British took with them to their colonial outposts. It was shipped to the country in 1912 by the great-aunt of one of Argentina's most famous authors, Victoria Ocampo (1890–1979). Cultural evenings are often dedicated to Indian music, dance and philosophy, which were of particular interest to Ocampo. Born into an aristocratic family and a vehement anti-Peronist, Ocampo became a leading feminist and literary critic, counting Borges, Camus, Greene and Tagore among her close friends.

IMAGES OF MARDEL: FISHING BOATS AND SEA LIONS

Second only to the Rambla Casino, with its stone sea lions, Mar del Plata's favourite postcard image is that of the striking orange **fishing boats** that depart every morning from its **port**, about 3km south of the city centre. In the early evening you can watch them returning to the Banquina de Pescadores (Fishermen's Wharf) full of crates bursting with sea bass, sole and squid, which are hauled onto the quayside by the fishermen. At the far end of the wharf is the Lobería, a colony of around 800 real-life **sea lions** – they are all males as you can tell by their distinctive giant manes and loud bark. These *lobos* can be observed from an incredibly close (and smelly) distance – a metre or so – all year round, though the colony shrinks in January and February, when large numbers head for the Uruguayan coast to mate. There are also a number of good **seafood restaurants** (see p.169) around the port, mostly grouped around the Centro Comercial. Buses from the centre of Mar del Plata head to the fishing port; both #551 and #553 can be caught anywhere along Avenida Luro.

2

Archivo Museo Histórico Municipal Roberto T. Barili

Lamadrid 3870 • Mon–Fri 8am–5pm, Sat & Sun 2–6pm • $4 • ☎ 0223 495 1200 • Take bus #511 from Av Luro or the Blvd Marítimo and get off on the corner of Alsinas and Formosa

The excellent **Archivo Museo Histórico Municipal**, in a fine villa one block southwest of Villa Victoria, is a goldmine of interesting information on Mar del Plata's history. Its archives include some wonderful photos of the resort's early days when the cognoscenti from Buenos Aires flocked to the *Hotel Bristol*, as well as copies of the strict rules enforced on bathers: single men could be fined or arrested for being within 30m of women bathers or for using opera glasses on the beach.

Punta Magotes

Following the coastal road south of the fishing port will take you along the **Costanera Sur** (officially Av Martínez de Hoz) and past an area known as **Punta Magotes** – easy to distinguish, with the city's iconic red-and-white-striped lighthouse, the Faro de Punta Magotes, at its extremity. Here you'll find quieter beaches and *balnearios*, including several popular with the surf crowd and a naturist beach, as well as most of the city's campsites.

Aquarium Mar del Plata

Av Martínez de Hoz 5600 • Jan & Feb daily 10am–8pm; March daily 10am–7pm; April–Nov Fri–Sun 10am–6pm; Dec daily 10am–6pm • $105 (cheaper online) • ☎ 0223 467 0700, ⓦ mdpaquarium.com.ar

Punta Magotes is home to **Aquarium Mar del Plata**. There are the inevitable sea lion and dolphin shows, but the aquarium's foundation carries out serious conservation and educational work to try and ensure it's not just a theme park. If you won't be heading to Patagonia or the Antarctic you may want to take this opportunity to see Magellanic and Emperor penguins in the flesh.

ARRIVAL AND DEPARTURE
MAR DEL PLATA

Mar del Plata is well connected by public transport to most points in Argentina, particularly during the summer, when services increase dramatically. From the combined bus and train terminal, bus #511 gets you into the centre of town.

By plane The airport, named for the city's most famous son, tango musician Astor Piazzolla, is 8km northwest of the city centre along Autovía 2; local bus #542 will take you into town. There are flights to Buenos Aires (1–2 daily; 55min), with more laid on in the height of summer. Aerolíneas Argentinas have their offices at Moreno 2442 (☎ 0223 496 0101), LADE at Rambla Casino Loc. 5 (☎ 0223 491 1484).

By train Trains from Buenos Aires (Constitución) arrive at Estación Norte, to the northwest of the town centre at Luro and Italia; services are operated by Ferrobaires (☎ 011 4306 7919). The main destination is Buenos Aires (3 daily; 6hr).
By bus The bus terminal is located beside the train station at San Juan 152.
Destinations Bahía Blanca (5 daily; 6hr); Bariloche (1 daily; 20hr); Buenos Aires (hourly; 7hr); Córdoba (3 daily; 18hr).

2

By car If you are travelling by car from Buenos Aires, you have a choice of three routes. Mind-numbingly straight Autovía 2 is the most direct of these, but is also by far the busiest route during the summer. The RP-29 via Balcarce and the coastal RP-11 are quieter, have lower tolls and meander through more attractive landscape, but add 80km (and a couple of hours) or more to your journey.

GETTING AROUND

Buses Local buses are efficient and routes are well marked at bus stops. Useful routes include #551, #552 and #553, all of which run between Avenida Constitución – the centre of the city's nightlife – downtown and the port. Some buses only accept cards, with prepaid credit on them ($1.50 a journey; card $5 available at most kiosks), so check before boarding.

Taxis Taxis are easy to come by and cheap; try Taxis Mar del Plata (☎ 0223 483 1111) or Tele Taxi (☎ 0223 475 8888).

Bike rental Madrid, at H. Yrigoyen 2249 ☎ 0223 494 1932.

INFORMATION

Tourist information The main office for Emtur, Mar del Plata's tourist information service, is centrally located on Belgrano 2740 (daily: summer 8am–10pm, winter 8am–8pm; ☎ 0223 494 4140, ⓦ turismomardelplata.gov.ar). There's also a useful office by the coast, on the northwest corner of the old *Hotel Provincial* on the Blvd Marítimo, on the inland side by Av Colón (daily: summer 8am–10pm; winter 8am–8pm; ☎ 0223 495 1777).

Travel agents and tour operators You'll find several travel agents in Galería de las Américas at San Martín 2648. Surf school: Playa Grande Balneario 8 ☎0223 15 455 4829; paragliding: Arcángel ☎0223 463 1167 (suitable for beginners).

ACCOMMODATION

Book ahead if you plan to stay in Mar del Plata during high season. Most of the **budget accommodation** is around the bus terminal, although you can also find some good deals in La Perla, a pleasant barrio with hilly streets just to the north of the town centre. There are numerous **campsites**, many of them just out of town along the Costanera Sur/RP-11 that heads south to Miramar. You can reach the Costanera Sur via bus #511, which passes by the bus and train terminals.

HOTELS AND HOSTELS

Calash Falucho 1355 ☎0223 486 2354, ⓦ entodalacosta.com.ar/calash. On a quiet street near the centre, this friendly, mock-Tudor hotel has rambling hallways, a wooden staircase and simple but light and attractive rooms. There's also a café and a shady seating area outside. $465

Costa Galana Blvd Marítimo 5725 ☎0223 410 5000, ⓦ hotelcostagalana.com. Modern luxury hotel overlooking Playa Grande, with a private tunnel running to the beach. Large, attractively decorated rooms with a/c; all with sea views. $1300

Etoile Santiago del Estero 1869 ☎0223 493 4968, ⒺHotedeletoile@hotmail.com. Three-star hotel with five-star pretensions. The comfortable, spacious, if slightly dog-eared rooms are very reasonably priced. In a central spot; facilities include a gym. $540

Franci Sarmiento 2742 ☎0223 486 2484, Ⓔinfo@hotelfranci.com. Right by the bus terminal, this is a good-value hotel. Rooms have TV and private bathroom, and there's a 24hr bar. $290

Hermitage Av Colón 1643 ☎0223 451 9081, ⓦ hermitagehotel.com.ar. A classically elegant hotel, almost lost amid the surrounding modern buildings. Popular with visiting celebrities, the *Hermitage* has suitably luxurious rooms, a pool and spa, and an excellent location. $1100

★ **NH Gran Hotel Provincial** Av Peralta Ramos 2502 ☎0223 499 5900, ⓦnh-hotels.com. The city's swishest hotel is housed in the original 1946 building beside the casino, overlooking the seafront. Services include massages, cable TV, 24hr room service, cocktail bar and swimming pool. $1000

Palacio Alberti 2056 ☎0223 495 6546, ⓦ hotelpalacio.com.ar. This pretty hotel, with its colourful artefacts the owner has collected from around the world, stands out from its rather dingy neighbours near the bus terminal. Private bathrooms and breakfast are included. $280

Peninsular 9 de Julio 2987 ☎0223 495 4151, ⓦ peninsular.com.ar. Colourful hotel located in La Perla neighbourhood. Rooms are functional but comfortable. Discounts offered when paying in cash. $460

Playa Grande Hostel Quintana 168 ☎0223 451 7307, ⓦ hostelplayagrande.com.ar. In a large, bright house a couple of blocks from the sea, this is one of Mar del Plata's most reliable hostels. Shared dorms are decent, and there's an on-site surf school. Private doubles available as well. Closed April–Nov although sister establishment *Playa Grande Suites* (at Alem 3495) is open all year. Dorms $120, doubles $350

CAMPING

Camping Del Faro Costanera Sur 400 ☎0223 467 1168, ⓦ autocampingdelfaro.com.ar. Located near the lighthouse and some of the best beaches, the site is well equipped with pool, store, laundry, restaurant and shower blocks, and there are also simple *cabañas* and bungalows. Camping $55, *cabañas* and bungalows $200

EATING, DRINKING AND NIGHTLIFE

There's a huge number of reasonable **restaurants** in the microcentro, though in high season if you want to avoid queuing up you may prefer to head for the otherwise quiet streets around Castelli and Yrigoyen, southwest of the microcentro, where there are some attractive small bars and restaurants. For many visitors, Mar del Plata's summer **nightlife** is at least as important as its beaches – and if you want to keep up with the locals, you'll need both stamina and transport. The densest concentration of **bars** is along lively Calle Alem, which also has a good selection of late-night restaurants and is swamped by a young crowd, intent on showing off their tans during the summer. Their next port of call is likely to be Constitución, an enormous avenue 4km north of the town centre, housing numerous **clubs**, none of which really gets going until well after 2am.

RESTAURANTS AND CAFÉS

★ **Cabaña del Bosque** El Cardenal s/n, Bosque Peralta Ramos ☎0223 467 3007, ⓦlacabaniadel bosque.com.ar; bus #521 or #522. Mar del Plata's most famous café is in a wooden building set in lush grounds within a residential district around 10km south of the city centre. The wildly exotic and rambling interior, decorated with fossils, carved wooden sculptures and stuffed animals, is worth a visit on its own, though the café's fantastic cakes are a pretty enticing attraction too. Summer daily 2–9pm.

Chichilo Centro Comercial Puerto, Local 17 ☎0223 489 6317. One of a clutch of cheap and excellent seafood restaurants that serve up the fresh catch of the day in the port's Centro Comercial; try local *rabas* (squid rings), *lenguado* (sole) or *langostinos* (prawns). Daily 11am–midnight.

Chiquilin Castelli and H. Yrigoyen 2899. Attractive, oak-panelled pub with an eclectic menu that gives an inventive twist to standard dishes. The dish of the day goes for $45, while the house special, beef goulash, is priced at $72. There's live music some evenings too. Daily 8am–2am.

La Fontanella Rawson 2302 ☎0223 494 0533. Named for its pretty fountain, *La Fontanella* specializes in *pizza a la piedra* as well as fish and pasta. Daily 11am–midnight.

Manolo de la Costa Castelli 15. Offering good sea views, *Manolo de la Costa* is a Mar del Plata institution that does upmarket fast food such as pizzas and a delicious *brochette mixto* (kebab), but it is for its fabulous range of filled *churros* (fried dough) that it is best known. The sister branch at Rivadavia 2371 is busy, too, and a popular spot for *chocolate con churros* after a hard night's clubbing. Daily 11.30am–midnight.

La Placita de Arenales Arenales 2184 ☎0223 493 2794. Cosy pizza restaurant with photos of the owner with local celebrities hanging from the walls. Serves twelve different types of empanada and specializes in delicious *calzones*. Daily 8pm–1am.

BARS AND CLUBS

Bar Ramona Castelli 291 and H. Yrigoyen. A slightly posey but attractive bar, popular with the young and well-to-do. Daily 6pm–late.

Chocolate Constitución 4445. Large, glossy club, consistently one of Mar del Plata's most highly rated dance destinations. Fri & Sat midnight–6am.

★ **La Cuadrada** 9 de Julio and Mitre. A café-bar and theatre that's worth a visit for its decor alone. The interior is covered with paintings, sculptures and antiques, and with a basement that is a rabbit warren of tiny rooms filled with wooden tables and stone seats. It's a mesmerizing place to while away an hour over a beer or a cup of its extensive range of teas. The food is also excellent and served with great style. Daily 11am–late.

Dickens Pub Diagonal Pueyrredón 3017. A pub that holds regular jazz evenings and is popular with foreign visitors. Daily 7pm–1am.

Mr Jones Alem, between Matheu and Quintana. One of Alem's most popular bars, heaving with bronzed bodies on summer evenings. Next to it is the softer lit, sit-down *Mr Lounge*. Daily 7pm–late.

Pinar de Rocha Av Constitución 5470. One of the city's big dance clubs, with two floors, featuring different styles of music, and a *cena-show* (dinner with show). Thurs–Sun midnight–late.

La Princesa B. de Irigoyen 3820. Long-running surfer bar and restaurant, with a good range of *milanesas* (both meat and soya), pizzas and salads to accompany your margarita. Daily 6pm–late.

Sobremonte Av Constitución 6690. Constitución's most popular club complex, featuring bars and dancefloors ranging from a mock-Mexican *cantina* to the laidback Velvet chillout room. The music is generally mainstream dance, although international DJs of the stature of Sasha and Deep Dish have played here. Thurs–Sun midnight–late.

Tijuana B. de Irigoyen 3966. An alternative hangout to *Mr Jones* around the corner – and in a very similar vein. Daily 6pm–late.

ENTERTAINMENT

Mar del Plata is well catered for as far as **theatres** and **cinemas** are concerned; most of them are in the downtown area. **Live music** concerts are a part of the fabric of summer too, with some popular national acts playing outdoors at the *balnearios*, as well as indoors in the theatres. In January and February many of the most successful plays on Buenos Aires' Corrientes strip move to Mardel and entertain hordes of holiday-makers.

2

Casa de Folklore San Juan 2543 ☎0223 472 3955, ⓦfolkloreclub.com.ar. This Mardel institution has a lively agenda, especially in the busy summer months, with gigs by national and international folk musicians nearly every night in Jan and Feb.

Cine Ambassador Córdoba 1673 ☎0223 495 7271. A modern multiplex, this is the resort's main cinema, mostly

screening blockbusters, but also the odd indie-style film.

Teatro Colón H. Yrigoyen 1665 ☎0223 499 6555, ⓦteatrocolonmdp.com.ar. Not as majestic or prestigious as its Buenos Aires namesake, Mar del Plata's main theatre, opened in 1893 and renovated three decades later, hosts all manner of shows, ranging from tango extravaganzas to jazz bands, plus folk, flamenco and classical music.

DIRECTORY

Banks and exchange There are many banks on avenidas Independencia, Luro and San Martín. Jonestur, at Luro 3185 (Mon–Fri 10am–7pm, Sat 10am–1pm), exchanges currency and travellers' cheques.

Hospitals Hospital Interzonal Mar del Plata, Juan B. Justo

6800 ☎0223 477 0265.

Laundry Laverap, Av Libertad 5519 ☎0223 474 6884.

Post office The main office is at Luro 2460, on the corner of Santiago del Estero, offering all the usual facilities ☎0223 499 1839; there are numerous other offices throughout the city.

Miramar and Mar del Sud

Heading south from Mar del Plata, the first resort you come to is popular **Miramar**, 45km further down the RP-11, a largely modern town, dominated by some rather grim high-rise buildings. A more appealing alternative to busy resorts like Mar del Plata is tiny **MAR DEL SUD**, a further 16km southeast. One of Argentina's least-developed beach resorts, Mar del Sud is in many ways one of its most appealing. Although it is increasingly courted by in-the-know Porteños looking for something a little different, the atmosphere remains tranquil, with a safe community feel and the occasional party to inject some life. Its beaches are far less frequented than those to the north and if you venture a shortway away from the small clutch of beachgoers grouped around the bottom of Avenida 100 you won't have much trouble finding a stretch of soft sand to yourself. The town's unassuming buildings are dominated by the crumbling faded-pink walls and steeply pitched roof of the ex-**Boulevard Atlantic Hotel**, an elegant, French-influenced construction built in 1886. It's now a wonderfully creepy old building, its once glamorous rooms taken over by doves and scattered with chunks of plaster. Guided visits are possible during the day on request from Eduardo Gambo, who runs the place and is something of a local personality; he also rents out bungalows.

ARRIVAL AND INFORMATION   MIRAMAR AND MAR DEL SUD

By bus Buses arrive at different terminals/offices in Miramar town centre – most are along Diagonal Fte de la Plaza, which leads south to Plaza General Alvarado. El Rápido del Sur, which serves Mar del Plata, and Expreso Mar del Sud, for Mar del Sud, leave from Av 23 and c/34, three blocks northwest of the plaza.

Destinations Buenos Aires (7 daily; 8hr); Mar del Plata (every 30min; 1hr); Necochea (2 daily; 2hr).

Tourist information There's a helpful tourist office in Miramar (daily: summer 7am–11pm; winter 8am–8pm; ☎02291 420190, ⓦmiramar-digital.com.ar) on c/12 between 19 and 21.

ACCOMMODATION

Camping La Ponderosa Av La Playa ☎02291 491118. This site, five blocks from the beach and to the west of Mar del Sud town centre, is well equipped, with showers, a restaurant and shops. **$35**

Hostería Villa del Mar Av 100, Mar del Sud ☎02291 491141. Open Jan & Feb only, this is the sole hotel on the seafront itself. It has small rooms with sea views and a lovely breakfast area with a hearth – useful for the odd cool day. **$320**

Hotel Marina Av 9 no. 744, Miramar ☎02291 420462, ⓦmiramar-digital.com/hotelmarina. One block back from the beach, this decent hotel offers some attractive rooms with balconies and sea views; these cost a few pesos more than the internal rooms but are well worth it. **$500**

La Posada Calles 15 and 98, Mar del Sud ☎02291 491274. A mere two blocks from the beach this posada has comfortable, simple rooms with shared bath and it's one of the few places open all year round. **$470**

Posada Las Camelias RP-77 at Km10.5, Miramar ☎ 011 15 5023 6642, ⓦ posadalascamelias.com.ar. This stunning posada set in large grounds is some way out of town. It has a gym and swimming pool and staff can organize horseriding along the oceanfront or in the hinterland. **$565**

EATING AND DRINKING

JR Café At the intersection of Av 100 and calles 11 and 13 ☎ 02291 491200. This family-friendly bar also houses the town's *locutorio*. Daily 8am–late.

Makarska Av 100 and c/13 ☎ 02291 491054. The best place in town is run by Argentines of Croatian origin; it does a delicious goulash as well as a tasty vegetable and ricotta strudel. Daily noon–4pm & 8pm–late.

2

Balcarce and the Museo Fangio

Around 60km northwest of Mar del Plata on RN-226, the modest agricultural town of **BALCARCE**, near the tabletop foothills of the Tandilia range, does not, at first glance, appear to have much to distinguish it from other provincial towns. However, it was the birthplace of legendary Formula One driver **Juan Manuel Fangio** and now houses a spectacular museum that is certainly worth the detour if cars and motor racing are your thing. You can easily visit Balcarce from Mar del Plata (buses every 2hr; 90min) or the other Atlantic resorts.

Museo Fangio

Dardo Rocha and Mitre • Daily Jan & Feb 10am–7pm; March–Dec 11am–5pm • $40 • ☎ 02266 425540, ⓦ museofangio.com • Take a taxi from Balcarce bus terminal (Teletaxi ☎ 02266 425076)

The **Museo Fangio** was built to honour the man who won the Formula One World Championship five times in the 1950s, a record not equalled until the twenty-first century (by Michael Schumacher, who notched up seven victories in all). The five floors of the museum are connected by a spiral ramp and tell Fangio's fascinating story in words, pictures and trophies. There are also displays on other prominent drivers, but the cars are the star here – around fifty of them, in fact, including a red 1954 Maserati 250 and the Brabham BT36 driven by Argentine ex-Formula One driver Carlos Reutemann, now a Peronist politician. The most impressive, though – and saved for the top floor – is the Mercedes-Benz Silver Arrow that Fangio drove to victory in 1954.

Córdoba and the Central Sierras

HORSE AT ESTANCIA LOS POTREROS

Córdoba and the Central Sierras

The Central Sierras are the highest mountain ranges in Argentina away from the Andean cordillera. Their pinkish-grey ridges and jagged outcrops alternate with fertile valleys, wooded with native carob trees, and barren moorlands, fringed with pampas grass – a patchwork that is one of Argentina's most varied landscapes. Formed more than 400 million years before the Andes and gently sculpted by the wind and rain, the sierras stretch across some 100,000 square kilometres, peaking at Cerro Champaquí. Colonized at the end of the sixteenth century by settlers heading south and east from Tucumán and Mendoza, Córdoba was the region's first city. The Society of Jesus and its missionaries played a pivotal part in its foundation, establishing it at a strategic point along the Camino Real ("Royal Way"), the Spanish route from Alto Perú to the Crown's emerging Atlantic trading posts on the Río de la Plata.

From that point on, the Jesuits dominated every aspect of life in the city and its hinterland, until King Carlos III kicked them out of the colonies in 1767. You can still see their handsome temple in the city centre, among other examples of **colonial architecture**. Further vestiges of the Jesuits' heyday, **Santa Catalina** and **Jesús María**, are two of Argentina's best-preserved **Jesuit estancias**, located between Córdoba city and the province's northern border. Slightly north of Santa Catalina is one of the country's most beguiling archeological sites, **Cerro Colorado**, which has hundreds of pre-Columbian petroglyphs.

Northwest from Córdoba city is the picturesque **Punilla Valley**, along which are threaded some of the country's most traditional holiday resorts, such as **La Falda** and **Capilla del Monte**. At the valley's southern end, close to Córdoba city, are two nationally famous resorts: noisy, crowded **Villa Carlos Paz** and slightly quieter **Cosquín**. By contrast, the far north of the province, particularly a stunningly unspoilt area roughly between Capilla del Monte and Santa Catalina, remains little visited: the dramatic rock formations at **Ongamira** and the lovingly restored hamlet of **Ischilín** are just two of the highlights. South of Córdoba, the **Calamuchita Valley** is famed for its popular holiday spots, sedately Germanic **Villa General Belgrano** and rowdy **Santa Rosa de Calamuchita**. **Alta Gracia**, at the entrance to this increasingly urbanized valley, is home to an outstanding historical museum housed in an immaculately restored estancia; Che Guevara spent much of his adolescence in the town.

Southwest of Córdoba a high mountain pass cuts through the sierras, leading to the generally more placid resorts of the **Traslasierra**, a handsome valley in western Córdoba Province, and some stunning scenery in the lee of Cerro Champaquí, accessed from the pretty village of **San Javier**. Along this route lies the province's only national park, the **Quebrada del Condorito**, whose dramatic ravines provide a breeding site for the magnificent condor.

Highlights

❶ Córdoba city Argentina's second city is home to some important colonial architecture as well as one of South America's oldest universities. **See p.176**

❷ Jesuit history The province of Córdoba owed its early importance to the Jesuits, whose legacy lives on in the form of estancias, churches and museums, which offer a fascinating insight into early colonial Argentina. **See p.189**

❸ Cerro Colorado Intriguing pre-Columbian pictures are etched onto the side of a cliff in the Reserva Cultural Natural Cerro Colorado. See p.192

❹ Estancias Ride on handsome horses, swim or just relax and enjoy breathtaking views in the unspoilt countryside on an estancia. One of the best is the Anglo-Argentine *Los Potreros*. See p.193

❺ Hang-gliding The province's rugged sierras and professional infrastructure make it a great place for adventure sports, especially hang-gliding. **See p.196**

❻ Parque Nacional Quebrada del Condorito This national park offers spectacular mountain views and is a major condor breeding ground. **See p.204**

HIGHLIGHTS ARE MARKED ON THE MAP ON P.176

GETTING AROUND   **CORDOBA AND THE CENTRAL SIERRAS**

Córdoba Province is well served by **public transport** and nearly everywhere is within striking distance of the city of Córdoba, but it would be a shame to miss out staying at some of the region's excellent estancias. Renting a **car**, however, does give you a bit more freedom, particularly if you want to visit some of the more off-the-beaten-track destinations like Ongamira or Ischilín. The province gets overcrowded in the summer, so try and go in the cooler, drier and quieter months; although night temperatures are low in winter (June–Aug), the days can be mild, sunny and extremely pleasant.

Córdoba

Around 700km northwest of Buenos Aires, the bustling, modern metropolis of **CÓRDOBA** sits on a curve in the Río Suquía, at its confluence with the tamed La

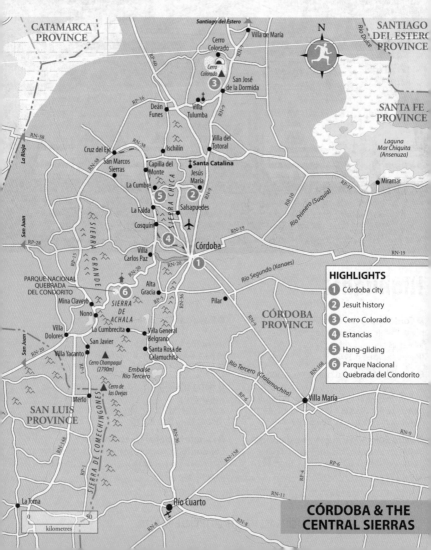

HIGHLIGHTS

1 Córdoba city
2 Jesuit history
3 Cerro Colorado
4 Estancias
5 Hang-gliding
6 Parque Nacional Quebrada del Condorito

CÓRDOBA & THE CENTRAL SIERRAS

Cañada brook. The jagged silhouettes visible at the western end of its broad avenues announce that the cool heights of the sierras are not far away, and it's here that many of the 1.3 million Cordobeses take refuge from the valley's sweltering heat during summer. Because it lacks the dynamism and style of Rosario, its rival for the title of Argentina's second city (see p.248), many people spend only an hour or two here before sprinting off to the nearby resorts. But Córdoba has a wide range of services, and its excellent location makes it an ideal base for exploring the region, while the colonial architecture at its heart remains an attraction in its own right. Moreover, the city is reputed nationwide for its hospitable, elegant population and its caustically ironic sense of humour, something you'll come to appreciate the longer you stay.

Brief history

On July 6, 1573, **Jerónimo Luis de Cabrera**, Governor of Tucumán, declared a new city founded at the fork in the main routes from Chile and Alto Perú to Buenos Aires, calling it Córdoba la Llana de la Nueva Andalucía, after the city of his Spanish ancestors. The Monolito de la Fundación, on the north bank of the Río Suquía nearly a kilometre northeast of the Plaza San Martín, supposedly marks the precise spot where the city was founded and commands panoramic views.

The Society of Jesus

Almost from the outset the **Society of Jesus** played a crucial role in Córdoba's development (see box, p.189), and King Carlos III of Spain's order to expel the Jesuits from the Spanish empire in 1767 inevitably dealt Córdoba a serious body blow. That, plus the decision in 1776 to make Buenos Aires the headquarters of the newly created Viceroyalty of the Río de la Plata, might well have condemned the city to terminal decline had it not then been made the administrative centre of a huge Intendencia, or viceregal province, stretching all the way to Mendoza and La Rioja. Like so many Argentine cities, Córdoba benefited from the arrival of the railways in 1870 and a period of prosperity followed, still visible in some of the city's lavishly decorated banks and theatres. By the close of the nineteenth century, Córdoba had begun to spread south, with European-influenced urban planning on a huge scale, including the **Parque Sarmiento**. This all coincided with a huge influx of immigrants from Europe and the Middle East.

The twentieth century

In the first half of the twentieth century Córdoba emerged as one of the country's main manufacturing centres. Sadly, the post-2001 crisis boom that occurred in other parts of the country never reached Córdoba, and the industries that once ruled here are now shadows of their former selves. However, despite the recent global economic downturn, the local government has invested heavily in arts and culture in the last few years, with the opening of several new museums and cultural spaces, such as the **Museo Superior de Bellas Artes Evita** and the **Paseo del Buen Pastor**.

The microcentro

You can see most of the sights in Córdoba's compact centre in a couple of days. The city's **historic core**, or **microcentro**, wrapped around leafy **Plaza San Martín**, contains all the major **colonial buildings** that sealed the city's importance in the seventeenth and eighteenth centuries. Its elegant **Cabildo** (colonial headquarters), now houses the city museum, which sits conveniently adjacent to the **cathedral**, one of the oldest in the country. Nearby, beyond a handsome Baroque convent, the **Monasterio de Santa Teresa** is a group of several well-preserved Jesuit buildings, including the temple and university buildings, that form the **Manzana Jesuítica** ("Jesuits' Block"). East of the Plaza San Martín, the eighteenth-century home of Governor Sobremonte (and the city's oldest

3

CÓRDOBA

RP-53, Airport (12km) & Salsipuedes
Alta Córdoba, 1 & 2
RN-9 & Jesús María
EL ABASTO
LAS HERAS
PUENTE ANTÁRTICA
Río Suquía
0 — 250 metres
N
Cerro de las Rosas & Parque San Martín (3km)
RN19, San Francisco & Santa Fe
9 DE OCTUBRE
IGUALDAD
RINCÓN
BV MITRE
HUMBERTO 1º
TABLADA
LIBERTAD
LA RIOJA
MERCADO NORTE
CÓRDOBA ANEROCENTRO
MAP FOR DETAIL
ONCATIVO
SANTA ROSA
SARMIENTO
9 DE JULIO
AVENIDA COLON
RÍO SARMIENTO
CATAMARCA
DEAN FUNES
LIMA
AVENIDA OLMOS
Mandolio de la Fundación (300m)
MICROCENTRO
PLAZA SAN MARTÍN
25 DE MAYO
Manzana Jesuítica
R. DE SANTA FE
SAN JERÓNIMO
DUARTE QUIROS
ENTRE RÍOS
BV SAN JUAN
CORRIENTES
Terminal de Minibuses
Ex-railway Station
BV A. ILIA
Bus Terminal
MONTEVIDEO
SAN LUIS
LA CAÑADA
LAPRIDA
PIE OLIVER
1
RN-9 & Buenos Aires
Paseo del Buen Pastor
BUENOS AIRES
3
Iglesia de los Capuchinos
LAN
SAN LORENZO
GÜEMES
2
NUEVA CÓRDOBA
5
4
Museo Superior de Bellas Artes Evita-Palacio Ferreyra
OBISPO ORO
Parque Sarmiento
DEROUI
Museo Provincial de Ciencias Naturales
Museo Provincial de Bellas Artes Emilio Caraffa
Zoo
AVENIDA POETA LUGONES
ESTRADA
CRISOL
AVENIDA OLMOS
RP-5, Alta Gracia & Villa General Belgrano
RN-20, Villa Carlos Paz & Pmilla San Luis

● **RESTAURANTS AND CAFÉS**
El Arrabal — 2
Las Rías de Galicia — 1

■ **BARS AND CLUBS**
Carreras — 3
Dorian Gray — 1
Infierno — 4
Johnny B Good — 5
Voodoo Lounge — 2

■ **ACCOMMODATION**
Hotel de la Cañada — 2
Le Grand Hostel and Suites — 3
N'aike — 1
Tango Hostel — 4

standing residential building) has been turned into the **Museo Histórico Provincial**, and contains some outstanding colonial paintings, while some interesting examples of nineteenth- and twentieth-century Argentine art are on display in a splendid French-style house, the **Museo Municipal de Bellas Artes**, a couple of blocks northwest of the plaza.

The city's regular Hispano-American grid, centred on Plaza San Martín, is upset only by the winding **La Cañada** brook a few blocks west of the centre, on either side of which snakes one of the city's main thoroughfares, acacia-lined Avenida

Marcelo T. de Alvear, which becomes Avenida Figueroa Alcorta after crossing Deán Funes. Street names change and numbering begins level with the Cabildo.

Plaza San Martín

The **Plaza San Martín** has always been the city's focal point. The square is at its liveliest during the *paseo* hour in the early evening, although it becomes a less appealing place to wander after dark, when it fills with homeless people. Originally used for military parades, the shady square was granted its recreational role in the 1870s when the Italianate marble fountains were installed and semitropical shrubberies planted: lush palm-fronds, the prickly, bulging trunks of the *palo borracho* and, in the spring, blazing pink *lapacho* and purple jacaranda blossoms. Watching over all the activity is a monumental bronze **sculpture** of the Liberator himself, victorious on a splendid mount and borne aloft on a huge stone plinth, which was unveiled in 1916 to mark the centenary of the declaration of independence.

The square's southern edge is dominated by the dowdy Banco Nación and the Teatro Real; more banks sit along the eastern edge. Wedged between shops and the modern municipal offices on the pedestrianized northern side is the diminutive **Oratorio del Obispo Mercadillo**, all that remains of a huge colonial residence built for Bishop Manuel Mercadillo. He had the seat of Tucumán diocese moved from Santiago del Estero to Córdoba at the beginning of the eighteenth century, before becoming the city's first bishop.

The Cabildo

Mon 4–9pm, Tues–Sun 9am–1pm & 4–9pm • Free • ☎ 0351 428 5856

On the pedestrianized western side of Plaza San Martín is the **Cabildo**, or colonial headquarters, a sleekly elegant two-storey building whose immaculate white facade dates to the late eighteenth century. Fifteen harmoniously plain arches, enhanced at night by lighting, alleviate the otherwise sober exterior. Old-fashioned lamps hang in the **Recova**, a fan-vaulted colonnade held up by slender pillars, in front of a row of wooden doors alternating with windows protected by iron grilles. On the pavement in front of the Cabildo, as elsewhere in the historic centre, a clever *trompe-l'oeil* device of mock shadows has been incorporated into the flagstones.

The original Cabildo was built on the same spot at the end of the sixteenth century, but the present facade was added when the Marqués de Sobremonte became governor-mayor in 1784. Put to many different uses throughout its long history – law court, prison, provincial parliament, government offices and police headquarters – nowadays the building and its inner courtyards are mainly used for exhibitions and official receptions. The Recova, meanwhile, houses the tourism office (see p.186) and a souvenir shop.

The cathedral

Daily 8am–noon & 4–7pm • Free • ☎ 0351 422 3446

Immediately south of the Cabildo, and completing the western flank of Plaza San Martín, is Córdoba's eighteenth-century **cathedral**. One of Argentina's oldest if not its most beautiful cathedrals, it is part Baroque, part Neoclassical – its most imposing external feature, the immense **cupola**, is surrounded by stern Romanesque turrets that contrast pleasingly with its Baroque curves. However, the building's highly porous, cream-coloured stone has suffered badly from ambient pollution and its sooty black facade required extensive cleaning in 2009.

The cathedral's **bell towers** are decorated at each corner with angelic trumpeters dressed in skirts of exotic plumes. You enter the cathedral first through majestic filigreed wrought-iron gates, past Deán Funes' solemn black mausoleum to the left, and then through finely carved **wooden doors** transferred here from the Jesuit temple at the end of the eighteenth century. The first thing you notice is the almost tangible gloom of the interior: scant daylight filters through small stained-glass windows onto an

3

CÓRDOBA MICROCENTRO

ACCOMMODATION
Aldea Hostel	2
Azur Real Hotel Boutique	3
Dorá	4
NH Panorama	5
Palenque Hostel	1
Windsor	6

SHOP
Librería Blackpool	1

RESTAURANTS AND CAFÉS
La Alameda	3
Alfonsina	6
Bursátil Café	2
Mandarina	4
Novecento	1
La Vieja Esquina	5

ornate but subdued **floor** of Belgian tiles. The ornate Baroque **pulpit**, in the left-hand aisle, momentarily lifts the atmosphere, as does the decoration of the **ceiling** and **chancel**. This was inspired by the Italian Baroque, but executed in the early twentieth century by local artists of Italian origin, supervised by Emilio Caraffa, whose pictures are displayed at the Museo de Bellas Artes Dr Genaro Pérez (see p.183).

Monasterio de Santa Teresa

Independencia 146 • Matins daily 7.30am • Free

Immediately southwest of Plaza San Martín, across Calle 27 de Abril from the cathedral, the lavish pink and cream-coloured **Monasterio de Santa Teresa** is part of a set of buildings dedicated to St Teresa. As it is a working nunnery, only the soberly decorated **Iglesia Santa Teresa**, built in the mid-eighteenth century, is open to the public. Founded by local dignitary Juan de Tejeda, great-nephew of St Teresa of Ávila, the monastery was built out of gratitude for the miraculous recovery of one of his daughters from a fatal disease; after Tejeda's death, his widow and two daughters became nuns and never left. It was designed by Portuguese architects brought over from Brazil, whose influence can be seen in the ornate cross and gabled shape of the church's two-dimensional bell tower.

Museo de Arte Religioso Juan de Tejeda

Independencia 122 • Wed–Sat 9.30am–12.30pm • $10 • ☎ 0351 15 671 3218, ⓦ museotejedacordoba.com.ar

Housed in the northern side of the complex, in a part no longer used by the holy order, the impressive **Museo de Arte Religioso Juan de Tejeda** is entered through an intricate, cream-coloured Baroque doorway, which contrasts with the pink outer walls. Informative guides, some of whom speak English, will show you around the partly restored **courtyards**, the garden of hydrangeas, orange trees, jasmine and pomegranates, and the rooms and cells of the former nuns' quarters. On display alongside all manner of religious artefacts and sacred relics are a very fine polychrome wooden statue of St Peter and some striking paintings from Cusco. Also from Alto Perú is a seat with carved armrests in the shape of jaguars, a symbol of power in pre-Columbian Perú; the original Spanish shield on the seat back was later removed and replaced with the Argentine one. The nuns' devout asceticism and utter isolation is evident in their bare **cells**, lit only by ground-level vents and blocked off by forbidding grilles. Apart from these vents, the austere confessionals positioned against so-called communicating walls were the sisters' only means of contact with the outside world. Life for members of the Carmelite Order, still in residence next door, has barely changed.

The museum was closed for renovations at the time of research, but should have reopened (probably with an increased entry fee) by the time you read this.

Manzana Jesuítica

Obispo Trejo 242 • Summer Tues–Sun 9am–1pm & 5–8pm; winter Tues–Fri 9am–1pm & 4–8pm, Sat & Sun 9.30am–12.30pm & 3.30–6.30pm • $10 • 1hr guided Spanish-language tours 10am, 11am, 5pm & 6pm; call ahead to organize English-language tours • ☎ 0351 433 2075

Two blocks west and south of Plaza San Martín is the **Manzana Jesuítica**, a whole block, or *manzana*, apportioned to the Society of Jesus a decade after Córdoba was founded. The complex is home to the main offices of the **Universidad Nacional de Córdoba**, the oldest in the country, dating from 1610. Most of the students are now based elsewhere in the city, and much of the campus has been turned into the **Museo Histórico de la Universidad Nacional de Córdoba**. Beyond the harmonious cream- and biscuit-coloured facade are shady patios, ablaze with bougainvillea for much of the year. The **libraries** contain a priceless collection of maps, religious works and late fifteenth-century artefacts, while a ceiling fresco in the **Salon de Grados** shows naked students reaching out to the Muses. Fittingly, this was where applicants for doctorates were quizzed for eight hours a day for three days by their seniors – one wrong answer and they were out.

3

3

The Templo de la Compañía de Jesús

The complex is also home to Argentina's oldest surviving Jesuit temple, the **Templo de la Compañía de Jesús**, built by Felipe Lemaire between 1640 and 1675. The almost rustic simplicity of its restored facade, punctuated only by niches used by nesting pigeons, is a foretaste of the severe, single-naved interior, with its roof of Paraguayan cedar in the shape of a barrel. Fifty painted canvas panels huddled around the ceiling and darkened by time depict the figures and legends of the Society of Jesus – at 10m above ground level they're hard to make out without the aid of binoculars. Even more striking is the handsome **Cusqueño altarpiece** and the floridly decorated pulpit. The chapel to the side is dedicated to Our Lady of Lourdes and was known as the Capilla de los Naturales: it was a roofless structure where indigenous churchgoers were graciously allowed to come and pray until the nineteenth century, when it was covered and lined with ornate marble.

The Capilla Doméstica

Another part of the complex is the **Capilla Doméstica**, the residents' private chapel and "gateway to heaven" – at least according to the inscription over the doorway. Its intimate dimensions, finely painted altarpiece and remarkable ceiling are in total contrast with the grandiose austerity of the main temple. The ceiling is a primitive wooden canopy, decorated with rawhide panels that have been painted with natural vegetable pigments. While the main temple is easily accessible, you have to ask the concierge to let you into the chapel.

The Colegio Nacional de Nuestra Señora de Montserrat

The last of the complex's three main Jesuit buildings is the prestigious **Colegio Nacional de Nuestra Señora de Montserrat**, founded at a nearby location in the city in 1687 but transferred to its present site in 1782, shortly after the Jesuits' expulsion; the building had been their living quarters, arranged around quadrangles. This all-male bastion of privilege finally went co-ed in 1998 despite fierce opposition. The building's studiously Neocolonial appearance – beige-pink facades, a highly ornate doorway, grilled windows and a pseudo-Baroque clock tower looming at the corner with Calle Duarte Quirós – dates from remodelling in the 1920s. Through the embellished doors and the entrance hall with its vivid Spanish majolica floor tiles are the original, seventeenth-century Jesuit cloisters.

Teatro del Libertador General San Martín

Av Vélez Sarsfield 365 • ☎ 0351 433 2323

A block southwest of the Colegio Nacional Montserrat, the austere Neoclassical **Teatro del Libertador General San Martín** is of world-class calibre, with outstanding acoustics and an elegant, understated interior. It was built in 1887 and inaugurated four years later, making it the oldest of its kind in the country. The creaking wooden floor, normally steeply tilted for performances, can be lowered to a horizontal position and the seats removed for dances and other social events.

Museo Histórico Provincial Marqués de Sobremonte

Rosario de Santa Fe 218 • Mon–Fri 8.30am–2pm • $2 • ☎ 0351 433 1661

East of Plaza San Martín, the **Museo Histórico Provincial Marqués de Sobremonte** is a well-preserved and carefully restored showpiece residence and the city's last private colonial house. Built in the middle of the eighteenth century, it was the home of Rafael, Marqués de Sobremonte, between 1784 and 1796. As governor of Córdoba he was responsible for modernizing the city, securing its water supplies and extending it westwards beyond La Cañada.

The building's unassuming exterior, sturdily functional with thickset walls, is embellished by a wrought-iron balcony resting on finely carved wooden brackets, while delicate whitewashed fan-vaulting decorates the simple archway of the entrance.

Guarding the door are two monstrous creatures, apparently meant to be lions, made of *piedra sapo*, a relatively soft stone quarried in the nearby sierras. The leafy **patio** is shaded by a pomegranate tree, supposedly planted when Sobremonte lived here.

The collections

Downstairs, the first rooms to the right house collections of silver and arms, while the rest have been arranged to reflect a nineteenth-century interior; each has an information sheet in English narrating how a typical day there may have passed. Best of all is the museum's outstanding set of paintings of the **Cusco School**, scattered throughout the house. Some of them, such as the *Feast of King David* and *Santa Rita de Cascia*, both downstairs, have been recently and very successfully restored, but others are still in dire need of attention. The portrait of Bishop Salguero de Cabrera displayed in the chapel, dated 1767 and painted at Arequipa, Perú, is a minor masterpiece, while upstairs there is a *Descent from the Cross* featuring a wonderfully contrite Mary Magdalene. Also upstairs, the relentless religious imagery is given a more secular counterpoint by a huge map of South America from 1770 that gives an idea of perceptions of regional geography in the era, and a surprisingly irreverent, scarlet four-poster bed in the "female" bedroom.

Museo de Bellas Artes Dr Genaro Pérez

Av General Paz 33 • Tues–Sun 10am–8pm • Free • ☎ 0351 434 1646

To take in Argentine art from the nineteenth and twentieth centuries, head for the **Museo de Bellas Artes Dr Genaro Pérez**, a block west of the Legislatura Provincial. This municipal gallery is housed in a handsome, early twentieth-century building, designed in a French style for the wealthy Dr Tomás Garzón, who bequeathed it to the city in his will. Impeccably restored, and with fine iron and glass details including an intricate lift, the museum is worth a visit for its interior alone, an insight into how the city's prosperous bourgeoisie lived a century ago. Most of the paintings on display belong to the **Escuela Cordobesa**, a movement whose leading master was the museum's namesake **Genaro Pérez** and which produced brooding portraits and local landscapes, some imitating the French Impressionists. Other names to watch out for are those of the so-called **1880s Generation** such as Fidel Pelliza, Andrés Piñero and Emilio Caraffa, the last famous for his supervision of the paintings inside Córdoba cathedral. The **1920s Generation**, markedly influenced by their European contemporaries including Matisse, Picasso and de Chirico, is represented by Francisco Vidal, Antonio Pedone and José Aguilera.

Cripta Jesuítica

Rivera Indarte and Av Colón • Mon–Fri 10am–3pm, Sat 10am–1pm • $3

At the point where pedestrianized Calle Rivera Indarte intercepts noisy, traffic-infested Avenida Colón, steps lead down into one of the city's previously hidden treasures. Beneath the hectic street lies the peaceful and mysterious **Cripta Jesuítica**, all that remains of an early eighteenth-century Jesuit novitiate razed to the ground in 1928 during the enlargement of Avenida Colón, and rediscovered by accident in 1989 when telephone cables were being laid under the avenue. The rough-hewn **rock walls** of its three naves, partly lined with bare brick, are a refreshing counterpoint to the cloying decoration of some of the city's other churches, and the space is used to good effect for exhibitions, plays and concerts.

Nueva Córdoba and around

South of the historic centre and sliced diagonally by Avenida Hipólito Yrigoyen, **Nueva Córdoba** was laid out in the late nineteenth century. It was designed as an exclusive residential district, but many of Nueva Córdoba's villas and mansions were taken over by bars, cafés, restaurants and offices after the prosperous middle classes moved to the northwestern suburb of Cerro de las Rosas in the 1940s and 1950s.

Architectural styles here are eclectic, to say the least: Neo-Gothic churches, mock-Tudor houses, Georgian facades and Second Empire mini-palaces. Today, Nueva Córdoba's bars are frequented by the city's large student population.

Parque Sarmiento

Southeast of the microcentro **Parque Sarmiento** is Córdoba's breathing space. The centre of the park occupies high ground, affording it panoramic views of otherwise flat Nueva Córdoba and the surrounding city. Designed by French landscape architect **Charles Thays** (see box, p.88), work was completed by 1900, and included the boating lake and the planting of several thousand native and European trees. This huge open area, crisscrossed by avenues of plane trees, is where the city's main **sports facilities** are located, including tennis courts, jogging routes and an Olympic-sized swimming pool.

Paseo del Buen Pastor

Av Hipólito Yrigoyen 325 • **Art Gallery** Daily 10am–10pm • Free • **Dancing Waters** Mon–Thurs & Sun 5pm, 7pm, 9pm & 10pm, Fri & Sat 5pm, 7pm, 9pm, 10pm & 11pm • Free • **Chapel** Tues–Sun 9am–8pm • Free • ☎ 0351 428 5856

On Avenida Hipólito Yrigoyen, between Independencia and Buenos Aires, the **Paseo del Buen Pastor** is a two-storey cultural centre made of stone and glass on the site of a former women's prison. A source of much civic pride, the building houses a small art gallery, temporary exhibitions on the walls of the covered passage that winds around the building's upper level, and several cafés and restaurants, as well as a tourist information office. There are also much hyped **"dancing water"** displays when the fountains around the centre's northern end are lit up in garish colours, set to a musical accompaniment. The area around the fountains is the hangout of choice for lovestruck teenage couples. The **chapel** is perhaps of most interest, hosting regular music concerts and film screenings. Designed by José Montbanch and completed in 1906, its lavishly decorated interior, with murals depicting religious scenes, is a fine example of Italian-influenced *neomanierismo*.

Iglesia de los Capuchinos

c/Buenos Aires and Obispo Oro • No fixed opening times • Free

Opposite the Paseo del Buen Pastor is the **Iglesia de los Capuchinos**, an impressive church mixing Neo-Gothic and Romanesque styles, built between 1927 and 1933, which dominates the Nueva Córdoba skyline. Designed by Italian architect Augusto Ferrari, the church's most interesting features adorn its exterior, in particular images of spiders, scorpions and other animals carved out of stone at the base of the columns beside the main entrance. Most notable are statues of hunched men, representing earthly sin, struggling to support the weight of the godly apostles above them. Above the church's central rose window a statue of St Francis keeps watch over the city.

Museo Provincial de Bellas Artes Emilio Caraffa

Av Poeta Lugones 411 • Tues–Fri 10am–8pm, Sat & Sun 10.30am–7pm • $3 • ☎ 0351 434 3348, ⓦ museocaraffa.org.ar

On the eastern side of the busy Plaza España roundabout is the **Museo Provincial de Bellas Artes Emilio Caraffa**, a ponderous Neoclassical pile inaugurated in 1916, and recently enlarged with the addition of a modernist new block. It was designed by Johan Kronfuss, architect of the city's Legislatura Provincial, and is named for the influential 1880s Generation artist who oversaw the decoration of the cathedral interior. Its airy galleries and shady gardens are used for temporary exhibitions, mostly featuring local artists.

Museo Provincial de Ciencias Naturales

Av Poeta Lugones • Tues–Sun 10am–5.30pm • $8 • ☎ 0351 434 4070

The **Museo Provincial de Ciencias Naturales**, the city's natural sciences museum, is geared up for children and families. There are numerous dinosaur skeletons, as well as exhibits on South American megafauna and the province's varied topography.

Museo Superior de Bellas Artes Evita

Av Hipólito Yrigoyen • Tues–Sun 10am–8pm • $10 • ☎ 0351 434 3636

Housed in the Palacio Ferreyra, one of Nueva Córdoba's finest buildings, the **Museo Superior de Bellas Artes Evita** is surrounded by large French-influenced gardens, designed by Charles Thays. Once the private residence of the wealthy Ferreyra family, the Palacio was built between 1912 and 1916 in an opulent Neo-Bourbon style. It passed into public ownership in 2004 and the museum, which controversially gutted most of the impressive interior of the house, opened in 2007, mixing original features like the grand central staircase with new flooring, lighting and a third floor that feels more chic bar than major art gallery. The result is a bold mix of old and new with spacious rooms featuring five hundred works of art.

The collection

The ground floor focuses on local artists and nineteenth-century Spanish painters while the upper two floors house portrait collections, local landscapes painted between 1920 and 1950 and the eclectic modernist period that followed. Heading up the staircase to the second floor, you pass a silver sculpture of **Evita's head**, a replica made by local artist Juan Carlos Pallarols of the death mask ordered by General Perón following his wife's death in 1952. Other museum highlights include two graphic sketches by Picasso on the top level, and a powerful exhibition about the abuses of the 1970s military dictatorship by Carlos Alonso.

Güemes

Paseo de las Artes: Sat, Sun & public holidays, from 5pm

Bordering the lively commercial area of Nueva Córdoba, the tranquil barrio of **Güemes** has an altogether different feel. The oldest part of town, it's here that Córdoba's mainly Italian population first settled in the 1860s, originally naming the neighbourhood Pueblo Nuevo. Today many of the old low-rise buildings still stand, although some are in desperate need of restoration work. Lined with antique shops and restaurants, Güemes is Córdoba's bohemian neighbourhood, comparable to San Telmo (see p.78) in Buenos Aires. Every weekend it hosts the **Paseo de las Artes**, when the streets around calles Belgrano and Archaval Rodríguez are overtaken by an excellent evening market, with handicraft stalls selling everything from *mate* holders to jewellery. It's the best time to visit the neighbourhood and when its bars and restaurants are at their liveliest.

Cerro de las Rosas and Chateau Carreras

The fashionable and prosperous northwestern suburbs of **Cerro de las Rosas** and **Chateau Carreras** are home to many of Córdoba's trendiest nightclubs (see p.188). Avenida Figueroa Alcorta leads out of the El Abasto area, on the northern bank of the Río Suquía, becomes Avenida Castro Barros and eventually turns into **Avenida Rafael Núñez**, the wide, main street of Cerro de las Rosas, lined with shops, cafés and restaurants. Otherwise, it's a mainly residential area of shaded streets and large villas, built on the relatively cool heights of a wooded hill.

Parque San Martín and the Centro de Arte Contemporáneo

Tues–Sun 2–7pm • Free • ☎ 0351 485 8876

On a peninsula formed by the river the leafy district of **Chateau Carreras** is named after a Neo-Palladian mansion built in 1890 for the influential Carreras family. This picturesque building, painted the colour of Parma violets, save for a row of slender white Ionic columns along the front portico, houses the **Centro de Arte Contemporáneo**, which stages temporary exhibitions of contemporary paintings and photographs. The mansion is tucked away in the landscaped woods of **Parque San Martín**, another of the city's green spaces, which, like Parque Sarmiento, was designed by Charles Thays. Incidentally, the area immediately around the museum is regarded as unsafe and it's best not to linger here alone or after dusk. To the east of the park is Córdoba's massive football stadium, built for the 1978 World Cup finals. Along the avenue, just south of here, are clustered a number of the city's most popular nightclubs (see p.188).

ARRIVAL AND DEPARTURE

CÓRDOBA

By plane Córdoba's Aeropuerto Internacional Taravella (☎ 0351 475 0874) is at Pajas Blancas, 11km north of the city centre. There are numerous daily flights to Buenos Aires, regular ones to Bariloche, Mendoza and Rosario, and several international services to Brazil, Chile and Perú. Minibuses (☎ 0351 475 3083) and taxis (around $100) connect the airport with central Córdoba. The Aerolíneas Argentinas office is at Av Colón 520 (☎ 0810 2228 6527, ⓦ aerolineas.com.ar); LAN is at San Lorenzo 309 (☎ 0351 425 3030, ⓦ lan.com).

By bus The long-distance bus terminal (☎ 0351 428 4141) is at Blvd Perón 380, several blocks east of the city centre, so you might need to take a bus or a taxi to get to and fro, especially if laden with luggage; stops for city buses and taxi ranks are close to the exit. The terminal has an array of facilities including banks and ATMs, a pharmacy, travel agency, telephones, restaurants, showers and dozens of shops. Tickets for destinations throughout the region and

the rest of the country are sold in the basement – advance booking is advisable. Local buses serving some provincial destinations such as Santa Rosa de Calamuchita, Jesús María and Cerro Colorado leave from the cramped Terminal de Minibuses behind Mercado Sur on Blvd Arturo Illia, between calles Buenos Aires and Ituzaingó.

Destinations Alta Gracia (every 15min; 1hr); Buenos Aires (44 daily; 9–11hr); Capilla del Monte (hourly; 1hr 30min); Cosquín (every 30min; 40–50min); Jesús María (every 30min; 1hr 30min); La Cumbre (every 30min–1hr; 2hr 30min); La Falda (every 30min–1hr; 1hr); La Rioja (5 daily; 6hr); Mendoza (hourly; 9–10hr); Mina Clavero (around 5 daily; 3hr); Nono (around 14 daily; 3hr); Rosario (hourly; around 6hr); Salta (10 daily; 11–12hr); San Juan (5 daily; 8hr–8hr 30min); Santa Rosa de Calamuchita (18–20 daily; 2hr 20min); Villa Carlos Paz (every 30min; 40min); Villa General Belgrano (every 45min–1hr; 2hr).

GETTING AROUND

By taxi Most of the city sights are within easy reach of each other, in the microcentro; to venture further afield you're advised to take a taxi rather than brave the city's crammed buses. For *remises* (radio taxis) try Tala Car Remis (☎ 0351 494 7000) or Taxi-Com (☎ 0351 464 4444).

By bus The local bus network is pretty poor, but if you do decide to use it, note that you must first buy a token (*cospel*; $2), available at kiosks and newsstands.

By car For car rental, try Avis, Av Jujuy 235 (☎ 0351 424 6185, ⓦ avis.com), or Localiza, Entre Rios 70 (☎ 0351 422 4867).

INFORMATION AND TOURS

Tourist information The main tourist office is in the Cabildo (daily 8am–8pm; ☎ 0351 434 1200, ⓦ cordoba turismo.gov.ar). Though not the most helpful of offices, it nonetheless has piles of maps and flyers, and there are useful weekly events and walking-tour lists pinned on a board. There are also several smaller (and often more amenable) information offices dotted around town, including at the bus station (daily 7am–9pm; ☎ 0351 433 1982), the airport (daily 8am–8pm; ☎ 0351 434 8390) and the Paseo del Buen Pastor (daily 8am–8pm; ☎ 0351

434 2727).

Tours The municipal tourist authority run regular free walking tours of downtown sights with English-language guides; pop in to the main tourist office to find out what's on. The privately run City Tour (☎ 0351 424 6605) offers sightseeing tours on a red double-decker bus starting from the Plaza San Martín near the cathedral. For day-trips and tours of the province, as well as city tours, try Nativo Viajes, Independencia 174 (☎ 0351 424 5341, ⓦ cordobanativo viajes.com.ar).

ACCOMMODATION

Córdoba has several good hostels and a classy boutique hotel, but the majority of accommodation options in the city are functional at best, with the more expensive places catering mainly to business travellers. Rates for all the hotels and guesthouses listed below include breakfast; the hostels tend to charge extra for it.

HOSTELS AND GUESTHOUSES

★ **Aldea Hostel** Santa Rosa 447 ☎ 0351 4261312, ⓦ aldeahostelcordoba.com; map p.180. This bright, ambitious hostel has space for 100 or so people and is bursting with extras, including a lively bar, two games rooms, a TV lounge, a leafy patio, and a roof terrace. Discounts for longer

stays. Dorms $55, doubles $200

Le Grand Hostel and Suites c/Buenos Aires 547 ☎ 0351 422 7115, ⓦ legrandhostel.com; map p.178. The city's biggest and brashest hostel is based in a French-style building. It has low-cost four-, six- and eight-bed dorms, some simple private rooms, a communal kitchen, a TV lounge, and a pool table. The attached *Le Grand Suites* annexe has smarter, private, en-suite rooms. Dorms $60, doubles $200

N'aike Fresnal 5048 ☎ 0351 589 0501, ⓦ naike.com.ar; map p.178. This friendly, well-run guesthouse is located in the quiet Villa Belgrano neighbourhood, a few kilometres northwest of the city centre. There are just six rooms, all with colourful but tasteful decor; four have private bathrooms. Guests have access to a kitchen, living room, plunge pool and jacuzzi. $290

Palenque Hostel Av General Paz 371 ☎ 0351 423 7588, ⓦ palenquehostel.com.ar; map p.180. Noisy but fun hostel in a pretty converted nineteenth-century townhouse that has retained such features as a black-and-white-tiled floor, stained-glass windows and wrought-iron banisters. The dorms and private rooms (with shared bathrooms) are decent value, and the wood-panelled common areas are good for meeting other backpackers. Dorms $60, doubles $165

Tango Hostel Fructuoso Rivera 70 ☎ 0351 425 6023, ⓦ tangohostelcordoba.com.ar; map p.178. In a good location, near the Paseo de las Artes, this popular hostel has a collection of no-frills dorms, as well as a few private rooms (with shared or private bathrooms). Staff can organize excursions and the atmosphere is friendly and sociable. Dorms $60, doubles $150

HOTELS

★ **Azur Real Hotel Boutique** San Jerónimo 243 ☎ 0351 424 7133, ⓦ azurrealhotel.com; map p.180.

This swish boutique hotel is easily the best place to stay in Córdoba. Located in the microcentro, it has stylish *norteño* decor in a beautifully converted building, with a small outdoor splash pool, a sun lounge, a gym and spa, and a restaurant. $840

Dorá Entre Ríos 70 ☎ 0351 421 2031, ⓦ hoteldora.com .ar; map p.180. Despite the drab decor straight out of the 1970s – check out the leopard-print sofa in the lobby – this mid-range hotel is a decent choice, with reasonable rooms, plus a pool, gym and restaurant. $400

Hotel de la Cañada Av Marcelo T. de Alvear 580 ☎ 0351 421 4649, ⓦ hoteldelacaniada.com.ar; map p.178. Frequented mainly by business travellers, this hotel, which is housed in a looming tower block, has comfortable, if unremarkable en suites, as well as a pool, sauna and gym, and a restaurant-bar. $600

NH Panorama Av Marcelo T. de Alvear 251 ☎ 0351 410 3900, ⓦ nh-hotels.com; map p.180. As the name suggests, the hotel – part of the Spanish NH chain – enjoys fine views from its pleasant en suites, roof garden and small pool. The slightly cheaper sister establishment, *Urbano*, is on the same street at no. 363. $600

Windsor c/Buenos Aires 214 ☎ 0351 422 9164, ⓦ windsortower.com; map p.180. One of the few hotels with charm in this category, opting for a resolutely British style. Rooms in the classy new wing are more expensive, and the bathrooms are more modern. There's a sauna, pool and gym, plus a slightly pretentious restaurant. $600

EATING

Interesting **restaurants** and **cafés** are disappointingly thin on the ground, though Córdoba cranks up a gear during university term time. With a couple of notable exceptions, the city centre has little to offer in the evenings, even becoming rather seedy. Nueva Córdoba and the cooler heights of the Cerro de las Rosas feel safer and have a number of restaurants, but they can also be rather colourless.

★ **La Alameda** Obispo Trejo 170; map p.180. With a great bohemian ambience, *Alameda* serves reasonably priced food (most mains $25–40) including empanadas and *humitas* alongside cold beers. Patrons leave scribbled notes and minor works of art pinned to the wall. Mon–Sat noon–4/5am.

★ **Alfonsina** Duarte Quirós 66 ☎ 0351 427 2847, ⓦ alfonsinaweb.com.ar; map p.180. Busy student restaurant-bar with economical snacks, meals ($30–60) and alcoholic drinks. It's a particularly popular spot for an early evening *mate*, generally served with home-baked bread, and there are often live folk-music performances. There are two other branches: at Belgrano 763 and at calles Viamonte and Lima. Mon–Sat 8am–2pm & 6pm–2am, Sun 6pm–2am.

El Arrabal Belgrano 899 and Fructuoso Rivera ☎ 0351 460 2990, ⓦ elarrabal.com.ar; map p.178. Good-value meals – including excellent steaks – but the main reason

to come is for the brilliant tango and *milonga* classes and shows; a three-course meal and tango show costs $139. Mon–Sat 10.30am–1.30am, Sun 10.30am–5pm & 6.30pm–1.30am.

Bursátil Café Ituzaingó and San Jerónimo ☎ 0351 571 9971; map p.180. In Córdoba's small financial district, this café takes its name from the Spanish for "stock exchange", and names its main dishes for international exchanges. Food includes classics like *locro* (stew) and international dishes such as Caesar salad. Mains $30–70. Mon–Fri 7am–7/8pm, Sat noon–7/8pm.

Mandarina Obispo Trejo 171 ☎ 0351 426 4909; map p.180. This central restaurant has a menu that's a touch more inventive than the norm, with Chinese, Japanese and Southeast Asian dishes, alongside pizzas, pastas and steaks. The decor features orange walls and an array of Buddhist imagery– there are also New-Age quotes from the likes of Eckhart Tolle to ponder while you wait for your food. Mains $30–110. Daily 8am–2am.

Novecento Deán Funes 33 ☎0351 423 0660, ⓦnovecento.com; map p.180. This atmospheric restaurant, part of the Cabildo complex, styles itself as an "American bistro" and delivers quality food on a menu featuring burgers, pastas, risottos, steaks and fresh fish – try the rainbow trout. Mains $50–90. Daily 11.30am–4pm & 8pm–1am.

Las Rías de Galicia Montevideo 271 ☎0351 428 1333; map p.178. You can choose from top-quality, Spanish-influenced seafood, fish and meat dishes at this swish restaurant; mains cost $45–100, though there's also a good-value weekday dish of the day for $35–40. Daily noon–3pm & 8.30pm–12.30am.

La Vieja Esquina Caseros and Belgrano ☎0351 424 7940; map p.180. This tiny local joint serves up excellent empanadas (around $5), *humitas* and *locro*; you can eat them at one of the counters, take them away or even have them delivered to your room. Mon–Sat 11am–3pm & 7.30pm–midnight.

DRINKING, NIGHTLIFE AND ENTERTAINMENT

Most of the **nightlife** has moved to two outlying areas: El Abasto, a revitalized former warehouse district close to the centre on the northern banks of the Río Suquía that buzzes with **bars**, clubs and **live-music venues**, many along Blvd Las Heras, and the even trendier Chateau Carreras area, just south of Cerro de las Rosas, which has a number of flash **clubs**. Córdoba also has a fine theatre, though you will need a good grasp of Spanish to get the most out of its productions.

BARS AND NIGHTCLUBS

Carreras Cárcano and Av del Piamonte, Chateau Carreras ☎0351 15 676 2342; map p.178. One of the city's biggest and liveliest clubs, *Carreras* is styled up to look like a "beach" and focuses on house and electro, though early on in the evening the sounds are a bit more varied. Fri & Sat 11pm–6am.

Dorian Gray Blvd Las Heras and Av Roque Sáenz Peña, El Abasto ☎0351 15 403 1626; map p.178. One of Córdoba's most popular clubs, playing techno and house on Fridays, with poppier edge on Saturdays. Prominent international DJs, including former *Space* resident Steve Lawler, have played here in the past. Fri & Sat 11pm–6am.

Infierno Cárcano and Av del Piamonte, Chateau Carreras ☎0351 15 509 8349; map p.178. This large, very popular, commercial dance venue features a slightly odd mix of cutting-edge music (especially house and techno, though also sometimes Latin and drum'n'bass) and fashion parades. Sat midnight–6am.

Johnny B Good Av Hipólito Yrigoyen 320, Nueva Córdoba, and Av Rafael Núñez 4791, Cerro de la Rosas

☎0351 424 3960, ⓦjbgood.com; map p.178. This busy, rather cheesy restaurant-bar serves up good North American-style food, a wide range of *tragos* (alcoholic drinks; from $20) and a rock-dominated soundtrack (live music most weekends). Mon–Thurs 7.30pm–2am, Fri 7.30pm–4am, Sat 11pm–4am, Sun 6pm–3am.

Voodoo Lounge Jerónimo Luís de Cabrera 565, Alta Córdoba ☎0351 15 030993, ⓦvoodoocba.com.ar; map p.178. Billing itself as a "glamour bar", this sleek venue plays everything from house and pop, to 1980s crowd pleasers and salsa. International DJs – such as Carl Cox – sometimes play sets here. Fri & Sat 10pm–6am.

THEATRE

Teatro del Libertador General San Martín Duarte Quirós 135 ☎0351 433 2323. One of Argentina's best theatres, the Teatro del Libertador General San Martín dates back to the 1890s and puts on excellent dance shows, operas, musicals and concerts, as well as (Spanish-language) theatrical performances. Box office daily 9am–8pm.

DIRECTORY

Banks and exchange The best banks for exchanging money are Citibank, at Rivadavia 104, and BBVA, at 9 de Julio 450. ATMs are everywhere, especially around Plaza San Martín.

Bookshop Librería Blackpool, Deán Funes 395 (Jan Mon–Fri 9am–1pm, Sat 9.30am–1.30pm; March Mon–Fri 8.30am–8.30pm, first and second Sat also 4.50–8.30pm; rest of year Mon–Fri 9am–1pm & 4–8pm, Sat 9.30am–1.30pm; ☎0351 481 5403, ⓦblackpoolcerro .com.ar), has a selection of English-language novels,

nonfiction and travel guides.

Consulates Bolivia, Bellas Artes 56 ☎0351 411 4489; Chile, c/Buenos Aires 1386 ☎0351 469 2010; Germany, Elíseo Canton 1870 ☎0351 489 0900; Uruguay, San Jerómino 167, piso 20 ☎0351 424 1028.

Internet access CyberUNO, at c/Duarte Quirós 201.

Laundry There are several branches of Laverap, including a conveniently located one at c/Chacabuco 313 (☎0351 423 6678).

Post office Av General Paz 201.

The Camino de la Historia

The first 150km stretch of **RN-9** that runs north from Córdoba city towards Santiago del Estero is promoted by the provincial tourist authority as the **Camino de la Historia** ("Historical Route"), as it coincides with part of the colonial Camino Real ("Royal Way"), the Spanish road from Lima and Potosí to present-day Argentina. This was the route taken, albeit in the opposite direction, by the region's first European settlers – the founders of Córdoba city – and the **Jesuit missionaries** who quickly dominated the local economy and culture. Eastwards from the road stretch some of Argentina's most fertile cattle ranches; to the west the unbroken ridge of the Sierra Chica runs parallel to the highway. One of the country's finest Jesuit estancias, now host to the well-presented **Museo Jesuítico Nacional**, can be visited at **Jesús María**, while beautiful **Santa Catalina**, lying off the main road to the north in a bucolic hillside setting, is still inhabited by descendants of the family who moved here at the end of the eighteenth century. Further north, in **Villa Tulumba**, a timeless little place well off the beaten track, the nondescript parish church houses a masterpiece of Jesuit art, the altarpiece that once adorned the Jesuits' temple and, later, Córdoba cathedral, until it was moved up here in the early nineteenth century. As they developed their intensive agriculture, the Jesuits all but wiped out the region's pre-Hispanic civilizations, but some precious vestiges of their culture, namely intriguing rock paintings, can be seen in the far north of the province, just off RN-9 at **Cerro Colorado**, one of Argentina's finest pre-Columbian sites.

Jesús María

Lying just off the busy RN-9, 50km north of Córdoba, **JESÚS MARÍA** is a sleepy little town that comes to life for the annual Festival Nacional de la Doma y el Folklore,

---

THE JESUITS IN CÓRDOBA PROVINCE

Even today the city of **Córdoba** owes its importance largely to the **Jesuits** who founded a college here in 1613. It would later become South America's second university, the Universidad San Carlos, in 1621, making Córdoba the de facto capital of the Americas south of Lima. In 1640, the Jesuits built a temple (see p.182) at the heart of the city, and for the next 120 years the Society of Jesus dominated life there. Their emphasis on education earned the city the nickname *La Docta* ("the Learned"), and even today Córdoba is still regarded as an erudite kind of place – albeit politically radical.

But while the Jesuits and other missionaries turned Córdoba into the cultural capital of this part of the empire, their presence elsewhere resulted in the decline in numbers of the native population. The indigenous Sanavirones, Comechingones and Abipones resolutely defended themselves from the invaders. Finally conquered, they thwarted attempts by the Spanish to "civilize" them under the system of *encomiendas*, a forced labour system in which indigenous populations were taught Catholicism and Spanish in "exchange" for their toil. Nonetheless, devastated by influenza and other imported ailments, the indigenous population dwindled from several thousand in the late sixteenth century to only a few hundred a century later. Apart from a few archeological finds, such as rock paintings, the only signs of their former presence are the names of villages, rivers and the mountain range to the south of the city, and discernible indigenous features in the *serranos*, or rural inhabitants of the sierras.

Despite their profound effect on the area's original inhabitants, the Jesuits were relatively enlightened by colonial standards, educating their workforce and treating them comparatively humanely. In addition to various monuments in the city itself, you can still visit their estancias, whose produce sustained communities and boosted trade in the whole empire. The Jesuit buildings in Córdoba and four of the remaining estancias around the province – including **Santa Catalina** (see p.190), **Alta Gracia** (see p.199), **Jesús María** (see p.190) and **Caroya**, near Jesús María – are all UNESCO World Heritage Sites.

a gaucho fiesta with lively entertainment held every evening during the first fortnight of January.

Museo Jesuítico Nacional

Just north of town, near the amphitheatre • Summer Tues–Fri 8am–7pm, Sat & Sun 10am–noon & 3–7pm; winter Tues–Fri 8am–7pm, Sat & Sun 2–6pm • $5 • Guided tours 9am, 10am, 11am, 2.30pm, 3.30pm & 5.30pm • ☎ 03525 420126 • Jesús María is reached by regular bus from Córdoba (every 30min; 1hr 30min)

On the town's northern outskirts is the **Museo Jesuítico Nacional** housed in the former residence and the bodega, or wineries, of a well-restored **Jesuit estancia**. Next to the missionaries' living quarters and the adjoining eighteenth-century church are a colonial *tajamar*, or reservoir, and apple and peach orchards – all that remain of the estancia's once extensive territory, which in the seventeenth and eighteenth centuries covered more than a hundred square kilometres.

In contrast to the bare, rough-hewn granite of the outside walls of the complex, a whitewashed courtyard lies beyond a gateway to the right of the church. Its two storeys of simple arches on three sides set off the bright red roofs, which are capped with the original ceramic tiles, or *musleros*. These slightly convex tiles, taking their name from *muslo*, or thigh, because the tile-makers shaped the clay on their legs, are common to all the Jesuit estancias. The U-shaped *residencia* contains the former missionaries' cells, storehouses and communal rooms, now used for temporary exhibits and various permanent displays of archeological finds, colonial furniture, sacred relics and religious artwork from the seventeenth and eighteenth centuries, along with farming and wine-making equipment. The local wine, Lagrimilla, is claimed to be the first colonial wine served in the Spanish court – Argentina's earliest vineyards were planted here at the end of the sixteenth century.

Santa Catalina

Estancia Tues–Sun: summer 10am–1pm & 2.30–7.30pm; winter 10am–1pm & 3–6pm • $5 • ☎ 03525 428505 • A taxi from Jesús María costs around $100

West of Jesús María, the RP-66 leads to Ascochinga, from where an easily passable trail heads north through thick forest to **SANTA CATALINA** 20km to the northwest. Almost completely hidden among the hills, Santa Catalina is the biggest, and undoubtedly the finest, Jesuit **estancia** in the region, an outstanding example of colonial architecture. A sprawling yet harmonious set of early eighteenth-century buildings, it is dominated by its church, whose elegant silhouette and symmetrical towers suddenly and unexpectedly appear as you emerge from the woods. Whitewashed to protect the porous stone from the elements, the brightness of the building almost dazzles you when you approach.

The **church** is dedicated to St Catherine of Alexandria, whose feast day is celebrated with pomp every November 25; the sternly imposing facade is reminiscent of the Baroque churches of southern Germany and Austria. Inside, the austere single nave, whitewashed like the exterior, is decorated with a gilded wooden **retable** that houses an image of St Catherine, and a fine carob-wood pulpit. On the right-hand flank of the church is an overgrown little cemetery, whose outer wall bears a plaque commemorating the Italian composer and organist Domenico Zípoli, who died here in 1726.

ACCOMMODATION AND EATING

SANTA CATALINA

Posada Camino Real 10km north of Santa Catalina • ☎ 0351 15 552 5215, ⬤ posadacaminorealweb.com.ar. The rooms at this modern guesthouse are extremely comfortable; horseriding and other activities in the unspoilt countryside are laid on and a swimming pool and massages provide welcome relaxation. It's also worth visiting for the gourmet food served in the restaurant (open to nonguests). Rates include breakfast, dinner and horseriding. **$650**

Villa Tulumba

A taxi from Córdoba costs $250–350

Ninety-five kilometres north of Santa Catalina, **VILLA TULUMBA** is a tiny hamlet that's home to a Baroque masterpiece: a subtly crafted seventeenth-century **tabernacle**, complete with polychrome wooden cherubs and saints, and decorated with just a hint of gold, inside the otherwise nondescript parish church. Soon after Argentina's independence, Bishop Moscoso, a modernizing anti-Jesuit bishop of Córdoba, decided that the city's cathedral should have a brand new altarpiece, and asked all the parishes in his diocese to collect funds for it. The citizens of Villa Tulumba were the most generous, and were rewarded with this tabernacle, which had been transferred to the cathedral from the city's Jesuit temple after the Society of Jesus was expelled from the Spanish empire by King Carlos III in 1767.

Cerro Colorado

Around 120km north of Jesús María, at the far northern end of the Camino de la Historia

The village of **CERRO COLORADO**, no more than a few houses dotted along a riverbank, nestles in a deep, picturesque valley, surrounded by three looming peaks, Cerro Colorado (830m), Cerro Veladero (810m) and Cerro Inti Huasi (772m), all of which are easily explored on foot and afford fine views of the countryside. The main attraction, though, is the **Reserva Cultural Natural Cerro Colorado**, home to one of Argentina's finest collections of **petroglyphs**.

La Reserva Cultural Natural Cerro Colorado

Compulsory guided tours leave 3–5 times daily from the guard post at the entrance to the village • $2

La Reserva Cultural Natural Cerro Colorado is home to some fascinating vestiges of pre-Columbian culture, notably its extensive collection of petroglyphs, several thousand drawings that were scraped and painted by the indigenous inhabitants onto the pink rock face at the base of the mountains and in caves higher up between 1000 and 1600 AD.

Some of the petroglyphs depict horses, cattle and European figures as well as native llamas, guanacos, condors, pumas and snakes, but few of the abstract figures have been satisfactorily or conclusively interpreted – though your guide will offer convincing theories. The deep depressions, or *morteros*, in the horizontal rock nearby were caused over the centuries by the grinding and mixing of paints. Of the different **pigments** used – chalk, ochre, charcoal, oils and vegetable extracts – the white and black stand out more than the rest, but climatic changes, especially increased humidity, are taking their toll, and many of the rock paintings are badly faded. The petroglyphs are best viewed very early in the morning or before dusk, when the rock takes on blazing red hues and the pigments' contrasts are at their strongest.

There's also a small, free archeological museum, next to the guard post, with photos of the petroglyphs and native flora.

ARRIVAL AND DEPARTURE

CERRO COLORADO

By bus Direct buses (3hr 30min) from Córdoba to Cerro Colorado are scheduled on weekends only, but several daily ones (3hr 15min) run from Córdoba to Santa Elena, 11km from Cerro Colorado village; from there you need to take a taxi ($40–50) to the village.

By car The reserve is next to Cerro Colorado village, 10km down a meandering dirt track off the RN-9, west of Santa Elena. Drivers beware: there's a deep ford lurking round a bend, 1km before you enter the village, followed by another in the village itself.

ACCOMMODATION

Hotel Cerro Colorado RP-21 ☎ 03522 15 648990, ⌨ hotelcerrocolorado.com. This simple, whitewashed hotel is a good-value choice, though not the most inspiring place in the world. It offers clean, if rather bare, en-suite rooms, a TV lounge, and a restaurant-bar. Rates include breakfast. $180

La Italiana ☎ 0351 15 687 0445, ⌨ cab-laitaliana .com. The friendly, rustic *La Italiana* has a collection of ochre-coloured *cabañas* that sleep up to eight people; each comes with bedrooms, private bathroom, kitchenette and dining area. A good option for families or groups. Breakfast costs extra. **$250**

The Punilla Valley

Squeezed between the continuous ridge of the Sierra Chica to the east, and the higher peaks of the Sierra Grande to the west, the peaceful **Punilla Valley** is Argentina's longest-established inland tourist area, with idyllic mountain scenery and fresh air, family-friendly resorts and numerous top-class outdoor pursuits.

The RN-38 to La Rioja bisects the valley, which stretches northwards for about 100km from horrendously noisy **Villa Carlos Paz**, the self-styled "Gateway to the Punilla", some 35km along the RP-34 west of Córdoba. Tens of thousands of Argentines migrate to this brash inland beach resort every summer in an insatiable quest for sun, sand and socializing – the town is renowned for its mega-clubs and crowded bars. Just north and overlooked by a sugar-loaf hill, El Pan de Azúcar, is **Cosquín**, a slightly calmer place with an annual folk festival. The further north you go, the more tranquil the resorts become: **La Falda**, **La Cumbre** and **Capilla del Monte** have all retained their slightly old-fashioned charm while offering a mixture of high-quality services and a propensity for New Age pursuits. Relatively less crowded, they make for better bases from which to explore the mountains on foot, on horseback or in a vehicle, or to try out some of the adventurous sports on offer. Anyone looking for remote locales to explore should head for the dirt roads between Capilla del Monte and Santa Catalina, where from **Ongamira** and **Ischilín** you can discover some of the region's most remarkable landscapes.

Villa Carlos Paz

Brash **VILLA CARLOS PAZ** lies at the southern end of the Punilla Valley, on the southwestern banks of a large, dirty reservoir, the Lago San Roque. It sits at a major junction, that of the RP-34, which heads south to Mina Clavero, and the RN-38

ESTANCIAS AROUND THE SIERRA CHICA

Although the Jesuit **estancias** in the Sierra Chica do not generally allow the opportunity to stay the night, there are a number of estancias around Santa Catalina and in the Punilla Valley that have opened their doors to visitors. These places can make excellent spots to laze away a few days in the countryside, horseriding and swimming; they can also be used as a base for visiting the area's other attractions.

★**Estancia Dos Lunas** Near Ongamira ☎011 6219 5390, ⓦdoslunas.com.ar. Lying discreetly off this road in extensive grounds, *Estancia Dos Lunas* is one of the best places to stay in the region. Simple but comfortable rooms are housed in English-style long houses, while the large pool offers views of the dramatic surroundings, including the peak of Cerro Uritorco. Gourmet cooking, excellent horserides (including full-moon outings), massages and a personal touch are the estancia's major assets. Rates include full board and activities. **$1650** per person

★**Estancia Los Potreros** Outside Río Ceballos, 1hr drive northwest of Córdoba ☎011 6091 2692, ⓦestancialospotreros.com. An authentic working estancia that has been owned by the Anglo-Argentine Begg family for four generations, *Los Potreros* is the place to come if you want to ride horses – the friendly owners will take you on wonderful trips around the area, organize polo lessons, and allow you to observe or help with farm activities. The animals are so well looked after and trained that even reluctant riders *usually* end up happily on horseback. Accommodation is in the attractive adobe *casco*, and you dine with the family. Trail rides, staying at local homesteads, and "learn to play polo" weeks also take place throughout the year, but must be arranged in advance. Rates include transfers, horseriding trips and full board; three-night minimum stay. **$2050** per person

toll road, which goes north through the valley towards Cruz del Eje and La Rioja. Nationally famous, but now spoilt by chaotic construction, pollution and overcrowding, the resort is frequently compared with Mar del Plata (see p.163), only without the ocean. It started out in the 1930s as a holiday centre for well-off Cordobeses, with sandy beaches created along the lakeside. Nowadays people whiz around the lake in catamarans and motorboats, or on water skis. In the town centre, dozens of amusement arcades and theme parks blare music, while most of the bars and *confiterías* show video clips or offer karaoke. The town sprawls in a disorderly way around the lake – the western districts are generally greener, airier and more attractive. The local population of around 72,000 more than doubles at the height of summer.

ARRIVAL AND INFORMATION

By bus Villa Carlos Paz's busy and cramped bus terminal is on Av San Martín, between Belgrano and Maipú.
Destinations Buenos Aires (19 daily; 10–12hr); Córdoba (every 30min; 40min).

Tourist information The tourist office is right in front of the bus terminal, at Av San Martín 400 (daily: Jan & Feb 7am–10.30pm; March–Dec 7am–9pm; ☎ 03541 421624).

ACCOMMODATION AND EATING

Accommodation During peak periods finding a place to stay can be difficult, even though there are many hotels, but residents often stand by the road advertising rooms for rent.

Eating There are dozens of places to eat, mostly pizzerias and *parrillas*; many are clustered around Av General Paz in the centre.

Cosquín

Some 25km north of Villa Carlos Paz, and barely more appealing, the small but bustling town of **COSQUÍN** nestles in a sweep of the river of the same name and in the lee of the 1260m **Pan de Azúcar**. It's one of the region's oldest settlements – dating from colonial times – and has been a holiday resort since the end of the nineteenth century. The summit of the sugar-loaf mountain, which affords panoramic views of the valley and mountains beyond, can be reached by a chairlift (*aerosilla*) from the well-signposted Complejo Aerosilla, which sits about 8km north of town and also houses a bronze monument to **Carlos Gardel**, the legendary tango singer, as well as the inevitable *confitería*. Alternatively, you can skip the chairlift and use your legs – from the Complejo Aerosilla it's about half an hour up a steep path. Cosquín has always been associated nationwide with the **Festival Nacional de Folklore** (☎aquicosquin.org), held annually in the second half of January and attended by folk artists, ballet troupes and classical musicians from across the country, although it has declined in quality in recent years. The festival takes place in the so-called Plaza Nacional del Folklore (actually the Plaza Próspero Molina) just off RN-38, which threads through the centre of town.

ARRIVAL AND INFORMATION

By bus The bus station, with regular services to and from Córdoba (every 30min; 40–50min) and other Punilla resorts, lies one block west of Plaza San Martín on Presidente Perón.

Tourist information The tourist office is at Plaza San Martín 560 (summer daily 7am–10pm; winter Mon–Fri 7am–2pm & 2.30pm–7pm; Sat & Sun 10am–1pm & 3pm–7pm; ☎ 03541 454644, ☎ cosquinturismo.gob.ar).

La Falda and around

Twenty kilometres north of Cosquín and a little more peaceful still, **LA FALDA** serves as a base from which to explore the nearby mountains – a taste of the far finer scenery to come some way up the valley. Today the town is best known for its annual three-day tango festival (☎festivaldetangolafalda.com) in July.

Hotel Edén

Av Edén 1400 • Guided tours daily 9.30am–6pm; guided night tours are also offered Jan–Feb and at Easter • $25 • ☎ 03548 426643, 🌐 hoteledenlafalda.com

In the early twentieth century, La Falda was an exclusive resort, served by the newly built railway and luring the great and the good from as far afield as Europe. A major advertising campaign was conducted here by a German-run luxury hotel, **Hotel Edén**, a magnificent holiday palace built in the 1890s, now a dilapidated and unusual tourist attraction. Much of Argentine high society stayed here in the 1920s and 1930s, as well as such famous international guests as the Prince of Wales and Albert Einstein, and some say even Adolf Hitler. The state confiscated it from its German owners in the 1940s, after which it fell into decline, but its grandiose design and opulent decor are still discernible, especially in the newly renovated lobby, wine cellar and *confitería*. The guided tours take you around the faded rooms; night tours, which are good, creepy fun, are also run during the summer and Easter, though you'll need decent Spanish to understand the ghost stories.

Cerro Banderita

From La Falda, follow Av Edén to its end and then take c/Austria

For exhilarating views of the valley, head for **Cerro Banderita**, where the El Chorrito, a small waterfall among lush vegetation, is the starting point of the steep one-hour climb to the peak, which many people do on horseback, before riding along the mountaintop. Of the longer routes, one of the most impressive takes you east over the Sierra Chica towards **Río Ceballos**; the views into the Punilla Valley from the peak at **Cerro Cuadrado**, 2km from La Falda, are stunning.

ARRIVAL, INFORMATION AND TOURS

LA FALDA

By bus The bus station is on Av Buenos Aires, just north of the intersection of avenidas Presidente Kennedy and Edén; all buses from Córdoba (every 30min–1hr; 1hr) and Carlos Paz (every 30min–1hr; 45min–1hr) to San Juan and La Rioja stop here.

Tourist information The tourist office, several blocks south of the bus station at Av España 50 (summer daily 10am–10pm; winter Mon–Sat 8am–9pm, Sun 10am–5pm; ☎ 03548 423007), has stacks of information, including where to hire horses or rent motorbikes or mountain bikes.

Tours Several agencies offer tours in the surrounding area, including Polo Tour at Av Edén 412 (☎ 03548 426101, 🌐 polotours.com.ar).

ACCOMMODATION AND EATING

Las Ardillas Las Lomas and El Rodeo ☎ 03548 426254, 🌐 lasardillas.net. This complex has a series of spacious, self-contained *cabañas* sleeping up to six people, as well as several "suites" – essentially more traditional hotel rooms – with hydrotherapy baths and balconies. There's an outdoor pool, and ample grounds to relax in. Breakfast included. *Cabañas* $360, suites $440

Camping Club del Lago 500m from the Siete Cascadas waterfalls, west of the bus terminal ☎ 03548 15 578511, 🌐 campingclubdel-lago.com. In a pleasant lakeside location, *Camping Club del Lago* provides both spots to pitch your tent and wooden cabins sleeping up to six people, plus a restaurant, a pool, and cooking facilities. Camping $48, cabins $200

Hostal L'Hirondelle Av Edén 861 ☎ 03548 422825, 🌐 lhirondellehostal.com. One of the best places to stay in town, the attractive *L'Hirondelle* offers comfortable en suites (each named after a famous writer or poet), a heated swimming pool, spa and jacuzzi, and a restaurant and bar. Check out the website for promotions. Breakfast included. $418

La Cumbre and around

Just east of the RN-38, 14km north of La Falda, **LA CUMBRE** is a small, leafy town, a great spot for fishing, exploring the mountains, participating in adventure pursuits or just relaxing. Over 1140m above sea level, it enjoys mild summers and cool winters, though is occasionally blanketed in snow. Several trout-rich streams run through town, among them the Río San Gerónimo, which runs past the central Plaza 25 de Mayo. A British community was established here when the railways were built in the nineteenth century, and La Cumbre's prestigious golf club, its predominantly mock-Tudor villas and manicured lawns testify to a long-standing Anglo-Saxon presence. But despite the resort's genteel appearance it has become synonymous with **hang-gliding**; every March international competitions are held here. Cerro Mirador, the cliff-top launching-point for hang-gliding and parasailing, is near the ruined colonial estancia and chapel of **Cuchi Corral**, 8km due west of La Cumbre and worth visiting for the views alone.

El Paraíso

Cruz Chica, 2.5km north of La Cumbre • Guided visits daily: Jan & Feb 10.30am–1pm & 4–8pm; April–Sept 2–6pm; March & Oct–Dec 3–7pm • $10 • ☎ 03548 15 630043, ⊛ fundacionmujicalainez.org

Anyone with a literary bent will enjoy the small museum at **El Paraíso**. This handsome Spanish-style house, built in 1915 and with an exquisite garden designed by Charles Thays (see box, p.88), was home to hedonistic writer Manuel "Manucho" Mujica Laínez, whose novel *Bomarzo* is regarded as an Argentine classic. Written in 1962, it was turned into an opera whose premiere at the Teatro Colón in Buenos Aires in 1967 was banned by the military dictatorship. The house, where it is said he held frequent orgies, contains a delightful collection of his personal effects, including 15,000 books, paintings, photographs and all manner of objects.

Camino de los Artesanos

Running roughly parallel to the RN-38 as it heads south to Villa Giardino is the winding **Camino de los Artesanos**, along which you'll find over two dozen establishments selling all manner of crafts – silver- and pewterware, macramé, ceramics, woollens – along with breweries, shops serving *dulce de leche* and home-made cakes, and even places offering yoga and massages.

Candonga

45km south of La Cumbre; you'll need your own car or to take a taxi • Wed–Fri 11.30am–7.30pm, Sat & Sun 11.30am–8.30pm • Free • ☎ 0351 15 529 4778, ⊛ candonga.com.ar

Some 45km from La Cumbre is the old **Estancia Santa Gertrudis**, featuring the splendid eighteenth-century Jesuit chapel of **Candonga** – a historic national monument – with its pristine walls, ochre-tiled roof and rough-hewn stone steps. The majestic curve of its porch, the delicate bell tower and lantern-like cupola fit snugly into the bucolic valley setting, set off by a fast-flowing brook that sweeps through the pampas fields nearby. The estancia serves food, and there are generally several rural activities on offer.

ARRIVAL, INFORMATION AND ACTIVITIES

LA CUMBRE

By bus The terminal is at Caraffa and General Paz; there are regular services to and from Córdoba (every 30min–1hr; 2hr 30min) and Capilla del Monte (every 30min–1hr; 30–45min).

Tourist information In the former train station at avenidas San Martín and Caraffa, 300m southwest of the main square (daily 8am–10pm; ☎ 03548 452966, ⊛ lacumbre.gov.ar).

Activities There's hang-gliding with Aeroclub La Cumbre (☎ 03548 452544), Camino a los Tronco s/n, or Aeroatelier (☎ 03548 452544, ⊛ aeroatelier.com); horseriding with El Rosendo, Juan XXIII s/n (☎ 03548 15 565150); and rock-climbing with Escuela de Montaña y Escalada George Mallory, 25 de Mayo 65 (☎ 03548 451393, ✉ jorgemallory @yahoo.com).

ACCOMMODATION

Posada de la Montaña 9 de Julio 753 ☎ 03548 451028, ⊛ posadadelamontana.com.ar. La Cumbre is somewhat lacking in decent budget and lower-mid-range hotels; *Posada de la Montaña* is one of the better (fairly) economical options, with homely, en-suite rooms and a small pool in the back garden. Rates include breakfast. **$310**

Posada San Andrés Benitz and Monteagudo ☎ 03548 15 56246. A lovely stone-built home dating back to the 1930s, *Posada San Andrés* has tasteful en suites overlooking a flower-filled garden. There's a pool and jacuzzi, and the breakfast (included in the rates) is excellent. **$460**

Capilla del Monte

Lively **CAPILLA DEL MONTE**, 17km north of La Cumbre, sits at the confluence of the rivers Calabalumba and Dolores against the bare-sloped Cerro Uritorco, at 1979m the highest peak of the Sierra Chica. It was a resort for Argentina's bourgeoisie at the end of the nineteenth century, as testified by the many luxurious villas, some of them now very dilapidated. These days it attracts more alternative vacationers, as you can tell from the number of hotels and restaurants calling themselves *naturista*, or back to nature. The town has few sights, but serves as an appealing base for treks into the mountains or hang-gliding and other pursuits. The central Plaza San Martín lies only a couple of blocks east of the RN-38, which runs through the west of the town, parallel to the Río de Dolores. From the plaza, Diagonal Buenos Aires, the busy commercial pedestrian mall, runs southeast to the quaint former train station on Calle Pueyrredón; it's claimed to be South America's only roofed street, an assertion nowhere else has rushed to contend. A number of **balnearios** can be found along the Río Calabalumba, including *Balneario Calabalumba*, at the northern end of General Paz, and *Balneario La Toma*, at the eastern end of Sabattini.

In addition to the fresh air, unspoilt countryside and splendid opportunities for sports pursuits, such as trekking and fishing, many visitors are also drawn to the area by claims of **UFO sightings**, "energy centres" and numerous local **legends**. One such myth asserts that when Calabalumba, the young daughter of a witch doctor, eloped with Uritorco, the latter was turned into a mountain while she was condemned to eternal sorrow, her tears forming the river that flows from the mountainside.

Cerro Uritorco

The path starts 3km from the *Balneario Calabalumba*, northeast of Plaza San Martín • Open daily; you must register at the base of the mountain and set off between 8am and 12.30pm and start your return by 3.30pm • $50 • Ⓦ cerrouritorco.com.ar

The **Cerro Uritorco**, the focus for Capillo del Monte's supposed paranormal activity, is well worth the climb (about 4hr to the top) up a steep, well-trodden path for the grandiose views across the valley to the Sierra de Cuniputo to the west. Only part of the climb is shaded, so take water with you.

NATURE'S MEDICINE IN THE CENTRAL SIERRAS

A bewildering variety of vegetation grows on the mountainsides of the Central Sierras and is representative of three of the country's principal phytogeographic zones – the Andes, the Pampas and the Chaco. Many of these plant species are reputed to possess remarkable **medicinal properties**. Perhaps best known is the *peperina*, of which there are two varieties: *Mintostachys verticillata* and *Satureja parvifolia* (the latter often known as *peperina de la sierra*). Both are highly aromatic and extremely digestive but, in men, diminish sexual potency. The *yerba del pollo* (*Alternanthera pungens*), on the other hand, is a natural cure for flatulence, while ephedrine, a tonic for heart ailments, is extracted industrially from *tramontana* (*Ephedra triandra*), a broom-like bush found all over the highlands at altitudes of 800–1300m.

Anyone suffering from problems of the gall bladder might do well to drink an infusion of *poleo* (*Lippia turbinata*), a large shrub with silvery foliage and an unmistakeable aroma. Appropriately enough, since Santa Lucia is the patron saint of the blind, the *flor de Santa Lucia* (*Commelina erecta*), whose intense blue or lilac blooms carpet the ground to astonishing effect, exudes a sticky substance that can be used as effective eye drops. The *cola de caballo* (*Equisetum giganteum*) – or "horsetail" – is used to control arterial pressure thanks to its diuretic powers; its ribbed, rush-like stems grow alongside streams and are crowned with hairy filaments that give it its popular name. Whatever you do, however, steer clear of *revienta caballos* (*Solanum eleagnifolium* or *S. sisymbrifolium*), a distant relative of the deadly nightshade. Its pretty violet flowers give way to deceptively attractive yellow berries, but the whole plant is highly toxic.

Obviously, you should **seek expert advice** before putting natural cures to the test, and they should not be used instead of conventional medicine for the severest of complaints. Pharmaceutical herbs, known as *yuyos*, are sold (usually in dried form) in pharmacies and in stores selling dietetic products throughout the region.

Los Terrones

15km outside Capilla del Monte; drive 8km north of town, along the RN-38, then head east at Charbonier along a small track towards Sarmiento • Daily 9am–dusk • $20 • ⊛ losterrones.com

Los Terrones is an amazing formation of multicoloured rocks on either side of a 5km dirt track. You can drive through the privately owned park quickly enough, but it's far better to walk along the signposted path that winds in between the rocks (a 1hr 30min circuit), to more clearly admire the strange shapes, all gnarled and twisted, some of them resembling animals or human forms.

ARRIVAL AND INFORMATION   CAPILLA DEL MONTE

By bus The bus station is at the corner of Corrientes and Rivadavia, 200m south of Plaza San Martín; there are regular services to Córdoba (every 1hr; 1hr 30min).

Tourist information The dynamic tourist office in the old railway station at Pueyrredón s/n (daily 8am–8pm; ☏ 03548 481903) has details of guides and operators offering treks, horseriding and hang-gliding.

ACCOMMODATION AND EATING

Hostel Los Tres Gómez 25 de Mayo 452 ☏ 03548 482 647, ⊛ hostelencapilladelmonte.com. HI-affiliated joint with a bright (some might say lurid) colour-scheme – orange walls, lime-green cupboards and a pink pool table are just some of the features. The dorms and private rooms, by contrast, are plain and a little bare. There's a communal kitchen, garden and a restaurant-bar. Breakfast included.

Dorms $70, doubles $200

Hotel Montecassino La Pampa s/n ☏ 03548 482572, ⊛ hotelmontecassino.com. A stately hotel, in a building dating back to 1901, with comfortable en suites (some with excellent mountain views), a swimming pool and a fine restaurant (open to nonguests). Yoga sessions are on offer, and rates include breakfast. $435

Ongamira

ONGAMIRA, 25km northeast of Capilla del Monte and 1400m above sea level, is a remote hamlet famed for its **Grutas**, strange caves amid rock formations sculpted by wind and rain in the reddish sandstone, and painted with black, yellow and white pigments by indigenous tribes some six hundred years ago. The drawings depict animals, human figures and abstract geometric patterns, and must be surveyed from a special viewpoint as the extremely fragile stone is gradually crumbling away and many of the paintings have already been lost.

The **Parque Natural Ongamira** (daily 9am–8pm, weekends only in winter; $10) is a privately owned reserve affording breathtaking views of the cerros Pajarillo, Áspero and Colchiquí; you can see condors, go on horseback rides and follow a 3km trail up to the top of Cerro Colchiquí.

Ischilín

Some 20km north of Ongamira, a dirt road snakes through mesmerizing rocky landscapes and past a polo ground to the once-abandoned village of **ISCHILÍN**. Its spectacular **Plaza de Armas**, not unlike an English village green, is dominated by a venerable algarrobo tree, its gigantic gnarled trunk host to epiphytic cacti and skeins of moss, and by the early eighteenth-century Jesuit church, **Nuestra Señora del Rosario**, with a mustard-yellow facade and a delightfully primitive interior, with a rickety choir balcony made of algarrobo wood.

Casa Museo Fernando Fader

8km south of the village • Thurs–Sun noon–5pm • Free

Eight kilometres outside Ischilín is the **Casa Museo Fernando Fader**, a brick house built by the painter Fernando Fader, an adoptive Argentine born of German parents who settled here in the vain hope of curing his chronic tuberculosis. His paintings, well executed if strongly influenced by Van Gogh and at times Monet, are best seen at the provincial fine-arts museum near Mendoza (see p.350). Only one is on show at this museum, alongside various personal effects and furniture, but the mock-Italianate garden is worth a visit.

ACCOMMODATION AND EATING ISCHILÍN

La Rosada ☎ 0351 15 558 7085, ⓦ ischilinposada.com .ar. This charming guesthouse is run by Fernando Fader's grandson and family; you can stay the night or just enjoy the fine food in the restaurant and swimming pool. Don't miss the chance of being shown around the village by the owners. Rates include full board. **$650**

The Calamuchita Valley

Long established as one of Córdoba Province's major holiday destinations, and where many cityfolk have weekend or summer homes, the green **Calamuchita Valley** begins 30km south of Córdoba city at the Jesuit estancia town of **Alta Gracia** – a popular day-trip destination from Córdoba – and stretches due south for over 100km, between the undulating Sierra Chica to the east and the steep Sierra de Comechingones to the west. The varied vegetation that covers the valley's sides provides a perfect habitat for hundreds of species of birds and other fauna. Two large and very clean reservoirs, Embalse Los Molinos in the north and Embalse Río Tercero in the south, both dammed in the first half of the twentieth century for water supplies, electricity and recreational angling, give the valley its alternative name, sometimes used by the local tourist authority: **Valle Azul de los Grandes Lagos** ("Blue Valley of the Great Lakes"). It's believed that the area's **climate** has been altered by their creation, with noticeably wetter summers than in the past.

The valley's two main towns could not be more different: **Villa General Belgrano** is a chocolate-box resort with a predominantly Germanic population, whereas **Santa Rosa de Calamuchita**, the valley's rather brash capital, is youthful and dynamic but far less picturesque. Both, however, are good bases for exploring the beautiful Comechingones mountains, whose Camiare name means "mountains and many villages". One of these villages, the quiet hamlet of **La Cumbrecita**, would not look out of place in the Swiss Alps, and is the starting-point for some fine highland walks. All the villages offer a wide range of accommodation and high-quality places to eat, making them ideal for anyone wanting to avoid big cities like Córdoba.

Alta Gracia

The historic **ALTA GRACIA**, less than 40km south of Córdoba and 3km west of busy RP-5, lies at the northern entrance of the Calamuchita Valley. It is now rather nondescript, but in the 1920s and 1930s its location made it popular with the wealthy bourgeoisie of Buenos Aires and Córdoba, who built holiday homes in the town – Che Guevara, spent some of his youth here, and revolutionary composer Manuel de Falla fled here from the Spanish Civil War. The original colonial settlement dates from the late sixteenth century, but in 1643 it was chosen as the site for a Jesuit estancia around which the town grew up. After the Jesuits' expulsion in 1767, the estancia fell into ruin but was inhabited for a short time in 1810 by Viceroy Liniers, forced to leave Córdoba following the Argentine declaration of independence.

Museo Casa del Virrey Liniers

Plaza Manuel Solares • Summer Tues–Fri 9am–8pm, Sat & Sun 9.30am–8pm; winter Tues–Fri 9am–1pm & 3–7pm, Sat & Sun 9.30am–12.30pm & 3.30–6.30pm • $5 • Free guided English-language tours on request • ☎ 03547 421303, ⓦ museoliniers.org.ar

The **Museo Casa del Virrey Liniers** is housed in the Residencia, the Jesuits' original living quarters and workshops. Entered through an ornate Baroque doorway on Plaza Manuel Solares, the town's main square, the beautifully restored Residencia, with its colonnaded upper storey, forms two sides of a cloistered courtyard. Exhibits consist mainly of furniture and art dating from the early nineteenth century, but there are also some magnificent examples of colonial religious paintings and sculptures. Perhaps the most interesting sections of the museum are the painstakingly re-created kitchen and the *herrería*, or forge, the oldest part of the estancia. The church adjoining the Residencia, though in pitifully poor repair, is used regularly for Mass; it lies immediately to the south.

Tajamar

North of Plaza Manuel Solares, the **Tajamar**, or estancia reservoir, is one of Argentina's earliest hydraulic projects, dating from 1659; it both supplied water for the community and served as a millpond. In its mirror-like surface is reflected the town's emblematic clock tower, erected in 1938 to mark 350 years of colonization in the area.

Villa Carlos Pellegrini

Avenida Sarmiento leads up a slope from the western bank of the Tajamar into **Villa Carlos Pellegrini**, an interesting residential district of quaint timber and wrought-iron dwellings, dating from when rich Porteños built summerhouses here in the fashionable so-called *estilo inglés*, a local interpretation of mock-Tudor. Many of them, however, are now sadly dilapidated.

CHE GUEVARA

Despite being one of Argentina's most famous sons, **Ernesto "Che" Guevara** is little celebrated in his homeland, with nothing like the number of monuments and museums you might expect for such an international icon. This is no doubt at least in part due to Che fighting his battles elsewhere – primarily, of course, in Cuba, where he is idolized, but also in places like the Congo and Bolivia. It is hard to know whether Argentine authorities ignore his legacy because he was, well, anti-authoritarian, or whether they feel offended that he had the cheek to go and instigate revolution outside of *la gran Argentina*. Whatever his claims to supra-nationality may be, though, Che was certainly Argentine – a fact reflected even in his nickname ("che" being a common interjection, more or less meaning "hey", and very characteristic of the River Plate region).

Che was born to a middle-class family in **Rosario** (see p.250) in 1928, and moved to **Alta Gracia** with his family at the age of 5, going to Deán Funes college in Córdoba before moving on to the Universidad de Buenos Aires to study medicine. Three years later, he set off on his famous **motorbike trip** around South America, during which he was exposed to the continent's poverty and inequalities, as well as the cultural similarities that led him to believe in the need to foster a sense of regional rather than national identity. He did return to Buenos Aires to finish his studies, but a month after graduating he was back on the road, this time heading to Guatemala and a meeting with local radicals which eventually led him to Fidel Castro, Cuba and his status as one of the great revolutionary figures of the twentieth century.

Che, however, saw the Cuban revolution as just the first step in a continent-wide **revolt against US control**, and in 1965 he formally resigned his Cuban citizenship, ministerial position and rank of comandante, and left the country. After an unsuccessful spell leading a Cuban guerrilla contingent supporting rebels in the Congo, Che set off with a small band of supporters for **Bolivia** in 1966 with the aim of fomenting a revolution that would spread throughout the neighbouring states, including Argentina. Bolivia, however, proved to be an exceptionally poor choice; it was the only South American country to have carried out radical land reform, and as such the revolutionary potential of its peasants was fairly low.

Che's group attracted little local support, and soon found itself on the run. On October 8, following a series of gun battles, he was captured by US-trained Bolivian soldiers, and the following day **executed** in the remote hamlet of La Higuera. According to legend, Che's last words were: "Shoot, coward, you are only going to kill a man."

Museo Casa de Ernesto "Che" Guevara

Avellaneda 501 • Jan & Feb daily 9.30am–7pm; March–Dec Mon 2–7pm, Tues–Sun 9am–7pm • $75 • ☎ 03547 428579

One of Villa Carlos Pellegrini's houses, Villa Beatriz, was for several years in the 1930s home to the family of **Che Guevara**. His doctor recommended the dry continental climate of the sierras, and his family rented various houses in Alta Gracia during his adolescence in the vain hope of curing his debilitating asthma. Homage is paid to the young revolutionary-to-be here in the **Museo Casa de Ernesto "Che" Guevara** where photographs, correspondence and all manner of memorabilia are lovingly displayed.

Museo Manuel de Falla

Av Carlos Pellegrini 1011 • Summer daily 9am–8pm; winter 9am–7pm • $20 • ☎ 03547 429292

Another house in Villa Carlos Pellegrini, Los Espinillos, was Spanish composer **Manuel de Falla's home** for four years until his death in 1946; like Che Guevara, he came to the sierras for health reasons, in his case because he suffered from chronic tuberculosis. Now the **Museo Manuel de Falla**, exhibiting his piano and other personal effects, the well-preserved house affords fine views of the nearby mountains. Piano and other music recitals are given, normally on Saturday evenings, in the small concert hall in the garden.

ARRIVAL AND INFORMATION   ALTA GRACIA

By bus Regular buses from Córdoba (every 15min; 1hr) use the bus terminal on Calle P. Butori and Av Presidente Perón, around eight blocks west of the Tajamar.

Tourist information The tourist office is in the clock tower at the corner of Av del Tajamar and c/del Molino (Dec–Feb daily 8am–11pm; March–Nov Mon–Thurs 8am–8pm & Fri–Sun 8am–9pm; ☎ 03547 428128, ⓦ altagracia.gov.ar).

Villa General Belgrano

Around 50km south of Alta Gracia and reached along attractive corniches skirting the blue waters of the **Embalse Los Molinos** is the demure resort of **VILLA GENERAL BELGRANO**. The unspoiled alpine scenery of its back country, the folksy architecture and decor and the Teutonic traditions of the local population all give the place a distinctly alpine feel. Many of the townspeople are of German, Swiss or Austrian origin, some of them descended from escapees from the *Graf Spee*, the pocket battleship scuttled by its captain off the Uruguayan coast on December 13, 1939, after it was surrounded by Allied cruisers during World War II's landmark Battle of the River Plate. The older generations still converse in German, maintain a Lutheran outlook and read the local German-language newspaper, while souvenir shops sell cuckoo clocks, tapes of oompah music and other such curios.

Whether or not the place's kitsch cosiness holds appeal, Villa General Belgrano is a decent base for the region if you'd rather avoid Córdoba, with plentiful and varied accommodation choices and easy access to the great Sierra de Comechingones. However, if adventure sports or nightclubs are what you're after, you're better off heading for nearby Santa Rosa de Calamuchita (see p.202).

ARRIVAL AND INFORMATION   VILLA GENERAL BELGRANO

By bus Regular services from Buenos Aires (8 daily; 11hr), Córdoba (every 45min–1hr; 2hr) and Santa Rosa de Calamuchita (every 15–30min; 30min) arrive at the small bus terminal on Av Vélez Sarsfield, 5min northwest of Plaza José Hernández. Pájaro Blanco (☎ 03546 461709; call for the latest timetable) runs a minibus service several times a day to and from La Cumbrecita (30min); its bus stop is on Av San Martín, 100m north of Plaza José Hernández.

Tourist information Villa General Belgrano's busy tourist office is in the German town hall at Av Julio A. Roca 168 (daily 8.30am–8.30pm; ☎ 03546 461215, ⓦ vgb .gov.ar).

ACCOMMODATION

You're spoilt for choice when it comes to accommodation in Villa General Belgrano, although if you're planning to attend the Oktoberfest you should book well ahead and be prepared for steeper prices.

VILLA GENERAL BELGRANO'S FESTIVALS

Essentially a sedate place favoured by families and older visitors attracted by its creature comforts and hearty food – especially welcome during winter snow – Villa General Belgrano shifts up a gear or two during one of its many **festivals**. While the Feria Navideña, or Christmas festival, the Fiesta de Chocolate Alpino, in July, and the Fiesta de la Masa Vienesa, a Holy Week binge of apple strudel and pastries, are all eagerly awaited, the annual climax, during ten days at the beginning of October, is the nationally famous **Oktoberfest**, Villa General Belgrano's answer to Munich's world-renowned beer festival. Stein after stein of foaming Pilsener is knocked back, after which merry revellers stagger down Villa Belgrano's normally genteel streets to their hotels.

Hostel Rincón c/Alexander Fleming 347 ☎ 03546 461323, ⓦ hostelrincon.com.ar. This laidback, HI-affiliated hostel offers dorms, en-suite private rooms, and a place to pitch your tent, as well as kitchen access and a small pool. Breakfast costs extra. Camping $20, dorms $65, doubles $110

Posada Nehuen Av San Martín 17 ☎ 03546 461412, ⓦ elsitiodelavilla.com/nehuen. This central guesthouse has a selection of comfortable en suites with TVs, mini-fridges and phones, though the decor throughout is a bit twee and old fashioned. Rates include breakfast but a/c costs extra. $270

Rincón de Mirlos 9km west of the centre, off the RP-5 ☎ 03456 15 516 4254, ⓦ rincondemirlos.com.ar. The best of several campsites around town, signposted 7km west of the centre on the road towards La Cumbrecita; from there it is another 2km through handsome farmland and woods to the bucolic riverside setting, where there are clean dorms, isolated camping pitches among the trees, a restaurant-bar, and long stretches of sandy beach. Breakfast costs extra. Camping $35, dorms $60

Tantra Posada Palotti 36 ☎ 03546 462142, ⓦ posada tantra.com.ar. In a pleasant whitewashed home with a well-kept garden and a small, curvy swimming pool, this mid-range guesthouse provides a warm welcome and clean and spacious en suites. Rates include a good breakfast. $350

EATING

Café Rissen Av Julio A. Roca 36 ☎ 03546 464100. This café is the place for German-style cakes and pastries (from $20) – try the Black Forest gâteau (*selva negra*), strudel and fruit crumbles. If you're in a decadent mood, go for a rich hot chocolate too. Daily 8am–midnight.

Ciervo Rojo Av Julio A. Roca 210 ☎ 03546 461345, ⓦ confiteriaciervorojo.com. Dating back almost fifty years, this appealing restaurant serves up an array of German and Central European dishes (mains $40–80) including schnitzel, goulash, *spätzle*, sausages and sauerkraut. There's live German music on Saturday nights. Daily 9am–11pm/midnight.

Santa Rosa de Calamuchita and around

In 1700, a community of Dominicans built an estancia and a chapel dedicated to the patron saint of the Americas, Santa Rosa of Lima, after which nothing much else happened in **SANTA ROSA DE CALAMUCHITA**, 11km south of Villa General Belgrano, until the end of the nineteenth century. Then, thanks to its mountainside, riverbank location and its mild climate, the place suddenly took off as a holiday resort, an alternative to its more traditional neighbour to the north. Now it's a highly popular destination, swamped by thousands of visitors from many parts of the country in the high season, and makes an excellent base for exploring the relatively unspoilt mountains nearby. Many of Santa Rosa de Calamuchita's visitors use it as a springboard to experience all kinds of outdoor activities, from diving and kayaking to jet-skiing and flying, all located at Villa del Dique, 17km away. Noticeably less sedate than Villa General Belgrano but more bearable than Villa Carlos Paz, from Christmas until Easter Santa Rosa throbs with disco music blaring from convertibles packed with holiday-makers.

The town's compact centre is built in a curve of the Río Santa Rosa, just south of where the Arroyo del Sauce flows into it. There's no main plaza, but a number of busy streets run off the main Calle Libertad.

Museo de Arte Religioso

Libertad • Jan & Feb daily 10am–1pm; March–Aug Wed–Sun 10am–1pm; Sept–Dec Thurs–Sun 10am–1pm • Free

The ruined estancia was demolished at the beginning of the twentieth century, but the beautifully restored **Capilla Vieja** (Old Chapel) now houses the **Museo de Arte Religioso**, where you can see a superb, late seventeenth-century wooden Christ, crafted by local Jesuit artisans, and other works of colonial religious art.

ARRIVAL, INFORMATION AND TOURS

By bus Regular buses from Córdoba (18–20 daily; 2hr 20min) and Villa General Belgrano (every 15–30min; 30min) drop off and pick up passengers at stops along Av Gómez.

Tourist information The tourist office is at Córdoba and Entre Ríos (daily 8am–10pm; ☎ 03546 429654).

SANTA ROSA DE CALAMUCHITA

Tours Naturaleza y Aventura (☎ 03546 464144, ⊚ naturalezacba.com.ar) organizes single- and multi-day treks into the Comechingones range, as well as a range of horseriding, 4WD and mountain-biking trips.

ACCOMMODATION AND EATING

Camping Vacacional Miami Outside town on the road to Yacanto ☎ 03546 499613, ⊚ campingmiami.com.ar. This campsite is a good option for budget travellers, offering a mix of camping spots, dorms, wooden huts with shared bathrooms, and larger en-suite apartments. Guests have access to cooking facilities, and there's a restaurant-bar. Camping $35, dorms $50, huts $140, apartments $250

Hostería Ana Mar Libertad 594 ☎ 03546 420248, ⊖ hosteria_anamar@yahoo.com.ar. Although the rooms at this bungalow-style guesthouse are on the small side, they are well kept and come with private bathroom and TV. Breakfast included. $260

Hotel Yporá 1km outside town on the RP-5 ☎ 03546 421233, ⊚ hotelypora.com. This stylish 1930s hotel has seven hectares of grounds, two pools, a tennis court, and a restaurant and bar. The en-suite rooms are smart, if sparsely furnished; all have a/c and plasma TVs. Breakfast included. $320

La Pulpería de los Ferreyra Libertad 578 ☎ 03546 421 769, ⊚ lapulperiaferreyra.com.ar. Aping the look of a *pulpería* (traditional bar), this reliable restaurant focuses on sizeable *asados*, though there are some good trout dishes too. Mains $45–90. Daily noon–3pm & 8pm–midnight.

La Cumbrecita

Around 35km northwest of Villa General Belgrano along a winding scenic track, **LA CUMBRECITA** is a small, peaceful alpine-style village in the foothills of the Comechingones range. Benefiting from a mild microclimate and enjoying views of wild countryside, it has developed as a relatively select holiday resort ever since it was built in 1934 by Swiss and Austrian immigrants.

Two paths wind their way through La Cumbrecita, parallel to the Río del Medio that cuts a deep ravine below. The lower one passes a mock-medieval *castillo* on the way to the Río Almbach, which flows into the Río del Medio north of the village; the upper trail climbs the hill to the west of the village, cutting through a well-tended cemetery from where you can enjoy wonderful views of the Lago Esmeralda and the fir-wooded mountains behind.

For some more great vistas, take Avenida San Martín, which leads north from Plaza José Hernández, and keep going until you reach the edge of town; from here the dirt road swings in a westerly direction and climbs through hills that open to views of the Río Segundo Valley.

Mountain walks and balnearios

La Cumbrecita is a perfect base for some of the region's most rewarding **mountain walks**, including some well-trodden but uncrowded trails reaching 2000m or more. Signposted treks lasting between one and four hours each way head off to the eyrie-like *miradores* at Casas Viejas, Meierei and Cerro Cristal, while one of the most popular trails climbs from the *castillo*, past *Balneario La Olla*, with its very deep pools of crystal-clear water created by the gushing waterfalls, to the 1715m summit of Cerro Wank.

Other **balnearios** include *Lago de las Truchas and Confluencia* – the former named for the plentiful trout in the stream and the latter renowned for its caves – both with bucolic settings and views up the craggy mountaintops: perfect for cooling off on a hot day.

ARRIVAL AND INFORMATION
LA CUMBRECITA

By bus Pájaro Blanco (☎ 03546 461709; call for the latest timetable) runs several daily minibuses (30min) between Villa General Belgrano and La Cumbrecita.

By car Private motor vehicles are banned from the whole village during the day (summer 9am–7pm; winter 10am–6pm), and many people rent electric buggies to get around.

Distances are walkable, however, and visitors are allowed to drive to their hotel's car park.

Tourist information La Cumbrecita's tourist office is across the bridge over the Río del Medio (daily: summer 9am–9pm; winter 10am–6pm; ☎ 03546 481088, ⓦ lacumbrecita.gov.ar).

ACCOMMODATION AND EATING

Bar Suizo Near the river ☎ 03546 481067. As you might expect given the kitsch Germanic design of the place, *Bar Suizo*'s focus is on hearty Central European fare (mains $40–50): expect lots of pork-based dishes, fondue and raclette, plus good cakes and pastries. Mon–Sat 9/10am–10/11pm.

Hotel Solares Pública s/n ☎ 03546 481019, ⓦ grupo solares.com.ar. The self-catering apartments come with TVs, private bathrooms and kitchenettes, and guests can make use of the complex's outdoor barbecue and big swimming pool. There's a children's play area, and massages are also on offer. $450

The Traslasierra

Easily the most rewarding route from Córdoba to San Luís, capital of the neighbouring province of the same name, is by the RP-34 and then the RN-20 beyond Villa Carlos Paz. The winding **Nueva Ruta de las Altas Cumbres** climbs past the **Parque Nacional Quebrada del Condorito**, a deep ravine where condors nest in cliffside niches, climbing over a high mountain-pass before winding back down a series of hairpin bends. The serene, sunny valleys to the west of the high Sierra Grande and Sierra de Achala, crisscrossed by streams and dotted with oases of bushy palm trees, are known collectively as the **Traslasierra**, literally "across the mountains".

The self-appointed capital of the sub-region, **Mina Clavero**, is a popular little riverside resort. Near **Nono**, a tiny village at the foot of the northern Comechingones to the south of Mina Clavero, is the oddball **Museo Rocsen**. In a long valley parallel to the Sierra de Comechingones lies the picturesque village of **San Javier**, from where you can climb the highest summit in the Central Sierras, **Cerro Champaquí**.

Parque Nacional Quebrada del Condorito

Around 65km from Villa Carlos Paz, just south of the RP-34 • Mon–Fri 9am–5pm, Sat & Sun 8am–6pm; the park generally closes a bit earlier in the winter • Free • ☎ 03541 433371, ⓦ condoritoapn.com.ar

The **PARQUE NACIONAL QUEBRADA DEL CONDORITO** takes its name from the Quebrada de los Condoritos, a misty canyon eroded into the mountains that, in turn, gets its name from the baby condors reared in its deep ravines.

To get to the park, take the RP-34 that sweeps across the **Pampa de Achala**, an eerily desolate landscape, ideal for solitary treks or horse rides. For the first 15km or so, this road, which starts southwest of Villa Carlos Paz, is quite narrow, but several viewpoints have been built at the roadside. From them, you have unobscured vistas of the Icho Cruz and Malambo valleys to the northwest, the distant peak of **Cerro Los Gigantes** (at 2374m the highest mountain in the Sierra Grande) to the north, and the **Sierra de Achala** to the south. Some 20km further on, are the bleak granite moorlands of the Pampa de Achala, reaching just over 2000m above sea level. Here condors, some with wingspans exceeding 3m, can be seen circling majestically overhead.

Hikes within the park

Hikes in the park take between two hours and several days, and there are designated areas where camping (free) is permitted. You should register at the Interpretation Centre (1.5km from the park entrance) before setting out; the centre is also a good place to get useful information about the park and the latest weather conditions. There's little shade and currently no food or drink on sale within the park boundaries, so bring a hat, sun-cream and sustenance.

The hike route is clearly marked with numbered posts, getting steadily more difficult after you pass number ten, which takes you down steep and sometimes slippery paths towards the bottom of the canyon. Many kinds of trees, shrubs and ferns can be spotted, including some endemic species such as rare white gentians, while among the plentiful fauna are various wild cats, frogs, foxes and lizards. Birdlife is prolific but the stars are the condors themselves, especially their young; if you're lucky you might see condors and their chicks bathing in the water at the bottom of the gorge.

Fundación Cóndor

RP-34, around 9km east of the Interpretation Centre • Daily 9am–5/6pm • Free • ☎ 0351 464 6537, ⓦ fundacion-condor.com.ar

The **Fundación Cóndor** is an independently run centre that provides information on the condors and has a striking photo exhibition of the park's flora and fauna. It also has a café, organizes condor-feeding spectacles in the evenings, and can arrange transport to and from the park itself.

3

ARRIVAL AND ACTIVITIES · PARQUE NACIONAL QUEBRADA DEL CONDORITO

By bus If you're not taking a tour, and haven't hired a car or a taxi, you can reach the park by bus: services (around 5 daily; 1hr 30min) between Córdoba and La Pampilla pass by the park; ask the driver to drop you off at the entrance.

Guides Guides can be hired in advance from the park's main office, the Intendencia del Parque Nacional Quebrida del Condorito (Resistencia 30 ☎ 03541 15 631727) in Villa Carlos Paz.

Activities Horseriding trips through the surrounding countryside are offered by Estancia La Granadilla (☎ 03547 48880, ⓦ lagranadilla.com.ar), located close to the park in San Clemente. Trekking, mountain biking and rock climbing can be arranged through agencies in Córdoba and other tourist centres in the province.

ACCOMMODATION

La Posta del Qenti 17km from the park entrance on the RP-34 ☎ 03541 495715, ⓦ laposta.qenti.com. The best accommodation in the area is provided in this tastefully converted nineteenth-century post house. Its remote location lends it an almost eerie atmosphere, offset by the design-magazine interior, snug en suites, gym and good food. There's an extensive range of activities on offer too. Full board. **$550**

Mina Clavero and around

Some 15km west of the Quebrada de los Condoritos, the RP-34 begins to snake along narrow corniche roads, which offer stunning views of the Traslasierra Valley and a cluster of extinct volcanic cones in the distance. Just 1.5km up the RP-15 north of the junction with the RP-34 is **MINA CLAVERO**, wedged between the Sierra Grande and the much lower Sierra de Pocho, to the west. A transport hub at the northern end of the Punilla Valley, it's also a boisterous riverside resort. The place is noteworthy for little else, though, other than its attractive black **ceramics**, made at workshops in and around the town. The nearby mountains lend themselves to mountain biking, horseriding, trekking and climbing, while trout-fishing is possible in the many brooks.

The balnearios

Mina Clavero is packed during January and February, when people come to relax at the many **balnearios** along the three rivers – Los Sauces, Mina Clavero and Panaholma – that snake through the town. The cleanest bathing area is the Nido de Aguila, set among beautiful rocks on the Río Mina Clavero 1km east of the centre, along Calle Urquiza.

By bus The terminal is on Av Mitre, next to the town hall. There are regular services between here and Córdoba (around 5 daily; 3hr).

Tourist information The tourist office is seven blocks south of the bus terminal, on Av San Martín (daily: summer 8am–10pm; winter 9am–8pm; ☎ 03544 470171, ⊛ mina clavero.gov.ar). There's also a small information office in the bus station (summer only daily 9am–9pm).

ACCOMMODATION AND EATING

Mina Clavero has a wide choice of **hotels**; out of season, prices can be half the cost of the high summer season ones quoted here. **Restaurants** selling the usual trio of pasta, pizza and *parrilla* line avenidas San Martín and Mitre.

Colina del Valle Olmos Sur s/n ☎ 03544 471177, ⊛ colinadelvalle.com. This mid-range hotel has pleasant en suites with high ceilings and jacuzzi-style baths, a huge outdoor pool, and a tennis court. Bike rental, hiking, horse-riding and yoga sessions can all be arranged. **$390**

Oh La La Hostel J.B. Villanueva 1192 ☎ 03544 472634, ⊛ ohlalahostel.com.ar. This hostel is the best in the town, with colourful decor, a large (though pretty bare) garden, a small pool, and a communal kitchen. Accommodation is provided in simple dorms and private rooms. Dorms **$72**, doubles **$240**

Los Serranitos Cura Gaucho 350, 2km north of town ☎ 03544 470817, ⊛ losserranitos.com.ar. Family-oriented complex with a range of camping spots, basic huts and more comfortable bungalows, plus a large pool, cooking areas, a shop selling provisions, and a cybercafé. Camping **$125**, huts **$184**, bungalows **$200**

Nono

From the junction with the RP-15, the RN-20 heads due south through rolling countryside, in the lee of rippling mountains, whose eroded crags change colour from a mellow grey to deepest red, depending on the time of day. Their imposing peak, Cerro Champaquí, lurks to the southeast at the northern end of the Comechingones range. Some 10km south of Mina Clavero you reach the sleepy village of **NONO**, a huddle of picturesque brick buildings around a little plaza. Its name is a corruption of the Quichoa *ñuñu*, meaning breasts, an allusion to the bosom-shaped hills poking above the horizon.

Museo Rocsen

Alto de la Quinta, 5km outside the village; take a taxi from Nono or walk • Daily 9am–sunset • $20 • ☎ 03544 498218, ⊛ museorocsen.org

One of Argentina's weirdest museums is the hallucinatory **Museo Rocsen**. Its imposing pink-sandstone facade is embellished with a row of 49 statues – from Christ to Mother Teresa, the Buddha to Che Guevara – representing key figures who, according to the museum's owner and curator, Juan Santiago Bouchon, have changed the course of history. After many years as cultural attaché at the French embassy in Buenos Aires, Bouchon opened his museum in 1969, with the intention of offering "something for everybody". The result is an eclectic collection of more than 30,000 exhibits, from fossils and mummies to a two-headed calf, clocks and cars.

ARRIVAL AND ACCOMMODATION

NONO

There are regular **buses** (around 14 daily) between Nono and Córdoba (about 3hr) via Mina Clavero (10min).

★ **Arabela Casas de Campo** Just outside Villa de Las Rosas, a 20min drive south of Nono ☎ 03544 459018, ⊛ complejoarabela.com. Opened in 2012, this excellent complex has four very stylish, fully fitted and secluded *casas de campo* (country houses). There's a pool, viewing tower offering lovely vistas, and lots of green space. Birdwatching (55 species have been spotted in the grounds), horseriding and mountain biking are among the activities on offer. **$1210**

Estancia La Lejanía 3km beyond Museo Rocsen ☎ 03544 498960, ⊛ lalejania.com. This outstanding French-run hotel has comfortable rooms in a secluded setting with a private riverside beach. The restaurant (open to nonguests) serves delicious Gallic cuisine, accompanied by select Argentine champagnes and wines from the cellar, and the hotel also offers trekking and horseriding in the nearby mountains. Full board. **$700**

San Javier

Some 35km south of Mina Clavero, the RP-148 branches off the RN-20 and heads due south towards **SAN JAVIER**, another 12km away. The tree-lined road takes you through some of the province's most attractive scenery and settlements. If you're driving, though, watch out for the often treacherous *badenes*, very deep fords that suddenly flood after storms; even when dry their abrupt drop and rough surface can damage a car's undercarriage or tyres.

San Javier is a pretty little place, set amid peach orchards, and serves as a base for climbing to the 2884m summit of **Cerro Champaquí**, directly to the east. It has developed as an exclusive tourist centre in recent years, offering a variety of services including massages, reiki and even "solar shamanism".

ARRIVAL AND ACCOMMODATION | SAN JAVIER

There are irregular **buses** between San Javier and Mina Clavero (around 30min); ask locally for the latest timetable.

La Constancia 7km east of San Javier on the road to Cerro Champaquí ☎ 011 5354 0487, ⓦ laconstancia .net. This superb hotel – an 1895 building augmented with some modern designer touches – is set in stunning environs. Horseriding, trekking, mountain biking and fishing are all possible, you can swim in the nearby river, and the food is excellent. Full board. The restaurant is open to nonguests. **$1310**

The Litoral and the Gran Chaco

GARGANTA DEL DIABLO WATERFALL, IGUAZÚ

The Litoral and the Gran Chaco

The defining feature of northeastern Argentina is water. Dominated by two of the continent's longest rivers, plus several of the country's other major waterways, it's a land of powerful cascades and blue-mirrored lagoons, vast marshes and fertile wetlands. The riverine landscapes of the Litoral (meaning "Shore" or "Coastline") – a term generally used to refer to the four provinces of Entre Ríos, Corrientes, Misiones and Santa Fe – range from the caramel-coloured maze of the Paraná Delta, just north of Buenos Aires, via the gentle sandy banks of the Río Uruguay and the jungle-edged Río Iguazú to the wide translucent curves of the upper Río Paraná. All of them exude a seductive subtropical beauty enhanced by the unhurried lifestyle of the locals and a warm, humid climate. The Northeast is also famed for *mate* and *chamamé*. Litoraleños, as the inhabitants are called, are fanatical consumers of Argentina's national drink, while the infectiously lively *chamamé* music can be heard in the highly traditional province of Corrientes.

4

The **Iguazú Falls**, shared with Brazil, in the far north of Misiones Province, are the region's major attraction by a long chalk: Iguazú's claim to the title of the world's most spectacular waterfalls has few serious contenders. Running a remote second, in terms of the number of visitors, **San Ignacio Miní** is one of the best-preserved ruins in the huge Jesuit Mission region – though some may find picking their way through nearby gothically overgrown **Loreto** and **Santa Ana** a more magical experience. Less well known than Iguazú and San Ignacio, but increasingly visited as the infrastructure improves, are two of Argentina's most unusual attractions: the strange and wonderful – but capricious – **Saltos del Moconá**, the world's most extensive longitudinal waterfalls; and the **Esteros del Iberá**, a vast bird-filled wetland reserve at the heart of Corrientes Province.

Further south, the region's biggest city, and Argentina's third largest, is **Rosario**. It is home to a vibrant cultural life, including its own laidback version of **tango**, fabulous restaurants and some exquisite late nineteenth- and early twentieth-century architecture.

SAN IGNACIO MINÍ

Highlights

❶ Colón This picturesque riverside resort has it all: sandy beaches, hot springs, and even a winery. **See p.217**

❷ Esteros del Iberá Glide in a boat across a mirror-like lagoon where capybaras splash, deer trampoline on spongy islets and thousands of birds fly overhead. **See p.222**

❸ Estancia Santa Inés A splendid colonial-style mansion, near its own *yerba mate* plantation, offering hospitality, relaxation, delicious food – and a monkey colony. **See p.232**

❹ San Ignacio Miní The best preserved of all the Jesuit settlements is set among impeccably mown lawns worthy of a cricket pitch. **See p.235**

❺ Garganta del Diablo Of the 250 waterfalls at Iguazú, the "Devil's Throat" is the most powerful, most dramatic – and wettest. **See p.238**

❻ Fogón de los Arrieros Visited over the years by leading artists and artistes, Resistencia's top culture club offers tango, folk and poetry recitals. **See p.269**

HIGHLIGHTS ARE MARKED ON THE MAP ON PP.212–213

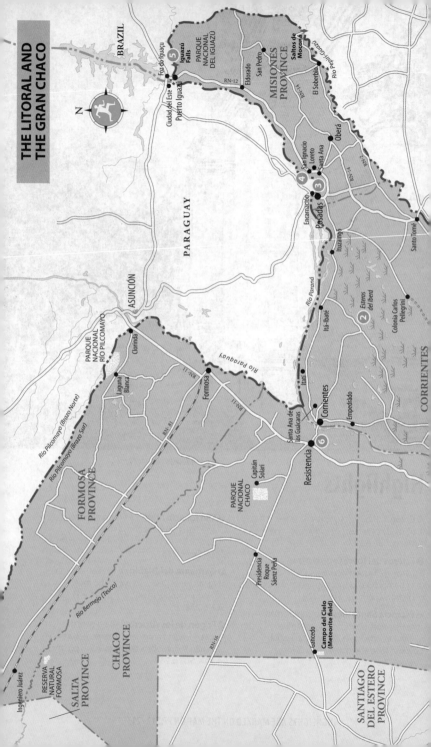

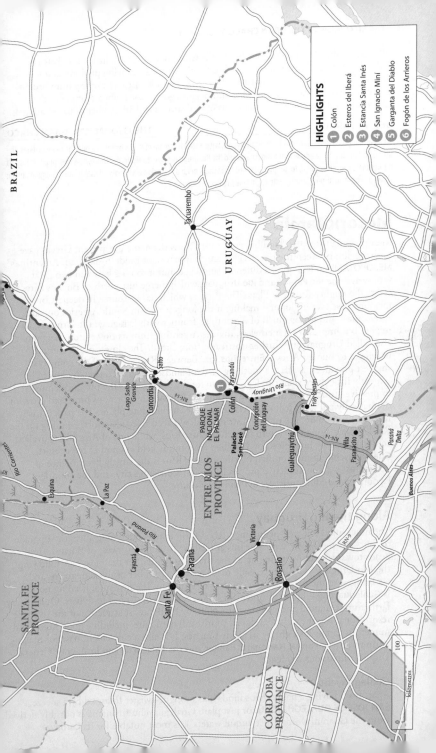

BRAZIL

URUGUAY

Tacuarembó

Salto

Payandú

Concordia

Lago Salto Grande

PARQUE NACIONAL EL PALMAR

Colón

Palacio San-José

Concepción del Uruguay

Río Uruguay

Fray Bentos

Gualeguaychú

Villa Paranacito

Paraná Delta

Buenos Aires

RN-9

Río Corrientes

Bovril

La Paz

Río Paraná

Cayastá

Paraná

Santa Fe

Victoria

Rosario

ENTRE RÍOS PROVINCE

SANTA FE PROVINCE

CÓRDOBA PROVINCE

RN-14

RN-14

RN-12

0 — 100 kilometres

1

Bordering the Litoral to the northwest, the **Gran Chaco** is a vast, little-visited area of flatlands forming the central watershed of South America and lying predominantly in western Paraguay and the far north of Argentina. With landscapes varying from brutally desiccated scrub to saturated marshes and boggy lagoons, the main attraction of the Chaco is its **wildlife**, including hundreds of bird species and all manner of native animals.

GETTING AROUND   **THE LITORAL AND GRAN CHACO**

Travel around the Litoral is relatively straightforward, with a steady stream of buses heading along the main arteries, the RN-12 and the RN-14, shadowing the Río Paraná and the Río Uruguay respectively. In the Chaco, however, public transport is rather less convenient and, to get the most out of a visit, a guided excursion is strongly advisable. All the region's major cities also have an airport, mostly with flights only to Buenos Aires.

Mesopotamia

Mesopotamia (literally, "land between rivers") was the name the ancient Greeks gave to the region between the rivers Tigris and Euphrates, or modern-day Iraq. Argentina's **MESOPOTAMIA** offers quite a different landscape, but it too lies between two great waterways, the **Río Paraná** and **Río Uruguay**, which merge just north of Buenos Aires to create the mighty Río de la Plata. The Paraná, which has its source in deepest Brazil, measures just over 4700km – making it the longest river in South America outside Amazonia – and forms much of Argentina's frontier with Paraguay; the Uruguay, less mighty but impressive nonetheless, divides Argentina from its tiny eastern neighbour, also called Uruguay, and further upstream, from Brazil. The closest of the Litoral's provinces to Buenos Aires is **Entre Ríos**, or "Between Rivers": one of the country's smallest provinces, it offers a soothing verdant landscape characterized by low hills – mostly little more than ripples – known locally as *cuchillas*. The province's most impressive attraction is the **Parque Nacional El Palmar**, an enormous protected grove of dramatically tall *yatay* palms towering over the surrounding plains. The park is easily reached from **Colón**, the pick of a string of slow-paced riverside resorts running up the Río Uruguay along the eastern border of Entre Ríos; while one of Argentina's liveliest **carnivals**, heavily influenced by Brazilian customs, is held at another river resort, **Gualeguaychú**, in the summer. North of Entre Ríos is the largely flat province of **Corrientes**, with an attractive provincial capital, **Corrientes city**, and the countless lagoons and wildlife treasures of **Iberá** at its centre.

Along the Río Uruguay

The much-used but well-maintained RN-14 toll road (undergoing a lengthy upgrade to four-lane motorway status) begins at Ceibas, 160km northwest of Buenos Aires, and heads towards Iguazú, ending up at the Brazilian border, for the most part following the Río Uruguay at a distance. Side roads lead to a number of riverside towns and, via bridges, to the neighbouring country of Uruguay. The first stop, heading north, is **Gualeguaychú** – home of Argentina's most renowned carnival festivities. Quite a way farther up is languid and picturesque **Colón**, by far the most attractive of the riverside resorts, boasting the most developed tourist infrastructure, including good hotels and numerous campsites right by its sandy beaches. It is also a convenient base for making a trip to nearby **Parque Nacional El Palmar** and the **Palacio de San José**, once General Urquiza's luxurious residence.

Gualeguaychú

Apart from having a name that sounds like a tongue-twister followed by a sneeze, **SAN JOSÉ DE GUALEGUAYCHÚ**, or just plain Gualeguaychú (its name is possibly derived from the Guaraní words for "tranquil waters"), is most notable for its **Carnaval**,

RESTAURANTS
Campo Alto	3
Dacal	2
La Paisanita	1

ACCOMMODATION
Abadía	3	Ñandubaysal	5
Aguay	4	La Posada	
Alemán	6	del Charrúa	7
Amalfi	2	Puerto Sol	8
Catedral	1		

GUALEGUAYCHÚ

generally regarded as Argentina's most important (though most towns in the Litoral celebrate with gusto); during January and February, the town is mobbed with people, particularly at weekends. Gualeguaychú's passion for processions is given further vent in October, when local high-school students take part in the **desfile de carrozas**, in which elaborate floats, constructed by the students themselves, are paraded around the streets. During the rest of the year – with the exception of long weekends, when it still attracts holiday-makers from Buenos Aires – Gualeguaychú is a tranquil town with some handsome old buildings and a pleasant *costanera* (riverfront) and park, plus decent accommodation and numerous campsites.

Gualeguaychú's two focal points are the streets surrounding its main square, **Plaza San Martín**, where the majority of hotels and shops are, and – particularly in the summer – the **Costanera**.

Casa de Aedo
Rivadavia and San José • Jan & Feb Wed–Sat 9am–noon & 5–8pm, Sun 9am–noon; April–Dec Wed–Sun 9am–noon • $5 • ☎ 03446 432643

The main building of interest on central Plaza San Martín is the **Casa de Aedo**; officially Gualeguaychú's oldest building, it dates from around 1800. Built in a primitive colonial style, the simple whitewashed building opens onto a garden of grapevines and orchids. Inside, the wood-floored rooms are filled with original furniture and objects belonging to the Aedos (sometimes written Haedos), one of Gualeguaychú's early patrician families. Among other exhibits, there's a beautiful Spanish representation of the Virgen del Carmen, made of silver and real hair, and a number of fine pieces of French porcelain. The house is also notable for having been occupied by Italian hero Giuseppe Garibaldi in 1845, when he ransacked Gualeguaychú for funds and provisions to assist General Oribe, who was under siege in Montevideo.

THE PAPER-PULP CONFLICT

The building of **paper-pulp plants** by European companies on the Río Uruguay in the first years of the millennium, including one just opposite Gualeguaychú, on Uruguay's side of the river, has caused great anger here. Argentines claim the plant is polluting their air and water, and the spat has seriously soured diplomatic relations between the two countries. Argentine protestors often block the General San Martín International Bridge, which connects the city with Fray Bentos in Uruguay – if you want to cross, you might need to travel 100km upriver to Colón (see opposite). Feelings still run very high in town about the plant – you'll see *"No a las papeleras"* signs everywhere – and the roadblock, which not everyone approves of; it is a topic of conversation that should not be lightly entered into.

Costanera J.J. de Urquiza

The **Costanera J.J. de Urquiza**, quiet during the day and out of season, heaves with life on summer evenings, when locals and holiday-makers indulge in an obligatory evening stroll or simply while away the hours on a bench, sipping a *mate*. The southern end of the Costanera leads to the **old port** and if you head down this way just before the October *desfile de carrozas* (float parade) you will come across scenes of frenetic activity as students – many of whom barely sleep for the last few days – put the finishing touches to their floats, which are assembled in huge riverside warehouses. The port was the termination point for the old railway tracks, which reached Gualeguaychú in 1873. If you follow the tracks round along Avenida Irazusta, you will come to the old train station, now the open-air **Museo Ferroviario**, or railway museum, where an old steam locomotive is displayed along with other relics; access is unrestricted.

Corsódromo

Ayacucho s/n • Every weekend in Jan & Feb • Carnival tickets can be bought on the door, or beforehand via Ticketek (⟨W⟩ ticketek.com.ar), and vary in price from $20 on wooden benches at the back to $850 for a seat in the VIP area with the best view • ☎ 03446 430528

Just next door to the railway museum is the **Corsódromo**, South America's second biggest purpose-built carnival stadium (after Río de Janeíro's), where almost 40,000 spectators pile in to watch Gualeguaychú's *comparsas*, or processions, during Carnaval. Though not as spectacular as Rio's carnival, the processions here are well worth experiencing – a huge effort is put into the colourful, skimpy costumes, loud music and thematic floats, and the crowd is always extremely enthusiastic. Compared with Brazilian carnivals the safety levels are far higher, too.

El Patio del Mate

Méndez 284 • Open daily until late • ☎ 03446 424371

Gualeguaychú's most original retail experience is provided by **El Patio del Mate** down by the Costanera: a shrine to Litoraleños' most pervasive habit, it sells *mates* carved out of every material imaginable – from simple and functional calabazas or gourds (generally regarded as the best material for *mates*) to elaborate combinations of hoof and hide, best described as gaucho kitsch.

ARRIVAL AND INFORMATION

By bus Gualeguaychú's bus terminal (☎ 03446 427987) is at the corner of Blvd Pedro Jurado and Av General Artigas, 2km from the centre – taxis into town cost about $30.

Destinations Buenos Aires (hourly; 3hr 30min); Colón (8 daily; 2hr); Corrientes (3 daily; 12hr); Paraná (7 daily; 5hr); Rosario (4–5 daily; 8hr); Santa Fe (5 daily; 6hr).

Tourist information Tourist information is available at the bus terminal (daily 8am–8/10pm; ☎ 03446 440706), but the main tourist office (same hours; ☎ 03446 423668, ⟨W⟩ gualeguaychuturismo.com) is on the Plazoleta de los Artesanos, Paseo del Puerto, down by the port; it keeps a list of families who rent rooms, plus an up-to-date price list of cabins and bungalows in the area. The staff can also offer information on excursions on the Río Gualeguaychú – such as regular catamaran trips and canoe rental – and on the *jineteadas*, or rodeo events, held in the vicinity throughout the year.

ACCOMMODATION

Gualeguaychú has a good selection of mostly budget **accommodation**. You'll need to book in advance if you plan to stay during Carnaval, and probably on long weekends, too, when most places also raise their prices. At these times, a number of impromptu notices spring up around town offering rooms to rent. There are numerous **campsites** in Gualeguaychú and the surrounding area; most are along the banks of the Río Gualeguaychú, or out towards the Río Uruguay.

Abadía San Martín 588 ☎ 03446 437502, ⊛ milashoteles .com.ar. An attractive *residencial* in an old building with pleasant rooms done out in pastel shades. $295

Aguay Av Costanera 130 ☎ 03446 422099, ⊛ hotel aguay.com.ar. Smart, modern hotel with top-floor swimming pool and *confitería* overlooking the river, and a reliable ground-floor restaurant, *Di Tulia*, that specializes in fish dishes. Spacious, bright rooms all have river-view balconies. Copious buffet breakfasts. $780

Alemán Bolívar 535 ☎ 03446 426153, ⊛ hotelaleman .com.ar. Professionally run and centrally located hotel with well-equipped rooms. The suitably Germanic facade and liberal use of Gothic script signal cleanliness and reliability in these parts. Rates include breakfast and parking. $495

Amalfi 25 de Mayo 571 ☎ 03446 426818, ✉ amalfihotel @yahoo.com.ar. One of the best of the budget hotels, located on the main drag, with some particularly spacious – though slightly dark – rooms at the front and cable TV. $425

Catedral Mitre 25 ☎ 03446 425469, ⊛ hotelcatedral gchu.com.ar. Guale's first boutique hotel is in the former governor's mansion, built in the 1870s. It has a beautiful Italianate facade, and many of the original features, including the marble staircase, tiled floors and ceiling frescoes, have been preserved. The rooms are light and spacious and it's in a good location close to the main plaza. $860

Ñandubaysal ☎ 03446 423298, ⊛ nandubaysal.com. Located on the banks of the Río Uruguay, 15km east of the town by RP-42, this is an extensive campsite forested with *ñandubay*, a thorny plant typical of the region whose fruit is a favourite of the ñandú (rhea or South American ostrich) – hence the name. $130

La Posada del Charrúa Av del Valle 250 ☎ 03446 426099. A rustic name somewhat belied by the hotel's appearance, which is bland and modern. It is spick and span, though, and well located by the Costanera, and with parking. $310

Puerto Sol San Lorenzo 477 ☎ 03446 434017, ⊛ hotel puertosol.com.ar. This friendly hotel has comfortable rooms, some looking onto the hotel's interior patio. You can also be taken across the river by boat to the hotel's private section of the Isla Libertad opposite, for quiet relaxation and a drink. $550

EATING

In terms of eating, at least, Gualeguaychú is a town with a split personality – in the summer (Dec–March) all life is centred on the Costanera, which is lined with *parrillas* specializing in freshwater fish, while the rest of the year the action gravitates to the town centre, around 25 de Mayo.

Campo Alto San Lorenzo and Concordia. Unlike its rivals along the Costanera, *Campo Alto* specializes more in meat than fish, but both are top quality. It has seating in a roomy *quincho*-style building or outside in a secluded garden-terrace. Daily noon–4pm & 8pm–late.

Dacal Andrade s/n. Wonderfully retro and pleasingly reliable, this classic riverside *parrilla* has a wide-ranging menu dominated by river fish. Daily noon–4pm & 8pm–late.

La Paisanita 25 de Mayo 1176. This down-to-earth place is extremely popular with locals for its *parrilla* and pasta dishes. Daily noon–4pm & 8pm–late.

Colón and around

Thanks to its setting, variety of activities (see box, p.219) and attractive hotels and restaurants, **COLÓN** is easily the most appealing of Entre Ríos' resorts. It also makes a good base for visiting the wonderfully exotic-looking **Parque Nacional El Palmar**, just 50km north, or the European-style splendour of **Palacio San José**, about 40km southwest. Moreover, Colón is linked to the major Uruguayan city Paysandú, 15km southeast, via the Puente Internacional General Artigas. Every February Colón hosts an important craft fair, the **Fiesta Nacional de la Artesanía**, with over five hundred exhibitors from Argentina and further afield. The rest of the year, there's no shortage of stores selling **artesan goods** ranging from *mates* and *asado* tableware to local cheese and salami.

Colón spreads along the Río Uruguay, with a narrow strip of beach running for several kilometres alongside its alluring riverside avenue, the **Costanera Gobernador Quirós**. The town's central square, **Plaza Washington**, where you will find the municipalidad, is twinned with Plaza Artigas and together they cover four blocks, ten blocks inland from the riverside; far more elegant and closer to the Uruguay, however, is smaller **Plaza San Martín**, east of Plaza Washington along Colón's main commercial street, Avenida 12 de Abril – named after the town's foundation date in 1863. The most distinctive district is the sleepy **port area**, a small but charming cobbled quarter lined with a clutch of handsome colonial-style buildings which slopes down to the riverbank, immediately to the north of Plaza San Martín; if you are driving, watch out for the huge toads that often hop across the street here.

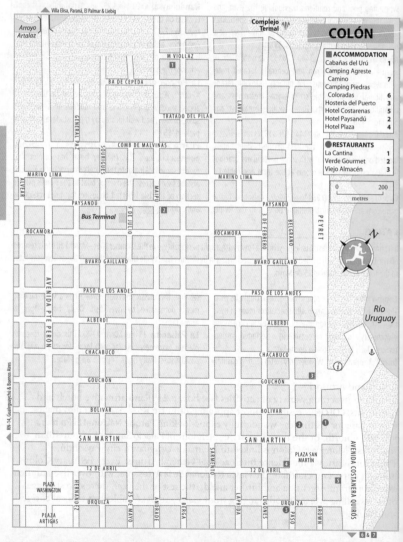

COLÓN

ACCOMMODATION

Cabañas del Urú	1
Camping Agreste Camino	7
Camping Piedras Coloradas	6
Hostería del Puerto	3
Hotel Costarenas	5
Hotel Paysandú	2
Hotel Plaza	4

RESTAURANTS

La Cantina	1
Verde Gourmet	2
Viejo Almacén	3

SIGHTS ALONG THE RÍO URUGUAY

To while away the time in relaxing Colón you can take memorable boat trips on the enticing **Río Uruguay**, swim at a riverine **beach**, taste wine at the region's only commercial **vineyard**, or tour a vestige of the area's once-thriving beef export industry. A day's exploration is well rewarded with a soak in the city's thermal springs, or with a visit to the **Termas Villa Elisa**, only a short distance north.

A few hundred metres from Colón's "coast", in the middle of the Río Uruguay, are some lush **islands** flanked with dense vegetation and pristine sandbanks: both offer opportunities for observing local flora and fauna, especially birdlife, and for sunbathing on a private beach.

Excursions to the islands in motorized dinghies (1–3hr; take sunscreen, bathing clothes, insect repellent and a sweater on cool evenings) can be made with ★ Ita-i-Corá (☎ 03447 423360, ⊕ itaicora.com), a wonderfully dynamic outfit whose larger than life co-owner, Charlie Adamson, speaks excellent English. Its office is at San Martín 97, on the corner of Plaza San Martín, but it also has an information stand on the corner of the Costanera and General Noailles, three blocks south. The same operator runs land-based trips (2–3hr) to see petrified tree trunks, a display of locally discovered semiprecious stones and the sadly disused **Pueblo Liebig** (open to the public every afternoon), a former meat-packing plant 12km north of town, where beef extract was invented. The surprisingly interesting stones are on display at the **Reservorio de Piedras Semipreciosas** (daily 9am–8pm; $5); RP-130 Km3.5; Selva, queen of the agates, is always delighted to show visitors the collection.

Villa Elisa

30km northwest of Colón, 15km off the fork of the RN-14 and the RN-130 • Daily 8am–10pm • $90 • ☎ 03447 480687, ⊕ termasvillaelisa.com

Although there's a thermal spa complex right in the middle of town, the best place hereabouts for a relaxing, therapeutic soak is at **Villa Elisa**, some way to the northwest. This huge, spacious, state-of-the-art thermal complex has seven pools with mineral waters especially good for sufferers from rheumatism, with massages and refreshments available; the restaurant is decent.

ARRIVAL AND INFORMATION

COLÓN AND AROUND

By bus Colón's bus terminal (☎ 03447 421716) lies fifteen blocks or so northwest of Plaza San Martín, on the corner of Paysandú and 9 de Julio.

Destinations Buenos Aires (hourly; 5hr 30min); Corrientes (2 daily; 10hr); Gualeguaychú (8 daily; 2hr); Paraná (9 daily; 5hr); Santa Fe (6 daily; 6hr).

Tourist information The busy and mostly helpful tourist office (daily 6am–10pm high season, 6am–8pm out of season; ☎ 03447 421233, ⊕ colon.gov.ar) is in an attractive mansion down in the port area, two blocks north of the plaza, on the corner of Av Costanera and Gouchón: it provides useful accommodation information, plus details of the sights around Colón and ways of exploring the river.

ACCOMMODATION

Colón has a fine range of accommodation at all budget levels, though it does become severely overstretched on summer weekends, when bookings should be made weeks ahead. There are also plenty of **campsites**, spread out along the length of Colón's waterfront – if you're looking for something quieter and more rustic go as far away from the town centre as possible.

Cabañas del Urú Mauricio Viollaz 330 ☎ 03447 424029, ⊕ cabaniasdeluru.com.ar. Six-bed thatched *cabañas* in a small garden with an equally small swimming pool; well-appointed "rustic chic" and in a quiet, away-from-it-all location, but a shame they are crammed into a tiny plot. $525

Camping Agreste Camino Costero Sur y Arroyo de la Leche ☎ 03447 1545 7787. Living up to its name ("rustic"), the *Agreste* campsite is an attractive wooded site especially popular with fishing enthusiasts. $40

Camping Piedras Coloradas ☎ 03447 423548. At the southern end of General Belgrano; it has volleyball and

basketball courts plus the usual facilities. The site is very well organized but it might be too noisy for many campers. $20

★ **Hostería del Puerto** Gouchón and Alejo Peyret 158 ☎ 03447 422698, ⊕ hosteriadecolon.com.ar. Remarkably good value, this *hostería*, housed in a pink colonial building just one block from the port, has a refreshing swimming pool. The mostly large, attractively decorated rooms are arranged around a central courtyard with an unusual well; some rooms have a river view, but try and avoid the noisy street-side ones. $475

4

COLÓN'S UNIQUE WINERY

In defiance of Colón's subtropical climate, usually regarded as totally hostile to wine grapes, in 1857 a Swiss immigrant named **Joseph Favre** planted a few **vines** from his homeland just outside the city. Seventeen years later, with his vines not only succeeding, but thriving, he added a handsome **bodega** (winery) in the Piedmontese style – an Italianate villa with ochre walls that would not look out of place in the countryside around Turin. In 1936, the national government banned the commercial production of wine anywhere outside the Cuyo and the Andean Northwest, but Favre's descendants continued making wine for their own consumption. When the law was finally repealed in 1998, Jesús Vulliez, a local descendant of other Swiss immigrants, bought the nineteenth-century bodega and began producing wine for commercial distribution under the label **Vulliez Sermet**, planting five hectares with chardonnay, malbec, merlot, cabernet sauvignon, tannat, syrah and sangiovese vines. If you call ahead, you can visit the beautiful bodega, with its impeccably restored interior and cool cellars, taste the fine red and white wines, and eat at the bodega restaurant (closed Tues). The attractive grounds nearby house a large swimming pool and three luxurious **cabañas** sleeping up to six (☎ 03447 156 45925, ⓦ bodegavulliezsermet.com.ar; $520). To reach the complex from the RN-14, take the RP-135 Colón–Paysandú road and stay on it for another 200m after the turn-off to Colón.

Hotel Costarenas Av Quirós and 12 de Abril ☎ 03447 425050, ⓦ hotelcostarenas.com.ar. Undoubtedly Colón's most luxurious hotel, enjoying a prime location overlooking the river. The spa is enticing, the indoor pool a mini-oasis, the gym functional and the restaurant bright and efficient. The rooms are spacious, comfortable and tastefully decorated, though the place lacks character. $820

Hotel Paysandú Maipú and Paysandú ☎ 03447 421140, ⓦ hotelpaysandu.com.ar. A good option near the bus terminal, this spruce modern place has clean, comfortable rooms, parking and very friendly owners; breakfast is included. $310

Hotel Plaza Belgrano and 12 de Abril ☎ 03447 421043, ⓦ hotel-plaza.com.ar. A hotel with an older side, in existence since 1913, offering small, fairly run-of-the-mill but perfectly acceptable rooms, and a newer part with much larger, smartly furnished rooms with LCD TVs and private jacuzzis – for rather higher rates. All guests can use the outdoor pool and communal jacuzzi and there's a good breakfast served. $490

EATING

La Cantina Alejo Peyret 79. A long-established and homely place where you can get good, cheap pasta and decent freshwater fish, with tables outside on a quiet street. Daily noon–3pm & 8.30pm–late.

Verde Gourmet Belgrano 75 ☎ 03447 1545 3354, ⓦ verdegourmet.com. For something a bit different, *Verde Gourmet* (booking essential) is a small, informal restaurant space, based in the living room of Martín and his family, who lovingly prepare delicious three-course tailor-made vegetarian meals at a very reasonable price. Daily noon–4pm & 8.30pm–late.

★ **Viejo Almacén** Urquiza and J.J. Paso ☎ 03447 422216. An excellent choice, one block southeast of Plaza San Martín, the *Viejo Almacén* is a stylishly old-fashioned place that does excellent river fish – try the grilled *surubí* or *pacú*. Daily noon–4pm & 8pm–late.

Palacio San José

40km southwest of Colón and a short way off the RP-39 • Mon–Fri 8am–7pm, Sat & Sun 9am–6pm; Jan & Feb also Fri 9pm–12.30am; 1hr guided visits, in Spanish, at 10am, 11am, 3pm & 4pm, plus noon & 2pm at weekends • $25 • ⓦ palaciosanjose.com.ar

When it was built in the middle of the nineteenth century for General Justo José de Urquiza, the **Palacio San José** was Argentina's most luxurious private residence. *Caudillo* of Entre Ríos Province in the early nineteenth century and its governor from 1841, Urquiza was also the province's largest and wealthiest landowner, possessing a huge *saladero* (meat-salting plant). Restrictions imposed by Buenos Aires on the provinces' freedom to trade led Urquiza to revolt against dictator General Rosas, finally defeating him at the Battle of Caseros, outside Buenos Aires, in 1853. The lavishness of the palace seems clearly intended as a challenge to the Buenos Aires elite's idea of provincial backwardness – it had running water before any building in the capital. The architect was Pedro Fosatti – who also designed the Italian hospitals in Buenos Aires and

Montevideo – and, despite the colonial watchtowers that dominate its facade, it shows a strong Italian influence in its elegant Tuscan arches.

The entrance to the palace is at the back of the building, now painted the deep pink of national monuments; to your right as you enter stands a tiny **chapel** lined with spectacular frescoes by nineteenth-century Uruguayan academic painter Juan Manuel Blanes and an imposing 3m-high baptismal font, entirely carved from Carrara marble, a gift from Pope Pius IX (who kept a copy in the Vatican). The palace's 38 rooms are laid out around two vast courtyards. The first of these, the **Patio del Parral**, is named for its grapevines, many of which were brought for Urquiza from France. The rooms in the second courtyard, the **Patio de Honor**, were occupied by Urquiza's most immediate family and important guests. Its most significant room is the dramatically named **Sala de la Tragedia** (Room of Tragedy), Urquiza's bedroom where, on April 11, 1870, he was assassinated by followers of rival *caudillo* López Jordán. It was turned into a shrine by Urquiza's widow, and traces of blood can still be seen on the door, along with bullets embedded in the wall. Beyond the Patio de Honor extends a small French-style **garden**, from where the Palacio's harmonious facade appears to best advantage.

ARRIVAL AND TOURS
PALACIO SAN JOSÉ

By remise/bus A *remise* will cost around $80, or take a bus from Concepción del Uruguay (just south of Colón) to Caseros or Paraná and ask to be let off at the turn-off to the Palacio San José, from where it's a 3km walk.

Tours During the high season (Jan, Feb & Easter), various tour companies offer trips from Colón, such as LDL, 12 de Abril 119 (☎ 03447 422222).

Parque Nacional El Palmar and around

The park entrance lies 50km north of Colón, along the RN-14. There is a *guardaparques'* post at the entrance where you pay and pick up a map and information leaflet • Daily 8am–6pm • $25 • It's a 10km walk from the entrance to the visitors' centre and campsite, though it should be possible to get a lift with someone entering the park. There are also organized trips – usually half-day tours – from Colón with companies such as LDL

As you head north from Colón along the RN-14, the first sign that you are approaching **PARQUE NACIONAL EL PALMAR** is a sprinkling of tremendously tall palm trees towering above the flat lands that border the highway. The 85-square-kilometre park was set up in 1966 to conserve examples of the **yatay palm**, which once covered large areas of Entre Ríos Province, Uruguay and southern Brazil. Intensive cultivation of the region almost wiped out the palm, and the national park is now the largest remaining reserve of the *yatay*; it is also one of the southernmost palm groves in the world. Though the terrain itself is nondescript rolling grassland, the sheer proliferation of the majestic *yatay* – with many examples over three hundred years old and up to 18m in height – makes for a wonderfully exotic-looking landscape. Bordering the Río Uruguay along its eastern fringe, the park is composed of **gallery forest**, dense pockets of subtropical vegetation formed when seeds and sediment are borne downstream from Brazil and Misiones. It is best appreciated on an overnight stay – the extensive acres of palm forest are absolutely stunning in the late afternoon light, when their exotic forms sing out against the deepening blue sky and reddish gold of the earth.

There are a number of well-signposted trails in the park, taking you along the streams and through palm forests; the longer of these are designed for vehicles, though if you don't mind trekking along several kilometres of gravel road, there's nothing to stop you from doing them on foot. There are great views from **La Glorieta**, a gentle bluff from where you can take in the surrounding sea of palms. Wildlife in the park includes ñandús, armadillos, foxes and capybaras and, particularly around the campsite, *vizcachas* and monitor lizards.

ACCOMMODATION
PARQUE EL PALMAR AND AROUND

Aurora del Palmar ☎ 03447 1543 1689, ⓦ auroradel palmar.com.ar. Just outside the park, set well back from the

RN-14 at Km202, on the opposite side to the park entrance, this is an ecology-minded accommodation complex. The 1.5

square kilometres of preserved land host a mini-grove of *yatay* palms, plus a set of disused train carriages that have been converted into accommodation; there are also more spacious rooms in a colonial-style building nearby, overlooking citrus orchards and a large swimming pool. Guests and nonguests can eat simple meals here and go on excursions such as horse rides, canoe trips, birdwatching and treks into the Palmar. Even as you have lunch on the terrace you are treated to a

bucolic scene and effortless sightings of several bird species. Camping is also allowed. Camping $60, doubles $510

Camping El Palmar ☎ 03447 423378. The only place to stay inside the park is a spacious and shady campsite with showers and a provisions store; the best pitches have a great view over the Río Uruguay. There is also a decent restaurant in the park (open to all visitors), next door to the interpretation centre. $55

Central Corrientes: the Esteros del Iberá

Covering nearly 13,000 square kilometres (one-sixth of Corrientes Province), the delicate ecosystem of the **ESTEROS DEL IBERÁ** is a magical landscape that offers some of the best opportunities in the country for close-up observation of wildlife. An elongated sliver of land running through the centre of Corrientes Province, the *esteros* (marshes) are bordered to the north by the RN-12, to the east by tributaries of the Aguaypey and Miriñay rivers and to the west by tributaries of the Paraná. The southern tip touches the RN-123, which runs east–west from the border town of Paso de los Libres, joining the RN-12 150km south of Corrientes city. In addition to the *esteros* that give the area its name, you will see a good many lakes, ponds, streams and wonderful floating islands, formed by a build-up of soil on top of intertwined water lilies.

For many years this was one of Argentina's wildest and least-known regions – a local legend even had it that a tribe of pygmies lived on the islands – harbouring an isolated community who made their living from hunting and fishing the area's wildlife. Since the **Reserva Natural del Iberá** was created in 1983, hunting has been prohibited in the area and many locals have been employed as highly specialized guides, or *baqueanos*, and park rangers, thus helping to preserve the unique environment. The ban on hunting has led to an upsurge in the region's abundant bird and animal population, with an amazingly diverse range of species thriving here (see box, p.225).

In the heart of the reserve, beside the ecosystem's second largest lake, the Laguna del Iberá, is the spread-out village of **Colonia Carlos Pellegrini** ("Pellegrini"). The main gateway to the *esteros*, though is **Mercedes**, a picturesque traditional town 120km southwest of Pellegrini. If **driving**, note that the road linking Pellegrini to Posadas in a northeasterly direction is not always viable, especially after rain (in any case, best in a 4WD); whatever you do, enquire about its current state before attempting it.

Mercedes

MERCEDES is unlikely to impress at first sight. Set among the flatlands of central Corrientes Province, approximately 200km southeast of the city of Corrientes, it appears as a sprawling modern settlement with little to tempt you into staying. Head into the centre, though, and you'll find an appealing agricultural town given a distinctive flavour by a mix of old-fashioned adobe and galleried-roof buildings plus some elegant late nineteenth-century architecture. The town is a real hub of country life, too: horses and carts are a common sight on its streets and on Saturdays gauchos come to town, traditionally dressed Corrientes-style, with shallow, wide-brimmed hats, ornate belts and wide *bombachas* (trousers) and accompanied by their wives, who wear frilly, old-fashioned dresses. Around 9km west of town, along the RN-123, there is a roadside shrine to a popular local hero, **Gauchito Gil**, now worshipped nationwide as a saint (see box opposite).

The town, built on a regular grid pattern, is centred on **Plaza 25 de Mayo**, a densely planted square with little fountains. At its southern end stands the rather unusual **Iglesia Nuestra Señora de las Mercedes**, a lofty, late nineteenth-century red-brick church whose towers are topped with Moorish domes. Along the southern side of the square runs Juan Pujol, an attractive street lined with some fine buildings.

Fundación Manos Correntinas

San Martín 487 • Mon–Fri 8am–1pm & 5–8pm, Sat 9am–noon • ☎ 03773 422671

Three blocks east of Plaza 25 de Mayo, on the corner of San Martín and Batalla de Salta, there's a beautifully preserved example of the local building style: a low whitewashed adobe-walled construction with a gently sloping red-tiled roof which overhangs the pavement, supported on simple wooden posts. This building houses the **Fundación Manos Correntinas**, a nonprofit enterprise that functions as an outlet for locally produced crafts. The small but superior collection of goods includes basketwork, simple gourd *mates*, heavy woollens and hand-turned bone and horn buttons.

ARRIVAL AND INFORMATION

MERCEDES

By bus Mercedes' bus terminal is six blocks west of Plaza San Martín, on the corner of Av San Martín and El Ceibo, with a left luggage and general information office (open 24hr).
Destinations Buenos Aires (10 daily; 10hr); Colonia Carlos Pellegrini (2 daily; 4hr); Corrientes (10 daily; 3hr); Posadas

(3 daily; 4hr); Resistencia (6 daily; 3hr 30min).
Tourist information The tourist office (daily 8am–noon & 4–8pm; ☎ 03773 15414384), inconveniently located in an isolated building at the western entrance to town, can provide useful information and a map.

ACCOMMODATION AND EATING

★ **La Casa de China** Fray Luís Beltrán 599 and Mitre ☎ 03773 1562 7269, ⓦ corrientes.com.ar/lacasadechina. This fabulous B&B in a tastefully furnished, quiet, patrician villa has four double rooms, a beautifully tended garden behind, and China herself will prepare delicious meals if given notice. $380

Hostel Delicias del Iberá Dr Rivas 688 ☎ 03773 423167, ⓦ corrientes.com.ar/deliciasdelibera. The best budget option in town, its rooms are a little small and tatty but the ambience is ultra-friendly. $160
Hotel Sol San Martín 519 ☎ 03773 420283, ⓦ corrientes .com.ar/hotelsolmercedes. This quaint and modest hotel is

4

GAUCHITO GIL

Along roadsides throughout Argentina you'll see mysterious **shrines** of varying sizes, smothered in red flags, red candles, empty bottles and other miscellaneous bits and pieces. These are erected in homage to the semi-mythical **Gauchito Gil**, a kind of nineteenth-century gaucho Robin Hood – one of those folkloric figures whose story has some basis in reality yet has undoubtedly been embellished over the years.

Born – perhaps – in 1847 in Corrientes, Antonio Gil refused to fight in that province's civil war and fled to the mountains, robbing from the rich, helping the poor and healing with his hands. Captured by the police, he claimed that he had deserted from the army as he had been told in a dream by a Guaraní god that brothers shouldn't fight each other. An unimpressed sergeant took him out to a spot near Mercedes to execute him. Gil told the sergeant that when he returned to town he would find that his son was seriously ill, but as Gil's blood was innocent it could perform miracles, so the sergeant must pray for his intervention. Unmoved, the sergeant cut Gil's throat. When he returned to town, he found that the situation was indeed as the gaucho had described, but – after fervent prayer – his son made a miraculous recovery.

The sergeant put up the first shrine to thank him, and Gauchito Gil has since been credited with numerous **miracles** and honoured with many **shrines**, all bedecked in the distinctive **red flags** – which may represent his neck scarf soaked in blood – making the shrine look like the aftermath of a left-wing political demonstration after all the protesters have gone home. The shrine erected near **Mercedes**, on the place where he was killed, presumably began life as a simple affair, but such is the popularity of **Gauchito Gil** that the site has mushroomed over time into a vast *villa* of humble restaurants, makeshift sleeping areas and souvenir stalls; there is even a kind of museum exhibiting the offerings made to the Gauchito, such as football shirts, wedding dresses and children's bicycles, along with more conventional rosaries. Simpler offerings, often made by passing motorists to ensure a safe journey, include ribbons and candles. January 8 sees Gauchito Gil pilgrims flock to the main shrine from the whole country. There is a close parallel with the folk-saint shrines to the Difunta Correa, whose main pilgrimage site lies near San Juan (see p.374) but is also honoured by smaller versions nationwide.

situated a few blocks east of Plaza San Martín in a lovely old building with spotless if dingy rooms – all of them en suite with TV and fans – set around an attractive flower-filled courtyard. $290

Sabor Único San Martín 1240 ☎03773 420314. The food is not exactly prize winning but you can get a decent steak and a salad at reasonable prices served in an attractive house with a patio – and everything is scrupulously clean. Daily noon–4pm & 8pm–1am.

DIRECTORY

Craft shops There are various craft outlets throughout town: try the shops along San Martín and Juan Pujol selling belts, gaucho knives, *mates* and the like – all with a sturdy utilitarian feel and far less gimmicky than the pieces on sale in more touristy towns.

Banks and exchange There's an ATM at the Banco de Corrientes, on the corner of Pedro Ferre, three blocks west of Plaza San Martín; stock up here if you are heading to Pellegrini, in the heart of the *esteros*, as it has no banking facilities or decent stores.

Colonia Carlos Pellegrini and around

About 120km northeast of Mercedes, **COLONIA CARLOS PELLEGRINI** lies at the heart of the Reserva Natural del Iberá, and is mainly accessed via the unsealed but well-maintained RP-40. The journey there takes you through flat, unremarkable land, reminiscent of the African savannah, but with little to prepare you for the wonderfully wild, watery environment of the *esteros* themselves. The village sits on a peninsula on the edges of the Laguna del Iberá, a 53-square-kilometre expanse of water. The banks of the sparkling lake (*iberá* means "shining" in Guaraní) are spread with acres of water lilies, most notably the striking lilac-bloomed *camalotes* and yellow *aguapés*, and dotted with bouncy floating islands formed of matted reeds and grass, known as *embalsados*.

If you come from Mercedes by bus or with your own transport, access to the village is over a temporary-looking – and sounding – narrow bridge constructed of earth and rock. Short trails on either side of the road lead through a small forested area south of the visitors' centre; the densely packed mix of palms, jacarandas, *lapachos* and willows here is a good place to spot and hear black howler monkeys. They typically slouch in a ball shape among the branches or swing from tree to tree on lianas. Easiest to see are the yellowish young, often ferried from tree to tree on the backs of their mothers. Birds and butterflies abound, while capybaras often graze on the grass.

The village itself is composed of a small grid of sandy streets, centred on grassy **Plaza San Martín**. There are few services, and no banking facilities, so make sure you bring enough cash with you for your stay (nobody takes credit cards).

The Esteros del Iberá

Wildlife-spotting excursions are organized through the posadas, which take visitors out in their small motorboats, with the boatmen acting as guides. After speeding across the centre of the lake, the boats dip under the causeway bridge, calling in at the visitors' centre to register, before cutting their engines to drift through the narrow streams that thread between the islands on the other side of the laguna. This silent approach allows you an incredibly privileged view of the *esteros'* wildlife (see box opposite); turning a corner you suddenly find yourself among a wonderful landscape of water lilies and verdant floating islands, the whole of it teeming with bird and animal life. Sometimes guides will take you onto the floating islands themselves; it's a particularly bizarre experience to feel the ground vibrating beneath your feet as you move. Another trip takes you along the Río Miriñay, home to slightly different varieties of flora and fauna to the lake. Enquire also about **horse rides** in the nearby marshes, another excellent way to see birds and the like, especially in the morning.

INFORMATION

Tourist information There's a small visitors' centre (open daily during daylight hours) immediately to the left just before you cross the bridge, where you can see a small display on the *esteros* and their wildlife.

WILDLIFE IN THE ESTEROS DEL IBERÁ

Home to well over three hundred species of **bird** and a mindblowing variety of **reptiles** and **mammals**, the Esteros del Iberá are a paradise for any visitor with an interest in animals. Armed with binoculars and a guidebook to South American species, you stand an excellent chance of observing dozens of different varieties in just an hour or two; a good guide will help, too.

BIRDS

A common sight and sound around the Laguna del Iberá are *chajás* (**Southern screamers**), large grey birds with a patch of red around the eyes and a look of bashful nervousness. They frequently perch on the trees on the lakeside, nonchalantly chanting "aha-aha" but occasionally emitting a piercing yelp (hence the English name) similar to the sound a dog makes when trodden on. Other large birds include sleek, black **Olivaceous cormorants**; **Maguari storks**, with striking black and white plumage, and a tendency to soar on the thermals above the lake; and **Striated herons**, characterized by a black crown and a lazy disposition. A particularly impressive sight during the spring nesting period is that of the *garzales*, where hundreds of normally solitary herons unite in a spectacular mass gathering. Another magical, if rarer, sight is the elegant *jabirú*, a long-legged relative of the stork with a white body, bright crimson collar and a black head and beak. Different species of **kingfisher** also put on a show of aviation prowess, swooping across the water or diving into it. **Wattled jacanas**, on the other hand, prefer to scuttle over water lilies and floating weeds, seldom showing off their lemon-tipped wings. Another strange-moving bird is the **Giant wood-Rail**, or *ipacaá*, whose Guaraní name is onomatopoeic; it croaks plaintively as it tiptoes around near houses, grabbing any food left out for it and scampering off to peck away at it.

REPTILES AND INSECTS

Birds are not the only wonders around the *esteros*. Among the reed beds at the edges of the lake you may catch sight of large **snakes**, such as the handsome **yellow anaconda**, its golden skin dotted with black patches; they can reach up to 3m in length. As you approach the edges of the floating islands, in particular, charcoal-grey **caymans**, or *yacarés*, freeze, often with their ferocious-looking jaws stuck open, or else they suddenly slither into the water, where they observe you with only their eyes peeking above the surface. Another startling spectacle is provided by creepily large **spiders**, which lurk in huge webs among bushes and reeds, waiting for their helpless insect prey. Some guides delight in making it look as though the boat is heading straight for them, so arachnophobes be warned. Rather more appealing are the hundreds of **butterflies**, in every colour imaginable, an enchanting sight you will see all over the region.

MAMMALS

Mammals are well represented, too. **Howler monkeys** – which really growl rather than howl – are much easier to hear than to see, but you might, if you are patient, observe their antics near the visitors' centre or in other tall trees in the area. Listen, too, for the sudden splash of a **capybara**, or *carpincho*, diving into the water. On land, this guinea-pig-like mammal, the world's largest rodent, looks almost ungainly, but they are incredibly graceful as they glide through the water. The floating islands are where the capybaras go to sleep and graze. There, and on the marshy lands and pastures around the more isolated extremes of the lake, you may also spot the rare **marsh deer**, South America's largest, equally at home in the water and on dry land. If you approach them gently, these astonishingly beautiful animals seem to accept your presence and continue grazing lazily on aquatic plants. Rarest of all of the *esteros*' wildlife, and certainly the hardest to spot, is the endangered *aguara-guazú*, or **maned wolf**, a reddish long-legged creature that awkwardly lopes through the vegetation, moving first its two left legs and then the two right ones – or so they say.

ACCOMMODATION

The best **accommodation** is provided by various posadas, most of which offer full board with at least one **boat trip** to the lagoon included and other activities laid on. For those on a budget, there are a couple of hostels and a municipal **campsite** immediately to the left as you enter the village from the bridge; it's a pleasant riverside site with showers but is almost entirely bereft of shade.

Don Justino ☎03773 499415, ✆corrientes.com.ar /donjustinohostel. Decent hostel in an attractive converted house overlooking the lake, with simple rooms and a basic restaurant; the friendly staff will help arrange excursions and onward travel. $320

Estancia Rincón del Socorro ☎03782 497073, ✆rincondelsocorro.com. Five kilometres from the main road, this converted working estancia is efficiently run by the hospitable Cook family. The traditional main building and luxurious rooms are all decorated with handsome furnishings and splendid photos of Iberá flora and fauna. Food includes home-grown, organic fruit, vegetables and herbs. A small plane can take you to a sister estancia, *San Alonso*, on the shores of Laguna Paraná, bang in the middle of the *esteros*, where it is also possible to spend the night. $1400

Irupé Lodge ☎03773 15 440 2193, ✆irupelodge.com .ar. Handsome wooden *hostería* with five down-to-earth, brightly decorated rooms overlooking the lagoon, with its own jetty and launch. $850

Posada Aguapé ☎03773 499412, ✆iberaesteros.com .ar. A traditional building set in spacious grounds with twelve appealing en-suite rooms overlooking the lake. There's also a swimming pool and a cosy bar area. $540

★ **Posada de la Laguna** ☎03773 499413, ✆posadadelalaguna.com. Particularly well situated in a quiet lakeside spot at the eastern edge of the village, this pioneering posada offers pared-down luxury with a rustic feel. The elegant and spacious but simple en-suite rooms are in a galleried building whose veranda provides a good vantage point for observing the birds that gather around the lake; food and service are top-notch and the swimming pool is another great spot for some laidback birdwatching. $960

Posada Rancho de los Esteros ☎03773 15 493041, ✆ranchodelosesteros.com.ar. Just two handsomely decorated suites in a wonderful ranch with a traditional gallery. $1100

Puerto Valle Just off the RN-12 between Posadas and Corrientes city ☎03786 425700, ✆hotelpuertovalle .com. Not in Carlos Pellegrini but allowing access to the northern reaches of the *esteros*, this small luxury hotel is on a large timber estate. The spacious, very comfortable rooms in a single-storey building – all overlooking trimmed lawns that run down to the edge of the Paraná river – are perfect for those who don't like their rural encounter to be too rustic, and there is a lovely pool and boat trips on the river and into the *esteros* included in the price. $1150

Rancho Inambú Yeruti and Peguajó ☎03773 436159, ✆ranchoinambu.com.ar. Recently converted from a hostel to a budget posada, *Inambú* is a typical mudbrick house, with attractive rooms of various sizes, an airy breakfast room and a bar with a pool table. Packages including boat and horseriding excursions can be arranged for around $650 per person. $490

Misiones Province

The proboscis-shaped territory of **Misiones**, in the extreme northeast of the country, is one of Argentina's smallest, poorest but most beautiful provinces. **Posadas**, the relaxed capital, is usually bypassed by most travellers, but the province has a lot more to offer than the juggernaut that is **Iguazú Falls**, the only place most visitors ever see, zipping in and out by plane. What looks odd on the map makes perfect sense on the ground: Misiones' borders are almost completely defined by the wide Paraná and Uruguay rivers and one can even imagine that the province's sierras were formed by the land being compressed by neighbouring Brazil and Paraguay. The province's distinctive iron-rich **red earth** ends abruptly just over the border with Corrientes, while the torrent of water that hurtles over the waterfalls at Iguazú must surely mark one of the world's most dramatic and decisive frontiers. Along the Brazilian border, formed by the upper reaches of the Río Uruguay, you can see one of the world's most unusual, if not most powerful, sets of cascades, the **Saltos del Moconá**, weather conditions permitting.

GUARANÍ: VESTIGES OF INDIGENOUS CULTURE IN THE LITORAL

As in parts of neighbouring Corrientes Province, a strong **Guaraní** influence remains in Misiones (known as Tapé or Guayrá in the native tongue), thanks to small pre-European communities scattered throughout the territory, and this cross-cultural phenomenon is echoed above all in the speech of inhabitants in the more rural areas, where a mix of Guaraní and Spanish can frequently be heard. Throughout the Litoral, even in urban districts, Guaraní words are a common feature of speech: for example, you may hear a child referred to as a "*guri*" or a woman as a "*guaina*". Toponyms like San Ignacio Miní, Iguazú, Moconá and Teyú Cuaré are all Guaraní.

The territory was named for the Jesuit settlements that flourished in the region in the seventeenth and eighteenth centuries; the most impressive mission on Argentine soil is the much-photographed ruins of **San Ignacio Miní**. Misiones became a centre of considerable immigration in the early twentieth century: mostly Ukrainians, Swedes, Japanese and Germans. The province's wildlife-filled **jungle** and its emerald fields and orchards – pale tobacco, vivid lime trees, darker manioc and neatly clipped tea plantations, painting the landscape endless shades of green – are further attractions that make wandering off the beaten tracks that are the RN-12 and the RN-14 infinitely rewarding.

Away from Iguazú tourist facilities are few and far between, but a number of **estancias** and **lodges** make for some of the country's most enjoyable accommodation experiences.

Posadas

If you arrive in **POSADAS** expecting your first taste of the jungle, you'll be disappointed: the provincial capital sits on a rather bare patch of land bordering the Río Paraná, which – bar the red earth – has more in common with northern Corrientes than with the luscious emerald sierras of central and northern Misiones Province. However, while not exactly postcard-worthy, Posadas is a pleasant and prosperous place with a lively feel, some attractive buildings tucked away among the centre's mostly modern constructions, and a revamped Costanera, or riverside esplanade, a wonderful place for a stroll on a summer's evening.

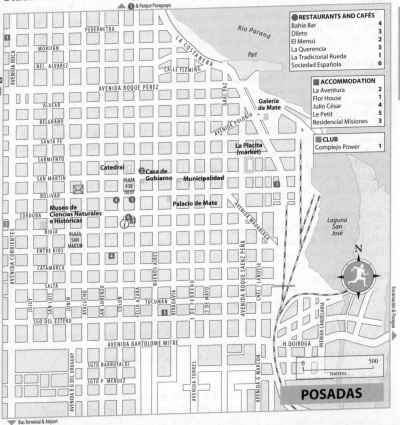

RESTAURANTS AND CAFÉS

Bahía Bar	4
Dileto	3
El Mensú	2
La Querencia	5
La Tradicional Rueda	1
Sociedad Española	6

ACCOMMODATION

La Aventura	2
Flor House	1
Julio César	4
Le Petit	5
Residencial Misiones	3

CLUB

Complejo Power	1

POSADAS

4

Posadas is primarily a **stopover city** and appears to do little to reap any benefit from the modest but steady stream of tourists who pass through. While there's a handful of mildly interesting **museums** here, there is little – bar the odd craft shop – specifically aimed at the holiday-maker. The town hosts a lively provincial festival, known as the **Estudiantina**, which runs over three weekends in September. During the festival local schools prepare and perform dance routines – all with a strong Brazilian influence.

The centre of Posadas is demarcated by four main avenues – Sáenz Peña, Guacurarí, Corrientes and B. Mitre, the last of which leads towards the international bridge. Within this area you will find the majority of hotels and points of interest. The main reason for heading further northeast is to visit the **Parque Paraguayo**, where there is a crafts market and the Museo Regional Aníbal Cambas, and the **Costanera**, a popular hangout in the evenings.

Brief history

The first recorded settlement in the vicinity of modern-day Posadas was a **Jesuit mission**, founded in 1615. In 1879, the fledgling city was named after **José Gervasio de Posadas**, who, in 1814, had become the first Supreme Director of the Provincias Unidas del Río de la Plata – a title that rather outdid his reign, which lasted only until January of the following year. In 1884 Posadas, by far the most important settlement in the region, became Misiones' provincial capital. Since then it has largely been a quiet backwater, whose fortunes in recent years have been tied to its proximity to the massive **Yacyretá Dam** and the linked construction of a road to Paraguay via the **Puente Roque González de Santa Cruz**. The dam has led to a significant rise in the water level of the Paraná, submerging beaches, campsites and docks in Posadas (and further afield) in 2009, while the link with Paraguay has dramatically swelled the town's population.

Plaza 9 de Julio

Posadas' central plaza, the **Plaza 9 de Julio**, is flanked to the north by the early twentieth-century **Iglesia Catedral**, a work by super-prolific Alejandro Bustillo, who designed Buenos Aires' Banco Nación, among many other buildings. The plaza's best-looking building, however, is the **Casa de Gobierno**, a sugar-pink Rococo construction on Félix de Azara. The building sits perfectly alongside the manicured splendour of the square, where there's a healthy selection of local vegetation, including *pindó* palms and *lapacho*, neatly displayed in densely packed flowerbeds that are like little urban squares of jungle. Throughout the town you will find examples of the bright red and yellow *chivato* tree, originally imported from Madagascar, together with ficus or rubber trees, whose enormous leaves provide welcome shade.

Calle Bolívar

The city's **commercial centre** is concentrated on the streets west of the plaza, with Calle Bolívar in particular forming the hub of the clothes shops that make up much of the town's retail activity. There's usually a huddle of street traders here.

Palacio de Mate

Rivadavia 1846, two blocks east of Plaza 9 de Julio • Daily 9am–6pm • $5

The rather grandly named **Palacio de Mate** houses temporary exhibitions by local artists, alongside a permanent collection of small wooden carvings of laidback Chaco life by Juan de Dios Mena – look out for *Empleado Publico* (Public Employee) asleep, with his feet up on his desk. On the patio in front of the building, check out the scrap metal sculpture of a *cebador* preparing his *mate* (see box opposite).

Bajada Vieja and the port

Just beyond Avenida Roque Pérez, Calle Fleming, more commonly known as the **Bajada Vieja**, is one of Posada's most picturesque streets, lined with original

MATE: MORE THAN JUST A DRINK

The herby leaves used in making **mate**, Argentina's national beverage, come from an evergreen tree, *Ilex paraguayensis*, a member of the holly family that grows in northeastern Argentina, southern Brazil and Paraguay. Its leaves and buds are harvested with machetes in the dry southern winter (June–Aug) and used to make the *yerba* or *mate* herb. The **preparation** process for good *yerba* is complex and subtle: first comes the *zapecado*, literally "opening of the eyes", when the *mate* leaves are dry-roasted over a fire, to prevent fermentation and keep the leaves green. They are then coarsely ground, bagged and left to mature in dry sheds for nine months to a year, though this is sometimes artificially accelerated to two months or even less. A milling process then results in either coarse *caá-guazú* "big herb", or the more refined *caá-mini*.

The **vessel** you drink it out of is also called a *mate*, or *matecito*, originally a hollowed-out gourd of the climbing species *Lagenaria vulgaris*, native to the same region. It's dried, hollowed out and "cured" by macerating *yerba mate* inside it overnight. These gourds are still used today and come in two basic **shapes**: the pear-shaped *poro*, traditionally used for *mate* sweetened with sugar, and the squat, satsuma-shaped *galleta*, meant for *cimarrón*, literally "untamed", or unsweetened *mate*. Many *mates* are **works of art**, intricately carved or painted, and often made of wood, clay or metal – though connoisseurs claim gourds impart extra flavour to the brew. The *bombilla* – originally a reed or stick of bamboo – is the other vital piece of equipment. Most are now straw-shaped tubes of silver, aluminium or tin, flattened at the end on which you suck, and with a spoon-shaped protruberance at the other; this is perforated to strain the *mate* as you drink it. Optional extras include the *pava hornillo*, a special kettle that keeps the water at the right temperature. A thermos-flask is the modern-day substitute for this kettle, and can be replenished at shops and cafés; "hot water available" signs are a common sight all over Argentina but especially in the Litoral.

Mateine is a gentler **stimulant** than the closely related caffeine, helping to release muscular energy, pace the heartbeat and aid respiration without any of the side effects of coffee. In the 1830s it even met with the approval of a wary Charles Darwin, who wrote that it helped him sleep. It's a tonic and a **digestive agent**, and by dulling the appetite can help you lose weight. Its laxative, diuretic and sweat-making properties also make it very effective at purging toxins, perfect after excessive *asado* binges.

THE DOS AND DON'TS OF *MATE* DRINKING

If you find yourself in a **group** drinking *mate*, it's just as well to know how to avoid gaffes. The *cebador* – from *cebar* "to feed" – is the person who makes the *mate*. After half-filling the *matecito* with *yerba*, the *cebador* thrusts the *bombilla* into the *yerba* and trickles very hot – but not boiling – water down the side of the *bombilla*, to wet the *yerba* from below. The *cebador* always tries the *mate* first – the "fool's *mate*" – before refilling and handing it round to each person present, in turn – always with the right hand and clockwise. Each drinker drains the *mate* through the *bombilla*, without jiggling it around, sipping gently but not lingering, or sucking too hard, before handing it back to the *cebador*. Sucking out of the corner of the mouth is also frowned upon. A little more *yerba* may be added from time to time but there comes a moment when the *yerba* loses most of its flavour and no longer produces a healthy froth. The *matecito* is then emptied and the process started afresh. Saying "*gracias*" means you've had enough, and the *mate* will be passed to someone else when your turn comes round.

4

nineteenth-century houses. The street leads down to the **port**, where boats formerly departed to Paraguay and Brazil, though the rising level of the Paraná has put all ferry services on hold for the immediate future.

The Costanera

The riverside walkway known, as in most Argentine towns that boast one, as the **Costanera** is lined with bars and restaurants and is a lovely spot to watch the sunset or wonder about life in Encarnacíon, Paraguay, clearly visible on the opposite bank. Currently stretching about twenty blocks from north to east, it has been much improved in recent years, and is popular with joggers and dog-walkers; plans are in place to extend it as far as the international bridge.

ADDRESSES IN POSADAS

Posadas' streets were **renumbered** in the 1990s but, confusingly, both systems are still in use. You will generally find that the **address** will be written as the new number (usually four digits), with the old number (usually three digits) in brackets, while either may be used on the building itself – where necessary, we have followed this custom.

Parque Paraguayo

The small **Parque Paraguayo,** ten blocks northwest of the Plaza 9 de Julio, hosts a crafts market in the mornings and late afternoons, where you can see examples of Guaraní basketwork made from local wild cane and carved wooden animals, among other items.

Museo Regional Aníbal Cambas

Alberdi 600 • Tues–Fri 7.30am–noon & 3–7pm, Sat 9am–noon • Free

By the park, the **Museo Regional Aníbal Cambas** is housed in a handsome century-old brick building and loyally maintained by its friendly staff in the face of an obvious shortage of funds. There are some interesting and well-labelled exhibits in the **historical and ethnographical collection**, such as objects culled from the ruins of Jesuit missions and artefacts produced by the region's indigenous populations: the Guayaquí, the Chiripá, the Mbyá and the Guaraní. The last are particularly strongly represented, with a large collection of clay funerary urns, known as *yapepo*, meaning "handmade" in Guaraní.

There are also a number of musical instruments, notably the *mimby*, a kind of wooden flute used by men and the *mimby reta*, similar but much smaller and used by women. The importance of music to the Guaraní is documented as far back as Alvar Núñez Cabeza de Vaca's first incursion into the Paraná region, when he noted that the Indians "received them covered in many-coloured feathers with instruments of war and music". You can reach the museum on local buses, including #4 and #14 from Colón and Catamarca.

ARRIVAL AND INFORMATION

POSADAS

By plane The quiet airport is around 7km southwest of the centre; bus #28 runs into town from here, or you could take a taxi (around $50). There are two daily flights to and from Buenos Aires (1hr 30min).

By bus Posadas' bus terminal (☎ 03752 454887) is about 4km south of the centre at the intersection of Av Santa Catalina and the RN-12. It's a modern building with good facilities, though no ATM machine. From the terminal there are numerous local buses (including #24, #25 and #21) heading into the centre; the taxi ride will cost about $40.

Destinations Buenos Aires (hourly; 14hr); Corrientes (9 daily; 5hr); El Soberbio (7 daily; 4hr); Formosa (1 daily; 7hr); Puerto Iguazú (hourly; 6hr); Resistencia (hourly; 5hr 30min); Rosario (5 daily; 15hr); San Ignacio (9 daily; 1hr).

Tourist information Posadas' well-stocked tourist office, at Colón 1985 (Mon–Fri 7am–8pm, Sat & Sun 8am–noon & 4.30–8pm; ☎ 03752 447539, ⓦ posadas.gov.ar), has fairly decent maps of both the town and the province, though it doesn't have an awful lot of information on anything beyond the well-worn Posadas/San Ignacio/Iguazú groove.

ACCOMMODATION

The majority of people seeking **accommodation** in Posadas are businessmen, so many of the hotels are fairly bland with a couple of worthy exceptions. Note that Posadas can be extremely hot and sticky during the summer, so plan on spending more than your normal budget in order to get air conditioning. Alternatively, if you have your own transport, consider staying at one of the excellent **estancias** in the surrounding countryside, where you can get to know the locals and enjoy the province's flora and fauna; booking ahead is vital.

IN TOWN

★ **La Aventura** Avenidas Urquiza and Zapiola ☎ 03752 465555, ⓦ complejoaaventura.com; buses #3 and #13 go from the corner of San Lorenzo and Sarmiento. Swish holiday complex on the outskirts of town, complete with good recreational facilities – including tennis courts and a swimming pool. Dorms around $̶5̶0̶, doubles $̶4̶9̶5̶

★ **Flor House** Av Roca 962 ☎ 03752 438053, ⓦ flor house.com.ar. Charming, traditional B&B in a lovely family house – the larger rooms are immaculate and spacious,

with mountains of frilly pillows and balconies. The breakfasts are top notch and there is an outdoor pool set in a garden filled with birdsong. $290

Julio César Entre Ríos 1951 ☎ 03752 427930, ⊛ juliocesarhotel.com.ar. Posadas' most upmarket hotel – four-star comfort including a swimming pool and gym. That said, the hotel is aimed mostly at the business traveller and for the same amount you are far better off at one of the nearby estancias. $760

Le Petit Santiago del Estero 1630 ☎ 03752 436031, ⊜ lepetithotel@ciudad.com.ar. On a quiet, tree-lined street away from the centre, this small, prettily decorated place has light and spacious rooms. Facilities include TV, telephone and a/c, and breakfast is provided. The friendly owner is also a good source of tourist information. Reservations advisable. $245

Residencial Misiones Félix de Azara 1960 (382) ☎ 03752 430133. This is just about the cheapest recommendable place in the centre of town: an old-fashioned hotel with rooms around a central patio. The whole family mucks in with the running of the hotel and there's a friendly atmosphere, although some of the rooms are in serious need of an overhaul. $185

ESTANCIAS AROUND POSADAS

Estancia Santa Cecilia Candelaria, 30km northeast of Posadas ☎ 03752 493018, ⊛ santa-cecilia.com.ar. Built in 1908 on a bluff overlooking the Río Paraná, this patrician house has six delightful rooms full of colonial charm, with a refined but not snobbish atmosphere. It provides horses for rides along the riverbanks, puts on impressive displays of gaucho horsemanship and horse-related crafts and serves traditional regional cuisine. The grounds are subtly landscaped, but the general feeling is one of open space – the swimming pool is fabulous. $1200

★ **Estancia Santa Inés** 20km southeast of Posadas ☎ 03752 156 60456, ⊛ estancia-santaines.com.ar. With a marvellous, old-fashioned interior, displaying a fantastic collection of silver *mate* paraphernalia, the estancia's trump card is its exotic setting within a mini-jungle of luxuriant vegetation. You can ride through the *mate* plantations to the huge outdoor pool, 5km away, fed by a natural spring, or visit the family's private chapel, containing handsome Jesuit carvings. Prices range from $80 for an afternoon visit, including tea (or *mate*), to $650 per person for an overnight stay, including all activities and meals. $1300

EATING, DRINKING AND NIGHTLIFE

There aren't a huge number of places to choose from for **eating** in Posadas, though there are a couple of exceptions. The town does have a thriving **nightlife**, however, which from Thursday to Saturday goes on until around 7am (not starting before well after midnight). In addition to home-grown rock and *cumbia*, the musical mix usually includes a bit of *marcha* (commercial dance) and Brazilian music.

Bahía Bar Bolívar 1911. Centrally located café-bar, popular with the locals and a great place for reasonably priced snacks such as juicy hamburgers and generous *lomos*. Daily noon–5pm & 9pm–late.

Complejo Power Corrientes and Centenario ⊛ complejopower.com.ar. Megadisco complex that towers over all

the other discos that Posadas has to offer. Fri & Sat midnight–6am.

Diletto Bolívar 1929 ☎ 03752 443 5514. Sophisticated à la carte restaurant specializing in fish – try the delicious grilled *surubí* and the reasonably priced pasta and steaks. Occasional live music. Tues–Sun noon–4pm & 8pm–late.

REGIONAL FOOD SPECIALITIES

The food you find around Argentina is remarkably homogeneous for such a huge country. However, there are **regional variations** that reflect the culinary influence of neighbouring nations more than most Argentines realize or care to admit. The most notable of these cross-border gastronomic influences can be found in the northern reaches bordering **Paraguay**. In the Chaco, northern Corrientes and much of Misiones you will find dishes that are part of the staple diet in Asunción and the rest of Paraguay. **Chipás** – savoury cheese-flavoured lumps of manioc-flour dough – are extremely popular snacks sold on the street, served in restaurants instead of bread and cooked in people's homes. **Sopa paraguaya** is actually not a soup at all, but a hearty maize and cheese dish, said to have been invented during the War of the Triple Alliance, when the beleaguered Paraguayan soldiers needed more sustenance than was provided by their traditional chicken broth, so army cooks thickened it with corn flour. **Borí borí**, on the other hand, *is* a soup, made from chicken, with little balls of maize and cheese floating in it. Last but not least, **tereré**, or cold *mate*, made with iced water or orange juice, is hugely popular in Paraguay, but can also be tasted in the borderlands of northeast Argentina, and is wonderfully refreshing on a hot summer's day.

El Mensú Coronel Reguera and Fleming ☎03752 434826. Regarded by some locals as the best restaurant in Posadas, *El Mensú* specializes in excellent home-made pasta and seafood and has a very good wine list – plus the bonus of being on the corner of Posadas' prettiest street. Mon–Fri 8pm–midnight, Sat & Sun noon–4pm & 8pm–1am.

La Querencia Bolívar 1849 ☎03752 443 7117. A bustling place that's a surprisingly good deal, particularly as you can easily share some of the dishes. Try the juicy *bife de chorizo* – shipped in from Buenos Aires Province, as local beef is of poorer quality – and accompany it with fried manioc for a local touch, or go for the excellent *galetos*, a kind of chicken and vegetable kebab. Mon–Sat 12.30pm–midnight, Sun noon–4pm.

Sociedad Española Córdoba between Colón and Félix de Azara. Very popular lunchtime spot – not surprising, as the basic two-course menu, which goes for next to nothing ($35), could possibly feed a small family. There are also more Spanish – and more expensive – dishes available à la carte. Daily noon–4pm & 8pm–late.

La Tradicional Rueda Costanera and Arrechea. This two-storey wooden building, decorated with facsimiles of historic photos of the city, does a mean, moderately priced *parrilla* and good river fish. There are great views of the Río Paraná across to Paraguay from the upstairs dining room. Daily noon–3.30pm & 8.30pm–late.

The Jesuit missions

After Iguazú Falls, the province's major tourist attractions are the **Jesuit missions**, north of Posadas. The largest, **San Ignacio Miní**, is also the best preserved in the whole of the missions region, which extended beyond the Paraguay and Uruguay rivers to Paraguay and Brazil, and also into Corrientes Province. Far less well preserved – and much less visited – are the ruins of **Santa Ana** and **Loreto**, south of San Ignacio; these crumbling monuments, set amid thick jungle vegetation, are less dramatic but appealing if only because they attract fewer visitors. All three missions can be visited on a day-trip from Posadas, though it's well worth spending a night in San Ignacio, visiting the ruins in the morning light – the best time for photographs, when the low light enhances the buildings' deep reddish hues – and again at night. In addition to the attractive village, there's a stunning area of forest with perhaps the finest stretch of river scenery in the whole region.

Santa Ana

Approximately 40km from Posadas • Daily 7am–7pm • A ticket can be bought at the mission entrance ($60), which gives you entry to all the missions and is valid for two weeks

Heading northeast from Posadas along the RN-12, the first mission site you come to is **Santa Ana**. A signposted, unsealed road just south of Santa Ana village leads to the mission entrance and a small visitors' centre. Originally founded in the Tapé region in 1633, Santa Ana was refounded, with a population of two thousand Guaraní, on its present site after the *bandeirante* attacks of 1660 (see box, p.234).

Like all the *reducciones*, Santa Ana is centred on a large square, to the south of which stand the crumbling walls of what was once one of the finest of all Jesuit churches, built by the Italian architect Brazanelli, whose body was buried underneath the high altar. A lot of work has been carried out on the site, yet the roots and branches of trees are still entangled in the reddish sandstone of the buildings around the plaza, offering a glimpse of the way the ruins must have appeared when they were rediscovered in the late nineteenth century. North of the church, on the site of the original orchard, you can still make out the channels from the *reducción*'s sophisticated irrigation system.

Loreto

Around 12km north of Santa Ana • Daily 7am–7pm • A ticket can be bought at the mission entrance ($60), which gives you entry to all the missions and is valid for two weeks

The ruins of **Loreto** are even wilder than those of Santa Ana. This site, founded in 1632, was one of the most important of all the Jesuit missions, housing six thousand Guaraní by 1733 and noted not only for its production of cloth and *yerba mate* but also for having the missions' first printing press. Like Santa Ana, Loreto has a small visitors' centre at its entrance, reached via a 6km stretch of unsealed road (impassable after heavy rain), which branches off the RN-12. Restoration work is being carried out

THE JESUITS AND THEIR MISSIONS

The first Jesuit **missions** in Argentina were established in 1609, three decades after the order founded by San Ignacio de Loyola first arrived in the region. Though the Jesuits tried to evangelize other parts of the country over the next 150 years, it was in the subtropical Upper Paraná where they had their greatest success. Known in Spanish as **reducciones**, these missions were largely self-sufficient settlements of Guaraní Indians who lived and worked under the tutelage of a small number of Jesuit priests. Missions were initially established in three separate zones: the **Guayrá**, corresponding mainly to the modern Brazilian state of Paraná; the **Tapé**, corresponding to the southern Brazilian state of Río Grande do Sul, present-day Misiones Province and part of Corrientes Province; and the **Itatín**, lying between the Upper Paraná and the sierras to the north of the modern Paraguayan city of Concepción.

ENLIGHTENED SLAVE DRIVERS

If the Jesuits were essentially engaged in "civilizing" the natives, they did at least have a particularly enlightened approach to their task – a marked contrast to the harsh methods of procuring native labour practised elsewhere in Latin America. Work was organized on a cooperative basis, with those who could not work provided for by the rest of the community. **Education** and culture also played an important part in mission life, with Guaraní taught to read and write not only in Spanish but also in Latin and Guaraní, and music and artisanship actively encouraged; however, coercion and violence were not unknown, and epidemics periodically ravaged these communities.

The early growth of the missions was impressive, but in 1660 *bandeirantes*, slave traders from São Paulo, attacked, destroying many of the missions, and carrying off their inhabitants, leading the Jesuits to seek more sheltered areas to the west, away from the Guayrá region in particular. The mission population soon recouped – and then surpassed – its former numbers, and also developed a strong standing **army**, making it one of the most powerful military forces in the region. Their most important crop proved to be *yerba maté*, which had previously been gathered from the wild but was now grown on plantations for export; other products sold by the missions included cattle and their hides, sugar, cotton, tobacco, textiles, ceramics and timber. They also exported musical instruments, notably harps and organs from the Reducción de Trinidad in Paraguay.

DECLINE AND FALL

By the end of the seventeenth century, the *reducciones* were among the most populous and successful areas of Argentina. By the 1730s, the larger missions such as Loreto (see p.233) had over six thousand inhabitants – second only to Buenos Aires. Nonetheless, the mission enterprise was beginning to show cracks: a rising number of epidemics depleted the population, and the Jesuits were becoming the subject of **political resentment**. Settlers in Paraguay and Corrientes were increasingly bitter at the Jesuit hold over the "supply" of Guaraní labour and domination of the market for *yerba maté* and tobacco. Simultaneously, the previous climate of Crown tolerance towards the missions' almost complete autonomy also began to change, with the Jesuits' power and loyalty questioned. Local enemies of the missions took advantage of this, claiming that the Jesuits were hiding valuable silver mines and that foreign Jesuit priests were agents of Spain's enemies. In 1750, an exchange treaty between Spain and Portugal was proposed, according to which Spain would give up its most easterly mission. The Jesuits and Guaraní put up considerable military resistance and the treaty was abandoned. The victory proved a double-edged sword, however; the resistance against the Crown only reinforced their image as dangerous rebels and, following earlier expulsions in France, Portugal and Brazil, the Jesuits were **expelled from Argentina** in 1767. Their magnificent buildings fell into disuse – lumps of stone were used for other constructions and the jungle did the rest – resulting in the ruins that can be visited today.

with the assistance of the Spanish government. When you head out from the visitors' centre to the *reducción* itself, it's actually difficult at first to work out where the buildings are. After a while, though, you begin to see the walls and foundations of the settlement, heavily camouflaged by vegetation and lichen, on which tall palms have managed, fantastically, to root themselves.

San Ignacio Miní

Daily 7am–7pm • Sound and light show 8pm in summer, 6pm rest of year • A ticket can be bought at the mission entrance ($60), which gives you entry to all the Argentine missions in the province and is valid for two weeks

The most famous of all the *reducciones*, **San Ignacio Miní** was originally founded in 1610 in the Guayrá region (see box opposite), in what is now Brazil. After the *bandeirantes* attacked the mission in 1631, the Jesuits moved thousands of miles southwards through the jungle, stopping several times en route at various temporary settlements before finally re-establishing the *reducción* at its present site in 1696.

The ruins occupy six blocks at the northeastern end of the village of San Ignacio: from the bus stop head east along Avenida Sarmiento for two blocks and turn left onto Rivadavia. Follow Rivadavia, which skirts around the ruins, for six blocks and then turn right onto Alberdi, where you'll find the entrance to the site. At the entrance, there's a small but worthwhile museum with a series of themed rooms depicting various aspects of Guaraní and mission life, plus a detailed maquette of the entire *reducción*. The site itself is dotted with panels lending context to the ruins, with audio provided in various languages, including English. Free, more detailed tours in rapid-fire Spanish depart regularly from the museum. There are also popular **sound and light shows** each evening.

The ruins

On entering the settlement itself, you'll come first to rows of simple *viviendas*, or living quarters, a series of six to ten adjoining one-roomed structures, each of which housed a Guaraní family. Like all the mission settlements, these are constructed in a mixture of basaltic rock and sandstone. Passing between the *viviendas*, you arrive at the spacious Plaza de Armas, whose emerald grass provides a stunning contrast with the rich red hues of the sandstone. At the southern end of the plaza, and dominating the entire site, stands the magnificent facade of San Ignacio's **church**, designed, like Santa Ana's, by the Italian architect Brazanelli. The roof and much of the interior have long since crumbled away, but two large chunks of wall on either side of the entrance remain, rising out of the ruins like two great Baroque wings. Though somewhat eroded, many fine details can still be made out: two columns flank either side of the doorway and much of the walls' surface is covered with decorative bas-relief sculpture executed by Guaraní craftsmen. Most striking are the pair of angels that face each other high up on either side of the entrance, while a more austere touch is added by the prominent insignia of the Jesuit order on the right-hand side of the entrance.

To the left of the main entrance, you can wander around the **cloisters** and **priests' quarters**, where a number of other fine doorways and carvings remain. Particularly striking is the doorway connecting the cloisters with the church baptistry, flanked by ribbed columns with heavily moulded bases and still retaining a triangular pediment over the arched doorway.

San Ignacio

Considering it's home to such a major attraction, the grand Jesuit ruins of San Ignacio Miní, **SAN IGNACIO**, is a remarkably low-key place – away from the restaurants and souvenir stands around the ruins themselves, the town has little in the way of tourist facilities. There are, however, a few worthwhile attractions southwest of the village.

Casa de Horacio Quiroga

Sarmiento 557 • ☎ 03752 470130 • Daily 8am–7pm • $10

The western extremity of San Ignacio is bounded by Avenida Horacio Quiroga, and if you head south along it for a kilometre or so, you'll come to the **Casa de Horacio Quiroga**, a museum to the Uruguayan writer, who made his home here in the early twentieth century. Quiroga, famed for his rather Gothic short stories and Kipling-inspired jungle tales for children (see Contexts, p.564), first visited the region in 1903, taking some of the earliest pictures of the then little-known ruins. He moved to San Ignacio in 1910, where the tropical setting further fired his imagination, inspiring stories of sunstroke and giant snakes. The museum is composed of two houses – a replica of the first wooden house built by the writer, containing many of his possessions, and a later stone construction also built by him. Though the buildings are pleasant to wander around, much of the museum's charm is derived from its wonderful setting, amid thick vegetation. At the back of the wooden house there's a small swimming pool built by the writer for his second wife (the first committed suicide, as would Quiroga himself in 1937, and his children after his death). She later left him, at which point Quiroga filled the pool with snakes.

Parque Provincial Teyú Cuaré

10km south of San Ignacio via a good unsealed road

The **Parque Provincial Teyú Cuaré** is accessed from the southern end of Bolívar. It's a small but stunning park of less than a square kilometre, notable for its golden-hued rocky formations, which jut out over the Paraná, and dense vegetation. The name Teyú Cuaré, meaning "the lizard's cave", refers to a local legend about a giant reptile that inhabited the region, attacking passing boats. The park's most publicized feature is its high rocky cliff, the **Peñón Reina Victoria**, named for its supposed similarity to the profile of the British monarch. There is a wild **campsite** within the park.

En route to the park, a small **private reserve**, the **Osununú**, is set in a wonderful wild patch of forest with some fantastic views over the river and islands and to the Parque Provincial.

4

ARRIVAL AND INFORMATION

SAN IGNACIO

By bus Buses to San Ignacio all arrive at the western end of Av Sarmiento. It's not a terminal, but there's a kiosk where you may be able to leave luggage for a few hours.

Tourist information The tourist office (daily 7am–7pm) is at the main entrance road, the turn-off from the RN-12.

ACCOMMODATION

Adventure Hostel San Ignacio Independencia 469 ☎03752 470955, ⊕sihostel.com.ar. Among the many hostels in Río is this place, run by the same outfit behind *La Aventura* in Posadas (see p.230). It has a pool and hammocks – very welcome after a day tramping round ruins. Dorms $80, doubles $275

Club de Pesca y Deportes Acuáticos Puerto Nuevo ☎03752 1568 3411. The best campsite in town, where tents can be pitched on a bluff with a great view over the river to Paraguay. $55

Club de Río ☎03755 1557 0843, ⊕clubderio sanignacio.com.ar. Several kilometres south of the settlement, signposted from the centre, with comfortable *cabañas* set around a huge swimming pool, at a quiet location. $280

San Ignacio San Martín and Sarmiento 823 ☎03752 470042, ⊖hotelsanignacio @arnet.com.ar A slick, modern place with comfortable en-suite rooms, all with a/c. There's also an adjoining restaurant. $210

EATING

Carpa Azul Rivadavia 1295 ☎0376 4470 0096. This is perhaps the most popular in a clutch of very similar large restaurants geared up for day-trippers around the entrance to the ruins, all of which serve snacks plus some more substantial dishes such as *parrilla*. It even boasts a swimming pool and shower facilities. Daily noon–3.30pm & 8.30pm–late.

Lo de Lenguaza Located conveniently – and strategically – at the village entrance this place provides a variety of food and drink, including pizza and river fish. Daily noon–late.

Iguazú Falls

Composed of over 250 separate cascades, and straddling the border between Argentina and Brazil, the **Iguazú Falls** (or "Cataratas", as they are known locally) are quite simply the world's most dramatic waterfalls. Set among the exotic-looking subtropical forests of **Parque Nacional Iguazú** in Argentina, and **Parque Nacional do Iguaçu** in Brazil, the

Falls tumble for a couple of kilometres over a complex set of cliffs from the Río Iguazú Superior to the Río Iguazú Inferior below. At their heart is the dizzying **Garganta del Diablo**, a powerhouse display of natural forces in which 1800 cubic metres of water per second hurtle over a 3km semicircle of rock into the boiling river canyon 70m below.

The first Europeans to encounter the Falls, in 1542, were members of a Spanish expedition led by Cabeza de Vaca, who named them the Saltos de Santa María. For nearly five hundred years, however, they remained practically forgotten in this remote corner of Argentina, and it wasn't until the early twentieth century that tourism began to arrive, encouraged by the then governor of Misiones, Juan J. Lanusse. The first hotel was constructed in 1922, right by the Falls, and by the mid-twentieth century Iguazú was firmly on the tourist map. Today, the Falls are one of Latin America's major tourist attractions, with around two million visitors each year.

The Argentine side

The vast majority of the **Iguazú Falls** lie on the **Argentine side** of the border, within the **Parque Nacional Iguazú**. This side offers the most extensive experience of the *cataratas*, thanks to its well-planned system of trails and catwalks taking you both below and above the waters – most notably to the Garganta del Diablo. The surrounding forest also offers excellent opportunities to view the region's wildlife. The main settlement on this side, **Puerto Iguazú**, lies approximately 18km northwest of the park entrance with a slightly sleepy, villagey feel, though its popularity with backpackers has livened it up a bit in recent years.

4

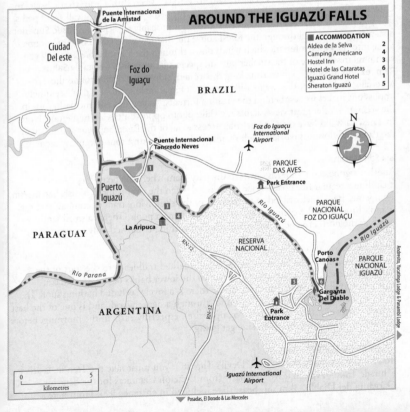

AROUND THE IGUAZÚ FALLS

ACCOMMODATION

Aldea de la Selva	2
Camping Americano	4
Hostel Inn	3
Hotel de las Cataratas	6
Iguazú Grand Hotel	1
Sheraton Iguazú	5

THE FOREST AROUND IGUAZÚ

The Falls are not the only attraction in the parks. The surrounding subtropical **forest** – a dense, lush jungle – is packed with animals, birds and insects, and opportunities for spotting at least some of them are good. Even on the busy catwalks and paths that skirt the edges of the Falls you've a good chance of seeing gorgeously hued, bright blue butterflies as big as your hand (just one of over 250 varieties that live around the Falls) and – especially on the Brazilian side – you will undoubtedly be pestered for food by greedy coatis (a raccoon relative). For a real close-up encounter with the parks' varied wildlife, though, head for the superb **Sendero Macuco**, a tranquil nature trail that winds through the forest on the Argentine side. Commonly spotted species along here include various species of toucan and shy capuchin monkeys.

Parque Nacional Iguazú

18km southeast of Puerto Iguazú, along the RN-12 • $130 (for foreigners); keep your ticket and have it stamped on the way out, which will entitle you to a fifty-percent discount the following day • Daily 8am–6pm • ⓦ iguazuargentina.com

As you get off the bus at the **Parque Nacional Iguazú**, you're greeted by the sound of rushing water from the Falls, the first of which lies just a few hundred metres away. There's a **visitors' centre** to the left of the bus stop, where you can pick up maps and information leaflets. There's also a small but interesting museum here with photographs and stuffed examples of the park's wildlife.

The Sendero Verde trail

From the visitors' centre, the so-called Sendero Verde ("Green Path") leads to the Estación Cataratas, from where two well-signposted trails, formed by a series of catwalks and paths, take you past the Falls. A recommended approach is probably to tackle the **Paseo Superior** first, along a short trail through the forest above the first few waterfalls. For more drama, segue into the **Paseo Inferior**, which winds down through the forest before bringing you within metres of some of the smaller but still spectacular waterfalls – notably **Saltos Ramírez** and **Bossetti** – which run along the western side of the river. Around the waterfalls, look out for the swallow-like *vencejo*, a remarkable small bird that, seemingly impossibly, makes its nest behind the gushing torrents. As you descend the path, gaps in the vegetation offer great views across the Falls: photo opportunities are numerous. Note that new catwalks have made **wheelchair access** to all of the Paseo Superior and much of the Paseo Inferior possible, although there is little room to turn round in many sections.

Isla San Martín

Another signposted trail leads down to the jetty from where the boat rides depart, including a regular free boat service (suspended when the river is high) for **Isla San Martín**, a gorgeous, high, rocky island in the middle of the river. More trails circumnavigate the island, through thick vegetation and past emerald green pools. There's a small sandy beach at the northern end of the island, though bathing is allowed only in summer.

The Sendero Macuco trail

Heading west from the visitors' centre, a well-marked trail leads to the start of the **Sendero Macuco**, a 4km nature trail down to the lower banks of the Río Iguazú, past a waterfall, the **Salto Arrechea**, where there is a lovely secluded bathing spot. The majority of the trail is along level ground, through a dense wood, and is one of the best places to spot the area's fauna (see box opposite), especially early in the morning, before the helicopters on the Brazilian side get going.

Garganta del Diablo

To visit the **Garganta del Diablo** ("Devil's Throat"), you must take the Tren de la selva ("Jungle Train"), which leaves regularly from Estación Cataratas for the Estación Garganta del Diablo, 3km southeast (fare included in entrance fee). From here a

FLORA AND FAUNA AROUND THE FALLS

Despite appearances, the jungle landscape around the Falls is not virgin forest. In fact, it is in a process of recuperation: advances in the navigation of the Upper Paraná – the section of the river that runs along the northern border of Corrientes and Misiones – in the early twentieth century allowed access to these previously impenetrable lands and economic exploitation of their valuable timber began. In the 1920s, the region was totally exploited and stripped of its best species and traversed by roads. Only since the creation of the park in 1943 has the forest been protected.

FLORA

Today, the forest is composed of several layers of **vegetation**. Towering above the forest floor is the rare and imposing *palo rosa*, which can grow to 40m and is identifiable by its pale, straight trunk that divides into twisting branches higher up, topped by bushy foliage. At a lower level, various species of palm flourish, notably the *pindó* palm and the palmito, much coveted for its edible core, which often grows in the shade of the *palo rosa*. Epiphytes, which use the taller trees for support but are not parasitic, also abound as does the *guaypoy*, aptly known as the strangler fig, since it eventually asphyxiates the trees around which it grows. You will also see lianas, which hang from the trees in incredibly regular plaits and have apt popular names such as *escalera de mono*, or "monkey's ladder". Closer still to the ground there is a stratum of shrubs, some of them with edible fruit, such as the pitanga. Ground cover is dominated by various fern species.

FAUNA

The best time to spot **wildlife** is either early morning or late afternoon, when there are fewer visitors and the jungle's numerous birds and mammals are at their most active: at times the screech of birds and monkeys can be almost cacophonic. At all times, you have the best chance of seeing wildlife by treading as silently as possible, and by scanning the surrounding trees for signs of movement. Your most likely reward will be groups of agile **capuchin monkeys**, with a distinctive black "cowl", like that of the monks they are named after. Larger, lumbering **black howler monkeys** make for a rarer sight, though their deep growl can be heard for some distance. Along the ground, look out for the tiny **corzuela deer**. Unfortunately, you've little chance of seeing the park's most dramatic wildlife, large cats such as the puma and the jaguar, or the tapir, a large-hoofed mammal with a short, flexible snout. **Toucans**, however, are commonly spotted; other birds that can be seen in the forest include the solitary **Black cacique**, which makes its nest in the *pindó* palm; various species of woodpecker and the striking Crested yacutinga. Of the forest's many butterflies, the most striking are those of the *Morphidae* family, whose large wings are a dazzling metallic blue.

4

catwalk with a small viewing platform takes you to within just a few metres of the staggering, sheer drop of water formed by the union of several immensely powerful waterfalls around a kind of horseshoe. As the water crashes over the edge, it plunges into a dazzling opaque whiteness in which it is impossible to distinguish mist from water. The *vencejos* often swirl around the waterfall in all directions, forming giant swarms that sometimes swoop up towards you and perform miraculous acrobatic twists and turns – quite a sight. If you're bringing your camera, make sure you've an airtight bag to stash it in, as the platform is invariably showered with a fine spray.

THE ARGENTINE SIDE: PARQUE NACIONAL IGUAZÚ

ARRIVAL AND TOURS

By bus A bus (30min) runs to the park every hour from the bus terminal in town, with the first one leaving at 7.30am and the last one returning at 8pm. The bus takes you all the way to the visitors' centre, but stops first at the entrance to the park.

Tours Various operators, such as Iguazú Jungle Explorer (☎ 03757 421696, ⌨ iguazujungle.com), will accost you and tempt you with different trips and tours, involving trucks, boats and walks, ranging from $80 to $500, depending on their length and the transport involved. The jeep rides are a little too noisy to allow for much wildlife observation, but the boat rides (around $200) are a thrill – albeit somewhat short-lived – not to be missed, providing the exhilarating experience of coming close up to the gush of the Falls.

Puerto Iguazú

Just under 300km northeast of Posadas, sitting high above the meeting of the Paraná and Iguazú rivers, at the most northern extremity of Misiones Province, **PUERTO IGUAZÚ** is a strange place. Originally a rather dull, backwater town, its popularity with Falls visitors has increasingly given it the feel of a lively resort in recent years and, though it has little in the way of notable architecture, it has a certain simple charm that can grow on you. Its tropical vegetation and quiet streets seem more in keeping with the region than the high-rise concrete of the Brazilian city of Foz, and of the three border towns (the commercial settlement of Ciudad del Este in Paraguay, notoriously unsavoury and unsafe, is definitely best avoided) Puerto Iguazú is the only one to have a really secure and accessible riverfront area from which you can take in the surrounding panorama.

The town is bisected diagonally by **Avenida Victoria Aguirre**, which runs from Puerto Iguazú's modest **port** out towards the RN-12 and the national park. You wouldn't exactly call Iguazú's **town centre** bustling, but most of its activity takes place around the intersection of Avenida Aguirre, Calle Brasil and Calle Ingeniero Gustavo Eppens. From here the Avenida Tres Fronteras runs west for 1.5km to the **Hito Argentino de las Tres Fronteras**, a vantage point over the rivers with views over to Brazil and Paraguay that is marked by an obelisk painted in the colours of the Argentine flag; similar markers across the rivers in the neighbouring countries are painted in their national colours, too. An alternative route to the Hito is via Avenida Aguirre, which forks right just before the town's triangular grassy plaza. From here, Avenida Aguirre snakes down through a thickly wooded area of town to the port area; you can then follow the pleasant Avenida Costanera, popular with joggers and cyclists, left uphill towards the Hito.

La Aripuca

RN-12 4.5km • 8am–7pm • $25, children free • ⓦ aripuca.com.ar

There is an unusual attraction on the outskirts of town: just over 4km along the RN-12 towards the national park, rustic signposts direct you to **La Aripuca**. An *aripuca* is an

PUERTO IGUAZÚ

■ ACCOMMODATION	
Hostería La Cabaña	3
Hostería San Fernando	4
Hotel Esturión	2
Hotel Saint George	5
Iguazú Jungle Lodge	1
Lilian	6
Residencial Noelia	7
La Strada	8

◆ RESTAURANTS AND CAFÉS	
Boca Mora	1
Maria Preta	2
Pizza Color	4
El Quincho del Tío Querido	3
La Rueda	5

■ BAR	
La Barranca	1

0 — 500 metres

indigenous wooden trap used in the region to catch birds; La Aripuca is a giant replica of such a trap, standing over 10m high and constructed out of 29 species of trees native to Misiones Province (all obtained through unavoidable felling or from victims of thunderstorms). Above all, La Aripuca is a kind of eco-symbol: the friendly German- and English-speaking family who constructed the strange monument hope to change visitors' conscience about the environment through tours designed to explain the value and significance of these trees. Some very good crafts are on sale – mostly made of tropical wood – and you can snack, have a drink or try *mate*-flavoured ice cream.

ARRIVAL AND DEPARTURE
PUERTO IGUAZÚ

By plane Puerto Iguazú's international airport lies around 20km southeast of the town, along the RN-12 just past the entrance to the park; a taxi to town or one of the nearby lodges will cost around $130. There are 3–5 daily flights to and from Buenos Aires (2hr). Aerolíneas Argentinas/Austral has offices at Av Aguirre and B. Brañas (☎03757 420168) and at the airport (☎03757 420915).

By bus The recently modernized bus terminal is central, on the corner of avenidas Córdoba and Misiones. There's no official tourist information kiosk here, though there are plenty of private companies who tout for your custom as

you get off the bus. The most helpful of the numerous kiosks offering information is probably friendly Agencia Noelia (☎03757 422722), which also sells the tickets for the bus to the national park. There's a restaurant in the terminal, a *locutorio* and a left-luggage service.

Destinations Buenos Aires (7 daily; 14hr 30min–19hr); Córdoba (2 daily; 22hr); Corrientes (1 daily; 10hr); Posadas (hourly; 6hr); Rosario (2 weekly; 18hr); San Ignacio (hourly; 5hr).

Car rental Rent a Car/Europcar, Av Aguirre 211 ☎03757 420289.

INFORMATION AND TOURS

Tourist information Puerto Iguazú's tourist office is at Av Aguirre 311 (Mon–Fri 7am–1pm & 2–9pm, Sat & Sun 8am–noon & 4–8pm, sometimes open longer in high season; ☎03757 420800). It has some good maps and information, though most answers to practical transport and accommodation queries can just as easily be answered by the kiosks in the bus terminal.

Travel agents and tour operators Aguas Grandes, Entre Ríos 66 ☎03757 425500, ⊕aguasgrandes.com; Cuenca del Plata, Paulino Amarante 76 ☎03757 421062, ⊕cuencadelplata.com; Sol Iguazú Turismo, Av Aguirre 316 ☎03757 421147, ⊕soliguazu.com.ar; Turismo Dick, Av Aguirre 226 ☎03757 420778, ⊕dickturismo.com.ar.

4

ACCOMMODATION

Puerto Iguazú's budget **accommodation** tends to be located in town, while the more upmarket places are set back among jungle vegetation on the road to the park and in the surrounding area. You may get a better deal at some of the more expensive hotels by booking a package, with flight, from a travel agency in Buenos Aires. Note that camping inside the national parks is forbidden.

IN TOWN

Hostería La Cabaña Av Tres Fronteras 434 ☎03757 420564, ⊕lacabanahotel.com.ar; map p.240. A quiet, motel-style place with comfortable if slightly musty rooms. **$320**

Hostería San Fernando Av Córdoba and Guaraní ☎03757 421429; map p.240. Friendly hotel opposite the bus terminal. Simple, pleasant rooms all with fan, much improved following renovation. Breakfast included. **$320**

Hotel Esturión Av Tres Fronteras 650 ☎03757 421429, ⊕hotelesturion.com; map p.240. With fine river views, a large swimming pool, spacious, cool rooms and decks and gardens brimming with native flora, this extremely professional hotel has a definite tropical feel to it. **$1230**

Hotel Saint George Av Córdoba 148 ☎03757 420633, ⊕hotelsaintgeorge.com; map p.240. A courteous hotel and one of the most comfortable in town, with some

exceptionally light and attractive first-floor rooms with balconies overlooking the swimming pool. Good restaurant downstairs and buffet breakfast with fresh fruit included in room rate. **$800**

★ **Iguazú Jungle Lodge** Hipólito Irigoyen and San Lorenzo ☎03757 420600, ⊕iguazujunglelodge.com; map p.240. Simply fabulous *cabañas* sleeping up to seven – plus a couple of doubles – in a landscaped plot overlooking the jungle at the edge of the village. Extremely well equipped and tastefully appointed, they are really luxurious houses, with ample verandas, a huge kitchen and barbecue facilities. Large swimming pool and decent breakfasts served either poolside or in the *cabañas*. **$890**

Lilian Fray Luis Beltrán 183 ☎03757 420968, ⊕hotel lilian@yahoo.com.ar; map p.240. Spotless, light and airy rooms with good fans and modern bathrooms. **$310**

Residencial Noelia Fray Luis Beltrán 119 ☎03757 420729, ✉residencialfamiliarnoelia@yahoo.com.ar; map p.240. The best deal in Iguazú, this friendly, family-run place largely caters to backpackers. Scrupulously maintained three- and four-bed rooms with fans and private bathroom, and breakfast of toast, fruit and coffee brought to your room or the shady patio. $170

La Strada Pombero 166 ☎03757 427156, ✇lastrada residencial.com.ar; map p.240. Simple but tasteful bungalows with wooden floors, a/c and TVs, set around a pool and garden; friendly staff. $365

OUT OF TOWN

Aldea de la Selva Selva Iriapú ☎03757 425777, ✇laaldeadelaselva.com; map p.237. Wooden *cabañas* that are comfortable but retain a rustic, jungle-lodge feel, with much creative use of local woods and tree roots such as *quebracho* and *loro negro*. All have verandas with hammocks from where you can listen to the noises of the forest, and there's also a tiered pool and good restaurant that does river fish served with local ingredients such as manioc and palm hearts. $1050

Camping Americano RN-12, 5km from town ☎03757 420190, ✇complejoamericano.com.ar; map p.237. In a great leafy location off the main road towards the national park, the campsite has showers, a shop, telephones and large swimming pool. Enquire also about *cabañas* and a hotel next to the complex. $75

Hostel Inn RN-12, 5km from town ☎03757 421823, ✇hiiguazu.com; map p.237. A large, well-run place with different-sized dorms, doubles and triples, in enormous grounds with a large swimming pool. Dorms $90, doubles $345

Iguazú Grand Hotel RN-12 Km1460 ☎03757 498050, ✇iguazugrandhotel.com; map p.237. This is the place to stay for film-star glamour – a fabulously luxurious hotel with enormous suites boasting everything from CD players to glossy picture books on Misiones. Landscaped outdoor pool and two very good restaurants. Weekends are reserved for high-rolling gamblers whom the hotel flies in from São Paulo and Buenos Aires to play at the adjoining casino. US$560

Sheraton Iguazú Parque Nacional Iguazú ☎03757 491800, ✇starwoodhotels.com; map p.237. Big, ugly modern hotel inside the national park. The crime of its construction is compounded by the fact that you only get a decent view of the Falls from a few of its rooms (for which you pay more), but it has to be admitted it is well located from the guests' viewpoint, with the Falls in walking distance and the possibility of exploring the jungle before most visitors arrive. US$520

ESTANCIAS AND LODGES AROUND IGUAZÚ

Las Mercedes Just outside El Dorado, 100km south of Iguazú ☎03751 420939, ✇estancialasmercedes.com. A 1920s property founded as a ranch by a family of British origin and now both a working farm and an ecotourism resort. The five charming rooms, delicious food (call ahead if you just want to visit or have lunch or tea) and beautiful swimming pool, set among immaculate lawns, make this a superb spot for a few days' relaxation. You can also go horseriding and canoeing on the nearby river. $990

Panambí Lodge 50km east of Puerto Iguazú within the national park ☎03757 497418, ✇panambilodge .com.ar. On the jungle-clad banks of the Río Iguazú, this rugged stone-and-timber lodge has five large rooms with picture windows and all mod cons, and offers birdwatching opportunities along with horse-drawn carriage rides. $1340

★ **Yacutinga** 60km east of Iguazú airport via a dirt road that runs parallel to the Río Iguazú ✇yacutinga .com. This eco-lodge is a great place to stay while visiting the Falls, tucked away amid one of the last remaining patches of unspoilt jungle. The main building is beautifully designed, while the rooms are in twenty well-camouflaged cabins. Expert multilingual guides take you on walks, pointing out all kinds of wildlife, including an astounding array of birds and butterflies. Full board, three-day, two-night packages US$2000

EATING, DRINKING AND NIGHTLIFE

The development of Puerto Iguazú has seen some fairly sophisticated **eating** places appear alongside the standard greasy spoons serving *milanesas* with loud TV as a backdrop. For **drinking** and **nightlife**, many locals head over to Brazil for a good night out. In town itself, there's a handful of bars-cum-nightclubs on Avenida Brasil close to the junction with Avenida Aguirre.

La Barranca Av Perito Moreno 269; map p.240. Puerto Iguazú's only really fun bar, *La Barranca* offers, in addition to a plentiful supply of cold beer, powerful cocktails and sangría, gigs occasional live music, mostly electronic and Brazilian pop-rock. Daily 8.30pm–late.

Boca Mora Costanera 39 ☎03757 420550; map p.240. This grill and fancy restaurant is superbly located in a colonial-style house overlooking the river. On weekend nights it metamorphoses into the town's main disco. Daily noon–3.30pm & 8.30pm–late.

María Preta Av Brasil 39 ☎03757 420221; map p.240. A stylish bar-restaurant with outdoor seating and a comprehensive menu that includes *yacaré* (cayman) as well as more conventional pasta and *parrilla*; it also has live

Brazilian music some evenings. The service can be quite slow. Daily noon–4pm & 9pm–late.

Pizza Color Av Córdoba 1354 ☎ 03757 420206; map p.240. This local institution does excellent *pizza a la piedra* and good salads, plus decently priced *parrillas*. You can sit inside or out. Daily noon–midnight.

El Quincho del Tío Querido Bompland 110 ☎ 03757 420151; map p.240. This spacious and airy restaurant always has huge skeins of sausages and *morcillas* (blood sausages) garlanded over the vast grill, a sign of the plentiful barbecued meat on offer, all served by a vast team of black-clad waiters. Daily 12.30–3.30pm & 8pm–late.

La Rueda Av Córdoba 28 ☎ 03757 422531; map p.240. Undoubtedly the best *parrilla* in town, though the menu also features an enticing range of salads, fish dishes and succulent pasta, all served in especially congenial surroundings – all rustic wood and old photos. The wine list is admirable. Daily noon–3.30pm & 8.30pm–late.

DIRECTORY

Banks and exchange There are several ATMs in Puerto Iguazú.

Consulates Brazil, Córdoba 264 ☎ 03757 421348 (Mon–Fri 8am–1pm).

Internet access Cybercafé at Aguirre and Alvar Núñez.

Post office Av San Martín 780.

Telephones Cybercafé at Aguirre and Alvar Núñez.

The Brazilian side

To complete your trip to Iguazú, you should also try and visit the **Brazilian side**. You'll only need a few hours but it's worth crossing in order to take photos of the Falls – particularly in the morning – as it provides you with a superb panorama of the points you will have visited close up in Argentina, as well as its own close encounter with the Garganta del Diablo. Though it offers a more passive experience, the view is more panoramic and the photo opportunities are amazing. You can cross for the day but, if you want to stay in Brazil, the city of **Foz do Iguaçu** lies a good 20km northwest of the access to the park. Much larger than **Puerto Iguazú** and with a modern, urban feel, Foz is neither the most beautiful nor most exotic of Brazilian cities, but if you've been travelling in Argentina for a while it'll give you the chance to hear another language, try some different food and sample some lively nightlife. Foz definitely feels less safe than its Argentine counterpart – a fact much exaggerated by Argentines, but nonetheless you should be on your guard in the city.

Parque Nacional do Iguazú

Around 20km southeast of Foz • Daily 9am–5pm • R$41.10 (pesos or dollars accepted) • ⓦ cataratasdoiguacu.com.br

The **Parque Nacional do Iguazú** has a visitor centre at the entrance with a restaurant and other facilities. Shuttle buses, included in the price, pass drop-off points for boat and trail tours (see p.244) before stopping at the head of the waterfalls trail, just opposite the *Hotel das Cataratas*. From here a walkway takes you high along the side of the river; it is punctuated by various viewing platforms from where you can take in most of the **Argentine Falls**, the river canyon and **Isla San Martín**. The 1.5km path culminates in a spectacular walkway offering fantastic views of the **Garganta del Diablo** and of the **Brazilian Santo Salto Maria**, beneath the viewing platform and surrounded by an almost continuous rainbow created by myriad water droplets. You are likely to get soaked here – enterprising locals sell ponchos, for what they're worth; carry a plastic bag to protect your camera. At the end of the walkway you can take an elevator to the top of a cliff for more good views. A little further along, the Porto Canoas complex has a shuttle bus stop, souvenir stores and restaurants, plagued by stripe-tailed coatis that accost visitors, begging for food.

Parque Das Aves

300m north of the park entrance • Daily 8.30am–5.30pm • US$17 • ☎ (0055)45 3529 8282, ⓦ parquedasaves.com.br

If you've not been lucky enough to see some of Iguazú's exotic birds at the Falls themselves, head for the **Parque Das Aves**, where walk-through aviaries allow for close encounters with some of the most stunning. The first of these is populated with various smaller species such as the noisy Bare-throated bellbird, with a weird resonant call, the bright blue Sugar bird and the Blue-black grosbeak. For most people, though, the highlight is a sighting of the bold toucans – almost comically keen to have their photo taken.

CROSSING THE BRAZILIAN BORDER   PARQUE NACIONAL DO IGUAZÚ

You will need to cross to Brazil via the Ponte Presidente Tancredo Neves, the bridge that crosses the Río Iguazú between the two towns and where immigration formalities take place. Certain nationalities may need **visas** to enter Brazil, which can be obtained (for a fee) at the consulate in Puerto Iguazú; check beforehand. When returning to Argentina make sure you have enough days to continue your journey, as passport control often gives only thirty days here – though you can ask for the normal ninety.

BY BUS

If you are staying in Puerto Iguazú, the most convenient buses are run by Crucero del Norte, which go direct from Puerto Iguazú's bus terminal to the Brazilian falls and back (every 45min; $35 either one way or return; approx 1hr).
International buses Cheaper ($10) but more time consuming are the international buses that depart regularly from Puerto Iguazú to Foz do Iguaçu, from where you can take the local bus (see opposite). You should be able to get by with pesos or dollars if you are just using the buses and visiting the park, but if you want to do any more in Foz you'll need a supply of the Brazilian currency, the real – change can be obtained from various kiosks at Foz's terminal. There's also a change facility and an ATM at the Falls visitors' centre.
Time difference Note that between Nov and Feb Brazil is one hour ahead of Argentina – this time difference could be vital for making sure you catch the last bus back into town.

TOURS

Helicopter flights From near the visitor centre, you can get helicopter flights over the Falls. The view from the helicopters is of course superb, but they're a noisy and intrusive presence in the surrounding area and seriously disruptive to local wildlife: Argentina has banned them from flying over its side.

Other excursions Less controversial excursions are offered by Macuco Safari (❶ 0055 45 3574 4244, ⓦ macuco safari.com.br) and Macuco Ecoaventura (❶ 0055 45 3529 9627), which run a variety of jeep, boat and trekking tours in the Parque Nacional do Iguaçu; these can also be booked at an information kiosk at the visitors' centre.

Foz do Iguaçu (Brazil)

The modern city of **FOZ DO IGUAÇU** faces its Argentine counterpart, Puerto Iguazú, across the Río Iguazú and is separated from the unappealing Paraguayan city of Ciudad del Este, 7km northwest across the Río Paraná, by the Ponte da Amizade/Puente de la Amistad. Until the 1970s, Foz had only around 30,000 inhabitants, but its population soared with the construction of the titanic Itaipú Dam. Today, the city has over 400,000 residents and though the dam is still an important source of employment, the vast majority of them are involved in the tourism industry. In addition to servicing the hundreds of thousands of tourists who pass through every year on their way to the Falls, Foz gains a lot of business as a retail outlet for Argentines and Brazilians in search of bargain clothes and shoes. The town's growth is evident around its sprawling outskirts and in its scattering of high-rise buildings, but the city centre remains a modest and compact area.

Foz is laid out on a fairly regular grid, with the main access route from Argentina being via the **Avenida das Cataratas**, which heads into town from the southeast, joining up with Avenida Jorge Schimmelpfeng, off which the town's main drag, Avenida Juscelino Kubitschek (often referred to as Avenida JK – *jota ka*) runs north towards Paraguay. The main shopping centre, where you'll also find plenty of banks, is Avenida Brasil, which runs parallel to Avenida Juscelino Kubitschek, one block east.

You'll hear a lot about the supposed dangers of Foz on the Argentine side, but the central area around the local bus terminal and shops is normally safe during the day, and the vast majority of people are welcoming and friendly in a way that belies the volume of tourists they are accustomed to seeing. You should, however, avoid heading down to the river below the bus terminal, where there is a shantytown whose inhabitants may be less hospitable.

ARRIVAL AND INFORMATION

FOZ DO IGUAÇU

By bus Foz's local bus terminal, the arrival point for buses from Argentina, is at the intersection of avenidas Juscelino Kubitschek and República Argentina. From here, Transbalan buses leave approximately every 20–30min for the airport and Falls (7am–6pm; $35).

On foot The city centre is easy to walk around, though a taxi is a good idea at night if you feel cautious.

Tourist information There are various tourist information offices throughout the town but the best is on the corner of Av Jorge Schimmelpfeng and Rua Benjamin Constant (Mon–Fri 8am–2pm; ☎ 0055 45 574 2196, or toll free ☎ 0800 451516, ⓦ iguassu.tur.br).

ACCOMMODATION

Accommodation is abundant in Foz but the continuing strength of the Brazilian real makes it expensive compared with Argentina. You can easily visit the Brazilian side from Argentina in any case – the only accommodation really worth it (and even it is over-priced) is the top-end *Cataratas*, for its before-your-eyes proximity to the Falls.

Foz Presidente Rua Xavier da Silva 1000 ☎ 0055 45 3572 4450, ⓦ fozpresidentehoteis.com.br. This modern hotel has spacious rooms with big comfortable beds and an attractive outdoor swimming pool and sunbathing area. **US$60**

Hotel das Cataratas Parque Nacional do Iguazú ☎ 0055 45 3521 7000, ⓦ hoteldascataratas.com; map p.237. Unbeatable for its location right inside the national park, just metres from the Falls, the famed *Cataratas* run by the luxury Orient Express group is housed in a charming pink-walled old building, with cool tiled floors and elegantly decorated rooms. It packs in all the style that the *Sheraton* on the Argentine side lacks, though do beware the smaller, pokier rooms. There's also a great outdoor swimming pool and an excellent restaurant (just as well as you are stranded there in the evening). **US$790**

Hotel del Rey Rua Tarobá 1020 ☎ 0055 45 3523 2027, ⓦ hoteldelreyfoz.com.br. Close to the terminal, this decent hotel offers clean, uncluttered en-suite rooms with good a/c and a tiny outdoor swimming pool; an excellent buffet breakfast is included. **US$85**

Paudimar Campestre Rua Rui Barbosa 634 ☎ 0055 45 3529 6061, ⓦ paudimar.com.br. The best youth hostel in the city is conveniently near the local bus terminal; it's a secure and very friendly place with hotel-style bedrooms, an outdoor pool, a kitchen and internet facilities. Dorms **US$20**, doubles **US$50**

EATING AND DRINKING

In town, there are plenty of inexpensive buffet-style restaurants along central Rua Marechal Deodoro, while the route out to the Cataratas is lined with **churrascarias**, Brazil's answer to the *parrilla*. If you've been travelling in Argentina, you're less likely to be impressed by the meat, much of it from the zebu – a kind of humped ox, originally from India, and far less appetizing than Argentina's beef – than by the buffet accompaniment of fresh salads, rice, beans and plantain.

The Saltos del Moconá

The quiet village of **El Soberbio** lies in one of Missiones Province's most striking areas, with some of the finest scenery in the whole region; at this border Brazil and Argentina sit like plumped-up cushions on either side of the curvaceous Río Uruguay. The village is the point of access for the **Saltos de Moconá**, an unusual but decidedly uncooperative set of waterfalls. One of Argentina's strangest sights, the **Saltos del Moconá** are made up of nearly 3km of immensely powerful waterfalls which spill down the middle of the Río Uruguay, tumbling from a raised riverbed in Argentina into a 90m river canyon in Brazil.

The split-level waterfalls – the longest of their kind in the world – are formed by the meeting of the Uruguay and Pepirí-Guazú rivers just upstream of a dramatic gorge. As the waters encounter this geological quirk, they "split" once again, with one branch flowing downstream along the western side of the gorge and the other plunging down into it. This phenomenon is visible only under certain conditions: if water levels are low, all the water is diverted into the gorge, while if water levels are high the river evens itself out. At a critical point in between, however, the Saltos magically emerge, as water from the higher level cascades down into the gorge running alongside, creating a curtain of rushing water between three and thirteen metres high. The incredible force of the water as it hurtles over the edge of the gorge before continuing downstream explains its Guaraní name – *moconá* means "he who swallows everything".

El Soberbio

About 322km south of Iguazú, **EL SOBERBIO**, the main gateway to the Saltos del Moconá, is perched on the banks of the Río Uruguay. The village's charm is derived not so much from its buildings, which are unassuming modern constructions, but from its gorgeous riverside setting, amid lush undulating sierras. There's also an intriguing **mix of cultures** – sunburnt, blond-haired Polish and German immigrants rub shoulders with Argentines of Spanish and Italian descent, all with a hefty dose of Brazilian culture thrown in. Locals have a refreshingly cavalier attitude to the idea of national boundaries, popping over to Brazil for Saturday-night dances and listening to Brazilian country music on the radio; indeed, in many homes Portuguese is often the main language.

ARRIVAL AND INFORMATION

By bus El Soberbio's modest bus terminal is right in the village centre at the intersection of avenidas San Martín and Rivadavia. There are seven daily buses to and from Posadas (4hr).

Tourist information There's a sporadically open tourist information kiosk on Av Rivadavia as you head into the centre.

ACCOMMODATION

If you can afford them, you're best off staying at one of the posadas and lodges deep in the nearby jungle (see box opposite). Otherwise there are a few passable accommodation choices in and around the village itself. There's no ATM, so bring enough money to cover all your expenses (none of the lodgings take credit cards).

Cabañas Saltos del Moconá Av San Martín 800 ☎03755 495179, ✉ saltosdelmocona@gmail.com.ar. On the way to the Saltos, the *Cabañas Saltos del Moconá* offers fairly plain but comfortable *cabañas* for up to four people. ＄300

Camping El Maynó Around 3km northwest of the village off RP-13 towards San Vicente ☎03755 15 434617. In a lovely riverside spot, this low-priced site has toilets, electricity and barbecue facilities. ＄35

Hostería Puesto del Sol High above the village at the southern end of c/Suipacha ☎03755 495161, ⊛ h-puestadelsol.com.ar. The least offensive of the poor accommodation in the village itself. It is run-down and the rustic rooms (with very noisy a/c) have French windows opening onto a veranda from where there are great views over the valley and the river, its only saving grace. ＄290

The Parque Provincial Moconá and the waterfalls

The **Saltos del Moconá** themselves lie just over 80km northeast of El Soberbio in the **Parque Provincial Moconá**, currently accessed via a partly unsealed road, although the paved the RN-2 is being gradually extended all the way to the Falls. They can be seen from both Argentina and Brazil (where they are known as Yucumã), the latter only by taking a boat trip from El Soberbio (unless you make arrangements on the Brazilian side directly). As with Iguazú, the better view is from Brazil, while the Argentine side wins out in the adventure stakes. Before setting out for the Saltos, you should check the state of the river with the police, who maintain a post nearby (☎03755 441001), and with locals in El Soberbio as to the condition of the road and for precise directions.

The first 40km of the road north takes you through tobacco plantations and communities of Polish and German immigrants clustered around numerous simple wooden Lutheran, Adventist and Evangelical churches. Despite the incredible lushness of the landscape, this is a region afflicted by considerable poverty, and local small farmers carry out much of their work using old-fashioned narrow wooden carts, pulled by oxen. Various side-trips can be made en route, including to the **Salto El Paraíso**, a gentle waterfall with swimming spots and camping facilities, and to the simple **perfume distilleries** (*alambiques*) where locals extract essential oils from native plants. If you are taking a **boat trip**, your guide will drive you down to the river and you will complete the journey by water – a fabulous experience in itself. Having surveyed the waterfalls from the spectacular Brazilian side, you will be transferred to land on the Argentine side, where you can look across the apparently "normal" river from the shore, swim in the shallows and admire the butterflies, and, if possible, wade over to view the waterfalls from above.

POSADAS AND LODGES IN THE SELVA MISIONERA

To experience the awe-inspiring beauty of this area of remote, virgin jungle at its best, it is worth treating yourself to a couple of days being pampered at one of the lodges or posadas tucked away in the forest. Access is difficult, even in a 4WD, so you're advised to fork out the extra for a transfer to and from your accommodation; if you have a vehicle they will arrange for its safekeeping while you are away.

★**Don Enrique Lodge** 011 4723 7020, donenriquelodge.com.ar. Just beyond *La Bonita* on the aptly named *Río Paraíso*, this place is run with dedication and affection by hospitable hostess Bachi and her family, offering fabulous service, delicious meals and, above all, peace and quiet. The individual wooden lodges, each with a balcony and sundeck, are furnished with impeccable taste. You can explore the jungle with a guide – on one side of the river up to a lookout, on the other to a waterfall to admire tree-ferns and all manner of flora and fauna. $1100

Posada La Bonita 30km north of El Soberbio 011 1544 908386, posadalabonita.com.ar. A fabulous construction smack in the middle of the jungle, this pioneering posada offers half-board deals. Built from stone and timber, and furnished with rustic pieces made of dead wood, it sets the trend for the other lodges in the region. The three isolated units stand apart from the main house and have their own little verandas. $1340

Posada La Misión Ruta Costera 2, Km40, Puerto Paraíso 03755 1552 0783, posadalamision.com .ar. Two nights minimum and full board only – vital as there are no eating options within a large radius. Located 45km north of El Soberbio on the banks of the Río Uruguay, *La Misión* is extremely convenient for visits to the Falls; you can also use its mountain bikes or kayaks, or go fishing. The six *cabañas* are handsome cedar and stone constructions, the food is good, the welcome warm and the views of the river and jungle are fantastic. $1400

4

The park

Forty kilometres from El Soberbio the road strikes into the heart of an area of secondary forest, the last stretch of which is protected as the park, which was created in 1988. As yet, little work has been done on registering the park's flora and fauna; sighted species of bird include the condor and the peculiarly noisy Bare-throated bellbird. It is thought (despite no recent sightings) that the park is one of the last refuges in Argentina of the rare *yaguareté*, or jaguar, whose presence has been registered on the Brazilian side. The Brazilian park is far older (created in 1947) and larger (its total area is approximately seventeen square kilometres) and the degree of protection is higher – surveys of its wildlife have confirmed the presence not only of the *yaguareté*, but also the capuchin monkey, the tapir and over two hundred species of bird, including various toucans. After another 40km or so, you arrive at the *guardaparques'* post, from where there are a number of short trails through the forest. A trail of just over a kilometre leads to the edge of the Río Uruguay, from where – compulsorily accompanied by a *guardaparque* or local guide, and conditions permitting – you can embark on an adventurous wade across 300m of knee-high water to reach the edge of the waterfalls.

ARRIVAL AND TOURS

By 4WD For the current road a 4WD is best, and the only option for periods when sections of the road are flooded, but once the RN-2 extension is complete it should be straightforward to drive there in an ordinary car – check at the tourist information office in El Soberbio or Posadas.

Organized tours Without your own transport, the easiest option for seeing the falls is to arrange an organized tour: some companies in Posadas and Puerto Iguazú offer packages involving at least an overnight stay, but these are expensive and only really worthwhile for a group. Better value is to make your own way to El

THE PARQUE PROVINCIAL MOCONÁ

Soberbio and then arrange a tour from there. The *Hostería Puesto del Sol* (see opposite) does packages including accommodation and excursions (from $450), while a number of agencies in El Soberbio, such as Yabotí Jungle, at Av Corrientes 481 (03755 495266), offer 4WD and boat tours to the waterfalls for around $300 per person. Otherwise, if you are prepared to hang around in El Soberbio for a few days, it may be possible to catch a lift to the waterfalls; vehicles do travel regularly to and from the site, taking provisions and sometimes school parties.

Up the Río Paraná: Rosario to Corrientes

The mighty **Río Paraná** is an attraction in itself, with its lush islands, delicious fish and relaxing aquatic landscapes. Anyone looking for urban pleasures should head for **Rosario**, the country's third largest city, whose famously handsome people, active cultural life and fascinating architecture make it one of Argentina's most attractive cities. Nearby **Santa Fe**, the much-overshadowed provincial capital, is at first sight less enticing, but its faded grandeur and revived dock area merit a stopover. Opposite, the dynamic city of **Paraná** shares not only its name with the river, but also its slow pace and a certain subtropical beauty. To the south, since it was linked to Rosario by a splendid bridge, the traditional town of **Victoria**, famous for its monastery, has been opening itself up to tourism. Some way to the north is the provincial capital of **Corrientes**, named for the strong currents in a sweeping loop of the Paraná. One of the region's oldest and most dynamic cities, it is also the gateway to the Gran Chaco (see p.267).

Rosario and around

I've always said that Rosario has beautiful women and good football. What more could an intellectual ask for?

Roberto Fontanarrosa

Confident and stylish, with a vibrant cultural scene and a lively nightlife, **ROSARIO** dominates the whole region. With a little over one million inhabitants, it is Argentina's third biggest city – Córdoba just beats it for second place. However, Rosario likes to see itself as a worthy rival to Buenos Aires, 300km southeast – in some ways it is a far smaller version of the capital, but without the hordes of foreign visitors or the political clout. Geographically the comparison certainly holds: Rosario is a flattish riverside city and major **port**, lying at the heart of a vital agricultural region. Its cobbled streets lined with handsome buildings and leafy trees – both with a tendency to flake – manage to be decadent and dynamic at the same time. Unlike Buenos Aires, however, whose back has until recently been firmly to the water, Rosario has always enjoyed a close relationship with the **Río Paraná**; the attractive riverfront area runs for 20km along the city's eastern edge, flanked by parks, bars and restaurants and, to the north, popular beaches. One of its main attractions is the splendidly unspoilt series of so-called "**delta islands**" with wide sandy beaches, just minutes away from the city by boat. Packed with locals during the sweltering summers that afflict the region, they give Rosario the feel of a resort town, despite the city's little-developed tourist industry.

Rosario may not have any of the impressive ecclesiastical and colonial architecture of, say, Salta or Córdoba. However, as the legacy of its late nineteenth-century wealth, it does boast some particularly handsome examples of rather more worldly constructions. You can see some of Argentina's finest turn-of-the-century **architecture** here, with an eclectic spread of styles ranging from English chalets to Catalan Modernism. The dawn of the new millennium saw a rash of architectural and art projects, such as the **Museo de Arte Contemporáneo**, housed in a conspicuously converted grain silo on the riverside. Rosario has a handful of conventional museums and galleries, while its most famous sight, nationally at least, is the monolithic **Monumento a la Bandera**, a 70m marble paean to the Argentine flag.

Brief history

Unusually for a Hispano-American city, Rosario lacks an official founding date. Having slowly grown up around a simple chapel, built in the grounds of an estancia in the late seventeenth century and dedicated to the **Virgen del Rosario**, the original settlement became known as La Capilla del Rosario. Despite its strategic location as a port for goods from Córdoba and Santa Fe provinces, early growth was slow: as in the whole region, Rosario's progress was hindered by Buenos Aires' stranglehold on the movement of trade

ROSARIO

ACCOMMODATION	
Anamundana Guesthouse	7
Boulevard	2
Esplendor Savoy	4
Garden	1
Nuevo Imperio	3
La Paz	5
Puerto Pirata	8
Río Grande Apart Hotel	6

RESTAURANTS AND CAFÉS	
Alma	11
Bruno	9
Café de la Opera	10
Davis	1
Escauriza	3
Espacio Once	12
Pampa	7
Pobla del Mercat	5
Señor Arenero	2
Victoria	6
El Viejo Balcón	4
Wembley	8

BARS, CLUBS AND LIVE-MUSIC AND TANGO VENUES	
Berlin	8
El Cairo	5
Contramambo	6
Tango Club	9
Gotika City Club	1
Madame	4
Pasaporte	7
Peña La Amistad	2
Piluso	3
La Sede	

4

Monumento al Che Guevara

RN-9 & Buenos Aires

Granja de la Infancia (7km)

Airport, RN-9, Córdoba & Santa Fe

MONUMENTO AL CHE GUEVARA

Acknowledgement of Rosario's most famous son, the revolutionary **Ernesto "Che" Guevara**, was a long time in coming; compared with Cuba, where Che is a hero of gigantic proportions, the Argentine authorities have seemed rather embarrassed about him, and it took until 2008 for a monument to him to be erected in his hometown. The bronze statue was unveiled to commemorate what would have been his 80th birthday, but even then, it was funded by thousands of small donations from around the world rather than the government, though they did contribute the space – an out of the way, rather forlorn plaza on 27 de Febrero and Laprida, twelve blocks east of Parque de la Independencia. The statue itself depicts a larger-than-life though not, in truth, very lifelike Che striding purposefully, mounted on a concrete plinth covered in suitably socialist graffiti.

between the interior and foreign markets through blockades of the Río Paraná. After 1852 when river traffic was freed up, Rosario was finally set on course for expansion and the city's population ballooned from 3000 in 1850 to 23,000 in 1869, boosted further when the **Central Argentine Railway**, owned and largely financed by the British, was completed in 1870, providing a link to Córdoba. By 1895, Rosario was Argentina's second city, with 91,000 inhabitants – many of them immigrants attracted by the promise of the by now flourishing port, giving the city its soubriquet, "**Hija de los Barcos**" (Daughter of the Ships). By the early twentieth century, the city had an important banking district populated by representatives from the world's major financial institutions, and a growing number of industries. Like Buenos Aires, Rosario also had its sleazy side, one that won it another nickname, the "Chicago of the South": during the late nineteenth and early twentieth centuries, the city was claimed to be a centre of white slave traffic with a notorious zone of **prostitution** known as the Barrio de Pichincha.

Progress and personalities

The latter half of the twentieth century was a period of intense political conflict and saw a steady decline in Rosario's fortunes, with the city suffering one of the country's highest unemployment rates. However, with the aid of forward-thinking local government policies, Rosario turned itself around, so that by the 2000s the city was once again a vital link between its hinterland's rejuvenated farmland (producing beef, dairy goods, soya, wheat and maize) and the outside world. Tourists came, attracted by the boomtown's dynamic cultural offering and catered to by a constantly improving set of hotels and even Latin America's biggest casino. The pace of growth has slowed in recent years, but Rosario remains an attractive and progressive city that has been home to a number of well-known Argentine names. Revolutionary **Che Guevara** was born in an apartment block on the corner of Santa Fe and Urquiza (and is commemorated by a modest monument; see box above), while arguably the greatest footballer of the twenty-first century, Barcelona superstar **Lionel Messi** was born here and began his career at local club Newell's Old Boys. Other **Rosarino celebrities** include leading artists Antonio Berni and Lucio Fontana, three of Argentina's most popular singers – Fito Páez, Juan Carlos Baglietto and Litto Nebbia – and the late cartoonist Roberto Fontanarrosa, whose most famous creation was the luckless gaucho Inodoro Pereyra.

Plaza 25 de Mayo

Constructed on the site of the first modest chapel built to venerate the Virgen del Rosario, **Plaza 25 de Mayo** sits on the edge of the city, near where it slopes down to Avenida Belgrano and the river. The plaza itself is a pleasantly shady space laid out very formally around its central marble monument, the **Monumento a la Independencia**. Around the square lie a number of grand public buildings, including the imposing **Palacio del Correo** on the corner of Córdoba and Buenos Aires and, on the northeast

corner, the terracotta-coloured Municipal Palace, also known as the **Palacio de los Leones**, in reference to the majestic sculptured lions that flank the main entrance.

Catedral de Rosario

Buenos Aires 789 • Mon–Sat 9am–12.30pm & 4.30–8.30pm, Sun 8am–1pm & 5–9.30pm • Free

South of the Palacio lies the **Catedral de Rosario**, a late nineteenth-century construction in which domes, towers, columns and pediments are mixed to particularly eclectic effect. Inside, there's a fine Italianate altar carved from Carrara marble and, in the crypt, the colonial wood-carved image of the Virgin of Rosario, brought from Cádiz in 1773.

Museo Municipal de Arte Decorativo Firma y Odilo Estévez

Santa Fe 748 • Tues–Fri 3–8pm, Sat & Sun 10am–8pm • Free • W museoestevez.gov.ar

Housed in a fantastically ornate mansion, whose facade reflects the early twentieth-century fashion for heavily ornamental moulding, this museum exhibits the collection of the building's former occupants, the Estévez family, Galician immigrants who made their fortune by growing *mate*. It's a stunning display – every inch of the interior is furnished and ornamented with objects seemingly chosen to exemplify the wealth and taste of the owners, from Egyptian glassware and tiny Greek sculptures to Flemish tapestry and Limoges porcelain, via pre-Columbian ceramics and Spanish ivory figures. There's a small but impressive **painting collection**, too, including *Portrait of a Gentleman* by French Neoclassicist Jacques Louis David and a Goya portrait, *Doña María Teresa Ruiz de Apodaca de Sesma*, with strikingly piercing black eyes.

Monumento a la Bandera

Santa Fe 581 • W monumentoalabandera.gov.ar

Your first sight of the **Monumento a la Bandera** is likely to be its depiction on the ten-peso note. The country's monument to its own flag (*bandera*), created in the city in 1812 by General Manuel Belgrano, and lending Rosario the official title of "Cuna de la Bandera" (Birthplace of the Flag), it is a huge allegorical sculpture based on the idea of a ship – representing Argentina – sailing towards a glorious future. The country's major Flag Day celebrations are held at the monument on June 20 each year. Finished in 1957 under the direction of architect Ángel Guido, it is reached from Plaza 25 de Mayo via the Pasaje Juramento, lined with dramatic marble figures by the great sculptress Lola Mora (see box below).

LOLA MORA

Dolores Mora Vega de Hernández – better known as **Lola Mora** – was born on November 17, 1866, at El Tala, a tiny village in Salta Province very close to the Tucumán border. She completed her studies in Italy and took to working in **marble**, a medium used for much of her prolific oeuvre of statues and monuments. In addition to works in various towns and cities around the country, she is best known for her invaluable contribution to the Monumento a la Bandera in Rosario (see above); the magnificent Nereidas fountain adorning the Costanera Sur in Buenos Aires (see p.76); and the voluptuous set of allegorical figures – Peace, Progress, Justice, Freedom and Labour – intended for the National Congress building (see p.69) but never placed there, as they were considered too shocking. Instead the five naked forms can be admired at the Casa de Gobierno in Jujuy (see p.295). Hailed as the country's foremost **sculptress**, Lola had a tragic life, losing her parents at an early age, enduring a turbulent marriage and facing social rejection owing to her bohemian lifestyle and her predilection for portraying shapely female forms (leading to comparisons with Camille Claudel). Towards the end of her life, she suffered from ill health and psychological problems. She died in poverty, on June 7, 1936, shortly after reconciliation with her husband after seventeen years of estrangement and only a few months after the national government agreed to grant her a pension.

The Costanera

Stretching over 20km from north to south, Rosario's **Costanera**, or riverfront, is one of the city's most appealing features, offering numerous green spaces and views over the Río Paraná. You'll find this area's most central park, the **Parque Nacional de la Bandera**, a narrow wedge of grass lining the river, just to the east of the Monumento a la Bandera. At the southern end of the park lies the **Estación Fluvial** from where regular boat services run to the river islands (see p.254). Every Saturday and Sunday evening around Av Belgrano 500, which runs past the western edge of the park, there is a flea market, the **Mercado de Pulgas del Bajo**, where you can browse through a selection of crafts, antiques and books. The park merges to the north with the **Parque de España**, where a cultural and exhibition centre, the **Complejo Cultural Parque de España**, has been imaginatively installed above some old nineteenth-century tunnels.

Balneario La Florida

Around 8km north of the centre, Rosario's most popular mainland beach, **Balneario La Florida** (bus #101 from Rioja) is packed on summer weekends, and has bars, restaurants and shower facilities. At the southern end of the *balneario* you'll find the **Rambla Catalunya** and Avenida Carrasco, lined with glitzy bars, smart restaurants and see-and-be-seen nightclubs that are the summertime focus of Rosario's famed *movida*.

Parque de la Independencia

Dissected by various avenues and containing several museums, a football stadium – Newell's Old Boys, known affectionately as "El Coloso" – and a racetrack, the **Parque de la Independencia** feels like a neighbourhood in itself. The park was inaugurated in 1902 and is an attractively landscaped space with shady walkways and beautifully laid-out gardens such as the formal **Jardín Francés**, just west of the main entrance on Boulevard Oroño. Just south of the entrance there is a large lake which is the setting for a rather kitsch but not unattractive spectacle known as the **Aguas Danzantes** (literally the "dancing waters"), a synchronized fountain display complete with coloured lights and music (Fri–Sun 8–11pm). Parque de la Independencia can easily be reached on foot from the city centre – it's a particularly attractive walk along the Paseo del Siglo and Oroño, or you can take buses #129 and #123 from Rioja.

Museo Municipal de Bellas Artes Juan B. Castagnino

Av Pellegrini 2202 • Mon & Wed–Fri 2–8pm, Sat & Sun 1–7pm • $5 • ⓦ museocastagnino.org.ar

Within the Parque de la Independencia, you'll find the **Museo Municipal de Bellas Artes Juan B. Castagnino**, regarded as the country's most important fine-arts museum after the Museo de Bellas Artes in Buenos Aires (p.93). The museum has two permanent collections: European painting from the fifteenth to the twentieth centuries, with works by Goya, Sisley and Daubigny, among others; and Argentine painting with examples from major artists such as Spilimbergo and Quinquela Martín, plus Antonio Berni and Lucio Fontana, both born in Rosario. The museum, arranged on two floors with large, well-lit rooms, also puts on some excellent temporary exhibitions – it's well worth looking out for exhibitions featuring local artists, who are producing some of Argentina's most interesting contemporary work.

Museo Histórico Provincial Dr Julio Marc

Av del Museo s/n • Tues–Fri 9am–5pm, Sat & Sun 2–6pm, closed during football matches • $5 • ⓦ museohistoricomarc.org.ar

Just west of Parque de la Independencia's lake, the large **Museo Histórico Provincial Dr Julio Marc** is not just any provincial museum, but houses a vast and splendid number of exhibits spanning the whole of Latin America. Among its most notable collection-s are those dedicated to **Latin American religious art**, with a stunning eighteenth-century silver altar from Alto Perú, which was used for the Mass given by Pope John Paul II when he visited the city in 1987, and some fine examples of polychrome works in wood,

KIDS' ROSARIO

Rosario's city government has a justified reputation for progressiveness, and one of its most positive achievements is the provision of entertainment for children, a rarity in Argentina. Everywhere you go in the city you see children's playgrounds, kids' menus and entertainment aimed at smaller people. One of the best long-running initiatives is the **Isla de los Inventos** (Fri–Sun 3–8pm; $7), housed in the stunning, former central train station at Corrientes and Wheelwright. Literally the "Island of Inventions", it features a series of interactive exhibits based on Rosario and its history – such as a contraption representing fluvial navigation on the Río Paraná – plus workshops where visitors can help assemble toys. Adults will enjoy some of the more abstract sections, such as one dedicated to infinity, and may need to hold toddlers' hands when they enter the magical dark chamber that comes to life to explain the history of the universe since the Big Bang.

Inside the **Parque de la Independencia** (see p.253), the former zoo is another kids' attraction, the **Jardín de los Niños** ("Children's Garden") mostly aimed at youngsters aged 4 and above (Fri–Sun 2–7pm; $7). An ingenious theme park whose only (strictly non-commercial) theme is enabling young people to discover everyday phenomena such as sound, mystery, flight and balance, it is adventurous but safe and great fun.

There are two museums aimed at children: a hands-on experimental **science museum** located in the town's planetarium in Parque Urquiza (Sat & Sun 5.30–8.30pm; $3), and the privately run **Museo de los Niños** in Shopping Alto Rosario (Tues–Sun 1–8pm; adults $10, children $35 Tues–Fri, $45 Sat & Sun; ⓦmuseodelosninos.org.ar), which leads children around a play version of a town, albeit one with a commercial flavour.

Finally, the **Granja de la Infancia** – "Youngsters' Farm" – is some way out of the centre at Av Perón 8100 (Tues–Fri 9am–5pm, Sat & Sun 10am–6pm; $7). Aimed at urban youth, it is so well designed that even the most field-wise kids get something out of it and, like all the other child-targeted venues, it will keep grown-ups entertained for a while too.

wax and bone, representing the famed Quiteña School (named after the capital of Ecuador). There's also an important collection of **indigenous American ceramics**, including some valuable musical pieces known as whistling glasses (*vasos silbadores*) from the Chimú culture of northern Perú and some well-preserved and delicate textiles. Colonial-era furniture is also well represented – look for the beautifully worked travel desk featuring carvings of conquistadores and native Americans.

Museo de Arte Contemporáneo de Rosario (MACRo)

Estanislao López 2250 • Thurs–Tues: summer 3–9pm; rest of year 2–8pm • $5 • ⓦ macromuseo.org.ar

West of the northern reaches of the elegant Boulevard Oroño lies the former red-light district, the Pichincha. This barrio has undergone earnest gentrification in recent years and is now home to trendy bars, fashionable restaurants and, above all, antique shops, the latter mostly clustered along Avenida Rivadavia. At the far end of the boulevard, on the waterfront, set among the verdant Parque Sunchales, is an unmissable hulk of a building, looking like a row of upturned giant liquorice allsorts. Once a grain silo belonging to the Davis family, it has been turned into a museum of contemporary art, the **Museo de Arte Contemporáneo de Rosario**, or **MACRo**. The most striking aspects of the museum are its exterior, especially the huge silo cylinders painted in vibrant pink, purple and azure shades, and its riverside location – both the top-floor viewpoint and the Perspex lift-shaft leading to it offer fine views of the majestic Paraná. The exhibitions are mostly dedicated to up-and-coming local and national artists, but even if the art leaves you cold the museum is worth a visit for the building, location and café-restaurant, *Davis* (see p.256), where you can enjoy watching boats, barges and bits of vegetation float past.

The Alto Delta islands

Known as the **Alto Delta**, the low-lying riverine **islands** off Rosario's "coast" in fact fall under the jurisdiction of the neighbouring province, Entre Ríos. Like the islands of the

Tigre Delta in Buenos Aires (see p.132), they host subtropical vegetation fed by sediment from the Upper Paraná River. The Alto Delta is far less developed than Tigre, however. With the exception of the remote island of **Charigüé**, where there is a small settlement with its own school, police station and a handful of restaurants, the islands are largely uninhabited, though plenty of pleasure boats ply the waters in the summer.

ARRIVAL AND GETTING AROUND | ROSARIO

BY PLANE

Rosario's airport lies around 10km northwest of the city centre, along the RN-9 (📞 0341 451 3220), with 1–6 daily flights to and from Buenos Aires (1hr). There is no bus service to the centre from the airport – the half-hour taxi ride will cost around $70.

Airlines Aerolíneas Argentinas/Austral, Santa Fe 1410 📞 0341 424 9332 and at the airport 📞 0341 451 1470; Lan Chile, San Lorenzo 1116 📞 0341 424 8205; Sol 📞 0810 444 4765.

BY BUS

Long-distance buses arrive at Rosario's clean and user-friendly Terminal de Omnibus Mariano Moreno, twenty blocks west of the city centre, at Santa Fe and Cafferata (📞 0341 437 3030). An information kiosk (daily 9am–7pm) can provide you with a list of hotels and a map. At the terminal you can buy a magnetic card (*tarjeta magnética*)

used instead of cash on the city's local buses – walk one block north along Cafferata to catch buses #116 or #107 to the centre from the corner with San Lorenzo. Otherwise, plenty of taxis pull up outside the front entrance, and will set you back $25 or so to the city centre.

Destinations Buenos Aires (2–3 hourly; 4hr); Córdoba (hourly; 6hr); Corrientes (5 daily; 10hr); Posadas (5 daily; 15hr); Puerto Iguazú (1 daily; 18hr); Resistencia (hourly; 8–10hr); Salta (9 daily; 16hr); Tucumán (hourly; 12hr); Victoria (5 daily; 1hr 20min).

BY BOAT

Passenger boats run to the various islands throughout the week, with regular services from Nov to March, from 9am to dusk; out of season, services are less frequent. All boats depart from the Estación Fluvial (📞 0341 447 3838, 🌐 lafluvialrosario.com.ar).

INFORMATION AND TOURS

Tourist information There's a dynamic tourist information office (ETUR) down by the riverfront, at Av Belgrano and c/Buenos Aires (daily 9am–7pm; 📞 0341 480 2230, 🌐 rosario turismo.com). It produces an informative map covering most of the city, together with accommodation and restaurant lists. Note that some of Rosario's attractions have slightly different winter (usually mid-March to mid-Nov) and summer (mid-Nov to mid-March) hours; it's always worth checking ahead, especially if you arrive on the cusp.

Bicycle/kayak tours For bicycle tours, as well as bike or kayak rental, contact Bike Rosario at Zeballos 327 📞 0341 155 713812, 🌐 bikerosario.com.ar. English and French spoken.

River tours One long-established river trip is a 2hr river cruise on the sightseeing boat, *Ciudad de Rosario* (Sat & Sun: winter 2.30pm & 5pm; summer 5pm & 7.30pm; $47; 📞 0341 449 8688, 🌐 barcocr1.com), while the more intimate *Island Explorer* dinghies do 90min trips (Mon–Fri 11am, Sat & Sun noon, 2pm & 4pm; $120; 🌐 islandexplorer .com.ar). Bike Rosario runs kayak excursions on the river, and the English-speaking Rosario Sail (📞 0341 156 289287, 🌐 rosariosail.com.ar) offers sailboat trips.

Travel agent ASATEJ, Shopping Del Siglo piso 2, Córdoba 1643 📞 0341 425 6002.

ACCOMMODATION

⭐ **Anamundana Guesthouse** Montevideo 1248 📞 0341 424 3077, 🌐 anamundahostel.com. Attractive guesthouse/hostel run by friendly ex-backpacker Ana, with beautiful stained-glass windows and polished wooden floors, as well as clean dorms with comfortable beds and a/c. Dorms $60, doubles $180

Boulevard San Lorenzo 2194 📞 0341 447 5795, 🌐 hotelboulevard.com.ar. Great B&B in a converted 1920s villa on the majestic Boulevard Oroño. Rooms share a bathroom, except for the bridal suite, which has its own. $220

⭐ **Esplendor Savoy** San Lorenzo 1022 📞 0341 429 6007, 🌐 esplendorsavoyrosario.com. Rosario's *belle époque*

Savoy hotel has been given a respectful makeover by the Fën group, creating a beautiful boutique hotel that incorporates many of its original features, including the marble staircases, chandeliers and the crowning cupola, where you can sit and contemplate the street scene below. $540

Garden Callao 45 📞 0341 437 0025, 🌐 hotelgardensa .com. An attractive modern hotel in a quiet area of town. Rooms have large, comfortable beds, a/c and cable TV, and rates include breakfast and use of a swimming pool. Spacious bar area. $395

Nuevo Imperio Urquiza 1264 📞 0341 448 0091, 🌐 hotelimperio.com.ar. A bland 1970s construction grafted on to a venerable old hotel (part of the stunning

4

but dilapidated Moorish interior survives but is not in use). Rooms are spotless, with cable TV and a/c, and there's a bar and restaurant and a pool. $235

La Paz Cortada Barón de Mauá 36 ☎0341 421 0905, ⓦhotellapazrosario.com.ar. Plain but adequate rooms with TV and private bathroom, some with balconies. Prices include breakfast. $230

Puerto Pirata Isla de los Mástiles ☎0341 156 933464, ⓦparadorpuertopirata.com.ar. On the Alto Delta island, this *parador* rents out *cabañas* (plus you can camp) and has

a good bar and restaurant with great views over the river from its terrace and long strip of beach. It can also be visited as a day-trip; boats ($25 return) leave hourly from 11am from Bajada Formosa. Camping $20, *cabañas* $250

★ **Río Grande Apart Hotel** Dorrego 1261 ☎0341 4241144, ⓦriograndeapart.com.ar. The best of the city's *apart-hotels*, with bright, roomy suites in a smart, renovated building in a fairly quiet part of the city. Outstanding buffet breakfasts, reliable internet and a safe garage. $530

EATING AND DRINKING

Rosario has plenty of **restaurants** to suit all budgets, both in the city centre and along the Costanera. In addition to pasta, pizza and *parrillas*, there are some adventurous places that easily rival the best in the capital, as well as a number of excellent fish restaurants specializing in *boga*, *dorado* and *surubí*. The city has always excelled in a **bar culture** – there are so many stylishly revamped bars around the city centre that you're spoilt for choice when it comes to drinking. The best spots for bar-hopping are just north of the centre, roughly between Santa Fe and Avenida Belgrano, and to the west, in the Pichincha, centred on an oblong formed by calles Ricchieri, Suipacha, Salta and Güemes.

RESTAURANTS AND CAFÉS

Alma Montevideo 2394 ☎0341 449 2397. Quiet, toned-down place in a charming corner house, all done in soothing lime-green and pastel shades, with mellow music, laidback service and interesting fusion fare – try the rabbit stuffed with bacon ($60) or the suckling-lamb tajine ($65). Tues–Sat 6pm–2am.

Bruno Ovidio Lagos 1599 ☎0341 421 2396. Long-established, family-run Italian restaurant serving excellent home-made pasta. Tues–Fri 8pm–late, Sat & Sun noon–3pm & 8pm–late.

★ **Café de la Ópera** Laprida and Mendoza 787 ☎0341 421 9402. Beautiful old-fashioned café adjoining the Teatro El Círculo, serving specials like tarragon chicken, along with pasta, omelettes and salads; or you can just have a coffee and a slice of date tart. Also hosts lively musical or cabaret events on Fridays and Saturdays from 10pm. Daily 8am–midnight.

★ **Davis** Blvd Oroño s/n ☎0341 435 7142. Named for the silo that was converted into the fabulous MACRo museum, this waterside bar-restaurant enjoys an incredible location and lively ambience, serving staples such as river fish and salads, as well as a good-value $65 three-course set menu. Daily 8am–late.

Escauriza Paseo Ribereño and Escauriza ☎0341 454 1777. Highly regarded *parrilla* specializing in fish, on the riverfront near the access to the Victoria road bridge. *Surubí*, *boga* and *dorado* are on the menu as well as more conventional meat, and the prices are very reasonable. Daily noon–3pm & 8pm–midnight.

Espacio Once Av de la Libertad 10. This large café on the southern Costanera is a popular early-evening pit-stop for Rosarinos on their way back from a walk around Parque Urquiza. The outside tables are good for a spot of people-watching. Daily 8am–midnight.

Pampa Moreno 1206 ☎0341 449 4303. Elegant tables in a trendy restaurant with a consciously industrial look, bare brickwork and all. Food is more conventional, though some dishes have a twist, such as the signature turkey, mozzarella and nut sorrentinos. Daily 8pm–late.

Pobla del Mercat Salta 1424 ☎0341 447 1240. A wine club and gourmet grocery with a smart restaurant attached. Attentive service, an impressive wine list and all manner of culinary wonders – from the fish carpaccio to the peach tart – make this one of the top restaurants in the city. Accordingly, it's not cheap. Daily 8pm–1am.

Señor Arenero Av Carrasco 2568 ☎0341 453 4267. Big glitzy restaurant specializing in fish, in the popular Rambla Catalunya area; prices are above average. Daily 8pm–late.

Victoria San Lorenzo & Pte Roca ☎0341 425 7665. Old-fashioned corner café-bar and restaurant with a sober wooden interior and tables on the pavement. Good-value *menú ejecutivo* ($55) with a main dish such as pork chops, a dessert and drink. Mon–Sat 9am–6pm & 8pm–late, Sun 8pm–midnight.

El Viejo Balcón Wheelwright and Italia ☎0341 425 5611. One of the city's best *parrillas*, serving up all the usual cuts (such as a *bife de chorizo* for $65) at an attractive riverside location. Daily noon–4pm & 8.30pm–late.

Wembley Av Belgrano 2012 ☎0341 481 1090. Busy, upmarket restaurant opposite the port. Daily specials include the likes of salmon with capers ($55), though the most successful dishes are the more simply executed grilled river fish ($50) or *parrillada* ($95 for two). Daily 8.30pm–late.

BARS

El Cairo Sarmiento and Santa Fe. A Rosarian institution, the high-ceilinged *Cairo* fleshes out its claim to be a literary café with a library at the back and theatrical-looking velvet drapes; it's also well known in town for being where the great cartoonist Roberto Fontanarrosa came to work. As well as full-blown meals, there is a huge cocktail menu and a *mate* bar serving Argentina's favourite brew. Daily 8am–late.

Pasaporte Maipú and Urquiza. Stylish bar with outside tables on a pleasant corner down near the riverfront. Coffee, alcoholic drinks and a large selection of filled crêpes. Board games available. Daily 9am–midnight.

Piluso Alvear and Catamarca. Pleasing wood-panelled bar on an attractive corner in Pichincha, serving a good range of beers and also fruity nonalcoholic drinks. Daily 11am–1am.

La Sede San Lorenzo and Entre Ríos. Elegant and rather literary bar in a fabulous Art Nouveau building – a favourite meeting-place for Rosario's artistic celebrities. Theatrical/cabaret evenings. Daily 7pm–1am.

NIGHTLIFE AND ENTERTAINMENT

Rosario is noted for its nightlife, **la movida**, but its **clubs** can be a little disappointing and in summer, when all the action moves to the Rambla Catalunya, a beachfront avenue at the northern end of town, you're limited to one or two very popular but faceless megadiscos, whose names but not character change with the seasons. You'll be far better off checking out one of the city's popular *milongas*, a more authentic experience: Rosario has a hard core of **tango** enthusiasts – who dance a slightly showier version of the tango than Porteños – and most nights of the week there is something going on. The tourist office has a list of current *milongas*.

Berlín Pje Zabala 1128, between the 300 block of Mitre and Sarmiento. Regular cabaret and musical events from Thursday to Sunday at this popular bar. Tues–Sun 6pm–late.

Contramambo Tango Club Mendoza and Corrientes ☏ 0341 426 5338. Tango classes followed by a *milonga* every Wednesday from 8.30pm, at the *Olimpo* bar. Daily 9pm–late.

Gotika City Club Mitre 1739. A loft, three bars and a garden are all features at the city's main gay disco, with regular shows and events. Thurs–Sun 11pm–late.

Madame Brown 3126. This megaclub aimed at the over-25s claims to be the biggest in Argentina. Fri & Sat only, 11pm–late.

Peña La Amistad Maipú 1121 ☏ 0341 411 0339. A good spot to listen to folk music, especially *chamamé* and other regional styles. Snacks such as empanadas and tamales are served. Fri & Sat 11pm–late.

Teatro El Círculo Laprida 1235 ☏ 0341 448 3784, ⓦ teatro-elcirculo.com.ar. Rosario's best-known theatre has an extensive programme of plays, music, opera and dance; check the website for full listings.

Victoria

Since a stunning road **bridge** across the Río Paraná was inaugurated in 2003, the somnolent little market town of **VICTORIA**, 58km northeast of Rosario, has been cajoled into life. Founded by immigrants from northern Italy and the Basque country, it has been brought physically much closer to the city and seems to relish its prospects as an up-and-coming holiday resort, with a new casino and a thermal baths complex. The RN-11 Paraná–Gualeguaychú road bypasses the town to the north, while Avenida Costanera Dr Pedro Radio skirts round the southern edge, following the contours of the riverbanks, where summer tourists flock to bathe along the sandy beaches.

Abadía del Niño Dios

RN-11 · Guided visits daily at 10am · Free · ⓦ abadiadelninodios.com.ar

Victoria's main tourist attraction is the **Abadía del Niño Dios**, home to Latin America's oldest Benedictine foundation, dating from 1899. The modern monastery and cheerfully designed church are certainly worth seeing, and include the chance to hear the monks singing Gregorian chant. The highlight for most visitors, however, is the excellent shop selling delicious, and mostly healthy, products, true to the Benedictine tradition, ranging from unusual jams and bee products to liqueurs and cheeses. The abbey sits alongside the main RN-11 artery, 3km from Victoria, between the turn-off to the Rosario bridge and the town proper.

ARRIVAL AND INFORMATION   VICTORIA

By bus Victoria's small bus terminal is halfway between the main northern entrance and the central plaza, just four blocks north of the latter, at Junín and L.N. Alem. Taxis to the centre are $5.

Tourist information The helpful little tourist office (daily 8am–8pm; ☎ 03436 421885, ⊛ turismovictoria.com.ar) is conveniently situated at the northern access, on the corner of main drag 25 de Mayo and Blvd Sarmiento.

ACCOMMODATION

Los Altos RN-11 Km114 ⊛ los-altos.com.ar. At the lower end of the budget scale, on the RN-11 near the abbey, these simple but attractive self-catering bungalows have access to a pool and gardens. **$250**

Casablanca Blvd Moreno s/n ☎ 03436 424131, ⊛ hotel casablancavictoria.com. A hospitable, medium-sized establishment in the southern neighbourhood of Barrio Quinto Cuartel, with large, slightly kitsch rooms, a beautiful garden and swimming pool, plus ample parking space. **$390**

Sol Victoria Mastrangelo s/n ☎ 03436 424040, ⊛ hotelsolvictoria.com.ar. The smartest accommodation option in town, this hotel also houses the casino. The spacious, well-appointed rooms are extremely comfortable, and there is a fine dining room and swimming pool, with views down to the river. Various promotional packages including drinks, spa treatments and the like are often available; check the website. **$795**

EATING AND DRINKING

Club de Pescadores Av Pedro Costanera Radio s/n ☎ 03436 15 416338. Enjoy Victoria's slow pace of life down on the riverfront over a lengthy *parrilla*. Next to the anglers' club and a stone's throw from the casino, fish and meat are both thrown on the barbecue here. Daily noon–4pm & 8.30pm–late.

Jockey Club L.N. Alem 91 ⊛ eljockeyvictoria.com.ar. One block north of the central square, this large restaurant is Victoria's classic eating place for simple but tasty fish dishes, though the pasta is not so great. Daily noon–3.30pm & 8pm–late.

4 Santa Fe

The capital of its namesake province, **SANTA FE** is of interest to visitors mainly as a stopover, although nearby Rosario and Paraná are both more appealing. Located 475km north of Buenos Aires, along the banks of the Río Paraná, the city of around 400,000 inhabitants is an important commercial centre for the surrounding agricultural region. Apart from a particularly hot and humid climate in summer, owing to its low-lying riverside location, Santa Fe's main handicap is a rather sprawling and disjointed layout that makes getting to and from the city's modest attractions a bit of a slog.

Plaza 25 de Mayo

Like the rest of the city, Santa Fe's main square, the **Plaza 25 de Mayo**, is an architecturally disjointed kind of place, with the styles of its surrounding buildings leaping from colonial through French Second Empire to nondescript modern. The square is somewhat unusual in having two churches, a simple eighteenth-century cathedral, of which only the massive, studded wooden entrance doors are still original, and the more interesting seventeenth-century Iglesia de Nuestra Señora de los Milagros.

Iglesia de Nuestra Señora de los Milagros

Plaza 25 de Mayo s/n • Mon–Fri 6.30am–noon & 6.30–8.30pm, Sat & Sun 6–8.30pm • Free

On the east side of the square, the **Iglesia de Nuestra Señora de los Milagros** has a pleasingly simple and typically colonial facade looking rather overwhelmed by the more modern constructions around it. Built between 1667 and 1700, it is the oldest church in the province; look inside to see the fine carvings produced by Guaraní in the Jesuit Missions – most notably the impressive Altar Mayor, produced in Loreto.

Museo Histórico Provincial Brigadier General Estanislao López

Plaza 25 de Mayo • Tues–Fri 8.30am–7pm, Sat & Sun 3–6pm • Free • ☎ 0342 457 3529

On the southeastern corner of the square you'll find the **Museo Histórico Provincial Brigadier General Estanislao López**. Housed in a late-colonial family house, the museum's collection comprises furniture, paintings, silverwork, religious icons and everyday items from the seventeenth century. Its most notable items are carvings from

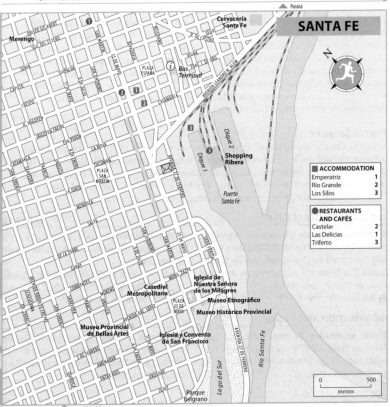

the missions and paintings from the Cusco School, a sixteenth- to eighteenth-century art movement named after the Peruvian city, where indigenous craft workers produced mainly religious art for their colonial masters.

Museo Etnográfico y Colonial Juan de Garay

25 de Mayo 1470 • Tues–Fri 8.30am–noon & 2–7pm, Sat & Sun 3.30–6.30pm • Free • ☎ 0342 457 3550

One block east of the main plaza, the bulk of the **Museo Etnográfico y Colonial Juan de Garay**'s well-organized and coherently displayed collection comprises pieces recovered from the site of **Santa Fe La Vieja** at Cayastá. The most commonly recovered pieces were *tinajas*, large ceramic urns – many of them in a surprisingly complete state considering they spent around three hundred years underground – and delicate amulets in the form of shells or the *higa*, a clenched fist symbol, used to ward off the evil eye. There's also a fine collection of **indigenous ceramics** with typical zoomorphic forms ranging from birds – especially parrots – and bats, to capybaras, cats and snakes.

Iglesia y Convento de San Francisco

Amenábar 2557 • Mon–Sat 8am–noon & 4–7pm • Free

Built in 1676, the **Iglesia y Convento de San Francisco,** one block south of Plaza 25 de Mayo, is notable for its incredible solid but rustic construction: the walls are nearly 2m thick and made of adobe, while the stunning and cleverly assembled interior **ceiling** was constructed using solid wooden beams of Paraguayan cedar, *lapacho*, *algarrobo* and *quebracho colorado* held together not with nails but with wooden pegs.

The intricate dome at the centre of the church is a particularly impressive example of the application of this technique and also has a rather light-hearted touch: at the centre a beautifully carved pine cone is suspended. Of the various icons around the church the most notable is that of **Jesús Nazareno**, immediately to your left as you enter. The beautifully detailed image was produced by one of Spain's most famous *imagineros*, or religious image-makers, Alonso Cano, in 1650. It was presented to the church by the Queen of Spain when the city was moved from Cayastá, to show sympathy for the repeated Indian attacks.

Puerto Santa Fe

Lying just to the southeast of the city centre where the Paraná forks towards Laguna Setúbal, the old dock area, **Puerto Sante Fe**, is being enthusiastically developed. Its two **diques** (docks) are home to a casino and upmarket hotel, housed in a giant former grain silo (see below), while the nearby warehouses have been converted into a smart, relatively upmarket shopping centre, with some good fish restaurants.

ARRIVAL AND DEPARTURE
SANTA FE

By plane Santa Fe's airport is at Sauce Viejo, 7km south of the city along the RN-11 ☎ 0342 4750386). There are 1–4 daily flights to and from Buenos Aires (1hr). The local bus marked "L" or "aeropuerto" runs between the airport and c/San Luís in the city centre (45min).
By bus The bus terminal is on the corner of Av Belgrano

and Hipólito Yrigoyen (☎ 0342 455 3908), just northeast of the town centre and within walking distance of most accommodation.
Destinations Buenos Aires (hourly; 6hr); Córdoba (hourly; 5hr); Posadas (8 daily; 14hr); Puerto Iguazú (2 daily; 20hr); Resistencia (hourly; 7hr); Rosario (hourly; 2hr 20min).

INFORMATION AND TOURS

Tourist information The main tourist office (daily 7am–8pm; ☎ 0342 457 4124) is in the bus terminal. Don't expect much, though the staff should at least be able to provide you with a map.

Boat tours At weekends, catamaran trips (☎ 0342 456 4381) leave from dock one in the port to explore the local waters (Sat & Sun 11am; $60 return) or visit Paraná (Sat & Sun 2pm; $90 return).

ACCOMMODATION

Emperatriz Hotel Irigoyen Freyre 2440 ☎ 0342 453 0061, ⓦ empatrizhotel.wordpress.com. Housed in a 1920s, Mudéjar construction – combining Moorish and Gothic features – with arched wooden doors and a tiled interior; all rooms come with private bathroom, but some may find the hotel a bit run-down. **$250**
Río Grande San Jerónimo 2586 ☎ 0342 450 0700, ⓦ hotel-riogrande.com.ar. Has less character than *Los*

Silos but its comfortable rooms are spotless, with cable TV, safe and a/c; there's a good buffet breakfast and the staff are courteous. **$457**
Los Silos Dique 1, Puerto Santa Fe ☎ 0342 450 2800, ⓦ hotellossilos.com.ar. Easily the best hotel in town, this luxury hotel is housed in an enormous former grain silo, complete with bar, swish rooms with fantastic views and a very high rooftop pool. **$700**

EATING AND DRINKING

Santa Fe is home to one of South America's largest **breweries**, the *Cervecería Santa Fe* (free guided visits are possible with prior booking on ☎ 0342 450 2201) and the city's beer is renowned throughout the country – locals ask for a *liso*, a draught lager served in a straight glass. You can try a *liso* or two at the lively bars found around the intersection of San Martín and Santiago del Estero, all with tables on the pavement and a fun atmosphere on summer evenings.

Castelar Shopping La Ribera, Dique 1, Puerto Santa Fe ☎ 0342 457 2110. Done out in soothing dark wood and tiles, this restaurant in the port's shopping centre serves a good-value set meal at lunchtime; it also has an attached bodega, where you can try and buy wine. Mon–Sat 1– 4pm & 8pm–1am, Sun 1–4pm.
Las Delicias San Martin and Hipólito Yrigoyen. A traditional *confitería* serving good sandwiches and

cakes – also a good place to sup a *liso*. Daily 8am– midnight.
Merengo San Martín and Cortado Falucho. As well as its beer, Santa Fe is famous in Argentina for *alfajores merengo*, a particularly tempting version of Argentina's favourite *alfajor* cake, coated in crispy, white sugar frosting and produced in the city for more than 150 years; they can be tasted at this long-running corner café. Daily 8am–11pm.

Paraná

PARANÁ is more appealing as a stopover than Santa Fe, its larger cross-river neighbour. Favoured by a gentle hilly terrain and a handsome, pedestrian-friendly riverfront area, the city is a pleasant place to chill out for a day or two. Like Rosario, Paraná lacks a true **foundation** date: the area was simply settled by inhabitants from Santa Fe, who regarded the higher ground of the eastern banks of the Paraná river as providing better protection from Indian attack. It is now the largest city in Entre Ríos Province, with a population of around 250,000. In addition to some fine sandy **beaches**, it has a particularly attractive park, the **Parque Urquiza**, whose shady walkways and thick vegetation provide welcome respite in the summer.

Plaza 1 de Mayo

The main square is the **Plaza 1 de Mayo**, ten blocks inland. The single most outstanding building here is the **cathedral**, built in 1887, a superficially handsome if somehow rather awkward Neoclassical edifice distinguished by an intense blue brick-tiled central dome and rather exotic, almost Byzantine bell towers.

Museo Histórico de Entre Ríos Martiniano Leguizamón

Buenos Aires 285 • Tues–Fri 8am–noon & 4–8pm, Sat 9.30am–noon & 4.30–7pm, Sun 9.30am–noon • $3 • ☎ 0343 420 7869

Pedestrianized Calle San Martín leads from the main square to Plaza Alvear, three blocks north, on the southwestern corner of which you'll find the mostly well-organized **Museo Histórico de Entre Ríos Martiniano Leguizamón**. Devoted to the history of Entre Ríos Province from pre-Columbian times to the present day, the informative panels are sometimes more interesting than the objects themselves, which are often notable mainly for their illustrious owners – they include such highlights as a 1976 Julio Iglesias LP and a wheelbarrow used by builders of the railways.

4

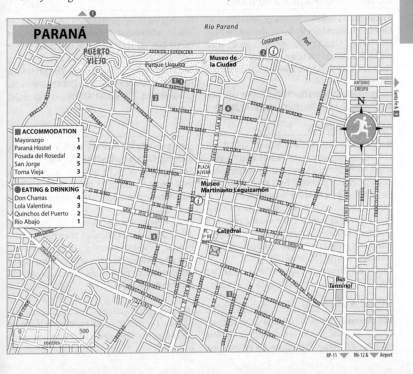

PARANÁ

ACCOMMODATION
Mayorazgo	1
Paraná Hostel	4
Posada del Rosedal	2
San Jorge	5
Toma Vieja	3

EATING & DRINKING
Don Charras	4
Lola Valentina	3
Quinchos del Puerto	2
Río Abajo	1

The museum does have an excellent collection of *criollo* silverwork. Among the more interesting pieces are vicious-looking spurs known as *lloronas* – *llorar* means "to cry", and it's debated whether they were thus called for the sound they made when the horse was moving or for the fact that they made the animal "cry blood". There's also a fine collection of gaucho *facónes*, or knives, with inscriptions such as "do not enter without cause nor leave without honour". Look out, too, for the beautifully crafted *yesqueros*, elaborate precursors of the cigarette lighter formed by a stone and chain contraption – the last two creating a spark to light the tinder – made out of materials as diverse as silver and the tail of an armadillo.

Parque Urquiza

Flanking Paraná's riverside, the **Parque Urquiza** is on a fairly narrow but hilly stretch of ground which slopes up from Avenida Laurencena, Paraná's Costanera, to the higher ground of the city. Designed, like so many of Argentina's parks, by landscape gardener Charles Thays, it's particularly attractive and verdant, traversed by serpentine walkways and with great views over the river, although the area is best avoided at night. At its western end, there's a picturesque little neighbourhood called the **Puerto Viejo**, distinguished by its winding cobbled streets and handsome old-fashioned residences.

Costanera

The real hub of Paraná life on summer evenings, the **Costanera** itself, is lined with a handful of bars and restaurants and some good public **beaches**; you can also become a member for the day of various clubs, giving you access to the smartest beaches and facilities such as swimming pools and showers.

ARRIVAL, INFORMATION AND TOURS

By bus Paraná's confusing Terminal de Omnibus is at Av Ramírez 2550, around nine blocks east of central Plaza 1 de Mayo (☎0343 431 5053, ⊛turismoparana.gov.ar); in the middle of it, a helpful bus-information-cum-tourist-office (daily 8am–2pm & 4–8pm) offers accommodation lists and maps.

Destinations Buenos Aires (hourly; 7hr); Corrientes (3 daily; 8hr); Posadas (7 daily; 10hr); Puerto Iguazú (3 daily; 14hr);

Rosario (2 hourly; 3hr); Santa Fe (every 20min; 50min).

Tourist information The central tourist office is at Buenos Aires 132 (daily 8am–8pm; ☎0343 423 0183 or ☎0800 555 9575).

Tours For river trips, kayak rental, half-day tours to Santa Fe and Victoria and other local tours, contact Costanera 241 at Buenos Aires 212 (☎0343 4234385, ⊛costanera241 .com.ar).

ACCOMMODATION

Mayorazgo Av Etchevere and Miranda ☎0343 423 0333, ⊛hjmayorazgo.com.ar. Paraná's most luxurious hotel is the *Mayorazgo*, towering over the Costanera; now run by the Howard Johnson chain, it has two swimming pools as well as great views over the river. $\overline{\underline{\$720}}$

Paraná Hostel Andrés Pazos 159 ☎0343 455 0847, ⊛paranahostel.com.ar. A truly wonderful place in a converted townhouse. The hostel has dorms and doubles with TV, plus a laundry, fully equipped kitchen and extensive library. Dorms $\overline{\underline{US\$16}}$, doubles $\overline{\underline{US\$34}}$

Posada del Rosedal Santiago del Estero 656 ☎0343 422 3148, ⊛posadadelrosedal.com.ar. A welcoming

guesthouse, with just three neat rooms and an enticing garden filled with flowers and birdsong. $\overline{\underline{\$460}}$

San Jorge Belgrano 368 ☎0343 422 1685, ⊛sanjorge hotel.com.ar. The pick of the cheaper places, in a lovely old building with tiled floors, a small garden and kitchen facilities. $\overline{\underline{\$280}}$

Toma Vieja Av Blas Parera, 4km northeast of the centre ☎0343 433 1721; bus #5 every hour from the terminal. The best place to camp, a huge site with several swimming pools and views over the Paraná. Hot showers and electricity are provided and there's a grocery store just down the road. $\overline{\underline{\$30}}$

EATING & DRINKING

Don Charras Av Uranga 1127 ☎0343 433 1760. Long-running traditional *parrilla* Don Charras has excellent meat, but also throws river fish on the barbecue too.

It also has a newer *Asador Criollo* branch at San Martín and San Lorenzo. Tues–Sun noon–late; Asador Criollo daily noon–late.

ESTANCIAS OF CORRIENTES PROVINCE

En route between Paraná and Corrientes are a couple of outstanding **estancias** that take in guests – often providing horse rides or hands-on experiences of genuine ranch life. You cannot just turn up on spec but must book ahead; sometimes they will arrange for you to be picked up at the nearest town, airport or bus terminal, even if you have your own car – often the lengthy approach roads are impassable other than by 4WD.

Estancia Buena Vista ☎ 011 4815 9305, ⊕ estancia buenavista.com.ar. A few kilometres north of Esquina, off the road to Corrientes, *Estancia Buena Vista* is a traditional working estancia, with large numbers of cattle and sheep but specializing in game, which can be sampled here at dinner. Run by a Swiss Argentine, Sara Röhner, and her German-born husband, the estancia combines a high level of comfort with old-fashioned *correntino* hospitality. The German-style teas are memorable. Full board, 20-percent discount for *Rough Guide* readers. **$900**

★ **Estancia La Rosita** ☎ 011 4312 6448, ⊕ estancialarosita.com.ar. Near the small town of Esquina some 250km north of Paraná, *Estancia La Rosita* lies among huge pastures dotted with ever-changing lakes and marshes, and is very much a working estancia, with lots of cattle and horses – galloping is a definite option. The house is an agreeable low-rise farmstead, with shady galleries and a noble dining room, while the guest rooms are simple and homely. Alicia Cometta de Landgraf runs the place with her sons, who are avid polo players – take a look at the impressive pitch even if you never get to see or participate in a game. An Australian tank swimming pool and barbecue facilities are added attractions; the food is authentic *criollo*. **$1200**

Lola Valentina Near Parque Urquiza at Mitre 302 ☎ 0343 423 5234. *Lola Valentina* serves up enormous and tasty river fish dishes – try the *dorado* in a rich cream and spring onion sauce. Mon–Fri 10am–2pm & 8pm–midnight, Sat & Sun 10am–3pm & 8pm–1am.

Quinchos del Puerto Av Laurencena and Santander ☎ 0343 423 2045. In a rustic thatched construction by the river, this highly rated if pricey *parrilla* fills up quickly – reservations are advised on summer weekends. Tues–Sun 10am–3pm & 8pm–1am.

Río Abajo Av Estrada 3582 ☎ 0343 4218023. Several kilometres west of the Puerto Viejo, in a splendid riverside setting with tropical decor and large terraces, *Río Abajo* is the place to be seen in Paraná; specializing in fusion cuisine, fish, pasta and cocktails. Daily noon–3pm & 8pm–midnight.

Corrientes

Sensual, sultry, subtropical and sitting on a bend in the Río Paraná, **CORRIENTES** is one of the region's oldest and most attractive cities, founded in 1588 as an intermediary port along the river route between Buenos Aires and Asunción. Its charm is derived largely from the number of traditional *correntino* buildings in its crumbling – but very handsome – centre, based around the **Plaza 25 de Mayo**. These Neocolonial edifices, with overhanging roofs supported on wooden posts, are interspersed with more elaborate late nineteenth-century Italianate architecture. Corrientes' modest museums, most notably the original **Museo de Artesanía**, where you can see fine examples of the province's distinctive crafts, are given added appeal by being housed in these traditional buildings, and its central streets make it a pleasant place to just wander around for a day or two. If you visit from November to February, though, be aware that both temperatures and humidity can be very high. As a result, locals take the siesta very seriously, not emerging from indoors until dusk on the hottest days: if you must hit the streets on a summer afternoon, head for Corrientes' attractive **Costanera**, curving for 2.5km around the northwest of the city centre where native *lapacho* trees, with exquisite pink blossom in spring, provide a welcome bit of shade – though mosquitoes like it here, too.

Corrientes is linked to Resistencia, the capital of Chaco Province, 20km to the west, via the Puente General M. Belgrano, a suspension bridge across the Río Paraná. The city itself is reasonably compact: all the major points of interest lie within the streets north of Avenida 3 de Abril, which runs east–west through the city towards Puente General Belgrano. The whole of this approximately triangular area is bordered to the northwest by the **Avenida Costanera General San Martín**. There are two centres: the centro histórico, with **Plaza 25 de Mayo** at its heart, lies to the north and is where you'll find most of Corrientes' historic buildings and museums, while the less interesting Centro Comercial is focused on Plaza Cabral, ten blocks southeast of Plaza 25 de Mayo and Corrientes' main pedestrianized shopping street, Calle Junín.

Plaza 25 de Mayo

An old-fashioned leafy square surrounded by some of Corrientes' most striking buildings, **Plaza 25 de Mayo** encapsulates the city's sleepy subtropical ambience. The square lies one block south of the Costanera, to which it is linked by the narrow streets of Buenos Aires and Salta, the former in particular lined with fine examples of late nineteenth-century architecture.

Casa de Gobierno

One of the most striking buildings on the square itself, the pink **Casa de Gobierno**, on the eastern side, was constructed in 1886 in the ornate Italianate style that replaced many of the older, colonial buildings at the end of the nineteenth century. Particularly attractive are the delicate filigree window grilles, best admired on the building's northern wall, along Fray José de la Quintana.

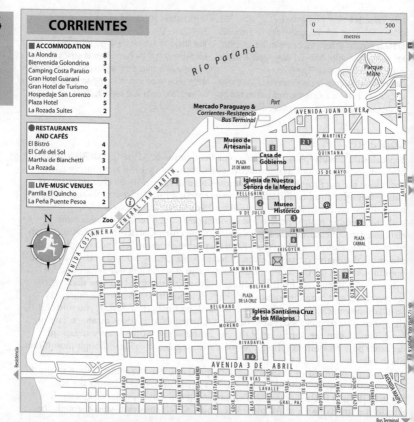

CORRIENTES

0 500
metres

ACCOMMODATION
La Alondra	8
Bienvenida Golondrina	3
Camping Costa Paraíso	1
Gran Hotel Guaraní	6
Gran Hotel de Turismo	4
Hospedaje San Lorenzo	7
Plaza Hotel	5
La Rozada Suites	2

RESTAURANTS AND CAFÉS
El Bistró	4
El Café del Sol	2
Martha de Bianchetti	3
La Rozada	1

LIVE-MUSIC VENUES
Parrilla El Quincho	1
La Peña Puente Pesoa	2

Iglesia de Nuestra Señora de la Merced

Daily 7am–noon & 4–8pm • Free

At the southern end of the square, the nineteenth-century **Iglesia de Nuestra Señora de la Merced** houses a handsome hand-carved wooden retable, or altar screen, with twisted wooden pillars and rich golden inlay work.

Museo de Artesanías Tradicionales Folclóricas de la Provincia

Fray José de la Quintana 905 • Mon–Fri 7am–noon & 4–7pm • Free

On the corner of Fray José de la Quintana and Salta, you'll find the **Museo de Artesanías Tradicionales Folclóricas de la Provincia** and its craft workshops, or *talleres*. The museum is housed within a typical colonial Corrientes building, built in the early nineteenth century; a low, whitewashed residence constructed around a central patio flanked by a gallery, providing shade from the fierce summer sun. Inside you'll find a selection of local crafts, including fine examples of leather, ceramics and basketwork. Perhaps the most intriguing pieces, sold by craftsmen working in the workshops within, are the carvings of San La Muerte (literally "Saint Death"). These solemn little skeletons, carved of wood, gold or bone are carried around – or, in the case of the smallest figures, inserted under the skin – to ensure the bearer a painless death; they're a typical example of the popular cults, many of them inherited from the Guaraní, which coexist in Corrientes with profound Catholic beliefs.

Iglesia Santísima Cruz de los Milagros

Plaza de la Cruz s/n • Daily 9am–noon • Free

The **Iglesia Santísima Cruz de los Milagros** is at the southern end of the Plaza de la Cruz, several blocks south of Plaza 25 de Mayo. Both the square and the church – an austere Italianate construction dating from 1897 – are named after Corrientes' first cross, brought by the Spaniards on the city's founding in 1588. The cross gained its epithet, the "Cross of Miracles", when, according to legend, it proved impervious to native attempts to destroy it with fire. A piece of the original cross is preserved as part of the altar within the church.

The Costanera

Corrientes' attractively maintained riverside avenue, the **Avenida Costanera General San Martín**, but generally just referred to as "the Costanera", runs from the small **Parque Mitre**, at the northern end of the city, as far as the Puente General Belgrano. Lined with fine examples of native trees, it's a lovely spot on summer evenings, when the heat dissipates a little and locals leave the cool refuge of their homes to pack its promenades for a jog or a stroll, or simply sit sipping *mate* or *tereré* on stone benches – but be prepared to share the experience with persistent mosquitoes. Just to the west of Parque Mitre, you'll find the port buildings and the **Mercado Paraguayo** – a standard fixture in northern Argentine cities – selling all manner of cheap imported Paraguayan goods, from shoes to stereos. Beyond here, the wide avenue sweeps southeast, with various panoramic points jutting out over the river, from where there are views to the flat Resistencia "coast".

| ARRIVAL AND INFORMATION | CORRIENTES |

By plane Corrientes' Aeropuerto Fernando Piragine Niveyro (☎03783 458340) lies 10km northeast of the city, along the RN-12. There is one daily flight to and from Buenos Aires (1hr 30min).

By bus The bus terminal (☎03783 442149) is around 4km southeast of Plaza 25 de Mayo, along one of the city's main access roads, Av Maipú. Various local buses, including the #103, run between the terminal and the centre, or a taxi will cost around $20.

Destinations Buenos Aires (6 daily; 12hr); Córdoba (1 daily; 14hr); Posadas (9 daily; 5hr); Puerto Iguazú (1 daily; 10hr); Resistencia (hourly; 30min); Rosario (5 daily; 10hr).

Tourist information Corrientes' tourist office (daily 7am–9pm) is down on the Costanera, where it meets Pellegrini, but is one of the country's least helpful and worst equipped – you'll probably find your hotel reception a more useful source of information. Look out too for the little booklets given out in hotels and stores that, alongside advertising, provide maps and what's-on guides.

ACCOMMODATION

Thanks to a decent hostel and two excellent boutique hotels there is a good choice of accommodation on offer in Corrientes. There are also some cheaper and just passable hotels around the bus terminal but – unless you are just spending a night in transit – this area is too far away from anything. The city's particularly hot and humid summers make air conditioning almost a necessity – though a shady room with a good fan can be acceptable.

HOTELS AND HOSTELS

★ **La Alondra** 3 de Abril 827 ☎03783 430555, ⓦ laalondra.com.ar. Truly original small hotel in a converted family house, with a library, reception and restaurant/bar stacked with antique travel trunks, chandeliers, globes, leather chairs and mahogany bookshelves. The rooms vary a great deal so ask to look at several if possible – they are all decorated in a similar *belle époque* style, though in a nod to modernity they also have a/c and flatscreen TVs. There's a small gym plus a plunge pool in the main patio. **$590**

Bienvenida Golondrina La Rioja 455 ☎03783 435316. The town's first hostel is the *Bienvenida*, with fairly ordinary dorm rooms: the pricier ones have a/c. The building, however, is very pleasant – a restored nineteenth-century house with original tiled floor and ceiling frescoes, and walls painted soothing lilac – and the friendly staff can help arrange river excursions. Dorms **$100**

Gran Hotel Guaraní Mendoza 970 ☎03783 433800, ⓦ hguarani.com.ar. The doyen of Corrientes' hotels, this is a business-oriented establishment in a modern glass-fronted building, with an inviting pool and bar area. There are several categories of rooms ranging from standard to VIP and two categories of suites; all have a/c and cable TV. **$350**

Gran Hotel de Turismo Entre Ríos 650 ☎03783 429112, ⓦ ghturismo.com.ar. This quaintly old-fashioned place (Graham Greene stayed here in the 1960s) is in a good location down by the Costanera. The rooms are showing their age a bit as is the very noisy a/c, but there's a great outdoor pool. Rates include breakfast. **$295**

Hospedaje San Lorenzo San Lorenzo 1136 ☎03783 421740. One of the best of the cheaper places to stay, friendly *San Lorenzo* offers basic, well-kept rooms on a quiet central street. Fans and private bathrooms. **$195**

Plaza Hotel Junín 1549 ☎03783 466500, ⓦ hotel-corrientes.com.ar. The *Plaza* overlooks the animated Plaza Cabral and is a shiny modern block blessed with a refreshing pool and bright rooms, but noisy a/c. **$420**

La Rozada Suites Placido Martínez 1223 ☎03783 433001, ⓦ larozada.com.ar. Beautifully furnished hotel, with local artworks and harmoniously blended features of the original 1890s building (a disused warehouse) giving the place character. The larger suites are duplexes with proper kitchens; the classic rooms are quite a bit smaller, but still elegant, with great views over the Paraná. **$610**

CAMPING

Camping Costa Paraíso Ruta 12 ☎03783 425046; local bus #109 from the terminal goes there every 10min or so, taking about 45min. The best campsite around, with showers, electricity and barbecue facilities, is located around 10km northeast of town at Laguna Soto. **$75**

EATING AND DRINKING

El Bistró La Alondra, 3 de Abril 827 ☎03783 430555. This hotel restaurant is popular with well-heeled locals and, unusually for Argentina (let alone Corrientes), does a Sunday brunch. Open for lunch, dinner and afternoon tea or coffee, it is elegant and beautifully decorated and the food is delicious if fairly unadventurous. There is a good wine list and the bar is well stocked. Daily noon–late.

El Café del Sol Rioja 708. One of the more traditional café-bars in the city – a great place for an espresso or a refreshing beer. Daily 8am–late.

La Costa Costanera and Pago Largo ☎03783 443846. One of the city's best *parrillas* – like many such establishments in Corrientes it specializes in grilled river fish such as *pacú* and *sirubí*, with plentiful supplies of *chipá*. Daily noon–4pm & 8pm–late.

Martha de Bianchetti Mendoza and 9 de Julio. Snacks, light meals, fruit juices, cakes and coffees are on offer at this wonderfully kitsch and extremely popular *confitería*. The walls drip with over-the-top decoration, gilded mouldings and all manner of baubles. Daily 8am–late.

CORRIENTES' FESTIVALS

Like many other cities in the region, Corrientes has an important **carnival**, held throughout January and February until Mardi Gras in the Corsódromo – a kind of open-air stadium specially constructed for the festival. A more locally authentic affair, though, is the **Festival del Chamamé**, a celebration of the region's most popular folk music with plenty of live music and dancing, held on the second weekend in December.

La Rozada Placido Martínez 1223 ☎03783 433001. This hotel has a very decent restaurant where, in addition to plentiful breakfasts, you can tuck into a perfectly grilled river fish – with a succulent salad on the side – or on (perhaps overly) elaborate pork and beef dishes. Not the most elegant dining in the city but very convenient if you're staying at the hotel. Daily noon–late.

NIGHTLIFE AND ENTERTAINMENT

A popular nightlife option in Corrientes is a **chamamé show** held at various restaurants; *chamamé* (see p.560) is perhaps Argentina's most infectious folk music, a lively danceable rhythm punctuated by a rather bloodcurdling cry, known as the *sapucay*.

Parrilla El Quincho Av Juan Pujol and Pellegrini ☎03783 446832. Open daily for lunch and dinner, this large *parrilla* is popular with locals for its food and live *chamamé* shows. Renowned for its *parrillada*, with plenty of juicy *chorizo* sausage and a wide variety of offal, it prides itself on being open until 3am. Full *parrilla* costs around $90 per person. Daily noon–4pm & 8.30pm–late.

La Peña Puente Pesoa At the intersection of the RN-12 with Av P. Ferrer (the continuation of Av 3 de Abril). This place does a very reasonable *tenedor libre parrilla* and has live chamamé shows on Fridays and Saturdays from about 10pm. Daily noon–4pm & 8pm–late.

The Gran Chaco

One of Argentina's forgotten corners and poorest regions, the **GRAN CHACO** is a land of seemingly unending alluvial plains, with areas of arid thornscrub in the dry west, and subtropical vegetation and palm savannah in the humid east. It has little in the way of dramatic scenery, no impressive historical monuments and few services for the visitor, but if you have a special interest in **wildlife** or like to get far away from the gringo trail you will find it rewarding, provided you avoid the blistering heat of summer. In the sizeable sectors not yet cleared for agriculture, it harbours an exceptional diversity of **flora and fauna** (see box, p.268), making it worth your while to break your journey for a day or two as you cross the region. Birdwatchers fare best: more than three hundred bird species have been recorded in the dry Chaco; and anglers come from all over the world in search of fish such as the *dorado*.

Wet Chaco scenery is mostly found near the **river systems** of the **Río Paraguay** and the **Río Paraná**, where the rainfall can be as high as 1200mm a year, causing heavy flooding at times. It is characterized by palm savannahs, patches of jungle and plantations of sugar cane, soya and fruit. Narrow strips border the main rivers that cross the region from west to east: the Río Pilcomayo and the Río Bermejo, which, after a fairly energetic start in the Bolivian highlands, grow weary with the heavy load of sediment they carry by the time they reach the Chaco plains. They meander tortuously, frequently change course, and sometimes lose their way entirely. In some places they dissipate into swamps called *esteros* or *bañados*, or **lagoons** that can become saline in certain areas owing to high evaporation. Rainfall diminishes the further west you travel from the Paraná and Paraguay rivers and the habitat gradually alters into dry Chaco scenery, typified by dense **thornscrub** that is used to graze zebu-crossbreed cattle, but cleared in those areas where irrigation has made it possible to cultivate crops such as cotton.

This zone was known to the conquistadors as **El Impenetrable**, less because of the thornscrub than for the lack of water, which only **indigenous groups** seemed to know how to overcome. Indeed, Formosa and Chaco provinces still have one of the most numerous and diverse indigenous populations in the country, including the Komlek, who are members of the Guaraní group and make a living from manual labour and crafts such as basket-weaving and pottery; and the Wichí, who still rely on hunter-gathering for their economic and cultural life but also sell beautifully woven *yica* bags made of a sisal-like fibre.

WILDLIFE-VIEWING IN THE CHACO

The main reason for visiting the Chaco is to see its varied and fascinating **wildlife**. Despite the vast lists of elusive, endangered mammals given in the region's tourist literature, though, only the very luckiest or most patient observers will see a **jaguar**, maned wolf, giant armadillo or *mirikiná* (nocturnal monkey). The surest bet for seeing any animals is to hire the services of one of the region's few but excellent **tour operators**; recommendations are listed in a separate box on p.271.

PARQUE NACIONAL COPO

In the northeast corner of Santiago del Estero Province, the **Parque Nacional Copo** is the best remaining chunk of prime dry Chaco left in the country and the only area of protected land in the Argentine Chaco big enough to provide a sustainable habitat for some of the region's most threatened wildlife, including the elusive **Wagner's peccary**. Giant and honey anteaters also inhabit the park, as do the threatened crowned eagle, the greater rhea and the king vulture. Frequently parched, it's a huge expanse of approximately 1140 square kilometres, with 550 square kilometres of provincial reserve attached to the west.

PARQUE NACIONAL RÍO PILCOMAYO

The edges of the woodland patches of the **Parque Nacional Río Pilcomayo**, to the north of Formosa city, can be great for glimpsing the larger mammals, including giant anteaters, honey anteaters, peccaries, deer, three types of monkey and pumas. Capybara, the two species of cayman, and even tapir live in the wetter regions of the park. Jaguars are believed to be extinct here, but the maned wolf can, very occasionally, be found – indeed, this park offers one of your best chances of seeing one. Almost three hundred species of **birds** have been recorded here, including the **bare-faced curassow** and **thrush-like wren**, both highly endangered in Argentina.

COMPLEJO ECOLÓGICO

The **Complejo Ecológico** (daily 8am–7.30pm; ☎03732 424284; $14), on the RN-95 near **Presidente Roque Sáenz Peña**, however, is really the best place for guaranteed viewing of the endangered beasts of the Chaco, including the maned wolf, jaguar, puma, tapir, honey anteater, bare-faced curassow, giant anteater and giant armadillo. This zoo fulfils an important educational role in an area where ecological consciousness is sometimes acutely lacking. Poorly funded, it nonetheless does an excellent job at rescuing, releasing or housing wounded or impounded specimens that are the victims of road traffic accidents, fires, illegal hunting and unscrupulous animal trading.

When to go

The Gran Chaco records some of the highest **temperatures** anywhere in the continent from December to February, often reaching 45°C or more. At these times, the siesta becomes even more sacred and people take to drinking chilled *tereré*. The best times to see wildlife are in the early morning or late afternoon and the best time of year to visit is from June to September: although night frosts are not unknown in June and July, daytime temperatures generally hover in the agreeable 20–25°C bracket. Moreover, the deciduous trees lose their leaves, so you've more chance of seeing wildlife. The **rainy season** generally lasts from October to May but violent downpours are possible throughout the year. For outdoor activities arm yourself with insect repellent, sunscreen and a hat, especially in summer; and make sure you have plentiful drinking-water supplies.

Chaco Province

The **easternmost strip of Chaco Province**, along the Paraná and Paraguay rivers, is the heartland of the wet Chaco. Most of the original forests and swamps have fallen victim to agricultural developments, dedicated to the production of beef cattle and crops such as fruit, soya and sugar cane. The main highway through this region is the RN-11, which connects Santa Fe with **Resistencia**, the starting point for trips along the RN-16 to **Parque Nacional Chaco** and the interior of the province.

Resistencia

RESISTENCIA is Chaco Province's sprawling administrative capital, with about half a million inhabitants, and the principal gateway to the Gran Chaco. Despite its commercial importance and lack of colonial architecture, the city is a pleasant enough place; it has a feeling of spaciousness about it and is known for the outstanding friendliness of its inhabitants. The city's self-styled nickname is "Ciudad de las Esculturas" ("City of Sculptures"), owing to over two hundred outdoor statues scattered throughout town.

Fogón de los Arrieros

Brown 350 • Daily 8am–noon & 9pm–12.30am • $12 • ☎ 03722 426418

Aldo Boglietti, the man behind the sculpture project, aimed at using art to instil civic pride, also founded (in 1943) a remarkable cultural centre called the **Fogón de los Arrieros**, the city's most famous attraction. Its name means "The Drovers' Campfire", and it's where artists traditionally came to meet, share their particular art form and then continue their journey. You can visit during the day to look round the eclectic mix of paintings (including works by Fontana and Soldi) and sculptures left behind by visiting artists, but it's more fun in the evening, when you can have a drink or empanada at the cosy bar. Best of all, try to catch one of the **events** – concerts, poetry recitals and the like – staged once or twice a week in the main salon or, weather permitting, the patio.

Museo del Hombre Chaqueño

Arturo Illia 655 • Daily 8am–noon & 5–9pm • Free

The **Museo del Hombre Chaqueño** has a clearly presented collection detailing provincial history, with information on the region's pre-Columbian cultures – before the arrival of the Spanish, the Gran Chaco was a melting pot of indigenous cultures from across the continent. The museum's highlights include models of figures from Guaraní mythology and beautiful nineteenth-century silver *mate* gourds.

Museo de Antropología

Las Heras 727 • Mon–Fri 9am–noon & 4–8pm • Free

Resistencia's most extensive archeological and ethnographical collection is housed in the **Museo de Antropología**; it displays objects recovered from the ruins of the failed sixteenth-century settlement of Concepción del Bermejo, the only serious attempt by the Spanish to colonize this area of hostile terrain and equally hostile natives.

Fundación Chaco Artesanal

Pellegrini 272 • Mon–Fri 8am–1pm & 4–8pm, Sat & Sun 9am–noon & 5–8pm • ☎ 03722 459372

The best place in the Chaco to purchase crafts made by the area's indigenous groups is the **Fundación Chaco Artesanal**, a smart, nonprofit outlet that sells items such as Wichí pottery, Komlek basketware and graceful *palo santo* crucifixes.

ARRIVAL AND INFORMATION   RESISTENCIA

By plane There are three daily flights to and from Buenos Aires (1hr 40min).

By bus The bus terminal (☎ 03722 461098) is at the junction of avenidas Malvinas Argentinas and MacLean, 4km south-west of the main square Plaza 25 de Mayo. A *remise* from here to the centre costs around $35. You can get a *remise colectivo* to Corrientes ($6) from the south side of the plaza at Alberdi.

Destinations Buenos Aires (hourly; 12hr 30min–14hr); Corrientes (hourly; 30min); Formosa (hourly; 2hr 15min); Posadas (hourly; 5hr); Puerto Iguazú (1 daily; 10hr); Santiago del Estero (3 daily; 10–11hr).

Tourist information There is a small tourist information kiosk on the Plaza 25 de Mayo (Mon–Fri 7.30am–12.30pm; ☎ 03722 458291).

ACCOMMODATION

Amerian Hotel Casino Gala J.D. Perón 330 ☎ 03722 452400, ⓦ hotelcasinogala.com.ar. Knocking spots off the competition, the *Amerian Hotel Casino Gala*, in a converted Neoclassical building, has comfortable and enormous rooms that are all effectively suites, a glorious swimming pool and an efficient spa offering massages and foot-rubs. **$515**

"EL CHACO" AND THE CAMPO DEL CIELO METEORS

An estimated five thousand years ago an asteroid shattered on impact with the earth's upper atmosphere, sending huge chips of matter plummeting earthwards, where they fell on a 15km band of the Chaco. This cataclysmic spectacle and the subsequent fires that would have been triggered must have terrified the locals. When the Spanish arrived in South America, the Komlek called the area *Pigüen Nonraltá* – or Field of the Heavens – Campo del Cielo in Spanish. They venerated the "stones from the sky", whose surface, when polished, reflected the sun. Mysterious legends reached Spanish ears, arousing an insatiable curiosity for anything that smacked of precious metal, and even sparking illusions of the fabled City of the Caesars, a variant of the El Dorado myth. In 1576, Hernán Mexía de Miraval struggled out here hoping to find gold but, instead, he found iron. The biggest expedition of all came in 1783, when the Spanish geologist and scientist Miguel Rubín de Celis led an expedition of two hundred men to find out if the **Mesón de Fierro** – a 3.5m-long curiosity and the most famous of the **meteors** – was in fact just the tip of a vast mountain of pure iron. When they dug below, they found only dusty earth. The latitude was recorded, but since there was no way of determining its coordinate of longitude, the Mesón de Fierro was subsequently lost – it's probable that the indigenous inhabitants reburied their "sunstone".

The largest of the meteorites you can see today, "**El Chaco**", has been reliably estimated to weigh 33,700kg, a strong contender for the second biggest in the world (the biggest, almost twice the size, is in Namibia). El Chaco and the Campo del Cielo (⊚ campodelcielo.com.ar) both lie in the southwestern corner of Chaco Province, 15km south of the town of Gancedo, in the Reserva Natural Pigüen N'onaxá.

4

Hotel Colón Santa María de Oro 143 ☎ 03722 422861, ⊕ hotelcolon@gigared.comi. A decent enough budget place, with pleasant albeit poorly lit rooms. **$305**

Hotel Covadonga Güemes 200 ☎ 03722 444444, ⊚ hotelcovadonga.com.ar. A well-run if rather old-fashioned place with smart rooms and comfy beds. **$445**

EATING AND DRINKING

Don Angelo Güemes 183. A café-cum-bar, with a varied choice of beers, whose sedate ambience is ideal for chatting. Daily 8am–late.

Kebon Güemes and Don Bosco ☎ 03722 442385. Resistencia has a very poor choice of restaurants, but this local favourite is definitely the best option: it has a tasteful ambience and serves well-cooked classics and tasty river fish.

Daily noon–4pm & 8.30pm–late; closed most of Jan.

Peña Nativa Martín Fierro 9 de Julio and Hernández ☎ 03722 423167. If a full *parrilla* with all the trimmings is what you are after, or maybe just a filling empanada or two, this traditional place is the right choice, plus you sometimes get live music thrown in. Daily noon–3.30pm & 8.30pm–late.

Parque Nacional Chaco

The paved **RN-16** shears straight through Chaco Province, northwest from Resistencia, clipping the northeastern corner of Santiago del Estero Province, before reaching Salta Province; it's the route taken by all trans-Chaco buses. Much of the land has been cleared to plant bananas, while *caranday* palms grow in the drier land between streams and reed- and lily-beds. Dedicated naturalists can spend a few days trying to track down the region's fauna in the **PARQUE NACIONAL CHACO** in the province's humid east. Within easy striking distance of Resistencia, the park conserves a mix of threatened wet and semi-dry Chaco habitat around the banks of the Río Negro. In quick succession, you can pass from riverine forest to open woodland, palm savannah and wetlands. Its 150 square kilometres are too restricted a space to provide a viable habitat for the largest Chaco predator, the jaguar, but plenty of mammals still inhabit the park, even if your chances of seeing them are slight. Birdlife, however, is plentiful and easy to spot.

The park has a camping area with toilets, fire pits and electricity, but there's no **food** to buy, and little in Solari, so bring supplies. A board by the park headquarters displays the trails, which are also marked on a pamphlet available from the *guardaparques*. A good introduction to the park is the well-shaded, nature-trail loop that leads from a suspension bridge behind the park headquarters (1.5km). But the most popular walk is the one to the lookouts at the ox-bow lagoons of **Laguna Carpincho** and **Laguna Yacaré** (6km), with a deviation to see an enormous *quebracho*, El Abuelo, which is an estimated five hundred years old. A longer walk (9km) is to **Laguna Panza de Cabra**, a swamp choked with lilac-bloomed *camalote* water lilies and offering excellent birdwatching opportunities.

ARRIVAL AND DEPARTURE

PARQUE NACIONAL CHACO

By bus/remise The turn-off to the park is 56km west of Resistencia along the RN-16, from where the paved RP-9 heads 40km north to Capitán Solari, 6km from the park

headquarters. There are regular buses from Resistencia to Solari, from where you can pick up a *remise* to the park.

Formosa Province

Formosa Province is dominated by its eponymous **capital city**, at its eastern end and second in importance to Resistencia in the Argentine Chaco; it's really a base for visiting the province's wildlife – but not in the height of summer. To the north are the nasty border town of Clorinda, best avoided; the internationally significant wetland site of **Parque Nacional Río Pilcomayo**, on the border with Paraguay; and the Paraguayan capital, Asunción, effectively the historical and spiritual nerve centre of the whole Gran Chaco. For those set on seeing deepest Argentina, the aptly named **El Impenetrable** poses a real challenge – the weather, bad roads and virtually nonexistent infrastructure being the main obstacles. The **Bañado La Estrella** is a remote wetland that rewards the most intrepid and determined with fine birdlife, but go on an organized tour to make it worthwhile.

4

Formosa city

The city of **FORMOSA**, the provincial capital, seems as though it has been pressed flat by the heat: few buildings rise above a single storey and many exhibit the grey mouldy stains of subtropical decay. Situated on a great loop in the Río Paraguay, it acts as a **port** for the entire province. Not a particularly attractive place, despite its name (an archaic form of *hermosa*, "beautiful"), it's given a pink facelift when the *lapacho* trees flower in September, the best time to see it. Graham Greene, in *Travels With My Aunt*, wrote that "there was a pervading smell of orange petals, but it was the only sweet thing about Formosa", for him "an ignoble little town".

The main commercial district is concentrated within a block or two either side of the **Avenida 25 de Mayo**, east of the Plaza San Martín. A block inland from here, on the corner of 25 de Mayo and Belgrano, is the pink, hacienda-style **Museo Histórico** (Mon–Fri 8am–7.30pm; free), housed in the former residence of General Ignacio Fotheringham, the Southampton-born first governor of what was then Formosa Territory. It is an eclectic and poorly organized collection, and exhibits include a stuffed Swiss bear and Komlek artefacts, plus information on early exploration of the region.

TOURS IN THE GRAN CHACO

The logistics of **visiting the parks and reserves** in the Gran Chaco region, and Formosa Province in particular, are complicated to say the least. Argentina's hottest climate, poorest roads and most inaccessible terrain are likely to frustrate even the most adventurous of travellers. Signposts are erratic and wildlife lurks where you least expect it. You will certainly need a helping hand if you are to get the most out of the Chaco and you will be best off going on an **organized tour** with a reputable company. **Aventura Formosa**, Paraguay 520, Formosa (☎03717 433713, ✉fiznardo@hotmail.com), has extremely reliable tours run by an experienced local guide with a tremendous in-depth knowledge of the region, its geography, wildlife and culture. **El Jabiru** (☎03715 432435, ✉eljabiru.com.ar) does birdwatching trips into the Bañado de la Estrella and other trips in Formosa, including to the Parque Nacional Río Pilcomayo; English spoken.

ARRIVAL AND INFORMATION

By plane There is one daily flight to and from Buenos Aires (1hr 50min).

By bus Arriving in Formosa from the southwest, you'll be welcomed by La Cruz del Norte, a white Meccano-style cross that's a common reference point. The bus terminal is to the east of here on Av Gutnisky, a multilane thoroughfare that changes its name to Av 25 de Mayo before it reaches the Plaza San Martín, the start of the town centre and nearly 2km from the terminal.

Destinations Buenos Aires (7 daily; 14hr); Corrientes (10 daily; 3hr); Jujuy (1 daily; 14hr); Posadas (1 daily; 6hr); Puerto Iguazú (1 daily; 10hr); Resistencia (15 daily; 2hr); Salta (1 daily; 14hr); Santa Fe (5 daily; 10hr).

Tourist information There's a small tourist office on Plaza San Martín, at Uriburu 820 (Mon–Fri 8am–noon & 4–8pm; ☎ 03717 425192), which can help with accommodation in the province, including a handful of tourism estancias.

ACCOMMODATION AND EATING

Asterión Acceso Sur s/n ☎ 03717 452999, ⓦ asterion hotel.com.ar. The best place to stay in Formosa is the *Asterión* on the RN-11 just before you reach the Cruz del Norte roundabout when arriving from Resistencia; the hotel's name comes from a Borges short story about the Minotaur, and you will find a small collection of Borges memorabilia on display in the lobby. As for the rooms, they are bright, spacious and appealingly decorated, with an ethnic touch, and all the facilities are impeccable, from the safe garage to the shady swimming pool. **$525**

Casa Grande González Lelong 185 ☎ 03717 431612, ⓦ casagrandeapart.com.ar. An attractive little complex whose well-equipped rooms have kitchenettes. Its facilities include a pool and garden, massages and a gym, plus one of the best restaurants for miles, *Mirita*, which specializes in delicious fish dishes and has a very decent wine list. **$450**

SHOPPING

Casa de la Artesanía San Martín and 25 de Mayo. The Casa de la Artesanía, a nonprofit organization, is the best outlet for the province's indigenous crafts. It stocks a good selection of Wichí *yica* bags, Pilagá woollen carpets, tightly woven Komlek basketwork, plus *palo santo* carvings and *algarrobo* seed jewellery. Mon–Sat 8am–noon & 4–8pm.

Parque Nacional Río Pilcomayo

The national park administration office (Mon–Fri 7am–4pm; ☎ 03718 470045), for information and permits, is on the RN-86 at the entrance to the village

The 519-square-kilometre **PARQUE NACIONAL RÍO PILCOMAYO** was created in the 1950s to protect some of the best remaining subtropical wet Chaco habitat. Extensive areas are subject to spring and summer flooding, whereas in the winter months it is prone to droughts. The park is protected under the international Ramsar Convention – designed to protect the planet's key wetland ecosystems – and its biological diversity was safeguarded by a concerted and largely successful campaign in the 1990s to get rid of most of the semi-wild cattle left by former settlers. In addition to swampy wetlands, it conserves some remnant gallery forest along the Río Pilcomayo, and large swathes of savannah studded with copses of mixed woodland.

The best times to **visit the park** are sunset and dawn, when it's cooler and you stand a better chance of seeing the wildlife. The park has **two entrances** – to the Estero Poí and the more compact Laguna Blanca sectors – both within striking distance of **Laguna Blanca**, a village 52km west of Clorinda.

The turn-off to **Estero Poí** lies 2km from Laguna Blanca village in the direction of Clorinda, from where 9km of dirt road leads to the *guardaparques'* house. An interpretation trail runs from a bush campsite through the adjacent scrub, and within easy walking distance is a pair of swamps, dominated by the attractive *pehuajó* reed with its banana-palm leaves, along with bulrushes, horsetails and the mauve-flowered water lilies. Further into the park lie swathes of savannah grassland and the gallery forest of the Río Pilcomayo – good for spotting wildlife.

Laguna Blanca sector

At Naick Neck, 12km east of Laguna Blanca village, a dirt track (5km) leads to the **Laguna Blanca Sector**. Next to the *guardaparques'* dwelling is a pleasant free **campsite**, shaded by *algarrobos* and palms, with drinking water and showers; bring all your own food supplies. From behind the toilet block, there's a 300m **nature trail** where you have a good chance of seeing howler monkeys, while an excellent boardwalk from the campsite takes you 500m through reedbed marshland to lookout points and a 10m **tower** on the shore of the shallow lagoon itself. If you swim here, wear shoes so the piranhas don't snack on your toes. There are excellent opportunities for **birdwatching**, especially at dawn.

El Impenetrable

The straight RN-81 runs northwest of Formosa through an area so difficult to enter it has been dubbed **El Impenetrable**. For those with a specialist interest in wildlife – especially birdlife – the route gives access to the **Bañado La Estrella**, a fascinating wetland near Las Lomitas, 300km from Formosa. Otherwise, avoid it: if you want to cross the Chaco region, take the much faster RN-16 from Resistencia.

Bañado La Estrella

As you head west, the scenery becomes drier, with some virulently green wetland. The land is mainly used for grazing cattle and goats, but charcoal is also produced – witness the roadside ovens. About 45km north of the village of Las Lomitas, via unsealed RP-28, is the **Bañado La Estrella**, a huge swathe of swamp in the central northern part of the province, fed by the waters of the Río Pilcomayo, a river that dissipates into numerous meandering channels.

The RP-28 crosses the Bañado by means of a long causeway (*pedraplén*), usually just beneath the water line. The scenery looks like a Dalí painting: tree skeletons (*champales*) swaddled in vines, as if the floodwaters had once completely submerged them and then receded, leaving them snagged with weed; beneath their branches shines the mirror-smooth blue water, dotted with rafts of lilac-flowered *camalote* water lilies. You might even get to see members of the **Pilagá community**, an indigenous people that number about five thousand, fishing for *sábalo* with spears; note they are generally reluctant to be photographed, especially without permission.

ARRIVAL AND DEPARTURE   EL IMPENETRABLE

By bus Buses pass regularly in both directions (north to Tartagal and Pocitos; south to Embarcación, Jujuy and Salta) and can be flagged down.

By car Driving times on unsealed roads in this area of the world are dependent on rainfall. Many vehicles can't negotiate the mud, and the ones that do often take far longer than they would in good conditions (if in doubt, call the Vialidad Provincial in Formosa; ☏ 03717 426040).

The Northwest

THE QUEBRADA DE HUMAHUACA

5

The Northwest

Argentina's Northwest (El Noroeste Argentino – often referred to as NOA or simply "El Norte") is infinitely varied: ochre deserts where llamas roam, charcoal-grey lava flows devoid of any life form, blindingly white salt flats and sooty-black volcanic cones, pristine limewashed colonial chapels set against striped mountainsides, lush citrus groves and emerald-green sugar plantations, impenetrable jungles populated by peccaries and parakeets. The Northwest is also the birthplace of Argentina – a Spanish colony thrived here when Buenos Aires was still an unsteady trading post on the Atlantic coast. One of the colonial cities, Salta, is indisputably the region's tourism capital, with some of the country's best hotels, finest architecture and a well-earned reputation for hospitality. From here, you can meander in a northwesterly direction up the enchanting Quebrada del Toro on a safari or on the Tren a las Nubes (Train to the Clouds), one of the world's highest railways. Heading due northeast across the subtropical lowlands will lead you to jungle-clad cloudforests, or *yungas*, poking out of fertile plains into the raincloud that gives them their name: a birdwatcher's paradise. Or you could head south, via the surreal canyon of the Quebrada de Cafayate, to visit some of the world's highest vineyards.

To Salta's northwest huddles boot-shaped Jujuy Province, one of the federation's poorest and remotest, shoved up into the corner of the country against Chile and Bolivia, where in the space of a few kilometres humid valleys and soothingly green jungles give way to the austere, parched altiplano (or *puna*), home to flocks of flamingoes, herds of llamas and very few people. **San Salvador de Jujuy**, the slightly oddball provincial capital, cannot rival Salta for its amenities or architectural splendours, but it's the best starting-point for exploring the many-hued **Quebrada de Humahuaca**.

Whereas Salta and Jujuy have a well-established international tourist industry, the provinces to the south remain far less known. Domestically the provinces of Tucumán and Catamarca are dismissed as poor, dull backwaters, but the city of **San Miguel de Tucumán** has an addictively lively atmosphere and the province does contain some real treasures, including impressive pre-Inca ruins at **Quilmes**, a marvellous museum dedicated to Pachamama, or Earth Mother, at **Amaicha**, and dramatic trekking around **Tafí del Valle**.

Highlights

❶ Incan mummies Controversially displayed in high-tech fridges, three impeccably preserved Incan children, discovered up a lofty volcano, can be seen in the Northwest's best museum, MAAM. **See p.282**

❷ Train to the Clouds This magical train ride takes you up a magnificent gorge to cloud nine, via countless tunnels, bridges and loops, hauling you higher and higher to an iconic viaduct in the altiplano. **See p.292**

❸ Tilcara You'll find charming hotels, an abundance of arts and crafts, a massive colonial church and even a pre-Incan fortress in this village, the best base for visiting the Quebrada de Humahuaca. **See p.300**

❹ Cuesta del Obispo Spiral up (or down) a mind-boggling mountain road, zigzagging between the sultry plains of the Valle de Lerma and the rarefied air of Cachi and the Valles Calchaquíes. **See p.310**

❺ Vineyards of Cafayate Try fruity cabernet sauvignons, earthy malbecs and heady torrontés at the world's highest wineries. **See p.314**

❻ Antofagasta de la Sierra Miles from anywhere, this high-altitude village huddles among out-of-this world volcanic landscapes. **See p.327**

HIGHLIGHTS ARE MARKED ON THE MAP ON P.278

Equally impressive are the eternally snowy peaks that give their name to the Nevados del Aconquija, the natural border with neighbouring Catamarca Province, where a plethora of picturesque villages, each more isolated than the previous, reward patient visitors with rural hospitality, wondrous natural settings and some fabulous handmade crafts: **Belén** and **Londres** stand out. Try and make it all the way to **Antofagasta de la Sierra**, an amazingly out-of-the-way market town set among rock and lava formations and reached via some of the emptiest roads in the country.

If you can, time your visit for the Argentine spring or autumn. Summers can be steamy in the valleys, making large cities like Tucumán unbearable, while heavy summer rains around Salta can wipe out roads and make exploring the area difficult. On the other hand, in July and August night-time **temperatures** at altitude are bitterly low, so your first purchase will probably be an alpaca-wool poncho.

GETTING AROUND   **THE NORTHWEST**

Salta and Jujuy are both well linked by **public transport**, as are the stops along the Quebrada de Humahuaca as far as Humahuaca town. Beyond this, transport is more sparse and you will have to plan in advance, or else rent a car or use tour agencies. Bear in mind that the nature of the roads – hairpin bends along steep climbs – means that buses that do run can take a long time to travel relatively short distances.

Salta and around

SALTA, historic capital of one of Argentina's biggest and most beautiful provinces, easily lives up to its well-publicized nickname of *Salta la Linda* (Salta the Fair), thanks to its festive atmosphere, handsome buildings and dramatic setting. In a region where the landscape and nature, rather than the towns and cities, are the main attractions, Salta is the exception. Fifteen hundred kilometres northwest of Buenos Aires, at the eastern end of the fertile Valle de Lerma, nationally famous for its tobacco plantations, and bounded by the Río Vaqueros to the north and Río Arenales to the south, the city is squeezed between steep, rippling mountains; at 1190m above sea level, it enjoys a relatively balmy climate. In recent years, Salta has become the Northwest's undisputed tourist capital, and its top-quality services include a slew of highly professional tour operators, some of the region's best-appointed hotels and liveliest youth hostels and a handful of very good restaurants. In addition to a cable car and a tourist railway, its sights include the marvellous Neoclassical **Iglesia San Francisco**, and a raft of excellent **museums** dedicated to subjects as varied as pre-Columbian culture, anthropology, local history and modern art. A generous sprinkling of well-preserved or well-restored **colonial architecture** has survived, giving the place a pleasant homogeneity and certain charm.

San Lorenzo, a self-contained suburb of Salta only fifteen minutes west, enjoys a slightly cooler mountain climate and is awash with lush vegetation, making it alluring for both visitors and locals who want to escape from the big city, especially in the summer.

Brief history

Governor Hernando de Lerma of Tucumán, who gave his name to the nearby valley, founded the city of Salta on April 16, 1582, following the instructions of Viceroy Toledo, to guarantee the safety of anyone entering or leaving Tucumán itself. The site was chosen for its strategic mountainside location, and the streams flowing nearby were used as natural moats. In 1776, the already flourishing city was made capital of a huge administrative region that took in Santiago del Estero, Jujuy and even the southern reaches of modern Bolivia, becoming one of the major centres in the viceroyalty. During the war of independence General Güemes posted his anti-royalist forces in the town, creating the now traditional red-and-black-poncho uniform for his

5

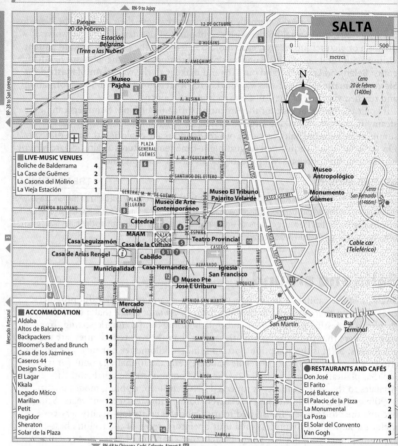

▲ RN-9 to Jujuy

SALTA

LIVE-MUSIC VENUES
Boliche de Balderrama	4
La Casa de Güemes	2
La Casona del Molino	3
La Vieja Estación	1

ACCOMMODATION
Aldaba	2
Altos de Balcarce	4
Backpackers	14
Bloomer's Bed and Brunch	9
Casa de los Jazmines	15
Caseros 44	10
Design Suites	8
El Lagar	3
Kkala	1
Legado Mítico	5
Marilian	12
Petit	13
Regidor	11
Sheraton	7
Solar de la Plaza	6

RESTAURANTS AND CAFÉS
Don José	8
El Farito	6
José Balcarce	1
El Palacio de la Pizza	7
La Monumental	2
La Posta	4
El Solar del Convento	5
Van Gogh	3

▼ RN-68 to Chicoana, Cachi, Cafayate, Airport & 15

gaucho militia. However, once Buenos Aires became the capital of the young country, Salta went into steady decline, missing out on the rest of the country's mass immigration of the mid- and late nineteenth century; the railway didn't arrive here until 1890. A belated urban explosion in the 1920s and 1930s has left its mark on the predominantly Neocolonial style of architecture in the city. Since the turn of the millennium, Salta has joined the ranks of Argentina's fastest growing and most dynamic metropolises, and its increased wealth can be seen in the sophistication of its inhabitants and the services they share with visitors.

Plaza 9 de Julio

Salta's central square, **Plaza 9 de Julio**, is one of the country's most harmonious, especially since it was spruced up in the early years of the new millennium. Surrounded on all four sides by graceful, shady *recovas*, or arcades, under which several café terraces lend themselves to idle people-watching, it's a great place to while away an hour or two. The well-manicured central part of the square is a collection of palms and tipas, fountains and benches, plus a quaint, late nineteenth-century bandstand. Around it stand the city's Neoclassical **cathedral**, the snow-white **Cabildo**, a number of popular cafés and two of the city's best **museums**.

The cathedral

España 537 • Mon–Fri 6.30am–12.30pm & 4.30–8.30pm, Sun 7.30am–1pm & 5–9.30pm • Free

Towering over the northern side of the Plaza 9 de Julio and mirrored in the innocuous plate-glass building next door, the brightly painted **cathedral** dates from 1882, the city's third centenary year. It's an Italianate Neoclassical pile of the kind found all over the region, with some well-executed interior frescoes – the one of the Four Apostles around the cupola is particularly fine. Inside, and immediately to the left of the entrance, is the grandiose Panteón de los Heroes del Norte, where local liberator General Güemes is buried. The Capilla del Señor del Milagro and Capilla de la Virgen del Milagro, at the far end of the left and right aisles respectively, house the sacred images that are the centrepieces of major celebrations every September (see box below).

Museo de Arte Contemporáneo (MAC)

Zuviría 90 • Tues–Sat 9am–8pm, Sun 4–8pm • $2 • Ⓦ macsaltamuseo.org

Housed on the first floor of a handsomely renovated Neocolonial building on the northeast corner of Plaza 9 de Julio, the outstanding **Museo de Arte Contemporáneo (MAC)** – all sleek white walls and dark parquet – puts on exhibitions of mainly local artists, from up-and-coming wannabes straight out of art school to more established local names, who are often given shows of their own. Painting dominates but sculpture, video and photography are also often on display.

Teatro Provincial

Zuviría 70 • Mon–Fri 9am–1.30pm & 4.30–9pm • ☎ 0387 422 4515, Ⓦ teatroprovincial.gob.ar

Salta's world-class **Teatro Provincial** is a beautifully renovated masterpiece with a plush interior, next to the MAC. Home to one of Argentina's best-regarded classical orchestras, the Sinfónica de Salta, which attracts leading musicians from around the globe, the theatre also hosts plays, dance and folklore concerts.

EARTHQUAKES AND THE FIESTA DEL MILAGRO

No earthquake as destructive as those that flattened the cities of Mendoza in 1861 and San Juan in 1944 has struck the Northwest region of Argentina within recent history, but this part of the country lies along the same fault line that was responsible for that seismic activity and is prone to occasional tremors, some of them violent. The **Nazca plate**, beneath the eastern Pacific, and the **South American plate**, comprising the whole continent, are constantly colliding – a continuation of the tectonic activity that formed the Andean cordillera. To make matters worse, the Nazca plate is subducting – nudging its way beneath the landmass – an action that accounts for the abundance of **volcanoes** along the range; some of them are extinct, others lie dormant, but none in the Northwest is very active. Nonetheless, frequent **earthquakes** of varying strength (but mostly mild for geological reasons) rock Northwest Argentina, accounting for the repeated displacement of many settlements and the absence of colonial architecture in some.

Salta still thanks its lucky stars for **El Milagro**, the legend according to which two sacred images have spared the city the kind of destruction caused by seismic disasters. An image of **Christ** and another of the **Virgin Mary** were found floating in a box off the coast of Perú in 1592, exactly a century after the Americas were discovered by Columbus, and somehow ended up in Salta. Precisely one century later, on September 13, 1692, a series of tremors began to shake the city, damaging some public buildings and houses. During that night, a priest named José Carrión dreamed that if the images of Christ and Mary were paraded through the streets for nine days the earthquakes would stop and Salta would be spared forever. Apparently it worked and, ever since, the **Fiesta del Milagro** has been a major event in the city's calendar. Festivities and religious ceremonies starting on September 6 reach a climax on September 15, when the now-famous images, which are kept in the cathedral, are paraded through the city's streets in a massive, solemn but colourful procession.

5

Museo El Tribuno Pajarito Velarde

Pueyrredón 106 and España • Mon–Fri 10.30am–2pm & 3.30–6pm • $10

Two blocks east of the MAC, the curious **Museo El Tribuno Pajarito Velarde** was the home of a colourful local personality, Guillermo Velarde Mors (born 1895), who died in his magnificent wooden bed here in 1965. Nicknamed "Pajarito" ("little bird"), this controversial bohemian was born into a wealthy, influential family, then worked in turn as a lawyer, journalist and banker, but retired from his last job, at the Banco Provincial de Salta, at the age of 37 to create a kind of arts club. While promoting artists, writers and musicians, especially local folk singers and groups, at a time when they lacked social kudos, he also went out of his way to cause scandals – he particularly liked provoking the nuns who ran the girls' school opposite his house. Respected as a great patron of the arts, he was also marginalized by local society, owing to his outlandish lifestyle – he never married, had lots of affairs and his music sessions often degenerated into drunken orgies. Crammed full of his fascinating belongings – including a hat donated by an admiring Carlos Gardel (two tangos were composed in Pajarito's honour) – this humble adobe house is a fitting tribute to both an original local character and the history of Salta's socio-cultural life in the twentieth century. The mischievous curator, Carol, delights in shocking visitors with some of Pajarito's prize trinkets, several of which are in dubious taste, but unfortunately her lively explanations are in Spanish only.

Museo de Arqueología de Alta Montaña (MAAM)

Mitre 77 • Tues–Sun 11am–7.30pm • $40 • ⓦ maam.gob.ar

In an attractive Neo-Gothic building on the western side of the plaza, the **Museo de Arqueología de Alta Montaña (MAAM)** is the one museum in Salta that you should not miss. It was specially created to present to the public the discovery of the so-called **Llullaillaco Children**, one of the most important archeological finds ever made in Argentina. In 1999, three naturally mummified Inca children were uncovered by an expedition of mountaineers and scientists on top of **Volcán Llullaillaco**, due west of Salta on the Chilean border and 6740m above sea level. They are a 6-year-old girl, visibly struck by lightning some time after her burial, her hair arranged in two small braids and with a metal plaque as an adornment (which attracted the lightning); a teenage girl whose face was painted with a red pigment and who had small fragments of coca leaves above her upper lip; and a 7-year-old boy wearing a white feather ornament tied around his head. Their incredibly well-preserved corpses – all three lived around 1490 AD – were at first kept in a university laboratory in the city while tests on their tissue and other remains were completed. They are now shown, one at a time, in specially refrigerated cases and the effect is startling.

The jury is still out as to whether it is sacrilegious to display the bodies in a public museum: the decision to do so provoked a furore, including demonstrations by representatives of local indigenous groups, so bear in mind that this is a sensitive issue. Certainly the fainthearted will want to skip the room where they are shown, as expressions of fear are clearly shown on their young faces – the children were sacrificed to the Inca deities, possibly in a fertility ceremony or as an offering to the gods of the sun and moon. They were probably knocked out with a blunt weapon (so their bodies were not rendered imperfect by wounds) and then left to die of the lack of oxygen and the extreme cold.

Over a hundred **artefacts**, part of the remarkably intact treasure-trove buried with the children at the end of the fifteenth century, are on display in the museum's other rooms, where the temperature and humidity are kept artificially low – bring something warm to wear. The exhibit is both scientific and didactic, including a video about the expedition, displays of textiles and the like, but it is no musty old-fashioned museum. The ground-floor bookshop is prime hunting ground for souvenirs, mostly of very high quality, while the marvellous **cafeteria**, offering local specialities, is open daily from 8am to midnight.

Cabildo (Museo Histórico del Norte)

Caseros 549 • Tues–Fri 9am–7pm, Sat & Sun 9am–1.30pm & 3–7pm • $10, free before 10am Wed • Ⓦ museonor.gov.ar

Opposite the cathedral, on the southern side of the plaza, stands the white-facaded **Cabildo**. Originally built in the early seventeenth century, it took on its current appearance in the late eighteenth, when the city became capital of the *intendencia* (administrative region). It underwent a facelift that left its slightly lopsided structure – the two rows of graceful arches don't quite tally – essentially intact in the middle of the twentieth century, over a hundred years after it ceased to be the colonial headquarters. It now houses the highly eclectic **Museo Histórico del Norte**, whose collections range from coins and eighteenth-century paintings to wooden saints and archeological finds to wonderful horse-drawn carriages parked in the cobbled courtyards, among them an elegant nineteenth-century hearse. Of the religious art in the first two rooms, the moving *San Pedro de Alcántara*, by eighteenth-century Altoperuvian artist Melchor Pérez de Holguín, stands out. Excellent temporary exhibitions, usually of regional art, are staged in the beautifully restored building, but the superb views across the plaza from the upper-storey veranda alone make a visit worthwhile.

Casa de Arías Rengel and around

La Florida 20 • Mon–Fri 9am–7.30pm, Sat 10am–6pm • $5

More colonial and Neocolonial buildings are clustered in the few blocks to the west of Plaza 9 de Julio, including, just 100m west of the Cabildo, the **Casa de Arias Rengel**. The pedestrianized street allows you an unrestricted view of its brilliant white facade, with an elaborate arched doorway and handsome green door. Erected towards the end of the eighteenth century, and virtually intact, albeit well restored, it's the finest viceregal building left in the city. The home of Sergeant-Major Félix Arias Rengel, who conquered the Argentine Chaco and had the house built, it has splendid patios, full of lush trees and plants, while the fine interior details include verandas, banisters and rafters of red *quebracho* timber. Inside there are temporary exhibitions of local arts, as well as a permanent display of African tribal pieces and African-inspired art.

Casa Leguizamón and the Municipalidad

Next door to the Casa Rengel, the **Casa Leguizamón** at Caseros and La Florida (undergoing refurbishment at the time of writing) was constructed at the beginning of the nineteenth century for a rich merchant. It's painted a deep raspberry pink, and its plain two storeys are set off by fine detailing, a delicate wrought-iron balcony and zinc gargoyles. A few steps south is the **Municipalidad**, whose unusual twelve-columned oval patio is worth investigating.

Casa Hernández (Museo de la Ciudad)

La Florida 97 • Mon–Sat 9am–1pm & 4–8.30pm • Free • Ⓦ museociudadsalta.gov.ar

Opposite Casa Rengel, the **Casa Hernández** is a typical Neocolonial corner house with a chamfered angle. Built around 1870, with a delightful patio at its heart, it now houses the **Museo de la Ciudad**, a rather motley collection of local donations of artefacts and documents tracing the city's history.

Museo Pte. José E. Uriburu

Caseros 417 • Tues–Fri 9am–7pm, Sat & Sun 9am–1.30pm & 3–7pm • $10

Calle Caseros, a busy thoroughfare leading east from the southern side of Plaza 9 de Julio, takes you past a number of striking Neocolonial buildings and a fine, late eighteenth-century house built to a simple design and with one of the most charming patios in the city: the Casa Uriburu, housing the **Museo Pte. José E Uriburu**, a museum of period furniture and Uriburu memorabilia. It was once home to the influential Uriburu family,

5

who produced two presidents of Argentina. The most impressive room is undoubtedly the reconstructed kitchen, with its polished copper and earthenware pots.

Iglesia San Francisco

Casero and Córdoba • Daily 8am–noon & 5–9pm • Free

One of the most beautiful religious buildings in the country, the **Iglesia y Convento San Francisco** takes up a whole block at the corner of Caseros and Córdoba. Built between 1750 and 1850 by architect **Luigi Giorgi**, it's an extravaganza of Italianate Neocolonial exuberance, displaying a textbook compliance with architectural principles combined with clever idiosyncrasies. The first thing that strikes you is the colour: pure ivory-white columns stand out from the vibrant ox-blood walls, while the profuse detailing of Latin inscriptions, symbols and Neoclassical patterns is picked out in braid-like golden yellow.

The church's most imposing feature is its slender **campanile**, towering over the low-rise Neocolonial houses of downtown Salta and tapering off to a slender spire. The highly elaborate **facade** of the church itself, behind a suitably austere statue of St Francis in the middle of the courtyard, is lavishly decorated with balusters and scrolls, curlicues and pinnacles, Franciscan inscriptions and the order's shield, but the most original features are the organza-like **stucco curtains** that billow down from each of the three archways, nearly touching the elegant wrought-iron gates below. Inside, the decoration is subdued, almost plain in comparison, but the most eye-catching elements are the three eighteenth-century Portuguese-style jacaranda-wood **armchairs** behind the altar. The **cloisters** of the convent sometimes shelter exhibitions and sales of local arts and crafts. If you can, do go on a **guided tour** (Spanish only; Mon, Wed & Fri 9.30am, 10.30am, 11.30am, 5pm & 6pm), which will also get you into the fascinating **Museo del Convento** (☎0387 431 0830 for opening times) – where the surprising archeological section features a perfect terracotta Etruscan head dating from the fourth century BC.

Paseo Güemes and around

Tree-lined **Paseo Güemes**, which begins three blocks north of the Iglesia San Francisco and five east, is the main thoroughfare of a leafy, well-to-do barrio crammed with later Neocolonial houses, and climbs up towards a bombastic **monument** of General Güemes, Salta's local hero. Surrounded by a grove of eucalyptus, the bronze equestrian statue, dating from 1931, is decorated with bas-reliefs depicting the army that defended newly independent Argentina from several last-ditch invasions by the Spanish.

Museo Antropológico Juan Martín Leguizamón

Ejército del Norte and Ricardo Sola • Mon–Fri 8am–7pm, Sat 10am–6pm • $5

Immediately behind the Güemes monument, where the streets begin to slope up the lower flanks of the mountain, you'll find an anthropological museum, the **Museo Antropológico Juan Martín Leguizamón**. The varied collection could be better presented, and many of the explanations in Spanish are sketchy, but some of the items on display are worth seeing. The centrepiece of the extensive ceramics collection is a set of finds from Tastil (see p.292), along with a petroglyph known as the **Bailarina de Tastil**, a delightful figure carved onto rock, removed from the *pukará*, or pre-Columbian fortress, to the safety of a glass case. A well-executed reconstruction of a pre-Columbian burial shows how the local climate preserved textiles and wood in perfect condition for centuries, and a row of decorative urns is a highlight of the museum.

Cerro San Bernardo

Cable car: Daily 10am–7.30pm • $35 return, $15 for children

Immediately behind the Museo Antropológico Juan Martín Leguizamón, a steep path zigzags up the overgrown flanks of **Cerro San Bernardo** (1458m), but you might prefer to take the **teleférico**, or cable car, from the base station on Avenida Hipólito Yrigoyen, between Urquiza and Avenida San Martín, at the eastern end of Parque San Martín. The smooth cable-car gondolas take you to the summit in less than ten minutes, and from them and the small garden at the top you can admire panoramic **views** of the city and the snowcapped mountain range to the west. A **café** with a terrace serves drinks and simple meals, and there is also a well-equipped children's play area ($3).

Museo de Bellas Artes

Av Belgrano 992 • Mon–Fri 9am–7pm, Sat 11am–7pm • $5

The **Museo de Bellas Artes** was inaugurated in December 2008 in the landmark Casona Usandivaras, an Art Nouveau mansion standing majestically at the corner of avenidas Sarmiento and Belgrano, just west of downtown. Its eleven beautifully restored rooms house a rich patrimony of local, national and international art, ranging from paintings from Cusco to twentieth-century sculpture. Highlights are a *St Matthew* of the **Cusqueña School** (see p.90); the eighteenth-century polychrome *Asunción de la Virgen* from the Jesuit missions; the large *The City of Salta*, painted in 1854 by Giorgio Penutti; and some fine engravings by nineteenth-century artists Basaldúa, Spilimbergo and Quinquela Martín.

Calle Balcarce and around

The liveliest and trendiest part of the city is the area around **Calle Balcarce**, especially the pedestrianized blocks north of Avenida Entre Ríos, near the Estación Belgrano, known as Paseo Belgrano. Arts and crafts are on sale in the evenings and on weekends, and this is also where you'll find the largest number of restaurants, bars, discos and folk-music venues.

Museo de Arte Étnico Americano Pajcha

20 de Febrero 831 • Mon–Sat 10am–1pm & 4–8pm • $20 • ⊛ museopajchasalta.com.ar

Proof that the Balcarce district is not all about eating and drinking, the **Museo de Arte Étnico Americano Pajcha** is a strong contender for the best museum of American ethnic art in the country. The result of the lifelong work of Liliana Madrid de Zito Fontán, a local ethnologist, this magnificent collection is arranged thematically and geographically in seven rooms, each with its own music. Native Argentine art and handicrafts loom large, but there are many outstanding items from all over South America, along with some beautiful photographs. Painting, textiles, religious objects (Christian and pre-Columbian) and wooden articles represent all the main ethnic groups; the silver jewellery crafted by the Mapuche of Chile and Andean ceramics are undoubtedly the highlights. There is also a fine example of a *pajcha*, an Inca offering tray with several compartments, looking not unlike an ancient muffin-mould. A selection of contemporary crafts is on sale at the reception, and there's also an excellent café on site.

| ARRIVAL AND GETTING AROUND | SALTA |

BY PLANE

Salta's Martín Miguel de Güemes International Airport (☏0387 424 2904) is in El Aybal, about 10km southwest of the city centre, along the motorway-like RN-51. Buses #8A and #6 run between the airport and central Av San Martín; a taxi will set you back about $45.

Airlines Aerolíneas Argentinas, Caseros 475 ☏0387 431 1331; AeroSur, España 414 ☏0387 432 0043; Andes, España 478 ☏0810 1222 6337; LAN, Caseros 476 ☏0810 999 9526.

Destinations Buenos Aires (6 daily; 2hr); Jujuy (1 daily; 20min).

BY BUS

Buses from all across the region and throughout the country use the modernized bus terminal at Av Hipólito Yrigoyen (☏0387 401 1143), just east of the Parque San Martín, five blocks south and eight east of central Plaza 9 de Julio.

5

Destinations Buenos Aires (hourly; 18hr); Cachi (2 daily; 5hr); Cafayate (7 daily; 3hr 30min); Córdoba (10 daily; 12hr); Jujuy (hourly; 1hr 30min); Resistencia (1 daily; 13hr); Tucumán (10 daily; 4hr).

BY TRAIN

Bus #5 links the bus terminal with the train station, at Ameghino 690, via Plaza 9 de Julio, though the only passenger train serving Salta these days is the privately run tourist train, Tren a las Nubes (see box, p.292).

BY TAXI

Taxis (with red-and-black livery) are plentiful and fairly inexpensive; try Remises Sol (☎0387 431 7317), or Balcarce (☎0387 421 3535).

INFORMATION

Provincial tourist office Buenos Aires 93 (Mon–Fri 8am–9pm, Sat & Sun 9am–8pm; ☎0387 431 0950, ⓦturismosalta.gov.ar). Dispenses maps and accommodation information; some staff members speak English. There is also a small branch at the base of the cable car.

ON FOOT

Getting around on foot is not difficult and it's hard to get lost, since the grid system is almost perfect in the microcentro; north–south streets change name at Calle Caseros; east–west streets on either side of avenidas Virrey Toledo and Hipólito Yrigoyen.

BY CAR

Heavy traffic and the related noise and exhaust pollution are a growing problem in Salta. There's little point in renting a car to see the city but if you're planning on touring the region, Salta is a good place to begin.
Car rental Marina Turismo, Caseros 489 ☎0387 431 2097, ⓦmarina-semisa.com.ar.

City tourist office Caseros 711 (daily 8am–9pm; ☎0387 421 6285). Attractively located in a converted Neoclassical building, the city tourist office has a few leaflets and a good city map.

TOURS FROM SALTA

A number of outfits offering a wide variety of highly professional **tours**, **expeditions** and other **activities** in the Northwest region are based in and around Salta city. The following is a selection of the best.

★ **Clark Expediciones** Mariano Moreno 1950, San Lorenzo ☎0387 497 1024, ⓦclarkexpediciones.com. Supremely experienced and professional team that specializes in birdwatching trips in Northwest Argentina, to Calilegua and El Rey national parks, to the Laguna de los Pozuelos and further afield (Chile, Bolivia, Paraguay and Brazil, plus other parts of Argentina). Based at the *Hostería Selva Montana*, San Lorenzo.

Marina Turismo Caseros 489 ☎0387 431 2097, ⓦmarina-semisa.com.ar. One of the most professional outfits in the region, Marina's friendly and dynamic team will bend over backwards to get you a vehicle (and driver-guide, should you need one), find a guided excursion, book your hotel, change your flight or even just give you useful tips about where to eat, sleep or drink. English spoken.

MoviTrack Buenos Aires 28 ☎0387 431 6749, ⓦmovitrack.com.ar. Offers the "Safari a los Nubes", a fun and adventurous way of discovering the Quebrada del Toro; there's an optional extension via the Quebrada de Humahuaca, in a special vehicle giving all passengers panoramic views. It also does trips to Cachi and Cafayate.

Norte Trekking Gral Güemes 265 oficina 1 ☎0387 431 6616, ⓦnortetrekking.com. Federico Norte and his experienced team are a fount of knowledge on the local area and can take you on a safari into the *puna*, to the Valles Calchaquíes, to the Parque El Rey and elsewhere; they also run longer tours into Chile and Bolivia.

★ **Salta Rafting** Caseros 177 ☎0387 421 3216, ⓦsaltarafting.com. Highly professional, youthful team of operators specializing in rafting in a bucolic setting on the Río Juramento, grade III rapids about a 2hr drive from the city. It also runs "canopy" (zipwire) rides over the canyon, and can organize horseriding and mountain-biking excursions.

Socompa Balcarce 998, 1st floor ☎0387 416 9130, ⓦsocompa.com. Excellent operator working out of Salta (and connected with the *Finca Valentina*, see p.291) but specializing in the Puna Catamarqueña.

Tastil Caseros 468 ☎0387 431 0031, ⓦturismo tastil.com.ar. Professionally run but mostly routine trips to the Salinas Grandes, Humahuaca, Cafayate, the cloudforest national parks, Laguna de Pozuelos and even as far as Chile. Expect to waste lots of time collecting and dropping off passengers and not much English in the commentary.

ACCOMMODATION

As you might expect of such a regional hub, Salta has a wide variety of **places to stay**, everything from five-star international hotels to exquisite boutique hotels to lively youth hostels and decent mid-range hotels, though prices reflect the area's popularity with tourists. As well as downtown, there is a cluster of hotels around Cerro San Bernardo, affording more space and good views if you don't mind the 1km or so walk or taxi into town. If you have your own transport and would rather avoid the city entirely, you'll also find a number of excellent accommodation options in nearby San Lorenzo (see p.290), only fifteen minutes' drive from the city centre, plus a good many **fincas** and **estancias** (see box, p.291) in the surrounding countryside. Holiday times and weekends can get busy in Salta, and it's a good idea to book ahead at these times.

CENTRAL SALTA

Altos de Balcarce Balcarce 747 ☎0387 431 5454, ⓦaltosdebalcarce.com.ar. Despite its location on Salta's liveliest night-time street, this first-rate, professionally run hotel is safe and quiet. The fine rooms are decorated with traditional touches, the public areas are bright and appealing, and there is a pleasant swimming pool. $556

★ **Bloomer's Bed and Brunch** Vicente López 129 ☎0387 422 7449, ⓦbloomers-salta.com.ar. The five suites around a colonial patio – all with mod cons like flat-screen TVs – ooze charm. Run by a British–Peruvian couple, this B&B serves brunch rather than breakfast, is welcoming, comfortable and brightly decorated. $480

Caseros 44 Caseros 44 ☎0387 421 6761, ⓦcaseros44 bandb.com.ar. Homely little B&B just like a private house. All the rooms have ceiling fans and en-suite bathrooms, and there's internet access. No credit cards. $370

Design Suites Pasaje Castro 215 ☎0387 439 5962, ⓦdesignsuites.com. Housed in the carefully renovated Palacio Usandivaras, a 1913 mansion with a rather ugly modern adjunct. Inside it is all modern art and minimalism, with the best suites in the old palace, also home to a top-rate restaurant. US$144

El Lagar 20 de Febrero 877 ☎0387 421 7943, ⓦellagarhotel.com.ar. A Neocolonial boutique hotel with an exquisite art collection. It's exclusive but not snobbish, and is undoubtedly one of the most tastefully appointed hotels in the region, though some of the installations are a little old-fashioned. There is a fine pool to relax in or by, and breakfast is served in a wood-panelled dining room. Reservations required. US$150

★ **Legado Mítico** Mitre 647 ☎0387 422 8786, ⓦlegadomitico.com. Wonderfully inviting themed hotel in a well-located converted townhouse – each of the huge, sumptuously decorated rooms is named after a figure of regional importance such as a writer, a gaucho or the member of an indigenous tribe. US$230

Marilian Buenos Aires 176 ☎0387 421 6700, ⓦhotel marilian.com.ar. Professionally run, attractively decorated central hotel with both heating and a/c, a decent *confitería* and room service. It has an *apart-hotel* branch at España 254. $470

Regidor Buenos Aires 10 ☎0387 431 1305, ⓦhotel regidorsalta.com.ar. Charming place with character, a rustic

confitería and very pleasant rooms. Rooms overlooking the square tend to be noisy. $450

★ **Solar de la Plaza** Leguizamón 669 ☎0387 431 5111, ⓦsolardelaplaza.com.ar. Definitely one of the classiest acts in the city, *Solar* is housed in a converted Neocolonial mansion with beautifully furnished, large rooms, rooftop pool, professional service and outstanding buffet breakfast featuring delicious local products. $800

OUT OF THE CENTRE

Aldaba Mitre 910 ☎0387 421 9455, ⓦaldabahotel .com. A wonderful boutique hotel with six rooms, each with its own decor and style, including lots of crisp white linen, antique furniture and attention to detail. $355

Backpackers Buenos Aires 930 ☎0387 423 5910, ⓦbackpackerssalta.com. The city's veteran hostel now has a pool, as well as a very friendly, international atmosphere and a strong tendency to have fiestas. There are simple doubles as well as cramped dorms. Dorms $50, doubles $75

La Casa de los Jazmines RN-51 Km11, La Merced Chica, near Salta airport ☎0387 431 5454, ⓦhouseof jasmines.com. The House of Jasmins is a colonial house tastefully transformed into a luxury lodge with discreet service. It has just seven suites and a scattering of private dining areas. The food and wine are memorable, making it just the place for a romantic treat. US$330

★ **Kkala** Las Higueras 104 ☎0387 439 6590, ⓦhotelkkala.com.ar. Fabulous boutique hotel in Tres Cerritos, a well-heeled barrio close to the centre but far from the hustle and bustle. The enticing rooms are beautifully furnished while the views from the hotel, its pool/deck and homely public areas are stunning. US$200

Petit Hipólito Yrigoyen 225 ☎0387 421 3012, ⓦpetit hotel.salta.com.ar. Budget hotel, seven blocks from the centre, with clean rooms and good service. You can enjoy views of the Cerro San Bernardo from its café terrace and small swimming pool. $340

Sheraton Av Ejército del Norte 330 ☎0387 432 3000, ⓦsheraton.com/salta. Although part of the international chain, this impeccably run hotel near Cerro San Bernardo has real personality – the decor is unmistakeably North-western, based on Andean rugs and indigenous masks. There's a handsome pool, a fine restaurant and a decent gym. US$170

5

PEÑAS

Salta is famed for its lively **peñas**, informal folk-music clubs mainly found in the Northwest. Opening times are informal but most open around 8pm to serve food – mainly local fare such as *locro* and empanadas. The musicians turn up and start jamming later, often at around 10pm but in some cases not till midnight. Many *peñas*, particularly the more touristy ones, charge extra for the music/show.

Boliche de Balderrama San Martín 1126 ☎0387 421 1542, ⓦ boliche-balderrama.com.ar. One of the most popular *peñas*; well known as a bohemian hang-out in the 1950s, nowadays it's a more conventional place, attracting tourists and local folk singers alike.

La Casa de Güemes España 720 ☎0387 431 0950. A mellow atmosphere combines with decent food and spontaneous music-making starting at midnight at the earliest.

★ **La Casona del Molino** Luís Burela and Caseros 2500 ☎0387 434 2835. Empanadas, *locro*, *guaschilocro*, tamales, *humitas*, sangría and improvised live music much later on, all in a handsomely restored Neocolonial mansion.

La Vieja Estación Balcarce 885 ☎0387 421 7727, ⓦ la-viejaestacion.com.ar. Modern *peña* in one of the city's trendiest streets, dishing out food, draught beer and music shows nightly.

EATING AND DRINKING

Salta has plenty of eating places to suit all pockets, ranging from simple **snack bars** where you can savour the city's famous **empanadas** to a growing number of classy **restaurants** where people dress smartly for dinner. The most traditional **cafés** huddle together around the Plaza 9 de Julio, while the city market (Mercado Central) at Florida and San Martín has a number of stalls selling snacks at super-cheap prices.

Don José Urquiza 484 ☎0387 431 4469. Cheap and cheerful restaurant serving up home-cooking in a laidback atmosphere; the paintings on the walls are Don José's too. Daily 8pm–late.

El Farito Caseros 509 ☎0387 421 5035. Tiny empanada joint on the main plaza, dishing out Salta's classic delicious piping-hot cheese and meat pasties all day long. Daily 10am–late.

José Balcarce Mitre and Necochea ☎0387 421 1628. José López presides over the kitchen at this charming – if slightly costly – Neocolonial corner restaurant and uses regional products like quinoa and grain amaranth (another Andean cereal) to accompany llama; also try llama carpaccio or, for the less adventurous, the steak and roast potatoes. Mon–Sat 8pm–late.

La Monumental Entre Ríos 202 ☎0387 421 7653. This *parrilla* with an extensive menu that includes pasta, rice and fish dishes is so popular that it has opened a second branch in a more attractive ex-government building on the opposite corner, though locals maintain the smaller

original is still best. Daily 8pm–late, other branch also open 12.30–3pm.

El Palacio de la Pizza Caseros 117 ☎0387 421 4989. This place, recently remodelled and enlarged, has been living up to its name for years, serving the best pizzas in Salta by far. It also does good empanadas. Daily noon–late.

La Posta España 456 ☎0387 421 7091. A moderately priced *parrilla*, in a large, airy dining room, with the usual no-nonsense steaks and desserts. Daily 8.30pm–late.

★ **El Solar del Convento** Caseros 444 ☎0387 421 5124. Elegant surroundings, classical music and a free glass of champagne set the tone for this high-class but not so expensive restaurant, serving juicy steaks and with an excellent wine list. Daily 11am–3pm & 8pm–midnight.

Van Gogh Plaza 9 de Julio. The best coffee in town, excellent cakes, quick meals, appetizing snacks and the local glitterati are the attractions, plus live music late at weekends. Daily 8am–late.

DIRECTORY

Banks and exchange Banco de la Nación, Mitre 151; Masventas, España 610. There's nowhere reliable to change travellers' cheques, but there are plenty of ATMs around town.

Consulates Bolivia, Mariano Boedo 32 ☎0387 422 3377; Paraguay, Mariano Boedo 38.

Internet There are *locutorios* all around the city offering reasonably priced internet and phone services.

Laundry Tía María, Av Belgrano 236; Laverap, Santiago del Estero, 363.

Post office Deán Funes 170.

CLOCKWISE FROM TOP LEFT CHEESE, TAFÍ DEL VALLE (P.320); FESTIVAL CELEBRATING PACHAMAMA, SALTA PROVINCE; HORSES BY A STREAM NEAR TAFÍ DEL VALLE (P.320); MUSEO PACHAMAMA, AMAICHA (P.322) >

5

San Lorenzo

Just 11km northwest of Salta along the RP-28, little **SAN LORENZO** is part dormitory town, part retreat for many Salteños, appreciated for its spotlessly clean *ceibo*-lined avenues and patrician villas. Plentiful walking and riding opportunities, a private nature reserve and an excellent range of **accommodation** make it an ideal alternative to staying in downtown Salta.

ARRIVAL AND DEPARTURE
SAN LORENZO

By bus Buses run at regular intervals from central Salta to the Camino de la Quebrada, just before the gorge, stopping along Avenida San Martín and Juan Carlos Dávalos.

ACCOMMODATION

Even if you don't have your own transport, it's worthwhile bedding down for the night in the calm fresh air of San Lorenzo, with accommodation ranging from the basic and rustic to the positively luxurious. Some of these lodgings are located outside the village itself, but the staff at these places can arrange transport to and from the city and/or the airport for those who need it.

Cabañas del Sol RP-28 Km11.5 ☎0387 492 2072, ⓦsaltacabanasdelsol.com. Wonderful complex of *cabañas*, some of them right down by the riverside, in a fabulous rural setting some way out of San Lorenzo; ideal for anyone who wants to have self-catering accommodation and good value for a group, with the cabins sleeping up to seven. *Cabañas* from $530

Casa de Campo Arnaga Aniceto la Torre, on the road to Lesser ☎0387 492 1478, ⓦredsalta.com/arnaga. This wonderfully located, handsome Basque-style patrician home drips with old-world charm and Salta's new-world colonial tradition. The slightly old-fashioned rooms are comfortable and the mountain views breathtaking. $520

Los Ceibos 9 de Julio and España ☎0387 492 1675, ⓦhlosceibos.com.ar. This relatively modest *hostería* in an attractive Neocolonial building has clean if uninspiring rooms, as well as sports facilities. $290

Cerros de San Lorenzo Joaquín V. Gonzales s/n, Loteo los Berros ☎0387 492 2500, ⓦcerrosdesanlorenzo .com.ar. Built in a fabulous Neocolonial style around a shady patio; the rooms are commodious and most attractive, and the bathrooms modish. The high location makes for breathtaking views. $450

★ **Eaton Place** Av San Martín 2457 ☎0387 492 1347, ⓦeatonplacesalta.com.ar. As the name hints, this exquisite hotel – whose English-speaking owner has a collection of antiques that reflect his impeccable taste – is inspired by London mansions, though what townhouse in Belgravia boasts a palm-lined driveway? The plush rooms, classy service, dreamy swimming pool, toothsome food and marvellous grounds make this a plum choice. $430

★ **Posada Don Numas** Pompilio Guzmán 1470 ☎0387 492 1918, ⓦdonnumas.com.ar. This home-from-home posada has spacious rooms with modern bathrooms, ultra-friendly service, two swimming pools, a fully equipped spa and a prime setting affording mountain views. The breakfast, complete with home-made cakes and pies, will keep you going all day, but other simple meals or *asados* are offered on request. $425

WALKS AND TOURS AROUND SAN LORENZO

It's a pleasant one- to two-hour walk up the **Quebrada de San Lorenzo**, a rocky gorge down which a stream flows, sometimes forming falls and pools; the walk takes you through unspoilt woodland to the foot of the hulking mountains that form a natural barrier behind the village.

Another enticing stroll can be taken through the **Reserva del Huaico** (daily 8am–noon & 2–6pm, by prior appointment only; guided walk $60; ☎0387 497 1024, ⓦreservadelhuaico .org.ar), a nature reserve set up to protect the native forest and its endogenous flora and fauna (especially its birds); the exploration of its trails culminates at a viewpoint from where you can take in the whole valley to Salta city and beyond.

Turismo San Lorenzo at Juan Carlos Dávalos in the town (☎0387 492 1757, ⓦturismosanlorenzo.com) offers guided walks up the Quebrada de San Lorenzo as well as other local walking and horseback trips. It also runs excursions further afield, such as to the Quebrada de Humahuaca or Cafayate.

ESTANCIAS AND FINCAS IN SALTA AND JUJUY PROVINCES

Salta and, to a lesser degree Jujuy, are provinces with a very long colonial history, which has left behind many **estancias** (traditional ranches), known locally as *fincas*, some of which now offer rooms to guests. Estancia stays are a wonderful way of combining rest – and sometimes even luxury – with a chance to get to know locals, tune in to nature and experience *criollo* customs and farming activities. In all cases, reserve ahead.

El Bordo de las Lanzas Rivadavia s/n, General Güemes ☎0387 490 3070, ⓦestanciaelbordo.com. A historic tobacco farm located 80km northeast of Salta. The early seventeenth-century house maintains its colonial structures – the furniture and artefacts come from Jesuit missions in the Northwest, Perú and Bolivia – but with all modern conveniences. Full board US$400

Finca Valentina RN-51 Km11, La Merced Chica ☎0387 15 4523490, ⓦfinca-valentina.com.ar. Conveniently close to Salta's airport, this delightful, modern *finca* is run by an utterly stylish couple from Milan who combine flair (Valentina is an architect) with professional know-how (Fabrizio is an economist). Its handful of charming rooms are set among a green park near wonderful walking and riding country. There's memorably delicious food, too. US$140

Puerta del Cielo Las Costas ☎0387 492 1757. Remote *finca* up in the Andean foothills not far from the city of Salta. Reachable only on horseback, it's a difficult place to get to, but rewarding once you're there, famous for its round-the-bonfire *asados*. You need to book your stay through a tour operator, such as Turismo San Lorenzo in San Lorenzo (see box opposite). Full-board prices are per person, including all activities and transfers. $1300

Santa Anita Piedras Moradas s/n, Coronel Moldes ☎0387 490 5050, ⓦsantaanita.com.ar. Located around 60km south of Salta by the RN-68, on the west bank of the huge Embalse Cabra Corral reservoir. As well as swimming in the pool or taking organized horserides, you can watch tobacco being processed and visit the tobacco museum on the premises. $360

EATING AND DRINKING

Confitería Don Sanca Juan Carlos Dávalos 1450 ☎0387 492 1580. A charming place serving delicious food, including a very good stab at tea, which can be enjoyed with a slice of cake inside or on the grassy patio. Daily noon–9pm.

El Duende de la Quebrada Juan Carlos Dávalos 2309 ☎0387 492 2053. At the entrance to the Quebrada, this tearoom is in an attractive rustic construction, with seemingly endless wooden balconies overlooking the

stream; it serves very decent fare, with emphasis on local specialities, plus cakes, teas, coffees, juices and the like. Daily 9am–noon.

Lo de Andrés Juan Carlos Dávalos and Gorriti ☎0387 492 1600. In a galleried building with a large terrace, the extensive menu of this *parrillada* includes empanadas, delicious *locro*, fresh trout (best simply grilled, rather than smothered in sauce) and pasta. Daily noon–3pm & 8pm–midnight.

Quebrada del Toro

Whether you travel up the magnificent **Quebrada del Toro** by train – along one of the highest railways in the world (see box, p.292) – in a tour operator's jeep, in a rented car or, as the pioneers did centuries ago, on horseback, the experience will be unforgettable, thanks to the gorge's constantly changing dramatic mountain scenery and multicoloured rocks. It is named after the **Río Toro**, normally a meandering trickle, but occasionally a raging torrent and as bullish as its name suggests, especially in the spring. The road and rail track swerve up from the tobacco fields of the Valle de Lerma, southwest of Salta, through dense thickets of **ceibo**, Argentina's national tree, ablaze in October and November with their fuchsia-red spring blossom, and end at the dreary but strategic mining settlement of **San Antonio de los Cobres**.

TOURS

QUEBRADA DEL TORO

Tour operators Many tour operators in Salta (see box, p.286) offer tours of the Quebrada del Toro by road, which

shadows the train for part of the way, offering passengers the chance to photograph the handsome locomotive if it is

5

THE TRAIN TO THE CLOUDS

Travelling through the Quebrada del Toro gorge on the Tren a las Nubes, or **Train to the Clouds**, is an unashamedly touristic experience. Clambering from the station in Salta (it never exceeds 35 km/hr) to the magnificent Meccano-like **La Polvorilla viaduct**, high in the altiplano, the smart train – with a leather-upholstered interior, shiny wooden fittings, spacious seats, a dining car, a post office and even altitude-sickness remedies – was originally built to service the borax mines in the salt flats of Pocitos and Arizaro, 300km beyond La Polvorilla. The viaduct lies 219km from Salta, and on the way the train crosses **29 bridges** and **twelve viaducts**, threads through **21 tunnels**, swoops round two gigantic **360° loops** and chugs up **two switchbacks**. La Polvorilla, seen on many posters and in all the tour operators' brochures, is 224m long, 64m high and weighs over 1600 tonnes; built in Italy, it was assembled here in 1930. The highest point of the whole line, just 13km west of the viaduct, is at Abra Chorrillos (4475m). Brief stopovers near La Polvorilla, where the train doubles back, and in San Antonio de los Cobres, allow you to stretch your legs and meet some locals, keen on selling you llama-wool scarves and posing for photos (for a fee). Folk groups and solo artists interspersed with people selling arts, crafts, cheese, honey and souvenirs galore help while the time away on the way down, when it's dark for the most part.

The train leaves (and returns to) Salta's Ferrocarril Belgrano station once or twice a week from late March to early December, with more frequent departures in July. It's a long day – the train departs Salta at 7am and gets back just before midnight – though many people now take the speedier bus back (see p.291). **Tickets** cost $830 for the round trip and should be reserved in advance at ⓦ trenalasnubes.com.ar. The **Ferrocarril Belgrano** station in Salta is at Ameghino 690, ten blocks north of the central Plaza 9 de Julio, and can be reached by buses #5 and #13 from downtown, the bus terminal and the campsite.

---

running that day. MoviTrak can meet you at a station on the way back to guide you around the altiplano in a jeep; you miss out on the return train journey and the folk show (a possible blessing) but get the best of both worlds – the train ride up in daylight plus a chance to explore the area more independently. It is also possible to combine excursions up the Quebrada del Toro with a return leg down the Quebrada de Humahuaca.

Alforcito

If you travel up the Quebrada by vehicle your first chance to stretch your legs (other than viewpoints) comes at the hamlet of **Alforcito**, about 100km northwest of Salta. There's a decent restaurant here – *Comedor La Griselda*, just past the village – and a crafts store, next to the church, sells products made of alpaca wool and *cardon* cacti, the flora and fauna most characteristic of the area.

Santa Rosa de Tastil

The minute village of **Santa Rosa de Tastil**, a few minutes' drive past Alforcito, has only eleven inhabitants but is the location of a **pre-Inca site**. The well-restored remains of one of the region's largest pre-Inca towns, ancient Tastil, signposted 3km west of the village, was inhabited by some three thousand people in the fourteenth century AD. The **mirador**, on once-fortified heights commanding fabulous valley and mountain views, overlooks the clearly terraced farmland from which the people eked out a living. Two tiny, related museums are set beneath the gorge's cactus-clad rocks – the **Museo del Sitio** (daily 10am–6pm; $2), which contains finds from nearby excavations, and the **Museo Regional Moisés Zerpa** (daily 10am–6pm; $2), decorated like a traditional local house, complete with cooking utensils, ceramics and textiles. If you're lucky, the curator of both the museums may also take you round the ruins.

San Antonio de los Cobres and around

A major regional crossroads at a dizzying 3775m above sea level, **SAN ANTONIO DE LOS COBRES** is the small, windswept "capital" of an immense but mostly empty portion of the altiplano, rich in minerals, as its name ("of the coppers") suggests, and little else, except some breathtaking **scenery**. The **Salinas Grandes**, to the north of San Antonio de los Cobres, are among the continent's biggest salt flats, a huge glistening expanse surrounded by brown mountains, snow-peaked volcanoes and sparse pasture.

Most people only ever see San Antonio de los Cobres from its train station – the Tren a las Nubes makes a short stop here on its way back down to the plains, during which the blue and white Argentine flag is hoisted and the national anthem played. You won't be missing much if you don't hop off: the town's low houses (many of them built by the borax and lithium mining firms for their workforce in a highly utilitarian style), dusty streets and lack of vegetation make for a rather forlorn little town, not especially inviting and displaying few signs of the wealth generated by the valuable metals running in rich veins through the nearby mountains.

ARRIVAL AND INFORMATION   SAN ANTONIO DE LOS COBRES

By bus El Quebracho runs a twice-daily bus service between Salta and San Antonio; there are also services onwards to San Pedro de Atacama (Chile) via the Paso de Jama.

Tourist information The police next to the train station can give you news about the state of the road and any weather hazards.

ACCOMMODATION AND EATING

Hostería de las Nubes Caseros 441 ☏ 0387 490 9059, ⊕ hoteldelasnubes.com. Fairly basic, but the plumbing works, the meals are fine, and it's the only really recommendable place in town. **$500**

Salinas Grandes

The aptly named **Salinas Grandes** are one of the country's biggest salt flats and certainly the most impressive, ringed by mountains on all sides and beneath almost perennial blue skies. From San Antonio de los Cobres, the recently renovated RP-38 passes by the glistening expanse of the flats about 50km northeast of the town, or they can be accessed from Purmamarca, Jujuy Province, via the fabulous Cuesta de Lipán (see p.299). This huge rink of snow-white crystals, forming irregular octagons, each surrounded by crunchy ridges, crackling like frozen snow under foot, acts as a huge mirror. The salt, shimmering in the nearly perpetual blazing sunshine, often creates cruel water mirages, though there are in fact some isolated pools of brine where small groups of flamingoes and ducks gather. This is a likely place for spotting vicuñas and llamas, too, flocks of which often leap across the road to reach their scrawny, yellow pastureland, or *tola*, on either side of the road.

San Salvador de Jujuy

SAN SALVADOR DE JUJUY is a tranquil place and, at 1260m above sea level, enjoys an enviably temperate climate. Just over 90km north of Salta by the direct and scenic but rather slow RN-9, it is the capital of the country's most remote mainland province, a small but intensely beautiful patch of land, ostensibly having more in common with next-door Chile and Bolivia than with the rest of Argentina, and little with Buenos Aires, nearly 1600km away. It is the most Andean of all Argentina's cities: much of its population is descended from indigenous stock, either *mestizos* or recent Bolivian immigrants. A day or two will suffice to see the town's modest attractions, and it does not have the tourist infrastructure that Salta enjoys, but it has an up-and-coming yet

5

authentic feel, with an excellent spread of restaurants and a thriving cultural scene, that makes it a good stopover or possible base to visit the rich hinterland that surrounds it. Dramatically situated, the city (usually known as San Salvador, or, simply, Jujuy) lies in a fertile bowl, with the spectacular multicoloured gorge of the **Quebrada de Humahuaca**, a major reason for heading in this direction, immediately north. The Cerro de Claros (1704m) and Cerro Chuquina (1987m) loom just to the southeast and southwest, and the city is wedged between two rivers, the Río Grande and Río Chico or Xibi Xibi, both bone dry for most of the year.

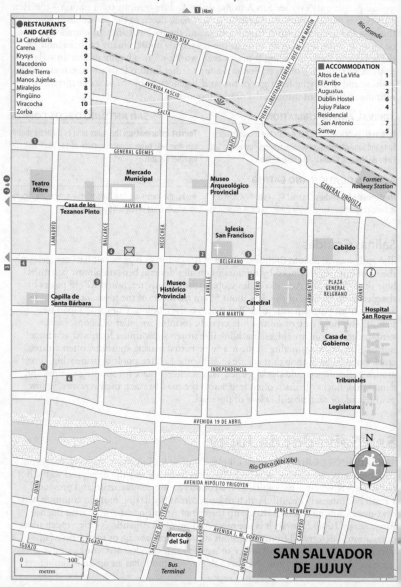

RESTAURANTS AND CAFÉS

La Candelaria	2
Carena	4
Krysys	9
Macedonio	1
Madre Tierra	5
Manos Jujeñas	3
Miralejos	8
Pingüino	7
Viracocha	10
Zorba	6

ACCOMMODATION

Altos de La Viña	1
El Arribo	3
Augustus	2
Dublin Hostel	6
Jujuy Palace	4
Residencial San Antonio	7
Sumay	5

SAN SALVADOR DE JUJUY

Though not a conventionally beautiful city, the central streets have a certain atmosphere – while the main Plaza Belgrano has a definite subtropical charm. Scratch the surface and you'll unearth some real treasures, among them one of the finest pieces of sacred art to be seen in Argentina, the **pulpit** in the **cathedral** – and the interior of **Iglesia San Francisco** is almost as impressive.

Brief history

Jujuy was founded, after a couple of early false starts, on April 19, 1593. Earthquakes, the plague and conflict all conspired to hamper the city's growth during the seventeenth and eighteenth centuries and have deprived it of any of its original buildings. General Belgrano ordered the **Jujuy Exodus** on August 23, 1812 – an event every Argentine schoolchild learns about – at the height of the Wars of Independence; the city's entire population was evacuated and Jujuy was razed to the ground to prevent its capture. Jujuy continued to bear the brunt of conflict, sacked by the royalists in 1814 and 1818. It then remained a forgotten backwater throughout the nineteenth century, and the railway did not reach it until 1903. Since the 1930s, its outskirts have spilt across both rivers and begun to creep up the hillsides, and it now has a sizeable immigrant population, mostly from across the Bolivian border to the north. The province – and therefore the city, which lives off the province's agricultural production – have traditionally grown rich on sugar and tobacco, but earnings have declined in recent years and forced farmers to diversify into other crops. Tourism has so far been exploited only half-heartedly, but is growing in importance.

Plaza General Belgrano

Most of the city's main sights are near **Plaza General Belgrano**, at the eastern extremity of the compact microcentro. Planted with orange trees and palms, it was the colonial settlement's central square or Plaza Mayor and is still the city's hub, partly occupied by craftsmen, mainly potters, displaying their wares. The elegant, white, arched Cabildo runs along its northern side, now housing the city's main police station.

Casa de Gobierno

Plaza General Belgrano s/n · Mon–Fri 9am–noon & 4–8pm · Free

Plaza General Belgrano is dominated to the south by the **Casa de Gobierno** with its extremely Gallic-looking slate mansard roof, where the national flag donated to the city by General Belgrano, as a tribute to the Exodus, is proudly guarded. In the grounds of the government house, dotted around the building, stand five large **statues** by renowned sculptress **Lola Mora** (see box, p.252). Representing Peace, Progress, Justice, Freedom and Labour, the set was originally designed for the Congreso Nacional in Buenos Aires, inaugurated in 1906, but the reactionary federal government vetoed the project and had the statues dumped in a store room. Luckily Jujuy's government at that time was less intransigent and in 1915 it appointed Lola Mora as the city's director of parks and squares, in order to erect the statues in their present position.

The cathedral

Plaza General Belgrano s/n · Daily 8am–1pm & 5–8pm · Free

On the west side of the plaza stands Jujuy's late eighteenth-century **cathedral**, topped by an early twentieth-century tower and extended by an even later Neoclassical atrium. The exterior is unremarkable, but the interior, a layer of painted Bakelite concealing the original timber structure, is impressively naive: a realistic mock-fresco of sky and clouds soars over the altar, while above the nave is a primitive depiction of the ceremony in which Belgrano awarded the Argentine flag to the people of Jujuy.

Two original doors and two confessionals, Baroque masterpieces from the eighteenth century, immediately catch the eye, thanks to their vivid red and sienna paint, picked

5

out with gilt, but the undisputed highlight – and the main attraction of the whole city – is the magnificent **pulpit**. Decorated in the eighteenth century by local artists, it easily rivals those of **Cusco**, its apparent inspiration, with its harmonious compositions, elegant floral and vegetable motifs and the finesse of its carvings. Its various tableaux in gilded, carved wood, gleaming with an age-old patina, depict subjects such as Jacob's ladder and St Augustine along with biblical genealogies from Adam to Abraham and David to Solomon. One curiosity is the error in the symbols of the four **apostles**: Matthew and John are correctly represented by a human figure and an eagle respectively, but Mark, symbolized by a bull, and Luke, by a lion, are the wrong way round.

Iglesia San Francisco

Belgrano and Lavalle • Mon–Sat 9am–noon & 5–7.45pm • Free

Not quite the same calibre as the cathedral's, but very striking nonetheless, is the Spanish Baroque **pulpit** in **Iglesia San Francisco**, two blocks west of the plaza; also inspired by the pulpits of Cusco and almost certainly carved by craftsmen in eighteenth-century Bolivia, it drips with detail, with a profusion of little Franciscan monks peeking out from row upon row of tiny columns, all delicately gilded. Although the church and separate campanile are built to the traditional colonial Franciscan design, in a Neo-Baroque style, the church was built in the 1930s.

Teatro Mitre

Alvear 1009 • ☎ 0388 442 2782, ⓦ teatromitrejujuy.gov.ar

Several blocks to the northwest of the Iglesia San Francisco, Jujuy's theatre and opera house, the beautiful Italian-style **Teatro Mitre**, was built in the 1890s and boasts a gleaming white exterior and a plush interior. Plays and classical concerts are regularly staged here, and are often of a high standard.

ARRIVAL AND DEPARTURE

By plane Jujuy's airport, Dr Horacio Guzmán (☎ 0388 491 1109), is over 30km southeast of the city, along the RN-66 near Perico; the taxi fare is around $150. The Aerolíneas Argentina office is at Senador Pérez 355 (☎ 0388 422 7198). Destinations Buenos Aires (3 daily; 2hr 10min); Salta (1 daily; 20min).
By bus The rudimentary bus terminal, at Iguazú and Av Dorrego (☎ 0388 422 6299), just south of the centre,

across the Río Chico, serves all local, regional and national destinations, and also runs a service to Chile. There's a left-luggage facility.
Destinations Buenos Aires (hourly; 20hr); Córdoba (10 daily; 13hr); Humahuaca (hourly; 3hr); La Quiaca (hourly; 7hr); Purmamarca (hourly; 1hr 15min); Resistencia (1 daily; 14hr); Salta (hourly; 1hr 30min); Tilcara (hourly; 2hr); Tucumán (10 daily; 5hr 30min).

INFORMATION

Tourist information For basic information, head for the Dirección Provincial de Turismo (Mon–Fri 7am–10pm, Sat &

Sun 9am–9pm; ☎ 0388 422 1325, ⓦ turismo.jujuy.gov.ar), at the northeastern corner of central Plaza General Belgrano.

ACCOMMODATION

Altos de la Viña Pasquini López, La Viña ☎ 0388 426 1666. On the heights of La Viña, 4km northeast of the city centre, this successfully refurbished hotel, with large, comfortable rooms and a shady garden, commands fabulous views of the valley and mountains. Shuttle service to and from downtown. **$522**
El Arribo Belgrano 1263 ☎ 0388 422 2539, ⓦ elarribo .com. A short walk from the centre, a remodelled nineteenth-century house, retaining original tiles and doors, has been turned into this pleasant and peaceful boutique hotel.

Friendly service, a small garden and a (rather cold) swimming pool are bonuses. **$400**
Augustus Belgrano 715 ☎ 0388 423 0203, ⓦ hotel augustus.com.ar. Extremely friendly place, with clean rooms, spacious bathrooms and good breakfasts. The snack bar serves delicious sandwiches and *lomitos*. **$485**
Dublin Hostel y Bar Independencia 946 ☎ 0388 422 9608, ⓦ dublinhostel.com.ar. Long-running Jujuy hostel, recently moved to larger premises. There's a handful of high-ceilinged dorms as well as a couple of doubles, and,

to the side, a bar with a good range of beers (closes at midnight). Dorms $60, doubles $200

Jujuy Palace Belgrano 1060 ☎0388 423 0433. Top-range hotel in central Jujuy, with stylish decor and charm. Professionally run, with a pleasant restaurant. $484

Residencial San Antonio Lisandro de la Torre 993 ☎0388 422 5998. Small, modern and very close to the bus terminal – the only non-squalid place in the vicinity. $140

Sumay Otero 232 ☎0388 423 5065. By far the nicest lower-range hotel, it's roomy, comfortable, and very popular, so book ahead. Can be noisy. $280

Las Vertientes RN-9 Km17 ☎0388 498 0030. Excellent campsite in an area near the village of Yala, north of the city, that used to be a tobacco plantation. The complex has its own pool and restaurant. $10

EATING, DRINKING AND NIGHTLIFE

La Candelaria Alvear 1346 ☎0388 15 4219781. This very stylish *parrilla*, ten blocks or so out to the west of the city, offers you mountains of meat until you burst. Heavenly desserts, too. Tues–Sat noon–3pm & 8.30pm–1am, Sun noon–3pm.

Carena Balcarce and Belgrano ☎0388 423 5109. Mellow *confitería*, serving snacks and acting as a community centre – concerts, seminars and group meetings are held here. Tues–Sat noon–3pm & 8.30pm–midnight.

Krysys Balcarce 272 ☎0388 423 1126. Trout is the speciality on an otherwise not very inventive meat-dominated menu, but the service is impeccable. Mon–Sat noon–3pm & 8pm–1am, Sun noon–3pm.

★ **Macedonio** Lamadrid and Güemes ☎0388 424 1606. Wonderful cultural centre and café-bar in an 1860s adobe house built in the colonial style, with a palm-fringed patio where folk and jazz bands play Wed–Sat. Inexpensive meals – hearty sandwiches, salads and pasta – are served. Mon 6pm–2am, Tues–Sat 10am–2am, Sun 10am–6pm.

★ **Madre Tierra** Belgrano 619 ☎0388 422 9578. Delightful, airy vegetarian lunch-only spot with a $60 set menu that will keep you going for hours. Even if you're not a vegetarian, you'll find the fresh salads, meatless empanadas and delicious fruit juices a great change from the meat overdose, and you can stock up on all manner of goodies for a picnic. Mon–Sat noon–3pm.

★ **Manos Jujeñas** Senador Pérez 379 ☎0388 424 3270. Absolutely fabulous Northwestern food, including memorable *locro* and delicious empanadas, accompanied by jugs of honest wine and, from time to time, by live folk music. Incredibly friendly service too. Mon 8pm–late, Tues–Sat noon–3pm & 8pm–late, Sun 8pm–late.

Miralejos Sarmiento 268 ☎0388 422 4911. Classic Northwestern gastronomy at its best in this popular place, with a few tables out on the plaza. Mon 8pm–1am, Tues–Sun 11.30am–1am.

Pingüino Belgrano 718. This is Jujuy's finest *heladería*, scooping out delicious ice cream by the bucketful. You can enjoy every flavour imaginable from the outdoor seating on a pedestrianized stretch, and watch the town in full swing. Daily noon–8pm.

★ **Viracocha** Independencia and Lamadrid ☎0388 15 4382605. Unusual dishes like llama in dark beer sauce, or smoked llama ravioli, plus delicious classic Andean fare – lots of quinoa and native potatoes – make this one of Jujuy's top places to eat. Mon–Wed & Sun 11am–4pm, Thurs–Sat 11am–4pm & 7pm–12.30am.

Zorba Belgrano and Necochea ☎0388 424 3048. Reasonably priced Greek food – feta salads, moussaka, *pastitsio* and stuffed vine leaves – along with Argentine favourites and delicious sandwiches in a bright, modern venue with a real buzz that would not look out of place in Kolonaki. Mon–Sat 8am–2am, Sun 6pm–1am.

DIRECTORY

Banks and exchange Quilmes, Belgrano 902; for exchange and travellers' cheques: Masventas, Balcarce 223 (Mon–Fri 8am–1.30pm & 5–8pm). Several ATMs are dotted around.

Consulate Bolivia (the most helpful in the Northwest),

Av Senador Pérez and Independencia.

Internet Telecentro, Güemes and La Madrid.

Laundry Laverap, Belgrano 1214.

Post office Belgrano, between Necochea and Balcarce.

Telephones Telecom, Belgrano and Lavalle.

Quebrada de Humahuaca

Although the intense beauty of the **Quebrada de Humahuaca** gorge features so often in tourist literature, posters and coffee-table books that some of the surprise element is taken away, a trip along it is nonetheless an unforgettable and moving experience. Stunning, varied scenery is on display all the way up from the valley bottom, just northwest of San Salvador de Jujuy, to the namesake town of **Humahuaca**, 125km north of the provincial capital. While most day-trips along the gorge from Jujuy and

5

Salta take you up and down by the same route, the RN-9, you're actually treated to two spectacles: you'll have your attention fixed on the western side in the morning, and on the eastern flank in the afternoon, when the sun lights up each side respectively and picks out the amazing geological features: polychrome strata, buttes and mesas, pinnacles and eroded crags. What's more, the two sides are quite different, the western mountains rising steeply, often striped with vivid colours, while the slightly lower, rounded range to the east is for the most part gentler, more mellow, but just as colourful.

Most (day) tours organized out of Jujuy and Salta only go as far as Humahuaca and then head back, but this still gets you two tracking-shot views of multicoloured mountains, the highlight of which is the photogenic **Cerro de los Siete Colores**, overhanging the picturesque village of **Purmamarca**. From Purmamarca a dramatic side road leads across splendid altiplano landscapes, via pretty little **Susques**, to the Chilean border at the Paso de Jama, high in the Andes. Purmamarca has enough accommodation options to make it a possible stopover, especially if you are forging on towards Chile. Two-thirds of the way to Humahuaca, the small town of **Tilcara** is another possible stopover; it boasts the best range of lodgings and eateries in the whole area, plus an interesting archeological museum and a beautiful pre-Inca fortress, or *pukará*. Beyond Humahuaca, the RN-9 crosses bleak but stunningly beautiful altiplano landscapes all the way up to La Quiaca on the Bolivian border, nearly 2000m higher yet only 150km further on. A side road off the RN-9 climbs to the incredibly isolated and highly picturesque hamlet of **Iruya**, if you really want to get off the beaten track. The whole of the RN-9 and some of the side roads are accessible by regular **buses** from Jujuy, many of them also serving Salta.

Tumbaya

As you climb the first stretch of the Quebrada beyond Yala, you soon leave the subtropical forest behind and enter an arid, narrow valley, gouged out by the Río Grande. Some 47km from Jujuy, you come to **TUMBAYA**, a tiny village with a handsome colonial church, the first of many along the Quebrada.

Iglesia de Nuestra Señora de los Dolores y Nuestra Señora de la Candelaria

Plaza General Manuel Belgrano • Free

The **Iglesia de Nuestra Señora de los Dolores y Nuestra Señora de la Candelaria** houses some fine colonial art, including a painting of *Nuestra Señora La Aparecida*, another of *El Cristo de los Temblores*, and a *Jesús en el Huerto*. Originally built at the end of the eighteenth century, it was partially rebuilt after two earthquakes in the nineteenth century and restored in the 1940s; its design is typical of the Quebrada, a solid structure clearly influenced by the Mudéjar churches of Andalucía. The domed campanile is particularly elegant.

Purmamarca

About 13km north of Tumbaya, the region's main trans-Andean route, the RN-52, forks off to the left, heading northwest towards Susques and the Chilean border. Lying 4km to the west of the RN-52, the tiny, picturesque village of **PURMAMARCA**, at the base of the gorge of the same name, is no longer quite as peaceful and quiet as it once was, due to an increase in traffic resulting from stronger trading links with Chile.

Plaza Principal

The main square is still a haven of tranquillity, where locals have erected a few tables to sell ponchos, alpaca toys and the like to passing tourists. The pretty seventeenth-century church, the **Iglesia Santa Rosa de Lima** (Mon–Fri 9am–1pm, Sat 9am–noon) is built to the typically plain, single-towered design of the Quebrada. At the northeast corner of the plaza, the four graceful arches of the **Cabildo** (daily 10am–noon & 5–7pm; free) embellish its otherwise simple white facade.

Cerro de los Siete Colores

Purmamarca's chief attraction is the famous **Cerro de los Siete Colores**, a dramatic bluff of rock overlooking the village. The mountain's candy stripes range from pastel beiges and pinks to orangey ochres and dark purples, though you may not be able to make out all seven of the reputed shades. A signposted route marked "Los Colorados", following an irrigation canal, takes you round the back of the village for the best views of the polychrome mountainside.

ARRIVAL AND INFORMATION   PURMAMARCA

By bus Frequent buses to Tilcara, Humahuaca and Jujuy leave from a block east of the main square.

Tourist information There is a helpful little tourist office (daily 8am–8pm) just off the main plaza.

ACCOMMODATION

Casa de Adobe RN-52 Km4 ☎ 0388 490 8003, ⓦ casadeadobe.com.ar. A small set of hyper-luxurious *cabañas*, affording magnificent mountain views and with a terrific display of good taste and technological progress. Gorgeous materials and textiles, plus plasma-screen TVs with international satellite channels. **$540**

La Comarca RN-52 Km3.8 ☎ 0388 490 8001, ⓦ lacomarcahotel.com.ar. In a stunning setting with unbeatable views of the coloured mountains, this stylish adobe-and-stone complex has huge rooms, a beautiful heated pool, a mini-spa and a top-rate gourmet restaurant (open to non-residents) with a cellar worth visiting in its own right. **$715**

★ **Hostería del Amauta** Salta s/n ☎ 0388 490 8043, ⓦ hosteriadelamauta.com. Oozing with charm, this well-designed *hostería* has a selection of rooms impeccably decorated with soft linens, local timber and wrought-iron detailing. Breakfasts are delicious, healthy and copious. **$480**

Manantial del Silencio RN-52 Km3.5 ☎ 0388 490

8080, ⓦ hotelmanantial.com.ar. This delightful, convent-like Neocolonial building in parkland a short distance out of the village houses small but comfortable rooms. The restaurant varies in quality, the swimming pool is unheated and the service leaves a lot to be desired, but as the pioneer boutique hotel in the area it has its merits. **$880**

La Posta de Purmamarca Pantaleón Cruz s/n ☎ 0388 490 8029, ⓦ postadepurmamarca.com.ar. Sturdy wooden beds in a white room – not exactly luxury but a great central location. **$550**

Residencial Bebo Vilte Salta s/n and Rivadavia ☎ 0388 490 8038. A classic B&B that still offers some of the best inexpensive rooms in the village; it's cheaper still in low season. **$350**

El Viejo Algarrobo Salta s/n ☎ 0388 490 8286, ⓔ elviejoalgarrobo@hotmail.com. A cosy *hospedaje* named after an ancient *algarrobo* tree (sadly destroyed by lightning in a freak storm in 2009) behind the church, with small but adequate rooms. **$300**

EATING AND DRINKING

Los Morteros Salta s/n. The area's best restaurant by far, a short way from the church. The gourmet food, using the region's excellent natural produce, including goat's cheese empanadas and chicken fricassee with broad beans and quinoa, is served in a classy decor, adorned with traditional textiles and other crafts. Noon–3pm &

8pm–late; closed Tues.

La Posta Plaza Principal. Next to the Cabildo, *La Posta* serves simple meals, snacks and drinks, and sells local crafts, in a rich red-ochre-walled building. Daily noon–3pm & 8pm–midnight.

Cuesta de Lipán

Leading west from Purmamarca, the RN-52 follows the Río Purmamarca, quickly climbing up the remarkable zigzags of the **CUESTA DE LIPÁN**, one of the most dramatic roads in the region. This road heads towards the Chilean border at Paso de Jama crossing some of the country's most startling landscapes – barren steppe alternating with crinkly mountains, often snow-peaked even in the summer. Some 30km west of Purmamarca, just after the Abra de Potrerillos pass, you reach the road's highest point, at nearly 4200m, and enter majestic altiplanic landscapes: ahead you have open views to gleaming salt-flats

5

and to the north, beyond the valley of the Río Colorado, the shallow, mirror-like **Laguna de Guayatayoc** glistens in the sun. Beyond the junction with the RP-38, which runs north–south from San Antonio de los Cobres (see p.293) to Abra Pampa (see p.306), the pastures on either side of the road are home to considerable communities of *vicuña*. Where the road snakes between the **Cerro Negro** and the valley of the Río de las Burras, through the **Quebrada del Mal Paso**, it crosses the Tropic of Capricorn several times, before reaching Susques, some 180km from Purmamarca.

Susques

A minute but wonderfully picturesque village, formerly belonging to Chile, **SUSQUES** is now where the Argentine customs point is located; expect lengthy clearance procedures, especially if coming from Chile. While waiting, take a look at the sumptuous church, with its delicate thatched roof and rough adobe walls, like those of all the houses in the village, and the naive frescoes on the inside.

ARRIVAL AND DEPARTURE — SUSQUES

By bus Pullman (☎ 0388 422 1366) runs buses from Salta, via Jujuy, Purmamarca and Susques, to San Pedro de Atacama and on to Antofagasta, Iquique and Arica, in Chile, twice a week, leaving Salta at 7am and arriving at San Pedro in the evening.

ACCOMMODATION

Pastos Chicos ☎ 0388 423 5387, ⓦ pastoschicos.com.ar. Probably the best place to stay; conveniently next to the fuel station, with rooms that are comfortable and warm. The restaurant is cosy with tasty meals. **$320**

La Vicuñita ☎ 03887 490207. Very basic but clean, serving simple food and located close to the village centre. **$150**

Maimará

From Purmamarca, the RN-9 continues north, climbing through the Quebrada de Humahuaca past coloured mountainsides, ornamented with rock formations like organ-pipes or elephants' feet with painted toes. One highly photogenic sight, conveniently visible from the main road, is the extraordinary cemetery at **MAIMARÁ**, 75km from Jujuy; a honeycombed mountain of a graveyard, surrounded by rough-hewn walls and covered with a jumble of centuries-old tombs of all shapes and sizes; crowned with bouquets of artificial flowers and rickety crosses, it appears even bigger than the village it serves. Behind it, the rock formations at the base of the mountain resemble multicoloured oyster-shells. The multiple shades of creams and reds, yellows and browns have earned the rocks the name La Paleta del Pintor ("the artist's palette").

ACCOMMODATION — MAIMARÁ

Hostal Posta del Sol Rodríguez and San Martín ☎ 0388 423 5387, ⓦ postadelsol.com. Maimará isn't the most happening place in the Quebrada, but if you choose to stay this is your best bet. The hotel has a number of very smart, simply decorated rooms, a restaurant and a pool, and the owners can take you on trips into the surrounding area. **$270**

Tilcara

Only 5km from Maimará along the RN-9 you are treated to your first glimpse of the great pre-Inca *pukará*, or fortress, of **TILCARA**. Just beyond it is the side road off to the village itself. At an altitude of just under 3000m and yet still dominated by the dramatic mountains that surround it, this is one of the biggest settlements along the Quebrada and the only one on the east bank; it lies just off the main road, where the Río Huasomayo runs into the Río Grande. The pleasant, easy-going village is always very lively, but even more so during **Carnival**. Like the rest of the Quebrada, it also celebrates **El Enero**

Tilcareño, a procession and feast held during the latter half of January, **Holy Week**, and **Pachamama**, or the Mother Earth festival, in August. The festivities feature wild games, music, noisy processions and frenzied partying. If you dislike crowds and have not booked accommodation well ahead, though, then these times are best avoided.

Nuestra Señora del Rosario

Alberro 447 • Wed–Fri 9–11am & 5.30–7pm • Free

The impressively massive colonial church, **Nuestra Señora del Rosario**, stands one block back from the main square, Plaza C. Alvarez Prado, on a smaller square of its own. Founded in the 1790s, it was rebuilt a century later. *Cardón* cactus replaces timber in the doorway and interior furnishings, while the beige walls blend agreeably with the mountain backdrop.

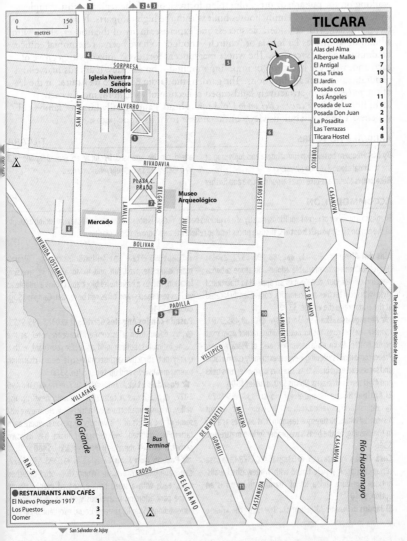

TILCARA

ACCOMMODATION
Alas del Alma	9
Albergue Malka	1
El Antigal	7
Casa Tunas	10
El Jardín	3
Posada con los Ángeles	11
Posada de Luz	6
Posada Don Juan	2
La Posadita	5
Las Terrazas	4
Tilcara Hostel	8

RESTAURANTS AND CAFÉS
El Nuevo Progreso 1917	1
Los Puestos	3
Qomer	2

5

Museo Arqueológico

Plaza C. Alvarez Prado • Daily 10am–6pm • $30 combined ticket for museum, *pukará* and botanical garden, Mon free

Housed in a beautiful colonial house on the south side of the main plaza, you'll find the **Museo Arqueológico**. The well-presented collection includes finds not only from the region but also from Chile, Bolivia and Perú, such as anthropomorphic Mochica vases, a bronze disc from Belén and assorted items of metal and pottery, of varying interest. The simple patio is dominated by a humanoid standing stone from the *pukará* of Rinconada, far up in the north of the province.

Pukará and Jardín Botánico de Altura

Acceso al Pukará • Daily 10am–6pm • $30, combined ticket for museum, *pukará* and botanical garden, Mon free

A kilometre or so southwest of the plaza, the University of Buenos Aires has long been working on the **pukará**, or pre-Columbian fortress, one of the region's most complex, with row upon row of family houses built within the high ramparts. It has reconstructed, with considerable success and expertise, many of the houses, along with a building known as La Iglesia or "church", thought to have been a ceremonial edifice, no doubt used for sacrifices. The whole magnificent fortress is spiked with a grove of cacti and, with the backdrop of imposing mountains on all sides, it affords marvellous panoramic views in all directions. The garden, the **Jardín Botánico de Altura**, in the lee of the *pukará*, is an attractively landscaped collection of local **flora**, mostly cacti, including the hairy *cabeza del viejo* ("old man's head") and equally hirsute "lamb's tail" varieties. There are fabulous views of the *pukará* from its stone paths.

ARRIVAL AND TOURS

TILCARA

By bus Frequent buses from Humahuaca and Jujuy stop at the terminal along Avenida Alvear.

Bike tours Mountain-bike tours around Tilcara and further

afield can be arranged by Jujuy en Bici, Belgrano 763 ☏ 09388 504 5335, ⓦ jujuyenbici.com.ar.

ACCOMMODATION

Thanks to a number of recent additions, mostly of a luxurious nature, Tilcara is not short of places to stay, including a couple of the region's best **youth hostels**, though prices tend to reflect the area's growing popularity.

Alas del Alma Padilla 437 ☏ 0388 495 5572, ⓦ alas .travel. Extremely comfortable adobe-and-stone *cabañas* sleeping two or four, done out in an appealing traditional style with local textiles and ceramics, conveniently located at the entrance to the village. $300

★ **Albergue Malka** San Martín s/n ☏ 0388 495 5197, ⓦ malkahostel.com.ar. An outstanding, rather upmarket youth hostel, 400m up a steep hill, east of Plaza Alvarez Prado, commands sweeping views, is extremely comfortable and serves excellent breakfasts. The friendly owner runs treks and 4WD tours in the area. Dorms $70, doubles $300

El Antigal Rivadavia and Belgrano ☏ 0388 495 5020, ⓔ lantigaltilcara@yahoo.com.ar. A basic but decent *residencial* with a picturesque tearoom that doubles as a bar in the evening; all the beds have proper sprung mattresses. $380

Casa Tunas Padilla 765 ☏ 0388 154 045784, ⓦ casa tunas.com.ar. A simple house with whitewashed walls, antique furniture and a lot of charm; half-board is an option. $250

El Jardín Belgrano 700, 1km northwest of the village

☏ 0388 495 5128, ⓦ eljardintilcara.com.ar. Tilcara's main campsite, well run and in an attractive riverside location. There's a basic hotel block and cabins available as well as tent spaces, and bikes can be rented. Camping $30, doubles $110

Posada con los Ángeles Gorriti s/n ☏ 0388 495 5153, ⓦ posadaconlosangeles.com.ar. Heavenly hotel, as the name intimates, built around an idyllic courtyard, with a quirky but attractive architectural-style decor, charming rooms, great views and tip-top service. $380

★ **Posada de Luz** Ambrosetti and Alverro ☏ 0388 495 5017, ⓦ posadadeluz.com.ar. Panoramic views up the valley, original architecture and a friendly welcome are just some of the assets of this wonderful posada, where each tastefully furnished and decorated room has its own cachet. Book well ahead as it fills up quickly. $460

★ **Posada Don Juan** Lavalle s/n ☏ 0388 495 5422, ⓦ posadadonjuan.com.ar. Wonderful semi-detached units, each with a small terrace, spaced evenly around a fine park affording marvellous views of Tilcara and its surroundings. Simple, tasteful decor, excellent breakfasts and professional staff. **$310**

La Posadita La Sorpresa s/n ☏ 0388 154 472 9997, ⓦ laposadita.com.ar. In a similar style to its "mother", *Posada de Luz*, but a little smaller and cheaper; the bright airy rooms have huge picture windows that look over to the coloured mountains to the west. **$290**

Las Terrazas Las Sorpresas and San Martín ☏ 0388 495 5589, ⓦ lasterrazastilcara.com.ar. Set up on landscaped stepped terraces near the edge of town, this boutique hotel has large rooms with balconies and a small pool and sundeck, all of which command fantastic views of the rippling mountains. **$570**

★ **Tilcara Hostel** Bolívar 166 ☏ 0388 495 5105, ⓦ tilcarahostel.com. This hostel has established a good reputation for safety, cleanliness and comfort in its dorms and *cabaña*-style doubles. It has a pleasant common room, barbecue facilities (the village market is just next door) and the owners organize local excursions. Dorms **$70**, doubles **$200**

EATING AND DRINKING

El Nuevo Progreso 1917 Lavalle 351 ☏ 0388 495 5237. An ideal place for good food – including more unusual dishes such as lamb cooked in dark beer as well as plentiful salads – and occasional excellent folk music, on the smaller plaza opposite the church. Daily 8pm–late.

Los Puestos Belgrano and Padilla ☏ 0388 495 5100. For a meal in exceptionally beautiful surroundings, with handsome photos on the walls, *Los Puestos* rules supreme:

the varied menu features tender grilled llama, mouth-watering empanadas, juicy *humitas* and succulent pasta, all at reasonable prices. Daily 11.30am–3pm & 8.30pm–midnight.

Qomer Belgrano 417 ☏ 0388 495 5439. An excellent place for a coffee, a snack or a more elaborate meal, such as a hearty *locro* – plus top-rate breakfast. Daily 8am–late.

Huacalera

After a short, steep climb beyond the side road from Tilcara, the RN-9 levels off and crosses the Tropic of Capricorn – marked by a giant sundial monument built in the 1980s and meant to align with the noon shadow at the solstice, but curiously installed at the wrong angle by mistake – a kilometre south of **Huacalera**, a tiny hamlet dominated by its seventeenth-century chapel. The road then climbs past Cerro Yacoraite, a polychrome meseta to the west, streaked with bright reds and yellows.

Uquía

Picturesque **UQUÍA**, around 20km north of Tilcara, is worth a stopoff to visit its fine colonial-era church, typical of churches in these parts – utterly simple design, plain whitewashed facade, embellished with an arch, and a single squat tower. There are also a couple of pleasant accommodation options if you want to spend the night.

Iglesia de San Francisco de Paula

Plaza Principal • Open on demand • Free

Set against a vivid backdrop of brick-red mountains and surrounded by lush *quebrachos*, behind a delightful square, is the seventeenth-century **Iglesia de San Francisco de Paula**, with its separate tower integrated in the churchyard wall, all painted pristine white, except the smart green door. Inside, the simple nave directs your gaze to the fine **retable**, the original, with its little inset painted canvases. Nine beautiful and unusual **paintings**, also from the seventeenth century, line the walls; these are unique to Collao, Alto Perú, and depict warrior-like *ángeles militares*, or angels in armour, holding arquebuses and other weapons. Formerly they numbered ten, but one went missing while they were being exhibited in Buenos Aires, where the remaining nine were restored, excessively to some tastes – they seem to have lost their centuries' old patina. If the church is closed – which is likely – ask around for the elderly woman who keeps the key, apparently the 300-year-old original.

ACCOMMODATION

Hostal de Uquía Belgrano and Lozano ☎03887 490508. In the village itself, this delightful hotel has a big homely sitting room, is done out in colonial pink, and has a fine dining room. **$350**

Huasadurazno Set back slightly from the RN-9, about 1km north of the village ☎0388 154 398457, ✉huasadurazno.com.ar. Attractive *hostería* with bright rooms, some with bath, arranged along a traditional galleried, whitewashed house. Delicious meals, using home-grown vegetables, are served to order. **$180**

Humahuaca

The main town in the area, **HUMAHUACA**, 125km north of Jujuy, spills across the Río Grande from its picturesque centre on the west bank. Its enticing cobbled streets, lined with colonial-style or rustic adobe houses, lend themselves to gentle ambling – necessarily leisurely at this altitude, a touch below 3000m. Most organized tours arrive here for lunch and then double back to Jujuy or Salta, but you may like to stay over, and venture at least as far as the secluded village of **Iruya**; Humahuaca is also an excellent springboard for trips up into the desolate but hauntingly beautiful landscapes of the altiplano or **Puna Jujeña**.

Statue of San Francisco Solano

Plaza Principal • Daily noon & midnight

Most tours to and around the town aim to deliver you at the beautifully lush main square at midday on the dot, in time to see a kitsch **statue of San Francisco Solano** emerge from a niche in the equally kitsch tower of the whitewashed **Municipalidad**, give a sign of blessing, and then disappear behind his door. A crowd gathers, invariably serenaded by groups of folk musicians; the saint repeats his trick at midnight to a smaller audience.

Iglesia de Nuestra Señora de la Candelaria y San Antonio

Plaza Principal • Daily noon–1pm • Free

Opening each day after the statue show is over, and far more impressive, is the **cathedral**, the Iglesia de Nuestra Señora de la Candelaria y San Antonio, built in the seventeenth century on the western side of the square, and much restored since. Within its immaculate white walls is a late seventeenth-century retable, and another on the north wall by Cosmo Duarte, dated 1790, depicting the Crucifixion. The remaining artworks include a set of exuberantly Mannerist paintings called the *Twelve Prophets*, signed by leading Cusqueño artist Marcos Sapaca and dated 1764.

Monumento a la Independencia

Jujuy and Córdoba

Looming over the church and the whole town is the controversial **Monumento a la Independencia**, a bombastic concoction of stone and bronze, built in the 1940s by local artist Ernesto Soto Avendaño. Triumphal steps lead up to it from the plaza, but the best thing about it is the view across the town and valley to the mountainside to the east. The 20m-high monument is topped by a bronze statue of an Indian in a ferociously warrior-like pose. Behind it, and far more appealing, framed by two giant cacti, is an adobe tower decorated with a bronze plaque, all that remains of the Iglesia Santa Bárbara, whose ruins were destroyed to make way for the monument.

ARRIVAL AND DEPARTURE

By bus Buses from Jujuy, Salta, La Quiaca and Iruya arrive at the small bus terminal a couple of blocks southeast of the main square, at Belgrano and Entre Ríos.

By car If you're travelling by car, be prepared for the local boys who will approach you at the RN-9 turn-off and offer to guide you. They'll show you around for a small tip, but speak only Spanish.

ACCOMMODATION

Many people tend to prefer staying in Tilcara, as Humahuaca is at considerably higher altitude and has less choice of accommodation. However, you should still have no problems finding somewhere to stay should you decide to base yourself here, and prices are generally low. A couple of the best options are some way from the village centre, across the Río Grande, in the Barrio Medalla Milagrosa, but if you call ahead they will come and collect you from the bus terminal.

Azul Barrio Medalla Milagrosa ☎03887 421596, ⓦhostalazulhumahuaca.com.ar. The location is a bit out of town and the rooms are a little cramped, but they are exquisitely decorated and built around a tranquil patio according to traditional techniques. The bread and jams served at breakfast are home-made. **$300**

Inti Sayana La Rioja 83 ☎03887 15 409 9806, ⓦintisayanahostal.com.ar. Lively, clean little B&B that organizes all kinds of cultural events – mostly music and dance. **$310**

Kuntur Wasi Santa Fe 520 ☎03887 421337, ⓔcarlos .kuntur@yahoo.com.ar. The rustic stone exterior is matched by a rustic stone interior, but the rooms are comfortable, albeit a little offbeat in design. The excellent restaurant is open only to patrons. **$320**

Residencial Humahuaca Córdoba 401 and Corrientes ☎03887 421141. Conveniently located close to the bus terminal, this homely *residencial* has very reasonable doubles, triples, quadruples and even quintuples. Breakfast is served in the *confitería* and there is a sunny patio. **$170**

★ **El Sol** Barrio Medalla Milagrosa ☎03887 421466, ⓦelsolhosteldehumahuaca.com. Fun little posada that doubles up as a youth hostel, with dorm bunks and neat doubles. The house is built of adobe brick with a straw roof, and the atmosphere is young, with lots of guitar-centred evenings. Dorms **$45**, doubles **$170**

Solar de la Quebrada Santa Fe 450 ☎03887 421986, ⓦsolardelaquebrada.com.ar. Gorgeous *hostería* with fabulous views, six stylishly appointed rooms with excellent mattresses, and appealing, bright decor. **$360**

EATING AND DRINKING

Casa del Tantanakuy Salta 370 ☎03887 421538. Serves regional dishes, wines and real espresso coffee and holds literary, artistic and musical events. In its marvellous little projection room it screens non-blockbuster films by the likes of Orson Welles and Wong Kar Wai. Daily noon–3pm & 8pm–midnight.

Casa Vieja Buenos Aires and Salta ☎03887 421181. A rustic interior belies some very fine cooking, with the emphasis on Andean ingredients, and the stage is regularly graced by leading folklore singers and musicians. Daily noon–3pm & 8pm–midnight.

Pacha Manka Buenos Aires 457 ☎03887 421265. Peaceful, friendly place offering lots of takes on quinoa – cheese- and quinoa-stuffed ravioli, quinoa stew and so on – as well as some spicier Bolivian dishes. Daily noon–late.

Peña de Fortunato Ramos San Luís and Jujuy ☎03887 421040. Delicious, plentiful regional food accompanied by live folk music – albeit aimed at tour groups. Daily 8pm–late.

El Rosedal Buenos Aires 175 ☎03887 421318. Authentic, delicious fare based on llama and quinoa. Daily 8am–11pm.

Iruya

The Andean hamlet of **IRUYA** fits snugly into the side of the valley of the Río Iruya, in the far northern corner of Salta Province, around 75km northeast of Humahuaca. Reminiscent of certain Greek island villages, its fortified walls, steep cobbled streets, whitewashed houses and timeless atmosphere, accentuated by the rarefied air – at an altitude of 2780m – make it worth a visit. The road here from Humahuaca is dramatic, crossing a couple of oases and stony riverbeds before winding up a stunningly beautiful narrow valley, and then down again, via a dramatic corniche road along which you wonder how two buses can pass each other. The point where you cross the border into Salta Province is the Abra del Cóndor pass, at a giddying and often gale-blown 3900m.

On the first Sunday of October, its beautiful little **Iglesia de Nuestra Señora del Rosario y San Roque** – a typical Quebrada chapel built to the familiar Mudéjar design – is the focal point for a wonderfully picturesque festival, half-Catholic, half-pre-Columbian, culminating in a solemn procession of weirdly masked figures, some representing demons. Of all the Northwest's festivals, this is the most fascinating and mysterious.

ARRIVAL AND ACCOMMODATION

Two or three Empresa Mendoza **buses** (☎03887 421016) a day make the at-least-3hr trip from Humahuaca.

Iruya San Martín 641 ☎03887 482002, ⓦhoteliruya
.com. Other than the hostel, the only really decent place
to stay is this comfortable but overpriced *hostería*, where
the food is agreeable. **$415**

Milmahuasi Hostel Salta s/n ☎03887 15 445 7994,
ⓦmilmahuasi.com. Warm blankets are on offer at this
friendly hostel with views over the river. Dorms $80,
doubles $320

The Puna Jujeña

Due north of Humahuaca and the turn-off to tiny Iruya, the RN-9 begins its long,
winding haul up into the remote **altiplano** of northern Jujuy, known as the **Puna
Jujeña**; this is a fabulously wild highland area of salt flats, **lagoons** speckled pink with
flamingoes and tiny hamlets built of mud-bricks around surprisingly big Quebrada-
style chapels. Some 30km north of Humahuaca, the RN-9 enters the **Cuesta de Azul
Pampa**, a dramatic mountain pass peaking at 3730m and offering unobstructed views
across to the huge peaks to the east. Past the bottleneck of the Abra de Azul Pampa,
where fords along the road sometimes freeze, causing extra hazards, the road winds
along to the bleak little mining town of **Tres Cruces**, where there's a major *gendarmería*
post – personal and vehicle papers are usually checked. Nearby, but out of sight,
are some of the continent's biggest deposits of lead and zinc, along with silver mines,
while overlooking the village is one of the strangest rock formations in the region, the
so-called **Espinazo del Diablo**, or "Devil's Backbone", a series of intriguingly beautiful
stone burrows, clearly the result of violent tectonic activity millions of years ago, ridged
like giant vertebrae. This road continues all the way to the Bolivian border at **La Quiaca**
– an ideal base for visiting the remote corners of the province, such as **Yavi**, and its
superb colonial church, and **Laguna de los Pozuelos**, with its sizeable wildfowl colony.

La Quiaca

Almost 165km north of Humahuaca, **LA QUIACA**, the largest settlement in the Puna
Jujeña, is a border town that has seen better days. Immediately to the north, the river
of the same name, gushing through a deep gorge, forms the natural frontier with
Bolivia; on the other side of it the twin town of Villazón thrives on cross-border trade,
while La Quiaca stagnates because its shops are losing trade to cheaper stores in Bolivia.

> ### CASABINDO AND THE FEAST OF THE ASSUMPTION
>
> If you have your own transport, and are looking to get well off the beaten track, you may want
> to take a diversion to the unspoilt village of **Casabindo**, particularly if you can time your visit
> to coincide with the August 15 **Feast of the Assumption**, among the most fascinating and
> colourful of all the Northwest's festivals. Some 80km north of Humahuaca you pass through
> the crossroads village of **Abra Pampa**, a forlorn place of llama herdsmen living in adobe
> houses, from where the rough-surfaced RP-11 leads to Casabindo, 60km southwest. The tiny
> village is dwarfed by a huge church, the **Iglesia de la Asunción**, so large it's nicknamed
> La Catedral de la Puna ("the cathedral of the *puna*"). It houses a collection of Altoperuvian
> paintings of *ángeles militares*, or angels in armour, similar to those in Uquía (see p.303). Its
> several chapels are the theatre of major celebrations on the August 15 festival. Plume-hatted
> angels and a bull-headed demon lead a procession around the village, accompanied by
> drummers. The climax of the festival is a bloodless *corrida*, a colonial custom. The bull,
> representing the Devil, has a rosette hung with coins stuck on his horns and the Virgin's
> "defenders" have to try and remove it. Coca leaves and fermented maize are buried in another
> ceremony on the same day, as an offering to Pachamama, the Earth Mother.

Although there's nothing to do here, except get used to the altitude – 3445m – and perhaps plan your trip into Bolivia, its accommodation makes it a possible base for exploring this furthest corner of Argentina. La Quiaca livens up a little on the third and fourth Sundays of October, when the **Manca Fiesta**, also known as the Fiesta de la Olla, or cooking-pot festival, is staged; ceramists and other artisans show off their wares, while folk musicians put on concerts.

ACCOMMODATION
LA QUIACA

Crystal Sarmiento 539 ☎ 03885 422255, ⓦ hotelcrystal laquiaca.com. Very basic rooms leading off a stark court-yard, with decent food served at low prices. **$160**

Hostería Munay Tierra de Colores Belgrano 51

☎ 03885 423924. La Quiaca's best place to stay, this well-run *hostería* has pleasant rooms in a modern building and a safe garage. **$190**

Yavi

Across the rolling Siete Hermanos mountain range, 17km east of La Quiaca, sits the charming altiplanic village of **YAVI**, with sloping cobbled streets, adobe houses and a splendid, working flour mill. There are also pre-Columbian petroglyphs and cave paintings in the nearby mountains, although the walk to get to them, through stunning countryside, is more worthwhile than the sites themselves.

Casa del Marqués de Tojo
Plaza Mayor • Opening hours erratic • $5

From a mirador at the top of main drag Avenida Senador Pérez, to the north of the village, you have a panoramic view, taking in the dilapidated but attractive eighteenth-century **Casa del Marqués de Tojo**, the erstwhile family home of the region's ruling marqués, the only holder of that rank in colonial Argentina. The house is a museum of sorts, with a motley collection of artefacts and junk, such as the bedstead used by the last marqués, arranged in various rooms around a fabulous patio shaded by a willow and an elm.

Iglesia de Nuestra Señora del Rosario y San Francisco
Plaza Mayor • Opening hours erratic, ask for the lady who keeps the key • Free

Behind its harmonious white facade, the village's seventeenth-century church, **Iglesia de Nuestra Señora del Rosario y San Francisco**, is one of the region's best-preserved colonial interiors, lit a ghostly lemon-yellow by the unique wafer-thin onyx-paned windows. Some of the church's treasures were stolen during the border conflict with Chile – when *gendarmes* left the village to guard Argentine territory – and were recently traced to a private collection in the US. The ornate Baroque pulpit, three retables decorated with coloured wooden statuettes of saints and a fine sixteenth-century Flemish oil painting that must have been brought here by early colonizers, look wonderful in the simple white nave.

ACCOMMODATION AND EATING
YAVI

Apart from some grimly basic *hospedajes*, there are a couple of recommendable places to stay, offering food as well as lodging – which is just as well, as there are no restaurants to speak of. You can also **camp** across the *acequia* (irrigation channel) from the church, but the site has no facilities.

Hostería Pachama Senador Pérez s/n ☎ 03887 490508, ⓦ pachamahosteria.net. The village's best place to stay, though the ultra-plain rooms come as a disappointment after the appealing decor of the main building. Staff can concoct a basic but tasty meal if required, served in an attractive dining room. **$150**

El Mirador Acceso a Yavi ⓦ elmiradordeyavi.com.ar. New, smart hostel in *cabaña*-style buildings at the top of the town, with both dorm beds and private rooms and a restaurant serving up local fare and pizzas. Dorms **$35**, doubles **$140**

5

The cloudforest national parks

A trio of the Northwest's cloudforests, or *yungas* – areas of dense jungle draped over high crags that thrust out of the flat, green plains of lowlands on either side of the Tropic of Capricorn – are protected by national park status. The microclimates of all three *yungas* are characterized by clearly distinct dry and wet seasons, winter and summer, but relatively high year-round precipitation. The peaks are often shrouded in cloud and mist, keeping most of the varied plant-life lush even in the drier, cooler months. They are difficult to access, and a visit requires time and planning, but they reward with dramatic scenery, though the incredibly varied fauna that live amid the dense vegetation are perhaps the main attraction.

The biggest of the three, the **Parque Nacional Calilegua**, is also the most accessible and best developed – it's the pride and joy of Jujuy Province – and within easy reach of San Salvador de Jujuy. **Parque Nacional El Rey**, in Salta Province, is much closer to the provincial capital, but its access roads are sometimes impassable after the heavy seasonal rains. **Parque Nacional Baritú**, away to the north in a far-flung corner of Salta Province, is the hardest to get to, and therefore the least spoilt. The parks are best visited between May and October, as the summer months – December to March or April – can see sudden cloudbursts cut off access roads and make paths much too slippery for comfort. At all times bring **insect repellent** since mosquitoes and other nasty bugs are plentiful.

Parque Nacional Calilegua

Aguas Negras, Jujuy • Daily 9am–6pm • Free • ⓦ calilegua.com

Spread over 760 square kilometres, just south of the Tropic of Capricorn, the **PARQUE NACIONAL CALILEGUA** sticks up above rich fertile land that is home to some of the country's biggest sugar farms. It's the setting for amusing anecdotes in Gerald Durrell's book *The Whispering Land*; his tales of roads cut off by flooding rivers can still ring true but his quest for native animals to take back to his private zoo cannot be imitated – the park's rich flora and fauna (see p.552) are now strictly protected by law. The land once belonged to the Leach brothers, local sugar barons of British origin, whose family donated it to the state to turn it into a national park in the 1970s. This was a shrewd business move: sugar plantations need a lot of clean water and the only way to keep the reliable supplies which run through the park free of pollution, uncontrolled logging and the general destruction of the fragile ecosystem was through the state regulations that come with national park status.

The **park entrance** is at Aguas Negras, 120km from Jujuy city via the RN-34. The nearest major settlement, around 5km southeast of the park entrance, is **Libertador General San Martín**, an uninviting little town, dominated by the huge Ledesma

---

TREKKING IN THE PARQUE NACIONAL CALILEGUA

You will need to walk off the beaten track, well away from noisy trucks, if you want to have the slightest chance of spotting any of the wildlife. **Trekking** around Calilegua takes time and it's a very good idea to spend a night or two in the park. Morning and late afternoon are the best times to see animals and birds by streams and rivers. A number of trails of varying length and difficulty have been hacked through the dense vegetation; ask the rangers for guidance.

The summits of the **Serranía de Calilegua**, marking the park's northwestern boundary, reach heights of over 3300m, beyond which lie grassland and rocky terrain. The trek to the summit of Cerro Amarillo (3320m) takes three days from the park entrance; the nearby shepherds' hamlet, **Alto Calilegua**, is certainly worth a visit. From the tiny settlement of San Francisco within the park it's even possible to link up with **Tilcara** (see p.300), a four-day trek; some of the organized trips arranged in Salta and Tilcara itself, including horse rides, offer this amazing chance to witness the stark contrast between the verdant jungle and the desiccated uplands.

industrial complex – the world's biggest sugar refinery – and usually referred to as Libertador or LGSM on signs. From the town, the RP-83 leads to the park and is paved as far as Aguas Negras. The tiny village of Calilegua, 2km from the park entrance, has a *hostería* and park information, but otherwise no facilities.

ARRIVAL, INFORMATION AND TOURS   PARQUE NACIONAL CALILEGUA

By car Cars can make it along the main road through the park, punctuated by numerous viewpoints, as far as the Mesada de la Colmenas, near a rangers' headquarters, but a 4WD will be required beyond here.

By bus Buses from Salta (2 daily) or Jujuy (frequent) stop at Libertador's terminal on Av Antartida Argentina, 200m east of the RN-34. Buses from Libertador to Valle Grande pass through the park, leaving the terminal at 8.30am and returning at 2pm.

Tourist information The *intendencia* is in the village of Calilegua (San Lorenzo s/n ☎03886 422046, ✉calilegua @apn.gov.ar). It's definitely worth a visit before you head in for maps and extra information about the park.

Tours You may wish to visit the park on an organized tour; Clark Expediciones (see box, p.286) regularly runs expert birdwatching safaris to the park.

ACCOMMODATION

Camping Aguas Negras Near to the park entrance. This free campsite offers only basic facilities; take enough insect repellent and drinking water.

Complejo Termal Aguas Calientes RP-1 ☎0388 156 50699, ⓦtermasdecaimancito.com.ar. In a bucolic setting, this spa resort offers excellent meals and clean rooms, camping and the opportunity to splash around in various curative mineral pools. Located 30km northeast of Libertador along the RP-1, which turns eastwards off the RN-34 past the straggly village of Caimancito, this is an excellent place to rest, conveniently near Calilegua in an area rich in trails and scenery. **$240**

El Jardín Colonial San Lorenzo s/n, Calilegua ☎03886 430334, ✉eljardincolonial@hotmail.com. The only place to stay in Calilegua village, close to the park entrance, is this simple but attractive and well-appointed *hostería*, with wi-fi, a pool and a/c, housed in a pink 1910s building that once belonged to Ledesma. **$135**

Posada del Sol Av Los Ceibos 747, Libertador ☎03886 424900, ⓦposadadelsoljujuy.com.ar. Plush posada offering top-notch service and excursion possibilities, with inviting rooms arranged around an attractive courtyard and swimming pool. **$380**

Parque Nacional El Rey

RP-20, Salta/Jujuy border · Daily 9am–dusk · Free

PARQUE NACIONAL EL REY straddles the borders of Salta and Jujuy provinces, nearly 200km by road from the city of Salta. Covering 400 square kilometres of land once belonging to Finca El Rey near the provincial border with Jujuy, the national park perches at an average of 900m above sea level and nestles in a natural horseshoe-shaped amphitheatre, hemmed in by the curving **Crestón del Gallo** ridge to the northwest, and the higher crest of the **Serranía del Piquete**, to the east, peaking at around 1700m. A fan-shaped network of crystal-clear brooks, all brimming with fish, drains into the Río Popayán. The handsome **toucan** (*Ramphastos toco*) is the park's striking and easily recognizable mascot, but other birdlife abounds, totalling over 150 species. Despite this, it is not that easy to see birds here; however, the park is the best place in the region for spotting tapirs, peccaries and wild cats. A road of sorts follows the Río La Sala, while a path will take you on the two-hour climb from the rangers' station to **Pozo Verde**, a lakelet coloured green by lettuce-like *lentejas de água*, and a nearby pond where birds come to drink. The only **accommodation** option is to pitch your tent in the clearing in the middle of the park.

ARRIVAL AND TOURS   PARQUE NACIONAL EL REY

By car If you plan to come under your own steam, make sure you have a 4WD. The park's only access road is the RP-20, branching left from the RP-5, which in turn leads eastwards from the RN-9/34, near the village of Lumbrera halfway between Metán and Güemes. *Guardaparques* at the entrance can advise you on how to get around in your vehicle.

Tours Public transport to the park is nonexistent and through traffic very slight, so an organized trip is the best option if you do not have your own vehicle. Norte Trekking

5

(see box, p.286) can take you on an informative and enjoyable safari to the park; equally professional Clark Expediciones (see box, p.286) specializes in natural history and birdwatching trips here.

Parque Nacional Baritú

Los Toldos, Salta/Bolivia border • Open border • Free

Located in an isolated corner of northeastern Salta Province, the all but inaccessible **Parque Nacional Baritú** is one of the country's least visited national parks. Baritú's mascot is the red **yunga squirrel** (*ardilla roja*), but you will find most of the cloudforest animal life here, enjoying the relative seclusion. In addition to the typical flora (see p.552), the virgin vegetation includes large numbers of the impressive **tree-fern**, a dinosaur of a plant surviving from the Paleozoic era, whose scaly trunk and parasol of fronds can reach five or six metres in height; they are hard to see, however, preferring the densest parts of the forest for their habitat. Less pleasant is the *maroma*, a parasite that ungratefully strangles its host tree to death.

The lack of public transport, the need to cross into Bolivia in order to enter the park, zero on-the-spot facilities and challenging terrain all but rule out individual travel and no tour operators go there regularly, but if you're really determined Clark Expediciones or Norte Trekking in Salta (see box, p.286) should be able to help you arrange a visit.

Valles Calchaquíes

The **Valles Calchaquíes** are a series of beautiful highland valleys that enjoy over three hundred days of sunshine a year, a dry climate and much cooler summers than the lowland plains around Salta. The fertile land, irrigated with canals and ditches that capture the plentiful snowmelt from the high mountains to the west, is mostly given over to vineyards – among the world's highest – that produce the characteristic Torrontés grape. The valleys are named after the Río Calchaquí, which has its source in the Nevado de Acay (at over 5000m) near San Antonio de los Cobres, and joins the Río de las Conchas, near Salta's border with Tucumán.

Organized tours from Salta squeeze a visit into one day, stopping at the valleys' main settlement, the airy village of **Cafayate**, for lunch. However, by far the most rewarding way to see the Valles Calchaquíes is under your own steam, by climbing the amazing **Cuesta del Obispo**, through the **Parque Nacional Los Cardones**, a protected forest of gigantic *cardón* cacti, to the picturesque village of **Cachi**; then follow the valley south through some memorable scenery via **Molinos** and **San Carlos**, on to Cafayate, where plentiful accommodation facilitates a stopover. The scenic road back down to Salta through the **Quebrada de Cafayate**, or Cuesta de las Conchas, snakes past some incredible rock formations, optimally seen in the late afternoon or early evening light. All along the valleys, you'll see typical *casas de galería*: long, single-storey houses, some with a colonnade of rounded arches, others decorated with pointed ogival arches or straight pillars.

The Cuesta del Obispo

To get to the northern Calchaquí settlement of Cachi, 170km southwest of Salta, you go along the partly sealed RP-33, a scenic road that squeezes through the dank Quebrada de Escoipe, before climbing the dramatic mountain road known as the **Cuesta del Obispo**, 20km of hairpin bends, offering views of the rippling Sierra del Obispo. These beautiful mountains, blanketed in olive-green vegetation and heavily eroded by countless brooks, are at their best in the morning light; in summer, cloud and rain descends in the afternoon and evening storms can make the road impassable.

5

Valle Encantado

Just before you reach the top of the *cuesta*, a signposted track leads south down to the **Valle Encantado**, 4km away; this is a fertile little valley, set around a marshy lagoon, that becomes a riot of colour in September and October, when millions of wild flowers burst into bloom, but it's a rewarding detour all year round; its cool temperatures and delightfully pastoral scenery make it a good place for a short rest, especially if you're driving. Foxes, vizcachas and other small animals are often spotted here.

Back on the main road the **Abra Piedra del Molino**, a narrow mountain pass at 3347m, is marked by the mysterious "millstone" that gives the pass its name.

Parque Nacional Los Cardones

Av San Martín s/n, Payogasta • Open border • Free

Some 20km west of the Abra Piedra del Molino, the road cuts through the **Parque Nacional Los Cardones**, an official reserve recently set up to protect the forest of *cardón* cacti that covers the dusty valley and creeps up the arid mountainside, mingled with the parasol-like *churquis* and other spiny trees typical of desert regions. There are no facilities and you can wander as you like among the gigantic cacti, many of them more than 5m tall. *Cardones* grow painfully slowly, less than a couple of millimetres a year, and their wood has been excessively exploited for making furniture and crafts and for firewood; it's now protected, so don't remove any specimens.

Cachi

At the tiny village of **Payogasta**, where the RP-33 joins the RN-40, you have a choice of roads. You can either head north to explore the furthest reaches of the Valles Calchaquíes, with dramatic high mountains on either side and beguiling desert-like scenery accompanying you all along the rough track to La Poma, 40km north; or, especially if time is short or night is drawing in, you can head straight south for **CACHI**. This picturesque village, 2280m above sea level, is overshadowed by the permanently snowcapped **Nevado del Cachi** (6380m), whose peak looms only 15km to the west. Cachi is a pleasant place to wander, investigating the various local crafts, including ponchos and ceramics, or climbing to the **cemetery** for wonderful mountain views and a panorama of the pea-green valley, every arable patch of which is filled with vines, maize and capsicum plantations.

Plaza Mayor

The village is centred around the delightful Plaza Mayor, shaded by palms and orange trees. On the north side of the plaza stands the much-restored **Iglesia San José**, with its plain white facade, fine wooden floor and unusual cactus-wood altar, pews and confessionals. On the east side, in a Neocolonial house around an attractive whitewashed patio, is the **Museo Arqueológico Pío Pablo Díaz** (Mon–Fri 9am–6pm, Sat 10am–2pm, Sun 10am–1pm), displaying a run-of-the-mill collection of locally excavated items.

Walks from Cachi

Scenic tracks to **Cachi Adentro** and **La Aguada**, each 6km west of the village, lead from the end of Calle Benjamín Zorrilla and take you through fertile farmland where, in late summer (March–May), the fields are carpeted with drying paprika peppers, a dazzling display of bright red that features in many postcards on sale in the region.

ARRIVAL AND INFORMATION

CACHI

By bus Buses from Salta (and local buses from various villages) arrive very close to the main plaza.

Tourist information There's a tourist office in the municipalidad, Plaza Mayor (Mon–Fri 8am–9pm, Sat & Sun 9am–3pm & 5–9pm; ☎ 03868 491053). The staff should be able to find you guides to take you up into the mountains.

ACCOMMODATION

El Cortijo Av del Automóvil Club Argentino s/n ☎03868 491034, ⓦelcortijohotel.com. In a colonial house at the bottom of the hill, this is good value, with its unusual native-style decor combined with sophisticated Neo-colonial furnishings and very attentive service. **$460**

Hostería ACA Sol del Valle Av del Automóvil Club Argentino s/n ☎03868 491105, ⓦsoldelvalle.com.ar. Nearer the village proper but a distant second to *La Merced del Alto* (see below). The *hostería* has a swimming pool with a view and a passable restaurant. **$500**

Llaqta Mawka Ruíz de los Lanos s/n ☎03868 491016, ⓦhotelllaqtamawka.todowebsalta.com.ar. This welcoming inn uses local building and decoration customs and techniques to create simple but comfortable rooms and offers interesting tours of the immediate region. **$280**

La Merced del Alto Fuerte Alto s/n ☎03868 490030, ⓦlamerceddelalto.com. In a converted convent, this is Cachi's most comfortable accommodation; set in lush gardens with a pool and a spa, it enjoys outstanding views of the surrounding countryside, and has a very decent bar and restaurant serving top-notch breakfasts. **$720**

EATING AND DRINKING

Confitería del Sol Ruíz de los Llanos s/n ☎03868 491222. Upmarket, atmospheric place that serves a range of classic Argentine dishes and local specialities such as goat. Daily 8am–1am.

Oliver Plaza Mayor ☎03868 491903. For real espresso coffee and all manner of snacks, charming little *Oliver*, on the main square just along from the *Confitería del Sol*, has no rivals. Daily 8am–midnight.

From Cachi to Cafayate

The mostly unsealed RN-40 from Cachi to Cafayate takes you along some stupendous corniche roads that wind alongside the Río Calchaquí itself, offering views on either side of sheer mountainsides and snowcapped peaks. It's only 180km from one town to the other, but allow plenty of time as the narrow track slows your progress and you'll want to stop to admire the views, take photographs and visit the picturesque valley settlements en route, oases of greenery in an otherwise stark landscape. The last stretch of the road to Cafayate threads its way through extensive **vineyards**, affording views of the staggeringly high mountains – many of them over 4000m – to the west and east.

Molinos

Some 60km south of Cachi, **MOLINOS** lies a couple of kilometres west of the main road, in a bend of the Río Molinos, and is worth the side-trip for a peek at its lovely adobe houses and the eighteenth-century **Iglesia de San Pedro Nolasco**. The village's artisan products are also regarded as among the finest in the region. Opposite the church, the refurbished Finca Isasmendi, the eighteenth-century residence of the last royalist governor of Salta, is now a beautiful rural inn, *Hacienda de Molinos* (☎03868 494094, ⓦhaciendademolinos.com.ar; US$130), with eighteen enchanting rooms, some with four-poster beds, set around a marvellous patio.

Quebrada de las Flechas

Around 50km or so south of Molinos, the already impressive scenery becomes even more spectacular as you enter the surreal **Quebrada de las Flechas**, where the red sandstone cliffs form a backdrop for the flinty arrowhead-like formations on either side of the road that give the gorge its name. For 10km, weird rocks like desert roses dot the landscape and, beyond the natural stone walls of **El Cañón**, over 20m high, the road squeezes through **El Ventisquero**, the "wind tunnel".

San Carlos

The oldest settlement in the valley, dating from 1551, is picturesque **SAN CARLOS**, 35km further on from the Quebrada de las Flechas, straddling the RN-40; it's a wine-growing village and the several bodegas welcome visitors at all times, but do not provide proper guided visits. The nineteenth-century **Iglesia San Carlos Borromeo** has interior walls decorated with naive **frescoes** depicting the life of St Charles Borromeo himself.

5

Cafayate

The self-appointed capital of the Valles Calchaquíes and the main settlement hereabouts, the sprawling village of **CAFAYATE** is the centre of the province's wine industry and the main tourist base for the valleys, thanks to its plentiful, high-quality accommodation, and convenient location at a crossroads between Salta, Cachi and Amaicha. It's a small but lively, modern place, originally founded by Franciscan missionaries who set up *encomiendas*, or Indian reservations with farms attached, in the region. Apart from exploring the surroundings on foot, by bike or on horseback, you can shop for artisan goods and learn all about wine making – trying out the final product – at an impressive wine museum and at numerous bodegas (see box below). The late nineteenth-century **Iglesia Catedral de Nuestra Señora del Rosario** dominates the main plaza but is disappointingly nondescript inside; more interesting, perhaps, is the small daily crafts market that adjoins the northern side.

Museo de la Vid y el Vino

Güemes and Perdiguero · Daily 10am–9pm · $30

Given a twenty-first-century makeover in 2010, this enjoyable museum of Cafayate wine-making uses poetry and audiovisuals to bring to life the oenologist's craft and explain why the climate in the area is so good for the grapes. Highlights include a scale model of the town that moves through day and night, a re-creation of the fantastic starry skies the region enjoys, and a walkway over rushing "water". A small shop and café where you can taste *picadas* and, of course, wine, rounds things off.

Museo de Arqueología Calchaquí

Calchaquí and Colón · Daily 10am–9pm · Free

The **Museo de Arqueología Calchaquí**, one block southwest of the plaza, comprises one room piled with **ceramics** of the Candelaria and Santamaría cultures, including some massive urns, followed by another room cluttered with *criollo* antiques and curios.

Local craft workshops

About 2km south of the town, on the RN-40 to Santa María, you'll find the workshop and salesroom of one of the region's finest artisans, Oscar Hipaucha. He sells wonderfully intricate wood and metal boxes, made of *quebracho*, *algarrobo* and copper, at justifiably high prices. Way up to the north of the town, the Cristofani ceramic workshop makes elegant urns, but most tend to be too big to make practical souvenirs.

THE CAFAYATE VINEYARDS

While Mendoza and, increasingly, San Juan are the names most associated with wines from Argentina, supermarkets and wine shops around the world are selling more and more bottles with the name **Cafayate** on their labels. These **vineyards**, which at around 1700m are some of the highest in the world, are planted with the malbec and cabernet varieties for which Mendoza is justly famous, but the local speciality is a grape thought to have been brought across from Galicia: the torrontés. The delicate, flowery white wine it produces, with a slight acidity, is the perfect accompaniment for the regional cuisine, but also goes well with fish and seafood. You can try some excellent samples and see how the wine is made at one of the many bodegas in and around Cafayate, where tastings and wine sales round off each tour (Spanish only). Bodegas including Domingo Hermanos, Etchart, La Banda, Don David, Nanni, and Finca Las Nubes open their doors every weekday and sometimes at weekends too (daily 9am–1pm; sometimes they also open 3–7pm).

ARRIVAL AND INFORMATION

By bus Frequent buses from Salta and less frequent ones from Cachi, via Molinos, plus daily services from Tucumán via Amaicha arrive at the cramped terminus just along Belgrano, half a block east of the plaza, or sometimes deposit passengers at their local office.

Tourist information A kiosk (daily 8am–9pm) on the plaza dispenses information about where to stay, what to do and where to rent bikes or hire horses.

ACCOMMODATION

You'll have little trouble finding a room except during the popular, but not very exciting, **folk festival**, the Serenata Cafayateña, held on the first weekend of Lent. The range extends from the humblest *residencial* to a couple of truly memorable establishments. Be warned that there have been reports of theft and other unpleasant experiences at a number of places in the village – to our knowledge there have been none concerning our recommendations.

Asturias Av Güemes 154 ☎ 03868 421328, ⓦ cafayate asturias.com. This centrally located, recently refurbished hotel with a northern-Spanish facade has a swimming pool, a reliable restaurant and tasteful rooms. $630

Casa de la Bodega RN-68 Km18.5 ☎ 03868 421555, ⓦ lacasadelabodega.com.ar. Off the road to San Carlos that branches off the Quebrada road (RN-68), but only 15min from Cafayate, this sumptuous wine-boutique hotel has only eight rooms, some of which are giant suites; the decor, comfort, service and, of course, the wine are all top-notch. $625

El Hospedaje Camila Quintana de Niño and Salta ☎ 03868 421680, ⓦ elhospedaje.todowebsalta.com.ar. Great little *hospedaje* that boasts a swimming pool in its grounds – a charming Neocolonial house, with comfortable rooms. $400

El Portal de las Viñas Nuestra Señora del Rosario 165 ☎ 03868 421098, ⓦ portalvinias.com.ar. Traditional *hospedaje* just off the main square – large rooms sleeping up to four, with en-suite bathrooms. $250

Hostal del Valle San Martín 243 ☎ 03868 421039, ⓔ hostaldelvalle@nortevirtual.com. Wonderful family-run B&B in an impeccably clean house. Rooms are comfortable but the highlight is a top-floor conservatory set aside for reading, listening to music and admiring the all-round views. Home-made jams are served at breakfast. $300

Hostel Ruta 40 Av Güemes 178 ☎ 03868 421689, ⓦ hostel-ruta40.com. Look for the handsome yellow front just a block south of the main plaza. This is the best hostel in Cafayate, without a doubt, with comfortable dorm beds and some decent doubles too. Dorms $90, doubles $260

★ **Killa** Colón 47 ☎ 03868 422254, ⓦ killacafayate.com .ar. Only a block from the central plaza, this splendid hotel is charming, comfortable and incredibly classy – it successfully combines Neocolonial elegance with rustic cosiness; some of the upstairs rooms have dream-like views of the surrounding mountains. There is a fair-sized pool. $450

Los Patios de Cafayate RN-40 and RN-68 ☎ 03868 421747, ⓦ patiosdecafayate.com. Handwoven carpets, chandeliers, colonial tapestries, native textiles and local arts and crafts all give this beautiful hotel a feeling of luxury, enhanced by the swimming pool and the fabulous spa, housed in a modern annexe and offering wine and grape massages. US$360

Portal del Santo Silverio Chavarría 250 ☎ 03868 422500, ⓦ portaldelsanto.com.ar. New hotel built in a Neocolonial style – note the arched galleries. The handsome rooms are well equipped, with minibars and cable TV, while breakfasts are delicious and generous, using home-made products. There's a swimming pool with jacuzzi. $585

Los Sauces Calchaquí 62 ☎ 03868 421158, ⓦ hotel lossaucessa.com. A pleasant, modern hotel, only a couple of blocks from the central plaza, with attractively decorated rooms looking onto a garden – avoid those facing the noisy street – and a bright *confitería* where breakfast is served. $430

Los Toneles Camila Quintana de Niño 38 ☎ 03868 422301, ⓦ lostoneleshostal.com.ar. Friendly budget hotel half a block from the plaza with barrels of character – literally, with giant beer barrels serving as decoration, as tables in the small patios off each room and for a children's play area. A yard with benches that resembles an English pub garden completes the picture. $160

Villa Vicuña Belgrano 76 ☎ 03868 422145, ⓦ villa vicuna.com.ar. Picturesque, slightly quirky hotel in a mustard-yellow Neocolonial house right next to the bus terminal. The rooms are delightful, as is the central patio where you can have breakfast or tea, weather permitting. $620

EATING AND DRINKING

El Almacén Camila Quintana de Niño 59 ⓦ elalmacen hostelbar.com. This remodelled house has retained many antique fittings, providing an atmospheric setting for enjoying the house *picadas* and very reasonable torrontés, made from vines that grow just behind. The building also houses a decent hostel ($55 for a dorm bed). Daily noon–11pm.

Carreta de Don Olegario Plaza Mayor ☎ 03868 421004. Much frequented and well-priced eating place on the east side of the plaza with regional fare. Daily noon–3pm & 8pm–late.

5

Heladería Santa Bárbara Güemes, half a block north of the plaza. Good gourmet ice creams; as well as the usual *dulce de leche*, chocolate etc, this small ice-cream parlour serves wine sorbets, both cabernet and torrontés. Daily noon–10pm.

El Rancho Güemes and Toscano ⓦelranchocafayate.com.ar. Reliable – and popular, so grab tables while you can – on the southern flank of the main plaza, this place also specializes in regional cooking. Daily noon–3pm & 9pm–1am.

Quebrada de Cafayate

The RN-68 forks off the RN-40 only 2km north of Cafayate, north of the Río Chuschas, before heading across fertile land, some of it given over to vineyards. It soon begins its winding descent, following the Río de las Conchas through the **QUEBRADA DE CAFAYATE** north to the Valle de Lerma and onwards to Salta. The gorge is seen at its best on the way down, in the mellow late afternoon or early evening light; organized tours aim to take you down this way and you should follow suit if travelling under your own steam. Leave plenty of time, as once in the gorge you'll be tempted to make several stops, to admire the views and take pictures.

The gorge entrance

At the northernmost part of the gorge you enter an invariably windy stretch, where you're better off inside your vehicle unless you want to be sandblasted. One positive result of frequent sandstorms, though, is the formation of wonderful sand dunes, **Los Médanos**, like gigantic piles of sawdust by the road. This is where the canyon proper begins, and the road snakes its way down alongside the riverbed. The majestic Sierras de Carahuasi – the northernmost range of the Cumbres Calchaquíes – loom behind as a magnificent backdrop, while in the foreground rock formations have been eroded and blasted by wind and rain to form buttresses, known as **Los Castillos**, or "the castles", and a huge monolith dubbed **El Obelisco**. The reds, ochres and pinks of the sandstone make it all look staggeringly beautiful.

La Yesera and the ravines

Just past the Obelisco, **La Yesera**, or "chalk quarry", is actually a strange group of eerily grey and yellow rocks exposed by millions of years of erosion, while a monk-like figure, skulking in the cliff-side, has earned the name **El Fraile**.

Just off the road, about 50km from Cafayate, two semicircular ravines carved in the mountainside are called **La Garganta del Diablo** (Devil's Throat) and **El Anfiteatro**, while the animal-like figure nearby is **El Sapo** (Toad).

The valley bottom

Still passing through delightful scenery, you leave the stupendous canyon, spiked with cacti, behind you to enter the forested valley bottom. Halfway between Cafayate and Salta, a convenient stopoff is provided by the excellent ★ *Posta de Las Cabras*, where in addition to the goat's cheese suggested by its name, you can sample all kinds of local delicacies, buy fine crafts, or just have a cup of coffee.

From La Viña, 100km northeast of Cafayate and just south of Embalse Cabra Corral, the enormous reservoir serving Salta, it's another 90km or so to the city, along the relatively busy RN-68.

San Miguel de Tucumán

In the humid valley of the Río Salí, in the eastern lee of the high Sierra de Aconquija, **SAN MIGUEL DE TUCUMÁN** (or simply **Tucumán**) is Argentina's fourth largest city, 1190km northwest of Buenos Aires and nearly 300km south of Salta by the RN-9. It hasn't changed much, it seems, since Paul Theroux was here in 1978 and wrote, in

The Old Patagonian Express, that it "was thoroughly European in a rather old-fashioned way, from the pin-striped suits and black moustaches of the old men idling in the cafés or having their shoes shined in the plaza, to the baggy, shapeless school uniforms of the girls stopping on their way to the convent school to squeeze – it was an expression of piety – the knee of Christ on the cathedral crucifix"; it still looks a bit like a European city caught in a time warp.

The capital of a tiny but heavily populated sugar-rich province, known popularly as the Garden of the Nation, Tucumán is by far the biggest metropolis in the Northwest, the region's undisputed **commercial capital** and one of the liveliest urban centres in the country, with a thriving business centre, a youthful population and even a slightly violent undercurrent, by Argentine standards. Tucumán certainly has a boisterous image, perhaps partly since it's Argentina's rugby capital, but its confidence has been trimmed over the past two or three decades by municipal political and economic crises – and the city seems to have taken longer than the rest of the country to recover from the turmoil of 2001.

Despite its narrow, traffic-clogged streets and the slightly down-at-heel pedestrianized shopping area northwest of the centre, Tucumán lends itself to a gentle stroll and you could easily spend a full day visiting its few sights, including a couple of decent museums.

Brief history

Originally founded in 1565 by Diego de Villarroel, Tucumán's first home was near the town of Monteros, 50km southwest of the present city, but mosquitoes proved an

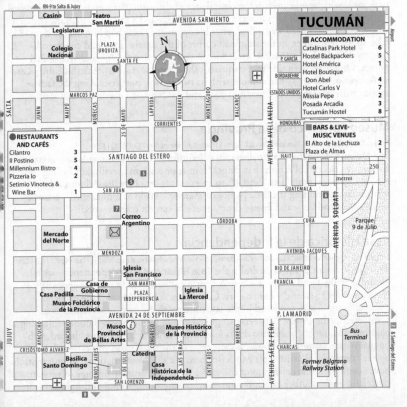

5

intolerable nuisance, and the settlement was moved to its current drier spot in 1685. The etymology of the name Tucumán is something of a mystery – it is probably a corruption of the Quichoa for "place where things finish", a reference to the abrupt mountains that loom above the fertile plains, but may have been derived from the Kana word *yukuman* meaning "welling springs". For a while, the city flourished and its name was applied to a whole region of Spanish America corresponding to southern Bolivia and the northwestern quarter of today's Argentina. Soon, though, the city was eclipsed by Salta and Córdoba, whose climates were found to be more bearable.

Then came its moment of glory, on July 9, 1816, when the city hosted a historic Congress of Unitarist politicians at which Argentina's independence from Spain was declared. British investment and climatic conditions favoured Tucumán's sugar industry, and most of the city's wealth, built up around the end of the nineteenth century, accrued from this "white gold". A slump in international sugar prices and shortsighted over-farming have now forced local sugar growers to branch out into alternative money earners, such as tobacco and citrus fruit. Tucumán has become the world's biggest lemon-producing area, but also grows mandarins, grapefruit and kumquats. With a climate similar to that around Santa Cruz de la Sierra in Bolivia, much of the area has also been given over to growing blueberries and strawberries – with large numbers of Bolivian workers helping local farmers at harvest time.

Plaza Independencia

Oozing tropical lushness **Plaza Independencia** is the city's focal point; a grove of native trees jostle with orange trees in the central area of the main plaza, each helpfully labelled, while a large pool with a fountain, a statue to Liberty and a monolith marking the spot where Avellaneda's head was spiked, after his opponent Rosas had him executed in 1841, take up the remainder. In the southeast corner of the square is the mid-nineteenth-century Neoclassical **cathedral**, its slender towers topped with blue-and-white-tiled domes. On the western side of the square is the imposing, early twentieth-century **Casa de Gobierno**, pleasingly harmonious with its two rows of porticoes along the facade, topped with an elegant slate mansard roof, and Art Nouveau detailing.

Museo Folclórico de la Provincia

Av 24 de Septiembre 565 • Tues–Sun 8am–1pm & 4–8pm • $1 (voluntary contribution) • ☎ 0381 421 8250

The **Museo Folclórico de la Provincia**, in a beautiful Neocolonial townhouse, contains a quaintly eclectic collection that ranges from *mate* ware and textiles, including the typical local lace, known as "randas", to an exquisite set of traditional musical instruments, including the little banjos or *charangos* made of mulita shell – a small species of armadillo – and *bombo* drums made of cardón (cactus wood).

Casa Histórica de la Independencia

Congreso 151 • ⊕ museocasadetucuman.com.ar • Daily 9am–7pm • $10; free guided tours at 9am, 10am & 11am • ☎ 0381 431 0826

Two blocks south of the cathedral is the **Casa Histórica de la Independencia**, with its gleaming white facade. This is where Argentina officially declared its independence from Spain in 1816 and where its first Congress was held. Most of the patrician colonial house was demolished in the late nineteenth century – this replica was completed in the 1940s. Between two grilled windows and mock-Baroque spiralling columns, the mighty *quebracho* doors lead into a series of large patios, draped with bougainvillea, jasmine and tropical creepers – in the third patio you can see bas reliefs by the famous local artist, Lola Mora (see box, p.252). Now a national monument, the house contains a fine collection of colonial armour, furniture, paintings, silverware and porcelain, while a rather kitsch but nonetheless interesting sound-and-light show in

Spanish (daily except Thurs 8.30pm; $10, tickets on sale shortly before each performance) re-enacts the story of how the country gained its independence.

ARRIVAL AND DEPARTURE   SAN MIGUEL DE TUCUMÁN

By plane Tucumán's international airport, Aeropuerto Benjamín Matienzo (☎0381 426 4906) serves Buenos Aires (6 daily; 1hr 50min) and is 9km east of the centre of town; a taxi will cost about $50. Tucumán is quite fog-prone and flights are sometimes inconveniently re-routed as far away as Santiago del Estero.

By bus Tucumanos are justifiably proud of their modern and efficient bus terminal (☎0381 422 2221), at Brígido Terán 350, six blocks east and two south of Plaza Independencia. It has sixty wide-berthed platforms, a shopping centre ("Shopping del Jardín") and supermarket,

restaurants, bars, post office, telephone centres, left-luggage and even a hairdresser – but no working ATMs: try the supermarket for cash withdrawals. Most city buses run between the centre and the bus terminal, and you'll need a token for each trip, on sale at all kiosks.

Destinations Buenos Aires (10 daily; 15hr); Córdoba (6 daily; 8hr); Jujuy (10 daily; 5hr 30min); Salta (10 daily; 4hr); Tafí del Valle (6 daily; 3hr).

By train Trains still run to and from Buenos Aires via Santiago del Estero from the station (☎0381 431 0725) at Catamarca and Corrientes.

INFORMATION

Tourist information is available at the provincial office at 24 de Septiembre 484 (Mon–Fri 7am–1pm & 5–9pm, Sat & Sun 9am–1pm & 5–9pm), on Plaza Independencia.

The branch at the bus station (same hours) can sometimes scrape a map together.

ACCOMMODATION

Rather than stay in the city, especially in the unbearable summer heat (Nov–March), you may well prefer to do as the locals do and stay in the cooler heights of Tafí del Valle (see p.320) or near the archeological site of Quilmes (see p.322). Downtown Tucumán has a wide selection of **hotels**, but the quality is poor – you're better opting for one of the boutique hotels in leafy Yerba Buena. In town, many mid-range hotels are conveniently clustered around the central Plaza Independencia, but even they are shoddily run and overpriced. At the budget end, you can choose from a number of decent **residenciales** and a couple of excellent **youth hostels**.

Catalinas Park Hotel Av Soldati 380 ☎0381 450 2250, ⦿catalinaspark.com. Rather bland and aimed mainly at the conference and business market, but worth trying, nonetheless, for its fine location overlooking Parque 9 de Julio, large roof-top pool, saunas and all mod cons; rates are cut at weekends. **$605**

Hostel Backpackers Laprida 456 ☎0381 430 2716, ⦿backpackerstucuman.com. Excellent hostel with an outdoor bar and swimming pool, in a beautiful Neocolonial townhouse. The owners also organize tours and special offers combining accommodation with excursions. There are some double rooms. Dorms **$70**, doubles **$180**

Hotel América Santiago del Estero 1064 ☎0381 430 0810, ⦿hotelamerica.com.ar. Averagely priced hotel well known for its bar, which is open till the early hours, but it also has smart rooms, with bright bathrooms. The restaurant serves decent food for those who can't be bothered to venture out. **$310**

Hotel Boutique Don Abel Güemes 35, Yerba Buena ☎0381 425 1230, ⦿hotelboutiqueabel.com.ar. Hand-some small hotel, with an attractive garden; the rooms are named after precious gems such as sapphire and ruby. **$640**

Hotel Carlos V 25 de Mayo 330 ☎0381 431 1666, ⦿hotelcarlosv.com.ar. Extremely well run, with a friendly

reception and comfortable, classy rooms with reproduction furniture and a decent restaurant. **$530**

Missia Pepe Av Aconquija 978, Yerba Buena ☎0381 425 1120, ⦿hotelmissiapepe.com. Unusually decorated suburban bungalow filled with artwork and set in stunning grounds, with a fine pool. There are just a couple of rooms available, so you get highly personalized treatment. The charming owners will lay on dinner if booked in advance. **$545**

Posada Arcadia Güemes 480, Yerba Buena ☎0381 425 22140, ⦿posadaarcadia.com.ar. One of a trio of excel-lent boutique hotels in this leafy suburb, *Arcadia* lives up to its name. The four rooms have Quechua names meaning beauty, wind, pretty woman and blooming. There is a swimming pool in the handsome garden and the owners can arrange for trips to pottery workshops nearby or horseriding in the surrounding hills. **$360**

Tucumán Hostel Buenos Aires 669 ☎0381 420 1584, ⦿tucumanhostel.com. Another exceptional Tucumán hostel, with rooms and dorms named after local mountain peaks. You get kitchen-use, bar service and internet access and a chance to book local tours, including adventure activities. Some double rooms, with and without private bath. Breakfast included. Dorms **$70**, doubles **$170**

5

EATING, DRINKING AND NIGHTLIFE

There are plenty of places to **eat**, some trendy **bars** and **cafés** in downtown, especially along Calle 25 de Mayo, and a number of **nightspots** mostly located in the chic neighbourhood of **Yerba Buena**, three or four kilometres west of the centre, on slightly higher ground. **Discos** change name and location at the drop of a sombrero, so ask around.

★ **El Alto de la Lechuza** 24 de Septiembre 1199 ☎ 0381 15 477 9527. One of the oldest *peñas*, or traditional music venues, in the country – there's great improvised music in an ancient building where the empanadas are particularly succulent. Wed–Sun 8pm–late.

Cilantro Monteagudo 541 ☎ 0381 430 6041. Fusion food and an excellent wine list at this highly regarded – and very fashionable – restaurant. Leave room for dessert and one of the delicious liqueurs on offer. Mon–Sat noon–3pm & 8pm–midnight, Sun noon–3pm.

Millennium Bistró Av Aconquija 1702, Yerba Buena ☎ 0381 425 4651. A popular, trendy pre-disco Mediterranean restaurant, bar and tearoom all rolled into one, with fashionable decor, in the cool heights of suburban Yerba Buena. Daily noon–3pm & 8pm–midnight.

Pizzeria Io Salta 602 ☎ 0381 435 4411. Vying for the city's best pizza award, this place bakes its pizzas in a wood oven and shows more than usual imagination with the toppings. Daily 8pm–late.

★ **Plaza de Almas** Maipú 791 ☎ 0381 430 6067. Popular place where locals flock to see the latest art exhibition, or just have a drink among friends. It also serves sandwiches, pizzas and other simple dishes. Tues–Sun 9pm–late.

Il Postino Córdoba 501 and 25 de Mayo ☎ 0381 421 0440. A reliable pizzeria that also serves good pasta, in attractive surroundings and with a laidback atmosphere. Daily 8am–2am.

Setimio Vinoteca & Wine Bar Santa Fe 512 ☎ 0381 431 2792. As the full name suggests, this pricey place takes its wine seriously – either sample it by the glassful with a hearty *picada* or enjoy the braised lamb and other fine dishes with a bottle of top-quality malbec or syrah. Daily 8pm–late.

DIRECTORY

Exchange Noroeste Cambios, San Martín 771.
Internet access *Locutorios* all around the city offer internet services.

Laundry Lavadero 25, 25 de Mayo 950.
Post office 9 de Julio and Córdoba.

The Selva Tucumana

The RP-307 – which turns off the RN-38 at Acheral, 42km southwest of the provincial capital – lifts you on a dramatic journey out of the moist lowlands of eastern Tucumán Province, where emerald-green sugar plantations stretch as far as the eye can see, up through the tangled mass of **Selva Tucumana** – a dense tropical forest ablaze with tree blossom from September to December – to the dry steppe of a highland valley. As the RP-307 snakes up steep jungle-clad cliffs, it offers fewer and fewer glimpses of the subtropical plains way below, where the sugar fields look increasingly like paddy fields and the individual trees of the citrus orchards resemble the dots of a pointillist painting.

At 2000m above sea level, the road levels off in more open, highland terrain and skirts the eastern bank of **Dique La Angostura**, a large reservoir; the often-snowy peak of extinct volcano **Cerro Pelao**, 2680m, is mirrored in the lake's normally still surface. If you head in a westerly direction towards Potrerillo along the RP-355, a signposted turning to El Mollar brings you to the **Parque de los Menhires**, where a number of engraved **monoliths**, deceptively Celtic-looking in appearance – but in fact the work of the Tafí tribes who farmed the area around two thousand years ago – have been planted haphazardly in a field. They used to be scattered decoratively on an exposed hill overlooking the lake at La Angostura, but weathering and graffiti led the authorities to move the historic standing stones to a safer, but not aesthetically pleasing, location.

Tafí del Valle

From the turn-off to Potrerillo, the RP-307 continues north to reach **TAFÍ DEL VALLE**, 128km west of Tucumán, favoured by locals and tourists alike as a day-trip destination or longer retreat from the provincial capital, especially in the summer when the city swelters. Tafí is a rather sprawling village located in a mountain-side valley (from which it takes its name) in the western lee of the Sierra del Aconquija, sandwiched between the Rio del Chusquí and the Río Blanquita, both of which flow into the Río Tafí and then into the Dique La Angostura. This is where Tucumanos come to escape the city – the average temperature is 12°C lower than in the city. Blue and sunny skies are virtually guaranteed year-round, though occasionally thick fog descends into the valley in the winter, making its alpine setting feel bleak and inhospitable.

Apart from relaxing, the main attraction is the opportunity to explore the beautiful mountain scenery and unspoilt riverbanks; the trekking hereabouts is very rewarding. Popular trails go up **Cerro El Matadero** (3050m; 5hr), **Cerro Pabellón** (3770m; 4hr), **Cerro Muñoz** (4437m; one day) and **Mala-Mala** (3500m; 8hr); go with a guide, as the weather is unpredictable.

The village's main streets, lime-tree-lined Avenida San Martín, and avenidas Gobernador Critto and Diego de Rojas (Av Perón on some maps), converge on the semicircular plaza, around which most of the hotels, restaurants, cafés and shops are concentrated.

Famous for its delicious cow's and goat's cheese, available at small farms and stalls all around the town, Tafí holds a lively **Fiesta Nacional del Queso**, with folk music and dancing and rock bands, in early February.

Capilla Jesuítica de la Banda

La Banda s/n • Mon–Fri 10am–6pm, Sat & Sun 9am–noon • $5; guided tours • ☎ 03867 421685

Tafí's only attraction apart from its scenery – and a good way to while away some time if the weather turns bad – lies across the Río Tafí in "La Banda", the name usually given to locations across rivers from main settlements. Just over 1km from the village main square, the **Capilla Jesuítica de la Banda** is a late eighteenth-century Jesuit building now housing archeological finds, mostly ceramic urns, from nearby digs, plus some items of furniture and modest paintings from the colonial period.

ARRIVAL AND INFORMATION

TAFÍ DE VALLE

By bus Buses from Tucumán, Santa María and Cafayate arrive at the terminal on the corner of avenidas San Martín and Gobernador Campero (☎ 03867 421025).

Tourist information Information can just about be gleaned from the tourist office on the southeastern edge of the main square (☎ 03867 421020, ☮ tafidelvalle.com), though you may find *La Cumbre* hostel (see below) more useful.

ACCOMMODATION

Accommodation in Tafí is plentiful, and often very good, ranging from a very comfortable hostel to luxurious lodgings offering haute cuisine. Rooms can get booked up at weekends in the summer, and during the cheese festival (early Feb) will be like gold dust.

Camping Los Sauzales Los Palenques ☎ 03867 421084. This is a municipal campsite, attractively located at Los Palenques on the banks of Río El Churqu, at the edge of the village. **$45**

Estancia Las Carreras RP-325 Km13 ☎ 03867 4214732, ☮ estancialascarreras.com. Rather away from the village centre, this traditional Jesuit estancia is very much a family-oriented place. Guests have contact with farm animals, dogs and horses; there's a cheese dairy on the premises; and the rooms are large and beautifully decorated, with lots of locally produced textiles. **$500**

Estancia Los Cuartos Juan Calchaquí ☎ 03867 421444, ☮ estancialoscuartos.com. A truly *criollo* estancia experience – you can even visit for the day (including lunch and

horseride, for $400) – at this traditional family home conveniently located right next to the bus terminal. There are seven charming rooms in the long galleried *casco* or in a more recent extension. **$550**

Hospedaje Celia Correa Belgrano 443 ☎ 03867 421170. The pick of the budget options, this place has basic but en-suite rooms. **$230**

Hostel La Cumbre Av Presidente Perón 120 ☎ 03867 421768, ☮ lacumbretafidelvalle.com. Tafí's hostel – highly recommended – is in a Neocolonial house built on two floors around a bright patio, all painted yellow; it doubles up as a de facto information office, much better than the official one, plus an adventure-travel tour company, Yungas. **$175**

5

Hostería ACA Sol del Valle San Martín and Gobernador Campero ☎03867 421027, ✆soldelvalle.com.ar. This well-refurbished institution is excellent value, with bright, clean and comfortable rooms. There is also a very good restaurant on the premises. $520

★ **Hostería Castillo de Piedra** La Banda s/n ☎03867 421199, ✆castillodepiedra.com.ar. This fabulously professional place is a quaint, stone, mock castle on the outside, but has designer rooms on the inside, with exquisite

furnishings, great views, a swimming pool, a sauna and, above all, a gourmet restaurant – call ahead if you are not staying at the *hostería* but want to come for a meal. $900

Hostería Huayra Puca Los Menhires 71 ☎03867 421190, ✆huayrapuca.com.ar. This unpretentious place has characterful, spacious, centrally heated rooms, soothing decor and unobjectionable artwork. There is a very decent *confitería* on site, too. $280

EATING AND DRINKING

El Blanquito Maipu 1236 ☎0381 421 0894. This fabulous tearoom serves scrumptious coffees, teas, cakes, scones and, above all, *alfajores*, with outside tables, on the road towards Amaicha. Daily 9am–2pm.

El Parador Tafinista Avenidas Gobernador Critto and Diego de Rojas. This typical local joint dishes up hefty portions of pasta and grilled meat – good no-nonsense fare. Daily noon–3pm & 8pm–midnight.

Amaicha

The village of **AMAICHA**, located at the edge of Tucumán Province, is a peaceful, nondescript little place that livens up once a year during the **Fiesta de la Pachamama** in carnival week, when dancers and musicians lay on shows while locals put on a kind of pre-Columbian Passion Play, acting the roles of the different pagan deities, including Pachamama, or Mother Earth. The goddess is also the inspiration for one of the region's most impressive museums, the Museo Pachamama, an ambitious project whose main aim is to show off a local artist's commercial success.

Amaicha can be reached from Tafí via the RP-307, which zigzags northwards offering fine views of the *embalse* and the mountains and heaves you over the windswept pass at Abra del Infiernillo (3042m). From here, the road steeply winds back down, along the banks of the Río de Amaicha, taking you through arid but impressive landscapes thickly covered with a forest of *cardón* cacti.

Museo Pachamama

200m along the road from the village centre, near the junction with the RP-357 • Daily 8.30am–1pm & 2–6pm • $10 • ☎03893 421004, ✆museopachamama.com • The regular buses from Tafi to Quilmes and Cafayate will drop you off by Amaicha's museum

The brainchild of local artist Héctor Cruz, the splendid **Museo Pachamama** is actually several museums rolled into one, and it's worth a look to see the structure itself, built around fabulous cactus gardens and incorporating eye-catching stone mosaics, depicting llamas, pre-Hispanic symbols and geometric patterns. Each large room in turn displays an impressive array of local archeological finds, the well-executed reconstruction of a mine along with impressive samples of various precious and semiprecious ores and minerals extracted in the area, plus paintings, tapestries and ceramics from Cruz's own workshops, to modern designs inspired by pre-Columbian artistic traditions.

Quilmes

From the RP-357/RN-40 junction, 15km north of Amaicha, via a dirt road heading in a westerly direction • Daily 9am–dusk • $20 • Buses to Cafayate running along the RN-40 will drop you at the junction, leaving you with the 5km trek along the dusty side-road to the site

The major pre-Inca **archeological site** of **Quilmes** is one of the most extensively restored in the country. Inhabited since the ninth century AD, the settlement of Quilmes had a population of over 3000 at its peak in the seventeenth century, but the whole Quilmes tribe was punished mercilessly by the Spanish colonizers for resisting evangelization and enslavement. Walls and many buildings in this terraced **pukará**, or pre-Columbian fortress, have been thoroughly, if not always expertly, excavated and reconstructed, and the overall effect is extremely impressive, especially in the morning light, when the mountains behind it are illuminated from the east and turn bright orange. The entrance fee also entitles you to visit the site **museum**, which contains some items found here, such as ceramics and stone tools, and displays more expensive modern crafts by local artist Héctor Cruz.

Belén

The Catamarqueño settlement of **BELÉN** is squeezed between the Sierra de Belén and the river of the same name. Olive groves and plantations of capsicum – paprika-producing peppers (*pimentones*) – stretch across the fertile valley to the south. Belén offers the area's best accommodation and a couple of very decent restaurants, a handsome church and an interesting archeological museum, and it's also a base for **adventure tourism**, including trekking and horseriding. Since Belén promotes itself as the **Capital del Poncho** you might like to visit the many excellent *teleras*, or textile workshops, dotted around the town; they also turn out beautiful blankets and sweaters made of llama, vicuña and sheep's wool, mostly in natural colours. The wool is sometimes blended with walnut bark, to give the local cloth, known as *belichas* or *belenistos*, its typical rough texture.

As for **festivals**, every January 6 a pilgrimage procession clambers to a huge statue of the Virgen de Belén, overlooking the town from its high vantage point to the west, the Cerro de la Virgen.

Iglesia Nuestra Señora de Belén

Plaza Presbítero • Free

On the western flank of its main square, **Plaza Presbítero Olmos de Aguilera**, shaded by whitewashed orange trees and bushy palms and ringed by cafés and ice-cream parlours, stands the Italianate **Iglesia Nuestra Señora de Belén**, clearly inspired by the cathedral in Catamarca and designed and built by Italian immigrants at the beginning of the twentieth century. Its brickwork is bare, without plaster or decoration, lending it a rough-hewn but not displeasing look.

Museo Provincial Cóndor Huasi

San Martín and Belgrano • Mon–Fri 9am–noon & 5–9pm • $2

Housed on the first floor of a rather grim commercial arcade (Galería Misael), half a block from the main square, the **Museo Provincial Cóndor Huasi** has one of the country's most important collections of **Diaguita** artefacts, but is poorly laid out. The huge number of ceramics, and some bronze and silver items, trace the Diaguita culture through all four archeological "periods": the Initial Period, 300 BC–300 AD, is represented by simple but by no means primitive pieces, often in the shape of

---

RHODOCHROSITE

Rhodochrosite is a semiprecious stone, similar to onyx but unique to Argentina. It is mined only from a generous seam in the Capillitas mine, to the north of Andalgalá in Catamarca Province. Known popularly as the Rosa del Inca – and believed by the indigenous people to be the solidified blood of their ancestors – rhodochrosite is reminiscent of Florentine paper, with its slightly blurred, marble-like veins of ruby red and deep salmon-pink, layered and rippled with paler shades of rose-pink and white. Its rarity has made it Argentina's unofficial **national stone**. Much of it is sold in Buenos Aires, in luscious blocks suitable as paperweights or book ends, or worked into fine, expensive jewellery, or into animal and bird figures, many of them kitsch.

5

squashes or maize-cobs; in the Early Period (Cóndor Huasi and Ciénaga; 300–550 AD), anthropomorphic and zoomorphic ceramics dominate, including naive representations of llamas and pumas; the Middle or Aguada Period, 650–950 AD, produced some of the museum's most prized pieces, such as a ceramic jaguar of astonishing finesse; and the Late Period, from 1000 AD onwards, includes the so-called Santa María culture, when craftsmen produced large urns, vases and amphoras decorated with complex, mostly abstract geometric patterns, with depictions of snakes, rheas and toads. There are a few Inca artefacts, too.

ARRIVAL AND INFORMATION   BELÉN

By bus Regular but infrequent buses from Catamarca city, Salta and Santa María arrive at the corner of Sarmiento and Rivadavia, near the museum.

Tourist information For information ask at the municipalidad, one block to the east.

ACCOMMODATION

Hotel Belén Belgrano and Cubas ☎ 03835 461501, ⊕ belencat.com.ar. The best place to stay in the area, this impressive hotel is part of a large complex that includes a convention centre and a games-room-cum-cybercafé – rooms are divided into sullka (small) and suma (large), but both are decorated in pristine white, with dark wood furnishings and amusing ethnic bathrooms, with lots of stone and ceramic tiling; there is also a clean hostel-style dorm. Breakfast is extra. Dorms $40, doubles $300

Hotel Samai Urquiza 349, one block east and south of the main square ☎ 03835 461320. Clean, and warm in winter (fans cool it enough in the summer), this modest place is certainly not luxurious but makes a useful back-up if the *Hotel Belén* is fully booked. $230

EATING

1900 Belgrano 390 ☎ 0381 461100. At the best restaurant here by far, smart waiters serve up lovingly prepared lunches and dinners in a cheery brightly-coloured decor – try the huge *bife de chorizo* with cheese and a potato tortilla plus the earthy house wine. It often gets filled up at midday with regulars. Daily noon–3pm & 8pm–midnight.

Parrillada El Único Sarmiento and General Roca, one block north of the church. If *1900* is closed or full, you can fall back on this classic favourite housed in a rustic hut; it serves excellent empanadas and does a great *locro*. Daily noon–3pm & 8pm–midnight.

Londres and around

Fifteen kilometres west of Belén and even more charming, with its partly crumbling adobe houses and pretty orchards, **LONDRES** lies 2km off the RN-40 along a winding road that joins its upper and lower towns, on either side of the Río Hondo, a usually dry river that peters out in the Salar de Pipanaco. Known as the Cuna de la Nuez, or Walnut Heartland, the town celebrates the **Fiesta de la Nuez** with folklore and crafts displays during the first few days of February. Londres de Abajo, the lower town, is centred on Plaza José Eusebio Colombres, where you'll find the simple, whitewashed eighteenth-century **Iglesia de San Juan Bautista**, in front of which the walnut festival is held. The focal point for the rest of the year is Londres de Arriba's **Plaza Hipólito Yrigoyen**, overlooked by the quaint **Iglesia de la Inmaculada Concepción**, a once lovely church in a pitiful state of repair but noteworthy for a harmonious colonnade and its fine bells, said to be the country's oldest. As yet, there's no accommodation in the town, but ask around, just in case someone has a room to let.

Londres' humble present-day aspect belies a long and prestigious history, including the fact that it's Argentina's second oldest "city" (*ciudad*), founded in 1558, only five years after Santiago del Estero. **Diego de Almagro** and his expedition from Cusco began scouring the area in the 1530s and founded a settlement which was named in honour of the marriage between Philip, heir to the Spanish throne, and Mary Tudor: hence the tribute to the English capital in the village's name.

Museo Arqueológico

Plaza Hipólito Yrigoyen s/n • Mon–Fri 8am–1pm • $3

Alongside the municipalidad, on the wall of which is a quaint fresco testifying to the town's glorious past, is the small but interesting **Museo Arqueológico** displaying pre-Columbian ceramics and other finds, including arrowheads and tools, from the impressive **Shinkal ruins**.

Shinkal

5km west of Londres • Daily: Dec–April 9am–1pm & 4–7pm; May–Nov 10am–5pm • $10

To find the ruins of Shinkal just follow the well-signposted scenic road, next to the Iglesia de la Inmaculada Concepción. Amazingly intact, though parts of it are over-restored in a zealous attempt to reconstruct the fortress, it was the site of a decisive battle in the **Great Calchaquí Uprising** (see box below). After Chief Chelemín cut off the water supplies to Londres and set fire to the town, forcing its inhabitants to flee to La Rioja, he was captured and had his body ripped apart by four horses. Shinkal gives you an insight into what Diaguita settlements in the region must have looked like: splendid steps lead to the top of high **ceremonial mounds**, with great views of the oasis and Sierra de Zapata.

THE CALCHAQUÍ WARS

After the European invasions of this region in the late sixteenth and early seventeenth centuries, the indigenous tribes who lived along the **Valles Calchaquíes**, stretching from Salta Province in the north, down to central Catamarca Province, steadfastly refused to be evangelized by the Spanish invaders and generally to behave as their aggressors wanted; the region around Belén and Londres proved especially difficult to colonize. Even the Jesuits, usually so effective at bringing the "natives" under control, conceded defeat. The colonizers made do with a few *encomiendas*, and more often *pueblos*, reservations where the Indians were forced to live, leaving the colonizers to farm their "own" land in peace. After a number of skirmishes, things came to a head in 1630, when the so-called **Great Calchaquí Uprising** began. For two years, under the leadership of **Juan Chelemín**, the fierce *cacique* of Hualfín, natives waged a war of attrition against the invaders, sacking towns and burning crops, provoking ever more brutal reactions from the ambitious new governor of Tucumán, Francisco de Nieva y Castilla. Eventually Chelemín was caught, drawn and quartered, and various parts of his body were put on display in different villages to "teach the Calchaquíes a lesson", but it took until 1643 for all resistance to be stamped out, and only after a network of fortresses was built in Andalgalá, Londres and elsewhere.

War broke out once more in 1657, when the Spanish decided to arrest "El Inca Falso", also known as Pedro Chamijo, an impostor of European descent who claimed to be Hualpa Inca – or Inca emperor – under the *nom de guerre* of **Bohórquez**. Elected chief at an impressive ceremony attended by the new governor of Tucumán, Alonso Mercado y Villacorta, amid great pomp and circumstance, in Pomán, he soon led the Calchaquíes into battle, and Mercado y Villacorta, joined by his ruthless predecessor, Francisco de Nieva y Castilla, set about what today would be called ethnic cleansing. Bohórquez was captured, taken to Lima and eventually garrotted in 1667, and whole tribes fell victim to genocide: their only remains are the ruins of Batungasta, Hualfín and Shinkal, near Londres. Some tribes like the **Quilmes**, whose settlement is now an archeological site near Amaicha (see p.322), were uprooted and forced to march to Buenos Aires. Out of seven thousand Quilmes who survived a long and distressing siege in their *pukará*, or fortress, despite having their food and water supplies cut off, before being led in chains to Buenos Aires, where they were employed as slaves, only a few hundred were left. These few remaining survivors, however, were wiped out in a smallpox epidemic at the end of the eighteenth century.

5 The Puna Catamarqueña

The altiplano of northwestern Catamarca Province, known as the **Puna Catamarqueña** (*puna* is the Quichoa word for altiplano, a word of Spanish coinage), stretches to the Chilean border and is one of the remotest and most deserted, but most outstandingly beautiful parts of the country. **Antofagasta de la Sierra**, a ghostly town of adobe-brick miners' houses and whispering womenfolk, is far flung even from Catamarca city in this sparsely populated region, but the tiny **archeological museum** is worth seeing for its fantastic mummified infant. Dotted with majestic ebony volcanoes and scarred by recent lava-flows, with the Andean cordillera as a magnificent backdrop, the huge expanses of altiplano and their desiccated vegetation are grazed by hardy yet delicate-looking **vicuñas**, while **flamingoes** valiantly survive on frozen lakes.

This is staggeringly unspoilt country, with out-of-this-world landscapes, and a constantly surreal atmosphere, accentuated by the sheer remoteness and emptiness of it all; the trip out here is really more rewarding than the main destination, **Antofagasta**, which is primarily a place to spend the night before forging on northwards, to San Antonio de los Cobres in Salta Province (see p.293), or doubling back down to Belén. As you travel, look out for *apachetas*, little cairns of stones piled up at the roadside as an offering to the Mother Goddess, Pachamama, and the only visible signs of any human presence.

Although a **bus** shuttles back and forth between Catamarca and Antofagasta twice a week, the surest way to get around is by 4WD, along the RP-43, one of the quietest roads in Argentina; it's quite possible not to pass another vehicle all day. Take all the necessary precautions including plenty of fuel, and don't forget warm clothing as the temperature can plummet several degrees below freezing at night in July. By far the best (and safest) way to explore this difficult region is with the Salta-based Socompa tours (see p.286), which also runs the *hostería* in El Peñón, easily the best accommodation this side of Belén.

Hualfín

In **HUALFÍN**, a tiny village where RP-43 branches northwestwards from the RN-40, 60km north of Belén, you can find rooms for rent, if you need **accommodation**, but most people use Hualfín as their last **fuel stop** before the long haul to Antofagasta de la Sierra; provisions can also be bought here. The village itself is famous for its paprika, often sprinkled on the delicious local goat's cheeses, and a fine **colonial church**, dedicated to Nuestra Señora del Rosario and built in 1770; ask for the key at the municipalidad to see the pristine interior adorned with delicate frescoes. Hualfín was also the birthplace and stronghold of Chelemín, the Calchaquí leader who spearheaded the Great Uprising in the 1630s (see box, p.325). **Thermal springs** with rudimentary facilities, and slightly better ones 14km north at **Villavil**, are open from January to April only.

Up to Antofagasta de la Sierra

Between **Corral Quemado** and **Villavil**, the first stretch of the RP-43 to Antofagasta de la Sierra, all of 200km from Hualfín to the northwest, takes you through some cheery if understated countryside, planted with vines and maize, with feathery acacias and tall poplars acting as windbreaks, and dotted with humble mud-brick farmhouses. Potentially treacherous fords at Villavil and, more likely, at **El Bolsón**, 10km further on, are sometimes too deep to cross even in a 4WD, especially after spring thaws or summer rains; you'll either have to wait a couple of hours for the rivers to subside or turn back. Just over 70km from the junction at Hualfín, the road twists and climbs through the dramatic **Cuesta de Randolfo**, hemmed in by rocky pinnacles and reaching

5

an altitude of 4800m before corkscrewing back down to the transitional plains. The good news is that from here to Antofagasta the road is now paved.

Reserva Natural Laguna Blanca

Along the flat section of the RP-43, you're treated to immense open views towards the dramatic crags of the Sierra del Cajón, to the south, and the spiky rocks of the Sierra Laguna Blanca, to the north. Impressive white **sand dunes**, gleaming like fresh snow against the dark mountainsides, make an interesting pretext for a halt. Down in the plain, the immense **salt lakes** stretch for miles and this is where you'll probably spy your first **vicuñas** – the shy, smaller cousins of the llama, with much silkier wool – protected by the **Reserva Natural Laguna Blanca**. All along this road, with photogenic ochre mountains as backdrops, whole flocks of vicuña graze off scrawny grasses, less timid than usual, perhaps because the flocks are so big and they feel the safety of numbers. You'll also see nonchalant llamas and shaggy alpacas and, if you're very fortunate, the ostrich-like suris or ñandús, before they scurry away nervously. You could make a short detour to visit the shores of **Laguna Blanca** itself, a shallow, mirror-like lake fed by the Río Río and home to thousands of teals, ducks and **flamingoes**; it's clearly signposted along a track off to the north.

Portezuelo Pasto Ventura

After the Reserva Laguna Blanca, the road climbs steadily again up the often snow-streaked Sierra Laguna Blanca to reach the pass at **Portezuelo Pasto Ventura** (4000m), marked by a sign: this is the entrance to the altiplano, or *puna* proper. From here you have magnificent panoramas of the Andes, to the west, and of the great volcanoes of northwestern Catamarca, plus your first glimpse of wide-rimmed **Volcán Galan** (5912m), whose name means "bare mountain" in Quichoa. It's an incredible geological feature: some 2,500,000 years ago, in a cataclysmic eruption, blasting over 1000 cubic kilometres of material into the air, its top was blown away, leaving a hole measuring over 45km by 25km, the largest known crater on the Earth's surface – or in the solar system, as locals like to boast.

El Peñón

Intriguing **El Peñón**, 135km from Hualfín, is the first altiplano settlement you reach along RP-43: just a few gingerbread-coloured adobe houses, a good *hostería* (run by Socompa tours; see p.286), some proud poplar trees, and an apple orchard, surprising given the altitude. The village nestles in the **Carachipampa Valley**, which extends all the way to the Cordillera de San Buenaventura, to the southwest, and its striking summit **Cerro El Cóndor** (6000m), clearly visible from here in the searingly clear atmosphere.

Soon the chestnut-brown volcanic cones of **Los Negros de la Laguna** come into view, a sign that you're in the final approaches to Antofagasta. One of twin peaks, **La Alumbrera** deposited enormous lava flows when it last erupted, only a few hundred years ago. The huge piles of visibly fresh **black pumice** it tossed out, all pocked and twisted, reach heights of 10m or more. Just before Antofagasta, the road swings round **Laguna Colorada**, a small lake often frozen solid and shaded pink with a massive flock of altiplanic flamingoes which somehow survive up here.

Antofagasta de la Sierra

Perched 3440m above sea level, 260km north of Belén, **ANTOFAGASTA DE LA SIERRA** lies at the northern end of a vast, arid plain hemmed in by volcanoes to the east and south, and by the cordillera, which soars to peaks of over 6000m, a mere 100km over to the west. With a population of under a thousand it exudes a feeling of utter

5

remoteness, while still managing to exert a disarming fascination. It's a bleak yet restful place, an oasis of tamarinds and green alfalfa fields in the middle of the *meseta altiplánica* – a harsh steppe that looms above the surrounding altiplano. Two rivers, Punilla and Las Paitas, meet just to the south, near the strange volcanic plug called **El Torreón**, adopted as the town's symbol. Named after the Chilean port-city, this is a tough town with a harsh climate, where night temperatures in midwinter drop well below freezing, accompanied by biting winds and a relentless sun during the day: its name means "home of the Sun" in the language of the Diaguita. Salt, borax and various minerals and metals have been mined in the area for centuries and Antofagasta has the hardy feel of a mining town, but most of its people are now subsistence farmers and herdsmen, scraping a living from maize, potatoes, onions and beans or rearing llamas and alpacas, whose wool is made into textiles. The people here are introverted and placid, hospitable but seemingly indifferent to the outside world.

The best views of the immediate surroundings can be enjoyed from the top of the Cerro Amarillo and Cerro de la Cruz, two unsightly mounds of earth that look like part of a huge building-site and dominate the town's humble streets of small mud-brick houses. The **Cerro de la Cruz** is the destination of processions held to honour Antofagasta's patron saints, St Joseph and the Virgin of Loreto, from December 8 to 10. In another sombre ceremony, the town's dead are remembered on November 1 and 2, when villagers file to and from the cemetery before a feast, talking in whispers so as not to disturb the spirits. And every March the town comes to life, for the **Feria Artesanal y Ganadera de la Puna**, a colourful event attended by craftspeople and herdsmen from all over the province.

If hard pushed you can stay, eat and fill up your vehicle at the municipal *Hostería de Antofagasta* (❶03835 471001) – but it is best avoided, having fallen into what seems to be permanent decline; you are much better off staying in El Peñón (see p.327).

Museo Arqueológico

Mon–Fri 8am–6pm • $2

The only tourist attraction in the town is the beautifully presented **Museo Arqueológico**, recently created primarily to house a perfectly preserved, naturally mummified baby, found in the mountains nearby and believed to be nearly two thousand years old; surrounded with jewels and other signs of wealth, suggesting the child belonged to a ruling dynasty, it exerts a morbid fascination. The museum's other exhibits, few in number but of extraordinary value, include an immaculately preserved pre-Hispanic basket, the pigment colouring and fine weave still intact.

ARRIVAL AND INFORMATION   ANTOFAGASTA DE LA SIERRA

By bus The twice-weekly bus (usually Mon & Wed) from Catamarca will drop you in the main street.

By car Fuel can be bought at inflated prices from the pump opposite the municipalidad, so it's better to fill up before making this trip.

Tourist information Antofagasta has no tourist office; for visiting the immediate and farther-flung surroundings ask at the municipalidad for the town's most experienced guides, Catalino Soriano, Antolín Ramos and Jesús Vásquez. Better still, contact Socampa travel (see p.286).

Around Antofagasta de la Sierra

The mostly unsealed and sometimes very bumpy RP-43 (in Catamarca Province, becoming RP-17 in Salta Province) leads north from Antofagasta to **San Antonio de los Cobres** (see p.293), 330km away via Caucharí. Antofagasta could therefore be visited as part of a gigantic loop, taking in vast, lonely yet dramatically memorable tracts of Salta and Catamarca provinces, but allow plenty of time and take far more provisions and fuel supplies than you think you'll need – in other words reckon on two or three days' food and several jerry-cans of petrol in reserve.

DAY-EXCURSIONS FROM ANTOFAGASTA

Within easy excursion distance of Antofagasta are a number of archeological and historical sites, such as the ruins at **Campo Alumbreras**, 5km south, and **Coyparcito**, 3km further away. The pre-Columbian **pukará**, or fortress, on the flanks of the Alumbrera volcano, a few kilometres south of Antofagasta, and nearby **petroglyphs** (mostly depicting llamas and human figures) are also worth a visit; you'll definitely need the services of a guide to find them, and for the necessary explanations to make a visit worthwhile, but they are all open to the public at all times and no entrance fee is charged. Ask at Antofagasta's museum for archeological information and guided visits. The abandoned onyx, mica and gold **mines** in the region are another interesting attraction, while long treks on mule-back are the only way of seeing **Volcán Sufre** (5706m) on the Chilean border. If you want quieter recreation than climbing mountains or scrambling through disused mines you might try a day's **trout fishing** at **Paicuquí**, 20km north of Antofagasta. In the crystal-clear streams you can catch delicious rainbow trout.

Salar del Hombre Muerto salt flats

The same road leads to the desolate, disorientingly mirage-like landscapes of the great **Salar del Hombre Muerto salt flats**, 75km to the north of Antofagasta and best explored using the services of a *baqueano*, or guide. **Cerro Ratones** (5252m) and Cerro Incahuasi (4847m) form a breathtaking backdrop to the bright whiteness of the flats.

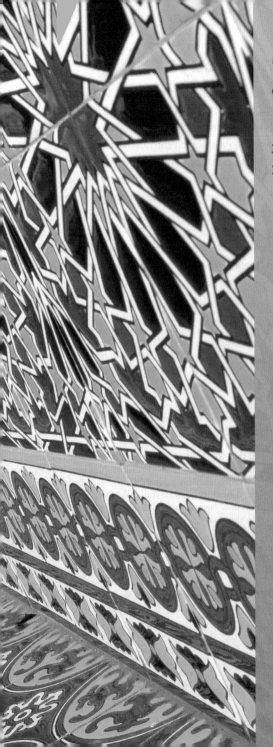

Mendoza
and El Cuyo

PLAZA DE ESPAÑA, MENDOZA

Mendoza and El Cuyo

Argentina's midwestern region, generally known as EL CUYO, is formed by the provinces of Mendoza, San Juan and La Rioja plus the neighbouring province of San Luís. This massive territory stretches all the way from the chocolate-brown pampas of La Payunia, on the northern borders of Patagonia, to the remote highland steppes of the Reserva Las Vicuñas, on the edge of the altiplano, more than a thousand kilometres to the north. Extending across vast, thinly populated territories of bone-dry desert, they are dotted with vibrant oases of farmland and the region's famous vineyards: the sophisticated metropolis of Mendoza, one of Argentina's biggest cities, is the epicentre of the country's blossoming wine – and wine tourism – industry, while the two smaller provincial capitals, San Juan and La Rioja, continue to be quiet backwaters by comparison.

The region's dynamics are overwhelmingly about its highly varied **landscapes** and **wildlife**. In the west of the provinces loom the world's loftiest peaks outside the Himalayas, culminating in the defiant **Aconcagua**, whose summit is only a shade under 7000m. Ranging from these snowy Andean heights to totally flat pampas in the east, from green, fertile valleys to barren volcanoes – including the world's second-highest cone, extinct **Monte Pissis** – the scenery also includes two of the country's most photographed national parks: the sheer red-sandstone cliffs of **Talampaya** and the moonscapes of **Ischigualasto**. All this provides a backdrop for some of Argentina's best opportunities for **extreme sport** – from **skiing** in exclusive **Las Leñas**, to whitewater rafting, rock climbing, and even the ascent of Aconcagua or the **Mercedario** and **Tupungato** peaks.

European settlers have wrought changes to the environment, bringing the grape vine, the Lombardy poplar and all kinds of fruit trees with them, but the thousands of kilometres of irrigation channels that water the region existed long before Columbus "discovered" America. Pumas and vicuñas, condors and ñandús, plus hundreds of colourful bird species inhabit the thoroughly unspoilt wildernesses of the region, where some of the biggest known dinosaurs prowled millions of years ago. Countless flowering **cacti** and the dazzling yellow **brea**, a broom-like shrub, add colour to the browns and greys of the desert in the spring.

GETTING AROUND

Tourism is well developed in Mendoza Province so it's possible to visit most places by **public transport** or on tours from Mendoza and other towns. In the two other provinces getting around is more difficult, though operators will take you to places like Talampaya from San Juan or La Rioja. To see the region at your own pace (and have much of it to yourself), consider renting a vehicle, preferably a **4WD**, since many of the roads are, at best, only partly sealed.

BODEGA SALENTEIN

Highlights

❶ Mendoza city Argentina's wine capital has a lot to offer, from top-class dining to a vibrant nightlife. **See p.335**

❷ Whitewater rafting Exhilarating trips on the region's feisty rivers. **See p.344**

❸ Bodega Salentein Who said the Dutch can't make wine? This "Wine Cathedral" is one of the continent's most impressive wineries. **See p.346**

❹ Mountain climbing If Aconcagua – one of the world's tallest peaks – is too crowded, then take your tent and ropes to Mercedario or another of the Andes' great challenges. See p.356 & p.375

❺ La Payunia A secluded region of ancient volcanoes, dark and rust-red lava flows, and photogenic guanacos. **See p.367**

❻ Ischigualasto and Talampaya The pride and joy of San Juan and La Rioja provinces – the first an eerie moonscape and dinosaur graveyard, the second an awe-inspiring canyon with mighty red-sandstone walls. See p.382 & p.384

❼ Laguna Brava Head up into the strikingly coloured cordillera of La Rioja to see flamingoes on this wild, high-mountain lagoon. **See p.386**

HIGHLIGHTS ARE MARKED ON THE MAP ON P.334

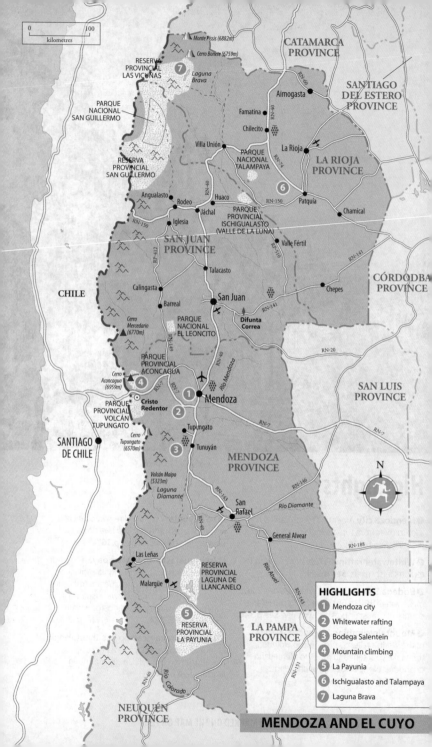

MENDOZA AND EL CUYO

0 — 100 kilometres

CATAMARCA PROVINCE

SANTIAGO DEL ESTERO PROVINCE

Monte Pissis (6882m)

Cerro Bonete (6759m)

RESERVA PROVINCIAL LAS VICUÑAS

Laguna Brava

PARQUE NACIONAL SAN GUILLERMO

RESERVA PROVINCIAL SAN GUILLERMO

Aimogasta

Famatina

Chilecito

Villa Unión

La Rioja

LA RIOJA PROVINCE

PARQUE NACIONAL TALAMPAYA

Angualasto

Rodeo

Huaco

Jáchal

Patquía

Chamical

Iglesia

PARQUE PROVINCIAL ISCHIGUALASTO (VALLE DE LA LUNA)

SAN JUAN PROVINCE

Valle Fértil

Talacasto

CHILE

Calingasta

Barreal

San Juan

Chepes

CÓRDOBA PROVINCE

Cerro Mercedario (6770m)

PARQUE NACIONAL EL LEONCITO

Difunta Correa

RN-20

Cerro Aconcagua (6959m)

PARQUE PROVINCIAL ACONCAGUA

SAN LUIS PROVINCE

Cristo Redentor

Mendoza

PARQUE PROVINCIAL VOLCÁN TUPUNGATO

SANTIAGO DE CHILE

Cerro Tupungato (6570m)

Tupungato

Tunuyán

MENDOZA PROVINCE

Volcán Maipo (5323m)

Laguna Diamante

San Rafael

Río Diamante

General Alvear

RN-188

Las Leñas

RESERVA PROVINCIAL LAGUNA DE LLANCANELO

Malargüe

Río Atuel

RESERVA PROVINCIAL LA PAYUNIA

LA PAMPA PROVINCE

N

Río Colorado

NEUQUÉN PROVINCE

HIGHLIGHTS

1 Mendoza city
2 Whitewater rafting
3 Bodega Salentein
4 Mountain climbing
5 La Payunia
6 Ischigualasto and Talampaya
7 Laguna Brava

EL CUYO – OUT WITH THE OLD AND IN WITH THE NEW

Mendoza, San Juan and La Rioja provinces – plus the less interesting province of San Luís, to the east – make up the region known as **El Nuevo Cuyo**, or "New Cuyo", formed by a 1988 treaty. The much older term *Cuyo* and the adjective *Cuyano*, which originally did not include present-day La Rioja, are widely used in the names of travel companies, newspapers and other businesses, for example. The etymological **origins** of the word *cuyo* are not entirely clear, but it probably comes from the native Huarpe word *xuyu*, meaning (sandy) riverbed. The original core area of the Intendencia del Cuyo, basically corresponding to the modern Mendoza Province, has strong historical ties with **Chile** from where it was first colonized, and among other things the local accent still reflects this – with, for example, the "-ll" and "-y" being pronounced as the "y" in yellow, as in Chile, rather than the "j" sound you hear in Buenos Aires.

6

Mendoza Province

The southern half of El Nuevo Cuyo is taken up by **Mendoza Province**, the self-styled Tierra del Sol y del Buen Vino, the "land of sunshine and good wine". Within its borders are some of the country's most dramatic **mountain landscapes**, where you can try a host of adventure pursuits, from kayaking to hang-gliding. Its lively capital city, **Mendoza**, can satisfy yearnings for creature comforts after treks, climbs into the Andes or a day of whitewater rafting. While Mendoza Province shares many things with San Juan and La Rioja – bleak wildernesses backed by snow-peaked mountains, remarkably varied flora and fauna, an incredibly sunny climate prone to sudden temperature changes and pockets of rich farmland mainly used to produce beefy red wines – it differs in the way it exploits them. Mendoza leads the way in **tourism** just as it does in the **wine industry**, combining professionalism with a taste for the avant-garde. The two industries come together for Mendoza's nationally famous **Fiesta de la Vendimia**, or Wine Harvest Festival, held in early March, a slightly kitsch but exuberant bacchanalia at which a carnival queen is elected from candidates representing every town in the province.

Mendoza Province can be divided into three sections, each with its own base. The north, around the capital, has the country's biggest concentration of vineyards and top-class **wineries**, clustered around **Maipú** and **Luján de Cuyo**, while the scenic **Alta Montaña** route races up in a westerly direction towards the high Chilean border, passing the mighty **Cerro Aconcagua**, an increasingly popular climbing destination. Not far to the southwest are the much more challenging **Cerro Tupungato** (6570m) and the remote **Laguna Diamante**, a choppy altiplanic lagoon in the shadow of the perfectly shaped **Volcán Maipo**, which can only be visited from December to March. Central Mendoza is focused on the laidback town of **San Rafael**, where you can taste more wine, and from where several tour operators offer whitewater-rafting trips along the nearby **Cañón del Atuel**, or rivers like the Sosneado and **Diamante**. If you've always wanted to ski or snowboard in July, try the winter sports resort at **Las Leñas**, where you'll be sharing pistes with South America's jet-set. The third, least-visited section of the province wraps around the southern outpost of **Malargüe**, a final-frontier kind of place promoting itself as a centre for nature, scientific discovery and adventure. Within easy reach are the **Laguna de Llancanelo**, home to an enormous community of **flamingoes**, the charcoal-grey and rust-red lava deserts of **La Payunia** and the karstic caves of **Caverna de las Brujas**.

Mendoza and around

MENDOZA is a mostly low-rise city, spread across the wide valley of the Río Mendoza, over 1000km west of Buenos Aires and less than 100km east of the Andean cordillera – whose perennially snowcapped peaks are clearly visible from downtown. Its airy microcentro is less compact than that of most comparable cities, partly because the streets, squares and avenues were deliberately made wide when the city was rebuilt in the late nineteenth century (see p.338), following a major earthquake. Every street is lined by bushy sycamore and plane trees – providing vital shade in the scorching summer, they are watered by over 500km of *acequias*, or irrigation ditches, which form a natural, outdoor air-cooling system. Watch out when you cross the city's streets, as the narrow gutters are up to a metre deep and often full of gushing water, especially in the spring when the upland snows melt.

The centre of the urban layout is the vast **Plaza Independencia**, and its four orbital squares, **plazas Chile**, **San Martín**, **España** and **Italia**, each with its own distinctive character. The **Museo del Pasado Cuyano** offers an insight into late nineteenth-century life for the city's richer families, while the **Museo de Ciencias Naturales y Antropológicas** is a natural history museum. The latter sits in the handsome **Parque General San Martín**, which commands views of the city and its surroundings. The park is also the venue for the city's major annual event, the **Fiesta de la Vendimia**, held every March.

RESTAURANTS AND CAFÉS	
1884 Francis Mallmann	4
Basilika	1
La Carmela	2
Don Mario	3
El Patio de Jesús	5

MENDOZA

The ruins of colonial Mendoza's nucleus have been preserved as the **Área Fundacional**, where there's another small museum. The most impressive sight is the historic **Bodega Escorihuela**, a beautiful **winery** in a southern suburb.

Most people visit Mendoza principally to do a **wine-tasting tour** at the many **bodegas** in or near the city (see box, pp.346–347). Within easy reach to the south of the city are two small satellite towns, **Luján de Cuyo** and **Maipú**, where, in addition to the majority of the region's wineries, you'll find a couple more interesting museums, one displaying the paintings of Fernando Fader – a kind of Argentine Van Gogh – and the other focusing on the wine industry. The city also acts as a base for some of the world's most thrilling **mountain-climbing** opportunities.

Brief history

Mendoza started out as part of the **Spanish colony of Chile**. In 1561 García Hurtado de Mendoza, captain-general of Chile, sent over an expedition led by Pedro del Castillo to

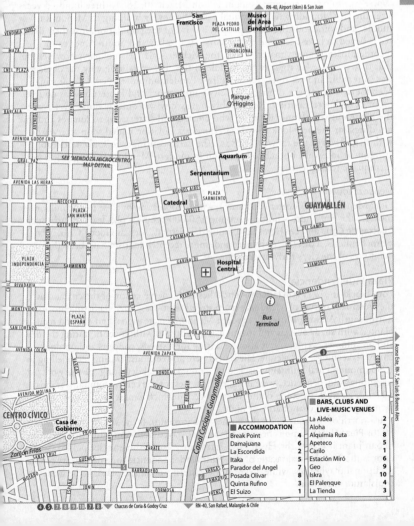

ACCOMMODATION		BARS, CLUBS AND LIVE-MUSIC VENUES	
Break Point	4	La Aldea	2
Damajuana	6	Aloha	7
La Escondida	2	Alquimia Ruta	8
Itaka	5	Apeteco	5
Parador del Angel	7	Carilo	1
Posada Olivar	8	Estación Miró	6
Quinta Rufino	3	Geo	9
El Suizo	1	Iskra	10
		El Palenque	4
		La Tienda	3

establish a colony from which to "civilize" the indigenous Huarpe; Castillo named the town he founded after his boss. Soon flourishing, Mendoza continued to be ruled from across the Andes, though its isolation enabled it to live a life of its own. The extensive network of pre-Hispanic **irrigation canals** was exploited by the colonizers, who planted **vineyards** that soon became South America's most productive. By 1700, the city's merchants were selling wine to Santiago, Córdoba and Buenos Aires. After the Viceroyalty of the River Plate was created in 1777, Mendoza was incorporated into the huge **Córdoba Intendencia**. Mendocinos are still proud of the fact that San Martín's Army of the Andes was trained in their city before thrashing the Spanish royalist troops at the Battle of Maipú, Chile, in 1818. Once Argentina gained its independence, however, Mendoza began to suffer from its relative isolation, stagnating by the mid-nineteenth century.

The 1861 earthquake

Worse was to come, though: as night fell on March 20, 1861, three hundred years after the city's founding, an **earthquake** smashed every building in Mendoza to rubble, and some four thousand people, a third of the population, lost their lives. It's believed to have been one of the worst ever to have hit South America in recorded history, an estimated 7.8 on the Richter scale. Seismologists now believe that the epicentre lay right in the middle of the city, explaining why the damage was so terrible and yet restricted in radius. Pandemonium ensued, God-fearing Mendocinos seeing the timing – the city's anniversary and Eastertide – as double proof of divine retribution. Remarkably, a new city was quickly built, overseen by the French urban planner **Ballofet**, who created wide streets, open squares and low buildings for the new-look Mendoza. The city's isolation ended soon afterwards, with the arrival of the railway in 1884. The earth continues to shake noticeably at frequent intervals, but all construction in modern Mendoza is designed to be earthquake resistant.

Mendoza today

Gran Mendoza (or "Greater Mendoza"), with a population of close to one million, includes the city centre – home to around 150,000 people – plus leafy suburbs such as **Chacras de Coria** and **Las Heras**, and industrial districts, such as Godoy Cruz. Wine, petrochemicals, a thriving university and, more recently, **tourism** have been the mainstays of the city's thriving economy.

Plaza Independencia

Four blocks in size, **Plaza Independencia** lies at the nerve-centre of the city and at the crossroads of two of Mendoza's main streets, east–west Avenida Sarmiento and north–south Avenida Mitre. It's modern Mendoza's recreational and cultural focus, planted with shady acacias and magnolias, and bustles with life both during the day and on summer evenings. It is also the setting for festivals, concerts and outdoor cinema-screenings, and a crafts fair is held here at weekends. During remodelling in 1995, monumental fountains, backed by a mosaic mural depicting the story of Argentina's independence, were installed. Just west of the central fountains stands a 17m-high steel structure, dating from 1942, on which a mass of coloured lights form the national coat of arms at night.

Just north of the square, on the corner of Sarmiento, is the site of the illustrious 1920s **Plaza Hotel**, famous because the Peróns stayed here soon after first meeting in San Juan; it is now the Hyatt's five-star luxury establishment (see p.345). Next door is the Neoclassical facade of the **Teatro Independencia**, one of the city's more traditional playhouses, while, over on the eastern side of the plaza, is the grim **Legislatura Provincial**.

Plaza España

The small plaza that lies a block east and a block south of Independencia's southeast corner, called Plaza Montevideo until 1949, is now known as **Plaza España**. It's the most beautiful of all Mendoza's plazas – its benches are decorated with brightly coloured Andalucian ceramic tiles, and the paths are lined with luxuriant trees and shrubs. Although Mendoza's population is of overwhelmingly Italian origin, the city's old, traditional families came from Spain, and they had the square built in the late 1940s. The mellow terracotta flagstones, picked out with smaller blue and white tiles,

6

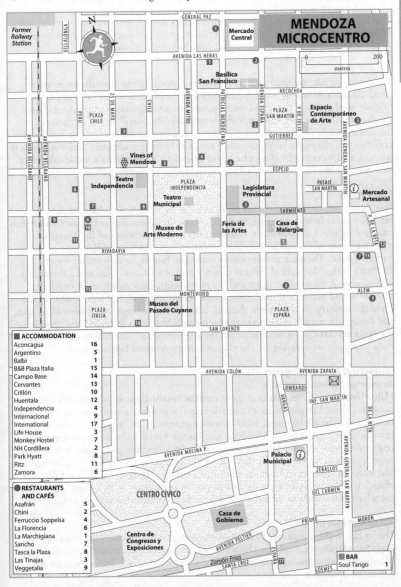

MENDOZA MICROCENTRO

6

and the lily ponds and fountains set off the monument to the Spanish discovery of South America, standing at the southern end of the plaza. It comprises a *zócalo* or brightly tiled pedestal, decorated with scenes from *Don Quixote* and the Argentine gaucho epic *Martín Fierro*, along with Columbus's "discovery" and depictions of missionary work. At the centre of the plinth stand two female statues: one is a Spanish noblewoman clasping a book, the other a *mestiza* (part Spanish, part Native American) woman, a Mendocina, holding a bunch of grapes. Dancing and folk music take place here on October 12, the **Día de la Raza**, a celebration of *mestizo* culture.

Plaza Italia

Four blocks west of Plaza España's northwest corner along Calle Montevideo – an attractive street lined with plane trees and picturesque Neocolonial houses with brightly coloured facades – is **Plaza Italia**. A monument on the south side of the square is a bronze statue of the mythical Roman wolf feeding Romulus and Remus, next to a marble pillar. The main monument in stone and bronze, to its west, represents La Patria – The Motherland – flanked by a statue of an Amerindian and a Roman philosopher. A frieze running around the monument, showing scenes of building, ploughing and harvesting, is a tribute to the Italian immigrants whose labour helped build the country. In November, the park blazes with the bright red flowers of its *tipas*, and during the week leading up to the Fiesta de la Vendimia in March, the plaza hosts the **Festa in Piazza**, a big party at which stalls representing every Italian region serve their local culinary specialities. The climax is an extravagant fashion parade.

Museo del Pasado Cuyano

Montevideo 544 • Mon–Fri 9am–12.30pm • $5

Half a block east of Plaza Italia is the **Museo del Pasado Cuyano**. It's the city's history museum, housed in part of an aristocratic late nineteenth-century mansion, the Quinta de los Civit. The adobe house, built to resist earthquakes, belonged to the family of Francisco Civit, governor of Mendoza, and his son Emilio, who was a senator and was responsible for many of Mendoza's civic works, including the great park. It contains a large amount of San Martín memorabilia and eighteenth-century furniture, artworks and weapons, all rescued from the earthquake rubble. The most valuable exhibit, in the chapel, is a fifteenth-century polychrome **wooden altarpiece**, with a liberal dose of rosy cherubim that somehow turned up here from Sant Andreu de Socarrats in Catalonia.

Plaza San Martín

The square to the northeast of Plaza Independencia is the relatively nondescript **Plaza San Martín**; it's dominated by an early twentieth-century statue of General San Martín on a horse, looking towards the Andes, which he crossed with his army to defeat the Spanish.

Basílica de San Francisco

April–Oct Tues–Sat 7.45am–5pm, Sun 9am–6.30pm; Nov–March Mon–Sat 9am–noon • Free

Near the plaza's northwest corner is the city's only church of note, the **Basílica de San Francisco**, one of the first buildings to go up after the 1861 quake. Its Belgian architect modelled it on Paris's Église de la Trinité, but part of the structure had to be demolished after another earthquake in 1927, leaving the church looking a bit truncated. It's venerated locally, as some members of San Martín's family are buried in simple tombs inside. A special chamber up the stairs next to the altar contains a revered image of Our Lady of Carmen, the patron saint of the Army of the Andes, along with San Martín's stylish rosewood staff, with a topaz hilt and a silver tip – it, too, has the status of a religious relic among the people of Mendoza.

6

The City district and Espacio Contemporáneo de Arte

9 de Julio and Gutiérrez • Mon–Sat 9am–1pm & 4–9pm, Sun 4–9pm • Free • ☏ 0261 429 0117

The district surrounding the basilica is Mendoza's small "**City**", or financial district, whose opulent banks and insurance-company offices, most built in a "British" style, are among the city's most impressive buildings. Both the Banco de Galicia and the Banco de la Nación were built in the 1920s and 1930s, the city's heyday, as was the ex-Banco de Mendoza, lying on the eastern side of Plaza San Martín, diagonally opposite the basilica. The latter now houses the **Espacio Contemporáneo de Arte**, worth a look for its contemporary art exhibitions, its tasteful arts and crafts shop, and the eight-sided lobby crowned with a huge stained-glass cupola.

Museo del Área Fundacional

Alberdi and Videla Castillo • Tues–Sat 8am–7pm, Sun 3–8pm • $5

The **Museo del Área Fundacional** is built on the Plaza Mayor, where the city was originally founded, 1km northeast of Plaza Independencia. The modern building houses an exhibition of domestic and artistic items retrieved from the rubble after the mammoth earthquake of 1861. It's built over part of the excavated colonial city foundations, which you can peer at through a glass floor. The exhibition relates the story of Mendoza's foundation and development before and after the great disaster. Nearby, across landscaped Plaza Pedro del Castillo, named for the city's founder, are the eerie ruins of the colonial city's Jesuit temple, popularly but erroneously known as the Ruinas de San Francisco.

Parque General San Martín

Av Sarmiento • Always open

Just over 1km due west of Plaza Independencia, on a slope that turns into a steep hill overlooking the city, **Parque General San Martín** is one of the most beautiful parks in the country, although you're advised not to visit after dark. As well as large areas of open land, used for impromptu football matches and picnics, its four square kilometres are home to the main football stadium, the amphitheatre where the finale of the Fiesta de la Vendimia is staged, a meteorological observatory, a monument to the Army of the Andes, a rowing lake, a tennis club, a hospital, the university campus, the riding club, an agricultural research centre, several restaurants, Mendoza's best jogging routes, a rose garden and an anthropological museum – in short, a city within the city.

The park was first created in 1897 by French botanist and landscape artist, **Charles Thays** (see box, p.88). It contains over fifty thousand trees of 750 varieties, planted, among other reasons, to stop landslides from the Andean foothills. The aristocratic Avenida de los Plátanos and Avenida de las Palmeras, lined with tall plane trees and Canary Island palms, and the romantic Rose Garden, with its five hundred rose varieties and arbours of wisteria, are popular walks.

6

FIESTA DE LA VENDIMIA

Mendoza's main festival is the giant **Fiesta de la Vendimia**, or Wine Harvest Festival, which reaches its climax during the first weekend of March every year. Wine takes over the city and the tourist trade shifts into high gear. On the Sunday before the carnival proper (the last Sun in Feb), the *Bendición de los Frutos*, or Blessing of the Grapes, takes place, in a ceremony involving the bishop of Mendoza. During the week leading up to the grand finale, events range from folklore concerts in the *centro cívico* to Italian food and entertainment in the Plaza Italia. On Friday evening is the **Vía Blanca**, a parade of illuminated floats through the central streets, while on Saturday it's the *Carrusel*, when a carnival parade winds along the same route, each department in the province sending a float from which a previously elected beauty queen and her entourage of runners-up fling local produce, ranging from grapes and flowers to watermelons and packets of pasta, into the cheering crowds lining the road. On Saturday evening, the *Acto Central* is held in an amphitheatre in the Parque San Martín; it's a gala performance of song, dance and general kitsch-o-rama, hosted by local TV celebs, eventually leading up to a drawn-out vote – by political leaders representing each department in the province – to elect the queen of the festival. The same show is re-run, minus the election, and therefore less tedium, on Sunday evening. The spectacle costs millions of pesos and is a huge investment by the local wine-growers, but as it's attended by some 25,000 people it seems to be financially viable. The organizers boast that it's the biggest such festival in South America and one of the most lavish wine-related celebrations in the world. For more information contact the city's tourist office (see opposite).

The gates

The main entrance is through magnificent bronze and wrought-iron **gates**, topped with a rampant condor, at the western end of Avenida Emilio Civit. They were not, as a popular legend would have it, ordered for Ottoman Sultan Hamid II, who couldn't pay the bill; the crescent motif in their fine lace-like design, which led to the apocryphal anecdote, was simply a fashionable pattern at the time. The gates were actually ordered by city authorities in 1910 to celebrate the country's centenary, and were made by the McFarlane ironworks in Glasgow.

Caballitos de Marly and Fuente de los Continentes

A road open to traffic skirts the northern edge of the park after going round the **Caballitos de Marly**, an exact reproduction in Carrara marble of the monumental horses in the middle of Paris's Place de la Concorde. From here you can rent a bike, take a horse and cart or catch a bus to the park's furthest points (remember, it is huge). A short walk southwest of the entrance, near the northern shores of the rowing lake, the recently restored **Fuente de los Continentes** is a dramatic set of sculptures meant to represent the diversity of humankind, and a favoured backdrop for wedding photographs.

The zoo

Av Libertador s/n • Tues–Sun 9am–5pm • $25, reductions for young visitors under 13 • ☎ 0261 428 1700, ✆ zoo.mendoza.gov.ar

A good 2km west of the park entrance you'll find the city's **zoo**, one of the best in the country for its variety of animals and, more to the point, for the conditions in which they are kept. It's a landscaped forest of eucalyptus, *aguaribay* and fir trees, built into the lower slopes of the Cerro de la Gloria, from which you also get sweeping views of the city.

Monumento al Ejército Libertador

A popular destination is the top of the Cerro de la Gloria, where there's an imposing 1914 monument to the Army of the Andes, the **Monumento al Ejército Libertador**. All cast in bronze, a buxom, winged *Liberty*, waving broken chains, leads General San Martín and his victorious troops across the cordillera. Around the granite plinth are bronze friezes depicting more picturesque scenes: the anti-royalist monk Luis Beltrán busy making weapons for the army, and the genteel ladies of Mendoza donating their jewellery for the good cause – these "Patricias Mendocinas", after whom a city street is named, were rumoured to have been particularly excited by the presence of so many soldiers billeted in the city; babies and infants sadly watch their valiant fathers head off to battle.

Museo de Ciencias Naturales y Antropológicas

Tues–Fri 8am–1pm & 2–7pm, Sat & Sun 3–7pm • $5 • ☎ 0261 428 7666

At the southern tip of the park's 1km-long, serpentine rowing lake, in its southeastern corner, is the **Museo de Ciencias Naturales y Antropológicas**. Built in the 1930s to imitate the shape of a ship's bridge by local architects who introduced German Rationalism to Argentina, the museum is a series of mostly private collections of stuffed animals, ancient fossils, indigenous artefacts and mummies. The most interesting exhibits are a female mummy discovered at over 5000m in the Andes – along with a brightly coloured shawl – shrunken heads from Ecuador and fossils or skeletons of dinosaurs unearthed near Malargüe in southern Mendoza.

ARRIVAL AND DEPARTURE   MENDOZA AND AROUND

BY PLANE

Officially called Aeropuerto Internacional Ingeniero Francisco J. Gabrielli, but known popularly as "Plumerillo" after the suburb where it's located, Mendoza's modern and efficient airport (☎ 0261 520 6000 ext 101) is only 7km north of the city centre, just off the RN-40. Taxis and *remises* ($30) are in plentiful supply, or buses #6/63 ($4) can also take you downtown; for information, ask at the Atención al Cliente office. Heading back to the airport, be sure to catch a bus that has an "Aeropuerto" sign in the windscreen.

Airlines Aerolíneas Argentina and Austral, Paseo Sarmiento 82 ☎ 0261 420 4101, and at the airport ☎ 0261 448 7065; LAN, España 1002 ☎ 0261 448 7387 or ☎ 0810 9999 526; United, Espejo 183 1st floor ☎ 0261 423 4683.

Destinations Buenos Aires (4 daily; 1hr 50min); Córdoba (1–2 daily; 1hr 20min); Rosario (1–2 daily; 2hr 40min); Santiago (2–3 daily; 55min).

BY BUS

Mendoza's very busy bus station (☎ 0261 431 5000) is slightly drab, but has plenty of facilities, including a small tourist office (7am–10pm). There are buses to and from just about everywhere in the country, plus Santiago de Chile, Lima and Montevideo. It's due east of the microcentro, on the edge of the suburb of Guaymallén, at the corner of avenidas Gobernador Videla (usually referred to as the Costanera) and Acceso Este (RN-7); this is less than 1km from the city centre but if the walk is too much, the "Villa Nueva" trolley-bus ($2) is a cheaper alternative to a taxi.

Destinations Buenos Aires (15 daily; 13hr); Córdoba (25 daily; 9–10hr); General Alvear (10 daily; 4hr 30min); La Rioja (16 daily; 8hr 30min); Las Leñas (June–Sept 2 daily; 5hr); Los Penitentes (3 daily; 4hr); Malargüe (8 daily; 4–5hr); Neuquén (12 daily; 12hr); Río Gallegos (1 daily; 40hr); Salta (9 daily; 19hr); San Juan (hourly; 2hr 20min); San Luís (hourly; 3hr 40min); San Rafael (hourly; 3hr 15min); Santiago de Chile (12 daily; 6–7hr); Uspallata (7 daily; 2hr); Valparaíso, Chile (5 daily; 8hr 30min).

GETTING AROUND AND INFORMATION

On foot The tourist office runs guided walks with themes such as history or religion – ask for the latest timetable. A number of tour operators run half-day city tours (see box, p.344).

By bike There's bike rental at Bikes and Wines, 25 de Mayo 981 ☎ 0261 410 6686, ⊚ bikesandwines.com; City Bike, San Martín 1070 ☎ 0261 423 2103.

By bus For finding your own way around, there are buses and trolley-buses – the latter mostly serving the inner suburbs plus the bus station. They have a complex numbering system, with a logic that escapes most people; study the map displayed at each stop. You pay a flat $2 fare for both – no change given – except for much longer distances such as the airport.

By car For car rental, head to Alamo, Primitivo de la Reta 928 ☎ 0261 429 3111; Avis, Primitivo de la Reta 914 ☎ 0261 429 6403; Budget, Primitivo de la Reta 923 ☎ 0261 425 3114; Hertz, Espejo 391 ☎ 0261 423 0225; Localiza, Primitivo de la Reta 936 ☎ 0261 429 6800. There are also branches at the airport.

By taxi Mendocar ☎ 0261 423 6666; Radiomóvil ☎ 0261 445 5855; Radiotaxi ☎ 0261 430 3300; Veloz del Este ☎ 0261 423 9090.

Tourist information The main tourist office (Mon–Fri 8am–9pm, Sat & Sun 9am–9pm; ☎ 0261 413 2101 or ☎ 0261 420 2800, ⊚ turismo.mendoza.gov.ar) is at San Martín 1143, a building that was previously the Jockey Club;

6

TOUR OPERATORS

Popular tours include ones to wine bodegas, Alta Montaña and Villavicencio. Mountain-bike tours in the foothills and whitewater rafting on the Río Mendoza are also possible. Many operators also offer longer trips to La Payunia, Cañón del Atuel, Talampaya and Ischigualasto, but Malargüe, San Rafael, San Agustín de Valle Fértil and Villa Unión are much closer bases for these.

Argentina Mountain Lavalle 606, San José, Guaymallén ☎ 0261 431 8356, ⓦ lagunadeldiamante .com. One of the few companies to offer trips to places like Laguna Diamante and Tupungato.

Argentina Rafting Primitivo de la Reta 992 ☎ 0261 429 6325, ⓦ argentinarafting.com. This outfit is the regional expert at rafting, but also offers a wide range of adventure activities such as rappels, parachute jumps and, for the less ambitious, horseriding.

Aymará 9 de Julio 1023 ☎ 0261 420 4304, ⓦ aconcaguaaymara.com.ar. With years of experience leading expeditions up Aconcagua, Aymara has also turned to other mountains in the region, as well as offering horse rides through upland terrain.

Campo Base Adventures and Expeditions Peatonal Sarmiento 229 ☎ 0261 425 5511, ⓦ campobase.com .ar. Aimed at the younger, budget-end market this

adventure-tour specialist focuses on mountaineering expeditions.

Cata Las Heras 601 ☎ 0261 425 1750, ⓦ cataturismo .com.ar. This Mendoza-based agent offers a wide range of tourist services, with the emphasis on getting groups around the region.

El Cristo Espejo 228 ☎ 0261 429 1911, ⓦ turismo -elcristo.com.ar. A highly professional team, El Cristo puts together excursions as far away as Malargüe, including interesting bodega tours.

Mendoza Viajes Sarmiento 129 ☎ 0261 438 0480, ⓦ mdzviajes.com.ar. This well-established agency offers reasonable wine tours throughout the province.

Sepean Primitivo de la Reta 1088 ☎ 0261 420 4162, ⓦ sepean.com. A general tour and travel agency, offering hotel packages in the region and across the border in Chile.

this is also the place to obtain Aconcagua climbing permits (see p.356). Another city tourist office is at Edificio Municipal, 9 de Julio 500 (Mon–Fri 8.30am–1.30pm; ☎ 0261 449 5185),

as well as one in the satellite town of Luján de Cuyo (see p.350) at Sáenz Peña 1000 (Mon–Fri 8.30am–6pm, Sat & Sun 10am–4pm; ☎ 0261 498 1912).

ACCOMMODATION

Mendoza is very well off for places to stay, with more than enough beds for its needs, except during the Fiesta de la Vendimia in early March. It has several luxurious **hotels**, including branches of top-class international chains, as well as over a dozen **youth hostels**, plus a fair number of **B&Bs**. In the middle range are countless nondescript but decent smaller hotels. At the higher end, particularly interesting options are **bodega hotels** or **posadas**, many of which are in the swish suburbs of Chacras de Coria and Maipú. The quiet, suburban location of these bodega hotels does mean that unless you have your own car you may be more or less limited to the delights the bodega has to offer. Always book bodega accommodation ahead, and let your hosts know if you don't have your own transport, as they will usually pick you up from Mendoza city or airport. If you haven't got anything booked, the best street to head for is Arístides Villanueva (usually referred to as Arístides), three blocks south and four blocks west of the Plaza Independencia – it's packed with both hostels and more upmarket options. You can also ask at the tourist office for its list of rooms to rent in private houses.

HOSTELS

Break Point Av Arístides Villanueva 241 ☎ 0261 423 9514, ⓦ breakpointhostel.com.ar; map pp.336–337. At the heart of the city's *movida* zone, this lively hostel offers free internet, all kinds of tours, a large TV lounge and a small pool. An added bonus is the excellent-value *parrilla*. Dorms $70, doubles $230

Campo Base Mitre 946 ☎ 0261 429 0707, ⓦ campobase.com.ar; map p.339. The youth hostel traditionally preferred by Aconcagua climbers, as the owners organize their own treks. Clean, friendly and very laidback, with lots of barbecues, parties and general fun, though some of the

dorms are slightly cramped. $80

Damajuana Arístides Villanueva 282 ☎ 0261 425 5858, ⓦ damajuanahostel.com.ar; map pp.336–337. Airy hostel in one of the city's main nightlife areas. One of its best features is the garden, with its decent-sized pool; the dorms are plain but clean. Organizes tours. $75

Independencia Mitre 1237 ☎ 0261 423 1806, ⓦ hostelindependencia.com.ar; map p.339. Nicely located in an attractive townhouse near the plaza of the same name, this has a fully equipped kitchen, a games room, a patio, and pleasant dorms. The staff organize bodega tours and treks. Dorms $70, doubles $180

★ **International** España 343 ☎0261 424 0018, ⓦhostelmendoza.net; map p.339. The best-established of all the hostels, with a bright patio, welcoming ambience, small dorms with private bathroom and an excellent kitchen; the staff can also fix you up with tours and sports activities in the whole region. Its *El Carajo* bar is a popular meeting-place, and there's an *asado* cook-out most Fridays. Private rooms available. Dorms $75, doubles $200

Itaka Av Arístides Villanueva 480 ☎0261 423 9793, ⓦitakahouse.com; map pp.336–337. Fun and friendly place with pretty patio and leafy garden, above-average kitchen facilities and a small pool. In addition to excursions they lay on a weekly wine tasting with nibbles. Dorms $60, doubles $180

Life House Gutiérrez 565 ☎0261 420 4294, ⓦlifehouse .com.ar; map p.339. Two-, four- and six-bed rooms with their own bath, decent kitchen, barbecue area and small swimming pool, at this friendly if rather neglected hostel. Dorms $60, doubles $160

Monkey Hostel Sarmiento 681 ☎0261 423 1148, ⓦmonkeyhostel.com; map p.339. Clean, friendly and central hostel with a small pool and bar. Staff can help you organize tours. Dorms $55, doubles $170

B&BS AND HOSPEDAJES

B&B Plaza Italia Montevideo 685 ☎0261 423 4219, ⓦplazaitalia.net; map p.339. Genuine, English-speaking B&B run by locals in a comfortable family house with en-suite rooms, a/c, a delicious breakfast and parking. Also organizes wine tours. $590

La Escondida Julio A. Roca 344 ☎0261 425 5202, ⓦlaescondidabb.com; map pp.336–337. Wonderfully welcoming B&B in a quiet residential part of the city, with a superb swimming pool at the end of a long lush garden; rooms are extremely comfortable. $420

Quinta Rufino Rufino Ortega 142 ☎0261 420 4696, ⓦquintarufinohostel.com.ar; map pp.336–337. A converted house (definitely not a youth hostel, despite the website) in a quiet neighbourhood, with pleasant en-suite rooms; friendly staff and the owners, who are outdoor specialists, can arrange adventure-sport outings. $270

Zamora Perú 1156 ☎0261 425 7537, ⓦhotelzamora .netfirms.com; map p.339. A Neocolonial villa with clean rooms around a leafy patio; ask for the room with a roof terrace. Also rooms with four or five beds, and group discounts available. Popular with Aconcagua climbers. $290

HOTELS

Aconcagua San Lorenzo 545 ☎0261 520 0500, ⓦhotel aconcagua.com; map p.339. Professionally run, modern hotel, with small but comfortable rooms with TV and minibar; it's worth paying extra for a room with a glorious mountain view. A swimming pool and sauna are welcome facilities in the summer and winter, respectively. $680

Argentino Espejo 455 ☎0261 405 6300, ⓦargentino -hotel.com; map p.339. Shiny place on the Plaza Independencia aimed squarely at the foreign tourist dollar, with ultra-stylish rooms, a small gym, a mini-swimming pool and highly attentive service; breakfast is served in an airy *confitería*. $720

Balbi Av Las Heras 340 ☎0261 423 3500, ⓦhotelbalbi .com.ar; map p.339. Hotel with old-fashioned decor, a lavish reception space, huge breakfast area and large rooms. There is an attractive swimming pool and terrace. $480

Cervantes Amigorena 65 ☎0261 520 0400, ⓦhotel cervantes.com.ar; map p.339. Traditional-style, comfortable three-star hotel, with plain decor and slightly old-fashioned bathrooms. In addition it has one of the best hotel restaurants in town, the *Sancho* (see p.339). $670

Crillón Perú 1065 ☎0261 429 8494, ⓦhcrillon.com.ar; map p.339. An above-average three-star hotel, the *Crillón* has efficient service. Bathrooms are well kept, although showers are rather cramped. $700

Huentala Primitivo de la Reta 1007 ☎0261 420 0766, ⓦhuentala.com; map p.339. Trendy, verging on glitzy, four-star boutique hotel with stylish lobby and plush rooms, with a pool and terrace plus a rather pretentious French restaurant, *Chimpay Bistro*. $880

★ **Internacional** Sarmiento 720 ☎0261 425 5606, ⓦhinternacional.com.ar; map p.339. The best in its class in Mendoza, this hotel has understated, tasteful furnishings in spacious a/c rooms. A swimming pool and parking are two further assets. $495

NH Cordillera España and Gutiérrez ☎0261 441 6464, ⓦnh-hotels.com; map p.339. Jazzy hotel, one of the nicest of the Spanish chain in Argentina, with professional reception service, sleek rooms, agreeable bathrooms; plus a gym, sauna and swimming pool; breakfasts are copious. $730

Parador del Angel Jorge Newbery 5418, Chacras de Coria ☎0261 496 2201, ⓦparadordelangel.com.ar; map pp.336–337. A handsome guesthouse built around a century-old adobe house. The owners are keen art collectors and share their exquisitely decorated home and peaceful garden with a great sense of hospitality. The breakfasts are memorable. $270

Park Hyatt Chile 1124 ☎0261 441 1234, ⓦmendoza .park.hyatt.com; map p.339. The most central of Mendoza's luxury hotels, this modern block is located on the site of the *Plaza Hotel* where Perón and Eva once stayed; the Neoclassical facade is a replica of its predecessor. Apart from the much vaunted casino, facilities include a luxurious spa specializing in wine treatments, a large outdoor pool, the stylish *Uvas* cocktail bar and *Bistro M*, one of the classiest restaurants in the city. Rooms are spacious, with luxurious bathrooms. $1540

Posada Olivar Besares 978, Chacras de Coria ☎0261 496 0061, ⓦposadaolivar.com; map pp.336–337. Set in fine grounds giving an insight into the typical *chacras* (smallholdings) that gave this leafy Mendoza suburb its name, this friendly posada run by an enthusiastic young English-speaking couple combines simplicity with comfort. There is a large pool in the garden. $890

Ritz Perú 1008 ☎0261 423 5115, ⓦritzhotelmendoza .com; map p.339. This place tries very hard to look British, and partly succeeds with its chintz furnishings and plush fitted carpets. Rooms have a/c. $480

BODEGA ACCOMMODATION

★ **Cavas Wine Lodge** Costa Flores s/n, Alto Agrelo ☎0261 410 6927, ⓦcavaswinelodge.com. Impeccably designed luxury lodge near Luján de Cuyo. Each of the fourteen individually designed rooms comes with its own wooden deck, pool and circular terrace with unobstructed views of the cordillera. The final Bacchanalian touch is a red-wine spa bath in an ancient tub; this and other wine-based spa treatments, such as a crushed malbec scrub, can be booked by nonguests, too. $4200

Club Tapiz Pedro Molina s/n, Maipú ☎0261 496 4815, ⓦtapiz.com.ar. Affiliated with *Bodega Tapiz* in Maipú, *Club Tapiz* has seven tastefully appointed rooms in a renovated villa dating from 1890, as well as a spa, pool, gaucho-style *pulpería* bar and its own gourmet restaurant, *Terruño*, surrounded by a vineyard. $900

Finca Adalgisa Pueyrredón 2222, Chacras de Coria ☎0261 496 0713, ⓦfincaadalgisa.com.ar. Small *finca*

BODEGAS IN AND AROUND MENDOZA

There are dozens of **wineries** in the **Mendoza area** that are open to visitors. The easiest way to visit bodegas is on a **tour** organized by an agency in Mendoza (see box, p.344). A typical half-day trip visits two or three bodegas, while a full day visits five or six and includes lunch; full-day trips are better value. Wine enthusiasts willing to splurge should contact Grapevine (☎0261 429 7522, ⓦthegrapevine-argentina.com), which does a range of small-group "premium" tours led by native English speakers who are also expert tasters; lunch is included.

Alternatively you can rent a car and **drive** yourself; using **public transport** only works if you're planning on seeing a limited number of bodegas. Another option is to rent a **bike**, but always double-check the bike, take an emergency number in case of punctures, and ask which routes are the safest, as it's no rural idyll – some busy roads have bike lanes, but on others you are exposed to industrial traffic. In Maipú, try the friendly Bikes and Wines, at Urquiza 1606 (☎0261 410 6686, ⓦbikesandwines.com); or Maipú Bikes, Urquiza y Gómez (☎0261 487 3311, ✉maipubikes@gmail.com).

If you're going under your own steam, call ahead to check times, to book a visit and to ask for an English-speaking guide, if necessary. The bodegas are concentrated in **Guaymallén**, in **Maipú** (see p.352) and in **Luján de Cuyo** (see p.350). For transport to Maipú and Luján de Cuyo, see the respective town accounts. Buses referred to below stop at the Mendoza bus terminal or along Avenida San Martín.

Some visits and tastings are **free**, but you're pointedly steered to a sales area at the end (cash only; surcharge for the best tipples). Try and see different kinds of wineries, ranging from the old-fashioned, traditional bodegas to the highly mechanized, ultramodern producers; at the former you're more likely to receive personal attention and get a chance to taste finer wines. Best of all is staying the night at one of the several wineries offering accommodation – some of it highly luxurious (see above).

BODEGA TOURS

Chandón Agrelo 5507, Luján de Cuyo ☎0261 490 9966, ✉visitorcenter@chandon.com.ar; bus #380. A modern bodega, somewhat lacking in character but with excellent wine-tasting. The tours start with a video and end up at the salesroom. English or premium-tasting tours should be requested ahead. Feb, March & July Mon–Fri 9.30am–4.30pm, Sat 9.30am–12.30pm; rest of year Mon–Fri 10.30am–4pm; free.

Domaine St Diego Franklin Villanueva 3821, Maipú ☎0261 499 0414, ✉juanmendoza@sinectis.com.ar; bus #20. Small, fairly intimate winery specializing in cabernet sauvignon. Visitors can try good-quality wines after an hour in the vineyards and an hour in the bodega (6 people max). Mon–Fri 9am–5pm, Sat 9am–2pm; reserve 24hr ahead; free.

Escorihuela Belgrano 1188 and Presidente Alvear, Godoy Cruz ☎0261 424 2744. Just 2km south of Mendoza's city centre, this historic bodega was founded in 1884. It is famous for its enormous barrel from France, housed in a cathedral-like cellar. The sumptuous buildings include huge vaulted storage rooms stacked with aromatic casks and a gourmet restaurant, *1884 Francis Mallmann* (see p.348). Mon–Fri 9.30am–12.30pm & 2.30–3.30pm; free.

Giol ("La Colina de Oro") Ozamis 1040, Maipú

(ranch) now geared more towards tourism than wine production, though still with its own vineyard. The attractive rooms are in an annexe with a jasmine-covered veranda running alongside; there's a swimming pool among the vines. **$1200**

Posada Salentein RP-89 and E. Videla, Tunuyán ☎ 02622 429 090, ⓦ bodegasalentein.com/bodega /posada/english/index.html. A posada belonging to the Salentein winery, which can also be visited on a tour (see box below). The price of a room includes a horseriding tour and a wine tasting in the fabulous bodega, plus free entrance to the art gallery. **$1750**

Tupungato Divino Ruta 89 and Calle Los Europeos ☎ 0261 15 601 4424, ⓦ tupungatodivino.com.ar. A

beautifully located hotel, surrounded by young vines, and with fabulous Andean views. Its rooms blend rustic charm with eye-catching modernity, and the outstanding food served in the restaurant complements the fine wines made at the nearby bodegas. **$850**

CAMPING

El Suizo El Challao, Av Champagnat, 6km northwest of the city centre ☎ 0261 444 1991, ⓦ campingsuizo.com .ar; bus #110 runs out to El Challao from the corner of Salta and Av Alem; map pp.336–337. A campsite set among shady woods up in the cool heights above the city. It has a swimming pool, a small restaurant and even an open-air cinema; tent pitches and *cabañas* are available. **$90**

6

☎ 0261 497 2592; bus #160. A wonderfully old-fashioned place, with its fair share of antique barrels – including one of the biggest in South America – alongside the Museo Nacional del Vino y la Vendimia. Mon–Sat 9am–6.30pm, Sun & public holidays 11am–2pm; free.

★ **El Lagar Carmelo Patti** San Martín 2614, Luján de Cuyo ☎ 0261 498 1379. Known as "El maestro del vino", local personality Carmelo has been working in the wine trade since 1971. His enthusiasm and knowledge make him one of the best wine guides in the area (Spanish only). Visits are informal (and free), but call ahead to arrange a mutually convenient time.

Lagarde San Martín 1745, Luján de Cuyo ☎ 0261 498 0011, ⓦ lagarde.com.ar. Lagarde is a major producer, and well worth visiting. There's also an impressive vintage car exhibition and a gourmet restaurant on this enormous site. Mon–Fri 10am–noon & 2.30–3.30pm, Sat 10am–12.30pm; $30 to taste three wines.

Luigi Bosca San Martín 2044, Luján de Cuyo ☎ 0261 498 1974, ⓦ luigibosca.com.ar. One of the best-known wine brands in Argentina, Luigi Bosca appears on many of the agency-run trips. The professional guides are keen to emphasize the winery's family credentials, but it all feels a bit too commercial. Mon–Fri 10.30am & 3.30–5pm, Sat noon; free.

Nieto Senetiner Guardia Vieja, Ruta Panamericana, Chacras de Coria ☎ 0261 498 0315, ⓦ nietosenetiner .com.ar. Some of Argentina's finest wines are produced by this traditional winery. The 12.30pm tour can be followed by a delicious lunch (reserve in advance). Tours Mon–Sat 10am–12.30pm & 3pm; $40.

Norton RP-15, Perdriel, Luján de Cuyo ☎ 0261 488 0480, ⓦ norton.com.ar; bus #380. A prize-winning producer, making top-class if slightly old-fashioned wines, but well worth the visit (reservations essential). Also has a restaurant. Mon–Sat 9am–4.30pm; $50.

★ **Salentein** RP-89 and E. Videla, Tunuyán

☎ 02622 423 550, ⓦ bodegasalentein.com. One of the most beautiful wineries in the country. Visiting this magnificent state-of-the-art building, known as the "Cathedral to Wine", makes for a memorable experience; the wines are also outstanding. Tours daily 11am–3pm (English); $20.

San Felipe ("La Rural") Montecaseros s/n, Coquimbito, Maipú ☎ 0261 497 2013; bus Línea 10 #171, #172 or #173 F. This magnificent traditional bodega stands among its own vineyards and has its own small museum. An interesting contrast with some of the more urban wineries. Free hourly tours (bilingual) Mon–Sat 9am–noon & 2–5pm.

Santa Ana Roca and Urquiza, Villa Nueva, Guaymallén ☎ 0261 421 1000, ⓔ avivas@bodegas-santa-ana.com .ar; bus #20. One of the closest good bodegas, near the city centre, with an enchanting mix of old-style and ultra-modern. Tours are especially friendly; English spoken. Mon–Fri 9.30am–noon & 2.30–5pm; free.

Viña El Cerno Moreno 631, Coquimbito, Maipú ☎ 0261 481 1567, ⓦ elcerno.com.ar. Satisfying boutique winery, in a small traditional country house with a tiny vineyard. The malbec and chardonnay are delicious and the tour highly personalized and enthusiastic. Does *parrilla* lunches noon–5pm ($100). Mon–Sat 10am–5pm, and weekend tours (Spanish only) can be arranged; $25.

Weinert San Martín 5923, Chacras de Coria ☎ 0261 496 0409, ⓦ bodegaweinert.com. One of Argentina's oldest and best wine producers, with an enormous antique barrel still in use, a fabulous cellar and mud-and-cane buildings – characteristic of the area's indigenous population – used to provide the perfect temperature for fermentation. Tasting tours are family-friendly, with grape juice on hand for the kids. Mon–Fri 9am–12.30pm & 2.30–4.30pm, Sat 10am–12.30pm & 2.30–3.30pm; free.

EATING

Mendoza is the prosperous capital of Argentina's western region, and the produce grown in the nearby oases is tiptop; as a result, the city's many, varied and often highly sophisticated **restaurants** and **wine bars** are usually full, and serve some of the best food and drink in the country, thanks to the nearby vineyards, the fertile valley produce and the relative proximity to the fishing ports of Chile.

★ **1884 Francis Mallmann** Belgrano 1188, Godoy Cruz ☎ 0261 424 2698, ⊛ 1884restaurante.com.ar; map pp.336–337. This ultra-chic wine bar and award-winning restaurant with fashion-model staff, swish decor and crystal wine-glasses – rare in Argentina – is considered one of the country's finest. It is next to the Bodega Escorihuela, and serves its fine wines with a balanced menu that includes Patagonian lamb ($90), trout from Malargüe ($85) and cooked plums from General Alvear ($55). Daily 7.30pm–1am.

Azafrán Sarmiento 765 ☎ 0261 429 4200; map p.339. A deli-cum-restaurant with an excellent cellar (you can walk in and choose a bottle), colourful decor and delicious food – specialities include smoked venison ravioli ($65) – plus home-brewed beer; portions are a bit on the miserly side, but the service is efficient and the quality is high. Daily noon–4pm & 7.30pm–1am.

Basilika Av Arístides Villanueva 332; map pp.336–337. One of the best pizzerias in the city, dishing up an array of appetizing toppings on delicious crusts until the early hours. There's also a giant screen showing football matches on Sundays. Wed–Sat noon–3pm & 7pm–1am.

La Carmela Av Arístides Villanueva 298; map pp.336–337. Great, no-fuss Argentine cooking with a menu that changes daily, speedy service and an attractive outdoor seating area from which to watch the lively Arístides streetlife. Daily noon–4pm & 7.30pm–midnight.

Chini Av España and Las Heras; map p.339. One of the best ice-cream parlours in the city, with dozens of flavours. Daily 11.30am–1am.

Don Mario 25 de Mayo 1324, Guaymallén ☎ 0261 431 0810; map pp.336–337. An institutional *parrilla* in the neighbourhood of Guaymallén (east of the city centre), frequented by Mendocino families in search of comforting decor and an old-fashioned *parrillada*. The meat comes in gargantuan portions at $70 a head. Daily noon–4pm & 7.30pm–1am.

Ferruccio Soppelsa Emilio Civit esq Belgrano, Espejo 299; map p.339. This chain of *heladerías*, run for years

by the same Italian family, is guaranteed to give you enough calories to last you to the top of Aconcagua. Branches elsewhere in and around the city. Daily 11am–midnight.

La Florencia Sarmiento 698 esq Perú; map p.339. A no-nonsense *parrilla* that's popular with tourists and locals alike. Sit inside or streetside, and check out the extensive local wine list. Daily noon–4pm & 8pm–1am.

★ **La Marchigiana** Patricias Mendocinas 1550 ☎ 0261 423 0751; map p.339. This is *the* Italian-Argentine restaurant in the city, run by the same family for decades. You can eat fresh *caprese* salad, followed by delicious cannelloni ($35) and finish with one of the best tiramisus ($30) in the country. Daily noon–3pm & 7.30pm–1am.

El Patio de Jesús María Viamonte 4961, Chacras de Coria; map pp.336–337. Well-known and respected classic *parrilla* out in Chacras. There are also other branches in the city, such as at the junction of Av Arístides Villanueva and Boulogne sur Mer. Daily noon–4pm & 8pm–midnight.

Sancho Amigorena 65; map p.339. Conventional meals such as *milanesas* and steaks, together with pasta and fish dishes, are on offer at this smart institutional establishment with an appealing patio seating area. Daily noon–4pm & 8pm–1am.

Tasca la Plaza Montevideo 117; map p.339. Intimate little bistro, or *tasca*, conveniently located on the Plaza España and serving appropriately Hispanic fare, including tapas, along with sangría and good wines; charming service. Tues–Sat noon–3pm & 7.30pm–1am.

Las Tinajas Lavalle 38; map p.339. Good-value *tenedor libre* in the city centre. The food quality is a cut above the usual all-you-can-eat establishments – there's an excellent *asado* and heaving salad bar. Daily noon–4pm & 7.30pm–1am.

Veggetalia Alem 43 ☎ 0261 15 625 0355; map p.339. This agreeable vegetarian restaurant serves a wide variety of well-prepared food by the kilo. Mon–Sat noon–3pm & 7pm–1am.

DRINKING AND NIGHTLIFE

Mendoza's **bars** are lively and it has a well-developed café-terrace culture, with Avenida Arístides Villanueva, to the west of the centre, a hotspot; **nightlife** is also vibrant, and is mostly concentrated in outlying places such as El Challao, to the northwest, and Godoy Cruz and fashionable Chacras de Coria to the south.

BARS

La Aldea Av Arístides Villanueva 495; map pp.336–337. A lively pub-style bar that does great sandwiches. Daily 10am–midnight.

★ **Apeteco** San Juan and Barraquero; map pp.336–337. A city institution, this pre-club bar used to be called *El Rancho*, and still hosts "El Rancho" nights on Wed – an essential stop on a midweek night out. Daily 8pm–late.

ARGENTINE WINE

Argentina is now the world's fifth largest wine producer (after Italy, France, Spain and the US), with three-quarters of the country's total production coming from **Mendoza** Province, focused on Maipú and Luján de Cuyo in the south of the city. **San Rafael**, **La Rioja** and **San Juan** are also major wine-growing centres.

Many wine experts would agree that Argentina's vintages are improving rapidly as a result of both a domestic market that's fast becoming more discerning and the lure of exports. **Table wines** still dominate, often sold at the budget end of the market in huge, refillable flagons called *damajuanas*, and sometimes marketed under usurped names such as *borgoña*, or burgundy, and chablis. Younger Argentines often only drink wine on special occasions, plumping for lighter **New Wave** wines such as Chandón's **Nuevo Mundo**. Many upmarket restaurants offer extensive wine lists including older vintages – but beware of exorbitant corkage charges. Commonly found bodega names to look for include **Chandón**, **Graffigna**, **Navarro Correas**, **Salentein**, **Finca Flichmann** and **Weinert**.

Although the most attractive wineries to visit are the old-fashioned ones, with musty cellars crammed with oak barrels, some of the finest vintages are now produced by growers using the latest equipment, including storage tanks lined with epoxy resin and computerized temperature controls. They tend to concentrate on making varietal wines, the main grape varieties being riesling, chenin blanc and chardonnay, for whites, and pinot noir, cabernet sauvignon and malbec, for reds – the reds tend to be better than whites. **Malbec** is often regarded as the Argentine grape par excellence, giving rich fruity wines, with overtones of blackcurrant and prune that are the perfect partner for a juicy steak. The latest trend is for a balanced combination of two grapes: for example, mixing malbec for its fruitiness and cabernet for its body, while toning down the sometimes excessive oakiness that used to characterize Argentine wines. Growers have also been experimenting with varieties such as tempranillo, san gervase, gewürztraminer, syrah and merlot, and very convincing sparkling wines are being made locally by the *méthode champenoise*, including those produced by Chandón and Mumm, the French champagne-makers.

El Palenque Av Arístides Villanueva 287; map pp.336–337. A *pulpería*-style bar with bags of old-fashioned pampas atmosphere and a range of empanadas and wines; popular with the city's youth. Daily noon–midnight.

Soul Tango Rivadavia and 9 de Julio; map p.339. Fun little place that plays both soul and tango music, as the name suggests, and hosts occasional tango classes and live bands. Tues–Sun 8pm–late.

La Tienda Av Arístides Villanueva 341 ☎0261 423 6050; map pp.336–337. Smart, modern café and resto-bar serving uncomplicated snacks until 2am, plus cocktails till later, to an eclectic mix of popular Latin and Western hits. Daily 10am–late.

Vines of Mendoza Espejo 567 ⓦvinesofmendoza.com; map p.339. Not a bar as such, but rather a sophisticated wine-tasting room in the city centre. The friendly and knowledgeable staff can recommend wines to try and bodegas to visit, and also make the necessary reservations – it's an ideal starting point for anyone thinking of heading off on the viniculture trail. Daily noon–midnight.

NIGHTCLUBS

Aloha Ruta Panamericana s/n, Chacras de Coria; map pp.336–337. Extremely fashionable club (best on Sat) playing Argentine rock music, frequented by a 30s crowd. Fri–Sun midnight–late.

Alquimia Ruta Panamericana s/n, Chacras de Coria; map pp.336–337. Restaurant-bar-club with disco on one floor, varied electronica on another and patios at which to eat throughout. One of the most popular places to dance the night away. Fri & Sat midnight–late.

Carilo Av Champagnat s/n, El Challao; map pp.336–337. The über-fashionable club during the summer season (Sept–March), spinning house and techno. Fri & Sat midnight–late.

Estación Miró Ejército de los Andes 656, Dorrego, Guaymallén; map pp.336–337. The city's main gay nightclub, open every weekend night, although Sunday is the best night to go. Cocktails, shows and even an alternative Fiesta de la Vendimia in March. Fri–Sun 11pm–late.

Geo San Martín Sur 576, Godoy Cruz; map pp.336–337. Trendy club playing a mix of electronica, rock and reggaeton. Thurs–Sat midnight–late.

Iskra San Martín Sur 905, Godoy Cruz; map pp.336–337. Varied mix of rock, reggaeton and dance music for a young crowd, most of whom are in their late teens and 20s. Thurs–Sat midnight–late.

DIRECTORY

Banks and exchange Banex, Av San Martín 1190; Boston, Necochea 165; Citibank, Av San Martín 1092; Banco Mendoza, Av España 1340; Banco de la Nación, Necochea 101. ATMs everywhere.

Consulates ⓦ ccmdz.consul.org.ar; Bolivia, M. Lemos 635 ☎ 0261 423 0413; Brazil, Perú 789 ☎ 0261 423 0939; Chile, Belgrano and Liniers ☎ 0261 425 5024; Ecuador, Francisco Moyano 1587 ☎ 0261 429 6416; France, Houssay 790 ☎ 0261 429 8339; Germany, Montevideo 127 ☎ 0261 429 6539; Italy, Necochea 712 ☎ 0261 520 1400; Perú, Huarpes 629 ☎ 0261 429 9831; Spain, Agustín Alvarez 455 ☎ 0261 425 3947; UK/Netherlands, Av Boulogne Sur Mer 889, 6th floor ☎ 0261 425 2823.

Internet WH at Sarmiento 219, Colón 136 and Las Heras 61.

Laundry Lavasec Colón 470 ☎ 0261 423 8866.

Police Tourist police, San Martín 1143 ☎ 0261 413 2135 or in Maipú ☎ 0261 15 502 0277.

Post office San Martín and Colón.

Luján de Cuyo

Bus #200 from downtown Mendoza or the bus terminal runs to Luján de Cuyo

Immediately south of Mendoza are two satellite towns, the first of which, sitting where the Guaymallén Canal meets the Río Mendoza, is **LUJÁN DE CUYO**. Lying just west of the Ruta Panamericana, or the RN-40, it's part residential, part industrial, with a huge brewery and some of the city's major **wineries**.

Iglesia de le Carrodilla

Carrodilla 11 • Mon–Fri 10am–noon & 4–8pm • Free

The northern district, known as Carrodilla, 7km south of downtown Mendoza, is an oasis of the colonial city that survived the 1861 earthquake. Here you'll find the **Iglesia de la Carrodilla**, usually included in the city's wine tours. Built in 1840, it's now a museum of seventeenth- and eighteenth-century religious art as well as the parish church. The naive frescoes depict scenes of grape harvesting, and the church's main relic is an oakwood statue of the Virgin and Child, star of the religious processions that precede Mendoza's Fiesta de la Vendimia. Artistically, the finest exhibit is the moving *Cristo de los Huarpes*, an exceptional piece of *mestizo* art carved out of *quebracho* wood in 1670 by local indigenous craftsmen.

Chacras de Coria

The western district of Luján de Cuyo is **Chacras de Coria**, a leafy suburb of European-style villas, golf courses, bodegas and several new, upmarket hotels. It's also full of outdoor *parrillas*, bars and nightclubs, frequented at weekends and in the summer by affluent Mendocinos.

Museo Provincial de Bellas Artes Emiliano Guiñazú

San Martín 3651 • Tues–Fri 8.30am–7pm, Sat & Sun 3–8pm • $5

On the town's eastern edge, in a rural area called Mayor Drummond, is Mendoza's **Museo Provincial de Bellas Artes Emiliano Guiñazú**, also known as the **Casa de Fader** after Fernando Fader (see p.198), the artist who decorated the interior. It's housed in a grandiose red-sandstone villa, which was built at the end of the nineteenth century for Emiliano Guiñazú, an influential landowner and socialite, in a style influenced by Art Nouveau, and is set off by a luxuriant garden of cacti, cypresses, magnolias and roses, among which you will find Neoclassical marble statues. Having heard that Fader had been to art school in France, Guiñazú commissioned him to decorate the house interior. Fader's **Impressionistic murals** – especially appealing are the frescoes of tropical vegetation painted on the walls of the bathroom, alongside Art Nouveau tiles – are the main attraction here. His paintings also dominate the museum's collection of nineteenth- and early twentieth-century Argentine art. Temporary exhibits are staged from time to time.

6

Maipú

Buses #150, #151, #170, #172, #173 and #180 all go to Maipú, taking slightly different routes from downtown Mendoza; once there, you can rent bikes for exploring the area at Urquiza 2288 (☎ 0261 497 4067)

The self-styled "Cuna de la Viña", or birthplace of the grapevine, **MAIPÚ**, lying some 15km southeast of Mendoza via the RN-7, is the city's other small satellite town. Founded in 1861 by the Mercedarian monks Fray Manuel Apolinario Vásquez and Don José Alberto de Ozamis as a new site for the earthquake-levelled Mendoza, it quickly became the centre of wine-making in the region, and is where many of the city's **wineries** are located today (see box, pp.346–347). The wine-growing district, to the north of the town's centre, is called Coquimbito, where vineyards alternate with dusky olive groves.

Museo del Vino

Bodega La Rural at Montecaseros • Mon–Sat 9am–6pm, Sun 10am–1pm • $5 • ☎ 0261 497 7763

The large Bodega La Rural at Montecaseros is where you'll find Mendoza's **Museo del Vino**, a summary explanation of the region's wine industry housed in a fabulous Art Nouveau villa, with elegant fittings and detailing, including some delicate stained glass – the venue far outstrips the contents, which won't teach you anything you won't find out in far more interesting bodegas.

Alta Montaña

The Andean cordillera, including some of the world's tallest mountains, loom a short distance west of Mendoza, and its snow-tipped peaks are visible from the city centre almost all year round, beyond the picturesque vineyards and fruit orchards. Even if you've come to the region for the wine, you'll want to head up into the hills before long: the scenery is fabulous, and skiing, trekking and highland walks are all possible, or you can simply enjoy the views on an organized excursion.

The so-called **Alta Montaña Route** – the RN-7 – is also the international highway to Santiago de Chile, via the upmarket Chilean ski resort of Portillo, and one of the major border crossings between the two countries, blocked by snow only on rare occasions in July and August. If you're in a hurry to get to or from Santiago, try to travel by day, to see the stunning scenery in the area. However, if you've more time to explore, possible stop-offs along the RN-7 include the pretty village of **Potrerillos** and **Vallecitos**, a tiny ski resort that caters for a younger crowd than exclusive Las Leñas (see p.363). As the road climbs further up into the mountains it passes another village, **Uspallata**, and then a variety of colourful rock formations – look for the pinnacle-like **Los Penitentes**. Closer to the border, **Puente del Inca** is a popular place to pause, both for its sulphurous thermal spring and its location – near the trailhead, base camp and muleteer-post for those brave enough to contemplate the ascent of mighty **Aconcagua**, the continent's tallest peak, just to the north. The last settlement before you travel through a tunnel under the Andes and into Chile is **Las Cuevas**, from where an old mountain pass can be ascended, weather permitting, to see the **Cristo Redentor**, a huge statue of Christ, erected as a sign of peace between the old rivals, and for the fantastic mountain views.

Potrerillos

Some 40km along the RN-7 is the village of **POTRERILLOS**, which styles itself as a centre for adventure tourism. Its picturesque valley is dotted with poplar trees that turn vivid yellow in March and April, while the views up to the precordillera are fabulous: the colours form a blurred mosaic from this distance.

ARRIVAL AND TOURS   **POTRERILLOS**

By car To reach the RN-7, the Alta Montaña road from Mendoza, first head south along the RN-40, and turn westwards 15km south of the city, beyond Luján de Cuyo and Perdriel.

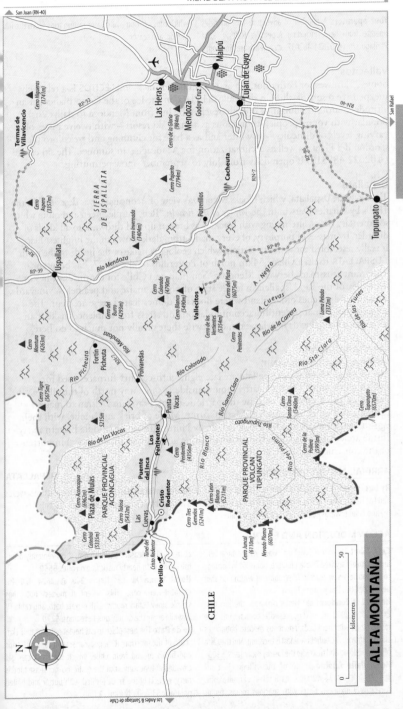

ALTA MONTAÑA

Tour operators A number of adventure-tour agencies operate from here, including Argentina Rafting, Ruta Perilago s/n (☎02624 482037, ⓦargentinarafting.com), which runs exciting whitewater-rafting trips down the Río Mendoza in season.

Vallecitos

Some 25km west of Potrerillos, via an unnumbered track, **VALLECITOS** is a relatively inexpensive resort nestling in the Valle del Plata, in the lee of the Cerro Blanco, at an altitude of around 3000m. It is easily reached by bus from Mendoza (3 daily; 2hr). Popular with young people, it functions as a small ski resort – with twelve pistes of varying levels of difficulty – in winter and as a base for climbing and treks into the Cordón del Plata, as well as acclimatization for Aconcagua, in summer. The ski centre (☎02622 488810) is open daily from July to September, snow permitting.

Uspallata

The **Sierra de Uspallata**, which blocks Mendoza's view of Aconcagua, was described in the 1830s by Charles Darwin in the *Voyage of the Beagle*: "Red, purple, green and quite white sedimentary rocks, alternating with black lavas broken up and thrown into all kinds of disorder, by masses of porphyry, of every shade, from dark brown to the brightest lilac. It really resembled those pretty sections which geologists make of the inside of the earth."

USPALLATA itself, a village 54km north of Potrerillos by the RN-7, has been an important crossroads between Mendoza, San Juan and Chile for centuries. It lies in the valley of the Río Uspallata, a fertile strip of potato, maize and pea fields, vineyards, pastures and patches of farmland where flocks of domesticated geese are kept. The village's cool climate, plentiful accommodation and stress-free ambience make it an ideal place for a few days' relaxation; otherwise there's really not much to do here.

Bóvedas de Uspallata

Tues–Sun 10am–7pm • $3 • ☎02624 420045

The unusual **Bóvedas de Uspallata** are late eighteenth-century furnaces used for smelting iron mined in the nearby mountainside, a short way north of the village. Famously, the ovens were used by the patriotic monk Fray Luis Beltrán to make cannons and other arms for San Martín's army. Made of brick and adobe, with their egg-shaped white domes they look decidedly North African or Middle Eastern in style. Inside are exhibitions about the region's mining activity and the historical importance of the construction.

ARRIVAL AND INFORMATION
USPALLATA

By bus The centre of Uspallata is the junction of the RN-7 and Las Heras, where buses arrive from Mendoza (7daily; 2 hr) and head towards Puenta del Inca and into Chile.

Tourist information A hut right by the junction serves as a rudimentary tourist office (daily 8am–10pm).

ACCOMMODATION AND EATING

Café Tibet Near the junction. Good coffee in a very imaginatively stylized Tibetan temple, done out in homage to the movie *Seven Years in Tibet*, some of which was shot near Uspallata. Daily 8am–10pm.

Hostal Los Cóndores Las Heras s/n, near the junction ☎02624 420002, ⓦloscondoreshotel.com.ar. Has nice rooms albeit with hard beds, enormous modern bathrooms and a *confitería*. The buffet breakfast is excellent, and they also offer horseriding and treks into the nearby mountains. $500

Hotel Valle Andino South of the village, just off the RN-7 ☎02624 420095, ⓦhotelvalleandino.com. A relatively luxurious hotel with spacious rooms, tennis courts and a pleasant sitting-room; it conveniently offers full board, with hearty rustic fare on offer. $550

Hotel Viena Av Las Heras 240 ☎02624 420046, ⓦhotel-viena.com. This decent if modest hotel has simple almost stark rooms, with private bath, and cable TV to while away the deadly quiet evenings. $270

Lo de Pato The best place to eat hereabouts, located 1km south of the junction; it's a popular stopoff for coach trips and buses to and from Chile, which means it can get crowded at lunchtime, but the rustic, no-nonsense food is tasty, especially the trout (grilled with butter and boiled potatoes; $35). Daily 8am–11pm.

Up to Los Penitentes

From Uspallata, the RN-7 swings round to the west and rejoins the Río Mendoza, whose valley it shares with the now-disused rail line all the way to its source at Punta de Vacas. The road follows an ancient Inca trail; several mummified corpses have been found in the mountains to the south and are displayed in Mendoza at the Museo de Ciencias Naturales y Antropológicas (see p.343). The scenery is simply fantastic: you pass through narrow canyons, close by the Cerro del Burro (4293m) and the Cerro División (4603m) to the south, with the rugged ridges of the Cerros del Chacay culminating in the Cerro Tigre (5700m) to the north. Stripes of different coloured rock – reds, greens and yellows caused by the presence of iron, copper and sulphur – decorate the steep walls of the cordillera peaks, while the vegetation is limited to tough highland grass and *jarilla*, a scruffy, gorse-like shrub gathered for firewood. The road climbs a gentle slope, slips through a series of tunnels, takes you through the abandoned hamlet of Polvaredas and past the police station at Punta de Vacas, at 2325m above sea level; the public customs post is further on at Los Horcones.

Los Penitentes ski resort

☎ 0261 428 3601, ⊛ penitentes.com

Some 65km from Uspallata is the small ski resort of **LOS PENITENTES**, or more properly Villa Los Penitentes. The "penitents" in question are a series of strange pinnacles of rock, high up on the ridge atop Cerro Penitentes (4356m), towering over the small village of typical, brightly coloured ski-resort buildings to the south. The pointed rocks are thought to look like cowled monks, of the kind that traditionally parade during Holy Week in places such as Seville – hence the name. The resort's 25 pistes vary from nursery slopes to the black "Las Paredes", with most of the runs classified as difficult and the biggest total drop being 700m. The modern ski lifts also run at weekends in the summer, so you can enjoy the fabulous mountain and valley views from the top of Cerro San Antonio (3200m); the fissured peak looming over it all is the massive Cerro Leña (4992m).

ACCOMMODATION

LOS PENITENTES

Ayelén Hotel de Montaña RN-7 Km160 ☎ 0261 423 4848, ⊛ lospenitentes.com/hotel-ayelen.html. Functional hotel aimed specifically at winter sports enthusiasts, with games and TV rooms to keep skiers entertained in the evenings, plus a decent restaurant. $720

Hostería Ayelén RN-7 Km160 ☎ 0261 423 4848. The best budget accommodation within comfortable reach of the pistes, this place is aimed at the youth market, with its bunk-bed dorms and party ambience. It has a canteen serving mostly fast food. Dorms $70, doubles $200

Hostería Los Penitentes RN-7 Km160 ☎ 0261 420 2137. This is the main alternative to the *Ayelén Hotel de Montaña*, and more amenable to one-night as opposed to full-week bookings in season. It is more about location than luxury, but is nonetheless comfortable, clean and efficient. $680

Puente del Inca

Just 6km west of Los Penitentes is **PUENTE DEL INCA**, a traditional stop for anyone heading along the Alta Montaña route. At just over 2700m, this natural **stone bridge** is an impressive sight, featuring on many a postcard. Formed by the Río de las Cuevas, it nestles in an arid valley, overlooked by majestic mountains; just beneath the bridge are the remains of a once sophisticated spa resort, built in the 1940s but swept away by a flood. The ruins, the bridge itself and the surrounding rocks are all stained a nicotine-yellow by the very high sulphur content of the warm waters that gurgle up nearby. Stalls sell souvenirs here, including all kinds of objects that have been left to petrify and yellow in the mineral springs: shoes, bottles, hats, books, ashtrays and statues of the Virgin Mary have all been treated to this embellishment, and are of dubious taste, but the displays make for an unusual photograph. Only 4km west of Puente del Inca is the dirt track that heads into the Parque Nacional Aconcagua.

Hostería Puente del Inca ☎ 02624 429993. This decent *hostería* has a number of slightly cramped but acceptable rooms – if you don't mind pink bedspreads. It offers half-board – a good idea in view of the lack of places to eat here. $480

Refugio La Vieja Estación 100m from the RN-7 ☎ 0261 452 1103. This mountaineers' refuge has basic bunk beds and shared bath but is a perfectly fine place to rest your head if the *hostería* is full or too expensive. The views are breathtaking. $60

Aconcagua

At 6962m – or 6959m according to some maps – **CERRO ACONCAGUA** is the highest peak in both the western and southern hemispheres, or outside the Himalayas. Its glacier-garlanded summit dominates the Parque Provincial Aconcagua, even though it is encircled by several other mountains that exceed 5000m: cerros Almacenes, Catedral, Cuerno, Cúpula, Ameghino, Güssfeldt, Dedos, México, Mirador, Fitzgerald, La Mano, Santa María and Tolosa, some of which are easier to climb than others, and many of which obscure views of the great summit from most points around. The five glaciers that hang around its faces like icy veils are Horcones Superior, Horcones Inferior, Güssfeldt, Las Vacas and Los Polacos.

Although **climbing** Aconcagua is technically less demanding than climbing many lower-altitude peaks, it is still a challenge to be taken seriously. Fitness, patience and acclimatization are key, and, unless you're fairly experienced at high-altitude treks, you shouldn't even consider going up; despite what the agencies may tell you, both independent climbers and people climbing as part of organized treks often end up turning back.

ACONCAGUA ESSENTIALS

Equipment Given the huge amount of supplies needed to make the ascent most people invest in a mule.

Hazards The two biggest obstacles are coping with the altitude and the cold – temperatures can plummet to -40°C at night even in the summer – and fickle weather is also a major threat. Expeditions always descend when they see milky-white clouds shaped like the lenses of eyeglasses, known as *el viento blanco*, which announce violent storms. On average, some two people a year die trying to climb Aconcagua. Frostbite and altitude sickness are the main health hazards, but proper precautions can usually prevent both.

Permits Unless you are arranging everything through a tour operator, the first place you need to go is the Dirección de Recursos Naturales Renovables (Mon–Fri 8am–6pm,

Sat & Sun 9am–1pm; ☎ 0261 425 2090, ⓦ aconcagua .mendoza.gov.ar), located on the first floor of Mendoza's main tourist office at Av San Martín 1143. This is where you must apply for the compulsory permits to enter the Aconcagua reserve. For foreign trekkers these cost from US$95 for a single day's access to as high as US$1000 for a twenty-day permit to climb to the summit in winter.

Seasons The main climbing season runs from mid-November to mid-March; January is the most popular month, and therefore most expensive, as it coincides with Argentine summer holidays and is when the weather is usually most settled. Allow two to three weeks for an expedition, since you should acclimatize at each level, and take it easy throughout the climb; many of the people who don't make it to the top fail because they try to rush.

Brief history

Aconcagua may be the highest Andean mountain, but for many mountain purists, it lacks the morphological beauty of Cerro Mercedario to the north or Volcán Tupungato to the south; it's also not as difficult a climb to the summit as some of the other Andean peaks. Nevertheless, ever since it was conquered by the Italian–Swiss mountaineer Mathias Zurbriggen in 1897 – after it had been identified by German climber Paul Güssfeldt in 1883 – Aconcagua has been one of the top destinations in the world for expeditions or solo climbs. In 1934, a Polish team of climbers made it to the top via the Los Polacos glacier now named after them; in 1953, the southwest ridge was the route successfully taken by a local group of mountaineers; and in 1954, a French team that had successfully conquered Cerro Fitz Roy made the first ascent of Aconcagua up the south face, the most challenging of all – Plaza Francia, one of the main base camps, is named after them. In recent years, Aconcagua has become a major

> ### ACONCAGUA IN PRE-COLUMBIAN HISTORY
> The origins of the name Aconcagua are not entirely clear, although it probably comes either from the Huarpe words *Akon-Kahuak* ("stone sentinel") or from the Mapuche *Akonhue* ("from the beyond"). That it was a holy site for these and/or other indigenous peoples is evidenced by the discovery in 1985 of an Inca mummy – now in the Museo del Área Fundacional, Mendoza (see p.341) – on the southwest face. Found at an altitude of 5300m, the presence of the mummy shows that ceremonies, including burials and perhaps sacrifices, took place at these incredible heights.

6

attraction for less experienced mountaineers, and of the seven thousand-odd people who try to reach the summit every year, about half make it.

Routes

Of the three **approaches** – south, west or east – the western route from the Plaza de Mulas (4230m) is the most accessible and most used, and is known as the Ruta Normal. Very experienced climbers take either the Glaciar de los Polacos route, with its base camp at Plaza Argentina, reached via a long track that starts near Punta de Vacas, or the very demanding south face, whose Plaza Francia base camp is reached from Los Horcones, branching off from the Plaza de Mulas trail at a spot called Confluencia (3368m). For more details of the different routes, advice on what to take with you and how to acclimatize, consult the Aconcagua website (ⓦaconcagua.com.ar). For more specialist information, especially for serious climbers who are considering one of the harder routes, the best publication is R.J. Secor's *Aconcagua, A Climbing Guide* (1994).

ARRIVAL AND TOURS ACONCAGUA

By bus To get to either Los Horcones or Punta de Vacas, you can take the twice-daily buses from Mendoza, or hop off a through bus headed to Santiago de Chile.

By organized tour It's definitely preferable, whether trekking or climbing, to go with local guides on an organized trip, if only because of the treacherous weather. Several outfits in Mendoza specialize in tours, which cost around US$3500 per person plus US$1000 each for equipment rental and permits. These include Aconcagua Trek, at Barcala 484 (ⓣ0261 429 5007, ⓦaconcaguatrek.com); Aconcagua Xperience, at Av Mitre 1237 (ⓣ0261 423 1806, ⓦaconcagua-xperience.com.ar); Campo Base Expeditions, at Pt Sarmiento 229 (ⓣ0261 425 5511, ⓦcampobase.com.ar); Aymará Viajes, at 9 de Julio 1023 (ⓣ0261 420 2064); and Fernando Grajales (ⓣ0261 428 3157, ⓦgrajales.net), where you can also hire mules if climbing independently.

ACCOMMODATION

Hostel Arco de las Cuevas ⓣ0264 420185, ⓦarcodelascuevas.com.ar. This hostel with comfortable dorms and rooms with en-suite baths in an attractive Alpine-style stone building, arching over the RN-7, is popular with Aconcagua climbers; it also has a restaurant. Dorms $80, doubles $280

Cristo Redentor

From January to March, but usually not for the rest of the year because of snowfalls or frost, you can drive up the several hairpin bends to the **Monumento al Cristo Redentor**, an 8m-high, six-tonne statue of Christ as the redeemer. It was put here in 1904 to celebrate the so-called May 1902 Pacts, signed between Argentina and Chile, under the auspices of British King Edward VII, to determine once and for all the Andean boundary between the two countries. Designed by Argentine sculptor Mateo Alonso, the statue was made from melted-down cannons and other weapons, in a reversal of Fray Luis Beltrán's project a hundred years before (see p.354). Nearby is a disused Chilean customs post – the Paso de la Cumbre, no longer used by international traffic. The views towards Cerro Tolosa (5432m), immediately to the north, along the cordillera and down into several valleys, are quite staggering; make sure you have something warm to wear, though, as the howling winds up here are bitterly cold. When the road is open, most Alta Montaña tours bring you up here as the grand finale to the excursion; would-be Aconcagua conquerors often train and acclimatize by clambering to the top on foot.

South of Mendoza

The cordillera south of Mendoza city contains two remote and little visited but stunning provincial parks – the fabulous **Parque Provincial Tupungato**, 80km southwest from Mendoza and dominated by the soaring volcano of the same name, and the **Reserva Provincial Laguna Diamante**, with a turquoise altiplanic lake, the **Laguna Diamante**, at its heart. The latter is a further 140km southwest of Tupungato and only open during the summer; both are well worth the effort it takes to reach them.

Tupungato and Parque Provincial Tupungato

Now that Aconcagua has become almost a victim of its own success, anyone looking for a challenging mountain trek with fewer people crowding the trails and paths should head for the better-kept secret of Cerro Tupungato, an extinct volcano peaking at 6570m. Its hulking cone dominates the **PARQUE PROVINCIAL TUPUNGATO**, which stretches along the Chilean border to the south of the RN-7 at Puente del Inca. The virgin countryside within the park is utterly breathtaking, completely unspoilt and unremittingly stark. The park is most accessible from the town of **TUPUNGATO**, reached from Mendoza via the RN-40 and the RP-86. There's little to see in the small market town, but this is where you can contract guides to take you to the top of the mighty volcano; you'll need plenty of time as the treks last between three and fifteen days, depending on how long you're given to acclimatize at each level – the longer the better. Calculate on US$1000 per person.

ARRIVAL AND INFORMATION
TUPUNGATO

By bus Buses run fairly regularly to and from Mendoza (hourly; 1hr 15min), stopping at Plaza General San Martín and other halts along the main road.

Tourist information Ask at the *Hotel Turismo* (see below), which also acts as the town's tourist office (daily 9am–6pm), about trips to the volcano.

Tours Apart from the companies recommended for Aconcagua, which also arrange tours to Tupungato (see p.357), check out Rómulo Nieto at the *Hostería Don Rómulo* (see below).

ACCOMMODATION AND EATING

Camping de Correa La Costa s/n ☎02622 1567 3299. The best of a bunch of campsites around the village – there's an excellent barbecue grill. $\overline{75}$

Hostería Don Rómulo Almirante Brown 1200 ☎02622 489020, ⊛donromulo.com.ar. Not only does owner Rómulo arrange reasonably priced tours in the area, including excellent highland horse treks, but you can stay at his small, plain but comfortable *hostería*, with decent rooms. There is an excellent *parrilla* attached. $\overline{320}$

Hotel Turismo Av Belgrano 1050 ☎02622 488 007. This spacious hotel offers smart bedrooms, modern bathrooms and a full-board option, thanks to its excellent restaurant – where local kid is a speciality. $\overline{290}$

Pizzeria Ilo Belgrano and Sargento Cabral. This place is very popular with the locals and serves up an excellent margarita plus delicious home-made pasta; the wine-list is surprisingly good for a pizzeria. Daily 12.30–4pm & 7.30–11.30pm.

Reserva Provincial Laguna Diamante

Some 220km southwest of Mendoza, **LAGUNA DIAMANTE** is the destination of one of the least-known but most unforgettable excursions in the area. The source of the Río Diamante, the lake is so called because the choppy surface of its crystalline waters suggests a rough diamond. One reason for its relative obscurity is that weather conditions make it possible to reach Laguna Diamante only from mid-December to the end of March. At Pareditas, 125km south of Mendoza by the RN-40, take the reliable, unsealed RP-101, which forks off to the southwest; the drive is one marvellous panoramic view of the Andean precordillera, following Arroyo Yaucha through fields of gorse-like *jarilla* and gnarled *chañares*, affording views of the rounded summits of the frontal cordillera, before entering the Cañón del Gateado, through which the Arroyo Rosario flows past dangling willows. At another fork in the road, 20km on, take the right fork to the Refugio Militar General Alvarado, the entrance to the **Reserva Provincial Laguna Diamante**. Here, you'll catch your first sight of **Cerro Maipo** (5323m), the permanently snowcapped volcano that straddles the frontier, some 4000m above sea level. Nestling beneath the Cordón del Eje, a majestic range of dark ochre rock, and towered over by the snow-streaked Maipo opposite – a perfect cone worthy of a Japanese woodcut – this ultramarine lake is constantly buffeted into white horses by strong breezes and its waves noisily lap the springy, mossy banks. The silence is broken only by the howl of the wind.

6

ARRIVAL AND INFORMATION

RESERVA LAGUNA DIAMANTE

By 4WD No public transport reaches this remote spot, so you'll need a 4WD.

By organized tour Some tour agencies also come; try Nicolás García at Argentina Mountain, Lavalle 606, San José, in Guaymallén, Mendoza (☎0261 431 8356, ⓦlagunadeldiamante.com), who offers day-trips from Mendoza ($500 per person), as well as longer horse treks and climbs up Maipo and Tupungato. You may also be able

to pick up a tour from San Rafael, which is closer. Since it's in an area under military control, near a strategic point on the Chilean border, take your passport.

Tourist information Rangers at the *guardería*, which you pass on the final approach to the lagoon, can offer some information on the reserve and its wildlife, and appreciate the chance to share a *mate*.

San Rafael and around

The small city of **SAN RAFAEL** is the de facto capital of central Mendoza Province; around 230km south of Mendoza via the RN-40 and the RN-143, it's a kind of mini-Mendoza, complete with wide avenues, irrigation channels along the gutters and scrupulously clean public areas. The town was founded in 1805 on behalf of Rafael, Marqués de Sobremonte – hence the name – by militia leader Miguel Telles Meneses. Large numbers of Italian and Spanish immigrants flocked here at the end of the nineteenth century, but the so-called Colonia Francesa expanded further when the railway arrived in 1903. Favoured by French immigrants during the nineteenth century, San Rafael built its prosperity on vineyards, olives and fruit, grown in the province's second biggest oasis.

In all, there are nearly eighty wine **bodegas** in San Rafael department, most of them tiny, family-run businesses, some of which welcome visitors. Tourism has been a big money-spinner over the past couple of decades, especially since adventure tourism has taken off. The **Cañón del Atuel**, a short way to the southwest, is a great place for gentle whitewater rafting, or you can try the much more challenging, dramatic **Río Diamante**. If exploring the southern parts of the province, there's a wider choice of accommodation in San Rafael than in Malargüe, although the latter still makes a far more convenient base.

San Rafael has a flat, compact centre that lends itself to a gentle stroll, but otherwise there aren't any sights to speak of – the town is essentially a base for visiting the surrounding area. The main drag, with most of the shops and hotels, is a continuation

---

RAFTING IN SAN RAFAEL

Rafael is an excellent base for **rafting** with the Cañón del Atuel being the most sedate option. More challenging experiences are available with rapids as tough as Grade IV–V in season, such as the Río Sosneado (booked through Bruni Aventura, Av Balloffet 98 ☎0260 442 3790, ⓦbruniaventura.com.ar; season Dec–Feb, min 4 people, $800 per person); and one- or multi-day adventures down the splendid and rarely visited canyon of the **Río Diamante**, or the Río Grande (Exoticandes Expediciones, San Luís 336 ☎0260 440 7602, ⓦexoticandes.com; season Dec–Feb, min 5 people; prices from $1000 per person).

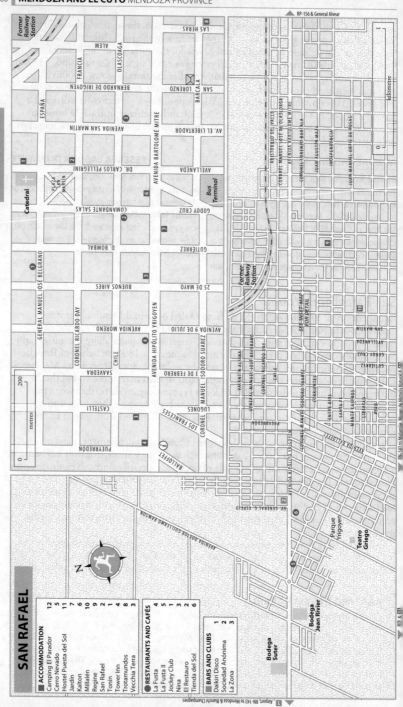

SAN RAFAEL

ACCOMMODATION	
Camping El Parador	12
Cerro Nevado	5
Hostel Puesta del Sol	11
Jardín	7
Kalton	6
Millalén	10
Regine	9
San Rafael	2
Tonin	1
Tower Inn	4
Trotamundos	8
Vecchia Terra	3

RESTAURANTS AND CAFÉS	
La Fusta	4
La Fusta II	5
Jockey Club	1
Nina	3
El Restauro	2
Tienda del Sol	6

BARS AND CLUBS	
Daikiri Disco	1
Sociedad Anónima	2
La Zona	3

of the RN-143 from Mendoza, called **Avenida Hipólito Yrigoyen** west of north–south axis **Avenida General San Martín** and **Avenida Bartolomé Mitre** to the east. Streets change name either side of both axes.

Museo de Historia Natural

Mon–Fri 8am–1pm & 3–8pm, Sat & Sun 8am–8pm • $2 • Take a taxi or a bus marked "Isla Diamante" from Av Hipólito Yrigoyen

To fill an hour or so, head to Isla Diamante, a large island 6km south of the town centre, in the middle of the river of the same name, and is home to the **Museo de Historia Natural**. Among masses of bedraggled stuffed birds, moth-eaten foxes and lumps of rock, you'll find some fabulous pre-Columbian ceramics, the best of which are statues from Ecuador; there's also a small collection of crafts from Easter Island and some particularly fine ceramics from northwestern Argentina. You'll also see a mummified child dating from 40 AD and a gorgeous multicoloured leather bag decorated with striking, very modern-looking geometric designs, found in the Gruta del Indio in the Cañón del Atuel.

6

ARRIVAL AND INFORMATION

By plane San Rafael's small airport, with daily flights to and from Buenos Aires (1hr 50min), is 5km west of the town centre, along the RN-143 towards Mendoza. There are no buses, but taxi rides into town won't break the bank ($25).
By bus The bus terminal is central, wedged in between calles Almafuerte and Avellaneda, at Coronel Suárez. It's surrounded by shops and cafés and has its own tourist information kiosk (Mon–Fri 9am–2pm).

SAN RAFAEL AND AROUND

Destinations Buenos Aires (4 daily; 13hr); General Alvear (3 daily; 1hr 20min); Las Leñas (June–Sept 3 daily; 2hr 40min); Malargüe (2 daily; 2hr 30min); Mendoza (hourly; 3hr 15min); Neuquén (2 daily; 12hr); San Juan (2 daily; 5hr 30min); San Luís (2 daily; 3hr).
Tourist information The city's main tourist office is at the corner of avenidas Hipólito Yrigoyen and Balloffet (daily 8am–9pm; ☎ 0260 442 4217, ✆ sanrafaelturismo.gov.ar).

ACCOMMODATION

Camping El Parador Isla Río Diamante, 6km south of the centre ☎ 0260 442 0492. Set in an attractive wooded location on an island in the middle of the river, the campsite has excellent facilities and also offers *cabañas*. Camping $80, cabañas $420
Cerro Nevado Hipólito Yrigoyen 376 ☎ 0260 442 8209, ✆ cerronevadohotel.com.ar. This spotless place with rather stark rooms with white walls and plain bedding has a pleasant restaurant, but avoid the streetside rooms, as they can be noisy. $280
★ **Hostel Puesta del Sol** Deán Funes 998 ☎ 0260 454 0042, ✆ complejopuestadelsol.com. One of the most stunning hostels in the country, with modern facilities, a huge swimming pool amid landscaped grounds, and a lively atmosphere, thanks to the owner, who's a real character. It's 2.5km from the bus terminal – $15 in a *remise*. Dorms $55, doubles $220
Jardín Hipólito Yrigoyen 283 ☎ 0260 443 4621. Very comfy rooms, all en suite, arranged around a lush patio shaded by an impressive palm tree. It's let down by details like the under-par breakfast and the minuscule TVs. $385
Kalton Hipólito Yrigoyen 120 ☎ 0260 443 0047, ✆ kaltonhotel.com. Typical mid-range town hotel near the bus station, with well-kept, albeit unremarkable, rooms. One of its plus points is the plentiful buffet breakfast, featuring home-baked cakes and breads. $520

Millalén Ortíz de Rosas 198 ☎ 0260 442 2776, ✉ ricardoloparco@hotmail.com. Modern hotel with pleasantly understated rooms, sparkling bathrooms and unfussy decor. The service cannot be faulted and staff will organize wine tours around town. $275
Regine Independencia 623 and Colón ☎ 0260 442 1470, ✆ hotelregine.com.ar. The mid-sized rooms are well furnished and charming, while the rustic dining room serves reliably good food; there's a beautiful lush garden and a small pool. The a/c works well and there is covered parking. $400
San Rafael Coronel Day 30 ☎ 0260 443 0127, ✆ hotel sanrafael.com.ar. One of San Rafael's most comfortable mid-range hotels; this one has a bar, reception with log fire and cable TV in the rooms, some of which are triples and quadruples. $455
Tonin Pellegrini 330 ☎ 0260 442 2499, ✆ sanrafael -tour.com/tonin/. Very pleasant, good-value rooms with modish stainless-steel washbasins in gleaming bathrooms. They are very helpful at putting together excursions in the region. $280
Tower Inn Hipólito Yrigoyen 774 ☎ 0260 442 7190, ✆ towersanrafael.com. This sandy-hued tower of stone and plate glass may be a bit of an eyesore, but the interior is comfortable and well run, and a large swimming pool, spa, gym and patio bar make it San Rafael's only four-star hotel. $880

6

BODEGAS IN AND AROUND SAN RAFAEL

Though Mendoza is undeniably Argentina's wine capital, **San Rafael's wineries** are among the finest in the country. Several open their doors willingly to visitors, although tours are more informal than in Mendoza and often don't run at set times; don't be surprised if no one speaks English. Some of the best include:

Champañera Bianchi Hipólito Yrigoyen s/n ☎ 0260 443 5353. An interesting contrast with its old downtown bodega, this ultramodern, sparkling wine-production unit, housed in a postmodern steel and glass building, is 4km west of the town centre. Excellent sparkling wines made according to the *méthode champenoise*. English spoken. Free 20min tours Mon–Sat 9am–noon & 2–5pm.

Jean Rivier Hipólito Yrigoyen 2385 ☎ 0260 443 2675, ⓦ jeanrivier.com. Friendly, small winery, founded by Swiss wine-makers; their tiptop wines include an unusual cabernet sauvignon–fer blend.

Delicious chardonnays, too. Free, Mon–Fri 8–11am & 3–6.30pm, Sat 8–11am.

Simonassi Lyon 5km south of San Rafael, at Km657 of RN-143, at Rama Caída ☎ 0260 443 0963, ⓦ bodega simonassi.com. Family-run, prize-winning winery, in an attractive farmhouse. Free guided visits Mon–Fri 8am–5pm, but phone 1hr in advance to reserve.

Suter Hipólito Yrigoyen 2850 ☎ 02627 421 076, ⓔ turismo@sutersa.com.ar. Slightly mechanical guided visits every 30min, but you're given a half-bottle of decent wine as a gift. Traditional-style winery. Mon–Sat 9am–5pm; free.

Trotamundos Barcala 300 ☎ 0260 443 2795, ⓦ trotamundoshostel.com.ar. A rather cramped hostel that's popular with young Argentines, and conveniently located for the bus station if you're just passing through town. Dorms $50, doubles $210

Vecchia Terra Castelli 23 ☎ 0260 442 4169, ⓦ vecchiaterra.com.ar. A high-quality *apart-hotel* with apartments for up to six people. Luxuriously furnished throughout, with modern kitchens and great showers. Better value for money than the *Tower*, although it lacks the pool. $530

EATING, DRINKING AND NIGHTLIFE

RESTAURANTS AND CAFÉS

★ **La Fusta** Hipólito Yrigoyen 538 ☎ 0260 442 8776. By far the town's best *parrilla*, serving succulent steaks, full *parrilladas* (from $80 per person) and local wines at very reasonable rates. Daily noon–4.30pm & 7.30pm–midnight.

La Fusta II Hipólito Yrigoyen and Beato Marcelino Champagnat ☎ 0260 442 8776. Sister restaurant to the above, serving similar fare in ultramodern surroundings with fine decor and a large terrace. Daily noon–4.30pm & 7.30pm–midnight.

Jockey Club Belgrano 330 ☎ 0260 446 7671. Good old-fashioned service and hearty food, with a good-value *menú turista* (for $65) at lunchtime. Daily noon–4pm & 8pm–midnight.

Nina San Martín and Olascoaga ☎ 0260 468 5173. Very smart cocktail bar doubling as a café and tearoom, so one of the best places to come for a shot of caffeine. Daily 10am–midnight.

El Restauro Chile and Salas ☎ 0260 444 5482. Friendly service and creative, interesting but inexpensive cuisine

using local ingredients such as trout with almonds ($55), kid and quinoa at this ample restaurant. Daily noon–4pm & 7pm–midnight.

Tienda del Sol Hipólito Yrigoyen 1663 ☎ 0260 442 5022. Trendy, postmodern resto-bar, serving seafood and pasta dishes (such as spaghetti with trout for $60) alongside cocktails and other drinks, at slightly inflated prices. Daily noon–4.30pm & 7.30pm–late.

BARS AND CLUBS

Daikiri Disco Hipólito Yrigoyen 3177. New, large club that's the place to go out in the city on a Friday night, with a sizeable garden area and outside bars. Fri midnight–late.

Sociedad Anónima Hipólito Yrigoyen 1530. This bar is one of San Rafael's more trendy options – and a great place to people-watch, especially on its lively terrace. Daily 8pm–late.

La Zona Deán Funes 1000. Ultra-hip dance club, very popular with young crowds, especially on Saturday nights. Fri & Sat midnight–late.

Cañón del Atuel

The **CAÑÓN DEL ATUEL** is one of San Rafael's main attractions, a beautifully wild canyon linking two man-made lakes along the Río Atuel, to the southwest of the town. Visits begin at the reservoir furthest away, the **Embalse del Nihuil**, reached along the winding RN-144 towards Malargüe, up the Cuesta de los Terneros to the 1300m summit, which offers great views of the valley below; and then via the RP-180, which forks off to the south. The lake lies 92km southwest of San Rafael.

The gorge

The partly sealed RP-173 then squeezes in a northeasterly direction through a narrow gorge whose cliffs and rocks are striped red, white and yellow, contrasting with the beige of the dust-dry mountainsides. Wind and water have eroded the rocks into weird and often rather suggestive shapes that stimulate the imagination: tour guides attach names like "the Nun" or "the Toad" to the strange formations. The road then passes a couple of dams, attached to power stations, before swinging round the other reservoir, the **Embalse Valle Grande**. Sticking out of these blue-green waters are more strange rock formations, one of which does indeed look like the submarine its nickname suggests. From the high corniche roads that skirt the lakeside you are treated to some grand views of the waters, dotted with kayaks and other boats, and the mountains beyond. Near here starts the stretch of the Río Atuel used for **whitewater rafting**. Raffeish, at RP-173 Km35, Valle Grande (☎0260 443 6996, ⊛raffeish.com.ar), is the most reliable and ecologically conscious operator, and has an office here. Trips last an hour, along an easy stretch for beginners, or a couple of hours or more, taking in a tougher Grade II section of the river; take a change of clothes, as you get soaked. The scenery along the way is pleasantly pastoral along the more open parts and staggeringly beautiful in the narrower gorges. Further downstream, Hunuc Huar is a wonderful crafts workshop (daily 9.30–1pm & 4–9pm) run by an indigenous family, specializing in fine ceramics, set in an idyllic garden.

ARRIVAL AND DEPARTURE   CAÑÓN DEL ATUEL

By organized tour San Rafael is only 25km from the canyon by RP-173, but unless you have your own transport, you'll have to get here on an organized tour: try Risco Viajes, Av Hipólito Yrigoyen 284, in San Rafael (☎0260 443 6439, ⊛riscoviajes.com).

ACCOMMODATION

Hotel Valle Grande RP-173 Km35 ☎0260 155 80660, ⊛hotelvallegrande.com. This upmarket hotel offers all kinds of sports facilities and a fine swimming pool, but can get very crowded during the summer months; the hotel also has four-bed *cabañas* for rent that can sleep up to seven. Doubles $610, *cabañas* $800

Las Leñas and around

To Argentines, **LAS LEÑAS** means chic: this is where the Porteño jet set come to show off their winter fashions, to get photographed for society magazines and to

RELIVING *ALIVE*

In 1972, a group of young **rugby players from Uruguay** caught the attention of the world after they survived an **air crash** and over two months of brutal subzero temperatures in the Andes, at a place on the Argentine–Chilean border in the mountains west of the Cerro Sosneado and Río Atuel, now called the **Glaciar de la Lágrimas** (glacier of tears). The students survived by consuming snow and their colleagues' corpses and fashioning sleeping bags from the insulation in the plane's tail, before two of them finally made it west over the mountains and alerted the Chilean authorities, who had long since given them up for dead. Their incredible story was told in the 1993 movie *Alive* and the documentary *Alive: 20 Years Later*. It is now possible to **visit the site** of the crash, where parts of the plane are still scattered. Some may find the idea macabre, and getting there is obviously no walk in the park – count on at least three days of trekking and horseriding through the snow, although you'll also get to take a unique hot bath in the warm blue waters bubbling up out of the ground at the ruins of the old *Hotel Sosneado*. Tours are run by Risco Viajes in San Rafael (see above) or with guides from Malargüe – such as Karen Travel (see p.366).

6

SKIING IN LAS LEÑAS

Las Leñas is no Gstaad or St Moritz: it's a purpose-built **resort** built at an altitude of 2200m, with excellent **skiing** and **snowboarding** – when there is enough snow – and a breathtaking backdrop of craggy mountain-tops, of which Cerro Las Leñas is the highest (4351m) and Cerro Torrecillas (3771m) the most daintily pinnacled. The whole area covers more than 33 square kilometres, with 28 pistes, ranging from several gentle nursery slopes to a couple of sheer black runs; cross-country and off-piste skiing are also possible.

Experienced skiers will want to head direct for **El Marte** lift, the only one which accesses the harder runs, but be aware that this is often closed due to the resort's characteristic high winds, which can be a source of some frustration. Contact the Ski School for information about off-piste excursions into the area's impressive **back-country** (from $800 per person for a half-day). Nature is, of course, unpredictable, but **August to early September** is probably your best bet for serious powder, as well as for lower winds (and prices) and thinner crowds. Lessons are available in several languages, including English. The equipment-rental service (next to the *Hotel Acuario*) is pricey, as are the lifts – day-passes cost upwards of $200, depending on the season – though many hotels offer discounts on these as part of packages. Your ski pass includes cover for getting you off the mountain in the event of an accident on piste, but only as far as the resort's medical centre. An early start to the day definitely pays off – the slopes are relatively empty, as many people are recovering from all-night partying.

---

have a good time. **Skiing** and **snowboarding** are only part of the fun – as in all exclusive winter resorts, the *après-ski* is just as important as the snow conditions. More seriously, many ski champions from the northern hemisphere head down here during the June to October season, when there's not a lot of snow in the US or Europe; the Argentine, Brazilian and South American skiing championships are all held here in August, while other events include snow-polo matches, snow-rugby, snow-volleyball and fashion shows. But even though Las Leñas is a playground for the rich and famous, it's possible to visit without breaking the bank; you could stay in the least expensive accommodation, or overnight elsewhere nearby, such as in Los Molles or Malargüe (see opposite). Las Leñas is also trying to branch out into **summertime adventure travel**, such as mountain biking, rafting and horseriding, making the most of its splendid upland setting and pleasant daytime temperatures. Note that the resort is completely **closed** down, however, from March to May and October to the end of December.

Pozo de las Animas

The road to Las Leñas heads due west from the Mendoza-to-Malargüe section of the RN-40, 28km south of the crossroads settlement of El Sosneado. It climbs past the ramshackle spa resort of Los Molles, and the peculiar **Pozo de las Animas**, a set of two huge well-like depressions that make for a diverting photo stop (scheduled bus services don't stop, and they can't be seen from the road). Caused by underground water erosion, each is several hundred metres in diameter, with a pool of turquoise water in the bottom. The sand-like cliffs surrounding each lake have been corrugated and castellated by the elements, like some medieval fortress, and the ridge dividing the two looks in danger of collapse at any minute.

ARRIVAL AND DEPARTURE

LAS LEÑAS

By plane The resort lies 50km from the RN-40, a total of nearly 200km southwest of San Rafael. If you are booked at the resort, look to get a transfer from Malargüe airport (once-weekly charter flight from Buenos Aires, June to mid-Sept; $4000 return), Mendoza or San Rafael.

By bus During the ski season you can take the daily buses run by Iselín and CATA from Mendoza, a 7hr journey ($200 one way), or the daily public bus or agency transfers from Malargüe – best to buy tickets from the terminal the night before and ask if they'll pick you up from your hotel. Otherwise you need your own transport.

ACCOMMODATION, EATING AND NIGHTLIFE

Las Leñas resort 4th floor Bartolomé Mitre, Buenos Aires ☎011 4819 6060, ⊛laslenas.com. All accommodation booking in Las Leñas is organized centrally through this resort. Usually booked as weekend or eight-day packages, the resort accommodation is within tramping distance of the slopes and costs upwards of US$1200 per person per night (half-board & ski passes included) in the peak weeks of July and August, though prices tend to drop by some fifty percent at either end of the season. The hotels are all rather functional in their aesthetic while more economical options are the "dormy houses", chalets grouped at the edge of the village that can sleep up to five and have simple kitchens and bedrooms.

Eating and nightlife There are several expensive restaurants to choose from and a couple of on-site discos.

Malargüe and around

MALARGÜE is a laidback town 186km south of San Rafael by the RN-144 and the RN-40. The biggest settlement in the southernmost section of Mendoza Province, it's less of a destination in itself, and more – like San Rafael – a base for exploring the prime tourist sites in this region. It's more conveniently located for most of these than San Rafael, although it has a far more limited choice of accommodation.

The town is within day-trip distance of the black and red pampas of **La Payunia**, a nature reserve where flocks of guanacos and ñandús roam over lava flows. Far nearer – and doable as half-day outings – are some remarkable underground caves, the **Cueva de la Brujas**, and **Laguna Llancanelo**, a shining lagoon flecked pink with flamingoes and crammed with other aquatic birdlife. You could also consider staying here in order to go skiing at **Las Leñas**, 77km away (see p.363).

The core of the town lies on either side of the RN-40, called Avenida San Martín within the town's boundaries, a wide, rather soulless avenue along which many of the hotels are located, as well as a couple of cafés, the bank and telephone centres. **Plaza General San Martín** is the focal point, with its benches shaded by pines and native trees, but it's nothing to get excited about. The town is extremely easy to find your way around, although it's fairly spread out. Its handful of attractions are clustered together at the northern reaches, beyond the built-up area.

Centro de Convenciones y Exposiciones Thesaurus

Av San Martín s/n • Daily 10am–8pm • Free • ☎0260 447 0027

Malargüe's pride and joy is the fine little **Centro de Convenciones y Exposiciones Thesaurus**, subtly plunged underground in the middle of the garden. Its postmodern design, incorporating some fine workmanship, is certainly impressive for a town of this size. The centre also houses an art gallery with small exhibition rooms linked by corridors, intended to echo a cave's labyrinth.

Observatorio Pierre Auger

Av San Martín Norte 304 • Guided visits Mon–Fri 5pm • Free • ⓦ auger.org.ar

The convention centre complements the **Observatorio Pierre Auger**, opposite, part of a fascinating twenty-year astrophysics project to measure the mysterious ultra-high-energy cosmic rays that bombard Earth. A grid of 1600 cream-coloured water tanks serving as particle detectors have been placed 1.5km apart across an area of the pampas fifteen times the size of Buenos Aires – look out for them as you drive into town. It makes hunting for a needle in a haystack seem like child's play: only one such particle is likely to hit a square kilometre of the Earth's surface per century.

Museo Regional

Av San Martín s/n • Daily 9am–1pm & 4–9pm • Free

The town's **Museo Regional** consists of a four-room display in a neatly refurbished building, including objects as varied as ammonites, guanaco leather, clay pipes for religious ceremonies, jewellery and dinosaur remains. A new annexe to the museum houses Mi Viejo Almacén, a shop selling local artisan goods.

ARRIVAL AND DEPARTURE

By bus Buses from Mendoza and San Rafael stop at the bus terminal at Esquibel Aldao and Av General Roca, six blocks south and two west of central Plaza San Martín, but will

MALARGÜE AND AROUND

also drop off and collect passengers at the plaza en route. Destinations Las Leñas (June–Sept daily; 1hr 15min); Mendoza (6 daily; 4–5hr); San Rafael (10 daily; 2hr 30min).

INFORMATION AND TOURS

Tourist information Malargüe's excellent tourist office (daily 8am–10pm; ☎ 0260 447 1659, ☯ malargue.gov.ar), in a fine rustic building on the RN-40 by the Parque de Ayer, four blocks north of the plaza, has loads of information on what to see and do, and on places to stay, tour operators and fishing in nearby rivers. It also issues the Malargüe Card, which can be used at various businesses around town to get discounts.

Tour operators Choique, Av San Martín and Rodríguez, 1st floor (☎ 0260 447 0391, ☯ choique.net), know the terrain inside out and offer excellent excursions to La Payunia and all the main sights of southern Mendoza; the long-established Karen Travel, Av San Martín 54 (☎ 0260

447 0342, ☯ karentravel.com.ar), can get you to just about any site you might wish to see, in a group or on a more personalized tour.

Ski equipment Equipment, including snowboards, can be rented from a number of outlets along Av San Martín, including Aires de Libertad or Fuera de Pista at #129 (☎ 0260 447 2430), which has a good range of skis. It makes sense to rent gear in Malargüe rather than at Las Leñas – it's cheaper and you'll avoid the queues, but try to avoid travelling with a second pair of footwear that you can't pop in a daypack as lockers at Las Leñas are expensive. Kitting yourself out fully will cost some US$70 or more a day, depending on the quality of skis; and rental shops are open late.

ACCOMMODATION

The range of accommodation in Malargüe is expanding with every year, though higher-end options are still limited. Additionally, twice a year (in March and Nov), what decent options there are get packed out with physicists, who come for an international convention on the Pierre Auger experiment (see p.365). You get a fifty percent discount on a Las Leñas ski pass if you stay at least two nights in Malargüe during the season, but the benefits of this are cancelled out by the fact you have to rent your equipment at Las Leñas, which is more expensive.

El Capitán Telles Meneses 897 ☎ 0260 447 1534. Decent, family-run hostel eight blocks from the bus terminal. There is a kitchen for communal use but they also serve hearty meals. Dorms $50, doubles $70

Cisne Civit and Villegas ☎ 0260 447 1350. Clean, functional hotel in the centre of town, located in a rather cuboid block. Rooms are well heated in the winter months. $400

Kathmandú Hostel Saturnino Torres 121 ☎ 0260 15 441 4899. A basic but homely place whose owner is very helpful, just half a block from Plaza San Martín. Dorms $70

Maggio Hotel Manuel Ruibal 592 ☎ 0260 447 2496, ☯ maggiohotel.com. The most pristine mid-range option with large, well-furnished rooms in a contemporary style. The whole hotel is done out in refreshing green tones and the bed linen is luxurious. $520

Nord Patagonia Fray Inalicán 52 ☎ 0260 447 1151, ☯ vallesaventura.com.ar. Pleasant, compact hostel right on the main square, whose staff also run adventure tours in the region, specializing in mountaineering. Dorms $50, doubles $280

Río Grande ☎ 0260 447 1589, ☯ hotelriogrande @rucared.com.ar. Friendly owners, a choice between decent but very plain rooms and more commodious, tastefully decorated ones, and a restaurant serving delicious food, including local specialities such as trout and roast kid. $545

Rioma Fray Inalicán 68 ☎ 0260 447 1065, ☯ hotel riomacom.ar. Reasonable, if rather nondescript, hotel in the centre of town. There is an outdoor swimming pool and the owners lay on barbecues on request. $385

EATING AND DRINKING

La Cima Av San Martín 886 (where the RN-40 enters town from the north) ☎ 0260 447 2583. This *parrilla*, by far the best in Malargüe, serves up huge hunks of beef, lamb and goat – you can walk off the calories getting back into town. Daily 12.30–4pm & 8pm–midnight.

Cuyam-Co El Dique, 8km west of Malargüe ☎ 0260 447

1102. This is a commercial trout farm where you can catch your own fish though you can also eat fish caught by staff, so at least you know it is fresh. It is then perfectly cooked and served with an excellent local rosé; try the delicious smoked trout and fresh trout paté, too. It is worth booking ahead. Daily 12.30–10pm.

Reserva Faunística Laguna de Llancanelo

Access to the reserve is via the RP-186, which branches east off the RN-40 some 20km south of Malargüe; it's then another 20km to the reserve entrance, near the shallow cavern known as the Cueva del Tigre

The **RESERVA FAUNÍSTICA LAGUNA DE LLANCANELO** makes an easy half-day trip from Malargüe. It's an internationally recognized RAMSAR wetland, with large populations of waterfowl year round, although you'll find the greatest concentrations in spring and summer, as many species come here to nest. On windless days, the shallow saline lagoon's mirror-still waters in the middle of a huge dried-up lake bed make for a fantastic sight. You'd be very unlucky not to spot flocks of flamingo, at times so huge that whole areas of the lake's surface are turned uniformly pink. Other species of bird include black-necked swan, several kinds of duck, grebe and teal, gulls, terns and curlews. Parts of the reserve are out of bounds all year, and access to others is restricted to non-critical seasons. The park is patrolled by *guardaparques*, and it is best to go on an organized tour from Malargüe, as you'll get more out of visiting the lagoon with someone who knows the terrain and the fauna. Preferably come very early in the morning or in the late afternoon and evening, when the light is fabulous and the wildfowl more easily spotted.

Caverna de las Brujas

The best option is to go on an organized tour from Malargüe (average $110 per person plus $40 entrance each, minimum 5 people)

The **CAVERNA DE LAS BRUJAS** is a marvellous cave that plunges deep into the earth, just 73km southwest of Malargüe, 8km off the RN-40 along a marked track. The road climbs over the scenic **Cuesta del Chihuido**, which affords fantastic views of the Sierra de Palauco to the east, in a region of outstanding beauty enhanced by sparse but attractive vegetation. This area is covered by a thick layer of marine sedimentary rock, through which water has seeped, creating underground cave systems. The name Caverna de las Brujas literally means "witches' cave", and local legends say that it was used as a meeting-place for sorcerers. Las Brujas is a karstic cave, filled with rock formations, including some impressive **stalactites and stalagmites**; typically they have been given imaginative names such as "the Virgin's Chamber", "the Pulpit" and "the Flowers". Water continues to seep inside, making the walls slippery, as if they were awash with soapsuds. Although the tourist circuit is only 260m long and never descends more than 6m below the surface, the experience is memorable.

The *caverna* lies within a provincial park, and a small *guardería* stands nearby; ask here for the key to the padlocked gates that protect the grotto. It's compulsory to enter with a guide. Wear good walking shoes and take a sweater – the difference in temperature between inside and out can be as much as 20°C – and a pocket torch, though miners' helmets are also supplied; a highlight inside the cave is experiencing the total darkness by turning out all lights and getting used to the spooky atmosphere.

La Payunia

The highlight of any trip to southernmost Mendoza Province, yet overlooked by most visitors because of its relative inaccessibility, **LA PAYUNIA**, protected by the Reserva Provincial La Payunia, is a fabulously wild area of staggering beauty, sometimes referred to as the Patagonia Mendocina. Dominated by Volcán Payún Matru (3690m), and its slightly lower inactive neighbour Volcán Payún Liso, it is utterly unspoilt apart from some remnants of old fluorite and manganese mines plus some petrol-drilling derricks, whose nodding-head pump-structures are locally nicknamed "guanacos", after the member of the llama family they vaguely resemble in shape. Occasionally, you will spot real guanacos, sometimes in large flocks, standing out against the black volcanic backdrop of the so-called **Pampa Negra**. This huge expanse of lava in the middle of the reserve was caused by relatively recent volcanic eruptions, dating back hundreds or thousands of years rather than millions, as is the case of most such phenomena in the region. "Fresh" trails of lava debris can be seen at various points throughout the park, and enormous boulders of igneous rock are scattered over these dark plains, also ejected during the violent volcanic activity. The only vegetation is flaxen grass, whose golden colour stands out against the blackened hillsides. Another section of the reserve is the aptly named **Pampa Roja**, where reddish oxides in the lava give the ground a henna-like tint. The threatening hulk of Volcán Pihuel looms at the western extremity of the reserve – its top was blown off by a particularly violent explosion that occurred when the mountain was beneath the sea.

ARRIVAL AND DEPARTURE   LA PAYUNIA

By organized tour To visit the park, take one of the excellent day-trips run by Karen Travel in Malargüe (see p.366).
By 4WD If you plan to drive there independently, you'll

need a 4WD and a good map. You must also take a guide with you – ask in the travel agencies or tourist office in Malargüe.

ACCOMMODATION

Kiñe La Agüita, on RP-186 in the northeast corner of the reserve ☎ 0260 447 1344, ⓦ kinie.com.ar. Eco-conscious accommodation in a basic but comfortable little farmstead at the remote hamlet of La Agüita. In addition to simple but tasty meals the friendly family also lays on

treks in the mountains and horse rides across plains full of guanacos. There is no public transport to *Kiñe* but the owners will pick you up in Malargüe (consult in advance for transfer costs if not arriving in your own vehicle). Full board; trips cost extra. **$500**

San Juan and La Rioja

San Juan and **La Rioja** provinces share some memorable countryside, with range after range of lofty mountains alternating with green valleys of olive groves, onion fields and vineyards, but they're the poorer cousins, in every sense, of Mendoza Province. The provinces' **bodegas**, for example, continue to take a back seat to those of Mendoza and San Rafael, even though their wine can be just as good and they export much of their grape harvest to Mendoza's wineries. **Tourism** has not fully got off the ground here, either, partly owing to poor transport services. To engineer tourist circuits you'll need your own transport, preferably a 4WD.

Outside the capital, La Rioja's population density barely reaches one inhabitant per square kilometre, while San Juan, where the equivalent ratio is around three, is on average half as densely populated as Mendoza Province. Leaving the cities behind to scout around the outback, you'll experience a real sense of setting off into uncharted territory. Some unpaved roads peter out into tracks barely passable in the hardiest jeep, and the weather conditions can be inclement. However, this inhospitable nature does offer up fantastic opportunities for alternative tourism, such as 4WD trips or hiking.

Club-sandwiched between the pre-cordillera and the two rows of cordillera – known as main and frontal ranges, a geological phenomenon unique to this section of the Andes – are successive chains of valleys. The higher ones over 1500m above sea level are known as the *valles altos*, of which the **Valle de Calingasta** is an outstanding example. Between them the two provinces have four natural parks. The highly inaccessible **Parque Nacional San Guillermo** in San Juan Province adjoins the **Reserva Provincial Las Vicuñas** across the boundary in La Rioja; respectively, they give you a sporting chance of spotting wild pumas and vicuñas, along with a host of other Andean wildlife, amid unforgettable landscapes. Further east are the provinces' star attractions: **Parque Nacional Talampaya**, with vertiginous red cliffs that make you feel totally insignificant and – only 70km south – its contiguous, unidentical twin, **Parque Provincial Ischigualasto**, more commonly referred to as the Valle de la Luna, an important dinosaur graveyard in a highly photogenic site.

PARQUE NACIONAL TALAMPAYA (P.384) >

San Juan and around

Some 165km north of Mendoza, the city of **SAN JUAN** basks in the sun-drenched valley of the Río San Juan, which twists and turns between several steep mountain ranges. The city revels in its pet name, Residencia del Sol. In some of its barrios it has rained only a couple of times over the past decade, and the provincial average is less than 100mm a year. When it does rain, it's usually in the form of violent storms, as savage as the *zonda* wind that occasionally stings the city (see box below). All this sunshine – more than nine hours a day on average – quickly ripens the sweetest imaginable grapes, melons and plums, irrigated by pre-Columbian canals, that have helped the city to prosper over the years. But nature is also a foe: periodic tremors remind Sanjuaninos that they live along one of the world's most slippery seismic faults; the Big One is dreaded as much here as in California.

One of South America's strongest-ever recorded earthquakes flattened the city in 1944 and as a result the city has hardly any buildings more than 70 years old. It's modern and attractive, but San Juan is also quite conservative compared with its much bigger rival Mendoza. Around a third of a million people live in Greater San Juan, but in the compact microcentro everyone seems to know everyone else. Broad pavements, grand avenues and long boulevards shaded by rows of flaky-trunked plane trees lend the city a feeling of spaciousness and openness, making San Juan a comfortable starting-point for touring some of the country's finest scenery. Destinations close to the city include an **archeological museum** in the southern suburbs and the mind-bogglingly grotesque pilgrim site of **Difunta Correa**, to the east.

The total area of San Juan city is extensive but easy to find your way around, as the grid is fairly regular and the streets don't change name. In all directions from the point zero, the intersection of Calle Mendoza and Avenida San Martín, the cardinal directions are added to the street name; for example, Avenida Córdoba oeste (west) or este (east), or Calle Tucumán norte (north) or sur (south).

Brief history

The city was founded by the Spanish aristocrat Juan Jufré as San Juan de la Frontera on June 13, 1562, during an expedition from Santiago de Chile, and since then it has had a persistently troubled history. In 1594, the settlement was washed away by floods, and in 1632 it was again destroyed, this time in attacks by natives. The following year an uprising by the indigenous inhabitants was brutally put down; seventeen were hanged on the Plaza Mayor as an example. In the middle of the nineteenth century, San Juan found itself at the heart of the country's civil war when its progressive leader, Dr Antonino Aberastain, was assassinated by federalist troops. In 1885 the arrival of

---

THE *ZONDA* EFFECT

San Juan, like the rest of the Cuyo, though even more so, is prone to the **zonda**, a legendary dry wind that blows down from the Andes and blasts everything in its path like a blowtorch. It's caused by a **thermal inversion** that arises when wet, cold air from the Pacific is thrust abruptly up over the cordillera and suddenly forced to dump its moisture, mostly in the form of snow, onto the skyscraper peaks before helter-skeltering down the other side into the deep chasm between the Cordillera Principal and the pre-cordillera, which acts like a very high brick wall. Forced to brake, the *zonda* rubs against the land like tyre-rubber against tarmac, and the resulting friction results in **blistering temperatures** and an atmosphere you can almost see. Mini-tornadoes can sometimes also occur, whipping sand and dust up in clearly visible spirals all along the region's desert-like plains. The Cuyo's answer to the *Föhn*, mistral or sirocco, ripping people's nerves to shreds, the *zonda* is one of the world's nastiest meteorological phenomena. Although it can blow at any time of year, the *zonda* is most frequent in the winter months, particularly August, when it can suddenly hike the temperature by ten to fifteen degrees in a matter of hours.

RN-20 to Difunta Correa, Airport & **12**

ACCOMMODATION
Albertina	9
Alhambra	5
Alkázar	4
América	11
Camping Municipal	3
Camping El Pinar	13
Gran Hotel Provincial	6
Jardín Petit	1
El Refugio	2
San Francisco	7
Suizo	8
Viñas del Sol	12
Zonda Hostel	10

RESTAURANTS AND CAFÉS
Abuelo Yuyi	5
Baró & De Sánchez	4
Bonafide	7
Freud Café	8
Hostal de Palito	2
Las Leñas	1
Maloca	9
Rigoletto	6
Soychú	3

BARS AND CLUBS
Aptko	2
Aruba	1

SAN JUAN

RN-40 to Mendoza & Museo Arqueológico

Antigua Bodega 1920 & Museo Bodega Graffigna

San José de Jáchal

Parque de Mayo

Museo de Ciencias Naturales

Museo de Bellas Artes

Mercado Artesanal

Museo Casa de Sarmiento

Convento de Santo Domingo

Catedral

Former Railway Station

Museo Histórico

Bus Terminal

Bus Stop

BARRIO MITRE

BARRIO JUAN XXIII

VILLA RIPOLL

0   250   metres

the railways heralded a change to San Juan's backwater status, as Basque, Galician and Andalucian immigrants began arriving.

Like Mendoza, the city has had terrible luck with seismic shocks: several violent earthquakes struck the city in the 1940s, but the strongest of all, reaching around 8.5 on the Richter scale, hit San Juan on January 15, 1944. It flattened the city and killed more than ten thousand people; during a gala held in Buenos Aires to raise funds for the victims shortly afterwards, an as yet relatively unknown army officer, Juan Domingo Perón, met an equally obscure actress, Eva Duarte.

Plaza 25 de Mayo

Plaza 25 de Mayo is the city centre, surrounded by terraced cafés and shops. The controversial **cathedral**, too modern for many tastes, on the northwest edge of the plaza, has a 50m brick campanile, built in the 1960s, that takes its inspiration from the tower of St Mark's in Venice. You can climb or take the lift almost to the top of the **bell tower** (daily 9.30am–1pm & 5–9.30pm; $5) – which plays the national anthem on special occasions – for panoramic views.

Museo Casa de Sarmiento

Sarmiento 21 sur • Tues–Fri 9am–7pm, Mon & Sat 9am–2pm, Sun 10am–7pm; guided tours every 30min, some in English • $5 • ⓦ casanatalsarmiento.gov.ar

Opposite the tourist office is the city's most famous historical site, the **Museo Casa de Sarmiento**. The house where Sarmiento, Argentine president and Renaissance man, was born on February 15, 1811, was only slightly damaged in the 1944 earthquake, thanks to its sturdy adobe walls and sandy foundations, and has since been restored several times, to attain its present gleaming state – for the Sarmiento centenary in 1911 it was declared a national historic monument, Argentina's first. It's a beautiful, simple whitewashed house built around a large patio, with a neat fig tree. The rooms contain an exhibition of Sarmiento relics and personal effects, plenty of portraits and signs of sycophancy, echoed by the gushing commentary of the guides who steer you round.

Museo de Ciencias Naturales

Avenidas España and Maipú • Daily 9am–1pm • Free • ☎ 0264 421 6774

Housed in a well-restored train station, the highly academic **Museo de Ciencias Naturales** contains an exhibition focusing on the remarkable **dinosaur skeletons** unearthed at Parque Provincial Ischigualasto (see p.382), and features models showing how the dinosaurs may have looked. You can also see the lab where the finds are analyzed. Rock fans will delight in the well-displayed collection of minerals and semiprecious stones, mostly mined in the province.

Museo Santiago Graffigna

Colón 1342 norte • Mon–Sat 9am–5.30pm, Sun 10am–4pm • Free • ☎ 0264 421 4227 • Bus #12A from Av Libertador San Martín, ($5)

The most notable bodega to visit is the **Bodega Graffigna**, now incorporating a wine museum – the **Museo Santiago Graffigna**. Located in a beautiful brick reconstruction of the pre-quake winery, it still produces red and white wines, among the best in the province. The displays use audiovisual techniques to give a guided tour (English included), and are a tribute to the Graffigna family, who went on producing wine despite major setbacks, not least the 1944 quake. The company is now owned by the French drinks company Pernod Ricard.

Museo Arqueológico Profesor Mariano Gambier

On the RN-40 between Progreso and c/ 5 • Mon–Fri 8am–8pm, Sat 10am–6pm • $5 • ☎ 0264 424 1424 • Take a taxi if you don't have your own transport

Some 6km south of San Juan centre, the **Museo Arqueológico Profesor Mariano Gambier** in the Rawson neighbourhood is worth the trek. Don't be put off by its location in an industrial warehouse – inside, the highly academic presentation, by San Juan University, takes you through the pre-history and history of the provinces' cultures, from the so-called Cultura de la Fortuna (10,000–6000 BC), of which there are just a few tools as evidence, to the Ullum-Zonda civilization of the Huarpe people, whose land was invaded first by the Inca in the fifteenth century and then by colonizers from Chile in the sixteenth. A number of digs near the city of San Juan have uncovered a treasure of ceramics and domestic items from the latter, well displayed here.

The museum's highlight, though, is a set of **mummified bodies** dating from the first century BC through to the fifteenth century AD, with the most impressive of all discovered in 1964 at over 4500m in the cordillera, in northern San Juan Province. Kept in an antiquated fridge is **La Momia del Cerro el Toro**, probably the victim of an Inca sacrifice; the body is incredibly well preserved, down to her eyelashes and leather sandals. Other items worth a mention are a 2000-year-old carob-wood **mask**, some fine **basketwork** coloured with natural pigments and ancient ponchos with geometric patterns. All the exhibits are labelled in Spanish and English.

6

ARRIVAL AND INFORMATION

SAN JUAN AND AROUND

By plane Las Chacritas airport, small but functional, is 12km east of the city, just off the RN-20 (☎ 0264 425 4133); there are plenty of taxis and *remises* to the centre ($35). There are two daily flights to Buenos Aires (1hr 40min).

By bus The city's user-friendly bus station, with regular services all over the province, region and country, is twelve blocks east of the central Plaza 25 de Mayo, at Estados Unidos 492 sur (☎ 0264 422 1604).

Destinations Barreal (2 daily; 5hr); Buenos Aires (13 daily;

16hr); Córdoba (5 daily; 8hr 30min); Huaco (daily; 3hr); La Rioja (7 daily; 6hr); Mendoza (hourly; 2hr 20min); Rodeo (daily; 3hr); Salta (5 daily; 16hr); (San Agustín de) Valle Fértil (3 daily; 4hr); San José de Jáchal (6 daily; 2hr 15min); San Rafael (2 daily; 5hr 30min).

Tourist information The extremely helpful, main provincial tourist office is at Sarmiento 24 sur (Mon–Fri 7.30am–8pm, Sat & Sun 9am–8pm; ☎ 0264 421 0004, ⊛ turismo.sanjuan.gov.ar).

ACCOMMODATION

Albertina Mitre 31 este ☎ 0264 421 4222, ⊛ hotel albertina.com. Tastefully decorated, comfortable, if rather cramped rooms in a refurbished hotel on the main square, with parking. Breakfasts are disappointing. $380

Alhambra General Acha 180 sur ☎ 0264 421 4780, ⊛ alhambrahotel.com.ar. Medium-sized rooms, each with bath, in this well-run but rather stuffy establishment with friendly staff. $390

Alkázar Laprida 84 este ☎ 0264 421 4965, ⊛ alkazar hotel.com.ar. One of San Juan's few luxury hotels; although on the impersonal side, it does have extremely smart rooms, with ultramodern bathrooms and sweeping views across the city, and a swimming pool in the grounds. The decor is quite dated, though. $580

América 9 de Julio 1052 este ☎ 0264 421 4514, ⊛ hotel -america.com.ar. Agreeable, traditional, small hotel. Popular, so call ahead to reserve. All rooms have an en-suite bathroom. Guests are entitled to use a swimming pool located a 20min walk away. $270

Camping Municipal Rivadavia RP-12 ☎ 0264 433 2374. Located opposite the racetrack, with a swimming pool and very decent facilities, this well-kept site is popular with families from San Juan. $80

Camping El Pinar Within the grounds of the Parque

Sarmiento, along the RP-14 just before the Dique Nivelador ☎ 0264 433 2374. Set amid a refreshing wood of pines, cypresses and eucalyptus, this shady site has a bathing area, a canteen and well-kept facilities. $85

Gran Hotel Provincial José Ignacio de la Roza 132 ☎ 0264 422 7501, ⊛ granhotelprovincial.com. An old-fashioned hotel with old-fashioned polite service, right at the centre of San Juan, a few steps from the Plaza 25 de Mayo. Beige is the predominant colour. $560

Jardín Petit 25 de Mayo 345 este ☎ 0264 421 1825, ⊛ jardinpetithotel.com.ar. Small, functional rooms with bath, and a bright patio overlooked by the breakfast room. Lots of bright colours in the public areas; the rooms are much duller. $300

El Refugio Ramón y Cajal 97 norte and San Luís ☎ 0264 421 3087, ✉ elrefugio@uolsinectis.com.ar. Attractive, professionally run *apart-hotel*, with car park, a refreshing little pool, and tastefully decorated duplex apartment-like rooms, with kitchenettes, bright bathrooms and breakfast served in the room or outside. $480

San Francisco Av España 284 sur ☎ 0264 422 3760, ⊛ nuevo-sanfrancisco.com.ar. Very reliable place, with smart, simply decorated rooms, modern bathrooms and friendly service; the bar is open 24hr. $285

Suizo Salta 272 sur ☎0264 422 4293. An odd mixture, with a rather chaotic entrance and twee bedrooms, in a Swiss style as the name suggests; good value, though. **$200**

Zonda Hostel Caseros 486 sur ☎0264 420 1009, ⊚zondahostel.com.ar. San Juan's newest youth hostel offers clean dorm rooms and a small garden, with breakfast included – whenever you want it. Dorms **$55**, doubles **$170**

EATING, DRINKING AND NIGHTLIFE

San Juan has a wide range of **places to eat**, including one of the region's best vegetarian restaurants, as well as plenty of pizzerias, *parrillas* and *tenedor libre* joints. Most of the best places are in the western, residential part of the city, near the Parque de Mayo. **Café** life is all part of the *paseo* tradition, imported lock, stock and barrel from Spain, but later in the evening most Sanjuaninos entertain themselves in their gardens, round a family *asado*. There are also a couple of decent **discos**, mostly in the outskirts.

RESTAURANTS AND CAFÉS

Abuelo Yuyi Av José Ignacio de la Roza and Urquiza ☎0264 422 1101. The most popular pizzeria in town, offering delicious thick-crust pies with a variety of toppings. Daily noon–4pm & 6pm–midnight.

★ **Baró** and **De Sánchez** Rivadavia 55 & 61 oeste respectively ☎0264 420 3670, ⊚desanchezrestoran .com.ar. Two of San Juan's most fashionable restaurants, under the same ownership and right next door to each other: the first serving tasty Italian food; the second a chic *belle époque*-style restaurant which serves imaginative contemporary cuisine and displays a connoisseur's selection of books, albums and CDs, many of which are for sale. Good-value lunch-time menus. Daily noon–4.30pm & 7.30pm–1am.

Bonafide Plaza 25 de Mayo, esq Mendoza y Rivadavia. A bustling meeting-place for the city's movers and shakers near the cathedral. Part of an upmarket café chain famous for its chocolate and decent strong coffees. Daily 9am–midnight.

Freud Café Plaza 25 de Mayo. A popular establishment on the eastern side of the main square where the locals come for coffee, drinks, lots of gossip and football chat. Daily 8am–late.

Hostal de Palito Av Circunvalación 284 sur ☎0264 423 0105. This is one of the best gastronomic restaurants in town, with a wide selection of international dishes and a delightful garden terrace. Daily 12.30–4pm & 7.30pm–midnight.

Las Leñas Av San Martín 1670 oeste ☎0264 423 5040. Cavernous dining room often packed with large parties and serving delicious meat. Daily noon–4pm & 7pm–midnight.

Maloca Del Bono sur 321 ☎0264 426 5740. Offbeat place with psychedelic decor, Latino music and a range of Mexican tacos, Colombian *arepas* and Cuban rice dishes, plus tropical cocktails. Daily 7.30pm–midnight.

Rigoletto Paula A. de Sarmiento 418 sur ☎0264 426 4331. This place offers a cosy atmosphere and friendly service, as well as delicious pizzas and pasta. Daily 12.30–4.30pm & 7pm–midnight.

★ **Soychú** Av José Ignacio de la Roza 223 oeste ☎0264 422 1939. Delightful vegetarian restaurant serving fabulous dishes, in a bright, airy space; office workers flock here to take food away, so come early. Daily noon–4.30pm.

BARS AND NIGHTCLUBS

Aptko Av San Martín 1369 oeste. Not terribly aesthetically appealing, but still the city's trendiest nightspot, where San Juan's affluent youth come to be seen, chat and dance the night away to a mixed soundtrack, dominated by house. Fri & Sat midnight–late.

Aruba Rioja and Maipú. A disco with a bar and *confitería* attached, playing salsa and Latin rhythms. Daily 8am–11pm, disco Fri & Sat midnight–late.

El Santuario de la Difunta Correa

Some 65km east of San Juan by RN-141 • ⊚visitedifuntacorrea.com.ar • Regular buses to Vallecito stop here, but unless you're really curious, it's only worth the short stop you get on the bus route from San Juan to La Rioja, or if you're travelling under your own steam between San Juan and Ischigualasto

The most unusual site around San Juan lies some 65km east of the city: **EL SANTUARIO DE LA DIFUNTA CORREA** is both a repellent and an intriguing place and one of the most concrete examples of how Amerindian legends and Roman Catholic fanaticism have melded together into one belief. All around Argentina you'll come across mini-Difunta **shrines**, sometimes little more than a few bottles of mineral water heaped at the roadside – and easily mistaken for a particularly bad bout of pollution. But the original shrine is here. Past the suburbs, the landscape turns into desert-like plains, complete with sand dunes; to the north the reddish Sierra Pie de Palo ripples in the distance, relieving the monotony. Suddenly, in the middle of nowhere, amid its own grim complex of hotels, *confiterías* and souvenir shops and on top of a small hill, is Argentina's answer to Lourdes.

DIFUNTA CORREA

As legend would have it, during the Civil War in the 1840s, a local man named Baudilio Correa was captured, taken to La Rioja and killed; his widow Deolinda decided to walk to La Rioja with their baby boy to recover Baudilio's corpse. Unable to find water she dropped dead by the roadside, where a passer-by found her, the baby still sucking from her breast. Her grave soon became a holy place and lost travellers began to invoke her protection, claiming miraculous escapes from death on the road. The story of the widow Correa is believed to be Amerindian in origin but has been mingled with Catholic hagiography in a country where the borderline between religion and superstition can often be very faint. The **Difunta Correa** – *difunta* meaning deceased – is now the unofficial saint of all travellers, but especially bus- and truck-drivers. Thousands of people visit the shrine every year, over 100,000 of them during Holy Week alone, many of them covering part of the journey on their knees; National Truck-Drivers' Day in early November also sees huge crowds arriving here. Some people visit the shrine itself – where a hideous statue of the Difunta, complete with sucking infant, lies among melted candles, prayers on pieces of paper and votive offerings including people's driving licences, the remains of tyres and photographs of mangled cars from which the occupants miraculously got out alive – while others just deposit a bottle of mineral water on the huge mountain of plastic built up over the years.

Valle de Calingasta

In the west of San Juan Province is the marvellous, fertile **VALLE DE CALINGASTA** – a bright green strip of land around 90km west of the city of San Juan as the crow flies, on the other side of the Sierra del Tontal range, but reached by a long road detour. Its major settlement of interest is **Barreal**, a pleasant, laidback little town set amid fields of alfalfa, onions and maize, with a stupendous backdrop of the sierra, snowcapped for most of the year. Barreal's environs are home to the **Complejo Astronómico El Leoncito**, one of the continent's most important space observatories, and the clay flats of the **Barreal del Leoncito**, used for wind-cart championships. To the east of town is a series of mountains, red, orange and deep pink in colour, known aptly as the **Serranías de las Piedras Pintadas**. To the southwest of Barreal, the RP-400 leads to the tiny hamlet of Las Hornillas, the point of departure for adventurous treks and climbs to the summit of **Cerro Mercedario** (6770m), said by many mountaineers to be the most satisfying climb in the cordillera in this region. In the sedate town of **Calingasta** itself, north of Barreal, the main sight is a fine seventeenth-century **chapel**.

Since the closure of the old RP-12, the main paved route from San Juan is to drive north along the RN-40 to Talacasto, then take the RP-436 for 23km, and branch left to Calingasta at the main RN-149 junction.

Barreal

The small oasis town of **BARREAL**, set alongside the Río Los Patos, 1650m above sea level, at the southern extreme of the Valle de Calingasta, is a fast up-and-coming, friendly place which makes a great base for adventure tourism in the surrounding area. The central square, **Plaza San Martín**, is the focal point, at the crossroads of Avenida Presidente Roca and General Las Heras. The town enjoys a pleasant climate, and the views to the west, of the cordillera peaks, including the majestic **Cerro Mercedario**, El Polaco, La Ramada and Los Siete Picos de Ansilta, seen across a beautiful plain, shimmering with onion and maize fields, are superb. Barreal makes a good base if you want to conquer **Mercedario** – one of the Andes' most challenging yet climbable mountains. To the east you can climb up into the coloured mountains, or up to the **Cima del Tontal**, which affords one of the most famous of all views of the cordillera, as well as panoramas across to San Juan city.

ARRIVAL, INFORMATION AND TOURS   BARREAL

By bus Buses from San Juan stop in Plaza San Martín.

Tourist information There's a helpful tourist office (Mon–Fri 9am–9pm, Sat & Sun 9am–midnight). The

offices for Parque Nacional El Leoncito (see p.376) are at Cordillera Ansilta s/n (☎ 0264 844 1240).

Tours For trips in the surrounding area try Fortuna

Viajes (☎ 0264 404 0913, ⓦ fortunaviajes.com.ar), which organizes treks and climbs, including that of Mercedario

(US$4500 per person for a 12-day expedition from Barreal, all-inclusive except food; 2 people min).

ACCOMMODATION

Barreal has a surprisingly wide choice of excellent accommodation. As this is spread out over a couple of kilometres – some of it on the northern and southern approaches into town – ask the bus driver to drop you as close to your lodging as possible.

Cabañas Doña Pipa Mariano Moreno s/n ☎ 0264 844 1004, ⓦ cdpbarreal.com.ar. Rents out *cabañas* for up to five people in pleasant grounds and has a simple hotel annexe. *Cabañas* $250 per person, doubles $210

Cabañas Kummel Presidente Roca s/n ☎ 0264 844 1206, ⓔ cabaniaskummel@infovia.com.ar. A good option with friendly owners who are very knowledgeable about the area and can also help arrange trips. Sleeps up to seven people. $500

Eco Posada El Mercedario Av Presidente Roca esq Los Enamorados ☎ 0264 15 509 0907, ⓦ elmercedario .com.ar. A lovingly restored adobe farmhouse, with high, cane ceilings, swept brick floors and wood-fired stoves in the rooms, which are all tastefully themed around famous Argentine women. There's a homely restaurant, and the owner runs 4WD tours. $390

Hostel Barreal Av San Martin s/n ☎ 0264 844 1144, ⓔ hostelbarreal@hotmail.com. An excellent and restful hostel whose owner organizes rafting trips on the Río Los Patos. Rooms are spotless and there is a convivial atmosphere. Dorms $50, doubles $190

Hostel Don Lisandro Av San Martín s/n ☎ 0264 15 505 9122, ⓦ donlisandro.com.ar. A well-equipped, wonderfully

sociable hostel set in attractive grounds where there's also space for tents. Camping $60, dorms $50, doubles $210

★ **Posada de Campo La Querencia** 4km south from the main plaza on Calle Florida ☎ 0264 15 436 4699, ⓦ laquerenciaposada.com.ar. In a beautifully designed building, this posada offers charming, appealingly designed rooms with fabulous views of open country – it's worth paying a little extra for the west-facing ones, looking towards the cordillera. Breakfasts and other meals are irreproachable, as is the friendliness of the welcome. $700

★ **Posada Don Ramón** 8km north of the village on Av Presidente Roca ☎ 0264 15 404 0913, ⓦ posadadon ramon.com.ar. All of the huge rooms are designed to maximize the splendid panoramic views of the cordillera, including Aconcagua and Mercedario. Lie back in your bathroom jacuzzi – or the swimming pool – and enjoy. The place is luxuriously, if simply, furnished, and has a lovely bodega stocked with organic Sanjuanino wines. The proprietor also owns and guides for Fortuna Viajes (see above). $550

Posada San Eduardo Av San Martín s/n ☎ 0264 844 1046. Large, simple rooms set around an old, wisteria-lined colonial-style patio. Its restaurant serves well-cooked, if slightly unimaginative food, and there's a garden pool. $450

EATING AND DRINKING

El Alemán Belgrano s/n ☎ 0264 844 1193. The German-descended owners dish up huge servings of sauerkraut, smoked hams and slabs of pork with well-prepared vegetables

from the garden and German-style beer in a bucolic setting – follow signs from the *Posada San Eduardo*. The owners also rent *cabaña* accommodation. Daily 7.30pm–midnight.

Barreal del Leoncito

Immediately south of Barreal along the western side of the RN-149 is a huge flat expanse of windswept, hardened clay, the remains of an ancient lake, known as the **Barreal del Leoncito**, the Pampa del Leoncito, or simply the Barreal Blanco. Measuring 14km by 5km, this natural arena, with a marvellous stretch of the cordillera as a background, is used for **wind-car** championships (*carrovelismo* in Spanish) – the little cars with yacht-like sails have reached speeds of over 130km an hour here; contact Sr Rogelio Toro in Barreal if you want to have a go (☎ 0264 15 671 7196, ⓔ dontoro .barreal@gmail.com; main season Nov–Dec; $200 for 2hr with an instructor).

Parque Nacional El Leoncito

Park entrance open 24hr daily, information 8am–6pm

Some 15km or so further south along the RN-149 is a turn-off eastwards up into the **Parque Nacional El Leoncito**, which is symbolized by the suri, or Andean rhea. Up on nearby hills are two space **observatories**, among the most important in the world because of the outstanding meteorological conditions hereabouts – averaging more than 320 clear nights a year. About 12km up this track is the park entrance: announce your presence to the *guardaparques*.

Complejo Astronómico El Leoncito

Visits 10am–noon & 3–5.30pm; not permitted for people under 4 or over 70; no wheelchair access • $20 • ☎ 0264 844 1088, 🌐 casleo.gov.ar

Visible from far around thanks to its huge white dome, the **Complejo Astronómico El Leoncito**, at an altitude of over 2500m, affords fabulous views of the valley and the cordillera. Inaugurated in 1986, this space observatory was built to resist earthquakes registering 10 or higher on the Richter scale, an absolute necessity in this area of violent seismic activity. The primary telescope weighs some 40 tonnes and its main 2.15m-diameter mirror has to be replaced every two years. The guided tour, led by enthusiastic staff members (English spoken), takes you through the whole process; take warm clothing as the inside is kept cold. Night visits, with food and lodging, are sometimes allowed: call or email at least 24hr in advance (☎ 0264 421 3653 ext 123, ✉ kdominguez@casleo.gov.ar), and turn up for 5pm.

Estación Astronómica Dr Carlos U. Cesco

Daily 10am–noon & 4–6pm; night visits 7.30–11pm • $20 • 🌐 oafa.fcefn.unsj-cuim.edu.ar

Off a turn-off 3km back down the track is the relatively modest-looking **Estación Astronómica Dr Carlos U. Cesco**, where the staff will also be only too happy to show you the visitors' centre and explain the observatory's work. You can also make night visits: either simply turn up at 7.30pm for a visit that will last to about 11pm or stay the night (see below). You actually get to use telescopes; take a torch and warm clothing.

ACCOMMODATION   **PARQUE NACIONAL EL LEONCITO**

Estación Astronómica Dr Carlos U. Cesco ☎ 02648 441 087. Located inside the space observatory (see above), these rooms make it easier to stay the night and gaze at the nocturnal sky; don't expect any great comfort and certainly not luxury, but everything works. Prices include breakfast; dinner is $50 extra. **$260**

Las Hornillas and Mercedario

Frustratingly, there are no public buses south from Barreal or the national park along the RN-149 – still mostly unpaved on this stretch – to Uspallata in Mendoza Province (see p.354). The scenic RP-400 strikes out in a southwesterly direction from Barreal to **Las Hornillas**, over 50km away. This tiny hamlet is inhabited mostly by herdsmen and their families amid pastureland and gorse scrub and is effectively the base camp for the mighty **Mercedario**, which looms nearby. If you want to climb this difficult but not impossible mountain, regarded by many as the most noble of all Argentina's Andean peaks, contact Fortuna Viajes in Barreal (see opposite). The nearby rivers are excellent for fishing for trout; ask at the tourist office in Barreal.

Cerros Pintados

The mountainsides to the immediate east of Barreal, accessible by clear tracks, are a mosaic of pink, red, brown, ochre and purple rocks, and the so-called **Cerros Pintados**, or "Painted Mountains", live up to their name. Among the rocky crags, tiny cacti poke out from the cracks, and in the spring they sprout huge wax-like flowers, in translucent shades of white, pink and yellow, among golden splashes of broom-like *brea* shrubs. About 8km north of Barreal, another track heads eastwards from the main road, climbing for 40km past some idyllic countryside inhabited only by the odd goatherd or farming family, to the outlook atop the **Cima del Tontal**, at just over 4000m. To the east there are amazing views down into the San Juan Valley, with the Dique de Ullum glinting in the distance, or west and south to the cordillera, where the peak of Aconcagua and the majestic summit of the Mercedario are clearly visible.

Calingasta and around

CALINGASTA itself is a peaceful place, 37km north of Barreal; its only attraction apart from its idyllic location is the seventeenth-century **Capilla de Nuestra Señora**

6

del Carmen, a simple whitewashed adobe building, with an arched doorway and a long gallery punctuated by frail-looking slender pillars. The bells are among the oldest in the country and the iron and wooden ladder leading onto the roof is a work of art, too.

From Calingasta it's 125km along the RP-412 north to Iglesia, along a dry valley, through the occasional ford, with the Sierra del Tigre to the east and the Cordón de Olivares providing stupendous views to the west. No public transport runs on this stretch.

ACCOMMODATION   CALINGASTA

Hotel Nora Aldo Cantoni s/n ☎02648 421 027, ✉calingasta22@hotmail.com. This comfortable but simple central hotel is by far the best in the region; extras include cable TV and parking. **$300**

Valle de Iglesia

The **VALLE DE IGLESIA** is named after one of its main settlements, **Iglesia**, a sleepy village of adobe houses. It is a fertile valley separated from the Valle de Calingasta by the dramatic Cordón de Olivares range of mountains. You can get there directly from San Juan via the RN-40, which forks off to the northwest at Talacasto, some 50km north of the city. From there a mountain road, the RP-436, joins up with the RN-149 heading north. From Calingasta you can get to Iglesia direct along the rugged, unsealed RP-412. More interesting than Iglesia itself are the small market town and windsurf hangout of **Rodeo** to the northeast, along the RN-150, and further north still, the idyllic village of **Angualasto**, along the dirt track that leads to one of the country's most recent national parks, **San Guillermo**, the place in Argentina where you are most likely to spot pumas in the wild.

Rodeo and around

The RN-150 arches round the pleasant, easy-going market town of **RODEO**. Windsurfing enthusiasts come from afar to take advantage of the superb, consistent winds on the local reservoir, the **Dique Cuesta del Viento** during the high season (Oct–April). Rodeo hosts one of the region's major folk festivals in the first weekend of February, the **Fiesta de la Manzana y la Semilla**, when you can try local specialities, such as empanadas and *humitas*, and watch dancing and musical groups in the Anfiteatro, just off Santo Domingo in the heart of the town.

North of Rodeo, you can head off towards Angualasto and the Parque Nacional San Guillermo (see opposite), while to the east the RN-150 takes you to Jáchal (see p.380); it is an impressive, winding cliff-side road that follows the stark valley of the Río Jáchal.

ARRIVAL AND INFORMATION   RODEO AND AROUND

By bus Buses to and from San Juan (1–2 daily; 3hr) stop at the main plaza.

Tourist information The town's tourist office is at Plaza de la Fundación s/n (daily 8am–9pm; ☎02647 493193).

ACCOMMODATION AND EATING

50 Nudos ☎011 155 703 3743, ⊚50nudos.com. For relatively luxurious accommodation, also aimed at the surfing crowd, this waterside posada offers comfortable rooms and a good restaurant and will get you kitted out to hit the reservoir's azure waters. **$490**

Finca El Martillo 2.5km from the plaza at the town's northernmost end ☎02647 493 019, ⊚fincaelmartillo .com. This marvellous farm, producing all kinds of herbs, fresh and preserved fruit and excellent jam and honey (sold at its shop and used in the onsite restaurant, which also specializes in trout and goat), rents out several delightful eight-bed *cabañas*. **$450**

Hostel Rancho Lamaral ☎0264 15 660 1197, ⊚rancholamaral.com. An excellent place to base yourself if you're keen on joining the windsurfistas for real, this atmospherically breezy farmstead is set a short walk from the reservoir's northeastern shore; take a *remise* from town. The owner and staff exude a highly positive vibe, they give lessons and will help sort you out with surfing rental gear. Dorms **$85**, doubles **$220**

Angualasto

From Rodeo, the RP-407 heads north, cutting through a ridge of rock and sloping down into the valley of the Río Blanco. The little village of **ANGUALASTO**, which has preserved a delightful rural feel, seemingly detached from the modern world, is set among rows of poplars, fruit orchards and small plots of maize, beans and other vegetables. It is proud of its little **Museo Arqueológico Luis Benedetti** (daily 8am–8pm), whose tiny collection of mostly pre-Columbian finds includes a remarkable 400-year-old mummified corpse, found in a *tumbería*, or burial mound, nearby.

El Chinguillo

The road northwards follows the Río Blanco valley, fording it once – often impossible after spring or summer rains or heavy thaws – to the incredibly remote hamlets of Malimán and **El Chinguillo**, the entrance to the Parque Nacional San Guillermo, in a beautiful valley surrounded by huge dunes of sand and mountains scarred red and yellow with mineral deposits. The Solar family's delightful farmhouse (no phone; $220) provides the only **accommodation** hereabouts, as well as delicious empanadas and roast lamb.

Parque Nacional San Guillermo

The **Reserva Provincial San Guillermo**, in the far northern reaches of San Juan Province, was the first region in the country to be declared a **UNESCO Biosphere Reserve**, in 1980. Part of the Provincial Reserve, on great heights to the west of the Río Blanco valley, later attained national park status, in 1998: the **PARQUE NACIONAL SAN GUILLERMO**. The Parque Nacional is home to a huge variety of wildlife. Guanacos and vicuñas abound, along with suris or ñandús, eagles, condors, several different kinds of lizard, foxes and all kinds of waterfowl, including flamingoes, which match the seams of jagged pink rock that run along the mountainsides like a garish zip-fastener. Above all, this is a part of Argentina where if you stay for a number of days you stand an extremely good chance of spotting a puma – a very rare occurrence elsewhere in the country. For some reason the pumas living here are less shy of humans and often approach vehicles; treat these powerful and potentially dangerous creatures with caution. The highest peaks, at well over 5000m, are permanently snowcapped, and the high altitude of the park's roads – as high as 3700m – affects some visitors.

PARK ESSENTIALS

Planning a visit Visiting requires advance preparation – the park is isolated and the weather can be capricious. You'll need at least three days, and must register with the park office on the western outskirts of Rodeo on Calle La Colonia (Mon–Fri 7am–2pm; ☎ 02647 493 214, ✉ sanguillermo@apn.gov.ar). You will require a 4WD and a guide (roughly $400 a day), as negotiating the fords can be dangerous, plus you'll have to travel with at least one other vehicle in case of breakdown. Make sure you travel with adequate clothing, fuel and supplies. Motorcycles and horses are not allowed. Registered guides include Alberto Ramírez (☎ 0261 15 658 1527) and Ramón Ossa (☎ 0264 844 1004; book as far in advance as possible).

Accomodation You can overnight in bunkbeds in the *Refugio Agua del Godo* in the centre of the park (bring suitably warm bedding and provisions; free).

San José de Jáchal and around

The sleepy little town of **San José de Jáchal** is most famous for a handful of nineteenth-century flour mills scattered about attractive farmland immediately north of the town, in a landscape rather like that of North Africa. From Jáchal you can head northeast for 145km on the **RN-40** to **Villa Unión**, in La Rioja Province (see p.383). You squeeze along the Cuesta de Huaco, a mountain road with magnificent views of the arid valleys to the north. From Huaco the road runs through the Río Bermejo Valley, bone dry for most of the time but suddenly flooding after storms. Beware of the many deep fords (*badenes*) along the road: if they are full of water, wait for the level to drop before attempting to cross; even when dry they can rip tyres if taken too fast.

San José de Jáchal

SAN JOSÉ DE JÁCHAL (usually called simply Jáchal) lies in the fertile valley of the Río Jáchal, 155km due north of San Juan by the RN-40; it's also 45km due east of Rodeo via the scenic RN-150 (see p.378). The town was founded in the seventeenth century on the site of a pre-Columbian village. Destroyed in a severe earthquake in 1894, the town was rebuilt using mud-bricks in an Italianate style, with arched facades and galleried patios, focused on the Plaza San Martín.

Jáchal itself isn't much to write home about, but it makes for a convenient stopover. If you have a moment to spare, visit the astonishingly eclectic **Museo Arqueológico Prieto** (☎02647 420298 to arrange visit), at 25 de Mayo 788 oeste, signposted along the RN-150. It is a motley collection of all manner of odds and ends, but among the curios are some fine pre-Columbian artefacts, painstakingly collected and displayed by a local who handed it all over to the police. During the first fortnight in November, the town stages the **Fiesta de la Tradición**, a festival of folklore, feasts and music.

ARRIVAL AND INFORMATION   SAN JOSÉ DE JÁCHAL

By bus Buses from San Juan stop at the terminal seven blocks southeast of the main plaza.

Tourist information There's a helpful tourist office on the plaza at San Juan 133 (daily 7am–9pm; ☎02647 420003); ask here for updates on which flour mills are open for visits. They'll also help sort out a *remise* for a tour of the mills (one recommended driver is Jorge Saleme at Rivadavia 525 ☎02647 420736).

ACCOMMODATION AND EATING

Hualta Picum Apart-Hotel Sarmiento 749 ☎02647 420774. The best place to stay in town has spacious, bright, well-furnished apartments for up to eight people. Thankfully, given the eating options in town, you can self-cater, so bring food. **$380**

Tata Viejo San Martín, Echegaray and General Paz. The only real restaurant in Jáchal offers hearty, inexpensive food, although service is unexceptional – if not downright unfriendly – and the old papa of the name is nowhere to be seen. Daily 12.30–3pm & 8pm–midnight.

The flour mills around Jáchal

North of Jáchal, the RN-40 suddenly swerves to the east and the road continuing straight ahead, the RP-456, cuts through Jáchal's rural northern suburbs amid bucolic farmland, used to grow wheat, maize, alfalfa and fruit. With the stark mountain backdrop of the Sierra Negra to the east, Sierra de la Batea to the north and Cerro Alto (2095m) to the west, this dazzlingly green valley, dotted with adobe farmhouses, some of them with splendid sun-faded wooden doors, looks like parts of Morocco in the lee of the Atlas. Canals and little ditches water the fields, using snow melt from the cordillera and pre-cordillera, as rain is rare here.

In the nineteenth century, a number of **flour mills** were built, and they are now rightly recognized as historic monuments. Their beige or whitewashed walls, wonderfully antiquated machinery and enthusiastic owners or managers make for a memorable visit; always offer guides a tip if shown around. **El Molino del Alto** (also called El Molino de García) is the best, as it is fully functioning, and – if he's around – the passion of Dionício Pérez, the manager, is a joy to behold (Spanish only). Also worth visiting if you can find the charming owner is the **Molino de Sardiña** (no longer in operation) at the corner of calles Maturrango and Mesias, just to the south of El Molino del Alto.

Huaco

Back on the RN-40, the road hugs the Sierra Negra, before skirting the Dique Los Cauquenes reservoir. Then you hit the Cuesta de Huaco, a narrow mountain road accurately described as a place "where the reddish dawn lingers on the even redder clay of the mountainside". Those words were sung by deep-voiced crooner **Buenaventura Luna**, real name Eusebio de Jesús Dojorti Roco, who was a highly popular star in the 1940s and 1950s, and is buried in nearby **HUACO**. This small village, shaded by *algarrobos* and eucalyptus, is no more than a cluster of mud-brick houses, but just before you get to the village you pass a splendid adobe **flour mill**, similar to those north of Jáchal. Built in the nineteenth century, it belonged to the Docherty family, descendants of an Irishman who fought in the British army that invaded Buenos Aires, was captured and decided to settle in Argentina; Buenaventura Luna was one of their descendants.

ACCOMMODATION   HUACO

Hostería Huaco 0264 421 9528, ◍ hosteriahuaco .com.ar. This *hostería* sitting just back from the main through road is an airy adobe-style building offering pleasant a/c rooms and spacious, airy *cabañas*, with a garden featuring a pool and outdoor jacuzzi. Doubles $240, *cabañas* $290

6

Parque Provincial Ischigualasto and Parque Nacional Talampaya

San Juan and La Rioja provinces boast two of the most-photographed protected areas in the country, which together have been declared a UNESCO World Heritage Site, as the only place on the Earth's surface where you can see all stages of the Triassic geological era, which witnessed the emergence of the first dinosaurs. In San Juan is **Parque Provincial Ischigualasto**, better known as Valle de la Luna – Moon Valley – because of its out-of-this-world landscapes and apocryphal legends. The province has jealously resisted repeated attempts to turn it into a national park, and the authorities are doing a good job of providing easy access and looking after the fragile environment. While he was in office, President Menem, on the other hand, made sure that his native province of La Rioja got its first national park: **Parque Nacional Talampaya**, best known for its giant red-sandstone cliffs, which are guaranteed to impress even the most jaded traveller. It's also the country's best example of desert *monte* scrub – a vulnerable ecosystem with rare fauna and flora, and the only habitat endemic to Argentina.

While you can visit both parks in the same day from either **Villa Unión** in La Rioja (see p.383) or the more appealing town of **San Agustín de Valle Fértil** in northeastern San Juan Province, you can get more from the parks by splitting your visits; Talampaya especially merits a longer visit. In many ways it is wise to go to Talampaya in the morning, when the sun lights up the coloured rocks and illuminates the canyon, whereas Ischigualasto is far more impressive in the late afternoon and at sunset in particular. If possible avoid the gruelling day-trips offered from San Juan, or even La Rioja.

San Agustín de Valle Fértil

Set among enticing landscapes some 250km northeast of San Juan by the RN-141 and the RP-510, the oasis town of **SAN AGUSTÍN DE VALLE FÉRTIL** is the best base for visiting Parque Provincial Ischigualasto, about 80km to the north, via Los Baldecitos. It's built around a mirror-like reservoir, the Dique San Agustín just up in the hills – cacti and gorse grow on its banks, and a small peninsula juts artistically into the waters. The town prospered in the nineteenth century thanks to the gold, iron and quartz mines and marble quarries in the mountains nearby, but it has now turned to tourism as its source of income, to supplement meagre farm earnings. The fertile valley that gives it its name – sometimes it's referred to simply as "Valle Fértil" – is a patchwork of maize fields, olive groves and pasture for goats and sheep – and the local cheese and roast kid are recommended.

ARRIVAL, INFORMATION AND TOURS   SAN AGUSTÍN DE VALLE FÉRTIL

You can visit Ischigualasto in your own vehicle, but you'll need to join a tour to visit Talampaya. Visiting it by public transport is complicated and not advised.

By bus Buses from San Juan and La Rioja arrive at the terminal at Santa Fe and Entre Ríos.
Destinations La Rioja (3 weekly; 4hr); San Juan (3 daily; 3hr 30min–4hr).
Tourist information The tourist office (daily 7am–

midnight; 02646 420104) on Plaza San Agustín is extremely helpful and can fix you up with guides and transport both to Ischigualasto and to other less-dramatic sites in the nearby mountains, including pre-Hispanic petroglyphs.

Tour operators For tours to Ischigualasto, contact Paula Tour at Tucumán s/n (☎ 0264 642 0096, ⓦ paula-tour.com .ar); it organizes a number of circuits in the park, including night-time ones around the time of the full moon. You'll need to reserve an English-speaking guide in advance ($80 extra). It also offers tours of the town, the wider province, and Talampaya – the latter often in combination with the Runacay agency in Villa Unión (see opposite).

ACCOMMODATION

Campo Base Valle de la Luna Tucumán and San Luis ☎ 02646 420063, ⓦ hostelvalledelaluna.com.ar. This is a very good youth hostel, which can help organize reasonably priced tours in the area. Dorms $65, doubles $170

Eco Hostel Mendoza s/n, half a block from the main plaza ☎ 02646 420147. There's nothing specifically "eco" about it apart from the name, but it's nevertheless a decent option. Tango and Spanish lessons available. Dorms $60

Fatme Rivadavia s/n ☎ 02646 420014, ⓔ fatmehotel @yahoo.com.ar. Just three blocks from the central plaza, this is an extremely clean and friendly place with very reasonably priced rooms, but no meals apart from breakfast are served. $200

Hostería Valle Fértil Rivadavia s/n ☎ 02646 420015, ⓦ alkazarhotel.com.ar/vallefertil. A full seven blocks from the plaza, the *hostería* is situated on a high bluff, overlooking the Dique. A comfortable, three-star place, it has a decent restaurant (daily 8pm–midnight), specializing in casseroled kid, and good, if cramped, rooms – the more expensive ones with reservoir views. It is a bit run down though, and the bunker-like design has not aged well. $410

Posada Los Olivos Santa Fe s/n ☎ 02646 420115, ⓦ posadalosolivos.alojar.com.ar. This friendly posada offers decent hostel-style accommodation, plus a spacious wood-beamed patio restaurant area, serving plain but well-prepared food. $225

Rustico Cerro del Valle Santa Fe s/n ☎ 0264 642 0202, ⓦ cerrodelvalle.com.ar. This aptly named *hostería*, conveniently located over the road from the bus terminal, has very comfortable rooms, a fine garden pool, hospitable owners and friendly dogs. $390

EATING AND DRINKING

A lo de Pepe Rivadavia and Sarmiento. One of the best restaurants in town (not that there are that many to compete with), *A lo de Pepe* is an intimate little place that serves a fine *parrilla*. Daily 12.30–4.30pm & 7pm–midnight.

El Serranito By the bus terminal, this simple but convenient place cooks up cheap and tasty *milanesas* and snacks. Daily noon–midnight.

Parque Provincial Ischigualasto

Some 80km north of Valle Fértil, the **PARQUE PROVINCIAL ISCHIGUALASTO**, also known as the Valle de la Luna, or Moon Valley, is San Juan's most famous feature by far, covering nearly 150 square kilometres of desolate but astonishingly varied terrain.

For paleontologists, Ischigualasto's importance is primarily as a rich dinosaur burial ground: two of the world's very oldest species of dinosaur, the diminutive *Euraptor lunesis* and *Herrerasaurus ischigualastensis*, both dating back some 230 million years, were found here, among many others. The park is also a joy for geologists, as most strata of the 45-million-year Triassic era are on plain view.

The park is in a desert valley between two ranges of high mountains, the Sierra Los Rastros to the west and Cerros Colorados to the east. As witnessed by the mollusc and coral fossils found in the cliffsides, for a long time the whole area was under water. Over the course of millions of years the terrain has been eroded by wind and water, and sections built of volcanic ash have taken on a ghostly greyish-white hue. A set of red-sandstone mountains to the north acts as a perfect backdrop to the paler stone formations and clay blocks, all of which are impressively illuminated in the late evening.

At the entrance, an excellent **museum** exhibits some wonderful stories of forensic paleontology, unravelling some curious examples of dinosaur death (Spanish only) – useful while you wait for a tour.

The rock formations

The majority of visitors come to admire the spectacular lunar landscapes that give the park its popular nickname, and the much publicized and alarmingly fragile **rock formations** – some have already disappeared, the victims of erosion and the occasional flash floods that seem to strike with increasing frequency. **Cerro El Morado**

(1700m), a barrow-like mountain that according to local lore is shaped like an Indian lying on his back, dominates the park to the east. A segmented row of rocks is known as El Gusano (the Worm); a huge set of vessel-like boulders is known as El Submarino; a sandy field dotted with cannon-ball-shaped stones is dubbed the Cancha de Bolas (the Ball-court). One famous formation, painfully fragile on its slender stalk, is El Hongo (the Mushroom), beautifully set off against the red sandstone cliffs behind.

Flora and fauna

Another of the park's attractions is its wealth of flora and fauna. The main plant varieties are the native broom-like *brea*, three varieties of the scrawny *jarilla*, both black and white species of *algarrobo*, the *chañar*, *retamo* and *molle* shrubs and four varieties of cactus. Animals that you are likely to spot here include European hares, Patagonian hares, the vizcacha, the grey fox, armadillos and small rodents, plus several species of bat, frog, toad, lizard and snake. Condors and ñandús are often seen, too, while guanacos may be spotted standing like sentinels atop the rocks, before scampering off.

Routes through the park

The main driving tour follows a set **circuit**, beginning in the more lunar landscapes to the south. Panoramic outlook points afford stunning views of weird oceans of hillocks. These are the typical moonscapes, but they look uncannily like the famous landscapes of Cappadocia, with their Gaudí-esque pinnacles and curvaceous mounds. The whole tour takes at least a couple of hours to be done at all comfortably. But be warned that sudden summer storms can cut off the tracks for a day or two, in which case you may not be able to see all the park. Apart from the main vehicle circuit (which you can also arrange to do at night around full-moon time), there are a couple of other options: a **mountain bike** circuit or a **trek** to climb Cerro El Morado (contact an agency in Valle Fértil, such as Paula Tour, see opposite). In 2012, the RN-150 that skirts the park's southern boundary is due to join up Los Baldecitos with San José de Jáchal (see p.380), which would make a much-needed tourist circuit possible, providing an alternative route to Villa Unión. But don't hold your breath on the timing.

ARRIVAL AND INFORMATION PARQUE PROVINCIAL ISCHIGUALASTO

Arrival The park can be visited only in a vehicle – either your own or that of a tour operator. You'll be assigned a *guardaparque* – many of whom only speak Spanish – who will accompany your convoy. Convoys leave every hour, and at busy times (Jan–March) can sometimes involve more than thirty vehicles. If you're seeking more solitude, arrive very early or late in the day; big convoys can also generate a lot of dust and considerably reduce the time you get to spend at each stop.

When to visit The optimal time of day for visiting the park

is in the mid- to late afternoon, when the light is the most flattering. That way you also catch the mind-boggling sunsets that illuminate the park, turning the pinkish orange rock a glowing crimson, which contrasts with the ghostly greyish white of the lunarscapes all around.

Tourist information The *guardería* (daily: Oct–March 8am–5pm last entrance; April–Sept 9am–4pm last entrance, you must leave by dusk; ☏ 02646 491 100; $40) lies at the entrance to the park, along a well-signposted lateral road off the RP-510 at Los Baldecitos.

ACCOMMODATION AND EATING

There is no camping or accommodation and most people stay at either Villa Unión (see below) or, to be closer, Valle Fértil (see p.381). There's a restaurant at the entrance.

Villa Unión and around

The small town of **VILLA UNIÓN**, essentially strung out along the main RN-76 in the parched Valle de Vinchina, 120km northeast of Huaco, isn't much to write home about, but is fast developing as a convenient base for tours to Parque Nacional Talampaya 70km south, but also to the staggeringly desolate Reserva Provincial Las Vicuñas, wrapped around the beautiful Laguna Brava (see p.386), over 150km northwest. The town, formerly called Hornillos, received its name in the nineteenth century in recognition of the hospitality of its people towards peasants thrown off a nearby estancia by the ruthless *estancieros*.

Cuesta de Miranda

Agencies like Runacay do tours, or you can catch the local Ivanlor buses that travel once a day in each direction; from Chilecito, buses continue to La Rioja

A popular trip from Villa Unión is east along the RN-40, over the 2025m mountain pass that crosses the Sierra de Famatina and down the fabulous **Cuesta de Miranda**, a sinuous, parapet-like mountain road, on towards Sañogasta and the old mining town of Chilecito. The Río Miranda snakes through a deep gorge, hemmed in by multicoloured cliffs and peaks, striped red, green, blue and yellow with oxidized minerals and strata of volcanic rock.

ARRIVAL, INFORMATION AND TOURS   VILLA UNIÓN

By bus A couple of blocks east of the main square is the bus station, serving La Rioja, Chilecito and planned routes to Valle Fértil and Huaco. Coop Transporte Talampaya (☎ 03825 15 662086) runs transfers to the park, as well as a couple of circuits within it.
Destinations Chilecito (daily; 4hr 30min); La Rioja (4 daily; 4hr); Patquía (4 daily; 3hr); Vinchina (4 daily; 1hr).
Tourist information There's an obliging tourist office on the main square, Plaza San Martín s/n (daily 8am–10pm; ☎ 03825 470543). The park office for Talampaya (Mon–Fri

7am–2pm; ☎ 03825 470356, ⊚ talampaya.gov.ar) is at San Martín 150, half a block from the plaza.
Tours Runacay is a first-rate travel agency, located on the main plaza at Hipólito Irigoyen esq J.V. González (☎ 03825 470368, ⊚ runacay.com). It runs a variety of tours, prime among them being its walking tours of Talampaya (including a night-time option around full moon), but also other Talampaya options and adventure trips into the cordillera, such as to Laguna Brava. Tours are available in English, French and Portuguese.

ACCOMMODATION

As with many provincial towns, the accommodation is spread out in the town and its approach roads, so get the bus driver to drop you off as close as possible to where you're staying. The less expensive options can be found in town, while the most luxurious accommodation is a couple of kilometres to the south of town on the RN-76, near the RN-40 junction.

Cañón de Talampaya RN-76 ☎ 03825 470753, ⊚ hotel canontalampaya.com. This modern hotel built around a rather arid patio houses earth-toned rooms, with rustic furniture, a very decent restaurant and an extremely exposed swimming pool. It's owned by Rolling Travel, who run the minibus circuits in the Talampaya park, so they can get you to the park and back. Don't expect the friendliest of welcomes, though. $510
Hospedaje Doña Gringa Nicolás Dávila 103 ☎ 03825 470528. This tiny *hospedaje* has very clean rooms around a delightful leafy patio. The laidback atmosphere is one of its assets. $220
Hostel Laguna Brava Honorato Guerrero, Alem and

Independencia ☎ 0261 15 591 3559. This excellent hostel is located in a beautiful if slightly rundown Andalucian-style villa. It is far better value than most of the other budget lodgings in town. Dorms $55, doubles $200
Noryanepat Joaquín V. González 150 ☎ 03825 470133. Just about acceptable rooms with cramped bathrooms, where the toilets have a tendency to break away from their fittings. Conveniently located just one block east of the main plaza. $410
Pircas Negras RN-76 ☎ 03825 470611, ⊚ hotelpircas negras.com. This modern hotel built to a contemporary design offers smart rooms, ample parking and a passable restaurant, although service can be sloppy. $550

EATING AND DRINKING

La Palmera 2km south of town by the junction of the RN-40 and the RN-76. Atmospheric place where they do fabulous *asados*, including delicious kid, or *chivito* ($60), to be washed down with their fine selection of local wines.

Service is excellent, and the decor is authentically *riojano* rustic – even if the puma and wildcat pelts might not be to everyone's taste. Daily noon–4pm & 7–11.30pm.

Parque Nacional Talampaya

The park's main entrance is a few kilometres down a well-signposted turn-off from the RN-76 at the Puerta de Talampaya • Daily May–Sept 8.30am–5.30pm; Oct–April 8am–6pm • $40 • ⊚ talampaya.gov.ar

The entrance to **PARQUE NACIONAL TALAMPAYA** is 55km down the RN-76 from Villa Unión, and then along a signposted road to the east. Coming from the south, it's 93km north of Ischigualasto and 190km from Valle Fértil. The park's main feature is a wide-bottomed canyon flanked by 180m-high, rust-coloured sandstone cliffs, so smooth and sheer that they look as if they were sliced through by a giant cheese-wire. Another section of the canyon is made up of rock formations that seem to have been created as part of a surreal Gothic cathedral. Added attractions are the presence of several bird species, including condors and eagles, as well as rich flora and some pre-Columbian petroglyphs. The park's name comes from the indigenous peoples' words *ktala* – the locally abundant *tala* bush – and *ampaya*, meaning dry riverbed. Avoid Easter if possible, when the park is at its busiest; the middle of the day in the height of summer, when it can be unbearably hot; and the day after a storm, when the park closes because of floods. The *zonda* wind (see box, p.370) can also cause the park to close. In midwinter, it can be bitterly cold. The best time of day by far to visit is soon after opening, when the dawn light deepens the red of the sandstone.

The cliffs and canyon

Talampaya's cliffs appear so frequently on national tourism promotion posters and in coffee-table books, you think you know what you're getting before you arrive. But no photograph really prepares you for the belittling feeling you have when standing at the foot of a massive rock wall, where the silence is shattered only by the wind. Even the classic shots of orange-red precipices looming over what looks like a toy jeep, included for scale, don't really convey the astonishment. The national park, covering 215 square kilometres, was created in 1997 to protect the canyon and all its treasures. Geologically it's part of the Sierra Los Colorados, whose rippling mass you can see in the distance to the east. The sandstone cliffs were formed at the beginning of the Triassic period, nearly 250 million years ago, and have gradually been eroded by torrential rain and various rivers that have exploited geological faults in the rock, the reason why the cliffs are so sheer.

The rock paintings and jardín botánico

Just south of the entrance to the canyon, huge sand dunes have been swept up by the strong winds that frequently howl across the Campo de Talampaya to the south. The higgledy-piggledy rocks at the foot of the cliffs host a gallery of white, red and black **rock paintings**, made by the Ciénaga and Aguada peoples who inhabited the area around a thousand years ago. The pictures include animals such as llamas, suris and pumas, a stepped pyramid, huntsmen and phallic symbols, and the nearby ink-well depressions in the rock are formed by decades of grinding and mixing pigments. There is a huge *tacu*, or carob tree, here, thought to be more than one thousand years old. Inside the canyon proper, the so-called **jardín botánico**, or more accurately the *bosquecillo* – thicket – is a natural grove of twenty or so different native cacti, shrubs and trees. They include *algarrobos*, *retamos*, *pencas*, *jarillas* and *chañares*, all labelled; occasionally grey foxes and small armadillos lurk in the undergrowth and brightly coloured songbirds flit from branch to branch. Nearby, and clearly signposted, is the **Chimenea** (chimney), also known as the Cueva (cave) or the Canaleta (drainpipe), a rounded vertical groove stretching all the way up the cliffside; guides revel in demonstrating its extraordinary echo, which sends condors flapping.

The rock formations

Wonderfully shaped formations in the park have been given imaginative names, mostly with a religious slant, but many of them do fit. **El Pesebre** (Crib) is a set of rocks supposed to resemble a Nativity scene, and appropriately nearby are **Los Reyes Magos**, the Three Kings, one of them on camel-back. A cluster of enormous needles and pinnacles is known as **La Catedral** – the intricate patterns chiselled and carved by thousands of years of erosion have been compared variously with Albi cathedral or the facade of Strasbourg cathedral, both built of a similar red sandstone. A set of massive rock formations is known as **El Tablero de Ajedrez**, or the Chessboard, complete with

6

rooks, bishops and pawns, while a 53m-high monolith, resembling a cowled human figure is El Cura, the Priest, or El Fraile, the Monk, depending on whom you ask. **El Pizarrón**, or the Blackboard, is 15m of flat rock-face of darker stone etched with more suris, pumas, guanacos and even a seahorse – suggesting that the peoples who lived here a thousand years ago had some kind of contact with the ocean.

ARRIVAL AND TOURS

By bus If you don't mind the walk, you could get a bus from La Rioja or San Juan to drop you off on the main road. **By organized tour** Private vehicles are not allowed into the park, so if you arrive here under your own steam you must choose between various guided tours. These should generally be arranged in advance, especially at busy times. Rolling Travel (☎ 03825 470397, ✆ talampaya.com) operates the two most commonly travelled vehicle circuits inside Talampaya, leaving roughly hourly, with the last tour of the day leaving an hour or so before the park's closure. Both circuits visit the main points of interest – the shorter is 2hr 30min and the longer 4hr 30min. Runacay (see p.384) offers

PARQUE NACIONAL TALAMPAYA

a variety of excellent walking circuits, which enable you to avoid congested minibuses and explore the park at a much more sedate pace, as well as getting into some of its lesser-known recesses. The local Cooperativa de Transporte Talampaya (☎ 03825 1566 2086, ✆ turismoentalampaya .com.ar) offers transfers from Villa Unión, plus tours to the Ciudad Perdida and Cañón Arco Iris sectors of the park.

By bike Mountain-bike tours are also possible – enquire at the entrance or contact the park guides' association (☎ 03822 1550 8816, ✉ sergiolei_guiatur @hotmail.com), but you need your own transport. Bring sun cream, headgear and water.

ACCOMMODATION AND EATING

Accommodation The closest (and very basic) accommodation to the park is in the village of Pagancillo, 27km north of the park entrance, which is served by a local bus from Villa Unión, but it is far preferable to stay in Villa Unión (see p.383). You can pitch a tent at the basic campsite

(☎ 03825 470397; $20) here, but bear in mind that it's often windy (and dusty) and can get extremely cold at night.

Eating There's a *confitería* serving simple, reasonably priced snacks and small meals, open during park hours.

Reserva Provincial Las Vicuñas and around

The **RESERVA PROVINCIAL LAS VICUÑAS** is nearly 150km northwest of Villa Unión, via the RN-76 and then a numberless track that twists and turns to the park's central feature, the wild and shallow **Laguna Brava**. The main attractions are fabulous altiplanic scenery – most of the terrain is at over 4000m – the magnificent, strikingly coloured mountainous backdrops and the abundant wildlife, mainly vicuñas, as the name suggests. Large flocks of this smaller cousin of the llama graze on the reserve's *bofedales*, the typical spongy marshes watered by trickles of run-off that freeze nightly. The best time to visit is in spring and autumn, since summer storms and winter blizzards cut off roads and generally impede travel.

Villa San José de Vinchina to the reserve

On the way to the reserve you pass through **Villa San José de Vinchina**, 65km north of Villa Unión, a nondescript village near which are six large, low, circular mounds. Made of a mosaic of pink, white and purple stones, these mysterious **Estrellas de Vinchina** form star-shapes and are thought to have had a ceremonial purpose for the pre-Columbian indigenous people of the area, perhaps serving as altars. Otherwise head on through the Quebrada de la Troya, a magnificent striped canyon, into the Valle Caguay, dominated by the majestic cone of Volcán Los Bonetes. From here the road is best negotiated in a 4WD – in any case it is wise to visit the reserve on an organized tour from Villa Unión (see p.383). You'll need to pull off the main road into **Alto Jagüe** to show your passport at the checkpoint and pay the park entrance fee ($25 per person plus $15 for the vehicle; ☎ 03825 1544 0879; don't forget to check back in when leaving the park so they know you're safe).

The track heads through to the southern banks of the Laguna Brava, a deep blue lake 17km by 10km, whose high potassium-chloride levels make it undrinkable. When it's blowing a gale, huge waves can be whipped up; when there is no wind, the mirror-like waters reflect the mountains behind. Behind stretches a panorama of 6000m peaks, including the enormous Pissis – the second highest volcano in the world (6793m). Other lakes in the reserve are the smaller Laguna Verde – a green lake as its name suggests – and the Laguna Mulas Muertas, often covered with pink flamingoes, Andean geese and other wildfowl. There's no public transport, no *guardería* and nowhere to stay: just you and the wilds.

La Rioja and around

LA RIOJA – or Todos los Santos de la Nueva Rioxa, as it was baptized at the end of the sixteenth century – is an indolent place, built in a flat-bottomed valley, watered by the Río Tajamar, 517km northeast of San Juan. It is not a sightseers' city, but you can find enough to occupy a full day if passing through. Among the highlights are two of the country's best **museums** of indigenous art, one archeological and the other with a folkloric slant. It is best visited in the spring (Oct–Nov), when the jacaranda trees are abloom, and the city is perfumed by the blossom of orange trees that have earned it the much-bandied sobriquet "Ciudad de los Naranjos". In spite of the plentiful shade of this luxuriant vegetation, the blistering summer heat is refracted off the brutally arid mountains looming to the west and turns the city, notoriously one of the country's hottest, virtually into a no-go zone. Whatever you do, avoid the midsummer, when temperatures can get up to 45°C.

Brief history

La Rioja came into being on May 20, 1591, when the governor of Tucumán, Juan Ramírez de Velasco, a native of La Rioja in Castile, founded the city in its strategic valley location. Today's main Plaza 25 de Mayo coincides exactly with the spot he chose. Ramírez de Velasco had set out on a major military expedition to populate

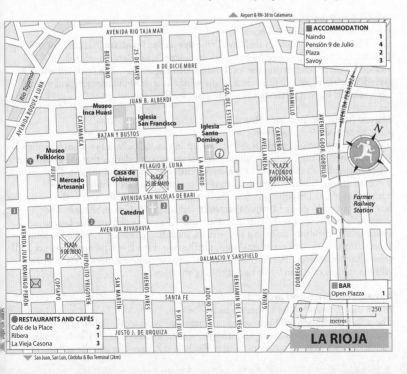

the empty spaces of the Viceroyalty and subdue the native Diaguitas, who had farmed the fertile oasis for centuries. La Nueva Rioxa, the only colonial settlement for leagues around, soon flourished and Ramírez de Velasco felt justified in boasting in a letter that it was "one of the finest cities in the Indies".

From it, mainly Franciscan missionaries set about fulfilling Ramírez de Velasco's other aim of converting the indigenous peoples. Their convent and that of the Dominicans, one of the oldest in Argentina, both miraculously survived the earthquake that flattened most of the old colonial city in 1894. The whole city was rebuilt, largely in a Neocolonial style that was intended to restore its former glory, but long decades of neglect by the central government were to follow. La Rioja did not even benefit as much as it hoped it would when Carlos Menem, scion of a major La Rioja wine-producing family was elected president in 1990. There are signs that La Rioja is beginning to diversify away from its agricultural base, although the city, with a current population of about 150,000, is still regarded by most Argentines as a rather arid backwater.

Catedral San Nicolás de Bari

Plaza 25 de Mayo • Daily 8am–9pm • Free

La Rioja's microcentro really is small and all the places of interest are grouped around the two main squares, Plaza 25 de Mayo, and, two blocks west and one south, Plaza 9 de Julio. On the west side of the former is the striking, white Casa de Gobierno, built in a Neocolonial style with a strong Andalucian influence, which contrasts with the **Catedral San Nicolás de Bari** on the south of the plaza. This Neoclassical hulk of a church, built at the beginning of the twentieth century in beige stone, with a huge Italianate cupola, Neo-Gothic campaniles and Byzantine elements in the facade, is primarily the sanctuary for a locally revered relic: a seventeenth-century walnut-wood image of St Nicholas of Bari, carved in Perú (kept locked in a side room; to see it, ask in the cathedral for the key).

Iglesia San Francisco

25 de Mayo and Bazán y Bustos • Daily 9am–noon & 5–9pm • Free

One block north of Plaza 25 de Mayo is the **Iglesia San Francisco** itself, an uninspiring Neoclassical building visited by St Francisco Solano, who played a key role in the sixteenth century converting the local indigenous population. The stark cell where he stayed, containing only a fine statue of the saint and a dead orange tree, said to have been planted by him, is treated as a holy place by Riojanos.

Museo Arqueológico Inca Huasi

Juan B. Alberdi 650 • Tues–Fri 9am–1pm & 4–8pm, Sat 9am–1pm • $2

The **Museo Arqueológico Inca Huasi** was set up in the 1920s by a Franciscan monk who was interested in the Diaguita culture – rather ironic, considering that the Franciscan missionaries did all they could in the seventeenth century to annihilate it. One of the pieces of art on display is a quite hideous seventeenth-century painting of the conversion of the Diaguita people by St Francisco Solano, but the rest of the exhibition is a fabulous collection of **Diaguita ceramics** and other pre-Columbian art. The dragon-shaped vase near the entrance is around 1200 years old; another later piece, inside one of the dusty cases, is a pot with an armadillo climbing it, while fat-bellied vases painted with, among other things, phalluses and toads – symbols of fertility and rain – line the shelves. The current director is striving to give a more pre-Christian context to the collection while not offending the friars.

Museo Folklórico and around

Pelagio B. Luna 811 • Tues–Fri 9am–1pm & 5–9pm, Sat & Sun 9am–1pm • $5

The wonderful **Museo Folklórico** contains a large display on local mythology; a set of beautiful terracotta statuettes representing the various figures brings to life the whole pantheon, such as Pachamama, or Mother Earth, and Zapam-Zucum, the goddess of children and the carob tree – she has incredibly elongated breasts the shape of carob-pods. Zupay is the equivalent of the Devil, while a series of characters called Huaira personify different types of wind. The museum also contains a reconstruction of a nineteenth-century Riojano house. Opposite, on the corner of Pelagio B. Luna and Catamarca, is one of the region's best **crafts markets** (Tues–Fri 8am–noon & 4–8pm, Sat & Sun 9am–1pm); the *artesanía*, all of it local, is of high quality, especially the regional *mantas*, or blankets.

Iglesia Santo Domingo

Pelagio B. Luna and Lamadrid • Daily 9am–noon & 5–9pm • Free

One block east of Plaza 25 de Mayo, the **Iglesia Santo Domingo** is the only building of interest to have survived the 1894 earthquake; it's one of the oldest buildings in Argentina, dating from 1623. The extremely long, narrow, white nave is utterly stark, apart from a fine altar decorated with seventeenth-century statuary, as is the simple whitewashed facade – but the carob-wood doors, carved by Indian craftsmen in the late seventeenth century, are a fine example of **mestizo art**.

6

ARRIVAL, INFORMATION AND TOURS

LA RIOJA AND AROUND

By plane La Rioja's small airport, Vicente Almandos Almonacid, is 7km east of town along RP-5 (☎0380 446 2160), and the only transport from it into town is by *remise*. There are flights to and from Buenos Aires daily except Sat (1hr 40min).

By bus The new bus terminal is some 2.5km south of the central Plaza 25 de Mayo, at Av F.O. de la Colina s/n (☎0380 446 8459; buses #2 or #8 to centre, $1.50), and serves the whole province plus other cities in the country.

Destinations Buenos Aires (6 daily; 14hr); Catamarca (20 daily; 2hr); Chilecito (4 daily; 3hr); Córdoba (hourly; 6hr 30min); Salta (21 daily; 10hr); San Juan (17 daily; 6hr); Valle Fértil (3 weekly; 4hr); Villa Unión (4 daily; 4hr).

Tourist information In the city centre, the provincial tourist office is at Pelagio B. Luna 345 (daily 8am–9pm; ☎0380 442 6384, ⓦturismolarioja.gov.ar).

Tours If you only have time for a day-tour to Talampaya or Ischigualasto, contact Ramón Pío Molina (☎0380 15 431 5674); Corona del Inca, Pelagio B. Luna 914 (☎03822 422142); or Terra Riojana, Lamadrid 93 (☎0380 442 0423).

ACCOMMODATION

You're unlikely to want to stay long in La Rioja, but it's good to know that it's not badly off for accommodation, covering the whole range with a few reliable options. Enquire about B&B-style *casas de familia*, the best bet at the budget end, at the tourist office.

Naindo San Nicolás de Bari and Joaquín Victor González ☎0380 447 0700, ⓦnaindoparkhotel.com. This sparkling five-star luxury hotel, comprising a modern plate-glass block stuck on top of a handsome Neocolonial mansion, offers comfortable if characterless rooms and has its own restaurant, a decent-sized pool and a well-stocked bar. **$850**

Pensión 9 de Julio Copiapó 197 ☎0380 442 6955. Your best bet for basic, budget accommodation. The leafy patio gives some atmosphere and the rooms are cramped but acceptably clean. Streetside rooms are extremely noisy, especially at weekends. **$160**

Plaza San Nicolás de Bari and 9 de Julio ☎0380 442 5215, ⓦplazahotel-larioja.com. Everything is squeaky clean, almost clinically so, but the rooms are smart and the roof-top pool and terrace enjoy views of the cathedral and mountains beyond. Its well-located *confitería* is one of the places to be seen in La Rioja. **$580**

Savoy San Nicolás de Bari and Av Roque A. Luna ☎0380 442 6894, ⓦhotelsavoylarioja.com.ar. This classic hotel is pulled down by its unimaginative neutral decor, but the staff are friendly and the rooms are quite spacious, with decent, functional bathrooms. **$350**

EATING AND DRINKING

Café de la Place Rivadavia and Hipólito Yrigoyen. One of the most strategically located places to have a drink or snack – the service is a bit nonchalant, and the decor is resolutely late 1990s, all brushed metal and diffused lighting. Daily 8am–late.

Open Piazza Rivadavia and F. Quiroga. A pub-bar with a summer terrace, men-in-black waiters and decent music, it serves delicious pizzas with a good range of toppings and a range of salads. Daily 11am–late.

Ribera Av Perón and Pelagio B. Luna ☎0380 446 0434. This is a classic pizzeria with decades of tradition but a polished, fresh setting set off by attractive wooden tables. Big pizzas start at $45. Daily noon–3pm & 7pm–midnight.

La Vieja Casona Rivadavia 427 ☎0380 442 5996. La Rioja's best *parrilla*, serving outstanding meat (around $80 per person) and delicious home-made pasta, with an excellent wine list from local bodegas. Daily 12.30–4pm & 7pm–1am.

The Lake District

LAGO ESPEJO

The Lake District

Argentina's Lake District – the northwestern wedge of Argentine Patagonia – is a land of picture-perfect glacial lakes surrounded by luxuriant forests, jagged peaks and extinct volcanoes. Not so long ago it was a wilderness controlled by indigenous peoples, but the undisputed modern capital, Bariloche, now sees annual invasions of Argentine and foreign holiday-makers. Thanks to excellent transport links, they descend on the town in droves year-round for the fresh air and outdoor adventures. The supposed lure is the alpine flavour of this "Argentine Switzerland" – a moniker borne out to some extent thanks to the Mitteleuropa-like setting, wooden chalet architecture and the region's breweries, dairies and chocolate shops. Yet the real attraction is the sheer unspoilt beauty of the goliath Parque Nacional Nahuel Huapi, the grandfather of all Argentina's national parks, packed with enough trekking and other outdoor activities to last any enthusiast weeks.

North of Bariloche is the upmarket resort of **Villa La Angostura**, and the stunning **Seven Lakes Route**, while to the south is the more alternative resort of **El Bolsón** and the splendid **Parque Nacional Los Alerces**, home to more fabulous lakes and ancient *alerce* trees. Further south still lurks a trio of curiosities: **Butch Cassidy's cabin**, the Welsh settlement of **Trevelin** and the historic railway at **La Trochita**.

In the northern swathes of the Lake District the main hub is family-oriented **San Martín de los Andes**, Bariloche's nearest regional rival, with an admirable lakefront location. Both it and neighbouring **Junín de los Andes** – renowned nationwide for its angling opportunities – are perfect bases for exploring the rugged **Parque Nacional Lanín**, whose focus is **Volcán Lanín**, a conical peak popular with mountaineers. **Neuquén**, the namesake capital of Argentina's only palindromically named province, is a pleasant enough city to relax in, but its indisputable draw has to be the nearby treasure-trove of giant dinosaur fossils, earning it the nickname of **Dinosaur Paradise**. In recent years vines have been planted with considerable success in the desert-like areas to the north and east of the city; **wineries** with dramatic names like Valle Perdido ("lost valley") and Bodega del Fin del Mundo ("winery at

HIKING CERRO CATEDRAL

Highlights

❶ Bariloche The region's principal town boasts plenty of amenities – plus it has some of the most handsome Lake District landscapes right on its doorstep. **See p.395**

❷ Lake District beer The El Bolsón and Blest breweries serve a variety of highly drinkable real ales from palest *rubia* to dark stout. **See p.399 & p.412**

❸ Cerro Catedral Whether you choose to hike it in summer, or ski it in winter, this peak in Nahuel Huapi park affords fabulous views of craggy mountains and rich blue lakes. **See p.404**

❹ Ruta de los Siete Lagos The scenic Seven Lakes Route swings past at least a dozen meres

whose waters range from deep ultramarine to delicate turquoise. **See p.408**

❺ La Trochita A much-loved steam-train that featured in Paul Theroux's *The Old Patagonian Express* – follow his example and take a trip down the memory tracks. **See p.415**

❻ Volcán Lanín Climb the slopes of a woodcut-perfect volcano that reigns over its namesake national park – or just admire the views from a peaceful lakeside vantage point. **See p.430**

❼ Giant dinosaurs Gawp up at some of the biggest dinosaur remains ever found or check out a clutch of unique titanosaur eggs – all within reach of Neuquén city. **See p.437**

HIGHLIGHTS ARE MARKED ON THE MAP ON P.394

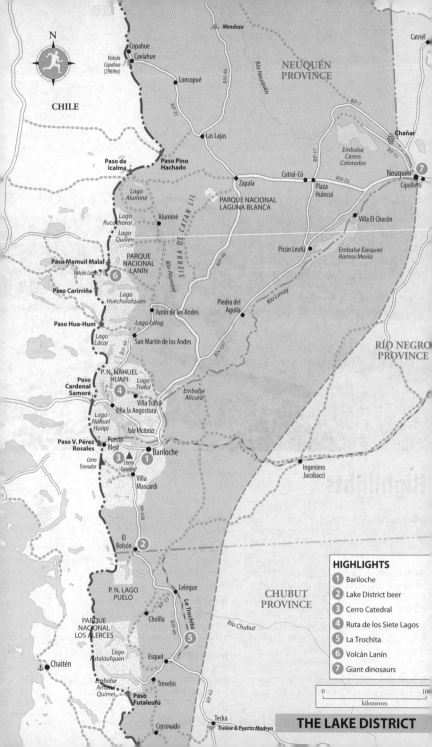

THE LAKE DISTRICT

HIGHLIGHTS

1 Bariloche
2 Lake District beer
3 Cerro Catedral
4 Ruta de los Siete Lagos
5 La Trochita
6 Volcán Lanín
7 Giant dinosaurs

0   100
kilometres

CHILE

NEUQUÉN PROVINCE

RÍO NEGRO PROVINCE

CHUBUT PROVINCE

Mendoza

Catriél

Copahue
Caviahue
Volcán Copahue (2969m)
Loncopué
Las Lajas
Chañar
Paso de Icalma
Paso Pino Hachado
Zapala
Cutral-Có
Plaza Huincul
Neuquén
Cipolletti
Lago Aluminé
Parque Nacional Laguna Blanca
Embalse Cerros Colorados
Lago Rucachoroi
Aluminé
Villa El Chocón
Lago Quillén
Picún Leufú
Embalse Ezequiel Ramos Mexia
Paso Mamuil Malal
Parque Nacional Lanín
Volcán Lanín
Paso Carirriñe
Lago Huechulafquen
Piedra del Aguila
Paso Hua-Hum
Junín de los Andes
Río Limay
Lago Lolog
Lago Lácar
San Martin de los Andes
Paso Cardenal Samoré
P. N. Nahuel Huapi
Lago Traful
Embalse Alicurá
Villa Traful
Villa la Angostura
Lago Nahuel Huapi
Isla Victoria
Paso V. Pérez Rosales
Puerto Blest
Bariloche
Cerro Tronador
Cerro Catedral
Villa Mascardi
Ingeniero Jacobacci
El Bolsón
Leleque
P. N. Lago Puelo
La Trochita
Cholila
Río Chubut
Parque Nacional Los Alerces
Lago Futalaufquen
Esquel
Chaitén
Embalse Amutui Quimei
Trevelin
Paso Futaleufú
Tecka
Trelew & Puerto Madryn
Corcovado

RN-40, RP-21, RP-17, RP-7, RP-51, RN-22, RN-237, RP-15, RN-62

the end of the world") have started making fabulous semillons and syrahs that you can go and taste on the premises.

GETTING AROUND THE LAKE DISTRICT

The Lake District is a popular Argentine tourist destination and served by generally excellent public transport links during the high season (roughly Christmas to Easter and the July–Sept ski season); buses are fewer out of season but most routes are still served, weather permitting. Consider renting a car if you want to visit some of the more off-the-beaten-path locations, such as Moquehue or the Chanar wineries.

Bariloche

The holiday capital of the Argentine South, **SAN CARLOS DE BARILOCHE** is one of those places that Argentines always tell you not to miss, the kind of hype that can easily lead to disappointment. Europeans familiar with the Alps – or North Americans or New Zealanders used to similar scenery – are unlikely to travel thousands of miles to see a simulacrum of Switzerland. Yet the city, the capital of Río Negro state, is undeniably worth the trip because it is the main base for visiting the stunningly pristine landscapes that surround it.

Bariloche, as it is nearly always called, rests up against the slopes of Cerro Otto, behind which rear the spire-tipped crests of the Cerro Catedral massif. Everything in Bariloche faces the mesmerizing Lago Nahuel Huapi, one of the scores of lakes that give the region its name, but something went massively wrong with the urban planning – the main road artery was built along the shore, severing the centre from the town's best feature. The **Parque Nacional Nahuel Huapi**, the prime reason for winging your way here, surrounds the town and you'll want to head out to discover its many treasures as soon as possible. The town's **beach** is narrow but pleasant enough and the views are predictably spectacular, but the water is cold even in summer.

The town's lifeblood is tourism, with getting on for a million visitors arriving annually. This is a place of secular pilgrimage for the nation's students, who flood here in January and February on their summer breaks, plus coachloads of young Israelis and Brazilians. None of these necessarily comes in search of the true mountain experience, but they often end up having one, pushed out of town by the inflated high-season prices of hotels and clubs. In winter, it's specifically the nearby **ski resort** of Cerro Catedral that draws the crowds. At peak times, in particular, the excesses of commercialization and crowds of tourists may spoil your visit. Nevertheless, the place does offer remarkably painless access to many beautiful and genuinely wild sections of the Andean cordillera, and out of season (May–June or Sept–Nov) the town is still big enough to retain some life of its own.

Brief history

Before the incursions of the Mapuche and Spanish, the area was the domain of indigenous tribes, whose livelihood largely depended on the lake and trade with their western, Mapuche, counterparts. The discovery of their mountain passes (the name Bariloche is derived from a native word meaning "people from beyond the mountains") became an obsession of early Spanish explorers in Chile, many of whom were desperate to hunt down the wealth of the mythical City of the Caesars. Knowledge of the passes' whereabouts was a closely guarded secret until the 1670s. The history of the non-autochthonous presence in the region really began when the Jesuit **Nicolás Mascardi** was dispatched by the Viceroy to found a **mission** around that time. The natives put paid to Mascardi and his successors and, in 1717, the mission was abandoned. The local indigenous groups took one Jesuit introduction more to their hearts than Christianity: the apple (*manzana*). Used for cider, wild apples became so popular that the region's Mapuche tribes became known as **Manzaneros**.

Modern Bariloche has its roots in the arrival of German settlers from southern Chile in the early twentieth century, but was tiny until the creation of the national park in 1937. In recent decades, the population has skyrocketed, and the town is now a major urban centre, though the homogeneity of its original alpine-style architecture has sadly been swamped by a messy conglomerate of high-rise apartment blocks. In 2011, the eruption of **volcano Pueyehue** in Chile, just over 90km from Bariloche, carpeted the surrounding area in ash. There were severe disruptions to flights as far as Buenos Aires for some months and the mess took time to clear up, with some people shutting up shop altogether and leaving town. By 2013, however, the volcano was slumbering again and life had largely returned to normal.

The centro cívico

Bariloche's focal point is the **centro cívico**, a set of buildings constructed out of timber and the local greenish-grey stone, resolutely facing the lake. Dating from 1939, it's a noble architectural statement by Ernesto de Estrada, who collaborated with Argentina's most famous architect, Alejandro Bustillo (after whom the main lakeside avenue is named), in the development of an alpine style that has come to represent the region. In the centre of the main plaza, around which these buildings are grouped, stands a graffiti-strewn equestrian **statue** of General Roca, whose horse looks suitably hangdog after the Campaign of the Desert. People bring Saint Bernards along, often with the obligatory cask around their necks, in readiness for photo opportunities at a small price. The pavement is adorned with painted white scarves, symbols of the Madres de la Plaza de Mayo (see p.63) and the names of local *desaparecidos*.

Museo de la Patagonia

Tues–Fri 10am–12.30pm & 2–7pm, Sat 10am–5pm • Free • ⓦ bariloche.com.ar/museo

Of the plaza's attractions, the most interesting is the **Museo de la Patagonia**, which also rates as one of the very best museums on things Patagonian, from wildlife to modern history. Look out for the caricature of Perito Moreno as a wet nurse guiding the infant Theodore Roosevelt on his trip through the Lake District in 1913. Superb, too, are the engraved Tehuelche tablet stones that experts speculate may have been protective amulets, Aónik'enk painted horse-hides and playing cards made of guanaco skin, one of the Mapuche's famous lances and Roca's own uniform.

Catedral Nuestra Señora del Nahuel Huapi

On the lake shore • Mon–Sat 8.30am–9pm, Sun 11.30am–9pm • Free

On the lake shore to the east of the Museo de la Patagonia is the Bustillo-designed **Catedral Nuestra Señora del Nahuel Huapi**, whose attractive stained-glass windows illustrate Patagonian themes such as the first Mass held by Magellan – the oppression of the indigenous peoples is clearly evident.

ARRIVAL AND DEPARTURE | BARILOCHE | 7

BY AIR

Bariloche's airport (☎0294 442 6162) is 14km east of town. Shuttle buses meet most flights and drop passengers off at their destination in town ($35). There are always *remises* hanging around (approx $90 to town), or you can take local bus #72, which runs every 2hr (7am–10pm).

Airlines Aerolíneas Argentinas, Mitre 185 ☎0294 443 3304; LADE, John O'Connor 214 ☎0294 442 3562.

Destinations Buenos Aires (6–8 daily; 2hr); Córdoba (1 daily; 2hr); Esquel (5 weekly; 30min); Mendoza (1 daily; 1hr 30min); Puerto Madryn (2 weekly; 3hr); Trelew (2 weekly; 1hr 15min).

BY BUS

The main bus terminal is next door to the train station, 3km east of the city centre along Av 12 de Octubre (RN-237). The best local buses for the centre are #10 or #20 (every 15–20min; 10min; $7, buy ticket in advance). Taxis to town from the terminal will cost around $40.

Destinations Buenos Aires (7 daily; 23hr); Córdoba (2 daily; 22hr); El Bolsón (10 daily; 2hr); Esquel (5 daily; 4hr 30min); Junín de los Andes (5 daily; 4hr); Mendoza (1 daily; 19hr); Neuquén (12 daily; 6hr); Puerto Madryn (1 daily; 14hr); Salta (2 daily; 39hr); San Martín de los Andes (7 daily; 4hr); Trelew (1 daily; 13–16hr); Villa La Angostura (hourly; 1hr); Villa Traful (1 daily; 2hr).

GETTING AROUND AND INFORMATION

By car Rental outlets include Avis, Av San Martín 162 (☎0294 443 1648), and Budget, Mitre 717 (☎0294 442 2482).

By bus You must buy bus tickets in advance from kiosks and supermarkets ($7 per journey); there is a kiosk next to the park *intendencia*. The exception is the "Catedral" bus, which you pay for on board ($10).

Tourist information Expect to queue in summer at the busy tourist office, in the centro cívico (daily 8am–9pm; ☎0294 442 9850, ⓦbarilochepatagonia.info). It keeps a

list of available accommodation.

Park information The *intendencia* of the Parque Nacional Nahuel Huapi is by the centro cívico at Av San Martín 24 (Mon–Fri 8am–5pm, Sat–Sun 10am–5pm; ☎0294 442 3111), which should be your first point of call if you are planning a visit to the park. A block behind is the Club Andino Bariloche, at 20 de Febrero 30 (daily 8am–8pm; ☎0294 442 2266, ⓦclubandino.org), which can offer more detailed information on trekking routes.

ACTIVITIES AND TOURS AROUND BARILOCHE

A host of tour agencies offer **activities** in the surrounding region. Exploring the rivers and lakes via raft and boat is popular, as is fishing. Rafting can be arranged at Aguas Blancas, Morales 564 (☎0294 443 2799, ⓦaguasblancas.com.ar), and other trips of various stripes at Del Lago Turismo, Mitre 660 (☎0294 443 0056, ⓦdellagoturismo.com.ar), and Turisur, Mitre 219 (☎0294 442 6109, ⓦturisur.com.ar). If you prefer to take to the water in a kayak, try Senzalimiti, Julio Cortazar 5050 (☎0294 452 0597, ⓦslimiti.com). Inland, you can rent mountain bikes at Dirty Bikes, Lonquimay 3908 (☎0294 444 2775). Bikes for doing the Circuito Chico (see p.402) are best rented at Bike Cordillera, Av Bustillo Km18.6 (☎0294 452 4828, ⓦcordillerabike.com).

ACCOMMODATION

Accommodation in Bariloche is plentiful but pricey, and you should reserve in advance throughout the year for the cheaper options, which fill rapidly – and in high season for all accommodation.

DOWNTOWN

La Bolsa del Deporte Palacios 405 ☎ 0294 442 3529, ⓦ labolsadeldeporte.com.ar. Excellent wooden cabin-style hostel with thirty beds and good attention to detail (eg bunk-bed reading lights). Kitchen facilities and internet access available. Dorms $80, doubles $280

El Gaucho Belgrano 209 ☎ 0294 452 2464, ⓦ hostel elgaucho.com. Recently renovated backpacker strong-hold, this is a basic but essentially good hostel for budget travellers. Dorms and double rooms are available, as is excellent information on local excursions. Dorms $90, doubles $160

La Pastorella Av Belgrano 127 ☎ 0294 442 4656. Tasteful French decor gives this place a homely feel. Rooms are tidy and spacious but lack the charm of the rest of the hotel. There's a small tranquil garden and free parking. $280

★ **Periko's Hostel** Morales 555 ☎ 0294 452 2326, ⓦ perikos.com. Best of the youth-hostel-type accommodation, this excellent, well-built and well-run place is loaded with information about trips. Reserve well in advance. Dorms $90, doubles $280

Piuké Beschtedt 136 ☎ 0294 442 3044. An attractive chalet-style hotel with flowery gardens just a block from the cathedral. Rooms are simple but comfortable and breakfast is included. $300

Plaza Vice Almirante O'Connor 431 ☎ 0294 442 4100, ⓦ hotelplazabariloche.com.ar. Nothing flashy, but good value for its lakeside location. A simple breakfast is included, served in the dining room with panoramic views over the lake and cathedral. Popular with students, particularly in the winter. $200

Tirol Libertad 175 ☎ 0294 442 6152, ⓦ hoteltirol.com .ar. Ideally located a block from the centro cívico, this is a modern but tastefully decorated hotel. Rates include breakfast served in a dining room with stunning lake views – the huge glass windows will shield you from any cold wind blowing from the lake. $500

AROUND THE LAKE

Avenida Bustillo runs for 25km along the lake shore to Puerto Pañuelo (served by bus #10) and is packed, at least for the first dozen kilometres, with bungalows and cabins, some of which have sensational lake views, though most have been gentrified in the worst possible taste; below is a small selection of some of the best, along with one or two places to stay a little farther afield.

Aldebaran Av Bustillo Km20.4 ☎ 0294 444 8678, ⓦ aldebaranpatagonia.com. Named after one of the brightest stars in the night sky, this hotel stands out for its stunning lakeside location, its spacious understated rooms and the original decor, which continues the astronomical theme. All rooms enjoy breathtaking views of the mountains and lake. US$290

Alun Nehuen Av Bustillo Km32 ☎ 0294 444 8005, ⓦ alunnehuenbariloche.com.ar. This slightly old-fashioned lakeside hotel boasts spectacular views; you can fish or take a boat trip from its dock. Big discounts offered in the low season. B&B $600, full board $900

Cabañas del Arroyo Av Bustillo Km4050 ☎ 0294 444 2082, ⓦ delarroyo.com.ar. Comfortable and functional cabins, with well-equipped kitchens, in a convenient location, situated over the *arroyo* (brook) that gives them their name, providing natural cooling on hot summer days. $620

★ **Casco** Av Bustillo Km11.5 ☎ 0294 446 3131, ⓦ hotel elcasco.com/es. Belonging to one of the country's leading art dealers, this fabulous hotel, whose grounds are lapped by the lake's waters, is like staying in a private art gallery – indeed, the mouthwatering works, mostly by native artists of the highest calibre, are on sale. Every detail refers back to this arty theme, without becoming heavy-handed; even the cocktails at the bar are inspired by specific painters and their palettes. US$200

Charming Luxury Lodge and Private Spa Hua Huan 7549, Av Bustillo Km7.5 ☎ 0294 446 2889, ⓦ charming -bariloche.com. The name says it all: it is charming and luxurious, and each room has its own private spa, with jacuzzi, sauna, steam bath, aromatherapy and chromo-therapy. It's pricey, though. US$360

★ **Estancia Peuma Hue** Entrance RN-40 Km2014 towards El Bolsón ☎ 0294 445 7349, ⓦ peuma-hue.com. Aptly named (it means "place of dreams" in Mapundungun), *Peuma Hue* is idyllically located at the head of the sapphire Lago Gutiérrez, and offers supreme comfort, exquisite and well-balanced food and the possibility of kayaking, horse-riding, birdwatching, walking or just lapping up the beauty of the place. The owner and staff are helpful and friendly. $2220

Hostería Lonquimay Lonquimay 3672, Barrio Melipal ☎ 0294 444 3450, ⓦ hosterialonquimay.blogspot.com. Nicely appointed chalet-style hotel with an intimate feel not far from the Cerro Otto chairlift. Breakfast included. $300

Llao Llao Av Bustillo Km28 ☎ 02944 448530, ⓦ llao llao.com. One of Argentina's most famous hotels, designed and built (twice) by Alejandro Bustillo along the lines of an enormous Canadian cabin (see p.402). Excellent views and services, including indoor and outdoor pools, a golf course and even a presidential suite. US$220

La Selva Negra Av Bustillo Km2.95 ☎ 0294 444 1013. A campsite within easy reach of the city, whose facilities include above-average bathrooms, a bar and café, wi-fi and the use of stoves. $80

EATING

Bariloche has a large and excellent selection of places to eat, most within walking distance of the centre. Calle Mitre is also lined with stores selling local specialities such as chocolate – including penguins and St Bernard dogs – smoked trout, ice cream and *alfajores*. Catering for large numbers of tourists, restaurants tend to have extended opening hours, with lunch from noon until past 3pm and dinner 7.30pm to past midnight.

El Boliche de Alberto Villegas 347 ☎0294 443 1433 and Av Bustillo 8800 ☎0294 446 2285. The juiciest and largest (and not the priciest) *parrillas* in town: prepare to gorge yourself – and to wait for a table (reservations not accepted). Also runs a pasta restaurant under the same name at Elflein and Villegas for a respite from meat. Daily noon–3pm & 7.30pm–midnight.

Covita O'Connor 511 ☎0294 442 1708. Small, wholesome vegetarian and fish restaurant that does a good-value $50 lunch with plentiful food and a glass of elderflower or raspberry juice. Mon–Thurs noon–3pm, Fri & Sat noon–3pm and 8–11pm.

Dias de Zapata Morales 362 ☎0294 442 3128. Mexican-run Mexican restaurant, so you're guaranteed the real deal. Portions are large, moderately priced and of high quality. Daily noon–3pm & 8pm–late.

La Esquina Urquiza and Perito Moreno ☎0294 442 8900. Corner by name and corner café by nature, this popular local haunt is a good place to have a drink and while away the time with a newspaper or book at outdoor tables sheltered from the summer sun. Daily 8am–1am.

Familia Weiss Palacios and O'Connor ☎0294 443 5789. A perennial hit with visitors, especially for its *ciervo a la cazadora* (venison in a creamy mushroom sauce) or *picada* selection of smoked specialities. Moderate prices. Daily 8pm–3am.

Friends Mitre and Rolando ⊛friendsbariloche.com. Well suited for night owls with the munchies. Burgers, pizzas, beers and spirits are served, all at competitive prices. Daily 24hr.

La Marmite Mitre 329 ☎0294 442 3685. Not a bargain by any means, the intimate, old-fashioned *Marmite* is nonetheless worthwhile for its regional and Swiss specialities, especially its fondues. Daily noon–4pm & 8pm–midnight.

Vegetariano 20 de Febrero 730 ☎0294 442 1820. If you've had your fill of *parrillas* this excellent mid-range veggie restaurant will provide relief. Vegans beware though – most dishes contain egg and dairy products, and there are also fish dishes. Mon–Fri noon–3pm & 8–11pm, Sat noon–3pm.

DRINKING AND NIGHTLIFE

With the constant influx of Argentine students mixing with an onslaught of thirsty backpackers, Bariloche has a lively *movida*. **Bars** are scattered around town but the majority of the action is in the area between Elflein and the waterfront. However, drinking can be expensive – plan on spending about a third more than elsewhere in Argentina in the trendiest bars, while many **discos** charge $50-plus entry fee for non-Argentines.

Antares Elflein 47 ☎0294 443 1454. Bar/restaurant with a wide variety of Austrian-style homebrews on tap. Beer is included in some of the dishes on the menu – such as the venison stew with stout – and "minipints" are even served with desserts. Daily 7pm–late; happy hour 7–8.30pm.

★ **Blest Microcervecería** Av Bustillo Km11.6 ☎0294 446 1026. This out-of-town microbrewery has an excellent selection of very good home-made brews – its potent strawberry beer is worth sampling as are all the ales. It also serves moderately priced meals, mostly with a Germanic flavour. Daily noon–1am.

Grisu Av Juan Manuel de Rosas 574 ☎0294 442 2269, ⊛grisubariloche.com.ar. Disco pumping out Latin and pop music, popular with Argentine tourists. Sat 10pm–late.

Roket Av Juan Manuel de Rosas 424 ☎0294 443 1940, ⊛roket.com. The best club in town, spread over three floors, featuring dance DJs of various stripes with top-notch acoustics and lighting. Fri & Sat 10pm–late; closed March–Nov.

Wilkenny Irish Pub San Martín 435 ☎0294 442 4444. Wannabe Irish bar that's the most famous party pub in Patagonia. Drinks are not cheap, although happy hour on selected drinks brings the price down a bit. Daily 7pm–late; happy hour 7–9pm.

DIRECTORY

Banks and exchange Bank hours vary depending on season: April–Nov 9am–2pm; Dec–March 8am–1pm. Banco de la Nación, Mitre 178; Banco Francés, San Martín 336; Banco de Galicia, Moreno 77; Cambio Sudamericana, Mitre 63.

Laundry Patagonia, Palacios 191.
Post office Moreno 175 (Mon–Fri 8.30am–1pm & 4–7pm, Sat 9am–1pm).

Parque Nacional Nahuel Huapi

Neuquén–Río Negro border • Open park border • $50 entrance fee charged at various points within

The main goal of any trip to Bariloche is to see the natural wonders contained within the **PARQUE NACIONAL NAHUEL HUAPI**. The doyen of the Argentine national park system rewards **trekkers** of all degrees of stamina and hardiness with a highly developed infrastructure of trails and refuges, while a plethora of lakes, waterfalls, boat trips and chairlifts will entertain anyone not so keen on hiking.

Protecting a glorious chunk of the Andean cordillera and its neighbouring steppe, most of the park falls within the watershed of the immense **Lago Nahuel Huapi**, an impressive expanse of water that can seem benign one moment and a froth of seething whitecaps the next. Of glacial origin, it's 557 square kilometres in area, but highly irregular in shape with peninsulas, islands and attenuated, fjord-like tentacles that sweep down from the thickly forested border region. The lake's name comes from Mapuche for Isle (*huapi*) of the Tiger (*nahuel*) and refers to the jaguars that once inhabited regions even this far south. Heavy rainfall permits the growth of temperate rainforest and species such as the *alerce*, here at the northernmost extent of its range in Argentina. Other species typical of the sub-Antarctic Patagonian forests also flourish: giant *coihues*, *lengas* and *ñire* among others. The dominant massif of the park is an extinct volcano, **Cerro Tronador**, whose three peaks straddle the Argentine–Chilean border in the south. Glaciers slide off its heights in all directions, though all are in a state of alarmingly rapid recession.

Snow can fall as late as December and as early as March at higher altitudes: it's not advisable to hike certain trails outside the high season. Bear in mind the area is a long way west of Buenos Aires despite being in the same time zone, so the sun is overhead in summer closer to 3pm, rather than midday. Average temperatures are 18°C in summer and 2°C in winter. The strongest winds blow in spring, which is otherwise a good time to visit, as is the calmer autumn, when the deciduous trees wear their spectacular late-season colours.

VISITING THE PARQUE NACIONAL NAHUEL HUAPI

THE CENTRAL ZONE

The most visited sites within the central zone, around Lago Nahuel Huapi, lie within easy reach of Bariloche. The numerous excursions available from here can be roughly divided into two categories, land and water, with the town's travel agents (see box, p.397) offering more or less identical packages and prices, though you may prefer to do it at your own pace on public transport or by private car. One popular excursion heads to Isla Victoria, the elongated, thickly forested island northwest of the city, and then on to the Bosque de los Arrayanes (see p.408), which can also be reached from the exclusive upmarket resort of Villa La Angostura (see p.406). At the western end of Brazo Blest, the outpost of Puerto Blest is surrounded by some of the park's most impressive forest, where a scenic trail takes you to the Cascada Los Cántaros, a series of waterfalls in the forest.

THE SOUTHERN ZONE

It is in the south where you'll find most of the longer and more mountainous treks, either around Cerro Catedral or Pampa Linda; again, Bariloche can be used as a base. A dirt road runs south for 3km to Puerto Alegre at the northern

---

WILDLIFE IN THE PARQUE NACIONAL NAHUEL HUAPI

Nahuel Huapi park has abundant **birdlife**, with species such as the Magellanic woodpecker, the green-backed firecrown, the ground-dwelling Chucao tapaculo and the Austral parakeet. You'll hear mention of rare **fauna** such as the *huemul* (see box, p.419) and the *pudú*, though you have only a slightly greater chance of seeing them than you do of spying Nahuelito, Argentina's answer to the Loch Ness monster. Animals that make their home in the steppe regions of the park (guanaco, rheas and foxes) are more easily seen. Of the non-native species, the most conspicuous are the **red deer** (*ciervo colorado*) and the **wild boar** (*jabalí*), introduced by hunt-loving settlers. In an effort to cull their numbers, the authorities issue shooting permits, which continue to serve as a source of revenue for the park – expect to see roast boar and venison carpaccio on many a local menu.

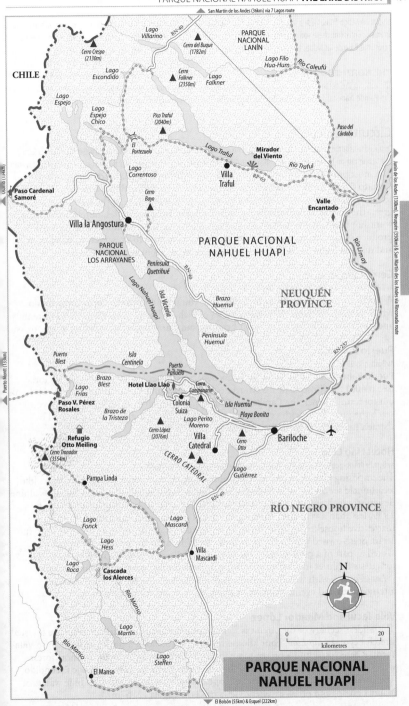

PARQUE NACIONAL
NAHUEL HUAPI

end of tiny Lago Frías, with a launch crossing the lake daily to Puerto Frías: from here you can cross to Chile or hike south across the Paso de las Nubes towards the southern zone.

THE NORTHERN ZONE

The zone to the north of Lago Nahuel Huapi, bordering on the Parque Nacional Lanín, centres around Lago Traful. Its big attraction is the Seven Lakes Route, which runs from Villa La Angostura to San Martín de los Andes (see p.420). *Guardaparques* stationed at points along the route are helpful when it comes to recommending day-treks in their particular sectors. The *Guía Sendas & Bosques de Lanín y Nahuel Huapi* is a very useful guide (in Spanish only) and comes with two reasonably reliable maps (1:200,000) of the region.

Circuito Chico

Organized tours do the circuit (4 hr; $90) or bus #20 goes to Cerro Campanario, Puerto Pañuelo and *Llao Llao* and #10 or #11 to Colonia Suiza. To do it by bike, take the bus and get off at Av Bustillo Km18.6, from where you can rent a bike (see p.397); this cuts out the initial traffic-heavy part

The most popular, if not the most exciting, excursion from Bariloche is the short **Circuito Chico**, a 65km road course that follows Avenida Bustillo westwards. The first ten or so kilometres of the circuit are underwhelming: although the lake views are great, they are accompanied by a steady stream of twee boutiques, hotels, restaurants, workshops and factory outlets for cottage industries. It's great for buying regional produce – you can get everything from woollen sweaters to preserves, smoked trout and meats, ceramics, chocolates and wood-carvings – but for very little else.

Cerro Campanario

Av Bustillo Km17.5 • Chairlift daily 9am–6.30pm • $60 return

A chairlift or stiff thirty-minute climb takes you up 200m to the **Cerro Campanario**, which offers panoramic 360-degree views of Nahuel Huapi, *Llao Llao*, Cerro Catedral and more – a good way to get your bearings and warm up before tackling longer treks.

Puerto Pañuelo

Av Bustillo Km25

Puerto Pañuelo is the location for boats departing for excursions to the Isla Victoria (see p.406), the Bosque de los Arrayanes (see p.408) and Puerto Blest (see p.406). Look out for a tiny chapel, the **Capilla San Eduardo**, on the left-hand side just before you reach the port. Built with cypress and tiled with *alerce* shingles, it was designed by Estrada under the supervision of Bustillo.

Hotel Llao Llao

Av Bustillo Km28 • Booking essential for guided tours • Free • ☎ 02944 448530, ⓦ llaollao.com

The imposing **Llao Llao**, one of Argentina's most famous hotels (see p.398), looks like a carbuncle set on top of a verdant knoll from below, though Alejandro Bustillo's alpine design strangely improves the closer you get. The original building burnt down in 1939, less than a year after completion, in a closed-season blaze caused by an inattentive housekeeper. The forests were plundered again, and the hotel reopened in 1940. State-owned until 1991, it is now owned by a private company and can be visited as part of a **guided tour**. The sensational views are worth a hike up alone, but for guests facilities include an indoor pool, gym, tennis courts and a fine restaurant – *Los Césares* – with superbly cooked regional cuisine. The restaurant is open for afternoon tea and evening dinner to nonguests – reservations are a must.

Villa Tacul and Mirador López

The wildest scenery of the circuit is found along the road that runs through the forested stretch beyond *Llao Llao*. Four kilometres beyond the hotel a track heads north to **Villa Tacul**, where you'll find a pretty, sandy beach. There are also a couple of short forest walks, one around Cerro Llao Llao, the other between *Llao Llao* and **Lago Escondido**. The latter walk brings you to **Mirador López**, which overlooks the deep blue waters of Nahuel Huapi and offers excellent views of **Cerro Capilla** (2167m).

TREKKING IN PARQUE NACIONAL NAHUEL HUAPI

To say **Parque Nacional Nahuel Huapi** is an ideal destination for **trekking** would be a sizeable understatement. Myriad spectacular trails lace the park, though its principal trekking region is the sector southwest of Bariloche, where the two foremost points of interest are **Cerro Catedral** and the **Pampa Linda** area, southeast of Cerro Tronador.

THE TREKS

In the **Cerro Catedral** area, a popular one- or two-day hike takes you to **Refugio Frey**, reached by taking the ski lift to Refugio Lynch and then a rocky traverse (4hr); the terrain is wearing on the legs but the spectacular mountain vistas make it worthwhile. You can make it a circular trek by descending through magical forest and meadow back to the base of the lift in Villa Catedral (4hr). In the **Pampa Linda** sector the classic hike is to **Refugio Otto Meiling**, above even the summer snowline and with views of Cerro Tronador, where you can stay or camp. Much less frequented is the trek to **Refugio Tronador**, also with great views, usually done as a three-day hike, overnighting near the Chilean *carabineros*. You'll need a permit from both the Pampa Linda *guardaparque* and the nearby *gendarmaría*, since the trek takes you into Chile. The Club Andino also runs its own trekking tour to Pampa Linda (summer 8.30am, runs on demand; $250, book in advance), which visits the Ventisquero glacier and then takes you on a guided 4.5-hour trek.

As a rule, trails or *sendas* to refuges are well marked; the high-mountain trails (*sendas de alta montaña*) are not always clearly marked, though, while the less-frequented paths (*picadas*) are not maintained on a regular basis, and close up with vegetation from time to time.

PRACTICALITIES

Before you set out, you should visit the Club Andino Bariloche (see p.397), which has extensive info and sells trekking **maps**. It is also obligatory to fill out a *registro de trekking* at the *guardaparque* station on entering the park and to check out again before leaving. The **trekking season** is basically between December and March, but you should always heed weather conditions and come prepared for unseasonal snowfalls. An impressive network of well-run **refuges** ($90–100 per person; reservations not possible) makes trekking appealing: you'll need to bring a sleeping bag, but can buy **meals** and basic supplies en route. In high season, refuges and trails in the more popular areas can get very busy so carry a tent with you. There are authorized **camping sites**, but you need to get a camping **permit** from the *intendencia* or any *guardaparque* in order to use them; the park has suffered a series of devastating **fires** in recent years, so restrictions have tightened up and you must now carry your own stove for cooking. **Campsites** include: *Lago Roca* (☎0294 4443 0154) near the Cascada Los Alerces; *Los Rápidos* (☎0294 446 1861) at Lago Mascardi; and *Los Vuriloches* (☎0294 4446 1861) at Pampa Linda.

At Pampa Linda there's more luxurious **accommodation** at *Hostería Pampa Linda* (☎0294 449 0517, ⓦhosteriapampalinda.com.ar; closed May & June; $840 half-board). Nearby there's also upmarket *Hotel Tronador*, at the northwestern end of Lago Mascardi (☎0294 444 1062, ⓦhoteltronador.com; closed May–Oct; $720 full board).

7

Colonia Suiza

The last point of call on the circuit is **Colonia Suiza**, a pretty village originally settled by Swiss immigrants. There's nothing particular to see here, but it's a good place for gorging yourself on *curanto*, a sort of stew of mussels, meat and vegetables, prepared in a pit with hot stones in the village centre twice a week (Wed & Sun 11am; ☎0294 444 8605).

Circuito Grande

Renting a car is the ideal way to do the Circuito Grande, though full-day organized tours ($235) are also available

The **Circuito Grande** is a 240km loop that leads east out of Bariloche on the RN-237 past the incredible rock formations of the **Valle Encantado** ("Enchanted Valley"). Here you'll see pine forests lining the steep valley outcrops and stone fingers pointing skywards while the blue waters of the Río Limay flow below. The Río Traful joins the Río Limay at Confluencia, 70km from Bariloche. Here the RN-237 continues on towards Neuquén while the RP-65 turns northwest towards Villa Traful. Past the lake, at El Portezuelo pass, the circuit joins the southern section of the Ruta de los Siete Lagos (see p.408) near Lagos Correntoso and Espejo, and then returns southwards to Bariloche via Villa La Angostura. Alternatively, you could turn right when you meet the Ruta de los Siete Lagos and head to San Martín de los Andes (see p.420).

Cerro Catedral

Cable car daily 9.30am–4.45pm • $120 return • Buses (marked "Catedral") leave from Moreno 470 in Bariloche to Villa Catedral; alternatively, you could take a half-day organized trip to the village ($90; 4hr 30min)

Some 20km south of Bariloche is **Cerro Catedral**, named after the Gothic steeples of rock that make up its craggy summit (2405m). In summer, the village of **Villa Catedral**, at the foot of the bowl, is the starting-point for a couple of fantastic treks up and around Cerro Catedral (see box, p.403), though you could just take a cable car and then a chairlift to reach Refugio Lynch near the summit (1870m). A short but steep climb takes you to the ridge, where the views are superb, and you just might catch a glimpse of condors.

Lago Mascardi and Cerro Tronador

Day-tours ($150–250) are run by several travel agents, with some also offering the possibility of a boat trip on Lago Mascardi

In 2003, the path of the famous RN-40 (see box, p.488) was diverted to head through Nahuel Huapi rather than its original less-scenic route further east, although some maps still show the old route numbers (RN-258 and 237). Leading south from Bariloche, it goes past handsome **Lago Gutiérrez** to the southernmost point on **Lago Mascardi**, where a dirt road strikes west around the lake shore and you must pay the park entrance fee. Further along, at Los Rápidos (where there's an organized campground), the road forks. Both roads here become single-track, necessitating a timetable for travelling in each direction; check with the tourist office before setting out, as this changes seasonally. One fork takes you west along the southern Río Manso to Lago Hess and the Cascada de los Alerces – a 20m plunge of white water that is said to resemble a seated nineteenth-century lady with her dress spread out. The other fork takes you north

---

SKIING IN THE LAKE DISTRICT

Along with Las Leñas (see p.363), Bariloche and the Lake District is Argentina's premier **ski destination**, packed in the winter with ski and snowboard fans from Argentina, Brazil and further afield. While it does get busy in peak season (July & Aug), the quality of the powder, infrastructure and après-ski is very good, with Bariloche acting as a hub for the surrounding area. The main ski resort is **Cerro Catedral** (ⓦ catedralaltapatagonia.com) served by Villa Catedral at its base, with plenty of accommodation, equipment rental, restaurants, comfortable lifts and easy access to the après-ski in nearby Bariloche – not to mention outstanding views. There are 67km of runs in all, of varying grades of difficulty, some with descents of up to 4km in length. Other resorts in the area include the smaller, more upmarket **Cerro Bayo** (ⓦ cerrobayoweb.com) 10km east of Villa La Angostura (see p.406), and **La Hoya** (ⓦ skilahoya .com) some 13km northeast of Esquel (see p.413), a low-key family centre with moderately challenging pistes, nine lifts and good powder.

For five days in August, Bariloche celebrates the **Fiesta Nacional de la Nieve**, with ski races, parades and a torchlit evening descent on skis to open the season officially, although the season actually lasts from around mid-June to mid-October. If you want the probability of good snow conditions but prefer quieter slopes, go in September.

towards **Pampa Linda**, with terrific views of the glaciers on **Cerro Tronador**. The "thundering" in its Spanish name refers to the echoing roar heard when vast chunks of ice break off the hanging glaciers and plunge down to the slopes below. The road goes on to the Ventisquero Negro lookout, a moraine-encrusted glacier and offshoot of Glaciar del Manso on the upper slopes of Cerro Tronador. Some tours include short walks to the 50m-high Saltillo de las Nalcas or Garganta del Diablo, while there are plenty of longer hiking options from Pampa Linda itself (see box, p.403).

Isla Victoria

Trips run by Turisur twice daily · $280 plus $70 transfer from Bariloche and $15 port tax

A very popular boat trip within the park heads to **Isla Victoria** from **Puerto Pañuelo** (see p.402), where there are rock paintings, beaches and a chairlift to Cerro Bella Vista with the requisite stunning views. The boat then continues north to the Bosque de los Arrayanes (see p.408).

Puerto Blest

Trips run by Turisur twice daily · $280 plus $70 transfer from Bariloche and $15 port tax

Less crowded than the Isla Victoria boat but equally worthwhile, the boat-and-bus excursion to **Puerto Blest** in the western fringes of the Parque Nacional Huapi takes in lake vistas along the way and starts with a 75-minute boat trip from Puerto Pañuelo. A minibus continues the trip to the shores of Lago Frías, with its peppermint-coloured waters. During the early morning and late afternoon you can see condors gathering at their nearby roost. Returning to Puerto Blest, the boat crosses the channel to dock on the north shore, after which there is a forty-minute stroll to the stepped Cascada Los Cántaros waterfall.

Villa La Angostura

Spread along the northern lake-shore of Nahuel Huapi, **VILLA LA ANGOSTURA** has grown enormously in the past decade, capitalizing on the Lake District's surging popularity. The settlement originally swelled owing to its proximity to the trout-fishing at Río Correntoso, one of the world's shortest rivers, but today caters mostly to upper-end tourists, with whole new areas of wooded hills giving way to luxury hotels, cabins and spas. The almost ubiquitous log-cabin architecture can feel a bit forced, rather like a mountain-village theme park, and the constant flow of traffic rather ruins the peace. However, it is smaller than Bariloche, has some top-notch accommodation (though not many budget options), and provides the only land access to **Parque Nacional Los Arrayanes** (see p.408).

The town sprawls along the lakeside, with the centre known as **El Cruce**. Avenida Arrayanes transects the town; everything you are likely to need during your stay is concentrated in a 200m stretch between Boulevard Nahuel Huapi and Cerro Bayo. The park is reached by crossing the isthmus at **La Villa**, a 3km-long peninsula west of the centre – the old harbour.

Other than visiting the park or going on fishing trips, you can get good views from the summit of **Cerro Bayo**, 10km east from the centre of Villa Angostura; you can hike up in summer but you'll need a guide – ask at the tourist office. Another good local hike (or short drive) is to **Mirador Belvedere** and Cascada Inacayal, a delightful waterfall, both along the southeast shore of Lago Correntoso.

ARRIVAL AND DEPARTURE   **VILLA LA ANGOSTURA**

By bus The cute wooden bus station (☎ 0294 449 4961) is just off Av Arrayanes at Av Siete Lagos. Empresa 15 de Mayo

(☎ 0294 449 5104) runs seven daily buses between La Villa and El Cruce. Quetrihue (Inacayal 13 1st floor, Villa

La Angostura ☎ 0294 449 4803) does transfers to Bariloche airport ($180), while Bariloche agencies offer day-trips to Villa La Angostura (around $200).

Destinations Bariloche (approx hourly; 1 hr); San Martín de los Andes (5 daily; 2hr 30min).

INFORMATION AND ACTIVITIES

Tourist information The tourist office is opposite the bus station (daily 8am–9pm; ☎ 0294 449 4124, ⓦ villa laangostura.gov.ar), which can help find accommodation if you haven't made reservations in advance.

Bike rental Bikes can be rented at Aquiles, Av Arrayanes 96 (☎ 0294 449 4303).

Activities Fishing can be organized through Banana Fly, at Av Arrayanes 282 (☎ 0294 449 4634), while horseriding is offered by Cabalgatas Correntoso, Cacique Antriao (☎ 0294 15 451 0559, ⓦ cabalgatacorrentoso.com.ar). Patagonia Sailing (☎ 0294 15 461 9781, ⓦ patagoniasailing.com.ar) runs sailing trips, from 1hr to a full day, on Nahuel Huapi lake for small groups.

ACCOMMODATION

The most affordable accommodation in Villa La Angostura tends to be in El Cruce, with more upmarket choices in the northern and southern suburbs – prices increase as the lake view improves.

La Angostura Barbagelata 157 ☎ 0294 449 4834, ⓦ hostellaangostura.com.ar. The best and most central hostel, two blocks from the bus station, with modern and tastefully designed four- to six-bed dorms, two double rooms and a pleasant communal area. Dorms $90, doubles $290

Las Balsas Bahía Las Balsas s/n ☎ 0294 449 4309, ⓦ lasbalsas.com. Part of the Relais et Chateaux group, *Las Balsas* epitomizes Angostura, renowned for its sybaritic qualities: beautiful rooms, a relaxing spa and a perfect location, though the restaurant is disappointing. US$350

Camping Unquehué Av Siete Lagos 727 ☎ 0294 449 4103, ⓦ campingunquehue.com.ar. The most convenient campsite, 500m west of the bus terminal. $72

Correntoso Av Siete Lagos 4505 ☎ 0294 15 461 9727, ⓦ correntoso.com. Overlooking Río Correntoso, the settlement's original fishing lodge, dating from 1917, has completely renovated before reopening in 2003. Making the most of its spectacular setting, the *Correntoso*'s historic charm, created by abundant natural light and highly tasteful decor, mixes well with its modern services, which include a herbal spa and gourmet restaurant. US$250

La Escondida Av Arrayanes 7014 ☎ 0294 447 5218, ⓦ hosterialaescondida.com.ar. Exquisite *hostería* lounging in sumptuous grounds that slope down to the lakeside, where a heated pool, loungers, kayaks, boats and even beds beckon. The rooms, named after typical Argentine game, are stylish in an understated fashion; each enjoys breathtaking views and is distinctly decorated and furnished. US$210

Hostería del Francés Lolog 2057 ☎ 0294 448 8055, ⓦ lodelfrances.com.ar. A beautiful cabin with lake views and double rooms with wooden bathrooms and balconies 4km from the tourist office. $350

Río Bonito Tora Topa 260 ☎ 0294 449 4110, ⓦ riobonito patagonia.com.ar. This spotlessly clean and pleasant *residencial* offers airy rooms, among the cheapest in town. $300

Traunco Las Frambuesas 52 ☎ 0294 449 5518, ⓦ traunco .com.ar. Pleasant *hostería* in typical local style – wooden floors throughout, with tree trunks curling around the stairs and bar. The location is handy for the bus station and main street and the rooms have balconies and are comfortable, if small. $515

★ **Verena's Haus** Los Taiques 268 ☎ 0294 449 4467, ⓦ verenashaus.com.ar. White, wooden-clad and homely establishment run with tender loving care. The breakfasts are excellent, with a selection of home-made breads, cakes and jams. $420

EATING AND DRINKING

Most of Villa La Angostura's **restaurants** are located along a 200m stretch of El Cruce. Prices are high by Argentine standards – don't expect much change from $200 per head for a full meal with wine – and the gentrification can be a bit over the top, but the quality of food is generally good.

Hub Arrayanes 256 ☎ 0294 449 5700. Trendy bar-restaurant with imaginative variations on a typically Patagonian theme. Live music some nights. Daily noon–late.

Lado Sur Los Taiques 55 ☎ 0294 449 4829. The tables here have views over the restaurant's beautiful garden. Dishes include reasonably priced (by Angostura standards) wild boar and venison. Daily noon–3pm & 8pm–late.

Loncomilla Arrayanes 176 ☎ 0294 449 5345. With high wooden ceilings hung with Spanish-style hams, this is an excellent place for a meat feast, particularly Patagonian lamb. Daily 8pm–late.

★ **La Luna Encantada** Belvedere 69 ☎ 0294 449 5436. Great home-brewed beer and wood-fired artisanal pizzas served in a well-appointed cabin. Popular with locals – a sure sign that the prices are keen. Daily noon–3pm & 8pm–late.

7

Parque Nacional de los Arrayanes

Daily 8am–2pm; stays open to 4.30pm for those arriving by boat • $50 • Hike or cycle from Villa La Angostura (12km each way), or take a boat – Futaleufú (☎ 0294 449 4405) runs three daily catamaran trips from Bahía Mansa ($210) and Patagonia Argentina (☎ 0294 449 4463) three daily trips from Bahía Brava ($190). Turisur (see p.397) runs two daily boat trips from Bariloche via Victoria ($280)

The **PARQUE NACIONAL DE LOS ARRAYANES** is a park within a park, home to the **Bosque de los Arrayanes**, the world's best stand of myrtle woodland. The park is located on the Península Quetrihué, a narrow-necked peninsula that juts out from Barrio La Villa in Villa La Angostura, with the Bosque situated at its far tip. The peninsula is covered with forests of *coihue*, *radal* and uncommon species such as *palo santo*, which sports rich, glossy foliage and an ashy grey bark. These forests provide cover for native fauna such as Des Mur's wiretail.

Quetrihué in Mapudungun means "place of the *arrayanes*" and it is those trees that are the real draw here. The **arrayán**, a member of the myrtle family, is a slow-growing tree characterized by flaky, cinnamon-coloured, paper-like bark and amazing spiralling trunks, which look rather like barley-sugar church columns. It can reach heights of up to 15m and live for three hundred years (although some specimens here may be as much as 600 years old), and it only grows close to cool water. The canopy of the *arrayán* is made up of delicate glossy clusters of foliage, and in late summer it flowers in dainty white blossoms, with the edible blue-black berries maturing in autumn.

Boulevard Nahuel Huapi terminates in La Villa with the stretch that connects the two bays on either side of the peninsula's narrow neck: **Bahía Mansa** ("Peaceful Bay"), on the eastern side and **Bahía Brava** ("Wild Bay") on the western side, both used as departure points for the catamarans. When seen from the lake, the Bosque doesn't look much different from the surrounding forest – it's when you're underneath the canopy that its magic envelops you. The much-told story that Walt Disney took his inspiration for the forest scenes in *Bambi* from this enchanted woodland is apocryphal (he actually took it from photographs of birch forests in Maine), but that doesn't much matter as the place certainly does have a fairytale feel, as you walk around the 600m **boardwalk** at your leisure while the contorted corkscrew trunks creak against each other in the breeze and the light plays like a French Impressionist's dream.

Ruta de los Siete Lagos

The classic **Ruta de los Siete Lagos** ("Seven Lakes Route") connects **Villa La Angostura** with **San Martín de los Andes** (see p.420) in spectacular fashion, passing through forested valleys and giving access to many more than the eponymous seven lakes, which are lagos Nahuel Huapi, Espejo, Correntoso, Escondido, Villarino, Falkner and Machónico. You'll also pass several fishing spots – buy permits before setting off (from tourist offices, YPF stations or campsites). The route is mostly paved, but be warned that the unsealed section – between Lago Espejo and Lago Villarino – can get extremely dusty, especially in summer, although it is being gradually tarred. Note that the entire route is now considered part of the classic RN-40; previously, it was the RN-231 in the southern half and RN-234 in the northern half, and older maps still mark it as such.

Lago Nahuel Huapi to Lago Correntoso

Soon after leaving Angostura, the paved RN-40 crosses Río Correntoso, famous for its fishing and, at barely 250m long, one of the planet's shortest rivers; the road then skirts the northernmost tip of **Lago Nahuel Huapi**, by far the largest lake on the route. As you turn north, you quickly sight **Lago Espejo** ("Looking-glass Lake"), renowned as the warmest and smoothest (hence the name) lake hereabouts. Alongside the Seccional Espejo *guardaparque* post is a free campsite, by a beach that's good for swimming. Just before the *guardaparque's* house is another campground, with spacious pitches and a beach, while opposite is an easy forest trail (30min) through the woods to an isolated spot on the western shore of magical **Lago Correntoso**. Beyond here you trace Lago Correntoso's northern shores and pass a lakeside campground, run by one of the area's original indigenous families and offering *tortas fritas*, meals and provisions.

Cascadas Ñivinco

After the road swings sharply north you'll reach the RP-65 turn-off via the Portezuelo pass to Villa Traful (see below). You then pass through a magnificent valley with sheer cliffs towering over 600m. It's worth stopping at the signposted track to a series of five waterfalls known collectively as **Cascadas Ñivinco**. Reaching them involves an easy 2km walk through *ñire* and *caña colihue* forest, but you'll get your feet (and possibly knees) wet when you ford the river.

Lago Escondido, Lago Villarino and Lago Falkner

Further north is pint-sized **Lago Escondido**, the most enchanting of all the lakes, hiding its emerald-green charms demurely in the forest. Before crossing the limpid waters of Río Pichi Traful, you pass through Seccional Villarino (8am–8pm), where the *guardaparque* will give you information on recommended walks, such as the trek up Cerro Falkner.

Continuing north you come to the eastern point of **Lago Villarino**, a popular place for fishing, with Cerro Crespo (2130m) as a picturesque backdrop and a free lakeside campground. On the other side of the main road, **Lago Falkner** is a perennial favourite of fishermen, sitting at the foot of **Cerro Falkner** (2350m) and a campground here (see below) provides accommodation. Just to the north of Lago Falkner you pass Cascada Vulliñanco, a 20m waterfall to the west of the road.

Lago Machónico to San Martín

Continuing on the RN-40, you cross from Parque Nahuel Huapi into the neighbouring Parque Lanín (see p.428). You then skirt the eastern shore of **Lago Machónico** and, in the final meanders of the route, pass through handsome *ñire* and *coihue* woods. Make sure you stop at the Mirador de Pil Pil to take in the superb panorama of mighty Lago Lácar, whose waters lap San Martín de los Andes, the route's northern terminus.

ARRIVAL AND ACCOMMODATION　　　　　　　　**RUTA DE LOS SIETE LAGOS**

By bus Several daily bus services travel the route between Villa La Angostura and San Martín; be sure you get a bus that goes the "7 lagos" route and not the alternative "Rinconada" route. La Araucana (☎02972 420285, ⓦaraucana.com.ar) runs minibuses twice a day (AR$50) with various pick-up points along the way. Albus also operates buses.

By organized tour Many agencies in San Martín offer trips along the route, including Siete Lagos Turismo at

Villegas 313 (☎02972 427877, ⓦsietelagosturismo.com .ar). Birdwatching tours are available with Aves Patagonia (☎02972 422022, ⓦavespatagonia.com.ar). Bariloche-based tour operators (see p.397) also come here.

Camping Falkner On the shores of Lago Falkner ⓦcampingfalkner.com.ar. This large lakeside campsite has lots of facilities, including a restaurant and shop; it's popular with Argentine students and young families, who come to cool off in the lake, camp and party. **$40**

Lago Traful

A popular destination for trout and salmon fishermen, **LAGO TRAFUL** is a pure, intense blue, like a pool of liquid Roman glass. It's best accessed along the RP-65, which follows its entire southern shore, with the most beautiful approach from the Ruta de los Siete Lagos, crossing the pass of El Portezuelo and heading through the **Valle de los Machis** (with its majestic *coihue* trees), beneath the heights of Pico Traful (2040m).

Midway along the lake on the RP-65 is **Villa Traful**, a loose assemblage of houses spread out along several kilometres of the shoreline. Five kilometres east of the village on the RP-65 is a particularly impressive lookout point: the **Mirador Pared del Viento** (or Mirador del Traful), a precipitous rock-face with superb views over the azure waters 75m below.

Trekking options include hikes to various waterfalls, climbing **Cerro Negro** behind the village (1999m; 7–9hr) or making a trip to **Laguna Las Mellizas** on the northern side of the lake to see indigenous rock paintings. You'll need to hire a boat for the fifteen-minute crossing, preferably with a driver who can also guide you through the multiple tracks to the paintings (5hr return); the *Hostería Villa Traful* (see below) can often put you in contact with someone. There is a free wild campsite at Paloma Araucana, by the foot of the Mirador Pared del Viento.

ARRIVAL AND INFORMATION

LAGO TRAFUL

By bus Albus buses (☎0294 442 3552) run four times a week between Villa Traful and Bariloche (2hr).

Park information Set back from the village's main jetty, a *guardaparque* post (daily 9am–8pm; ☎0294 447 9033) can provide you with information on local hikes – register

before setting out.

Tourist information To the east of the village, near the YPF fuel station, is the tourist office (daily 9am–9pm; ☎0294 447 9099). As well as advising on accommodation, it sells fishing permits and has information on fishing guides.

ACCOMMODATION AND EATING

Hostería Villa Traful RP-65, Villa Traful ☎0294 447 9005, ⓦhosteriavillatraful.com. Homely, log-cabin style hotel with a real fire and windows looking out onto expansive gardens. Also rents out cabins for up to four people. $320

Ñancú Lahuen RP-65, Villa Traful ☎0294 447 9017. Popular tearoom and restaurant, serving high-quality

chocolates and cakes, as well as pasta and trout. Daily noon–11pm.

La Vulcanche Los Sorbus 67 ☎02944 494015, ⓦvulcanche.com. A pleasant budget complex with good-value self-catering cabins sleeping up to five. There's a restaurant on site and staff can help you organize fishing excursions. $430

El Bolsón

The 123km trip southwards along the RN-40 from Bariloche to **EL BOLSÓN** offers yet more stunning mountain and lake views. Just inside Río Negro Province and set in the bowl of a wide, fertile valley, hemmed in by parallel ranges of mountains, El Bolsón is a thriving tourist centre with numerous trekking opportunities close at hand. It was Latin America's first town to declare itself nuclear free and an "ecological municipality". Owing to the claim that the jagged peak of the nearby **Cerro Piltriquitrón** is one of the earth's "energy centres", El Bolsón became a popular hippy hangout in the 1960s, and while it's a bit more commercial these days, the laidback atmosphere persists. In summer it's particularly popular with young Argentine backpackers, since it's far easier on the wallet than nearby Bariloche.

OUTDOOR ACTIVITIES IN EL BOLSÓN

The Club Andino Piltriquitrón (CAP; Mon–Fri 6–8pm; ☎0294 449 2600), at Roca and Sarmiento, can guide you through **trekking** possibilities in the area, most of which consist of considerable ascents – they will also mind your bags for you for a small fee. Among the most popular is the **Cerro Hielo Azul Circuit** (4–6hr), which brings you high enough to present glacier vistas. Further north you can make side treks to less visited areas of **Cerro Dedo Gordo** (4–5hr) and **Los Laguitos** (6–8hr). To the south, the hike to *Refugio Cerro Lindo* (5–7hr) takes in the lake of the same name with beautiful blue waters encased by sheer cliffs. Another interesting, relatively gentle hike to **Cajón Azul** (4–5hr) starts from the same point as Dedo Gordo and passes an excellent *refugio* that serves hot food. The Cajón (gorge) itself is an opening 1m wide and 40m deep; the Río Azul roars through the bottom. Local tour operators offer guided treks as well as horseriding, rafting and boating. Particularly good is Grado 42, at Av Belgrano 406 (☎0294 449 3124, ⓦgrado42.com), which offers tours to the Bosque Tallado and other sights locally.

Spiritual life in El Bolsón is cosmopolitan, and you'll find Buddhist temples as well as a variety of practitioners of alternative paths. Unsurprisingly, UFOs and spirits (*duendes*) are also said to stop off regularly, being guaranteed an especially sympathetic reception on the last Saturday of February, when the town's main party, the **Fiesta del Lúpulo** (Hops Festival) celebrates the harvest of an important local crop (and in particular the heady brew made from it), with music in the main square and an enjoyable, well-lubricated atmosphere.

The town is also worth visiting for its **crafts market** (Tues, Thurs, Sat & Sun 10am–dusk) on the Plaza Pagano, famous throughout the Lake District for the quality of its merchandise, including locally brewed beers. A small **ornithological museum** (daily 10am–8pm; $10) two blocks east of the plaza, on Saavedra and Feliciano, features over one hundred exhibits of stuffed Patagonian birds.

Bosque Tallado
Taxi to Cerro Piltriquitrón plus a 40min uphill walk

East of town, on the wooded slopes of **Cerro Piltriquitrón** (2260m), is an unconventional and interesting site – the **Bosque Tallado** (Sculpted Forest) – 31 tree stumps carved by local craftsmen into a variety of fascinating and often grotesque figures.

7

ARRIVAL AND DEPARTURE   EL BOLSÓN

Arriving from the north, the RN-40 is called Av Sarmiento; its southern end is called Av Belgrano. These two converge on the ACA fuel station in the centre of town on **Av San Martín**, the town's backbone. If you come in a car it's worth filling your tank – fuel is cheaper in El Bolsón than in nearby localities.

By bus Local buses drop you off at their respective offices, most of which are on or just off Av Sarmiento.
Destinations Bariloche (14 daily; 2hr); Esquel (6 daily);
Lago Puelo (5–10 daily; 30min).
By taxi Taxis can be hard to find and should be booked in advance: try Remises Patagonia (☎0294 449 3907).

INFORMATION AND TOURS

Tourist information On the north side of the plaza, at the corner of San Martín and Roca, is the useful tourist office (Mon–Sat 8am–11pm, Sun 9am–11pm; ☎0294 449 2604, ⓦ elbolson.gov.ar).

Tours Bariloche agencies run day-trips to El Bolsón ($215). Fran's Remises (☎0294 449 3041) offers return services to local attractions such as Cascada Escondida and Bosque Tallado.

ACCOMMODATION

Albergue Gaia 7km north of the centre ☎0294 449 2143, ⓦ alberguegaia.com.ar; take a Transporte Urbano bus to Km118. A stellar hostel, the airy, ecologically minded *Gaia* boasts laundry facilities, a swimming pool and a kitchen. There's an extra charge for breakfast. Dorms $80, doubles $250

Cabañas Paraiso Subida a Piltriquitrón 2005 ☎0294 449 2766, ⓦ cabaniasparaiso.com.ar. Ideally located for the Bosque Tallado, with well-equipped cabins for up to six people, and a heated indoor pool. The staff can organize rafting, trekking and horseriding excursions. $660

La Posada de Hamelin Granollers 2179 ☎0294 449 2030, ⓦ posadadehamelin.com.ar. A lovely brick building

in town, with hops growing up the walls, adobe interiors and four tastefully furnished rooms. $400

El Pueblito Comarca Andina del Paralelo 42 ☎0294 449 3560, ⓦ elpueblitohostel.com.ar. Located 4km north of the centre and reached by Transporte Urbano bus or a taxi, the well-run, HI-affiliated *El Pueblito* has a bar serving local beers, restaurant and open fires, as well as great views of the surrounding area. There's an extra charge for breakfast. Dorms $70, en-suite doubles $250

★ **Valle Nuevo** 25 de May and Berutti ☎0294 449 2087. Small but clean, bright rooms with stunning mountain views. Well maintained (and renovated in 2009) with excellent customer care – there are even fire escapes. $180

EATING AND DRINKING

El Bolsón is one of the few towns in Argentina where finding **vegetarian food** is not a problem. The valleys around are chock-a-block with *chacras* or smallholdings that produce organic vegetables, and fruits and berries for jams or desserts; local honey and cheeses are also good. In summer, the plaza heaves with open-air **bars**.

El Bolsón Brewery Km124 on the main road north ☎0294 449 2595, ⍈cervezaselbolson.com. The aficionado owner serves up a variety of beers, including fruity brews (if you like the similar ales from Belgium, you'll love these). Free guided tours of the brewery are sometimes given. Mon–Sat 9am–midnight, Sun 10am–10pm.

Humus de la Montaña Camino los Nagales ☎0294 449 2702. Famed for its organic yogurt, cheese and ice cream. Tours of the dairy are given a couple of times a day (10.30am & noon). Mon–Fri 9am–1pm & 3–9pm, Sat 9am–1pm.

★ **Jauja** San Martín 2867 ☎0294 449 2448. Patagonian restaurant, ice-cream parlour and artisanal chocolate shop all in one; the ice cream, especially the red fruits flavours, is fantastic. The original home of what is now a small chain. Daily noon–late.

Cholila and around

Sitting amid prairie grasslands, 3km east of the junction of the RP-71 and the RP-15, the hamlet of **CHOLILA**, with its spectacular backdrop of savage peaks, seems to belong in the American West. So there's no better setting for one of Patagonia's most idiosyncratic sights – the **cabin** of Wild West outlaw **Butch Cassidy**. From Cholila, you can continue southwest through a glorious lush valley hemmed in by snowcapped mountains towards the northern gate of Parque Nacional Los Alerces (see p.416).

Butch Cassidy's cabin

To get to the cabin head 12km north of Cholila along the RP-71 towards Leleque, and turn left at the police commissionaire's white house at El Blanco towards *La Casa de Piedra* teahouse. The cluster of three buildings is around 250m down the track

The area's main tourist attraction lies 12km north of the village itself along the RP-71 towards Leleque. This is the site of the **cabin** of **Butch Cassidy**, who fled incognito to

---

BUTCH CASSIDY AND THE SUNDANCE KID

Butch Cassidy, Etta Place and the **Sundance Kid** were fugitives together in the Argentine frontier town of Cholila between the years 1901 and 1906, as attested to by both the Pinkerton Agency and provincial records of the time. Butch and Sundance had begun to grow weary of years of relentless pursuit, and had heard rumours that Argentina had become the new land of opportunity, offering the type of wide-open ranching country they loved, and where they could live free from the ceaseless hounding of Pinkerton agents.

It appears that, at first, the *bandidos* tried to go straight, even living under their real names – Butch as "George Parker" (an old alias derived from his name at birth, Robert Leroy Parker), and Etta and Sundance as Mr and Mrs Harry Longabaugh – and in this they succeeded, for a while at least. They were always slightly distant from the community and were evidently viewed as somewhat eccentric, yet decent, individuals. Certainly no one ever suspected they had a criminal past.

Various theories are mooted as to why the threesome sold their ranch in such a rush in 1907, but it seems as though the arrival of a Wild Bunch associate, the murderous Harvey "Kid Curry" Logan, following his escape from a Tennessee jail, had something to do with it. The robbery of a bank in Río Gallegos in early 1905 certainly had the hallmarks of a carefully planned Cassidy job, and a spate of robberies along the cordillera in the ensuing years have, with varying degrees of evidence, been attributed to the *bandidos norteamericanos*.

What happened to Cholila's outlaws next is a matter of conjecture. Etta returned to the US, putatively because she needed an operation for acute appendicitis, but equally possibly because she was pregnant, as a result of a dalliance with a young Anglo-Irish rancher. The violent deaths of Butch and Sundance were reported in Uruguay, and in several sites across Argentina and Bolivia. The least likely scenario is the one depicted by Paul Newman and Robert Redford in the famous 1969 Oscar-winning film. Bruce Chatwin in his classic *In Patagonia* proposes that the Sundance Kid was shot by frontier police in Río Pico, south of Esquel. Countless books have been written on the trio, including *In Search of Butch Cassidy*, by Larry Pointer, and most recently *Digging Up Butch and Sundance*, by Anne Meadows.

this isolated area at the start of the twentieth century with his partner, the **Sundance Kid**, who also lived here for a short while with his beautiful gangster moll, **Etta Place**. The buildings were already in a lamentable state of repair when Bruce Chatwin (*In Patagonia*) visited in the 1970s and were about to collapse when the local authorities finally set about restoration in 2007 – overdoing the job, to some tastes. Still, there is no visitors' centre, entrance fee, or much to do as such, other than take in the atmosphere, the remoteness, and conjure up the ghosts of the famous outlaws.

Museo Leleque

RN-40 Km1440 • Daily except Wed: Jan & Feb 11am–7pm; March, April, July, Aug, Oct & Dec 11am–5pm • $10 • ☎ 02945 455151

A couple of kilometres off the RN-40 along a track that leads east from the RP-15 turn-off to Cholila, the estancia Leleque lies within the Benetton estate, one of the largest private properties in the country, owned by the Italian fashion family. The only part of the estancia open to the public is the fabulous **Museo Leleque**, housed in a beautifully restored outbuilding. The handsome exhibits spread over four rooms trace the history of the indigenous peoples, local pioneers and the relations between them by means of a collection of memorabilia collected by the late Pablo Korscheneweski, born in Odessa in 1925. The highlight, though, is the *boliche* – a typical rural inn combined with general store and canteen, where you can have a drink and something to eat while admiring a set of remarkably well-preserved old bric-a-brac. Save some money for the excellent museum catalogue.

ARRIVAL AND DEPARTURE

CHOLILA AND AROUND

By bus Cholila's bus terminal is on the main square (☎ 02945 498173).

Destinations El Bolsón (daily; 1hr 40min–2hr); Esquel

(3 daily or 5 weekly depending on season; 2hr 30min–3hr 45min).

ACCOMMODATION

Hostería El Trebol 2.7km from the terminal along the RP-15 ☎ 02945 498055, ⓦ hosteriaeltrebol.com.ar. Comfortable, tranquil hotel, with simple rooms in lime-green

cabins, and a bar area with homely hearth. There's a half-board option, with the meals featuring vegetables grown in the hotel's orchard. B&B $360, half-board $560

Esquel and around

Heading south beyond Cholila you'll notice a distinct change in the scenery, as the lush pine forests are replaced by drier terrain that is home to the stunted *meseta*-style vegetation more typical of Patagonia proper. Some 90km south of the Cholila/Leleque turn-off, **Esquel**, the main town in the area, is a starting-point for visits to **Parque Nacional Los Alerces**, as well as a scattering of Welsh villages of which **Trevelin** is the most appealing. This is also the stage through which the steam train **La Trochita**, one of the region's most enduring attractions, plies its trade.

Esquel

For a place so close to exuberant Andean forests, **ESQUEL** is surprising for the aridity of its setting. Enclosed in a bowl of dusty ochre mountains, it is a stark contrast to Bariloche and El Bolsón. The town itself is pretty drab and uninteresting – most people make the trip to access the nearby **Parque Nacional Los Alerces** (see p.416), with the trip on *La Trochita* (see box, p.415) as the next biggest attraction; it's also a popular place to stay for skiing in winter (see box, p.404). If you're looking to kill some time in town, the **Museo de Arte Naif**, next to the post office on Avenida Alvear, hosts a display of pictures by local artists, charmingly childlike in their simplicity. It's also worth

7

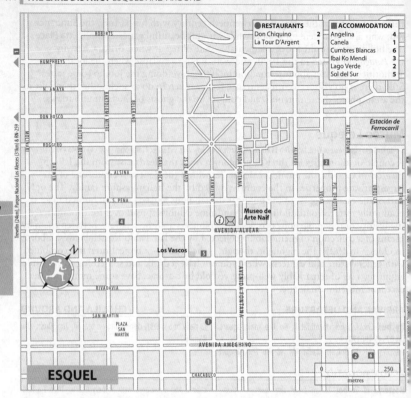

RESTAURANTS
Don Chiquino	2
La Tour D'Argent	1

ACCOMMODATION
Angelina	4
Canela	1
Cumbres Blancas	6
Ibai Ko Mendi	3
Lago Verde	2
Sol del Sur	5

ESQUEL

popping into the old-fashioned *almacen de ramos generales* (general store) Los Vascos at 9 de Julio 1000. Such stores were once common sights in the Argentine countryside, providing a one-stop shop for pioneers and estancia workers to get their supplies. The 90-year-old store, with its wooden shelves and stepladders, still sells everything from shampoo and talc to trousers and hats.

ARRIVAL AND DEPARTURE
ESQUEL

By air The town's airport (☎ 02945 451676) is 19km east of the centre; you can take a *remise* to town ($80).
Destinations Bariloche (5 weekly; 1hr); Buenos Aires (3 weekly; 3hr); Trelew (Wed–Fri 1 or 2 daily; 2hr).
By bus The stylish bus terminal (☎ 02945 451566) is on the main boulevard, Av Alvear, at no. 1871, about 1km from

the town centre.
Destinations Bariloche (15 daily; 4hr 30min); Cholila (3 daily or 5 weekly depending on season; 2hr 30min–3hr 45min); El Bolsón (15 daily; 2hr 30min); Trevelin (hourly; 30min).
By train The *La Trochita* train station (see box opposite) is at Roggero and Brun, nine blocks northeast of the bus terminal.

INFORMATION AND TOURS

Tourist information The excellent and busy tourist office, just past the post office, at Alvear and Sarmiento (daily 7am–11pm; ☎ 02945 451927, ⚑ esquel.gov.ar) can help you find accommodation if you haven't reserved.

Tours Brazo Sur, Rivadavia 891 (☎ 02945 456359, ⚑ brazosur .com.ar), operates tours in the region, including trips to the Parque Los Alerces, horseriding and rafting.

ACCOMMODATION

There's a wide range of accommodation in town while *cabaña* complexes are found 2–3km from the centre. Outside summer (Dec–Feb) and the skiing season (July & Aug) you'll get large discounts.

Angelina Alvear 758 ☎02945 452763, ⊚hosteria
angelina.com.ar. This comfortable, family-run *hostería* is
modern with stone-clad walls and a fountain. Ask for a
room at the back, as the front can be a bit noisy. $500
★ **Canela** Los Notros s/n ☎02945 453890, ⊚canela
esquel.com. Veronica and Jorge run a fabulous British-style
B&B in a pleasant residential area a short way out of town.
The tastefully decorated rooms are extremely comfortable,
the house is charming – as are the hosts – and the breakfast
will keep you up and running all day. $750
Cumbres Blancas Av Ameghino 1683 ☎02945 455100,
⊚cumbresblancas.com.ar. A classy motel feel pervades
this upmarket establishment. Large airy rooms come with
free internet connection and safe, and there's a sauna and
"Scottish shower" (lateral water jets). $860

★ **Ibai Ko Mendi** Rivadavia 2965 ☎02945 451503,
⊚ibaikomendi.com.ar. Extremely attractive wood and
stone cabins, plus delightful rooms in the main *hostería*
building, all set in a tranquil complex that includes a pool
and spa. Doubles $600, *cabañas* $700
Lago Verde Volta 1081 ☎02945 452251, ⊚patagonia
-verde.com.ar. Peaceful and welcoming guesthouse (its
owners also run the Patagonia Verde travel agency) with
clean rooms overlooking a rose garden. Reserve in advance
in high season. $200
Sol del Sur 9 de Julio 1086 ☎02945 452189,
⊚hsoldelsur.com.ar. A dependable mid-range choice,
with standard, comfortable rooms and amenities (TV and
fridge). Breakfast is included. $300

EATING

Don Chiquino Av Ameghino 1641 ☎02945 450035.
This reliable restaurant serves tasty Italian food in a cosy
atmosphere, though it gets packed in high season. Daily
10.30am–late.
La Tour d'Argent San Martín 1063 ☎02945 454612.

Cheap and filling menus of pastas and chicken, as well as
a more adventurous, appetizing à la carte selection that
includes trout with a variety of sauces. Daily noon–3pm
& 8pm–late.

Trevelin

The main Welsh settlement along the Andes (most of the Welsh towns in Patagonia are
closer to the ocean), **TREVELIN** is a small, easy-going place that retains a pioneering feel,

---

LA TROCHITA: THE OLD PATAGONIAN EXPRESS

A trip on the **Old Patagonian Express** rates as one of South America's classic journeys.
The steam train puffs, judders and lurches across the arid, rolling steppe of northern Chubut,
like a drunk on the well-worn route home, running on a track with a gauge of a mere 75cm.
Don't let Paul Theroux's disparaging book *The Old Patagonian Express* put you off: travelling
aboard it has an authentic Casey Jones aura and is definitely not something that appeals only
to train-spotters. Along the way you'll see guanacos, rheas, maras and, if you are lucky, condors,
as you traverse the estate of Estancia Leleque, owned by Italian clothes magnate Benetton,
Argentina's biggest landowner.

Referred to lovingly in Spanish as **La Trochita**, from the Spanish for "narrow gauge", or *El Trencito*,
the route has had an erratic history. It was conceived as a branch line to link Esquel with the main
line joining Bariloche to Carmen de Patagones on the Atlantic coast. Construction began in
Ingeniero Jacobacci in Río Negro Province in 1922, but it took 23 years to complete the 402km to
Esquel. Originally, it was used as a mixed passenger and freight service, carrying consignments of
wool, livestock, lumber and fruit from the cordillera region. The locomotives had to contend with
snowdrifts in winter, and five derailments occurred between 1945 and 1993, caused by high
winds or stray cows on the track. Proving unprofitable, the line was eventually closed in 1993. The
Province of Chubut took over the running of the 165km section between Esquel and El Maitén
soon afterwards, and *La Trochita* has matured into a major tourist attraction.

For most people, a ride on *La Trochita* means the half-day trip north from Esquel to Nahuel
Pan, 22km away ($180). The train departs every Saturday at 10am and puts on up to ten further
journeys weekly depending on demand and the season – ask at the tourist office for the latest
timetables or call ☎02945 451403. There is also an occasional sporadic service running the
165km to El Maitén and returning the following day. Renovations or strikes sometimes close
the line completely so check before you come to Esquel if the train ride is the main objective
of your journey.

with several low brick buildings characteristic of the late nineteenth century and early twentieth. Lying 24km south of Esquel, it has beautiful views across the grassy valley to the peaks in the south of Parque Nacional Los Alerces. The town was founded by Welsh settlers from the Chubut Valley following a series of expeditions to this region that began in 1885 with a group led by Colonel Fontana of the Argentine army and John Evans; *tre* being Welsh for town, *velin* mill, in reference to the flour mill that was built by the settlers. The town's Welsh heritage is evoked in the celebration of a minor **Eisteddfod** (two days in the second week of October), and **casas de té**, the best one being *Nain Maggie*, at Perito Moreno 179 (daily 3.30–8.30pm; ☎ 02945 480232; $90 for Welsh tea with cakes): the teahouse is named after owner Lucia Underwood's grandmother, who was born in Trelew, came to Trevelin in 1891 and died in the town ninety years later at the age of 103.

Museo Cartref Taid

200m northeast of the plaza • Daily 3–7pm • $20

Clery Evans, granddaughter of the village's founder John Evans, relates the origins of the settlement in Spanish at the **Museo Cartref Taid** (Welsh for "grandfather's home"). In the garden is the **Tumba de Malacara**, part of the grave of her granddad's faithful horse, El Malacara – who leapt heroically down a steep scarp to save his master from the same grisly fate that befell his companions. They had been killed by enraged Mapuche warriors who, following an atrocity committed against their tribe during the Campaign of the Desert, were bent on reprisals against any Europeans. The house attracts a steady stream of Bruce Chatwin pilgrims, as the story features in his classic travelogue, *In Patagonia* (see p.562).

ARRIVAL, INFORMATION AND TOURS
TREVELIN

By bus Buses run to Esquel every 1–2hr (30min), dropping you off near the main plaza.

Tourist information The RN-259 from Esquel arrives at the octagonal Plaza Coronel Fontana at the north end of town, where you'll find the tourist office (Jan–Feb & July–Aug daily 8am–10pm; rest of year Mon–Fri 8am–8pm;

☎ 02945 480120, ⊛ trevelin.gob.ar).

Tours Gales Al Sur, Av Patagonia 186 (☎ 02945 480427, ⊛ galesalsur.com.ar), runs excursions to Los Alerces national park, horseriding trips and other local interest tours; it also has internet access.

ACCOMMODATION AND EATING

El Chacay Cacique Nahuel Pan s/n ☎ 02945 1540 7376. This campsite has showers and a shop, has a rural feel and a decent view of the hills; near the south end of San Martín, turn left one block beyond *Oregón* restaurant. $60

Estefania Perito Moreno 215 ☎ 02945 480148, ⊛ hosteriaestefania.com.ar. This *hostería* has frill-bedecked

rooms, a small heated pool and serves a buffet breakfast. $350

Oregón San Martín and John Thomas ☎ 02945 480408, ⊛ oregontrevelin.com.ar. Good *cabañas* with a kitchen in an orchard and a decent *parrilla* restaurant, eight blocks south of the plaza. $400

Parque Nacional Los Alerces

Established in 1937, the huge **PARQUE NACIONAL LOS ALERCES** in Chubut Province protects some of the most biologically important habitats and scenic landscapes in the region. Its superb lakes are famous for both their rich colours and their fishing, while most have a backdrop of sumptuous forests that quilt the surrounding mountain slopes. In the northeast of the park these lakes form a network centred on **lagos Rivadavia**, **Menéndez** and **Futalaufquen**, whose waters drain south to the dammed reservoir of **Embalse Amutui Quimei**, and from here into the Río Futaleufú (also called Río Grande). The western two-thirds of the park up against the Andes are off-limits, being designated a "strict scientific reserve".

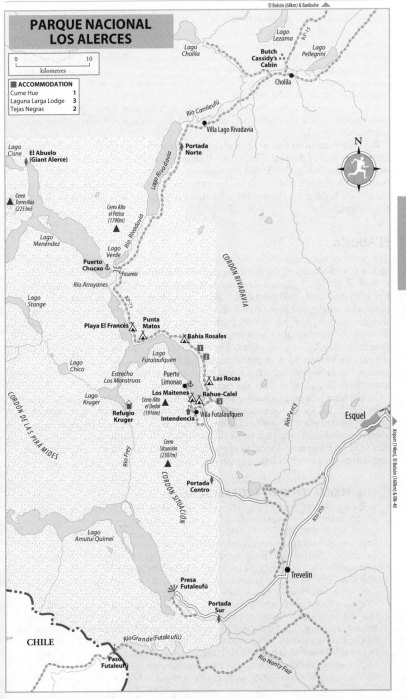

PARQUE NACIONAL
LOS ALERCES

0   10
kilometres

■ ACCOMMODATION
Cume Hue	1
Laguna Larga Lodge	3
Tejas Negras	2

El Bolsón (68km) & Bariloche

Lago Lezama
Lago Cholila
Lago Pellegrini
Butch Cassidy's Cabin
RP-15
Cholila

Río Carrileufú

Villa Lago Rivadavia

Lago Cisne
El Abuelo (Giant Alerce)

Portada Norte

Cerro Torrecillas (2253m)

Lago Rivadavia

Cerro Alto el Petiso (1790m)

Lago Menéndez

Río Rivadavia

Lago Verde

Puerto Chucao

Pasarela

Río Arrayanes

Lago Stange

RP-71

CORDÓN RIVADAVIA

N

7

Playa El Francés
Punta Matos
Bahía Rosales
1
2

Lago Futalaufquen

Lago Chico
Estrecho Los Monstruas
Puerto Limonao
Las Rocas

Lago Kruger
Los Maitenes
Rahue-Calel
3

Refugio Kruger
Cerro Alto el Dedal (1916m)
Intendencia
Villa Futalaufquen

CORDÓN DE LAS PIRÁMIDES

Río Frey

Cerro Situación (2307m)

CORDÓN SITUACIÓN

Río Percy

Esquel

Airport (14km); El Bolsón (160km) & RN-40

Lago Amutui Quimei

Portada Centro

RN-259

Trevelin

Presa Futaleufú

Portada Sur

CHILE

Río Grande (Futaleufú)

Paso Futaleufú

Río Nanty Fall

The vegetation changes considerably as you move east from the Chilean frontier into the area affected by the rain shadow cast by the cordillera. Near the border, rainfall exceeds 3000mm a year, enough to support the growth of dense **Valdivian temperate rainforest** (*selva valdiviana*) and, most interestingly, the species for which the park is named: the **alerce**. The ground is dominated by bamboo-like *caña colihue*, while two species of flower are everywhere: the orange or white-and-violet *mutisias*, with delicate spatula-like petals, and the *amancay*, a golden-yellow lily growing on stems 50cm to 1m high. In contrast, the eastern margin of the park is much drier. Cypress woodland and *ñire* scrub mark the transitional zone here between the wet forests and the arid steppe near Esquel.

The **northeastern section** of the park is the most interesting for the visitor, especially around the area of the beautiful but small **Lago Verde**. The transcendental **Río Arrayanes** drains Lago Verde and a suspension bridge gives access to a delightful hour-long loop walk that takes you along the riverbank to Puerto Chucao. For most visitors the highlight is the trip from Puerto Chucao across Menéndez to see **El Abuelo**, the ancient *alerce*.

El Abuelo

The most popular excursion in the park is the lake trip ("Safari Lacustre") to the far end of Lago Menéndez's northern channel to see **El Abuelo** ("The Grandfather", also named *El Alerzal*), a gigantic *alerce* 2.2m in diameter, and 57m tall. This magnificent tree is an estimated 2600 years old, making it a sapling when Pythagoras and Confucius taught, but at the end of the nineteenth century it almost became roof shingles: only the fact that settlers deemed its wood rotten inside saved it from the saw. To see it you need to take a **boat trip**; the earlier sailing crosses Lago Futalaufquen and goes down Río Arrayanes to Puerto Mermoud followed by a thirty-minute walk across the isthmus to meet up with the later sailing at Puerto Chucao. The excursion is guided, but in Spanish only; if you want an English translation, you'll need to organize a tour from Esquel rather than just turn up at the pier.

On the ninety-minute trip across the pristine blue waters of **Lago Menéndez** you get fine views of the Cerro Torrecillas glacier, which is receding fast and may last only another seventy years. To get to El Abuelo, a 3km trail takes you through dense Valdivian temperate rainforest (*selva valdiviana*), a habitat distinguished from the surrounding Patagonian forests by the presence of different layers to the canopy, in addition to the growth of lianas, epiphytes, surface roots and species more commonly

---

THE *ALERCE* (*FITZROYA CUPRESSOIDES*)

Similar in appearance to the Californian redwood, the **alerce**, or Patagonian cypress, can reach heights of 57m and is one of the four oldest species of tree in the world. To the Mapuche it is *lahuán*, meaning "long-lived" or "grandfather", and the oldest specimens are an estimated four thousand years old. They grow in a relatively narrow band of the central Patagonian cordillera, on acidic soils by lakes and only in places where the annual rainfall exceeds 3000mm, so are more common on the wetter Chilean side of the Andes than in Argentina. Growth is extremely slow (0.8–1.2mm a year), and it takes a decade for a tree's girth to gain 1cm in diameter – though the trunk may eventually reach 3m across.

From the late nineteenth century onwards, the *alerce* was almost totally logged out by pioneers: the reddish timber is not eaten by insects and does not rot, so was highly valued for building, especially for roof shingles. Other uses included musical instruments, barrels, furniture, telegraph poles and boats. In Argentina, the only trees to survive the forester's axe were the most inaccessible ones, or those like El Abuelo, a titanic millennial specimen whose wood was bad in parts. In Argentina, a few stands exist north of Los Alerces, in Parque Nacional Lago Puelo and the Lago Frías area of Nahuel Huapi, and the trees that remain are generally well protected.

THE *HUEMUL (HIPPOCAMELUS BISCULUS)*

If you spend any time in the Argentine Lake District it won't be long before you hear talk of the almost legendary **huemul**. This little deer, which stands 1m at the shoulder, was declared a "National Monument" in 1996 in response to an alarming decline in population. A secretive denizen of high Patagonian forests, it once played an important role in the livelihood of indigenous groups who relied on it for food and often depicted it in cave paintings. The arrival of the Europeans and their firearms had disastrous consequences for the remarkably tame species, and there are even tales about them being killed with knives. With the increasing destruction of their forest habitat, their numbers declined rapidly and today only an estimated six hundred remain in Argentina. Your best chance of glimpsing one is in winter, when harsh weather may drive them down to lower altitudes and more open areas in search of food.

One of the likeliest locations to spy a *huemul* is near Playa El Francés on the northeastern shore of Lago Futalaufquen in the Parque Nacional Los Alerces – but even there you'll need luck on your side. They are also sometimes spotted further south, in Los Glaciares national park (see p.466) or Chile's Torres del Paine.

The *huemul* shows a series of adaptations to its tough environment, possessing a thick, dense coat to protect against the cold and short, strong legs that help it gain a foothold on rocky slopes. They are also remarkably good swimmers, and can cross lakes and rivers with ease.

7

found in Chile. Here a mass of vegetation is engaged in the eternal struggle of the jungle: height equals light. In addition to the *alerces*, look out for fuchsia bushes and *arrayan*es (see p.408). Despite its name **Lago Cisne** is no longer home to any Black-necked swans; they were wiped out by mink.

ARRIVAL AND INFORMATION

PARQUE NACIONAL LOS ALERCES

By boat Boat trips leave from Puerto Limonao, 3km north of the *intendencia* at 9am ($320), or from Puerto Chucao halfway round the Lago Verde/Río Arrayanes trail loop at 11.30am ($270); book in advance at Brazo Sur (see p.414).

Access points and entrance fees Entrance to the park is via three points of access: the most practical is the Portada Centro (or "central gate"; 33km from Esquel and 12km before the small village of Villa Futalaufquen), which gives access to the park headquarters and the useful information centre. The most scenic route is to take the RP-71 to the Portada Norte, by the headwaters of Lago Rivadavia near Cholila (see p.412), although it is 55km from the central gate. The third entrance, Portada Sur (or Futaleufú), is in the southeast corner of the park, 14km southwest of Trevelin. There is a $50 entry fee.

Getting around Transportes Esquel (☎02945 453429, ⓦtransportesesquel.com.ar) runs a useful daily bus service (summer only) along the RP-71 between Esquel and Cholila, while Transportes Martín runs five times a week

between Trevelin and Villa Futalaufquen. Out of season, you'll need your own transport.

Information Set on manicured lawns alongside the bus stop in Villa Futalaufquen is the *intendencia* (daily 8am–9pm in high season, 9am–4pm low season; ☎02945 471020) and visitors' centre which supplies useful information on hikes, accommodation and fishing, and sells fishing permits.

Services Services in the village are limited and all food and provisions are far cheaper in Esquel; the sale of fuel within the park has been prohibited, so fill your tank in the nearby towns first.

When to visit Hordes of people descend on the park each year, most from late Nov until Easter, and it gets extremely busy in Jan and Feb – so visit off-peak, if possible. The park is accessible year-round, although the RP-71 can, albeit rarely and temporarily, be cut off by snow, and most accommodation closes outside the fishing season (mid-Nov to Easter). The autumn months are perhaps best, as the deciduous trees put on a blaze of colour, but spring is also very beautiful, if subject to some fierce winds.

ACCOMMODATION

During the fishing season, there's a wide choice of accommodation in the park, especially along Lago Futalaufquen's eastern shore, but most establishments close off-season. There are plenty of **campsites**, including a free one with fine swimming at Punta Matos, Km21. Those who don't want to camp must splash out heavily on private **hotels** and **lodges** or rent a **cabin** (the ones north of the park in Villa Lago Rivadavia are a good bet and often better value), though these tend to be geared towards groups of fishermen or families. All accommodation should be reserved in advance, especially in summer.

TREKKING IN LOS ALERCES

There are 130km of **public trails** in the Parque Nacional Los Alerces, which are generally well maintained and marked at intervals with red spots. You are required to **register** with the nearest *guardaparque* before setting off (remember to check back in afterwards). In times of drought, some trails are closed, while others can only be undertaken with a guide. Bring plenty of water, sun protection, and adequate clothing as the weather changes rapidly and unseasonal snowfalls occur in the higher regions. Insect repellent is worthwhile, especially after several consecutive hot days in December and January, as that's when the fierce horseflies (*tábanos*) come out.

THE TREKS

The super-easy pastoral 1200m **Pinturas Rupestres** circuit passes eroded indigenous geometric designs painted about three thousand years ago on a hulk of grey rock that's surrounded by *caña colihue* and *maitén* trees; the lookout from the top of the rock affords a fine view. A more challenging trip is to the *hostería* and campsite at the southern end of **Lago Kruger**. This can be reached in a fairly stiff day's trekking (12hr), returning next day either the same way or by launch (cost depends on number of passengers). However, it's better to make it into a three- or four-day excursion, breaking the outward-bound trek by putting up a tent by the beautiful beach at Playa Blanca – get permission at the visitors' centre. Fires are strictly prohibited and there are no facilities.

One of the most popular treks is the **El Dedal Circuit**. It involves some fairly tough climbs but you'll be rewarded with excellent panoramic views. The path starts as the "Sendero Cascada" (which runs up behind the visitors' centre) through thick *maitén* and *caña colihue*. It then enters impressive mature woodland and scrubland, from where you have a panoramic view of the scarified, rust-coloured **Las Monjitas** range opposite. The path continues along the ridge northwest towards the craggy El Dedal massif. Up here you'll see delicate celeste and grey-blue *perezia* flowers, and possibly even condors. Passing gorgeous **Lago Futalaufquen**, whose turquoise body is fringed, in places, by a frill of Caribbean-blue shallows, you'll dip down into an oxide-coloured glaciated cwm (valley). A tiring scramble takes you back up to the top of the ridge, which overlooks the *Hostería Futalaufquen* and Puerto Limonao. From the ridge, a poor path leads up to the summit of **Cerro Alto El Dedal** (1916m), about forty minutes away; don't attempt it in poor weather.

Cume Hue ☎02945 453639, ⊛cumehue.patagonia express.com. This pretty white house on the eastern shore of Lago Futalaufquen is popular with anglers and offers full-board packages. The delicious teas include home-made scones and fabulous jams made with local fruit. $510, camping $40

★ **Laguna Larga Lodge** ☎02322 402231, ⊛laguna largalodge.com. Impeccably run by Andrés, an enthusiastic sports fisherman and lover of excellent wine and fine dining – hence the top-rate restaurant and enticing cellar – this secluded fishing lodge set on the shore of the

attractive Laguna Larga is well worth the slightly difficult trip to get here (make sure you ask for clear directions when you book). $1460

Los Maitenes 400m from the *intendencia* ☎02945 451006. The closest campsite to Villa Futalaufquen is generally good, with great views of Lago Rivadavia. It can get packed, though. $50

Tejas Negras Lake Futalaufquen ☎02945 471012, ⊛tejasnegras.com.ar. Attractive cabins for rent all year round, which sleep up to four people comfortably. $300

San Martín de los Andes and around

The southern belle of Argentine towns and the northern terminus of the famous **Ruta de los Siete Lagos** (see p.408), **SAN MARTÍN DE LOS ANDES** is Neuquén Province's most-visited destination by far and gets very busy indeed in the high midsummer and midwinter seasons. Nestled between mountains on the eastern shores of jewel-like Lago Lácar, the relaxing resort of chalets and generally low-key architecture is an excellent base for exploring much of Parque Nacional Lanín (see p.428). There's a sandy, if often windy, beach on the lake's shores, and in spring, the introduced broom (*retama*) daubs the scenery on the approach roads a sunny yellow. Expansion has been rapid, but – with the exception of the hideous derelict Hotel Sol de los Andes that overlooks town – by no means uncontrolled. Whereas the larger rival resort of Bariloche caters to the young party crowd, San Martín attracts a more sedate type of small-town tourism, aimed at families and professionals rather than students and backpackers. **El Trabún** (meaning the "Union of the Peoples") is the main annual **festival**, held in early December on the Plaza San Martín. Local and Chilean musicians hold concerts (predominantly folklore), and mighty bonfires are lit at the corners of the square to prepare delicious *asados* of lamb and goat.

Museo de los Primeros Pobladores

Centro Cívico • Mon & Wed–Sat 2–6pm • Free

There is little to do in town itself apart from bar-hopping, sunning yourself on the small beach by the lake or popping into the **Museo de los Primeros Pobladores** on the main square. The tiny museum has three rooms – one on the Mapuche, one on skiing, and one on the town's history and architecture, featuring photos from the early days of San Martín, which was founded in 1898.

Mirador Bandurrias

Take the bridge across Arroyo Pocahullo on c/ Juez del Valle, pass the water treatment plant and keep heading northwest through the woods

If you can muster the energy, it's worth dragging yourself away from the bars to take in the stupendous views. The compelling **Mirador Bandurrias** (named after the buff-necked ibis), is 3km along the northeast shore of Lago Lácar, with marvellous views of the lake along its length.

Mirador Arrayán

Taking the track from the lake shore, pass Hotel Sol de los Andes and take the right fork following the signs

Mirador Arrayán is another viewpoint, this time overlooking the town, with lovely mountain backdrops. If you can't face the climbing, the town's tour bus – an old red London double-decker – leaves twice daily from Plaza San Martín ($80) and goes as far as the Hotel Sol de los Andes.

La Pastera Museo del Che

Sarmiento and Roca • Daily except Tues 10am–1pm & 5–8pm • $20 • Ⓦ lapastera.org.ar

A historical curiosity, **La Pastera Museo del Che**, behind a whitewashed wall, is a simple building where Che Guevara spent a night or two at the end of January 1952 during his first trip across South America – later immortalized in *The Motorcycle Diaries*. Well restored, perhaps overly so, it now functions as a community and cultural centre with regular poetry recitals and music performances. The permanent exhibit is a tribute to Che and includes a bale of hay, on which the future freedom-fighter apparently slept during his stay here.

ARRIVAL AND DEPARTURE   SAN MARTÍN DE LOS ANDES

By air Chapelco Airport (Ⓣ 02972 427636) lies 25km away in the direction of Junín de los Andes and serves both towns. La Araucana minibuses connect the airport with San Martín ($50), or you can take a *remise*. If flying out of Chapelco, you could catch the hourly bus run by Castillo (Ⓣ 02944 15 328659; $5), which runs in both directions

between Junín and San Martín and will drop you off at the airport on request.

Destinations Buenos Aires (1–2 daily in high season, 3 weekly rest of year); Mendoza (3 weekly in high season only); Comodoro Rivadavia (3 weekly in high season only).

SAN MARTÍN DE LOS ANDES

La Pastera
Museo del Che

National
Park Office

Museo de
los Primeros
Pobladores

Bus
Terminal

Dock for Boats to
Hua Hum &
Quila Quina

Lago
Lácar

Mirador
Arrayán

Mirador Bandurrias

Bariloche, Cerro Chapelco & RN-40

0   250
metres

N

● RESTAURANTS AND CAFÉS	
Casino Magic	4
Corazón Contento	1
La Barra	6
La Costa del Pueblo	5
Ku	3
Pulgarcito	2

■ ACCOMMODATION	
Aparthotel Cascadas	9
Caupolicán	6
Hueney Ruca	8
Intermonti	7
Laura	4
Lolen	5
Las Lucarnas	3
Puma	1
Secuoya	2

By bus The bus terminal is scenically located in the southwest of town, across the road from Lago Lácar and the pier. Nearly everything you need is found along avenidas Roca and San Martín, or the parallel Villegas.

Destinations Bariloche (7 daily; 3hr 30min); Junín de los Andes (hourly; 1hr); Villa La Angostura (2 daily; 2hr 30min).

INFORMATION AND TOURS

Tourist information On the Plaza San Martín, the tourist office (daily 8am–9pm; ☎02972 427347, ⓦ sanmartin delosandes.gov.ar) will lend a hand if you can't find a room in high season.

Park information The *intendencia* of Parque Nacional Lanín (daily 8am–9pm; ☎02972 429106, ⓔ lanin@apn .gov.ar) is on the plaza, opposite the tourist office – it should be your first stop if you are planning on trekking.

It also sells fishing permits, as do all the fishing shops in town.

Tours AndesX3 at Coronel Pérez 830 (☎02972 414404, ⓦ andesx3.com) offers guided trekking, kayaking, biking, rafting and diving excursions, as well as hikes up Volcán Lanín. Siete Lagos, Villegas 313 (☎02972 427877), and a handful of other local agencies do tours to Huahum, Quila Quina and other places of interest.

ACCOMMODATION

During the peak summer and skiing seasons you should **reserve rooms** as far in advance as possible. If you haven't, the tourist office keeps a daily list of vacancies, though you may find these choices limited. Some hotels have three or four price brackets, with the ski season often more expensive than summer. Out of season, room prices can be as much as halved.

Aparthotel Cascadas Obeid 859 ☎02972 420133, ⓦapartcascadas.com.ar. Great-value, aesthetically pleasing six-person *cabañas* on a quiet street with superb facilities for the price. Includes a heated pool, hydromassage and PC with internet connection in every cabin. $\overline{\$700}$

Caupolicán San Martín 969 ☎02972 427658, ⓦinterpatagonia.com/caupolican. Fancy three-star hotel in the centre of town with a range of facilities, including a sauna and a living room with log fire. $\overline{\$650}$

Hueney Ruca Obeid and Coronel Pérez ☎02972 421499, ⓦhueneyrucahosteria.com.ar. Spacious and airy with attractive minimalist decor and modern bathrooms. Some rooms accommodate up to five people and breakfast is included. $\overline{\$700}$

Intermonti Villegas 717 ☎02972 427454, ⓦhotel intermonti.com.ar. Functional, comfortable, well-lit rooms in an excellent location a block from the main plaza and surrounded by eating options. $\overline{\$500}$

Laura Mascardi 632 ☎02972 427271. Simple but pleasant with airy, wood-panelled rooms, this budget hotel is close to the town centre and among the cheaper places in town in summer. $\overline{\$300}$

Lolen 4km southwest of town, 1km off the RN-234 at Km78 and down a very steep track to Playa Catritre. A lakeside campsite with superb views, run by the Curruhuinca Mapuche community. $\overline{\$50}$

★ **Las Lucarnas** Coronel Pérez 632 ☎02972 427085, ⓦhosterialaslucarnas.com.ar. The best of the cheaper spots, *Las Lucarnas* boasts excellent, spacious rooms in a family-run, central but tranquil place. $\overline{\$360}$

Puma Fosbery 535 ☎02972 422443, ⓦpumahostel .com.ar. Small, well-scrubbed and modern hostel with a couple of double rooms, kitchen and washing facilities. Dorms $\overline{\$90}$, doubles $\overline{\$290}$

Secuoya Rivadavia 411 ☎02972 424485. The best hostel in town has some double rooms and is modern, safe and friendly. Dorms $\overline{\$80}$, doubles $\overline{\$180}$

EATING, DRINKING AND NIGHTLIFE

La Barra Brown and Costanera ☎02972 425459. A superb wood-cabin restaurant on the lakeside. Patagonian specialities (not always that cheap) are the order of the day and the wine list is extensive. Artisanal pasta and stone-baked pizza will appeal to those who have had enough of trout and lamb. Daily 8pm–late.

Casino Magic Villegas and Elordi ☎02972 427142. This casino restaurant has a dated, 1970s feel but is good for cheap eats late at night. Daily 2pm–4am.

Corazón Contento San Martín 467 ☎02972 412750. Buzzing café and takeaway joint offering a delicious and varied menu of sandwiches, burgers, *milanesas* and so on,

though it's the veggie-stuffed quiches that are the biggest hit with the locals. Daily 9am–11.30pm.

La Costa del Pueblo Costanera and Villegas ☎02972 429289. With good, if slightly obscured lake views, *La Costa del Pueblo* is an excellent place to grab a snack while waiting for a bus. The food is abundant and cheap. Daily noon–3pm & 7.30pm–late.

★ **Ku** San Martín 1053 ☎02972 427039. This moderately priced restaurant offers a varied menu that includes *parrillas* and pastas as well as regional trout, venison and wild boar dishes in a rustic setting decorated with wine barrels and bottles. Daily noon–3pm and 7.30pm–late.

Lago Lácar and around

Southwest of San Martín, **LAGO LÁCAR** ("Lake of the Sunken City"), which lies entirely within the Parque Nacional Lanín (see p.428), is best explored by combining boat or road trips with the odd hike.

San Martín to Huahum

From San Martín's pier Naviera Lácar Nonthue runs boat excursions to Huahum and back (daily at 12.30pm; $360; ☎02972 427380), which stop off at Quila Quina and the Chachin waterfall. Buses run twice daily along the route ($34), or you could rent a car

The unsurfaced RP-48 runs for 46km along the northern shore of Lácar and the adjoining **Lago Nonthue** to **Huahum**, a small settlement at the western end of the lake used as a base for walks and fishing. The beautiful trip there takes in lakeside views and white beaches. Around 13km from San Martín is the trailhead for an excellent two-hour hike up **Cerro Colorado** (1774m). You'll go towards a broad V-shaped valley, then along the banks of a stream – a steep climb with views of the valley and lake below. A few kilometres from Huahum is a 20m-high waterfall, Chachin; follow the signs to the car-park and then there's a thirty-minute walk through forest to reach the falls.

Paso Huahum
Customs open year-round daily 8am–8pm

Around 10km from Huahum village the road continues on to the international border crossing, **Paso Huahum**. The crossing is one of the most enjoyable Andean routes through to Chile, leading towards the town of Villarrica, although there is no public transport behind Huahum so you will need your own vehicle. Following the Río Huahum northwest brings you to the slender, gorgeous Lago Pirehueico, which is crossed by **car ferry**. The car ferry timetable changes frequently; ask at the tourist office or call the Panguipulli tourist office in Chile (☎0056 63 310436).

Termas de Queñi
To the southeast of Huahum, 12km by dirt track, is the *guardaparque*'s post at **Lago Queñi**. The area around this lake is one of the wettest places in Parque Nacional Lanín, and is covered with Valdivian temperate rainforest and dense thickets of *caña colihue*. The star attraction here is the enchanting **Termas de Queñi** – unadorned hot springs, set in lush forest near the southern tip of the lake. Late September to early May is generally the best time to visit the springs: register with the *guardaparque*, and you can **camp** just past the post, on the other side of Arroyo Queñi. You can walk to the springs on an easy route from the campsite (1hr).

Quila Quina
Ferries leave San Martín's pier on the hour (last boat 7pm) • $120 return

Ferries head to the beautiful, sheltered bay at **Quila Quina**, an incongruous mix of agricultural smallholdings of the Curruhuinca Mapuche community and holiday homes on the southern shore of Lago Lácar. You can also reach the settlement by signposted dirt road off the RN-234. There's a beach and walks in the area, including a two-day trek to the western end of Lago Lácar at **Pucará**.

Junín de los Andes

Set in a dry, hilly area of the steppe at the foot of the Andes to the northeast of San Martín, **JUNÍN DE LOS ANDES** is aptly named – Junín means "grassland" in the Aymara language. It's a relaxed town popular with fishermen, largely owing to the rivers in the region that teem with trout. Though not as aesthetically attractive as its bigger neighbour, San Martín de los Andes (see p.420), Junín lacks the trappings of a tourist town and the high prices that generally accompany them. It is also better placed for making trips to the central sector of Parque Nacional Lanín (see p.428), especially if you plan to climb Volcán Lanín itself, or to explore the **Lago Huechulafquen** area. A good time to visit is mid-February, when the **Fiesta del Puestero**, with gaucho events, folklore music in the evenings, *artesanía* and *asados*, takes place.

Plaza San Martín and around

The few sites of interest in Junín are all within a couple of blocks of **Plaza San Martín**, the pleasant main square that is the hub of the town's activity. The **Paseo Artesanal** on the east side of the square is a cluster of boutiques selling a selection of crafts, among which Mapuche weavings figure heavily. More Mapuche artefacts and some dinosaur bones can be seen at the tiny **Museo Mapuche** at Ginés Ponte and Avenida Rosas (Mon–Fri 8am–1pm & 5–8pm; free).

THE MAPUCHE

Calling themselves the people (*che*) of the earth (*Mapu*), the **Mapuche** were, before the arrival of the Spanish in the sixteenth century, a loose confederation of tribal groups who lived exclusively on the Chilean side of the cordillera. The aspiring conquistadors knew them as Araucanos, and so feared their reputation as indomitable and resourceful warriors that they abandoned attempts to subjugate them and opted instead for a policy of containment. Encroachments into Araucania sparked a series of Mapuche migrations eastwards into territory that is now Argentina, and they soon became the dominant force in the whole region, their cultural and linguistic influence spreading far beyond their territories.

By the eighteenth century, four major Mapuche tribes had established territories in Argentina: the **Picunche**, or "the people of the north", who lived near the arid cordillera in the far north of Neuquén; the **Pehuenche**, or "the people of the monkey puzzle trees", dominant in the central cordillera; the **Huilliche**, or "the people of the south" of the southern cordillera region based around Lago Nahuel Huapi; and the **Puelche**, or "the people of the east", who inhabited the river valleys of the steppe. These groups spoke different dialects of **Mapudungun**, a tongue that belongs to the Arawak group of languages. Lifestyles were based around nomadic hunter-gathering, rearing livestock and the cultivation of small plots around settlements of *rucas* (family homes that were thatched, usually with reeds). Communities were headed by a *lonco*, or cacique, but the "medicine-men", or *machis*, also played an influential role.

SPANISH INFLUENCE

The arrival of the Spanish influenced Mapuche culture most significantly with the introduction of **horses and cattle**. Horses enabled tribes to be vastly more mobile, and hunting techniques changed, with the Mapuche adopting their trademark lances in lieu of the bow and arrow. As importantly, the herds of wild horses and cattle that spread across the Argentine pampas became a vital trading commodity.

Relations between the Mapuche and the Hispanic *criollos* in both Chile and Argentina varied: periods of warfare and indigenous raids on white settlements were interspersed with times of relatively peaceful coexistence. By the end of the eighteenth century, the relationship had matured into a surprisingly symbiotic one, with the two groups meeting at joint *parlamentos* where grievances would be aired and terms of trade regulated. Tensions increased after Argentina gained its independence from Spain, and the Mapuche resisted a military campaign organized against them by the dictator Rosas in the early 1830s, but they were finally crushed by Roca's Campaign of the Desert in 1879. Mapuche communities were split up and forcibly relocated onto reservations, often on marginal lands.

THE MAPUCHE TODAY

The Mapuche remain one of Argentina's **principal indigenous peoples**, with a population of some forty thousand divided among communities dotted around the provinces of Buenos Aires, La Pampa, Chubut, Río Negro and, above all, Neuquén. Most families still earn their livelihood from mixed animal farming, but increasingly, Mapuche communities are embarking on tourist-related ventures. These include opening campsites; establishing points of sale for home-made cheese or *artesanía* such as their fine woven goods, distinctive silver jewellery, ceramics and woodcarvings; offering guided excursions; or receiving small tour groups. Mapuche culture is not as visibly distinct or politically active in Argentina as it is in Chile; nevertheless, the Mapuche are one of Argentina's best-organized indigenous groups.

Santuario de la Beata Laura Vicuña

Ginés Ponte and Padre Milanesio • Opening hours vary • Free

The imposing, alpine-style tower of the **Santuario de la Beata Laura Vicuña**, also called by its old name of the Iglesia Nuestra Señora de las Nieves, is splendid in its simplicity. Dedicated to the beatified Laura Vicuña, it rates as the most refreshingly original church in southern Argentina. Its airy, sky-blue interior is suffused with light, and its clean-cut lines are tastefully complemented by the bold use of panels of high-quality Mapuche weavings, with strong geometric designs and natural colours. Laura Vicuña, born in Santiago de Chile in 1891, studied in Junín and died here, aged just 13, in 1904. As a rather macabre touch, one of her vertebrae resides in an urn at the entrance to the sanctuary.

ARRIVAL AND DEPARTURE
JUNÍN DE LOS ANDES

By air Chapelco airport serves both Junín and San Martín (see p.421).

By bus The RN-234, called Blvd Rosas/Roca (rather confusingly) for the stretch through Junín, cuts across the western side of town. Nearly all you'll need lies to the east,

including the bus terminal (📞02972 492038), one block over at Olavarría and F.S. Martín.

Destinations Aluminé (3 weekly; 3hr); Buenos Aires (7 daily; 20hr); San Martín de los Andes (9 daily; 1hr).

INFORMATION AND TOURS

Tourist information Padre Milanesio and Coronel Suárez (daily 8am–9pm; 📞02972 491160). The information centre can help book accommodation and also sells fishing licences. A small kiosk also operates at the bus station.

Park information Padre Milanesio 570 (Mon–Fri 8am–9pm; 📞02972 492748).

Tours Alquimia, O'Higgins 603 (📞02972 491355,

🌐 alquimiaturismo.com.ar), is a helpful travel agency that organizes professional day-tours in the region, including one to lakes Huechulafquen and Paimún with a visit to a Mapuche community; it specializes in adventure tourism, such as climbing Lanín and rafting on the Río Aluminé, and rents climbing equipment.

ACCOMMODATION

Junín's **hotel** tariffs rise somewhat in summer, when it's worth reserving in advance. There are some good places on the main road but often the best bet is to head for the streets east of the plaza.

Aparthotel Alina Ginés Ponte 80 and Felíx San Martín 📞02972 492636, 🌐apartalina.com.ar. Close to the bus terminal and ideal for small groups, with rooms and cabins for four to six people, but no double rooms. Tours can be arranged, and yoga and massages are also on offer. **$300** per person

Cabañas Las Bandurrias Lanín s/n 📞02972 491295, 🌐 lasbandurriasjunin.blogspot.com. Two delightful cabins sleeping up to five set in Jardines del Chimehuín, a quiet residential area of town. **$600**

⭐ **Chimehuín** Coronel Suárez and 25 de Mayo 📞02972 491132, 🌐interpatagonia.com/hosteriachimehuin. A rare gem, it combines excellent value with a cottage-like setting among well-tended gardens, and engenders great loyalty from its regular guests, especially fishing aficionados. A fine home-made breakfast is included in the price. Book well ahead in summer. **$330**

Complejo Caleufu Travel Lodge J. Roca 1323 📞02972 492757, 🌐caleufutravellodge.com.ar. Motel-style travel lodge on the main road, run by a fun-loving couple who lived in California for years – they have a true

sense of hospitality and an equally great sense of humour. **$455**

Estancia Huechehue RN-234 Km4 🌐huechehue.com. Just over 20km north of Junín, this working and largely self-sufficient estancia takes its guests fishing and on horserides to see condors and petroglyphs in the surrounding countryside; at cattle-rounding time you'll be taken along on horseback to help. Run by London-born Jane, the homestead offers large, comfortable rooms and plentiful food and there's a jacuzzi to soak in after a hard day's ranching. The price includes all meals, transfers and fishing. **US$820**

La Isla 📞02972 492029. Campsite on an island in the Río Chimehuín that can be accessed from the eastern extreme of Ginés Ponte, a few blocks from the centre, with shady pitches. **$50**

Marisa J.M. Rosas 360 📞02972 491175. The best of the budget options and just around the corner from the bus terminal, this *residencial* is a neat, amiable place, and not too noisy, despite having some rooms that face the main road. **$250**

EATING AND DRINKING

Roble Bar Ginés Ponte 331 📞02972 491111. The town's most happening pub serves a *menú del día* at lunch and burgers and the like in the evenings. Daily noon–3pm & 8pm–late.

⭐ **Ruca Hueney** Plaza San Martín 📞02972 491113. A local institution whose speciality is unforgettably delicious trout; it also offers some tasty Lebanese dishes and takeout options. Daily noon–3pm & 8pm–late.

Parque Nacional Lanín

Formed in 1937, **PARQUE NACIONAL LANÍN** (ⓦparquenacionallanin.gov.ar) protects 420 square kilometres of Andean and sub-Andean habitat that ranges from barren, semiarid steppe in the east to patches of temperate Valdivian rainforest pressed up against the Chilean border. To the south, it adjoins its sister park, Parque Nacional Nahuel Huapi (see p.400), while it also shares a boundary with Parque Nacional Villarrica in Chile.

The park's raison d'être and geographical centrepiece – the cone of **Volcán Lanín** – rises to 3776m and dominates the entire landscape. Meaning "choked himself to death" in Mapudungun, it is now believed to be extinct. The park's other trump card is the **araucaria**, or monkey puzzle tree (see box below), which grows as far south as Lago Curruhue Grande, but is especially prevalent in the northern sector of the park, an area known as the **Pehuenia region**. As well as the araucaria, other tree species endemic to the park are the *roble pellí* and the *raulí*, both types of deciduous *Nothofagus* southern beech. Parque Lanín also protects notable forests of *coihue* and, in the drier areas, cypress. Flowers such as the *arvejilla* purple sweet pea and the introduced lupin abound in spring, as does the flame-red *notro* bush. Fuchsia bushes grow in some of the wetter regions.

As for **fauna**, the park is home to a population of *huemules*, a shy and rare deer (see box, p.419). *Pudú*, the tiny native deer, and pumas are present, but rarely seen: you're more likely to glimpse a coypu, a grey fox or two species introduced for hunting a century ago, the wild boar and the red deer, which roam the semiarid steppes and hills of the east of the park. Birdwatchers will want to keep an eye out for the active White-throated treerunner, a bizarre bird with an upturned bill adapted for removing beech nuts, while the acrobatic Thorn-tailed rayadito is another regional speciality.

Lago Huechulafquen and around

The RP-61 branches west off the RN-40 (ex-RN-234) just north of Junín de los Andes, entering Parque Nacional Lanín and skirting the shores of **LAGO HUECHULAFQUEN**. Just 4km from the junction is the **Centro de Ecología Aplicada de Neuquén** (Mon–Fri

---

THE ARAUCARIA, OR MONKEY PUZZLE TREE

The distinctive and beautiful **araucaria** (*Araucaria araucana*), more commonly known as the **monkey puzzle tree**, is one of the world's most enduring species of tree. It grows naturally only in the cordillera of Neuquén Province and at similar latitudes in Chile, where it favours impoverished volcanic soils at altitudes between 600m and 1800m. This prehistoric survivor has been around for more than one hundred million years.

Araucarias grow incredibly slowly, though they can live for over **a thousand years**. Young trees grow in a pyramid shape, but after about a hundred years they start to lose their lower branches and assume their trademark umbrella appearance – mature specimens can reach 45m in height. Their straight trunks are covered by panels of thick bark that provide resistance to fire. The female trees produce huge, head-size cones filled with up to two hundred fawn-coloured pine nuts called *piñones*, some 5cm long, and rich in proteins and carbohydrates.

Known to the Mapuche as the *pehuén*, the tree was worshipped as the daughter of the moon. Legend has it that there was a time when the Mapuche, though they adored the *pehuén*, never ate its *piñones*, believing them to be poisonous. This changed, however, during a terrible famine, when their god, Ngünechén, saved them from starvation by sending a messenger to teach them both the best way of preparing these nutritious seeds (roasting them in embers or boiling), and of storing them (burying them in the earth or snow). *Piñones* became the staple diet of tribes in the area (principally the Pehuenche, named after their dependence on the tree), and have been revered by the Mapuche ever since.

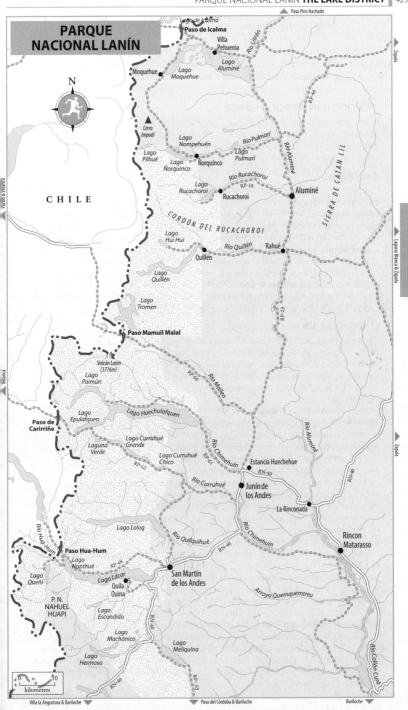

PARQUE
NACIONAL LANÍN

N

CHILE

Lago de Icalma
Paso de Icalma
Villa
Pehuenia
Río Litrán
Moquehue
Lago
Moquehue
Lago
Aluminé
Cerro
Impodi
Lago
Nompehuén
Río Pulmarí
Lago Piihué
Lago
Ñorquinco
Ñorquinco
Lago
Pulmari
Río Aluminé
RP-46
Río Rucachoroi
Lago
Rucachoroi
Rucachoroi
RP-18
Aluminé
SIERRA DE CATAN LIL
CORDÓN DEL RUCACHOROI
Lago
Hui Hui
Río Quillén
Rahué
Quillén
Lago
Quillén
Lago
Tromen
RP-23
Paso Mamuil Malal
Volcán Lanín
(3776m)
Lago
Paimún
RP-60
Río Malleo
Paso de
Cariririñe
Lago
Epulafquen
Lago Huechulafquen
Laguna
Verde
Lago Curruhué
Grande
Lago Curruhué
Chico
RP-62
Río Chimehuín
RP-61
Estancia Huechehue
Río Aluminé
Río Curruhué
RN-40
Lago Lolog
Río Quilquihué
Junín de
los Andes
La Rinconada
RN-40
Paso Hua-Hum
Río Hua-Hum
Lago
Nonthué
RP-48
Lago
Queñi
Lago Lácar
Quila
Quina
San Martín
de los Andes
Río Chimehuín
Rincon
Matarasso
RN-40
P. N.
NAHUEL
HUAPI
Lago
Escondido
RN-40
Arroyo Quemquemtreu
Zapala
Lago
Machónico
Lago
Meliquina
Lago
Hermoso
RN-40
RP-63
Río Collón Curá

0   10
kilometres

7

Zapala

Laguna Blanca & Zapala

Zapala

Pucón & Villarica

Villarica

Villa la Angostura & Bariloche   Paso del Córdoba & Bariloche   Bariloche

9am–1pm), which undertakes studies of regional fauna and has a trout farm that raises fish for restocking the area's rivers.

The park's largest lake, Huechulafquen is an enormous finger of deep blue water extending into the steppe, its northern shores black with volcanic sand. The mouth of the Río Chimehuín, at the lake's eastern end, is a notable fly-fishing spot.

TREKKING IN PARQUE LANÍN

Before planning **treks** in the park you should check thoroughly with park officials in Junín or San Martín and fill out a *registro de trekking*, which must be presented at the *guardaparque* post before departure and on your return. Make sure your map is new – this is an area of active volcanoes, and trails and refuges change constantly.

THE TREKS

One of the most popular walks within striking distance of Junín is the four-hour hike to **Cerro del Chivo**, which starts opposite *Camping Bahía Cañicul*. It's a steep climb and you'll need to concentrate not to lose the trail above the tree-line, but the views are spectacular. An excellent two-day option for losing the crowds is to cross the narrows linking the two lakes at La Unión near Puerto Canoa (there's normally a rowing-boat service) and head along the south shore of **Lago Paimún**. Initially, you strike inland skirting round the southern slopes of Cerro Huemules (1841m) before reaching the lake again midway along its length at **Don Aila**, where you can camp. From the *guardaparque* in Puerto Canoa there's another good, if somewhat arduous, day-hike to the **base of Volcán Lanín**. The last forty minutes are steep and there's no water source for the final hour. You can take a short detour to the waterfall at Cascada El Saltillo from *Camping Piedra Mala* at Km64, where there's space to pitch a tent.

CLIMBING LANÍN

If you wish to go all the way up Volcán Lanín you'll find it is a good mountain to climb: easy to access, it also retains the balance between being possible for inexpert climbers to ascend while still representing a real physical challenge. Nonetheless, do not undertake it lightly – you should take a guide and be reasonably fit. The most straightforward route is from Lago Tromen; the heavily glaciated south face is a much fiercer option that's suitable only for experienced climbers.

The route **from Lago Tromen** takes two or three days in good weather – the two-day option involves a very tiring second day that includes the summit push and a complete descent. Group climbing through an agency is possible: a good one to book with is Alquimia in Junín (see p.427), or else the park offices can email you a list of authorized guides. They also rent out all the essential mountaineering gear: good boots, waterproof clothing, helmet, ice axe, crampons, torch (or, better still, a headlamp) and cooker. UV sunglasses, high-factor sunblock, matches and an alarm clock are likewise essential. Optional items are gaiters (especially in late summer when you have to negotiate volcanic scree), black bin liners (for melting snow in sunny weather), candles, a two-way radio and emergency whistle. You are unlikely to need a compass or climbing rope, but an incense stick will help to counter pungent refuge odours. *La Guía Verde* (on sale locally) comes with a reasonable map and an aerial photo with the climbing route superimposed.

You'll need to register for the climb at the Lago Tromen **guardaparque's office** (daily 8am–6pm), and the *guardaparque* will check that you have all the equipment listed above. If permission is granted you'll need to start the climb by 1pm at the latest. It will be necessary to acclimatize for a night in one of the three refuges on the mountain. The *guardaparque* will assign one to you, and will try to accommodate your preference. In high season, get to Tromen early, as all refuges might otherwise be full. The first refuge that you reach following the main trail is **Refugio RIM**. Its big advantage is that it has meltwater close by (Jan & Feb; if climbing outside high summer, you'll need to melt snow for water anyway). You may prefer to try for the smaller **CAJA**, further up the slope, especially if you plan to make the final ascent and total descent in one day, as this saves you half an hour's climb in the early morning. The **BIM** refuge, down from *RIM* via a second path, has pleasant tables and chairs, but is the lowest down the slope.

Puerto Canoa

At the western end of the lake is the settlement and jetty of **Puerto Canoa**, where you can look up at the fantastic, crevassed **south face** of Volcán Lanín. Puerto Canoa is the base for treks and boat trips in the area, including a fun **boat trip** that plies a circuit that includes lakes Huechulafquen, Paimún and Epulafquen, where you'll see the solidified lava river of Volcán Achen Ñiyeu.

ARRIVAL AND INFORMATION

Access points The volcano, and the central sector of the park around lakes Huechulafquen, Paimún and Tromen are best accessed from Junín de los Andes, while the park's southernmost reaches, and the area around Lago Lácar (see p.423) are best visited from San Martín, or as part of the Siete Lagos circuit.

Entrance and fees The park has an open border. There is a $50 entrance fee, payable at the Lago Huechulafquen entrance only.

Maps and guides If you want to hike and can read Spanish, the *Guía Sendas & Bosques de Lanín y Nahuel Huapi* is very useful. Two reasonably reliable maps (1:200,000) accompany the guide.

PARQUE NACIONAL LANÍN

When to go The whole park can be covered in snow from May to October, and it can snow in the higher mountain regions at almost any time of year. The best time to visit is in spring (especially Oct–Nov) or autumn (March to mid-May), when the deciduous trees adopt a spectacular palette, particularly in the Pehuenia area. Trekking is possible between late October and early May, although the season for some of the higher treks is shorter, usually from December to March. January and February see an influx of Argentine holiday-makers, but in general it is less crowded than Nahuel Huapi even in high season.

Lago Huechulafquen Castelli (☏ 02972 491557) operates two daily bus services from Junín de los Andes.

ACCOMMODATION AND EATING

LAGO HUECHULAFQUEN

On the lake's north shore, between Km47 and Km60, there are plenty of places to camp, with no fewer than fifteen sites with varying facilities run by the Raquithué and Cañicul Mapuche communities.

Bahía Cañicul Halfway along the lake at Km54 ☏ 02972 490211. A campsite with good, secluded pitches but basic toilets on top of the peninsula. $60

Hostería Huechulafquen Km56 ☏ 02972 427598,

ⓦ hosteriahuechulafquen.com. A snug fishing-lodge in full view of Lanín. Its restaurant is open to the public. Half-board $1400

Hostería Paimún ☏ 02972 491211, ⓦ hosteriapaimun .com.ar. In a delightful spot on the shore of Lago Paimún, this peaceful inn offers half- and full-board options, as well as guided fishing and boat trips. Half-board $1200, full-board $1500

Aluminé and the Pehuenia Circuit

Northwards from Junín, the **RP-23** runs mostly parallel to the turbulent waters of the Río Aluminé, carving through arid rocky gorges, before continuing on to Lago Aluminé and Villa Pehuenia and the groves of araucaria trees along the river's upper reaches. To the east, parallel with the valley, lies the **Sierra de Catan Lil**, a harsh and desiccated range that's older and higher than the nearby stretch of the Andes. The nearby area is home to the **Pehuenia Circuit** and its trio of stunning lakes, northwest from slow-paced **Aluminé**, and offering a plethora of outdoor experiences – you can choose between mountain biking, rafting and horseriding, or just hike along rewarding trails through beautiful woodland.

Aluminé

ALUMINÉ itself is a small but growing riverside town with a gentle pace of life. For a week in March it celebrates the **Fiesta del Pehuén** to coincide with the Mapuche harvest of *piñones*, with displays of horsemanship, music and *artesanía*. Its main claim to fame, though, is as a summer **rafting centre**: organized trips are run by Aluminé Rafting (☏ 02942 496322, ⓦ interpatagonia.com/aluminerafting). A branch road heads west from the village to Rucachoroi and (28km away) the *guardaparque* post.

ARRIVAL AND INFORMATION

By bus Aluminé's bus terminal is on Av 4 de Caballería. Albus (☎02942 496041, ⊚albus.com.ar) runs services on a circuit from Neuquén to Zapala, on to Aluminé and Villa Pehuenia, and back to Zapala again.

Destinations Neuquén (3 daily; 5hr 30min); Villa Pehuenia (2 daily; 1hr–1hr 30min).

By taxi There is no public transport heading west of the village; you'll need to book a taxi (☎02942 496397) or ask at local travel agent Mali Viajes (☎02942 15 662984) about group transport – its office is just off the plaza.

Tourist information From the bus terminal it's half a block to the Plaza San Martín, where you'll find the tourist office, Cristian Joubert 326 (daily 8am–10pm; ☎02942 496001, ⊚alumine.gov.ar).

ACCOMMODATION AND EATING

Aluminé Cristian Joubert 336 ☎02942 496174, ⊚hosterialumine.com.ar. A clean, straightforward hotel open year-round that is just off the main square; the place has its own restaurant, where breakfast is served (extra cost). **$350**

Pehuenia RP-23 and Capitán Crouzeilles ☎02942 496340. A resort hotel a little out of place in the otherwise rustic village. Its rooms are comfortable, if a little twee, and some have river views. The hotel rents out mountain bikes and arranges horseriding. **$430**

La Posta del Rey Cristian Joubert 336 ☎02942 496174. A good place to try a sort of *piñones* paté, while imaginative home-made pastas are the house speciality. Daily noon–3pm and 8pm–late.

The Pehuenia Circuit

The area around Villa Pehuenia, north of Aluminé, is one of the least developed yet most beautiful parts of the Argentine Lake District. This "forgotten corner" of Mapuche communities, wonderful mountain lakes, basalt cliffs and araucaria forests has largely escaped the commercial pressures found further south in the park system, although locals and recent settlers are fast waking up to its potential and tourists are arriving in ever-increasing numbers. However, infrastructure links are still fairly rudimentary, and having your own transport is a boon – otherwise, you'll need to take a taxi, as there is almost nothing in the way of public transport. One of the most popular routes is the **Pehuenia Circuit**, which links **Villa Pehuenia** on the northern bank of Lago Aluminé with tiny **Moquehue**, at the southwest tip of the lake of the same name, and passes along **Lago Ñorquinco**, which forms the northernmost boundary of the Parque Nacional Lanín. Most people finish or start the circuit in **Aluminé**.

Trekking and other activities

The lack of convenient road routes acts as an encouragement to **trek**: there is great potential in the area around Moquehue and Ñorquinco, but local politics and unreliable weather mean you should carefully discuss your plans and route with local *guardaparques* or, even better, take a guide who knows the area. Remember that it is obligatory to register your departure with a *guardaparque* before setting out and clock in your arrival at the other end. If it's not safe, you will be refused permission to trek. The terrain is also ideal for **mountain biking**, and there's tremendous scope for other outdoor activities here as well, such as **horseriding** and **rafting** through the scenic gorge of the Río Aluminé.

Villa Pehuenia

Set among araucaria trees on the shores of pristine Lago Aluminé, **VILLA PEHUENIA** is a splendid, fast-growing holiday village. *Cabañas* are the boom industry here, springing up in both the main part of the village and on the lumpy, tree-covered peninsula that juts into the lake's chilly waters. From the tourist office it is 700m to the commercial centre – a cluster of buildings selling food and other provisions. If you're walking around town, note that there are no street names and that the map provided by the tourist office lacks distinguishing features. To the north is **Volcán Batea Mahuida**, a mountain that has a minuscule Mapuche-run ski resort and a picturesque crater lake.

ARRIVAL AND INFORMATION

VILLA PEHUENIA

By bus A limited number of buses run from the village centre.

Destinations Aluminé (3 daily; 1hr–1hr 30min); Neuquén (3 weekly; 5hr).

Tourist information The well-informed tourist office (daily: summer 9am–9pm; winter 10am–6pm; ☎ 02942 498011, ⓦ villapehuenia.gov.ar) is at Km11 on the main road to Aluminé.

ACCOMMODATION AND EATING

The higher-end accommodation is on the peninsula, a picturesque twenty-minute walk from the main village. Following the road that runs by the side of the tourist office and then branches left at the lake brings you to a cluster of eating options.

Anhedonia Golfo Azul ☎ 02942 498054. This romantic and good-value restaurant offers fondue and home-made pasta by candlelight with views over the lake. 8pm–late; closed Wed.

Camping Lagrimitas RP-13 ☎ 02942 498003. Fantastic, tranquil pitches beneath araucarias by the lake shore. **$30**

★ **Posada La Escondida** ☎ 02942 15 691166, ⓦ posadalaescondida.com.ar. Luxurious accommodation on the west coast of the peninsula, where the suite-like rooms all have their own sun decks. Half-board. **$1500**

La Serena ☎ 02942 15 665068, ⓦ complejolaserena .com.ar. A well-designed, rustic hotel. The rooms are on two levels, with enough space to sleep four, small kitchens and wonderful views. A breakfast with home-made jams and passes to the hotel spa are included in the price. **$650**

Moquehue and around

Villa Pehuenia is connected to the pioneer village of **MOQUEHUE** by an unsurfaced road (15km) that runs around the northwestern shores of **Lago Moquehue**, Lago Aluminé's sibling. The two lakes are joined at La Angostura by a 20m-wide, 500m-long channel of captivating turquoise waters.

A loose conglomeration of farmsteads set in a broad pastoral valley at the southwestern end of its lake, Moquehue is overlooked on both sides by splendid ranks of rugged, forested ranges and **Cerro Bella Durmiente**, so named because the summit supposedly looks like the profile of a sleeping beauty. As yet, there's none of the contrived feel that comes from an excess of holiday-makers, and most residents have deep roots here. There is also no electricity in the village, though some places have generators.

Hiking around Moquehue

Unguided **hiking** around Moquehue has created local political problems, with landowners complaining that hikers ignore private-property signs and are causing damage to the countryside. While the effects of hiking are probably exaggerated, the depth of feeling is not, and the tourist office strongly recommends all hikers be accompanied by an authorized guide. Once you've organized a guide (available through Destinos Patagonicos; ☎ 02942 498067), one of the best day-hikes takes you around the southeastern shores of **Lago Moquehue**, through land belonging to the **Puel Mapuche** community. The trail leads past several Puel farmsteads as well as diminutive, secluded lakes, including Cari Laufquén, and beautiful woodland of *ñire*, *radal*, *notro*, araucaria and *coihue*.

However, there are also some excellent local walks that you can do independently: one short leg-stretch (35min one way) leads to an attractive **waterfall** in mystical mixed araucaria woodland; a slightly longer option is the hike up **Cerro Bandera** (2hr one way), with excellent views to Volcán Llaima.

ARRIVAL AND ACCOMMODATION

MOQUEHUE

There is no public transport to Moquehue – you'll need to have your own car or organize a taxi from Villa Pehuenia.

Bella Durmiente RP-13 ☎ 02942 496172, ⓦ bdurmiente moquehue.com.ar. A wonderfully authentic, wood-built guesthouse with camping and commanding vistas of the

scenery and wood fires in every room. **$380**

Camping Trenel RP-11 ☎ 02942 15 664720, ⓦ villa pehuenia.org/campingtrenel. Campsite located at the southeast corner of the lake on a slightly raised area with glorious views. Treks, canopy, climbing, kayaking and more can be organized from here; owner Fernando López is a well-known hiking guide in the area. $60

Central and northern Neuquén

Central and northern Neuquén Province is an area of desert-like *meseta* and steppe, home to Argentina's most important reserves of natural gas and petroleum. **Neuquén**, the eponymous provincial capital, is a likeable city and a good base for visiting the area's dinosaur-related attractions (see box, p.436): the village of **El Chocón** has a world-class paleontology exhibit and some truly remarkable dinosaur footprints *in situ* by the turquoise-hued Embalse Ezequiel Ramos Mexía reservoir, while in **Plaza Huincul** you can see bones from the largest dinosaur ever discovered, the *Argentinosaurus huinculensis*. Further north at **Lago Barreales** you can watch paleontologists in action, while at **Rincón de los Sauces**, in the extreme north of the province, the world's first fossilized dinosaur eggs were unearthed. Wine buffs will be more interested in the region's award-winning **wineries** a short way north of Neuquén – you can even stay at one and sleep above the cellars.

Neuquén

The bustling provincial capital of **NEUQUÉN** sits at the confluence of the rivers Neuquén and Limay, whose waters unite to become the Río Negro. With a population of a quarter of a million or so, this plains metropolis functions as the commercial, industrial and financial centre of the surrounding fruit- and oil-producing region. It's a surprisingly attractive and friendly place to pass a day or two, with a couple of museums as good as any

NEUQUÉN

▲ Chañar & Wineries

ACCOMMODATION
El Cortijo	2
Residencial Inglés	3
Suizo	1

● **RESTAURANTS**
1900 Cuatro	3
La Birra	4
Franz y Peppone	2
La Nonna Francesca	1
Rosignano	5

Obelisk

Museo Gregorio Álvarez

Parque Central

Museo Paraje Confluencia

Sala de Arte Emilio Saraco

Malvinas Monument

Museo Bellas Artes

Disused Railway Line

Bus Station

Airport

0   100
metres

other in the region. You'll find everything you need in the **microcentro**, which comprises the area north of the RN-22, three blocks on either side of the central boulevard.

Parque Central

The centre of life in town is the vast **Parque Central**, bisected by an old railway line and home to four free museums, three of which are housed in abandoned railway buildings. From west to east these are: the **Museo Gregorio Álvarez** (Mon–Fri 8am–8pm, Sat & Sun 4–8pm), at San Martín and Misiones, which contains several works by the local sculptor for whom the museum was named, as well as a small display on Patagonian history; the **Sala de Arte Emilio Saraco** (Mon–Fri 9am–8pm, Sat & Sun 2–9pm), an old cargo shed featuring temporary exhibitions by local artists; the **Museo Paraje Confluencia** (Mon–Fri 9am–6pm, Sat & Sun 6–10pm), which specializes in the city's history; and, the pick of the bunch, the **Museo Nacional de Bellas Artes** (Tues–Sat 8am–9pm, Sun 4–8pm) at the southeast corner of the park. The permanent exhibition here features examples from all the major European art movements and works by all the great Argentine masters; the most valuable painting is *La Última Copla*, by the great Valencian artist, Joaquín Sorolla. Adjacent to the museum is an impressive **monument to the fallen** of the Malvinas/Falklands campaign of 1982 – the names of the dead are poignantly displayed on a glass wall that overlooks the serene fountain.

7

ARRIVAL AND DEPARTURE   NEUQUÉN

By air Neuquén's airport (☎02994 440448) is 5km west of town off the RN-22, with connections to Buenos Aires three times a day (1hr 30min). Indalo runs a bus to the city centre; it departs from the main road in front of the airport every 20min (pay on the bus).

By bus Neuquén is a major transport nexus for the whole region. Its modern bus terminal, 3.5km east of the city centre on the RN-22, is regarded as one of the best in the country; it's styled along airport lines (bags come through

on a conveyor belt and passengers have to check in to platforms). Ko-Ko (☎0800 333 5656) runs a bus service to the centre every 15min; buy tickets from Kiosk 39 before boarding. Alternatively, you can take a taxi.

Destinations Bariloche (21 daily mainly am; 6hr); Buenos Aires (hourly; 16hr 30min); Córdoba (7 daily; 18hr 30min); Mendoza (8 daily; 12hr 30min); San Juan (3 daily; 12hr); San Martín de los Andes (8 daily; 6hr); Villa Pehuenia (2 daily; 5hr).

GETTING AROUND AND INFORMATION

By bus To use Neuquén's city buses, you must buy a ticket in advance from marked kiosks scattered throughout the city.

Tourist information There are tourist information booths at both the airport and the bus terminal, but the

main tourist office (daily 7am–11pm; ☎02994 423386, ⓦneuquentur.gob.ar) is at Félix San Martín 182, two blocks east of Av Olascoaga. It is a mine of information on the whole province and runs an unusually informative and up-to-date website, although largely Spanish only.

ACCOMMODATION

Hotels in Neuquén are busy even during the week, so it's well worth booking in advance. Several unspectacular though centrally located mid-range places are clustered around avenidas Olascoaga and Argentina – a simple breakfast is generally included in the price.

El Cortijo Tierra del Fuego 255 ☎02994 421795. Decent mid-range option just off the Parque Central. Heated rooms are clean and well maintained, if a little plain, and are arranged around small sunny courtyards. **$310**

Residencial Inglés Félix San Martín 534 ☎02994 422252. Clean but dated and with slightly tatty rooms. Still, it's one of the cheapest options in town, and the

garden with a vine is quite pleasant. **$270**

Suizo Carlos Rodríguez 167 ☎0299 442 2602, ⓦhotelsuizo.com.ar. Good-value higher-end option with bright, stylish rooms for up to four people, all with minibar and spacious bathroom. The reception area plays on the Swiss-chalet theme, but this is a classy and modern hotel. **$580**

EATING AND DRINKING

Neuquén's best places to eat and drink are scattered around Avenida Argentina between San Martín and Roca, where there are a number of pool bars and pizzerias in addition to more upmarket restaurants.

7

THE DINOSAUR SITES AROUND NEUQUÉN

Since 1988, the area around Neuquén has become a hotbed of dinosaur fever, with paleontologists uncovering **fossils** of both the largest herbivorous sauropod and the largest carnivorous dinosaur ever found. As you cross the Neuquén environs en route for the sites of discovery it is easy to imagine dinosaurs roaming the stunted plains and pterodactyls launching themselves into the air from the imposing cliff-faces. Getting to the sites by public transport is awkward – if you don't have your own car, your best bet is to go on a tour from Neuquén. These vary, but generally visit several sites of paleontological interest, some combining with winery stopoffs; try Arauquén (H. Yrigoyen 720 ☎0299 442 6476, ⓦarauquen.com) or Rahue Viajes (Sargento Cabral 165 ☎0299 448 1645, ⓦrahueviajes.com.ar).

MUSEO ERNESTO BACHMANN

On the banks of the picturesque Embalse Ezequiel Ramos Mexía hydroelectric reservoir, 79km southwest of Neuquén along the RN-237, the little oasis of **Villa El Chocón** is home to the **Museo Ernesto Bachmann** (daily 9am–7pm; $20) where you can see a virtually complete, hundred-million-year-old skeleton of *Giganotosaurus carolinii*, discovered 18km away in 1993. This fearsome creature puts even *Tyrannosaurus rex* in the shade: it measured a colossal 13m long (its skull alone accounting for 1.8m), stood 4.7m tall and weighed an estimated eight tonnes.

PARQUE CRETÁCICO

Three kilometres further south along the RN-237, a left turn-off leads another 2km down to the shores of Embalse Ezequiel Ramos Mexía. Here, at the northwest corner of the lake, is the **Parque Cretácico**, where you'll find some huge, astonishingly well-preserved **dinosaur footprints**. Not realizing what they were, fishermen once used them as barbecue pits. The footprints resemble those of a giant rhea, but were probably left by an iguanadon – a 10m-long herbivore – or some kind of bipedal carnivore. Other kidney-shaped prints are of four-footed sauropods, and smaller prints were probably left by 3m-long theropods.

MUSEO CARMEN FUNES

Plaza Huincul, just over 110km west of Neuquén along the RN-22, is where the region's petroleum reserves were discovered in 1918. Memorabilia from those pioneering days is displayed at the **Museo Carmen Funes** on the main street (Mon–Fri 9am–7pm, Sat & Sun 10.30am–8.30pm; $10), though you'll find it impossible to concentrate on petroleum with the full-size reconstruction of *Argentinosaurus huinculensis* looming in the hangar next door. Walking between the legs of this beast – 40m long, 18m high and weighing 100 tonnes – is a bit like walking under a jumbo jet. The only fossils of this giant beast that have been found are the pelvis, tibia, sacrum and some vertebrae – the reconstruction of the rest is based on educated guesswork.

DINO PROJECT

Heading northwest from Neuquén 90km along the RP-51 or the RP-7 brings you to the shores of **Embalse Cerros Colorados**, where you can watch paleontologists at work on the "**Dino Project**" at Lago Barreales (☎0299 15 418 2295, ⓦproyectodino.com.ar). Considered a "complete ecosystem of the Mesozoic era", the project, overseen by the University of Comahue, gives you the chance to help with the excavation. The most important finds are displayed at the on-site museum.

MUSEO ARGENTINO URQUIZA

Further afield, 250km northwest of Neuquén along the RP-8, the isolated town of **Rincón de los Sauces** is home to the **Museo Argentino Urquiza** (Mon–Fri 8am–noon & 4–8pm, Sun 4–8pm; ☎0299 156 319080), whose collection features the only known fossils of a titanosaurus, including an almost complete specimen. There is also a set of fossilized titanosaur eggs from nearby Auca Mahuida: the first set of **dinosaur eggs** ever to be found, they are approximately 14cm in diameter and have thin, porous shells through which the embryonic dinosaurs are thought to have breathed.

1900 Cuatro First floor of the Hotel Del Comahue, Av Argentina 377 ☎0299 443 2040. Serves eclectic and imaginative foreign dishes and appetizing meals, though the overall ambience is somewhat formal and staid, and prices are predictably high. Daily noon–3pm & 8pm–late.

La Birra Santa Fe and Independencia ☎0299 443 4344. Housed in a beautiful warehouse-style building with Hollywood-themed interior, this restaurant serves an international menu and the pizza and pasta are superb – and not that expensive. Daily 8pm–late.

Franz y Peppone 9 de Julio and Belgrano ☎0299 448 2299. Another pizza, pasta and all things Italian restaurant, aimed squarely at those on a backpacker's budget. Daily noon–3pm & 8pm–late.

La Nonna Francesca 9 de Julio 56 ☎0299 430 0930. Atmospheric trattoria, on a similar theme to *Franz y Peppone*, though pricier. Large portions mean you won't go hungry. Mon–Sat noon–3pm & 8pm–midnight, Sun noon–4.30pm.

Rosignano Independencia and Buenos Aires. Hugely popular deli and takeout joint (there's no room for eating in) packed with office workers at lunch time. Varied and inventive menu includes fish, vegetarian offerings and grilled meats. Mon–Fri noon–3pm.

Chañar and the wineries

The RP-7 follows the mighty Río Neuquén northwestwards from Neuquén across alluvial plains whose fertile lands feed the city with all manner of fruit and vegetables, while a series of reservoirs provides it with much needed water. Artificial oases have been created in the desert-like terrain just west of tiny **SAN PATRICIO DEL CHAÑAR** (or **Chañar**), 41km from Neuquén, to support some of the country's newest and finest vineyards, producing highly palatable whites and reds, using grape varieties such as semillon and malbec.

A handful of outstanding wineries have sprung up in the region and some can be visited as part of the local **Ruta del Vino**, or wine route. Tours, tastings and fine dining are on offer; in all cases, reserve ahead. After leaving Chañar in the direction of Añelo, heading along the RP-7, watch out on the right-hand side for the numbered lanes (*picadas*).

Bodega Valle Perdido

Visits Mon, Wed & Fri 11am, daily 7pm • US$40 includes a free bottle of wine • ☎011 6091 7777, ⓦvalleperdido.com.ar

Picada no. 6 leads off towards **Bodega Valle Perdido**, a state-of-the-art winery that is also a luxury **hotel**. In addition to checking out the fabulous cellars and tasting a variety of wines, you can make use of the wine spa and pool (with water, not wine), or lunch or dine at the top-rate restaurant, drinking the house wines, of course.

Bodega Familia Schroeder

Visits daily 10am & 5pm • $20 • ☎0299 443 5917, ⓦfamiliaschroeder.com

Picada no. 7 strikes off in the direction of **Bodega Familia Schroeder**. One-hour tours with tastings include a visit to the "dinosaur cellar", where a dinosaur fossil was found during the winery's construction. The vineyard also has an acclaimed restaurant-bar, open daily for lunch.

Bodega del Fin del Mundo

Visits Tues–Fri hourly 10am–4pm, Sat 10am–5pm • Free • ☎0299 485 5004, ⓦbodegadelfindelmundo.com

Picada 12 leads to the dramatically named **Bodega del Fin del Mundo** ("Winery at the End of the World") – so called because these wineries are in close competition with one or two in New Zealand for the title of the world's most southerly vineyard. These are the emblematic Patagonian wines, found throughout Argentina and further afield.

Bodega NQN

Tours hourly Mon–Fri 9am–noon & 2–4pm, Sat & Sun 10.30am–4.30pm • Free • ☎0299 489 7500, ⓦbodeganqn.com.ar

Picada 15 is the approach to **Bodega NQN**, which has an excellent if pricey restaurant-bar on the premises serving lunch daily. "Malma", meaning "pride" in Mapudungun, is the name of the winery's flagship range of red and white varietals, such as pinot noir and sauvignon blanc.

Patagonia

GLACIAR PERITO MORENO

Patagonia

An immense land of arid steppe, seemingly stretching into infinity, Patagonia is famed for its adventures and adventurers, for marvellous myths and fabulous facts. Its geographical immensity is paralleled only by the size of its reputation – which itself has taken on legendary proportions, thanks partly to writers such as Chatwin, Hudson and Theroux, as well as Charles Darwin. As a region of extremes, it has few equals in the world: from the biting winds that howl off the Southern Patagonian Icecap – the planet's largest area of permanent ice away from the poles – to the hearthside warmth of old-time Patagonian hospitality; from the lowest point on the South American continent, the Gran Bajo de San Julián, to the savagely beautiful peaks of the Fitz Roy massif; from the mesmerizingly sterile plains along the coastline to the astoundingly rich marine fauna that thrives and breeds just offshore.

One of southern Argentina's principal arteries, the **RN-3** stretches from the capital all the way down to austral **Río Gallegos**. The highlight of this Atlantic fringe of Patagonia is the wildlife, most notably at the nature reserve of **Península Valdés**, famous for its **whale-watching**, but also at **Punta Tombo**, the continent's largest **penguin** colony. Further south, in Santa Cruz Province, colonies of sea birds perch on spectacular porphyry cliffs at **Puerto Deseado** and playful Commerson's dolphins frolic in the *ría*, or estuary, just outside the town. This coastal area was key in defining the Patagonian pioneering spirit: Welsh settlers landed on a beach just south of Península Valdés, at what is now the resort town of **Puerto Madryn**, and gradually ventured into the **Lower Chubut Valley**. You can explore their cultural legacy in settlements such as **Gaiman** and **Trelew**.

The second main road running through Argentine Patagonia is the famous **RN-40** (Ruta 40), which starts at Cabo Vírgenes, the most southerly point of mainland Argentina, and hugs the Andean backbone most of the way all the way up to the country's northerly tip. Some of the destinations in this western fringe are difficult to reach without your own transport (and not always that easy with it) but it is along or close by this route that you'll find Argentine Patagonia's hallmark features: a slew of impressive national parks brimming with wild beauty, a series of great mountain lakes,

CUEVA DE LAS MANOS PINTADAS

Highlights

❶ Whale-watching Enjoy close-up views of majestic Southern right whales off the Península Valdés, one of the most important marine reserves on Earth. **See p.451**

❷ Welsh tearooms For a little taste of Wales, visit the town of Gaiman, which is famous for wonderful tearooms. **See p.458**

❸ Magellanic penguins Watch tens of thousands of these charming birds waddling around their major nesting sites – the biggest is at Punta Tombo. **See p.459**

❹ Parque Nacional Los Glaciares The legendary Glaciar Perito Moreno dominates any visit to southern Patagonia, with world-class

trekking in the Fitz Roy sector a close second. **See pp.466–487**

❺ Lamb asados Succulent lamb cooked over an open fire defines Patagonia almost as much as the horizon-defying terrain and relentless gales. **See p.471**

❻ RN-40 Leave the crowds behind and head out onto the open road on the Patagonian stretch of Argentina's famous RN-40. **See p.488**

❼ Cueva de las Manos Pintadas Wonder at rock art executed hundreds or thousands of years ago, dramatically sited in the heart of a canyon. **See p.494**

HIGHLIGHTS ARE MARKED ON THE MAP ON P.442

PATAGONIA

HIGHLIGHTS

1. Whale-watching
2. Welsh tearooms
3. Magellanic penguins
4. Parque Nacional Los Glaciares
5. Lamb asados
6. RN-40
7. Cueva de las Manos Pintadas

the finest spit-roast lamb *asados* and some unique skies. The Cañón of Río Pinturas is home to one of Argentina's most famous archeological sites, the **Cueva de las Manos Pintadas**, with its striking, age-old rock art; to the west two beautiful, wind-whipped **lakes, Posadas and Pueyrredón**, lie in a seldom-visited area in the lee of stately San Lorenzo peak. Further north is an outstanding geological curiosity, the **Bosque Petrificado Sarmiento**, a beguiling collection of ancient fossilized trees, while to the south stretches the wilderness of **Parque Nacional Perito Moreno**, one of the most inaccessible – and, consequently, untouched – of Argentina's national parks, with some excellent hiking trails.

The region's climax is reached, however, with two of the country's star attractions: the trekking and climbing paradise of the **Fitz Roy** sector of **Parque Nacional Los Glaciares**, accessed from the laidback village of **El Chaltén**; and the patriotically blue-and-white hues of craggy **Glaciar Perito Moreno**, one of the world's natural wonders, within easy reach of the tourist hotspot of **El Calafate**.

Brief history

For over ten thousand years, before the arrival of European seafarers in the sixteenth century, Patagonia was exclusively the domain of nomadic **indigenous tribes**. It was Magellan who coined the name "Patagonia" (see p.462) on landing at **Bahía San Julián**. The tales related by these early mariners awed and frightened their countrymen back home, mutating into myths of a godless region where death often struck hard.

European colonization

Two centuries of sporadic attempts to colonize the inhospitable coastlands only partially ameliorated Patagonia's unwholesome aura. In 1779, the Spanish established **Carmen de Patagones**, which managed to survive as a trading centre on the Patagonian frontier. In doing so, it fared considerably better than other early settlements: **Puerto de los Leones**, near Camarones (1535); **Nombre de Jesús**, by the Magellan Straits (late 1580s); **Floridablanca**, near San Julián (1784); and **San José** on the Península Valdés, all failed miserably, the latter crushed by a Tehuelche attack in 1810 after braving it out for twenty years. Change was afoot, nevertheless. In 1848, Chile founded Punta Arenas on the Magellan Straits, and in 1865, fired by their visionary faith, a group of **Welsh Nonconformists** arrived in the Lower Chubut Valley. Rescued from starvation in the early years by **Tehuelche** tribespeople and Argentine government subsidies, they managed to establish a stable agricultural colony by the mid-1870s.

Sheep farming and the oil industry

In the late nineteenth century, Patagonia changed forever with the introduction of **sheep**, originally brought across from the Islas Malvinas/Falkland Islands. The region's image shifted from one of hostility and hardship to that of an exciting frontier, where the "white gold" of wool opened the path to fabulous fortunes for pioneer investors. The transformation was complete within a generation: the plains were fenced in and roads were run from the coast to the cordillera. Native populations were booted out of their ancestral lands, while foxes and pumas were poisoned en masse to make way for gigantic estancias. By the early 1970s, there were over sixteen million sheep grazing the fragile pastures on over a thousand of these ranches. Later, the region's confidence and wealth blossomed further with the discovery of oil, spurring the growth of industry in towns such as **Comodoro Rivadavia**.

Plummeting international wool prices and desertification, though, eventually brought sheep farming to its knees, with the final blow being the eruption of Volcán Hudson in 1991, which buried immense areas of grazing land in choking ash. To make matters worse, the oil industry also went through a massive downturn and shed thousands of jobs.

Patagonia today

The corner has since been turned, however, and today the picture is far from bleak. Although there are hundreds of abandoned estancias in Santa Cruz alone, the Patagonian economy is once again booming – wool prices have been steadily rising owing to rocketing demand in emerging economies and a worldwide interest in a return to natural fibres. Perhaps more importantly for the region's economic future, **tourist** numbers are also rising sharply, as visitors come looking for a wild experience in an almost mythical land. This swelling interest has helped rekindle regional pride to the point where locals boast of being NYC – Nacido y Criado (Born and Bred) – in Patagonia.

GETTING AROUND   **PATAGONIA**

Distances are huge in Patagonia, but most cities and towns are served by regular buses. However, to make the most of some of the more remote places, such as Península Valdés (see p.448) and a number of destinations along Ruta 40, you will really need to rent a car. Note also that some bus services do not operate out of season (Easter–Sept), above all along and around the Ruta 40, while others are severely curtailed.

The RN-3 coastal route

A journey along the seemingly endless RN-3, with a few detours just off it, offers many opportunities – albeit at great distances from one another – to marvel at magnificent wildlife; nowhere is this easier or more rewarding than at the world-class reserve of **Península Valdés**, best accessed from the seaside town of **Puerto Madryn**. In addition you can check out Patagonia's fascinating Welsh legacy in the villages of the Lower Chubut Valley near **Trelew**, while nature lovers will want to see the huge Magellanic penguin colony at **Punta Tombo**. The long trip can be broken up with stopovers in a trio of typical austral ports, **Puerto Deseado**, **Puerto San Julián** and **Puerto Santa Cruz**, each with its own wealth of marine wildlife and historical associations. A short way south of the last of these three, **Monte León**, the country's newest national park – and the first to be created on the coast – is well worth a visit even if the marvellous estancia in its midst is beyond your budget. With your own transport, you could also fit in a side-trip to the curious petrified forests of the **Monumento Natural Bosques Petrificados**, or the **Bosque Petrificado Sarmiento** (see p.461), closer to the Ruta 40 but accessible from the coast, too. The end of the road – and seemingly the end of the world – is reached at workaday **Río Gallegos**, a jumping-off point for travelling on to Tierra del Fuego or for starting a journey northwards along the RN-40.

Puerto Madryn

Sprawling along the beautiful sweep of the Golfo Nuevo, Argentina's self-styled diving capital, **PUERTO MADRYN**, is the gateway to the ecological treasure-trove of Península Valdés; indeed, the superb **Ecocentro**, just east of town, makes a great introduction to the area's abundant marine life. Though Puerto Madryn was where the Welsh first landed in Patagonia in 1865, little development took place until the arrival of the railway from Trelew two decades later, when it began to act as the port for the communities in the Lower Chubut Valley. With the explosion of tourism in recent years, Puerto Madryn has undergone rapid growth, and the town's small permanent population swells exponentially during the summer months.

Parque Histórico Punta Cuevas

Blvd Brown 3681, 4km south of the centre along the coast road • Daily 24hr • Free • ⓦ puntacuevas.org.ar • Bus #2 from the bus station

The **Parque Histórico Punta Cuevas** marks the first Welsh settlement in Patagonia with the **Monumento al Indio Tehuelche**, a statue erected both to celebrate the centenary of the arrival of the Welsh and pay homage to the Tehuelche (see box, p.446),

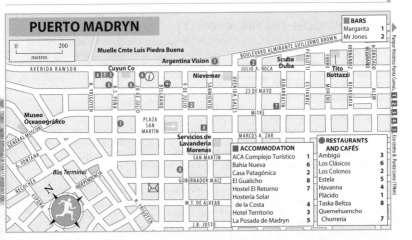

who provided invaluable help to the community. At sunset from here there is a glorious wide view of the arc of the Golfo Nuevo to the lights of the town. Close to the monument are the 3m-square **foundations** of the very first houses built by the pioneers, right above the high-water mark. There is also the small but fascinating **Museo del Desembarco** (daily except Tues: March–Nov 3–7pm; Dec–Feb 5–9pm; $8), which tells the story of the Welsh arrival in the region.

Ecocentro

Julio Verne 3784, just beyond Punta Cuevas • Jan & Feb daily 10am–1pm March & July–Sept daily except Tues 3–7pm; April–June Wed–Sun 3–7pm; Oct–Dec daily except Tues 3–8pm • $55 • ☎ 0280 445 7470, 🖥 ecocentro.org.ar • Bus #2 from the bus station

Round the headland past the Monumento al Indio Tehuelche is Puerto Madryn's prime attraction, the excellent **Ecocentro**. An interactive museum set up to promote respect and understanding for marine ecosystems, it also houses a stunning life-size model of the orca Mel, famous for catching sea-lion pups and returning them to the shore unharmed. Be sure to go up the tower as well, to relax on one of the comfy sofas while enjoying panoramic views of the bay. There's also a lovely café.

Museo Oceanográfico y de Ciencias Naturales

D. Garcia and Menéndez • Mon–Fri 9am–7pm, Sat 3–7pm • $10

The rather staid **Museo Oceanográfico y de Ciencias Naturales** is not in the same league as Ecocentro, but the location – in the elegant, turreted Chalet Pujol – is grand. You can feel a whale's baleen and view relics from Welsh pioneering days in addition to more sombre photos of sea-lion massacres.

ARRIVAL AND DEPARTURE

PUERTO MADRYN

By plane Puerto Madryn's airport is 10km outside the city (around $50 by taxi), but there is a far greater range of flights from Trelew airport, 65km south (see p.456). Aerolíneas Argentinas has an office at Roca 427 (☎ 0810 222 86527, 🖥 aerolineas.com.ar); LADE is at Roca 117 (☎ 0280 445 1256, 🖥 lade.com.ar).

By bus The bus terminal is at Ávila and Independencia,

a short walk from the city centre.

Destinations Bariloche (1–3 daily; 14hr); Buenos Aires (10–11 daily; 18hr); El Calafate (1 daily; 20–23hr); Puerto Pirámides (1–3 daily; 1hr 15min); Río Gallegos (4–5 daily; 16–19hr); Trelew (every 30min–1hr; 1hr).

By car There's car rental at Fiorasi, Roca 165 (☎ 0280 445 6300, 🖥 fiorasirentacar.com).

INFORMATION AND ACTIVITIES

Tourist information Much of what you'll need in Puerto Madryn lies within three blocks in any direction of

the first-rate tourist office at Roca 223 (April to mid-Dec Mon–Fri 7am–9pm, Sat & Sun 8am–9pm; mid-Dec to

THE TEHUELCHE: THE BRAVE PEOPLE

Once spread throughout much of Patagonia, the **Tehuelche**, whose name, meaning "brave people", is derived from the language of the Chilean Araucanian groups, actually consisted of three different tribes – the Gününa'küna, Mecharnúek'enk and Aónik'enk – each of whom spoke a different language but shared common bonds of culture. Great intertribal parliaments were held occasionally, but any alliances formed would be temporary, and sporadic intertribal warfare broke out.

CULTURE AND RELIGION

The Tehuelche's **nomadic culture** – centred on the hunting of rhea and guanaco – had probably existed for well over 3000 years by the time Magellan landed on Patagonian soil, but contact with Europeans soon brought change. By 1580, Sarmiento de Gamboa had reported use of the horse by the Tehuelche, and by the early eighteenth century the animal had become integral to Tehuelche life. Intertribal contact and intermarriage became more common and hunting techniques evolved, with **boleadoras** and lances increasingly preferred to the bow and arrow. The *boleadora* consisted of two or three stones wrapped in guanaco hide and connected by long thongs made from rhea or guanaco sinew. Whirled around the head, these were thrown to ensnare animals at close quarters. *Boleadoras* are the main physical legacy of Tehuelche culture in today's Argentina.

Tehuelche **religious beliefs** recognized a benign supreme god (variously named Kooch, Maipé or Táarken-Kets), but he did not figure greatly in any outward devotions. In contrast, the malign spirit, **Gualicho**, was a much-feared figure, the regular beneficiary of horse sacrifices and the object of shamanistic attentions. The main divine hero was **Elal**, the being who created man.

DECLINE AND FALL

The decline of **Tehuelche civilization** came fast: in 1870, there were estimated to be 1500 Tehuelche in Patagonia; a 1931 census in Santa Cruz Province (home to the greatest population of Tehuelche) recorded only 350. Wars with the *huincas* (white men) were catastrophic – above all, Julio Roca's Conquest of the Desert (see p.533) in 1879 – and were exacerbated by intertribal conflicts. Even peaceful contact with *huinca* civilization led to severe problems: disease wiped out whole tribal groups, while alcohol abuse led whites to replace one misconception (the "noble savage") with another (the "moral delinquent"), enabling them spuriously to justify attempts to settle ancestral Tehuelche lands as part of a greater plan to "civilize the *indio*".

Following the capitulation of the last rebel group to Roca in December 1884, the remaining Tehuelche were pushed into increasingly marginal lands. Guanaco populations plummeted and Tehuelche life became one of dependency. Many found the closest substitute to the old way of life was to join the estancias that had displaced them as *peón* shepherds. In this way, they were absorbed into the rural underclass. Whereas Mapuche customs and language have managed, tenuously, to survive, Tehuelche populations fell below that imprecise, critical number that is necessary for the survival of a cultural heritage. The last Gününa'küna speaker died in 1960. The Aónik'enk language can be spoken, at least partially, by fewer than a dozen people.

March Mon–Fri 7am–11pm, Sat & Sun 8am–11pm; ☎0280 445 3504, ⓦ madryn.gov.ar/turismo), where you can get good maps, leaflets in English, and a list of independent, multilingual guides.

Tour operators Dozens of agencies organize day-trips to the Península Valdés, all charging around $300 (excluding entrance fee and whale-watching trip): some of the best run are Argentina Vision, Roca 536 (☎0280 445 1427, ⓦ argentinavision.com); Cuyun Co, Roca 165 (☎0280 445 1845, ⓦ cuyunco.com); Tito Bottazzi, Blvd Brown and Martín Fierro (☎0280 447 4110, ⓦ titobottazzi.com); and Nievemar, Roca 549 (☎0280 445 5544, ⓦ nievemartours.com.ar).

Diving Diving trips that take in the area's offshore wrecks and abundant marine life start at around $350. The experienced

Madryn Buceo, on Blvd Brown by the third roundabout in Balneario Nativo Sur (☎0280 15 456 4422, ⓦ madrynbuceo .com), has English-speaking instructors and offers a wide range of dives (including one with sea lions; around $900) and courses. Scuba Duba, Blvd Brown 893 (☎0280 445 2699, ⓦ scubaduba.com.ar), is another good option.

Mountain biking Mountain bikes can be rented (from $60–80/day) from several places, including Vernadino Club de Mar (☎0280 447 4289), Blvd Brown 860. There are a couple of good bike excursions within easy reach of town: north along the old Puerto Pirámides road to Playa Doradilla (17km from Madryn), where you can often see whales late in the afternoon between June and September, and to the sea-lion colony at Punta Loma (19km in the other direction).

ACCOMMODATION

Puerto Madryn has a wide range of accommodation with good discounts available off season; high season (Oct–Dec), when prices are at their highest, is the best time for whale-watching. The better places tend to fill up quickly regardless of the time of year, however, so advanced bookings are recommended. Rates for all include breakfast, unless stated otherwise.

ACA Complejo Turístico Punta Cuevas Punta Cuevas ☎ 0280 445 2952, ⓦ acamadryn.com.ar. This well-run complex has camping spots (tents provided), simple rooms and self-contained apartments suitable for groups. There are plenty of facilities, including a restaurant-bar. Breakfast costs extra. Camping $\overline{$52}$, doubles $\overline{$300}$, apartments $\overline{$670}$

Bahía Nueva Roca 67 ☎ 0280 445 1677, ⓦ bahianueva .com.ar. Smart, red-brick hotel on the seafront, with comfortable rooms – try to get one of the few with an ocean view – and a nice lounge with an extensive library. The ample buffet breakfasts are also a cut above the rest. $\overline{$525}$

Casa Patagónica Roca 2210 ☎ 0280 445 1540, ⓦ casa-patagonica.com.ar. This cheerful, family-run B&B has a handful of rooms with shared bathrooms and one en suite; they are simply decorated, but comfortable and good value. Guests have access to a microwave and a fridge, and there's a living room to relax in. $\overline{$250}$

★ **El Gualicho** Marcos Zar 480 ☎ 0280 445 4163, ⓦ elgualicho.com.ar. Fantastic HI-affiliated hostel with a lovely garden, welcoming staff, a communal kitchen, and a good selection of private rooms and four-, six- and eight-bed dorms. Tours, diving trips and bike rental are also on offer. Dorms $\overline{$95}$, doubles $\overline{$420}$

Hostel El Retorno Mitre 798 ☎ 0280 445 6044, ⓦ elretornohostel.com.ar. An attractive hostel whose whitewashed exterior is mirrored by the spick-and-span rooms – both dorms and private rooms – heated bathrooms and spotless communal areas. Kitchen and laundry facilities, barbecue, table tennis and bike rental are all available too. Dorms $\overline{$70}$, doubles $\overline{$250}$

Hostería Solar de la Costa Brown 257 ☎ 0280 445 8822, ⓦ solardelacosta.com. A popular beachfront guesthouse at the eastern end of town, *Solar de la Costa* has tastefully furnished en suites, many of which look out over the Golfo Nuevo. Staff are friendly, and there's a peaceful garden out back. $\overline{$530}$

Hotel Territorio Blvd Brown 3251 ☎ 0280 447 0050, ⓦ hotelterritorio.com.ar. The top hotel in town, located close to Punta Cuevas, has slick, contemporary en suites with plenty of space and sea views. There's a gym, spa, restaurant-bar, and decor that features artwork, historic photos, and even a whale skeleton (a combination that works far better than you might think). $\overline{$1650}$

La Posada de Madryn Abraham Matthews 2951 ☎ 0280 447 4087, ⓦ la-posada.com.ar. A stylish guesthouse, located close to a wooded area, with compact, minimalist en suites that receive lots of natural light. There is also a comfortable communal lounge, plus an outdoor pool and a pleasant garden. $\overline{$550}$

EATING AND DRINKING

Puerto Madryn is known for its seafood, and there are several beachfront **restaurants** that serve nothing else, including the town's speciality, *arroz con mariscos* – a variant of paella usually containing prawns, squid and clams. Prices here – and in Patagonia as a whole – are higher than in the central and northern regions of the country.

Ambigú Roca and R.S. Peña ☎ 0280 447 2541, ⓦ ambigu resto.com.ar. The menu jumps from steaks, seafood and thinnish-crust pizzas to more exotic fare, such as curries and stir-fries. The walls are covered with old drinks posters and there are plenty of magazines to read, though the topless photos in the bathrooms are rather out of keeping with the restaurant's popularity with families. Mains $40–100. Daily noon–2pm & 8pm–midnight.

Los Clásicos 28 de Julio and 25 de Mayo ☎ 0280 447 1455. A typical Argentine café-restaurant where time seems to stand still: there's football on the TV, old photos of Puerto Madryn on the wall, and a steady stream of local customers. Pop in for a coffee (from $12) or a good-value lunch or dinner and watch the world go by. Daily 9am–10/11pm.

Los Colonos Roca and Estorini ☎ 0280 445 8486. A super-kitsch seafood restaurant in a building designed to look like a ship. Inside, the decor, naturally, has a maritime theme, with starfish, buoys, and rope tied in knots. The food is good too, and comes in hearty portions. Mains $41–90. Daily noon–3pm & 7.30pm–midnight.

Estela R.S. Peña 27 ☎ 0280 445 1573. This friendly, down-to-earth steakhouse serves top-notch *morcilla*, *chorizo* and *bifes de chorizo*, as well as a vast *parrilla*. Steaks cost around $55–90, and there are some good weekday lunch deals. Daily noon–2pm & 8pm–midnight.

Havanna Roca and 28 de Julio ☎ 0280 447 3373, ⓦ havanna.com.ar. The Puerto Madryn branch of the venerable Argentine coffeehouse chain is a reliable spot for coffee ($12–25) at any time of the day – if you need a treat, the sugary *alfajores* are good options too. Daily 8/9am–10/11pm.

Margarita Roca and R.S. Peña ☎ 0280 447 0885. This lively bar is a great place for a pre- or post-dinner drink – a beer will set you back around $20–25. Live bands often perform, and there's a happy hour (7.30–9pm) too. Mon–Sat 7.30pm–2/3am.

8

Mr Jones 9 de Julio 116 ☎0280 447 5368. A buzzing pub-restaurant, popular with locals and young gringos alike. Most of the diners – who fill up the wooden benches and spill out onto the street-side tables – are here for a beer (from around $20) and a *picada* (cold meat and cheese platter). Mon–Sat 7pm–1/2am.

Plácido Roca 506 ☎0280 445 5991, ⓦplacido.com.ar. Elegant and intimate restaurant directly overlooking the Golfo Nuevo: it serves fine seafood, including hearty paellas and delicious prawn kebabs, as well as home-made pasta dishes. There's an excellent wine list too. Mains $40–80. Daily noon–4pm & 8pm–1am.

Quemehuencho Churrería Roque Sáenz Peña 212 ☎0280 15 440 4016. This café has two specialities: delicious *churros*, filled with everything from *dulce de leche* to home-made jam, and the national drink, *mate*. For the novice *mate* drinker, the friendly staff are on hand to explain how everything works. Drinks $10–20. Mon–Fri 8am–noon & 4.30–8pm, Sat & Sun 4.30–8pm.

★ **Taska Beltza** 9 de Julio 461 ☎0280 447 4003, ⓦlataskabeeltza.com.ar. Unquestionably the best seafood restaurant in town, and very good value for money (mains $40–80). Ask for the daily special, or sample a few Basque tapas, followed by a mouthwatering *merluza* (hake) and wash it down with a chilled Chablis. Tues–Sun 7.30pm–midnight.

DIRECTORY

Banks There are plenty of ATMs, including at Banco de la Nación, 9 de Julio 117, and Banco del Chubut, 25 de Mayo 154. **Internet** There are numerous internet cafés, including TeleNetK on Belgrano and 25 de Mayo. **Laundry** Servicios de Lavandería Morenas, Sarmiento and Marcos Zar (☎0280 445 6969).

Península Valdés

The reserve entrance is halfway along the isthmus, 43km from Madryn • Daily 8am–8pm • $100 per person, plus $8 per car • ☎0280 445 0489, ⓦpeninsulavaldes.org.ar

PENÍNSULA VALDÉS, a sandy-beige, treeless hump of land connected to the mainland by a 35km isthmus, is one of the planet's most significant marine reserves, winning deserved UNESCO World Heritage status in 1999. It was beautifully evoked by Gerald Durrell in *The Whispering Land*: "It was almost as if the peninsula and its narrow isthmus was a cul-de-sac into which all the wildlife of Chubut had drained and from which it could not escape." No description, however, prepares you for the astonishing richness of the marine environment that surrounds it – most notably the **southern right whales** that migrate here each year to frolic in the waters off the village of **Puerto Pirámides** – nor the immense animal colonies that live at the feet of the peninsula's steep, crumbly cliffs.

The first attempt to establish a permanent settlement here was made in 1779 by Juan de la Piedra, who constructed a fort on the shores of the Golfo San José. A small number of settlers tried to scrape a living by extracting salt, but the colony was abandoned in 1810 after attacks by the local Tehuelche; an extremely limited salt-extraction industry exists to this day in the saltpans at the bottom of Argentina's second deepest depression, the **Salina Grande**, 42m below sea level, in the centre of the peninsula. However, it is nature tourism that's the pot of gold now, with **Punta Delgada**, **Punta Cantor** and **Punta Norte**, along with **Caleta Valdés** bay, providing some of the best opportunities on the continent for viewing marine mammals such as elephant seals and sea lions. How the recent discovery of oil and shale gas reserves in the vicinity of the reserve will affect this remains unclear at present.

Be warned not to collect your own shellfish in the area, because of the possibility of periodic **red-tide** outbreaks; all shellfish served in restaurants is safe for consumption.

Isla de los Pájaros

Some 22km beyond the reserve entrance, you pass a signposted turn-off north that takes you 5km to the lookout point for the **Isla de los Pájaros** (Bird Island), a strictly controlled area where access is only permitted for the purposes of scientific research. From the shore, telescopes enable you to view sea birds in the nesting colonies 800m away. The most active months are between September and March, when you can spot egrets, herons, waders, ducks, cormorants, gulls and terns.

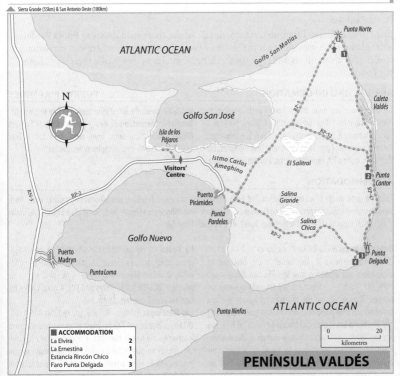

(Map of Península Valdés)

Punta Norte

ATLANTIC OCEAN

Golfo San Matías

1

Caleta Valdés

N

RP-3

RP-52

Golfo San José

Isla de los Pájaros

Istmo Carlos Ameghino

El Salitral

Visitors' Centre

Puerto Pirámides

Salina Grande

Punta Cantor

2

RP-47

Punta Pardelas

Salina Chica

RP-2

RN-3

RP-2

Golfo Nuevo

Puerto Madryn

Punta Loma

Punta Delgada

3

4

Punta Ninfas

ATLANTIC OCEAN

8

■ ACCOMMODATION	
La Elvira	2
La Ernestina	1
Estancia Rincón Chico	4
Faro Punta Delgada	3

0   20
kilometres

PENÍNSULA VALDÉS

▲ Trelew (17km)

0   20

Centro de Interpretaciones

Daily 8am–8pm • Free

Just past the turn-off to the Isla de los Pájaros is the **Centro de Interpretaciones**, which although poor by comparison with Puerto Madryn's Ecocentro (see p.445), still has some interesting old photos and the skeleton of a young southern right whale that washed up at Caleta Valdés.

Puerto Pirámides and around

At the end of the asphalt road, 105km from Puerto Madryn, lies the tiny settlement of **Puerto Pirámides**, named after the pointed cliff at the mouth of the bay. This is *the* place for whale-watching: between June and mid-December the nearby waters are temporarily home to the most famous of all the peninsula's visitors, the **southern right whale**. Few experiences beat the thrill of watching these massive animals approaching your boat, breaching (leaping out of the water) or jutting their tails above the surface as they dive to feed. There are also good **diving** opportunities for humans (see p.451), with some trips attracting the attention of sea lions and whales, though it's officially illegal to dive with whales; locals refer euphemistically to "*excursiones especiales*". You can walk to the **sea-lion colony** (Jan is the best time) at Punta Pirámides, 5km round the headland to the northwest.

With only three streets, the village's orientation is straightforward: the main one you come in on, Avenida de las Ballenas, runs parallel to the beach, with two perpendicular streets descending to the water – the shorter, busier Primera Bajada and the much longer Segunda Bajada.

Punta Pardelas

Just outside Puerto Pirámides, it's worth taking the short road down to **Punta Pardelas**, a delightful little spot right on the shore of Golfo Nuevo, from where you can often get spectacular close-up sightings of southern right whales as they make their way along the coast.

ARRIVAL AND INFORMATION
PUERTO PIRÁMIDES

By bus There are daily buses from Puerto Madryn to Puerto Pirámides (Mon–Fri departing 6.30am, 9.45am & 4pm, returning 8.10am, 1pm & 6pm; Sat & Sun departing 9.45am, returning 6pm; 1hr 15min; note that the timetable fluctuates quite a lot, especially outside of the high season, so double-check the latest information before setting off).

Tourist information There's a tourist office on Primera Bajada (daily 8am–6pm; open until 8pm Jan & Feb; ☎ 0280 449 5048, ⓦ puertopiramides.gov.ar).

ACCOMMODATION

There's a good range of accommodation, but book ahead in January and February when hordes of tourists arrive for a seaside-cum-partying experience, and throughout the whale-watching season (June–Dec). Some places close shop in the early winter months (May and sometimes June). Rates include breakfast.

Bahía Ballenas Av de las Ballenas s/n ☎ 0280 447 4110, ⓦ bahiaballenas.com.ar. This hostel is the best bet for backpackers and shoestring travellers. The two dorms – one male, one female – are clean and tidy, though not always the quietest. The owners run the Tito Bottazzi agency (see box opposite) and offer guests discounts on their tours. Dorms **$45**

★ **Hostería Ecológica del Nomade** Av de las Ballenas s/n ☎ 0280 449 5044, ⓦ ecohosteria.com.ar. This environmentally sensitive guesthouse is based in a handsome building and has eight lovely, minimalist en suites. Staff are ultra-friendly and the home-made breakfasts delicious. Big discounts offered for stays of two nights or more. **$800**

La Posta Av de las Ballenas s/n ☎ 0280 449 5036, ⓦ lapostapiramides.com.ar. A staggered line of good-value, if rather plain, apartments – sleeping up to six people – all with kitchenettes and TVs. A good choice for families or self-caterers. **$500**

Las Restingas Primera Bajada s/n ☎ 0280 449 5101, ⓦ lasrestingas.com. The smartest place in town in a great location on the beach. Most of the bright and airy (though overpriced) en suites have wonderful sea views, so you might even do some whale-spotting from the comfort of your bedroom. There's also a gym, spa and restaurant. **$1150**

VISITING PENÍNSULA VALDÉS

Many people see Península Valdés on a **day-trip** from Puerto Madryn (see p.444), following a fairly standard route that visits the lookout point for Isla de los Pájaros, Puerto Pirámides (where a whale trip costs from around $170) and Punta Cantor and Caleta Valdés and – depending on the operator – either Punta Norte or Punta Delgada. Be sure to find out exactly what sights you're visiting and how long you'll get in each place (most tours stay 1hr at each destination), whether the guide speaks English and the size of the group (some companies use large buses). Tours are long (10–12hr) so bring picnic provisions, though you can buy lunch in Puerto Pirámides.

If you want to visit the peninsula independently, the Mar y Valle **bus service** links Puerto Madryn with Puerto Pirámides (see p.449). However, it's difficult to get from Pirámides to the rest of Península Valdés without your own wheels.

Undoubtedly the best way to see the peninsula is to **rent a car** from Trelew or Puerto Madryn, allowing you to decide how long you want to spend wildlife-watching, and to time your arrival at Punta Norte or Caleta Valdés for high tide, when there's the best chance of seeing orcas; it also gives you the freedom to stay at an estancia, recommended for a better appreciation of what makes the peninsula so special (see opposite). Do not attempt to rush, however, especially if this is your first experience of driving on unsurfaced roads – serious crashes and fatalities happen with alarming regularity on the peninsula, especially after rain. When renting, check what happens if you break down or have a minor accident, as rescue bills can be hefty.

The whale-watching season runs from mid-June to mid-December, but the **best time to visit** the peninsula is from September to November, when elephant seals are also active, the penguin colonies have returned to breed and, if you're lucky, you stand a chance of seeing orcas cruising behind the spit at Caleta Valdés.

WHALE-WATCHING FROM PUERTO PIRÁMIDES AND OTHER ACTIVITIES

In season (June to mid-Dec), you are almost guaranteed to come within a few metres of a southern right whale. If you're here towards the end of the season, there will be fewer specimens and you'll have to go farther out to sea to spot them, but you're also likely to see mothers with calves. Outside these dates, boat trips generally spot dolphins and sea lions. During the whale-spotting season, half a dozen reliable and professional companies offer regular daytime and "sunset" **whale-watching** trips (from around $170) into the Golfo Nuevo: Hydrosport (📞 0280 449 5065, 🌐 hydrosport.com.ar), Tito Bottazzi (📞 0280 449 5050, 🌐 titobottazzi.com) and Whales Argentina (📞 0280 449 5015, 🌐 whalesargentina.com.ar) are all on Primera Bajada; Jorge Schmid (📞 0280 449 5012, 🌐 puntaballena.com.ar) and Peke Sosa (📞 0280 449 5010, 🌐 avistajespekesosa.com.ar) are both on Segunda Bajada; while Southern Spirit (📞 0280 449 50594, 🌐 southernspirit.com.ar) is marked by a model whale on Las Ballenas at the top of Primera Bajada. Services vary little, but check what type of boat you'll be using; the semi-rigid inflatable zodiacs allow you to get closer to the animals, but bounce more in rough waters. Remember, though, that boat operators are meant to observe strict regulations about keeping a respectful distance from the cetaceans; the whales, especially the young, are highly inquisitive, however, and will often come up close or even plunge beneath the boat.

DIVING AND KAYAKING

For **diving**, Buceo Aventura (📞 0280 449 5031) has decent equipment and friendly staff, as does Patagonia Scuba (📞 0280 449 5030, 🌐 patagonia-scuba.com.ar). Patagonian Brothers Expeditions on Avenida de las Ballenas (📞 0280 15 434 0618, 🌐 patagoniaexplorers.com) runs excellent guided small-group **kayak** trips in both gulfs, from half-day paddles to nine-day expeditions.

8

EATING AND DRINKING

⭐ **La Estación** Opposite the petrol station 📞 0280 449 5047. One of the best bars in the area with a cosy ambience, laidback vibe and mix of old-time memorabilia and rock iconography. It also serves great home-made pastas and fresh fish and seafood. Mains $40–100. Daily 10am–11pm/midnight.

Hostería The Paradise Av de las Ballenas, on the corner with 2a Bajada 📞 0280 449 5030, 🌐 hosteria theparadise.com.ar. One of the best restaurants in Puerto Píramides: the fish and seafood dishes ($40–100) are highlights, and there's a varied wine list too. Daily noon–11pm.

Punta Delgada

From Punta Pardelas, it's another 70km to **Punta Delgada**, at the southeasterly tip of the peninsula, past the pinky-white salt deposits of the **Salina Grande** and **Salina Chica** depressions. Punta Delgada itself is a headland topped by a lighthouse, part of the *Faro Punta Delgada* hotel (see below). The area affords excellent opportunities to view **sea lions** and, in high season, **elephant seals**. However, it is private property, and can only be visited on tours run by Argentina Vision (see p.446), who own the hotel. Independent travellers are allowed to stop, but will need to buy lunch at the hotel's restaurant in order to access the beach on a short guided tour (free).

ACCOMMODATION   PUNTA DELGADA

⭐ **Estancia Rincón Chico** Just southwest of Punta Delgada 📞 0280 447 1733, 🌐 rinconchico.com.ar. This wonderful estancia blends traditional Patagonian architecture with attractive modern rooms. The food served in the handsome dining room is simple but delicious, while the lobby and living room are decorated with bric-a-brac, such as stranded whale-bones. The highlight of any stay is a guided visit to the large colonies of marine wildlife (up to 3500 sea lions and 10,000 elephant seals) that gather on the estancia's private beach. You can also rent bikes to explore the steppe

and admire the cliff-top ocean views. Closed Easter to mid-Aug. Rates include full board and excursions. **$2900**

Faro Punta Delgada 📞 0280 447 1733, 🌐 rinconchico .com.ar. Perched on a cliff and buffeted by winds, this converted lighthouse is a very atmospheric place to stay. Rooms are comfortable, and there's a restaurant and pub. As well as tours of the nearby elephant-seal reserve (included in the price of your room), staff can organize treks, bike rides and horseriding. Closed April–July. Rates include breakfast. **$1420**

Punta Cantor and Caleta Valdés

North along the coast from Punta Delgada are a string of beaches bustling with marine mammals. **Punta Cantor**, midway up the peninsula, is a colony of seven thousand elephant seals at the foot of a high cliff. Walk down the cliff face of sedimentary deposits and fossilised oysters (around a million years old) to the ridge just above the beach – don't try to climb down onto the beach, however, as it is strictly off limits. The best time to visit is from late September until early November, when the bull elephant seals fight for females – a display of bloodied blubbery bulk.

Two kilometres north is a viewpoint over the shifting curves of the shingle spits of **Caleta Valdés** – from September to November, orcas may be spotted entering the *caleta*, or bay behind the spit, at high tide – and there's a colony of Magellanic penguins 3km further on. This road is also one of the best for sighting *maras*, *choiques*, skunks and other terrestrial wildlife.

ACCOMMODATION	PUNTA CANTOR AND CALETA VALDÉS
La Elvira Near the Punta Cantor turn-off ☎0280 447 4248, ⓦlaelvira.com.ar. Although this working estancia isn't the most attractive from the outside – the main building is a rather ugly modern block – the rooms are decent (though	overpriced), and it's a relaxing place to spend a night. The restaurant's buffet-style food is popular with tour groups. Closed April–Aug. Rates include breakfast. $1500

Punta Norte

Wild **Punta Norte**, the northernmost point of the peninsula, is famous for the **orca attacks** on baby sea lions that occur there during March and early April. In a spectacle rivalling anything in the natural world, the eight-tonne orcas beach themselves at up to 50km per hour and attempt to grab a pup; most efforts are unsuccessful, and an orca will sometimes settle for a snack of penguin. Attacks usually occur with the high tides – if you're so inclined, check with the Centro de Interpretaciones (see p.449) for times and plan your arrival to coincide with the hour either side of high tide to stand the best chance of witnessing one. These aside, the sight of ominous black dorsal fins of a pod of killer whales cruising just off the coast is thrilling enough. Serious photographers can buy an expensive permit to descend to the beach (contact the Secretaria de Turismo in Rawson; ☎0280 448 1113), but the general viewing area can be as good a vantage point as any.

On the slope above the beach there's a small **visitors' centre and museum** (daily 8am–8pm; free); inside, you can identify the distinguishing features of the different individual orcas.

ACCOMMODATION AND EATING	PUNTA NORTE
La Ernestina Punta Norte ☎0280 447 1143, ⓦlaernestina.com. A charming but pricey estancia, *La Ernestina* has an excellent location right on the beach,	making it a favourite haunt of wildlife photographers. Rates include full board, all drinks and excursions. $2860

Chubut Province: the Welsh heartland

If you're coming to Chubut Province looking for Argentina's answer to Snowdonia, think again. Not only is there not a mountain in sight, but also the **Welsh**, like the Tehuelche before them, have been absorbed almost seamlessly into Argentina's diverse cultural identity. Under the surface, though, there remain vestiges of their pioneering culture and a real pride in both the historical legacy – evident in the number of fine **Welsh chapels** dotted across the farmlands of the **Lower Chubut Valley** – and the current cultural connection that goes well beyond the touristy trappings.

Halting Welsh is still spoken by some of the third- or fourth-generation residents in the main towns of **Trelew** and **Gaiman**, even if it isn't the language of common usage,

THE MARINE MAMMALS OF PENÍNSULA VALDÉS

Although diverse and significant populations of birds and terrestrial mammals exist on **Península Valdés**, it is the **marine mammals** here that are of particular interest.

SOUTHERN RIGHT WHALE

The **southern right whale** (*Ballena franca austral*) comes to the sheltered waters of the Golfo Nuevo and Golfo San José to breed. Weighing up to fifty tonnes and measuring up to 18m in length, these gentle leviathans are filter-feeders, deriving nutrients from plankton. Once favoured targets for the world's whalers – they were the "right" whales to harpoon, as they were slow, yielded copious quantities of oil and floated when killed – they have now been declared a "National Natural Monument", and are protected within Argentine territorial waters. This has enabled the present tourist industry to develop, reinforcing the economic value of keeping these creatures alive; their charming curiosity – a trait that once put them in danger – now makes them one of the most enjoyable cetaceans to view in the wild.

KILLER WHALES

The **killer whale**, or orca, is not in fact a whale at all, but the largest member of the dolphin family – it displays the high levels of intelligence we associate with such creatures, if not their cuteness. This is amply demonstrated in their unique hunting behaviour at Caleta Valdés and Punta Norte, where orcas storm the shingle banks, beaching themselves in order to snap up their preferred prey: baby sea lions and young elephant seals. Male killer whales have been known to measure over nine metres, and weigh some eight tonnes, although the ones off Valdés do not reach these sizes. The dorsal fin on an adult male is the biggest in the animal kingdom, measuring 1.8m, and its size and shape is one of the factors used to identify individual orcas, along with the shape of the saddle patch and colour variations. If you want to know more, contact Fundación Orca in Puerto Madryn (☎0280 445 4723, ⓦfundorca.org.ar).

SEA LIONS

Sea lions (*Lobos marinos*) were once so numerous on the peninsula that 20,000 would be culled annually for their skins and blubber – a figure that roughly equals the entire population found here today. They are the most widely distributed of the Patagonian marine mammals and their anthropomorphic antics make them a delight to watch. It's easy to see the derivation of the name when you look at a 300kg adult male, ennobled by a fine yellowy-brown mane.

ELEPHANT SEALS

Península Valdés is the only continental breeding ground for the southern **elephant seal** (*Elefante marino*). Weighing some three tonnes and measuring four to five metres, bull elephant seals mean business. Though the average size of a harem for a dominant male ranges between ten and fifteen females, some super-stud tyrants get greedy. One macho male at Caleta Valdés infamously amassed 131 consorts. October is the best month to see these noisy clashes of the titans, but be prepared for some gore, as tusk wounds are inevitable. Adult females, much smaller than the males, are pregnant for 11 months of the year, giving birth from about mid-September. Pups weigh 40kg at birth, but then balloon to weigh 200kg after only three weeks. The elephant seal's most remarkable attribute, however, is as the world's champion deep-sea-diving mammal. Depths of over 1000m are not uncommon, and it is reckoned that some of these animals have reached depths of 1500m, staying submerged for a (literally) breathtaking two hours.

and whereas it once seemed doomed to die out, the tongue now appears to be enjoying a limited **renaissance**. In municipal schools today, young students have the option to study the language of their forebears: a team of **Welsh teachers** works in Chubut, and **cultural exchanges** with Mam Cymru are thriving – two or three pupils are sent annually from Chubut to Welsh universities and numerous delegations from different associations ply across the Atlantic. It's not all one way either: scholars have come from Wales to study the manuscripts left by pioneers and seek inspiration from what they pronounce to be the purity of the language that was preserved in Patagonia.

Trelew

The medium-sized town of **TRELEW** – its Welsh name means the "village of Lewis", in honour of Lewis Jones, its founder – rose to prominence after the completion, in 1889, of the rail link to Puerto Madryn, which allowed easy export of the burgeoning agricultural yields. Today it is home to a couple of excellent museums, while its good transport connections make it a convenient base from which to explore the surrounding Welsh settlements of the **Lower Chubut Valley** and, to the south, the famous penguin colony at **Punta Tombo**. The only downside is the shortage of appealing accommodation – nearby Gaiman has a far better selection.

Museo Regional Pueblo de Luis

9 de Julio and Fontana • Mon–Fri 8am–8pm, Sat & Sun 2–8pm • $5 • ☎ 0280 442 4062

The railway has since disappeared, but the old station is now home to the **Museo Regional Pueblo de Luis**, which does a good job of tracing the area's **Celtic** history and also explores the coexistence of the Welsh and the Tehuelche as well as the eisteddfod (traditional annual Welsh) festivals. The museum was closed for renovation at the time of research, but is due to reopen in the future.

Museo Paleontológico Egidio Feruglio (MEF)

Fontana and Lewis Jones • April–Aug Mon–Fri 10am–6pm, Sat & Sun 10am–7pm; Sept–March daily 9am–8pm • $42 • Free English-language guided tours available • ☎ 0280 443 2100, ⓦ mef.org.ar

Across the road from the Museo Regional is the excellent **Museo Paleontológico Egidio Feruglio (MEF)**, one of South America's most important paleontological collections. It sets out to describe "300 million years of history" and contains beautifully preserved clutches of dinosaur eggs and skeletons from the region, including a 95-million-year-old argentosaurus, one of the world's largest dinosaurs.

8

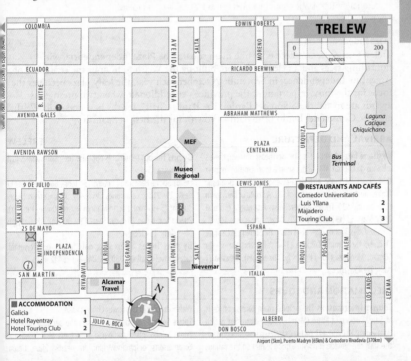

THE WELSH IN PATAGONIA

In July 1865, after two months at sea, 153 **Welsh** men, women and children who had fled Britain to escape cultural and religious oppression disembarked from their tea-clipper, the *Mimosa*, and took the first steps into what they believed was to be their Promised Land. Here they planned to emulate the Old Testament example of bringing forth gardens from the wilderness, but though the land around the Golfo Nuevo had the appearance of Israel, its parched harshness cannot have been of much comfort to those who had left the green valleys of Wales. Fired by Robert Fitz Roy's descriptions of the Lower Chubut Valley, they explored south and, two months later, relocated – a piecemeal process during which some groups had, in the words of one of the leading settlers, Abraham Matthews, to live off "what they could hunt, foxes and birds of prey, creatures not permitted under Mosaic Law, but acceptable in the circumstances".

The immigrants were mostly miners or small merchants from southeast Wales and had little farming experience. Doubts and insecurities spread, with some settlers petitioning the British to rescue them, but when all avenues of credit seemed closed, vital assistance came from the Argentine government by way of provisions and substantial monthly subsidies. And despite initial mistrust of the **Tehuelche**, the Welsh learned survival and hunting skills from their native neighbours, which proved invaluable when the settlers' sheep died and the first three harvests failed. By the early 1870s, 44 settlers had abandoned the attempt, and sixteen had died, but optimists pointed to the fact that ten new settlers had since arrived, and 21 Welsh-Argentines had been born into the community. They decided to stick it out.

With increasing awareness of irrigation techniques, the pioneers began to coax their first proper yields from the Lower Chubut Valley, and recruitment trips to Wales and the US brought a much-needed influx of new settlers in 1874, the year in which Gaiman (see opposite) was founded. Yet the best indicator of the settlement's progress was the international recognition received when samples of barley and wheat grown in Dolavon returned from major international expositions in Paris (1889) and the US (1892) with gold medals in their respective categories. The village's flour mill, built in the 1880s, still works today.

Plaza Independencia

Trelew's urban centrepiece is its fine main square, the **Plaza Independencia**, with flourishing trees and an elegant gazebo, built by the Welsh to honour the centenary of Argentine Independence; in September/October each year, the leafy plaza becomes the focus for the most important of the province's **eisteddfodau**, when two prestigious awards are made: the Sillón del Bardo (The Bard's Chair), for the best poetry in Welsh, and the Corona del Bardo (The Bard's Crown), for the best in Spanish.

ARRIVAL AND DEPARTURE
TRELEW

By plane Trelew's airport is 5km northeast of town; there's a Banco de Chubut ATM and a simple tourist-office counter that opens for flight arrivals. Passengers on all domestic flights must pay a departure tax of $32. A taxi to or from town costs around $30. There's an Aerolíneas Argentinas office at 25 de Mayo 33 (☎0280 442 0170, ⓦ aerolineas.com.ar).
Destinations Buenos Aires (1–3 daily; 1hr 50min); El Calafate (1 daily; 1hr 45min); Córdoba (1–4 daily; 1hr 20min–1hr 50min); Mendoza (10–11 weekly; 1hr 50min); Ushuaia (1 daily; 2hr 15min).

By bus The bus terminal is opposite the main square, just off Urquiza.
Destinations Bariloche (1 daily; 13–16hr); Buenos Aires (11 daily; 19–21hr); Camarones (3 weekly; 3hr); Gaiman (every 30min; 25–35min); Puerto Madryn (every 30min–1hr; 1hr); Puerto San Julián (5 daily; 10hr–11hr 30min); Río Gallegos (4–5 daily; 15–16hr).
By taxi There's a taxi rank outside the bus terminal. Alternatively, call ☎0280 442 0404 or ☎442 4445.

INFORMATION AND TOURS

Tourist information The helpful main tourist office is at San Martín and Mitre (Mon–Fri 8am–8pm, Sat & Sun 9am–9pm; ☎0280 442 6819, ⓦ trelewpatagonia.gov.ar); the staff can provide you with a good leaflet on the various

Welsh chapels of the Lower Chubut Valley.
Tours Several agencies run tours to the penguin colony at Punta Tombo, often combined with tours of Gaiman and Commerson's dolphin-watching in nearby Playa Unión.

Recommended outfits include Alcamar Travel, San Martín 146 (☎ 0280 442 1213, ⓦ argentinapatagonia.com.ar), and Nievemar Tours, Italia 98 (☎ 0280 443 4114, ⓦ nievemartours .com.ar).

ACCOMMODATION

Galicia 9 de Julio 214 ☎ 0280 443 3802, ⓦ hotelgalicia .com.ar. This well-run hotel, in a building that dates back to 1947, has a grand entrance and a lavish lobby but the en-suite rooms, while perfectly comfortable, are a little on the small side. Breakfast included. $\overline{$460}$

Hotel Rayentray San Martín 101 ☎ 0280 443 4702, ⓦ cadenarayentray.com.ar. Though somewhat anonymous, this is the smartest option in town. It has larger-than-average en suites and a range of facilities, including a top-floor swimming pool, a decent restaurant and a bar. Breakfast included. $\overline{$515}$

★ **Hotel Touring Club** Fontana 240 ☎ 0280 443 3997, ⓦ touringpatagonia.com.ar. *Little Prince* author Antoine de Saint-Exupéry and (reportedly) Butch Cassidy and the Sundance Kid have stayed at this faded Art Deco hotel, built in 1918. The compact en-suite rooms are pretty simple, but the atmosphere – especially in the high-ceilinged café-bar (see below) – is the real draw. Breakfast included. $\overline{$250}$

EATING AND DRINKING

Comedor Universitario Luis Yllana Just off 9 de Julio. If you're after an inexpensive breakfast, lunch or early dinner, join the students at this bustling university canteen, which serves simple, hearty dishes (around $30–40) at prices that won't break the bank. Daily 10am–8pm.

Majadero Av Gales 250 ☎ 0280 443 0548. Housed in an old mill, this smart restaurant has a concise, rather pricey menu featuring pasta, steak and chicken dishes ($56–100), plus a good range of wines and beers. There's live music on Thursday nights. Tues–Sun 11.30am–3pm & 8pm–midnight/1am.

★ **Touring Club** Fontana 240 ☎ 0280 443 3997, ⓦ touringpatagonia.com.ar. Lively *confitería* and bar with touches of grandeur, offering standard snacks and meals like *milanesas* – as well as an array of *tragos* (from $15) from the extensive range of bottles lining the back of the bar. Daily 6.30am–midnight.

8

The Lower Chubut Valley

West of Trelew is the broad **LOWER CHUBUT VALLEY**, a fertile ribbon of land amid some barren steppe, thanks to the Río Chubut, which flows through here from the Andes. The river derives its name from the Tehuelche word "*chupat*", meaning clean or transparent. The Welsh began using the Chubut to irrigate the valley in 1867, and it was dammed a hundred years later to ensure a more predictable flow to the farm plots, while also generating electricity for industrial development around Trelew. A string of well-maintained **Welsh chapels** (*capillas galesas*) line the Chubut, including – just south of Trelew – the Capilla Moriah; dating from 1880 it's the oldest in Argentina and many of the original settlers are buried in its cemetery. The small towns along the river's route are all charming and, though you won't exactly hear Welsh spoken in the streets, the legacy of pioneering times is still detectable.

Gaiman

The town of **GAIMAN**, 16km west of Trelew along the RN-25, sits amid lush pastures and poplar trees that – in clement weather, at least – form a landscape more like a Monet watercolour than typical Patagonia. It's a pleasant place and the most eminently "Welsh" of the area's settlements. A visit to a Welsh tearoom (see box, p.458) is a must, and there are various monuments built by or dedicated to the settlers dotted around town: keep an eye out for the handsome brick **Capilla Bethel**, a chapel dating back to 1913, and the squat stone **Primera Casa** (First House), which was built in 1874, and looks as if it has been transplanted from Snowdonia. Mini-**eisteddfodau** are held in Gaiman in mid-September and the first week of May.

Museo Histórico Regional

Sarmiento and 28 de Julio • Tues–Sun 3–7pm • $3

Gaiman's old train station now houses the **Museo Histórico Regional**, a small but very worthwhile museum that focuses on the challenges of pioneer life and the development of the Welsh community in the region; among the exhibits are some particularly evocative old photos. After visiting the museum, railway buffs should walk over to the nearby tourist office, close to which is an abandoned 300m-long **railway tunnel**, which is open for exploration.

Parque El Desafío

Almirante Brown 52 • Opening hours are somewhat erratic, but generally Mon–Wed 3–7pm, Thurs–Sun 9am–1pm & 3–7.30pm • $10

For all its Celtic heritage, Gaiman's most surprising monument has nothing whatsoever to do with tradition, Welsh or otherwise. **Parque El Desafío** (The Challenge Park) is a backyard where tens of thousands of **tin cans and plastic bottles** have been recycled and reincarnated. It's the work of Joaquín Alonso (who died at a ripe old age in 2007), dubbed by the local media as the Dalí of Gaiman. His fabulous constructions, such as the tower he erected "in homage to myself", stand alongside ironic mockeries of modern consumerist society.

ARRIVAL AND INFORMATION GAIMAN

By bus/taxi Regular buses (every 30min; 25–35min) travel between the terminal in Trelew and Gaiman's main square. A taxi for the same journey costs around $100.

Tourist information The helpful tourist office (Mon–Sat 9am–8pm, Sun 11am–7pm; ☎0280 449 1571, ⓦgaiman.gov .ar) is at Belgrano 574, a 5min walk from the central square.

ACCOMMODATION

Hostería Gwesty Tywi Chacra 202 ☎0280 449 1292, ⓦhosteria-gwestywi.com.ar. This cheerful guesthouse has a collection of comfortable en-suite rooms. There's a nice garden and (in the summer) guests can use the small swimming pool. It's a 10–15mins walk from the main square on the other side of the river. Breakfast included. **$250**

Plas y Coed Av Yrigoyen 320 ☎0280 449 1133, ⓦplasycoed.com.ar. The owners have done a good job of recreating the homely atmosphere that pervades their original property – Gaiman's first teahouse – which lies just around the corner. The spacious living room is a good spot to recover from the massive, high-calorie breakfast

(included in the rates). **$300**

Ty Gwyn 9 de Julio 147 ☎0280 449 1009, ⓦtygwyn .com.ar. Located one block away from the main square and attached to a *casa de té*, Ty Gwyn has clean and compact rooms with wooden floors and partial views of the Río Chubut. Breakfast included. **$300**

Yr Hen Ffordd Michael D. Jones 342 ☎0280 449 1394, ⓦyrhenffordd.com.ar. *Yr Hen Ffordd* (*The Old Way*) is a good, clean budget option, although it could do with a bit of a face-lift. There are several twins and doubles with private bathrooms, as well as a family room sleeping six ($90 per person). Breakfast included. **$200**

EATING

Gwalia Lân Jones and Av Tello. If you're after lunch or dinner, rather than a Welsh tea, head to this restaurant, located diagonally opposite the main square, where there's

a typical Argentine mix of steaks, pasta and pizza on offer. Mains $40–70. Tues–Sat 12.30–3pm & 7.30pm–midnight, Sun 12.30–3pm.

GAIMAN'S WELSH TEAROOMS

The highlight of a visit to Gaiman is working your way through a mountain of cakes over afternoon tea at a **Welsh tearoom** (*casa de té*), some of which are owned and run by descendants of the original Welsh settlers. They all serve similar arrays of cake, toast, scones and home-made jams (around $80–90 per person); the most traditional component is the *torta negra* (dark fruit cake), originally a wedding gift to be eaten on a couple's first anniversary. These three tearooms are among the best:

Plas y Coed Michael D. Jones 123 ☎0280 449 1133, ⓦplasycoed.com.ar. The walls of this charming *casa de té* are covered with a glorious array of Welsh-language posters, tea towels and photos. The cakes here are some of the best in town. Tues–Sun 3–7pm.

Ty Cymraeg Abraham Matthews 74 ☎0280 449 1010, ⓦcasagalesa.com.ar. At *Ty Cymraeg*, housed in a green-roofed building close to the river, a descendant of the pioneers serves tea in the original family home.

There are options available for children and coeliacs too. Tues–Sun 3–7pm.

Ty Nain Av Yrigoyen 283 ☎0280 449 1126. The ivy-clad *Ty Nain*, in a building dating back to 1890, is one of the most authentic of the teahouses. The abundant tea is served here by a descendant of the first Welsh woman to be born in Gaiman. Don't forget to check out the small museum at the back. Tues–Sun 3–7pm.

THE MAGELLANIC PENGUIN

The word "penguin", some maintain, derives from Welsh *pen gwyn* (white head), a name allegedly bestowed by a Welsh sailor passing these shores with Thomas Cavendish in the sixteenth century. In fact, **Magellanic penguins** don't have white heads and it's far more likely that the name comes from the archaic Spanish *pingüe*, or fat. The birds were a gift to the early mariners, being the nearest equivalent at that time to a TV dinner.

Though they're not exactly nimble on land, in water these birds can keep up a steady 8km an hour, or several times that over short bursts. An adult bird stands 50 to 60cm tall and weighs a plump 4–5.5kg. Birds begin arriving at their ancestral Patagonian nesting sites – which can be up to 1km from the sea – from late August, and by early October nesting is in full swing. Parents share the task of incubation, as they do the feeding of the brood once the eggs start to hatch, in early November. By early January, chicks that have not been preyed upon by sea birds, foxes or armadillos make their first sorties into the water. During the twenty-day February moult, the birds do not swim, as they lose their protective layer of waterproof insulation; at this time, penguin sites are awash with fuzzy down and sneezing birds. In March and April, they begin to vacate the nesting sites. Although little is known of their habits while at sea, scientists do know that the birds migrate north, reaching as far as the coast off Río de Janeiro, 3000km away.

Punta Tombo

107km south of Trelew; unless you have your own car, the easiest way to visit is on a day-trip with a travel agency in Puerto Madryn or Trelew • Sept to late March daily 8am–6pm • $60

Punta Tombo is by far the largest single colony of penguins on the continent, with a population of more than half a million birds; it is also one of the most commercialized. The noise from these black-and-white **Magellanic penguins** is immense; it's quite an experience to wander around this scrubland avian metropolis amid a cacophony of braying, surrounded on all sides by waddling, tottering birds. The penguins nest behind the stony beach in scrapes underneath the bushes, with a close eye on approaching strangers. Get too close and they'll indicate their displeasure by hissing or bobbing their heads from side to side like a dashboard dog – respect these warning signals, and remember that a penguin can inflict a good deal of pain with its sharp bill.

Late November to January is probably the best time to visit, as there are plenty of **young chicks**. The penguins are most active in the morning and early evening; tour agencies run morning trips from Trelew, allowing around one and a half hours with the birds. The nearby countryside is an excellent place to see **terrestrial wildlife**, such as guanacos, *choiques*, skunks, armadillos and *maras*.

Cabo Dos Bahías

260km south of Trelew • Daily 8am–6pm • $35

The remote coastal reserve of **Cabo Dos Bahías**, stuck out on a headland 30km from the tiny fishing village of **Camarones**, is home to 55,000 Magellanic penguins plus a colony of sea lions from August to April. Tame herds of guanacos are abundant in the park, which also has healthy populations of *choique* and *mara*.

ARRIVAL AND DEPARTURE   CABO DOS BAHÍAS

By bus Unless you have your own wheels or are on an organized tour, you'll have to take a bus (3 weekly; 3hr) from Trelew to Camarones and then a taxi from there to the park (around $80–100).

ACCOMMODATION

Indalo Inn Roca and Sarmiento, Camarones ☎0297 496 3004, ⦿indaloinn.com.ar. If you want to stay the night, try *Indalo Inn* in Camarones, which has no frills, rather cramped en-suite rooms and more comfortable *cabañas* with sea views, plus a restaurant. A rather meagre breakfast is included. Doubles **$250**, cabañas **$400**

The coast of Santa Cruz Province

The stretch of the RN-3 south of Cabo Dos Bahías encompasses some pretty dreary towns, not least the oil-hub of **Comodoro Rivadavia** – a dire place best avoided, though it does have some useful transport links, including an airport. While this section of eastern Patagonia must claim some of the most desolate scenery in Argentina, there are some natural gems threaded along it: the **Ría Deseado estuary** at **Puerto Deseado**, with its handsome porphyry cliffs and marvellous opportunities to view dolphins and penguins at close quarters; the tremendous trunks of fossilized araucaria monkey puzzles in the **Monumento Natural Bosques Petrificados**; and **Puerto San Julián**, a historic town with access to one of the most conveniently situated penguin colonies in Patagonia. Farther south you could also break the excruciatingly long distances of largely uneventful coastline into more manageable chunks by stopping at **Comandante Luis Piedra Buena**, known for its fishing, or **Parque Nacional Monte León**, Argentina's first coastal national park, in which a century-old estancia offers some of the area's finest lodgings.

Puerto Deseado and around

Avoiding grim Caleta Olivia, the first place worth visiting in Santa Cruz Province (albeit entailing a hefty detour) is easy-going **PUERTO DESEADO**, a straggly but engaging fishing and naval port on the flooded estuary, or *ría*, of the Río Deseado. Some spectacular coastal scenery and a couple of remarkable colonies of marine wildlife are within sight of town, most dramatically along the **estuary** itself. The town owes its name to the English privateer Thomas Cavendish, who baptized it **Port Desire**, in honour of his ship, when he put in here in 1586.

Museo Regional Mario Brozoski

Colón and Belgrano • Mon–Fri 8am–5pm, Sat & Sun 3–5pm • Free

By the seafront, the **Museo Regional Mario Brozoski** displays items brought up from the *Swift*, a small English warship that sank off the coast of Puerto Deseado in 1770 and was discovered by divers in 1982. Check out the gallon gin bottles.

Museo de la Estación del Ferrocarril

Arias s/n • Mon–Sat 4–7pm • Free, but donations welcome

Modern-day Puerto Deseado was largely shaped by the Ferrocarril Nacional Patagónico, a cross-country cargo route that ran northwest to Las Heras; the town's fine, porphyry-coloured, former train station operated as the route's terminus from 1911 until 1979. It now functions as the **Museo de la Estación del Ferrocarril** and houses a small collection of train memorabilia.

Ría Deseado

Stretching 45km inland from Puerto Deseado is the **RÍA DESEADO**, an astonishing sunken river valley, which, unlike most other estuaries on the continent, is flooded by the sea, like a shallow fjord. Opposite the town, its purple cliffs are smeared with guano

---

BOAT TRIPS FROM PUERTO DESEADO

Darwin Expediciones, based beside the Gipsy dock at España 2551, on the approach to town (❶0297 15 624 7554, ◗darwin-expeditions.com), runs some excellent **boat trips** around the Ría Deseado and, if the tide is high, up the **Cañadón Torcida**, a narrow and steep-sided channel of the estuary, dolphin-spotting on the way to **Isla de los Pájaros**, where passengers can disembark and observe the birdlife – dominated by Magellanic penguins – at close hand; to **Isla Pingüino**, one of the few places outside Antarctica where the punkish Rockhopper penguin can easily be spotted; and a trip up the estuary to the scenic **Miradores de Darwin**, retracing the scientist's 1833 journey and stopping to look at wildlife en route. The company also operates kayaking excursions and trips to the Monumento Natural Bosques Petrificados (see opposite).

from five species of **cormorant**, including the dapper, morning-suited Grey cormorant (*Cormorán gris*), whose dull-coloured body sets off its yellow bill and scarlet legs. These birds are seen in few other places, and nowhere else will you get such a sterling opportunity to photograph them. The estuary also hosts several penguin colonies, small flocks of dazzling white Snowy sheathbills (*Palomas antárticas)*, a colony of sea lions and an estimated fifty playful and photogenic **Commerson's dolphins** (*Toninas averas)*; the undisputed stars here, these beautiful creatures torpedo through the water to rollick in bow waves just feet from boats.

ARRIVAL AND INFORMATION   PUERTO DESEADO AND AROUND

By bus The bus terminal is inconveniently located at the far end of town. Try to disembark in the centre or, if leaving town, flag down the bus as it passes along Av España. Caleta Olivia has more frequent buses to Río Gallegos, as well as connections to Puerto Madryn and Trelew.

Destinations Caleta Olivia (5 daily; 3hr 30min); Río Gallegos (1 daily; 12hr).
Tourist information The main tourist office is at San Martín 1525 (daily: April–Oct 9am–4pm; Nov–March 9am–9pm; ☏ 0297 487 0220).

ACCOMMODATION

Hotel Los Acantilados España and Pueyrredón ☏ 0297 487 2167, ⌨ hotellosacantilados.com.ar. Occupying a bluff on the outskirts of town, this hotel has a good range of rooms (though they're not as stylish as the hotel's exterior might suggest). Those on the upper storey have good views, while the ground-floor options can be a bit noisy thanks to

their proximity to the restaurant-bar. $320
Residencial Los Olmos Gob. Gregores 849 ☏ 0297 487 0077. Shoestring travellers should head to this friendly little *residencial*, which has very clean, if rather drab and boxy rooms with wall-mounted TVs, heaters and compact private bathrooms. Rates include breakfast. $250

8

Monumento Natural Bosques Petrificados

50km down a branch road leading west off the RN-3, 80km south of the turn-off to Puerto Deseado; unless you have a rental car, you'll need to visit on an organized trip from Puerto Deseado or Puerto San Julián • Daily: April–Sept 10am–5pm; Oct–March 9am–8pm • Free

The fossilized tree trunks at the **MONUMENTO NATURAL BOSQUES PETRIFICADOS** (aka Jaramillo) are strangely beautiful, especially at sunset, when their jasper-red expanses soak up the glow, as though they're heating up from within. The sheer magnitude of the trunks is astonishing, too, measuring some 35m long and up to 3m across. The primeval Jurassic forest grew here 150 million years ago – 60 million years before the Andean cordillera was forced up, forming the rain barrier that has such a dramatic effect on the scenery we know now. In Jurassic times, this area was still swept by moisture-laden winds from the Pacific, allowing the growth of araucaria trees. A cataclysmic blast from an unidentified volcano flattened these colossi and covered the fallen trunks with ash. The wood absorbed silicates in the ash and petrified, later to be revealed when erosion wore down the supervening strata.

Surrounding the trunks is a bizarre **moonscape** of arid basalt *meseta*, dominated by the 400m-tall **Cerro Madre e Hija** (Mother and Daughter Mount). A 2km trail, littered by shards of fossilized bark as if it were a woodchip path through a garden, leads from the park office past all the most impressive trunks, while the small **museum** has displays of some fascinating fossils such as the araucaria pine cones.

Puerto San Julián and around

The small port of **PUERTO SAN JULIÁN**, just off the RN-3 some 260km south of the turn-off to Puerto Deseado, is another convenient place to break the long journey down to Río Gallegos. Puerto San Julián lies 3km off the RN-3, down a straight road that becomes Avenida San Martín, the town's main artery. This barren town, rich in historical associations owing to its shingle-banked **bay**, was once one of the few safe anchorages along the Patagonian coast. Today, there's little visible evidence of the port's history apart from a replica of Magellan's ship the *Victoria* moored along the *costanera*, but it's a good place to go on one of various **tours**, including a highly recommended trip to view the **marine life** of the bay. The penguins here live closer to human settlement than at any other site in the south, and are not afraid to assert ancestral privilege – indeed, local radio has been known to put out appeals to remove penguins from the town hall.

Museo Regional y de Arte Marino Rosa Novak

Magallanes s/n • Early March to mid-Dec Mon–Fri 9am–noon & 2–5pm; mid-Dec to early March daily 9am–noon & 3–7pm • Free

By far the most interesting exhibit at the small **Museo Regional Rosa Novak** is a paving slab that lay in the town square for many years until someone noticed that it had the distinct, prehistoric prints of a sauropod (a crocodile-like reptile) on it.

Bahía de San Julián

Pinocho Excursiones, Costanera and 9 de Julio (☏ 02962 454600, ⓦ pinochoexcursiones.com.ar) run boat trips around the bay (around $220)

The easiest tour from Puerto San Julián is also the best: a trip around **Bahía de San Julián** in a zodiac launch to see the most conveniently situated **penguin colony** in Patagonia and all manner of flying sea birds. In addition, you stand a good chance of spotting **Commerson's dolphins**, a graceful, fun-loving species that regularly play games with the boats. You'll also be taken to the protected island of **Banco Justicia** (Justice Bank) to see the cormorant colonies (home to four different species – Rock, Olivaceous, Guanay and Imperial), and other sea birds. Banco Justicia is thought by some to be where, in the sixteenth century, Magellan, and later **Francis Drake**, executed members of their crews who had mutinied while in the bay, although others maintain it was at **Punta Horca** (Gallows Point), on the tongue of land that encloses the bay, opposite the town. You're not allowed to disembark at either, though you are allowed to get off at the misleadingly named **Banco Cormorán** where there is a colony of Magellanic penguins but no cormorants.

The best time for seeing dolphins and cormorants is December to Easter, especially early on, though the guide will always give a scrupulously honest appraisal of your chances.

ARRIVAL AND INFORMATION

By bus Most bus services arrive at or depart from the terminal at San Martín 1552 in the early hours.
Destinations Comandante Luis Piedra Buena (6 daily; 1hr 30min); Río Gallegos (6 daily; 4–5hr); Trelew (2 daily;

10hr 30min).
Tourist information The tourist office is at San Martín and Rivadavia (Mon–Fri 7am–9pm, Sat & Sun 9am–9pm; ☏ 02962 452353, ⓦ sanjulian.gov.ar).

ACCOMMODATION

Hostel Costanera 25 de Mayo 917 ☏ 02962 452300, ⓦ costanerahotel.com. This low-rise hotel has a seafront location overlooking the Bahía San Julián. The en-suite rooms are neat and tidy – each one comes with a TV and phone, and those on the second floor have sea views – and there's a bar-restaurant. Breakfast included. **$350**

Hotel Bahía San Martín 1075 ☏ 02962 454028, ⓦ hotelbahiasanjulian.com.ar. As smart as it gets accommodation-wise in Puerto San Julián – though that isn't exactly a ringing endorsement – *Hotel Bahía* has decent en suites, though the decor could do with a freshen up. Breakfast included. **$385**

THE BIRTHPLACE OF PATAGONIA

Puerto San Julián can rightfully claim to be the **birthplace of Patagonia**. In 1520, during **Magellan**'s stay in the bay, the very first encounter occurred between the Europeans and the "giants" of this nameless land, when, it is believed, the explorer bestowed on them the name "patagon" (literally "big foot") in reference to their comparatively large build. As related by Antonio Pigafetta, the expedition's chronicler: "One day, without anyone expecting it, we saw a giant, who was on the shore of the sea, quite naked, and was dancing and leaping, and singing, and whilst singing he put sand and dust on his head... When he was before us he began to be astonished, and to be afraid, and he raised one finger on high, thinking that we came from heaven. He was so tall that the tallest of us only came up to his waist... The captain named this kind of people Patagon." On Palm Sunday, April 1, 1520, Magellan celebrated the first Mass on Argentine soil, near a site marked by a cross, down by the town's port.

Comandante Luis Piedra Buena

Around 50km south of Puerto San Julián, the desolate monotony of the steppe is lifted briefly by the **Gran Bajo de San Julián**, whose Laguna del Carbón – 105m below sea level – is the lowest point on the entire South American continent. It's another 70km from here to **COMANDANTE LUIS PIEDRA BUENA**, a sleepy town 1km off the RN-3, with little to detain visitors unless you've come specifically for the world-class **steelhead trout fishing** (licences available at the municipalidad, Avenida Gregorio Ibáñez 388, just down from the bus terminal).

The town is named after naval hero Piedra Buena, who was famed for his gentlemanly ways and determination to assert Argentine sovereignty in the south. In 1859, he made **Isla Pavón** (the island in the jade-coloured Río Santa Cruz) his home, building a diminutive house, from which he traded with the local Aónik'enk Tehuelche.

ARRIVAL AND DEPARTURE   COMANDANTE LUIS PIEDRA BUENA

By bus The bus terminal is at Gregorio Ibáñez Norte 130, near the town centre.

Destinations Puerto San Julián (2–4 daily; 1hr 30min); Río Gallegos (2–4 daily; 3hr).

ACCOMMODATION

Hostería El Alamo Lavalle 8 ⚊ 02962 497249. Accommodation options are pretty limited in Comandante Luis Piedra Buena, but El Alamo is a reasonable place to spend the night.

The rooms are simple and well kept, and there's a *confitería*. **$300**

Parque Nacional Monte León

33km south of Comandante Luis Piedra Buena • Daily: Nov–March 9am–7pm; April–Oct 10am–5pm • Free • ⚊ 02962 498184, ⓦ pnmonteleon.com.ar

Beyond Comandante Luis Piedra Buena, the Patagonian plateau continues with unabating harshness for some 250km to Río Gallegos. An early detour, 33km out of Piedra Buena, leads to the **PARQUE NACIONAL MONTE LEÓN**, Argentina's first coastal national park. Created in October 2004 on land donated by two conservation NGOs, the magnificent 627-square-kilometre reserve encompasses sweeping cliffs, rocky islands and picturesque bays and, between September and April, the waters are awash with wildlife, including sea-lion and penguin colonies (the fourth largest in Argentina) and three types of cormorant. The rugged cliffs that dominate the landscape are indented with vast caverns and rock windows – at low tide, you can walk out to **Isla Monte León**, a steep-sided islet chock-a-block with cormorants. Check first with the *guardafauna* office, 7km north of the park entrance on the RN-3 for tide schedules; you also have to register here before entering the park and even if you choose not to hire a guide (they have a list), it is worthwhile asking about what there is to see and how to get there.

ARRIVAL AND DEPARTURE   PARQUE NACIONAL MONTE LEÓN

Tours There's no public transport, so if you don't have your own car, you'll need to take a tour: try Kimiri Aike Tours

(⚊ 02966 15 625763, ⓦ martaboillos@hotmail.com) or Nievemar in Trelew (see p.455).

ACCOMMODATION

Monte León Lodge RN-3 ⚊ 011 4621 4780, ⓦ monte leon-patagonia.com. Unless you plan to camp, and if your budget will stretch, the best place to stay in the park is at the glorious *hostería* in the former estancia

homestead. It offers a taste of classy but simple, isolated country life in large rooms with wooden floors, fireplaces and old-fashioned bathrooms. Reservations necessary. Closed April–Oct. Half-board **$2300**

Río Gallegos

With its harsh climate and no-nonsense commercial feel, provincial capital **RÍO GALLEGOS** – 246km south of Piedra Buena – is not the kind of place where you'll want to stay for long, though there are a couple of museums and some attractive early twentieth-century buildings. It is, however, an important transport hub and many travellers pass through en route to or from El Calafate or Tierra del Fuego. The city's namesake river is also a top fly-fishing spot, with some of the world's biggest brown trout.

Avenida Kirchner (formally Av Roca) is the focus of city life; outdoor gear costs far less here than in the tourist hubs such as El Calafate, so stock up if you're off trekking. The attractive main square, **Plaza San Martín**, is marked by a fine equestrian **statue** of General San Martín and the quaint white-and-green Salesian **cathedral**, Nuestra Señora de Luján, a classic example of a pioneer church made from corrugated iron, and originally built in 1899 with a labour force composed of displaced Tehuelche.

Museo de Los Pioneros

Alberdi and Elcano • Daily 10am–7pm • Free • ☎ 02966 437763

The **Museo de Los Pioneros**, based in the city's oldest house, provides a great insight into life in the region at the beginning of the twentieth century, with curators playing ancient, crackly discs on a 1904 Victrola. There are some evocative old photos – look out for the one of a group of British settlers nursing their pints outside The White Elephant pub (which sadly no longer exisits).

Museo Regional Provincial Padre Jesús Molina

San Martín and Ramón y Cajal 51 • Mon–Fri 10am–5pm, Sat & Sun noon–7pm • Free • ☎ 02966 423290

The eclectic **Museo Regional Provincial Padre Jesús Molina** hosts temporary exhibitions of contemporary art, along with displays of Tehuelche artefacts, dinosaur remains and impressive reconstructions of Pleistocene mammals. There's also a weaving workshop selling woollens.

CROSSING THE CHILEAN BORDER TO TIERRA DEL FUEGO

It takes the best part of a day to travel overland from Río Gallegos to Río Grande (see p.522), the first major town in **Argentine Tierra del Fuego**, a tedious journey that involves crossing two borders and the **Magellan Straits**; you might well consider flying.

MONTE AYMOND BORDER CROSSING

At the Monte Aymond border crossing (April–Oct 9am–11pm; Nov–March 24hr), 67km south of Gallegos, formalities are fairly straightforward, but don't try to bring fresh vegetables, fruit or meat products into Chile, as they'll be confiscated. On the Chilean side, the road improves and heads to Punta Arenas, Puerto Natales and, down a turning at Kimiri Aike, 48km from the border, Tierra del Fuego. This road, the RN-257, takes you to Punta Delgada and the Primera Angostura (First Narrows) of the Magellan Straits.

BY FERRY ACROSS THE MAGELLAN STRAITS

The ferry that plies across the Magellan Straits leaves from 7/8am to 11pm/midnight, making the twenty- to thirty-minute crossing roughly every 45min (✪tabsa.cl /Eng/html /PrimeraAngostura.php; CH$1600 per person, CH$14,000 for a car). As early mariners found, the currents here can be ferocious, but they're unlikely to be as disruptive to your plans as they were to sea-goers in the past – only in extreme weather does the ferry not leave. While crossing history's most famous straits, look out for Commerson's dolphins.

ON TO USHUAIA

Heading for Ushuaia, the road then traverses Chilean Tierra del Fuego to the border settlement of San Sebastián (April–Oct 9am–11pm; Nov–March 24hr), 80km from Río Grande. Check times carefully, as there may be a time difference between the Argentine and Chilean sides. Buses depart regularly from Río Gallegos for Punta Arenas (5–7hr), Río Grande (10hr) and Ushuaia (12hr); ferry crossings are included in the fare.

ARRIVAL AND INFORMATION

RÍO GALLEGOS

By plane The airport is 7km west of town. Although there are no buses to the town centre – a taxi will cost around $60–70: bizarrely, there are direct buses from the airport to El Calafate (3hr 30min–4hr 30min), some 300km away. Destinations Buenos Aires (3–4 daily; 3hr); Ushuaia (1 weekly; 55min).

By bus From the bus terminal, near the edge of town on the RN-3, it's best to take a taxi 2km into the centre (around $30–35); alternatively, buses #1 or #12 will drop you on Av Kirchner in the heart of town.

Destinations El Calafate (4–5 daily; 4hr–4hr 30min); Puerto Madryn (4–5 daily; 16–19hr); Punta Arenas, Chile

(1–2 daily; 5–7hr); Río Grande (via Chile; 1–2 daily; 10hr); Trelew (4–5 daily 16–19hr); Ushuaia (via Chile; 2 daily; 12hr).

Tourist information Río Gallegos has two main tourist offices in the city centre, both helpful and efficient: one at Beccar 126 (Mon–Fri 8am–8pm, Sat & Sun 8am–noon & 4–8pm; ☎ 02966 436920, ⊚ turismo.riogallegos.gov.ar) and another in an old (formerly horse-drawn) wagon on the corner of Kirchner and San Martín (summer only: Mon–Fri 8am–8pm, Sat & Sun 8am–2pm & 4–8pm; ☎ 02966 422365). There's also a booth in the bus terminal (Mon–Fri 7am–8pm, Sat & Sun 4–8pm; ☎ 02966 442159).

ACCOMMODATION

Apart Hotel Austral Kirchner 1505 ☎ 02966 434314, ⊚ apartaustral.com. These spacious modern apartments – each with private bathroom, kitchenette and small dining area – are ideal for self-caterers or anyone planning to stay a few days, though the location can be a little noisy. Breakfast included. $370

Hotel Colonial Urquiza and Rivadavia ☎ 02966 420020, ⊚ ines_frey@hotmail.com. The warmest welcome in town is provided here by owner María Clark, a descendant of one of the first settlers in Río Gallegos. The rooms are spotless and very good value; all have TVs, and some have

private bathrooms. Breakfast included. $200

Hotel Patagonia Fagnano 54 ☎ 02966 444969, ⊚ hotel-patagonia.com. The smartest hotel in town, aimed at business travellers rather than tourists. The en suites are comfortable, though expensive for what you get, and there's a gym, spa, and a good restaurant. Breakfast included. $644

Sehuén Rawson 160 ☎ 02966 425683, ⊚ hotelsehuen .com. An efficiently run little hotel with a range of decent rooms; each has a TV, phone and boxy private bathroom, as well as a bilingual copy of the New Testament. Breakfast included. $230

EATING AND DRINKING

Club Británico Kirchner 935 ☎ 02966 432668, ⊚ britishclub.com.ar. A port of call for Bruce Chatwin, this atmospheric place has more than a hint of a gentleman's club about it and is still the favoured hangout for the declining community of those of British descent. The menu has some inventive lamb and seafood dishes, though prices are on the high side, with few mains under $70. Daily noon–midnight.

Freddo Kirchner 917 ☎ 02966 423302, ⊚ freddo.com.ar. This outpost of the famous Argentine chain serves the best *helado* (ice cream) in town – try the *maracuja* (passion fruit) cheesecake flavour. The coffee (from $11) is good too, and each cup comes with a little taster of ice cream. Tues–Sun 10am–10pm.

★ **Laguanacazul** Lista and Sarmiento ☎ 02966 444114, ⊚ laguanacazul.com.ar. The best restaurant in Gallegos, where the stylish setting is bettered only by the food: fresh Patagonian cuisine (both lamb and seafood) that varies with the season but is never short of excellent, though the prices ($60–90) do reflect this. The wine list is equally impressive. Tues–Sun noon–3pm & 8pm–midnight.

RoCo Kirchner 1157 ☎ 02966 420203. With a huge window overlooking the main street, this popular *parrilla* has an extensive menu; beyond the steaks, there's a wide selection of salads, pastas, seafood and chicken dishes (including chicken Kiev). Mains $37–95. Mon 8pm–midnight, Tues–Sat noon–3pm & 8pm–midnight, Sun noon–3pm.

8

RÍO GALLEGOS TO EL CALAFATE

Much of the landscape between Gallegos and **El Calafate** is gale-blasted steppe, though there is the odd oasis, plus fabulous views of the austral Andes, including the baroque peaks of Torres del Paine on the Chilean side in clear weather. There are two main routes: the more scenic but far longer **RN-40**, which passes several crossing points into the far south of Chile as it curves round the southwesternmost reaches of Argentina; and the quicker, more direct **RP-5**, the "busiest" of the roads that cross the deep south of Santa Cruz Province – in the early twentieth century this journey took up to six weeks by ox-cart, but you can now do it in less than four hours by bus and around three by car. About halfway along the RP-5 route is tiny **La Esperanza**, where you can refuel and eat.

Parque Nacional Los Glaciares

Declared a UNESCO World Heritage Site in 1981, the wild expanse of **Parque Nacional Los Glaciares** is a huge chunk of magical terrain shoved up against the Andes in the southwest corner of Santa Cruz Province. It encompasses a range of contrasting environments from enormous glaciers that ooze down from the heights of the gigantic Hielo Continental Sur icecap to thick, sub-Antarctic woodland of deciduous *lenga* and *ñire*, and evergreen *guindo* and *canelo*; and from savage, rain-lashed, unclimbed crags to dry, billiard-table Patagonian *meseta* stretching as far as the eye can strain. Most people will visit only the two sightseeing areas: the southern sector, around **Glaciar Perito Moreno**, one of the planet's most famous glaciers; and the **Fitz Roy** sector in the north for its superb trekking. Serving as bases for these two areas are, respectively, the towns of **El Calafate**, in the **south**, and **El Chaltén**, in the **north**, both lying just outside the boundary of the park itself, but catering well to a burgeoning influx of outdoor enthusiasts from across the world.

El Calafate

The overriding reason to visit **EL CALAFATE** is to make it your base for seeing **Glaciar Perito Moreno** and the other world-class attractions in the southern sector of **Parque National Los Glaciares** (see p.472). Once a primitive staging post between the area's estancias and Río Gallegos, the town is now one of Argentina's most-visited tourist destinations, with a hotchpotch of neo-pioneer architecture, scores of hotels and souvenir shops, and a huge casino. There has been significant investment here, not least because it is the fiefdom of President Cristina Fernández Kirchner, who owns several hotels in the region. Prices are high, and El Calafate has a sprawling feel, set in the shadow of its eponymous mountain and overlooking Lago Argentino. Apart from shopping, eating and planning your visits, there's little to do in the town itself.

The best **times to visit** are spring and autumn (Nov to mid-Dec & March–April), when there's a nice balance between having enough visitors to keep services running but not too many for the place to seem overcrowded; it can be uncomfortably busy in January and February. If you're planning to arrive any time outside winter (when access can be hard and many places are closed any way), it is advisable to book accommodation, flights and car rental well in advance.

The town's biggest festival, the **Festival del Lago Argentino**, takes place in the week leading up to February 15.

Museo Regional

Libertador 575 • Mon–Fri 8am–8pm • Free

The tiny **Museo Regional**, housed in a 1940s-era building, just east of the centre, has an eclectic range of exhibits including photos of the pioneers who founded El Calafate, a collection of fossils and stuffed birds, a stack of ancient typewriters, and some indigenous crafts. It's worth a quick look.

Calafate Centro de Interpretación Histórica

Brown and Bonarelli • Daily 10am–8pm • $40 • ☎ 02902 492799, ⓦ museocalafate.com.ar

A ten-minute walk north of the Museo Regional, the **Calafate Centro de Interpretación Histórica** attempts to trace 100 million years of natural and human history in Patagonia. There are displays on indigenous communities, rock art, the 1920–21 workers' strike (see box, p.474), glaciers and dinosaur skeletons, including part of a mylodon, the creature that inspired Bruce Chatwin's *In Patagonia*.

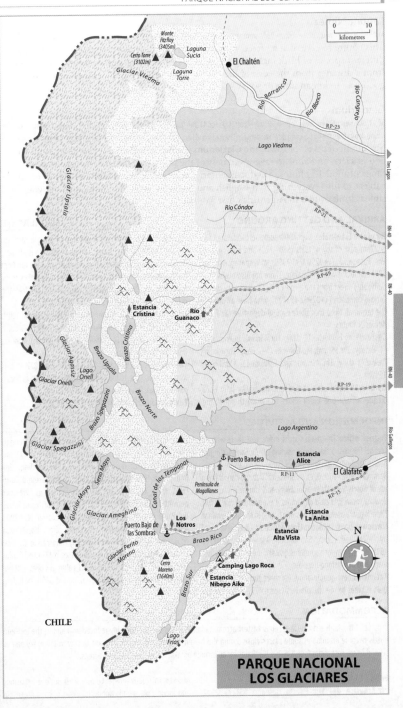

PARQUE NACIONAL
LOS GLACIARES

8

CHILE

Laguna Nimez

Just off L.N. Alem, north of the centre • Daily: summer 9am–9pm; winter 9am–7pm • $25

This nature reserve, just a fifteen-minute walk from the town centre, is home to eighty different species of bird, including flamingoes (though you can sometimes spot them from a distance from the edge of the reserve without paying the entry fee) and is a good way to kill an hour or so.

Glaciarium

RP-11, 6km west of town • Daily: Sept–April 9am–8pm; May–Aug 11am–7pm • $95 • ☎ 02902 497912, ⓦ glaciarium.com • Shuttle buses ($30 return) depart from the car park on 1 de Mayo, between Libertador and Roca, every hour on the hour 9am–6pm (reduced service May–Aug)

Six kilometres west of town, the **Glaciarium** is a modern museum that focuses on ice and glaciers, and aims to raise awareness of the impact of climate change. It uses a range of models, photos, 3D documentaries and interactive exhibits to help bring the subject to life (everything is in English and Spanish), and after looking round you can sink a drink or two in Argentina's first ice-bar.

ARRIVAL AND GETTING AROUND

By plane El Calafate's airport (ⓦ aeropuertocalafate.com) is 22km east of town; taxis ($80–120) and buses run by Ves Patagonia (☎ 02902 497355, ⓦ vespatagonia.com; $38) connect it with El Calafate. There are also buses (1–3 daily; 3hr) direct from the airport to El Chaltén with the Las Lengas company (☎ 02962 493023), who have an office in the terminal. Note that there's a $38 departure tax for all domestic flights.

Destinations Bariloche (1 daily; 1hr 45min); Buenos Aires (4–8 daily; 2hr 55min); Río Gallegos (1–2 daily; 1hr 15min); Trelew (1 daily; 1hr 45min); and Ushuaia (2–4 daily; 1hr 15min).

By bus All buses stop at the terminal on Av Julio Roca, on the hillside one block above the main thoroughfare,

EL CALAFATE

Av Libertador, to which it's connected by a flight of steps. Cal Tur, Chaltén Travel, Taqsa, TPS and Las Lengas all have daily services to El Chaltén (3hr), normally at 8am and 6pm (and sometimes around 1pm too). Generally only Cal Tur (☎ 02902 491368) operates a year-round service; the others tend only to run in the warmer months.

Destinations Bariloche (summer only; 1 daily; around 30hr); El Chaltén (2–3 daily; 3hr); Puerto Natales, Chile (1–2 daily; 6–7hr); Río Gallegos (4–5 daily; 4hr–4hr 30min); Ushuaia (via Chile; 1 daily; 16hr).

Car rental Avis, Libertador 1078 ☎ 02902 492877, ⓦ avis .com; Fiorasi, Libertador 1341 ☎ 02902 495330, ⓦ fiorasi rentacar.com. Prices start at around $500/day.

Taxis Cóndor, 25 de Mayo 50 ☎ 02902 491655.

INFORMATION AND ACTIVITIES

Tourist office The main tourist office is a short way up Coronel Rosales, a side street leading off Av San Martín just before the bridge (daily: summer 8am–10pm; winter 8am–8pm; ☎ 02902 491090, ⓦ turismo.elcalafate.gov.ar); it has a list of hotels with daily availability and can help you track down a room in a *casa de familia* if everywhere else is full. There is also a useful branch (same hours) in the bus terminal.

National park information office At Libertador 1302 (Mon–Fri 8am–6pm, Sat & Sun 9am–6pm; ☎ 02902 491545, ⓦ parquesnacionales.gov.ar); here you can get maps and buy fishing licences.

Activities Few people allow for more time in El Calafate than it takes to see the glaciers (see p.472), but there are

other worthwhile excursions if you're around for longer. The Cerro Frías agency, Libertador 1857 (☎ 02902 492808, ⓦ cerrofrias.com), runs daily trekking, horseriding, zip-lining and 4WD trips (from $250) in and around Cerro Frías, from which there are stunning views, weather permitting, of both Monte Fitz Roy to the north and Torres del Paine in the south. Calbagatas del Glaciar (☎ 02902 495447, ⓦ cabalgatasdelglaciar.com) offers horseriding trips (from $240) in the surrounding countryside. Several agencies, including Hielo y Aventura (see p.473) and Cal Tur (see above), run trips to Torres del Paine in Chile: a (long, rather rushed) day-trip costs from around $800, excluding entry fees.

ACCOMMODATION

Outside of the high season (Jan, Feb & Easter) accommodation prices are considerably reduced and all but the top-end hotels become affordable; some places close during the height of winter. If you don't want to stay in town, try one of several nearby estancias (see box, p.470). Rates for all include breakfast and wi-fi/internet access.

HOSTELS AND HOSPEDAJES

★ **América del Sur** Puerto Deseado 151 ☎ 02902

493525, ⓦ americahostel.com.ar. Well-designed, spacious and friendly place with wonderful views of Lago Argentino

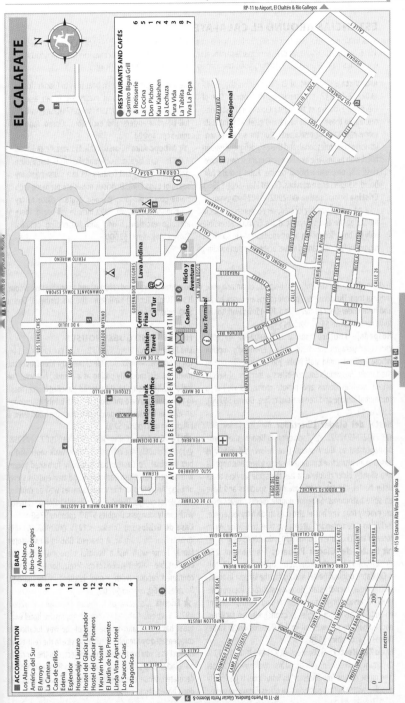

EL CALAFATE

RP-11 to Airport, El Chaltén & Río Gallegos

● RESTAURANTS AND CAFÉS

Casimiro Bigua Grill & Rotisserie	6
La Cocina	5
Don Pichon	1
Kau Kaleshen	2
La Lechuza	4
Pura Vida	3
La Tablita	8
Viva La Pepa	7

■ ACCOMMODATION

Los Álamos	6
América del Sur	3
El Arroyo	8
La Cantera	13
Casa de Grillos	1
Edenia	9
Esplendor	11
Hospedaje Lautaro	5
Hostel del Glaciar Libertador	10
Hostel del Glaciar Pioneros	12
I Keu Ken Hostel	14
El Jardín de los Presentes	2
Linda Vista Apart Hotel	7
Los Sauces Casas Patagónicas	4

■ BARS

Casablanca	1
Libro-bar Borges y Álvarez	2

Museo Regional

National Park Information Office

Hielo y Aventura

Casino

Bus Terminal

Lava Andina

Cerro Frías

Chaltén Travel

Cal Tur

RP-15 to Estancia Alta Vista & Lago Roca

RP-11 to Puerto Bandera, Glaciar Perito Moreno

0 — 200 metres

8

ESTANCIAS AROUND EL CALAFATE

In addition to the options listed below, staff at the office of Estancias de Santa Cruz, Libertador 1215 (☎02902 492858, ⓦestanciasdesantacruz.com), can provide information on many other estancias in the area and throughout the province, and make reservations.

Alta Vista 35km west of El Calafate on the RP-15 ☎02902 491247, ⓦhosteriaaltavista.com.ar. One of the more exclusive of the Santa Cruz tourist estancias, catering to those seeking peace and quiet. Airy, intimate rooms have tasteful, restrained decor; the service is non-intrusive and professional; and there's a delightful garden filled with lupins. The excellent restaurant serves simple, classically prepared regional cuisine. Rates include full-board, transfers and excursions. Closed May–Sept. __$2300__

Cristina Bahía Cristina ☎02902 491034, ⓦestancia cristina.com. Superbly located, very expensive estancia hidden at the end of remote Bahía Cristina, accessible only by boat. Top-notch accommodation – in spacious rooms with peak-framed views across the surrounding

meseta – is combined with boat trips to Glacier Upsala and hiking or horseriding excursions. It can also be visited on a day-trip to Upsala (see p.474). Rates include full-board, transfers and excursions. Closed June to mid-Sept. __$6000__

★ **Nibepo Aike** 60km outside El Calafate ☎02966 422626, ⓦnibepoaike.com.ar. Beautiful farmhouse dating from early last century set in a stunning valley south of Lago Roca. Delicious meals are prepared with home-grown produce; it's also a great place to try traditional lamb *asado*. Rates include full-board. There are also excellent hiking and horseriding options. Closed May–Sept. __$2000__

and knowledgeable staff who can help you organize a wide range of trips. The dorms and private rooms are clean, bright and have under-floor heating. It's a 10–15min walk to the town centre. Dorms __$100__, doubles __$420__

Hospedaje Lautaro Espora 237 ☎02902 492698, ⓦhospedajelautaro.com.ar. A super-friendly option whose well-informed staff make you feel just like one of the family, *Hospedaje Lautaro* offers a mixture of keenly priced, no-frills dorms and private rooms, as well as a communal lounge and free tea and coffee. Dorms __$97.50__, doubles __$220__

Hostel del Glaciar Libertador Av Libertador 587 ☎02902 491792, ⓦglaciar.com. Under the same management as the *Pioneros* (see below), *Libertador* is based in an attractive building closer to town, and appeals to a slightly older clientele. It has the same services as its sister hostel, though dorms are more spacious and have en-suite bathrooms. Superior double rooms, meanwhile, are exactly that. The hostel also runs its own travel service, including recommended alternative trips to Glaciar Perito Moreno and El Chaltén. Dorms __$105__, doubles __$435__

★ **Hostel del Glaciar Pioneros** Los Pioneros 255 ☎02902 491243, ⓦglaciar.com. Opened in 1987, this is Calafate's original hostel and by far the largest in town. Multilingual, friendly staff, decent restaurant, inexpensive laundry service, bright four- and six-bed dorms, excellent en-suite rooms (from singles to quads), kitchen facilities, and bargain lunchboxes all make *Pioneros* great value. Dorms __$83__, doubles __$308__

I Keu Ken Hostel F.M. Pontoriero 171 ☎02902 495175, ⓦpatagoniaikeuken.com.ar. This welcoming hostel (the name means "my ancestor" in Tehuelche) is justifiably popular, with a hilltop position that offers expansive views,

economical dorms and *cabañas*, and a sociable living room. It's a 10min (uphill) walk from the bus terminal. Dorms __$80__, cabañas __$300__

HOTELS AND GUESTHOUSES

Los Alamos Gob. Moyano and Bustillo ☎02902 491144, ⓦposadalosalamos.com. One of the most luxurious of the town's hotels, modestly posing as a *posada*, but with the feel of a village complex. It has wood-panelled rooms (those in the newer part are the biggest), with bright bathrooms, an excellent restaurant, gardens, tennis court and even a Lilliputian golf course. __$795__

★ **La Cantera** Calle 306 173 ☎02902 495998, ⓦlacanteracalafate.com.ar. A 10min walk south of the bus terminal, *La Cantera* has tastefully furnished rooms with huge beds, plush bathrooms and tremendous views of Lago Argentino or the mountains, as well as *cabañas* suitable for groups. There's also a sizeable balcony scattered with comfy loungers. Doubles __$730__, cabañas __$760__

Casa de Grillos Los Condores 1215 ☎02902 491160, ⓦcasadegrillos.com.ar. A peaceful B&B in a two-storey family home with just a handful of rooms, which are comfortable – albeit in need of modernization – and a self-contained *cabaña* (with a mini kitchen) in the garden. Doubles __$360__, cabaña __$420__

★ **Edenia** Manzana 642, Punta Soberana ☎02902 497021, ⓦedeniahoteles.com.ar. Impressive hotel with great bay views and whose out-of-the-way location is compensated by a regular minibus service to the centre and the fact that you are the last to be collected in the morning on glacier tours. The en suites are bright and simply decorated, while the excellent restaurant-bar means you don't have to trek into town in the evening. __$650__

Esplendor Perón 1143 ☎02902 492485, ⓦesplendor elcalafate.com. Sharp boutique hotel on the hill that overlooks town. The rather forbidding exterior belies a sun-filled interior: a huge lobby – complete with antler chandeliers – a minimalist bar-restaurant, and rustically cool bedrooms awash in the colours of the Patagonian steppe. Corner suites have 270-degree views of El Calafate and Lago Argentino. Free shuttle bus into town every 30min. Closed June to mid-Aug. Doubles $658, suites $855

El Jardín de los Presentes Guido Bonarelli 72 ☎02902 491518, ⓦlospresentes.com.ar. In a town with a real shortage of decent mid-range options, *El Jardín de los Presentes* stands out for its clean, simple and reasonably priced en-suite rooms and self-contained *cabañas*. It's a 15min walk from the town centre. Doubles $370, *cabañas* $445

Linda Vista Apart Hotel Agostini 71 ☎02902 493598, ⓦlindavistahotel.com.ar. A good option for couples or groups who are planning to self-cater, *Linda Vista* has a collection of very clean, self-contained apartments (sleeping up to five) with bedrooms, bathrooms, kitchenettes and TVs. $620

Los Sauces Casas Patagónicas Los Gauchos 1352/1370 ☎02966 495854, ⓦcasalossauces.com. One of El Calafate's top hotels, *Los Sauces* has impeccable en suites, all unique; a free bottle of champagne and a selection of fine chocolates are provided to help you to settle in. There's also a state-of-the-art spa and gym, as well as indoor and outdoor pools, a "club house" to relax in, a fine restaurant and bar, and expansive grounds. $1730

CAMPING

El Arroyo José Pantín 58 ☎02902 492233. This campsite, conveniently located one block behind the petrol station at the entrance to El Calafate, has a pleasant riverside setting and is a good choice (during the warmer months of the year at least). $40

EATING AND DRINKING

Most **restaurants** are clustered along or within a block of Avenida Libertador; with a few exceptions, prices are high by Argentine standards. Surprisingly the choice of **bars** and late-night hangouts is limited – perhaps because everyone has to get up so early for the excursions. The opening hours given here are for the high season; during the rest of the year, at many places, they are much reduced.

RESTAURANTS AND CAFÉS

Casimiro Biguá Grill & Rotisserie Libertador 963 ☎02902 492590, ⓦcasimirobigua.com. Top-end joint serving fine cuts of prime beef and succulent Patagonian lamb in a slick but congenial atmosphere. It has one of the best wine lists in town and while the prices (mains $70–130) are high, eating here is a real experience. It closes during the winter but there are two other branches (both open year-round) on Libertador, one, at no. 993, specializing in barbecued meat, and the other, at no. 1359, serving mainly Italian cuisine. Daily 10am–1am.

La Cocina Libertador 1245 ☎02902 491758. Cosy diner with a mouthwatering list of savoury tarts and pancakes ($30–65), as well as a selection of salads, pastas, fish and meat dishes. The place is a bit understaffed, so service isn't particularly quick. Noon–3.30pm & 6.30–11.30pm; closed Tues.

Don Pichon Puerto Deseado 242 ☎02902 492577. Top-notch *parilla* on a hill a 10min walk northeast of the centre (call ahead for a free transfer) whose wraparound windows offer panoramic views of the city and the lake. Steaks are the big draw, but if you're feeling indulgent, go for the fondue. Mains $45–90. Tues–Sun noon–3pm & 7pm–midnight.

Kau Kaleshen Gob. Gregores 1256 ☎02902 491188. This charming vegetarian restaurant/*casa de té* has a keenly priced, inventive menu that features wraps, pizzas, stir-fries and curries (all $35–60). There are also treats like chocolate fondue ($160) and a range of teas, coffees and home-made cakes that are ideal for a *merienda* (afternoon snack). Tues–Sun 4pm–midnight.

La Lechuza Libertador and Primero de Mayo ☎02902 491610, ⓦlalechuzapizzas.com.ar. This deservedly popular place serves up a huge range of pizzas ($45–75) from its wood-fired oven, plus pasta dishes, make-your-own salads

THE CALAFATE BUSH

Calafate, the indigenous name for what is known in English as the box-leaved barberry (*Berberis buxifolia*), is Patagonia's best-known plant. The bushes are protected by vindictive thorns, and the wood contains a substance known as *berberina*, which possesses medicinal properties and is used as a textile dye. From late October onwards, the bushes are covered with exquisite little bright yellow flowers. Depending on where they're growing, the berries mature between December and March. Once used by the indigenous populations for dye, they're nowadays often employed in delicious ice creams, appetizing home-made preserves or as a filling for *alfajores*. Remember the oft-quoted saying: "*El que come el calafate, volverá*" ("Eat calafate berries and you'll be back").

and huge sandwiches. There are a couple of other branches dotted around town too. Daily noon–midnight.

★ **Pura Vida** Libertador 1876 ☎02902 493356. The young owners provide traditional food with a modern touch in an A-frame *cabaña* with a purple roof and green walls. The menu has numerous vegetarian options along-side appetizing dishes such as country chicken pie and "Granny's" lentil stew. Prices (for El Calafate at least) are reasonable too, with mains around $56–76. It's a 10min walk from the centre. 7.30–11.30pm; closed Wed.

★ **La Tablita** Cnel. Rosales 28 ☎02902 491065. Legendary *asador*, deservedly popular with locals and tour groups alike, who come here to gorge on delicious, serious-sized lamb or beef grills (the mixed *parrilla* could feed a small army). Sides are fairly expensive but the massive mains ($70–105) are generally big enough for two. Noon–3.30pm & 7.30pm–midnight; closed Wed.

Viva La Pepa Emilio Amado 833 ☎02902 491880, ⓦvivalapepacalafate.com. Cheerful café with no less

than 69 different savoury and sweet crêpes ($36–70), as well as soups, sandwiches, fresh juices and coffees. There's a whimsical air to the place: crudités are served in mini watering cans and children's paintings cover the orange and green walls. Noon–8pm; closed Thurs.

BARS

Casablanca Libertador 1202 ☎02902 491402. Buzzing café-bar that serves fine coffee (from $12), as well as fifteen types of beer (around $20–25) and tasty *lomitos*. Classic film posters and signed rugby and hockey shirts cover the walls. Noon–midnight; closed Wed.

Libro-bar Borges y Alvarez Libertador 1005 ☎02902 491464. This small, first-floor café-bar is run by, and aimed at, bibliophiles. There's an extensive range of Argentine and South American books (mainly in Spanish) crammed onto overstacked shelves that you can flick through whilst sampling a coffee, hot chocolate or *trago* (alcholic drink; $20–25). 11am/noon–2/3am; closed Wed.

DIRECTORY

Internet There are several internet cafés in town, including Locutorio on the corner of Espora and San Martín.

Laundry Lava Andina, Cmte. Espora 88 (☎02902 493980).

Money and exchange There are several ATMs including

at the Banco de la Nación, Libertador 1133, and Banco de Santa Cruz, Libertador 1285. Thaler, 9 de Julio, exchanges all major international and South American currencies.

Post office Libertador 1133.

The southern sector of the park

The exalted glaciers in the **southern sector** of the Los Glaciares national park attract huge numbers of visitors from all over the world and it takes a bit of planning to find the magic and avoid the crowds. The main sites cluster around **Lago Argentino**, the largest of all exclusively Argentine lakes, and the third biggest in all South America, with a surface area of 1600 square kilometres.

The three hotspots in the southern sector of the park are: the easy-to-reach and not-to-be-missed **Glaciar Perito Moreno**, which slams into the western end of the **Península de Magallanes**; **Puerto Bandera**, from where boat trips depart to Glaciar Upsala and the other northern glaciers that are inaccessible by land; and, to the south down the RP-15, the much-less-visited **Lago Roca** and the southern arm of Lago Argentino, the **Brazo Sur**.

Within the boundaries, be especially aware of the dangers of fire – an area of forest near Glaciar Spegazzini that burnt in the 1930s still hasn't even remotely recovered. **Mammals** in the park include the *gato montés* wildcat, pumas and the endangered *huemul*, although you are highly unlikely to see any of these owing to their scarcity and elusive nature. There is plenty of enjoyable **flora** on display, though, such as the ubiquitous *notro* (*Embothrium coccineum*, known in English as the Chilean firebush or firetree), with its flaming red blooms between November and March. Commonly seen **birds** include the majestic black and red Magellanic woodpecker (*Carpintero patagónico*).

Glaciar Perito Moreno

The immense pack ice of the **GLACIAR PERITO MORENO** (also called Ventisquero Perito Moreno) is one of Argentina's greatest natural wonders. It's not the longest of Argentina's glaciers – nearby Glaciar Upsala is twice as long (60km) – and whereas the ice cliffs at its snout tower up to 60m high, the face of Glaciar Spegazzini can reach heights double that. However, such comparisons prove irrelevant when you stand on the **boardwalks** that face this monster. Perito Moreno has a star quality that none of the others rivals.

The glacier zooms down off the icecap in a great motorway-like sweep, a jagged mass of crevasses and towering, knife-edged séracs almost unsullied by the streaks of dirty moraine that discolour many of its counterparts. When it collides with the southern arm of Lago Argentino, the **Canal de los Témpanos** (Iceberg Channel), the show really begins: vast blocks of ice, some weighing hundreds of tonnes, detonate off the face of the glacier with the report of a small cannon and come crashing down into the waters below. These frozen depth-charges then surge back to the surface as icebergs, sending out a fairy ring of smaller lumps that form a protecting reef around the berg, which is left to float in a mirror-smooth pool of its own.

That said, it's more likely you'll have to content yourself with the thuds, cracks, creaks and grinding crunches the glacier habitually makes, as well as the wonderful variety of **colours of the ice**: marbled in places with streaks of muddy grey and copper-sulphate blue, while at the bottom the pressurized, de-oxygenated ice has a deep blue, waxy sheen. The glacier tends to be more active in sunny weather and in the afternoon, but early morning can also be beautiful, as the sun strikes the ice cliffs.

With the wind coming off the ice, the temperature at the glacier can be a lot colder than in El Calafate, so take **extra clothes**. Do not stray from the boardwalks: many deaths have been caused by ricocheting ice or wave surges.

Brief history

Perito Moreno is considered to be a "stable" glacier in the sense that it is neither advancing nor retreating. It is famous for the way it periodically pushes right across the channel, forming a massive dyke of ice that cut off the Brazo Rico and Brazo Sur from the main body of Lago Argentino. Isolated from their natural outlet, the water in the

8

TOURS OF GLACIAR PERITO MORENO

DAY-TOURS

Most people visit the Glaciar Perito Moreno on guided day-tours, which are offered by virtually all agencies in El Calafate and allow for around four hours at the ice face, the minimum required to fully appreciate the spectacle. They cost $170–200, plus the park entrance fee of $100. Rather than having a fixed point of departure, companies tend to drive round town collecting passengers from hotels; to avoid having to get up much earlier than you need to, try to arrange that you're the last pick-up or go to the office yourself just before the bus leaves. **Tour agencies** The trips with *Hostel del Glaciar Pioneros* (see p.470), Chaltén Travel (Libertador 1174 ☎02902 492212, ⓦchaltentravel.com) and Rumbo Sur (Libertador 960 ☎02902 492155, ⓦrumbosur.com.ar) are recommended for their knowledgeable, friendly guides and time spent at the glacier.

BOAT TOURS

An excellent way of seeing the ice face from another angle is to take one of the boat trips that chug along near the towering heights of the ice wall. Safari Náutico heads to the southern face from Puerto Bajo de las Sombras (daily: Oct–May hourly 10am–4pm; June–Sept noon; 1hr; $100).

ICE-TREKKING

For an even closer look, you can walk on the glacier with Hielo y Aventura, Libertador 935 (☎02902 492205, ⓦhieloyaventura.com), which organizes daily "Mini Trekking" trips (full day; 1hr 30min on the ice; $640 plus park entrance fee) and longer, more demanding "Big Ice" excursions (full day; 4hr on the ice; $850 plus park entrance fee), which include a boat trip across to the glacier. This is ice-trekking, not ice-*climbing* (try El Chaltén for that): you do not need to be a peak-bagging mountain man to do it. You'll be issued crampons, but bring sunglasses, sun cream, gloves and a packed lunch, and wear warm, weatherproof clothes.

> ## ESTANCIA ANITA
>
> About 30km from El Calafate, the RP-15 passes historical Estancia Anita, the scene of one of Patagonia's most grisly episodes. In 1921, 121 men were executed here by an army battalion that had been sent to crush a rural strike and the related social unrest; a monument by the roadside commemorates the victims.

brazos (arms) would build up against the flank of the glacier, flooding the surrounding area, until eventually the pressure forced open a passage into the canal once again. Occurring over the course of several hours, such a **rupture** is, for those lucky enough to witness it, one of nature's most awesome spectacles.

The glacier first reached the peninsula in 1917, having advanced some 750m in fifteen years, but the channel did not remain blocked for long and the phenomenon remained little known. This changed in 1939, when a vast area was flooded and planes made a futile attempt to break the glacier by bombing it. In 1950, water levels rose by 30m and the channel was closed for two years; in 1966, levels reached an astonishing 32m above their normal level. The glacier then settled into a fairly regular cycle, completely blocking the channel approximately every four years or so up to 1988; after that there was a sixteen-year gap until another rupture in 2004. Since then there have been major ruptures in March 2006, 2008 and, most recently, in March 2012.

ARRIVAL AND DEPARTURE   GLACIAR PERITO MORENO

By bus or remise If you don't want to be restricted to a tour (see p.473), Cal Tur runs a twice-daily bus service departing at 8am and 3pm and returning around 1pm and 8pm. If you get the 8am departure you'll probably be among the first to arrive at the glacier – it's worth the effort to beat the crowds and glimpse the early morning sun shining on the west-facing snout. The 3pm bus arrives at the park after most tour groups have left, though the boat trips will also have stopped running by this point. Alternatively, you could hire a *remise* taxi (around $500, including a 4hr wait at the glacier).

By car The other option is to rent a car (around $500/day) and drive along the lesser-used RP-15 towards Lago Roca or along the paved RP-11. The RP-15 is unsurfaced but by far the most picturesque. Turn right just after the tourist estancia *of Alta Vista* (see p.470), and then left after another 12km to the park's main entrance. The route along the RP-11 heads straight down Av Libertador and along a paved road that lines the lake shore, then dropping down to the park's main entrance; the right turning here, down the RP-8, leads to Puerto Bandera (see box opposite), for boat trips to Upsala and other glaciers.

INFORMATION

Visitors pay the entry fee ($100) at the main entrance to the park (daily 8am–7pm), which lies at the edge of the peninsula; the trees nearby are a favourite evening roost of the rabble-rousing austral parakeet (*cachaña*), the most southerly of the world's parrots. From here it's a 40min drive (around 30km) past picnic spots, a campsite, the exclusive *Los Notros* hotel (see below), and Puerto Bajo de la Sombras (see p.473) to a series of boardwalks in front of the glacier; there's also a café, a gift shop and public toilets here.

ACCOMMODATION

Los Notros Inside the park ☎ 011 4813 7285, ⊛ losnotros .com. The only hotel right up close to the Glaciar Perito Moreno (and with views of its left flank), *Los Notros* is a tastefully designed "rustic" wooden lodge built on private land within the park, with smart en suites and an excellent (if expensive) restaurant. Much cheaper if you book online in advance. Rates include full board, excursions and transfers. Closed June to mid-Sept. **US$914**

The Upsala, Spegazzini, Onelli and Agassiz glaciers

Glaciar Upsala is the undisputed heavyweight of the park, between 5km and 7km wide, with a 60m-high snout and a length of 60km. It's still South America's longest glacier, despite massive retrocession over the last decade or so, and covers a total area three times larger than that of metropolitan Buenos Aires. Upsala played an important role in consolidating Argentine claims to its Antarctic territory – expedition teams used to acclimatize by living for months in a base on the glacier.

Navigating **Brazo Upsala** is a highlight in itself, though trips here are often cancelled due to the increasing number of **icebergs** that bob, grind and even turn occasional flips around you. As any good student of the *Titanic* will know, for every one part of iceberg above the surface, it has six to seven parts below, which gives an idea of the tremendous size of these blocks. Even in flat light, the icy blues shine as if lit by a neon strip-light – an eerie, incredible, cerulean glow.

Glaciar Spegazzini is many visitors' favourite glacier, with an imposing ice cascade to the right and the most dizzying snout of all the glaciers in the park (between 80 and 135m high). The **Onelli** and **Agassiz glaciers** are less impressive – but beautiful nonetheless – and are reached by an easy 800m walk to **Laguna Onelli**, a chilly lake dotted with small bergs. The walk itself is likely to appeal only to those who haven't had the opportunity to see Patagonian forest elsewhere, since the beauty of these woodlands is not enhanced by the presence of crowds of day-trippers.

Lago Roca

Overshadowed by the nearby glaciers, **Lago Roca**, a southern branch of Lago Argentino, tends to be frequented mainly by keen fishermen. Lying 52km from El Calafate, it offers good horseriding and trekking possibilities in stunning areas of open woodland and among the neighbouring hills of the Cordón de los Cristales. It also has examples of rock art dating back three thousand years, which can be seen along a signposted trail to the left of the main road just before *Lago Roca* campsite (see p.476); from here, you can continue the four-hour hike to the summit of Cerro Cristales, with fine views of Torres del Paine to the south. Note that there's no entry fee for this area of the park.

8

ARRIVAL AND DEPARTURE
LAGO ROCA

By bus/taxi Cal Tur runs buses to Lago Roca (summer only: Mon, Wed & Fri–Sun; leaving El Calafate at 8.30am, returning 6pm), while a taxi from town costs about $400–500. Alternatively several travel agencies (see p.473) run day-trips taking in Lago Roca.

GLACIER CRUISES

FROM PUERTO BANDERA

Boat trips to see the Upsala, Spegazzini and Onelli glaciers are run from Puerto Bandera by Solo Patagonia (Libertador 867; ☎02902 491298, ⓦ solopatagonia.com). When the weather's fine, the full-day excursion ($560 plus $100 park entrance fee) is an unforgettable experience; when it's rough, it can be memorable for the wrong reasons – if badly affected by motion sickness, take precautionary seasickness tablets. Dress in warm, waterproof and windproof clothing, and take your own food as prices on board are high.

Before booking, remember that your scope for refunds is limited: the weather has to be exceptionally foul for the trip to be cancelled entirely, and the company fulfils its legal obligations if only one main part of the trip is completed; in windy weather especially, icebergs can block the channels, and in recent years, Upsala has been frequently inaccessible.

Mar Patag (9 de Julio 57; ☎02902 492118, ⓦ crucerosmarpatag.com) in El Calafate runs excellent day-long cruises (from $1125, plus $100 park entry fee), as well as the extended three-day "The Spirit of the Glaciers" tour; prices are high, but the service and the experience justify them. The trips give you close-quarter views of the Upsala and Spegazzini glaciers – as well as Perito Moreno – anchoring at Puerto las Vacas, off the Brazo Spegazzini, for the night.

TOURS OF BAHÍA CRISTINA

The one- and multi-day trips ($400–1850, excluding transfers and the $100 park entry fee) run by *Estancia Cristina* (see p.470) give you access to the central sector of the park and the windswept, desolate Bahía Cristina area. Boats visit Glacier Upsala before heading up Bahía Cristina to the isolated estancia, a favoured point of entry for explorers of the icecap, including Padre de Agostini and Eric Shipton, the famous mountaineer and explorer of the 1960s. Trekking, horseriding and 4WD excursions can be added on.

ACCOMMODATION

Camping Lago Roca Lago Roca ☎02902 499500. This site has a mix of camping pitches and simple *cabañas*; the latter are heated and sleep two to four people. There's also a restaurant-bar, and you can rent fishing equipment and bikes. Camping $50, cabañas $250

El Chaltén

EL CHALTÉN, 90km west of the RN-40 and 220km north of El Calafate, has undergone a convulsive expansion since it was established in 1985 in a (successful) attempt to claim the area from Chile. Today, it's a thriving tourist centre showing regrettable signs of uncontrolled development: whereas some hotels have been built in a style sympathetic to their surroundings, others would look more at ease in the beach resort of Mar del Plata. That said, the atmosphere in the town is extremely pleasant and relaxed, with a friendly mix of Argentines and foreign visitors of all ages.

Rearing up on the opposite bank of the **Río de las Vueltas** is the curiously stepped, dark-grey cliff face of **Cerro Pirámide**, while you can glimpse the tips of the park's most daunting peaks, **Fitz Roy** and **Cerro Torre**, from the southern and eastern fringes of the village. In terms of specific sights, there is only the classically uncluttered alpine **chapel** on the western edge of the village. Built by Austrian craftsmen with Austrian materials, it's a fitting memorial to the climbing purist Toni Egger (see box, p.484), as well as to others who have lost their lives in the park.

ARRIVAL AND DEPARTURE

EL CHALTÉN

By bus All buses arrive and depart from the bus terminal in the southeastern end of the town, on Güemes and Perito Moreno. Cal Tur, Chaltén Travel, Taqsa, TPS and Las Lengas all have services to El Calafate; generally only Cal Tur operates a year-round service. Las Lengas has services to and from El Calafate's airport; and during the summer, daily buses travel to Perito Moreno. Buy tickets at least a day in advance for all services.

Destinations Bariloche (Nov–April; 1–2 daily; around 27hr); El Calafate (2–10 daily; 3hr); El Calafate airport (1–3 daily; 3hr); Perito Moreno (Nov–April; 1–2 daily; 13hr).

To Chile There are several ways to reach Chile: many travel agencies (see box, p.478) organize trips to Torres del Paine national park; there are bus services to Puerto Natales (3 weekly; 5hr); and, for those with a real sense of adventure, it is possible to cross to Villa O'Higgins (during Nov–March only) via a two-day trip by bus, boat and on foot (or a bike) – ask at the tourist office for more details on the route.

INFORMATION

National park visitors' centre Just under 1km south of the town, the national park visitors' centre (daily: Dec–Feb 8am–6pm; March–Nov 9am–5pm; ☎☎02962 493004) is a necessary point of call; helpful volunteers advise visitors of the park's regulations and the various hiking routes. Inside are wildlife exhibits, a message board and a useful information book for climbers, all of whom must register here, as should anyone planning to stay at the Laguna Torre campsite to the south. Fishing licences can be purchased here too.

Tourist information There's a small tourist office in the bus station (daily: Dec–Feb 8am–8pm; March–Nov Mon–Fri 9am–2pm & 5–7pm, Sat & Sun 10.30am–noon & 5–7pm; ☎0292 493370).

Websites Two useful websites are ⓦlacachania.com.ar and ⓦelchalten.com.

LA LEONA: A HISTORIC WAYSIDE INN

En route from El Calafate to El Chaltén, by a modern bridge over the Río La Leona, stands one of the RN-40's original inns, **Hotel La Leona** (☎011 5032 3415, ⓦhoteldecampolaleona.com.ar; daily 8.30am–9.30pm; cakes around $13–25). It's a wonderfully atmospheric place (despite heavy restoration) worth stopping at for a slice of home-made lemon meringue or apple pie or maybe just a tea or coffee; it also sells crafts and useful maps. You could try your hand here at the **juego de la argolla**, an old gaucho drinking game where you take turns to land a ring that's attached by a string to the ceiling over a hook mounted on the wall opposite: the first person to succeed wins a drink – try one of the **typical gaucho tipples**, such as sweet *caña ombú* or *caña quemada*. Buses travelling between El Calafate to El Chaltén generally make short stops here.

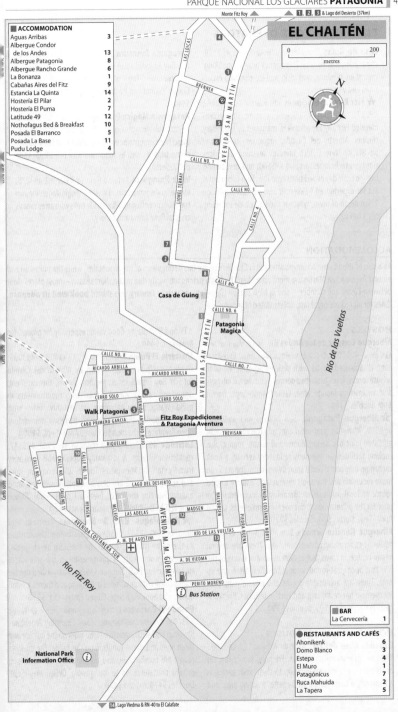

Monte Fitz Roy ▲   ▲ **1**, **2**, **3** & Lago del Desierto (37km)

EL CHALTÉN

0 ——————————— 200
metres

N

LAS LOICAS

BRENNER

AVENIDA SAN MARTIN

@

CALLE NO. 1

LIONEL TERRAY

CALLE NO. 3

CALLE NO. 4

CALLE NO. 5

Casa de Guing

CALLE NO. 6

Patagonia Magica

Río de las Vueltas

8

CALLE NO. 7

CALLE NO. 8

RICARDO ARBILLA

RICARDO ARBILLA

CERRO SOLO

CERRO SOLO

AVENIDA ANTONIO ROJO

Walk Patagonia

CABO PRIMERO GARCIA

RIQUELME

Fitz Roy Expediciones & Patagonia Aventura

TREVISAN

AVENIDA SAN MARTIN

CALLE NO. 12

CALLE NO. 9

CALLE NO. 10

CALLE NO. 11

HENSEN

MCLEOD

LAGO DEL DESIERTO

LAS ADELAS

AVENIDA M. M. GÜEMES

MADSEN

HALVORSEN

PIEDRA BUENA

AVENIDA COSTANERA NORTE

A. M. DE AGOSTINI

RÍO DE LAS VUELTAS

A. DE VIEDMA

PERITO MORENO

ⓘ **Bus Station**

AVENIDA COSTANERA SUR

Río Fitz Roy

National Park Information Office *ⓘ*

▼ **14**, Lago Viedma & RN-40 to El Calafate

EL CHALTÉN TOUR OPERATORS

Casa de Guias San Martín s/n ☎02962 493118, ⓦcasadeguias.com.ar. This agency provides trekking, mountain-climbing, and rock- and ice-climbing excursions and workshops.

★ **Fitz Roy Expediciones** San Martín 56 ☎02962 493178, ⓦfitzroyexpediciones.com.ar. The recommended Fitz Roy Expediciones, managed by legendary climber Alberto del Castillo, organizes ice-trekking on Glaciar Torre (which involves teaching basic ice-climbing techniques; around AR$500) and demanding five- to nine-day expeditions onto the Hielo Continental Sur for experienced trekkers. It also runs an eco-lodge 17km north of town, which is used as a base for many of its treks.

Patagonia Aventura San Martín 56 (same office as Fitz Roy Expediciones) ☎02962 493110, ⓦpatagonia aventura.com. Runs boat trips across Lago Viedma to Glaciar Viedma and ice-trekking trips on its flanks (from $440).

Patagonia Mágica Fonrouge s/n ☎02962 493066, ⓦpatagoniamagica.com. This agency offers everything from mountaineering expeditions to backcountry skiing trips, as well as mountain-bike rides from Lago del Desierto.

Walk Patagonia Antonio Rojo 62 ☎02962 493275, ⓦwalkpatagonia.com. Excellent Anglo-Argentine-run travel agency offering tailor-made treks with an emphasis on local flora, fauna and history.

ACCOMMODATION

As a rule of thumb, the accommodation in El Chaltén's centre has better views of the mountains, while the places on and around Avenida San Martín are more upmarket. The **high prices** are partly due to the short season – most places close between Easter and October – and in high season (Dec–Feb), especially January, you should **book well in advance**. Rates for all include breakfast, unless stated otherwise.

HOSTELS

Albergue Condor de los Andes Río de las Vueltas s/n ☎02962 493101, ⓦcondordelosandes.com. Excellent, cosy, HI-affiliated hostel with welcoming staff, en-suite private rooms, four- to six-bed dorms, a communal kitchen, and an inviting lounge area. Closed April–Sept. Dorms $90, doubles $380

★ **Albergue Patagonia** San Martín 493 ☎02962 493019, ⓦpatagoniahostel.com.ar. This homely, HI-affiliated joint has decent dorms and private rooms, plus cooking facilities, an inexpensive laundry service, a book exchange, bike rental and a snug living room. The staff can make excursion and transport reservations and are a good source of local information. Breakfast is included in the price for the private rooms, but not for dorm guests. Closed April–Sept. Dorms $70, doubles $220

Albergue Rancho Grande San Martín 724 ☎02962 493005, ⓦranchograndehostel.com. There are several better hostels in town, but as *Rancho Grande* is one of the few that open year-round, budget travellers often end up here. There are acceptable dorms and private rooms, an inexpensive bar-restaurant and kitchen facilities. Breakfast costs extra. Dorms $100, doubles $390

HOTELS AND GUESTHOUSES

Cabañas Aires del Fitz Ricardo Arbilla 124 ☎02962 493134, ⓦairesdelfitz.com.ar. Friendly, family-run set of split-level *cabañas* sleeping up to six people; each has a bedroom, a bathroom, a kitchenette, a dining area, and a TV and DVD player. Good value, especially for groups. No breakfast. $440

Hostería El Puma Lionel Terray 212 ☎02962 493095, ⓦhosteriaelpuma.com.ar. Run by Alberto del Castillo (of Fitz Roy Expediciones; see box above), this excellent, upper-end option was designed with mountaineers in mind. Warm, softly lit rooms are stylishly rustic, with wooden flooring throughout, and there's a tremendous open fireplace in the lounge. Closed April–Sept. $1000

Latitude 49 Güemes and Madsen ☎02962 493347, ⓦlatitude49.com. A justifiably popular B&B with very friendly staff and keen prices. The en-suite rooms are spick and span, and there are also a couple of self-contained apartments (for the latter, breakfast costs extra). Closed June & July. Doubles $290, apartments $420

★ **Nothofagus Bed & Breakfast** Hensen and Riquelme ☎02962 493087, ⓦnothofagusbb.com.ar. As the name (the Spanish for the southern beech genus) suggests, wood features prominently in the interior of this welcoming B&B. The good-value, sun-washed double rooms come with or without bathroom, and there's a small library and book exchange. Closed Easter–Oct. $250

Posada El Barranco Lionel Terray and Calle 2 ☎02962 493006, ⓦposadaelbarranco.com. Charming Argentine-Kiwi-run B&B with attractive stone work on the outside and clean lines and smart furniture on the inside. The en-suite rooms are comfortable, and there's also a self-contained *cabaña* that sleeps up to four people. Closed May–Sept. Doubles $470, *cabaña* $470

Posada La Base Hensen 16 ☎ 02962 493031, ⓦ elchalten patagonia.com.ar. This guesthouse has good-value rooms (especially for stays of two nights or more), several with mountain views. The owners are hospitable, and there are shared kitchen facilities (one for every two rooms), an inexpensive laundry service, and free film screenings in the attic sitting room. Closed May–Sept. $\overline{\underline{$440}}$

Pudu Lodge Las Loicas 97 ☎ 02962 493365, ⓦ pudulodge .com. A smart, modern hotel owned by Gabriel "Rapa" Rapaport, an experienced mountaineer. The spacious rooms and private bathrooms are done out in a pleasing contemporary style, and the breakfasts are copious. $\overline{\underline{$700}}$

OUT OF TOWN

Aguas Arribas Lago del Desierto, 37km from town ☎ 011 4152 5697, ⓦ estancialaquinta.com.ar. In a tranquil lakeside location, just 5km from the Chilean border, *Aguas Arribas* is a wonderful spot for travellers who want to get away from it all. Great food, swish en suites, superlative views, and excellent hiking and fishing opportunities are all on offer. Rates include full board and activities. Closed May to mid-Oct. $\overline{\underline{$1950}}$

Estancia La Quinta 5km south of town off the RP-23 ☎ 02962 493012, ⓦ estancialaquinta.com.ar. A working cattle ranch in a lovely location whose thoroughly modern refurbishment belies its considerable history. Rooms are neat and compact, there's a peaceful lounge with views across the valley, and beautifully home-cooked local dishes are served in the 100-year-old *casco*. Closed May–Sept. $\overline{\underline{$800}}$

★ **Hostería El Pilar** 15km north of town on the RP-15 ☎ 02962 493002, ⓦ hosteriaelpilar.com.ar. Delightful, old-fashioned corrugated metal *casco*, appealingly decorated in period style. Rooms are comfortable and peaceful, the homely living room has a wood-burning stove, and home-made treats are served in the tearoom, which has an enviable view of Fitz Roy. There is also a neat little garden, and the owner is a knowledgeable guide. Closed April–Oct. $\overline{\underline{$730}}$

CAMPING

La Bonanza RP-23 ☎ 02962 493366, ⓦ camping bonanza.com.ar. This charming campsite, around 8km north of town, is situated next to the Río de las Vueltas, where trees offer some shelter from the wind. There are hot showers and ample cooking facilities. $\overline{\underline{$50}}$

8

EATING AND DRINKING

El Chaltén has several very good **restaurants** (although prices are relatively high), plus a few little **bars**. Most hotels and restaurants make **lunchboxes** for day-treks. The opening times given below are for the high season, and should only be taken as a rough guide; many places close between Easter and October, and those that stay open have reduced hours.

Ahonikenk Güemes 23 ☎ 02962 493070. This no-nonsense little restaurant in the southern part of the town serves up a good range of pasta dishes, pizzas and simple meals at fairly low prices (mains $32–72). Daily 11.30am–3.30pm & 7–10.30pm.

La Cervecería San Martín 564 ☎ 02962 493109. Top-notch microbrewery whose crisp, clean pilsners (from around $25) provide relief after a day on the trail. Genial staff, the occasional live-music session, and tasty snacks such as pizza and empanadas add to the convivial atmosphere. Daily 12.30–3.30pm & 7.30pm–1am.

Domo Blanco San Martín 164 ☎ 02962 493036. Alongside arguably the town's best ice cream (from $15) – which features local berries and fruits – *Domo Blanco* also serves up an interesting range of paninis, wraps and sandwiches. Daily 11am–9/10pm.

Estepa Cerro Solo and Antonio Rojo ☎ 02962 493068. Welcoming restaurant-bar in an adobe-style building lying in the shadow of Fitz Roy. Good selection of lamb dishes, as well as hearty calzones and pizzas from the wood-fired oven. Mains $50–100. Tues–Sun noon–3.30pm & 7.30pm–midnight/1am.

El Muro San Martín 912 ☎ 02962 493248. The name –

El Muro means "The Wall" – comes from the climbing wall on its exterior. Inside you can build up your trekking calories with a range of tasty offerings like lamb chops with red berries, though service can be slow at times. Mains $50–110. Daily 12.30–3pm & 7.30–11.30pm.

Patagónicus Güemes and Madsen ☎ 02962 493025. Terrific range of pizzas ($26–80) – the best in town – served up at chunky wooden tables in a social, friendly atmosphere. There's a good range of beers on offer too. 12.30–3pm & 7–10.30pm; closed Wed.

Ruca Mahuida Lionel Terray 104 ☎ 02962 493018. This tiny *cabaña* is home to some of the most imaginative cooking in El Chaltén. The extensive menu covers regional and international dishes; among the highlights are lamb spare ribs with pear and apple chutney. Good vegetarian options too. Mains $45–120. Daily 7–11.30pm.

La Tapera Av Antonio Rojo s/n ☎ 02962 493195. Housed in an appealing log *cabaña*, *La Tapera* has ultra-friendly service, and offers a menu featuring delicious and filling dishes ($50–100) including excellent tapas (hence the name). The wine list is excellent and make sure you leave room for the unusual but lip-smacking house dessert, mint pancakes. Daily 12.30–3pm & 7.30–11.30pm.

DIRECTORY

Money and exchange There are no banks or official money-changing facilities in El Chaltén, though some restaurants will exchange US dollars. There is an ATM in the bus station, but it's not the most reliable, so bring some cash with you.

Internet There are several cybercafés, including El Informante, San Martín 820.

The northern sector of the park

The northern sector of Parque Nacional Los Glaciares, the **Fitz Roy sector**, is a trekking paradise. One of its main attractions is that those with limited time, or who are not in peak fitness, can still make worthwhile **day-hikes** using El Chaltén as a base.

The sector also contains some of the most breathtakingly beautiful mountain peaks on Earth. Two concentric jaws of jagged teeth puncture the Patagonian sky with the 3405m incisor of **Monte Fitz Roy** at the centre of the massif. This sculpted peak was known to the Tehuelche as El Chaltén, "The Mountain that Smokes" or "The Volcano", owing to the almost perpetual presence of a scarf of cloud attached to its summit. It is

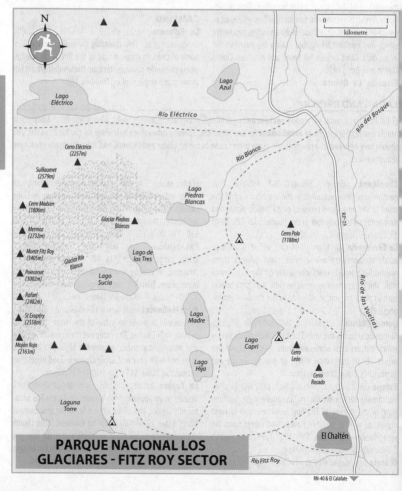

PARQUE NACIONAL LOS GLACIARES - FITZ ROY SECTOR

TREKKING TIPS

Adequate outdoor clothing is essential in the park at all times of the year, as snowstorms are possible even in midsummer. Note that there is a **ban on lighting campfires** in the park, so if you need your food hot, make careful use of gas stoves (and bring fuel with you, as it can be very difficult to get in town); **horses** are no longer allowed in the park, either, owing to the damage they were doing to the terrain but some operators now use environmentally friendly **llamas** as pack animals for treks. The best trekking **map** available is the 1:50,000 *Monte Fitz Roy & Cerro Torre* published by Zagier & Urruty, which includes a 1:100,000 scale map of the Lago del Desierto area. The informative *Trekking in Chaltén and Lago del Desierto* by Miguel A. Alonso is also worth a look.

not inconceivable, however, that the Tehuelche were using the term in a rather more metaphorical sense to allude to the fiery pink colour that the rock walls turn when struck by the first light of dawn. Francisco Moreno saw fit to name the pagan summit after the evangelical captain of the *Beagle*, who, with Charles Darwin, had viewed the Andes from a distance, after having journeyed up the Río Santa Cruz by whaleboat to within 50km of Lago Argentino. Alongside Monte Fitz Roy rise **Cerro Poincenot** and **Aguja Saint-Exupéry**, while set behind them is the forbidding needle of **Cerro Torre**, a finger that stands in bold defiance of all the elements that the Hielo Continental Sur (see box, p.482) hurls against it.

For those who enjoy camping, the quintessential three-day **Fitz Roy/Cerro Torre loop** at the centre of the park makes a good option, and can be done in either direction. The advantage of going anticlockwise is that you avoid the steep climb up to Lagunas Madre y Hija and you have the prevailing wind behind you when returning to El Chaltén. However, the biggest gamble is always what the weather will be like around Cerro Torre, so if this unpredictable peak is visible on day one, you might like to head for it first. The longer interlocking circuit to the north will add at least another two days. Detailed below are some of the shorter sections of the route, as well as a few other popular trails.

Note that there is **no entry fee** for this section of the park.

El Chaltén to Laguna de los Tres trail

The trek from **El Chaltén to Laguna de los Tres** (13km; 3–4hr; 750m ascent), at the very foot of **Monte Fitz Roy**, is one of the park's most scenic trails, and can be hiked either as a return trip or as part of the Fitz Roy/Torre loop.

The starting point for this classic hike is the house at the northern end of Avenida San Martín. The path is clearly indicated, climbing up through the wooded slopes of Cerro Rosado and Cerro León, until the scenery opens out with views of Fitz Roy. After heading up alongside the ravine of the Chorillo del Salto – where there is a plunging 20m waterfall – you come to a turn-off left (1hr–1hr 30min from El Chaltén), which leads after ten minutes to the **campsite** at **Laguna Capri** – there are great views, but the site (free) is rather exposed to the winds, and water from the lake should be boiled or treated. Better, if you have the time, to push on down the main path, crossing one stream just past the turn-off to Laguna Madre, and another brook until you reach **Campamento Poincenot** (1hr–1hr 15min from the Laguna Capri turn-off), named after one of the team of French climbers who made the victorious first ascent of Fitz Roy in 1952. According to the official story, Poincenot drowned while trying to cross the Río Fitz Roy before the assault on the mountain even took place, although another rumour hinted that this was no accident, but the work of a cuckolded estancia owner, enraged by his wife's infidelities with the Gallic mountaineer. The campsite (free) covers a sprawling area on the eastern bank of the Río Blanco. Choose your spot well and you won't need to get out of your tent to see the rosy blaze of dawn on the cliffs of Fitz Roy.

To Laguna de los Tres

From *Campamento Poincenot*, follow the crisscrossing paths to the wooden bridge that spans the main current of the Río Blanco. A second, makeshift bridge takes you to the far bank, from where the path heads up through the woods, passing the **Río Blanco campsite** (intended for the use of climbers), before pushing on past the tree line. The next section is tough going as the eroded path ascends a steep gradient, but mercifully it's not long before you come to the top of the ridge, cross a boggy meadow and then climb the final hurdle: a moraine ridge that hides a breathtaking panorama – perhaps the finest in the entire park – on the other side.

You now stand in the cirque of the rich, navy-blue **Laguna de los Tres** (1hr–1hr 15min from *Campamento Poincenot*) fed by a concertinaed glacier and ringed by a giant's crown of granite peaks, including Aguja Saint-Exupéry (named after Antoine de Saint-Exupéry, who drew on his experiences as a pioneer of Patagonian aviation when writing *Vol de Nuit*), Cerro Poincenot, Fitz Roy and a host of other spikes. Round the small rocky outcrop to the left for even more impressive views: this ridge separates the basins of Laguna de los Tres and Laguna Sucia, some 200m below the level of the first lake. The **Glaciar Río Blanco**, hanging above Laguna Sucia, periodically sheds scales of ice and snow, which, though they look tiny at this distance, reveal their true magnitude by the ear-splitting reports they make as they hit the surface of the lake. Retrace your steps and follow the path on the western (right-hand) bank of the Río Blanco (40min from the *Río Blanco* campsite).

Lagunas Madre y Hija trail

From *Campamento Poincenot*, there are two other trails: one crosses the Río Blanco and follows its western bank northward towards the Río Eléctrico and Piedra del Fraile (see p.486), while the path from **Campamento Poincenot to Campamento De Agostini** (6km; 2–3hr; 100m descent), at the eastern end of Laguna Torre, leads past **Lagunas Madre y Hija** (Mother and Daughter Lagoons); to do this, you'll need to double back towards Laguna Capri a little way, before finding the signposted route.

Walk due south of the campsite to the Chorrillo del Salto and follow the stream's eastern bank until you see a signpost directing horseriders left and hikers right. Take the right turning, which leads across a little bridge, and follow the boardwalk as it curves east to the turn-off to Laguna Madre, less than five minutes away. The route past the two lagoons makes for gentle walking and is easy to follow, pushing through knee-high bushes, and after a few hundred metres rising to and passing through the young forest to avoid the swampy ground for the most part. Look out for Upland Geese (*cauquenes*), who like to graze by the lake shore. The path curls round to the right, squeezing between the far end of Laguna Hija and Laguna Nieta (Granddaughter Lagoon), and continues through mixed pasture and woodland before coming to the lip of the valley of Río Fitz Roy. Here, the path descends the steep slope and, if you look to your right, you may get your first glimpses of Cerro Torre through the *lenga* forest. Emerging from the trees, the slope levels out and you link up with the path from El Chaltén to *Campamento De Agostini* (see p.485), a forty-minute walk away.

THE HIELO CONTINENTAL SUR

Blanketing massive expanses of Parque Nacional Los Glaciares, the **Hielo Continental Sur** (Southern Patagonian Icecap) is the largest body of ice outside the poles. Estimates vary as to exactly how big it is but most studies put the figure at around 17,000 square kilometres, some seventy percent of which is in neighbouring Chile. What is certain is that it is suffering from the effects of global warming. In 2003, *Science Magazine* published a report claiming over 16 cubic kilometres of ice was melting annually; Greenpeace puts the figure at 42 cubic kilometres annually, or "enough to fill 10,000 large football stadiums".

THE CERRO TORRE CONTROVERSY

Even members of the French team that first ascended Fitz Roy in 1952 thought that summitting **Cerro Torre** was an impossible task. The altitude wasn't the problem – at 3102m, it wouldn't reach even halfway up some Andean peaks – neither was the type of rock it was made out of – crystalline igneous diorite is perfect for climbing. Rather, it was the shape and the formidable weather: a terrifying spire dropping sheer for almost 2km into glacial ice, battered by winds of up to 200kph and temperatures so extreme that ice more than 20cm thick can form on rock faces. Not only that, but the peculiar glaciers – "mushrooms" of ice – which build up on the mountain's summit often shear off, depositing huge blocks of ice onto climbers below.

MAESTRI, EGGER AND FERRARI

The Italian alpinist **Cesare Maestri** became the first to make a serious attempt on the summit. In 1959, he and Austrian climber **Toni Egger** worked their way up the northern edge. Caught in a storm, Egger was swept off the face and killed by an avalanche. Maestri somehow made it to the bottom, and announced that he had **conquered the summit** with Egger. The world, however, demanded proof, something Maestri could not furnish – the camera, he claimed, lay entombed with Egger.

Angered by the doubters, Maestri vowed to return. This he did, in 1970, and it was clear he meant business. Among his equipment was a 150kg compressor for drilling bolts into the rock. Torre couldn't resist in the face of such a determined onslaught, and Maestri's expedition reached the summit, making very sure that photos were snapped on top. A stake had been driven through Torre's Gothic heart.

Or had it? The climbing world was riven by dispute. Were Maestri's tactics in keeping with the aesthetic code of climbing or had the use of a machine invalidated his efforts? Did this represent a true ascent? On top of this, Maestri's photos revealed that although he had reached the top of the rock, he had not climbed the ice mushroom – the icing that topped the cake.

Enter **Casimiro Ferrari**, another Italian climber. Using guile where Maestri had favoured strong-arm tactics, Ferrari sneaked up on the beast from behind, from the Hielo Continental Sur. In the space of two days, Ferrari achieved his goal, and, elatedly, his team brought down photos of them atop the summit, ice mushroom and all.

Toni Egger's body was recovered in 1975, but no camera was found with him (he is now commemorated in the name of a jagged peak alongside Cerro Torre and a simple chapel in El Chaltén). But despite the controversy at the time, the bolts drilled by Maestri were used for many years, forming the most common route to the summit.

A BITTERSWEET IRONY

Nevertheless, this irony was a bittersweet triumph for Maestri, who feels he has been cursed. In the 1990s, he reputedly voiced his hatred for the mountain, claiming he wanted it razed to the ground. History has added its own weight to that of the doubters. The mountain has been scaled by routes of tremendous technical difficulty by modern climbers with modern equipment, culminating in the Slovenians Silvo Karo and Janez Jeglic's ascent of the south wall in 1988. It wasn't until 2005 that a team of climbers managed to climb the route that Maestri claimed he and Egger took in 1959.

The controversy reignited in January 2012 when two climbers – American Hayden Kennedy and Canadian Jason Kruk – unilaterally decided to remove many of Maestri's bolts. On their return to El Chaltén, amid much local anger, they were briefly detained by the police, who confiscated the bolts. The reaction in the mountaineering community worldwide has been mixed: while some have praised their actions as returning the mountain to its natural state, many others have accused them of destroying a piece of climbing history.

El Chaltén to Laguna Torre trail

The most scenic route from **El Chaltén to Laguna Torre** (10km; 2hr 15min–3hr; 250m ascent), the silty lake in which – on perfect days – the imposing peak of **Cerro Torre** (3102m) is reflected, is reached by turning off Avenida San Martín by Viento Oeste and picking up the marked path at the base of the hill. This path climbs past the eerie skeleton of a large *lenga* tree (now a monument to the dangers of cigarettes), on to some rocks used by climbers for bouldering, and then weaves through hilly country before arriving, after an hour, at a viewpoint where, weather permitting, you'll catch your first proper view of Cerro Torre.

Along the Río Fitz Roy Valley

The path subsequently levels out along the Río Fitz Roy Valley, in whose ragged stands of southern beech you're likely to come across wrens and the Thorn-tailed Rayadito, a diminutive foraging bird. A signposted turn-off on the right leads to Lagunas Madre y Hija (see p.482), which you'll need to return to if hiking the central circuit in clockwise fashion. This path soon starts to climb a steep, wooded hillside, before levelling out, running along the right-hand (eastern) side of the shallow lakes and continuing on to *Campamento Poincenot* (1hr 30min–2hr 15min from turn-off).

Sticking on the trail towards Laguna Torre, the path climbs to another viewpoint, before dropping down onto the valley floor – covered here in puddles that, in good weather, mirror Cerro Torre. You'll see an area that burned in 2003, apparently due to a discarded cigarette. The last section crosses a hill in the middle of the valley and a small stream before coming to blustery *Campamento De Agostini*, the closest **campsite** to the mountain for trekkers. Occupying a beautiful wooded site on the banks of the Río Fitz Roy, it also acts as the base camp for climbers and can get very busy (especially in Jan), so plan accordingly. The only good views of Cerro Torre from the campsite are from a rocky outcrop at the back of the wood, where there's one extremely exposed pitch. Otherwise, follow the path alongside the river, which brings you after about ten minutes to the moraine at the end of **Laguna Torre**. On top of the moraine, you can gaze at the granite needles of Cerro Torre, **Aguja Egger** (2900m) and **Cerro Standhardt** (2800m). Here, too, you'll find a **cable crossing** of the river, used by climbers who go ice-trekking on **Glaciar Torre**. Although it looks easy enough to cross without a harness, be warned: a girl drowned here in 1998 while attempting to do just that – gusts of wind can be sudden and fierce.

To Mirador Maestri

You can get closer to the mountain by walking for forty minutes along the path that runs parallel to the northern shore of Laguna Torre to the **Mirador Maestri** lookout point, passing en route an expedition hut that contains moving commemorative dedications to climbers who never quite succeeded in their attempts on the various peaks (note that this is not a recognized camping spot). The mirador provides superb views of Cerro Torre and Cerro Grande, and the incredible peak-dotted ridge that runs between them.

Río Eléctrico, Piedra del Fraile and beyond

The area to the north of Fitz Roy, just outside the national park, makes for rewarding trekking and can be linked to the Fitz Roy/Torre circuit. Although much of this is private land, you are welcome as long as you observe the same regulations stipulated by the park, and camp only in designated sites.

The start of the trek

To get to the start of the trek from the **RP-23 to Piedra del Fraile** (6km; 1hr 45min–2hr 15min; 80m ascent), take a Las Lengas or El Huemel **minibus** bound for Lago del Desierto (2–3 daily; 15min) and get off right next to the bridge over the **Río Eléctrico**, a tempestuous river; this saves having to struggle for five to six hours against the prevailing winds that sweep down the valley from the north. The path starts to the left of the bridge, although its first section is imperilled every time the river is in spate. Soon you peel away from the river and, following the fairly inconspicuous cairns, cross the flat gravel floor of the Río Blanco valley. On the other side of the valley, the path joins the one heading south to Laguna Piedras Blancas and *Campamento Poincenot* (see p.481). Rather than turn south, aim right of the ridge ahead, into the valley of the Río Eléctrico, where you enter an enchanting, sub-Antarctic woodland, interspersed with grassy glades. Cross a brook and fifteen minutes further on you come to a gate in a ragged fence, followed shortly by another gate in another, equally dishevelled, fence. From the second gate, head right, towards the Río Eléctrico, and follow its bank. After approximately 35 minutes' gentle walk, you emerge from the woodland to be greeted with a terrific view of **Glaciar Marconi**; Piedra del Fraile is just five minutes further on.

Piedra del Fraile

At **Piedra del Fraile**, you'll find the *Los Troncos* campsite ($70 per pitch), scenically set alongside the swift-flowing Río Eléctrico and sheltered by a vast erratic boulder – the *piedra* of the name. The *fraile* (friar or priest) was Padre De Agostini (1883–1960), a Salesian priest who was one of Patagonia's most avid early mountaineers and explorers, and who lends his name to the campsite at Laguna Torre (see p.485). He was the first person to survey the area, and chose this site for his camp. There is a day-use *refugio* with a kitchen, possibly the hottest shower in Patagonia, and a small café.

To Glaciar Marconi

Two worthwhile treks lead from here, though you'll be charged $20 to continue your journey on through private land: the first, from **Piedra del Fraile to Glaciar Marconi** (10km return; 5hr–6hr 30min return; 35m ascent), takes you to the foot of the glacier, fording the Río Pollone and passing through the blasted scenery on the southern shore of Lago Eléctrico. There are fine views of the northern flank of Fitz Roy, especially from the Río Pollone Valley, but be warned that the trail is unmarked once you cross the river; keep tight to the shore of Lago Eléctrico as it curves right, then continue due north past *Campamento La Playita*, following the Río Eléctrico Superior upstream to Laguna Marconi and its glacier. Glaciar Marconi itself sweeps down off the **Hielo Continental Sur** (see box, p.482), and forms the most frequently used point of access for expeditions heading onto this frigid expanse, by way of the windy **Paso Marconi** (1500m).

To Paso del Cuadrado

The second hike, from **Piedra del Fraile to the Paso del Cuadrado** (6km return; 7–9hr return; 1200m ascent), involves a much more difficult climb and should only be attempted by those with comprehensive mountaineering experience. From the camp, cross the small stream on the south side, walk through a wood and strike towards the gap between two streams, to the right of the wooded hillside. The path zigzags steeply up, though eventually levels out. After one and a half to two hours, you pass an oddly shaped boulder with a tiny pool just above it and then the path peters out further up, once it reaches the scree. From here on you must make your own course, keeping the main stream to your right. When you reach the terminal moraine of the glacier, ford the river and work your way around the right-hand side of the col, two to two and a half hours from the boulder. Cross the exposed area of rock on your right and then make the tiring thirty-minute climb up the snow to the pass, which is not immediately obvious but lies in the middle of the ridge. Expect a ferocious blast of wind at the top of Paso del Cuadrado (approximately 1700m), but hold onto your headgear and look out at one of the most dramatic views you're likely to come across in Patagonia. Weather permitting, you'll be able to see Fitz Roy's north face, across to the steeple of Cerro Torre, and down, across deeply crevassed glaciers, to the peaks of Aguja and Cerro Pollone, named after Padre De Agostini's home village in the Italian Alps.

Piedra del Fraile to Campamento Poincenot trail

You can head back east from **Piedra del Fraile to Campamento Poincenot** (11km; 3hr–3hr 30min; 200m ascent) to join up with the Fitz Roy/Torre loop. The path follows the Vallé Río Blanco south but can be difficult to pick up due to a number of false trails created by meandering cattle. On leaving the woods and emerging into the valley plain of the Río Blanco, head back towards the RP-23 until you reach a stream (about 20min).

Turn right and follow its course until you see a faint path that heads south along the tree line. After about half an hour, you enter back into the national park and eventually pick up the line of under-ambitious cairns that mark the path: follow these until you come to the confluence of the Piedras Blancas stream and Río Blanco.

This area is strewn with chunks of granite. It's worth making a short detour right (west) up this valley, scrambling across the boulders to see the **Glaciar Piedras Blancas** tumbling into its murky lake, backed by a partial view of Fitz Roy (20–30min one way). Otherwise, ford the Piedras Blancas stream a little way up from where it meets the Río Blanco and cross the moraine dump to regain the trail. From this point, it's less than an hour's walk along the deteriorated if fairly easy path to *Campamento Poincenot* (see p.481).

The RN-40 and the Cordillera

The western boundary of Argentine Patagonia and the border with Chile are formed by the southern reaches of the Cordillera de los Andes, the world's longest mountain chain. These peaks are the feature that draws most visitors here, luring them along with a ring of beautiful lakes and a national park, albeit not as famous or as breathtaking as Los Glaciares. The nationally renowned RN-40 (often simply called "La Cuarenta") zigzags up this mountainside swathe of inland Patagonia; indeed it hugs the Andes all the way from the southern tip of the mainland to the Bolivian border in the far north. Most access roads for visiting the region run west from the RN-40: to the wild trekking areas around lakes Posadas and Pueyrredón and into Parque Nacional Perito Moreno. The main exceptions are the major archeological site of the Cueva de las Manos Pintadas in the canyon of **Río de las Pinturas**, just east of the RN-40; and the oasis town of **Sarmiento**, a very useful stopover for anyone travelling farther up to the Lake District.

The region's scenery is predominantly dry and flat, though some slopes are densely cloaked in southern beech woods, with a narrow fringe of scrubland separating forest from steppe. It's in these areas that you stand your best chance of seeing the area's outstanding **fauna**: condors, and perhaps even a puma or *huemul*. As for **flora**, the brush looks dreary and anonymous for most of the year. Some bushes liven up considerably in the spring, however, not least the thorny calafate, which blooms with a profusion of yellow flowers, and the *lengua de fuego* with its gloriously bright orange flowers like clam shells. The RN-40 also passes harsh meseta, rocky outcrops, patches of desert and the occasional river valley, usually accompanied by boggy pasture and lined in places with willow and poplar. Here you'll find the few people who live along the route, where old traditions and an unhurried pace still reign.

8

ARRIVAL AND GETTING AROUND   **THE RN-40 AND THE CORDILLERA**

By bus From November to April, Chaltén Travel (☎02962 493092, ⓦchaltentravel.com) operates buses (3–4 weekly) between Bariloche and Perito Moreno (around 13hr) and between Perito Moreno and El Chaltén (around 13hr). Also in

---

THE ESTANCIAS OF SANTA CRUZ

In many people's minds, Argentina is composed of a vast patchwork of immense *latifundias* presided over by their *estanciero* owners. Although this image is no longer entirely true, landowning is still deeply embedded in the national consciousness, and an opportunity to stay at an **estancia** provides an excellent glimpse into this important facet of Argentine culture. Indeed, a stay on one of these farmsteads can be a holiday destination in itself. In the sheep-farming province of Santa Cruz a group of estancia owners runs the **Estancias de Santa Cruz** (ⓦestanciasdesantacruz.com), which can make reservations at their estancias and produces an excellent booklet detailing them all, available from the offices at Suipacha 1120, Buenos Aires (☎011 4325 3098) and Libertador 1215, El Calafate (☎02902 492 8580). The best of their estancias are listed in the relevant sections of the guide.

8

THE LEGENDARY RUTA 40

Argentines fondly refer to the RN-40, or Ruta 40, the country's longest road, as La Cuarenta (The Forty). Stretching from Cabo Vírgenes, the southernmost point of the Argentine mainland, to northernmost Ciénaga, on the Bolivian border, it's more than just a highway. Like Route 66 in the US, the road has its own ethos – inspiring songs, books and arguments – and is as central to a visit to Argentina as a football match or a *milonga*.

By far the best way to approach Ruta 40 is to rent a vehicle and drive yourself – it's worth investing in a **4WD**, even for the paved sections. Special care is required, though, especially further south where strong crosswinds and poorly maintained gravel (*ripio*) roads make it extremely easy to flip over.

A LONG AND WINDING ROAD

La Cuarenta runs a staggering 5224km – the distance from Amsterdam to Afghanistan. Partly to make it more attractive for tourists, the road's itinerary has been changed over the years. Ruta 40 now starts at the ocean at Cabo Vírgenes and winds north through eleven provinces, past twenty national parks and across 24 major rivers, before reaching the altiplano. There it breaks a record: the dizzying **Abra de Acay**, at 5061m, is the highest point on a national road anywhere in the world. Although sections are relatively busy, notably around Bariloche and between Mendoza and San Juan, most of La Cuarenta runs through Argentina's magnificent open spaces, seldom more than 100km from the majestic peaks of the Andes. Many visitors are drawn by the road's rugged mystique – a result of its inaccessibility and frequently poor condition – while others are put off for the same reason. The Argentine government has pledged to pave the entire road, but hasn't completed the task yet.

SOUTH TO NORTH: THE ROUTE

Between a navy lighthouse at **Cabo Vírgenes**, La Cuarenta's starting point, and Chos Malal, in Neuquén Province, the road zigzags across the Patagonian steppe, a barren, windswept expanse thickly blanketed with snow during the winter.

North of Neuquén Province, Ruta 40 enters **El Cuyo**, Argentina's western midlands. It meanders through La Payunia, in Mendoza Province (see p.367), a land of rosy lava and ebony gorges, deep karstic caves and flamingo-flecked lagoons, before passing near **Laguna Diamante** (see p.358), an all-but-inaccessible lagoon from where you can admire the silhouette of Volcán Maipo. Further north, in La Rioja Province, the road skirts sunny valleys and hugs the **Cuesta de Miranda** (see p.384), a serpentine corniche winding through polychrome mountains.

La Cuarenta's last – and highest – stretch cuts through the historic **Northwest**. Rippling hills, herds of goats and crumbling adobe houses are typical sights here. For a top-notch poncho, stop off at **Belén**, in Catamarca (see p.323) – local methods of weaving have been maintained in this highland village since pre-Hispanic times. You'll also want to stop in **Cachi** (see p.312), for a photo of the surrounding snow-topped sierras and valleys. Just before Ruta 40 reaches Bolivia, it is spanned by the mighty **La Polvorilla viaduct** (see p.292), a fabulous feat of engineering.

the summer, Taqsa/Marga (⊛taqsa.com.ar) runs a daily bus between Bariloche and El Calafate via El Chaltén and Perito Moreno; the whole journey takes around 30 hours. A couple of smaller operators sometimes run services on these routes too. Timetables on this route are notoriously prone to change, so it's worth checking out the latest information before setting off.
By car To truly appreciate the mystique of the area, you can drive yourself. The RN-40 is just about passable in a normal sedan – if it doesn't rain, and if you don't mind having to drive at 30kph along some sections for fear of crunching the undercarriage. Although the government is steadily tarmacking the road, significant sections are still *ripio* (gravel), notably between Tres Lagos, Bajo Caracoles and Perito Moreno (though parts of this section have been improved in recent years). They require careful negotiating but add greatly to the sense of adventure.

Tres Lagos to Parque Nacional Perito Moreno

The taste of things to come, the paved RN-40 heading northeastwards from the El Chaltén turn-off is desolate and remote: the minuscule and rather depressing settlement of **TRES LAGOS**, 35km to the north, is little more than a road junction (unpaved tracks lead off the RN-40, west towards the Andes and east into the heart of the steppe) but it does have a few services for the traveller, useful in emergencies: a free municipal **campsite**, shaded by cherry trees along a small stream; a couple of tyre-repair places (*gomerías*); and a supermarket.

The next 340km stretch of the RN-40, between Tres Lagos and Bajo Caracoles, is the most rugged of all. High crosswinds can make driving hazardous, so always keep your speed under control and take breaks. There are virtually no fuel stations along this part of the route, and you should carry enough fuel for several hundred kilometres of motoring (invest in a jerry can or two) if you plan to make any side-trips. Journeys are now speedier thanks to the excellent tarmac section between the junction near Estancia La Verde – where you can make a detour to tiny **Gobernador Gregores** some 70km away for fuel and some basic accommodation – and **Las Horquetas**, the hamlet from which a road leads to the Parque Nacional Perito Moreno. Both tourist estancias in or near the national park – *Estancia Menelik* and *Estancia La Oriental* – sell petrol and diesel, but the former is often out and the latter's supply is intended for guests only; they will, however, help out in an emergency.

ACCOMMODATION
TRES LAGOS

Huentru Niyeu Tres Lagos ☎02962 495005. If you need somewhere to stay, and don't fancy sleeping under canvas, try the simple *cabañas* at *Huentru Niyeu*, located just beyond the municipal campsite in Tres Lagos. You can get home-cooked meals here, and have your laundry done. **$100**

Parque Nacional Perito Moreno

Extreme isolation means that, despite being one of Argentina's first national parks to be created, the **PARQUE NACIONAL PERITO MORENO** is also one of its least visited. Though replete with glorious mountains and beautiful lakes, this is not a "sightseeing" park like Nahuel Huapi or Los Glaciares. The bulk of the park's forested mountain scenery lies in its western two-thirds, which are reserved for **scientific study**, meaning that most of the area accessible to the public consists of arid steppe. Although visitor numbers are slowly increasing, the park still offers a solitude that few other places can match.

You can see much of the park by car in a day or two, but could equally spend much longer trekking through the starkly beautiful high pampas, past virulently colourful lakes and near the imperious snowcapped hulk of San Lorenzo – and still miss out on many of its hidden wonders. In the absence of humans, **wildlife** thrives here. Guanacos can be seen at close quarters, while the luckiest visitors may glimpse a puma (or at least its tracks) or an endangered *huemul*, of which about one hundred are thought to live in the park. Condors are plentiful as is other **birdlife** including the Chilean flamingo, Black-necked swan and the powerful black-chested Buzzard eagle (*águila mora*). One of the park's most biologically interesting features is its **lakes**: the ones here have never been stocked with non-endemic species – native fish are protected and no fishing is allowed.

The northern sector

From *Estancia La Oriental* (see p.491), a pass leads 10km on to the *guardaparque's* house at **El Rincón**, once one of Argentina's most isolated estancias, where you can **camp**. Just before the buildings, a track branches west towards Chile. The first 3km can be covered by car, and from here it's a 5km walk to the desolate shores of **Lago Volcán**, a milky-green glacial lake. Although a pass (Paso de la Balsa) is marked on some maps this is not a legal border crossing and you will be detained if caught.

From El Rincón, it's a stiff five- to six-hour walk to the **Puesto San Lorenzo** refuge, from where you can access the park's finest views of Monte San Lorenzo. Consult the *guardaparque* about conditions ahead before setting off. Take the winding track to the right of the house (traversable in a normal car for 5km; beyond you'll need a high-clearance 4WD and even that will only get you a bit further), leaving the park's northern boundary. After one particularly tight hairpin down a small gravel scarp, you must ford two streams and pick up the track on the other side. Eventually,

8

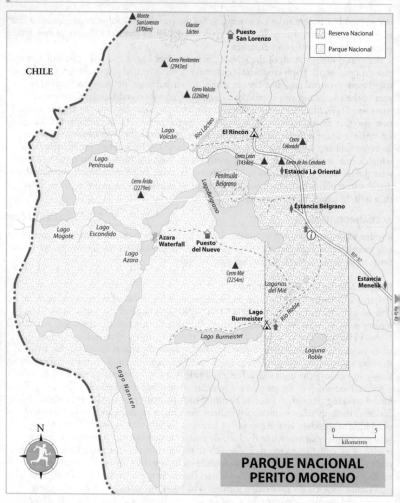

**PARQUE NACIONAL
PERITO MORENO**

you reach a bluff with a steep moraine scarp, which is as far as you can get with a vehicle (9km from El Rincón).

From here, you have a fine view of the turbulent **Río Lácteo**, which you must keep on your left. The track drops down the bluff, passes a windbreak and then gives up entirely in the woods some 200m beyond. From here on, there's always a temptation to drop down onto the flat gravel bed of the Río Lácteo, but resist this and stay high, at least until you have passed the huge alluvial moraine fan that pushes the river far over to the eastern side of the valley. After this, the path drops and wends its way through the marshy grassland bordering the river valley. A little further on, the tin shack of Puesto San Lorenzo is easily visible. A supply of firewood and rustic stove await inside, but make sure you replace any wood you use.

With care, you can ford the Río Lácteo here. Beyond, a path leads west up the valley towards **Glaciar Lácteo** and the 2000m fortress wall of **San Lorenzo's southeast face** – if you are lucky enough, that is, to catch this notoriously temperamental mountain in one of its more benevolent moods.

The central sector

A kilometre or two north of the park administration building, at Estancia Belgrano, the track forks left towards **Lago Belgrano**, the most remarkable of the lakes accessible to visitors, with one of the most intensely gaudy turquoise colours anywhere in Patagonia. After 8km you reach the scrub-covered **Península Belgrano**; a leaflet is available from the park administration building for a self-guided two-hour circular trail through the *mata negra* bushes, detailing the behaviour of its graceful guanaco inhabitants. Look out for the mounds of guanaco dung at the animals' communal toilets, and the piles of bones pumas have left behind. Although it only takes three to four hours to walk to the other side, you can **camp** on the peninsula allowing more time to take in the beauty – or worry about the predators.

A longer hike of two to three days can be made south of Lago Belgrano, accessed on a path that cuts through the Lagunas del Mié, but you must ask permission from park administration first to use the old shepherd's refuge, **Puesto del Nueve**, as a base. From here, you can visit the 10m waterfall that drains Lago Belgrano and explore the region around beautiful **Lago Azara**, where you stand a slim chance of finding footprints or traces of *huemules*, the endangered Andean deer that is the park's symbol. You may cook on the small stove in the refuge, but should replace all firewood used.

Back on the main track, heading north from *Estancia Belgrano*, you reach the well-marked turn-off to *Estancia La Oriental*, which lies on the edge of a tranquil valley (see below). About 3km further north, on the other side of the valley, stands **Cerro de los Cóndores**, a cliff face stained by great white smears, indicating the presence of condors' nests. About thirty of the giant birds use the *condorera* regularly. To gain a similar perspective, you can climb nearby **Cerro León** (1434m; 4hr return), which affords excellent views of the heartland of the park.

8

ARRIVAL, INFORMATION AND ACTIVITIES ⬥ PARQUE NACIONAL PERITO MORENO

Reached by a 90km *ripio* spur road, which joins the RN-40 just west of Las Horquetas, the park is open year-round but can be cut off by snow, sometimes for weeks on end; the weather changes moods like a spoilt child. Temperatures are bracing all year, and can drop to -25°C in winter, lower with wind chill. Note that there is no entry fee for the park.

By bus/taxi Without your own transport, getting to the park is difficult and expensive: guests at the estancias (see below) should be able to arrange a pick-up from the RN-40 ($500 or so). A taxi from Gobernador Gregores, where there is a national park office at San Martín 882 (☎ 02962 491477, ✉ peritomoreno@apn.gov.ar), will charge around $700–900, though don't rely on finding one willing to go all that way.

By organized tour Ruta-40, a travel agency based in Bariloche (Juramento 190; ☎ 0294 452 3378, ⓦ ruta-40 .com), has a ten-day RN-40 tour that visits the park.

Tourist information On arrival you'll need to register at the park administration building (daily 8am–8pm), 5km inside the park. You'll also be given a welcome talk and leaflets on the trails and wildlife (some in English); there are creative educational displays in the small museum. Apart from water, there are no facilities here.

Horseriding trips *Estancia Menelik* can organize one- to four-day horseriding trips in the surrounding area (from around $140).

ACCOMMODATION

There are a couple of free, basic **campsites** in great locations at Lago Burmeister and El Rincón. If you are heading for these, you must register first at the administration office. Note that it is strictly illegal to cross into Chile at Paso Cordoniz by Lago Nansen.

Estancia Menelik 10km outside the park, off the RP-37 ☎ 011 4765 8085, ⓦ cielospatagonicos.com. This English-style *casco viejo* dates back to the 1920s and offers cosy, wood-floored rooms with views across the steppe; dorm beds are provided in two separate buildings. Rates for the rooms include full board; those for the dorms only cover a bed for the night, though you can buy meals at the estancia. Closed April to mid-Oct. Dorms **$140**, doubles **$1700**

Estancia La Oriental 7km north of the administration building ☎ 011 4152 6901. *La Oriental* is a beautifully sited working estancia, looking out across the northern curl of Lago Belgrano. Standards of accommodation and service are not always as high as they should be, but you're severely limited for choice in this area. Room rates include half-board. Closed April–Oct. Camping **$120**, doubles **$450**

Bajo Caracoles

From the Parque Nacional Perito Moreno turn-off, the RN-40 swings north for around 110km across more desolate steppe – the Pampa del Asador to the west at least affords occasional glimpses of the cordillera as relief – to the tiny crossroads settlement of **BAJO CARACOLES**. This stretch of the road is currently being paved, leading to slight changes in the route. Nondescript Bajo Caracoles is only really useful for refuelling your vehicle (it's the first reliable petrol stop north of Gobernador Gregores or Tres Lagos) and grabbing a bite to eat.

Posadas

From Bajo Caracoles an unpaved road leads west to the larger village of **POSADAS**, which has better facilities, especially in terms of accommodation, and a petrol station. It is a loosely grouped assemblage of modern houses, and is listed on some maps as **Hipólito Yrigoyen** (or even, confusingly, as **Lago Posadas**), but locals use the old name of Posadas.

The village can used as a base for visiting the turquoise **Lago Posadas**, and the stunning lapis lazuli **Lago Pueyrredón**, set among splendid landscapes and famed for their fishing. The lakes are separated by the narrowest of strips of land, the arrow-straight **La Península**, which looks for all the world like a man-made causeway. It was actually formed during a static phase of the last Ice Age, when an otherwise retreating glacier left an intermediate dump of moraine, now covered by sand dunes, which cut shallow Lago Posadas off from its grander neighbour. Most places of interest around the lakes are accessible only to those with their own vehicle.

Cerro de los Indios

Three kilometres south of Posadas, the low, rounded wedge of **Cerro de los Indios** lies beneath the higher scarp of the valley. Bruce Chatwin's description of this rock in *In Patagonia* is unerring: "…a lump of basalt, flecked red and green, smooth as patinated bronze and fracturing in linear slabs. The Indians had chosen the place with an unfaltering eye for the sacred."

Indigenous **rock-paintings**, some almost 10,000 years old, mark the foot of the cliff, about two-thirds of the way along the rock to the left. The well-known depiction of a "unicorn" – now thought to be a *huemul* – is rather faded; more impressive are the wonderful concentric circles of a hypnotic labyrinth design. The red blotches high up on the overhangs appear to have been the result of guanaco hunters firing up arrows tipped in pigment-stained fabric, perhaps in an ancient version of darts. However, the site's most remarkable feature is the polished shine on the rocks, which really do possess the patina and texture of antique bronze. There's also no fence screening off the engravings and paintings here, leaving the site's magical aura uncompromised.

ARRIVAL, DEPARTURE AND TOURS   POSADAS

By bus There are just a couple of weekly buses: one to Bajo Caracoles (every Tues; 2hr), the other to Perito Moreno (every Tues; 4hr).
To Chile Five kilometres east of Posadas, the beautiful RP-41 runs north towards the Chilean border at Paso Roballos and Los Antiguos, though spring floods mean that it is usually only passable from mid-December to March.
Tours Las Loicas (☎ 02963 490272, ☞ lasloicas.com), Las Lengas and Condor Andino, offers a range of tours around Posadas and along the RN-40.

ACCOMMODATION AND EATING

La Posada del Posadas Near the village centre ☎ 02963 490250, ☞ delposadas.com.ar. A well-established place with both an old hotel with rooms set around a courtyard and, further out towards Lago Posadas, ten self-contained bungalows sleeping up to five people. The owners, Pedro and Susana Fortuny, also run the village's best restaurant and have excellent knowledge of local hikes and fishing. Doubles $430, bungalows $430

Lago Posadas

Do not try to drive around the south shore of **Lago Posadas**, even though a road is marked on many maps: cars can easily get bogged down near the Río Furioso. Instead, take the route running around the north shore, which passes through a zone of blasted, bare humps, crisscrossed by lines of *duraznillo* bushes. Known as **El Quemado** (The Burnt One), it's one of the most ancient formations in Argentina, dating back 180 million years to the Jurassic Age, and there are spectacular contrasts between minerals such as green olivina sandstone and porphyry iron oxides.

ACCOMMODATION · LAGO POSADAS

Lagos del Furioso At the southern end of La Península ☎ 02963 490253, ⓦ lagosdelfurioso.com.ar. The beautifully located, luxurious *Lagos del Furioso* has well-designed bungalows sheltered from the wind by a pocket of poplars, a Finnish sauna, and an airy communal dining room where freshly prepared cuisine is served, complemented by panoramic views of Lago Posadas and the Río Furioso canyon. Sailing, horseriding, hiking and mountain biking are all possible. Rates include half-board; minimum two-night stay. Closed May–Oct. **$1200**

Lago Pueyrredón and the Río Oro

Ambitious engineers have somehow managed to squeeze a dirt road between the southern shore of pristinely beautiful **Lago Pueyrredón** and the hills that press up against it, without having to resort to tiresome infill projects. This precarious arrangement is compromised only by the occasional spring flood (September is the worst month).

Just past the neat bridge over the **Río Oro**, a track wends its way up the mountainside and past the magnificent purple chasm of the **Garganta del Río Oro**.

Monte San Lorenzo

Further on, the road rises through the wild foothills of **Monte San Lorenzo** and towards the snowline. This is private land, and crossing the border here is illegal; climbers intending to ascend San Lorenzo from the Chilean side should cross over to Cochrane at one of the legitimate border posts further north and tackle the mountain from Padre De Agostini's base camp, owned by the mountain guide, Luís Soto de la Cruz. Alternatively, contact Pedro Fortuny (of *La Posada de Posadas*; see opposite), who can help organize an expedition up San Lorenzo. The best **maps** of the area are those from the Instituto Geográfico Militar in Buenos Aires (see p.51: #4772-27 *Cerro Pico Agudo* and #4772-33 y 32 *Lago Belgrano*).

ACCOMMODATION · LAGO PUEYRREDÓN AND THE RÍO ORO

Estancia Suyai Beside Lago Pueyrredón ☎ 02963 490242, ⓦ suyaipatagonia.com.ar. Set on a stunningly beautiful peninsula jutting out into the lake, this estancia has rooms, *cabañas* and a campsite, as well as a good restaurant (try the local trout). Staff can organize a range of activities in the surrounding countryside. Closed May–Oct. Camping **$100**, doubles **$500**, *cabañas* **$800**

Perito Moreno and around

With a little over four thousand inhabitants, **PERITO MORENO** is the biggest town in this part of the world, which shows just how thinly populated the region is. Lying 130km north of Bajo Caracoles, it's a typically featureless, spread-out Patagonian settlement whose main point of interest is as a base for excursions to places such as the **Cueva de las Manos Pintadas**, some 120km south. When there is enough water, Black-necked swans and flamingoes pass their time at the free wildlife refuge in town, the **Laguna de los Cisnes**.

ARRIVAL, INFORMATION AND TOURS

By bus The bus terminal is just north of town on the RP-43; from here, cross the road and walk down Av San Martín to reach the town centre in about 10min. Chaltén Travel buses (ⓦ chaltentravel.com) stop outside the *Hotel Belgrano*, at the far end of San Martín; between Nov and April, the company has services to Bariloche, El Chaltén and Puerto Madryn.

Destinations Bajo Caracoles (Tues; 2hr); Bariloche (Nov–April; 1–2 daily; 13hr); Comodoro Rivadavia (1–2 daily; 5hr); El Chaltén (Nov–April; 1–2 daily; 13hr); Puerto Madryn (Nov–April; 3–4 weekly; 14hr); Río Gallegos (1–2 daily; 14hr).

Tourist information The tourist office is at San Martín

PERITO MORENO AND AROUND

and Gendarmería Nacional (daily 8am–10pm; ☎ 02963 432732).

Tours English-speaking Guanacóndor, Perito Moreno 1087 (☎ 02963 432303, ✉ jarinauta@yahoo.com.ar), runs several trips to the Cueva de las Manos Pintadas, the best of which includes a 3hr walk down into the spectacular canyon floor ($250, plus entry fee). It also runs a recommended tour to Arroyo Feo ("Ugly Stream"; $250), an area of great beauty and archeological interest, 70km south of town; with its dramatic narrow canyon and 9000-year-old cave-paintings, it offers a wilder alternative to the Cueva de las Manos. From December, the company also runs three-day trips that take in the RP-41, a scenic road that skirts striking Monte Zeballos.

ACCOMMODATION

Estancia Telken 30km south of town ☎ 02963 432079, ✉ telkenpatagonia@yahoo.com.ar. This estancia, which dates back to 1915, provides a good insight into life on a working ranch. The rooms are comfortable enough, but far from fancy; you can also camp in the grounds. Hiking, birdwatching and horseriding trips can all be arranged. Room rates include breakfast. Closed May–Sept. Camping $90, doubles $400

Municipal Campsite Mariano Moreno and Paseo Julio A. Roca ☎ 02963 432130. Shoestring travellers should head to the town's campsite, which lies off the shore

of Laguna de los Cisnes in the southern part of Perito Moreno. As well as spots to pitch your tent, there are small, rustic *cabañas*, which are just about acceptable for a night. Camping $30, *cabañas* $120

Posada del Caminante Rivadavia 937 ☎ 02963 432204, ✉ posadadelcaminante@yahoo.com.ar. Accommodation in Perito Moreno is neither abundant nor particularly good value, but *Posada del Caminante* is a decent place to stay for a night. Its en-suite rooms are clean, homely and popular, so book in advance. $300

Cueva de las Manos Pintadas

120km south of Perito Moreno • Daily 9am–7pm • $50 • Guided walks: June–Sept on demand, Oct–May every 90min

The landscape between Perito Moreno and Bajo Caracoles best embodies most people's concept of Patagonia – sparsely populated and at times empty lands stretching to the horizon. Why most people venture to these parts at all is to see the magnificent **Cueva de las Manos Pintadas** (Cave of the Painted Hands), one of South America's finest examples of rock paintings and listed as a UNESCO World Heritage Site. It can be approached either by road along a sidetrack just north of Bajo Caracoles or, better, by walking or riding up the canyon it overlooks, the impressive **Cañón de Río Pinturas**.

From the canyon rim, it's a spectacular two-hour **walk** to the cave paintings. The path drops sharply to the flat valley bed, and continues to the right of the snaking river, nestling up against rock walls and pinnacles that display the region's geological history in bands of black basalt, slabs of rust-coloured sandstone and a layer of sedimentary rocks that range in hue from chalky white to mottled ochre. Bring binoculars for viewing the finches and birds of prey that inhabit the canyon, plus food, water, a hat and sunscreen.

At the point where the course of the Río Pinturas is diverted by a vast rampart of red sandstone, you start to climb the valley side again to reach the road from Bajo Caracoles and the **entrance building** to the protected area around the paintings, where there's a modest display. Unfortunately, some parts of the site have been tarnished by tourists etching modern graffiti on the rock – hence the fence that now keeps visitors at a distance – and you can only access the cave accompanied by a *guardaparque* on a one-hour **guided walk**.

The *cueva* itself is less a cave than a series of overhangs: natural cutaways at the foot of a towering 90m cliff face overlooking the canyon below, a vantage point from which

THE SIGNIFICANCE OF THE PAINTINGS

The earliest paintings were made by the Toldense culture and date as far back as 1100 BC, but archeologists have identified four later cultural phases, ending with depictions by early Tehuelche groups – notably geometric shapes and zigzags – from approximately 1300 AD. The significance of the paintings is much debated: whether they represented part of the rite of passage for adolescents into the adult world, and were thus part of ceremonies to strengthen familial or tribal bonds, or whether they were connected to religious ceremonies that preceded the hunt will probably never be known. Other tantalizing mysteries involve theories surrounding the large number of heavily pregnant guanacos depicted, and whether these herds were actually semi-domesticated. One thing is for certain: considering their exposed position, it is remarkable how vivid some of the colours still are – the colours were made from the berries of *calafate* bushes, earth and charcoal, with guanaco fat and urine applied to create the waterproof coating that has preserved them so well.

groups of Paleolithic hunter-gatherers would survey the valley floor for game. Despite the rather heavy-handed fence that now frames them, the collage of black, white, red and ochre **handprints**, mixed with gracefully flowing vignettes of guanaco hunts, still makes for an astonishing spectacle. Of the 829 handprints, most are male, and only 31 are right-handed. They are all "negatives", being made by placing the hand on the rock face, and imprinting its outline by blowing pigments through a tube. Interspersed with these are human figures, as well as the outlines of puma paws and rhea prints, and creatures such as a scorpion.

ARRIVAL AND TOURS

By car To get to the paintings, take the turn-off just to the north of Bajo Caracoles, a rough 45km stretch of *ripio* leading to a car park, 600m from the entrance building.

CUEVA DE LAS MANOS PINTADAS

Tours Alternatively, you can take a tour from Perito Moreno (see opposite).

ACCOMMODATION

Estancia La Cueva de las Manos 7km up a well-signed track off the RN-40 ☏ 011 5237 4043, ⊕ cuevas delasmanos.net. The *cueva* actually lies on land owned by the estancia, which has dorms, private rooms and a *cabaña*. There's a restaurant, and staff can organize horse rides, hikes and transport. The estancia also runs 4WD trips to the *cueva* as well as to nearby Charcamata, a similar rock-art site. Note that any visit to the paintings from the estancia side involves negotiating a steep and difficult climb down to the river valley and up again. Closed May–Oct. Dorms $150, doubles $640, *cabaña* $740

Sarmiento

North of Perito Moreno, the RN-40 has undergone some major rerouting, with much of it now tarmacked. It heads northeast from Río Mayo to meet the RN-26 at a junction 70km west of **SARMIENTO** (or Colonia Sarmiento), the first real town you reach if you travel up the whole RN-40 from El Calafate. Beyond the RN-26 intersection, the (paved, but badly potholed) RN-40 heads northwest again, crossing some particularly bleak Patagonian pampa, towards **Tecka** and, eventually, Esquel (see p.413) in the Argentine Lake District.

A rough-and-ready but not unappealing pioneering settlement, Sarmiento can also be accessed along the RN-26 from Comodoro Rivadavia, 150km to the east. Cutting through hilly steppe country covered in *duraznillo* bushes, this road provides ample evidence of the country's oilfields, with the nodding heads of hundreds of oil wells relentlessly probing the ground.

In addition to agriculture, Sarmiento, which has more than 10,000 inhabitants, services a large military presence (this is border country), but tourism is relatively underdeveloped despite the vicinity of the petrified forest (see p.461). If you're in town over the second weekend in February, don't miss the **Festival Provincial de Doma y Folklore**, with equestrian events in the afternoon and folk concerts in the evening.

Museo Regional Desiderio Torres

20 de Junio • Daily 9am–7pm • $10

The excellent **Museo Regional Desiderio Torres**, housed in the old train station, is worth a visit for its sizeable collection of indigenous artefacts and well-explained displays of weavings by the Mapuche (see p.426) and Tehuelche (see p.446), plus dinosaur bones and other fossils. Part of the museum is given over to the town's pioneering immigrant communities, and exhibits some fascinating photos.

Lago Colhué Huapi and Lago Musters

Sarmiento is irrigated by waters from the Río Senguer and the sizeable lakes it feeds, **Lago Colhué Huapi** (around 15km east of town) and **Lago Musters** (around 5km northwest of town), the latter named after a nineteenth-century English adventurer, Captain George Chaworth Musters, who put it on the map. Both lakes, shining royal blue on sunny days, are home to large numbers of birds, including flamingoes. The irrigation supports a strong farming community (try to be around for the cherry blossom in early October or the fruit harvest in December), originally founded by the Welsh, with an influx of Lithuanians and **Boers**, who fled here after the Boer War and soon took to the strenuous task of farming in relatively hostile conditions.

Bosque Petrificado Sarmiento

32km from Sarmiento; 2km from the town centre, a signposted gravel track off the RN-26 leads to the site • Daily: April–Sept 9am–6.30pm; Oct–March 8am–8pm • $20 • Taxis from town will run you to the park and back for around $150 including 90min waiting time; the tourist office can put you in touch with guides

The **BOSQUE PETRIFICADO SARMIENTO** is home to perfectly preserved 65-million-year-old tree trunks, randomly strewn across a near-lunar setting with a stunning purple-and-orange cliff backdrop. Formed by mineral-rich water permeating the wood over hundreds of thousands of years, effectively turning the trees into stone, the petrified forest has parallels with the Monumento Natural Bosques Petrificados (see p.461), but its bands of "painted desert" soils are more striking and erosion processes are much more visible here. Traversing the 2km circuit is rather like walking around a sawmill, the ground covered by splinters of bark and rotten wood that chink under foot, except that these woodchips are Mesozoic. The highlight is a famous and much photographed chunk of **hollow fossilized log** that looks like nature's take on a giant drainage pipe.

Take water, sunscreen and hats as the sun can be very strong, as can the winds. There are toilets in the park, but no other services.

ARRIVAL AND INFORMATION   SARMIENTO

By bus Sarmiento's main street, initially Av Regimiento de Infantería, later becoming Av San Martín, runs off the RN-26 at a right angle. Buses pull into the terminal at the far end, at avenidas San Martín and 12 de Octubre.
Destinations Comodoro Rivadavia (3 daily; 2hr 15min); Esquel (1–2 daily; 6hr).
Tourist information The tourist office at Pietrobelli 388

(daily: April to mid-Dec 8am–8pm; mid-Dec to March 8am–11pm; ☎0297 489 8220, ⊛coloniasarmiento.gov.ar) has a useful free map, sells trout-fishing permits (the season is Nov–April) and can provide details about visits to three local *chacras* or market gardens (Labrador, San José and San Cayetano).

ACCOMMODATION

Camping del Búlgaro 5km northwest of town ☎0297 489 3114, ✉ebulgaro@coopsar.com.ar. Located on the shores of Lago Musters, set among a strand of poplars,

Camping del Búlgaro is the most attractive of the town's campsites. There's a small shop selling provisions on site. __$30__

★ **Chacra Labrador** About 8km west of town on the RN-26 at Km146.5 ☎0297 489 3329, ⓦhosteria labrador.com.ar. The congenial owners of English, Boer and Dutch origins (English, German and Dutch spoken) have modelled their farmhouse on a British-style B&B, with four charming rooms, set in sixty hectares of land. Delicious food is on offer and the owners can arrange guided tours. $450

Hotel Ismar Patagonia 248 ☎0297 489 3293. The motel-like *Ismar* is the best of an inauspicious bunch of hotels in the town itself, with functional, rather cramped rooms (with private bathrooms and TVs) off a courtyard that is generally occupied by noisy oil-workers' trucks. $250

8

Tierra del Fuego

SEALS IN THE BEAGLE CHANNEL

9

Tierra del Fuego

Across the Magellan Strait from mainland Patagonia, Tierra del Fuego is a land of windswept bleakness, whose settlements seem to huddle with their backs against the elements: cold winters, cool summers, gales in the spring, frost in the autumn. Yet this remote and rugged archipelago, tucked away at the foot of the South American continent, exercises a fascination over many travellers. Some look to follow in the footsteps of the region's famous explorers, such as navigator Ferdinand Magellan, naturalist Charles Darwin or, more recently, author Bruce Chatwin. Others just want to see what it's like down here, at the very end of the world. While it may be expensive, fast-developing and time-consuming to reach, Tierra del Fuego offers up an easily-accessible national park, epic mountain scenery, diverse wildlife, a truly fascinating history, and an array of outdoor activities – from hiking and skiing to boat trips and dog-sledding. There's nowhere else quite like it on Earth.

Though comprising a number of islands, Tierra del Fuego is more or less the sum of its most developed part, **Isla Grande**, the biggest island in South America. Its eastern section, roughly a third of the island, along with a few islets, belongs to Argentina – the rest is Chilean territory. The major destination for visitors is the Argentine city of **Ushuaia**, a year-round resort on the south coast. Beautifully located, backed by distinctive jagged mountains, it is *the* base for visiting the tremendous **Beagle Channel**, rich in marine wildlife, and the wild, forested peaks of the **Cordillera Darwin**. With the lakes, forests and tundra of **Parque Nacional Tierra del Fuego** just 12km to the west, and historic **Estancia Harberton**, home to descendants of Thomas Bridges, an Anglican missionary who settled here in 1871, a short excursion from the city, you could easily spend a week or so in the area.

Lago Fagnano, and the village of **Tolhuin** at its eastern end, is the main focus of the island's central area, which is of considerably greater interest than the windswept plains and scrubby *coirón* grasslands in the north. The southeastern chunk of Isla Grande, **Península Mitre**, is one of Argentina's least accessible regions, a boggy wilderness with low scrub and next to no human habitation, while, to its east, lies the mysterious **Isla de los Estados**, known in English as Staten Island. It is an extremely difficult area to visit, even more than the great white continent of **Antarctica**, which can be reached from Ushuaia – at a price.

GETTING AROUND

Ushuaia is Tierra del Fuego's undisputed **transport hub**, with bus services to destinations throughout the region, a busy airport, and a dock served by numerous tour boats and cruise ships. A car can be useful for reaching some of the more remote places on the archipelago.

PARQUE NACIONAL TIERRA DEL FUEGO

Highlights

❶ Arriving in Ushuaia by plane The city's dramatic location – wedged between the tail-end of the Andes and the Beagle Channel – makes this a landing to remember. **See p.508**

❷ Fresh king crab Plucked straight from the Beagle Channel, *centolla* appears on menus throughout Ushuaia, and is delicious served in soups, baked in its shell or simply grilled. **See p.511**

❸ Wildlife in the Beagle Channel Spot albatrosses and sea lions, terns and whales as you brave the elements on a boat trip through

this stunningly beautiful, mountain-fringed waterway. **See p.512**

❹ Estancia Harberton Get a unique insight into the life of some of the early European settlers – and their interactions with the local indigenous communities – at Estancia Harberton. **See p.513**

❺ Parque Nacional Tierra del Fuego Parakeets and hummingbirds are some of the surprising inhabitants of this national park, which spans 630 square kilometres of mountains, lakes, forests and tundra. **See p.514**

HIGHLIGHTS ARE MARKED ON THE MAP ON PP.502–503

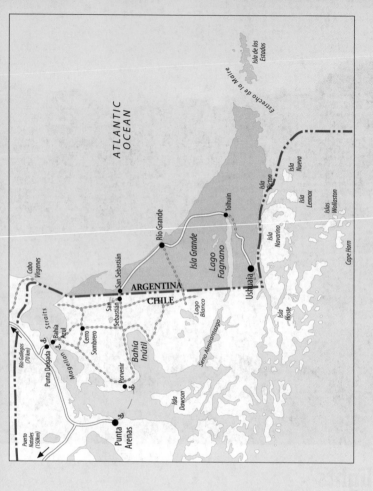
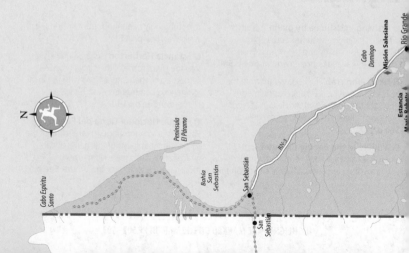

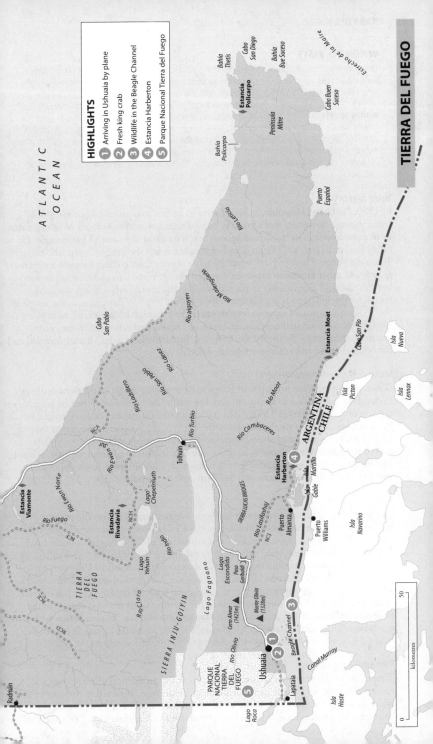

ATLANTIC
OCEAN

HIGHLIGHTS

1. Arriving in Ushuaia by plane
2. Fresh king crab
3. Wildlife in the Beagle Channel
4. Estancia Harberton
5. Parque Nacional Tierra del Fuego

Estancia Policarpo

Bahía Thetis
Cabo San Diego
Bahía Bue Suceso
Estrecho de la Maire

Cabo Buen Suceso

Bahía Policarpo
Península Mitre

Puerto Español

Río Lecrú

Cabo San Pablo

Río Malengüena

Río Irigoyen

Puerto San Pablo

Río Ladrillero

Río San Pablo

Río Turbio

Tolhuin

Río Cambaceres

Río Moat

Estancia Moat

Cabo San Pío

Isla Nueva

RCA

Estancia Viamonte

Río Ewan

Río Fuego

Río Ewan Norte

Sur

RCF

RCH

Estancia Rivadavia

Río Claro

Río Irigoyen

Lago Chepelmuth

RCH

RCl

RCE

Radmán

TIERRA
DEL
FUEGO

Lago Yehuin

Río Ladrillero

Río Turbio

ARGENTINA
CHILE

Isla Picton

Isla Lennox

SIERRA INJU-GOIYIN

Lago Fagnano

Lago Escondido
Paso
Garibaldi

SIERRA LUCAS BRIDGES

Río Lasifashaj

Puerto
Almanza

RCJ

Estancia
Harberton 4

Isla
Martillo

Isla
Gable

Puerto Williams

Isla Navarino

Cerro Alvear
(1425m)

Monte Olivia
(1326m)

Río Olivia

PARQUE
NACIONAL
TIERRA
DEL
FUEGO 5

Ushuaia 1
2

Beagle Channel 3

Canal Murray

Lapataia

Lago
Roca

Isla
Hoste

0   50
kilometres

TIERRA DEL FUEGO

9

Brief history

In 1520, **Ferdinand Magellan**, in his attempt to be first to circumnavigate the globe, sailed through the straits that were later named after him and saw clouds of smoke rising from numerous fires lit by the indigenous Selk'nam along the coast of Isla Grande. He called the land Tierra del Humo (Land of Smoke); it was the king of Spain who thought Tierra del Fuego (Land of Fire) would be more poetic. Early contact between indigenous groups and other **European explorers** was sporadic from the sixteenth century onwards, but this changed dramatically in the latter half of the nineteenth century, with tragic results for the indigenous population. When Robert Fitz Roy came here in the *Beagle* in the 1830s, an estimated three to four thousand Selk'nam and Mannekenk were living in Isla Grande, with some three thousand each of Yámana and Kawéskar in the entire southern archipelago. By the 1930s, however, the Mannekenk were virtually extinct, and the other groups had been effectively annihilated.

Missionaries and sheep farmers

White settlement came to Tierra del Fuego in three phases. Anglican **missionaries** began to catechize the Yámana in the south, and Thomas Bridges established the first permanent mission on Ushuaia Bay in 1871. From the late 1880s, the Italian Roman Catholic Salesian Order began a similar process to the north of the Fuegian Andes. From the mid-1890s came a new colonizing impetus: the inauspicious-looking northern plains proved to be ideal **sheep-farming** territory, and vast *latifundias* sprang up. Croat, Scottish, Basque, Italian and Galician immigrants, along with Chileans from across the border, arrived to work on the estancias and build up their own landholdings.

Border disputes

The issue of the international border has been a contentious one over the years, as it has been along other sections of the Argentina–Chile boundary. Frontier disputes at the end of the nineteenth century required the arbitration of Great Britain, who in 1902 awarded Argentina the eastern half of Tierra del Fuego; land squabbles were still going on over eighty years later, the two countries almost coming to war in 1984 over three islands in the Beagle Channel. This time it took the intervention of Pope John Paul II, who, possibly to even things up, gave the islands to Chile. A cordial peace has reigned since. In 1991, the Argentine sector gained full provincial status and is known as the **Provincia de Tierra del Fuego, Antártida e Islas del Atlántico Sur**. Its jurisdiction is seen to extend over all southern territories, including the Islas Malvinas/Falklands Islands (see box, p.542), which lie 550km off the coast, and the Argentine segment of Antarctica.

Tierra del Fuego today

Tierra del Fuego's **economy** is now dependent on the production of petroleum and natural gas, fisheries, forestry and technological industries, attracted to the area by its status as a duty-free zone. Meanwhile the tourist industry, centred on Ushuaia, continues to expand. Luxury items are comparatively cheap, but basic items such as food are much more expensive than in other parts of the country, owing to the huge distances involved in importing them.

Ushuaia and around

USHUAIA, the provincial capital and tourism hub for the whole of Tierra del Fuego, lies in the far south of Isla Grande. Dramatically situated between the mountains – among them **Cerro Martial** and **Monte Olivia** – and the sea, the city tumbles, rather chaotically, down the hillside to the encircling arm of land that protects its bay from the southwesterly winds and occasional thrashing storms of the icy **Beagle Channel**. Ushuaia is primarily a convenient base for exploring the rugged beauty of the lands that border the channel, a historically important sea passage, but be warned that it exploits tourism to the full – prices vary between high and astronomical.

Puerto Williams lies just across the channel, on the southern (Chilean) side of the straits, and there are other trips as well: to historic **Estancia Harberton**, to a small penguin colony, and to nearby **Parque Nacional Tierra del Fuego**. In winter, there's decent skiing in the **Sierra Alvear** region north of town; in warmer seasons, it's also good for **trekking**.

Every year on June 21 – the longest night of the year – the **Bajada de Las Antorchas** takes place, with the darkness celebrated by a torchlit ski descent of Cerro Martial's slopes, traditionally opening the season. Daylight lasts from about 9am until 4pm at this time of year.

Brief history

In 1869, Reverend Waite Stirling became Tierra del Fuego's first white settler when he founded his **Anglican mission** among the Yámana here; the city takes its name from the Yámana tongue, and means something akin to "bay that stretches towards the west". Stirling stayed for six months, before being recalled to the Islas Malvinas/Falklands Islands to be appointed Anglican bishop for South America. Thomas Bridges, his assistant, took over the mission in 1871, after which Ushuaia began to figure on mariners' charts as a place of refuge in the event of shipwreck. A modest **monument** to the achievements of the early missionaries can be found where the first mission stood, on the south side of Ushuaia Bay, and is reached by the modern causeway southwest of the town centre.

The penal colony

In 1884, Commodore Augusto Lasserre raised the Argentine flag over Ushuaia for the first time, formally incorporating the area into the Argentine Republic. From 1896, in order to consolidate its sovereignty and open up the region to wider colonization, the Argentine state established a **penal colony** here. Forced convict labour was used for developing the settlement's infrastructure and for logging the local forests to build the town, but the prison had a reputation as the "Siberia of Argentina" and Perón closed it in 1947.

Ushuaia today

Nowadays, Ushuaia has a quite different reputation: the most populous, and popular, city in Tierra del Fuego, it depends largely on its thriving **tourist** industry, capitalizing on the beauty of its natural setting. You'll soon catch on that this is the world's most southerly resort, allowing you to amass claims to fame galore – golf on the world's most southerly course, a ride on the world's most southerly train, and so on. Ushuaia has plenty of sites worthy of a visit on their own merits, but unfortunately tourism has been allowed to develop with scant regard for the unique character of the town, and has changed it almost beyond recognition in the last decade. At certain moments you can still get a sense of the otherworldliness that used to make Ushuaia special, but if you are coming expecting a Chatwin-esque frontier town, you will be disappointed.

9

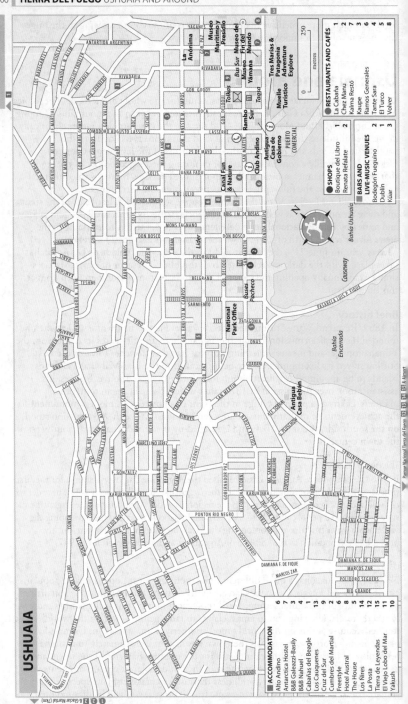

USHUAIA

■ **SHOPS**
| Boutique del Libro | 1 |
| Renata Refalate | 2 |

■ **BARS AND LIVE-MUSIC VENUES**
Bodegón Fueguino	2
Dublin	1
Küar	3

● **RESTAURANTS AND CAFÉS**
La Cabaña	1
Chez Manu	2
Kalma Restó	7
Kaupe	3
Ramos Generales	6
Tante Sara	4
El Turco	5
Volver	8

■ **ACCOMMODATION**
Alto Andino	6
Antarctica Hostel	7
B&B Galeazzi-Basily	3
B&B Nahuel	4
Cabañas del Beagle	1
Los Cauquenes	13
Cruz del Sur	9
Cumbres del Martial	2
Freestyle	6
Hotel Austral	8
The House	5
Los Ñires	14
La Posta	12
Tierra de Leyendas	15
El Viejo Lobo del Mar	11
Yakush	10

Antigua Casa de Gobierno

Maipú 465 • Mon–Sat noon–7pm • $50 (ticket also valid for Museo del Fin del Mundo) • Free guided Spanish-language tour 3.30pm

The best place to start wandering around Ushuaia is down by the pier, the **Muelle Turístico** (Tourist Dock), where an **obelisk** commemorates Augusto Lasserre's ceremony to assert Argentine sovereignty in this part of the world. Overlooking the sea from the other side of the street is the late nineteenth-century **Antigua Casa de Gobierno**, a stately building that was originally the governor's house before being used by the local government and then the police. It was restored in 2003 to reflect its original use and you can wander around to get an idea of how the wealthy would have lived in Ushuaia's early years.

Museo del Fin del Mundo

Maipú and Rivadavia • Oct–March daily 9am–8pm; April–Sept Mon–Sat noon–7pm • $50 (ticket also valid for Antigua Casa de Gobierno) • Free guided Spanish-language tour 2pm

The worthwhile **Museo del Fin del Mundo**, a five-minute walk from the Antigua Casa de Gobierno, has exhibits on the region's history and wildlife, including the polychrome figurehead of the *Duchess of Albany*, an English ship wrecked on the eastern end of the island in 1883, and a rare example of a Selk'nam–Spanish dictionary written by a Salesian missionary.

Museo Marítimo y Presidio

Yaganes and Gob. Paz • April–Oct daily except Wed 10am–8pm; Nov–March daily 9am–8pm • $90 • Free Spanish-language tours April–Oct 11.30am & 6.30pm, Nov–March 11.30am, 4.30pm & 6.30pm • ☎02901 437481, ☎museomaritimo.com

Ushuaia's former prison is now the must-visit **Museo Marítimo y Presidio**, and houses a motley collection of exhibits, the best of which are the meticulous scale-models of famous **ships** from the island's history in the maritime section as you first enter. The prison building itself, though, is the main draw, an example of the panopticon style popularized by English philosopher Jeremy Bentham, its wings radiating out like spokes from a half-wheel, most of which have now been opened to the public. The cells in wing four are complete with gory details of the notorious criminals who occupied them, and details of prison life, with informative panels in Spanish and English. The most celebrated prisoner was early twentieth-century anarchist Simón Radowitzsky, whose miserable stay and subsequent brief escape in 1918 are recounted by Bruce Chatwin in *In Patagonia*.

Upstairs, fairly dry displays tell something of Antarctica and the history of its exploration. Wing three has been given over to an art museum and a gift shop,

---

WINTER SPORTS AT THE END OF THE WORLD

In order to boast that you have been to the end of the world to **ski** or **snowboard**, you'll need to visit between late May and early September – June to August are the most reliable months. Most runs are for beginners and intermediates, but several companies, such as Gotama Expediciones (☎02901 1560 5301, ☎gotama-expediciones.com) offer guided back-country skiing for the more advanced. Equipment rental is reasonable and there are a couple of downhill (*esquí alpino*) pistes close to Ushuaia: the small Club Andino, 3km from town, and the more impressive one up by Glaciar Martial, 7km away.

Better runs are to be had, however, in the Sierra Alvear, the resorts of which are accessed from the RN-3. These include the modern Cerro Castor centre (☎02901 499301, ☎cerrocastor .com), 27km from Ushuaia, with 15km of pistes in runs, including a few black ones, up to 2km long. The Sierra Alvear is also an excellent area for **cross-country** skiing (*esquí de fondo* or *esquí nórdico*). In addition, there are several winter-sports centres (*centros invernales*) along the **Valle Tierra Mayor** where you can try out snowmobiles, snowshoes, ice-skating and dog-sled trips (*trineos de perros*), including Valle de Lobos and Nunatak (see p.519). Bear in mind that winter this far south entails short days, and it can be bitterly cold.

while wing two houses an art gallery of dubious quality and more exhibits and photos of early Ushuaia and its maritime history. Finally, wing one, which has not been restored and contains no exhibits at all, is in many ways the most interesting – the unheated and bare cells with peeling walls are quite spooky, and give something of an idea of what it must have been like to have been locked up or working here.

Museo Yámana

Rivadavia 56 • Daily: summer 10am–8pm; winter noon–7pm; generally closes July–Aug • $25 • ⓣ 02901 422874

The **Museo Yámana** is a charming little museum in a converted house that charts the arrival of pre-Columbian and European settlers in the archipelago. Beautiful dioramas give an idea of the native habitats and way of life, but the displays go rather easy on the European colonists; excellent descriptions in Spanish and English, though, more than validate its claim to be an interpretation centre.

Antigua Casa Bebán

Maipú and Plüschow • Mon–Fri 10am–6pm, Sat & Sun 11am–6pm • Free

At the southwestern end of town, the **Antigua Casa Bebán** is a lovely pavilion-style building with a steep roof and ornamental gabling that was prefabricated in Sweden in 1913. It hosts exhibitions of photos and artwork, as well as occasional films, and is the venue for the **Ushuaia Jazz Festival** every November.

Glaciar Martial

7km above town at the end of the steep Luis Martial road • Chairlift daily Nov–March 9.30am–4.45pm; June–Oct 10am–4.45pm • $50 • A taxi from the centre costs around $35–40

For first-rate views of the Beagle Channel and the islands of Chile, head up to the hanging (and fast receding) **Glaciar Martial**. A chairlift runs from beside the *Cumbres del Martial* hotel, which has a great tearoom (see p.511). During the winter, Glaciar Martial offers the closest decent skiing to Ushuaia (see box, p.507).

ARRIVAL AND DEPARTURE — USHUAIA AND AROUND

By plane The modern international airport, Malvinas Argentinas, is 4km southwest of town. There's no public transport into the city; a taxi to the centre costs around $30–40. Passengers on all domestic flights must pay a $28 departure tax. The Aerolíneas Argentinas office is at Maipú and 9 de Julio (ⓣ 02901 436338, ⓦ aerolineas.com.ar), and LADE is at Av San Martín 542 (ⓣ 02901 421123, ⓦ lade.com.ar). LAN (ⓣ 0810 999 9526, ⓦ lan.com) has an office at the airport.

Destinations Buenos Aires (3–5 daily; 3hr 30min); El Calafate (2–4 daily; 1hr 20min); Río Gallegos (1 weekly; 55min); and Trelew (1 daily; 2hr 15min).

By bus There's no single bus terminal in Ushuaia; instead buses depart from their respective company offices. Buses Pacheco (Av San Martín 1267; ⓣ 02901 437073, ⓦ buses pacheco.com) runs buses to Punta Arenas via Río Grande and Tolhuin. Bus Sur (Av San Martín 245; ⓣ 02901 430727, ⓦ bus-sur.cl) has services to Punta Arenas and Puerto Natales. Tecni Austral also has services to Punta Arenas and a single one to Río Gallegos; book through Tolkar (Roca 157; ⓣ 02901 431408, ⓦ tolkarturismo.com.ar). Lider (Gob. Paz 921; ⓣ 02901 436421, ⓦ lidertdf.com.ar) has buses to Río Grande via Tolhuin. Taqsa (Godoy 41; ⓣ 02901 435453, ⓦ taqsa.com.ar) has a single daily bus (5am) to Río Gallegos. Note that these are the summer-season timetables; out of season, services are reduced drastically.

Destinations Puerto Natales (4 weekly; 15hr); Punta Arenas (2–3 daily; 12hr); Río Gallegos (2 daily; 12hr); Río Grande (every 30min–1hr; 3hr 30min); Tolhuin (every 30min–1hr; 1hr 30min).

By car Avis (ⓣ 02901 433323, ⓦ avis.com) and Hertz (ⓣ 02901 432429, ⓦ hertz.com) both have offices at the airport. Most companies do not permit you to take your rental car out of the Argentine part of the island. Roads are fairly reliable from Oct to early May; outside this period, carry snow chains and drive with caution.

By boat Cruceros Australis (ⓣ 011 5199 6697, ⓦ australis .com) operates luxury, three- to four-night cruises (from around US$1000 per person) between Ushuaia and Punta Arenas in Chile.

FROM TOP USHUAIA (P.505); PENGUINS ON ISLA MARTILLO (P.513) >

INFORMATION AND TOURS

Tourist information The main commercial street, Avenida San Martín, runs parallel to and one block uphill from Maipú; at no. 674, you'll find the tourist office (Mon–Fri 9am–10pm, Sat & Sun 9am–8pm; ☎02901 432001, ✆turismoushuaia.com). The well-informed staff have lots of information on the region, can help you find accommodation and will even frank your passport with an "End of the World" stamp. There are also tourist offices at the Muelle Turístico (☎02901 437666; daily 9am–6pm) and the airport (opens to meet incoming flights).

Trekking and climbing information Serious trekkers and climbers should contact the Club Andino Ushuaia, at Fadul 50 (Mon–Sat 10am–1pm & 3–7pm; ☎02901 422335, ✆clubandinoushuaia.com.ar), which can advise on longer treks outside the normally visited areas of the Parque Nacional Tierra del Fuego and put you in touch with qualified guides. Registering here or at one of the tourist offices before embarking on any trek or climb is advisable.

Tours Canal Fun & Nature, 9 de Julio 118 (☎02901 437345, ✆canalfun.com), and Rumbo Sur, Av San Martín 350 (☎02901 421139, ✆rumbosur.com.ar), both offer a range of tours and day-trips, from kayaking to beaver-spotting.

ACCOMMODATION

Ushuaia has a wide range of **hotels, guesthouses** and **hostels**, many of which are clustered along the first four streets parallel to the bay. Nonetheless, most manage to get booked up in the height of summer, and have become increasingly expensive. The most attractive options tend to be up the mountainside on the road to Glaciar Martial or west towards the national park; some of these have occasional shuttle buses running to town and back but you're still bound to need taxis from time to time. Be aware that hotels in Tierra del Fuego are the main culprits when it comes to charging **higher rates for non-residents**, often as much as three times more – in such cases, we have quoted the non-resident rate. Rates for all include breakfast.

HOSTELS

Antarctica Hostel Antártida Argentina 270 ☎02901 435774, ✆antarcticahostel.com. One of Ushuaia's best hostels, with a sociable atmosphere, sunny lounge area, loft kitchen, coin-operated washing machines, and a lively bar. The simple upstairs dorms are a bit of a hike from the downstairs bathrooms though. Dorms $90, doubles $290

Cruz del Sur Gob. Deloqui 242 ☎02901 434099, ✆xdelsur.com.ar. A reliable hostel with a well-equipped kitchen and a laidback lounge area. The dorms are on the small side but are clean, and each has a view. Dorms $70

Freestyle Gob. Paz 866 ☎02901 432874, ✆ushuaia freestyle.com. A delightful hostel with spacious four- and six-bed dorms, swish bathrooms, a beanbag-filled TV room, and a relaxing top-floor lounge with superb views across the bay. The adjoining Alto Andino (see below) is a considerable step up in comfort (and price). Dorms $90

La Posta Perón Sur 864 ☎02901 444650, ✆laposta-ush .com.ar. Although it's a 20min walk from the city centre, this hostel remains a fine choice; the dorms are well kept, and there are two kitchens, a laundry room and helpful staff. It also has private rooms with shared bathrooms and self-contained apartments. Dorms $100, doubles $320, apartments $490

Yakush Piedrabuena 118 ☎02901 435807, ✆hostelyakush .com.ar. High-ceilinged hostel with a central location – the breakfast room overlooks busy Av San Martín – and a couple of good communal areas: an attic lounge room and a backyard with panoramic views. As well as the four- and six-bed dorms there are a few private rooms. Dorms $90, doubles $280

HOSTERÍAS, B&BS AND HOTELS

Alto Andino Gob. Paz 868 ☎02901 430920, ✆alto andinohotel.com. Slick boutique hotel with a mix of contemporary suites (some with jacuzzi) and apartments with their own mini kitchens; both have plasma-screen TVs. There's also a bar with wraparound windows affording great views of the Beagle Channel and the Martial Glacier. Suites $845, apartments $890

B&B Galeazzi-Basily Gob. Valdez 323 ☎02901 423213, ✆avesdelsur.com.ar. Welcoming B&B with two spick-and-span doubles sharing a spotless bathroom; guests have access to the kitchen and a TV lounge. The owners rent out cabañas (each with private bathrooms and mini kitchens) that sleep up to four people. Doubles $320, cabañas $550

B&B Nahuel 25 de Mayo 440 ☎02901 423068, ✆bybnahuel.com.ar. The bright green exterior make this B&B easy to spot; inside are homely, rather frilly rooms (one of which has shocking-pink walls you'll either love or hate) with either shared or private bathrooms. There's also a small TV lounge. $295

Cabañas del Beagle Las Aljabas 375 ☎02901 432785, ✆cabanasdelbeagle.com. Self-contained cottages beautifully constructed in local stone and wood, with floor-to-ceiling windows that make the most of their lofty location. Original fireplaces add to the cosiness, and there's under-floor heating throughout. Transfer from/to airport included. Good discounts for extended stays. $1295

Los Cauquenes Reinamora, 7km outside Ushuaia towards the national park ☎02901 441300, ✆los cauquenesushuaia.com.ar. Luxury wood-framed resort-style hotel at the far edge of Ushuaia, right on the Beagle Channel – the channel-facing rooms (others face the mountains) are so close that the sound of the waves lulls you to sleep. Entry to the spa, with its gorgeous indoor/outdoor pool and hot tub, is included in the rates. $1560

9

Cumbres del Martial Luis Martial 3560 ☎02901 424779, ⓦcumbresdelmartial.com.ar. Situated by the glacier chairlift, this excellent hotel boasts a fabulous position, which affords amazing views of the city and the Beagle Channel. Choose between tasteful rooms and luxurious split-level *cabañas* – the latter have their own private jacuzzis. There's also a spa and a teahouse (see p.508). Rooms $1270, cabañas $1826

★ **Hotel Austral** 9 de Julio 250 ☎02901 422223, ⓦhotel-austral.com.ar. This hotel is an excellent mid-range choice: as well as a convenient location in the centre of Ushuaia, it boasts very comfortable en-suite rooms with bright decor, queen-sized beds and TVs. Highly recommended. $540

★ **The House** Gob. Paz 1410 ☎02901 437576, ⓦthehouseushuaia.com. An elegant little hotel creatively designed by its welcoming Barcelona-born owner. The minimalist en-suites receive plenty of natural light and have attractive stoneware bathrooms, and there are good vistas from the tasteful living room. $600

Los Ñires Av de los Ñires 3040 ☎02901 445173, ⓦnires.com.ar. A quality mid-range place that has fewer frills but is not significantly different to its more luxurious neighbours on Ushuaia's outskirts. The en-suite rooms are cosy and have large windows that provide lots of light and views over the mountains or the channel. There's a decent restaurant too. $550

★ **Tierra de Leyendas** Tierra de Vientos 2448 ☎02901 443565, ⓦtierradeleyendas.com.ar. Charming couple Maía and Sebas have made this wonderful boutique hotel one of the best places to stay in Tierra del Fuego. There are just five rooms, all immaculately designed, with huge windows to make the most of the stunning views. The food – both at breakfast and in the restaurant (open to nonguests) – is outstanding, as is the service. It's a 10min taxi ride from the centre. $960

El Viejo Lobo del Mar Gob. Godoy 98 ☎02901 424850, ⓦhotelelviejolobodemar.com. *El Viejo Lobo del Mar* (The Old Sea Lion) is a centrally located *apart-hotel*, with neat apartments (sleeping up to four people) that each contain a bedroom, living room, bathroom and a simple kitchen. A good choice for families or groups planning to self-cater. $950

EATING, DRINKING AND NIGHTLIFE

The city centre has plenty of places to **eat** or grab a coffee, but many places are now tourist traps. You'll get better-quality food at lower prices – and, often as not, breathtaking views into the bargain – if you move around a bit. The quality of cuisine in Ushuaia has rocketed in recent years and there are several places where you can splash out on a memorable meal and sample the local gastronomic pride, *centolla* (king crab). **Prices** are high by Argentine standards, and those on a tight budget should consider self-catering.

RESTAURANTS AND CAFÉS

La Cabaña Luis Martial 3560 ☎02901 424779, ⓦlacabania.com.ar. Part of the *Cumbres del Martial* complex, this flowery, alpine-style casa de té serves up an inviting array of teas, cakes, sandwiches and main meals such as lentil and sausage stew, as well as fondue. Mains $40–80. Daily 10am–11.30pm.

Chez Manu Luis Martial 2135 ☎02901 432253, ⓦchezmanu.com. Stunning panoramic views from huge windows and gourmet French food using local produce – *centolla*, of course, plus melt-in-the-mouth lamb, fish and seafood – make this one of the city's most sought-after dining spots, though it is a bit expensive (mains $75–130). Daily noon–3pm & 8pm–midnight.

Kalma Restó Antártida Argentina 57 ☎02901 425786, ⓦkalmaresto.com.ar. Some of the most distinctive – and delicious – food in Ushuaia is served at this cool little joint. Dishes include a Tierra del Fuego-inspired paella, and *centolla* and roasted pumpkin ravioli. Mains $75–145. Mon–Fri 12.30–3pm & 7–11.30pm, Sat 7–11.30pm.

★ **Kaupe** Roca 470 ☎02901 422704, ⓦkaupe.com.ar. *Kaupe's* service is friendly, the food delicious and the decor unpretentious, in what is just a family home with a fabulous view (the tables are packed in together). Seafood is the star; try the sea bass in black butter sauce with capers. Reservations essential in the high season. Mains $75–130. Mon–Sat 8.30–11.30pm.

Ramos Generales Maipú 749 ☎02901 424317, ⓦramosgeneralesushuaia.com. An atmospheric bar-café-bakery decked out with an eclectic array of knick-knacks

---

THE KING OF THE CRUSTACEANS

A fixture on menus throughout Tierra del Fuego, the **centolla** (king crab) has spindly legs that can measure over a metre from tip to tip, but the meat comes from the body, with an average individual yielding some 300g. The less savoury practice of catching them with traps baited with dolphin or penguin meat has almost been stamped out by the imposition of hefty fines by both Chilean and Argentine authorities, but despite controls on size limits, they are still subject to rampant over-fishing. Canned king crab is served off-season, but is bland and not worth the prices charged; frozen *centolla* is only slightly better, so always make sure it is fresh.

including model ships, old lamps, typewriters and sewing machines, and rows of traditional penguin jugs (used for serving wine) behind the bar. As well as good cakes, sandwiches ($40–50) and *picadas*, there's a strong wine and beer list. Daily 9am–midnight.

Tante Sara Av San Martín 175 ☎02901 433710, ⓦtantesara.com. Popular *confitería* and *panadería*, which does a fine line in cakes, sandwiches and baguettes ($12–30), as well as decent coffee. There's another branch on the same road at no. 701. Mon–Thurs & Sun 8am–8.30pm, Fri & Sat 8am–9/10pm.

El Turco Av San Martín 1410 ☎02901 424711. Popular with locals, this low-key restaurant serves hearty portions of pizza, pasta, chicken and steak, as well as empanadas. The food is nothing to write home about, but prices (for Ushuaia at least) are very reasonable. Mains $30–70. Mon–Sat noon–3pm & 8pm–midnight.

Volver Maipú 37 ☎02901 444444, ⓦvolverushuaia .com.ar. The usual seafood menu at the usual prices (mains from around $70), but the portions are generous and well prepared. *Volver* is an Ushuaia original and the place is dripping with character and bric-a-brac, from faded newspaper cuttings to old tango shoes to a lifesize statue of Che – it's virtually a museum in itself. Tues–Sun noon–3pm & 7.30pm–midnight.

BARS AND LIVE MUSIC VENUES

Bodegón Fueguino Av San Martín 895 ☎02901 431972. A convivial place, its sheepskin-covered benches packed with gringos sampling the home-brewed beer; the food is also well worth a look – particularly the tasty lamb and pork dishes (mains $50–130). Tues–Sat 12.30–3pm & 8pm–midnight.

Dublín 9 de Julio 168 ☎02901 430744, ⓦdublin ushuaia.com. This green-walled, red-roofed pub is a good place for a draught beer (around $25), with a buzzing atmosphere and occasional live music. Apart from the Guinness posters, however, there isn't much in the way of Hibernian trappings. Daily 8pm–3/4am.

★ **Küar** Perito Moreno 2232 ☎02901 437396, ⓦkuar .com.ar. Set in an attractive stone-and-timber building right on the seafront, on the road out towards Río Grande, this youthful bar-restaurant has stupendous views and a blazing fire, as well as fish and pasta dishes and its own delicious home-brewed pale ale, amber ale and dark porter (each around $25). Daily 3pm–4am.

DIRECTORY

Banks and exchange Banco Tierra del Fuego, Av San Martín and Roca; Banco de la Nación, Av San Martín 190. There are several *casas de cambio* on San Martín.

Books Boutique del Libro, Av San Martín 1120 (Mon–Sat 10am–1pm & 4–8.30pm; ☎02901 424750, ⓦboutique dellibro.com.ar), has a selection of English-language books on Tierra del Fuego and Patagonia, plus a few novels.

Consulate Chile, Jainén 50 ☎02901 430909.

Hospital Hospital Regional, Maipú and 12 de Octubre

☎02901 421439 or ☎02901 421278; emergencies ☎107.

Laundry Qualis, Güiraldes 568.

Police Deloqui 492 ☎02901 421773; emergencies ☎101.

Post office Av San Martín and Godoy.

Souvenirs Renata Rafalak, Piedrabuenos 51 (Mon–Sat 10am–1pm & 3–5pm; ☎02901 437 254), sells some of the finest craft items in southern Patagonia; specialities include reproductions of the bark masks worn by the Selk'nam and Yámana in their Hain and Kina initiation ceremonies.

Beagle Channel

No trip to Ushuaia is complete without a voyage on the legendary **Beagle Channel**, the majestic, mountain-fringed sea passage south of the city. Most **boat excursions** start and finish in Ushuaia, and you get the best views of town looking back at it from the straits. Standard trips visit Isla Bridges, Isla de los Pájaros and Isla de los Lobos, looping around Faro Les Eclaireurs, sometimes erroneously called the Lighthouse at the End of the World – that title belongs to the beacon at the tip of Isla de los Estados – on their way back. On boat trips, look out for **sea birds** such as the Black-browed albatross, the thick-set Giant petrel, Southern skuas and the South American tern, as well as **marine mammals** such as sea lions, Peale's dolphin (with a grey patch on its flank) and the occasional minke whale.

ARRIVAL AND ACTIVITIES

BEAGLE CHANNEL

By boat Boats depart from the Muelle Turístico, where you'll find agents' booking huts; trips tend to depart daily at 9.30/10am and 3pm, last 3–4hr, and cost around $250, including drinks and snacks. Note that there is also a $7 per passenger dock tax. Recommended operators include Tres Marías (☎02901 436416, ⓦtresmariasweb.com),

whose trip includes trekking on Isla "H" to see Yámana shell middens (see p.521), and Patagonia Adventure Explorer (☎02901 15 465842, ⓦpatagoniaadvent.com.ar), who run the standard tour. These operators both use smaller boats; there are several other larger vessels available, but it is harder to see the wildlife close up.

ANTARCTIC CRUISES

Ushuaia lies 1000km north of **Antarctica**, but is still the world's closest port to the white continent – and most tourists pass through the city to make their journey across Drake's Passage, the wild stretch of ocean that separates it from South America. The grandeur of Antarctica's pack ice, rugged mountains and phenomenal bird and marine life will leave you breathless: whales, elephant seals, albatrosses and numerous varieties of penguin are just some of the species you can hope to see. Regular **cruise ships** depart from November to mid-March and most cruises last between eight and 21 days, some stopping at the **South Atlantic islands** (Islas Malvinas/Falklands, South Georgia, the South Orkneys, Elephant Island and the South Shetlands) en route.

COSTS AND INFORMATION

These cruises are very expensive (generally from at least US$5500), but you can sometimes get last-minute discounts in Ushuaia, especially on the newest ships. Ushuaia's **Oficina Antártica** at the Muelle Turístico (☎ 02901 430015) has details of current sailings and can advise on what each trip involves; otherwise, try contacting the following agencies: Antarpply, at Gob. Paz 633 (☎ 02901 436747, ⓦ antarpply.com), Canal Fun & Nature (see p.510), Rumbo Sur (see p.510), Puerto Williams-based Sim Expeditions (see p.518) or US-based Quark Expeditions (ⓦ quarkexpeditions.com).

Diving Ushuaia Divers (☎ 02901 444701, ⓦ ushuaiadivers .com.ar) runs diving trips into the channel to look for king crabs and sea lions among the seaweed forests.

Estancia Harberton and around

Patagonia's most historic estancia, **Estancia Harberton** is an ordered assortment of whitewashed buildings on the shores of a sheltered bay. Though Harberton is assuredly scenic, it's the historical resonance of the place that fleshes out a visit: this farmstead – or more particularly the family who settled here – played a role out of all proportion to its size in the region's history. It was built by Reverend Thomas Bridges, the man who authored one of the two seminal Fuegian texts, the *Yámana–English Dictionary*, and was the inspiration for the other, Lucas Bridges' classic, *Uttermost Part of the Earth*. Apart from being a place where scientists and shipwrecked sailors were assured assistance, Harberton developed into a sanctuary of refuge for groups of Yámana and Mannekenk.

Today the estancia is owned by Tommy Goodall, a great-grandson of Thomas Bridges, and is open to **guided tours** that take in the copse on the hill, where you learn about the island's plant life, authentic reconstructions of Yámana dwellings, the family cemetery and the old shearing shed. Housed in a building at the entrance to the farmstead is an impressive marine-mammal museum, **Museo Acatushún** (ⓦ acatushun .com), which displays the remains of all the main families of such animals – whales, dolphins, seals and the like – found in the surrounding waters.

Harberton is **accessed** via the **RCj** branch road, whose turn-off is 40km northeast of Ushuaia on the RN-3. Around 25km from the turn-off, you emerge from the forested route by a delightful lagoon fringed by the skeletons of *Nothofagus* beeches, and can look right across the Beagle Channel to the Chilean town of Puerto Williams. A few hundred metres beyond here the road splits: take the left-hand fork heading eastwards across rolling open country and past a clump of **flag trees**, swept back in exaggerated quiffs by the unremitting wind. The estancia is a further 10km beyond the turn-off, 85km east of Ushuaia.

Isla Martillo

While at Harberton you can cross to the Reserva Yecapasela on **Isla Martillo**, the only island in the Beagle Channel that **penguins** call home – biologists think it's because the softness of the soil is perfect for their burrowing, and the sea currents in which they feed lead here, too. There are two species – Magellanic, the same species but a different group from the larger colony in Punta Tombo (see p.459), and the orange-beaked sub-Antarctic Gentoo.

9

The RCj beyond Harberton

Beyond Harberton, the RCj runs for forty spectacular kilometres – accessible only with your own transport – to **Estancia Moat**, past the famous islands that guard the eastern mouth of the Beagle Channel: **Picton**, **Nueva** and **Lennox**. These uninhabited atolls have a controversial past, with both Chile and Argentina long claiming sovereignty over them. The track comes to an end at a naval outpost, beyond which Península Mitre (see p.520) stretches to Cabo San Diego, at the far tip of Tierra del Fuego.

ARRIVAL AND DEPARTURE

By bus From mid-Oct to mid-April several travel agencies (most based at the Muelle Turístico) run buses from Ushuaia to Harberton (1hr 30min).

By organized tour Travel agencies also offer guided day-trips (around $280–300) to Harberton, often combined with

ESTANCIA HARBERTON AND AROUND

a tour of the Beagle Channel. The only operator permitted to land boats on Isla Martillo is Piratour (☎02901 424834); note though that its half-day bus and boat trips ($285) depart from Ushuaia via Harberton but don't really visit the estancia. It's advisable to book at least a day in advance.

INFORMATION

Estancia opening times and entry fee Estancia Harberton (ⓦestanciaharberton.com) is open mid-Oct to

mid-April daily 10am–7pm. Entry is $60 (includes a 2hr guided tour and access to the museum).

ACCOMMODATION AND EATING

Estancia Harberton 85km east of Ushuaia. No phone; ⓦestanciaharberton.com. Simple accommodation is provided in the old *Shepherd's House*, which has two en-suite rooms (each sleeping up to three people), a small shared kitchenette and a large porch. Rates include tea on arrival,

dinner, breakfast and an extended guided tour. Camping is also permitted at three sites, though there are no facilities; you need to register first at the estancia's *Mánacatush* tearoom and obtain a permit. The tearoom itself serves delicious cakes and lunches. Camping **free**, rooms **$920**

Parque Nacional Tierra del Fuego

PARQUE NACIONAL TIERRA DEL FUEGO, 12km west of Ushuaia, is the easiest to access of southern Argentina's national parks. Protecting 630 square kilometres of jagged mountains, intricate lakes, southern beech forest, swampy peat bog, subantarctic tundra and verdant coastline, the park stretches along the frontier with Chile, from the Beagle Channel to the **Sierra Inju-Goiyin** (also called the Sierra Beauvoir) north of Lago Fagnano, but only the southernmost quarter of this is open to the public, accessed via the RN-3 from Ushuaia. Fortunately, this area contains much of the park's most beautiful scenery, if also some of the wettest – bring rain gear.

The quarter is broken down into three main sectors: Bahía Ensenada and Río Pipo in the east, close to the station for the Tren del Fin del Mundo; Lago Roca further west; and the Lapataia area south of Lago Roca, which includes Laguna Verde and, at the end

---

PARROTS AND HUMMINGBIRDS

Most visitors to South America associate parrots and hummingbirds more with the steamy, verdant jungles of the Amazon than the frigid extremes of Tierra del Fuego. However, it is also possible to see them both in Parque Nacional Tierra del Fuego. The unmistakeably garrulous **Austral parakeet** is the world's most southerly parrot, inhabiting these temperate forests year-round. The Selk'nam christened it *Kerrhprrh*, in onomatopoeic imitation of its call. Once upon a time, according to their beliefs, all Fuegian trees were coniferous, and it was *Kerrhprrh* who transformed some into deciduous forests, painting them autumnal reds with the feathers of its breast. The tiny **Green-backed firecrown** is the planet's most southerly hummingbird, and has been recorded – albeit rarely – flickering about flowering shrubs in summer. Known to the Selk'nam by the graceful name of *Sinu K-Tam* (Daughter of the Wind), this diminutive creature was, curiously, believed by them to be the offspring of *Ohchin*, the whale, and *Sinu*, the wind.

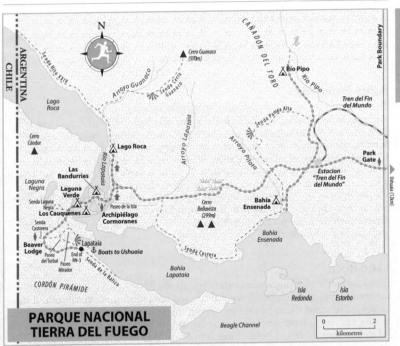

PARQUE NACIONAL TIERRA DEL FUEGO

of the RN-3, Bahía Lapataia. You can get a good overview of the park in a day, but walkers will want to stay two to three days to appreciate the scenery and the **wildlife**, which includes birds such as Magellanic woodpeckers (*Carpintero patagónico*), condors, Steamer ducks, Kelp geese – the park's symbol – and Buff-necked ibis; and mammals such as the guanaco, the rare Southern sea otter (*Nutria marina*), the Patagonian grey fox and its larger cousin, the native Fuegian red fox, once heavily hunted for its pelt.

Walking trails

The park is easy to walk around, with several relatively unchallenging though beautiful **trails** (*sendas*), many of which are completed in minutes rather than hours or days; the best is arguably the scenic Senda Costera (Coastal Path) connecting Bahía Ensenada with Lago Roca and Bahía Lapataia. The spectacular climb up Cerro Guanaco from Lago Roca is comparatively tough, though hardened trekkers will find sterner physical challenges in the Sierra Valdivieso and the Sierra Alvear (see p.519). Obey the signs warning you to refrain from collecting shellfish – which are sometimes affected by poisonous red tide – and light fires only in permitted campsites, extinguishing them with water, not earth.

Río Pipo

North of the train terminus is the pleasant wooded valley of Cañadón del Toro, through which runs the **Río Pipo**. A gentle 4km walk along an unsealed road brings you to *Camping Río Pipo* (see p.517), and a couple of hundred metres on you come to an attractive **waterfall**. Although a through-route north from here to Lago Fagnano is marked on some old maps, the area is now off-limits and you will be fined if caught there. If you're heading from Río Pipo back south to Bahía Ensenada, a more interesting alternative to walking between the two by road is to take the fairly

9

demanding **Senda Pampa Alta** (5km; 1hr 30min), which is signposted off west on the way back to the train-station crossroads. This offers fine views from a lookout over the Beagle Channel as it crosses the RN-3 towards Bahía Lapataia 3km west of the crossroads, and then drops to the coast on a poor path through thick forest.

Bahía Ensenada

Two kilometres south of the crossroads, **Bahía Ensenada** is a small bay with little of intrinsic interest. It does, however, have the jetty for boats to Bahía Lapataia and Isla Redonda, and is the trailhead for one of the park's most pleasant walks, the excellent **Senda Costera** (6.5km; 3hr). The route affords spectacular views from the Beagle Channel shoreline and takes you through dense coastal forest of evergreen beech, Winter's bark and *lenga*, some of their branches clad in *barba de viejo* (old man's beard), a hanging lichen that gives the trees a rather sorrowful appearance. Look out, too, for the *pan de Indio* (Indian bread), a bulbous orange fungus that clusters around the knots of branches. On the way, you'll pass grass-covered mounds that are the ancient campsite **middens** (see p.520) of the Yámana – these are protected archeological sites and should not be disturbed.

Lago Roca

Two kilometres after the Senda Costera rejoins the RN-3, a turn-off to the right takes you across the lush meadows of the broad Río Lapataia to **Lago Roca** and its campsite. Just past the campsite (see opposite) buildings, which include a *confitería*, there's a car park. From here, the gentle **Senda Hito XXIV** (8km return; 3hr) hugs the lake's northern shore and heads through majestic *lenga* forest to the Chilean border. This is a particularly good trail from which to spot the red-headed **Magellanic woodpecker** – most people hear it before they see it, hammering away at trees. Do not attempt to cross the border: it is under regular surveillance and you may be arrested if you try to do so.

Cerro Guanaco

A spectacular but demanding trek is the climb up 970m-high **Cerro Guanaco** (8km return; 7hr), the mountain ridge on the north side of Lago Roca. From here, the **views** of the angular landscape are superb: the swollen finger of Lago Roca, flanked by the spiky ridge of Cerro Cóndor, with the jagged Cordillera Darwin beyond; to the east, Ushuaia and its airport; and to the north, a vertiginous cliff plunges down to the Cañadón del Toro. Best of all, however, are the views to the south: the tangle of islands and rivers of the Archipiélago Cormoranes; Lapataia's sinuous curves; the Isla Redonda in the Beagle Channel; and across to the Chilean islands, Hoste and Navarino, separated by the Murray Channel. On a clear day, in the distance beyond the channel, you can make out the Islas Wollaston, the group of islands whose southernmost point is Cape Horn.

Note that the weather on Cerro Guanaco can turn capricious with little warning at any time of year, so bring adequate clothing, even if you set out in glorious sunshine.

The Lapataia area

The absorbing Lapataia area is accessed by way of the final 4km stretch of the RN-3, as it winds south from the Lago Roca junction, past **Laguna Verde**, and on to **Lapataia** itself, on the bay of the same name. This is one of the most intriguing sections to explore: a kind of "park within a park". In the space of a few hours, you can take a network of short trails past an incredible variety of scenery, including peat bogs, river islets, wooded knolls and sea coast.

Río Lapataia and the Archipiélago Cormoranes

A few hundred metres past the Lago Roca junction, you cross the **Río Lapataia** – over a bridge that's a favoured haunt of Ringed kingfishers (*Martín pescador grande*) – onto the **Archipiélago Cormoranes** (Cormorant Archipelago). Signposted left off the road here is a short circuit trail, the **Paseo de la Isla** (600m), a delightful walk through tiny, enchanting humped islets.

Laguna Verde and beyond

Next you pass **Laguna Verde**, which is actually a sumptuous, sweeping bend of the Río Ovando, and makes a lovely setting for the two campsites here, *Camping Laguna Verde* and *Camping Los Cauquenes* (see below). From Laguna Verde, it's only 2km to Lapataia, but there are several easy nature trails along the way, which you can stroll along in half an hour or so, allowing time to stop and study the signs with ecological and botanical information (in Spanish). Paseo Mirador (1km) takes you down to Bahía Lapataia via an impressive lookout over the bay; **Paseo del Turbal** (2km) takes you on a walkway across the peat bogs; and the **Senda Castorera** passes a **beaver dam**. You stand a good chance of spotting these rodents – which now number nearly 50,000 – if you arrive in the early morning or at dusk.

Bahía Lapataia and the end of the Pan-American Highway

The RN-3 comes to its scenic end – marked by a much-photographed sign – at Lapataia on **Bahía Lapataia**. For some this is not just the end of the RN-3, but the end of the entire **Pan-American Highway** – around a mere 49,958km from Prudhoe Bay, Alaska. Deriving its name from the Yámana for "forested cove", Lapataia is a serenely beautiful bay studded with small islets. Near the car park here is the **jetty** where boats arrive from Ushuaia.

ARRIVAL AND DEPARTURE

By boat There are limited boat services running to the park from Ushuaia, usually going to Bahía Lapataia as part of a combined boat-and-bus tour – enquire at the travel agency offices at the Muelle Turístico.

By bus Regular buses (20–30min) shuttle throughout the day from the corner of Maipú and Fadul, not far from the Muelle Turístico, to various points in the park; services are reduced, and sometimes halted, during the colder months.

By train You can also get to the park on the world's most southern railway, the Tren del Fin del Mundo (2–3 departures daily to the park, 1–2 from the park; 40min each way; $155 round trip; ticket office at the Muelle Turístico;

PARQUE NACIONAL TIERRA DEL FUEGO

⊕02901 431600, ⊛trendelfindelmundo.com.ar), which chugs its way through woodland meadows and alongside the Río Pipo to the park station, 2km from the main gate. Used to transport wood in the days of the penal colony, it's now little more than a tourist toy train, and you'll still need to get to the main station, 8km west of Ushuaia on the road to the national park; a taxi costs about $150.

By taxi A taxi to the park from Ushuaia costs around $220.

By organized tour The most popular way to access the park is along the good dirt road from Ushuaia. Virtually all travel agencies in Ushuaia offer tours of the park ($200, plus entrance fee); most last 4hr and stop at the major places of interest, including Bahía Lapataia.

INFORMATION

Opening hours and entry fees The park is open daily 8am–8pm; hours are slightly shorter in winter. Entrance is $85; if you plan to visit again the next day, let the park staff know, and you won't have to pay twice.

Information The staff can also provide a simple map of the park's trails here, as well as info on its attractions.

ACCOMMODATION

There are four main **camping** areas: the two nearest the entrance, *Río Pipo* and *Bahía Ensenada*, are free, but you're better off heading to Lago Roca and Laguna Verde, in the more exciting western section of the park. On Lago Roca, *Camping Lago Roca* is the only site with any facilities (and the only one that charges a fee), though the three free sites on Archipiélago Comoranes – *Camping Las Bandurrias*, *Camping Laguna Verde* and *Camping Los Cauquenes* – just edge it for beauty.

Camping Lago Roca Near Lago Roca ⊕02901 433313, ⊛confiterialagoroca.com.ar. This site sits near picturesque Lago Roca, where the lake bottlenecks into the Río Lapataia, and is the only one with facilities. There's also a *refugio* with dorm beds and a couple of self-contained *cabañas*. Camping $45, dorms $50, cabañas $80

9

Central and northern Tierra del Fuego

The second-largest settlement in Tierra del Fuego, **Río Grande** is also the only town of significance in Isla Grande's **central and northern sector**. The sterile-looking plains that surround it harbour fields of petroleum and natural gas that generate millions of dollars of wealth annually, with huge quantities of gas transported each year to Ushuaia and as far away as Buenos Aires. North of town, the RN-3 runs through monotonous scenery towards San Sebastián, where you cross the border into Chile or continue north on a dead-end route to the mouth of the Magellan Straits at Cabo Espíritu Santo. On the way to Río Grande from Ushuaia, the RN-3 winds up to **Paso Garibaldi**, where you have majestic views over **Lago Escondido**, and then bypasses **Tolhuin**, crossing the woodland scenery of the central region. This stretch is marked by a string of *ripio* branch roads, the **rutas complementarias**, which wiggle away from the RN-3; those headed west take you to a couple of fine estancias, and those headed east into the **Península Mitre**, the windswept land that forms Isla Grande's desolate tip.

One of the northern region's principal tourist draws is its world-class **trout-fishing**, especially for sea-running brown trout, which on occasion swell to weights in excess of 14kg. The river, also named Río Grande, currently holds several fly-fishing world

---

THE OTHER END OF THE WORLD: PUERTO WILLIAMS AND CAPE HORN

Nestled in a small bay on the north shore of **Isla Navarino** on Chile's side of the border, 82km due east and ever so slightly south of Ushuaia along the Beagle Channel, is **Puerto Williams**. "Williams" is something of a thorn in Argentina's toe, since despite all the publicity and hype about Ushuaia being **the most southerly town in the world**, that dubious privilege actually belongs to Puerto Williams. Founded as a military outpost and officially the capital of Chilean Antarctica, the town looks tranquil and idyllic on a fine day, with colourful roofs surrounded by the jagged peaks of Los Dientes. Though the settlement can easily be seen from the RN-3, actually getting there from Argentina is a bureaucratic headache, meaning that companies that do the trip are few and expensive.

ARRIVAL AND ACCOMMODATION

Zenit Explorer (Fadul 126; ☎02901 15 486161, ⓦzenitexplorer.com.ar) and Ushuaia Boating (Godoy 190; ☎02901 436193, ⓦushuaiaboating.com.ar) both operate daily boats (Nov–April, weather permitting) across the channel to Isla Navarino; passengers are then transported by bus to Puerto Williams. The whole journey takes around an hour and costs about US$125 one way. Alternatively, you could cross the land border with Chile (see box, p.523) and travel across from Punta Arenas. Aero Club Ushuaia (book via one of the travel agencies in Ushuaia) operates small planes that fly loops without landing over Puerto Williams and the surrounding area; in the past they have landed there and may do so again, so it's worth enquiring.

Among Puerto Williams' fairly limited accommodation options, *Residencial Pusaki* at Piloto Pardo 222 (☎061 621116, ✉pattypusaki@yahoo.es) stands out for its welcoming, family atmosphere, comfortable and economically priced dorms (CH$8500/$84) and private rooms (CH$25,00/$246), and tasty home-cooked food.

ROUNDING THE CAPE

Having come this far south, many travellers like to go the whole hog and "round the Cape", erroneously translated into Spanish as *Cabo de Hornos* ("Ovens Cape"). Ask around in Puerto Williams – SIM Expeditions (Casilla 6; ☎061 621150, ⓦsimexpeditions.com) on the main plaza is a good place to start – about **boat trips** to the most southerly point of the world's landmass, barring Antarctica. Weather permitting, you disembark on a shingle beach, climb a rickety ladder and visit the tiny Chilean naval base, lighthouse and chapel; there's not much to do otherwise and it's all quite desolate.

DAP (☎061 616100, ⓦaeroviasdap.cl) runs **flights** from Punta Arenas that make a loop over the headland and return without landing, or which land at Puerto Williams. These air excursions treat you to incredible views of Isla Navarino and the Darwin peaks, but, again, weather is a vital factor. The company also has flights over Antarctica.

records for brown trout caught with various breaking strains of line. The mouths of the Río Fuego and Río Ewan can also be spectacularly fruitful, as can sections of the Malengüeña, Irigoyen, Claro and Turbio rivers, and lakes Yehuin and Fagnano.

Ushuaia to Paso Garibaldi and the Sierra Alvear

The road from Ushuaia to **Paso Garibaldi** wends its way north and east through dramatic forested scenery, with great views of the valleys and savage mountain ranges that cross the southern part of the island. Many activity centres and refuges have sprung up along the route, primarily to cater to **winter-sports** enthusiasts, though they often also make excellent bases for adventurous **trekking** or horseriding. Above all, the rugged, serrated peaks of the **Sierra Valdivieso** and **Sierra Alvear ranges** make ideal bushwhacking territory. If rough-hiking independently, consult the Club Andino in Ushuaia (see p.510) and arm yourself with a copy of Zagier & Urruty's *Ushuaia Trekking Map*, but do not underestimate the need for orienteering skills or the unpredictable nature of the weather: blizzards can hit at any time. You must also be prepared to get thoroughly soaked when crossing bogs and streams, but you'll be rewarded by the sight of **beaver dams** up to 2.5m high, as well, in all probability, as their destructive constructors.

Heading northeast from Ushuaia, the RN-3 curls up around the foot of **Monte Olivia** and heads into the **Valle de Tierra Mayor**, a popular area for winter sports and a good spot for trekking in the Sierra Alvear.

Valle de Lobos and Nunatak

17km outside Ushuaia • Several travel agencies in Ushuaia run buses to Altos del Valle and Nunatak; check the latest timetable at the Muelle Turístico

One of the first places you come across, 17km from Ushuaia, is **Valle de Lobos** (📞02901 15 612319, 🌐valledelobos.com), an activity centre offering a range of activities, including dog-sledding trips. Nearby a relatively clear trail leads to attractive **Laguna Esmeralda** (4.5km; 2hr), where you can camp (free), and a more challenging hike to **Glaciar Alvear** (another 3.5km; 2hr 30min), which feeds the lake below. A kilometre or so beyond Valle de Lobos is the excellent Nunatak (📞02901 430329, 🌐nunatakadventure.com), a sports centre offering dog-sledding and snowmobile trips in the winter, and trekking and beaver-watching trips in the summer, among other activities. Ask about their tough but fascinating guided trek to **Lago Ojo del Albino** (10hr; guide, crampons and food included).

Lago Fagnano

Cresting the **Paso Garibaldi** some 45km out of Ushuaia, the RN-3 descends towards **Lago Escondido**, the first of the lowland lakes, accessible via a 4km branch road to the north, before heading alongside the southern shore of **LAGO FAGNANO**. This impressive lake, also called Lago Kami from its Selk'nam name, is flanked by ranges of hills, and straddles the Chilean border at its western end. Most of its 105km are inaccessible to visitors, apart from dedicated anglers who can afford to rent a good launch. Travelling along the RN-3 as it parallels the lake, you'll see several sawmills, denoted by their squat, conical brick chimneys, used for burning bark.

ARRIVAL AND INFORMATION — LAGO FAGNANO

By bus Transportes Pasarela (25 de Mayo and Maipú in Ushuaia; 📞02901 433712, 🌐transferpasarela.com.ar) runs a daily bus (departs 10am, returns 2pm; sometimes extra services run in the high season; 1hr 15min) to Lago Fagnano.

Tours Several agencies offer day-trips (around $250) to Lago Fagnano and Lago Escondido.

ACCOMMODATION

Cabañas Khami Eastern end of Lago Fagnano 📞02964 15 566045, 🌐cabaniaskhami.com.ar. Popular with anglers, this complex of cosy wooden *cabañas* is good value if you are in a big group. The *cabañas* sleep up to six people, and there's a heated indoor pool. Minimum three-night stay. **$800**

9

Tolhuin

Near the eastern end of Lago Fagnano, the road splits: the left fork is the more scenic, old, unsealed RN-3 route, which cuts north across the lake along a splendid causeway; the right is the RN-3 bypass, the more direct route to **TOLHUIN**, the region's oddest little town. Created in the 1970s, Tolhuin was designed to provide a focus for the heartland of Isla Grande – indeed, the name means "heart-shaped" in Selk'nam – but as a place of unassuming houses that hangs together with little focus, it has an artificial commune-like feel. It does, however, make a useful halfway point to break the journey – as most buses do – between Ushuaia and Río Grande.

ARRIVAL AND EATING

TOLHUIN

By bus There are regular buses to Tolhuin from both Ushuaia (every 30min–1hr; 1hr 30min) and Río Grande (every 30min–1hr; 1hr 30min).

Panadería La Unión Jeujepen 450 @ 02901 492202,

@ panaderialaunion.com. This bakery and restaurant acts as the hub of village life, and sells a range of delicious breads and other goodies, ideal if you are planning a picnic. Snacks from $10. Daily 24hr.

To Río Grande: the RN-3 and the rutas complementarias

The main route between Tolhuin and Río Grande is the fast, paved RN-3, but if you have the time it's worth exploring one or more of the unsealed **rutas complementarias** (RC) that branch off it – alphabetized roads that provide access to the heartland of Argentine Tierra del Fuego but are only really accessible to those with their own transport. Dotted around this inhospitable land are some hospitable **estancias**, worth the journey for the authentic experience of seeing a working Fuegian farm, or for the opportunity to gallop on horses across the steppe.

The RCh and RCf loop

The **RCh**, which branches off the RN-3 22km north of Tolhuin, and the connecting **RCf**, which joins the RN-3 some 10km south of the bridge over the Río Grande, form a 120km loop that passes through swathes of transitional Fuegian woodland and grassy pasture-meadows (*vegas*) populated by sheep. Along RCh you'll see cone-shaped Mount Yakush and pyramid-like Mount Atukoyak to the south before the road joins the RCf by **Lago Yehuin**, a popular fishing locale and a good place for spotting **condors**, which nest on Cerro Shenolsh between the lake and its shallow neighbour, **Lago Chepelmut**.

ACCOMMODATION

THE RCH AND RCF LOOP

Estancia Rivadavia Just off the RCh @ 02901 492186, @ estanciarivadavia.com. In a secluded location, this hospitable hotel has pleasant en-suites, a wonderfully

relaxed atmosphere, and 160 square kilometres of land across which you can go horseriding or hiking. Rates include full board. $1500

The RCa

Some 40km north of Tolhuin, the most beautiful of the central *rutas complementarias* – the **RCa** – branches east through golden pastureland towards the coast and the knobbly protrusion of **Cabo San Pablo**. A wonderful panorama stretches out from the south side of Cabo San Pablo, encompassing the wreck of the *Desdémona*, grounded during a storm in the early 1980s – at low tide, you can walk out to the ship – but the area is mainly of interest to fishermen. Beyond the cape, the road continues for 17km through wetlands and burnt-out "tree cemeteries" and past the odd beaver dam to the *Estancia Fueguina*, from where you'll need a high-clearance 4WD to progress any further.

Península Mitre

The public track eventually fizzles out at *Estancia María Luisa*, 18km further on, just beyond which run the famous fishing rivers, Irigoyen and Malengüeña. This is the beginning of the **Península Mitre**, the bleak toe of land that forms the southeastern

THE INDIGENOUS PEOPLES OF TIERRA DEL FUEGO

9

The lands at the end of the earth were home to several distinct societies before the arrival of the Europeans.

THE SELK'NAM

In 1580, Sarmiento de Gamboa became the first European to encounter the **Selk'nam**, one of the largest groups. He was impressed by these "Big People", with their powerful frames, guanaco robes and conical headgear. It wasn't long before their war-like, defiant nature became evident, though, and a bloody skirmish with a Dutch expedition in 1599 proved them to be superb fighters. Before the arrival of the Europeans, Selk'nam society revolved around the hunting of **guanaco**, which they relied on not just for meat – the skin was made into moccasins and capes, the bones were used for fashioning arrowheads and the sinews for bowstrings. Hunting was done on foot, and the Selk'nam used stealth and teamwork to encircle guanaco, bringing them down with bow and arrow, a weapon with which they were expert.

THE YÁMANA

The other sizeable group was the **Yámana** (Yaghan), a sea-going people living in the channels of the Fuegian archipelago. Their society was based on tribal groups of extended families, each of which lived for long periods aboard their equivalent of a houseboat: a canoe fashioned of *lenga* bark. Out on the ocean, work was divided between the sexes: the men hunted seals from the prow while the women – the only ones who could swim – took to the icy waters, collecting shellfish with only a layer of seal grease to protect them from the cold. When not at sea, the Yámana stayed in dwellings made of *guindo* evergreen beech branches, building conical huts in winter (to shed snow), and more aerodynamic dome-shaped ones in the summer (when strong winds blow). Favoured campsites were used over millennia, and, at these sites, **middens** of discarded shells would accumulate in the shape of a ring, since doors were constantly being shifted to face away from the wind.

THE IMPACT OF THE EUROPEAN SETTLERS

The arrival of European settlers marked the beginning of the end for both the Selk'nam and the Yámana. To protect colonists' **sheep farms in the late nineteenth century**, hundreds of miles of wire fencing were erected, which the Selk'nam, unsurprisingly, resented, seeing it as an incursion into their ancestral lands; however, they soon acquired a taste for hunting the slow animals, which they referred to as "white guanaco". For the settlers, this was an unpardonable crime, representing a drain on their investment. The Selk'nam were painted as "barbarous savages" who constituted an obstacle to settlement and progress, and isolated incidents of attack and retaliation soon escalated into bloody conflict. Reliable sources point to bounty hunters being paid on receipt of grisly invoices, such as a pair of severed ears. The assault on Selk'nam culture, too, was abrupt and devastating, led by the "civilizing" techniques of the **Salesian missions**, who "rehoused" them in their buildings. By the late 1920s there were probably no indigenous Selk'nam living as their forefathers had done and when pure-blooded Lola Kiepje and Esteban Yshton passed away in 1966 and 1969, respectively, Selk'nam culture died with them.

THE MEASLES EPIDEMIC

Meanwhile, the arrival of settlers in 1884 triggered a **measles epidemic** that killed approximately half the estimated one thousand remaining Yámana. Damp, dirty clothing – European castoffs given by well-meaning missionaries – increased the risk of disease. Missionaries promoted a shift to sedentary agriculture, but the consequent change of diet, from one high in animal fats to one more reliant on vegetables, reduced the Yámana's resistance to the cold, further increasing the likelihood of disease. Outbreaks of scrofula, pneumonia and tuberculosis meant that by 1911 fewer than one hundred Yámana remained. Abuela Rosa, the last of the Yámana to live in the manner of her ancestors, died in 1982. Nevertheless, a few Yámana descendants still live near Puerto Williams on Isla Navarino.

extremity of Tierra del Fuego. This semi-wilderness – primarily swampy moorland and thickets fringed by rugged coastal scenery – was once the territory of the indigenous Mannekenk, whose presence is attested to by old shell middens. Before the 1850s, the only white men who came ashore were sailors and scientists, such as Fitz Roy and Darwin, as well as shipwreck victims; the remains of many wrecks line the shore, including the late nineteenth-century *Duchess of Albany*, near **Bahía Policarpo**. Apart from a few gauchos, the peninsula is now effectively uninhabited, and the only way to explore the area is on guided **horseriding** excursions with Centro Hípico Ushuaia (Ruta 3, west of town; ☎02901 1556 8278, ⍟centrohipicoushuaia.com.ar), which runs trips down the Costa de los Naufragios, from *Estancia María Luisa* to *Estancia Policarpo* and back.

ACCOMMODATION
THE RCA

★ **Estancia Viamonte** Just off the RCa, 37km from the RN-3 turn-off ☎02964 430861, ⍟estanciaviamonte .com. The extremely atmospheric *Estancia Viamonte* was established against the odds by Lucas Bridges with the help of his Selk'nam friends and is still run by his descendants. It is one of the island's most historic farms and figures prominently in Bridges' epic work, *Uttermost Part of the Earth*. The three rooms are simple but thoughtfully furnished and the welcome is warm; it's a great place to gain a real insight into life on a working estancia – farm activities (and half-board) are included in the price. Closed April–Oct. **$1700**

The RCb to Chile

The scenery north of *Estancia Viamonte* (see above) undergoes an abrupt transition, from scraggly clumps of Fuegian woodland to the forlorn, bald landscape of the steppe. South of the town of Río Grande, a few kilometres before you cross the Río Grande itself, you pass the turn-off for the **RCb**, worth detouring along for 1km to see the tiny village of **Estancia José Menéndez**, whose shearing shed is emblazoned by the head of a prize ewe, its face obscured by an over-effusive wig of curls. The estancia was founded as Estancia Primera Argentina in 1896 by sheep magnate Menéndez. The most notorious of its first managers was a hard-drinking Scotsman by the name of MacLennan, who earned himself the sobriquet of "Red Pig" for taking pleasure in gunning down the Selk'nam. The RCb continues across the steppe for 70km to the Chilean frontier at **Radman**, where there's a little-used **border crossing**, known as Bella Vista (Nov–March 8am–9pm), which allows access to Lago Blanco, an excellent fishing destination, as well as providing an alternative route west to Porvenir in Chile.

Río Grande

RÍO GRANDE is a drab, sprawling city that grew up on the river of the same name as a port for José Menéndez's sheep enterprises. The treacherous tides along this stretch of the coast can reach over 15m at the spring equinox, and low tide exposes a shelf of mud flats better for sea birds than boats. The port, therefore, has virtually ceased to exist, having been superseded by the vastly superior one at Ushuaia. And in spite of the people's friendliness, the atmosphere here is as flat as the landscape: it's a place to pass through quickly, unless you're a trout fisherman, in which case it's a functional starting-point for exploring the region's fruitful rivers – the wonderful **Monumento a la Trucha**, a statue of a giant brown trout on the RN-3, leaves you in little doubt about what the town is famous for. The only sight worth visiting hereabouts is the nearby **Misión Salesiana Nuestra Señora de la Candelaria**, a mission turned agricultural school and museum.

ARRIVAL AND INFORMATION
RÍO GRANDE

By bus Buses arrive and depart from the terminal at Finocchio and Obligado, four blocks from the main avenue, San Martín.
Destinations Punta Arenas (1–2 daily; 9hr); Río Gallegos (1–2 daily; 10hr); Tolhuin (every 30min–1hr; 1hr 30min); Ushuaia (every 30min–1hr; 3hr 30min).
Tourist information The tourist office is at Plaza

Almirante Brown, Rosales 350 (Dec–March Mon–Fri 9am–8pm, Sat & Sun 2–9pm; April–Nov Mon–Fri 9am–5pm; ☎02964 431234).
Fishing information For fishing licences and information, visit the Asociación Argentina de Pesca con Mosca at Montilla 1040 (☎02964 421268).

ACCOMMODATION AND EATING

Posada de los Sauces El Cano 839 ☎02964 432895, ⓦposadadelossauces.com.ar. The city's most comfortable

option, across from the bus terminal, with reasonable en-suite rooms, a relaxed lounge bar and a decent restaurant. **$500**

Misión Salesiana Nuestra Señora de la Candelaria

Eleven kilometres north of the centre of Río Grande on the RN-3 stands the **Misión Salesiana Nuestra Señora de la Candelaria**, a collection of whitewashed buildings grouped around a modest but elegant chapel. Río Grande's first mission, it was founded in 1893 by two of Patagonia's most influential Salesian fathers, Monseñor Fagnano and Padre Beauvoir, but their first township burnt down in 1896, and was relocated to its present site. Originally, it was built with the purpose of catechizing the island's Selk'nam, but in effect it acted as part refuge and part prison, since local sheep magnates would round up the indigenous peoples on their land and pay the Salesians for their "conversion". In 1942, with virtually no Selk'nam remaining, the mission became an agricultural school, a role it has retained to this day.

Museo Monseñor Fagnano

Mon–Sat 9.30am–2.30pm & 3–7pm, Sun 3–7pm • $5 • ☎02964 430667 • Take the Línea B "Misión" bus from Av San Martín (hourly; 25min)

The **Museo Monseñor Fagnano** is in the building to the left of the chapel as you enter the compound. There's a medley of exhibits on local flora and fauna but more interesting are the homages to Don Bosco, the founder of the Salesian movement, among which you'll find some first-rate Fuegian indigenous items and a kerosene-lit projector that was used to entertain, and no doubt indoctrinate, the Selk'nam. Across the road is a fenced **cemetery** with some vandalized tombs of Salesian fathers and unmarked crosses indicating Selk'nam graves, testaments to a culture that had been completely depersonalized.

North to San Sebastián and the Chilean border

North of the Misión Salesiano rears **Cabo Domingo**, and beyond that, the unforgiving plains of Patagonian shingle begin again, dotted by shallow saline lagoons that sometimes host feeding flamingoes. The RN-3 is paved as far as the **San Sebastián border post**, 82km north of Río Grande (see opposite), on the bay of the same name. The Bahía San Sebastián itself is famous for its summer populations of migratory waders and shore birds and is a vital part of the **Hemisphere Reserve for Shorebirds**, designed to protect migratory birds along the coasts and interior wetlands of the Americas. Oil companies operate in the area, and access is therefore restricted, but there are some birdwatching spots on the mud flats at Río Grande.

TO CHILE AND PATAGONIA

If you're planning on heading north into Patagonia via land, you'll need to cross first into Chilean Tierra del Fuego and then across the **Magellan Straits** that separate Isla Grande from Patagonia. The main land **border crossing** between the Chilean and Argentine halves of the island is at **San Sebastián**, in the north of the island. The respective customs posts (April–Oct 7am–1am; Nov–March 24hr) are several hundred metres apart, 15km west of the Argentine village of the same name. Formalities are straightforward, if somewhat lengthy at times. There is also a smaller border post at Bella Vista. You may not take any fresh fruit, meat or dairy products into Chile, and Argentine officers sometimes reciprocate. Once in Chile, you can either continue to the town of Porvenir, where a long (2hr) and irregular crossing connects direct with Punta Arenas, or head to Bahía Azul, where there is a shorter (30min) and much more frequent crossing to Punta Delgada, although these ferries can't operate at low tide and involve a longer drive afterwards if you're planning to head further into Chilean Patagonia. Buses depart most days from Ushuaia (see p.505) or Río Grande (see opposite) to Punta Arenas and elsewhere in Patagonia.

EVA PERÓN'S TOMB, BUENOS AIRES

Contexts

History

Argentina's past might best be summed up as "chequered". The modern nation is essentially a product of Spanish colonialism initiated in the sixteenth century and immigration from all corners of Europe and the Middle East during the late nineteenth and early twentieth centuries. Relatively little of its pre-Columbian civilizations has survived, other than archeological finds, though there is more of an indigenous influence on present-day Argentine culture than initially meets the eye, especially in the north. After independence in 1810, Argentina repeatedly took one step forward to progressive democracy and two steps back into corrupt lawlessness.

Twentieth-century Argentina produced its fair share of international icons – with Evita and Che Guevara leading the way, followed closely by Maradona (and, in the twenty-first century, Messi) – and was often in the news for the wrong reasons. The country experienced a series of military dictatorships, including that of the late 1970s, whose widespread campaign of state-sponsored terror came to be known as the Dirty War. That regime eventually collapsed in 1983, after the Falklands/Malvinas fiasco. Argentina again hit the international headlines in a negative light when social unrest and economic recession lurched into chaos in late 2001. In 2003, Néstor Kirchner became president, overseeing an economic recovery and a period of relative calm. Four years later, his wife, Cristina Fernández de Kirchner, became the country's first woman to be elected head of state – and was re-elected in 2011.

Pre-Columbian Argentina

The earliest records for human presence in the territory that is now Argentina can be dated back to around 10,000 BC. Over the millennia that preceded the arrival of Europeans, widely varying cultures developed. From around 4000 BC, distinct nomadic cultures like that of the **Yámana** (see box, p.521) emerged in the Tierra del Fuego archipelago. Other groups, such as the **Guaraní** peoples of the subtropical northeast, evolved seminomadic lifestyles dependent on hunter-gathering and slash-and-burn agriculture.

The most complex cultures emerged, however, in the **Andean northwest**, where sedentary agricultural practices developed from about 500 BC. Irrigation permitted the intensive cultivation of crops like maize, quinoa, squash and potatoes and this, combined with the domestication of animals like the llama, facilitated the growth of rich material cultures. The most important early sedentary culture was the **Tafí**, whose people sculpted intriguing stone menhirs, which can be seen near Tafí del Valle, Tucumán Province. Later, this period saw the development of Catamarca's **Condorhuasi** culture, renowned for its distinctive, beautifully patterned ceramics. From about 600 AD, metallurgical technologies developed, and bronze was used for items such as ceremonial axes and chest-plates, perhaps best by the **Aguada** civilization, also centred

c.10,000 BC	c.4000 BC	c.500 BC
The earliest recorded human presence in the territory that is now Argentina.	Nomadic and seminomadic cultures appear in the extreme north and south.	The first sedentary peoples leave their mark in the Northwest of present-day Argentina.

on Catamarca. The increasing organization of Andean groups after 850 AD is demonstrated by the appearance of fortified urban settlements. Three important **Diaguita** cultures emerge: Sanagasta, Belén and **Santa María**, whose overlapping zones of influence stretched from Salta to San Juan, and which are notable for their painted ceramics, anthropomorphic funeral urns and superb metalwork.

Tiahuanaco and Inca empires

Trade networks expanded vastly once the area came under the sway of pan-Andean empires: first that of Bolivia's great city, **Tiahuanaco**, which probably influenced Condorhuasi culture; and, from 1480, that of the **Inca**, who incorporated the area into Kollasuyo, their southernmost administrative region. Incredibly well-preserved finds, such as **three ritually sacrificed mummies** at the summit of 6739m Cerro Llullaillaco – the world's highest archeological discovery (see p.282) – have revealed the extent of this influence in terms of customs, religion and dress.

Tribal groups on the eve of the European arrival

According to estimates, in the early sixteenth century Argentina's **indigenous population** was around half a million, two-thirds of whom lived in the Northwest. The central sierras of Córdoba and San Luís were inhabited by the **Comechingones** and Sanavirones. The Cuyo region was home to semi-sedentary Huarpe, while south and east of them lived various Tehuelche tribes (see p.446), often referred to generically by the Spanish as Pampas Indians or, further south, Patagones ("big feet") – giving rise to the name Patagonia. Tierra del Fuego was sparsely inhabited by Selk'nam, Mannekenk and the Yámana (see p.521). The Gran Chaco region was home to the nomadic Chiriguano, Lule-Vilela, **Wichí**, Abipone and Qom, while the northeastern areas were inhabited by Kaingang, Charrúa and Guaraní.

The first group to encounter the Spanish, however, were probably the nomadic **Querandí** of the Pampas. They lived in temporary shelters and hunted guanaco and rhea with *boleadores* (lassos with heavy balls attached). Though they put up determined resistance to the Spanish for several decades, their culture was eliminated during the subsequent colonial period – a fate shared by many others.

Early Spanish settlement

In 1516, Juan Díaz de Solís, a Portuguese mariner in the employ of the Spanish Crown, led a small crew to the shores of the River Plate in search of a trade route to the Far East. He was killed by the Querandí, or possibly the Charrúa, who inhabited what is now Uruguay. Another brief exploration of the region was made in 1520 by **Ferdinand Magellan**, who continued his epic voyage south to discover the famous straits that now bear his name, and the next significant expedition to this part of the world was made by an explorer of Italian descent, **Sebastian Cabot** (see box opposite).

The first foundation of Buenos Aires

In 1535, Pedro de Mendoza was authorized by the Spanish Crown to colonize the River Plate to pre-empt Portuguese conquest. In February 1536, he founded Buenos Aires, naming it Ciudad de la Santísima Trinidad y Puerto de Santa María de los

600–850 AD	**c. 1500 AD**
Andean groups begin to produce ceramics and other crafts, whose remains grace the nation's many museums.	The Northwest comes under the sway of the great Tiahuanaco and Inca empires and is incorporated into the latter.

CABOT – ARGENTINA'S UNWITTING BAPTIZER

Explorer **Sebastian Cabot** reached the River Plate in 1526 and built a small, short-lived fort near modern Rosario. He misleadingly christened the river the Río de la Plata ("River of Silver"), after finding bullion and believing there to be deposits nearby. Ironically, the metal had probably been brought here by a Portuguese adventurer, Aleixo García. In 1524, García had reached the eastern fringes of the Inca empire, but was killed with his Andean booty on his return journey.

Cabot's silver had its most lasting legacy in the word "Argentina" itself, which derives from the metal's Latin name, **argentum**. Its first recorded use was in a Venetian atlas of the New World produced in the middle of the sixteenth century. Martín del Barco Centenera, a member of a later expedition, published an epic poem in 1602 called *La Argentina*. The name also appeared in Ruy Díaz de Guzmán's 1612 book *Historia del descubrimiento, población y conquista del Río de la Plata* (History of the discovery, population and conquest of the River Plate), where he referred to the territory as Tierra Argentina, or "Land of Silver". However, "Argentina" was not adopted as the name of the Republic until the middle of the nineteenth century.

Buenos Ayres, after the sailors' favourite saint, the provider of fair winds. However his plans soon went awry, as it proved impossible to subjugate the Querandí. Mendoza was forced to send Pedro de Ayolas upstream to find a more suitable site for settlement, and in August 1537, Ayolas founded **Nuestra Señora de la Asunción del Paraguay** (Asunción). Mendoza died at sea on the way back to Spain, and authority for the colony devolved to Domingo de Irala, who ordered the evacuation of Buenos Aires in 1541. Spanish interest in colonizing this area of the world had decreased significantly after **Pizarro**'s conquest, in 1535, of Perú.

The creation of the Viceroyalty of Perú

In 1543, the new Viceroyalty of Perú, with its capital at Lima, was given authority over all of southern Spanish America. The northwest region of Argentina was first tentatively explored in the mid-1530s, but the impulse for colonizing the area came with the discovery, in 1545, of enormous **silver deposits** in **Potosí**, Alto Perú (modern-day Bolivia). This led to the establishment of the **Governorship of Tucumán**, covering a territory embracing most of today's Northwest. Conquistadors crossed the Andes to press the locals into labour and find overland routes to the Potosí mines. Francisco de Aguirre founded Santiago del Estero, Argentina's earliest continually inhabited town, on St James' Day 1553, while other settlements were established at Mendoza (1561), San Juan (1562), Córdoba (1573), Salta (1582), La Rioja (1591) and San Salvador de Jujuy (1593).

Meanwhile, the Spanish in Asunción sent an expedition under the command of Juan de Garay down the River Paraná, founding Santa Fe in 1573 and **resettling Buenos Aires** in 1580 – this time, for good. Settlers benefited from one vital legacy of the Mendoza settlement – the feral **horses and cattle** that had multiplied in the area. Few then realized the significance these animals would have on most of Argentina's future.

Colonial developments

Buenos Aires and its environs were largely overlooked by the Spanish Crown until the late eighteenth century. Direct trade with Spain from the River Plate was prohibited

1516	**1526**	**1536**
Portuguese sailor Solís discovers the River Plate before being killed by the native inhabitants.	Venetian navigator Cabot finds silver treasures on its shores, giving the River Plate its name.	The city of Buenos Aires is established by Pedro de Mendoza, but is not settled for four decades.

from 1554, and all imported and exported goods traded via Lima, which restricted growth of the port, but encouraged **contraband** imports. The potential of the Governorship of the River Plate was limited: there was no market in preindustrial Europe for agricultural produce, and the indigenous populations could not easily be yoked into the **encomienda** system of forced labour. It was the Society of Jesus – the Jesuits – who effectively pioneered Spanish colonization of this region (see box, p.190).

The economies of Buenos Aires, Santa Fe, Entre Ríos and Corrientes engendered strife with the native peoples. Mounted raids by indigenous tribes from the Gran Chaco, such as the Abipone, terrorized the northeastern provinces well into the eighteenth century, and Buenos Aires, dependent on its Wild West-style round-ups of wild cattle (*vaquerías*) for its **hide and tallow industries**, frequently came into conflict with groups of Tehuelche and, increasingly from the eighteenth century, Mapuche (Araucanians). These peoples relied on the same feral cattle and horses, driving vast herds of them to the northern Patagonian Andes for the purpose of trading with white settlers and other indigenous groups in present-day Chile. This period also saw the emergence and apogee of **gauchos**, nomadic horsemen, often of *mestizo* origins, who roamed in small bands and lived off the wild herds of livestock.

The Viceroyalty of the River Plate

By the late eighteenth century, the British controlled the Caribbean and were blocking the Lima sea routes, so the establishment of another route to Potosí became vital. Owing to the obstacle that was Brazil, the River Plate seemed the logical choice, and the growing value of Buenos Aires as a market and strategic post gained the recognition of the Spanish Crown, which, in 1776, made it the capital of the new **Viceroyalty of the River Plate**, whose jurisdiction included Alto Perú (modern Bolivia), Paraguay and the Governorship of Montevideo. Commercial restrictions were gradually loosened, and trade permitted with ports in Spain and Spanish America, but the Crown still clung to its monopoly on colonial commerce, prohibiting the sale of silver to foreign powers.

SLAVERY IN THE NEW COLONY

More important than the River Plate in the seventeenth and eighteenth centuries was the Governorship of Tucumán. The *encomienda* system of institutionalized slavery was more effective here and, to a lesser extent, in the Sierra de Córdoba, as the lands were more densely settled. Though some trade from this area was directed towards Buenos Aires, the local economy was run so as to provide the Potosí mine with mules, sugar, cotton textiles and wheat. Indigenous resistance to the colonizers erupted on occasion, as with the Diaguita rebellion of 1657, which was actually led by a Spanish rebel, Pedro Bohórquez. The rebellion was brutally crushed in 1659 and survivors were displaced from their ravaged communities and forcibly resettled as workers on haciendas. By the second half of the eighteenth century, demand for labour from both Potosí and the towns of Tucumán was so great that it led to the importation of **black slave labour**. It is estimated that by 1778 one in ten of Tucumán's regional population was a slave, while well over a quarter were of pure indigenous blood. Racial divisions were strongly demarcated, and the rights of whites to control land and political offices were reinforced by a dress code and a weapons ban for the non-white castes.

1553	1659	1776
Santiago del Estero – Argentina's second oldest city – is founded on July 25.	The Diaguita uprisings are quashed, presaging future moves to eradicate the region's indigenous peoples.	The Spanish create the Viceroyalty of the River Plate – corresponding to much of northern Argentina.

THE BRITISH INVASIONS

In **June 1806**, a force of 1600 men led by **General William Beresford** stormed into Buenos Aires hoping to assert British imperial control over the entire Viceroyalty. The Viceroy, the **Marqués de Sobremonte**, fled the city, and the remaining Spanish authorities grudgingly swore allegiance to the British Crown. Among the ordinary inhabitants, though, there was a sense of offended honour at the way such a tiny force had been allowed to overrun the city's defences.

The locals regrouped under a new commander-in-chief, the French-born **Santiago Liniers**, and ousted their invaders during the **Reconquista** of August 12. Undaunted, the British captured Montevideo, from where they launched a second assault on a better-prepared Buenos Aires in July 1807. This battle led to the surrender of the British and came to be known as **La Defensa**, a name imbued with the bravura of Liniers' hastily assembled militia, whose cannon- and musket-fire peppered the enemy, while women poured boiling oil from the tops of the city's buildings onto the hapless British soldiers.

Tensions between **monopolist traders** and advocates of **free trade** were becoming entrenched. The European wars of the late eighteenth century forced the Crown to loosen control and, in 1797, allowed its colonies to trade with neutral countries. To the dismay of monopolists, cheap European manufactures flowed freely into Buenos Aires courtesy of contraband merchants. Monopolists trading on the traditional Cádiz route suffered, and exports to Spain plummeted. It proved difficult to reinstate restrictions and attempts to do so caused anger among merchants, such as **Manuel Belgrano**, who argued for free trade with all nations, but not rebellion against the Crown. Although news of the French Revolution and the American Declaration of Independence circulated among Buenos Aires' elite, there was no significant revolutionary feeling against Spain. The **British**, however, caught wind of the commercial tensions in Buenos Aires, and, mistakenly interpreting them as revolutionary, **invaded** the city in 1806 (see box above).

Other changes in the economy of Buenos Aires became increasingly apparent during the Viceroyalty. Rich merchants (*comerciantes*) helped finance the growth of **estancias** (ranches) in the province, a shift away from the earlier practice of *vaquerías*. By the end of the eighteenth century, these estancias had become highly profitable enterprises.

The May revolution and independence

The victory over the British showed the people of Buenos Aires that they could manage their own affairs and not rely on the viceregal authorities. They had been united against a foreign invader and the feeling of pride carried over into defiance against the monarchy.

In 1808, **Napoleon Bonaparte's troops** invaded the Iberian Peninsula. Napoleon forced the rival Spanish Bourbon kings – Carlos IV and his son, Ferdinand VII – to **abdicate**, and installed his own brother, Joseph Bonaparte, on the throne. This had massive repercussions in the Latin American colonies, ushering in two decades of upheaval. A new viceroy, **Viscount Balthasar de Cisneros** – appointed by a Spanish junta in Seville loyal to Ferdinand – was unable to curb tensions between Spanish and *criollo* (creole) elites, and parallel tensions between various trading interests. The authority of Cisneros was fatally undermined, when news came through of the fall of Seville to French troops.

1778	1797
José de San Martín, the country's future liberator, is born in Yapeyú, now Corrientes Province.	The Spanish Crown relaxes trade restrictions in the Viceroyalty, leading to a sharp rise in smuggling.

The Primera Junta

On May 25, 1810, supporters of self-government gathered in front of the Cabildo in Buenos Aires, allegedly sporting sky-blue and white ribbons, the colours of the future **Argentine flag**. Inside, Cisneros was ousted and the **Primera Junta** sworn in. However, deposition of the viceroy and the establishment of self-government did not necessarily mean advocating republicanism. The new authority continued to proclaim loyalty to the deposed Ferdinand VII, although in reality this was a convenient fudge designed to win over conservatives.

The Primera Junta was headed by **Cornelio Saavedra**, who believed in sharing power with the provinces. Other members of the Junta, including Belgrano and **Mariano Moreno**, were avowed free-trade enthusiasts, intent on bringing the rest of the territory under the central control of Buenos Aires. Moreno's views came to represent what was

---

JOSÉ DE SAN MARTÍN

National hero **José de San Martín** is as ubiquitous as George Washington in the US, and has countless villages, barrios, streets, plazas, public buildings and even a mountain named after him, as well as innumerable statues in his honour. He's often simply referred to as **El Libertador** (The Liberator) and is treated with saint-like reverence. Yet he didn't even take part in the country's initial liberation from Spain, helped to free traditional rival Chile and spent the last 23 years of his life in self-imposed exile in France. This last fact is celebrated with streets and barrios named after **Boulogne-sur-Mer**, the town where he died on August 17, 1850. A slightly larger-than-original replica of his Parisian mansion, Grand Bourg, built on the edge of leafy Palermo Chico, is now the Instituto Sanmartiniano, a library-cum-study-centre.

San Martín was born in 1778 in Yapeyú, Corrientes Province. He was sent to military school in Spain and later served in the royal army, taking part in the Spanish victories against Napoleon. He returned to his homeland soon afterwards, and assisted in training the rag-bag army that was trying to resist Spain's attempt to cling onto its South American empire. After replacing Manuel Belgrano as leader of the independence forces in 1813, he became increasingly active in politics, as a conservative, and attended the Tucumán Congress in 1816. He formed his own army, known as the **Ejército de los Andes**, basing himself in Mendoza. From there he crossed the Andes and obliterated royalist troops at Chacabuco, **freeing Chile** from the imperialist yoke – though his comrade-in-arms Bernardo O'Higgins got most of the credit – finally mopping up the remaining royalist resistance at Maipú in 1818, before moving on to Lima.

San Martín was not at all interested in political power, but was in favour of setting up a constitutional monarchy in the emerging South American states. In 1821, he signed the Punchanca agreement with the viceroy of Perú to put a member of the Spanish royal family on the throne, but when the royalists did not respond, he declared Perú's independence on July 12, 1821. Unable to hold the country together in the face of royalist resistance, he called upon **Simón Bolívar**, the liberator of Venezuela, to come to his assistance. The only meeting between the two occurred in Guayaquil, Ecuador, in 1822. Bolívar's radical ideals clashed with San Martín's conservative mindset and San Martín opted to withdraw from Perú. Frustrated by a nascent Argentina that was a patchwork of disunited provinces led by brutish *caudillos*, San Martín took off to Europe, ending his days in **France**, slipping into obscurity; all this changed after his death, however, and the national hero's remains were repatriated later that century. He now lies buried in Buenos Aires' Metropolitan Cathedral, where his tomb is a national monument (see p.67). His death is commemorated annually with a national holiday on or around August 17.

1806–07	**1810**
British troops attempt invasions of the Viceroyalty two years running – but fail miserably both times.	Anti-colonial leaders form a government, known as the Primera Junta, on May 25.

to be the position of the **Unitarists** (or **Azules** – "Blues") who favoured centralism, while Saavedra's contained the first seeds of the ideas of **Federalists** (the **Colorados** – "Reds"), promoting the autonomy of the provinces within the framework of a confederation. This dispute was to dominate nineteenth-century Argentine politics, causing bitter division and **civil war**. While the Junta's internal disputes prevented unity in Buenos Aires, the May Revolution also failed to mark a clean break from the motherland. Royalists under the leadership of Martín de Alzaga continued to press for the return of a viceroyalty.

As Unitarist and Federalist interests continued to battle for control of the capital, clashes between pro-royalist forces and pro-independence forces flared up across the old viceroyalty. After 1810, in the interior these struggles saw the emergence of Federalist **caudillos**, powerful local warlords. They recruited – or press-ganged – militias from among the slaves, indigenous peoples and gauchos of the countryside. Back in Buenos Aires, the royalist factions were effectively crushed by 1812, and a *criollo* front led by **José de San Martín** (see box opposite), the Sociedad Patriótica, sought full emancipation from foreign powers.

Declaration of Independence

Two congresses were convened to discuss the future of the former viceroyalty, but these were dominated by Unitarists and failed to produce a cohesive plan for the country. However, at the second, held on **July 9, 1816**, in the city of Tucumán, the independence of the **United Provinces of the River Plate** was formally declared, a title first adopted in Buenos Aires in 1813. The date, July 9, has since come to be recognized as Argentina's official **Independence Day**.

Later that year, San Martín led five thousand men across the Andes to attack the Spanish in Chile, in one of the defining moments of Latin America's struggle against its colonial rulers. During this time, he was assisted in the north by another hero of Argentine independence, **Martín Miguel de Güemes**, an anti-royalist, Federalist *caudillo* whose gaucho army eventually liberated Salta. Though *caudillos* such as Güemes were in favour of independence, many resented the heavy taxes imposed to fund the struggle for autonomy, and tensions remained high.

Caudillismo and civil war

The 1820s began with infighting among *caudillo* groups but, in 1826, **Bernardino Rivadavia**, a Unitarist admirer of European ideals and bitter rival of San Martín, became the first outright president of what was then called the United Provinces of South America. He proposed a new constitution, which was rejected by the provinces, who objected to the call for dissolution of their militias and the concession of land to the national government. At the same time, conflict with Brazil over Uruguay led to a blockade of the River Plate and caused a financial crisis. These two issues brought Rivadavia's presidency to its knees by 1827. The bitter Unitarist/Federalist fighting that ensued only ceased when a *caudillo* from Buenos Aires, **General Juan Manuel de Rosas**, emerged victorious (see box, p.532). In 1829, he became governor of Buenos Aires, with power over the newly titled Confederation of the River Plate, or Argentine Confederation.

1816	**1826**
In the city of San Miguel de Tucumán, independence from Spain is officially declared on July 9.	Rivadavia becomes the first President of the United Provinces of South America – after six years of political squabbling.

ROSAS – THE "CALIGULA OF THE RIVER PLATE"

General Juan Manuel de Rosas, one of the most influential figures of Argentine history, was born into an influential cattle-ranching family, and was respected by his gauchos for his riding skills and personal bravery. He was an avowed Federalist, but his particular brand of Federalism had more to do with opposing intellectual Unitarism, with its gravitation towards foreign, European influence, than it did in respecting provincial autonomy per se. As it turned out, his platform was more about centralizing power in his own province, Buenos Aires.

He left office at the end of his term in 1832 but returned as dictator in 1835 as the country teetered on the brink of fresh civil war after the assassination of an ally of his, the *caudillo* of La Rioja, **Juan "Facundo" Quiroga**. For seventeen years Rosas ruthlessly consolidated power using the army and his own brutal police force, the **Mazorca**. The Mazorca used a network of spies and assassins to keep resistance in check. During this time, many opponents and intellectuals fled to Uruguay and Europe.

Rosas sought to improve his network of **patronage** through the expansion of territories available for farming in the Pampas. His **Desert Campaign** of 1833 against the indigenous peoples was the precursor to Roca's genocidal Conquest of the Desert of the late 1870s (see opposite). The vast landholdings that Rosas dealt out to "conquerors" ensured he retained powerful allies.

However, Rosas managed to alienate many of the interior provinces by not permitting free trade along the Paraná, by increasing taxes on provincial trade and by allowing the import of cheap foreign produce, such as French wine, into Buenos Aires. Rosas' bloody regime was brought to an end in 1852, at the Battle of Caseros. Defeat came at the hands of a one-time ally, the powerful *caudillo* governor of Entre Ríos, **Justo José de Urquiza**, who was backed by a coalition of interests who desired free trade on the Paraná, including the Brazilians, British and French. After defeat, Rosas left for England to become a farmer in Southampton, where he died in 1877.

The establishment of the Argentine Republic

The three decades that followed the defeat of Rosas in 1852 saw the foundations laid for the **modern Argentine state**. Economic expansion and the triumph of progressive Unitarism ensured the conditions for the boom that followed. Buenos Aires emerged from its struggles with the provinces and territorial conquest began in earnest, resulting in the subjugation of the south. Urquiza's attempt to establish a constitution sympathetic to Federalist interests foundered when Buenos Aires refused to renounce its privileged trading terms. Its rejection of the **1853 constitution** led to the de facto creation of two republics: one in Buenos Aires and the other, the Argentine Confederation, centred on Entre Ríos and headed by Urquiza himself.

The deadlock ended only in 1861, when the powerful governor of Buenos Aires, **Bartolomé Mitre**, defeated Urquiza. The 1853 constitution was then ratified nationwide, with significant amendments to please Buenos Aires, and the basic structure of Argentine government was set. In 1862, Mitre was elected the first president of the new **Argentine Republic**. Trade restrictions were lifted throughout the country while colonization of the interior was promoted, one result of which was the small Welsh settlements in Patagonia (see box, p.456).

Mitre aimed for rapid **modernization** of the country, focusing particularly on the capital. His achievements included the creation of a national army and postal system, and the expansion of the fledgling **railway network**. These initiatives were financed by foreign

1829	**1833**
Federalist *caudillo* Rosas, with his power-base in Buenos Aires, triggers lengthy civil wars.	Rosas undertakes his Desert Campaign, with the aim of ridding the Pampas of non-European inhabitants.

investment from Britain, which contributed the capital to build railways, and by greater export earnings – the result, particularly, of the important expanding trade in **wool**.

Sarmiento and Europeanization

A significant event of Mitre's presidency was the start of the War of the Triple Alliance (see box below), the end of which overlapped with the presidency (1868–74) of **Domingo Sarmiento**, the man most identified with the drive to "Europeanize" Argentina in the nineteenth century. Sarmiento was an avid opponent of *caudillismo* and famous for pillorying the likes of Rosas. He believed that they represented a "barbaric" era in Argentine history, and that their legacy impeded the country from adopting contemporary North American and European notions of progress and civilization. These theories of progress impacted heavily on the remaining indigenous populations of Argentina, as they sponsored those who believed in "civilizing the Indian", and helped underpin the doctrine of the so-called "Generation of the Eighties" (the 1880s) who subscribed to imposing the nation-state by force – its leaders included Julio Roca (see below) and Nicolás Avellaneda. Sarmiento is also remembered for his highly ambitious **education policy** and for encouraging European immigration on a grand scale.

The Conquest of the Desert

With the near disappearance of wild herds of livestock and the movement of settlers into the Pampas, Mapuche and Tehuelche groups found it increasingly difficult to maintain their way of life. Indigenous raids – called **malones** – on estancias and white settlements became more frequent, and debate raged in the 1870s as to how to solve the "Indian Problem". Two main positions crystallized. The one propounded by Minister of War **Alsina** consisted of containment, and aimed at a gradual integration of the indigenous tribes. The second, propounded by his successor, **General Julio Roca**, advocated uncompromising conquest and subjugation – Argentina could then concentrate on territorial expansion to the south, where it was believed the future of the nation lay.

Roca led an army south in 1879, and his brutal **Conquest of the Desert** was effectively over by the following year, leaving over 1300 indigenous dead and the whole of Patagonia open to settlement. Roca swept to victory in the 1880 presidential election on the back of his success. He believed strongly in a highly centralized government and consolidated his power base by using the vast new tracts of land as a system of patronage. With the southern frontier secure, he could, from the mid-1880s, back

---

THE WAR OF THE TRIPLE ALLIANCE

Starting during Mitre's presidency, the **War of the Triple Alliance** (1865–70) was a conflict that had its origins in the expansionist ambitions of Paraguay's dictators and disputes over navigation rights on the Paraná and River Plate. In it, Argentina allied with Uruguay and Brazil to defeat Paraguay, though much of the fighting, some of it farcical yet brutal, was left to the Brazilians, whose military ineptitude resulted in a prolonged campaign, during which most of the male population of Paraguay was decimated. By defeating its neighbour, Argentina secured control of the upper Paraná river and the territory (now Province) of Misiones.

1850	**1852**
General San Martín, hero of the wars of independence, dies in exile in Boulogne-sur-Mer, France, on August 17.	Rosas is defeated at the Battle of Caseros by Entre Ríos *caudillo* Urquiza and flees to England.

campaigns to defeat indigenous groups in the **Gran Chaco**, and thus stabilize the country's northern frontier with Paraguay.

Times of socioeconomic change

Agriculture and infrastructure continued to expand, benefiting from massive British investment. The first **railway** had been built in 1854, connecting Buenos Aires to the farms and estancias in its vicinity. In 1880, the railway network carried over three million passengers and over one million tonnes of cargo, and by 1890 nearly 10,000km of track had been built across the country. **Wool production** became such a strong sector of the economy in the second half of the nineteenth century that sheep outnumbered people, thirty to one. The rise in the number of sheep farms – small, privately owned or rented family concerns – saw the growth of a strong middle class in the provinces. Also transforming the countryside was the boom in **export crops** such as wheat, oats and linseed. Another development of importance had been the invention of **refrigerator ships** in 1876, which enabled Argentina to start exporting meat to the urban centres of Britain and Europe. In Buenos Aires and other areas, the age of **latifundismo** had begun as huge tracts of land were bought up by Argentine speculators hoping to profit by their sale to railway companies. In the interim period they were rented out to sheep farmers and sharecroppers.

The age of Radicalism

At the turn of the nineteenth century, pressure for political change was increasing. Power still rested in the hands of the landed and urban elite, a tiny minority, leaving the rapidly expanding urban professional and working classes unrepresented; electoral fraud was rife. From 1891, a new more progressive party, the **Radical Civic Union** (Unión Cívica Radical

---

A LAND OF IMMIGRATION

At the same time as Argentina was expanding its trade and improving its infrastructure, European immigration began to rocket. Significant numbers of French people had already arrived in the 1850s and 60s, followed later by isolated groups of Italians, Swiss and Germans driven by poverty and an enterprising spirit. Many came in search of land but often settled for work as sharecroppers in estancias or as lowly shepherds, labourers and artisans. Between 1880 and World War I, another six million **immigrants** came to Argentina. Half of these were Italians (mostly from the north) and a quarter Spaniards, while other groups included French, Portuguese, Russians, Ottoman subjects (mostly Syrians and Lebanese), Irish and Welsh. In 1895, immigrants represented nearly a third of the population of Buenos Aires city, which grew from 90,000 in 1869 to 670,000. This convulsive influx caused occasional resentment, particularly during periods of economic depression, which were usually sparked by events abroad. Growth depended largely on foreign investment and the country was susceptible to slumps like the one that affected Britain in the 1870s, prompting occasional debate about **protectionism** and tighter border controls. Immigrant participation in politics was not encouraged, and few took up Argentine citizenship on arrival, because citizens were obliged to perform military service. Generally, though, immigrants were welcomed as part of the drive towards economic expansion and colonization of the countryside.

1853	1854	1862
A new Constitution effectively creates an Argentine Republic for the first time.	The country's first railway links the capital to its agricultural hinterland.	Bartolomé Mitre (who founded *La Nación* in 1870) becomes President of the Republic.

THE CENTENARY CELEBRATIONS

In 1910, the **centenary anniversary** was cause for great celebration. In its first hundred years Argentina had gone from being a fairly small colonial backwater to one of the world's richest countries, still in the throes of an unprecedented immigration and building boom, bursting with confidence, and destined for great things on the world stage. Several foreign nations gifted statues and other monuments, many of which are still standing in Buenos Aires, including the Torre Monumental (Britain; see p.88) and the Monumento de los Españoles (Spain; see p.101).

or UCR), agitated for reform but was excluded from power. A sea change came with the introduction of **universal manhood suffrage** and secret balloting in 1912 by reformist conservative president, Roque Sáenz Peña, giving into Radical pressure. Four years later, this allowed the victory of the first Radical president, **Hipólito Yrigoyen**, ushering in thirteen unbroken years of Radicalism, under him and his associate, **Marcelo T. de Alvear**.

Turbulent labour relations

After World War I, economic growth picked up again, with the expansion of manufacturing industries, but its benefits were far from equally distributed. Confrontations between police and strikers in Buenos Aires led to numerous deaths in the **Semana Trágica** – or Tragic Week – of 1919. This was followed by the 1920–21 **workers' strikes** in southern Patagonia. Most strikers were immigrant *peón* farmhands from the impoverished Chilean island of Chiloe but there were also a few labour activists, Bolsheviks and anarchists. A first strike in 1920 was sparked by the fact that *peones* (estancia employees) had been unable to cash in or exchange the tokens with which they were paid by sheep barons. The protest expanded to include a raft of other grievances concerning working rights and conditions, and more extreme factions latched onto what was, at root, a fairly conservative phenomenon. Shaken, estancia owners promised to arrange payment, but when this was not forthcoming, a second strike was unleashed, this time releasing more in the way of pent-up anger and frustration. Incidents of **violent lawlessness** were used by opponents of the strike to panic the authorities, now better prepared, into **brutal repression**. The final tragedy came with the massacre in cold blood of 121 men by an army battalion at Estancia Anita. In response, the Radicals introduced social security and pro-labour reforms.

Before and after the Crash

By 1925, Argentina was one of the world's richest nations and confidence was sky-high. Britain remained the country's major investor and market – as revealed in a confidential report by Sir Malcolm Robertson, ambassador to Argentina, in 1929: "Argentina must be regarded as an essential part of the British Empire. We cannot get on without her, nor she without us." This was a nation predicted to rival the United States in economic power. Within two or three decades, however, Argentina had fallen to the status of a Third World state. The loss of this golden dream of prosperity has haunted and perplexed the Argentine conscience ever since. The decline in status was not constant, but the **world depression** that followed the Wall Street Crash of 1929 marked one of the first serious blows. The effects of the crash and the collapse of export markets left the Radical regime reeling and precipitated a **military takeover** in 1930 – an inauspicious

1865–70	1879	1880s
The War of the Triple Alliance is fought, together with Brazil and Uruguay, against the despots of Paraguay, with huge loss of life.	General Julio Roca undertakes his short-lived but brutal Conquest of the Desert.	The first waves of full-scale European immigration arrive on Argentine shores.

omen of events later in the century. The military restored power to the oligarchic elite, who ruled through a succession of coalition governments that gained a reputation for fraud and electoral corruption. By the late 1930s, the value of manufactured goods overtook that of agriculture for the first time. Immigration continued apace, with one important group being Jews fleeing persecution in Germany.

The rise and fall of Perón

One of the major political developments of twentieth-century Argentina was the rise of **Juan Domingo Perón** (1895–1974), a charismatic military man of relatively modest origins who had risen through the ranks during the 1930s to the status of colonel. The outbreak of **World War II** had repercussions in Argentina, severely affecting its international trade. It stayed neutral for most of the war, as a split developed in the armed forces, with one faction favouring the Allies and a larger one, the Axis powers, admired mainly for their military prowess.

Perón's involvement with politics intensified after a **military coup** in 1943, in which the army replaced a weak conservative coalition led by Ramón Castillo, whose government had been elected amid allegations of fraud and had come to be seen as self-serving; moreover, it had been veering towards a declaration of support for the Allies. Perón was appointed Secretary for Labour and used this minor post as a platform to cultivate links with trade unions. His popularity alarmed his military superiors, who arrested him in 1945. However, Perón's second wife, Eva Duarte or **Evita** (see box, p.538), helped to organize mass demonstrations that secured his release, generating the momentum that swept him to the **presidency** in the 1946 elections. His first term in government signalled a programme of radical social and political change, but his philosophy of government, which came to be known as Peronism, defies easy definition (see box below).

DEFINING PERONISM

Perón's brand of fierce **nationalism**, combined with an authoritarian cult of the leader, bore many of the hallmarks of Fascism. Nevertheless, he assumed power by overwhelming democratic vote, and was seen by the poor as a saviour. Perón's scheme involved a type of "corporatism" that offered genuine improvements to the lives of the workers while making it easier to control them for the smooth running of the capitalist system. Perón saw strong **state intervention** as a way of melding the interests of labour and capital, and propounded the doctrine of **justicialismo**, or social justice, better known as **Peronism**. His administration passed a comprehensive programme of social welfare legislation that, among other things, granted workers a minimum wage, paid holidays (often at specially built hotels) and pension schemes, and established house-building programmes.

Perón also supported nationalization and **industrialization**, in an attempt to render Argentina less dependent on foreign capital. One of the most significant acts of his administration was, in 1947, to nationalize the country's railway system, compensating its British owners to the tune of £150 million. In so doing, he also capitalized on popular anti-British sentiment, which had been fostered over preceding generations during a period of disproportionate commercial influence wielded by the tiny class of British farming and industrial oligarchs. Nevertheless, some believe that he paid over the odds for outdated stock.

1891	**1895**	**1912**
The Unión Cívica Radical (Radical Civic Union), or Radical Party, is founded.	Nearly 250,000 immigrants are living in Buenos Aires, one third of the population.	Universal suffrage (for men only) is made law, ushering in several Radical governments.

Authoritarian rule

Controversy surrounds many aspects of Perón's regime. Dissident opinion had no place in his scheme: these years were marked by a **suppression of the press**, increasingly heavy-handed control over institutions of higher education and the use of violent intimidation. Though it is unclear to what extent he was personally involved, Perón's apparent willingness to provide a haven for Nazi refugees has also done little for his or Argentina's international reputation. Adolf Eichmann was one of the most notorious war criminals to settle here and, much more recently, Erich Priebke was extradited from Bariloche to Italy to face trial for wartime atrocities. A recent report has revealed that fewer Nazis actually fled to Argentina than was previously thought, listing the number as 180, most of whom were Croats, not Germans – though others suggest that various regimes including Carlos Menem's (see p.543) had records relating to this period destroyed.

Perón's troubled second term

In 1949, Perón secured a constitutional amendment that allowed him to run for a **second term**. Though he won by a landslide in the 1951 elections, his position was severely weakened only one year later by the death of Evita, who had been a key political asset. It was becoming clear that his administration and the cult of personality that had swept him to power were losing impetus. He faced dissent within the army, resentful at what they saw as the subordination of their role during Evita's lifetime. He had also incited the wrath of the powerful Catholic Church, whose privileges he had attacked. In addition, his successful wealth-redistribution policies had alienated influential sectors of society while raising the expectations of the less well-off – expectations that he found increasingly difficult to fulfil. Agriculture had been allowed to stagnate in favour of industrial development, resulting in inflation and economic recession. Against a background of strikes and civil unrest, factions within the military rebelled in 1955, with the tacit support of a broad coalition of those interests that Perón had alienated. In the **Revolución Libertadora**, or Revolution of Liberation, Perón was ousted from power and went into **exile**, initially in Panama.

Military governments and guerrilla activity: 1955–73

The initial backlash against Peronism was swift: General Aramburu banned it as a political movement, Peronist iconography and statues were stripped from public places and even mention of his name was forbidden. There followed eighteen years of alternate military and short-lived civilian regimes that lurched from one crisis to another. All the civilian administrations were dependent on the backing of the military, which itself was unsure of how to align itself with the Peronist legacy and the trade unions.

The Cold War in Argentina

Much of the 1960s was characterized by economic stagnation, strikes, wage freezes and a growing disillusionment of the populace with the government, in an international climate dominated by the Cold War. Throughout this time, Perón hovered in the background, in exile in Spain, providing a focus for opposition to the anti-Communist military. In 1966, a **military coup** led by General Juan Carlos Onganía saw the imposition of austerity measures to stabilize the economy, and repression to keep a

1916	1920–21	1929
Hipólito Yrigoyen is elected President, the first Radical to hold the post.	Violent workers' protests in Patagonia lead to more liberal policies on welfare and labour relations.	The Wall Street Crash devastates the Argentine economy.

EVITA

Eva Perón, in true rags-to-riches style, began life humbly. She was born **María Eva Duarte** in 1919, the fifth illegitimate child of Juana Ibarguren and Juan Duarte, a landowner in the rural interior of Buenos Aires. She was raised in poverty by her mother, Duarte having abandoned the family before Evita – as she was universally known – reached her first birthday. At the age of 15, she headed to the capital to pursue her dream of becoming an actress, and managed to scrape a living from several minor roles in radio and TV before working her way into higher-profile leading roles through the influence of well-connected lovers. Her life changed dramatically in 1944 when she met Juan Perón. She became his mistress and married him a year later, shortly before his election to the presidency.

PUBLIC LIFE

As First Lady, Evita was in her element. She championed the rights of the working classes and underprivileged poor, whom she named her **descamisados** ("shirtless ones"), and immersed herself in populist politics and programmes of social aid. In person, she would receive petitions from individual members of the public, distributing favours on a massive scale through her powerful and wealthy instrument of patronage, the Social Aid Foundation. She played the role of the devoted wife, but was, in many ways, a pioneering feminist of Argentine society, and has been credited with assuring that women were finally granted suffrage in 1947. She yearned to legitimize her political role through direct election, but resentment among the military forced her to pull out of running for the position of Vice-President to her husband in the election of 1951.

Another role she revelled in was that of **ambassador** for her country, and she captivated a star-struck press and public during a 1948 tour of postwar Europe, during which she was granted an audience with the Pope. Hers was the international face of Argentina, dressed in Dior and Balenciaga, which assuredly compounded the jealousy of Europhile upper-class women at home. She was detested by the Argentine elite as a vulgar upstart who respected neither rank nor customary protocol. They painted her as a whore and as someone who was more interested in feeding her own personality cult than assisting the *descamisados*. Evita, for her part, seemed to revel in antagonizing the oligarchic establishment, whipping up popular resentment towards an "anti-Argentine" class.

EVITA'S DEATH

Stricken by **cancer of the uterus**, Evita died in 1952, at the age of only 33. Her death was greeted with mass outpourings of grief never seen in Argentina before or since. Eight people were crushed to death in the crowds of mourners that gathered, and over two thousand needed treatment for injuries. In death, Evita led an even more rarefied existence than she had in life. After the military coup of 1955, the military made decoy copies of her **embalmed corpse** and spirited the original away to Europe, all too aware of its power as an icon and focus for political dissent. There followed a truly bizarre series of burials, reburials and even allegations of necrophilia, before she was repatriated in 1974, during Perón's third administration and, later, afforded a decent burial in Recoleta Cemetery. To this day, Evita retains saint-like status among many traditionalist, working-class Peronists, some of whom maintain altars to her. Protests and furious graffiti greeted the casting of Madonna, fresh from a series of pornographic photo shoots, to portray her in the Alan Parker film musical, *Evita*. For many, this was sacrilege – an insult to the memory of the most important woman of Argentine history.

1939	1943	1946
The outbreak of World War II divides the country between supporters of the Allies and Fascist sympathizers.	Juan Domingo Perón enters government for the first time and builds a popular base among trade unions.	Perón becomes President for the first time, with the support of his second wife, Evita.

tight rein on political dissent. This was not without consequences, and, in the city of radical politics, Córdoba, tension eventually exploded into violence in May 1969. In what has become known as the **Cordobazo**, left-wing student protesters and trade unionists sparked off a spree of general rioting that lasted for two days, and left many people dead and the authorities profoundly shaken. Onganía's position became less and less tenable and, with unrest spreading throughout the country and an economic crisis that provoked devaluation, he was deposed by the army.

It was about this time that society saw the emergence of **guerrilla** organizations, which crystallized, over the course of the early 1970s, into two main groups: the People's Revolutionary Army (Ejército Revolucionario del Pueblo or ERP), a movement committed to radical international revolution in the style of Trotsky or Che Guevara; and the **Montoneros**, a more urban movement that espoused revolution on a more distinctly national model, extrapolated from left-wing traits within Peronism. Multinationals, landed oligarchs and the security forces were favoured Montonero targets.

The return of Perón and the collapse of democracy

By 1973, the army seemed to have recognized that its efforts to engineer some sort of national unity had failed. The economy continued to splutter, guerrilla violence was spreading and incidences of military repression were rising. Army leader General Lanusse decided to risk calling an election, and in an attempt to heal the long-standing national divide permitted the Peronist party – but not Perón himself – to stand. Perón, still exiled in Spain, nominated a proxy candidate, **Héctor José Cámpora**, to stand in his place. Cámpora emerged victorious in the June elections and forced a reluctant military to allow Perón himself to return to stand in new elections.

By this time, Perón had come to represent all things to all men. Left-wing Montoneros saw themselves as true Peronists – the natural upholders of the type of Peronism that championed the rights of the *descamisados* and freedom from imperialist domination. Likewise, some members of conservative landed groups saw him as a symbol of stability in the face of anarchy. Any illusion that Perón was going to be the balm for the nation's ills dissipated before his plane touched down at Ezeiza International Airport. His welcoming party dissolved into a violent melee, with rival groups in the crowd of 500,000 shooting at each other. It's not known how many people died in the fracas; the total is thought to be in three figures, though the official figure is 25. Cámpora quickly resigned and in May 1973 handed power to a stand-in, Raúl Lastiri, who called new elections in September. Perón was allowed to stand this time and as his running mate he chose his third wife, María Estela Martínez de Perón, a former dancer from La Rioja, commonly known by her stage name, **Isabelita**.

Perón's death and the doomed presidency of Isabelita

Perón was 78 and his health was failing; though he won the elections with ease, his third term lasted less than nine months, ending with his death in July 1974. Power devolved to Isabelita, who became the world's first female president. She managed to make a bitterly divided nation agree on at least one thing: her regime was a catastrophic failure. Rudderless, out of her depth and with no bedrock of support, Isabelita clung increasingly desperately to the advice of her Minister for Social Welfare, José López

1947	1949	1951
Women are granted the right to vote in elections on an equal footing with men.	Perón changes the Constitution so that presidents can run for a second term.	Evita dramatically decides not to run for Vice-President but Perón wins his second term.

Rega, a shadowy figure who had been Pérón's private secretary and who became known as the "Wizard", even being compared to Rasputin. Rega's prime notoriety stems from having founded the much-feared right-wing **death squads** (the Triple "A", or Alianza Argentina Anticomunista) that targeted intellectuals and guerrilla sympathizers. The only boom industry, it seemed, was corruption, and with hyperinflation and spiralling violence, the country was set to enter a dark phase in its history.

Totalitarianism: the Dirty War

The inevitable **military coup** finally came on March 24, 1976 (now commemorated every year as a national holiday). Ousted President Isabelita Perón was imprisoned, returning to exile in Spain several years later. Under **General Jorge Videla**, a military junta initiated what it termed the Process of National Reorganization (usually known as the **Proceso**), which is more often referred to as the Guerra Sucia, or **Dirty War**. In the minds of the military, any attempt to combat opposition through the normal judicial process was sure to result in failure, so there was only one response to it: an iron fist. The constitution was suspended, and a campaign of systematic violence backed by the full apparatus of the state was unleashed. In the language of chauvinistic patriotism, they invoked the Doctrine of National Security to justify what they saw as part of the war against international Communism. These events were set against the background of **Cold War politics**, and the generals received covert CIA support. Apart from guerrillas and anyone suspected of harbouring guerrilla sympathies, those targeted included liberal intellectuals, journalists, psychologists, Jews, Marxists, trade unionists, atheists and anyone who, in the words of Videla, "spreads ideas that are contrary to Western and Christian civilization".

The World Cup and the Madres movement

The military junta had the opportunity to demonstrate the "success" of their regime to the world, by hosting the **1978 football World Cup**. Though victory of the Argentine team in the final stoked national pride, few observers saw this as a reflection of the achievements of the military. Indeed, the event backfired on the military in other ways.

TORTURE AND DISAPPEARANCES

The most notorious terror tactic used by the dictators was to send hit squads to make people "disappear". Once seized, often by thugs driving unmarked cars, these **desaparecidos** simply ceased to exist – no one knew who had taken them or where they had gone. In fact, the *desaparecidos* were taken to secret detention camps – places like the infamous **Navy Mechanics School** (ESMA), now a national memorial – where they were subjected to horrific torture, rape and, usually, execution. Many were taken up in planes and thrown, drugged and weighted with concrete, into the River Plate, the perverse idea being that they were not murdered directly by their executors. Most victims were between their late teens and 30s, but no one was exempt, even pregnant women and the disabled. Jacobo Timerman, in *Prisoner Without a Name, Cell Without a Number*, an account of his experiences in a torture centre, gives an insight into the mind of one of his interrogators, who told him: "Only God gives and takes life. But God is busy elsewhere, and we're the ones who must undertake this task in Argentina."

1952	**1955**	**1966**
Evita dies of cancer of the uterus and mourners are trampled to death at her funeral.	In the Revolución Libertadora, Perón is sent into exile by the military, who do all they can to eradicate every trace of Peronism.	General Onganía heads one of the country's many military juntas, imposing strict censorship.

The vast expense of hosting the tournament compounded the regime's economic problems. In addition, it provided a forum for human-rights advocates, including a courageous group called the **Madres de Plaza de Mayo** (see box, p.63), to bring the issue of the *desaparecidos* to international attention. The Madres of the Plaza de Mayo were one of the few groups to challenge the regime directly, organizing weekly demonstrations in Buenos Aires' central square. Their protests continued until January 2006, when their leader said that they no longer had an enemy in the Casa Rosada.

Economic and military failure

A slight softening of Videla's extremist stance came when **General Roberto Viola** took control of the army in 1978 and then the presidency of the junta in 1981, but he was forced out later the same year by hardliners under **General Leopoldo Galtieri**. The military's grip on the country, by this time, was nonetheless increasingly shaky, with the economy in recession, skyrocketing interest rates and the first mass demonstrations against the regime since its imposition in 1976. Galtieri, with no other cards left to play, chose April 2, 1982 to play his trump: **an invasion of the Falkland Islands**, or Islas Malvinas as they are known to Argentines. Nothing could have been more certain to bring a sense of purpose to the nation, and the population reacted with delight. This, however, soon turned to dismay when people realized that the British government was prepared to go to war. The Argentine forces were defeated by mid-June (see box, p.542).

The military had proved themselves incapable of mastering politics and disastrous stewards of the economy, and now they had suffered ignominious failure doing what they were supposed to be specialists at: fighting. Perhaps the only positive thing to come out of this futile war was that it was the final spur for Argentines to throw off the shackles of the regime. While the junta prepared to hand over to civilian control, **General Reynaldo Bignone**, successor to Galtieri, issued a decree that pronounced an amnesty for all members of the armed forces for any alleged human-rights atrocities.

Alfonsín and the restoration of democracy

Democracy was restored with the elections of October 1983, won by the Radical **Raúl Alfonsín** – the first time in its four decades of existence that the Peronist party had been defeated at the polls. Alfonsín, a lawyer much respected for his record on human rights, inherited a precarious political panorama. He faced two great challenges: the first, to build some sort of national concord; and the second, to restore a shattered economy, where inflation was running at over 400 percent and the foreign debt was over US$40 billion. In the midst of this, he solved a politically sensitive border dispute with Chile over three islands in the Beagle Channel – **Picton, Nueva and Lennox**. Papal arbitration had awarded the islands to Chile, but Alfonsín ensured, in 1984, that a public referendum approved this.

The issue of prosecuting those responsible for crimes against humanity during the dictatorship proved an intractable one. Alfonsín set up a **National Commission on Disappeared People** (CONADEP), chaired by the respected writer Ernesto Sabato, to investigate the alleged atrocities. Their report, *Nunca Más* – or "Never Again" – documented nine thousand cases of torture and disappearance, although human rights groups believe the actual figure for the number of deaths during the Dirty War is

1969	1973	1974
Inspired by similar uprisings in Europe, the Cordobazo riots mark the growing polarization of Argentine society.	Perón returns from exile and is elected president but old age and ill health make him weak.	After Perón's death on July 1, his widow "Isabelita" takes over and embarks on a disastrous two-year term in the Casa Rosada.

A HISTORICAL DISPUTE: THE FALKLAND ISLANDS/ISLAS MALVINAS

The islands known to the British as the **Falklands**, and to Argentines as **Las Malvinas**, lie some 12,500km from Britain and 550km off the coast of Argentina. Disputes have raged as to who first discovered them, but the first verifiable sighting comes from a Dutch sailor in 1600. In 1690, Captain John Strong discovered the strait that divides the two major islands in the group, and christened the archipelago the "Falkland Islands", after Viscount Falkland, the commissioner of the British Admiralty at the time.

French sailors from St Malo made numerous expeditions to the islands from 1698, naming them the **Iles Malouines**, from which derives the Argentine name "Malvinas". The first serious attempt at settlement came when a French expedition established a base at Port St Louis in 1764. A year later, claiming ignorance of the French settlement, a party of British sailors settled **Port Egmont**, and claimed the islands for George III. The Spanish also believed they had legal title to the area, dating from the 1494 papal treaty that divided the Americas between Spain and Portugal. Reluctant to come to blows with an ally, the French negotiated a settlement, and, in 1767, Port St Louis was surrendered to Spain. In 1774, the British were persuaded to abandon their colony (although not, they would later maintain, their claims to sovereignty).

In 1820, the newly independent Argentine federation asserted what it saw as its right to inherit the sovereign Spanish title to the islands. This was not, initially, contested by the British, but in the late 1820s Britain started to make noises about reasserting its sovereignty claim. The Argentine federation, paralyzed by internal disputes, was powerless to prevent Britain from establishing a base on the islands, and its colony developed significantly after the founding, in 1851, of the **Falkland Islands Company** and with the beginnings of serious commercial exploitation such as sheep farming and whaling. By 1871, eight hundred people were living in Port Stanley.

In April 1982 General Galtieri saw the opportunity to divert attention away from his junta's failed policies (see p.541) by organizing a military campaign to "liberate" the islands. The British had been making preparations for the scrapping of its only naval presence in the South Atlantic, and Galtieri made a serious misjudgement in believing Britain would acquiesce in the face of an invasion. Following the arrival of a **British task force**, the conflict was short. The struggle was unequal: poorly equipped Argentine teenagers on military service were expected to combat professional paratroopers. In the worst atrocity of the war, the *General Belgrano* was torpedoed outside the British-imposed naval exclusion zone, leading to the death of hundreds – an event that is still viewed with considerable bitterness by many Argentines.

More than 900 people perished in the 74-day conflict, and negotiations on the sovereignty issue were set back decades. At the time of the invasion, the islands were essentially a forgotten British colony that had long suffered a dearth of development and were being gradually integrated into the Argentine economic sphere. This stopped abruptly with the war.

In some ways, old wounds are healing – in 2009, after years of wrangling, relatives of the Argentine war dead were allowed to visit the islands to dedicate a war memorial to their fallen. However, the issue of sovereignty remains a major obstacle. Britain says there can be no negotiations until the Falkland Islanders so wish and called a referendum in the territory. There have been a series of flare-ups in rhetoric: after British exploration companies began drilling for oil in the Falklands waters in 2010; when Prince William did his helicopter practice on the islands; and when the British sent a naval warship to the South Atlantic to coincide with the war's thirtieth anniversary in 2012.

1976	1978	1982
On March 24, the military overthrows Isabelita and ushers in six years of totalitarian dictatorship.	Argentina hosts and wins the football World Cup.	Argentine forces invade British island territories in the South Atlantic but are defeated by a UK Task Force.

closer to thirty thousand. It recommended that those responsible be brought to **trial**. Those convicted in the first wave of trials included the reviled Videla, Viola, Galtieri, and Admiral Emilio Massera, one of the most despised figures of the junta. All were sentenced to life imprisonment.

Alfonsín's concessions to the military

Military sensibilities were offended by the trials: defeat in the South Atlantic War had discredited them but they could still pose considerable danger to the fragile democracy and Alfonsín decided he couldn't risk full confrontation. In 1986, he caved in to military pressure and passed *Punto Final*, or "End Point", legislation, which put a final date for the submission of writs for human rights crimes. However, in a window of two months, the courts were flooded with such writs, and, for the first time, the courts indicted officers still in active service.

Several short-lived uprisings forced Alfonsín to pull back from pursuing widespread prosecutions. In 1987, the **Law of Due Obedience** (*Obediencia Debida*) was passed, granting an amnesty to all but the leaders for atrocities committed during the dictatorship. At a stroke, this reduced the number of people facing charges from 370 to fewer than fifty. This incensed the victims' relatives, who saw notorious Proceso torturers escape prosecution, including the "Angel of Death", **Alfredo Astiz**, who attained international notoriety for the brutal murder of two French nuns and a young girl.

Economic collapse and the early handover

Alfonsín managed to secure some respite by restructuring the national debt and, in 1985, introducing a platform of stringent austerity measures, which were angrily received by many sectors of the population. The government deemed the **Plan Austral**, named after the new currency it introduced, to be essential, with inflation running at over a thousand percent annually. The country continued to be crippled by **hyperinflation**, however, even after a second raft of belt-tightening measures, or *australito*, in 1987. The inflationary crisis came to a head in 1989, when the World Bank suspended all loans: many shops remained closed, preferring to keep their stock rather than selling it for a currency whose value disappeared before their eyes. In supermarkets, shoppers listened to the tannoy to hear the latest prices, which would often change in the time it took to take an item from the shelf to the checkout. Elections took place in 1989, but, with severe **civil unrest** breaking out across the country, Alfonsín called a state of emergency and stood down early, handing control to his elected successor, **Carlos Saúl Menem**. Even so, it was the first time since 1928 that power had transferred democratically from one civilian government to another.

Menem's decade in power: 1989–99

The 1990s were dominated by **Carlos Menem** – the son of Syrian immigrants – and were characterized by radical reforms and controversy. Menem had been governor of La Rioja at the outbreak of military rule in 1976 and had spent most of the dictatorship in detention. His **Justicialist Party** (*Partido Justicialista* or PJ) was theoretically Peronist but – once elected in 1989 – he embarked on a series of sweeping **neoliberal reforms**.

1983	1985	1987
Radical Raúl Alfonsín oversees the return to democracy but is forced to make humiliating concessions to the military.	*The Official Story*, a film about the dictatorship, wins an Oscar.	Amnesty laws are passed, resulting in the release of dozens of military officers found guilty of crimes against humanity.

His first major achievement was to destroy **inflation**. Backed by international finance organizations, Menem and his finance minister, **Domingo Cavallo**, introduced the Convertibility Plan (*Plan de Convertibilidad*), which pegged the restored peso, worth 10,000 australes, at parity with the US dollar, and guaranteed its value by limiting the Central Bank's power to print money. Inflation fell to eight percent by 1993 and remained in single figures throughout the 1990s.

Menem also abandoned the Peronist principle of state ownership and the dogma of state intervention, favouring the **privatization** of all the major utilities and industries: electricity, gas, telephones, Aerolíneas Argentinas and even the profitable YPF, the state-owned petroleum company, were sold off. Investment came primarily from European, mainly Spanish and French, corporations, and the sales allegedly benefited individuals (including politicians) rather than the state. All Federal railway subsidies ended in 1993, coinciding with massive **public spending cuts**. In 1995, regional trade barriers fell, as a consequence of the full implementation of the **Mercosur** trading agreement, creating a **free-trade block** of Southern Cone countries – Brazil, Argentina, Uruguay and Paraguay, with other countries joining or developing close ties later on. Unemployment rocketed and acute financial hardship resulted in strikes and sporadic civil unrest.

Playboy president

One thing about Menem's brand of Peronism that stayed faithful to the original was his style of government. A cavalier **populist**, Menem never stopped trying to develop the "cult of the leader". He modelled his image, mutton-chop sideburns and all, on that of provincial *caudillos* such as Facundo Quiroga, the La Rioja warlord of the 1830s. Not known for his modesty, he preached austerity while developing a penchant for the life of a playboy.

The president increasingly became associated with trying to rule by **decree**. One of the most controversial aspects of this policy was the issuing of executive **amnesties** in 1989 to those guilty of atrocities during the 1970s. Although the amnesty included ex-guerrillas, public outrage centred on the release of former members of the junta, including all the leading generals. To Menem it was the pragmatic price to pay to secure the military's cooperation; to virtually all the rest of the country, it was a flagrant moral capitulation. His apparent failure to launch a serious investigation into two terrorist attacks that targeted the **Jewish community** in 1992 and 1994 (see box, p.71) also showed him in a very poor light.

Menem's second term

In August 1994, Menem secured a **constitutional amendment** that allowed a sitting president to stand for a second term, though the mandate was reduced from six years to four. The voters, trusting his economic record, elected him to a second term the following year. **Human rights issues** continued to surface. One of the most important developments was the start of a campaign to prosecute those guilty of having "**kidnapped**" babies of *desaparecidos* born in detention, in order to give them up for adoption to childless military couples. Recognition of this crime, not covered by Alfonsín's Punto Final legislation, resulted in the successful interrogation and detention of many leading members of the old junta, including Videla and Massera. In the mid-1990s, the armed forces acknowledged their role in the atrocities of the

1989	1992	1994
Carlos Menem, a neoliberal Peronist, is elected President and takes office early after Alfonsín declares a state of emergency.	The Israeli embassy in Buenos Aires is attacked by Jihadist suicide bombers, resulting in 29 deaths.	Argentina's worst-ever terrorist outrage, the bombing of the HQ of AMIA, a Jewish association, leaves 85 dead and hundreds wounded.

dictatorship, making a **public apology** – a symbolic act that was followed by similar repentance by the Catholic Church.

Austerity measures seemed to apply to anyone not in government, and foreign debt continued to balloon. When, at the beginning of 1999, Brazil's currency lost half of its value, the government had to resist acute pressure to devalue the peso. Convertibility held, but Menem announced that Argentina ought seriously to consider the "**dollarization**" of the economy.

As the end of his second term approached, Menem mooted the possibility of running for a third consecutive term of office, shenanigans which alienated the populace from his Justicialist Party and contributed to the defeat of its eventual candidate, Eduardo Duhalde, in 1999. Duhalde was emphatically beaten by **Fernando de la Rúa**, the Córdoba-born mayor of the city of Buenos Aires, who headed up the **Alianza**, a coalition of the Radicals (UCR), of which he was leader, and **FREPASO**, itself a coalition party of left-wingers and disaffected Peronists.

The De la Rúa government and the 2001 meltdown

Known for his stolid reliability rather than his charisma, De la Rúa was a complete contrast to his predecessor. On taking office in 1999 he seemed to represent the **fiscal and moral probity** that Argentines felt their country – already starting to show signs of its worst-ever recession – needed. Once in charge, though, the Alianza coalition was hit by severe infighting, and public spending cuts forced by economic strictures led to large-scale demonstrations.

By early 2001, De la Rúa had already appointed his third finance minister – bringing back Domingo Cavallo, Menem's henchman, who announced an unrealistic "zero deficit" drive to meet stiff IMF targets and protect convertibility. The country still wasn't pulling out of recession, with industrial production and exports dismally low owing to the phoney exchange rate, unemployment soaring and financial confidence on the wane. Then, in the national elections of October 2001, the Peronists gained control of both houses of Congress. Private depositors began to pull their money out of banks, afraid the peso-dollar peg would be abolished. Under severe pressure to abandon convertibility and devalue the peso, Cavallo stood firm.

Corralito and chaos

In early December 2001, in a desperate bid to avoid devaluation and stop the cash drain from banks, Cavallo announced restrictions severely limiting access to private deposits, including salaries. This measure, known as the **corralito**, or "playpen", riled Argentines of all classes, though the wealthiest managed to get their money out in dollars and into accounts abroad. To cap it all, the IMF then announced the withdrawal of support owing to lack of confidence in the economy.

On December 13, a general strike was staged against the *corralito* by the Peronist-controlled unions and acts of looting were reported in the suburbs of Buenos Aires, a Peronist bastion. Despite De la Rúa's announcement of a state of emergency to deal with the crisis, on the evening of December 19 tens of thousands of protestors bashing pots and pans (the first of many noisy "**cacerolazos**", or saucepan protests) marched on the Plaza de Mayo. Although the police dispersed the huge crowd,

1995	1996
Menem is elected for a second term and forces the armed forces and the Catholic Church to apologize for their roles in the Dirty War.	Protests face Madonna when she shoots the film *Evita*, but she gets to appear on the balcony of the Casa Rosada.

more demonstrations took place the following day. De la Rúa found himself politically isolated, while brutal police efforts to clear the Plaza de Mayo and halt **demonstrations** in other cities ended in a bloodbath, with at least 25 people dead nationwide. De la Rúa left office ignominiously, fleeing the Casa Rosada by helicopter.

The Duhalde presidency: an interregnum

After a farcical series of short-lived presidential appointments, Congress finally opted for **Eduardo Duhalde**, the Peronist presidential candidate defeated by De la Rúa in 1999, who was sworn in on January 1, 2002. He heavily **devalued the peso** within days and then negotiated a new agreement with the IMF to avoid a humiliating default with international lending agencies. After militant jobless groups known as *piqueteros* (see box opposite) clashed with police, leaving two people dead, in June 2002 he announced early **presidential elections** for 2003, pledging that he and his ministers would not stand for office.

After the worst of the crisis Duhalde's finance minister, **Roberto Lavagna**, calmed financial markets, avoiding hyperinflation and stabilizing the US dollar exchange rate at just over three pesos, after a peak of nearly four. He also reached a short-term agreement with the IMF and, by early 2003, signs of economic recovery – in particular, increased exports – began to show. The downside to this was a **sharp rise in poverty** across the country, as the price of basic products and imports soared.

Menem's failed comeback

The Peronists failed to unite ahead of the 2003 elections, and warring factions fielded three separate contenders: former presidents Menem and Rodríguez Saá (the latter was head of state for a few days at the height of the 2001 crisis) and Duhalde's protégé, **Néstor Kirchner**, who enjoyed a narrow lead in opinion polls. In the event, **Menem** came first, with just under a quarter of the vote, with Kirchner going through to the second round, only a couple of percentage points behind. But, as the run-off approached, opinion polls unanimously suggested that only three voters in ten would back Menem – who withdrew from the race to avoid a crushing defeat and, it was rumoured, spitefully deprive Kirchner of an overwhelming mandate.

Néstor Kirchner and new-look Peronism

When Néstor Kirchner took power the political and economic situation he inherited was still grave and few had any confidence that he had the skills or support to bring about recovery. However, against the odds, he grew to be a surprisingly powerful force in Argentine politics. He and his family began to dominate the country to an extent that led to talk of a "penguin" takeover; Kirchner, often known simply as "**K**" – easier on the tongue than his Swiss–German surname – was nicknamed "Pingüino", less for his bird-like appearance than for his Patagonian origins.

Kirchner soon emerged as one of a new generation of left-leaning **South American leaders**, including Hugo Chávez and Lula, set on forging regional independence and interdependence, strengthening Mercosur, limiting the influence of multinationals, defying the IMF and largely thumbing his nose at Washington. Helped by Duhalde's respected economy minister Lavagna, he oversaw an astonishing revival in the

1999	2001
Having failed to change the Constitution, Menem cannot run for a third term and De la Rúa takes over.	The government loses control of the economy and De la Rúa is airlifted from the Casa Rosada by helicopter.

PIQUETEROS AND CARTONEROS – THE TOUGHER SIDE OF ARGENTINE LIFE

Piqueteros – "picketers" – came to prominence in the late 1990s and especially around the time of the 2001 crisis, staging often violent protests outside the houses of former junta members or banks and businesses, blockading roads and major access points to cities, in order to draw attention to social injustices such as job losses, poor working conditions or hospital closures. They've become a feature of Argentine life, with some pickets being organized on the spur of the moment in response to specific grievances, and other groups being linked to political movements – mainstream or otherwise.

A new phenomenon for the new millennium, the **cartonero**, is now a common sight on the streets of the capital. *Cartoneros* are poor people who effectively act as semi-official refuse recyclers. They rummage through garbage bags, salvaging paper and cardboard to sell for scrap value. The sight of whole families, including young children, sorting out rubbish on the city pavements, does not exactly make for a good image and is an ongoing challenge faced by the authorities.

Argentine economy, as the devalued peso provided a platform for Argentina's export sector to flourish; from 2003, the country registered one of the world's highest **GDP growth rates** (averaging over eight percent a year for several years). Favourable settlements were hammered out with the majority of Argentina's international creditors, and the government paid back billions of dollars in defaulted loans. Joblessness figures started to drop, dipping below ten percent by 2007. Argentina also had a string of record years for **international tourism**, matched with huge numbers of Argentine holiday-makers forced to discover their own country.

"K" for Kirchnerism

As tax revenues swelled, Kirchner was able to reverse years of spending cuts in the education, welfare and public-service sectors, providing students with free computers, handing out child allowances and building better roads. While skilful macroeconomic management was a factor of the recovery, the government was helped along by record commodity and agriculture prices (especially **soya**) on world markets, and Kirchner became the most popular resident of the Casa Rosada for years.

He risked the wrath of some Peronists and the military, by repealing the **amnesty laws** that had made it impossible to prosecute anyone who had committed human rights atrocities. He closed the capital's **Escuela Mecánica de la Armada** (the Navy Mechanics School, which had been a key torture centre during the Dirty War) and had it turned into a monument to the dictatorship, excluding Peronist politicians with a dubious past from a memorial ceremony for the disappeared.

Meanwhile, as poverty persisted (witness the *cartoneros* on the streets; see box above) the government faced an upsurge in violent **crime** in the capital and other large cities. Critics accused the government of massaging inflation figures, through the state statistics office, **INDEC**, a situation that persisted for years. And a series of high-profile financial scandals hit the headlines in 2007. Rather than running for a second term that year, he stepped aside for his wife, **Cristina Fernández de Kirchner** (see box, p.548) to run as the candidate of their newly named Frente para la Victoria (Victory Front, or FPV). Beating rivals Elisa Carrió, a colourful ex-Radical, and Roberto Lavagna,

2002	2003
Argentina's economy collapses and caretaker president Duhalde devalues the peso and restores order.	Despite an attempted comeback by Carlos Menem, left-wing Peronist Néstor Kirchner is elected President.

the former economy minister, she swept to a resounding victory in the first round of the presidential election held in November 2007.

President Cristina Fernández de Kirchner

In many ways Cristina Fernández de Kirchner's electoral victory meant business as usual, with continued economic growth, booming exports and flourishing national and international tourism filling the government's coffers, aided by more efficient tax collection procedures. Cristina's first big hurdle loomed early in 2008, when she was forced to back down in a major dispute with farmers over attempts to raise export taxes on agricultural produce; when her vice president, ex-Radical Julio Cobos, cast his vote against the government she cut off all relations with him for the next four years. Her administration successfully expropriated US$26 billion in private pension funds, in order to boost the State's own fund, to the consternation of foreign investors.

Although Latin America was not as hard hit by the global recession of 2009 as many countries, it has not been entirely unscathed – Argentina's economy grew less than one percent in 2009, and has faltered ever since. Suddenly, Argentina was once again faced

---

LA PRESIDENTA

Cristina Fernández de Kirchner – commonly known simply as CFK or Cristina, and satirically as Kristina – has become Argentina's most high-profile female politician since Evita. Born in 1953 in La Plata, she became involved in political activism while studying law there in the 1970s. She met Néstor Kirchner through anti-military politics and, after they married, moved to his native **Santa Cruz Province**, where they practised law and embarked on their political careers. After serving several terms as a representative of Santa Cruz Province in the national Congress, Cristina was elected a senator for the province of Buenos Aires. In 2003, she became the country's First Lady or, as she preferred it, "First Female Citizen". Glamorous and extremely photogenic, she has a forthright manner and a sharp tongue – with a tendency to give long ad-libbed speeches laced with emotional outbursts and vitriolic rhetoric.

Both as the President's wife and as President of the Republic in her own right, since 2007, she has taken a firm and progressive stand on human rights (including justice for the victims of the dictatorship, same-sex marriage, transgender identity and gender equality) and the need for Latin America to assert itself on the world stage. Her popularity with the working classes (which secured her a landslide second electoral victory) and her high-profile **ambassadorial trips** abroad – together with a fashionable wardrobe – have led to inevitable comparisons with Evita. However, she told one newspaper early on, perhaps tongue-in-cheek, that she was both more intelligent and more beautiful.

She has also often been likened to **Hillary Clinton** – another clever, tough female politician not afraid to make enemies. But in another interview Cristina dismissed that too, saying that Hillary only became a force in national politics because she was married to Bill, where she is very much her own boss. Other observers, much to her horror, see her increasingly playing the role of an Argentine **Margaret Thatcher** – owing to her confrontational, anti-consensus approach and a tendency to listen only to an ever-shrinking inner core of sympathetic advisers. Ironically, history might see her more as a reincarnation of Perón himself – a clever demagogue with authoritarian tendencies who made the most of the death of a consort but suffered from not knowing when, or to whom, to hand over power.

2007	2009
Kirchner lets his wife, Cristina Fernández, stand in the elections, and she becomes the country's first elected female President.	Two Argentine films win Oscars – *The Secret in Their Eyes* and the animated movie *Logorama*.

LA CÁMPORA

Founded by Kirchner supporters during the 2003 presidential campaign, **La Cámpora** is a youth association that takes its name from the caretaker President whose short term paved the way for Perón's return to power three decades earlier. Modelling itself philosophically on the Montoneros, it uses social media and noisy street demos to contest the social order rather than the guerrillas' terror tactics of the 1970s. Dominated by the president's son Máximo and other up-and-coming politicians determined to honour the Kirchner legacy, it is mistrusted by the opposition as an all-pervasive, antidemocratic movement based on rampant nepotism and veiled threats.

with the prospect of raising money on sceptical international financial markets to keep levels of public spending high – the same markets that had been burned by Argentina's massive debt default during the 2001 crisis.

Problems for Kirchnerism

Kirchnerism – as the new branch of Peronism began to be called, backed by a powerful youth movement known as La Cámpora (see box above) – suffered defeat in the mid-term parliamentary elections of 2009, with its governing coalition losing its majority in both houses of Congress. Néstor Kirchner failed in his attempt to be elected as a member of the lower house of the national Congress for Buenos Aires Province and stood down as Justicialist party leader. The presidential couple faced growing allegations of nepotism – Néstor's sister Alicia has been a minister since 2003 – and repeated questions have been raised about how the Kirchners' personal declared assets have rocketed since they've been in power.

The 2010 bicentenary

One hundred years after its lavish *belle époque* centenary, Argentina hadn't exactly lived up to the heady promise of world domination and the bicentenary celebrations in 2010 were far more low-key. Even so the government organized all manner of military processions and music-led festivities to entertain the crowds and launched a series of high-minded projects with logos and slogans galore (see box, p.63). The 2016 anniversary – two hundred years after the official declaration of independence – is expected to be an excuse for more pomp and circumstance.

Life after Néstor

When Néstor Kirchner stood aside in 2007, it was generally assumed he would run again for the presidency at the end of his wife's term in 2011, and would stand a good chance of winning. Those carefully laid plans were wrecked when Néstor's poor health took a turn for the worse and he died of a heart attack on October 27, 2010. His widow set about beatifying her late husband, donned mourning black and referred to Néstor mystically as "Él" – He. A mausoleum was built in their Patagonian home town of El Calafate, streets and public buildings were named after the former leader and a hagiographic biopic was released along with myriad books on his life and politics.

Despite favourable opinion polls, Cristina left it until the very last minute before announcing that she would run for a second term as president. Undoubtedly benefiting from her widow status, plus a blip of good economic news and, above all, a divided

2010	2011
Low-key bicentenary celebrations are held in May; Néstor Kirchner dies unexpectedly on October 27, aged 60.	Now widowed and permanently clad in black, CFK wins a landslide election victory in November.

opposition, she won the first-round ballot by a landslide. On December 10, 2011, she swore the oath of office, with former economy minister, Amado Boudou, as her vice president.

Cristina's second term

Cristina's second honeymoon period came to a sudden end in February 2012, when a commuter train failed to stop at the capital's busy Once station, killing 51 and injuring hundreds. The ensuing public outrage led the government to promise long overdue modernization of the country's criminally neglected rail network.

The year continued to bring bad news, with a further string of corruption allegations printed in an increasingly hostile press, targeting the playboy Vice President in particular. As longstanding energy and transport subsidies were lifted and unions demanded massive wage hikes, inflation continued unabated. The official rate of ten percent was widely contested (unofficial sources put it at 25 percent or higher), though financial consultants who did so were fined. Argentina's middle classes were annoyed by tight currency controls that restricted their ability to take vacations in Punta del Este, Miami and Europe, but a parallel market started selling US dollars for fifty percent more (the "blue" rate) than the state-imposed rate of just shy of five pesos to the dollar.

At the end of 2012, the government drove legislation through Congress ostensibly designed to encourage plurality of the media, but opponents – above all, voices in the powerful *Clarín* media group – maintained that it was an attack on the free media intended to stifle legitimate dissent. A series of court appeals and counter-appeals further poisoned the already bitter relations between the President and her followers, on one side, and the media and judiciary on the other.

The prospects for a third term

Although Cristina's popularity ratings were at an all-time low early in 2013, the opposition, resigned to another three years of Kirchnerism, still seemed unable to unite behind a plausible leader. Political commentators warned that the only real opposition was coming from the media, the judiciary and alienated sectors of the trade union movement.

Meanwhile, the President and her followers began making it clear they would favour changing the Constitution to allow her to run for a third term. The only political figure with any chance of putting a spoke in her wheel seems to be her archrival, Mauricio Macri, currently *intendente* (mayor) of Buenos Aires. But voters with any memory will recall that the last time a mayor from the capital took over from a charismatic Peronist two-termer – namely De la Rúa – the result was utter chaos.

ARGENTINA'S POPE

Argentina's recent history, including the dark years of the dictatorship, came under close scrutiny in 2013 when **Jorge Bergoglio**, an Argentine of Italian descent, became **Pope Francis I**. Bergoglio was known as a modest man who travelled by bus and lived in a simple apartment in Buenos Aires, although his past was tainted by allegations that he withdrew protection from two Jesuit priests who were jailed after visiting the villas during the Dirty War. His defenders deny the claims, saying there is no proof. In more recent years, he had a tense relationship with the Kirchners, criticizing the 2010 gay marriage bill.

2012	2013
In February a crowded commuter train crashes into the buffers at Once station, in one of the worst such accidents in the country's history.	In January, the parallel peso slumps to $7.50 to the US dollar for the first time. In March, the former cardinal archbishop of Buenos Aires, Jorge Mario Bergoglio, becomes Pope Francis I.

Environment and wildlife

Argentina's natural wonders are some of its chief joys. Its remarkable diversity of habitats, ranging from subtropical jungles to subantarctic icesheets, is complemented by an unexpected juxtaposition of species: parrots foraging alongside glaciers, or flamingoes surviving bitter subzero temperatures on the stark Andean altiplano. Though the divisions are too complicated to list fully here, we've covered Argentina's most distinctive habitats, along with the species of flora and fauna typical to each.

Pampas grassland

The vast alluvial plain that centres on Buenos Aires Province and radiates out into the surrounding provinces was once pampas grassland, famous for its clumps of brush-tailed *cortadera* grass. However, its deep, extremely fertile soil has seen it become the agricultural heart of modern Argentina, and this original habitat has almost entirely disappeared, transformed by cattle grazing and intensive arable farming.

Once, these plains were the home of **pampas deer** (*venado de las pampas*), but today only a few hundred individuals survive, mainly in Samborombón and Campos del Tuyú in Buenos Aires Province. The **coypu** (*coipo*) is a large rodent commonly found in the region's wetlands, especially in places like the Paraná Delta. The great vizcacha dens described in the nineteenth century by famous natural history writer W.H. Hudson have all but disappeared, but you may see an endemic bird named for the writer, Hudson's canastero, along with **Greater rheas**, **Burrowing parrots** (*loro barranquero*), and **Ovenbirds** (*horneros*). Named after the domed, concrete-hard mud nests they build on posts, Ovenbirds have always been held in great affection by gauchos and country folk.

Bordering the pampas to the north and west is a semicircular fringe of **espinal woodland**, a type of open wooded "parkland". Common species of tree include **acacia** and the **ceibo**, Argentina's national tree, which in spring produces a profusion of scarlet blooms.

Mesopotamian grassland

The humid Mesopotamian grasslands extend across much of Corrientes and Entre Ríos provinces and into southernmost Misiones. Here you will find *yatay* palm savannah and some of Argentina's most important **wetlands**, most notably the Esteros de Iberá.

The wetlands have a remarkable diversity of birdlife, including numerous species of duck, rail, ibis and heron. Some of the most distinctive species are the **Wattled jacana** (*jacana*); the **Southern screamer** (*chajá*), a hulking bird the size of a turkey; **Roseate spoonbills** (*espátula rosada*); and **Jabirus** (*yabirú*), the largest variety of stork, measuring almost 1.5m tall, with a bald head and shoe-horn bill. Up above fly **Snail kites** (*caracoleros*), which use their bills to prise freshwater snails from their shells.

In the shallow swamps, among reed beds and long grasses, you will find the **Marsh deer** (*ciervo de los pantanos*), South America's largest native deer, with multi-horned antlers. One of the most common wetland animals is the **capybara** (*carpincho*), the world's biggest rodent, weighing up to 50kg. **Reptiles** include the **Black cayman** (*yacaré negro*), which grows up to 2.8m in length, and is the victim of illegal hunting.

Subtropical Paraná forest

Subtropical Paraná forest (*Selva paranaense*) is Argentina's most biologically diverse ecosystem, a dense mass of vegetation that conforms to most people's idea of a jungle. The most frequently visited area of Paraná forest is Parque Nacional Iguazú, but it is also found in patches across the rest of Misiones, and parts of Corrientes. It has over two hundred tree species, including the **palo rosa** (one of the highest canopy species, at up to 40m); the **strangler fig** (*higuerón bravo*); the **lapacho**, with its beautiful pink flowers; and the **Misiones cedar** (*cedro misionero*), a fine hardwood species that has suffered heavily from logging. Lower storeys of vegetation include the wild **yerba mate** tree, first cultivated by the Jesuits in the seventeenth century; the **palmito** palm, whose edible core is exploited as palm heart; and endangered prehistoric **tree ferns**. Festooning the forest are lianas, mosses, ferns and epiphytes, including several hundred varieties of **orchid**.

More than five hundred species of bird inhabit the Paraná forest, and you stand a good chance of seeing the **Toco toucan** (*tucán grande*), with its bright orange bill.

This part of the country is also one of the few places you just might see the highly endangered **jaguar** (*yaguareté* or *tigre*). Weighing up to 160kg, this beast is the continent's most fearsome predator.

The dry chaco

The dry chaco refers to the parched plain of thorn scrub that covers most of central and western Chaco and Formosa provinces, northeastern Salta and much of Santiago del Estero. To early explorers and settlers, much of this area was known simply as the **Impenetrable** for its aridity. Everything, it seems, is defensive: the *vinal* shrub, for instance, is dreaded by riders for its brutal spikes, up to 20cm long. In places, there is a dense undergrowth of **chaguar** and **caraguatá**: robust, yucca-like plants that the Wichí process to make fibre for their *yica* bags.

Perhaps the hardest wood is that of the endangered, slow-growing **palo santo** (meaning "holy stick"). Its fragrant, green-tinged wood can be burnt as an insect repellent. The **palo borracho** (or *yuchán*) is the most distinctive tree of all, with a bulbous, porous trunk to store water; the tree protects itself, especially when young, with rhino-horned spikes.

The dry chaco is home to forty percent of Argentina's mammal species. An estimated two hundred **jaguars** hang on here. Less threatened are the **puma** and the **Geoffroy's cat** (*gato montés*). One of three species of native Argentine wild pig, the famous **Chacoan peccary** (*chancho quimilero*) was thought to be extinct until rediscovered in Paraguay in 1975, and later in a few isolated areas of the Argentine dry chaco. Another high-profile living fossil is the nocturnal **giant armadillo** (*tatú carreta*). Weighing as much as 60kg, a full-grown one is strong enough to carry a man.

The yungas

Yungas is the term applied to the subtropical band of the Argentine Northwest that lies between the chaco and the Andean precordillera, from the Bolivian border through

Jujuy, Salta, Tucumán and into Catamarca. Abrupt changes of altitude give rise to radical changes in the flora here, creating wildly different ecosystems. The lowest altitudes are home to transitional woodland and lowland jungle (*selva pedemontana*), up to about 600m. Most of the trees and shrubs in these lower levels are deciduous and have showy blossoms: jacaranda, *palo blanco* and *amarillo*, *lapacho* and the **ceibo**. Much of this forest has been hard hit by clearance.

Above 600m starts the most famous *yungas* habitat, the **montane cloud-forests** (*selva montaña* or *nuboselva*), best seen in the national parks of Calilegua, Baritú and El Rey. These forests form a gloomy canopy of tall evergreens, beneath which several varieties of cane and bamboo compete for sunlight. The tree trunks are covered in moss and lichen; lianas hang in a tangle; epiphytes and orchids flourish; and bromeliads, heliconias and succulents all add to the dank atmosphere.

More than three hundred varieties of **bird** inhabit the *yungas* forests. Species include the **Toco toucan**; the rare **Black-and-chestnut eagle** (*águila poma*); the **King vulture** (*jote real*), with a strikingly patterned head; and numerous varieties of **hummingbird**.

The streams are favourite haunts of crab-eating **raccoons** (called *mayuatos* here). Other mammals found close to the water include South America's largest native terrestrial mammal, the **Brazilian tapir** (*tapir*, *anta* or *mborevi*). The strange **tree-porcupine** (*coendú*) clambers around the canopy with the help of its tail, while the **three-toed sloth** (*perezoso*) depends on its sabre-like claws for locomotion. Felines are represented by **jaguars**, **margays**, **pumas** and **Geoffroy's cats**, but you will be lucky to see anything other than their tracks. This also applies to the most famous regional creature of all: the **taruca**, a stocky, native Andean deer.

The puna

The pre-*puna* and higher **puna** of the Andean Northwest encompass harsh, arid habitats. The most distinctive plant is the **cardón cactus** (also called *pasakán*), which indigenous folklore holds to be the reincarnated form of ancestors. On the higher slopes, you'll also find a type of rock-hard cushion-shaped prehistoric moss called **yacreta** that grows incredibly slowly – perhaps a millimetre a year – but lives for hundreds of years. It has been heavily exploited – partly for medicinal teas, but mainly because it is the only fuel found at these altitudes.

Of the fauna, birds are the most prolific; you can see all three varieties of **flamingo** – Andean, Chilean and James' – wading or flying together. Mammals spotted in the *puna* include **vizcachas**, looking like large rabbits with long, curly tails, and camelids (see box below).

THE CAMELIDS

The animals most people associate with the Andes are the four species of South American **camelids**, especially the **llama**, a domesticated species. The local people use llamas as beasts of burden, as well as for meat and wool. The other domesticated camelid is the slightly smaller **alpaca**, which produces finer wool. The two other South American camelids are both wild. The short-haired antelope-like **guanaco** inhabits a wide area, from the northwest *puna* to the mountains and steppe of Tierra del Fuego; listen for their eerie, rasping call. The guanaco population is still relatively healthy, although it is hunted for its meat and skin. The guanaco's diminutive cousin, the **vicuña**, is the most graceful, shy and – despite its appearance – hardy of the four camelids, capable of living at the most extreme altitudes. It's usually found between 3500m and 4600m, as far south as northern San Juan Province, although the biggest flocks are in Catamarca Province. Hunting brought them to the brink of extinction, but protection measures have helped ensure that their numbers have risen to safe level. Attempts are being made to exploit their valuable fur (the second finest natural fibre in the world after silk) on a sustainable commercial level.

Patagonian steppe

Typified by brush scrub and wiry *coirón* grassland, the Patagonian steppe (*estepa*) covers the greatest extent of any Argentine ecosystem. This vast expanse of semi-desert lies south of the pampas and east of the Andean cordillera. Vegetation is stunted by gravelly soils, high winds and lack of water, except along rivers, where you find marshlands (*mallines*) and startlingly green willows (*sauces*). Just about the only trees, apart from the willows, are non-native Lombardy poplars, planted to shelter estancias.

Much of the scrubby brush is composed of monochrome *mata negra*, but in places you'll come across the resinous, perfumed *mata verde*, or the ash-grey *mata guanaco*, which blooms with dazzling orange flowers. You'll also see spiky **calafate** bushes, and *molle* – one of the largest bushes, covered with thorns and parasitic galls.

Your best chance of sighting some of the steppe's key species is in places such as Chubut's Península Valdés and Punta Tombo. **Guanacos** abound here. Look out too for the **mara** (Patagonian hare), the largest of Argentina's endemic mammals. This long-legged rodent, the size of a small dog, is becoming ever rarer. The **grey fox** (*zorro gris*) is regularly found around national park gates, waiting for scraps thrown by tourists. *Pichi* and *peludo* **armadillos** are often seen scampering across the plains.

Another characteristic bird of prey is the Black-chested buzzard-eagle (*águila mora*), a powerful flier with broad wings and splendid plumage. The classic bird of the steppe, though, is the Lesser or Darwin's rhea (*ñandú petiso* or *choique*). These long-legged, ashy-grey birds lay their eggs in communal clutches.

Patagonian forests

The eastern slopes of the Patagonian cordillera are cloaked in forests of **Nothofagus southern beech**. Two species run from northern Neuquén to Tierra del Fuego: the **lenga** (upland beech) and the **ñire** (lowland or Antarctic beech). In autumn both species turn a variety of hues. Associated with them are three intriguing plant species: false mistletoe (*farolito chino*), a semi-parasitic plant; verdigris-coloured **lichen beards** (*barba del indio* or *toalla del indio*); and **llao llao** tree fungus, also called *pan de indio* ("Indian's bread"). The *llao llao* produces brain-like knots on trunks and branches that are beloved of local artisans.

One of Argentina's most remarkable trees, the **araucaria monkey puzzle**, grows in central Neuquén on volcanic soils (see box, p.428). But the most diverse type of forest in the region is the rare **Valdivian temperate rainforest** (*selva Valdiviana*), found in patches of the central Patagonian Andes from Lanín to Los Alerces, usually around low passes where rainfall is heaviest. Another tree species found only in the central

---

ENVIRONMENTAL PROTECTION

Despite the protection afforded by a relatively well-managed national park system, the country's precious environmental heritage remains under threat. The most pressing issues are **habitat loss** and the protection of threatened forest, such as the Paraná forest in Misiones – a habitat that's been decimated over the border in Brazil and Paraguay. **Hydroelectric projects** in the northeast have destroyed valuable habitats along the Uruguay and Paraná rivers, and **overfishing** has also severely depleted stocks in the latter. The phenomenal rise of **genetically modified soya** production in Argentina has also alarmed environmental campaigners, with particular concerns about the effects of monoculture on the country's biodiversity.

That said, **environmental consciousness** is slowly gaining ground, especially among the younger generation. Greenpeace has thousands of members in Argentina; the national parks system is expanding with the help of international loans; and committed national and local pressure groups such as the Fundación de Vida Silvestre in Buenos Aires (see p.40) are ensuring that ecological issues are not ignored.

Patagonian Lake District is the mighty **alerce**, or Patagonian cypress, which resembles a Californian redwood and is one of the world's oldest and grandest species.

Many of the birds that inhabit the steppe are also found in the cordillera. Typical woodland species include the world's most southerly parrot, the **Austral parakeet** (*cachaña* or *cotorra*) and two birds that allow you to get surprisingly close – the **Magellanic woodpecker** (*carpintero negro gigante*), and the **Austral pygmy owl** (*caburé*). Finally, if any bird has a claim to symbolizing South America, it's the **Andean condor**. With eyesight eight times better than a human's, and the longest wingspan of any bird of prey, it's the undisputed lord of the skies from Venezuela to Tierra del Fuego.

The principal predator of cordillera mammals is the **puma**, which has an extensive range in Argentina but is rarely seen. Perhaps the most endangered creature is the **huemul**, a thick-set native deer (see box, p.419). Almost as endangered is the **pudú**, the world's smallest deer, measuring 40cm at the shoulder. It has small, single-pointed horns, and is difficult to spot, as it inhabits the dense undergrowth of the central cordillera forests.

Introduced species include the European **red deer** (*ciervo colorado*) and **wild boar** (*jabalí*), both of which have reached plague proportions in some parts of the central Lake District. The **beaver** (*castor*), introduced to Tierra del Fuego in an attempt to start a fur-farming industry, has had devastating effects on the environment.

The Atlantic seaboard

Argentina has 4725km of **Atlantic coastline**, with several coastal areas integrated into a shorebird reserve network, designed to protect migrant waders across the Americas. Birds like the **Hudsonian godwit** (*becasa de mar*) and the **Red knot** (*playero rojizo*) migrate from Alaska as far as Tierra del Fuego – over 17,000km. Other coastal species are **Magellanic penguins** (*pingüino magallánico*), whose major continental breeding colony is at Punta Tombo; **Chilean flamingoes**; and the **South American tern** (*gaviotín sudamericano*).

Península Valdés is the main destination for marine fauna. Its twin bays, Golfo Nuevo and Golfo San José (Latin America's first marine park), are where as much as a quarter of the world's population of **Southern right whales** (*ballena franca austral*) breed annually. The peninsula also hosts a forty-thousand-strong and growing colony of **Southern elephant seals** (*elefante marino*). Other sightings might include **sea lions** (*lobos del mar*), found in colonies along the whole Atlantic coast, and possibly even a **killer whale** (*orca*). Further down the coast at Cabo Blanco, you can see the endangered **fur seal** (*lobo de dos pelos*); while Puerto Deseado and San Julián are fine places to catch the piebald **Commerson's dolphins** (*toninas overas*). Sea trips on the Beagle Channel offer a slim chance of seeing **minke whale**, or even perhaps an endangered **marine otter** (*nutria marina* or *chungungo*).

Music

With the obvious exception of tango, Argentina's music has a low international profile. The country has a tradition that doesn't quite fit the popular concept of "Latin American" music: there is little of the exhilarating tropical rhythms of, say, Brazil, nor is there much of the pan-pipe sound associated with Andean countries. Within Latin America, however, Argentina is famed for its rock music, or rock nacional – a term which embraces an eclectic bunch of groups and musicians. Folk music, or folklore, is also popular throughout the country and provides a predominantly rural counterpoint to tango.

Tango

The great Argentine writer Jorge Luis Borges was a tango enthusiast and something of a historian of the music. "My informants all agree on one fact," he wrote. "The Tango was born in the brothels." Borges' sources were a little presumptuous, perhaps, for no one can exactly pinpoint **tango**'s birthplace, but it certainly had roots in Buenos Aires. Early tango was a definitively urban music: a product of the melting pot of European immigrants, *criollos*, blacks and natives, drawn together when the city became the country's capital in 1880. Tango was thus forged from a range of musical influences that included Andalucían flamenco, southern Italian melodies, Cuban habanera, African candombé and percussion, European polkas and mazurkas, Spanish contradanse and, closer to home, the *milonga* – the song of the gaucho. In this early form, tango became associated with the bohemian life of bordello brawls and *compadritos* – knife-wielding, womanizing thugs. By 1914 there were over one hundred thousand more men than women in Buenos Aires, and machismo and violence were part of the culture. Men would dance together in cafés and bars, practising new steps and keeping in shape while waiting for their women, often the *minas* of the bordellos. Their dances tended to have a showy yet predatory quality, often revolving around a possessive relationship between two men and one woman. In these surroundings, the *compadrito* danced the tango into existence.

The original **tango ensembles** were trios of violin, guitar and flute, but around the end of the nineteenth century the **bandoneón**, the tango accordion, arrived from Germany, and the classic tango orchestra was born. The box-shaped button accordion, now inextricably linked with Argentine tango, was invented around 1860 in Germany to play religious music in organless churches, and was reworked as the *bandoneón*.

In Argentina, an early pioneer of the instrument was **Eduardo Arolas**, remembered as the "Tiger of the Bandoneón". He recognized its immediate affinity with the tango – indeed, he claimed it was an instrument made to play tango, with a deep melancholy feeling that suited immigrants nostalgic for the homeland. It is not, however, an easy instrument to play, demanding a great deal of skill, with its seventy-odd buttons each producing one of two notes depending on whether the bellows are being compressed or expanded.

Vicente Greco (1888–1924) is credited as the first bandleader to standardize the form of a tango group, with his **Orquesta Típica Criolla** of two violins and two *bandoneones*. There were some larger bands but the instrumentation remained virtually unchanged until the 1940s.

First tango in Paris

By the first decade of the twentieth century, the tango was an intrinsic part of the popular culture of Buenos Aires, played on the streets by organ grinders and danced in tenement courtyards. Its association with whorehouses and the low-down Porteño lifestyle, plus its saucy, sometimes obscene and fatalistic lyrics, didn't endear it to the aristocratic families of Buenos Aires, though, and they did their best to protect their children from the new dance, but it was a losing battle.

A number of upper-class playboys, such as poet and writer **Ricardo Güiraldes**, enjoyed mixing with the *compadritos* and emulating their lifestyle – from a debonair distance. It was Güiraldes who, on a European grand tour in 1910, is said to have been responsible for bringing the dance to Europe. The following year Güiraldes gave an impromptu performance in a Paris salon to a fashionable audience, for whom tango's risqué sexuality ("the vertical expression of horizontal desire", as one wag dubbed it) was highly attractive. Despite the local archbishop's admonition that Christians should not in good conscience tango, they did, and in large numbers. And, once it was embraced in French salons, its credibility at home greatly increased. Back in Argentina, from bordello to ballroom, everyone was soon dancing the tango.

And then came **Rudolph Valentino**, a charismatic Hollywood star whose image tango fitted to a T. A tango scene was gratuitously added to his film *The Four Horsemen of the Apocalypse* (1926): dressed in a gaucho's wide trousers, Valentino danced with a carnation between his lips (his own invention) and a whip in his hand. The scene was the hit of the film, and, travesty though it was, it meant the dance was now known all over the world. Tango classes and competitions were held in Paris, and tango teas in England, with young devotees togged up as Argentine gauchos. Even the greatest tango singer of all time, **Carlos Gardel**, when he became the darling of Parisian society, and later starred in Hollywood films, was forced to perform dressed as a gaucho. To this day, this image remains many people's primary perception of tango.

Tango's golden age

Back in Argentina, in the 1920s, the tango moved out of the cantinas and bordellos and into cabarets and theatres, entering a classic era under bandleaders like **Roberto Firpo**, **Julio de Caro** and **Francisco Canaro**. With their *orquestas típicas* they took the old line-up of Vicente Greco (two *bandoneones*, two violins, a piano and flute) and substituted a double bass for the flute, thereby adding sonority and depth. It was during this period that some of the most famous of all tangos were written, including Uruguayan **Gerardo Hernán Matos Rodríguez**'s *La Comparsita* in 1917.

CARLOS GARDEL

Carlos Gardel (1887–1935) was – and still is – a legend in Argentina. He was a huge influence in spreading the popularity of tango round the world, and came to be seen as a symbol of the fulfilment of the dreams of poor Porteño workers.

In Argentina, it was Gardel above all who transformed tango from an essentially low-down dance form to a song style popular among widely differing social classes. Everything about Gardel – his suavity, his arrogance and his natural machismo – spelt tango. The advent of radio, recording and film all helped his career, but nothing helped him more than his own voice – a voice that was born to sing tango and which became the model for all future singers of the genre.

His arrival on the scene coincided with the first period of tango's golden age and the development of *tango-canción* in the 1920s and 1930s. During his life, Gardel recorded some nine hundred songs and starred in numerous films, notably *The Tango on Broadway* in 1934. He was tragically killed in an air crash in Colombia at the height of his fame, and his legendary status was confirmed. His image is still everywhere in Buenos Aires, on plaques and huge murals, and in record-store windows, while admirers pay homage to his life-sized, bronze statue in Chacarita cemetery (see p.102).

After Gardel, the split between the **evolutionists**, who wanted to develop new forms of tango, and the **traditionalists**, who thought it was fine as it was, became more pronounced. Bands, as elsewhere in the world during this period, became larger, in the mode of small orchestras, and a mass following for tango was enjoyed through dance halls, radio and recordings until the end of the golden age around 1950.

Early **tango-canciónes** (tango songs) used the language of the ghetto and celebrated the life of ruffians and pimps. **Angel Villoldo** and **Pascual Contursi** introduced the classic lyric of a male perspective, placing the blame for heartache firmly on the shoulders of a fickle woman. In its **dance**, tango consolidated a contradictory mix of earthy sensuality and middle-class kitsch. It depended on an almost violent and dangerous friction of bodies, which collided often in a passion that seemed controlled by the dance itself.

The second golden age

As an expression of the working classes, the progression of the tango has inevitably been linked with social and political developments in Argentina. The music declined a little in the 1930s as the army took power and suppressed what was seen as a potentially subversive force, but it enjoyed a second golden age with the rise of Perón and his emphasis on nationalism and popular culture. By the late 1940s Buenos Aires was a city of five or six million, and each barrio boasted ten or fifteen amateur tango orchestras, while the established orchestras played in the cabarets and nightclubs in the city centre. Sometime in this era, however, tango began to move away from working class and into middle-class and intellectual milieus. It became a sort of collective reminiscence of a world that no longer existed – essentially nostalgia.

In the 1950s, with the end of Peronism and the coming of rock'n'roll, tango slipped into the shadows once again.

Astor Piazzolla and tango nuevo

Astor Piazzolla dominates the recent history of tango, much as Carlos Gardel was the key figure of its classic era. From 1937, Piazzolla played second *bandoneón* in the orchestra of the master Aníbal Troilo, where he developed his feel for arrangements. (The first *bandoneón* takes the melody, and the second *bandoneón* the harmony.)

Troilo left Piazzolla his *bandoneón* when he died, and Piazzolla went on to ensure that tango would never be the same again. Piazzolla's idea was that tango could be a serious music to listen to, not just for dancing, and for many of the old guard this was a step too far. As he explained: "Musicians hated me. I was taking the old tango away from them. The old tango, the one they loved, was dying. And they hated me, they threatened my life hundreds of times. They waited for me outside my house, two or three of them, and gave me a good beating. They even put a gun at my head once." In the 1970s, Piazzolla was out of favour with Argentina's military regime and he and his family moved to Paris, returning to Argentina only after the fall of the junta. His influence, however, had spread, and his experiments – and international success – opened the way for other radical transformations.

Chief among these, in 1970s Buenos Aires, was the fusion of **tango-rockero** – tango rock. This replaced the flexible combination of *bandoneón*, bass and no drums, as favoured by Piazzolla, with a rock-style rhythm section, electric guitars and synthesizers. It was pioneered by **Litto Nebbia**, whose album, *Homage to Gardel and Le Pera*, is one of the most successful products of this fusion, retaining the melancholy of the traditional form in a rock format. Tango moved across to jazz, too, through groups such as the trio **Siglo XX**, while old-guard figures like **Roberto "Polaco" Goyeneche** and **Osvaldo Pugliese** kept traditional tango alive.

These days in Argentina, the tango scene is a pretty broad one, with rock and jazz elements along with the more traditional sound of acoustic groups. There is no shortage of good *tangueros* and they know each other well and jam together often. Big tango orchestras, however, are a thing of the past, and tango bands have returned to their roots, to an intimate era of trios, quartets and quintets – a sextet is serious business. Two of the best sextets, the **Sexteto Mayor** and **Sexteto Berlingieri**, joined together in the 1980s to play for the show *Tango Argentino*, and subsequent shows which revived an interest in tango across Europe and the US. The Sexteto Mayor, founded in 1973 by the virtuoso *bandoneonistas* **José Libertella** (1933–2004) and

Luis Stazo (born 1930), is one of the best tango ensembles in Argentina today, though some of its founding members are no longer with us.

In a more modern idiom, singers like **Susana Rinaldi** and **Adriana Varela** are successfully renovating and re-creating tango, both at home and abroad. They are names to look out for along with *bandoneonistas* **Osvaldo Piro**, **Carlos Buono** and **Walter Ríos**; singer **José Ángel Trelles**; and **Grupo Volpe Tango Contemporáneo**, led by Antonio Volpe.

Latterly, tango is enjoying an upsurge of popularity in Argentina and other parts of the world, thanks in part to TV shows like *Strictly Come Dancing*, and the likes of Buenos Aires' Parakultural outfit and Bajofondo, which successfully melds tango with drum'n'bass and other forms of electronic music, are once again reinventing tango for a new generation. Incidentally, Gustavo Santaolalla, one of the founders of Bajofondo, won the Academy Award (or Oscar) for Original Score in 2005 for *Brokeback Mountain* and again the following year for *Babel*.

Text courtesy of Jan Fairley

Rock nacional

Listened to passionately throughout the country, Argentina's home-grown rock music – known simply as **rock nacional** – began to emerge in the 1960s with groups such as **Almendra**, one of whose members, **Luis Alberto Spinetta**, went on to a solo career and until his death in 2012 was one of Argentina's most successful and original musicians, and **Los Gatos**, who in 1967 had a massive hit with the eloquent *La Balsa*. From a sociological point of view, though, the significance of *rock nacional* really began to emerge under the military dictatorship of 1976–83. At the very beginning of the dictatorship, there was an upsurge in rock concerts, during which musicians such as **Charly García**, frontman of the hugely popular **Serú Girán** and now a soloist, provided a subtle form of resistance with songs such as *No te dejes desanimar* (Don't be discouraged), which helped provoke a collective sense of opposition among fans. It wasn't long, however, before the military rulers clamped down on what it saw as the subversive atmosphere generated at such concerts. The government issued recommendations that stadium owners should not let their premises be used for rock concerts, and by the end of the 1970s many bands had split up or gone into exile.

By 1980, cracks had begun to appear in the regime and a subtle freeing-up of the public sphere began. In December 1980, a concert by Serú Girán attracted sixty thousand fans to La Rural in Palermo: led by Charly García, the fans began to shout, in full view of the television cameras *"No se banca más"* (We won't put up with it anymore).

By 1982 the rock movement was a loudly cynical voice, creating massively popular songs such as **Fito Páez**'s self-explanatory *Tiempos difíciles* (Difficult times), Charly García's *Dinosaurios*, whose title is a clear reference to the military rulers, and *Maribel* by Argentina's finest rock lyricist, Spinetta, dedicated to the Madres de Plaza de Mayo.

Post-dictatorship rock

After the dictatorship ended, rock returned to a more apolitical role, typified by the lighthearted approach of 1984's most popular group, **Los Abuelos de la Nada**. One of the founding members of Los Abuelos, **Pappo**, went on to a solo career in heavy rock, appealing to a predominantly working-class section of society who felt that their lot had improved little with democracy; Pappo's music seemed to sum up their frustrations. One of the most popular groups of the 1980s was **Sumo**, fronted by charismatic **Luca Prodan**, an Italian raised in the UK who had come to Argentina in an attempt to shake off his heroin addiction. Sumo made sometimes surreal, noisy, reggae-influenced tracks, expressing distaste for the frivolous attitudes of Buenos Aires' upper-middle-class youth on tracks such as *Rubia tarada* (Stupid blonde). Luca Prodan ultimately died of a heroin overdose in 1987, but is still idolized by Argentine rock fans.

Like Sumo, the strangely named and massively popular **Patricio Rey y Sus Redonditos de Ricota** (literally: Patricio Rey and His Little Balls of Ricotta) made noise with enigmatic tracks such as *Aquella vaca solitaria cubana* (That solitary Cuban cow), often touching on the dissatisfactions felt by many young Argentines in the aftermath of the dictatorship. Another success story of the 1980s and 1990s – albeit in a very different vein – was **Fito Páez**, whose 1992 album *El Amor después del amor*, with its sweet melodic tunes, one of them inspired by the film *Thelma and Louise*, sold millions throughout Latin America. One of Argentina's most original bands also emerged in the 1980s – **Los Fabulosos Cadillacs**, with their diverse and often frenetic fusion of rock, ska, dub, punk and rap. An irreverent and ironic sense of humour often underlies their politicized lyrics, all belted out by their charismatic, astringently-voiced lead singer, Vincentico, and backed up with a tight horn section and driving Latin percussion. Their classic album is *El León* (1992), on which you'll find their most famous anthem, *Matador*, a savage indictment of the military dictatorship.

Rock nacional's most enduring figures still include Charly García, whose wild exploits fill the pages of gossip magazines, while standout newcomers include the internationally popular "sonic rock" band **Babasónicos**; experimental **Catupechu Machu**; punky **Attaque 77**; **Las Pelotas**, incorporating former Sumo members; melodic indie rockers **Los Estelares**; and the tropical rock sound of **Bersuit Vergarabat**.

Chamamé, cuarteto and folklore

Tango aside, Argentine music is mostly rooted in the rural dance traditions of the countryside, an amalgam of Spanish and immigrant Central European styles with indigenous music. Many of these dances – *rancheras*, *milongas*, *chacareras* and more – are shared with the neighbouring countries of Chile, Perú and Bolivia, while others like **chamamé** are uniquely Argentine. Argentina's Amerindian roots are explored by **Atahualpa Yupanqui**, which grew new shoots in the politicized *nueva canción* (new song) movement.

Chamamé

Chamamé is probably Argentina's most popular roots music. It has its origins in the rural culture of Corrientes – an Amerindian area that attracted nineteenth-century settlers from Poland, Austria-Hungary and Germany. These immigrants brought with them Middle European waltzes, mazurkas and polkas, which over time merged with music from the local Guaraní Amerindian traditions, and African rhythms from the music of the region's slaves. Thus emerged *chamamé*, a music of poor rural *mestizos*, many of whom looked more Indian than European, and whose songs used both Spanish and the Indian Guaraní languages.

Chamamé's melodies have a touch of the melancholy attributed to the Guaraní, while its history charts the social, cultural and political relationships of *mestizo* migrants. Until the 1950s, it was largely confined to Corrientes, but during that decade many rural migrants moved to Buenos Aires, bringing their music and dances with them. *Chamamé* began to attract wider attention – in part, perhaps, because it was a rare folk dance in which people dance in cheek-to-cheek embrace.

The essential sound of *chamamé* comes from its key instrument – the large **piano accordion** (on occasion the *bandoneón*). It sweeps through tunes which marry contrasting rhythms, giving the music an immediate swing. Its African influences may have contributed to the music's accented weak beats so that bars blend and swing together. The distinctive percussive rhythms to the haunting, evocative melodies are the music's unique, compelling feature.

Argentina's reigning king of *chamamé* is **Raúl Barboza**, an artist who has also notched up a certain degree of success in Europe. Barboza's *conjunto* features a typical *chamamé* line-up of one or two accordions, a guitar and *guitarrón* (bass guitar). Perhaps one of the best-known *chamamé* artists internationally is **Chango Spasiuk**, an Argentine of Ukrainian heritage, who has been successful in producing a sort of *chamamé*-rock crossover, with a more modern feel that still preserves the music's essence.

Cuarteto

The Argentine dance style known as *cuarteto* first became popular in the 1940s. Named after the original **Cuarteto Leo** who played it, its line-up involved a solo singer, piano, accordion and violin, and its dance consisted of a huge circle, moving counterclockwise, to a rhythm called *tunga-tunga*. In the 1980s it underwent a resurgence of interest in the working-class "tropical" dancehalls of Buenos Aires, where it was adopted alongside Colombian *guarachas*, Dominican merengue and Latin salsa. It slowly climbed up the social ladder to reach a middle-class market, notching up big record sales. The most famous contemporary singer of *cuarteto* is **Carlos "La Mona" Jiménez**.

Folklore

In a movement aligned to *nueva canción*, dozens of folklore singers and groups emerged in the 1960s and 1970s – their music characterized by tight arrangements and four-part harmonies. The big *nueva canción* star was **Mercedes Sosa**, who passed away in 2009; other leading artists of these decades included the group **Los Chalchaleros**, guitarist **Eduardo Falú**, and **Ariel Ramírez**, notable for his *zambas* and Creole Mass. In more recent years groups have come through experimenting and re-evaluating the folk dance traditions, including the *zamba*, a national dance that involves the couple taking slow steps back and forth while waving handkerchiefs. Among this new wave are **Los Trovadores**, **Los Huanca Hua** and **Cuarteto Zupuy**. The best place to see folklore music is at the annual **Cosquín national folklore festival** (see p.194), which has been a fixture since the 1960s.

Books

Argentina's intellectual tradition is reflected in its many bookshops, especially the splendidly monumental ones in Buenos Aires. For non-Spanish-speakers, there are specialist sellers in the capital (see pp.125–127 for stockists), though if you're looking for specific books, such as the works listed below, your best bet is to get a copy before you depart. Glossy English-language coffee-table books that focus on subjects such as Patagonia, gauchos and indigenous peoples are widely available in tourist areas. A ★ preceding a title means that it is highly recommended.

TRAVEL

★ **Bruce Chatwin** *In Patagonia*. For many travellers, this is *the* Argentine travel book – in fact, the book that broke the mould for travel writing in general. Written in the 1970s, it's really a series of self-contained tales (most famously of the Argentine adventures of Butch Cassidy and the Sundance Kid) strung together by their connection with Patagonia. This idiosyncratic book has even inspired a "Chatwin trail", although his rather cold style and literary embellishments on the region's history have their detractors too.

Bruce Chatwin and Paul Theroux *Patagonia Revisited*, published in the US as *Nowhere is a Place*. The two doyens of Western travel writing combine to explore the literary associations of Patagonia. Wafer-thin and thoroughly enjoyable, this book throws more light on the myths of this far-flung land than it does on the place itself.

Che Guevara *The Motorcycle Diaries*. Ernesto "Che" Guevara's own account of his epic motorcycle tour around Latin America, beginning in Buenos Aires and heading south to Patagonia and then up through Chile. Che undertook the tour when he was just 23 and the resulting diary is an intriguing blend of travel anecdotes and an insight into the mind of a nascent revolutionary.

George Chaworth Musters *At Home with the Patagonians*. The amazing 1869 journey of Musters as he rode through Patagonia, becoming in the process the first outsider to be accepted into Tehuelche society. This book is our prime source for information on the Tehuelche, and gives a portrait of a culture about to be exterminated.

Paul Theroux *The Old Patagonian Express*. More tales about trains by the tireless cynic. In the four chapters on Argentina, which he passed through just before the 1978 World Cup, he waxes lyrical about cathedral-like Retiro station and has a surreal dialogue with Borges.

A.F. Tschiffely *Tschiffely's Ride*. An account of a truly adventurous horseback ride – described as the "longest and most arduous on record ever made by man and horse" – made by Tschiffely from Buenos Aires to Washington DC in the 1920s and providing an insight into rural Argentina at the time.

HISTORY, POLITICS AND SOCIETY

★ **Paul Blustein** *And the Money Kept Rolling In (and Out): Wall Street, the IMF, and the Bankrupting of Argentina*. The definitive account of the Argentine economic crisis of 2001. *Washington Post* journalist Blustein contends that, though Argentina's fate was always in the hands of its own politicians, the IMF worsened the situation by indulging their emerging market "poster child" long beyond the point when the debt burden had become unsustainable, while the unrestricted flows of the global finance market had their role to play, too. Authoritative, and a cracking read.

Lucas Bridges *The Uttermost Part of the Earth*. The genius of this classic text on pioneering life in Tierra del Fuego in the late nineteenth century lies less in its literary attributes than in the extraordinary tales of an adventurous young man's relationship with the area's indigenous groups, and the invaluable ethnographic knowledge he imparts about a people whose culture was set to disappear within his lifetime.

Jimmy Burns *The Hand of God*. A compelling read in which Anglo-Argentine journalist Burns charts the rise and fall of Diego Maradona, updated in 2010 as the bad-boy hero of football prepared to manage the national squad in the World Cup. Burns also wrote *The Land that Lost its Heroes*, a thoroughly researched account of the Falklands/Malvinas conflict.

★ **Uki Goñi** *The Real Odessa*. A thoroughly researched investigation into the aid given by Perón (and the Vatican) to Nazi war criminals; hundreds infamously settled in Argentina. The Argentine government and Peronist party in particular has done little to address its previous sheltering of these men – indeed, Goñi finds evidence that incriminating documents were being burnt as late as 1996.

John Lynch *San Martín: Argentinian soldier, American hero*. The first English-language biography of modern times of José de San Martín, arguably the greatest of all Latin American

THE DIRTY WAR IN BOOKS AND FILM

The tragedy of the bloody 1979–83 "Dirty War" has left deep scars on Argentine society that are yet to heal, and the experience and legacy of those years is a recurrent theme in books – fact and fiction – and films set in the country. As well as the works below, there's *Nunca Mas* (Never Again), the 1984 report (assembled by a truth commission – a model later used by other Latin American countries facing past demons), which was the first to reveal the horrors of what had taken place. It is available in English at @desaparecidos.org, with an excellent intro by novelist Ernesto Sabato.

BOOKS

Rita Arditti *Searching for Life*. Describes the ongoing search by their wider families for hundreds of children who disappeared, many given for adoption to military families after their parents were captured.

Nathan Englander *The Ministry of Special Cases*. A wry and tragic fictional story by a Jewish-American writer, which deals with the disappearance of a teenage son during the *proceso*.

Tomás Eloy Martínez *Purgatory*. Heart-wrenching semiautobiographical tale of a woman and a country still haunted by the ghosts of the past.

Jacobo Timerman *Prisoner Without A Name, Cell*

Without A Number. A first-person account written by a prisoner who survived; his son is currently Argentina's foreign minister.

Horacio Verbitsky *Confessions of an Argentine Dirty Warrior*. Infamous account of the horrific practice of pushing drugged prisoners into the River Plate, by one of the perpetrators of the state-backed repression.

Andrew Graham Yool *A State of Fear*. Written by the *Buenos Aires Herald* editor, this is a very readable account of this dark era by a journalist living through and reporting on it.

FILMS

Argentina's vibrant movie industry has received two foreign-language Oscars, both for movies that deal with this subject.

The Official Story (1985). A middle-class woman learns of events that have been hidden from her when she sets out to uncover her adopted daughter's real parents.

The Secret in Their Eyes (2009). Through the story of a federal agent revisiting an old murder case, this

asks the question pondered by many – isn't it time to move on now? The answer seems to be no – not while there are still people who have to live with the painful events three decades on, and who still have unanswered questions.

---

heroes, who led the continent's independence struggle against Spain in the nineteenth century. Lynch is a major Latin American scholar; his numerous books on the region also include essential biographies of nineteenth-century dictator Rosas and of San Martín's brother-in-arms Simón Bolívar.

★ **Gabriella Nouzeilles and Graciela Montaldo** (eds) *The Argentina Reader*. Compendium of essays and stories on Argentina's history and culture, including extracts from many of the books listed here. An excellent starting point for further reading, though a bit hefty for lugging around in a backpack or suitcase.

Domingo F. Sarmiento *Facundo, or Civilization and Barbarism*. Written in the form of a fictional biography of

real-life gaucho thug Facundo Quiroga, this is probably the most influential of all books written in Latin America in the nineteenth century. The essay defines one of Argentina's major cultural peculiarities – the battle between the provinces seeking to carve out their own power and a sophisticated metropolis more interested in what is going on abroad than in its vast hinterland.

Richard W. Slatta *Gauchos and the Vanishing Frontier*. Scholarly work that is the perfect cerebral accompaniment to the coffee-table tomes sold on the subject. Slatta charts the rise, fall and rise again of the gaucho, his lifestyle, his maltreatment by the upper classes and the myths that grew around him.

NATURE AND WILDLIFE

Charles Darwin *The Voyage of the Beagle*. Very readable account of Darwin's famous voyage, which takes him through Patagonia and the pampas. Filled with observations on the flora, fauna, landscape and people (including the dictator Rosas) that Darwin encounters, all described in the scientist's methodical yet evocative style.

Gerald Durrell *The Whispering Land*. A lighthearted read

detailing Durrell's observations while animal-collecting in Península Valdés, the Patagonian steppe and the *yungas*. Enduring good value, despite what now comes across as a colonial tone: his capacity for making animals into characters is unsurpassed. See also *The Drunken Forest*, about his trip to the Chaco.

W.H. Hudson *Far Away and Long Ago*. A nostalgic and gently ambling portrait of childhood and rural tranquillity in the Argentine pampas in Rosas' time. An early environmentalist, the author regrets the expansion of agriculture and the destruction of habitat variety in the pampas in the course of his lifetime.

THE ARTS

Simon Collier (ed) *Tango! The Dance, the Song, the Story* (o/p). A glossy coffee-table book with a lively account of the history of tango and its key protagonists, well illustrated with colour and black-and-white photos.

★ **Francis Mallman** *Seven Fires*. Beautifully illustrated recipe book, with a good dash of memoir, by top Argentine cook Francis Mallman, now a TV personality as well as owner of one of the country's most applauded restaurants

Martín R. de la Peña and Maurice Rumboll *Birds of Southern South America and Antarctica*. A useful companion for even the non-specialist birdwatcher. It would benefit from some indication of frequency and a few illustrations could do with more detail, but overall is recommended.

(see p.348). Mallman explains how to cook over wood, and includes dozens of recipes, from empanadas to *dulce de leche* flan.

Alberto Manguel *With Borges*. Accomplished Argentine writer Manguel recounts the time as a young man he spent reading to Borges. Absolutely charming essay, with the kind of gentle humour, subtle poetry and sharp insights into Buenos Aires life that characterize the great man's own work.

FICTION

Roberto Arlt *The Seven Madmen*. Until his tragically early death, Roberto Arlt captured the lot of the poor immigrant with his gripping, if idiosyncratic, novels about anarchists, whores and other marginal characters in 1920s Buenos Aires. *The Seven Madmen* is the pick of his works – dark and at times surreal, it's filled with images of the frenetic and alienating pace of urban life as experienced by the novel's tormented protagonist, Remo Erdosain.

★ **Jorge Luis Borges** *Labyrinths*. Not only Argentina's greatest writer, but one of the world's finest and most influential. His prose is highly original, witty and concise; rather than novels, he introduces his ideas through short stories and essays – ideal for dipping into – and *Labyrinths* is a good introduction to these, with selections from his major collections. It includes many of his best-known and most enigmatic tales, including *Library of Babel*, an analogy of the world as a never-ending library.

★ **Julio Cortázar** *Hopscotch*. Cortázar is probably second only to Borges in the canon of Argentine writers and *Hopscotch* is a major work, published in the 1960s. In this fantastically complex book, Cortázar defies traditional narrative structure, inviting the reader to "hop" between chapters (hence the name), which recount the lives of a group of friends in Paris and London.

Graham Greene *The Honorary Consul*. A masterful account of a farcical kidnapping attempt that goes tragically wrong. Set in the city of Corrientes and dedicated to Argentine literary doyenne Victoria Ocampo, with whom Greene spent time in San Isidro and Mar del Plata.

★ **Ricardo Güiraldes** *Don Segundo Sombra*. A tender and nostalgic evocation of past life on the pampas, chronicling the relationship between a young boy and his mentor, the novel's eponymous gaucho. Written in 1926, some decades after the gaucho era had come to a close, it was a key text in changing the image of the Argentine cowboy from that of a violent undesirable to a strong, independent man with simple tastes, at the heart of Argentina's national identity.

José Hernández *Martín Fierro*. The classic gaucho epic, written in verse and traditionally learnt by heart by many Argentines. Written as a protest against the corrupt authorities, it features a highly likeable gaucho outlaw on the run, who rails against the country's weak institutional structures and dictatorial rulers. Its rhyming verse and liberal use of gaucho lingo make translation difficult; one version is the classic Walter Owen translation from the 1930s, available in Argentine bookshops.

★ **Tomás Eloy Martínez** *The Tango Singer*. The late Tomás Eloy Martínez was one of modern Argentina's most insightful journalists and novelists. The evocative descriptions of contemporary Buenos Aires in this tale of an American seeking an elusive tango singer make this an ideal literary companion to a visit. See also his books *Santa Evita* and *The Perón Novel*, about Argentina's famous couple, which masterfully mix historical fact and fiction.

Manuel Puig *Kiss of the Spiderwoman*. Arguably the finest book by one of Argentina's most original twentieth-century writers, distinguished by a style that mixes film dialogue and popular culture with more traditional narrative. Set during the 1970s dictatorship, this is an absorbing tale of two cellmates, worlds apart on the outside but drawn together by gay protagonist Molina's recounting of films to his companion, left-wing guerrilla Valentín.

Horacio Quiroga *The Decapitated Chicken and Other Stories*. Wonderful if sometimes disturbing gothic tales of love, madness and death. Includes the spine-chilling "Feather Pillow", in which the life is slowly sucked from a young bride by a hideous blood-sucking beast, found engorged after her death within her feather pillow.

Colm Tóibín *The Story of the Night*. A moving tale of a young Anglo-Argentine trying to come to terms both with his sexuality and existential dilemmas in the wake of the South Atlantic conflict, and getting caught up in an undercover plot by the CIA to get Carlos Menem elected president.

Language

You'll find at least a decent smattering of Spanish very useful in Argentina. English-speakers are not uncommon, especially in big cities, but they are not ubiquitous and Argentines are appreciative of visitors who make the effort to communicate in Castellano, or Spanish. A good pocket dictionary is a vital accessory but if you really want to refine your grasp of the language, a comprehensive grammar such as *A New Reference Grammar of Modern Spanish* by John Butt and Carmen Benjamin is a worthwhile investment.

Argentine Spanish is highly distinctive, especially the unmistakeable Porteño accent, characterized by a musical lilt and peppered with colloquialisms, betraying the strong Italian influence, as does the irresistible tendency to gesticulate. Beyond the River Plate region (in or close to the capital), certain regional variations take hold, though most rules of pronunciation, grammar and vocabulary apply for the whole country. Nowhere in Argentina will you hear the Iberian lisp in words like *cerveza* ("beer" – pronounced "sehr-bessa"). What really sets the local lingo apart, though, is the unique pronunciation of y/ll in words such as *yo* ("I/me") and *llave* ("key") as "zh" (the English equivalent is the "s" in "treasure"): "zho", "zhabe". A notable grammatical difference is the use of *vos* as the second-person pronoun ("you" singular), in place of *tú*, with correspondingly different verb endings – eg *vos sabés* = "you know", instead of *tú sabes*. *Ustedes* is always used as the second-person plural pronoun (the plural of "you"); *vosotros* and its derivatives are unheard of. The use of "*che*" (used when addressing someone; it loosely translates as "hey mate") in particular is so much identified with Argentina that other Latin Americans sometimes refer to Argentines as "*Los Che*". The word was most famously applied as a nickname of Ernesto Guevara, who was popularly and universally known as "Che" Guevara.

Pronunciation

The Spanish pronunciation system is extremely phonetic – in other words spelling follows rigid rules, unlike English that seems to make them up as it goes along. Sounds in no two languages are exactly alike – be aware in particular that Spanish tends to be more fluid, less clearly enunciated and less staccato than English – but the following are examples of letters that are pronounced in a radically different way in (Argentine) Spanish and English. By the way, an (acute) accent written on a vowel denotes emphasis or stress – otherwise the tonic accent nearly always falls on the last syllable but one.

c is like "ss" before E and I, like "k" elsewhere.

g is like the h in "hill" before E and I, like "g" (as in "got") elsewhere.

h is silent, except after C when the two letters combine to make "ch" as in "Chile".

j is like the "ch" in "loch" but softer, closer to an aspirate H.

ll is like the "s" in "pleasure" (except in Corrientes and Misiones where it is pronounced "li" as in "pavilion"): *ella* sounds like "pleasure" (British pronunciation) without the "pl" but in the northeast sounds like "ell-ya".

ñ is pronounced "ni" as in "onion". Ñandú is pronounced "nyandOO".

r is trilled as in Italian or Scots; RR or R at the beginning of a word is doubly trilled (in parts of central and northwestern Argentina this sound is more like a "sh": *rosa* ("rose") and *barrio* ("district/neighbourhood").

s is always soft as in "sign", never like a Z and not slushy as in much of Spain.

u after G and Q is silent. Miguel, the name, is "Mig-el", not "Mig-well".

v is basically pronounced like a B, though softened to a sound closer to English V in between two vowels: eg *Eva*.

y as a consonant (eg in *yacaré* – "alligator") is like the "s" in "pleasure", even in Corrientes and Misiones. Y meaning "and" is an example of "y" as a vowel: it is pronounced like the "y" in "city".

z is a soft "ss" sound, never hard like an English Z: *zorro* (fox) sounds a little like the English word "sorrow".

ESSENTIALS

yes, no	sí, no	Great Britain	Gran Bretaña
please, thank you	por favor, gracias	Ireland	Irlanda
where, when	dónde, cuándo	New Zealand	Nueva Zelanda
what, how much	qué, cuánto	South Africa	Sudáfrica
here, there	acá, allá	United Kingdom	Reino Unido
now, later	ahora, más tarde/luego	United States	Estados Unidos
open, closed	abierto/a, cerrado/a	Scotland	Escocia
with, without	con, sin	Wales	Gales
good, bad	bueno/a, malo/a		
big	grande	**GREETINGS AND RESPONSES**	
small	chico/a (pequeño/a is used less)	hello, goodbye (adiós is used for goodbye, but is more formal)	hola, chau
more, less	más, menos		
a little, a lot	poco, mucho	good morning	buen día
very	muy	good afternoon	buenas tardes
today, tomorrow	hoy, mañana	good night	buenas noches
yesterday	ayer	see you later	hasta luego
nothing, never	nada, nunca	how are you?	¿cómo está(s)? ¿cómo anda/andás?
entrance, exit	entrada, salida		
pull, push	tire, empuje	(very) well, thanks	(muy) bien gracias
Australia	Australia	excuse me	(con) permiso
Canada	Canadá	sorry	perdón, disculpe
England	Inglaterra	cheers!	¡salud!

USEFUL PHRASES AND EXPRESSIONS

Note that when two verb forms are given, the first corresponds to the familiar *vos* form and the second to the formal *usted* form.

I (don't) understand	(No) entiendo	I'm hungry	Tengo hambre
Do you speak English?	¿Hablás inglés?/¿habla inglés?	I'm thirsty	Tengo sed
		I don't feel well	No me siento bien
I (don't) speak Spanish	(No) hablo castellano	What's up?	¿Qué pasa?
My name is…	Me llamo…	I don't know	No (lo) sé
What's your name?	¿Cómo te llamás?/¿cómo se llama (usted)?	What's the time?	¿Qué hora es?
I'm British/	Soy británico/a	**HOTELS AND TRANSPORT**	
…English	…inglés(a)	Is there a hotel/	¿Hay un hotel/banco cerca (de aquí)?
…American	…estadounidense/ norteamericano/a		
		How do I get to…?	¿Cómo hago para llegar a…?
…Australian	…australiano/a		
…Canadian	…canadiense	Turn left/right	Doblá/doble a la izquierda/derecha
…Irish	…irlandés(a)		
…Scottish	…escocés(a)	On the left/right	A la izquierda/derecha
…Welsh	…galés(a)	Go straight on	Seguí/siga derecho
…a New Zealander	…neocelandés/a	One block/two blocks	Una cuadra, dos cuadras
…South African	…sudafricano(a)		
What's the Spanish for this?	¿Cómo se dice en castellano?	Where is…?	¿Dónde está…?
		the bus station	la terminal de omnibus

the train station	la estación de ferrocarril	5	cinco
the toilet	el baño	6	seis
I want a (return) ticket to…	Quiero un pasaje (de ida y vuelta) para…	7	siete
		8	ocho
Where does the bus for …leave from?	¿De dónde sale el micro para…?	9	nueve
		10	diez
What time does it leave?	¿A qué hora sale?	11	once
How long does it take?	¿Cuánto tarda?	12	doce
far, near	lejos, cerca	13	trece
I want/would like…	quiero/quería…	14	catorce
Is there a discount for students?	¿Hay descuento para estudiantes?	15	quince
		16	dieciséis
Is there hot water?	¿Hay agua caliente?	17	diecisiete
Do you have…?	¿Tiene…?una	18	dieciocho
a (single, double)	habitación (single/	19	diecinueve
room with two beds	doble) con dos camas	20	veinte
with a double bed	con cama matrimonial	21	veintiuno
with a private bathroom	con baño privado	30	treinta
with breakfast	con desayuno	40	cuarenta
It's for one person/	Es para una persona/	50	cincuenta
one night/two weeks	una noche/dos semanas	60	sesenta
How much is it?	¿Cuánto es/Cuánto sale?	70	setenta
It's too expensive	Es demasiado caro	80	ochenta
Do you have anything cheaper?	¿Hay algo más barato?	90	noventa
		100	cien/ciento
Is there a discount for cash?	¿Hay descuento por pago en efectivo?	200	doscientos/as
		1000	mil
Is camping allowed here?	¿Se puede acampar aquí?	1,000,000	un millón
		2008	dos mil ocho
		Monday	lunes
NUMBERS AND DAYS		Tuesday	martes
0	cero	Wednesday	miércoles
1	uno/una	Thursday	jueves
2	dos	Friday	viernes
3	tres	Saturday	sábado
4	cuatro	Sunday	domingo

AN ARGENTINE MENU READER

BASICS

Spanish	English	Spanish	English
aceite de maíz	corn oil	desayuno	breakfast
aceite de oliva	olive oil	guarnición	side dish
agregado	side order or garnish	harina	flour
ají	chilli	huevos	eggs
ajo	garlic	lata/latita	can or tin
almuerzo	lunch	manteca	butter
arroz	rice	mayonesa	mayonnaise
azúcar	sugar	menú del día	set meal
carta/menú	menu	mermelada/dulce	jam
cena	dinner	mostaza	mustard
comedor	diner or dining room	pan (francés)	bread (baguette or French stick)
copa	glass (for wine)	pimentón dulce	paprika
cuchara	spoon	pimienta	pepper
cuchillo	knife	plato	plate or dish
cuenta	bill	queso	cheese

sal	salt
sanduich	sandwich (usually made with very thinly sliced bread: *sanduich de miga*)
servilleta	napkin
taza	cup
tenedor	fork
vaso	glass (for water)
vegetariano	vegetarian
vinagre	vinegar

CULINARY TERMS

parrilla	barbecue
asado	roasted or barbecued; *un asado* is a barbecue
a la plancha	grilled
ahumado	smoked
al horno	baked/roasted
al natural	canned (of fruit)
al vapor	steamed
crudo	raw
frito	fried
picante	hot (spicy)
puré	puréed or mashed potatoes
relleno	stuffed

MEAT (*CARNE*) AND POULTRY (*AVES*)

bife	steak
bife de chorizo	prize steak cut
cabrito	goat (kid)
carne vacuna	beef
cerdo	pork
ciervo	venison
codorniz	quail
conejo	rabbit
cordero	lamb
chivito	kid or goat
chuleta	chop
churrasco	grilled beef
fiambres	cured meats – hams, salami, etc
filete	fillet steak
jabalí	wild boar
jamón	ham
lechón/cochinillo	suckling pig
lomo	tenderloin steak
milanesa	breaded veal escalope
oca	goose
paletilla	shoulder of lamb
panceta	Italian-style bacon
pato	duck
pavo	turkey

pebete	sandwich in a bun or bread roll
pollo	chicken
ternera	grass-fed veal
tocino/beicon	bacon

OFFAL (*ACHURAS*)

bofes	lights (lungs)
chinchulines	small intestine
chorizo (blanco)	meaty sausage (not spiced like Spanish chorizo – *chorizo colorado*)
corazón	heart
criadillas	testicles
hígado	liver
lengua	tongue
mollejas	sweetbreads (thymus gland)
mondongo	cow's stomach
morcilla	blood sausage
orejas	ears
patas	feet or trotters
riñones	kidneys
sesos	brains
tripa gorda	tripe (large intestine)
ubre	udder

TYPICAL DISHES (*PLATOS*)

arroz con pollo	a kind of chicken risotto
bife a caballo	steak with a fried egg on top
bife a la criolla	steaks braised with onions, peppers and herbs
brochetas	kebabs
carbonada	a filling meat stew
cazuela de marisco	a seafood casserole
cerdo a la riojana	pork cooked with fruit
fainá	baked chickpea dough traditionally served with pizza
guiso	basic meat stew
locro	stew based on maize, beans and meat, often including tripe
matambre relleno	cold stuffed flank steak (normally filled with vegetables and hard-boiled eggs, and sliced; literally means "stuffed hunger killer")
matambrito	pork, often simmered in milk until soft

milanesa napolitana	breaded veal escalope topped with ham, tomato and melted cheese
milanesa de pollo	breaded chicken breast
mondongo	stew made of cow's stomach with potatoes and tomatoes
pastel de papa	shepherd's pie
provoletta	thick slice of provolone cheese grilled on a barbecue
puchero	a rustic stew, usually of chicken (*puchero de gallina*), made with potatoes and maize or whatever vegetable is to hand
vittel tonné	the Argentine starter par excellence: slices of cold roast beef in mayonnaise mixed with tuna

FISH (*PESCADO*)

abadejo	cod
atún	tuna
boga	large, flavoursome fish caught in the Río de la Plata
caballa	mackerel
corvina	sea bass
dorado	a large freshwater fish, with mushy flesh and loads of bones
lenguado	sole
lisa de río	oily river fish
manduví	river fish with delicate, pale flesh
manguruyú	oily river fish (best grilled)
merluza	hake
pacú	firm-fleshed river fish
pejerrey	popular inland-water fish
pirapitanga	salmon-like river fish
sábalo	oily-fleshed river fish
salmón	salmon
surubí	kind of catfish
trucha (arco iris)	(rainbow) trout
vieja	white, meaty-fleshed river fish

SEAFOOD (*MARISCOS*)

camarones	shrimps or prawns
cangrejo	crab
centolla	king crab
mejillones	mussels
ostras	oysters
vieira	scallop

VEGETABLES (*VERDURAS*)

aceitunas	olives
acelga	chard (like spinach but tougher and more bitter)
albahaca	basil
alcauciles	artichokes
apio	celery
arvejas	peas
aspárragos	asparagus
berenjena	aubergine/eggplant
berro	watercress
cebolla	onion
champiñon	mushroom
chauchas	runner beans
choclo	maize or sweetcorn
chucrút	sauerkraut
coliflor	cauliflower
ensalada	salad
espinaca	spinach
garbanzo	chickpea
habas	broad beans
hinojo	fennel
hongos (silvestres)	(wild) mushrooms
lechuga	lettuce
lentejas	lentils
morrón (dulce/ rojo/verde)	(sweet/red/green) pepper
palmito	palm heart
palta	avocado
papa	potato
papas fritas	chips/French fries
papines	small potatoes eaten whole
perejil	parsley
pimiento	green pepper
poroto	bean
puerro	leek
remolacha	beetroot
rúcula	rocket
tomate	tomato
tomillo	thyme
zanahoria	carrot
zapallito	gem squash – small green pumpkins that are a favourite throughout the country, usually baked stuffed with rice and meat
zapallo	pumpkin

FRUIT AND NUTS (*FRUTA Y FRUTOS SECOS*)

almendra	almond
almíbar	syrup
ananá	pineapple
arándano	cranberry/blueberry
avellana	hazelnut
banana	banana
batata	sweet potato
castaña	chestnut
cayote	spaghetti squash
cereza	cherry
ciruela (seca)	plum (prune)
damasco	apricot
dátiles	dates
durazno	peach
frambuesa	raspberry
frutilla	strawberry
higo	fig
lima	lime
limón	lemon
maní	peanut
manzana	apple
melón	melon
membrillo	quince
mora	mulberry
mosqueta	rose hip
naranja	orange
nuez	walnut
pasa (de uva)	dried fruit (raisin)
pera	pear
pomelo (rosado)	(pink) grapefruit
quinoto	kumquat
sandía	watermelon
uva	grape(s)
zarza mora	blackberry

DESSERTS (*POSTRES*)

arroz con leche	rice pudding
budín de pan	bread pudding
crema	custard or cream
dulce	sweet in general; candied fruit or jam
dulce de leche	thick caramel made from milk and sugar, a national religion (see box, p.35)
ensalada de fruta	fruit salad
flan	crème caramel
helado	ice cream
medialuna (dulce/salado)	(sweet/plain) croissant-like pastry, more like the Italian "cornetto"
miel (de abeja)	honey
miel (de caña)	molasses
panqueque/crêpe	pancake
sambayón	zabaglione (custard made with egg yolks and wine, a popular ice-cream flavour)
torta	tart or cake
tortilla/tortita	breakfast pastry

DRINKS (*BEBIDAS*)

agua	water
agua mineral (con gas/sin gas)	mineral water (sparkling/still)
aguardiente	brandy-like spirit
botella	bottle
cacheteado	Coke and red wine spritzer (very popular in Córdoba)
café (con leche)	coffee (with milk)
cerveza	beer
champán	sparkling wine, usually Argentine, or champagne
chocolate caliente/ submarino	hot chocolate (often a slab of chocolate melted in hot milk, served in a tall glass)
chopp	draught beer
cortado	espresso coffee "cut" with a little steaming milk (similar to macchiato)
Fernet (branca)	Italian-style digestive drink, popularly mixed with Coke (the gaucho drink par excellence)
gaseosa	fizzy drink
jugo (de naranja)	(orange) juice
lata	can
leche	milk
licuados	juice-based drinks or milkshakes
liso	small draught beer (Litoral)
mate cocido	infusion made with *mate*, sometimes heretically with a bag
sidra	cider
soda	fizzy water
té	tea
vino (tinto/blanco/ rosado)	wine (red/white/rosé)

Argentine idiom and slang

Anyone who has learnt Spanish elsewhere will need to become accustomed to the specific vocabulary in Argentina, as a familiarity with Argentine equivalents will certainly smooth things along. Many words for foodstuffs, especially fruit and vegetables, are not the same in Argentina as in other Spanish-speaking countries – you will find many of them in the Argentine menu reader (see p.567).

Though few terms used in Spain are actually taboo in Argentina, there is one major exception, which holds for much of Latin America. The verb **coger**, used in Spain for everything from "to pick up" or "fetch" to "to catch (a bus)", is never used in this way in Argentina, where it is the equivalent of "to fuck". In Argentina use *tomar* (to take) as in *tomar el colectivo* (to catch the bus) or *agarrar* (to take hold of or grab) as in *agarrá la llave* (take the key). Less likely to cause problems, but still one to watch, is **concha**, which in Spain is a perfectly innocent word meaning "seashell", but in Argentina is usually used to refer to the female genitals; the words *caracol* or *almeja* are always used instead for shells and Argentines never tire of finding the Spanish woman's name Conchita (short for Inmaculada Concepción) hilarious (it sounds like "little cunt").

Colloquial speech in Argentina, particularly in Buenos Aires, is extremely colourful, and it's good fun to learn a bit of the local lingo. There's a clear Italian influence in some words. Many colloquial expressions and words also derive from an Italian-flavoured form of slang known as *lunfardo*, originally the language of the Buenos Aires underworld (hence the myriad terms in *lunfardo* proper for police, pimps and prostitutes). There's also a playful form of speech, known as **vesre**, in which words are pronounced backwards (*vesre* is the word for *revés* – reverse, backwards); a few of these words, such as *feca* (coffee from *café*), have found their way into everyday speech. Though these expressions will sound odd coming from the mouth of a less-than-fluent foreigner, knowing a few of them will help you get the most out of what's being said around you. *Lunfardo* is also an important part of the repertoire of tango lyrics. Another feature to listen for is the widespread use of the prefix "re-", to mean "really" or "totally". *Re-lindo/a* means really good-looking; *re-malo/a* means really bad. *Recontra-* is even stronger: something that is *recontra-barato* means it is on sale at a rock-bottom price.

Words listed below that are marked with an asterisk (*) should be used with some caution as they are very familiar; those marked with a double asterisk (**) denote strong language and are best avoided until you are really familiar with local customs or know the person you are speaking to won't be offended.

afanar	to rob*	bombachas	knickers
almacén	grocery shop/store	bombilla	straw-like implement,
auto	car (*coche* is rarely		usually of metal, used
	used)		for drinking mate from
bancar	to put up with*; *no me*		a gourd
	lo banco ("I can't stand	bondi	bus
	it/him")	bronca	rage*, as in *me da bronca*
bárbaro/a	great!		("he/she/it makes me
barra brava	(group of) hardcore		angry")
	football fans	cana	police officer (cop)*;
birome	biro/ballpoint pen		prison*
birra	beer*	cancha	football stadium
boliche	nightclub; also some	canchero	smart (for clothes etc),
	times bar/store/shop		sharp-witted, (over-)
	in rural areas		confident, cool
boludo/pelotudo	idiot (equivalent to prat,	carpa	tent
	jerk etc)**	cartera	handbag/purse

cataratas	waterfalls, usually used to refer specifically to Iguazú Falls
caudillo	regional military or political leader, usually with authoritarian overtones
chabón	boy/lad*
chamuyo	conversation/chat*
chancho	ticket inspector*
chanta	braggart, unreliable person*
chata	pick-up truck*
chico/a	small (also boy/girl)
chorro	thief*
chupar	to drink (alcohol)*
colectivo	bus
combi	small minibus that runs urban bus routes
copado	cool, good*
despelote	mess*
estancia	farm, traditionally with huge areas of land
faso	cigarette*
feca	coffee*
fiaca	tiredness/laziness*, eg tengo fiaca ("I can't be bothered")
forro	condom/idiot**
gamba	leg*
gaucho	typical Argentine "cowboy" or rural estancia worker
gil	idiot*
guita/plata	money*
hincha pelotas	irritating person**
laburar	to work*
lapicera	pen
living	living room
luca	one thousand* (pesos)
mamado	drunk* (un mamado** means a blow-job)
mango	mango; peso*/monetary unit as in no tengo un mango ("I don't have a penny")
manyar	to eat*
mate	strictly the mate gourd or receptacle, but used generally to describe the national "tea" drink
medias	socks
micro	long-distance bus
milico	member of the military*
mina	woman/girl*
morfar	to eat*
negocio	shop (in general)
nene/nena	child
onda	atmosphere/character, as in tiene buena onda ("there's a good atmosphere" or "she's good-natured")
palo	one million (pesos)*; un palo verde is a million US dollars (greenbacks)
pato	Argentine national sport; similar to handball on horseback
patota	gang*
pedo (estar en)	fart** (to be drunk*)
pendejo	kid (mostly used derogatorily)**
petiso	small, also small person
pibe	kid
pinta	"it looks good"; la pinta means appearance, as in tiene pinta or tiene buena pinta
piola	cool, smart
pollera	skirt
pucho	cigarette*
quilombo	mess*
remera	T-shirt
subte	Buenos Aires' underground railway
suéter	sweater
tacho	taxi (tachero is taxi driver)
tapado	coat (usually woman's)
telo	short-stay hotel where couples go to have sex*
tereré	drink composed of yerba mate served with wild herbs (yuyos) and ice-cold water or lemonade/orange juice
trucho	fake, phoney
vereda	pavement
vidriera	shop window
vieja/viejo/viejos	mum/dad/parents*
zafar	to get away with*

A glossary of Argentine terms and acronyms

ACA (Automóvil Club Argentino) National motoring organization, which also runs decent hotels in many towns (pronounced A-ka).

Acampar To camp.

Aduana Customs post.

Aerosilla Chairlift.

Agreste Wild or rustic (often used to describe a campsite with very basic facilities).

Alerce Giant, slow-growing Patagonian cypress, similar to the Californian redwood.

Almacén Small grocery store, which in the past often functioned as a bar too.

Altiplano High Andean plateau.

Aónik'enk The southern group of Tehuelche, the last of whose descendants live in the province of Santa Cruz.

Araucaria Monkey puzzle tree.

Arepa Flat maize bread.

Arroba The @ sign on a computer keyboard.

Arroyo Stream or small river.

Autopista Motorway.

Bailanta Dance club, where the predominant sound is cumbia (see p.574).

Balneario Bathing resort; also a complex of sunshades and small tents on the beach, often with a bar and shower facilities, for which users pay a daily, weekly or monthly rate.

Baqueano Mountain or wilderness guide.

Barrio Neighbourhood.

Bofedal Spongy altiplano wetland.

Boleadoras/bolas Traditional hunting implement, composed of stone balls connected by thick cord, thrown to entangle legs or neck of prey. Traditionally used by gauchos, who copied it from Argentina's indigenous inhabitants.

Boletería Ticket office.

Boleto Travel ticket.

Bombachas de campo Baggy gaucho trousers for riding.

Bombilla Straw-like implement, usually of metal, used for drinking mate from a gourd.

Bonaerense Adjective relating to or person from Buenos Aires Province.

Bondi Colloquial term in Buenos Aires for a bus.

Botiquín Medicine kit.

C/ The abbreviation of calle (street); only rarely used.

Cabildo Colonial town hall; now replaced by Municipalidad.

Cabina telefónica Phone booth.

Cacique Generic term for the head of a Latin American indigenous community or people, either elected or hereditary.

Cajero automático Cashpoint machine (ATM).

Calafate Type of thorny Patagonian bush, famous for its delicious purple berries.

Camioneta Pick-up truck.

Campesino Country-dweller; sometimes used to refer to someone with indigenous roots.

Campo de hielo Icecap or ice field.

Caña colihue Native Patagonian plant of the forest understorey; resembles bamboo.

Cancha Football stadium.

Cantina Traditional restaurant, usually Italian.

Característica Telephone code (eg 011 for Buenos Aires).

Carretera Route or highway.

Cartelera Agency for buying discounted tickets for cinemas, theatres and concerts.

Casa de té Tearoom.

Casco Main building of estancia; the homestead.

Cataratas Waterfalls, usually used to refer specifically to Iguazú Falls.

Caudillo Regional military or political leader, usually with authoritarian overtones.

Cebar (mate) To brew (mate).

Ceibo Tropical tree with a twisted trunk, whose bright-red or pink blossom is the national flower of Argentina, Uruguay and Paraguay.

Cerro Hill, mountain peak (often used in names).

Chaco húmedo Wet chaco habitat.

Chaco seco Dry chaco habitat.

Chacra Small farm.

Chamamé Folk music from the Litoral region, specifically Corrientes Province.

Chango Common term in the Northwest for a young boy; often used in the sense of "mate"/"buddy".

Chaqueño Someone from the Gran Chaco (or Province of Chaco).

Chata Slang term for pick-up truck.

China A gaucho girl or woman (often used as nickname).

Choique Common term, deriving from Mapudungun, for the smaller, southern Darwin's rhea of Patagonia.

Churro Strip of fried dough, somewhat similar to a doughnut, often filled with dulce de leche.

Colectivo Urban bus.

Combi Small minibus that runs urban bus routes.

Comparsa Carnival "school".

Confitería Café and tearoom, often with patisserie attached.

Conventillo Tenement building.

Cordillera Mountain range; usually used in Argentina to refer to the Andes.

Cortadera Pampas grass.

Costanera Riverside avenue.

Country Term for exclusive out-of-town residential compound or sports and social club.

Criollo/a Historically an Argentine-born person of Spanish/European descent. Used today in two ways: as a general term for Argentine (as in *comida criolla*, traditional Argentine food) and used by indigenous people to refer to those of nonindigenous descent.

Cuadra The distance from one street corner to the next, usually 100 metres (see also *Manzana*).

Cuchilla Regional term for low hill in Entre Ríos.

Cuesta Slope or small hill.

Cumbia Popular Argentine "tropical" rhythm, inspired by Colombian *cumbia*.

Departamento Administrative district in a province; also an apartment.

Descamisados Term meaning "the shirtless ones", popularized by Juan and Evita Perón to refer to the working-class masses and dispossessed.

Despensa Shop (particularly in rural areas).

Día de campo Day spent at an estancia where traditional *asado* and empanadas are eaten and guests are usually given a display of gaucho skills.

Dique Dock; also dam.

E/ The abbreviation of entre (between), used in addresses.

Empalme Junction of two highways.

Encomienda Package, parcel; also historical term for form of trusteeship bestowed on Spaniards after Conquest, granting them rights over the indigenous population.

Entrada Ticket (for football match, theatre etc).

Estancia Argentine farm, traditionally with huge areas of land.

Estanciero An owner of an estancia.

Estepa Steppe.

Estero A shallow swampland, commonly found in El Litoral and Gran Chaco areas.

Facón Gaucho knife, usually carried in a sheath.

Federalists Nineteenth-century term for those in favour of autonomous power being given to the provinces; opponents of Unitarists (see p.576).

Feria artesanal/de artesanías Craft fair.

Ferretería Hardware shop (often useful for camping equipment).

Ferrocarril Railway.

Ficha Token.

Fogón Place for a barbecue or camp fire; bonfire.

Fonda Simple restaurant.

Galería Small shopping arcade.

Gaseosa Soft drink.

Gaucho The typical Argentine "cowboy", or rural estancia worker.

Gendarmería Police station.

Gomería Tyre repair centre.

Gomero Rubber tree.

Gringo/a Any white foreigner, though often specifically those from English-speaking countries; historically, European immigrants to Argentina (as opposed to *criollos*), as in *pampa gringa*, the part of the Pampas settled by Europeans. Often used as a nickname.

Guanaco Wild camelid of the llama family.

Guaraní Indigenous people and language, found principally in Misiones, Corrientes and Paraguay.

Guardaequipaje Left-luggage office.

Guardafauna Wildlife ranger.

Guardaganado Cattle grid.

Guardaparque National park ranger.

Gününa'küna The northern group of the Tehuelche, now extinct.

Hacer dedo To hitchhike.

Humedal Any wetland swampy area.

IGM (Instituto Geográfico Militar) The national military's cartographic institution.

Impenetrable Term applied historically to the area of the dry *chaco* with the most inhospitable conditions for white settlement, due to lack of water; the name of a zone of northwestern Chaco Province.

Intendencia Head office of a national park.

Intendente Administrative chief of a national park.

Interno Telephone extension number.

Isleta de monte Clump of scrubby mixed woodland found in savannah or flat agricultural land, typically in the Gran Chaco and the northeast of the country.

IVA (Impuesto de Valor Agregado) Value-added tax or sales tax.

Jacarandá Tropical tree with trumpet-shaped mauvish blossom.

Jarilla Thorny, chest-high bush.

Junta Military government coalition.

Kiosko Newspaper stand or small store selling cigarettes, confectionery and some foodstuffs.

Kolla Andean indigenous group predominant in the northwestern provinces of Salta and Jujuy.

Lancha Smallish motor boat.

Lapacho Tropical tree typical of the Litoral region and distinguished by bright-pink blossom.

Leña Firewood.

Lenga Type of Nothofagus southern beech common in Patagonian forests.

El Litoral Littoral, shore – used to refer to the provinces of Entre Ríos, Corrientes, Misiones, Santa Fe and sometimes Eastern Chaco and Formosa.

Litoraleño Inhabitant of the Litoral (see above).

Locutorio Call centre, where phone calls are made from cabins and the caller is charged after the call has been made.

Lomo de burro Speed bump.

Lonco Head or cacique (see p.573) of a Mapuche community.

Madrejón A swampy ox-bow lake.

Mallín Swamp, particularly in upland moors.

Manzana City block; the square bounded by four *cuadras* (see opposite).

Mapuche One of Argentina's largest indigenous groups, whose ancestors originally came from Chilean Patagonia and whose biggest communities are found in the provinces of Chubut, Río Negro and especially Neuquén.

Mapudungun The language of the Mapuche.

Marcha Commercial dance music.

Mataco See Wichí.

Mate Strictly the *mate* gourd or receptacle, but used generally to describe the national "tea" drink.

Menú del día Standard set menu.

Menú ejecutivo Set menu. Tends to be more expensive than the *menú del día* (see above), though not always that executive.

Mesopotamia The three provinces of Entre Ríos, Corrientes and Misiones, by analogy with the ancient region lying between the rivers Tigris and Euphrates, in modern-day Iraq.

Micro Long-distance bus.

Microcentro The area of a city comprising the central square and neighbouring streets.

Milonga Style of folk-guitar music usually associated with the pampas region; also a tango dance and a subgenre of tango, more uptempo than tango proper. Also a tango dancing event, often with tuition (see box, p.81).

Mirador Scenic lookout point or tower.

Monte Scrubby woodland, often used to describe any uncultivated woodland area. Also used to refer to the desertified ecosystem that lies in the rainshadow of the central Andes around the Cuyo region.

Mozarabic Spanish architectural style, originally dating from the ninth to thirteenth centuries and characterized by a fusion of Romanesque and Moorish styles.

Muelle Pier or jetty.

Municipalidad Municipality building or town hall.

Ñandú A common name, derived from Guaraní, for the Greater rhea, but also used to refer to its smaller cousin, the Darwin's rhea.

Ñire Type of Nothofagus southern beech tree common in Patagonian forests.

Ñoqui Argentine spelling of the Italian *gnocchi*, a small potato dumpling. Used to refer to phoney employees who appear on a company's payroll but don't actually work there, or idle civil servants; also slang for a punch (as in a fight).

Nothofagus Genus of Patagonian trees commonly called southern beech (includes lenga and ñire).

Ombú Large shade tree, originally from the Mesopotamia region and now associated with the Pampas, where it was introduced in the eighteenth century.

Paisano Meaning "countryman"; sometimes loosely used as equivalent to gaucho and often used by people of indigenous descent to refer to themselves, thus avoiding the sometimes pejorative *indio* (Indian).

Palmar Palm grove.

Palo borracho Tree associated especially with the dry-*chaco* habitat of northern Argentina; its name (literally "drunken stick") is derived from its swollen trunk in which water is stored.

Palometa Piranha/piraña.

Pampa(s) The broad flat grasslands of central Argentina.

Parquímetro Parking meter.

Parrillada The meat barbecued on a *parrilla* (barbecue).

Pasaje Narrow street.

Paseaperro Professional dog walker.

Pastizal Grassland, often used for grazing.

Pato The Argentine national sport; a kind of handball on horseback.

Payada Traditional improvised musical style, often performed as a kind of dialogue between two singers (*payadores*) who accompany themselves on guitars.

Peaje Road toll.

Peatonal Pedestrianized street.

Pehuén Mapuche term for monkey puzzle tree.

Peña Circle or group (usually of artists or musicians); a *peña folklórica* is a folk-music club.

Peón Farmhand.

Picada A roughly marked path; also a plate of small snacks eaten before a meal, particularly cheese, ham or smoked meats.

Planta baja Ground floor (first floor, US).

Playa Beach.

Playa (de estacionamiento) Parking area; garage.

Plazoleta/plazuela Small town square.

Porteño/a Someone from Buenos Aires city.

Prefectura Naval prefecture for controlling river and marine traffic.

Puesto Small outpost or hut for shepherds or *guardaparques*.

Pukará Pre-Columbian fortress.

Pulpería A type of traditional general-provisions store that doubles up as a bar and rural meeting-point.

Puna High Andean plateau (alternative term for altiplano, see p.573).

Puntano/a Someone from San Luís.

Quebrada Ravine, gully.

Querandí Original indigenous inhabitants of the Pampas region.

Quinta Suburban or country house with a small plot of land, where fruit and vegetables are often cultivated.

Qom An indigenous group, living principally in the east of Formosa and Chaco provinces. The word means "people" in their language.

Rancho Simple countryside dwelling, typically constructed of adobe.

Rastra Gaucho belt, typically ornamented with silver.

RC (Ruta Complementaria) Subsidiary, unsealed road in Tierra del Fuego.

Recargo Surcharge on credit cards.

Recova Arcade around the exterior of a building or courtyard, typical of colonial-era buildings.

Reducción Jesuit mission settlement.

Refugio Trekking refuge or hut.

Remise/remís Taxi or chauffeur-driven rental car, booked through a central office.

Remise colectivo Shared cab that runs fixed inter-urban routes.

Represa Dam; also reservoir.

Río River.

Rioplatense Referring to people or things (including language) from the region around the River Plate (Río de la Plata) – Buenos Aires Province, Santa Fe Province and Uruguay, plus slightly further afield.

Ripio Gravel; usually used to describe an unsurfaced gravel road.

RN (Ruta Nacional) Major route, usually paved.

RP (Ruta Provincial) Provincial road, sometimes paved.

Ruta Route or road.

Salto Waterfall.

Sapucay Bloodcurdling shriek characteristic of *chamamé* (see p.573).

Selk'nam Nomadic, indigenous guanaco-hunters from Tierra del Fuego, whose last members died in the 1960s. Also called Ona, the Yámana name for them.

Sendero Path or trail.

S/N Used in addresses to indicate that there's no house number (*sin número*).

Soroche Altitude sickness.

Sortija Display of gaucho skill in which the galloping rider must spear a small ring hung from a thread.

Subte Buenos Aires' underground railway.

Suri A type of rhea indigenous to Argentina.

Tanguería Tango club.

Tasa de terminal Terminal tax.

Taxímetro Taxi meter.

Tehuelche Generic term for the different nomadic steppe tribes of Patagonia, whom early European explorers named "Patagones".

Teleférico Gondola or cable car.

Tenedor libre All-you-can-eat buffet restaurant.

Tereré Common drink in the subtropical north of the country and Paraguay, composed of *yerba mate* served with wild herbs (*yuyos*) and ice-cold water or lemonade.

Terminal de ómnibus Bus terminal.

Terrateniente Landowner.

Tipa Acacia-like tree often found in northern *yungas* (and along urban avenues).

Toba See Qom.

Truco Argentina's national card game, in which the ability to outbluff your opponents is of major importance.

Unitarists Nineteenth-century centralists, in favour of power being centralized in Buenos Aires; opponents of Federalists (see p.574).

Villa Short for *villa miseria*, a shantytown.

Wichí Seminomadic indigenous group, living predominantly in the dry central and western areas of Chaco and Formosa provinces, and in the far east of Salta. Sometimes referred to pejoratively as Mataco.

Yahganes See Yámana.

Yámana Nomadic indigenous canoe-going people who lived in the islands and channels south of Tierra del Fuego, and whose culture died out in Argentina in the early twentieth century.

Yerba (mate) The dried and cured leaves of the shrub used to brew *mate*.

YPF (Yacimientos Petroleros Fiscales) The principal Argentine petroleum company, controversially renationalized. It is often used to refer to the company's fuel stations, which act as landmarks in the less-populated areas of the country.

Zona franca Duty-free zone.

Small print and index

Rough Guide credits

Editor: Ann-Marie Shaw
Layout: Nikhil Agarwal
Cartography: Ashutosh Bharti
Picture editor: Marta Bescos
Proofreader: Diane Margolis
Managing editor: Mani Ramaswamy
Assistant editor: Jalpreen Kaur Chhatwal
Production: Charlotte Cade
Cover design: Wilf Matos, Marta Bescos, Dan May and Nikhil Agarwal

Editorial assistant: Olivia Rawes
Senior pre-press designer: Dan May
Design director: Jason Mitchell
Travel publisher: Joanna Kirby
Digital travel publisher: Peter Buckley
Operations coordinator: Helen Blount
Publishing director (Travel): Clare Currie
Commercial manager: Gino Magnotta
Managing director: John Duhigg

Publishing information

This fifth edition published October 2013 by
Rough Guides Ltd,
80 Strand, London WC2R 0RL
11, Community Centre, Panchsheel Park,
New Delhi 110017, India
Distributed by the Penguin Group
Penguin Books Ltd,
80 Strand, London WC2R 0RL
Penguin Group (USA)
345 Hudson Street, NY 10014, USA
Penguin Group (Australia)
250 Camberwell Road, Camberwell,
Victoria 3124, Australia
Penguin Group (NZ)
67 Apollo Drive, Mairangi Bay, Auckland 1310,
New Zealand
Penguin Group (South Africa)
Block D, Rosebank Office Park, 181 Jan Smuts Avenue,
Parktown North, Gauteng, South Africa 2193
Rough Guides is represented in Canada by Tourmaline
Editions Inc. 662 King Street West, Suite 304, Toronto,
Ontario M5V 1M7
Printed in Singapore by Toppan Security Printing Pte. Ltd.

MIX
Paper from
responsible sources
FSC
www.fsc.org
FSC® C018179

Help us update

We've gone to a lot of effort to ensure that the fifth edition of **The Rough Guide to Argentina** is accurate and up-to-date. However, things change – places get "discovered", opening hours are notoriously fickle, restaurants and rooms raise prices or lower standards. If you feel we've got it wrong or left something out, we'd like to know, and if you can remember the address, the price, the hours, the phone number, so much the better.

Please send your comments with the subject line "**Rough Guide Argentina Update**" to @ mail@uk .roughguides.com. We'll credit all contributions and send a copy of the next edition (or any other Rough Guide if you prefer) for the very best emails.

Find more travel information, connect with fellow travellers and plan your trip on @ roughguides.com

Acknowledgements

Andrew Benson wishes to thank: Julie and Juliana in Buenos Aires, China, Julio, Elsa and Charlie in the Litoral, Javier Eppens – the best wine guide in Mendoza (if not the world), all my friends in Argentina, Shafik and Rosalba for being excellent colleagues, Mani for all-round support, Annie for hawk-eyed but dove-winged editing, and as ever Fernando for being a clown (when necessary).

Shafik Meghji wishes to thank: all the locals and travellers who helped out along the way. A special *muchas gracias* must go to: Andrew Benson and Rosalba O'Brien for all their help and advice; Ann-Marie Shaw for her sterling editing work; Mani Ramaswamy at RG HQ for the original commission; Julie Dallemagne of Destino Argentina; Laura

Rendell-Dunn of Journey Latin America; Louisa and Kevin Begg of Estancia Los Potreros; Anna Kaminski; Zoe Ximena Taylor of Walk Patagonia; Maria and Sebastian at Tierra de Leyendas; Soledad Fernandez at The House; Maria Salduna at Cumbres del Martial; Jean, Nizar and Nina Meghji; and Sioned Jones for all her love and support.

Rosalba O'Brien wishes to thank: my family in Argentina – Mimi, Amalia, Sebastian, Ernie & Santiago; James "Anakin" & Steve "Fingers"; Jane at Huechehue; Federico in Salta; ANDA travel; the Salta Rafting gang; Andrew for support and friendship and Fernando for help on the journey home! And most of all as always Esteban and my little travel companion Arwen.

Readers' updates

Thanks to all the readers who have taken the time to write in with comments and suggestions (and apologies if we've inadvertently omitted or misspelt anyone's name):

Michael Carpenter; Mikael and Virginia Lagarde; Jessica Rossell; Monty Roy; and Luca Toscani.

ABOUT THE AUTHORS

Danny Aebehard first headed out to Argentina in the early 1990s with a fistful of maps and a desire to immerse himself in all things Latin. He subsequently spent several years travelling and leading tours throughout Central and South America. He's now based in London and works for the BBC World Service, always looking for an excuse to zip off to Latin America for radio and writing projects.

Andrew Benson splits his time between Argentina and Europe, where he works for various UN agencies. His favourite activities in Argentina are riding a horse through a *yerba mate* plantation, then soaking in a Jesuit-style stone swimming pool in a bamboo grove and sipping *tereré* in the blazing Misiones sun.

Shafik Meghji, a travel writer, journalist and editor based in south London, first visited Argentina in 2004 and later returned to live in Buenos Aires for a year. He's travelled the country, snowboarding in the Andes, horseriding with gauchos, and ice-trekking across glaciers in the process. Shafik also co-authors the Rough Guides to Bolivia, Chile, India and Nepal, and contributes to several others. He blogs at ⓦunmappedroutes.com and you can follow him on Twitter @ShafikMeghji.

Rosalba O'Brien became interested in Latin America through her degree in Comparative American Studies, after which she spent a number of years travelling and leading adventure tours in Perú, Brazil and Argentina. She now divides her time between the UK and Latin America, working as a journalist. She lives with her Argentine husband and their daughter.

Lucy Phillips first travelled to Argentina in 1991, when she fell in love with Buenos Aires, tango and Boca Juniors. Since then, she has interspersed periods of employment at home with travel and work in Latin America. She now lives on the south coast of England, where she works as a photographer and translator.

Photo credits

All photos © Rough Guides except the following:
(key: t-top; c-centre; b-bottom; l-left; r-right)

p.1 Alamy/Yadid Levy
p.2 Alamy/AA World Travel Library
p.4 Alamy/imagebroker
p.7 Getty Images/Design Pics/Philippe Widling
p.8 Corbis/Yann Arthus-Bertrand
p.9 Alamy/Alex Bramwell (t); Dreamstime.com/Paop (c); Peter Stroh (b)
p.12 Alamy/LOOK Die Bildagentur der Fotografen GmbH
p.13 Alamy/GM Photo Images (t); Dreamstime.com/Adriel80 (b); Nico Smit (c)
p.14 Alamy/Genevieve Vallee (t); iStockphoto.com/© Eric R. Schroeder (b)
p.15 Alamy/Christian Kober 1 (b); Dreamstime.com/Marbar1974 (tl)
p.16 Alamy/Cindy Hopkins (t); Getty Images/M G Therin Weise (c); iStockphoto.com/Dmitry_Saparov (b)
p.17 Alamy/AA World Travel Library (t); WILDLIFE GmbH (c); Arterra Picture Library (b)
p.18 Alamy/Action Plus Sports Images (b); Corbis/Adam Burton/Robert Harding (t)
p.19 Yadid Levy (t); imagebroker (c); Alamy/Jeremy Hoare (b)
p.20 Alamy/Image Source RM (t); Getty Images/Guenter Fischer (b)
p.21 Getty Images/Gallo Images (t); Alamy/imagebroker (b)
p.22 Dreamstime.com/Thoron
p.24 Alamy/imagebroker
p.75 Getty Images/Don Klumpp (tl);Yadid Levy (tr); Dreamstime.com/Spectral-design (br); Alamy/Letterbox Digital (bl)
p.107 Corbis/Jon Hicks (b)
pp.128-129 Alamy/David R. Frazier Photolibrary, Inc.
p.131 Getty Images/AWL Images RM
p.149 Yadid Levy (tl); Fotolia/rrruss (tr); Alamy/Etcheverry Images (b)
pp.172–173 Alamy/Yadid Levy

p.175 Corbis/Christian Kober/Robert Harding
p.191 imagebroker (tl, bl); Emiliano Rodriguez (tr); Alamy/AA World Travel Library (br)
pp.208–209 Corbis/Radius Images
p.211 Alamy/ITPhoto
p.231 Norberto Lauria (t); Alamy/Didi (b)
p.251 Getty Images/AFP (t); Mariana Eliano (b)
pp.274–275 Alamy/Etcheverry Collection
p.277 Getty Images/Danita Delimont
p.289 Alamy/AA World Travel Library (tl); Javier Etcheverry (tr); Eduardo Pucheta Photo (br); Chris Howarth/Argentina (bl)
p.311 Corbis: Ocean (t); Alamy/Javier Etcheverry (b)
pp.330–331 Alamy/AA World Travel Library
p.333 Alamy/AA World Travel Library
p.351 Dreamstime.com/Pablo Caridad (t); Alamy Images/Marco Guoli (c); Getty Images/Flickr RF (b)
p.369 Alamy/AA World Travel Library
pp.390–391 Getty Images/John Elk
p.393 Alamy/AA World Travel Library
p.405 Getty Images/Gallo Images (t); Alamy/Javier Etcheverry (b)
p.425 Alamy/Javier Corripio (t); Getty Images/Imagebroker RF (b)
pp.438–439 Alamy/Renato Granieri
p.453 Alamy/Etcheverry Collection (t)
p.483 Alamy/James Cresswell (t); Getty Images/Picavet (b)
p.509 Gallo Images (t); Getty Images/age fotostock RM (b)
p.524 Getty Images/Gallo Images

Front cover Monte Fitz Roy, Parque Nacional Los Glaciares © 4Corners/Fridmar Damm
Back cover Shop sign in La Boca © eye ubiquitous/ Robert Harding Picture Library (t); Malbec vines © Imagebroker RF/ Getty Images (bl);Salt desert in Salinas Grandes © Flickr RF/ Getty Images (br)

Index

Maps are marked in grey

Map symbols

The symbols below are used on maps throughout the book

✈	International airport	⊞	Hospital	🛡	Ranger station	⛪	Church (regional maps)
✦	Domestic airport	⛳	Golf course	⛳	Guardaparque/park ranger HQ/ border crossing	⛪	Church (town maps)
★	Bus stop	⊙	Statue	⛏	Campsite	🕌	Mosque/muslim monument
P	Parking	🏛	Monument	⛺	Refuge	▨	Building
Ⓜ	Metro stop	∩	Arch	⛷	Ski area	▢	Market
⚓	Ferry/boat station	🌊	Waterfall	⛯	Lighthouse	○	Stadium
⛽	Petrol station	〰	Rocks	🍇	Vineyard	⊞	Christian cemetery
⊠	Gate	⋀	Mountains	∴	Ruin	▨	Park
◆	Place of interest	/\	Volcano	≈	Marshland	▢	Beach
@	Internet	▲	Peak	⤳	Bridge/pass	≈	Swamp
ⓘ	Tourist office	♒	Spring/spa	✡	Synagogue	▨	Glacier
🕐	Telephone	⌒	Cave	●-●-●	Cable car	▤	Salt flat
✉	Post office	⤊	Viewpoint	— -	Ferry route		

Listings key

■	Accommodation
●	Restaurant/café
■	Bar/club/nightlife/music venue
●	Shop

Let´s travel together
We are the best choice in Argentina

We offer unlimited mileage and a collision damage waiver
Contact us for conditions

Branches at main cities and airports throughout the country

Reservations Argentina: (5411) 4816-8001
reservas@milletrentacar.com.ar
www.milletrentacar.com.ar

CHAT ONLINE!

Hertz.

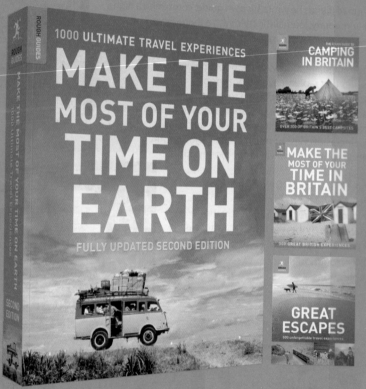